Dictionary of Literary Biography

1 *The American Renaissance in New England,* edited by Joel Myerson (1978)

2 *American Novelists Since World War II,* edited by Jeffrey Helterman and Richard Layman (1978)

3 *Antebellum Writers in New York and the South,* edited by Joel Myerson (1979)

4 *American Writers in Paris, 1920–1939,* edited by Karen Lane Rood (1980)

5 *American Poets Since World War II,* 2 parts, edited by Donald J. Greiner (1980)

6 *American Novelists Since World War II, Second Series,* edited by James E. Kibler Jr. (1980)

7 *Twentieth-Century American Dramatists,* 2 parts, edited by John MacNicholas (1981)

8 *Twentieth-Century American Science-Fiction Writers,* 2 parts, edited by David Cowart and Thomas L. Wymer (1981)

9 *American Novelists, 1910–1945,* 3 parts, edited by James J. Martine (1981)

10 *Modern British Dramatists, 1900–1945,* 2 parts, edited by Stanley Weintraub (1982)

11 *American Humorists, 1800–1950,* 2 parts, edited by Stanley Trachtenberg (1982)

12 *American Realists and Naturalists,* edited by Donald Pizer and Earl N. Harbert (1982)

13 *British Dramatists Since World War II,* 2 parts, edited by Stanley Weintraub (1982)

14 *British Novelists Since 1960,* 2 parts, edited by Jay L. Halio (1983)

15 *British Novelists, 1930–1959,* 2 parts, edited by Bernard Oldsey (1983)

16 *The Beats: Literary Bohemians in Postwar America,* 2 parts, edited by Ann Charters (1983)

17 *Twentieth-Century American Historians,* edited by Clyde N. Wilson (1983)

18 *Victorian Novelists After 1885,* edited by Ira B. Nadel and William E. Fredeman (1983)

19 *British Poets, 1880–1914,* edited by Donald E. Stanford (1983)

20 *British Poets, 1914–1945,* edited by Donald E. Stanford (1983)

21 *Victorian Novelists Before 1885,* edited by Ira B. Nadel and William E. Fredeman (1983)

22 *American Writers for Children, 1900–1960,* edited by John Cech (1983)

23 *American Newspaper Journalists, 1873–1900,* edited by Perry J. Ashley (1983)

24 *American Colonial Writers, 1606–1734,* edited by Emory Elliott (1984)

25 *American Newspaper Journalists, 1901–1925,* edited by Perry J. Ashley (1984)

26 *American Screenwriters,* edited by Robert E. Morsberger, Stephen O. Lesser, and Randall Clark (1984)

27 *Poets of Great Britain and Ireland, 1945–1960,* edited by Vincent B. Sherry Jr. (1984)

28 *Twentieth-Century American-Jewish Fiction Writers,* edited by Daniel Walden (1984)

29 *American Newspaper Journalists, 1926–1950,* edited by Perry J. Ashley (1984)

30 *American Historians, 1607–1865,* edited by Clyde N. Wilson (1984)

31 *American Colonial Writers, 1735–1781,* edited by Emory Elliott (1984)

32 *Victorian Poets Before 1850,* edited by William E. Fredeman and Ira B. Nadel (1984)

33 *Afro-American Fiction Writers After 1955,* edited by Thadious M. Davis and Trudier Harris (1984)

34 *British Novelists, 1890–1929: Traditionalists,* edited by Thomas F. Staley (1985)

35 *Victorian Poets After 1850,* edited by William E. Fredeman and Ira B. Nadel (1985)

36 *British Novelists, 1890–1929: Modernists,* edited by Thomas F. Staley (1985)

37 *American Writers of the Early Republic,* edited by Emory Elliott (1985)

38 *Afro-American Writers After 1955: Dramatists and Prose Writers,* edited by Thadious M. Davis and Trudier Harris (1985)

39 *British Novelists, 1660–1800,* 2 parts, edited by Martin C. Battestin (1985)

40 *Poets of Great Britain and Ireland Since 1960,* 2 parts, edited by Vincent B. Sherry Jr. (1985)

41 *Afro-American Poets Since 1955,* edited by Trudier Harris and Thadious M. Davis (1985)

42 *American Writers for Children Before 1900,* edited by Glenn E. Estes (1985)

43 *American Newspaper Journalists, 1690–1872,* edited by Perry J. Ashley (1986)

44 *American Screenwriters, Second Series,* edited by Randall Clark, Robert E. Morsberger, and Stephen O. Lesser (1986)

45 *American Poets, 1880–1945, First Series,* edited by Peter Quartermain (1986)

46 *American Literary Publishing Houses, 1900–1980: Trade and Paperback,* edited by Peter Dzwonkoski (1986)

47 *American Historians, 1866–1912,* edited by Clyde N. Wilson (1986)

48 *American Poets, 1880–1945, Second Series,* edited by Peter Quartermain (1986)

49 *American Literary Publishing Houses, 1638–1899,* 2 parts, edited by Peter Dzwonkoski (1986)

50 *Afro-American Writers Before the Harlem Renaissance,* edited by Trudier Harris (1986)

51 *Afro-American Writers from the Harlem Renaissance to 1940,* edited by Trudier Harris (1987)

52 *American Writers for Children Since 1960: Fiction,* edited by Glenn E. Estes (1986)

53 *Canadian Writers Since 1960, First Series,* edited by W. H. New (1986)

54 *American Poets, 1880–1945, Third Series,* 2 parts, edited by Peter Quartermain (1987)

55 *Victorian Prose Writers Before 1867,* edited by William B. Thesing (1987)

56 *German Fiction Writers, 1914–1945,* edited by James Hardin (1987)

57 *Victorian Prose Writers After 1867,* edited by William B. Thesing (1987)

58 *Jacobean and Caroline Dramatists,* edited by Fredson Bowers (1987)

59 *American Literary Critics and Scholars, 1800–1850,* edited by John W. Rathbun and Monica M. Grecu (1987)

60 *Canadian Writers Since 1960, Second Series,* edited by W. H. New (1987)

61 *American Writers for Children Since 1960: Poets, Illustrators, and Nonfiction Authors,* edited by Glenn E. Estes (1987)

62 *Elizabethan Dramatists,* edited by Fredson Bowers (1987)

63 *Modern American Critics, 1920–1955,* edited by Gregory S. Jay (1988)

64 *American Literary Critics and Scholars, 1850–1880,* edited by John W. Rathbun and Monica M. Grecu (1988)

65 *French Novelists, 1900–1930,* edited by Catharine Savage Brosman (1988)

66 *German Fiction Writers, 1885–1913,* 2 parts, edited by James Hardin (1988)

67 *Modern American Critics Since 1955,* edited by Gregory S. Jay (1988)

68 *Canadian Writers, 1920–1959, First Series,* edited by W. H. New (1988)

69 *Contemporary German Fiction Writers, First Series,* edited by Wolfgang D. Elfe and James Hardin (1988)

70 *British Mystery Writers, 1860–1919,* edited by Bernard Benstock and Thomas F. Staley (1988)

71 *American Literary Critics and Scholars, 1880–1900,* edited by John W. Rathbun and Monica M. Grecu (1988)

72 *French Novelists, 1930–1960,* edited by Catharine Savage Brosman (1988)

73 *American Magazine Journalists, 1741–1850,* edited by Sam G. Riley (1988)

74 *American Short-Story Writers Before 1880,* edited by Bobby Ellen Kimbel, with the assistance of William E. Grant (1988)

75 *Contemporary German Fiction Writers, Second Series,* edited by Wolfgang D. Elfe and James Hardin (1988)

76 *Afro-American Writers, 1940–1955,* edited by Trudier Harris (1988)

77 *British Mystery Writers, 1920–1939,* edited by Bernard Benstock and Thomas F. Staley (1988)

78 *American Short-Story Writers, 1880–1910,* edited by Bobby Ellen Kimbel, with the assistance of William E. Grant (1988)

79 *American Magazine Journalists, 1850–1900,* edited by Sam G. Riley (1988)

80 *Restoration and Eighteenth-Century Dramatists, First Series,* edited by Paula R. Backscheider (1989)

81 *Austrian Fiction Writers, 1875–1913,* edited by James Hardin and Donald G. Daviau (1989)

82 *Chicano Writers, First Series,* edited by Francisco A. Lomelí and Carl R. Shirley (1989)

83 *French Novelists Since 1960,* edited by Catharine Savage Brosman (1989)

84 *Restoration and Eighteenth-Century Dramatists, Second Series,* edited by Paula R. Backscheider (1989)

85 *Austrian Fiction Writers After 1914,* edited by James Hardin and Donald G. Daviau (1989)

86 *American Short-Story Writers, 1910–1945, First Series,* edited by Bobby Ellen Kimbel (1989)

87 *British Mystery and Thriller Writers Since 1940, First Series,* edited by Bernard Benstock and Thomas F. Staley (1989)

88 *Canadian Writers, 1920–1959, Second Series,* edited by W. H. New (1989)

89 *Restoration and Eighteenth-Century Dramatists, Third Series,* edited by Paula R. Backscheider (1989)

90 *German Writers in the Age of Goethe, 1789–1832,* edited by James Hardin and Christoph E. Schweitzer (1989)

91 *American Magazine Journalists, 1900–1960, First Series,* edited by Sam G. Riley (1990)

92 *Canadian Writers, 1890–1920,* edited by W. H. New (1990)

93 *British Romantic Poets, 1789–1832, First Series,* edited by John R. Greenfield (1990)

94 *German Writers in the Age of Goethe: Sturm und Drang to Classicism,* edited by James Hardin and Christoph E. Schweitzer (1990)

95 *Eighteenth-Century British Poets, First Series,* edited by John Sitter (1990)

96 *British Romantic Poets, 1789–1832, Second Series,* edited by John R. Greenfield (1990)

97 *German Writers from the Enlightenment to Sturm und Drang, 1720–1764,* edited by James Hardin and Christoph E. Schweitzer (1990)

98 *Modern British Essayists, First Series,* edited by Robert Beum (1990)

99 *Canadian Writers Before 1890,* edited by W. H. New (1990)

100 *Modern British Essayists, Second Series,* edited by Robert Beum (1990)

101 *British Prose Writers, 1660–1800, First Series,* edited by Donald T. Siebert (1991)

102 *American Short-Story Writers, 1910–1945, Second Series,* edited by Bobby Ellen Kimbel (1991)

103 *American Literary Biographers, First Series,* edited by Steven Serafin (1991)

104 *British Prose Writers, 1660–1800, Second Series,* edited by Donald T. Siebert (1991)

105 *American Poets Since World War II, Second Series,* edited by R. S. Gwynn (1991)

106 *British Literary Publishing Houses, 1820–1880,* edited by Patricia J. Anderson and Jonathan Rose (1991)

107 *British Romantic Prose Writers, 1789–1832, First Series,* edited by John R. Greenfield (1991)

108 *Twentieth-Century Spanish Poets, First Series,* edited by Michael L. Perna (1991)

109 *Eighteenth-Century British Poets, Second Series,* edited by John Sitter (1991)

110 *British Romantic Prose Writers, 1789–1832, Second Series,* edited by John R. Greenfield (1991)

111 *American Literary Biographers, Second Series,* edited by Steven Serafin (1991)

112 *British Literary Publishing Houses, 1881–1965,* edited by Jonathan Rose and Patricia J. Anderson (1991)

113 *Modern Latin-American Fiction Writers, First Series,* edited by William Luis (1992)

114 *Twentieth-Century Italian Poets, First Series,* edited by Giovanna Wedel De Stasio, Glauco Cambon, and Antonio Illiano (1992)

115 *Medieval Philosophers,* edited by Jeremiah Hackett (1992)

116 *British Romantic Novelists, 1789–1832,* edited by Bradford K. Mudge (1992)

117 *Twentieth-Century Caribbean and Black African Writers, First Series,* edited by Bernth Lindfors and Reinhard Sander (1992)

118 *Twentieth-Century German Dramatists, 1889–1918,* edited by Wolfgang D. Elfe and James Hardin (1992)

119 *Nineteenth-Century French Fiction Writers: Romanticism and Realism, 1800–1860,* edited by Catharine Savage Brosman (1992)

120 *American Poets Since World War II, Third Series,* edited by R. S. Gwynn (1992)

121 *Seventeenth-Century British Nondramatic Poets, First Series,* edited by M. Thomas Hester (1992)

122 *Chicano Writers, Second Series,* edited by Francisco A. Lomelí and Carl R. Shirley (1992)

123 *Nineteenth-Century French Fiction Writers: Naturalism and Beyond, 1860–1900,* edited by Catharine Savage Brosman (1992)

124 *Twentieth-Century German Dramatists, 1919–1992,* edited by Wolfgang D. Elfe and James Hardin (1992)

125 *Twentieth-Century Caribbean and Black African Writers, Second Series,* edited by Bernth Lindfors and Reinhard Sander (1993)

126 *Seventeenth-Century British Nondramatic Poets, Second Series,* edited by M. Thomas Hester (1993)

127 *American Newspaper Publishers, 1950–1990,* edited by Perry J. Ashley (1993)

128 *Twentieth-Century Italian Poets, Second Series,* edited by Giovanna Wedel De Stasio, Glauco Cambon, and Antonio Illiano (1993)

129 *Nineteenth-Century German Writers, 1841–1900,* edited by James Hardin and Siegfried Mews (1993)

130 *American Short-Story Writers Since World War II,* edited by Patrick Meanor (1993)

131 *Seventeenth-Century British Nondramatic Poets, Third Series,* edited by M. Thomas Hester (1993)

132 *Sixteenth-Century British Nondramatic Writers, First Series,* edited by David A. Richardson (1993)

133 *Nineteenth-Century German Writers to 1840,* edited by James Hardin and Siegfried Mews (1993)

134 *Twentieth-Century Spanish Poets, Second Series,* edited by Jerry Phillips Winfield (1994)

135 *British Short-Fiction Writers, 1880–1914: The Realist Tradition,* edited by William B. Thesing (1994)

136 *Sixteenth-Century British Nondramatic Writers, Second Series,* edited by David A. Richardson (1994)

137 *American Magazine Journalists, 1900–1960, Second Series,* edited by Sam G. Riley (1994)

138 *German Writers and Works of the High Middle Ages: 1170–1280,* edited by James Hardin and Will Hasty (1994)

139 *British Short-Fiction Writers, 1945–1980,* edited by Dean Baldwin (1994)

140 *American Book-Collectors and Bibliographers, First Series,* edited by Joseph Rosenblum (1994)

141 *British Children's Writers, 1880–1914,* edited by Laura M. Zaidman (1994)

142 *Eighteenth-Century British Literary Biographers,* edited by Steven Serafin (1994)

143 *American Novelists Since World War II, Third Series,* edited by James R. Giles and Wanda H. Giles (1994)

144 *Nineteenth-Century British Literary Biographers,* edited by Steven Serafin (1994)

145 *Modern Latin-American Fiction Writers, Second Series,* edited by William Luis and Ann González (1994)

146 *Old and Middle English Literature,* edited by Jeffrey Helterman and Jerome Mitchell (1994)

147 *South Slavic Writers Before World War II,* edited by Vasa D. Mihailovich (1994)

148 *German Writers and Works of the Early Middle Ages: 800–1170,* edited by Will Hasty and James Hardin (1994)

149 *Late Nineteenth- and Early Twentieth-Century British Literary Biographers,* edited by Steven Serafin (1995)

150 *Early Modern Russian Writers, Late Seventeenth and Eighteenth Centuries,* edited by Marcus C. Levitt (1995)

151 *British Prose Writers of the Early Seventeenth Century,* edited by Clayton D. Lein (1995)

152 *American Novelists Since World War II, Fourth Series,* edited by James R. Giles and Wanda H. Giles (1995)

153 *Late-Victorian and Edwardian British Novelists, First Series,* edited by George M. Johnson (1995)

154 *The British Literary Book Trade, 1700–1820,* edited by James K. Bracken and Joel Silver (1995)

155 *Twentieth-Century British Literary Biographers,* edited by Steven Serafin (1995)

156 *British Short-Fiction Writers, 1880–1914: The Romantic Tradition,* edited by William F. Naufftus (1995)

157 *Twentieth-Century Caribbean and Black African Writers, Third Series,* edited by Bernth Lindfors and Reinhard Sander (1995)

158 *British Reform Writers, 1789–1832,* edited by Gary Kelly and Edd Applegate (1995)

159 *British Short-Fiction Writers, 1800–1880,* edited by John R. Greenfield (1996)

160 *British Children's Writers, 1914–1960,* edited by Donald R. Hettinga and Gary D. Schmidt (1996)

161 *British Children's Writers Since 1960, First Series,* edited by Caroline Hunt (1996)

162 *British Short-Fiction Writers, 1915–1945,* edited by John H. Rogers (1996)

163 *British Children's Writers, 1800–1880,* edited by Meena Khorana (1996)

164 *German Baroque Writers, 1580–1660,* edited by James Hardin (1996)

165 *American Poets Since World War II, Fourth Series,* edited by Joseph Conte (1996)

166 *British Travel Writers, 1837–1875,* edited by Barbara Brothers and Julia Gergits (1996)

167 *Sixteenth-Century British Nondramatic Writers, Third Series,* edited by David A. Richardson (1996)

168 *German Baroque Writers, 1661–1730,* edited by James Hardin (1996)

169 *American Poets Since World War II, Fifth Series,* edited by Joseph Conte (1996)

170 *The British Literary Book Trade, 1475–1700,* edited by James K. Bracken and Joel Silver (1996)

171 *Twentieth-Century American Sportswriters,* edited by Richard Orodenker (1996)

172 *Sixteenth-Century British Nondramatic Writers, Fourth Series,* edited by David A. Richardson (1996)

173 *American Novelists Since World War II, Fifth Series,* edited by James R. Giles and Wanda H. Giles (1996)

174 *British Travel Writers, 1876–1909,* edited by Barbara Brothers and Julia Gergits (1997)

175 *Native American Writers of the United States,* edited by Kenneth M. Roemer (1997)

176 *Ancient Greek Authors,* edited by Ward W. Briggs (1997)

177 *Italian Novelists Since World War II, 1945–1965,* edited by Augustus Pallotta (1997)

178 *British Fantasy and Science-Fiction Writers Before World War I,* edited by Darren Harris-Fain (1997)

179 *German Writers of the Renaissance and Reformation, 1280–1580,* edited by James Hardin and Max Reinhart (1997)

180 *Japanese Fiction Writers, 1868–1945,* edited by Van C. Gessel (1997)

181 *South Slavic Writers Since World War II,* edited by Vasa D. Mihailovich (1997)

182 *Japanese Fiction Writers Since World War II,* edited by Van C. Gessel (1997)

183 *American Travel Writers, 1776–1864,* edited by James J. Schramer and Donald Ross (1997)

184 *Nineteenth-Century British Book-Collectors and Bibliographers,* edited by William Baker and Kenneth Womack (1997)

185 *American Literary Journalists, 1945–1995, First Series,* edited by Arthur J. Kaul (1998)

186 *Nineteenth-Century American Western Writers,* edited by Robert L. Gale (1998)

187 *American Book Collectors and Bibliographers, Second Series,* edited by Joseph Rosenblum (1998)

188 *American Book and Magazine Illustrators to 1920,* edited by Steven E. Smith, Catherine A. Hastedt, and Donald H. Dyal (1998)

189 *American Travel Writers, 1850–1915,* edited by Donald Ross and James J. Schramer (1998)

190 *British Reform Writers, 1832–1914,* edited by Gary Kelly and Edd Applegate (1998)

191 *British Novelists Between the Wars,* edited by George M. Johnson (1998)

192 *French Dramatists, 1789–1914,* edited by Barbara T. Cooper (1998)

193 *American Poets Since World War II, Sixth Series,* edited by Joseph Conte (1998)

194 *British Novelists Since 1960, Second Series,* edited by Merritt Moseley (1998)

195 *British Travel Writers, 1910–1939,* edited by Barbara Brothers and Julia Gergits (1998)

196 *Italian Novelists Since World War II, 1965–1995,* edited by Augustus Pallotta (1999)

197 *Late-Victorian and Edwardian British Novelists, Second Series,* edited by George M. Johnson (1999)

198 *Russian Literature in the Age of Pushkin and Gogol: Prose,* edited by Christine A. Rydel (1999)

199 *Victorian Women Poets,* edited by William B. Thesing (1999)

200 *American Women Prose Writers to 1820,* edited by Carla J. Mulford, with Angela Vietto and Amy E. Winans (1999)

201 *Twentieth-Century British Book Collectors and Bibliographers,* edited by William Baker and Kenneth Womack (1999)

202 *Nineteenth-Century American Fiction Writers,* edited by Kent P. Ljungquist (1999)

203 *Medieval Japanese Writers,* edited by Steven D. Carter (1999)

204 *British Travel Writers, 1940–1997,* edited by Barbara Brothers and Julia M. Gergits (1999)

205 *Russian Literature in the Age of Pushkin and Gogol: Poetry and Drama,* edited by Christine A. Rydel (1999)

206 *Twentieth-Century American Western Writers, First Series,* edited by Richard H. Cracroft (1999)

207 *British Novelists Since 1960, Third Series,* edited by Merritt Moseley (1999)

208 *Literature of the French and Occitan Middle Ages: Eleventh to Fifteenth Centuries,* edited by Deborah Sinnreich-Levi and Ian S. Laurie (1999)

209 *Chicano Writers, Third Series,* edited by Francisco A. Lomelí and Carl R. Shirley (1999)

210 *Ernest Hemingway: A Documentary Volume,* edited by Robert W. Trogdon (1999)

211 *Ancient Roman Writers,* edited by Ward W. Briggs (1999)

212 *Twentieth-Century American Western Writers, Second Series,* edited by Richard H. Cracroft (1999)

213 *Pre-Nineteenth-Century British Book Collectors and Bibliographers,* edited by William Baker and Kenneth Womack (1999)

214 *Twentieth-Century Danish Writers,* edited by Marianne Stecher-Hansen (1999)

215 *Twentieth-Century Eastern European Writers, First Series,* edited by Steven Serafin (1999)

216 *British Poets of the Great War: Brooke, Rosenberg, Thomas. A Documentary Volume,* edited by Patrick Quinn (2000)

217 *Nineteenth-Century French Poets,* edited by Robert Beum (2000)

218 *American Short-Story Writers Since World War II, Second Series,* edited by Patrick Meanor and Gwen Crane (2000)

219 *F. Scott Fitzgerald's* The Great Gatsby: *A Documentary Volume,* edited by Matthew J. Bruccoli (2000)

220 *Twentieth-Century Eastern European Writers, Second Series,* edited by Steven Serafin (2000)

221 *American Women Prose Writers, 1870–1920,* edited by Sharon M. Harris, with the assistance of Heidi L. M. Jacobs and Jennifer Putzi (2000)

222 *H. L. Mencken: A Documentary Volume,* edited by Richard J. Schrader (2000)

223 *The American Renaissance in New England, Second Series,* edited by Wesley T. Mott (2000)

224 *Walt Whitman: A Documentary Volume,* edited by Joel Myerson (2000)

225 *South African Writers,* edited by Paul A. Scanlon (2000)

226 *American Hard-Boiled Crime Writers,* edited by George Parker Anderson and Julie B. Anderson (2000)

227 *American Novelists Since World War II, Sixth Series,* edited by James R. Giles and Wanda H. Giles (2000)

228 *Twentieth-Century American Dramatists, Second Series,* edited by Christopher J. Wheatley (2000)

229 *Thomas Wolfe: A Documentary Volume,* edited by Ted Mitchell (2001)

230 *Australian Literature, 1788–1914,* edited by Selina Samuels (2001)

231 *British Novelists Since 1960, Fourth Series,* edited by Merritt Moseley (2001)

232 *Twentieth-Century Eastern European Writers, Third Series,* edited by Steven Serafin (2001)

233 *British and Irish Dramatists Since World War II, Second Series,* edited by John Bull (2001)

234 *American Short-Story Writers Since World War II, Third Series,* edited by Patrick Meanor and Richard E. Lee (2001)

235 *The American Renaissance in New England, Third Series,* edited by Wesley T. Mott (2001)

236 *British Rhetoricians and Logicians, 1500–1660,* edited by Edward A. Malone (2001)

237 *The Beats: A Documentary Volume,* edited by Matt Theado (2001)

238 *Russian Novelists in the Age of Tolstoy and Dostoevsky,* edited by J. Alexander Ogden and Judith E. Kalb (2001)

239 *American Women Prose Writers: 1820–1870,* edited by Amy E. Hudock and Katharine Rodier (2001)

240 *Late Nineteenth- and Early Twentieth-Century British Women Poets,* edited by William B. Thesing (2001)

241 *American Sportswriters and Writers on Sport,* edited by Richard Orodenker (2001)

242 *Twentieth-Century European Cultural Theorists, First Series,* edited by Paul Hansom (2001)

243 *The American Renaissance in New England, Fourth Series,* edited by Wesley T. Mott (2001)

244 *American Short-Story Writers Since World War II, Fourth Series,* edited by Patrick Meanor and Joseph McNicholas (2001)

245 *British and Irish Dramatists Since World War II, Third Series,* edited by John Bull (2001)

246 *Twentieth-Century American Cultural Theorists,* edited by Paul Hansom (2001)

247 *James Joyce: A Documentary Volume,* edited by A. Nicholas Fargnoli (2001)

248 *Antebellum Writers in the South, Second Series,* edited by Kent Ljungquist (2001)

249 *Twentieth-Century American Dramatists, Third Series,* edited by Christopher Wheatley (2002)

250 *Antebellum Writers in New York, Second Series,* edited by Kent Ljungquist (2002)

251 *Canadian Fantasy and Science-Fiction Writers,* edited by Douglas Ivison (2002)

252 *British Philosophers, 1500–1799,* edited by Philip B. Dematteis and Peter S. Fosl (2002)

253 *Raymond Chandler: A Documentary Volume,* edited by Robert Moss (2002)

254 *The House of Putnam, 1837–1872: A Documentary Volume,* edited by Ezra Greenspan (2002)

255 *British Fantasy and Science-Fiction Writers, 1918–1960,* edited by Darren Harris-Fain (2002)

256 *Twentieth-Century American Western Writers, Third Series,* edited by Richard H. Cracroft (2002)

257 *Twentieth-Century Swedish Writers After World War II,* edited by Ann-Charlotte Gavel Adams (2002)

258 *Modern French Poets,* edited by Jean-François Leroux (2002)

259 *Twentieth-Century Swedish Writers Before World War II,* edited by Ann-Charlotte Gavel Adams (2002)

260 *Australian Writers, 1915–1950,* edited by Selina Samuels (2002)

261 *British Fantasy and Science-Fiction Writers Since 1960,* edited by Darren Harris-Fain (2002)

262 *British Philosophers, 1800–2000,* edited by Peter S. Fosl and Leemon B. McHenry (2002)

263 *William Shakespeare: A Documentary Volume,* edited by Catherine Loomis (2002)

264 *Italian Prose Writers, 1900–1945,* edited by Luca Somigli and Rocco Capozzi (2002)

265 *American Song Lyricists, 1920–1960,* edited by Philip Furia (2002)

266 *Twentieth-Century American Dramatists, Fourth Series,* edited by Christopher J. Wheatley (2002)

267 *Twenty-First-Century British and Irish Novelists,* edited by Michael R. Molino (2002)

268 *Seventeenth-Century French Writers,* edited by Françoise Jaouën (2002)

269 *Nathaniel Hawthorne: A Documentary Volume,* edited by Benjamin Franklin V (2002)

270 *American Philosophers Before 1950,* edited by Philip B. Dematteis and Leemon B. McHenry (2002)

271 *British and Irish Novelists Since 1960,* edited by Merritt Moseley (2002)

272 *Russian Prose Writers Between the World Wars,* edited by Christine Rydel (2003)

273 *F. Scott Fitzgerald's* Tender Is the Night: *A Documentary Volume,* edited by Matthew J. Bruccoli and George Parker Anderson (2003)

274 *John Dos Passos's* U.S.A.: *A Documentary Volume,* edited by Donald Pizer (2003)

275 *Twentieth-Century American Nature Writers: Prose,* edited by Roger Thompson and J. Scott Bryson (2003)

276 *British Mystery and Thriller Writers Since 1960,* edited by Gina Macdonald (2003)

277 *Russian Literature in the Age of Realism,* edited by Alyssa Dinega Gillespie (2003)

278 *American Novelists Since World War II, Seventh Series,* edited by James R. Giles and Wanda H. Giles (2003)

279 *American Philosophers, 1950–2000,* edited by Philip B. Dematteis and Leemon B. McHenry (2003)

280 *Dashiell Hammett's* The Maltese Falcon: *A Documentary Volume,* edited by Richard Layman (2003)

281 *British Rhetoricians and Logicians, 1500–1660, Second Series,* edited by Edward A. Malone (2003)

282 *New Formalist Poets,* edited by Jonathan N. Barron and Bruce Meyer (2003)

283 *Modern Spanish American Poets, First Series,* edited by María A. Salgado (2003)

284 *The House of Holt, 1866–1946: A Documentary Volume,* edited by Ellen D. Gilbert (2003)

285 *Russian Writers Since 1980,* edited by Marina Balina and Mark Lipovetsky (2004)

286 *Castilian Writers, 1400–1500,* edited by Frank A. Domínguez and George D. Greenia (2004)

287 *Portuguese Writers,* edited by Monica Rector and Fred M. Clark (2004)

288 *The House of Boni & Liveright, 1917–1933: A Documentary Volume,* edited by Charles Egleston (2004)

289 *Australian Writers, 1950–1975,* edited by Selina Samuels (2004)

290 *Modern Spanish American Poets, Second Series,* edited by María A. Salgado (2004)

291 *The Hoosier House: Bobbs-Merrill and Its Predecessors, 1850–1985: A Documentary Volume,* edited by Richard J. Schrader (2004)

292 *Twenty-First-Century American Novelists,* edited by Lisa Abney and Suzanne Disheroon-Green (2004)

293 *Icelandic Writers,* edited by Patrick J. Stevens (2004)

294 *James Gould Cozzens: A Documentary Volume,* edited by Matthew J. Bruccoli (2004)

295 *Russian Writers of the Silver Age, 1890–1925,* edited by Judith E. Kalb and J. Alexander Ogden with the collaboration of I. G. Vishnevetsky (2004)

296 *Twentieth-Century European Cultural Theorists, Second Series,* edited by Paul Hansom (2004)

297 *Twentieth-Century Norwegian Writers,* edited by Tanya Thresher (2004)

298 *Henry David Thoreau: A Documentary Volume,* edited by Richard J. Schneider (2004)

299 *Holocaust Novelists,* edited by Efraim Sicher (2004)

300 *Danish Writers from the Reformation to Decadence, 1550–1900,* edited by Marianne Stecher-Hansen (2004)

301 *Gustave Flaubert: A Documentary Volume,* edited by Éric Le Calvez (2004)

Dictionary of Literary Biography Documentary Series

1 *Sherwood Anderson, Willa Cather, John Dos Passos, Theodore Dreiser, F. Scott Fitzgerald, Ernest Hemingway, Sinclair Lewis,* edited by Margaret A. Van Antwerp (1982)

2 *James Gould Cozzens, James T. Farrell, William Faulkner, John O'Hara, John Steinbeck, Thomas Wolfe, Richard Wright,* edited by Margaret A. Van Antwerp (1982)

3 *Saul Bellow, Jack Kerouac, Norman Mailer, Vladimir Nabokov, John Updike, Kurt Vonnegut,* edited by Mary Bruccoli (1983)

4 *Tennessee Williams,* edited by Margaret A. Van Antwerp and Sally Johns (1984)

5 *American Transcendentalists,* edited by Joel Myerson (1988)

6 *Hardboiled Mystery Writers: Raymond Chandler, Dashiell Hammett, Ross Macdonald,* edited by Matthew J. Bruccoli and Richard Layman (1989)

7 *Modern American Poets: James Dickey, Robert Frost, Marianne Moore,* edited by Karen L. Rood (1989)

8 *The Black Aesthetic Movement,* edited by Jeffrey Louis Decker (1991)

9 *American Writers of the Vietnam War: W. D. Ehrhart, Larry Heinemann, Tim O'Brien, Walter McDonald, John M. Del Vecchio,* edited by Ronald Baughman (1991)

10 *The Bloomsbury Group,* edited by Edward L. Bishop (1992)

11 *American Proletarian Culture: The Twenties and The Thirties,* edited by Jon Christian Suggs (1993)

12 *Southern Women Writers: Flannery O'Connor, Katherine Anne Porter, Eudora Welty,* edited by Mary Ann Wimsatt and Karen L. Rood (1994)

13 *The House of Scribner, 1846–1904,* edited by John Delaney (1996)

14 *Four Women Writers for Children, 1868–1918,* edited by Caroline C. Hunt (1996)

15 *American Expatriate Writers: Paris in the Twenties,* edited by Matthew J. Bruccoli and Robert W. Trogdon (1997)

16 *The House of Scribner, 1905–1930,* edited by John Delaney (1997)

17 *The House of Scribner, 1931–1984,* edited by John Delaney (1998)

18 *British Poets of The Great War: Sassoon, Graves, Owen,* edited by Patrick Quinn (1999)

19 *James Dickey,* edited by Judith S. Baughman (1999)

See also DLB 210, 216, 219, 222, 224, 229, 237, 247, 253, 254, 263, 269, 273, 274, 280, 284, 288, 291, 294, 298, 301

Dictionary of Literary Biography Yearbooks

1980 edited by Karen L. Rood, Jean W. Ross, and Richard Ziegfeld (1981)

1981 edited by Karen L. Rood, Jean W. Ross, and Richard Ziegfeld (1982)

1982 edited by Richard Ziegfeld; associate editors: Jean W. Ross and Lynne C. Zeigler (1983)

1983 edited by Mary Bruccoli and Jean W. Ross; associate editor Richard Ziegfeld (1984)

1984 edited by Jean W. Ross (1985)

1985 edited by Jean W. Ross (1986)

1986 edited by J. M. Brook (1987)

1987 edited by J. M. Brook (1988)

1988 edited by J. M. Brook (1989)

1989 edited by J. M. Brook (1990)

1990 edited by James W. Hipp (1991)

1991 edited by James W. Hipp (1992)

1992 edited by James W. Hipp (1993)

1993 edited by James W. Hipp, contributing editor George Garrett (1994)

1994 edited by James W. Hipp, contributing editor George Garrett (1995)

1995 edited by James W. Hipp, contributing editor George Garrett (1996)

1996 edited by Samuel W. Bruce and L. Kay Webster, contributing editor George Garrett (1997)

1997 edited by Matthew J. Bruccoli and George Garrett, with the assistance of L. Kay Webster (1998)

1998 edited by Matthew J. Bruccoli, contributing editor George Garrett, with the assistance of D. W. Thomas (1999)

1999 edited by Matthew J. Bruccoli, contributing editor George Garrett, with the assistance of D. W. Thomas (2000)

2000 edited by Matthew J. Bruccoli, contributing editor George Garrett, with the assistance of George Parker Anderson (2001)

2001 edited by Matthew J. Bruccoli, contributing editor George Garrett, with the assistance of George Parker Anderson (2002)

2002 edited by Matthew J. Bruccoli and George Garrett; George Parker Anderson, Assistant Editor (2003)

Concise Series

Concise Dictionary of American Literary Biography, 7 volumes (1988–1999): *The New Consciousness, 1941–1968; Colonization to the American Renaissance, 1640–1865; Realism, Naturalism, and Local Color, 1865–1917; The Twenties, 1917–1929; The Age of Maturity, 1929–1941; Broadening Views, 1968–1988; Supplement: Modern Writers, 1900–1998.*

Concise Dictionary of British Literary Biography, 8 volumes (1991–1992): *Writers of the Middle Ages and Renaissance Before 1660; Writers of the Restoration and Eighteenth Century, 1660–1789; Writers of the Romantic Period, 1789–1832; Victorian Writers, 1832–1890; Late-Victorian and Edwardian Writers, 1890–1914; Modern Writers, 1914–1945; Writers After World War II, 1945–1960; Contemporary Writers, 1960 to Present.*

Concise Dictionary of World Literary Biography, 4 volumes (1999–2000): *Ancient Greek and Roman Writers; German Writers; African, Caribbean, and Latin American Writers; South Slavic and Eastern European Writers.*

Dictionary of Literary Biography® • Volume Three Hundred One

Gustave Flaubert: A Documentary Volume

Dictionary of Literary Biography® • Volume Three Hundred One

Gustave Flaubert: A Documentary Volume

Edited by
Éric Le Calvez
Georgia State University

A Bruccoli Clark Layman Book

THOMSON
GALE

Detroit • New York • San Francisco • San Diego • New Haven, Conn. • Waterville, Maine • London • Munich

THOMSON
GALE

Dictionary of Literary Biography
Volume 301: Gustave Flaubert:
A Documentary Volume
Éric Le Calvez

Editorial Directors
Matthew J. Bruccoli and Richard Layman

For more information, contact
Thomson Gale
27500 Drake Rd.
Farmington Hills, MI 48331-3535
Or you can visit our Internet site at
http://www.gale.com

LIBRARY OF CONGRESS CATALOGING-IN-PUBLICATION DATA

Gustave Flaubert : a documentary volume / edited by Éric Le Calvez.
p. cm. — (Dictionary of literary biography ; v. 301)
"A Bruccoli Clark Layman Book."
Includes bibliographical references and index.
ISBN 0-7876-6838-9 (hardcover : alk. paper)
1. Flaubert, Gustave, 1821–1880. 2. Novelists, French—19th century—Biography. I. Le Calvez, Éric. II. Series.

PQ2247.G84 2004
843'.8—dc22
2004010067

Printed in the United States of America
10 9 8 7 6 5 4 3 2 1

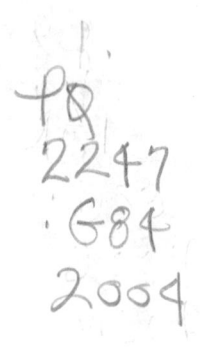

Contents

Plan of the Series xvii

Preface xix

Acknowledgments xxi

Permissions xxii

Books by Gustave Flaubert 3

Chronology 8

Flaubert's Youth: 1821–1844 19

Home, School, and Élisa Schlésinger 19

The Hôtel-Dieu–from Herbert Lottman, *Flaubert: A Biography*

Élisa–from Lottman, *Flaubert: A Biography*

Early Stories 26

A Lecture on Natural History–Genus: *Clerk*–from Robert Griffin, *Early Writings: Gustave Flaubert*

The *Bêtise* of Bourgeois Life–from Eric Gans, *The Discovery of Illusion: Flaubert's Early Works, 1835–1837*

Reading *Mémoires d'un fou*–from Shoshana Felman, "Gustave Flaubert: Living Writing, or Madness as Cliché," in *Writing and Madness*

Facsimile: First page of the manuscript of "Louis XIII"

Facsimile: Manuscript of "The Beautiful Explanation of Famous Constipation"

Flaubert's *Intimate Notebook* 43

A Writer's Ambitions–from Flaubert, *Intimate Notebook, 1840–1841*

Sartre on Flaubert's Nervous Attack 46

The Event–from Jean-Paul Sartre, *The Family Idiot, Gustave Flaubert 1821–1857*

Trouville–from Griffin, *Early Writings: Gustave Flaubert*

Facsimile: First page of the manuscript of "Smar"

A New Life: 1844–1851 58

A Tumultuous Year: 1846 58

Flaubert letter to Maxime Du Camp, 25 March 1846

Flaubert's Correspondence

Flaubert letter to Louise Colet, 6 or 7 August 1846

Flaubert letter to Colet, 18 September 1846

Facsimile: Flaubert letter to Colet, 7 March 1847

A Journey and a Revolution 69

Westward with Du Camp–from Herbert Lottman, *Flaubert: A Biography*

Writing *La Tentation de saint Antoine* 73

La Tentation de Saint Antoine (1848–9)–from Enid Starkie, *Flaubert: The Making of the Master*

Flaubert and the Representation of Memory–from Georges Poulet, *Studies in Human Time*

"A Long, Morose Meditation"–from *La Première Éducation sentimentale*

Flaubert in the Middle East 79

Flaubert letter to Anne-Justine-Caroline Flaubert, 17 November 1849

Du Camp's Photographs

Racing to the Sphinx–from Francis Steegmuller, *Flaubert in Egypt: A Sensibility on Tour*

Climbing the Great Pyramid–from Steegmuller, *Flaubert in Egypt: A Sensibility on Tour*

Flaubert letter to Anne-Justine-Caroline Flaubert, 5 January 1850

From Kena to Koseir and the Red Sea–from Steegmuller, *Flaubert in Egypt: A Sensibility on Tour*

The Long Journey Home

The Years of *Madame Bovary:* 1851–1857 92

Writing *Madame Bovary* 92

Flaubert letter to Louise Colet, 16 January 1852

Flaubert letter to Colet, 24 April 1852

Facsimile: One of the multiple drafts of the first page of *Madame Bovary*

Flaubert letter to Colet, 25 June 1853

Flaubert letter to Colet, 25 October 1853

Facsimile: Scenario notes for the preparation of the writing of part 2, chapter 1 of *Madame Bovary*

Flaubert letter to Colet, 23 December 1853

Facsimile: Flaubert's map of Yonville-L'Abbaye

Flaubert letter to Colet, 13 January 1854

Facsimile: One of the multiple sketches for the beginning of part 3 of *Madame Bovary*

The End of the Affair 101

A View of Flaubert–from Louise Colet, *Lui. A View of Him*

Flaubert on *Lui*–from Flaubert letter to Amélie Bosquet

Facsimile: Last letter from Flaubert to Colet, 6 March 1855

Haunted by Flaubert–from Francine du Plessix Gray, *Rage and Fire: A Life of Louise Colet*

On Colet's Death–from Flaubert letter to Edma Roger des Genettes

The Trial of *Madame Bovary* 109

Pinard for the Prosecution

Facsimile: Page from the publication of *Madame Bovary* in the *Revue de Paris*

Flaubert on Illustrations

Sénard for the Defense

Flaubert on the Trial–from Flaubert letter to Achille Flaubert, 30 January 1857

Reception of *Madame Bovary* 141

Sainte-Beuve on Flaubert's "New Literary Manner"–review, *Le Moniteur Universel,* 4 May 1857

Facsimile: Flaubert's inscription to Charles Asselineau

Facsimile: Flaubert's annotation on page 232 of *Madame Bovary*

Baudelaire on the Greatness of *Madame Bovary*–review, *L'Artiste,* 18 October 1857

Critical Views of *Madame Bovary* 155

Flaubert's Disagreeable Masterpiece–from Henry James, "Charles de Bernard and Gustave Flaubert," *Galaxy,* February 1876

Madame Bovary and the Battle for Zamboanga–from Patrick O'Connor, *Don't Look Back: A Memoir*

Art Remains: Nabokov's Notes on *Madame Bovary*–from Vladimir Nabokov, *Lectures on Literature*

Facsimile: The opening pages of Nabokov's annotated copy of *Madame Bovary*

Facsimile: Nabokov's notes on Charles Bovary's cap, with his drawing of the cap

Facsimile: Nabokov's annotations to pages 36 and 37 of his copy of *Madame Bovary*

Facsimile: One of Nabokov's lists regarding problems with the Aveling translation

Madame Bovary after a Century–essay by Benjamin F. Bart, in *Madame Bovary and the Critics: A Collection of Essays*

Windows and the Plunging View–from Jean Rousset, "*Madame Bovary* or the Book about Nothing," in *Flaubert. A Collection of Critical Essays*

Robbe-Grillet on Flaubert–from Alain Robbe-Grillet, *Ghosts in the Mirror*

Emma Bovary's Eyes–from Julian Barnes, *Flaubert's Parrot*

***Salammbô* and Antiquity: 1857–1863** 181

Research for a Novel of the Ancient World 181

Facsimile: Pages from Flaubert's travel book number 10

A Purple Novel 186

A Reading of *Salammbô*–from the Goncourts' *Journals,* 6 May 1861

Laure de Maupassant letter to Flaubert, 6 December 1862

Facsimile: Pages from drafts of Mâtho's encounter with Salammbô

Flaubert Responds to His Critics: The Polemics of *Salammbô* 190

Flaubert to Charles-Augustin Sainte-Beuve, 23–24 December 1862

The Popularity of *Salammbô*

Flaubert to Guillaume Froehner, 21 January 1863

Critical Views of *Salammbô* 203

The Harmony of *Salammbô*–Arthur Symons, "Gustave Flaubert," in *Figures of Several Centuries*

Salammbô as a Modern Historical Novel–from Georg Lukács, *The Historical Novel*

Salammbô Bound–from Naomi Schor, *Breaking the Chain*

***L'Éducation sentimentale:* 1863–1869** 222

A New Novel with an Old Title 222

Flaubert letter to George Sand, 2 February 1869

Sand letter to Flaubert, 11 February 1869

Sand as Defender 225

Sand letter to Flaubert, 30 November 1869

Facsimile: Preliminary notes for *L'Éducation sentimentale*

Flaubert letter to Sand, 3 December 1869

Flaubert letter to Sand, 7 December 1869

Sand letter to Flaubert, 9–10 December 1869

Flaubert letter to Sand, 10 December 1869

Sand letter to Flaubert, 10–11 December 1869

Critical Views of *L'Éducation sentimentale* 229

An Epic without Air: James on *L'Éducation sentimentale*–Henry James, "Gustave Flaubert," in *Notes on Novelists*

Stylistic Faults in *L'Éducation sentimentale*–John Middleton Murry, "Gustave Flaubert, 1821–1880," in *Countries of the Mind*

Flaubert's Politics–from Edmund Wilson, *The Triple Thinkers*

George Sand's First Magny Dinner–from Sand's diary, 12 February 1866

Facsimile: Page from Sand's diary, 12 February 1866

L'Éducation sentimentale: Profanation and the Permanence of Dreams–from Victor Brombert, *The Novels of Flaubert*

Facsimile: Page from a draft describing Nogent-sur-Seine

Scenes of Revolution

Facsimile: Page from a draft describing the people invading the Tuileries palace

Facsimile: Page from a sketch describing Frédéric and Rosanette's visit to Fontainebleau

Time in *L'Éducation sentimentale*–from Georg Lukács, *The Theory of the Novel*

Facsimile: Pages from notebook describing Fontainebleau forest

The Rhetoric of *L'Éducation sentimentale*–from John Porter Houston, "Flaubert," in *The Traditions of French Prose Style*

Facsimile: Page from a sketch of the Fontainebleau episode

Facsimile: Page from a draft describing the last encounter between Frédéric and Madame Arnoux

Facsimile: Flaubert's letter to Jules Duplan, 16 May 1869

***La Tentation de saint Antoine,* a Lifetime's Work: 1870–1874** 268

The Legacy of Louis Bouilhet 268

Gustave Flaubert, "Preface to the *Last Songs* of Louis Bouilhet" (1872)

The Failure of *Le Candidat* 274

Flaubert letter to Sand, 12 March 1874

Sand letter to Flaubert, 14 March 1874

Flaubert letter to Sand, 15 March 1874

Sand letter to Flaubert, 3 April 1874

Flaubert letter to Sand, 8 April 1874

Sand letter to Flaubert, 10 April 1874

Critical Views of *La Tentation de saint Antoine* 279

Flaubert's *Temptation of Saint Anthony*–review by Henry James in *The Nation,* 4 June 1874

Facsimile: Page of notes for *La Tentation de saint Antoine*

Facsimile: Page from manuscript of Ivan Turgenev's article on *La Tentation de saint Antoine*

The Last Confession of Flaubert–from Georg Brandes, "Gustave Flaubert," in *Creative Spirits of the Nineteenth Century*

Improving *La Tentation de saint Antoine*–from George Saintsbury, preface to *Tales from Flaubert*

A Monument to Erudition–from Michel Foucault, "Fantasia of the Library," in *Language, Counter-Memory, Practice*

Projection as Ego Defense: Flaubert's *Tentation de saint Antoine*–from Laurence M. Porter, *The Literary Dream in French Romanticism: A Psychoanalytic Interpretation*

Final Years: 1874–1880 311

Beginning *Bouvard et Pécuchet* 311

Flaubert letter to Turgenev, 25 July 1874

Flaubert letter to Turgenev, 22 September 1874

The Commanville Collapse 313

Sand letter to Flaubert, 15 August 1875

Flaubert letter to Sand, 18 August 1875

Flaubert letter to Sand, 3 October 1875

Sand letter to Flaubert, 8 October 1875

Flaubert letter to Sand, 11 October 1875

Sand's Death and *Trois Contes* 317

Turgenev letter to Flaubert, 18 June 1876

Flaubert letter to Turgenev, 25 June 1876

Turgenev letter to Flaubert, 19 December 1876

Flaubert letter to Turgenev, 24 December 1876

Facsimile: First manuscript page of Turgenev's translation of "Hérodias"

Last Years 322

Flaubert letter to Turgenev, 19 July 1877

Turgenev letter to Flaubert, 24 July 1877

Flaubert letter to Turgenev, 27 July 1877

Facsimile: Flaubert letter to his publisher Georges Charpentier, 16 February 1879

Sundays with Flaubert–from Henry James, "Gustave Flaubert," in *Notes on Novelists*

Flaubert letter to Turgenev, 9 August 1879

Flaubert letter to Turgenev, 7 April 1880

The Last Saint Polycarp Dinner–from Flaubert letter to Caroline Commanville, 28 April 1880

Facsimile: Menu for the last "Saint Polycarp" celebration, 27 April 1880

Facsimile: One of Flaubert's last letters to Guy de Maupassant

Flaubert's Death 330

Guy de Maupassant letter to Turgenev, 25 May 1880

Critical Views of *Trois Contes* and *Bouvard et Pécuchet* 332

Profane, Sacred: Disorder of Utterance in *Trois Contes*–Raymonde Debray-Genette, essay in *Flaubert and Postmodernism*

Facsimile: First page of the final manuscript of "Un cœur simple"

Facsimile: Two of the sketches Flaubert wrote for "Hérodias"

Fetishism and Allegory in *Bouvard et Pécuchet*–Charles Bernheimer, essay in *Flaubert and Postmodernism*

Facsimile: One of the research lists Flaubert made for *Bouvard et Pécuchet*

Facsimile: Notes on Dom Calmet's *Dissertation sur les apparitions*

Bouvard et Pécuchet and the End of Dialogue–Stirling Haig, essay in his *Flaubert and the Gift of Speech. Dialogue and Discourse in Four Modern Novels*

Facsimile: Page from a draft for *Bouvard et Pécuchet,* chapter 8

Checklist of Further Readings 361

Cumulative Index 367

Plan of the Series

. . . Almost the most prodigious asset of a country, and perhaps its most precious possession, is its native literary product—when that product is fine and noble and enduring.

Mark Twain*

The advisory board, the editors, and the publisher of the *Dictionary of Literary Biography* are joined in endorsing Mark Twain's declaration. The literature of a nation provides an inexhaustible resource of permanent worth. Our purpose is to make literature and its creators better understood and more accessible to students and the reading public, while satisfying the needs of teachers and researchers.

To meet these requirements, *literary biography* has been construed in terms of the author's achievement. The most important thing about a writer is his writing. Accordingly, the entries in *DLB* are career biographies, tracing the development of the author's canon and the evolution of his reputation.

The purpose of *DLB* is not only to provide reliable information in a usable format but also to place the figures in the larger perspective of literary history and to offer appraisals of their accomplishments by qualified scholars.

The publication plan for *DLB* resulted from two years of preparation. The project was proposed to Bruccoli Clark by Frederick G. Ruffner, president of the Gale Research Company, in November 1975. After specimen entries were prepared and typeset, an advisory board was formed to refine the entry format and develop the series rationale. In meetings held during 1976, the publisher, series editors, and advisory board approved the scheme for a comprehensive biographical dictionary of persons who contributed to literature. Editorial work on the first volume began in January 1977, and it was published in 1978. In order to make *DLB* more than a dictionary and to compile volumes that individually have claim to status as literary history, it was decided to organize volumes by topic, period, or genre. Each of these freestanding volumes provides a biographical-bibliographical guide and overview for a particular area of literature. We are convinced that this organization—as opposed to a single alphabet method—constitutes a valuable innovation in the presentation of reference material. The volume plan necessarily requires many decisions for the placement and treatment of authors. Certain figures will be included in separate volumes, but with different entries emphasizing the aspect of his career appropriate to each volume. Ernest Hemingway, for example, is represented in *American Writers in Paris, 1920–1939* by an entry focusing on his expatriate apprenticeship; he is also in *American Novelists, 1910–1945* with an entry surveying his entire career, as well as in *American Short-Story Writers, 1910–1945, Second Series* with an entry concentrating on his short fiction. Each volume includes a cumulative index of the subject authors and articles.

Between 1981 and 2002 the series was augmented and updated by the *DLB Yearbooks.* There have also been nineteen *DLB Documentary Series* volumes, which provide illustrations, facsimiles, and biographical and critical source materials for figures, works, or groups judged to have particular interest for students. In 1999 the *Documentary Series* was incorporated into the *DLB* volume numbering system beginning with *DLB 210: Ernest Hemingway.*

We define literature as the *intellectual commerce of a nation:* not merely as belles lettres but as that ample and complex process by which ideas are generated, shaped, and transmitted. *DLB* entries are not limited to "creative writers" but extend to other figures who in their time and in their way influenced the mind of a people. Thus the series encompasses historians, journalists, publishers, book collectors, and screenwriters. By this means readers of *DLB* may be aided to perceive literature not as cult scripture in the keeping of intellectual high priests but firmly positioned at the center of a nation's life.

DLB includes the major writers appropriate to each volume and those standing in the ranks behind them. Scholarly and critical counsel has been sought in deciding which minor figures to include and how full their entries should be. Wherever possible, useful refer-

**From an unpublished section of Mark Twain's autobiography, copyright by the Mark Twain Company* ences are made to figures who do not warrant separate entries.

Each *DLB* volume has an expert volume editor responsible for planning the volume, selecting the figures for inclusion, and assigning the entries. Volume editors are also responsible for preparing, where appropriate, appendices surveying the major periodicals and literary and intellectual movements for their volumes, as well as lists of further readings. Work on the series as a whole is coordinated at the Bruccoli Clark Layman editorial center in Columbia, South Carolina, where the editorial staff is responsible for accuracy and utility of the published volumes.

One feature that distinguishes *DLB* is the illustration policy–its concern with the iconography of literature. Just as an author is influenced by his surroundings, so is the reader's understanding of the author enhanced by a knowledge of his environment. Therefore *DLB* volumes include not only drawings, paintings, and photographs of authors, often depicting them at various stages in their careers, but also illustrations of their families and places where they lived. Title pages are regularly reproduced in facsimile along with dust jackets for modern authors. The dust jackets are a special feature of *DLB* because they often document better than anything else the way in which an author's work was perceived in its own time. Specimens of the writers' manuscripts and letters are included when feasible.

Samuel Johnson rightly decreed that "The chief glory of every people arises from its authors." The purpose of the *Dictionary of Literary Biography* is to compile literary history in the surest way available to us–by accurate and comprehensive treatment of the lives and work of those who contributed to it.

The *DLB* Advisory Board

Preface

Despite the persistence of a family legend that had Gustave Flaubert only learning to read when he was nine years old, just before he started attending school, Flaubert in fact was immersed in stories at an early age. During his childhood and adolescence he composed all kinds of texts, from small plays and essays to tales and short stories. Although he saved his juvenile manuscripts, he published little—a pattern that remained true in his later years as well. Later, when he was a law student and after he had abandoned legal studies because of the onset of a nervous disease, he continued to write regularly, producing travel narratives, novels, tales, and plays. He did not publish his first and most celebrated novel, *Madame Bovary,* until he was thirty-seven years old.

In his adult life, Flaubert never ceased devoting himself to his literary work. He read widely and deeply, studying Greek, Latin, and English writers as well as the French classics and contemporary works. He also did prodigious research, for he felt the need to know about all aspects of the topics touched on in the works he planned before he began writing. Fortunately for Flaubert, he did not need to earn money in order to live and could pursue his interests. Although Flaubert's family was not extraordinarily wealthy, his father was a respected surgeon and his parents made investments in real estate and farms, which provided stable income. He was thereby enabled to spend his life amid his books and manuscripts, which for him represented a freedom that was essential to carry out his craft.

While most readers first think of *Madame Bovary* when Flaubert's name is mentioned, it should be stressed that Flaubert's works are varied and that each is deserving of attention. The novels or long works—doubtless the most renowned and successful of his texts—alternate between contemporary topics, which are treated in his first, third, and fifth novels: *Madame Bovary* (1857), *L'Éducation sentimentale* (1869), and *Bouvard et Pécuchet* (1881); and ancient times, which are treated in his second and fourth works: the novel *Salammbô* (1862) and the difficult-to-classify *La Tentation de saint Antoine* (1874). Critics often relate this dichotomy to a tension between realism and Romanticism in Flaubert's writing. A similar variety appears in a condensed way in *Trois contes* (1877), inspired by three different periods: contemporary ("Un cœur simple"), medieval ("La Légende de saint Julien l'Hospitalier"), and ancient ("Hérodias").

Even if one takes into account the fact that Flaubert died before he was fifty-nine, his production of published works is modest—four major novels, the last left incomplete; *La Tentation;* a collection of three short tales; one *féerie* that he wrote with two others; and one play—especially when one considers his devotion to his literary avocation. Although some ill-intentioned critics have blamed Flaubert for his inability to write facilely, the real difficulty stems directly from his writing method. He spent approximately five years to complete a long work, polishing it until he obtained a final version that met his exacting standard. Flaubert always spent a long period planning and then spent enormous amounts of time rewriting and revising his work as he made slow but certain progress. His corrections and deletions are quite visible on the manuscripts; sometimes he wrote and corrected twenty pages in order to obtain one single page. There are some 4,800 pages of rough drafts for *L'Éducation sentimentale,* a novel that is about 400 pages long in its definitive version.

Flaubert believed that writing was an Art. He strongly adhered to the ideas of the writers—such as his friend Théophile Gautier—who defended the belief in Art for Art's own sake. His goal was always to reach Beauty, an ideal that he believed was independent from the chosen topic. Along with a constant search for the "mot juste" (the right word), he was also deeply concerned with images, rhythms, and sounds, for he focused simultaneously on all of the different levels of prose, as if he were writing poetry. While he was struggling with the sentences of *Madame Bovary,* he wrote to his mistress Louise Colet: "there are no noble subjects or ignoble subjects; from the standpoint of pure Art one might almost establish the axiom that there is no such thing as subject—style in itself being an absolute manner of seeing things." In another letter he wrote:

> I envision a style: a style that would be beautiful, that someone will invent some day, ten years or ten centuries from now, one that would be rhythmic as verse,

> precise as the language of the sciences, undulant, deep-voiced as a cello, tipped with flame: a style that would pierce your idea like a dagger, and on which your thought would sail easily ahead over a smooth surface, like a skiff before a good tail wind. Prose was born yesterday: you have to keep that in mind. Verse is the form par excellence of ancient literatures. All possible prosodic variations have been discovered; but that is far from being the case with prose.

Flaubert thought that only a single, specific form matches a given subject, so that each text should display a unique texture–the result of the artist's search for the "intrinsic poetics" of the work.

In the eyes of his contemporaries, Flaubert never again obtained the great success that he achieved with *Madame Bovary*. He even became so annoyed when people mentioned the novel to him that he came to wish he had not written it. The situation, though, especially in regard to his works subsequent to *Madame Bovary,* has changed. Thanks in particular to the publications from structuralists and literary theorists in the 1960s in France, Flaubert is now considered a master and is, along with Balzac and Proust, one of the French authors who attracts the most scholars around the world and on whom considerable research is still being conducted. Even more so, since the 1980s the genetic critics–who examine the writing process through the study of manuscripts–have developed a new dimension of studies into the writer's work. As almost all of his manuscripts have been preserved, geneticians can study, stage after stage, the multiple processes at work in Flaubert's rough drafts and show how the text came painstakingly into being: the future of Flaubertian studies is clearly guaranteed for a long time.

Flaubert is an appropriate choice as the first French writer to be included in the *Dictionary of Literary Biography* documentary series. Like other volumes in the series, *DLB 301: Gustave Flaubert* focuses on the writer at work throughout his entire career, presenting a suggestive variety of biographical sources and critical approaches. Although Flaubert hated illustrations and photographs (he even once said that he allowed no photograph to be taken of him, which is untrue, as can be seen from the volume), *DLB 301: Gustave Flaubert* includes a significant photographic record that opens up a literary life lived in nineteenth-century France. Besides personal and official documents, it comprises, for instance, photographs of Flaubert's manuscripts, of literary friends who, for the most, were Flaubert's faithful and longtime correspondents, and of places and things that inspired the writer. Together these illustrations provide the reader an excellent account of Flaubert's background during the years he composed his masterpieces.

This volume also reprints material concerning Flaubert's craft and his changing concerns as one project ended and the next began. Excerpts from his letters explain his work, his literary goals and doubts, his constant struggle to create a work of Art. His letters, too, show him engaged in a dialogue with important writers such as George Sand and Ivan Turgenev. Each section of the volume also includes substantial selections of literary criticism, as it testifies to the transformation that has affected the understanding of Flaubert since the nineteenth century. Some articles reveal the critical reception of the time, such as the reviews that Sainte-Beuve and Baudelaire wrote on *Madame Bovary;* others display contemporary misunderstandings. Moreover, as it seems that Flaubert has been rediscovered and newly appreciated during the second half of the twentieth century, it has been deemed desirable to reprint more-recent scholarly articles that approach the texts with diverse points of view and methods, particularly when they deal with what is the most significant in Flaubert's fictions: the change his Art and Style definitely brought to the novel as a genre.

–Éric Le Calvez

Acknowledgments

This book was produced by Bruccoli Clark Layman, Inc. George Parker Anderson was the in-house editor.

Production manager is Philip B. Dematteis.

Administrative support was provided by Ann M. Cheschi and Carol A. Cheschi.

Accountant is Ann-Marie Holland.

Copyediting supervisor is Sally R. Evans. The copyediting staff includes Phyllis A. Avant, Caryl Brown, Melissa D. Hinton, Philip I. Jones, Rebecca Mayo, Nadirah Rahimah Shabazz, and Nancy E. Smith.

Pipeline manager is James F. Tidd Jr.

Editorial associate is Joshua M. Robinson.

In-house prevetter is Catherine M. Polit.

Permissions editor is Amber L. Coker.

Layout and graphics supervisor is Janet E. Hill. The graphics staff includes Zoe R. Cook and Sydney E. Hammock.

Office manager is Kathy Lawler Merlette.

Photography editors are Mark J. McEwan and Walter W. Ross.

Digital photographic copy work was performed by Joseph M. Bruccoli.

Systems manager is Donald Kevin Starling.

Typesetting supervisor is Kathleen M. Flanagan. The typesetting staff includes Patricia Marie Flanagan, Mark J. McEwan, and Pamela D. Norton.

Walter W. Ross is library researcher. He was assisted by the following librarians at the Thomas Cooper Library of the University of South Carolina: Jo Cottingham, interlibrary loan department; circulation department head Tucker Taylor; reference department head Virginia W. Weathers; reference department staff Laurel Baker, Marilee Birchfield, Kate Boyd, Paul Cammarata, Joshua Garris, Gary Geer, Tom Marcil, Rose Marshall, and Sharon Verba; interlibrary loan department head Marna Hostetler; and interlibrary loan staff Bill Fetty, Nelson Rivera, and Cedric Rose.

The editor thanks the interlibrary-loan staff of Georgia State University's William Russell Pullen Library for diligently providing the requested volumes, as well as David Blumenfeld, Associate Dean of the College of Arts and Sciences, and John Austin, Chair of the Department of Modern and Classical Languages, for their support and encouragement.

I wish to thank Claude Bourret, curator at the Cabinet des Estampes, Bibliothèque nationale de France, Paris. In Rouen, I thank the staff of the *Réserve* at the Bibliothèque municipale de Rouen and Marie-Dominique Nobécourt Mutarelli, director of the ancient collection, for her welcome during my visit to the library. I also thank Sophie Demoy at the Musée Flaubert et d'Histoire de la Médecine: with a very good knowledge of the topic, she gave me a personal guided tour which was detailed and insightful.

I also wish to thank the following colleagues for providing always useful information: Guy Leach, librarian at Georgia State University, who helped me with great professionalism, Laurence M. Porter (Michigan State University), Mary Donaldson-Evans (University of Delaware), Jean-Max Guieu (Georgetown University), Jean-Pierre Leduc-Adine (ITEM-CNRS, Paris), Odile de Guidis (ITEM-CNRS, Paris), Stéphanie Dord-Crouslé (Lire-CNRS, Lyon), and finally Julia Mulatinho Simoes, my excellent graduate assistant. I am also very grateful to Matthew J. Bruccoli, Literary Personal Representative, for his constant advice during the preparation of the volume.

My special thanks go to Yvan Leclerc (Université de Rouen), who patiently answered my multiple questions.

Finally, my warmest thanks go to Bradley Deckert for his encouragement and exceptional technical support throughout this project.

Permissions

Bibliothèque de la Société de Géographie

Illustration on page 88, courtesy of the Bibliothèque de la Société de Géographie, Paris.

Bibliothèque de l'Institut de France

Illustrations on pages 109 and 238, courtesy of Bibliothèque de l'Institut de France, Paris.

Bibliothèque historique de la Ville de Paris

Illustrations on pages 143, 182, 183, 184, 185, 226, 252, and 253, courtesy of Bibliothèque historique de la Ville de Paris.

Bibliothèque municipale de Rouen

Illustrations on pages 27, 32, 36, 38, 43, 45, 48, 52, 59, 64, 74, 92, 94, 96, 98, 99, 181, 211, 213, 223, 231, 232, 260, 273, 286, 311, 327, 328, 330, 345, 348, and 351, cliché Bibliothèque municipale de Rouen.

Bibliothèque nationale de France

Illustrations on pages 7, 22, 24, 28, 34, 50, 54, 55, 56, 68, 69, 71, 80, 81, 84, 90, 100, 111, 114, 116, 118, 122, 133, 139, 142, 144, 148, 154, 186, 187, 188, 189, 190, 193, 196, 198, 201, 205, 206, 209, 215, 218, 219, 220, 222, 224, 225, 234, 236, 238, 240, 243, 246, 248, 250, 256, 257, 261, 265, 268, 269, 275, 280, 281, 283, 294, 299, 301, 312, 314, 321, 323, 326, 329, 336, 340, and 341, cliché Bibliothèque nationale de France, Paris.

Ilse Bischoff

Illustrations on pages 288, 303, 306, 307, and 308; from *The Temptation of Saint Antony,* by Gustave Flaubert (New York: Ives Washburn, 1930), wood engravings by Ilse Bischoff.

British Museum

Illustration on page 124, sketch by Jacques-Louis David; courtesy of the British Museum.

Royal S. Brown

Illustration on page 175; used by permission of Royal S. Brown.

Cambridge University Press

Stirling Haig, "Bouvard et Pécuchet and The End of Dialogue," in *Flaubert and the Gift of Speech. Dialogue and Discourse in Four Modern Novels* (Cambridge: Cambridge University Press, 1986), pp. 160–169. Reprinted with the permission of Cambridge University Press.

Columbia University Press

Salammbô Bound, Breaking the Chain. Women, Theory, and French Realist Fiction (New York: Columbia University Press, 1985), pp. 113–126. By permission of Columbia University Press.

Conseil Général de la Seine-Maritime, Rouen

Illustration on page 65, courtesy of Conseil Général de la Seine-Maritime, Rouen.

Cornell University Press

Excerpt from Michel Foucault, *Language, Counter-Memory, Practice. Selected Essays and Interviews,* edited by Donald F. Bouchard, translated by Bouchard and Sherry Simon (Ithaca, N.Y.: Cornell University Press, 1977), pp. 88–105. Reprinted with the permission of Cornell University Press.

Illustration on page 159; from *Nabokov at Cornell,* by Gavriel Shapiro (Ithaca, N.Y.: Cornell University Press, 2003), photograph by Robert L. Wegryn.

Editions José Corti

Jean Rousset, "Madame Bovary or the Book about Nothing," translated by Raymond Giraud, in *Flaubert. A Collection of Critical Essays,* edited by Giraud (Englewood Cliffs, N.J.: Prentice-Hall, 1964), pp. 123–131. Originally appeared in *Forme Et Signification* © José Corti, 1962. Reprinted with the permission of Editions José Corti.

Farrar, Straus & Giroux

Edmund Wilson, "Flaubert's politics," in his *The Triple Thinkers. Ten Essays on Literature* (New York: Harcourt, Brace, 1938): Excerpts from "Flaubert's politics," (pp. 100–121), pages 108–115 to be reprinted. Permission granted by Farrar, Straus & Giroux.

George Borschardt, Inc.

Haunted by Flaubert–from Francine du Plessix Gray, *Rage and Fire. A Life of Louise Colet* (New York: Simon & Schuster, 1994), pp. 349-351. © 1994 by Francine du Plessix Gray. Reprinted by permission of George Borschardt, Inc. on behalf of Francine du Plessix Gray.

Getty

Illustration on page 150; photograph by Étienne Carjat, courtesy of the BBC Hulton Picture Library © Getty/ Hulton Archive image #HE6538.

Harcourt, Inc.

Excerpts from *Lectures on Literature* by Vladimir Nabokov, copyright © 1980 by the Estate of Vladimir Nabokov, reprinted by permission of Harcourt, Inc. Illustrations on pages 160, 161, 164, and 165.

Harvard University Press/ McIntosh and Otis, Inc.

Excerpts reprinted by permission of the publisher from *The Letters of Gustave Flaubert: Volume I ~ 1830–1857,* selected, edited, and translated by Francis Steegmuller, Cambridge, Mass.: The Belknap Press of Harvard University Press, Copyright © 1980 by Francis Steegmuller. Reprinted with the permission of Harvard University Press and McIntosh and Otis, Inc.

Excerpts reprinted by permission of the publisher from *The Letters of Gustave Flaubert: Volume II ~ 1857–1880,* selected, edited, and translated by Francis Steegmuller, Cambridge, Mass.: The Belknap Press of Harvard University Press, Copyright © 1982 by Francis Steegmuller. Reprinted with the permission of Harvard University Press and McIntosh and Otis, Inc.

Harvill Press

Letters from *Flaubert ~ Sand: The Correspondence,* translated by Francis Steegmuller and Barbara Bray (New York: Knopf, 1993). Reprinted with the permission of Harvill Press.

Houghton Library, Harvard University

Illustration on page 156, used by permission of Houghton Library at Harvard University.

John Calder Publications

Robbe-Grillet on Flaubert–Alain Robbe-Grillet, *Ghosts in the Mirror,* translated by Jo Levy (London: John Calder, 1988), pp. 146–151. Reprinted by permission of John Calder Publications.

The Johns Hopkins University Press

Poulet, Georges. *Studies in Human Time,* pp. 258–261. © 1956, reproduced with permission of The Johns Hopkins University Press.

Éric Le Calvez

Illustrations on pages 30, 41, 62, 263, 266, 270, 273, 315, 318, 319, 331, 332, and 353; photographs by Éric Le Calvez, used with the permission of Le Calvez.

Herbert Lottman

Excerpts from Herbert Lottman, *Flaubert, A Biography* (Boston, Toronto & London: Little, Brown, 1989). Reprinted with the permission of Herbert Lottman.

Louisiana State University Press

Reprinted by permission of Louisiana State University Press from *The Tradition of French Prose: A Rhetorical Study* by John Porter Houston. Copyright © 1981 by Louisiana State University Press.

McIntosh and Otis, Inc.

Flaubert in Egypt: A Sensibility on Tour, edited by Francis Steegmuller. (Boston & Toronto: Little, Brown, 1972), pp. 51–54, 180–192. © 1972 by Francis Steegmuller. Reprinted with the permission of McIntosh and Otis, Inc.

Excerpts from Gustave Flaubert, *Intimate Notebook,* translated and edited by Francis Steegmuller (London: W. H. Allen, 1967), pp. 20–26, 49–50. Copyright © 1967 by Francis Steegmuller. Reprinted with the permission of McIntosh and Otis, Inc.

Merlin Press

Georg Lukács. "Salammbô." *The Historical Novel.* Translated by Hannah and Stanley Mitchell. (London: Merlin Press, Ltd., 1962), pp. 184–195. Reprinted by permission of Merlin Press, Ltd.

Musée Calvet

Illustration on page 102, courtesy of Musée Calvet, Avignon.

Musée Carnavalet

Illustrations on pages 105, 241, 245, 246, and 358, courtesy of Musée Carnavalet, Estampes.

Musée des Arts et Traditions Popularies

Illustration on page 28, courtesy of Musée des Arts et Traditions Popularies, Paris.

Musée Flaubert et d'Histoire de la Médecine

Illustrations on pages 20, 25, 61, 63, 316, and 356, courtesy of the Musée Flaubert et d'Histoire de la Médecine.

Musée Granet

Illustration on page 67, courtesy of Musée Granet.

Musée Picasso

Illustration on page 63, courtesy of Musée Picasso, Antibes.

Musées Nationaux

Illustration on page 131, cliché Musées Nationaux, Versailles.

New York Public Library

Illustrations on pages 82 and 86, courtesy of the New York Public Library.

New York University Press

"*Madame Bovary* after a Century," essay by Benjamin F. Bart–from *Madame Bovary and the Critics: A Collection of Essays,* edited by Bart (New York: New York University Press, 1966), pp. 180–197. Reprinted by permission of the New York University Press.

Penguin Putnam, Inc.

"Speech for the Defense" and "Speech for the Prosecution," in "The Trial of Madame Bovary," translated by Evelyn Gendel, in Gustave Flaubert, *Madame Bovary* (New York: Signet Classic, 1964), pp. 329–347, 363–400. Reprinted by permission of Penguin Putnam, Inc.

Laurence M. Porter

Laurence M. Porter, "Projection as Ego Defense: Flaubert's *Tentation de saint Antoine,*" in *The Literary Dream in French Romanticism. A Psychoanalytic Interpretation* (Detroit: Wayne State University Press, 1979), pp. 49–67. Reprinted by permission of Laurence M. Porter.

Princeton University Press

Victor Brombert, "*L'Éducation sentimentale:* Profanation and the Permanence of Dreams," in his *The Novels of Flaubert. A Study of Themes and Techniques* (Princeton: Princeton University Press, 1966), pp. 125–150. Copyright © 1966 by Princeton University Press. Reprinted by permission of Princeton University Press.

Random House, Inc.

"Emma Bovary's Eyes," from Julian Barnes, *Flaubert's Parrot* (London: Cape, 1984), pp. 74–81. Copyright © 1985 by Julian Barnes. Used by permission of Alfred A. Knopf, a division of Random House, Inc. and by permission of The Random House Group Ltd.

The Regents of the University of California

The "Bêtise" of Bourgeois Life–Eric Gans, *The Discovery of Illusion. Flaubert's Early Works, 1835–1837* (Berkeley: University of California Press, 1971), pp. 157–161. Copyright ©1971. By permission of The Regents of the University of California.

Simon & Schuster

La Tentation de Saint Antoine–Enid Starkie, *Flaubert: The Making of the Master* (New York: Atheneum, 1967), pp. 159–166. Reprinted by permission of Simon & Schuster.

Sotheby's New York

Illustration on page 141 from Sotheby's: The Maurice F. Neville Collection of Modern Literature, 13 April 2004, item 68, courtesy of Sotheby's New York.

Stanford University Press

Reading *Mémoires d'un fou*–from "Gustave Flaubert: Living, Writing, or Madness as a Cliche." From *Writing and Madness: Literature/Philosophy/Psychoanalysis* by Shoshana Felman, Translated by Martha Noel Evans and others (Stanford, Cal.: Stanford University Press, 2003), pp. 78–95. Reprinted by permission of Stanford University Press.

The University of Chicago Press

"The Event," a chapter from *The Family Idiot: Gustave Flaubert 1821–1857,* by Jean-Paul Sartre (Chicago: University of Chicago Press, 1991), volume IV, pp. 3–17. Reprinted by permission of the University of Chicago Press.

University of Georgia Press

Louise Colet, *Lui. A View of Him,* translated by Marilyn Gaddis Rose. Athens, Ga.: University of Georgia Press, 1986, pp. 14–15, 84–86, 253–263. Reprinted by permission of University of Georgia Press.

University of Nebraska Press

Excerpts from Robert Griffin, *Early Writings: Gustave Flaubert* (Lincoln & London: University of Nebraska Press, 1991). Original reprinted with the permission of Les Editions du Club de l'Honnête, S. A. and the English translation from University of Nebraska Press.

Raymonde Debray-Genette, "Profane, Sacred: Disorder of Utterance in *Trois contes,*" translated by Susan Huston (pp. 13–29) and Charles Bernheimer, "Fetishism and Allegory in *Boubard et Pécuchet*" (pp. 163–176); reprinted from *Flaubert and Postmodernism,* edited by Naomi Schor and Henry F. Majewski, by permission of University of Nebraska Press. Copyright 1984 by the University of Nebraska Press.

W. W. Norton and Company, Inc.

Excerpts from Flaubert & Turgenev. *The Complete Correspondence,* translated and edited by Barbara Beaumont (New York & London: Norton, 1985). Reprinted with the permission of W. W. Norton and Company, Inc.

Worshipful Company of Stationers and Newspaper Makers

Illustration on page 126; used by permission of Worshipful Company of Stationers and Newspaper Makers, London.

Dictionary of Literary Biography® • Volume Three Hundred One

Gustave Flaubert: A Documentary Volume

Dictionary of Literary Biography

Books by Gustave Flaubert

The textual reliability of much of Flaubert's work is less than satisfactory. Recognizing the importance of this problem and responding to readers' interest in Flaubert's private writings, Gallimard began publishing Correspondance, *edited by Jean Bruneau, the most definitive edition of Flaubert's letters. Four volumes of the so-called Pléiade edition were published between 1972 and 1998; the fifth and final volume, covering the years 1876 to 1880 and edited by Yvan Leclerc, is yet to be published. In the early 1990s Gallimard asked a group of Flaubert specialists working on his manuscripts at the Institut des Textes et Manuscrits Modernes in Paris to produce a new and complete edition of Flaubert's* Œuvres complètes *(Complete Works). In 2001 Gallimard published the first–and to date the only–volume of the Pléiade edition,* Œuvres de jeunesse *(Works of Youth), edited by Claudine Gothot-Mersch and Guy Sagnes, which includes all of Flaubert's writings from 1831 to 1845, excepting the correspondence. Five volumes are planned.*

The following bibliography is designed to guide the reader to editions of Flaubert's works that are historically significant and/or the most accurate now available. The first section, Books, lists the volumes that Flaubert intended to publish. With the exception of Bouvard et Pécuchet, *on which he was working when he died, Flaubert saw all of these books through the publication process–although his involvement did not guarantee accurate texts.*

When he finished a book, Flaubert considered that it did not belong to him anymore and quickly began working on a new project. His final manuscript went to a copyist, who produced a new manuscript that Flaubert then corrected. However, he often missed errors made by the copyist. The corrected manuscript then went to the printer, who introduced new errors in preparing proofs for the author to review. Flaubert again missed many errors. The second section of the bibliography, Recommended Editions of Works and Letters, includes new editions of Flaubert's texts in which editors have conscientiously attempted to catch or bring to the reader's attention the mistakes that were made in the transmission of the text from Flaubert's hand to the printed page.

The second section also includes works that Flaubert preserved but did not intend to publish, either because he felt that they were not good enough–only a very few of his Œuvres de jeunesse *escaped this judgment–or because he considered them private, such as his notebooks and his letters. After Flaubert's death, publishers began to print Flaubert's unpublished writings in* Œuvres complètes *editions. The first such edition, eight volumes published by A. Quantin in 1885, has been followed by many other multivolume editions, including three separate editions published by Louis Conard (eighteen volumes, 1910–1924; twenty-one volumes, 1923; twenty-eight volumes, 1954) as well as editions by Librairie de France (thirteen volumes, 1921–1925), Les Belles Lettres (ten volumes, 1945–1948), Éditions du Seuil (two volumes, 1964), and Éditions Rencontre (eighteen volumes, 1964–1965). The most complete of these* Œuvres complètes *is probably the sixteen-volume edition edited by Maurice Bardèche, which was published by Club de l'Honnête Homme in 1971–1975. All of these* Œuvres complètes *have many errors, and the Bardèche edition alone is listed, not because of its textual superiority, but because it provides the reader access to texts in some cases otherwise unavailable; it also includes the years of the* Correspondance *not yet covered by the Pléiade edition (1876–1880).*

The third section, Editions in English, lists translations of Flaubert's works that have been published since his death. It should be noted that in addition to the difficulties of capturing Flaubert's style, the translators often were working with inaccurate French texts.

Books

Madame Bovary. Mœurs de province, 2 volumes (Paris: Michel Lévy frères, 1857);

Salammbô (Paris: Michel Lévy frères, 1862);

L'Éducation sentimentale. Histoire d'un jeune homme, 2 volumes (Paris: Michel Lévy frères, 1869);

Lettre à la municipalité de Rouen (Paris: Michel Lévy frères, 1872);

Préface aux Dernières chansons de Louis Bouilhet (Paris: Michel Lévy frères, 1872);

Le Candidat, comédie en 4 actes (Paris: Charpentier, 1874);

La Tentation de saint Antoine (Paris: Charpentier, 1874);

Trois contes (Paris: Charpentier, 1877)–comprises "Un cœur simple," "La Légende de saint Julien L'Hospitalier," and "Hérodias";

Bouvard et Pécuchet (Paris: Alphonse Lemerre, 1881).

Recommended Editions of Works and Letters

Lettres inédites de Gustave Flaubert à son éditeur Michel Lévy, edited by Jacques Suffel (Paris: Calmann-Lévy, 1965);

Madame Bovary, edited by Claudine Gothot-Mersch (Paris: Éditions Garnier, 1971);

Œuvres complètes de Gustave Flaubert, 16 volumes, edited by Maurice Bardèche (Paris: Club de l'Honnête Homme, 1971–1975)–includes Flaubert's dramatic work *(Le Château des cœurs, Le Sexe faible, Le Candidat,* and sketches for unfinished plays), the unfinished *Conte oriental (Les Sept fils du derviche),* and other works Flaubert did not intend to publish ("Voyage en Orient," "Voyage à Cartrage," and his notebooks);

Correspondance, 4 volumes to date, edited by Jean Bruneau (Paris: Gallimard, Bibliothèque de la Pléiade, 1972–1998);

Bouvard et Pécuchet, edited by Claudine Gothot-Mersch (Paris: Gallimard, Folio, 1979);

Gustave Flaubert–George Sand: Correspondance, edited by Alphonse Jacobs (Paris: Flammarion, 1981);

La Tentation de saint Antoine, edited by Claudine Gothot-Mersch (Paris: Gallimard, Folio, 1983);

L'Éducation sentimentale, edited by Peter Michael Wetherill (Paris: Éditions Garnier, 1984);

L'Éducation sentimentale, edited by Claudine Gothot-Mersch (Paris: Garnier-Flammarion, 1985);

Cahier intime de jeunesse, edited by Jean-Pierre Germain (Paris: Nizet, 1987);

Le Candidat, edited by Yvan Leclerc (Paris: Le Castor Astral, 1987);

Par les champs et par les grèves, by Flaubert and Maxime Du Camp, edited by Adrianne J. Tooke (Genève: Droz, 1987);

Carnets de travail, edited by Pierre-Marc de Biasi (Paris: Balland, 1988);

Gustave Flaubert–Ivan Tourguéniev: Correspondance, edited by Alexandre Zviguilski (Paris: Flammarion, 1989);

Le Dictionnaire des idées reçues, edited by Marie-Thérèse Jacquet (Paris: Schena & Nizet, 1990);

Voyage en Égypte, edited by Pierre-Marc de Biasi (Paris: Grasset, 1991);

Gustave Flaubert–Guy de Maupassant: Correspondance, edited by Yvan Leclerc (Paris: Flammarion, 1993);

Le Dictionnaire des idées reçues, edited by Anne Herschberg Pierrot (Paris: Le Livre de Poche Classique, 1997);

Gustave Flaubert–les Goncourt, Correspondance, edited by Pierre-Jean Dufief (Paris: Flammarion, 1998);

Bouvard et Pécuchet, edited by Stéphanie Dord-Crouslé (Paris: Flammarion, GF, 1999);

Carnet de voyage à Carthage, edited by Claire-Marie Delavoye (Rouen: Publications de l'Université de Rouen, 1999);

Trois contes, edited by Pierre-Marc de Biasi (Paris: Le Livre de Poche classique, 1999);

Gustave Flaubert–Alfred Le Poittevin, Gustave Flaubert–Maxime Du Camp, Correspondances, edited by Yvan Leclerc (Paris: Flammarion, 2000);

Salammbô, edited by Gisèle Séginger (Paris: Flammarion, GF, 2001);

Œuvres complètes, volume 1: *Œuvres de jeunesse,* edited by Claudine Gothot-Mersch and Guy Sagnes (Paris: Gallimard, Bibliothèque de la Pléiade, 2001)–includes "Louis XIII"; "Trois pages d'un cahier d'écolier"; "Les Soirées d'étude"; "Narrations et Discours"; "Opuscules historiques"; "La Fiancée et la tombe"; "La Grande dame et le joueur de vielle"; "Un Parfum à sentir"; "Chronique normande au Xe siècle"; "La Femme du monde"; "Un Secret de Philippe le Prudent, roi d'Espagne"; "La Peste à Florence"; "Bibliomanie"; "Rage et impuissance"; "La Dernière heure"; "Une Leçon d'histoire naturelle: genre Commis"; "La Main de fer"; "Rêve d'enfer"; "'Quidquid Volueris'"; "Passion et vertu"; "Loys XI"; "Agonies"; "La Danse des morts"; "Ivre et mort"; "Les Mémoires d'un fou"; "Rome et les Césars"; "Étude sur Rabelais"; "Smar"; "Les Funérailles du Docteur Maturin"; "Mademoiselle Rachel"; "Pyrénées-Corse"; "Cahier intime de 1840–1841"; *Novembre; L'Éducation sentimentale* (1845); "Voyage en Italie"; "Deux rédactions d'histoire naturelle"; "Influence des Arabes d'Espagne sur la civilisation française du Moyen âge"; "Lutte du sacerdoce et de l'empire; Histoire; Histoire moderne"; "Les Arts et le commerce"; "De la littérature romantique en France"; and four scenarios from Flaubert's youth.

Editions in English

Madame Bovary. A Tale of Provincial Life, translated by John Sterling (Philadelphia: T. B. Peterson & Bros., 1881);

Salammbô, translated by M. French Sheldon (New York: Lovell, Coryell, 1885; London: Saxon, 1886);

The Temptation of Saint Anthony, translated by D. F. Hannigan (London: H. S. Nichols, 1895; Akron: St. Dunstan Society / Chicago: Magee, 1904);

Bouvard et Pécuchet, translated by D. F. Hannigan (London: H. S. Nichols, 1896; Akron: St. Dunstan Society / Chicago: Magee / New York: M. Walter Dunne, 1904);

Sentimental Education: A Young Man's History, translated by D. F. Hannigan (London: H. S. Nichols, 1898; Chicago: Magee, 1904);

The Candidate: A Humorous Political Drama in Four Acts (Chicago: S. P. Magee / New York: M. Walter Dunne, 1904);

Over Strand and Field: A Record of Travel through Brittany (Akron: St. Dunstan Society / New York & London: M. Walter Dunne, 1904);

Three Tales, translated by Arthur McDowall (London: Chatto & Windus, 1923; New York: Knopf, 1924);

Bibliomania: A Tale, translated by Theodore Wesley Koch (Evanston, Ill.: Northwestern University Press, 1929);

The First Temptation of Saint Anthony, translated by René Francis (London: Duckworth, 1910; New York: Privately printed for Rarity Press, 1932);

Bouvard and Pécuchet, translated by T. W. Earp and G. W. Stonier (New York: New Directions, 1954);

Flaubert's Dictionary of Accepted Ideas, translated by Jacques Barzun (London: Max Reinhardt, 1954);

Madame Bovary. Provincial Manners, translated by Eleanor Marx-Aveling and Paul de Man (New York: Norton, 1965);

Intimate Notebook, 1840–1841, translated and edited by Francis Steegmuller (London: W. H. Allen, 1967);

Sentimental Education (1845), translated by Douglas Garman (Berkeley: University of California Press, 1972);

Salammbô, translated by Allen J. Krailsheimer (New York: Penguin, 1977);

Flaubert in Egypt: A Sensibility on Tour: A Narrative Drawn from Gustave Flaubert's Travel Notes and Letters, translated and edited by Francis Steegmuller (Chicago: Academy Chicago Limited, 1979);

The Letters of Gustave Flaubert, 1830–1857, translated and edited by Francis Steegmuller (Cambridge, Mass.: Harvard University Press, 1980);

The Temptation of Saint Anthony, translated by Mrosovsky Kitty (Ithaca, N.Y.: Cornell University Press, 1981);

The Letters of Gustave Flaubert, 1857–1880, translated and edited by Francis Steegmuller (Cambridge, Mass.: Harvard University Press, 1982);

Flaubert and Turgenev. A Friendship in Letters. The Complete Correspondence, translated and edited by Barbara Beaumont (New York & London: Norton, 1985);

November, translated by Frank Jellinek (London: John Lane, 1934; New York: Carroll & Graf, 1987);

Early Writings: Gustave Flaubert, translated by Robert Griffin (Lincoln & London: University of Nebraska Press, 1991)–comprises "A Trip to Hell"; "Portrait of Lord Byron"; "A Fragrance to Smell; or, The Clowns"; "Rage and Impotence"; "A Lecture on Natural History–Genus: *Clerk*"; "Dream of Hell"; "Whatever You Want"; "Passion and Virtue"; "Dance of the Dead"; "Diary of a Madman"; and "Smarh";

Sentimental Education, translated by Robert Baldick (New York: Penguin, 1991);

Flaubert~Sand. The Correspondence, translated and edited by Francis Steegmuller and Barbara Bray (New York: Knopf, 1993);

Three Tales, translated by Allen J. Krailsheimer (New York: Oxford University Press, 1999);

Memoirs of a Madman, translated by Andrew Brown (London: Hesperus, 2002).

Gustave Flaubert (12 December 1821 – 8 May 1880). This photograph by Félix Nadar was probably taken during the 1860s (cliché [photograph] Bibliothèque nationale de France, Paris).

Chronology

1821

12 December — Birth of Gustave Flaubert at 4:00 A.M. in the Hôtel-Dieu, Rouen's hospital. His father is Achille-Cléophas Flaubert, chief surgeon of the hospital; his mother is Anne-Justine-Caroline Fleuriot, an orphan from Pont-L'Évêque, where her father was a physician. The couple already has a son, Achille, born 9 February 1813; three other children died in infancy.

1824

15 July — Birth of Caroline Flaubert, sixth and last child of the Flauberts.

1825

Béatrix Caroline Hébert, age twenty-one, enters the Flauberts' service. Called Julie by the family, she remains their servant until Flaubert's death. She dies in 1883, three years after the death of the man she served for fifty-five years.

1830

31 December — In his earliest surviving letter Flaubert, writing to his friend Ernest Chevalier, proposes that he will write comedies while Ernest will write his dreams.

1832

15 May — Begins to attend the Collège Royal of Rouen (now Lycée Corneille). With his sister Caroline, Ernest Chevalier, Alfred Le Poittevin and his sister Laure, and other friends, Flaubert acts in plays in his father's billiard room. He is already interested in literature: he admires Miguel de Cervantes's *Don Quixote de la Mancha* and discovers Gérard de Nerval's translation of *Faust.*

1833

August — Takes his first trip to Paris, visiting the Jardin des Plantes, Versailles, and Fontainebleau.

1834

Edits the handwritten newspaper *Art et Progrès* (Art and Progress) at the Collège Royal.

October — Meets Louis Bouilhet but does not then develop the close friendship they will later enjoy.

1835

The Flauberts begin to spend summer vacations at the fishing village of Trouville, which later develops into a fashionable resort. At school Flaubert writes "Portrait de lord Byron"

(Portrait of Lord Byron) and the sketch "Voyage en enfer" (A Trip to Hell), which is published in the literary journal *Art et Progrès.*

1836

Writes many short stories, including "Un Parfum à sentir" (A Fragrance to Smell), "La Femme du Monde" (The Mundane Woman), "Bibliomanie" (Bibliomania), and "Rage et impuissance" (Rage and Impotence); some of them are inspired by his passion for history: "Un Secret de Philippe le Prudent" (A Secret of Philip the Prudent), "La Peste à Florence" (The Plague in Florence), and "Chronique normande du Xe siècle" (History of Normandy in the Tenth Century).

Summer — On vacation at Trouville, Flaubert meets and conceives an intense passion for Élisa Schlésinger, who is married to the music publisher Maurice Schlésinger. She becomes the model for important characters in several of his later works.

1837

Writes the stories "Rêve d'enfer" (Dream of Hell), "La Main de fer" (The Iron Hand), and "La Dernière heure" (The Last Hour).

12 February — "Bibliomanie" is published in *Le Colibri,* a small literary newspaper in Rouen.

30 March — "Une Leçon d'histoire naturelle–genre: *commis*" (A Lecture on Natural History–Genus: *Clerk*) is published in *Le Colibri;* it is the last juvenile work Flaubert publishes in his lifetime.

1838

Writes a play in five acts, *Loys XI,* and three short stories: "Agonies," "La Danse des morts" (The Dance of the Dead), and "Ivre et mort" (Drunk and Dead). He finishes a long story, *Mémoires d'un fou* (Memoirs of a Madman), and begins *Smar.*

1839

Finishes *Smar* and writes the short story "Les Funérailles du Dr. Mathurin" (Dr. Mathurin's Funeral) as well as three essays: "Les Arts et le commerce" (Art and Commerce), "Rabelais," and "Rome et les Césars" (Rome and the Caesars). His brother Achille marries after completing his thesis in medicine.

December — During his last year at the Collège Royal, Flaubert is expelled because of his leadership in a student protest; Bouilhet is also involved.

1840

August — Passes his *baccalauréat,* for which he prepared himself through study at home. Flaubert leaves for a journey of some two months to the Pyrenees and Corsica with his father's colleague Dr. Jules Cloquet.

October — In Marseilles, Flaubert has a brief, intense affair with Eulalie Foucaud, a thirty-five-year-old daughter of an innkeeper. Returning from his trip, he works on his travel notes.

1 November — Travels to Paris. Back in Rouen a few days later, Flaubert finishes writing his travel notes.

1841

Reads for the entire year, taking vacations in Nogent-sur-Seine, where the Flauberts have relatives, and in Trouville. Begins writing his novel titled *Novembre,* probably during the summer.

November — Registers at the Law School in Paris but returns to Rouen.

1842

A reluctant student of the law, a subject he finds boring, Flaubert continues to work on *Novembre.*

July — Moves to Paris, returning to Trouville in September for his vacation.

25 October — Finishes *Novembre* (published as *Novembre,* 1885; translated as *November,* 1934). Flaubert finds an apartment in Paris, 19 rue de l'Est.

28 December — Passes the examinations for the first year of law school.

1843

February — Begins writing the novel titled *L'Éducation sentimentale.*

March — Meets Maxime Du Camp, who soon becomes one of his closest friends. He sees the Schlésingers and frequently visits the sculptor James Pradier's studio, where he meets poet Victor Hugo.

August — Fails the examinations for the second year of law school.

1844

January — Suffers a sudden nervous attack while driving a coach on the road from Pont-L'Évêque to Honfleur. His brother Achille, who is riding with him, at first believes he has dropped dead. Repeated attacks, though less severe, continue throughout his life; such an attack may have caused or contributed to his death. Flaubert's father decides that his son will not resume his law studies.

May — Flaubert's father buys Croisset, a property on the Seine four kilometers below Rouen, where the family moves in June for the summer. The two-story residence becomes Flaubert's primary residence for the rest of his life.

1845

7 January — Finishes "L'Éducation sentimentale" (published as *La Première Éducation sentimentale,* 1910; translated as *Sentimental Education (1845),* 1972).

March — Flaubert's sister marries Émile Hamard.

27 March — Flaubert and his parents accompany the newlyweds on their honeymoon to Paris, Nogent-sur-Seine, Provence, Italy, and Switzerland. At Genoa, Flaubert is fascinated by the painting *The Temptation of Saint Anthony,* attributed to Peter Brueghel the Younger, in the Balbi palace.

15 May — From Milan, Flaubert writes to Le Poittevin that he plans to base a work on Saint Anthony's life.

8 June — The Flaubert family arrives in Paris, where they stay for a couple of days before returning to Rouen on 12 June.

June — Studies Voltaire's plays and continues his reading of history.

November — Flaubert's father becomes ill with an infection on his thigh.

1846

15 January — Death of Flaubert's father at sixty-one. Achille succeeds his father as the chief surgeon at the Hôtel-Dieu.

21 January — Birth of Caroline Hamard, Flaubert's "niece Caroline," his sister's only child.

22 March — Death of Flaubert's sister Caroline at age twenty-one. Flaubert moves to Croisset with his mother and the baby.

6 July — Le Poittevin marries Louise de Maupassant, a decision Flaubert feels as both an artistic and personal betrayal.

26 July — In Pradier's Paris studio, where he goes to have the marble bust of his sister created by the sculptor, Flaubert meets the poet Louise Colet, wife of Hippolyte Colet and mother of a young daughter, Henriette. Three days after their first encounter, they become lovers. When Flaubert returns to Croisset a couple of days later, they begin a regular correspondence.

1847

May to August — Travels with Du Camp to Brittany, Normandy, and Touraine, and returns by the coast. During the trip they take notes for an account of their journey, *Par les champs et par les grèves;* Flaubert writes the odd-numbered chapters and Du Camp the others (published as *Par les champs et par les grèves (voyage en Bretagne),* 1885; translated as *Over Strand and Field: A Record of Travel through Brittany,* 1904).

1848

23 February — Accompanies his friend Bouilhet to Paris to witness the Revolution. A day later, Flaubert and Du Camp are at the Tuileries palace with the revolutionaries.

March — Breaks off relationship with Colet as she announces that she has another lover and is now pregnant.

3 April — Death of Alfred Le Poittevin. Flaubert spends two nights watching over his corpse, reading Creuzer's *Les Religions de l'Antiquité* (Religions of Antiquity).

24 May — Begins *La Tentation de saint Antoine.*

1849

12 September — Finishes *La Tentation de saint Antoine* (translated as *The First Temptation of Saint Anthony,* 1910). For four days Flaubert reads it to Bouilhet and Du Camp, who then horrify him with their harsh criticism. According to Du Camp, Bouilhet began by declaring, "We think you should throw that into the fire and never mention it again."

29 October — Flaubert and Du Camp leave for their long-planned oriental journey that had been postponed because of the writing of *La Tentation de saint Antoine.*

4 November — They sail from Marseilles aboard *Le Nil,* arriving in Alexandria on 15 November.

26 November — Arrive in Cairo, where they stay for more than two months visiting the city and the pyramids; Flaubert is fascinated by Egyptian mores.

1850

6 February — Depart Cairo, sailing up the Nile and reaching the second cataract on 22 March. They spend some four months on the river, returning to Cairo in June.

17 July — Embark from Alexandria to Beirut, traveling in the region to Jerusalem in August and arriving in Damascus on 1 September.

Fall — Arrive in Rhodes in October and in Constantinople in November.

19 December — Arrive in Athens. Flaubert and Du Camp travel around Greece for nearly two months.

1851

13 February — Embark at Patras to sail for Brindisi. In Italy, they visit Naples and reach Rome in April, where Flaubert meets his mother. Flaubert spends most of his time in museums, and Du Camp returns to Paris on his own. With his mother, Flaubert visits Florence and Venice.

June — Returns with his mother to Croisset. Shortly thereafter, Flaubert resumes his relationship with Colet, who wrote to him on his return to France.

19 September — Begins writing *Madame Bovary.*

25 September — Leaves with his mother and niece for England. In London Flaubert visits and takes detailed notes on The Great Exhibition of the Works of Industry of All Nations as well as the British Museum.

December — In Paris, Flaubert witnesses Louis-Napoléon Bonaparte's coup d'état.

1852

Flaubert works on *Madame Bovary,* through chapter 3 of part 2 by the end of the year, and corresponds with Colet, whom he sees rarely. His friendship begins to cool with Du Camp, who, now codirector of the *Revue de Paris,* urges him to move to Paris and publish right away.

October — Around mid month Flaubert visits Paris for a couple of days and sees Colet.

1853

Work continues on *Madame Bovary,* through the eighth chapter of part 2. Flaubert conceives a metaphysical novel, "La Spirale," which he will never write.

July — An English governess (probably Juliet Herbert) comes to Croisset to become Caroline's governess.

1854

Work continues on *Madame Bovary,* through the thirteenth chapter of part 2. Colet begins to irritate him: she wants to be introduced to his mother and even comes unexpectedly to Croisset, but he refuses to receive her. Bouilhet has moved to Paris, and he and Flaubert exchange a regular correspondence. Flaubert has a liaison with the actress Beatrix Person.

1855

Work continues on *Madame Bovary,* through the eighth chapter of part 3 by October. During this year Flaubert begins a discreet liaison with his niece's governess Juliet Herbert. The relationship continues even after her return to England in September 1857 and lasts until his death.

6 March — In Paris on a visit, Flaubert writes his last letter to Colet, who had tried to visit him the previous day: "I was not home. And in fear of the affronts that such persistence on your part might provoke on mine, good manners require that I warn you *that I shall never be here.*"

October — Flaubert goes to Paris and moves into an apartment on the fourth floor at 42, Boulevard du Temple.

1856

February	Colet's *Une Histoire de soldat* (The Story of a Soldier), a novel in which Flaubert is ridiculed through the portrayal of the character of Léonce, is published in five installments in *Le Moniteur;* it is published as a book in 1859.
April to October	*Madame Bovary* is completed. Flaubert rewrites *La Tentation de saint Antoine,* producing a second version of the novel.
May	Flaubert gives a copy of *Madame Bovary* to Du Camp for publication in the *Revue de Paris.*
October to December	*Madame Bovary* is serialized in the *Revue de Paris.* Because the editors require changes and impose cuts, Flaubert in the 15 December issue inserts a note of protest, warning his audience that what they are reading are mere fragments.
21 December	The first of four excerpts from the second version of *La Tentation de saint Antoine* is published in *L'Artiste* by his friend Théophile Gautier. Subsequent excerpts are published in the magazine on 28 December 1856, 11 January 1857, and 1 February 1857.

1857

January	Calling *Madame Bovary* an "outrage to public morals and religion," the government brings a suit against Flaubert as well as the directors and the printer of the *Revue de Paris.*
29 January	The trial takes place at the sixth division of police court.
7 February	Flaubert and the *Revue de Paris* are acquitted.
April	*Madame Bovary* is published by Michel Lévy. Some critics are hostile, but the publication is a great success for Flaubert, who becomes immediately famous.
Spring to Winter	In Paris a great part of the year, Flaubert develops friendly relationships with writers such as Edmond and Jules de Goncourt, Ernest Renan, Charles Augustin Sainte-Beuve, and Ernest Feydeau. Although *La Tentation de saint Antoine* is completed, he decides not to publish it from fear of a new scandal.
Summer	Begins to contemplate an historical novel and plans "Carthage," which will become *Salammbô.*

1858

12 April	Dissatisfied with his work on *Salammbô,* Flaubert leaves for Tunisia to study the ruins of Carthage and see the landscapes. Returning to Croisset on 9 June, he revises his plan for the novel and resumes writing.

1859

	Work continues slowly on *Salammbô,* through only chapter 7.
August to September	Colet's *Lui* (translated as *A View of Him,* 1986), the second novel in which she presents an unflattering view of Flaubert, is published in *Le Messager de Paris;* it is published in book form by Michel Lévy. Flaubert is bitter and ironic when he comments on Colet's novels.

1860

	Flaubert spends most of his time secluded in Croisset working on *Salammbô.* He rewrites the passage on the Macar battle nine times. At the end of the year, chapter 10 is in progress.

Winter — In Paris, Flaubert meets his literary friends, including the Goncourt brothers, Renan, and Paul de Saint-Victor.

1861

Work continues on *Salammbô,* reaching chapter 14 by the end of the year.

May — Visits Paris but decides to return to Croisset and stay there until his novel is finished.

1862

15 February — *Salammbô* is completed in Paris. During the summer, Flaubert works with Bouilhet to correct its final version.

24 November — *Salammbô* is published by Lévy. Critics in general are hostile, but the novel achieves great popular success.

23–24 December — Writes a long reply to Sainte-Beuve's criticisms of *Salammbô* that had been published in three December articles in *Le Constitutionnel.*

1863

Early January — More and more famous, Flaubert is received by Princess Mathilde Bonaparte. He becomes a frequent visitor to Prince Jérôme, her brother.

27 January — George Sand publishes in *La Presse* a review of *Salammbô* that marks the beginning of a long friendship and correspondence.

23 February — Meets the Russian writer Ivan Turgenev at one of the Magny restaurant dinners organized by Sainte-Beuve.

April — Considers and writes scenarios for two writing projects, which he has been thinking about since 1862: a Parisian novel *(L'Éducation sentimentale)* and the story of two clerks *(Bouvard et Pécuchet).*

June — Still hesitating between the two projects, he decides to plan another work, a *féerie* (a fairy play of the pantomime type), *Le Château des cœurs* (The Castle of Hearts).

Summer to Fall — With the collaboration of Bouilhet and Charles d'Osmoy, he writes *Le Château des cœurs,* finishing in October.

1864

6 April — Flaubert's niece Caroline marries Ernest Commanville, a wood merchant in Dieppe.

Summer — Travels to Montereau, Sens, and Nogent to take notes for the novel he has chosen to write: *L'Éducation sentimentale.* Returns to Croisset on 27 August and researches the history of the 1840s for the novel.

1 September — Begins writing *L'Éducation sentimentale.*

November — Flaubert is invited to the palace of Compiègne by the Emperor and the Empress.

1865

Completes the first part of *L'Éducation sentimentale.* Unlike his past practice, Flaubert no longer refuses social life. He regularly goes to the Magny dinners and visits Princess Mathilde, who offers him one of the watercolors she has painted.

February — Attends a great ball given by Prince Napoléon.

July	Visits London, where he again sees Juliet Herbert.

1866

	Work continues on *L'Éducation sentimentale.* Flaubert visits porcelain factories and takes notes for the novel.
1 July to 15 August	Publication of George Sand's last novel, *Dernier amour,* in the *Revue des Deux Mondes,* with a dedication to Flaubert; it is published as a book by Michel Lévy in 1867.
July	Visits London and sees Juliet Herbert, then to Princess Mathilde's at Saint-Gratien, then to Dieppe, at the summer home of the Commanvilles.
15 August	Receives the Legion of Honor. Returns to Croisset, where Sand visits him in August and November.

1867

	Continues to gather documentation and to write *L'Éducation sentimentale.* From February to May as well as in August and November he is in Paris.
June	Attends a ball at the Tuileries palace in honor of the Czar.
Fall	Travels to Nogent and Dieppe in September; goes to Paris to do research for the novel in November.

1868

	Continues to gather documentation and to write *L'Éducation sentimentale.* He is in Paris from January to May.
May	Sand comes to Croisset.
Summer	Visits Fontainebleau several times in order to write the episode in part 3, chapter 1, and also visits Ouville, Dieppe, Paris, and Saint-Gratien.
November	Turgenev comes to Croisset.

1869

January	Visits several places in Paris for the last chapters of *L'Éducation sentimentale,* including the Père-Lachaise cemetery to write the episode of Dambreuse's funeral.
16 May	*L'Éducation sentimentale* is completed. He reads it to George Sand and to Princess Mathilde; they are both enthusiastic. He leaves his apartment on Boulevard du Temple to rent another one on 4, rue Murillo, at the Parc Monceau.
June	Back in Croisset, Flaubert returns to work on *La Tentation de saint Antoine.*
18 July	Death of Louis Bouilhet in Rouen. Flaubert attends the funeral on 20 July; Bouilhet is buried in Rouen's Cimetière monumental, close to the graves of Flaubert's father and sister.
17 November	*L'Éducation sentimentale* is published by Lévy. In general, the critics are hostile; some of Flaubert's literary acquaintances even refuse to write a review to defend him.
22 December	George Sand publishes in *La Liberté* an article praising Flaubert's craft in *L'Éducation sentimentale.*
Christmas	Visits Sand in Nohant.

1870

Work continues on *La Tentation de saint Antoine* until Flaubert returns to Croisset.

May — After spending the winter in Paris, Flaubert returns to Croisset, where he begins to write his preface to Bouilhet's *Dernières chansons.*

20 June — Death of Jules de Goncourt. Flaubert attends his funeral in Paris on 22 June.

July — France declares war on Prussia.

1 September — The French are defeated at Sedan, and three days later the Republic is proclaimed.

December — The Prussians invade Rouen and Croisset; ten officers occupy Flaubert's house. He and his mother leave Croisset to go to Rouen.

1871

28 January — The armistice between France and Prussia is signed.

February — Accompanies his mother to his niece's home at Dieppe.

March — Travels to Brussels, where he visits Princess Mathilde in exile, and London, where he sees Juliet Herbert, returning to Dieppe.

April — Returns to Croisset and resumes his work on *La Tentation de saint Antoine.* He is disgusted by public affairs, politics, and by the Commune.

August — Visits Princess Mathilde in Saint-Gratien.

November — The fifth part of *La Tentation de saint Antoine* is completed.

15 November — Departs for Paris.

1872

January — Bouilhet's *Dernières chansons* is published with a preface by Flaubert.

26 January — Flaubert's "Lettre au Conseil municipal de Rouen," criticizing the city council for its rejection of a plan for a monument to Bouilhet, is published in *Le Temps.*

March — Quarrels with publisher Lévy.

25 March — Returns to Croisset, where his mother, whose health had been deteriorating since the war, dies on 6 April.

June — Completion of *La Tentation de saint Antoine* in Paris.

July and August — Visits the Commanvilles at Luchon. He returns to Croisset to begin researching for his next novel, *Bouvard et Pécuchet.*

September — Meets Georges Charpentier, who offers to become his new publisher.

23 October — Théophile Gautier dies. Flaubert, who had known him since 1849, learns about his death too late and cannot attend the funeral.

December — Departs for Paris.

1873

Ongoing research for *Bouvard et Pécuchet.*

April — Visits George Sand at Nohant, where Turgenev joins them.

May — Begins working on Bouilhet's *Le Sexe faible,* which the writer had left unfinished.

20 June — Charpentier comes to Croisset with a contract for new editions of *Madame Bovary* and *Salammbô.*

Summer — Flaubert tries to arrange a production of *Le Sexe faible.* He travels around Brie and Beauce to find a setting for *Bouvard et Pécuchet.*

September — While continuing his readings for *Bouvard et Pécuchet,* Flaubert begins writing a play, *Le Candidat.*

Early October — Turgenev visits Croisset.

November — *Le Candidat* is completed.

Early December — Departs for Paris, where he stays until May 1874. A contract is signed with Charpentier for the publication of *La Tentation de saint Antoine.*

1874

11 March — *Le Candidat* flops in its premiere at the Vaudeville; Flaubert withdraws the play after the fourth performance. It is published by Charpentier on 28 March.

31 March — *La Tentation de saint Antoine* is published by Charpentier; it sells well, but the critics are hostile.

June — Travels with his friend Laporte around lower Normandy for *Bouvard et Pécuchet.* On the advice of his physician, he spends two weeks in Switzerland at Kaltbad-Rigi before returning to Croisset.

1 August — Begins writing *Bouvard et Pécuchet.*

November — Travels to Paris for the rehearsal of Bouilhet's *Le Sexe faible.* He decides to withdraw the play. He remains in Paris until May 1875.

1875

Feels profoundly ill, without knowing the cause. Experiences chronic flu.

April — Flaubert is troubled by the financial disaster that overtakes the Commanvilles and fears that Croisset might be sold to help pay debts. He sells his farm at Deauville and abandons his Parisian apartment. Commanville's business is put into liquidation to avoid bankruptcy.

Summer — A depressed Flaubert sets *Bouvard et Pécuchet* aside.

September — At Concarneau, a small town on the seashore in Brittany where he has joined the naturalist Georges Pouchet, Flaubert begins writing the short story "La Légende de saint Julien l'Hospitalier," which he works on for five months.

November — Settles into the Commanvilles' apartment in Paris, 240, rue du Faubourg Saint-Honoré.

1876

February — Begins writing another tale, "Un cœur simple," for which he travels to Pont-L'Évêque and Honfleur. He completes the story in August.

7 June — Death of George Sand. Flaubert attends her funeral at Nohant.

November — At Croisset, Flaubert begins writing a third tale, "Hérodias," completing it in February 1877.

1877

February	Departs for Paris after finishing "Hérodias."
24 April	*Trois contes* is published by Charpentier.
June	At Croisset, Flaubert resumes writing *Bouvard et Pécuchet.*
September	Travels for two weeks with Laporte around lower Normandy for *Bouvard et Pécuchet.* He has reached the fourth chapter.
27 December	Departs Croisset to spend the winter in Paris.

1878

	Continues work on *Bouvard et Pécuchet.*
September	Travels to Etretat with his disciple Guy de Maupassant. He spends the rest of the year at Croisset, working on his novel.

1879

27 January	Slips and falls on ice, breaking his fibula: he has to stay in bed for six weeks. He obtains a yearly pension of 3,000 francs from Jules Ferry, the minister of Education and Fine Arts. He feels humiliated and asks that the incident remain confidential.
July	Charpentier begins preparing a new edition of *L'Éducation sentimentale,* published in November.
September	Visits Princess Mathilde at Saint-Gratien with Edmond de Goncourt.

1880

January	Flaubert reaches the tenth chapter of *Bouvard et Pécuchet:* this is the last of the first volume.
28 March	An Easter reception is given at Croisset: Goncourt, Zola, Daudet, Charpentier, Maupassant, and Flaubert's physician, Dr. Fortin, attend.
Early May	Flaubert plans a trip to Paris where he will finish the "second volume" of the novel, on which he needs to work six more months, as he says.
8 May	Death of Gustave Flaubert from apoplexy. His funeral is on 11 May at the church of Canteleu and his burial is at Rouen's Cimetière monumental.

1881

March	The unfinished *Bouvard et Pécuchet* is published by Alphonse Lemerre.
May	Caroline Commanville sells the Croisset property.

Flaubert's Youth: 1821–1844

Home, School, and Élisa Schlésinger

In 1810, after outstanding medical studies in Paris where he defended his thesis, Dissertation sur la manière de conduire les malades avant et après les opérations chirurgicales *(Dissertation on the Way to Treat Patients Before and After Surgical Operations), twenty-six-year-old Achille-Cléophas Flaubert became a surgeon at Rouen's hospital, the Hôtel-Dieu. His future wife, Anne-Justine-Caroline Fleuriot, an orphan from Pont-l'Évêque, was provided room and board by the chief surgeon of the hospital, Dr. Jean-Baptiste Laumonier. The couple married on 10 February 1812 and celebrated the birth of their first child, Achille, on 9 February 1813. In 1815 Achille-Cléophas Flaubert succeeded Laumonier as chief surgeon, a post his son Achille filled after him.*

This is the second chapter in Herbert Lottman's Flaubert: A Biography *(1989).*

The Hôtel-Dieu

The death of Dr. Laumonier at the beginning of 1818 freed the chief surgeon's quarters for the Flaubert family, which at that point meant Achille-Cléophas, his wife, and five-year-old Achille. This residence was a sturdy stone pavilion occupying a convenient corner on the town side of the hospital. It was here that two other male children were born to the couple, both to die in infancy. Between the birth of the second luckless infant on November 30, 1819, and his death on June 29, 1822, Gustave came into the Flauberts' world.[1]

We can almost seize that instant, we can almost photograph it, so little has the physical environment changed in the 170 years separating us from the birth of Gustave Flaubert. The generously proportioned hospital complex, completed at the end of the reign of Louis XV, resembles, as so many old French hospitals do, a palace and its dependencies. From the main gate on the town side, as one approaches on Rue de Crosne–now Avenue Gustave Flaubert–the visitor confronts an austere facade topped with slate tiles and dominated by the steeples of a chapel and of the Saint Madeleine church, where Gustave received his baptism. From this angle, the chief surgeon's residence stands on the left, its windows facing the main courtyard and the narrow Rue de Lecat. Gustave would have been born in his parents' bedroom, on the second floor; later he was to occupy a room of his own on a still higher, low-ceilinged service floor.[2]

His birth certificate specifies that Gustave joined the world at four A.M. on December 12, 1821.[3] The baptismal certificate adds that the infant's father was absent from the religious ceremony, and at least one writer attributes this to the doctor's anticlericalism.[4] Although they respected custom, Gustave's parents were not practicing Catholics; they have been described as deists, like so many of their bourgeois peers.[5]

One would love to be able to see the world as this child saw it. Lively, industrious Rouen began more or less at the Flauberts' doorstep. Although the hospital is only five hundred yards or so west of the Place du Vieux Marché, it was virtually outside of town when it was built, for its original function was to provide shelter for victims of the plague. The city center owes most of its imposing buildings to the Middle Ages and to the Renaissance, but by the first decades of Flaubert's century, thriving textile factories had caused Rouen to be called the Manchester of France. It contained some 90,000 inhabitants; with surrounding towns and villages, the figure rose to 225,000. The inner city boasted 470 streets, seventeen thousand houses, twenty-nine squares and markets, and fourteen churches (thirteen Catholic and one Protestant). Also "three barracks, three hospitals, two prisons, two theaters," as a local almanac put it.[6] The depth of the river allowed ocean-going vessels to dock in Rouen–up to twenty-five hundred of them each year.[7] In addition to its museums, botanical garden, and learned societies, Rouen also maintained a public library that stored thirty-two thousand books and twelve hundred ancient manuscripts.[8]

Achille was already eight years old when Gustave was born, and he was sent off to high school just as his brother was beginning to take notice of the world outside his nursery. Those were no-nonsense times, when youngsters lived at boarding school even if their parents resided in the same city. But when Gustave was only three, a sister was born, who was named Caroline, just as their parents' firstborn daughter had been.

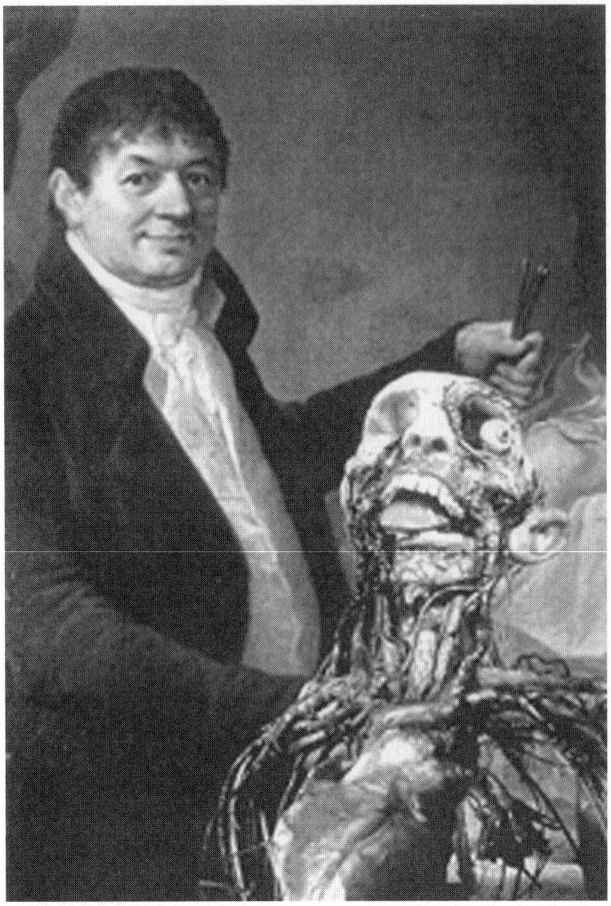

Dr. Jean-Baptiste Laumonier, chief surgeon at Rouen's hospital, the Hôtel-Dieu, with an anatomy model. After suffering a series of strokes, he was replaced in December 1815 by Flaubert's father, Achille-Cléophas Flaubert (courtesy of the Musée Flaubert et d'Histoire de la Médecine, Rouen).

Gustave and Caroline grew up together in a tender relationship interrupted only by her marriage. Then there was Julie, almost the cliché image of a faithful servant. Scholarship has more or less determined that she was born Béatrix Caroline Hébert, in the nearby Eure district; perhaps she was given the name Julie to avoid the confusion of having two Carolines in the same house. She would have been twenty-one when she entered the Flauberts' service in 1825.[9] A family fixture, Julie stayed with the family until her retirement, surviving even Gustave.

When Gustave's niece Caroline first recorded her reminiscences, she was forty years old, and the faithful servant Julie had been dead for four years. In these "Souvenirs intimes," she describes Gustave as a child, drawing on Julie as her prime source. The servant had grown up in a region "fertile in old stories of love and ghosts," and she would tell them to the boy. Thanks to a year spent in bed with a bad knee, Julie had read more than a young woman of her station normally did; these stories, too, she passed on to little Gustave.

Caroline had also been told a great deal about Gustave by his mother, who had been dead for fourteen years when Caroline set down these recollections. She remembered the description of Gustave as quiet, meditative, and with a naïveté he never shook off. He could spend hours with a finger in his mouth, lost in his thoughts, seeming stupid. Caroline repeats the following unkind anecdote: when Gustave was six an old servant named Pierre used to say to him when he got in the way, "Go look in the garden or the kitchen to see if I'm there." Gustave would obey, telling the cook, "Pierre told me to see if he is here."

There is also the story, again passed on by Caroline, that after teaching her older son to read, Gustave's mother tried to do the same for him, but he only cried. He would say, "Why learn to read, since Papa Mignot reads?" (Mignot was a favorite neighbor.) Gustave was almost nine, says the family legend, before he learned to read.[10]

We need not believe this; in fact the evidence is that it isn't true. But everything about a nineteenth-century childhood is hazy. Take Gustave's favorite neighbor, Papa or *père* Mignot: no one, not even any of his direct descendants, has ever come up with a first name for him. He was a retired farmer living just opposite the chief surgeon's house on Rue de Lecat. One of his sons, Amédée, born in 1801 and later an attorney and law professor, was an early admirer of young Gustave's (who, as we shall see, was more of a prodigy than a slow learner). And his daughter Lucie was the mother of Gustave's best childhood friend, Ernest Chevalier.[11]

Family legend has Gustave dashing across the street to sit on *père* Mignot's knee to hear his favorite stories again and again. The old man read *Don Quixote* to him, and here word of mouth is reinforced by a remark later made by Gustave himself. He knew *Don Quixote* by heart, he said–obviously in a popular abridgment–before he knew how to read.[12]

Then a recollection in a different key. The Place du Vieux Marché, where Joan was burned, was still used for executions in Gustave's time. Once when he was six or seven, on his way home from school, Gustave was passing by the guillotine and saw fresh blood on the paving stones; they were just detaching the basket containing the decapitated head when he got there. Years later, after having a tooth extracted, he crossed the square and recalled that childhood experience, and that night dreamed of the guillotine.[13]

Surely every child can call up at least one unbearable memory, even if guillotines and heads in baskets are harder to find now. But Gustave was in for more.

He lived in a hospital, where he could open a door and find himself in a ward filled with patients; the dissecting chamber adjoined the family's billiard room. Much later, one of Dr. Flaubert's students remembered seeing little Gustave inside that dissecting chamber, wearing a white smock and a padded ring around his head, of the sort children wore to avoid injury when they fell.[14] Gustave himself recalled it: "The anatomical theater faced our garden. How often my sister and I climbed up the trellis and, suspended between the vines, looked in at the laid-out corpses. . . . The same flies that flitted over us and the flowers entered the theater and returned. . . ."[15] Early in our century, a scholar sought to pin a "medical mentality" on Flaubert; it was a well-argued thesis.[16]

In his own version of Gustave's childhood, Jean-Paul Sartre (who preferred intuitive perception to tangible evidence), in the twenty-eight-hundred-page, three-volume study of Flaubert he left uncompleted on his death, paints a grim picture of Gustave's growing-up years. Sartre cites Flaubert's youthful writings as evidence, and one early story does present an adolescent who was persecuted, sullen, ferocious, and miserable.[17] But why not prefer Flaubert's "Mémoires d'un fou" ("Memoirs of a Madman"), written only a year after the story Sartre quotes? In this partly autobiographical tale, Gustave's hero remembers his childhood: "I was merry and cheerful, loving life and my mother. . . ." This child also had "moments of sadness and despair," but dare we build on this a hypothesis concerning Flaubert's childhood?[18]

Sartre paints Flaubert's father as a tyrant, based on analysis of the son's adolescent writings; his conclusion is that Gustave was relegated to the role of family idiot.[19] In his own diary, probably in the very period during which he was producing the stories on which Sartre based his analysis, Gustave wrote: "I loved only one man as a friend and only one other, my father."[20] (The friend, as we shall see, was Alfred Le Poittevin.) Later, after expressing scorn for the medical profession, Flaubert made an exception for his father, recalling how devoted he had been to his profession and to even the least privileged of his patients.[21] Flaubert's letters to his parents, and theirs to him, are further evidence that he was anything but the idiot of the family.

Indeed, we should go back a few years, to deal with a matter that has been questioned but not explained. Family legend dies hard. It was the servant Julie who apparently first told the tale of little Gustave's being unable to read until he was nine years old. She told it to Gustave's niece Caroline, who repeated it to Flaubert's disciple Guy de Maupassant; both he and Caroline published it as fact.[22] This is a piece of nonsense that modern biographers, including Sartre, repeat without questioning. What Flaubert himself would have thought of such a backward child is suggested by his comment on the ignorance of his brother's daughter: because of the abominable way she was being brought up, he complained, she still couldn't read, even though she was six years old.[23]

The truth is that Gustave read early, and well. He seems to have begun writing early, too; later he recalled that he would ask Julie to spell the words he was using in the sentences he invented.[24] The best evidence of Flaubert's capabilities is his own letters, two of them written when he was eight, a year before the legend says he learned to read. Or witness the letter written to his comrade Ernest Chevalier at the end of 1830, when he had just turned nine. He was not only a reader, he was an *author*. He and his friends were writing and performing their own plays. "I'll send you my comedies also," he wrote (true, his spelling is approximative). "If you want to collaborate with me, I will write the comedies and you will write up your dreams. . . ." Soon Gustave told Ernest that he had begun to compose stories in notebooks.

Gustave was all of ten when he informed Ernest that he was now a published writer. He had written a brief paper on Corneille and a still briefer (but funnier) description of constipation, and Ernest's uncle Amédée Mignot had reproduced these pieces in facsimile.[25]

–Herbert Lottman, *Flaubert: A Biography* (Boston, Toronto & London: Little, Brown, 1989), pp. 8–12

---

1. [Lucien] Andrieu, "Les Maisons de la famille Flaubert," [*Les Amis de Flaubert* (bulletin, published in Croisset, May 1967)], 10.
2. Charles Terrasse, "L'Hôtel-Dieu de Rouen," *Échanges-Actualités,* April 1984; Jean Hossard, "Le Musée Flaubert et d'Histoire de la Médecine," (brochure) (Rouen, n.d.).
3. *Album Flaubert* [(Paris: Gallimard, 1972)], 17.
4. Gilles Henry, *L'Histoire du monde c'est une farce* (Condé-sur-Noireau, Calvados: Corlet, 1980), 18, 96f.
5. Gustave Flaubert, *Correspondance,* vol. 1 (Paris: Gallimard-Pléiade, 1973), 844f. (note by Jean Bruneau).
6. *Almanach de Rouen* (Rouen: Periaux, 1834), 43.
7. Théodore Licquet, *Rouen, son histoire* (Rouen: Frère, 1839), 225.
8. *Almanach de Rouen,* 43.
9. Lucien Andrieu, "Les Domestiques de la famille Flaubert," *AF [Les Amis de Flaubert],* May 1974.
10. [Caroline] Franklin-Grout, "Souvenirs intimes," [in Gustave Flaubert, *Correspondance,* vol. 1 (Paris: Conrad, 1926)], x ff.
11. Georges Mignot, "Le Père Mignot," *AF* 14 (1959); letter from Georges Mignot, 1958, in Bibliothèque Municipale de Rouen, 92N4a Flaubert. Mignot warns that references to *père* Mignot may apply either to the old farmer or to his son Amédée.
12. Franklin-Grout, "Souvenirs intimes," xi.
13. GP 2 [Flaubert, *Correspondance,* published by Gallimard-Pléiade, Paris, volume 2]: 321.

Anne-Justine-Caroline Fleuriot, Flaubert's mother, in her youth (reproduction of an anonymous painting; cliché Bibliothèque nationale de France, Paris)

14. GP 1 [Flaubert, *Correspondance,* published by Gallimard-Pléiade, Paris, volume 1]: 660.
15. GP 2: 376.
16. René Dumesnil, *Flaubert: Son Hérédité, son milieu, sa méthode* (Paris, 1906; Geneva: Slatkine Reprints, 1977).
17. Jean-Paul Sartre, *L'Idiot de la famille,* vol. 1 (Paris: Gallimard, 1971), 137ff., 240ff.
18. Gustave Flaubert, *Œuvres complètes,* vol. 1 (Paris: Seuil, 1964), 230f.
19. Sartre, *L'Idiot* 1: 80ff., 98, 381ff.
20. Gustave Flaubert, *Souvenirs, notes et pensées intimes* (Paris: Buchet-Chastel, 1965), 52.
21. Edmond et Jules de Goncourt, *Journal,* vol. 2 (Paris: Fasquelle-Flammarion, 1956), 964.
22. Quoted in Gustave Flaubert, *Madame Bovary* (Paris: Conard, 1930), 540. When Maupassant asked for information for an article, Caroline Commanville informed him in November 1883 that Flaubert learned to read "only several months before entering the *lycée;* he was nine years old." Daniel Sickles Collection, courtesy of Thierry Bodin.
23. GP 1: 317.
24. Ibid., 110.
25. Ibid., 3ff.

* * *

Flaubert attended the Collège Royal in Rouen "solitary and bored, plagued by my teachers and jeered by my schoolmates," as he later wrote in Mémoires d'un fou *(written in 1838; translated as "Diary of a Madman," 1991). In his first year he became friends with Alfred Le Poittevin, with whom he talked about literature for hours. Five years older than Flaubert, Le Poittevin was like an elder brother to the writer. As a student Flaubert received many class prizes and was influenced by his indulgent French teacher, Henry Gourgaud-Dugazon, who encouraged him to write. In 1834 at the school, Flaubert compiled the manuscript newspaper "Art et Progrès," in which he inserted his own stories as well as information regarding ongoing plays at the theater.*

In the following excerpt–the fifth chapter in Flaubert: A Biography*–Lottman traces Flaubert's school experiences and his encounter with Élisa Schlésinger, a woman who represented a great source of inspiration for the romantic writer that Flaubert was as a teenager and young man. She became the main character of the romantic narrative* Mémoires d'un fou; *she reappears in the novel* Novembre, *written in 1842, in the first version of the novel titled* L'Éducation sentimentale, *finished in 1845, as well as in the second version of the novel, published with the same title in 1869.*

Elisa

In October 1835, when Gustave entered the eighth grade, he found another influential teacher in the person of the young historian Adolphe Chéruel. "His appearance alone imposed silence and respect," a student remembered; he was not another Gourgaud-Dugazon. Himself a former Rouen pupil, he had earned his teaching degree at the Ecole Normale in Paris. In Rouen he taught ancient Roman history, using a book just published by one of his professors, Jules Michelet, who was on his way to becoming one of the most respected historians of his time.

Chéruel took his students from Roman to medieval history–this in the ninth grade–and then to modern times, a course that included literary history. In the next-to-the-last year before graduation, his course was called "Philosophy of History." "His teaching has no equal in the provinces," his superior was to observe. An Inspector General admired the way he utilized geography to explain history, and concluded, "Mr. Chéruel knows how to maintain suspense in his class." [1]

If Gourgaud-Dugazon confirmed Flaubert as a writer, Chéruel gave him his material. All his life long, Gustave was happiest when writing or re-creating history; when necessary (as in the Carthage of *Salammbô*), he reinvented it. When he approached contemporary history, as in *A Sentimental Education,* he undertook research that was as thorough as that for any of his stories of antiquity. His history classes also produced some immediate results: short pieces that dealt with historical events, sometimes in the form of fiction. In exploring the past, he seemed to be testing subjects for his own future, though for the time being he seemed to favor assassins, ghosts, and ravished women, as in his tale called "La Fiancée et la Tombe" ("The Fiancée and the Tomb"), written at fourteen.[2] As he grew older, his taste for "cheap thrills"–eroticism, death and decay–intensified; someone once said that the reticence of the adult Flaubert to publish these adolescent works can be explained by their revelatory nature.[3] On the other hand, he did save them, and no other writer of his time left so much juvenile work. Later Flaubert was to manifest a certain fascination for the Marquis de Sade, but it is clear that his temperament was in place before he discovered that Sade could feed it.

Gustave went to school during the tail end of romanticism, which explains how romanticism was able to enter the classroom. It still needed defending, or so Gustave thought, for in a school paper he explained how difficult it was to win acceptance for the Romantics even now, even though "Victor Hugo has never wished to disown Corneille." He placed Hugo with Chateaubriand, Lamartine, Schiller, Goethe, and Byron as the greats of his time.[4] He would have discovered the classics in Dr. Flaubert's library (whose inventory we possess); at some point he picked up Goethe's *Faust* and gobbled it up while seated under a tree on the banks of the Seine, instead of going home.[5]

If we set aside daydreams, and masturbation in the toilets, schoolboys in Rouen had little time for living. But there were days away from school. In one of his most introspective adolescent pieces, Gustave described one such Thursday holiday during the month of November; he would have been thirteen years old at the time. He hurried from school to the family table to find two English girls already seated there. They were sisters, friends of his own sister, the younger of the two small, slender, with eyes livelier, wider, and more attractive than those of her elder sister. But his heart was won by the older girl all the same, with her round head, pink cheeks, and lovely chestnut hair parted down the middle. He watched her at play in the garden; soon they had reached the kissing stage. He enjoyed listening to her foreign accent. (Two other women who were to count in his life spoke French with English accents.) Research has turned up the identity of this young woman: she was Caroline Anne Heuland, born in London in September 1820, Gustave's senior by a year and then some.[6]

Gustave admired both sisters and liked the kissing of both–so he said in another fictional memoir. During the Easter vacation, he found himself alone with the sister he preferred. The day was hot, and she had been running, so when he kissed her on the neck, his lips "remained stuck on that silken skin. . . ." That afternoon he daydreamed about her braids, and about her already evident bustline, which he kissed as much of as her proper clothing allowed. He wrote his first and only poem for her, with appropriate reference to his bitter pain and deep melancholy. (Whether it was the real Gustave or merely the fictional one who wrote the poem is unknown.) She became increasingly provocative; one day she draped herself on his sofa in an inviting manner, but he decided not to take advantage of her, and when she kissed him, he found that she was crying. But time passed, and she was married off to her art teacher. (The real Caroline Heuland married a Rouen painter.)[7]

And then there were the summer holidays. Summer of course meant Trouville. One summer in that fishing village on the Channel–the year was most probably 1836, though this has been contested, but the event will have been no less important if it is found to have taken place in 1835 or in 1837–Gustave discovered that yearning could be as cruel for him as it had been for the English Caroline.

Gustave told the story several times, with variations. The common elements were a teenage boy and a married woman in her twenties, with ample breasts and hair parted in the middle. In all versions, including the historical one, the boy's infatuation remained undeclared.

In the summer of 1836 Gustave had just completed the eighth grade at the Collège Royal; he was four months from his fifteenth birthday. One day–this from his *Mémoires d'un fou,* written two years later but not published in his lifetime–the young man went out walking by himself, as he often did. Beyond the village, on the bathing beach, he noticed an attractive fur-lined cloak with red and black stripes lying on the sand. The tide was rising; already one wave had dampened the cloak's silk fringe. He gathered it up and carried it to drier sand. Then, during lunch at their inn, a woman seated with her husband at the next table addressed him: "Sir, I thank you for your kind gesture." He was embarrassed, and he lowered his eyes and blushed, but not before remarking how lovely she was. "She was tall, dark, with magnificent black hair that fell in tresses on her shoulders; her nose was Greek, her eyes burning, her eyebrows high and admirably arched, her skin was ardent and seemed coated with gold; she was slender and delicate, and there were blue veins climbing her brown and crimson neck." Had he seen all that with lowered eyes? "She could have been reproached for a bit of plumpness, or rather, artistic indifference. . . ."

The description has been quoted at length, for it is the portrait of the amply endowed older woman whom Gustave Flaubert would seek again and again and sometimes find.

In this early story the boy continues to observe the woman in the sea each day, envying the waves that strike her thighs and cover her panting breast with foam. He gazes at the shape of her limbs under the wet bathing dress. And when she approaches him, his "heart beat[s] with violence." Maria–he called her Maria in this first memoir–has an infant daughter. She nurses the baby at her breast, and one day he is there when it happens. He remarks that her breast is round and full; he catches sight of the blue veins again. He is troubled; never before has he seen a woman's nude breast. "It seemed to me that if I had placed my lips on it, my teeth would have bitten it with rage."

Gustave's relations with Maria and with her husband were to be pursued, but more calmly. Her husband was half artist, half traveling salesman; he sported a mustache, smoked cockily, and was lively, friendly; he enjoyed food, and young Gustave marveled when he walked three leagues to buy a melon in the nearest town. Later the real Gustave was to remind the real Maria–whose married name was Elisa Schlesinger–of the day her husband Maurice walked from Honfleur to Trouville with a gigantesque melon on his shoulder.[8]

She was born Elisa Foucault on September 23, 1810, in Vernon, another Seine town, this one thirty-five miles upstream from Rouen. Her father had served under Napoleon and retired a captain. She was raised in a local convent and at nineteen married a junior officer stationed in Vernon. Not long after that, her husband, by name Emile-Jacques Judée, went off for five years' duty in Africa. Somewhere, perhaps in Vernon, she met Maurice Schlesinger.[9]

But this is already more than Gustave knew, more than he was to know for a long time, and it is not yet the whole story.

He continued to see the Schlesingers in Trouville, finding ways to get conversations started, to join them on walks. In the memoir, one evening the husband suggests a boat ride; as they row, Maria talks, and Gustave, "intoxicated with love," abandons himself to the sound of her voice and the rocking of the boat. He accompanies her to her door, stays behind to look up at her window, and, when the lights are extinguished, decides that she has gone to sleep. But then, all of a sudden, he thinks otherwise, in a fit of rage and jealousy. He thinks of her husband, vulgar and jovial, "and the most hideous of images came to me": Maria belongs to that man.[10]

In *Mémoires d'un fou,* the author says goodbye at the end of the holidays, and it is an "adieu" forever. But

Dr. Achille-Cléophas Flaubert, chief surgeon of the Hôtel-Dieu (lithograph by Legal, printed by Lemercier, 1836; cliché Bibliothèque nationale de France, Paris)

this is because Gustave himself was still too close to the summer of 1836. In real life he was to see much more of the Schlesingers. Maurice Schlesinger was a Prussian from Berlin, born in October 1797, so that he was nearly thirty-nine when the young writer met him. He was Jewish but apparently converted to Catholicism when he married Elisa–so says Richard Wagner, who was notoriously sensitive to such things. Schlesinger's father had been a music publisher and founder of an influential musical magazine in Berlin. After serving in the Prussian army, notably in the final campaign against Napoleon, Maurice had moved to France, begun to sell sheet music and instruments, and founded a *Gazette et Revue Musicale de Paris.*[11]

If Elisa Schlesinger was Maria in that memoir of adolescence, she became Emilie in young Flaubert's first attempt at a book-length work, "A Sentimental Education"–the title used for a better and different book in his maturity. In the final, published *Sentimental Education,* which is also a final attempt by Flaubert to exorcise the vision on the beach at Trouville, Elisa is again called Maria, and the cloak recovered from the waves is a shawl that she wears on a boat ride, which would have blown away had the young man not rushed to save it. In the novel Elisa's husband, the music publisher, becomes Jacques Arnoux, an art dealer and the publisher of an art magazine.

Maxime Du Camp was the first to talk about Elisa. In his memoirs, in which Gustave Flaubert is the central character, Du Camp reproached Gustave for

The quarters of the Flaubert family on the second floor of the Hôtel-Dieu. Gustave Flaubert was born in a bedroom here. The painting on the easel is of Julie Flaubert, the wife of Gustave's brother, Achille (cliché Bruno Maurey, courtesy of the Musée Flaubert et d'Histoire de la Médecine, Rouen).

lacking tenderness, but he remembered the beach at Trouville. He got the dates wrong, he didn't mention Elisa's name, even though he knew it, but he described her. "She was pretty and above all curious," he began. He mentioned her headbands, her darkish complexion, her large, somber eyes.[12] At the beginning of his liaison with Louise Colet, another older woman with a generous bust, Gustave explained that he had loved one woman from the age of fourteen to the age of twenty, but without confessing his love.[13] Louise Colet and Elisa Schlesinger were both born in September 1810, only a week apart.

Yet no one outside Flaubert's family circle, and only a couple of his friends, ever got a glimpse of Elisa. One of the mysteries that has stirred the curiosity of writers closer to our own time is whether Gustave and Elisa consummated their love. In the first version of "A Sentimental Education," written when Flaubert was still in his early twenties, the character who stands for the author seduces and runs off with the married woman he desires. But the mature version of *A Sentimental Education* does not give the lovers a similar license. Had it happened in life, remarked an investigative writer who made Elisa something of a specialty, we should have discovered hints of it in the thousands of pages of Flaubert's correspondence.[14]

She did seem untouchable. But the young woman Gustave encountered in Trouville already had a past, and it is not certain that Gustave ever in his life learned much about it. Even her relationship with Maurice Schlesinger was less conventional than appearances might have suggested. For when Elisa left her first husband, Lieutenant Judée, she didn't divorce him right away. The daughter she nursed on the beach was Maurice's, conceived after the departure of her husband for Algeria, but in the summer of 1836 Elisa and Maurice were not yet legally married. Their child was declared as the daughter of Maurice Schlesinger and "an unnamed mother," for if Elisa had been registered as the mother, the child would have belonged to Lieutenant Judée. Yet there seemed to be nothing to fear from this officer, and even on his return to France he left Elisa in peace.[15]

How explain the passivity of Lieutenant Judée?

Elisa Foucault's marriage to the young officer, we know from the license, was celebrated late one night (at eleven-thirty, then a fashionable hour for a wedding). The groom's witnesses were fellow officers; one of the bride's witnesses was a colonel.[16] A man who made a career of investigating the story of Gustave and Elisa thought that he had discovered the truth about Elisa's marriage. It has not been published before, and is offered here as a possibility. During the wedding banquet—long past midnight—the groom's soldier comrades teased him about his virginity. Surely drunk by then, Lieutenant Judée offered to show what he could do by taking his bride then and there. But he was not up to the effort, and we are asked to believe that his comrades took over the job.

Elisa slipped away before dawn, taking refuge with her sisters in Vernon and then traveling down to Paris. The story is that she became a woman for hire. Schlesinger found her and took her in; when she gave birth, he could not be sure the child was his, but he recognized it all the same. When Gustave encountered Elisa in Trouville soon after that, she was already the good mother and unattainable spouse he could only yearn for.[17]

—Lottman, *Flaubert: A Biography,* pp. 23–28

---

1. [François-Valentin] Bouquet, *Souvenirs du Collège [de Rouen par un élève de pension (1829–1835)* (Rouen: Cagniard, 1895)], 74ff.; Labracherie, "L'Elève Flaubert," 4f.
2. [Jean] Bruneau, *Les Débuts [littéraires de Gustave Flaubert* (Paris: A. Colin, 1962)], 162ff., 167.
3. Victor Brombert, *Flaubert* (Paris: Seuil, 1971), 33ff.
4. Bibliothèque Nationale, manuscript NAF 18244.
5. André Dubuc, "La Bibliothèque générale du père de Flaubert," in *Les Rouennais et la famille Flaubert;* [Caroline] Franklin-Grout, "Souvenirs intimes" [in Gustave Flaubert, *Correspondance,* vol. 1 (Paris: Conard, 1926)], xxxix.
6. *OC* (S) [Flaubert, *Œuvres complètes,* published by Editions du Seuil, Paris]: 240ff.; Lucien Andrieu, "Un amour inconnu de Gustave Flaubert," *AF,* April 1963.
7. Andrieu, "Un Amour inconnu."
8. GP 2 [Flaubert, *Correspondance,* published by Gallimard-Pléiade, Paris, volume 2]: 637.
9. G. Tenon, "Un Amour de Flaubert: Elisa Foucault, une vernonnaise," *Les Cahiers Vernonnais,* April 1974.
10. *OC* (S) 1: 236ff.
11. [Emile] Gérard-Gailly, *Flaubert et "les fantômes de Trouville"* [Paris: La Renaissance du Livre, 1930)], 59ff.
12. Maxime Du Camp, *Souvenirs littéraires,* vol. 2 (Paris: Hachette, 1906), 336ff.
13. GP 1 [Flaubert, *Correspondance,* published by Gallimard-Pléiade, Paris, volume 1]: 279.
14. Gérard-Gailly, *Flaubert et "les fantômes de Trouville,"* 91ff.
15. [Emile] Gérard-Gailly, *L'Unique passion de Flaubert* (Paris: Le Divan, 1932), 3lff.
16. [Emile] Gérard-Gailly, *Le Grand amour de Flaubert* (Paris: Aubier, 1944), 49.
17. Dr. Germain Galérant was told the story by Emile Gérard-Gailly, who apparently obtained this version of events only after publishing his books on Flaubert. Letter from Dr. Galérant to the author.

Early Stories

As a youth Flaubert was constantly writing stories or imagining plays in which he acted with his younger sister, Caroline, his friend Ernest Chevalier, and other playmates. In 1836, for example, he wrote at least nine short stories, one of which, "Bibliomanie" (translated as Bibliomania: A Tale, *1929), was published in* Le Colibri *(12 February 1837), a small literary newspaper in Rouen.*

His essay-like story "Une leçon d'histoire naturelle—genre: commis,*" a translation of which follows, was also published in* Le Colibri *(30 March 1837).*

A Lecture on Natural History—Genus: *Clerk*

From Aristotle to Cuvier, from Pliny to Blainville, natural science has made great strides.[1] Each scientist has brought his aggregate of observations and studies to this field. Intrepid explorers have traveled the world over and have made important discoveries, but for the most part they have brought back only small black, yellow, or multicolored furs. It was helpful to learn that bears eat honey and have a weakness for cream tarts.

I admit that those are very great discoveries. But no one has yet thought about discussing the *Clerk,* the most interesting animal of our era. No one has specialized narrowly enough, or meditated, observed, and traveled sufficiently to be in a position to speak with reasonable authority on the Clerk.

Another obstacle arose: how should one classify this animal? For a long time people were undecided among the sloth, the howling monkey, and the jackal.

In short, the question remained undecided. The solution to this problem was left to the future, along with discovering the origin of the genus: *dog.*

Indeed, it was difficult to classify an animal so illogical in its makeup. Its otter hat would make your judgment lean toward an aquatic life, just like its shaggy brown frock coat, whereas its thick wool vest proved indisputably that this animal originated in the northern countries. Its curved nails would lead you to take it for a carnivore, if it had teeth to match. Finally, the Academy of Science stipulated that it was digitigrade. Unfortunately, people soon realized that it had an ironwood cane and that it occasionally paid visits on New Year's Day in a hackney coach and went to dine in the country in a one-horse chaise.[2]

My long experience has placed me in a position to instruct humankind. I can speak with the modest confidence of a zoologist. My frequent trips to various offices have left me enough impressions to describe the anatomy and customs of the animals that inhabit them.

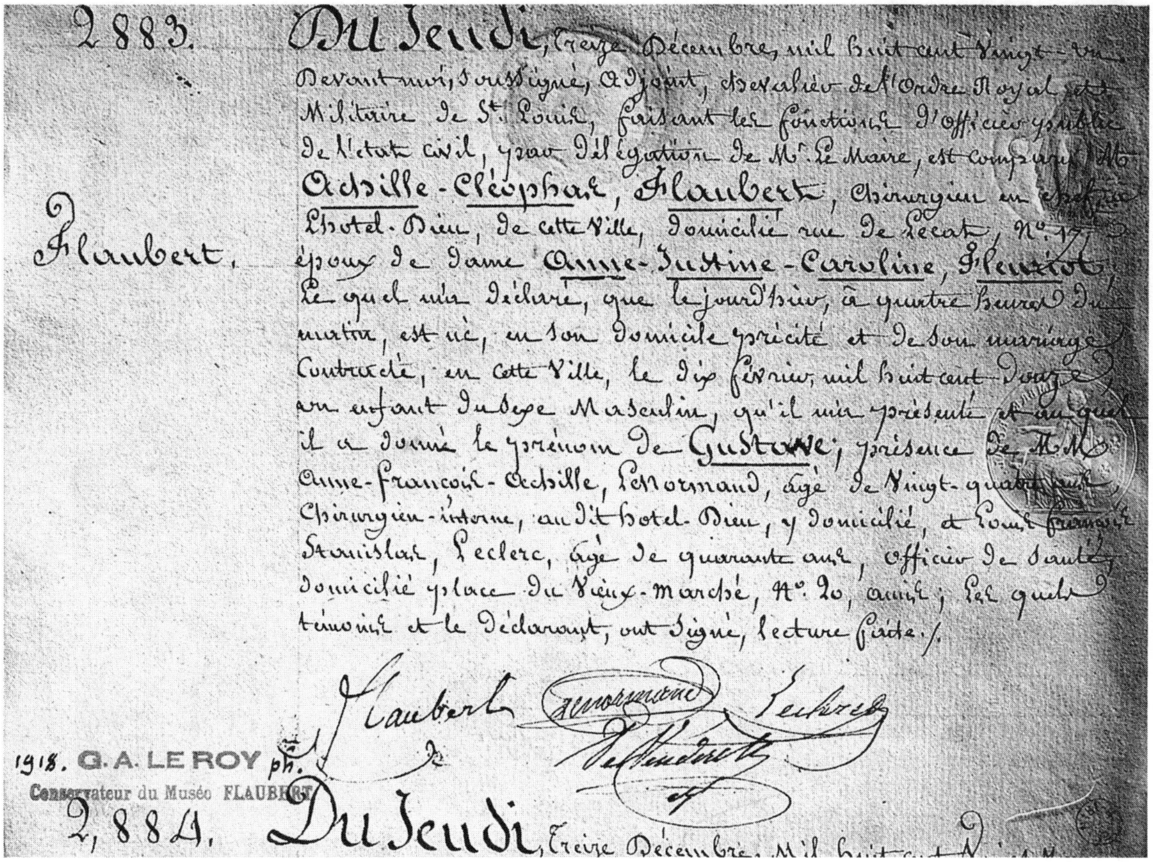

2883. Du Jeudi, treize Décembre, mil huit cent vingt-un.

Flaubert.

Devant moi, soussigné, Adjoint, chevalier de l'Ordre Royal et Militaire de St. Louis, faisant les fonctions d'officier public de l'état civil, par délégation de Mr. Le Maire, est comparu Mr. Achille-Cléophas, Flaubert, chirurgien en chef à l'hôtel-Dieu, de cette ville, domicilié rue de Lecat, No. 17, époux de dame Anne-Justine-Caroline, Fleuriot, Lequel m'a déclaré, que le jour d'hier, à quatre heures du matin, est né, en son domicile précité et de son mariage contracté, en cette ville, le dix février, mil huit cent douze, un enfant du sexe masculin, qu'il m'a présenté et auquel il a donné le prénom de Gustave; présence de MM. Anne-François-Achille, Lenormand, âgé de vingt-quatre ans, chirurgien-interne, au dit hôtel-Dieu, y domicilié, et Louis-François Stanislas, Leclerc, âgé de quarante ans, officier de santé domicilié place du Vieux-marché, No. 20, amis; les quels témoins et le déclarant, ont signé, lecture faite./

Flaubert Lenormand Leclerc

1918. G. A. LE ROY ph.
Conservateur du Musée FLAUBERT

2,884. Du Jeudi, treize Décembre, Mil huit cent vingt

Flaubert's birth certificate, established on Thursday, 13 December 1821, in the presence of his father, who declared that Gustave had been born at four in the morning the previous day (photograph from Rouen's official records; Collections de la Bibliothèque municipale de Rouen. Cliché Thierry Ascencio-Parvy)

I have seen all species of Clerks, from tax collectors to record keepers. Those trips have completely ruined me, and I ask my readers to sign the appropriate approval forms for a man who has devoted himself to science, in the process has worn out two umbrellas and a dozen hats (including their oilcloth rain protectors), and has had his boots resoled six times.

The Clerk is between thirty-six and sixty years old. It is short and pudgy with a ruddy complexion. It has a snuffbox called a "rat tail," a red wig, silver glasses for the office, and a cotton-print handkerchief.

It often spits, and when you sneeze it says, "God bless you!" It has its fur groomed differently, according to the season.

In the summer it wears a straw hat and light cotton pants over which it spreads a handkerchief to keep from getting ink spots on them. Its shoes are made of beaver and its vest is twill. Invariably it wears a detachable velvet collar. In winter it wears blue trousers with an enormous frock coat for protection against the cold. The coat is the element of clerks, as water is to fish.

Originating in Eurasia via Africa, it is unfortunately very widespread in these climes. It is mild-mannered but defends itself when attacked. It usually remains unmarried, so it leads a bachelor's life. The bachelor's life! In other words, when it goes to a cafe, it addresses the lady at the cashier's desk as "Miss," takes along the remaining sugar cubes on its saucer, and sometimes allows itself a cheap, slender cigar. Oh, but then the Clerk can be a hellion! The day it smokes its cigar, it is quarrelsome, cuts itself four pens before finding one suitable, is gruff with the office boy, drops its glasses, and smears ink on its ledger, which greatly upsets it.

In other instances, the Clerk is married. Then it is a peaceful and proper citizen, no longer a youthful hothead. It takes its turn standing guard, goes to bed at nine o'clock, and never goes out without an umbrella. On Sunday mornings it takes its coffee with milk, reads the *Constitutional,* the *Echo,* the *Parliamentary Register,* or some other paper of similar persuasion.[3]

Two views of the Rouen of Flaubert's youth. The bottom illustration, circa 1842, shows the considerable presence of industry (top, courtesy of the Musée des Arts et Traditions Populaires, Paris; bottom, lithograph by Bichebois and Adam, cliché Bibliothèque nationale de France, Paris).

It is a strong partisan of the Charter of 1830 and of the freedoms of the July Revolution. It respects the laws of its country, shouts "Long live the King!" with fireworks in the background, and cleans its sword belt every Saturday evening.

The Clerk supports the National Guard. Its heart is stirred when a drum roll summons it to the parade ground, tightly buckled up and choked by its collar as it hums the tune "Oh, what a joy a soldier's life is!"

As for its mate, she stays home to darn socks, makes him cloth oversleeves, reads melodramas from the Ambigu Theater, and–as her speciality–dunks bread in her soup.

Although it is chaste, the Clerk nevertheless has a licentious and playful mind, for it says "my pretty child" to young ladies entering its office. Moreover, it is a confirmed reader of Paul de Kock, especially sitting near the stove in the evening, wearing its slippers and its black silk cap.[4]

You ought to see this interesting biped in the office, copying its register. It has removed its coat and collar, working in shirtsleeves and wearing its wool vest.

It is hunched over the desk, with its quill tucked above its left ear. It writes slowly, savors the smell of ink, and enjoys watching it cover a huge sheet of paper. It repeats to itself what it writes, with its mumbling giving off a constant nasal sound. But when it is in a hurry, it hastily scatters periods, commas, dashes, "The Ends," and paragraphs. That is the height of talent. With its colleagues, it often discusses the return of snails after the frost, the replacing of the port, the iron bridge, and the use of natural gas. If it peers through the curtains that keep out the light and notices that the weather is rainy, it suddenly exclaims, "Damn, gonna be thick as pea soup!" Then it turns back to its work.

The Clerk has a mania for staying warm and lives in a perpetual oven. Its greatest pleasure is to get the stove near the cashier's desk red hot. Then its laughter echoes contentment. Steadily panting, it takes its handkerchief and joyfully wipes the sweat streaming down its face. But soon it is so stifled by the weight of its happiness that it cannot keep from exclaiming, "It's so nice here!" And when it rises to this bliss, it begins to copy with renewed vigor. Its pen goes faster than usual, its eyes sparkle, it forgets to put the lid back on its snuffbox, and rapt with heady joy, it suddenly gets up from its seat and hurries to the sanctuary to bring back an enormous log. It approaches the stove, backs away several times, opens the door by reaching out with a ruler, and then throws in the piece of wood, announcing, "One more match!" It just stands there for a few moments with its mouth open, listening to the flame rumble in the flue with a muffled and pleasing sound.

If you unfortunately leave the door open when you enter its office, the Clerk becomes furious, extends its nails, scratches its hair piece, stamps its foot, swears, and from the midst of the columns, the copies, and the numerous ledgers with their credits and debits, you can hear a voice yelping, "Close the door, fer Chrisake! Can't you read? Look at the sign on the cashier's desk! The heat's going to escape, dammit!"

Do not consider hailing it as "Clerk!" Instead, address it as "Mr. Employee."

The Employee has long nails because one of its favorite pastimes is filing them. In the morning it brings its small loaf of bread in its pocket, opens its desk, takes out its broad green visor, and waits for the office boy to bring it a breakfast of salted butter or its daily cheese.

When the day draws to a close, the Employee is thoroughly tickled to see the cashier's door crack open so that the person lighting the oil-burning lamps can be seen. For the Argand lamp furnishes the bureaucrat with a wondrous subject of conversation that inspires much debate among all the employees. As soon as the lamp is lit, it is scrutinized to see whether the wick is good or whether it has slipped out. If the knob gets turned too high or if a half-dozen lamp glasses get broken, it complains bitterly and repeats with the deepest sadness that the light hurts its eyes. That is why it wears the enormous visor that casts a shadow over its neighbor's sheet of paper. The neighbor declares that it cannot possibly write without any light and asks that the visor be removed. But the sly Clerk pulls the visor down more tightly over its ears and even fastens the chin strap.

At the theater every Sunday it sits in the loges or in the orchestra section. It whistles for the curtain to go up and applauds the vaudeville acts. In its youth it engages in a match of dominoes between acts. Whenever it loses, it goes home and breaks a couple of dishes, no longer refers affectionately to its mate as "my bride," neglects its dog Azor, gobbles down the boiled beef reheated from the previous evening, furiously salts its green beans, and then falls asleep to dream about columns of numbers, the weather, civic improvements, and its daily sums.

I believe that just about covers everything in general about the Clerk, or at least I am beginning to feel that the reader's patience is running short.

I still have numerous observations in my notes on the different species of this genus, such as the Clerk of the tax collector, the Clerk of the dry goods merchant, the Clerk of the customs official (who sometimes rises to supervisor, dabbles in literature, and writes billboard copy and serialized stories), the traveling salesman, the Employee of the mayor's office, and a thousand others.

Those are the uncompensated fruits of my studious nights. But if times get better and if the turbulent political climate improves, well, I might appear on the scene again and publish the conclusion to these zoology lectures as a huge slice of society extending from the Tax Clerk to the stockbroker's Cashier.

–translated by Robert Griffin in *Early Writings: Gustave Flaubert* (Lincoln & London: University of Nebraska Press, 1991), pp. 45–49

---

1. This opening sentence exemplifies the sort of ambiguous irony that shades *Bouvard et Pécuchet* throughout. The stature of Aristotle and Pliny as Greek and Roman natural scientists matches the Classical balance of the sentence, but not that of Cuvier and Blainville. Renowned for his *Lessons in Comparative Anatomy* and *Animal Kingdom,* Baron Georges Cuvier (1769–1832), became councillor of state under Napoleon until his death, five years before the composition of this text. His prize student, Henri Blainville (1777–1850), was a zoologist who lectured on mollusks and worms at the Museum of Natural History, and replaced Cuvier as chair of comparative anatomy at the Academy of Sciences, after publicly debunking some of his tutor's basic principles. The ideas of Blainville appear in the penultimate paragraph of this treatise.
2. The name used for the one-horse chaise (*coucou*) indicates that the Clerk is up to date in his post-1830 tastes.
3. The *Parliamentary Register* approximates the American *Congressional Record;* the other newspapers testify to the political volatility and dread of revolution that were belied and yet explained by bourgeois conservatism following the Hundred Days (as Napoleon's return from Elba is called). The *Constitutionnel,* for instance, was a child of that period (cf. sec.II of "Whatever You Want"), founded by former revolutionaries. Like Jacques Arnoux's *Art industriel* in *L'Education sentimentale,* the paper changed its name according to shifting political currents, to *L'Indépendant, L'Echo du Soir,* and back to *Le Constitutionnel* shortly after the restoration of the Bourbon family (June 28, 1815). Attacks on the government led to its decline, after which it became eminently bourgeois and conservative, as would befit the Clerk. His support of the July Revolution (next paragraph) places him in the camp of Louis-Philippe (the so-called Orleanist, bourgeois, or July monarch), in the golden age of the European middle class.
4. Paul de Kock (1793–1871) was a popular novelist who turned successfully to comic opera. The Théâtre de l'Ambigu-comique (Boulevard du Temple) mentioned in the preceding paragraph was newly inaugurated in 1828, primarily as a puppet theater.

* * *

In the following excerpt from his study of Flaubert's early writings, critic Eric Gans discusses "Une leçon d'histoire naturelle–genre: commis,*" comparing it to the contemporaneous fantastic tale "Rêve d'enfer" (translated as "Dream of Hell," 1991). Although Gans says that* Le commis *shows Flaubert's attitudes toward the* bêtise *(stupidity) of the bourgeois and their* idées reçues *(received ideas), he argues that part of Flaubert's fascination with the life of the clerk is that "in his bourgeois security [the commis] experiences not the slightest degree of alienation."*

The *Bêtise* of Bourgeois Life

Of all Flaubert's works before *Mémoires d'un fou, Le commis* has undoubtedly attracted the most general interest. One of the two early works published in the Rouen journal, the *Colibri,* and undoubtedly the most professional of the *œuvres de jeunesse,* it has been widely viewed[1] as a prefiguration of *Bouvard et Pécuchet* and as the first clear expression of Flaubert's "realist" tendencies.

The date of its composition is unknown. In a letter to Ernest Chevalier of March 24, 1837 (only three days after the termination of *Rêve d'enfer*), Flaubert mentions that he is about to correct the proofs of *Le commis.*[2] The story appeared in the *Colibri* six days later. Since Flaubert had spoken to the editor of the journal about the completed work on March 23, its composition must have antedated the completion of *Rêve d'enfer* (dated March 21), but we have no way of knowing by how much. In the absence of any other evidence, the most plausible hypothesis is that it was written at some time following the publication of *Bibliomanie* in the same journal on February 28, which would make it more or less contemporaneous with *Rêve d'enfer.*

. . . .

The *physiologie,* to which genre *Le commis* belongs, is less a work of fiction than a form of essay, although in such works as Balzac's *Physiologie du mariage* and particularly in his *Petites misères de la vie conjugale,* a great deal of fictional content can be brought in as illustrative material. The essence of the genre is its generally good-natured ridicule of the reified existence of the bourgeois–the portrayal of a type, usually a professional one, as the unreflective, unfree object of a "scientific" investigation. The depiction of the mannerisms and "idées reçues" of the type in question involves the sort of comic spirit analyzed by Bergson in *Le rire:* the assimilation of human activity to mere mechanism. An analogous critique of bourgeois social types was carried on in the popular lithographs (Monnier, Gavarni, Daumier) of the July monarchy.

Because *Le commis* contains no materials of directly personal significance, it is chiefly important as a manifestation of the keen interest that Flaubert had begun to take at this early stage of his career in the "bêtise" of bourgeois life.

. . . .

. . . *Le commis* can be said to participate in a general growth of Flaubert's concern with the unideal reality of the bourgeois milieu. But this concern is not sufficient to explain the great interest the author shows in *Le commis* for concrete, trivial manifestations of the *bêtise* of bourgeois life. Flaubert is not merely analyzing the unideality of the *commis* as a member of contemporary society; he is in a positive sense attracted to the minutiae of his "hero's" everyday existence. As has often been observed, *Le commis* represents the first clear-cut manifestation of a lifelong fascination with such details that led Flaubert to compile the *Dictionnaire des idées reçues* and the "Dossier" of *Bouvard et Pécuchet.*

. . . .

The story of the *commis* . . . cannot become the subject of a work of fiction because it is not a "story" at all, but a static description. Its source in the author's personality is not his interest in the praxial possibilities for movement through the world, but his fascination with the "being," the "matière" that already *is* in the world. The details of this being attract and tempt Flaubert because, like the "stupidity" of the childhood ideal, the *bêtise* of the *commis* places him in a form of paradise, secure from any possibility of alienation.

This unideal paradise can acquire a greater significance than the ideal one now that the unideal world has replaced the Romantic universe destroyed at the end of "Rêve d'enfer" as the locale of Flaubert's fictions. The reified career of the *commis,* and of the bourgeois in general, is an alternative to authentic praxis that exists not in an inaccessible past but in the real world itself. And in this sense, the *commis* offers . . . a genuine, permanent temptation for the author. The childhood ideal can exist only for the Romantic hero and accordingly plays no part in Flaubert's mature works; but the adult "paradise" of *la bêtise* first revealed in "Le commis" is never renounced.

—Eric Gans, *The Discovery of Illusion: Flaubert's Early Works, 1835–1837* (Berkeley: University of California Press, 1971), pp. 157–161

---

1. Notably by Edouard Maynial, *La jeunesse de Flaubert,* 2d ed. (Paris, 1913), pp. 95 ff.
2. "J'ai été hier [March 23] chez Degouve-Denuncques [editor-in-chief of the *Colibri*], mon "Commis" sera inséré jeudi prochain et mercredi je corrigerai avec lui les épreuves." [Yesterday I went to see Degouve-Denuncques, my *Commis* will be inserted next Thursday, and on Wednesday I will correct the proofs with him.] (*Correspondance* [Paris: Conard, 1910–1933], I, 24.)

* * *

The Place du Vieux Marché in Rouen in 2004, where Joan of Arc was burned. During Flaubert's life a guillotine still stood there. As a child of six or seven, he passed the square just after an execution and could see fresh blood on the paving stones as well as the basket containing a severed head (photograph by Éric Le Calvez).

Flaubert decided not to attempt to publish much of what he wrote, but he preserved the manuscripts, most of which have been published since his death. In the following excerpted essay on one of Flaubert's most important juvenile stories that went unpublished during his lifetime, critic Shoshana Felman is less interested in discussing the young author's fascination with Élisa Schlésinger than in his use of the idea of madness. In Mémoires d'un fou, *she argues that Flaubert–unlike Ariadne, who gives her lover a thread to follow out of the Minotaur's labyrinth–provides the reader with only a bewildering text.*

Reading *Mémoires d'un fou*

Seen as the first draft of what Flaubert will three versions later finally call the definitive, publishable text of his *Sentimental Education,* the *Memoirs of a Madman* has long been considered as merely the "preface to a writer's life." But can a writer's life really be said to have prefaces? Can the well-known oeuvre be clearly set off from the rest, which would serve as its hors d'oeuvre? Can one locate the point at which the author's real works begin? And can one, indeed, restrict those works to what are customarily and somewhat arbitrarily known as *master*works? It is perhaps time to attempt to read, among the texts of an author like Flaubert, those rafts of drafts that lie in the margins of the official oeuvre, in which writing can still be seen as a process of struggle and work. For doesn't "the production of meaning in Flaubert"[1] take place precisely in those folds where the text is actively sketching and scrapping itself, marking its boundaries only to bound over them?

The Flaubert that wrote *Memoirs of a Madman,* then, was a sixteen-year-old boy. The text is "romantic" to the hilt, but nevertheless sets out to attack the values and illusions of Romanticism: at once naïve and sophisticated, talky and declamatory, buzzing with awkwardness and intelligence, it disconcerts and ensnares readers, provoking them into becoming, in imitation or in reaction, either too ironic or too naïve. How can such a text be read? How is one to account for *both* its simplification *and* its sophistication, *both* its irony *and* its faith?

I shall propose here, successively, three directions for reading: 1) a "thematic" reading of "madness"; 2) a reading of the *ironic function* of "madness," of the irony the text directs toward the naïveté of Romantic "madness"; and 3) an *ironic* reading of the text's irony, which will bring out that irony's own naïveté: a reading generated by the irony that the text *writes,* so to speak, in its strata of silence, over and against the irony it *speaks.*

These three interpretations, all of which seem to me to be both suggested and authorized by Flaubert, will, however, prove contradictory, successively subverting each other to reveal the dynamics of the production of meaning in the text as inseparable from such questions of approach and from a general problematic of reading.

Flaubert at age nine, from a sketch by Eustache-Hyacinthe Langlois (Collections de la Bibliothèque municipale de Rouen. Cliché Thierry Ascencio-Parvy)

The Thematics of "Madness"

Let us then follow the Ariadne's thread of the *theme* of "madness," which instead of leading us out of the labyrinth, will lead us straight into it. We are warned at the beginning of the book: "it is a madman who has written these pages."[2] A madman in what sense? We read further: "I was in boarding school from the age of ten, and I soon developed there a profound loathing for my fellow man. . . . All my inclinations were found offensive: in class, it was my ideas; at recess, my uncivilized preference for solitude. From then on, I was a madman" (III, p. 232). Madness, then, is an uncivilized solitude, an "eccentricity," the difference that separates the young romantic from those around him. It is also a grand and unique love, the impossible desire for a woman one will never see again: "O, Maria . . . precious angel of my youth . . . adieu! And yet, how I would have loved you! . . . Oh, my soul melts with delight at every *madness* that my love invents" (XXII, p. 247). "No, I could never express to you what sweet sensations, what heartfelt intoxications, what bliss and *madness* there is in love" (X, p. 237).[3] Madness is thus the dream of an imagination overwrought in solitude. And it is sometimes terrifying: "I had frightening visions, enough to drive one *mad* with terror" (IV, p. 233). "It was just barely, if at all, that they granted me imagination, which was, according to them, a fever in the brain akin to madness" (V, p. 234).

According to them. Hence the term madness is borrowed from the language of others, in which it implies a judgment, a condemnation: "Youth! The age of *madness* and dreams, of poetry and foolishness, all synonyms on the lips of those who judge the world *sanely*" (III, p. 232; Flaubert's emphasis). The fact that the narrator calls himself "mad" suggests that he accepts the division such a judgment implies, that he judges himself to be different from the norm, to stand outside the values of bourgeois society: "They laughed at me . . . who would never have a positive idea, who would never display a propensity for any profession" (III, pp. 232–233). "Oh, how full of dreams my childhood was! What a poor *madman* I was, without set ideas or positive opinions!" (II, p. 230). Madness, then, in a positivistic world, is the rejection of positivity.

Here, in sum, is the essence of the narrative project of the *Memoirs of a Madman:* "I am therefore going to write the story of my life. . . . But have I lived? . . . My life is not a collection of facts; my life is my thought. . . . You will learn of the adventures of that life . . . so rich in feeling, so poor in facts" (II, pp. 230, 232). The lexical distribution of the term "madness" reflects this narrative project quite remarkably: the twenty-five occurrences of the term (or the related terms, "mad," "follies," etc.) found in the space of twenty-three chapters (eighteen pages in the "Intégrale" edition) are unevenly distributed; as if by chance, the term "madness" happens to be absent from three consecutive chapters, precisely the ones that relate the *facts* of the story–the encounter with the great love (chapters XI, XII, XIII). In the middle of the work, we find a kind of hole in this "madness." The term reappears when the woman departs. Madness, then, is not an event, it is not the *fact* of love, but rather what comes before–and after. "I put myself back in a past that would never return. . . . There was chaos in my heart, an immense buzzing, a madness. Everything had gone like a dream" (XIV, p. 239).

"Madness" is also an excess of remembrance. The *Memoirs of a Madman* is then perhaps the madness of memories, or of memory itself: a memory without a referent, a memory not of what is external, some event or fact, but of what is internal, a desire, a reminiscence–a memory not so much of the object of desire as of the desiring subject himself. We recognize here what is at stake in any Romantic project of "confession": the possibility of unveiling a subjective "identity," a project that entails both "sincerity" ("I made a vow to tell all," XV, p. 239) and expressivity ("these pages . . . contain an entire soul," Dedication, p. 230). This undertaking is, however, felt to be impossible; it is experienced as an unresolvable tension between an interior and anterior subject and a language whose exteriority renders it incapable of expressing that subject's real meaning or fundamental origins.

> I would tell you many other things, much more beautiful and sweet, if I could say all that I felt of love, of ecstasy, of regret. Can one say in words the beating of one's heart? (XXI, p. 247)

> How can one express in words those things for which there is no language, those things imprinted on the heart, those mysteries of soul unknown to the soul itself? (XIII, p. 238)

To "ex-press" oneself is thus an impossible task; one could never "press" words hard enough to "ex"-tract from their exteriority the nectar of the inner heart or mind.

> How high my mind flew in its delirium, high in those regions unknown to man where there are neither worlds, nor planets, nor sun! I possessed an infinity more immense, if that is possible, than God's, where poetry was cradled and tried its wings in an atmosphere of love and ecstasy; then came the inevitable descent back down from such sublimity to words,–and how can words express the harmony arising in the poet's heart, those Titan thoughts that make phrases bend beneath them . . . ? By what rungs climb down from the infinite to the empirical? . . . Then I had moments of sadness and despair, I felt my own force breaking me and my frailty bringing me shame, for language is only a feeble and distinct echo of thought. (II, p. 231)

To one who rejects all positivism, language itself seems too "finite," too empirical. And that is perhaps another, the ultimate, madness of the *Memoirs:* the desire to ex-press a "soul," an interiority that can never be externalized–the desire to de-limit the limitless. Madness is at once what is ineffable and the desire to *name* the ineffable.

The Ironic Function of "Madness"

While language is judged inadequate as the "expression" of the subject, it nonetheless retains one power: that of naming and, through naming, mastering the object. They name *me:* they judge me, they *categorize*

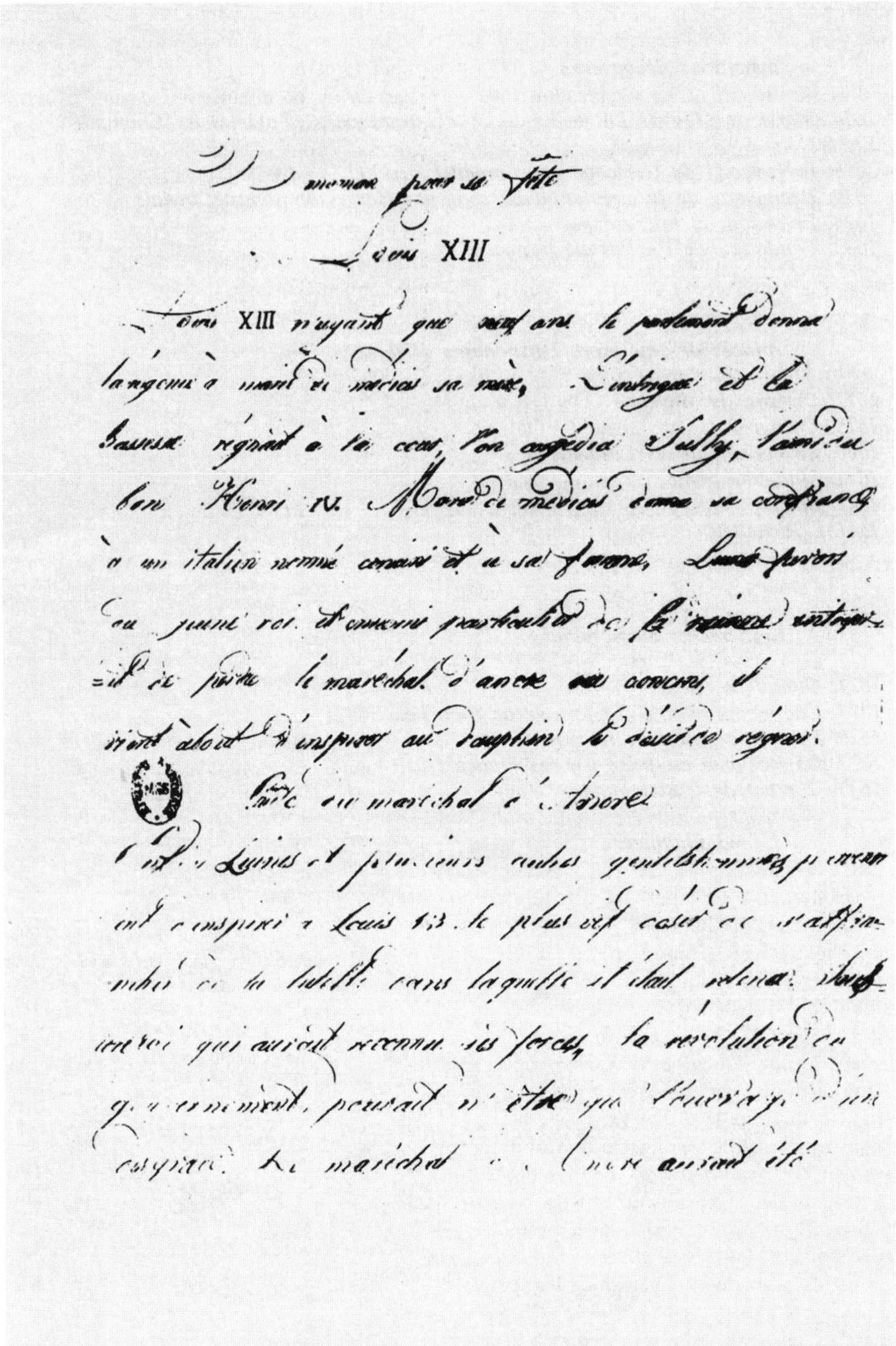

Pour maman pour sa fête

Louis XIII

Louis XIII n'ayant que neuf ans le parlement donna la régence à marie de médicis sa mère. L'intrigue et la bassesse régnait à la cour, l'on congédia Sully, l'ami du bon Henri IV. Marie de médicis donna sa confiance à un italien nommé concini et à sa femme. Luines favori du jeune roi et ennemi particulier de la reine intrigua: il fit périr le maréchal d'ancre ou concini, il avait abord inspiré au dauphin le désir de régner.

Mort du maréchal d'Ancre

C'est de Luines et plusieurs autres gentilshommes qui avaient inspiré à Louis 13 le plus vif désir de s'affranchir de la tutelle dans laquelle il était retenu. Ensuite un roi qui aurait reconnu ses forces, la révolution du gouvernement pouvait n'être que l'ouvrage d'un [illegible] espace. Le maréchal d'Ancre aurait été

First page of a short essay summarizing the reign of Louis XIII that Flaubert wrote at age nine. It is the earliest of Flaubert's writings known and was dedicated to his mother (cliché Bibliothèque nationale de France, Paris).

me as *mad.* But *I* can claim the power of mastery inherent in words as well; I can name, I can categorize them:

> Them, laugh at *me?* They who are so weak, so common, so narrow-minded! . . . At me, who felt as big as the world, who could have been reduced to dust by a single one of my grand thoughts, poor *madman!* (III, p. 232)

> A *madman!* That strikes horror. What then are you, reader? What category do you place yourself in? In the category of *fools* or of *madmen?*–Given a choice, your vanity would yet prefer the latter condition. (I, 230)

Is the narrator himself a madman, or a fool? The answer is not self-evident, nor is the question simply rhetorical: it will be raised quite seriously at another level of the text.

In any case, "madness" here turns into irony: it no longer adheres entirely to its meaning; it stands at a certain distance from itself, takes a strategic step back from the condemnation it suffers. Madness is no longer quite the image of a "soul," the profound essence or fundamental nature of the narrator's subjectivity, but a social mask, a *role to be played.* Beneath the mask of accusation, the accused becomes the accuser, pointing his finger at the exposed faces of the "fools": madness designates as its opposite not sanity, but stupidity. It is as though reason did not exist at all, or existed only as a term of negative comparison. What enters into *opposition* are two ways of *being opposed* to reason: either through pettiness, which characterizes the "category of fools" (what is commonly called reason–bourgeois good sense, the logic of self-interest); or through greatness, in the case of the "category of madmen." There is obviously in "madness" more than a touch of complacency and pride. Saying "I am a *madman,*" in this context, boils down to saying "I am not a fool." Madness thus constitutes the negation effected by the stigmatizing term "madness," and is expressed by a reversal of signs:

> You would be mistaken to see in this anything other than the diversions of a poor *madman!* A *madman!*

> And you, dear reader, perhaps you just got married or paid your debts? (I, p. 230)

The lexical choice has thus become a strategic operation.[4] "Madness" invokes the stigmatizing power of language, but that power, since it is based on the structure of *opposition,* is *reversible.* Flaubert's text will ceaselessly mobilize the ironic power of *antithesis* and chiasmus: first seen as a purely negative state, madness becomes an active force of negativity, merging with the dynamic of reversal inherent in language, with the very principle of negativity constitutive of language as such. Thus the king's fool, in a play by Flaubert from the same period as the *Memoirs of a Madman,* says to Louis XI:

> Isn't it true, uncle, that you are very pleased when you have called someone a *madman?* A convincing argument! A *madman!* Well now, a *madman* is a *wise man* and a *wise man* a *madman,* for what is a *madman?* . . . A *madman* is the cleverest invention of *wisdom.*[5]

So language, while incapable of externalizing the interiority of the subject, is able to reverse the very opposition between exterior and interior, to invert their power relations. The Flaubertian usage of the term "madness" demonstrates not only that the *outside* is, in reality, *inside*–that what society rejects under the name of "madness" as its *exterior,* in fact constitutes the very *interior* of subjectivity–but also that the non-mad are fools, that those who believe themselves to be *inside,* inside society and inside reason, are actually "out of it," in the realm of stupidity. Therefore, "a madman is a wise man and a wise man a madman." Though outside of society, the narrator nonetheless considers himself "in the know." In this inverted world, is he then inside or outside? Who's in and who's out? Who's mad? Who's not?

> What good, I ask myself in all sincerity, is a book that is neither instructive nor amusing . . . but tells of a madman, that is, the world, that strapping idiot, which has been spinning in space for centuries without ever taking one step forward? (I, p. 230)

"Madness" becomes generalized, but at the same time relativized: it is now nothing more than an effect of *perspective.* And the perspectives are many. "What a strange thing is this diversity of opinions, of systems, of beliefs and follies!" (XX, p. 244).

Here again, lexical frequency follows the ironic movement of the text: as the text progresses, "madman" disappears in favor of "follies": the essence of the substantive is subverted by the *plural,* which fragments and deconstructs it:

> There are in life so many loves for man! At four, he loves horses, the sun, flowers . . . at ten, he loves girls . . . at thirteen, a big, buxom woman, for I remember that what adolescents adore *madly* is a woman's bosom. . . . At sixty, he loves a prostitute . . . and casts her an impotent look, a regret for the past. . . . How many *follies* there are in a man! Oh! there is no question about it, a harlequin's suit is not more varied in its colors than the human spirit in its *follies.* (XV, p. 241)

Flaubert's mother; copy made in 1920 by Flaubert's niece, Caroline Franklin-Grout, from an 1831 drawing by Eustache-Hyacinthe Langlois (Collections de la Bibliothèque municipale de Rouen. Cliché Thierry Ascencio-Parvy)

Madness is the illusion of being able to salvage something from time, the belief in the possibility of eternity, of the absolute: in love, or in God. Madness, then, is *illusion* as such, *belief* inasmuch as it is always credulous; it is the loss of perspective, the relative mistaken for the absolute. Madness is not simply love, but *the belief in love.* If the thematics of madness say "I suffer" ("madness!"), then the irony of the narrator says "I don't believe it" ("follies!"): I *doubt* what I am suffering from.

> Doubt is the death of the soul: it is a leprosy that attacks enfeebled races, a sickness caused by science and leading to *madness. Madness* is the doubt of reason; it is perhaps reason itself! (XIX, p. 244)

In a strange synthesis, the text tries simultaneously to write Rousseau, Voltaire, and Descartes: I suffer; I don't believe in what I suffer from; I doubt it; I doubt, therefore I think. "Madness is the doubt of reason," "my life is my thought":

> Oh! How long my thought went on! Like a hydra, each of its headings devoured me. Thoughts of mourning and bitterness, thoughts of a weeping buffoon, thoughts of a philosopher in meditation. . . . Oh, yes! How many hours of my life have flowed past . . . *in thought, in doubt!* (II, p. 230)

The narrator himself indeed becomes the very image of the mad buffoon he describes:

> There is thus nothing but darkness around man; everything is empty, and he yearns for something solid; he himself tumbles through the formless vastness in which he would find rest; he clutches at everything, but everything slips away; homeland, liberty, belief, God, virtue, he has grasped at all these things and they have all fallen from his hands; he is like a *madman* who drops a crystal glass and laughs at all the fragments he has made. (XX, p. 244)

The Irony of Irony: The Rhetoricity of "Madness"

Flaubert's irony, as we have just seen, mobilizes the *rhetorical* power of language. The narrator is well aware of the rhetorical play of his writing, but sees it only as an exercise in eloquence:

> I am going to put down on paper . . . all that takes place in my mind and in my soul; laughter and tears . . . sobs that come *first from the heart* and then spread out like dough into *sonorous periods,* tears thinned in *romantic metaphor.* (I, p. 230)

In the narrator's view, the rhetorical figure is exterior and posterior to what it talks about, to the signified, the *theme* that precedes and founds it, just as language was external to the soul. The *theme* would thus be the soul of the text, the original meaning of the figure. And the text would be a figure whose truth is named by the theme. Since the play of signs is thus subordinated to the signified content, rhetoric seems to be *subordinate* to the theme, doubling it, reinforcing its effect in a flow of eloquent continuity.

This esthetics of emphasis, of eloquence and plenitude, tends naturally toward a kind of verbal delirium: toward the excesses of hyperbole. But the author denies the fact that his style is exaggerated: if he uses hyperbole, it is because the feeling itself (the theme) is hyperbolic, beyond the reach of language. If a word seems exaggerated, if the rhetorical figure seems to "surpass" the theme, it is because the theme is, in effect, much greater than the figure.

> But you will perhaps think that in many places the expression is *forced* and the picture is darkened at will; remember that it is a *madman* who has written these pages, and, if the *word* often seems to *surpass the feeling* it expresses, it is because, elsewhere, it has *bent* under *the weight of the heart.* (Dedication, p. 230)

This passage merits close reading: "remember that it is a *madman* who has written these pages, and if the word often seems to *surpass the feeling* it expresses . . ." The "word": What word? Wouldn't it be possible to read the clause, "a madman . . . has written these pages" not only as causal or explanatory, but as the *antecedent* of what follows: "and if the word surpasses the feeling"? To read, in other words: "remember that it is a madman who has written these pages, and if the word (the word I have just written: 'madman') often seems to surpass the sentiment it expresses, it is because, elsewhere, it has bent under the weight of the heart"? Nothing in the syntax rules out such a reading. "Madness," or "madman," would from the start be hyperbolic: a hyperbole that tries, of course, to justify or credit itself by invoking the pressure behind it, "the weight of the heart." But what if "the weight of the heart" were also, as it well might be, *already* a hyperbole, nothing but another "word" that often "surpasses the feeling"? Since it is the "word" that is in question–since it is a question *only* of words–how can we know what is word and what is feeling? Where is the feeling if not in the word? How can we separate the heart from the hyperbole, the theme from the *figure?* Things are not as simple as they seem. Once rhetoric comes into play, it snowballs, never stopping where we want it to, within the limits we try to assign it.

Rhetoric is a strange game: its only rule is to bend the rules, to surpass the code of the game. "If the word often seems to surpass the feeling it expresses, it is because, elsewhere, it has bent under the weight of the heart." If hyperbole is visible, it is because, *elsewhere,* there is a weight on the heart. *Here,* we have hyperbole. The weight of the heart is not here, but elsewhere. Elsewhere, but where? We will never know, except by drifting with the sign toward the figure of another sign, by agreeing to rediscover meaning within the hyperbole, "the weight of the heart." If the "weight of the heart" and the excessive word thus relate to each other through the reversals of a chiasmus, then it is impossible to *stop* the movement of reversal, to fix their places once and for all, to know which comes first, which founds the other. We will never know which it is, the "weight of the heart" or the word "madman," that often "surpasses the feeling"; we will never know which of the two is not a word, which one is not rhetorical, that is, at once excessive and external. The rhetoricity of "madness" makes the difference between inside and outside *undecidable:* it deconstructs the very system of their opposition. What we have here is clearly no longer a "rhetoric of madness" in the sense of an eloquent *expression* of "madness," but rather a madness of rhetoric itself: the madness of its unceasing and uncontrollable movement, of its infinite, indefinite relay from one sign to another.

It is a movement of *displacement* which breaks the continuity between theme and figure, interposing a gap, a pause. "There is a gap in the story, a verse missing in the elegy" (XV, p. 241).

Rhetoric is the relation of the infinite to the finite. But this relation is not the "impossible" relation of expression that the narrator imagines it to be: the "Titan thoughts that make phrases bend beneath them," and which oblige the poet to "climb down from the infinite to the empirical," to "shrink the giant who embraces the infinite" (II, p. 231). The infinite is not a thematic excess: It is, on the contrary, the rhetorical *lack* that makes the discourse function. The infinite is composed not of an excess of signified, but rather of a *missing signified,* of an *excess of signifier* that is constantly being displaced, replaced by another signifier.

The rhetorical figure is not a "phrase bent by a Titan's thought," a rhetorical wisp bent by the mass of the theme, but a mass of language through which the theme escapes the reader, a linguistic mass through which my thought, displaced, escapes me.

Meaning, then, can only be inscribed in the gap left by its own disappearance, by its own *castration.*

> At night I would listen for hours to the wind sighing dolefully through the long, empty corridors. . . . I had frightful visions, enough to drive one *mad* with terror. I was in bed in my father's house. . . . The door opened by itself, and they came in. There were many of them. . . . They were covered with rough, black beards, unarmed except for steel blades between their teeth, and, as they circled my bed, their teeth began to chatter, and it was horrible. . . . At other times, I was in a green countryside dotted with flowers, beside a river; I was with my mother who walked along the riverbank; she fell. I saw the water foam up, circles spreading and suddenly disappearing. . . . I lay down on my stomach in the grass to look, I saw nothing . . . and I heard the cry: "I'm drowning! I'm drowning! Help me!" The water flowed by, flowed by, transparent . . . (III, IV, p. 233)

Inscription is possible only because there is erasure. The castration of meaning, the drowning of the signified, determines the flow, the substitution and displacement of signifiers. The erasure of the mother determines the inscription of Maria, who is in effect found, by metonymy, under water, beside the sea (*mer*)–beside the mother (*mère*)?–and whose coat is "saved" in the beginning when the narrator retrieves it from the water.

> Each morning I went to watch her swim; I watched her from afar under the water. . . . I stared long at her footprints, and would have wept to see the waves slowly erase them. (X, p. 237)

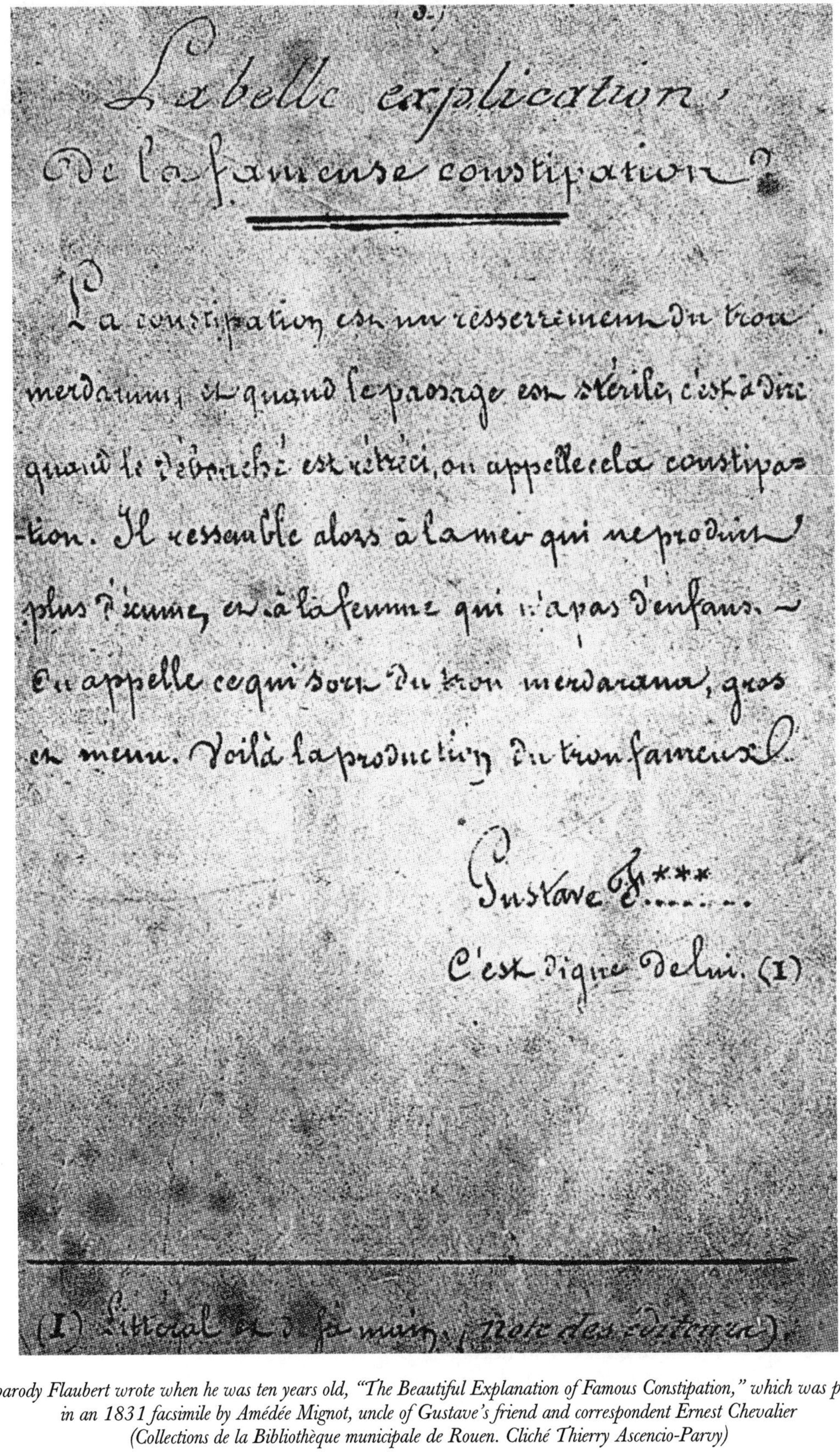

La belle explication
De la fameuse constipation

La constipation est un resserrement du trou merdarum, et quand le passage est stérile, c'est à dire quand le débouché est rétréci, on appelle cela constipation. Il ressemble alors à la mer qui ne produit plus d'écume, et à la femme qui n'a pas d'enfans. – On appelle ce qui sort du trou merdarum, gros en menu. Voilà la production du trou fameux.

Gustave F***

C'est digne de lui. (1)

(1) Littéral et de sa main. (Note des éditeurs).

A parody Flaubert wrote when he was ten years old, "The Beautiful Explanation of Famous Constipation," which was printed in an 1831 facsimile by Amédée Mignot, uncle of Gustave's friend and correspondent Ernest Chevalier (Collections de la Bibliothèque municipale de Rouen. Cliché Thierry Ascencio-Parvy)

Maria: a rhetorical inscription, an inscription in the signifier both of desire and of the law, because the name Maria encompasses both the mother–Mary, the Virgin Mother–and the name-of-the-father–*mari* [husband], *mariée* [married], the forbidden.

Hence, thought is first an unconscious rhetoric, an ordered blindness, a play of signifiers over which one has no mastery:

> You call yourself free, and each day your acts are determined by a thousand things. You see a woman, and you love her, you are dying of love for her; are you free . . . to calm the ardor that consumes you? Are you free from your thoughts? A thousand chains restrain you, a thousand goads drive you on, a thousand shackles stop you. (XX, p. 244)

But if one is so well aware and asserts so clearly that thought is determined–without knowing it, and under the illusion of freedom–by these goads, by these shackles and chains, by this rhetoric that functions through it and that it misapprehends and overlooks, how then can one in the same breath propose the meaning of one's own thought? How can one propose, in the same text, this project, this certitude: "I am going to tell the story of my life"; "My life is my thought"?

The narrator's discourse is clearly a contradictory one: the *theme* of thought is not transparent to itself; no more transparent, indeed, than the theme of madness. To say "I am mad" is already, logically, a contradiction in terms: either the speaker is "mad" and what he says (the theme) is non-sense, or else he is saying something meaningful, and is therefore sane (at least at the moment he says it). The act of enunciation contradicts and problematizes the statement it issues. The question then arises: *Who* is mad in the text? *Who* is thinking in the text? But the very formulation of this question, springing out of the contradiction within the theme, disqualifies a thematic answer; it disqualifies the theme *as* answer. In the logic of the theme, contradiction is inadmissable. But the rhetoric of the text *suspends* that logic: it *resides in* thematic contradiction, functioning according to a different logic, that of the unconscious, which, as we know, knows nothing of contradiction. Rhetoric is nothing other than a mode of contradiction in the text. The "theme" is never simple, never simply reversible in a dialectic with two terms. Rhetoric is precisely the non-simplicity, the non-self-transparency, of the theme. Or to put it another way, rhetoric is never external to the theme: it resides in it, pervades it, but in so doing decenters it, articulates it otherwise. Within the theme, rhetoric is a discourse that is radically other.

—

In order to attempt to isolate this other discourse–this discourse that the text articulates otherwise than in the theme–in order to bring out the irony of the writing, as opposed to that of the narrator–the silent irony and not the irony that speaks–one possible strategy would be to turn the text back upon itself. We can, as we have just done, turn the rhetorical categories (such as hyperbole) back on the theme; or we can turn the theme itself over to reveal its own gaps, to discover in what way it fails to coincide, precisely, with itself.

We can, for example, ask the following question: if the narrator's irony is the *madness of doubt,* what does this madness of doubt *forget to doubt?* There are several possible answers, of which the most obvious is: the narrator forgets to doubt . . . precisely *his own madness*–his madness as it constitutes his self-definition. For it does not suffice to call oneself a "madman" to *be* one. As Jacques Lacan suggests aphoristically: "Not all who would go mad, do go mad."[6] It is thus precisely the hero's "madness" that the reader must rigorously place in doubt. If there is "madness" in the text–and that can be maintained–it is not where the narrator thinks he sees it. It does not lie in the thematic meaning, but somewhere else.

The madness of the narrator is first of all negatively defined: it is a name for his being-other, his *difference* from the world. But since the narrator turns the accusation around and calls the world around him "mad," offering us a book that "tells of a madman, that is, the world" (I, p. 230), what the text underscores is not at all the would-be difference of the "I," but rather its *resemblance* to the world it denounces–a resemblance that the narrator, of course, fails to recognize, even though his own vocabulary, the lexicon of "madness," brings it to the fore. The narrator does not perceive that the world, like a mirror, sends back his own driving principle: what Hegel analyzed as the "law of the heart," self-affirmation as a resistance to others and an assertion of individual uniqueness. The narrator fails to recognize that the principle governing the "category of fools," for example, is not in fact a contingency foreign to his own nature, but indeed the same principle of narcissistic egoism that constitutes the "category of madmen" as well. Self-interest is the equivalent of pride: in the order of narcissism, "fools" and "madmen" are perhaps the same. As a result of this governing misapprehension, as a result of this thematic (but not thematized) blindness, the narrator is caught in the trap of his own self-image: the image of the "beautiful soul," auto-seductive and auto-destructive. He illustrates perfectly Hegel's definition of madness:

> The heart-throb for the welfare of mankind passes therefore into the rage of frantic self-conceit . . . by projecting outside of itself the perversion which it really is, and by straining to regard and to express that perversion as an other.[7]

The narrator, then, misapprehends the true nature of his madness, which is precisely *not to doubt,* thus *to believe in,* his madness as his mode of being different–*being other*–as his negative self-definition. But he also forgets to doubt his madness as his mode of *being-himself,* as his positive self-definition. It is the height of irony that his "poor madman without set ideas, without positive opinions" (II, p. 230), who would never display "a propensity for any profession" (III, p. 233), assumes the role of the Romantic "madman" as a positive attribute, as a trade, a vocation and indeed a career. "All Romanticism achieved," writes Georges Bataille, "was to make unhappiness a new form of career."[8] This also brings to mind an admirable passage in *Notes from the Underground,* where Dostoevski analyzes and demystifies the subtle workings of this Romantic "vocation":

> Oh, if I had done nothing simply from laziness! Heavens, how I should have respected myself because I should at least have been capable of being lazy; there would at least have been one quality, as it were, positive in me, in which I could have believed myself. Question: what is he? Answer: A sluggard; how very pleasant it would have been to hear that of oneself! It would mean that I was positively defined, it would mean that there was something to say about me. "Sluggard"–why, it is a calling and a vocation, it is a career. Do not jest, it is so. I should then be a member of the best club by right, and should find my occupation in continually respecting myself. . . . Then I should have chosen a career for myself, I should have been a sluggard and a glutton, not a simple one, but, for instance, one with sympathies for everything good and beautiful.[9]

Once more, the dialectic of madmen and fools boils down to the same: the negation of a negation is but a *denial* [dénégation], that is, in effect, a confirmation of the system. The refusal to choose an occupation is replaced by the analogous need to be "somebody," to assume a specific role. Whether it is in the category of "madman" or the category of "fools," the naming game is the same, and simply confirms the *rule* of "categories": the search for the security of being *categorized,* of having a *positive identity.* What is unbearable in either case is to remain uncategorized.

The *Memoirs of a Madman,* read from this angle, is the story of the illusion of an adjective made into a noun: "*mad* man" changed into "*madman,*" an attribute turned into an essence, a characteristic turned into a *character.* The narrator's mistake lay in putting madness *in the title,* believing he held *title* to madness. If there is one thing madness is not, it's a title: no one can ever be appointed to it. Contrary to what the narrator says, the text thus tells the story not of a man entitled to madness, but of a man mad about titles.

The title of madness gets its authority only from dreams and fantasy. "Madness" is not the assertion of a fact, but the locus of an aspiration: "madness" is the *desire* for madness, a blind rush toward meaning, a dream of excess and hyperbole, of plenitude and potency which, once again, seeks only to forget, to deny castration–the castration of meaning.

> I filled my lungs with that cool, salt ocean air which so fills the soul with energy. . . . I gazed upon the deep, upon space, the infinite . . .
>
> Oh! But that isn't where you will find the boundless horizon, the immense abyss. No, a wider, deeper abyss opened before me. *That abyss contains no tempests;* if it had a tempest, it would be *full*–and it is *empty!* (II, p. 231)

But to create the tempest of a madness, or the madness of a tempest, through a riot of writing, an intoxication with hyperbole, an orgy of language–isn't that precisely to create the illusion of a plenitude in the void?

"I was drunk," the narrator of *November* will later say:

> I was *mad,* I imagined myself a great man . . . I carried in my loins the very life of a god. . . . I made myself a temple to hold something divine, and the temple remained empty.[10]

"Madness" is a hyperbole of the self produced through an intoxication of language; it is the illusion of drunkenness which, in fact, masks an incapacity to be drunk, to "be mad." The narrator of the *Memoirs* may be fooling himself, but the fool in *Louis XI* does not:

> For what is a madman? It is he who sleeps in the wind and thinks it's hot, *drinks water and believes he is drinking wine.*[11]

Thus, while he dismantles the theme of illusion, the narrator himself falls victim to the supreme, ironic illusion of his own "madness": the illusion of a difference (a negative self-definition); the illusion of identity (a positive self-definition); the illusion of plenitude and intoxication. Madness is, once again, belief: the belief that one is identical to oneself and differs from others; the belief that one is dizzy with wine when one has only drunk water; the belief that one is mad, when one is not, or only ever so slightly. But this leads to a paradox: whoever believes himself mad when he is not, is mad by virtue of that very belief. Mad not because he believes himself mad, but because he *believes himself* at all–because he identifies with the shadow of an image in a lake or a mirror: because he *alienates himself* in the madness of a specular identification.[12]

The Collège Royal, the upper-elementary and secondary school in Rouen (now Lycée Corneille), which Flaubert attended from May 1832 to December 1839, when he was expelled because of his participation in a student protest (photograph by Éric Le Calvez)

Thus, in the very act of defusing illusion, the narrator's irony only reinforces the structure and effect of illusion, since it adds to the others the illusion of having no more illusions: the belief that one no longer believes. While the narrator's irony consisted in his madness of doubt, the naïveté of that irony–the irony of the text–consists in the fact that the narrator's true madness in effect escapes him.

In the same way, through what the narrator calls his "thought," he tells the story of that in him which is *not* thought: he narrates *himself* as *un*thought. "Desire," writes Emmanuel Levinas, "is only the fact of thinking more than you think."[13] Desire, and maybe madness, too. In this strange relation–constitutive of rhetoric–between thought and desire, between writing and madness, the text actively *unthinks* the narrator's thought. In his thematic "message," "I think that I doubt," the narrator still forgets to doubt the "I think." But the text thinks it for him, rhetorically turning what it *says*–"I think that I doubt"–into what it *writes*–"I doubt that I think." Paradoxically, the theme of madness is articulated in the text by the Cartesian formula: "I think, therefore I am." But the text's irony–not the way it speaks of "madness" but the way it is rhetorically traversed by it–is articulated on the contrary by a Lacanian formula: "I think where I am not, therefore, I am where I do not think . . . I am not wherever I am the plaything of my thought; I think of what I am, where I do not think to think."[14]

Thematics and Rhetoric

I have thus proposed three different readings of the *Memoirs of a Madman*. In this plurality of interpretations, it was not a matter of a simple "peaceful-co-existence" of various aspects of a text but, rather, a strategic confrontation of different *positions* of meaning. The text was treated as a field of forces and shifting intensities, and any one of the three readings was necessarily an intervention in the conflict; each successive reading indeed subverted the authority of the one that came before. Of these three readings, none can be considered exclusive or privileged, since all three are fundamentally interdependent: the more complex a reading becomes, the more it relies on another, which it must deconstruct by analyzing its specific mode of error or illusion. Although they were presented successively, the three interpretations do not constitute a chronology, or an evolution in the development of the text. They all exist side by side, simultaneously cohabiting the space of the text.

There are thus three different positions of meaning: 1) the *thematic* interpretation that the "I"-hero gives of his "madness"; 2) the *ironic* interpretation that the "I"-narrator proposes of the madness of the "I"-hero, rhetorically deconstructing his *thematic* reading; 3) the ironic interpretation of the narrator's irony, demonstrating how the irony of the text rhetorically deconstructs the irony *thematized* by the voice of the narrator.

While the voice of the narrator operated a reversal, a rhetorical-ironical chiasmus of the *theme* of the hero's madness, the narrator in turn *thematized* this gesture of reversal, explicitly articulating it as the *theme* of the madness of doubt. As a result, although the "I"-narrator ironically, rhetorically demystifies the "I"-hero, the narrator's relation to himself is still mystified, remaining thoroughly thematic: it is a relation of consciousness and of self-presence–of *presence to self*–within the very "madness" of his doubting.

The thematic and the rhetorical positions of meaning thus confront and contest each other in two different ways, on two different levels of reading: first in the narrator's irony and then in the irony of the text. Let us summarize from this angle the strategic movement of our three readings: first, we read along with the hero from the *thematic* point of view; then came the demystifying perspective of the narrator, his *rhetorical* (ironic) re-inscription of the hero's thematic reading, as well as the *thematization* of this rhetorical re-inscription; and finally, the irony *thematized* was displaced, *rhetorically,* by the irony *textualized:* it was, thus, Flaubert's *writing* that effected the (ironic) *rhetoricization* of the *thematization* of the narrator's irony.

Rhetoric and thematics are thus engaged in a dynamic that is not symmetrical, or dialectical. The theme has no hold over the rhetoric; it can only misapprehend it, and hence cannot deconstruct it. On the other hand, even though the rhetoric often effects the deconstruction or the decentering of the theme, it is always stalked by its own thematization, which steals away and cancels out its ironic force. Only a theme can exist in the mode of presence and consciousness. Rhetoric cannot become conscious of itself; if it does, it vanishes, losing what is specifically rhetorical in its effect. Rhetoric cannot itself express its own essence. It cannot *know* what it knows; it cannot complete its own trajectory or attain the calm of a final truth. Any rhetorical movement that reaches consciousness, that makes its meaning explicit, that ends its motion in a finite thought, is transformed into a theme, which in turn will have to be demystified by another textual rhetoric, by another unthought, unthinkable rhetorical movement.[15]

–Shoshana Felman, "Gustave Flaubert: Living Writing, or Madness as Cliché," in *Writing and Madness,* translated by Martha Noel Evans and others (Stanford, Cal.: Stanford University Press, 1985), pp. 78–95

---

1. Title of the colloquium for which this piece was originally written.
2. Gustave Flaubert, *Mémoires d'un fou,* in *Œuvres complètes,* "L'Intégrale" edition (Paris: Seuil, 1964), I, 30.
3. Here, as elsewhere, the italics are mine unless otherwise indicated.
4. Cf. a longer analysis of this same operation in Stendhal in S. Felman, *La Folie dans l'œuvre romanesque de Stendhal* (Paris: Corti, 1971), chaps. V, VI.
5. Flaubert, *Louis XI,* in *Œuvres complètes,* I, 132.
6. *Ecrits* (Paris: Seuil, 1966), p. 176.
7. *The Phenomenology of Mind,* trans. J. B. Baillie (New York: Harper & Row, 1967), p. 397. Translation modified.
8. *Œuvres complètes,* I, 526.
9. *Notes from the Underground,* trans. C. Garnett (New York: Dell, 1959), pt. I, chap. 6, pp. 39-40.
10. Flaubert, *Novembre,* in *Œuvres complètes,* I, 252.
11. Flaubert, *Louis XI,* p. 132.
12. Cf. the Lacanian aphorism which here takes on all its significance: "If a man who believes himself to be king is mad, a king who believes himself to be king is no less mad" (*Ecrits,* p. 170).
13. *Totalité et infini. Essai sur l'extériorité* (The Hague: M. Nijhoff, 1961).
14. Lacan, *Ecrits: A Selection* (New York: Norton, 1977).
15. Of course, this does not exclude my own critical discourse, which can only *thematize* the irony of the text, and remains, therefore, to be deconstructed itself. It is in this respect that the third reading *resembles* the first two: it is why the third reading is in no way privileged or definitive. There is no final reading.

Flaubert's *Intimate Notebook*

Flaubert, circa 1833. This painting is a 1920 copy by Berthon of an original painting that belonged to Flaubert's niece Caroline Franklin-Grout (Collections de la Bibliothèque municipale de Rouen. Cliché Thierry Ascencio-Parvy).

Flaubert continued to write: in 1838, apart from Mémoires d'un fou, *he wrote "Loys XI," "Agonies," and "La Danse des morts," among other short stories; in 1839, he completed* Smar *(subtitled "an old mystery"), an essay on* Rabelais, *and another historical study ("Rome et les Césars"). After passing his baccalaureate in 1840, he traveled to the Pyrenees and Corsica.*

In 1840, before being sent back home from the Collège Royal, Flaubert began to write a notebook, which he continued in a desultory fashion for a little while in 1841. It belongs to a period when the young writer was uncertain about his future, although he remained determined to write despite his law studies. Most pages of the notebook include short, undeveloped paragraphs that reveal Flaubert's view of humanity and his doubts about himself and his vocation. The following excerpts from this notebook are from a translation based on the 1967 French edition. A corrected French edition was published by Jean-Pierre Germain in 1987, but a new English edition has not yet been published.

A Writer's Ambitions

Friday, 28 February 1840

I have read over this notebook and pitied myself.

What is the matter with me today? Is it satiety, is it desire, disillusion, dreams of the future? My head aches, my heart is empty; ordinarily I have what is called a gay nature, but there are voids there, frightful voids into which I fall, crushed, battered, annihilated!

I no longer write–formerly I wrote, I was enthusiastic about my ideas, I knew what it was to be a poet, I was one, inside at least, in my soul, as all the generous-hearted are. The form was always faulty, it expressed my thought badly–but no matter–I was a sublime musician playing on a rebec; I was conscious of bursts of brilliance and of suave passages like noiseless kisses, silent whispers. If I had had a fine voice, how I would have sung! People would have laughed at me had they known how I was admiring myself, and they would have been right; all my accomplishment remained within me; I never wrote a line on the beautiful poem in which I took such delight. I remember that before I was ten I had already begun to write–I dreamed of the splendours of genius, a lighted hall, applause, wreaths–and now, although I am still convinced of my vocation, or else am full of immense vanity, I doubt more and more. If you knew what anguish that is! If you knew what my vanity is–what a savage vulture, how it eats my heart–how alone I am, isolated, suspicious, low, jealous, selfish, ferocious! Oh, the future I dreamed of–how marvellous it was! Oh, the life I used to build for myself, like a novel: what a life! How hard it is for me to renounce it!–and love, too, love!–I used to tell myself that when I was twenty someone would certainly love me, that I would meet someone, no matter whom, some woman, and I would know what it is, that beautiful word that was setting all the fibres of my heart, all the muscles of my flesh a-quiver with anticipation.

However, I fell in love like anybody else and no one knew anything about it. What a pity! How happy I might have been. I often find myself thinking of that, and scenes unfold amorously as in a dream. I imagine long embraces–sweet words that I repeat to myself, caress myself with–intoxicating glances. Ah, if you have had in your life something more than the caresses of whores, something more than glances that were sold, have pity on me.

Love, genius–that was the heaven that I felt, that I caught glimpses of, whose emanations came to me–visions that drove me insane; and then it closed over forever–so who will have me? It should have happened already; I have such need of a mistress, of an angel! . . .

People tell me I am conceited–but then why this doubt that I have about everything I do, this void that frightens me, all those lost illusions?

Oh, a woman, what a wonderful thing! Add two wings and you have an angel! I love to dream of her contours. I love to dream of the charm of her smiles, of the softness of her white arms, the shape of her thighs, her attitude as she bends her head.

Often I am in India, in the shade of banana trees, sitting on mats; bayaderes are dancing, swans are fluffing out their feathers on blue lakes, nature throbs with love.

A week ago I thought for two hours about a pair of dainty green shoes and a black dress; not to mention the other foolish things that keep my heart occupied for long periods–I toy with absurd notions, tickle myself to make myself laugh, imagine pictures for myself to look at, pictures with rosy horizons and splendid sunshine–everything in them is bliss and radiance.

Oh! The man writing this is the same man who might have been a genius, made a name for himself in the future. Ah! How wretched I am!

I'd love to be a mystic; it must give you a wonderful feeling to believe in paradise, to drown in waves of incense, to annihilate yourself at the foot of the Cross, take refuge on the wings of the dove. There is something naïve about First Communion; let us not laugh at those who weep on that occasion; an altar covered with sweet-smelling flowers is a lovely thing. The life of a saint is glorious, I should have liked a martyr's death; and if there is a God, a good God, a God who is the father of Jesus, let him send me his grace, his spirit, I will accept it and prostrate myself. I well understand that people who fast regale themselves with their hunger and enjoy their privations; it is a much more refined sensualism than the other kind; these are pleasures, thrills, raptures of the heart.

The so-called pleasure one takes in doing a good deed is a lie; it is no different from the pleasure felt by a man who is digesting. Heroism is different. But I say that when you have given a coin to a beggar and then say that you are happy, you are an imposter; you are deceiving yourself. Every good deed is more than three-quarters pride; that leaves one quarter to account for interestedness, irresistible animal impulse, need, actual appetite.

One incomprehensible thing is the infinite. But who doubts it? So there are things beyond the reach of our intelligence and we believe that they exist. Is there perhaps something which thinks, other than this same intelligence–something which is convinced that our reason—[1].

Why is it that when we do not share the feelings of people we are talking with, we feel clumsy and embarrassed? I recently saw a man who told me that his brother was dying; he pressed my hand affectionately, and I simply let him press it, and as I left him I gave a stupid laugh, as I might have smiled at a party.

I was annoyed at once; that man humiliated me. He was full of a certain feeling and I was quite devoid of it. I saw him again yesterday. He is a pathetically stupid fellow[2], but I remember how I hated myself and found myself detestable at that moment.

Sensual pleasure is pleased with itself; it relishes itself, like melancholy–both of them solitary enjoyments, all the more intense because in each case their subject is the same and their object themselves. Love, on the contrary, demands sharing. Sensual pleasure is selfish and deliberate and serious; such pleasures carried to the extreme are like orgasms of self-abuse; their self-contemplation and self-enjoyment are a kind of onanism of the heart.

There are great men whom one would have liked to see and admire; there are others with whom—[3] vile men in History. I enjoy that, and if I were to write a book it would be on the turpitudes of great men–I am glad that great men were capable of them.

To speak to me about the dignity of the human species is a mockery; I love Montaigne and Pascal for that.

The only thing that distinguishes man from the animals is that he eats when he is not hungry, drinks when he is not thirsty–free will.

I shun discipline–mathematician's mind, narrow mind–shopkeeper's heart, dry as the wood of his counter.

Modesty' in art is an idea that can have come only from a fool. Art in its most immodest flights is 'modest' if it is beautiful, if it is great. A nude woman is not immodest; a hand that hides, a veil that covers, a fold that is made–those are immodest.

Modesty' is a thing of the heart, not of the body; it is a varnish that glows with a velvety bloom.

There are people whose slightest gesture, whose most insignificant word, the mere sound of whose voice, disgusts and repels us.

Beauty is divine. Despite ourselves we love what is beautiful, we hate what is ugly; all dogs bark at beggars because they are ragged. Children are the same; you cannot convince them that someone they dislike, someone ugly, is good; for them this is impossible.

When artists sought to represent angels, they modelled them on female nudes.

I have already written a good deal, and perhaps I would have written well if instead of perching my feelings high in order to idealize them, and setting my thoughts up on a stage, I had let them run free in the fields, just as they are, fresh and rosy.

When you write, you feel how it must be, you know that at such a spot a certain thing is needed, at another spot something else; you compose pictures for yourself that you see, you have rather the feeling that you are going to bring something to flower; you feel in your heart like the distant echo of all the passions you are going to create; and the inability to render all that is the eternal despair of those who write; the poverty of languages, which have scarcely one word for a hundred thoughts; the weakness of man, who cannot find approximations–and to me particularly it is an eternal anguish.

— 20 —

4e *Accessit*... Auguste VIRET, pensionnaire au Collége Royal, déjà nommé (1 fois le premier).
5e......... Louis HAVÉ, Pension de MM. DUSSEAUX, déjà nommé (1 fois le premier).
6e......... Eugène REYNARD, élève royal, déjà nommé (1 fois le premier).

PRIX DE SEMESTRE.

1er *Prix*.... Alfred BUSQUET, Pension de M. MORTREUIL, déjà nommé.
2e......... Jules VIARD, Institution de M. LEMARDELÉ, déjà nommé.

SEPTIEME.

THÈME.

Prix....... Frédéric-Constant-Edouard FOUARD, d'Elbeuf, élève royal.
1er *Accessit*. Ernest-César BASTIDE, de Rouen, élève au Collége Royal.
2e......... Louis-Charles-Ferdinand MORIN, de Falaise, élève royal.
3e......... Gustave FLAUBERT, de Rouen, pensionnaire au Collége Royal.

VERSION.

Prix....... Auguste CASTILLON, de Valmont, pensionnaire au Collége Royal.
1er *Accessit*. Victor-Louis DURAND, de Beaumont-le-Roger, pensionnaire au Collége Royal.
2e......... Frédéric-Constant-Edouard FOUARD, élève royal, déjà nommé.
3e......... Auguste BRÉZOT, de Paris, élève royal.

EXERCICES FRANÇAIS.

Prix....... Frédéric-Constant-Edouard FOUARD, élève royal, déjà nommé.
1er *Accessit*. Victor-Louis DURAND, pensionnaire au Collége Royal, déjà nommé.
2e......... Louis-Charles-Ferdinand MORIN, élève royal, déjà nommé.
3e......... Gustave FLAUBERT, pensionnaire au Collége Royal, déjà nommé.

GÉOGRAPHIE.

Prix....... Louis-Charles-Ferdinand MORIN, élève royal, déjà nommé.
1er *Accessit*. Frédéric-Constant-Edouard FOUARD, élève royal, déjà nommé.
2e......... Gustave FLAUBERT, pensionnaire au Collége Royal, déjà nommé.
3e......... Georges-Henri DE MAUREPAS, de Louviers, élève royal.

A list of the prizes granted by the Académie de Rouen, Collège Royal (12 August 1833). For that semester, Flaubert earned the fourth prizes in "Theme" and "French Exercises," the third prize in "Geography," and the second prize in "Excellency" (Collections de la Bibliothèque municipale de Rouen. Cliché Thierry Ascencio-Parvy).

Oh my God, my God, why did you cause me to be born with so much ambition? For it is certainly ambition that I have. When I was ten, I was already thinking of fame–I began to compose as soon as I knew how to write; I painted ravishing pictures for myself–I dreamed of a hall, brightly lighted and glittering with gold, of hands that were clapping, of shouts, of wreaths. They call 'Author! Author!'–the author is myself, of course, he has my name, he is me, me, me; they seek me out in the corridors, in the boxes, they lean out to see me; the curtain goes up; I step forward–such ecstasy! They are looking at me, admiring me, envying me, almost loving me!

Ah! How pitiable, how pitiable to dream of it; how much more so to write it to yourself, say it to yourself. Yes, I am a great man who failed to make the grade; my kind is common today. When I consider what I have done, and all that I might have done, I tell myself that I have accomplished little, and yet what strength I have within me, if you knew all the flashes that illuminate my mind. Alas! Alas! I tell myself that at twenty I could already have created masterpieces–I have booed myself, humbled myself, down-graded myself, and I do not know even what to hope for, what I want, nor what is wrong with me–I shall never be anything but a despised scribbler, a poor conceited fool.

Oh! if I had someone to love, if there were someone who loved me! How happy I should be; glorious nights, glorious hours–some people actually do live that life! Why not me? Oh, my God, I want no other pleasures–my heart is full of sonorous chords, melodies sweeter than those of heaven: a woman's finger would make them sing, vibrate–to melt together in a kiss, in a look, am I never to know anything of all that? And yet I feel that my heart is far bigger than my head. Oh, how I would love! Come, then, come, mysterious soul, sister-soul to mine, I will kiss your footsteps; you will walk on me and I will embrace your feet and weep.

–Gustave Flaubert, *Intimate Notebook, 1840–1841,*
translated and edited by Francis Steegmuller
(London: W. H. Allen, 1967), pp. 20–26, 49–50

---

1. 'our reason—' These lines are one of several possible readings of an obscurely phrased paragraph which in both French texts is incomplete. Madame Chevalley Sabatier tells us in a footnote that in the original manuscript the paragraph is cancelled with a red line and that the word *bête* (stupid) is written across it.
2. 'a pathetically stupid fellow.' Madame Chevalley Sabatier tells us in a footnote that Flaubert refers here to his schoolmate and future brother-in-law, Emile Hamard, father of Madame Franklin Grout.
3. 'others with whom—' Broken or corrupt texts here.

Sartre on Flaubert's Nervous Attack

Flaubert left Rouen in early 1842 to study law in Paris. He hated law, preferring Greek and Latin as subjects, and fell into a state of complete boredom. He managed, however, to pass the tests for the first year and completed a longer narrative than any he had written, Novembre. *In 1843, he began* L'Éducation sentimentale *(first version). He met Maxime Du Camp and frequently went to the studio of the sculptor James Pradier and to the Schlésingers'. In August, he failed the exams for the second year of law.*

In early 1844, Flaubert experienced a first nervous attack–akin to if not actually epileptic in nature–that became one of the most important events in his life: later he said about it that in him one man died and another one was reborn. Sartre's interpretation of the attack and its consequences is subjective: he sees it as the moment when "neurosis was chosen."

The Event

One evening in January 1844, Achille and Gustave were returning from Deauville, where they had been to see the site of the new country house. It was pitch dark; Gustave was driving the cabriolet himself. Suddenly, in the vicinity of Pont-l'Evêque, as a wagon passed to the right of the carriage, Gustave dropped the reins and fell at his brother's feet as if struck by lightning. Seeing him motionless as a corpse, Achille thought he was dead or dying. In the distance, the lights of a house were visible. The elder son carried his brother to the house and gave him emergency treatment. Gustave remained for a few minutes in this cataleptic state; he had, however, retained full consciousness. When he opened his eyes, he may have had convulsions, but we have no firm evidence. In any case, his brother took him to Rouen that same night.

Before going further, we must determine the *date* of this attack. In a letter from Caroline written *17 January 1844* and addressed to rue de l'Est, we read: "Your letter reached us only at five last evening and we were afraid that you had been ill, so if we had not received news of you, you might well have had a visit from someone from the family." Since the Flauberts were worried on the 17th, Gustave must have departed at least three days before, hence, close to the date he had set in December. On the other hand, he writes to Ernest toward the end of January or the beginning of February: "I nearly popped off in the hands of my family (where I had gone to spend two or three days recovering from the awful scenes I had witnessed at Hamard's)."

Most commentators consider that the letter to Chevalier alludes to the *first* crisis, that is, to the one at Pont-l'Evêque. According to this supposition, Gustave would have left for Paris, nervous but unscathed, around 15 January. At Caroline's entreaty, he would have paid a visit to Hamard, who had just lost his mother, *after* 17 January.[1] Shaken by the "awful scenes," he would have returned to his family around the 20th to calm down a little before getting back to his studies.

The incident at Pont-l'Evêque would have happened during the two days that followed his arrival at Rouen, since he writes that he had "come to spend *two or three days*." We could then safely locate the event between 20 and 25 of January–closer to the 20th if Gustave left Paris without warning, in a sort of retreat; closer to the 25th if he had first wanted to inform his parents–by a note which is now lost.[2]

This commonly accepted thesis is countered by Jean Bruneau, who contends that the crisis of Pont-l'Evêque had taken place *before* the 15th, during Flaubert's first visit to Rouen. It "could not have inordinately worried the two doctors Flaubert," since they allowed him to leave again for Paris. The attack that felled him, which in his letter to Ernest he calls "a miniature apoplexy," would thus be a *second* crisis, more serious than the first, and would probably have occurred in the town itself, perhaps at the Hôtel-Dieu. In other words, the letter to Chevalier describing his "congestion" and that of 2 September '53 in which he recounts to Louise his accident at Pont-l'Evêque would not concern the same event. We would have to accept the following chronology: during the New Year's vacation, a first "apoplexy"; then, from around the 15th to the 20th, Paris; after that, between the 20th and the 25th–approximately–a second attack, of which we know only what Flaubert tells Ernest, that is, almost nothing: indeed, he mentions neither the circumstances, nor the moment, nor the place, nor the singular form of this new accident.

That Gustave *discovered* his illness at Pont-l'Evêque when he suffered the first seizures, no one doubts. The question–an important one, as we shall see–is to determine whether this discovery took place *before* his return to Paris or *during* his second visit to Rouen. We lack precise information on this point. However, unless Bruneau has evidence that he did not provide in his book, his hypothesis of *two* crises seems inadequately supported.

What argues in its favor is that Flaubert "had an epileptic fit" when returning from Deauville, where he had gone with Achille to examine the work the chief surgeon was having done on the recently acquired land. Wouldn't Gustave have wanted to see this "country house," which "was preventing" him "from working," and to see it *right away?* He arrives on New Year's Day. What is the family discussing? The country house. That is enough for him to fix a date with Achille: they will go to inspect the work in three days, or at latest by the end of the week. Therefore, according to Bruneau, probability requires that this unfortunate journey should take place in the first half of January, and as near as possible to New Year's Day. Caroline's letter alone would suggest it; it betrays the family's anxiety: "If you were not to go . . ." This is not her usual way: obviously something has happened. Having searched carefully, I see nothing else to support this conjecture except perhaps the fact that Gustave in '52, recounting the first accident, mentions simply "the house where my brother cared for me"; whereas in the letter of '44 to Ernest he writes that he was given three simultaneous bleedings.

What are we to make of these hypotheses? That they have very little foundation. We know that, on 20 December, Flaubert was delighting in the thought of the country house that his father was going to have built. Let us note in passing that in the two letters where he speaks of it he does not even say that he wishes to see the work in progress. Had it even begun? On 20 December, it seems they were still discussing the architect's plans. There is no evidence that Gustave wanted to go to Deauville, or that there was anything to see there. There is no evidence, either, that he did not go there twice: first before the 15th, and again on his return from Paris. It could even be that around the 20th, Achille-Cléophas, worried by his son's extreme nervousness, had the idea that a journey by cabriolet followed by a brief visit to the seashore would help calm him down. Thus, the attack could very well have taken place after the 15th, in the course of either a first or a second return from Deauville to Rouen.

There remains Caroline's anxiety. But no one doubts that during the New Year's vacation Flaubert appeared tormented, or that certain troubles of previous years recurred during his period at home. Besides, the postscript is curious: "Papa read your letter and said nothing to me about your arm, but here is my prescription: rest and grease." Flaubert was complaining of an arm: had he bruised a muscle? His father takes the letter from Caroline's hands, reads it in silence, and gives it back without a word; so the problem Gustave mentioned was a minor one. In any case, this is not the attitude of a doctor who feared the return of a "miniature apoplexy." Besides, is it conceivable that the two doctors Flaubert would have allowed Gustave to return if Achille had "thought for ten minutes that he was dead"? Maxime tells us that Achille, at Pont-l'Evêque,[3] "hoped, though he didn't really believe it, that the crisis would not be repeated," and that the father "was in despair." Certainly he is a doubtful witness and begins by mistaking the date and the place. But he had seen Flaubert during the winter of '44 and took this informa-

Pencil drawing of Flaubert, circa 1833, made by his brother, Achille (Collections de la Bibliothèque municipale de Rouen. Cliché Thierry Ascencio-Parvy)

tion from him. If the two doctors had allowed him to depart after the attack, Gustave's resentment would have prompted him to point out this huge professional error to Maxime, who would have taken pleasure in reporting it to us: Du Camp's testimony, in fact, aims at denigrating Achille-Cléophas by presenting him as a disciple of Broussais, "who doesn't know how to do anything but bleed people."

And then, if Gustave *had already* suffered his crisis by 17 January, his father's diagnosis would already have been made: cerebral congestion. In this case, the family's anxiety–as it becomes apparent through Caroline's letter–seems rather feeble: if he was in danger of a relapse, if to survive he urgently needed bleeding, it would not have sufficed to send someone to Paris; they should not have let him out of their sight. The words "we were afraid that you had been ill . . . , you might well have had a visit from someone from the family" are justified only in a case of *moderate urgency*. If Flaubert was really subject to bouts of apoplexy, this "someone from the family," at the end of a long journey, was in serious danger of finding a decomposing corpse at rue de l'Est. The sentence becomes clear, on the other hand, if we suppose that Gustave left his family without notable incident but in an alarming mental state. When he arrives at the Hôtel-Dieu, he has just spent a day at Vernon with the Schlésinger family; he is certainly relaxed, happy. But the next day, a change of scene: in Paris, Rouen was hope, happy expectation, escape; now the expectation remains but offers up its true meaning: it is the Parisian prison that he awaits, the dreadful repetition of the already done, the already seen. He wouldn't dream of resisting, but in the inflexible temporalization that leads him toward a future so near and so detested he sees the symbol of his entire life, drawn by that other-future, the *profession*. From one day to the next he grows more nervous, more irritable; he is sometimes depressed, sometimes overexcited, always anxious. We shall say that the disorders are nonsignifying because they are symptomatic of neither an identifiable illness, nor an enterprise, nor a hidden intention: they simply indicate that Flaubert lives with increasing exasperation a contradiction that can be neither borne nor transcended. If these disorders expressed anything, it would be the structural disarray of an unhappy young man who does not know what to do, who doesn't even take it into his head to devise a solution, who is at once convinced of the fate that awaits him and unable to believe in it; in sum, the disorders present themselves exactly for what they are: meaningless agitations that take the place of an impossible and even inconceivable behavior in a tormenting but unrealizable situation. Overexcitement feeds on itself: he sleeps badly, no doubt, scarcely eats, drinks too much. He flies into a rage over nothing. Maxime claimed that these disturbances were a consequence of his illness–rather quickly assimilated to epilepsy. "At the least incident disturbing the extreme quiet of his existence, he would go off his head. I have seen him shouting and running around his apartment because he couldn't find his penknife." But we have enough familiarity with his youthful works and the correspondence to know that these disorders long preceded the illness: Gustave's impulse to shout, to bellow, to smash everything, his sudden desire to throw himself on passersby and massacre them did not begin just yesterday. It seems certain that these "itchings"–as he himself calls them–or these panics probably grew in frequency and intensity at the beginning of January, to the point that the family finally took notice. For Achille-Cléophas, the tremors have *one* very precise meaning: they remind him of the "illness" which, from '39 to '42, compelled him to keep Gustave near him. Isn't his son cured, then? He lets him depart, nonetheless, but in this hypothesis his behavior is perfectly comprehensible; his paternal obstinacy aside, he does not want to "settle" his son into his illness by taking its vague symptoms too seriously: nothing could be worse for Gustave, he thinks, than to be authorized to interrupt his studies and once more sequester himself in his room. The father promises himself to watch over his son from a distance; after all, isn't Dr. Cloquet keeping an eye on him? For the moment, the paterfamilias intends to make no change of plans. Gustave must have left in a state of extreme despondency; for this reason his mother and sister are worried by his silence; and if it had lasted, one of them would have come to settle in at rue de l'Est; this is the meaning of "someone from the family." A woman to watch over him, to look after his needs while awaiting the father's decisions, and, *especially,* to "boost his morale." What the Flauberts dread, on 17 January, is not the return of a definite attack but the physical effects of solitude and anguish.

In the letter to Ernest of January-February 1844, we find a confirmation of our conjectures. This time *an* attack has taken place, and he says so. Is it the first? The second? What is certain is that the description he gives of it can be applied precisely to the attack at Pont-l'Evêque. For ten minutes Achille thought I was dead, he would write in '52; and in '44: "I almost popped off in the hands of my family." Then I was bled, he tells Louise. And to Ernest he speaks of a triple bleeding. In both letters he says that he "opened his eyes again." Both mention the bad case of nerves that follow the "resurrection," etc. It is not conclusive, of course, that both letters are describing the same attack; the first attacks, in any case, must have closely resembled each other. But if the accident he reports to Chevalier is not the first, why doesn't he tell him that an earlier one preceded it? To be sure, he is not always sincere with his old friend. But what need does he have to conceal this particular truth from Ernest? Subsequently, between February and June, he readily speaks to him of his attacks, in the plural: "My last major attack," etc. Why not mention the original one? The lie would not jibe with a certain attitude Gustave took toward his ailment, an attitude we shall discuss shortly; it would also be absurd because unmotivated. Forgetfulness? Negligence? Quite the contrary: although he nowhere says, "This was the first time it happened to me," everything suggests that it was. Gustave is still astonished; he tells of his adventure with the importance of someone who has had a brush with death. But the most significant thing is that he unreservedly adopts his father's diagnosis, although within eight days he will radically challenge it.[4] For him to believe he was the victim of a cerebral congestion, he must have been taken by surprise: this can be explained only by his stupefaction at an unfamiliar event, that is, an event which is unrecognizable, unique. In fact, he will very quickly understand. . . . And if by the end of January he had undergone *two* experiences of the same kind, separated by an interval of a fortnight, if before the second attack he had been able to spend two weeks thinking about

Trouville

In Mémoires d'un fou *Flaubert describes Trouville as the village of X.*

It would be impossible to tell you the precise year; but then I was very young–fifteen, I believe; that year we went to the seaside resort of X, a town in Picardy, utterly charming with its chockablock houses, black, gray, red, white, turned in all directions, without alignment or symmetry, like a pile of shells and pebbles that waves have driven onto the shore.

A few years ago no one went there, despite its having more than a mile of splendid beach and its charming location; but recently it has come back in vogue. The last time I was there I saw a quantity of yellow gloves and livery; there was even talk of building a theater.

Everything was simple and wild then; there was hardly anyone except artists and people from the area. The shore was deserted, and at low tide you saw silver-gray sand shimmering in the sun, still damp from the waves. To the left there were rocks where on somnolent days the sea lazily slapped the breakwater, blackened by seaweed; then in the distance you could see the blue ocean under a burning sun, bellowing indistinctly like a weeping giant.

And when you returned to the town there was the warmest and most picturesque scene. Black nets that had deteriorated from the water were spread out on the doors; everywhere half-naked children were walking on gray pebbles, which were the only pavement of the area; there were sailors in red and blue clothes; and all of that was simple and robust in its grace. Everything was imbued with a vigorous and energetic character.

I often went alone to walk on the strand. One day chance led me toward the place where people went swimming. It was a place not far from the last houses of the town, frequented mainly for this use; men and women swam together; they undressed on the bank or in their houses, and they left their robes on the sand. . . .

–translated by Robert Griffin in *Early Writings: Gustave Flaubert,* pp. 176–177

Scenes of Trouville, where the Flauberts began spending summer vacations in 1835. Flaubert met and fell in love with Élisa Schlésinger during a sojourn there (lithographs by Charles-Louis Mozin, circa 1845; clichés Bibliothèque nationale de France, Paris).

the first and doing some soul-searching, we can be certain that he would have seen the second in the light of the first and interpreted it quite otherwise.

To conclude: although firm proof remains impossible for lack of documentation, the strongest probabilities are that one evening at Pont-l'Evêque, between 20 and 25 January, Gustave fell victim to an affliction he had never before experienced. This shall be our working hypothesis. If the attack at Pont-l'Evêque had indeed taken place *before* 15 January, and if the two doctors Flaubert had treated it lightly, they would have found themselves in contradiction with the patient himself. For them, in effect, the second manifestation of illness would have been decisive. But for Gustave, the only one that counted was the first, which he still regarded ten years later as the chief event of his life. It was at Pont-l'Evêque, according to him, that his youth was "concluded," it was there that one man died and another was born. In the "attacks" that followed he never saw anything but weakened repetitions of this archetypal fulguration. Is such a misunderstanding likely? Is it believable that Achille-Cléophas regarded merely as a negligible incident what his son experienced as the "fatal moment" determining an entire existence? Of course, the good surgeon hardly knew his son. But in this case it was not a question of fathoming a heart: somatic disorders were manifest, and, for Gustave to have kept this terrifying memory of it, their intensity must have been extreme: he fell down, he says, in floods of fire, as if struck by lightning. To the credit of Achille and Achille-Cléophas, we refuse to believe that they could have been mistaken. For if there were *two* accidents–the first at Pont-l'Evêque before the 15th, the second after the 20th–and if they were similar, the *repetition* would most certainly have prompted them to change their diagnosis. It was after the attack at Pont-l'Evêque that they were able to settle on cerebral congestion. But a "miniature apoplexy" does not repeat itself after eight or ten days without being fatal. If the attack recurs, and if the patient survives it, other interpretations must be considered. This is precisely what Achille-Cléophas did in February: before the cyclical return of the problems, he abandoned apoplexies and congestions for the diagnosis of a "nervous illness" and, perhaps more precisely, epilepsy. He must be given credit for this correct aboutface: since it was made between the end of January and the beginning of February, he would have been capable of making it two weeks earlier. In short, it was perfectly excusable, if the first appearance of illness is situated around the 20th or the 25th, to reach the conclusion of congestion, and then, with its recurrence, of a nervous disorder; on the other hand, if the accident at Pont-l'Evêque had taken place before the 15th, it would have been absurd for him to begin by diagnosing a nervous illness and later, when it recurred, to decide that it was a cerebral congestion. And that is precisely what we cannot accuse Achille-Cléophas of doing: one more reason for situating at Pont-l'Evêque Gustave's first pathological experience and for dating it at the end of January 1844.

Toward the middle of the month, then, the young man once more finds himself in his Paris apartment, deeply shaken but still unscathed. For the neurosis to become structured, he needed to discover, during the trajectory of the return, the true meaning of passive activity: he does what repels him because he cannot find in himself the will not to do so. No sooner does he return to Paris than his despondence is transformed into a stupor: he *should not* be there, it is absurd since he cannot bear being there; and yet he is there; he came *willingly,* so he *must* be there. No contingency here: the necessary is indeed the impossible and the reverse is also true. Merely being present between these walls seems at once an objective truth and a nightmare. The denial is total but passive, and conscious of being so; obedience–passive also but subsumed by the appearance of activity–seems convincing to him, like an underlying determination of his life: this is what will determine his future. Thus posed, the contradiction can find a precise solution within him: his passivity must be charged with depriving him of the means to obey. This scheme is obscurely linked to this temptation to collapse, which will give that abstract, rigorous form its content. Nothing is said, however, nothing is known; and yet nothing is hidden, no choice is made: it is a matter of setting up an arrangement that may facilitate a future choice. At the heart of clear consciousness, by contrast, is resentment on the one hand (he did not find the strength to write immediately to his family that he had arrived–*as if* he wanted to enjoy their anxiety and prolong it awhile, *as if* he wanted to compel them to say to themselves: we were wrong to let him go),[5] and, on the other hand, a passionate desire suddenly to find himself at the Hôtel-Dieu again, in his room, and to stay there forever. But this desire is not only disputed by rancor; it can end only in dream: it poses itself as unrealizable since there is no conceivable means of satisfying it. Gustave said so in his letter of 20 December, and he certainly said the same thing to his father: on 15 January he will start preparing for his February exam. This is what was repeated at their farewells: "Good-bye, see you soon, we shall expect you on 1 March." The young man knows he will have no excuse to renege on his commitments. But of course–illness. Yet he is not ill, just desperate. Simulation would be revolt and would testify to a cynicism of which this inveterate boaster of vice is quite incapable. Besides, as he knows from experience, it would be merely an expe-

Gustave (right), about fifteen, and his brother Achille, about twenty-three (drawing by Delaunay, circa 1836; Collections de la Bibliothèque municipale de Rouen. Cliché Thierry Ascencio-Parvy)

dient. For those few days, between the four walls of his room in Paris, Gustave felt as Baudelaire would feel later, "brushed by the wing of imbecility": the inconceivable realizes and imposes itself but can be neither lived nor thought; one can only fall into the daze or escape into the imaginary. He does not touch his law books: this time he does not even find the strength to push obedience to the point of active complicity. He waits–for *nothing;* he vegetates, oversensitive, a stranger to himself, in the midst of a crisis of depersonalization.

This was the moment Caroline chose to advise him to pay a visit to Hamard: "The news of Madame Hamard's illness made me sorry for her son; in less than two years he will have lost everything he loved, poor Hamard; go see him, for he likes you and has often spoken to me about you."[6] The tone is new; a few years earlier, Gustave, Hamard's friend and Caroline's brother, was their only link. Now it is Caroline who acts as intermediary, informing Flaubert of Hamard's feelings and dictating how he should behave toward his comrade. From the beginning of June '43, Hamard, who shuttles between Rouen and Paris, is charged with transmitting Caroline's letters to Gustave. He sees the girl frequently and regularly. It is true, they will not announce their engagement until November '44, but in this new year there is already something between them that is more than friendship. Gustave, who will feign astonishment when he announces the "big news" to Ernest the following autumn, does not know, perhaps, precisely that they are in love: he cannot be unaware that they now have a personal relationship and that he has no place in it. We are already familiar with his jealous rages, and . . . he will make a clean break with his sister–without telling her–the day the two young people make known their engagement. It is therefore perfectly clear from this time that he harbored a vigorous personal resentment of Caroline. Of course, he could not help being jealous, but there is more: the little sister was his vassal; she lived in his dependence and was the object–he thought–of his inexhaustible generosity.

Here another man unexpectedly turns up: there is no question of sharing her; Gustave must be everything to her, or she must be nothing to him. A vassal's betrayal is more criminal than that of a friend: it is the denial of *homage*. And above all it casts doubt on the Lord: he perceives that his "man" was his objective truth; without fealty, no longer Lord, just a poor wretch. Vassal to his father and to Alfred, rejected by both, Gustave was sovereign only to Caroline. By breaking her bonds, she leaves him *destitute* and causes him to fall back into a dark, hopeless vassalage; she ravages his memory by sullying the remembrance of their common childhood; beside her he was *himself,* a subject, an agent of history: she has returned him to his other-being, to his relative-being. In short, in this moment of his life when the failures are accumulating, he experiences his sister's love affair as a new failure, more profound, perhaps, than all the others. We shall have no difficulty imagining his mood when he reads the letter in which she enjoins him, kindly but peremptorily, to go to her lover's home. He goes, nonetheless. Out of a masochism born of resentment; it is as if he were saying to his sister: I shall go, nervous and morose as I am; I shall do what you wish; but you will see what a state this visit will put me in.

He has another motive as well. According to him, Hamard is "pitifully stupid." Once, however, when he was telling Gustave about his brother's death throes, he was fascinating. . . . Flaubert observed then: "I didn't like it at all; that man humiliated me. He was full of feeling and I was empty . . . I recall how I hated myself and thought myself loathsome for a moment." This time it will be even worse. No sooner emerged from his first bereavement, Hamard sees his mother die and is about to find himself utterly alone. We know the effect these repeated shocks would produce in this unfortunate man: after Caroline's death, he went quite mad. Beginning in '44, at the bedside of his dying or already dead mother, suffering makes him fall into mental disarray. Gustave suspects it: half-mad himself, he goes to the home of a madman; unfeeling and wretched, he goes to contemplate a despair incommensurate with his own. Not that Hamard's unhappiness is deeper: it is *other*. Gustave's, most of the time, is lived intensely and for short periods: he calls it *ennui,* and at times must *summon* it by gestures in order to establish it inside him. The *other* has entered Hamard by breaking in: it imposes itself and sponges on him. Here again, Flaubert thinks, is the dichotomy of empty and full. In fact, he is mistaken. Mourning is an unlivable emptiness, and yet it must be lived, no matter how; it is a discourse that cannot cease to address the other; remaining a dialogue, it experiences itself as monologue. Lacking an answer, in these real moments when the living person, amputated, feels the mutilation internalized, there is some phantom of dark comedy that holds in derision the worst suffering. Then comes mental disarray, prompted by the unrealizable fracture of a reciprocal relation whose reciprocity the entire act of mourning maintains in a vacuum. In order to realize an impossible plenitude, one resorts to the craziest gestures or loses oneself in meaningless convulsions. Flaubert is unaware of all that: empty, and ashamed of being empty, he is about to contemplate a horrible void, which he takes for plenitude. He has understood for himself that our misfortune is to be *lacunary;* he has generalized in vain–he is unaware that this lacuna is characteristic of our condition and is to be found in all our feelings.[7]

Of course, the reality surpasses his hopes. Hamard is dazed, convulsive; he probably falls upon Gustave and clings to him; he may even be delirious. Flaubert abhors him and finds *himself* abhorrent. He is cold, stiff, exasperated: he doesn't "go along" with it, and yet this appearance of plenitude fascinates him. He would like to establish it inside himself, this beautiful suffering, this opaque block of unhappiness, in order to fill his emptiness at last, to *realize* Hell even as he scorns the man writhing before his eyes. It seems to him, in short–this is what disconcerts him–that Hamard does not deserve his suffering and that he, Gustave, who alone is worthy of it, is condemned not to feel it. At the same time, terror overtakes him: this fascination, already a temptation, may tomorrow be an attempt. He vaguely understands his pithiatism . . . ; he is afraid of autosuggestion, of letting himself go in an act of irreparable, fatal violence initiated by envy and self-loathing. Yes, he is transfixed by *his doom:* he wants to die and to survive, to play at once the role of mother and son, because he is sure that he can weep for only one death with that marvelous intensity–his own. He can no longer cut himself off from Hamard; apparently he returns several days in a row to the house of death, for he speaks to Ernest of *some* scenes that took place there. This will not be surprising if we recall that beginning in April '38, he evoked–out of a generalized prudence–the "natural feeling that impels man to become impassioned by what is hideous and bitterly grotesque." What is hideous, here, is agony and death; what is grotesque is that despair which has mistaken the sufferer and gives itself undeserved to Hamard, defrauding Gustave. Two words make Flaubert's real feelings manifest: "horrible scenes." He is rarely so pathetic where a death is concerned. These scenes, he says, so shook him that he needed to "recover" from them. Yet the word "horrible" betrays him: it implies a certain blame, a repugnance, which is not contained in "terrible." Hamard's *terrible* suffering *horrifies* Gustave. Precisely because it attracts him, it repels him. He must flee, flee

Élisa Schlésinger with her child, circa 1838. After their first meeting in Trouville in 1836, Flaubert saw the Schlésingers regularly. Long the object of Flaubert's unrequited desire, she served as a partial model for several of his important female characters (lithograph by Deveria; cliché Bibliothèque nationale de France, Paris).

these nightmarish days that he lives now at his friend's and now immured in his own room, trembling with fear. Here he has found the pretext for rejoining his family. But it is already too late. For what he flees is himself, the option that imposes itself on his shattered nerves. In vain: the choice is made. Barely two or three days after the return to Rouen, he will execute the sentence he has passed on himself. So it must *also* be understood that his haste is motivated by a presentiment: if the worst must happen, let it strike in the midst of his family. First of all because the "survival" will be less painful, and second because it will make his family eyewitnesses to the disaster they have provoked. We might say that he both retreats from this disaster and pursues it. Come tonight to Samarkand. This is what gives all its meaning to that sentence in the letter to Ernest: "I almost popped off *in the hands of my family*."

Before interpreting the attack at Pont-l'Evêque, we must ask what role it played in that curious neurosis from which Gustave was to suffer for nearly ten years. Was it a warning signal, a symptom, the first appearance of an illness that would run its course, intensifying to a *maximum* point, after which it would begin to abate? Would this first disorder, original and definite, be followed by others, equally definite but of a different nature, which cannot be identified with it because, although they might have been the effect and expression of the same morbid entity, they manifested it at different moments in its evolution? In short, was it the initial stage of a complex and unforeseeable development, or did it embody the entire illness in a flash of lightning? Would this illness grow, overwhelming other aspects of his being, or, to the contrary, would it mark time, be lost in repetitions, in replays? Would there be, at least for a few months, a progression of psychopathic inventiveness, or was the neurotic structure completed at Pont-l'Evêque once and for all? In order to answer these questions, it will suffice to examine the subsequent attacks.

On those that took place from January to June we have little information: Gustave tells us only that they were numerous at first and subsequently became less frequent. On 7 June he writes to Ernest: "As for your servant, he is doing all right without precisely doing well. Not a day passes without my seeing something now and then like bundles of hair or fireworks passing before my eyes. This lasts for quite a long time. Still, my last big attack was milder than the others." In short, the frequency and intensity are diminishing; several years later, Flaubert will write to Louise that his "attacks" are repeated about every four months.

Maxime was not an eyewitness to the attack at Pont-l'Evêque. But he witnessed several of those which followed, and we have no reason to doubt his testimony.

> He grew very pale . . . This state . . . sometimes went on for several minutes . . . He still hoped it was just a scare . . . Then he walked, he ran toward his bed, lay down, as dismal as if he were lying down alive in a coffin . . . He would cry: "Drop the reins; here comes the wagoner, I hear the bells! Ah! I see the lantern of the inn!" Then he would groan . . . and the convulsion would lift his body . . . a paroxysm in which his whole being would shake, [followed] invariably by a deep sleep and a fatigue that lasted several days.

This description calls forth several comments. First of all, the basic character of these attacks is that they are explicitly constituted as references to the first attack. In a way, they resurrect it. But these stereotypical repetitions of the archetypal event are also weakened reproductions. The attack at Pont-l'Evêque had jumped Gustave like a thief: now the young man has a *warning*. An unutterable malaise and the impression of seeing "fireworks" serve as alarms. He waits, *conscious* of

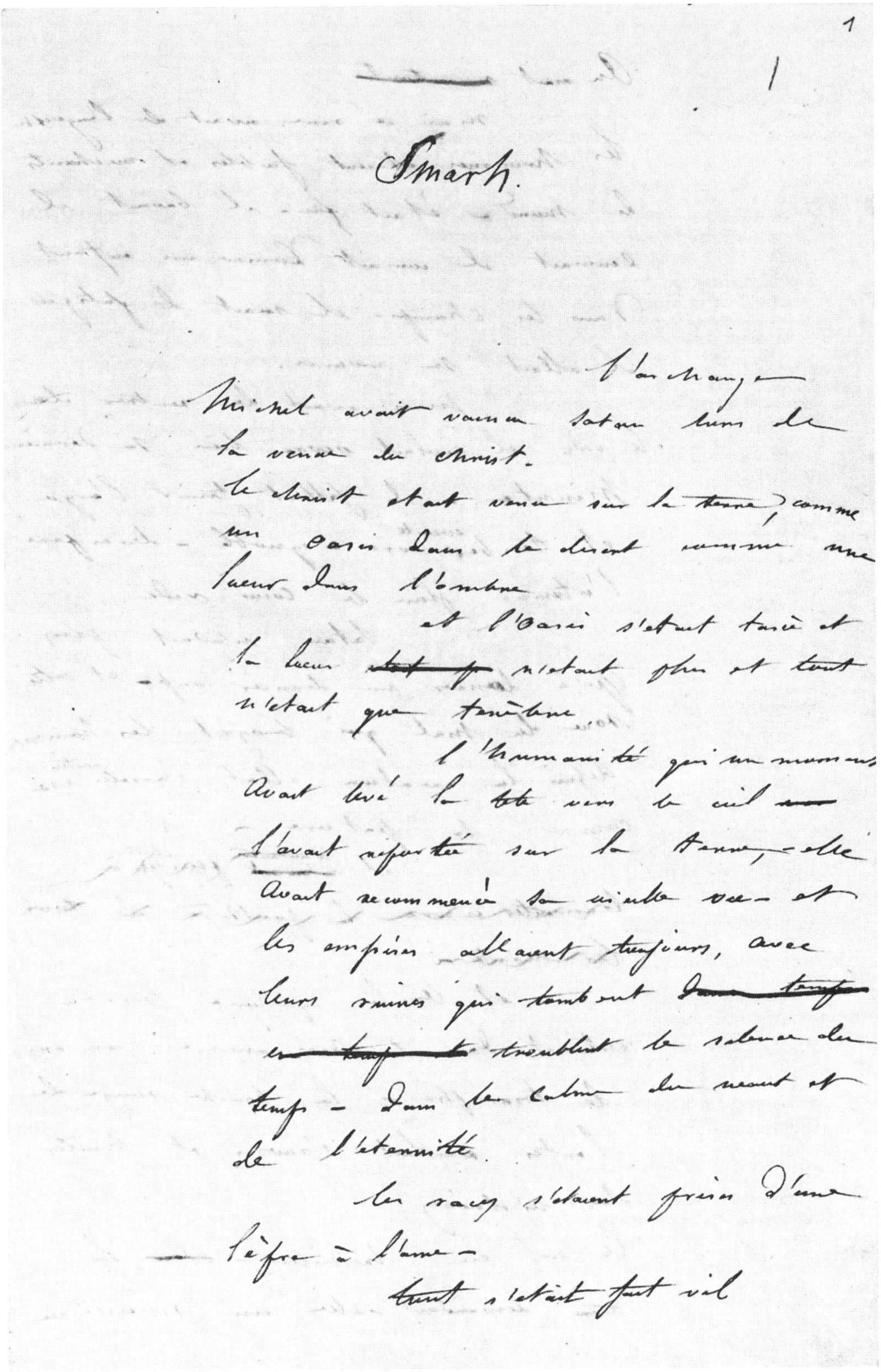
1

Smarh.

L'archange
Michel avait vaincu Satan lors de
la venue du christ.
le christ etait venu sur la terre, comme
un oasis dans le desert comme une
lueur dans l'ombre
et l'oasis s'etait tarie et
la lueur n'etait plus et tout
n'etait que tenebre
l'humanité qui un moment
avait levé la tete vers le ciel
l'avait reportée sur la terre, elle
avait recommencé sa misérable vie et
les empires allaient toujours, avec
leurs ruines qui tombent
troublent le silence du
temps – dans le calme du neant et
de l'eternité
les races s'etaient prises d'une
lèpre à l'ame –
tout s'etait fait vil

First page of the April 1839 manuscript for Flaubert's tale later titled "Smar," which prefigures his work on La Tentation de saint Antoine *(cliché Bibliothèque nationale de France, Paris)*

The village of Pont-L'Évêque in 1842. On the road returning from this village, in a coach with his brother, Flaubert was struck by his first nervous attack; he was so debilitated that Achille thought him dead (cliché Bibliothèque nationale de France, Paris).

the danger that threatens him, and instead of falling as if struck by lightning he has time to go and lie down on his couch. From this point on, the primal scene is relived *in the imaginary* on the basis of a few indices, always the same, provided by memory. "I see the wagoner, the lights," etc. In a sense, it is *played* and, above all, *spoken:* the psychopathic aggression that Flaubert suffered he reconstitutes here as a *role*. The content is, moreover, debased: Flaubert often spoke of the millions of images and ideas that rushed through his consciousness when he fell at his brother's feet; they were "all the ignited rockets of a fireworks display." This incommunicable richness of perception–illusory but experienced–contrasts with the poverty of discourse, and consequently of thoughts, in the referential attacks. The wagoner's noisy cart, the distant lights, etc., make up the meager bunch of auditory and visual images or, rather, the assortment of *words* that monopolize his consciousness. It is like a conjuring trick: the patient *invokes* and *convokes* the false death that felled him one night. But it doesn't come: Achille believed for ten minutes that he was dead; Maxime doesn't believe it for a moment. Cataleptic immobility is replaced by convulsions; these disordered movements, it seems, are born of the futile quest for a former state and the impossibility of reproducing it. Did the "fireworks" of thoughts light up at that moment in Flaubert's head? It is unlikely. He repeated, of course, that he never lost consciousness on those occasions. But the "catalepsy" at Pont-l'Evêque was favorable to "mentism" [the flight of ideas]. During convulsions, the jerks of the body suffice to occupy the consciousness; it is hard to imagine that they accelerate thought and foster ideas. *Physically* exhausted, the patient falls into a heavy sleep, and this is how it ends until the next time.

These referential attacks occur frequently in certain patients. Janet cites, among others, the case of a young girl who *reproduced* the terrible night she had kept vigil over her dead mother with her dead-drunk father close by. Autonomous systems, constituted *on one occasion,* reappear in progressively weakened form and are finally reduced to a symbolic skeleton, a few stereotypical movements. In Flaubert's case, a single moment seems to have assured the passage from a normal to a pathological state. The morbid creation and the *fiat* (the neurotic consent to the neurosis) are merged into a single moment on a moonless night in January 1844. After that night, the neurosis in Gustave invented nothing more; it seemed out of breath. As a result, no other disorder appended itself to the first ones; the illness did not develop, it had no history, it was maintained in the circular time of repetition: it was an *involution* rather than an evolution. Flaubert feels this; he feels that his illness *consumes him*. In a word, the only moment that counts is that of the archetypal event: in it, the neurosis is chosen, structured, realized; in the depths, a choice has taken place, four years in the making, which has willed itself to be irreversible or, rather, was none other than a consented irreversibility. Afterward, for nearly ten years, disorders will occur that no longer have the same meaning, precisely because their purpose is merely to reproduce the original choice, maintain it across the temporal flow. The convulsive attacks are suffered yet playacted ceremonies intended to commemorate the irreversible, to confirm the patient in his neurotic option. . . .

–Jean-Paul Sartre, "The Event," in *The Family Idiot, Gustave Flaubert 1821–1857,* volume 4, translated by Carol Cosman (Chicago & London: University of Chicago Press), pp. 3–17

---

1. Caroline's letter informs us that at this date, Madame Hamard lay dying.
2. This would not be the only one. For example, the letter that Caroline says she received on the 17th at five o'clock in the evening–which might allow a better understanding of Gustave's mental state at this date–has been lost or destroyed.
3. He writes "Pont-Audemer."
4. 9 February 1844, to the same Ernest: "[I am following] a stupid regimen." . . .
5. But his submission prevents him from making the pleasure last: after one day or, at the most, two, he sends a note to Caroline.
6. Letter of 17 January 1844.
7. It goes without saying that I do not mean to deny the *truth* of such suffering. I am saying only that this biologically *rational* fact, the death of the other, is lived *in irrationality* because it is unrealizable and that, for this reason, all our acts are transformed into gestures. To cite only one example, to carry out the last wishes of a dying man can lead to real and difficult endeavors. But they are derealized from the outset because they are born of the futile decision to keep him alive, to institute him as living by claiming that he is at the source of acts which are in fact born of our personal options. The carrying out is *in principle* incommensurate with the *intention* one claims to realize; the results will be always *other* than what the dead man had foreseen, and we cannot help being aware of it.

A New Life: 1844–1851

Gustave Flaubert benefited from his illness in that his father decided that he should not return to his law studies. In 1844 Achille-Cléophas Flaubert bought a house in Croisset—a small hamlet on the Seine a couple of miles downstream from Rouen—where the family went to spend the summer. The two-story home, which became Flaubert's primary residence for the rest of his life, proved conducive to a quiet life of contemplation and writing. While reading the classics, Flaubert managed in January 1845 to finish L'Éducation sentimentale *(published as* La Première Éducation sentimentale, *1910; translated as* Sentimental Education (1845), *1972), a novel that went unpublished during his lifetime and that has little in common with the work published as* L'Éducation sentimentale. Histoire d'un jeune homme *(1869; translated as* Sentimental Education: A Young Man's History, *1898).*

On 3 March 1845 Flaubert's sister Caroline married Émile Hamard, whom he had known since his years at the Collège Royal. Flaubert and his parents accompanied the newlyweds on their honeymoon trip to Italy. The journey was significant because in Genoa, Flaubert saw Peter Brueghel the Younger's The Temptation of Saint Anthony, *a painting that inspired the author to try to write the story of the saint over a period of almost thirty years.*

A Tumultuous Year: 1846

The year 1846 began tragically for Flaubert, who suffered through the deaths of his sixty-one-year-old father and his twenty-one-year-old sister in its first three months. Achille-Cléophas Flaubert succumbed to an infection on 15 January. Six days later Caroline gave birth to a daughter (Flaubert's niece, also named Caroline), but she never recovered from the delivery and died on 22 March. Soon after the death of his sister, Gustave, his mother, and the baby moved to Croisset for good.

In the aftermath of his sister's death and burial Flaubert wrote to his friend Maxime Du Camp on a Wednesday morning from Croisset. The two men's friendship had begun in Paris in March 1843. Born on 8 February 1822, Du Camp was two months younger than Flaubert. He had been raised independently, as his parents had died in his early youth. When Flaubert met him, he was a dilettante writer living on his fortune.

Flaubert to Maxime Du Camp, 25 March 1846

Mon cher vieux, I didn't want you to come here. I was afraid of your affection. It was enough for me to see Hamard, without seeing you. Perhaps you would have been even less calm than we were. In a little while I'll send you a call: I count on you. It was yesterday at eleven o'clock that we buried her, poor girl. They dressed her in her wedding-gown, with bouquets of roses, immortelles and violets. I watched beside her all night. She lay on her bed, in that room where you heard her play her piano. She seemed much taller and much more beautiful than when she was alive, with the long white veil coming down to her feet.[1] In the morning, when everything was done, I gave her a long last farewell kiss in her coffin. I bent over her, and as I lowered my head into the coffin I felt the lead buckle under my hands. It was I who attended to the casts. I saw the great paws of those louts touching her and covering her with plaster. I shall have her hand and her face. I shall ask Pradier to make me her bust and will put it in my room. I have her big colored shawl, a lock of her hair, her table and writing-desk. That is all—all that remains of those we love!

Hamard insisted on coming with us. There, in the cemetery (I used to walk just outside the walls with my class, and it was there that Hamard saw me for the first time), he knelt at the edge of the grave, threw kisses to her, and wept. The grave was too narrow, the coffin wouldn't fit. They shook it, pulled it, turned it this way and that; they took a spade and crowbars, and finally a gravedigger trod on it—just above Caroline's head—to force it down. I was standing at the side, holding my hat in my hand; I threw it down with a cry.

I'll tell you the rest when we're together, for I'd write it all too badly. I was as tearless as a tombstone, but seething with anger. I wanted to tell you all this, thinking it would give you pleasure. You are sufficiently intelligent, and love me enough, to understand that word "pleasure," which would make the bourgeois laugh.

Two views of the Seine at Croisset at about the time Flaubert's father bought the Croisset property for his family: top, pencil drawing by Eustache Bérat, 1840; bottom, painting by an unidentified artist (Collections de la Bibliothèque municipale de Rouen. Clichés Thierry Ascencio-Parvy)

Flaubert's Correspondence

Flaubert's correspondence is regarded as one of the jewels of French literature. Although many of the thousands of letters that Flaubert wrote between 1830 and 1880 were destroyed, more than 3,200 were preserved, and taken together they are an exceptional record of and commentary on nineteenth-century bourgeois and artistic life in Paris and in the provinces. The letters also reveal Flaubert's intellectual life and early interest in the arts and later his acquaintance with other artists and writers. He writes with sincerity, exposing his own life, giving advice, and confiding in certain correspondents. In short, Flaubert's letters provide a precious tool for understanding his complex personality.

Whereas the years 1830–1851 correspond to a period of formation, the letters of the author's maturity may be read as a long reflection on Art in general and on Flaubertian aesthetics in particular. During the time of his second relationship with Louise Colet (1851–1855), which corresponds to the period in which he was working on Madame Bovary, *he discusses his conception of prose, problems with literary forms, anxiety concerning creation, and his desperate search for Beauty. These letters bear witness to Flaubert's ambition to reach perfection in style, the most important aspect of his writing.*

After his separation from Colet, Flaubert never again engaged in such a dialogue. Although he still conveys his critical ideas in letters to literary correspondents such as Ernest Feydeau, the Goncourt brothers, Charles Baudelaire, and, later, Émile Zola, and to acquaintances, particularly Edma Roger des Genettes and Marie-Sophie Leroyer de Chantepie, these letters often turn into lists of details that Flaubert needed for his work, as he calls upon friends to obtain relevant information. Moreover, with the death of Louis Bouilhet in 1869 and then through the 1870s–when he was greatly affected by exigencies such as the Franco-Prussian war, the deaths of his mother and intimate friends, and finally the Commanvilles' bankruptcy in 1875–the letters reveal his flagging energy and increasing pessimism. One has the impression that Flaubert keeps repeating himself in succinct formulas, except in the letters to Ivan Turgenev and George Sand.

Soon after Flaubert's death, Caroline Commanville began to sell the rights to publish her uncle's literary papers. Selected letters hence appeared in four volumes published by Charpentier from 1887 to 1893. Conard later attempted to publish a more comprehensive edition of the letters, publishing 1,992 of them in nine volumes from 1926 to 1933. However, this edition was also far from complete and satisfactory, as many letters were not included and others were censored because of Flaubert's tone, considered "indecent" if not "obscene"; in addition, the text of the letters was often inaccurate because of reading mistakes, and many letters were incorrectly dated. Such problems led Conard in 1954 to publish four additional volumes of Flaubert's correspondence in the twenty-eight-volume edition of Flaubert's Œuvres complètes *(Complete Works), which included 1,296 previously unpublished letters.*

In 1972, Gallimard began publishing Correspondance, *the most definitive edition of Flaubert's letters. Four volumes, edited by Jean Bruneau, were published by 1998; the fifth volume, covering the years 1876 to 1880 and edited by Yvan Leclerc, is yet to be published. Thanks to patient research around the world, the editors for the Gallimard Pléiade edition have discovered and brought to light previously unpublished letters, and they have filled lacunae and corrected errors found in letters published in other editions.*

Unfortunately, the translation of Flaubert's letters into English has not kept pace with the strides French scholars have made in Correspondance. *The two volumes published as* The Letters of Gustave Flaubert, 1830–1857 *(1980) and* The Letters of Gustave Flaubert, 1857–1880 *(1982) include fewer than 400 letters and are often heavily edited. The only two unabridged books in English of the letters are* Flaubert and Turgenev. A Friendship in Letters *(1985) and* Flaubert~Sand. The Correspondence *(1993).*

We have been back in Croisset since Sunday. (What a journey, alone with my mother, and the baby crying!) The last time I left Croisset was with you: you remember. Of the four who lived here then, two remain. The trees are still leafless, the wind is blowing, the river is high; the rooms are cold and bare.

My mother is better than one would think she could be. She busies herself with her daughter's child, sleeps in her room, rocks her, does everything she can. She is trying to turn herself into a mother again. Will she succeed? The reaction has not yet set in, and I dread its coming.

We face some bad trouble because of the child.[2] It is no longer possible to settle things privately; we must go to court. Even if there is no hitch, it will take three months. Also–and this is the most pressing–we must find a place to live in Rouen.[3]

I am crushed, numb. I greatly need to resume a quiet existence: the grief and the worry have been suffocating. When can I return to my austere life of tranquil art and long meditation? I laugh with pity at the vanity of the human will, when I think that for the past six years I have wanted to learn Greek, and that circumstances have been such that I haven't yet got as far as the verbs.

Adieu, dear Maxime. Je t'embrasse tendrement.

It goes without saying that this letter is for you alone, and nothing in it should go any further.

–*The Letters of Gustave Flaubert, 1830–1857,* edited by Francis Steegmuller (Cambridge, Mass.: Harvard University Press, 1980), pp. 38–39

---

1. Recalling this scene in a later letter to Louise Colet, Flaubert adds the following: "I was reading Montaigne; my eyes kept turning from my book to the corpse; her husband and the priest were snoring: and I kept telling myself, as I saw all this, that forms disappear, that the idea alone remains; and I kept feeling thrills at turns of phrase in the Montaigne, and reflected that he too would be forgotten. It was freezing, the window was open because of the odor, and from time to time I got up to look at the stars, calm, radiant, eternal."
2. Hamard was showing signs of mental derangement.
3. For the following winter.

* * *

Flaubert suffered another loss when his closest friend, Alfred Le Poittevin, announced that he was going to marry Louise de Maupassant on 6 July 1846. Flaubert believed Le Poittevin was giving up his calling as a poet to become a bourgeois and felt personally betrayed. His life took another unexpected turn in the same month as his friend's wedding, for on a visit to sculptor James Pradier's studio he met and began an intense affair with Louise Colet. Born in Aix-en-Provence in 1810, Colet was a minor poet and a prolific writer. At the time, she was married to Hippolyte Colet and the mistress of the philosopher Victor Cousin. Flaubert returned to Croisset and, as Colet lived in Paris, the two lovers began to exchange letters in which they discussed art as well as love.

Flaubert to Louise Colet, 6 or 7 August 1846

I am shattered, numb, as though after a long orgy; I miss you terribly. There is an immense void in my heart. Formerly I was calm, proud of my serenity. I worked keenly and steadily from morning to night. Now I cannot read, or think, or write. Your love has made me sad. I can see you are suffering; I foresee I will make you suffer. Both for your sake and for my own I wish we had never met, and yet the thought of you is never absent from my mind. In it I find an exquisite sweetness. Ah! How much better it would have been to stop short after our first ride together! I had forebodings that things would turn out as they have! The next day, when I didn't come to Phidias', it was because I

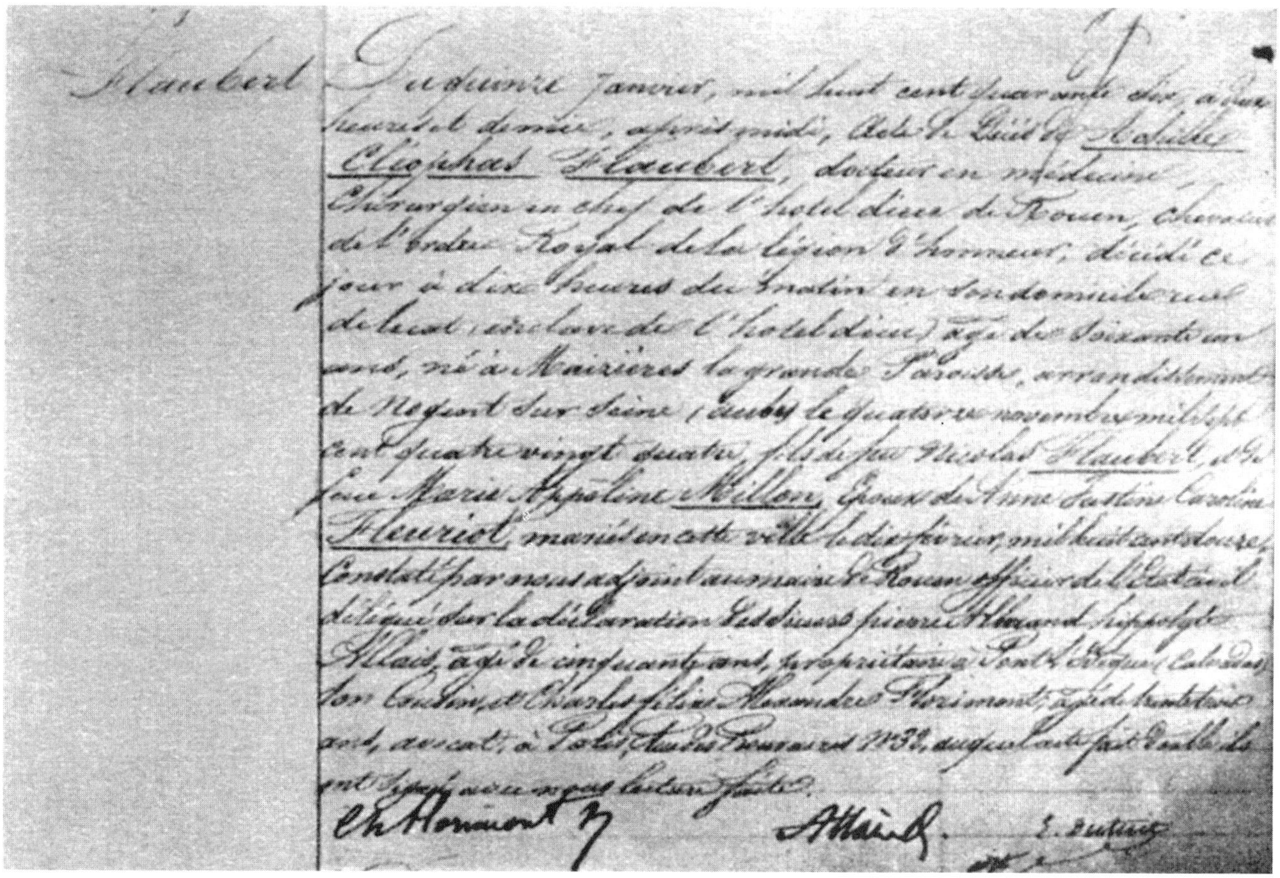

Flaubert

Du quinze janvier, mil huit cent quarante six, à deux heures et demie, après midi, Acte de Décès de Achille Cléophas Flaubert, docteur en médecine, Chirurgien en chef de l'hotel dieu de Rouen, Chevalier de l'ordre Royal de la légion d'honneur, décédé ce jour à dix heures du matin en son domicile rue de lecat (enclave de l'hotel dieu) agé de soixante un ans, né à Maizières la grande Paroisse, arrondissement de Nogent sur Seine (Aube) le quatorze novembre mil sept cent quatre vingt quatre, fils de feu Nicolas Flaubert, et de feue Marie Apolline Millon, Epoux de Anne Justine Caroline Fleuriot, mariés en cette ville le dix février mil huit cent douze; Constaté par nous adjoint au maire de Rouen officier de l'Etat civil [illegible] sur la déclaration des sieurs [illegible] Hippolyte Allais, agé de cinquante ans, propriétaire à Pont l'Evêque (Calvados) son cousin, et Charles Félix Alexandre [illegible], agé de trente [illegible] ans, avocat, à [illegible] [illegible] avec nous lecture faite.

Ch [illegible] Allais [illegible]

Death certificate for Flaubert's father, recipient of the Royal Order of the Legion of Honor, who died at 10 A.M. on 15 January 1846 (courtesy of the Musée Flaubert et d'Histoire de la Médecine, Rouen)

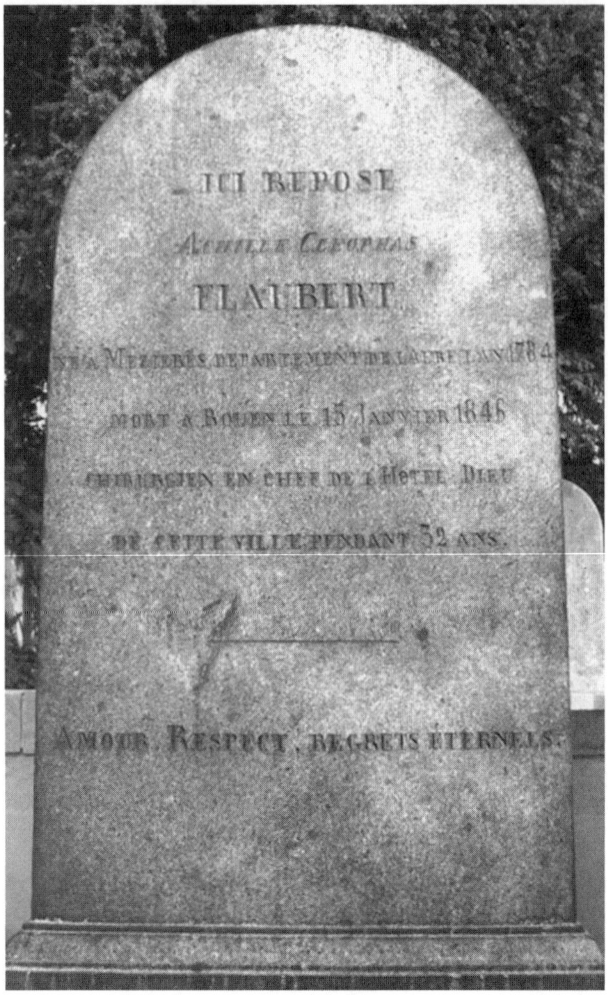

The graves of Flaubert's father and sister in Rouen. The inscription for Dr. Flaubert reads "chief-surgeon of the Hôtel-Dieu of this city during thirty-two years. Love, Respect, Eternal regrets." The inscription for his daughter mentions her husband, Émile Hamard, "who desires to see her again some day and remain eternally with her" (photographs by Éric Le Calvez).

already felt myself sliding down the slope. I wanted to stop: what pushed me? So much the worse! So much the better! God did not give me a merry constitution; no one senses more keenly than I the wretchedness of life. I believe in nothing–not even in myself, which is rare. I devote myself to Art because it gives me pleasure to do so, but I have no faith whatever in beauty, any more than in anything else. So the part of your letter in which you speak of patriotism, poor darling, would have made me laugh if I had been in a gayer mood. You will think that I am hard, I wish I were. All those who cross my path would benefit from my being so, and so would I, with my heart that's been cropped close–like meadow grass in autumn by all the passing sheep. You would not believe me when I told you I was old. Alas, yes, for every sensation that enters my soul turns sour, like wine poured into jars too often used. If you knew all the inner forces that have consumed me, all the mad desires that have passed through my head, everything I have tried and experienced in the way of sensations and passions, you would see that I am not so young! It is you who are a child, you who are fresh and new, you whose candor makes me blush. The grandeur of your love fills me with humility; you deserved someone better than I. May lightning strike me, may all possible curses fall upon me if ever I forget that! You ask me whether I despise you because you gave yourself to me too quickly. Have you really been able to suspect that? *Never, never:* whatever you do, whatever may happen, I am devoted to you for life, to you, to your daughter, to anything and anyone you wish. That is a vow. Remember it. Use it. I make it because I can keep it.

Yes, I desire you and I think of you. I love you more than I loved you in Paris. I can no longer do anything; I keep seeing you in the studio, standing

Marble busts of Flaubert's father and sister, sculpted by James Pradier. Flaubert kept the bust of his sister, made from a mold taken after her death, in his study throughout his life. During his days as a law student, Flaubert was a regular visitor to Pradier's Paris studio-salon. He met Louise Colet there when he traveled to Paris in July 1846 (left, courtesy of the Musée Flaubert et d'Histoire de la Médecine, Rouen; right, courtesy of the Musée Picasso, Antibes).

near your bust, your long curls stirring on your white shoulders, your blue dress, your arm, your face–everything. Ah! Now *strength* is beginning to circulate in my blood. You seem to be here; I am on fire, my nerves tremble . . . you know how . . . you know the heat of my kisses.

Ever since we said we loved each other, you have wondered why I have never added the words "for ever." Why? Because I always sense the future, the antithesis of everything is always before my eyes. I have never seen a child without thinking that it would grow old, nor a cradle without thinking of a grave. The sight of a naked woman makes me imagine her skeleton. As a result, joyful spectacles sadden me and sad ones affect me but little. I do too much inward weeping to shed outward tears–something read in a book moves me more than a real misfortune. When I had a family, I often wished I had none, so that I might be freer, free to live in China or among savages. Now that my family is gone, I long for it, and cling to the walls that still retain the imprint of its shadow. Others would be proud of the love you lavish on me, their vanity would drink its fill of it, and their male egotism would be flattered to its inmost depths. But after the moments of frenzy have passed, my heart swoons with sadness, for I say to myself: "She loves me and I love her too, but I do not love her enough. If she had never known me, she would have been spared all the tears she is shedding." Forgive me, forgive me in the name of all the rapture you have given me. But I have a presentiment of immense unhappiness for you. I fear lest my letters be discovered, that everything become known. *I am sick and my sickness is you.*

A drawing of the property at Croisset (Collections de la Bibliothèque de Rouen. Cliché Thierry Ascencio-Parvy)

Imagined view of Flaubert's Croisset residence, painted by Thomsen in 1937, long after the home had been destroyed. All that remains is the pavilion (far left), which in 1906 became a museum dedicated to the author (Collections de la Bibliothèque municipale de Rouen. Cliché Thierry Ascencio-Parvy).

You think that you will love me for ever, child. For ever! What presumption on human lips! You have loved before, have you not? So have I. Remember that you have said "for ever" before. But I am bullying you, hurting you. You know that my caresses are fierce. No matter: I should rather inject some disquiet into your happiness now than deliberately exaggerate its extent, as men always do, to make you suffer the more when it ends–who knows? You will thank me later, perhaps, for having had the courage not to be more tender. Ah! If I lived in Paris, if every day of my life could be passed at your side–yes, then I'd let myself be swept away by this current, without crying for help! I should find in you, for my heart, my body and my mind, a daily gratification that would never weary me. But apart, destined to see each other only rarely, how frightful! What a prospect! What can we do? Still–I cannot imagine how I was able to leave you. But that is how I am; there you see my wretched character. If you were not to love me, I should die; but you do love me, and I am writing you to stop. I am disgusted by my own stupidity. But in whatever direction I look I see only unhappiness! I wish I might have come into your life like a cool brook to refresh its thirst, not as a devastating torrent. At the thought of me your flesh would have thrilled, your heart smiled. Never curse me! Ah, I shall love you well before loving you no longer. I shall always bless you–your image will stay with me, all imbued with poetry and tenderness, as last night was bathed in the milky vapor of its silvery mist.

Sometime this month I'll come to see you and will stay an entire day. In two weeks or less I shall be with you. When Phidias writes[1] I will come at once, I promise . . .

You want me to send you something I have written. No, you would find everything too good. Have you not given me enough, without literary praise? Do you want to make me completely fatuous? Nothing I have here is legible; you couldn't decipher it, with all its crossings-out and inserts–I have never had anything properly recopied. Aren't you afraid of spoiling your style by associating with me? You'd like me to publish something immediately; you'd like to stimulate me; you'd end by getting me to take myself seriously (may the Lord preserve me from that!). Formerly the pen ran quickly over my paper; now as it runs it tears. I cannot write a sentence, I keep changing my pen, because I can express nothing of what I want to say. Come to Rouen with Phidias, pretend you met him here by chance, and visit me here. That will satisfy you more than any possible description. Then you'll think of my rug and of the great white bearskin I stretch out on during the day, as I think of your alabaster lamp and how I watched its dying light flickering on the ceiling. Did you understand, that night, that I was waiting for it to go out? I didn't dare; I am timid, despite my cynicism–or perhaps because of it. I told myself I'll wait till the candle dies. Oh! Such forgetfulness of everything! Such exclusion of the rest of the world! The smooth skin of your naked body! And the hypocritical pleasure I took in my resentment as your other guests stayed, and stayed! I shall always remember your look when you were at my knees on the floor, and your ecstatic smile when you opened the door and we parted. I went down through the shadows on tiptoe like a thief. Wasn't I one? And are they all as happy, when they flee with their loot?

I owe you a frank explanation of myself, in response to a page of your letter which makes me see that you harbor illusions about me. It would be cowardly of me (and cowardice is a vice that disgusts me, in whatever aspect it shows itself) to allow these to persist.

My basic character, whatever anyone may say, is that of the mountebank. In my childhood and my youth I was wildly in love with the stage. I should perhaps have been a great actor if I had happened to be born poorer. Even now, what I love above all else, is *form,* provided it be beautiful, and nothing beyond it. Women whose hearts are too ardent and whose minds too exclusive do not understand this religion of beauty, beauty considered apart from emotion. They always demand a

Gustave Flaubert at the time he met Louise Colet (pencil drawing by Desandré, circa 1845; courtesy of the Conseil Général de la Seine-Maritime, Rouen)

cause, an end. I admire tinsel as much as gold: indeed, the poetry of tinsel is even greater, because it is sadder. The only things that exist for me in the world are splendid poetry, harmonious, well-turned, singing sentences, beautiful sunsets, moonlight, pictures, ancient sculpture, and strongly marked faces. Beyond that, nothing. I would rather have been Talma than Mirabeau, because he lived in a sphere of purer beauty. I am as sorry for caged birds as for enslaved human beings. In all of politics, there is only one thing that I understand: the riot. I am as fatalistic as a Turk, and believe that whether we do everything we can for the progress of humanity, or nothing at all, makes no whit of difference. As for that "progress," I have but an obtuse comprehension of muddy ideas. I am completely out of patience with everything pertaining to that kind of language. I despise modern tyranny because it seems to me stupid, weak, and without the courage of its convictions. But I have a deep cult of ancient tyranny, which I regard as mankind's finest manifestation. I am above all a man of fantasy, caprice, lack of method. I thought long and *very seriously* (don't laugh, it is a memory of my best hours) of becoming a Mohammedan in Smyrna. The day will come when I will go and settle somewhere far from here, and nothing more will be heard of me. As for what ordinarily touches men most closely, and for me is secondary–I mean physical love–I have always kept it separate from this other. I heard you jeer at J.J.[2] on this account the other day: his case is mine exactly. You are the only woman whom I have both loved and possessed. Until now I used women to satisfy desires aroused in me by other women. You made me untrue to my system, to my heart, perhaps to my nature, which, incomplete in itself, always seeks the incomplete.

I loved one woman from the time I was fourteen until I was twenty, without telling her, without touching her;[3] and after that I went three years without feeling sexual desire. At one time I thought I should continue so until I died, and I thanked God. I wish I had neither body nor heart, or rather, I wish I might be dead, for the figure I cut on this earth is infinitely ridiculous. That is what makes me mistrustful and fearful of myself.

You are the only woman to whom I have dared to try to give pleasure, the only one, perhaps, to whom I have given it. Thank you, thank you for that! But will you understand me to the end? Will you be able to bear the burden of my spleen, my manias, my whims, my prostrations and my wild reversals? You tell me, for example, to write you every day, and if I don't you will reproach me. But the very idea that you want a letter every morning will prevent me from writing it. Let me love you in my own way, in the way my nature demands, with what you call my originality. Force me to do nothing, and I will do everything. Understand me, do not reproach me. If I thought you frivolous and stupid like other women, I would placate you with words, promises, vows. That would cost me nothing. But I prefer to express less, not more, than the true feelings of my heart.

The Numidians, Herodotus says, have a strange custom. They burn the scalps of their infant children with coals, to make them less sensitive to the action of the sun, which is so fierce in their country. And of all people on earth they are the healthiest. Imagine that I was brought up in the Numidian way. Wouldn't it be too easy to say to me: "You don't feel anything! The sun itself doesn't warm you!" Have no fear: my heart is none the worse for being calloused. Don't misunderstand me, however: when I probe myself I don't think myself better than my neighbor. Only, I have some perspicacity, and a certain delicacy in my manners.

Evening is falling. I have spent my afternoon writing to you. When I was eighteen, back from a trip to the Midi, I wrote similar letters for six months to a woman I didn't love.[4] I did it to force myself to love her, to play a role with conviction. Now it is the exact opposite; the antithesis is complete.

One last word: in Paris, there is a man[5] who is at my service, devoted to me unto death; active, bold, intelligent, a great and heroic nature compliant to my every wish. In case of need, count on him as you would on me. Tomorrow I expect your poems, and in a few days your two volumes. Farewell, think of me; yes, kiss your arm for me. Every evening now I read some of your poems. I keep looking for traces of yourself in them; sometimes I find them.

Adieu, adieu; I lay my head on your breasts and look up at you, as to a madonna.

11 P.M.

Adieu, I seal my letter. This is the hour when, alone amidst everything that sleeps, I open the drawer that holds my treasures. I look at your slippers, your handkerchief, your hair, your portrait, I reread your letters and breathe their musky perfume. If you could know what I am feeling at this moment! My heart expands in the night, suffused with a dew of love!

A thousand kisses, a thousand, *everywhere–everywhere.*

–*The Letters of Gustave Flaubert, 1830–1857,* pp. 46–50

---

1. About the bust of Dr. Flaubert. Because of his mother, Flaubert needed a pretext to go to Paris. "Phidias," of course, was Pradier.
2. The critic Jules Janin.
3. Elise [*sic,* for Élisa] Schlesinger.
4. Eulalie Foucault.
5. Maxime DuCamp.

* * *

Colet with her daughter, Henriette, in 1842, four years before she met Flaubert. She was thirty-two years old at the time (painting by Adèle Grasset; courtesy of the Musée Granet, Aix-en-Provence).

This excerpt is from a letter Flaubert dated "Friday, 10 P.M."

Flaubert to Colet, 18 September 1846

You tell me, my angel, that I have not initiated you into my inner life, into my most secret thoughts. Do you know what is most intimate, most hidden, in my heart, and what is most authentically myself? Two or three modest ideas about art, lovingly brooded over; that is all. The greatest events of my life have been a few thoughts, a few books, certain sunsets on the beach at Trouville, and talks five or six hours long with a friend now married and lost to me.[1] I have always seen life differently from others, and the result has been that I've always isolated myself (but not sufficiently, alas!) in a state of harsh unsociability, with no exit. I suffered so many humiliations, I so shocked people and made them indignant, that I long ago came to realize that in order to live in peace one must live alone and seal one's windows lest the air of the world seep in. In spite of myself I still retain something of this habit. That is why I deliberately avoided the company of women for several years. I wanted no hindrance to my innate moral precept. I wanted no yoke, no influence. In the end I no longer desired women's company at all. Stirrings of the flesh, throbbings of the heart, were absent from my life, and I was not even conscious of my sex. As I told you, I had an overwhelming passion when I was little more than a child. When it ended I decided to divide my life in two parts: to put on one side my soul, which I reserved for Art, and on the other my body, which was to live as best it could. Then you came along and upset all that. So here I am, returning to a human existence!

You have awakened all that was slumbering, or perhaps decaying, within me! I had been loved before, and intensely, though I'm one of those who are quickly forgotten and more apt to kindle emotion than to keep it alive. The love I arouse is always that felt for something a little strange. Love, after all, is only a superior kind of curiosity, an appetite for the unknown that makes you bare your breast and plunge headlong into the storm.

As I said, I have been loved before, but *never the way you love me;* nor has there ever been between a woman and myself the bond that exists between us two. I have never felt for any woman so deep a devotion, so irresistible an attraction; never has there been such complete communion. Why do you keep saying that I love the tinselly, the showy, the flashy? "Poet of form!" That is the favorite term of abuse hurled by utilitarians at true artists. For my part, until someone comes along and separates for me the form and the substance of a given sentence, I shall continue to maintain that that distinction is meaningless. Every beautiful thought has a beautiful form, and vice versa.[2] In the world of Art, beauty is a by-product of form, just as in our world temptation is a by-product of love. Just as you cannot remove from a physical body the qualities that constitute it–color, extension, solidity–without reducing it to a hollow abstraction, without destroying it, so you cannot remove the form from the Idea, because the Idea exists only by virtue of its form. Imagine an idea that has no form–such a thing is as impossible as a form that expresses no idea. Such are the stupidities on which criticism feeds. Good stylists are reproached for neglecting the Idea, the moral goal; as though the goal of the doctor were not to heal, the goal of the painter to paint, the goal of the nightingale to sing, as though the goal of Art were not, first and foremost, Beauty!

Sculptors who create real women, with breasts that can contain milk and thighs that suggest fecundity, are accused of sensualism. Whereas, were they to carve wads of drapery and figures flat as signboards, they would be called idealists, spiritualists. "Yes, he does neglect form, it's true," people would

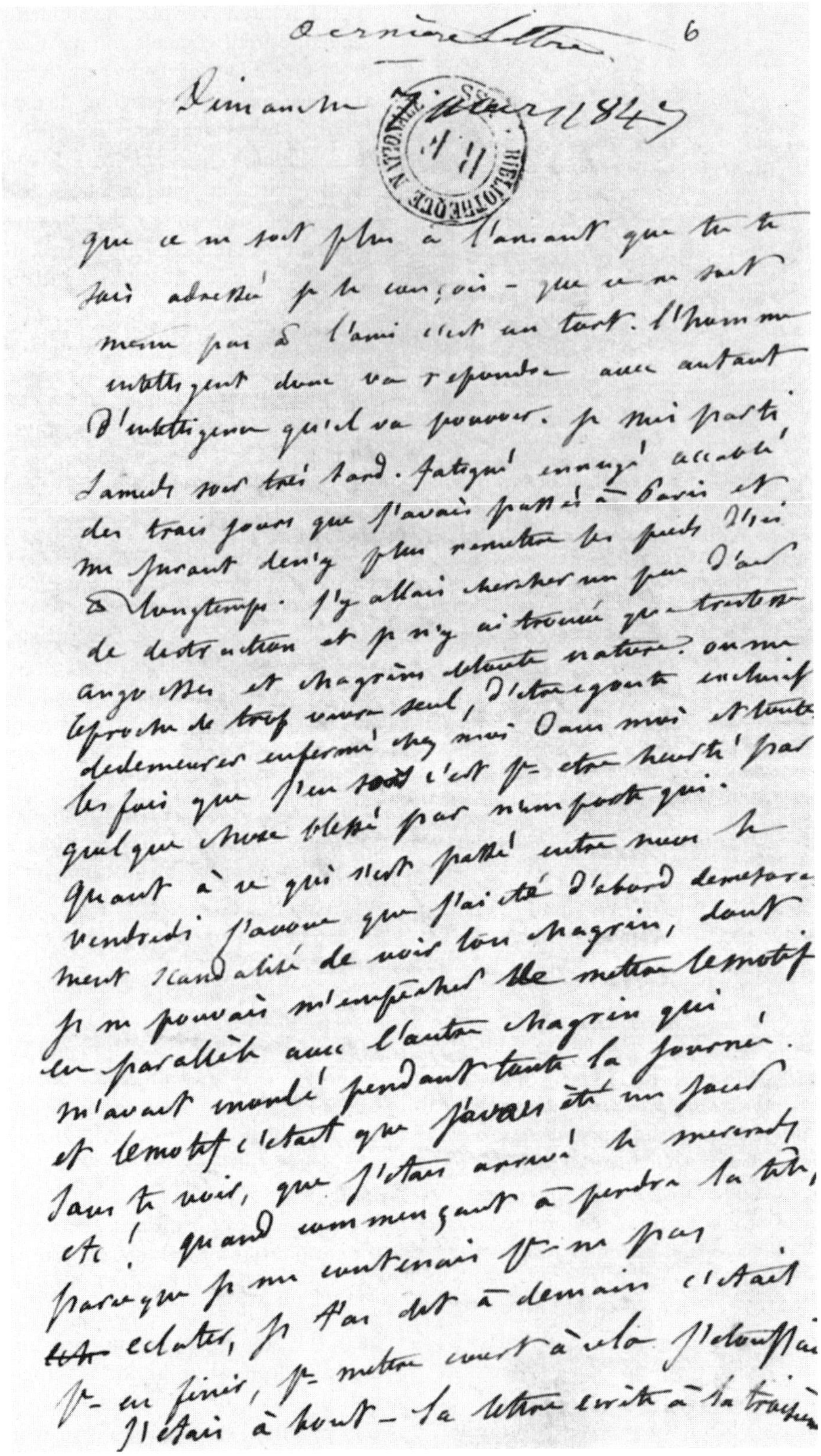

Dernière lettre 6

Dimanche 7 Mars 1847

que ce ne soit plus à l'amant que tu te
sois adressée je le conçois – que ce ne soit
même pas à l'ami c'est un tort. L'homme
intelligent donc va répondre avec autant
d'intelligence qu'il va pouvoir. Je suis parti
samedi soir très tard. fatigué ennuyé accablé
des trois jours que j'avais passés à Paris et
me jurant de n'y plus remettre les pieds d'ici
de longtemps. J'y allais chercher un peu d'air
de destruction et je n'y ai trouvé que tristesses
angoisses et chagrins de toute nature. on me
reproche de trop vivre seul, d'être égoïste exclusif
de demeurer enfermé chez moi dans moi et toutes
les fois que j'en sors c'est pour être heurté par
quelque chose blessé par n'importe qui.
Quant à ce qui s'est passé entre nous le
vendredi j'avoue que j'ai été d'abord démesurément
scandalisé de voir ton chagrin, dont
je ne pouvais m'empêcher de mettre le motif
en parallèle avec l'autre chagrin qui
m'avait inondé pendant toute la journée.
et le motif c'était que j'avais été un jour
sans te voir, que j'étais arrivé le mercredi
etc ! quand commençant à perdre la tête,
je me contenais pour ne pas
parce que je me suis dit à demain c'était
éclater, je [illegible] à cela j'étouffais
pour en finir, pour mettre [illegible] la lettre écrite à la tragédie
j'étais à bout –

First page from Flaubert's 7 March 1847 letter to Colet. He wrote this letter during a tense period in their relationship, when Colet was annoyed with Flaubert for spending most of his time at Croisset and not seeing her as often as she wished. The reproachful tone of this letter was so evident that she thought it was his "Last letter," as she wrote on the top of the page. In fact, they continued their correspondence until the end of that year and for a little while in 1848 (cliché Bibliothèque nationale de France, Paris).

Colet, circa 1845. She gave a copy of this engraving to Flaubert (etching by Franz Winterhalter; cliché Bibliothèque nationale de France, Paris).

say, "but he is a thinker!" Whereupon the bourgeois, with cries of joy, would outdo themselves to admire what bores them. It's easy, with the help of conventional jargon, and two or three ideas acceptable as common coin, to pass as a socialist humanitarian writer, a renovator, a harbinger of the evangelical future dreamed of by the poor and the mad. Such is the modern mania: one blushes to be a writer. If you merely write verse or a novel, merely carve marble, shame! That was acceptable previously, before the poet had a "social mission." Now every piece of writing must have its moral significance, must teach its lesson, elementary or advanced; a sonnet must be endowed with philosophical implications, a play must rap the knuckles of royalty, and a watercolor contribute to moral progress. Everywhere there is pettifoggery, the craze for spouting and orating: the muse becomes a mere pedestal for a thousand unholy desires. Poor Olympus! They'd be capable of planting a potato patch on its summit! If it were only the mediocrities who were involved, one would let them do as they liked. But no–vanity has banished pride, and caused a thousand little cupidities to spring up where formerly a single, noble ambition prevailed. Even men of parts, great men, ask themselves: "Why not seize the moment? Why not impress these people now, hour after hour, instead of being admired by them later?" Whereupon they mount the tribune. They join the staff of a newspaper, and there we see them lending the weight of their immortal names to ephemeral theories.

They intrigue to overthrow some minister who would topple without them–when with a single line of satirical verse they could make his name a synonym for infamy. They concern themselves with taxes, customs-duties, laws, peace and war! How petty all this is! How transient! How false and secondary! All these wretched things excite them–they attack all the crooks, gush over every decent action no matter how commonplace, cry their eyes out over every poor fellow who is murdered, every dog that's run over–as though this were the sole purpose of their lives. To me it seems finer to stand at a distance of several centuries and thrill whole generations, fill them with pure pleasures. Who can measure the ecstasy that Homer has inspired, or count the tears that the excellent Horace has changed into smiles? To speak only of myself, I am grateful to Plutarch because of evenings he gave me at the lycée, evenings filled with warlike ardor, as though the clash of armies were in my very soul.

–*The Letters of Gustave Flaubert, 1830–1857,* pp. 76–78

---

1. Alfred LePoittevin.
2. Flaubert had read Hegel's *Aesthetics.* (J.B.)

A Journey and a Revolution

In May 1847, Flaubert left with Maxime Du Camp for a three-month trip around Normandy and Brittany, visiting Blois and the châteaus of the Loire valley before returning by way of the coast. Traveling also meant for Flaubert a return to literature, for the two friends had decided to write an account of the trip, which became Par les champs et par les grèves *(translated as* Over Strand and Field, *1904). Flaubert wrote the odd-numbered chapters and Du Camp the even. The book was not published during Flaubert's lifetime, but he later extracted a fragment on Carnac that was published in the April 1858 issue of Théophile Gautier's journal* L'Artiste.

In this excerpt from the thirteenth chapter of Flaubert: A Biography, *Herbert Lottman describes Flaubert's trip with Du Camp and also his witness of the Revolution of 1848.*

Westward with Du Camp

Stay-at-home though he may have seemed to Louise, Gustave dreamed of travel. He told Ernest Chevalier, for example, that he would like to visit Corsica but did not dare wish it, for he would be free to travel only if the worst happened; Ernest would understand that he meant by this his mother's death.[1] He could not reach the Mediterranean, but he could visit Brittany. As Du Camp remembered it, the voyage was to be a prelude to the longer trips the friends intended to take together. Brittany itself was relatively far-off and remained somewhat removed from civilization, thanks to its peculiar customs and language.[2] One even needed a passport for such domestic travel. We have Gustave's. His profession was now given as landowner, his height as one meter, eighty-three centimeters; his hair and beard were dark chestnut, and he had an oval face, a high forehead, blue eyes, a vivid complexion. It was also noted that he had a scar under his left eye and another, caused by a burn, on his right hand.[3]

They left Paris at dawn on May 1, 1847, walking from Du Camp's apartment near the Place de la Madeleine to the Orléans station, where they would catch the train to Blois.[4] They had decided to write a travel diary; they would make notes and then prepare a final text on their return, with Gustave doing the odd-numbered chapters and Maxime the even.[5] The first chapter alerts the reader to the modest goals of these travelers: "Later on there will be long journeys across the world, on camelback with Turkish saddles." On this trip they sought only fresh air, a bit of wilderness, and vast sandy beaches. All the same, they began with the Loire valley castles, Blois, Chambord, and Amboise (this last owned by the reigning monarchy, with its "nouveau riche bad taste").[6] On their fourth day out, Du Camp revealed in his memoirs, Gustave suffered an attack. They were in Tours, and Du Camp summoned a local doctor of repute, who confessed his helplessness; he could do no more than prescribe a heavy dose of quinine to serve as a stimulant. It was the only such incident during their trip.

Du Camp also let us see the wildness of western Brittany, with its rough roads, its strange tongue, its rudimentary agriculture, humble villages, untidy houses, superstition, misery . . . they went so far out that they became emissaries of civilization and were called upon to treat wounds. Gendarmes who asked for their passports found it hard to believe that they were traveling for pleasure and not on some mission.[7]

Gustave's mother and tiny Caroline–then eighteen months old–joined them in Brest. Gustave and Maxime rode with them part of the way and then walked alone when it pleased them. Saint Malo was a pilgrimage site for these travelers. Although that quintessential romantic Chateaubriand was still alive, he had already built his tomb there. They went on to Chateaubriand's castle at Combourg and sat outdoors that evening reading his *René*.[8]

From Pontorson, near Mont-Saint-Michel, Gustave wrote Louise on July 14 to announce that he was returning to Croisset to prepare himself to write *The Temptation of Saint Anthony*. He would not begin right away, but he expected to work "rather violently" that winter.[9] But it was not going to be that easy. Louise had expected Gustave to come to Paris for the anniversary of their first encounter, and he had not even sent flowers. He told her that he had never promised to come. To her next letter, which was more tender, he replied with the news that he was suffering from his nervous condition, and that Le Poittevin, "whom I loved beyond measure in my youth," was incurably ill. There were family problems, money problems . . . he wished he were somewhere out of France. She offered to help with money, but he assured her that he would get along. One thing was certain: he intended never to work for a living, and certainly not with his pen.

He was then with his mother and niece in La Bouille, a village on the Seine some twelve miles downstream from Rouen; there was an epidemic of children's diseases in Rouen, and they thought it prudent to keep little Caroline out of the city. "If you knew what my life is like!" he wrote Louise at the end of August. "When I go downstairs in the evening after eight hours of work, my head filled with what I have been reading or writing, . . . I sit down to eat opposite my mother, who sighs when she thinks about the empty chairs, and the infant begins to scream or cry!"[10]

Home in Croisset in September, he set to work writing up his Brittany notes. Du Camp joined him in the middle of the month and was present when his friend had still another attack. Gustave thought it was because he was writing, something he had not done for quite a while. Soon he was telling Louise how he went about his work. "Style, which is something I take to heart, agitates my nerves horribly; I become anxious and angry. There are times when it makes me sick, and at night I have a fever." Or again, "I am always disgusted with what I do."[11]

The lovers continued their fruitless dialogue all the while. He warned Louise that he could not make any woman happy; he could not even play with a child. "My mother takes the baby away when I touch it, for I make it shout, and she is like you, she wants to be near me and calls me." In her reply, one of the rare letters of Louise's that has survived (though only in the copy she made), she returned to the more formal *vous* form to conclude with irony: "I cordially kiss your handsome eyes, which are dazzled by all those visions of the East, and to which I must appear rather bourgeois and dull when they deign to look at me. I remain your old, faithful, and platonic friend." He wrote her on his twenty-sixth birthday in December, suggesting that they return to the use of *tu*. Patience; they would meet and kiss again, though it would be worse than ever for her after that.[12]

He and his mother and Caroline took up winter quarters in Rouen. He pursued his sword lessons–three half hours a week. In a rare brush with politics, he accompanied Du Camp and Bouilhet to a banquet sponsored by the bourgeois reformists opposed to the regime of Louis Philippe. The July Monarchy, born of those "three glorious days" in 1830, was living its final hours, challenged by the radical left and by the upper middle class, which in France, as elsewhere in Europe, was demanding a share of the power. Perhaps Gustave and his friends did in fact sympathize with the opposition, but for the moment they professed horror at the political clichés they had to listen to.[13] Yet if the young men in Normandy were unable to take the reformist banquets seriously, Parisians felt differently. The banning of one such assembly on February 22, 1848, provoked demonstrations. Gustave and Louis Bouilhet rushed to Paris to pick up the thread of events "from the point of view of art," as they put it, and found themselves at the core of the revolution.

On the afternoon of February 23, after a day of agitation in the streets, Maxime Du Camp returned to his lodgings to find Gustave and Louis waiting for him. When the friends went out for dinner, it appeared as if the protest had died out; the crowd had dispersed, soldiers were patrolling, and there were even shouts of "Long live the king!" (By then Louis Philippe had gotten rid of his unpopular minister François Guizot.) But as they approached the Palais-Royal en route to a favorite restaurant, they passed groups carrying paper lanterns and chanting "Long live reform!" Returning to Du Camp's at nine-thirty that evening, they observed columns of marchers on the Boulevard des Capucines. Then, as Du Camp knocked on the street door of his building, they heard a violent explosion. Flaubert said it sounded like shooting and suggested that they take a look, but Du Camp laughed it off; he thought it must be children tossing firecrackers. So they went inside to listen to Bouilhet read the first part of a verse play he was writing on ancient Rome, which was to be *Melaenis*.

What they had turned their backs on was the historic gunning-down of demonstrators that set off a sequence of events concluding with the flight of Louis Philippe into exile. The next day Du Camp was watching the action in the street from his terrace when his Rouen friends arrived: they had walked from their nearby hotel just as barricades were going up. Du Camp remembered Bouilhet predicting, "Louis Philippe is lost; he won't sleep at the Tuileries palace tonight." They went out to see it happen. There was fighting around the Palais-Royal: there the friends lost each other, but Flaubert was tall and easily found again. He and Du Camp stood with their backs to a wall and watched a man fall at their feet from a bullet wound. An officer approached; addressing them as "Citizens," he announced that "tyranny has been overthrown." The Tuileries palace was open, he added, and anyone could go inside. So they took up the invitation. Within the royal dwelling they saw a table set in the state dining room, with silver coffeepots bearing the king's emblem and even bread in the breadbaskets. Some of the uninvited guests seated themselves at the table and said, "This is our reform banquet." The carousing became violence with the arrival of uniformed troops: by a ruse, Du Camp and Flaubert were able to save a group of municipal guards from the mob. Later they would witness scenes of pillage at the Palais-Royal. None of this was lost on Gustave, and the events of 1848 were to provide a story line for the later version of *A Sentimental Education*.

Maxime Du Camp, photograph by Félix Nadar (cliché Bibliothèque nationale de France, Paris)

Exhausted, the two friends returned to Du Camp's place, where they found Bouilhet waiting. He had been forced to work on the barricades until a paving stone fell on his foot. After dinner they pushed through the crowd to the Hôtel de Ville and witnessed the reading of the Provisional Government's decree calling for a republic.[14]

Louise found out that Gustave had been in Paris, and in the thick of it. She wrote a solicitous note that caught up with him in Croisset. "I don't know if the new form of government and the social state that will come out of it will be favorable to Art," he summed up his impressions of the February revolution. "One could not be more bourgeois, or more useless."[15] Long after these events Du Camp would remember the unnecessary violence and the futility of it all, for February 1848 led straight to Napoléon III and the Second Empire.[16] Flaubert in *A Sentimental Education* stresses the futility.

In her unexpected letter Louise also let drop a bit of news. She was pregnant, but not by Gustave. In the interregnum created by their falling-out, she had found other young men to love, and to this day we are not sure which of them was the father of her second child: the best scholars come up only with a first name. Gustave told Louise that she could count on him, whatever happened. He was, he pointed out, a decent human being: someday she would recognize that.[17] He was more preoccupied by another event: Alfred Le Poittevin had died on April 3. "I watched over him for two nights (the last night, all the night through)," Gustave wrote Du Camp. "I wrapped him in his sheet, I gave him a farewell kiss, and I watched them seal his coffin." While seated alongside his dying friend, he read a book for background material to be used in the writing of *The Temptation of Saint Anthony*.[18]

The revolution reached the provinces. In April Flaubert joined the local guard, and was part of a formation at a ceremony to plant a Tree of Liberty.[19] According to Du Camp, Gustave then traveled to Paris, found a hunting rifle, and enlisted in Du Camp's national guard company. They were being good citizens, protecting the new republican institutions from the mob. Popular reaction did not manifest itself until after Gustave left. In June the workers of Paris, disappointed that the new regime was not guaranteeing jobs, challenged the government. Du Camp served in the guard again, and this time he was shot in the leg while attacking a barricade in the Faubourg Poissonnière neighborhood. He was a hero now.[20]

Gustave and his mother had gone to Forges-les-Eaux, a peaceful village some twenty-five miles east of Rouen, to get away not from revolution but from little Caroline's father, Emile Hamard. Virtually no one knew where they were, not even Gustave's brother, Achille; Bouilhet forwarded their mail. Finally they won a court order that gave Madame Flaubert temporary custody of Caroline; they hoped Hamard would show himself to be totally insane, or be banned from the district, before the order expired.[21]

As soon as he could, Gustave went down to Paris to visit Du Camp, then convalescing. Du Camp remembered that Flaubert was fascinated by a neighborhood street fair, and one day entered the sickroom accompanied by a five-footed sheep, which he and the farmer who owned it had managed to cajole up the stairs. "No bourgeois would have thought of that!" Gustave exclaimed triumphantly. When Du Camp was on his feet–on crutches–he took the train to Rouen to visit Croisset, "where Flaubert was still working mysteriously on *The Temptation of Saint Anthony*."[22]

–Herbert Lottman, *Flaubert: A Biography* (Boston,Toronto & London: Little, Brown, 1989), pp. 78–83

---

1. GP 1 [Flaubert, *Correspondance,* published by Gallimard-Pléiade, Paris, volume 1]: 439f.
2. [Maxime] Du Camp, *Souvenirs littéraires* 1 [vol. 1 (Paris: Hachette, 1906)]: 241f.
3. Bibliothèque Municipale de Rouen, 92N7 Flaubert.
4. Du Camp, *Souvenirs littéraires* 1: 256f.
5. Bib. I [Bibliothèque de l'Institut de France], MS 1287.
6. *OC* (S) [Flaubert, *Œuvres complètes,* published by Éditions du Seuil, Paris] 2: 474ff.
7. Du Camp, *Souvenirs littéraires* 1: 257ff.; *OC* (S) 2: 515f.; GP 1: 457.
8. *OC* (S) 2: 535f.; GP 1: 459ff.
9. GP 1: 462f.
10. *Ibid.,* 463ff.
11. *Ibid.,* 470ff., 478.
12. *Ibid.,* 482ff., 488f.
13. *Ibid.,* 491f.
14. Maxime Du Camp, *Souvenirs de l'année 1848* (Paris: Hachette, 1876), 51ff., 75ff., 104ff.
15. GP 1: 492f.
16. Du Camp, *Souvenirs de l'année 1848,* 10; [Du Camp,] *Souvenirs littéraires* 1: 269f.
17. GP 1: 493, 1043.
18. *Ibid.,* 493ff.
19. *Ibid.,* 496.
20. Du Camp, *Souvenirs littéraires* 1: 277; [Du Camp,] *Lettres inédites [à Gustave Flaubert* (Messina: EDAS, 1978)], 135f.; BSL [Bibliothèque de l'Institut, Spoelberch de Lovenjoul collection], Correspondence Flaubert, B I: letter from Louis de Cormenin, June 1848.
21. GP 1: 499ff.
22. Du Camp, *Souvenirs littéraires* 1: 281f.

Writing *La Tentation de saint Antoine*

Flaubert began writing La Tentation de saint Antoine *soon after Le Poittevin's death in April 1848. He had been thinking of the work since seeing Brueghel's painting in 1845. As was typical for Flaubert, he required a long period of research and planning–in this case to immerse himself in the life of Saint Antoine and his world–before beginning the actual writing.*

This is the thirteenth chapter from Enid Starkie's Flaubert: The Making of the Master *(1967).*

La Tentation de Saint Antoine (1848–9)

There may have been some coldness between Flaubert and Le Poittevin in the period after the marriage of the latter, but, as soon as he died, all this changed, and he felt that here was the friend of all others whom he had most dearly loved. Suddenly he underwent a great change, and Alfred's influence became more marked on him after his death than it had ever been during his lifetime, and he tried then to become all the things that Alfred had wanted him to be. Flaubert was to utilize such a phenomenon later, the posthumous influence of those whom one had loved and, in *Madame Bovary,* he showed how Charles was influenced from beyond the grave by his dead wife, and how he then did his utmost to become all the things which she had wanted, in vain, for him to be when she was alive.

Flaubert now turned temporarily away from the more austere standards of the Art for Art's Sake movement, which he had tried to follow in his part of the book on Brittany, and became once more the most extreme Romanticist. He felt the urge to compose a Romantic work full of eastern exotic colour and overflowing with personal feeling.

He then remembered the emotion he had experienced when he had been composing *Smarh* at the height of his friendship with Alfred Le Poittevin; he recalled also how excited and moved he had been when he had seen the Breughel picture of the *Temptation of Saint Anthony* in the Balbi Palace in Genoa, and all he had written about it to Alfred in his letters from abroad, and all he had said after his return.

He had intended, when he got back, to start work immediately and his first idea had been to make a play on the subject.[1]

But then occurred all the tragic events of 1846 and he still did not start writing. In August, two years later, in 1847, he said that he was postponing composition as he did not feel that he had yet done sufficient reading for it.[2] In October the same year he said that he might begin his *Saint Antoine* some time the following year.[3] And he wrote to Laure de Maupassant that he had discussed his *Saint Antoine* with her brother Alfred Le Poittevin six months before he had died, which would have meant that it was in November 1847.[4]

What can, however, be accepted as certain is that *La Tentation de Saint Antoine* was not begun–the writing of it–until after Le Poittevin had died, and that it was his death which forced Flaubert to write it when he did, making it seem urgent. He began the work fifty days after the death of his friend. He wrote, on the manuscript, that it was begun on 24 May 1848, at a quarter past three, and that it was finished on Wednesday 12 September 1849, at twenty minutes past three o'clock in the afternoon, on a sunny and windy day.

Maxime Du Camp had long wanted to travel in the East with Flaubert, and he had managed to extract from Madame Flaubert permission for him to accompany him. Du Camp had wanted to start as early as possible, but Flaubert said that he could not leave until his *Tentation de Saint Antoine* was finished. It was then decided that, as soon as the book was completed, Flaubert should read it to his friends, Louis Bouilhet and Maxime Du Camp, and that they would after that be able to set out on their journey.

This time Flaubert wrote with excitement and a flow of inspiration, and he felt that he had regained the fluency of his youth. Writing later, he said:[5] "Never again shall I be able to recapture the abandonment of style which I indulged in for eighteen long months."

But, although he wrote with ease and pleasure, the months of writing cannot all have been joy and happiness. On a blank page in one of his unpublished *Carnets de Lecture,* he had written:[6] "Rouen, 23 November 1848, 9 o'clock in the evening; my dog died yesterday–I am more and more bored."

The book was finished on 12 September 1849, and the reading began soon afterwards.

Du Camp has given a vivid account of it in his *Souvenirs Littéraires.*[7]

For four days Flaubert read without stopping, from midday until four in the afternoon, and again from eight o'clock until midnight. It had been agreed between them that Du Camp and Bouilhet should keep their opinions to themselves as long as the reading continued, that they would not interrupt, and that, only when he had finished, would they make any comment. Before he began, Flaubert cried excitedly, waving his sheaf of papers:[8] "If you don't shriek with excitement, it will only mean that nothing is capable of moving you!"

Du Camp, when writing, over thirty years later, said that the memory of the long hours of reading had never faded from his mind, and they remained very painful in retrospect. He said that he and Bouilhet went on expecting the action to begin, but they were always disappointed, for the only unity that they could find was the unity of monotony, which was constant from the beginning. There were nothing but lyric phrases, fine in themselves, but meaning nothing; there was nothing but overwhelming lyricism. They could not grasp what he was aiming at, and they had the impression that three years' work was crumbling away into nothingness. After each reading Madame Flaubert

Louis Bouilhet, painting by R. Lelarge (Collections de la Bibliothèque municipale de Rouen. Cliché Thierry Ascencio-Parvy)

used to ask them what they thought of the work, but they did not dare answer.

Before the reading of the last part started Bouilhet and Du Camp decided between themselves that, at the end, they would tell him the unvarnished truth. They considered the matter urgent and that the whole of his literary future was at stake; they thought it necessary to restrain him before his talent had become completely liquefied. Utter frankness, they agreed, was the only possible policy.

At midnight, after the last reading, when he had ended, Flaubert said to them: "And now tell me frankly what you think of it."

Bouilhet, who was by nature gentle and shy, is said to have answered desperately:[9] "We think you should throw it in the fire and never mention it again!"

We have only Du Camp's testimony for this answer, written thirty years later, and it is hard to imagine that Bouilhet could ever have been so harsh.

Flaubert bounded up, uttering a cry of horror. Then, Du Camp tells us, there began a serious conversation, of the kind only possible between friends who trust and love one another. Every sentence was gone through, word by word, while Flaubert tried to defend his writing. They ended by advising him to choose a commonplace subject like, for instance, *La Cousine Bette* or *Le Cousin Pons* by Balzac. The struggle continued from midnight until eight o'clock the following morning, and the night had gone by in their discussions.

It was a shattering blow to Flaubert, all his hopes destroyed at one fell swoop, and the repercussion of it can be found in his correspondence, in the letters which he wrote during his eastern trip, when he described how depressed and low he was, though he was by then beginning to recover from the shock.[10] Later he was to admit to Du Camp, recognizing the value of the lesson he had received:[11]

> I was riddled with the cancer of lyricism; you operated on me, but it was only in the nick of time, and I howled with pain.

Nevertheless, although he accepted, on the whole, the verdict of his friends, he was not convinced that they had been entirely right. Three years later, while composing *Madame Bovary,* he said to Louise Colet that the book had been hastily judged:[12]

> And so you're definitely enthusiastic about *Saint Antoine!* Well, I'll have had one person for it, and that's something! Although I don't accept everything that you say about it, I believe that my friends weren't prepared to see what was in it. It was too lightly judged; I don't say unjustly, but too lightly.

Du Camp tells us that, at one moment during the day which followed the sad verdict on the work, as they sat in the garden, Bouilhet suddenly said to Flaubert:[13] "Why shouldn't you write the story of Delaunay?" And Flaubert raised his head, suddenly overjoyed, and answered: "What a good idea!"

Du Camp was writing thirty years after the events concerned, and it is not astonishing that there should be errors in his statement. The man he wanted Flaubert to write about was not called Delaunay but Delamare, and he had been an "officier de santé", one of Dr Flaubert's former students. Also it is certainly not true that, at this time, Flaubert was considering writing about Delamare and his wife, or that anyone had suggested the subject to him. It was only after his return from the eastern trip, when other circumstances brought it to his notice, that it seemed to him a possible topic for him. We now know, from his letters that, all through his eastern trip, and, even on his return, he was very undecided about what subject he should embark upon, and the Delamare story was not mentioned.

Many critics have blamed this verdict, and some have even accused the two friends of jealousy. This could certainly not have been true of Bouilhet, who was incapable of envy, and it is very unlikely to have been true either of Du Camp. He was still very much attached to Flaubert and wanted to help him in his career as a man of letters–his own was very much more advanced than that of his friend. But both men, as minor writers, saw more clearly than a genius could the way literature was going. Both of them realized that the days of Romanticism were over; and they understood that for a man who had literary pretensions to produce a work in the romantic vein of Quinet's *Ahasvérus* or Byron's *Cain,* at that time, was artistic suicide. The day for that kind of lush exuberance was long past in 1849.

Nowadays readers are less scandalized by Du Camp's and Bouilhet's verdict than were those who read it in the *Souvenirs Littéraires* when it appeared in 1883, and who had not yet had the opportunity to wade through the five hundred and thirty-one pages of the first *Tentation de Saint Antoine.* Many nowadays consider that the verdict was, on the whole, justified and that the work, except in isolated fragments, is unreadable. It is one of the most extreme manifestations of Romantic subjectivity, and Flaubert, according to his own testimony, became Saint Anthony as he wrote. He analysed himself, and the book became a personal confession.[14] "In the place of Saint Anthony, for instance, it is I who am there; the *Tentation* was for me and not for the reader." And again:[15] "Oh! happy time of *Saint Antoine,* where are you now? Then I wrote with my whole being." And also:[16] "It was a 'déversoir'; I had only pleasure in composing it, and the eighteen months that I spent in writing its five hundred pages, were the most deeply voluptuous of my whole life."

Bouilhet and Du Camp should, however, have realized the lyric beauty of certain portions–perhaps they did but they did not draw attention to them: as for instance the passage describing Simon the Magician's companion Helen.[17] Or the one where Death exclaims:[18]

> Où sont-elles maintenant toutes les femmes qui furent aimées, celles qui mettaient des anneaux d'or pour plaire à leurs maris, les vierges aux joues roses qui brodaient des tissus, et les reines qui se faisaient, au clair de lune, porter près des fontaines? Elles avaient des tapis, des éventails, des esclaves, des musiques amoureuses jouant tout à coup derrière les murs; elles avaient des dents brillantes qui mordaient à même dans les grenades, et des vêtements lâches qui embaumaient l'air autour d'elles. Où sont-ils donc les forts jeunes hommes qui couraient si bien, qui riaient si haut, qui avaient la barbe noire et l'œil ardent? Où sont leurs boucliers polis, leurs chevaux qui piaffaient, leurs chiens de chasse rapides qui bondissaient dans les bruyères? Qu'est devenue la cire des torches qui éclairaient leurs festins?
>
> Oh! comme il en a passé de ces hommes, de ces femmes, de ces enfants et de ces vieillards aussi. . . .
>
> Plus d'un couple d'amis a causé de moi bien souvent, seuls près du foyer, dont ils remuaient les cendres, tout en se demandant ce qu'ils deviendraient plus tard; mais celui qui s'en est allé ne revient point pour dire à l'autre s'ils s'étaient trompés jadis, et, quand ils se retrouveront dans le néant, rien d'eux ne se reconnaîtra, pas plus que ne se rejoindront les parties du morceau de bois qu'ils regardaient brûler.
>
> [Where are, now, all the women who were loved, those who put on gold rings to please their husbands, the virgins with pink cheeks who made embroidery and the queens who, by the light of the moon, were carried towards the fountains? They had carpets, fans, slaves, amorous music suddenly playing behind the walls; they had shiny teeth which bit into pomegranates, and loose clothes which perfumed the air around them. Where are, now, the strong young men who ran so well, who laughed so loud, who had black beards and burning eyes? Where are their polished shields, their horses who stamped the ground, their swift hunting hounds who jumped in the heathers? What became of the wax of the torches which gave light to their feasts?
>
> Oh! How many of these men, women, children and old men too went past . . .
>
> Quite often, more than a couple of friends talked about me, alone beside the hearth, of which they poked the ashes while wondering what they would become later; but the one who went away never comes back to tell the other that long ago they were mistaken, and, when they will meet again in the void, nothing of them will be recognizable, not any more than the pieces of burning wood they were watching will ever come together again.]

This passage might be the prose version of a poem by Victor Hugo in a collection from his first lyric period, between 1830 and 1840.

In *La Tentation de Saint Antoine,* Flaubert returned to the inspiration of *Smarh* of ten years before, to the epic tradition of the nineteenth century, with its symbolical picture of mankind–its miserable state of degradation, its restlessness as it longs forever for something beyond its grasp. The visions of Saint Anthony fascinated Flaubert, as they gave him the opportunity for philosophic reflections on the world, religion, the infinite, and so forth. Anthony discusses these matters with the vices and virtues; with the heresies; with logic and science; with various historical and legendary characters–Apollonius of Thyana, Helen of Sparta, Juno, Minerva, Zoroaster; with abstractions such as Death and the Earth; and the Devil.

There are here the same influences at play as in the earlier work–Byron's *Cain,* Goethe's *Faust* and especially Quinet's *Ahasvérus,* which . . . was the basis of the first work.

There is here, as there had been in *Smarh,* the summing-up of the universal tragedy of mankind, in all its stages, through all the ages, and Flaubert had intended to give a picture of the evolution of humanity as it passes through all the phases of doubt, and eventually reaches the same state as his Saint Anthony, a return to prayer. This gives a quality of mysticism to the first *Tentation de Saint Antoine* which is absent from the final version, which is more sceptical, more critical and historical. The first possesses some of the religious feeling which is found in Baudelaire, who was writing at the same time what the poet calls "spleen" and "idéal", the contrast between the baseness of the instinct in man, his leaning towards the ignoble, and his longing for the ideal.

In form, the work keeps the dramatic structure of *Smarh,* and there is the memory of the mediaeval mystery puppet play which he had seen as a child at the Foire Saint-Romain.

There is manifest here, in very marked form, the characteristic Flaubertian mixture of the serious and the grotesque, which is seen in his mature works, which we find in the meetings between the pig and the saint.

Although, taken as a whole, *La Tentation de Saint Antoine* is formless and diffuse, and largely unreadable today except for those with specialized knowledge, we have seen that there are fine lyrical passages which redeem it. The prose poem on death has been quoted and there is also the description of the earth as it was before the coming of man:[19]

> Moi, j'avais des forêts mystérieuses, j'avais des océans démesurés, j'avais des montagnes inaccessibles. Dans des eaux noires vivaient des bêtes dangereuses, et l'haleine des marécages comme un voile sombre se balançait sur ma figure. J'étais couverte de plantes, je tremblais comme un épileptique aux secousses de mes volcans. Durant les nuits le champignon large poussait au tronc des chênes; sur des mousses d'or, des grands serpents au soleil dormaient le corps plié, des odeurs suaves passaient dans les hautes herbes. Terrible d'énergies, enivrante de parfums, éblouissante de couleurs, immense; ah! j'étais belle, quand je sortis toute échevelée de la couche du Chaos! et que je portais encore sur moi la marque de ses étreintes.
>
> Débile et nu, l'homme alors pâlissait au bruit de mes abîmes, à la voix des animaux, aux éclipses de la lune; il se roulait sur mes fleurs, il grimpait dans mes feuillages pour se gorger de fruits vermeils, il ramassait sur les grèves les perles blondes et les coquilles contournées, il regardait au flanc des collines scintiller les minerais de fer et les diamants qui roulaient dans les ruisseaux; je l'entourais d'étonnements, je l'épuisais de travail, je l'accablais de volupté. A la fois Nature et Dieu, principe et but, j'étais infinie pour lui, et son Olympe ne dépassait point la mesure de mes montagnes.
>
> [Me! I had mysterious forests, I had immeasurable oceans, I had inaccessible mountains. In black waters lived dangerous beasts, and the breath of the swamps, like a dark veil, swung at my face. I was covered with plants, I was trembling like an epileptic from the shaking of my volcanoes. During the nights the large mushroom grew against the trunk of the oaks; on the golden moss, large snakes slept in the sun with their bodies folded, sweet scents passed among high grasses. Terrible with forces, heady with perfumes, dazzling with colors; ah! I was beautiful, when, quite tousled, I came out of the bed of Chaos! And I still had, on me, the marks of his embraces.
>
> At that time, frail and naked, Man grew pale from the noise of my abysses, from the voices of the animals, from the eclipses of the moon; he rolled on my flowers, he climbed in my foliages to gorge himself on red fruits, he collected on the shores blond pearls and twisted shells, he looked, on hillsides, at twinkling iron ores and diamonds rolling in the streams; I surrounded him with surprises, I exhausted him with work, I overwhelmed him with pleasure. Both Nature and God, principle and goal, for him I was infinite, and his Olympia could never attain the size of my mountains.]

Flaubert continued in low spirits and was unsure of himself, weighed down by the verdict of his friends. It was hoped that the complete change of the eastern trip might give him back a taste for life and raise him from his deep state of depression.

Maxime Du Camp and Flaubert set out on their journey on 29 October 1849; they were to be away for twenty-one months.

—Enid Starkie, *Flaubert: The Making of the Master* (New York: Atheneum, 1967), pp. 159–166

Starkie references the twenty-eight-volume Œuvres complètes de Gustave Flaubert *(Paris: L. Conard, 1954).*

1. *Correspondance,* Vol. I, p. 173, letter to Le Poittevin, 13 May 1845.
2. *Ibid.,* Vol. II, p. 33, letter to Louise Colet, August 1847.
3. *Ibid.,* Vol. II, p. 54, letter to Louise Colet, October 1847.
4. *Ibid.,* Vol. VI, p. 443, letter 30 October 1872.
5. *Ibid.,* Vol. II, pp. 344–5, letter to Louise Colet, 16 June 1852.
6. *Carnets de Lecture No. 3,* in Bibliothèque [Historique] de la Ville de Paris.
7. Vol. I, p. 427 *et seq.*
8. *Ibid.,* p. 428.
9. *Ibid.,* p. 450.
10. *Correspondance,* Vol. II, p. 146, letter to his mother, 5 January 1850.
11. *Souvenirs Littéraires,* Vol. I, p. 433.
12. *Correspondance,* Vol. II, p. 364, letter 8 February 1852.
13. *Souvenirs Littéraires,* Vol. I, p. 435.
14. *Correspondance,* Vol. II, p. 462, letter to Louise Colet, 6 July 1852.
15. *Ibid.,* Vol. III, p. 92, letter to Louise Colet, 29–30 January 1853.
16. *Ibid.,* Vol. III, p. 156, letter to Louise Colet, 6 April 1853.
17. *La Tentation de Saint Antoine,* pp. 264–5.
18. *Ibid.,* pp. 437–8.
19. *Ibid.,* p. 457.

* * *

Although Flaubert decided not to try to publish any of the novels he wrote in the 1840s, critic Georges Poulet argues that the posthumously published works La Première Éducation sentimentale *and* La Première Tentation de saint Antoine *(translated as* The First Temptation of Saint Anthony, *1910) show that he was advancing as an artist, progressing from a "lyrical" to a "methodical design" in his treatment of recalled experience.*

This excerpt is a translation of a portion of Poulet's chapter on Flaubert in his Études sur le temps humain *(1950).*

Flaubert and the Representation of Memory

There is in the *Première Éducation sentimentale* a passage that is particularly important because it seems to give us the profound reason for the difference, so visible in Flaubert, between the works of his youth and those of his maturity. This passage begins with a long, morose meditation that one of the characters pursues on the formlessness and dejection of his existence. Then gradually, the thought is transformed into images, and once again the past is put to unrolling a series of memory-pictures. But this time the dominating factor in this succession of images is neither the kind of spontaneous homogeneity which is given to the most disparate things by the current of emotions that carries them along nor, on the reverse side, the feeling of radical heterogeneity which reveals itself in them and between them when the current fails to link them together. This time, on the contrary, it is possible to

"A Long, Morose Meditation"

At the beginning of chapter 26 of La Première Éducation sentimentale *(Paris: L. Conard, 1910), Flaubert describes the thoughts of Jules—a passage that Georges Poulet argues prefigures the author's mature work.*

Injuste pour son passé, dur pour lui-même, dans ce stoïcisme surhumain il en était venu à oublier ses propres passions et à ne plus bien comprendre celles qu'il avait eues; s'il ne s'était pas senti chaque jour forcé, comme artiste, de les étudier et de les rechercher chez les autres, puis de les reproduire par la forme la plus concrète et la plus saillante, ou de les admirer sous la plastique du style, je crois qu'il les eût presque méprisées et il en serait arrivé à cet excès d'inintelligence.

Voilà d'où venait son étonnement, en retrouvant dans le bruit des feuilles mortes qu'il écartait avec ses pieds les restes des trésors qu'il croyait n'avoir jamais possédés. Il se dit qu'il avait été jeune cependant, que dans ce temps-là son corps et son âme étaient bien faits pour la vie, et que tout son être alors s'épanouissait au bonheur comme une plante au soleil; que si le ciel l'avait voulu il aurait pu vivre heureux, et qu'il y a des gens sur la terre qui s'en vont au bras de leur maîtresse en regardant les étoiles. D'autres que lui avaient-ils ces perpétuels tourments, qui font du cœur d'un homme un enfer qu'il porte avec lui? et peut-être était-il en ce moment la seule créature qui pensât ces choses-là. Puis revinrent successivement tous les amours qu'il avait eus, tous les airs de fêtes dont il avait été en rêves, tous les costumes qu'il avait aimés: écharpes qui pendent des balcons, longues robes à queue qui traînent sur les tapis, ses illusions d'enfant, ses illusions de jeune homme, son grand amour trompé, la sombre époque qui l'avait suivi, ses idées de mort, son appétit du néant, son redressement subit, ses résolutions gigantesques et l'éblouissement de la vue première de son intelligence, ses projets, ses aspirations, ses frissonnements divers à l'inspiration des belles œuvres, les avortements de sa pensée, ses évanouissements d'ennui, et toute l'humiliation de ses chutes, plus profondes chaque fois de la hauteur d'où il était tombé.

(Unfair to his past, harsh on himself, in the middle of this superhuman stoicism he came to forget his own passions and to misunderstand those he had had; if he had not felt forced, as an artist, to study them every day and to look for them in others, and then to reproduce them with most concrete and detailed form or to admire them with stylistic perfection, I believe that he would have almost despised them and would have reached an excess of unintelligence.

Here was where his amazement came from, finding again, in the noise of the fallen dead leaves his feet pushed away, some remains of treasures he believed he had never possessed. He thought that he had been young, however, that at that time his body and soul were made for life, and that his entire being bloomed in happiness like a plant in the sun; that if heaven had meant so, he could have been happy and that there are men on earth who walk away arm in arm with their mistress while looking at the stars. Did others than him feel this perpetual torment which turns the heart of a man into a hell he carries within him? and maybe he was, at that moment, the only creature who thought such things. Then came back, one by one, all the loves he had had, and all the festive tunes he had dreamt, all the costumes he had loved: scarves hanging from balconies, long evening dresses trailing on carpets, his illusions as a child, his illusions as a young man, his great love deceived, the dark period which had followed, his ideas of death, his appetite for the void, his sudden awakening, his gigantic resolutions and his bedazzlement at the first sight of his intelligence, his projects, his aspirations, his diverse shivers at the sight of beautiful and inspiring works, his failing thoughts, his faintings from boredom, and the great humiliation from his falls, deeper each time from the heights from which he had fallen.)

find there a certain coherence. For the first time one can distinguish not only sensory and imaginative events but also events penetrable by the mind:

> Nevertheless from all that there resulted his present state, and this state was the sum of all those antecedents, one which permitted him to review them; each event had of itself produced a second, every feeling had been fused into an idea. . . . Thus there was a sequence and a continuity to this series of diverse perceptions.[1]

It would be hard to imagine a reflection more ordinary or more commonplace. Nevertheless, it is around this reflection that Flaubert tried to reform a life and a work abandoned of themselves to the power of images. The solution he accepts is the middle solution, it is an option in favor of order–an order, moreover, which is perceived and which perhaps exists only when it is discovered as the order of accomplished facts. For it is discovered only in things that are completed and in the postulate that they are completed by reason of other things which have determined their completion: "The thought that comes to you now has been brought to you . . . by successions, gradations, transformations and rebirths."[2] Thus, the order does not depend on the assumption of any transcendence. It is an adequate relationship between what exists in this moment and what existed in all preceding moments. It is an *a posteriori* construction that the mind imposes upon the universe to make it hold together. Thanks to this formula, there are no more *gaps,* no more intervals between things, nor an abyss between the present and the past. We are in the kingdom of immanence, and of so integral an immanence that everything is representable and implied there. Beyond the chain of causes and effects as they are represented in the mind, there is the supposition that the same chain and the same interactivity of causes and effects persist indefinitely; there is nothing else; no mystery; nothing veiled or inexpressible. What the imagination cannot revive the mind can represent to itself.

Representative thought, therefore, chooses a particular moment of life. It perceives this moment and all the sense-data it contains as a relationship between the human being and its immediate environment. Then it proceeds to discern how those sensations are modified by the action of other images coming from the past. From this stage backward, reconstructive thought will begin an ascending movement. It will see how in their turn those images of the past were linked to objects of the past. Behind the environment in which the present self lives, it will discover the milieu in which it has lived and felt; and behind this double past, which is that of being and milieu, it will discover another, and then still another, always making sure of its discoveries and in this way creating a proportionate density of duration in which there is neither hiatus nor rupture; a movement which, by its direction as well as by its very nature, is the exact reverse of the "flight of memories," that is to say, the sudden jump by which the mind discovered itself, in the works of Flaubert's youth, thrown away, so to speak, into any moment of the past.

For it is no longer now a question of a sudden plunge into the depths of a former time, from whence one is allowed to descend haphazardly the course of existence. The design of Flaubert is no longer a lyrical but a methodical design. He sketched it in a passage in the *Première Tentation;* there he makes Science speak in the following terms:

> If I could penetrate matter, grasp idea, follow life through its metamorphoses, understand being in its modes, and thus from one to the other, reascending the ladder of causes like a series of steps, reunite in myself those scattered phenomena and put them back into motion in the synthesis from which my scalpel detached them.[3]

Thus, the first movement of the Flaubertian reconstruction is the ascending movement by which thought climbs, in a series of inferences, the stairway of causes, and so progressively withdraws from the domain of sensation or of actual images, in order to pass into that of the order of things, into the domain of law. It is a method strictly opposed to that of Balzac, who, starting with an *a priori* creature, posits at the outset the existence of a law-force, of which there remains simply to express next, in terms more and more concrete, the descending curve into real life. Balzac, novelist of the *determining;* Flaubert, novelist of the *determined.*

But precisely by reason of the fact that in Flaubert that which is first given is this *determined* actual, indubitable, and resisting object upon which the representative faculty can rest all its weight, the Flaubertian construction, as high as it may rise, never risks becoming abstract. The law is not a non-temporal thing. It does not exist in itself but in the action by which it is exercised. In proportion as one ascends to it, one gathers up, at each step, the perceptible matter with which the human being has remodified itself in each of the antecedent moments of its duration. Thus the human being is somehow found to exist in two ways: by its sensations, whether immediate or remembered, which form its variable, contingent reality, though in intimate contact with the reality of things; and on the other hand, by the synthetic order that the concatenating series of causes imposes upon its existence.

A double synthesis, or rather a recapture, in the framework of an objective synthesis, of what had always–but in a subjective, fragmentary, and fugitive fashion–been synthetically expressed in the works of Flaubert's youth.

This is what he himself seems to indicate in a note written in 1859:

> The artist not only carries humanity within him, but he reproduces its history in the creation of his work: first confusion, a general view, aspirations, bedazzlement, everything is mixed up [the barbarous epoch]; then analysis, doubt, method, the disposition of parts [the scientific era]; finally, he comes back to the first synthesis, made wider in the execution.

Having arrived at this peak of synthesis, thought turns itself about to begin its downward movement. If it raised itself up into the regions of causes and antecedents, that was in order to prepare itself to understand and show how, starting out from this region and from the past, the actual is organized. So then the descending movement of Flaubert's thought takes on the aspect of a prospective representation of life which, through a series of states, is brought out of the past up to the present and ends there by giving it the significance of being an effect that is the consequence of all the vast perceptible genetic travail in space and duration–a perspective similar to that which one has when, on the shore, one lifts his eyes slowly to the open sea in order to follow from out there the course of a wave that draws nearer and nearer, and finally perishes at one's feet–an experience that one also has when in writing, say, a periodic sentence (the periodic sentence of Flaubert) one finds that from the protasis to the apodosis the different elements are composed in a rising and falling synthesis which, in coming to its completion, affords the discovery in the written sentence of an indissoluble unity in which everything becomes present. From that point on, the problem of time is simply a problem of style.

–Georges Poulet, *Studies in Human Time,* translated by Elliot Coleman (Baltimore: Johns Hopkins University Press, 1956), pp. 258–261

---

1. *Première Éducation,* p. 244.
2. *Tentation* of 1849, p. 418.
3. *Ibid.,* p. 349.

Flaubert in the Middle East

Flaubert and Du Camp embarked for the "Orient"–a term then used for what is now called the Middle East–from Marseilles on 4 November 1849 and reached Alexandria eleven days later. Then, they remained in Cairo from 26 November to 6 February 1850, and left for a long trip along the Nile, to Upper Egypt and the Red Sea.

Flaubert's mother and Bouilhet were his main correspondents during his long trip. This excerpt is from a letter Flaubert wrote to his mother from Alexandria.

Flaubert to Anne-Justine-Caroline Flaubert, 17 November 1849

When we were two hours out from the coast of Egypt I went into the bow with the chief quartermaster and saw the seraglio of Abbas Pasha like a black dome on the blue of the Mediterranean. The sun was beating down on it. I had my first sight of the Orient through, or rather in, a glowing light that was like melted silver on the sea. Soon the shore became distinguishable, and the first thing we saw on land was a pair of camels led by their driver; then, on the dock, some Arabs peacefully fishing. Landing took place amid the most deafening uproar imaginable: negroes, negresses, camels, turbans, cudgelings to right and left, and ear-splitting guttural cries. I gulped down a whole bellyful of colors, like a donkey filling himself with hay. Cudgelings play a great role here; everyone who wears clean clothes beats everyone who wears dirty ones, or rather none at all, and when I say clothes I mean a pair of short breeches. You see many gentlemen sauntering along the streets with nothing but a shirt and a long pipe. Except in the very lowest classes, all the women are veiled, and on their noses they wear ornaments that hang down and sway from side to side . . . On the other hand, if you don't see their faces, you see their entire bosoms. As you change countries, you find that modesty changes its place, like a bored traveler who keeps shifting from the outside to the inside of the stage-coach. One curious thing here is the respect, or rather the terror, that everyone displays in the presence of "Franks," as they call Europeans. We have had bands of ten or twelve Arabs, advancing across the whole width of a street, break apart to let us pass. In fact, Alexandria is almost a European city, there are so many Europeans here. At table in our hotel alone there are thirty, and the place is full of Englishmen, Italians, etc. Yesterday we saw a magnificent procession celebrating the circumcision of the son of a rich merchant. This morning we saw Cleopatra's Needles (two great obe-

A January 1850 view of Cairo, where Flaubert and Du Camp spent two months before sailing up the Nile (photograph by Du Camp; cliché Bibliothèque nationale de France, Paris)

lisks on the shorefront), Pompey's column, the catacombs, and Cleopatra's baths. Tomorrow we leave for Rosetta, whence we shall return in three or four days. We go slowly and don't get overtired, living sensibly and clad in flannel from head to foot, even though the temperature indoors is sometimes thirty degrees.[1] The heat is not at all unbearable, thanks to the sea breeze.

Soliman Pasha,[2] the most powerful man in Egypt, the victor at Nezib, the terror of Constantinople, happens just now to be in Alexandria instead of Cairo. We paid him a visit yesterday, and presented Lauvergne's letter. He received us very courteously. He is to give us orders for all the provincial governors of Egypt and offered us his carriage for the journey to Cairo. It was he who arranged about our horses for tomorrow. He is charming, cordial, etc. He apparently likes the way we look. In addition, we have M. Galis, chief of the army engineers, Princeteau Bey, etc. Just to give you an idea of how we are

Du Camp's Photographs

Although Flaubert and Du Camp paid their own way, Du Camp was able to arrange for government sanction for their Middle Eastern journey. Their government passport stipulated that the two men were charged with a mission by the ministries of Education and Trade. Although Flaubert made little pretense to any "official" role, Du Camp performed an important service through his photography. His collection of photographs (actually calotypes) was the first such survey of the region to appear in France. He overcame great difficulties in transporting the heavy equipment needed–by the backs of mules, camels, and men–to take 220 calotypes, from which 125 were chosen and published in Égypte, Nubie, Palestine et Syrie. Dessins photographiques recueillis pendant les années 1849, 1850, et 1851, accompagnés d'un texte explicatif et précédés d'une introduction par Maxime Du Camp, Chargé d'une mission archéologique par le Ministère de l'Instruction Publique *(1852).*

Flaubert in a Nubian costume in front of the Cairo hotel where he and Du Camp stayed, 9 January 1850 (photograph by Du Camp; cliché Bibliothèque nationale de France, Paris)

to travel, we have been given soldiers to hold back the crowd when we want to photograph: I trust you are impressed. As you see, poor old darling, conditions couldn't be better. As for ophthalmia: of the people one sees, only the very lowest orders (as the expression goes) suffer from it. M. Willemin, a young doctor who has been in Egypt five years, told us this morning that he has not seen a single case among the well-to-do or Europeans. That should reassure you. Don't worry, I'll come back in good shape. I have put on so much weight since I left that two pairs of my trousers are with M. Chavannes, a French tailor, being let out to accommodate my paunch.

So–goodbye, old lady. I was interrupted during the writing of this letter by the arrival of M. Pastré, the banker who is to send us our money as we need it and will ship home any packages, in case we buy a mummy or two. Now we are going to our friend Soliman Pasha to pick up a letter from him about tomorrow's expedition: it is addressed to the Governor of Rosetta, seeing to it that he puts us up in his house–i.e., in the fort, apparently the only place to stay. We had intended to push on as far as Damietta. But as we have been told that would be too tiring on horseback because of the sand, we've given up the idea. We'll go to Cairo by boat. As you see, we're not stubborn; it's our principle to follow the advice of experts and behave like a pair of little saints. Goodbye, a thousand kisses, kiss the baby for me, send me long letters . . .

–*The Letters of Gustave Flaubert, 1830–1857,* pp. 101–103

---

1. Réaumur. 86° Fahrenheit.
2. François Sève, a former colonel in the French army, taken into the Egyptian service in 1815 (after Waterloo) by Mohammed Ali. The latter, viceroy of Egypt, revolted against his sovereign, the Turkish sultan; and his forces, under Soliman Pasha, defeated the Turks in the battle of Nezib (or Nisib) in 1839. A number of other officials mentioned by Flaubert were also Frenchmen, given the title "bey" or "pasha" in the Egyptian service.

The Sphinx, as photographed by Du Camp (courtesy of the New York Public Library)

Racing to the Sphinx

Flaubert took contemporary notes on many of his experiences and rewrote them properly after he returned to Croisset. Here, he recounts how on 7 December 1849, as they approached the Pyramids at 3:30 in the afternoon, he found that he could no longer contain himself and spurred his horse to a gallop. Soon he and Du Camp were in a "furious race," as the Sphinx, growing larger and larger, "rose out of the ground like a dog lifting itself up."

View of the Sphinx. Abu-el-Houl (Father of Terror). The sand, the Pyramids, the Sphinx, all gray and bathed in a great rosy light; the sky perfectly blue, eagles slowly wheeling and gliding around the tips of the Pyramids. We stop before the Sphinx; it fixes us with a terrifying stare; Maxime is quite pale; I am afraid of becoming giddy, and try to control my emotion. We ride off madly at full speed among the stones. We walk around the Pyramids, right at their feet. Our baggage is late in arriving; night falls.

–*Flaubert in Egypt: A Sensibility on Tour,* edited by Francis Steegmuller (Boston & Toronto: Little, Brown, 1972), p. 50

Back in Croisset, Flaubert wrote this description of his visit to the Great Pyramid.

Climbing the Great Pyramid

The tent is raised. (That was its inauguration. Today, 27 June 1851, I have just folded it up with Bossière–very badly. This is its finis.) Dinner. Effect of the little white cloth lantern hanging from the tent-pole. Our guns are stacked. The Arabs sit in a circle around their fire or sleep wrapped in their blankets in the holes they have scooped in the sand; they lie there like corpses in their shrouds. I fall asleep in my pelisse, savoring all these things. The Arabs sing a monotonous *canzone;* I hear one telling a story. Desert life.

At two o'clock Joseph wakes us, thinking that day is breaking, but it was only a white cloud on the opposite horizon, and the Arabs had mistaken Sirius for Venus. I smoke a pipe in the starlight, looking up at the sky; a jackal howls.

Ascent. Up at five–the first–and wash in front of the tent in the canvas pail. We hear several jackals barking. Ascent of the Great Pyramid, the one to the right (Kheops). The stones, which at a distance of two hundred paces seem the size of paving-blocks, are in reality–the smallest of them–three feet high; generally they come up to our chests. We go up at the left hand corner (opposite the Pyramid of Khephren); the Arabs push and pull me; I am quickly exhausted, it is desperately tiring. I stop five or six times on the way up. Maxime started before me and goes fast. Finally I reach the top.

We wait a good half hour for the sunrise.

The sun was rising just opposite; the whole valley of the Nile, bathed in mist, seemed to be a still white sea; and the desert behind us, with its hillocks of sand, another ocean, deep purple, its waves all petrified. But as the sun climbed behind the Arabian chain the mist was torn into great shreds of filmy gauze; the meadows, cut by canals, were like green lawns with winding borders. To sum up: three colors–immense green at my feet in the foreground; the sky pale red–worn vermilion; behind and to the right, a rolling expanse looking scorched and iridescent, with the minarets of Cairo, *canges* passing in the distance, clusters of palms.

Finally the sky shows a streak of orange where the sun is about to rise. Everything between the horizon and us is all white and looks like an ocean; this recedes and lifts. The sun, it seems, is moving fast and climbing above oblong clouds that look like swan's down, of an inexpressible softness; the trees in the groves around the villages (Gizeh, Matariyeh, Bedrashein, etc.) seem to be in the sky itself, for the entire perspective is perpendicular, as I once saw it before, from the Port de la Picade in the Pyrenees; behind us, when we turn around, is the desert–purple waves of sand, a purple ocean.

The light increases. There are two things: the dry desert behind us, and before us an immense, delightful expanse of green, furrowed by endless canals, dotted here and there with tufts of palms; then, in the background, a little to the left, the minarets of Cairo and especially the mosque of Mohammed Ali (imitating Santa Sophia), towering above the others. (On the side of the Pyramid lit by the rising sun I see a business card: '*Humbert, Frotteur*' fastened to the stone. Pathetic condition of Maxime, who had raced up ahead of me to put it there; he nearly died of breathlessness.) Easy descent down the opposite face.

Interior of the Great Pyramid. After breakfast we visit the interior of the Pyramid. The opening is on the north. Smooth, even corridor (like a sewer), which you descend; then another corridor ascends; we slip on bat's dung. It seems that these corridors were made to allow the huge coffins to be drawn slowly into place. Before the king's chamber, wider corridors with great longitudinal grooves in the stone, as though a portcullis or something of the kind had been lowered there. King's chamber, all of granite in enormous blocks, empty sarcophagus at the far end. Queen's chamber, smaller, same square shape, probably communicating with the king's chamber.

As we emerge on hands and knees from one of the corridors, we meet a party of Englishmen who are coming in; they are in the same position as we; exchange of civilities; each party proceeds on its way.

Pyramid of Khephren. Nobody climbs it except Abdullah. 'Abdullah five minutes climb.' At the tip its [limestone] encrustation still exists, whitened by bird-droppings.

Interior. Belzoni's chamber. At the far end, an empty sarcophagus. In it Belzoni found only a few ox-bones–perhaps the bones of Apis. Under Belzoni's name, and no less large, is that of a M. Just de Chasseloup-Laubat. One is irritated by the number of imbeciles' names written everywhere: on the top of the Great Pyramid there is a certain Buffard, 79 Rue Saint-Martin, wallpaper-manufacturer, in black letters; an English fan of Jenny Lind's has written her name; there is also a pear, representing Louis-Philippe. (Almost all the names are modern.) Also scratched in the stone are little holes forming an Arab abacus; it's a game–pebbles are put in the holes for calculation.

–*Flaubert in Egypt: A Sensibility on Tour,* pp. 51–54

* * *

This excerpt is from a letter Flaubert wrote to his mother from Cairo.

Flaubert to Anne-Justine-Caroline Flaubert, 5 January 1850

Your fine long letter of the 16th reached me as a New Year's present last Wednesday, dear old darling. I was paying an official call on our consul, when he was handed a large packet. He opened it immediately, and I seized the envelope that I recognized among a hundred others. (I was itching to open it, but manners, alas! forbade.) Fortunately, he showed us into his wife's salon, and as there was a letter for her too, from her mother, we gave each other mutual permission to read almost before saying how do you do . . .

. . . .

I'm bursting to tell you my name. Do you know what the Arabs call me? Since they have great difficulty in pronouncing French names, they invent their own for us Franks. Can you guess? Abu-Chanab, which means "Father of the Moustache." That word, *abu,* father, is applied to anyone connected with the chief detail under discussion–thus for merchants selling various commodities they say Father of the Shoes, Father of the Glue, Father of the Mustard, etc. Max's name is a very long one which I don't remember, and which means "the man who is excessively thin." Imagine my joy when I learned the honor being paid to that particular part of myself.

. . . Often when we have been out since early morning and feel hungry and don't want to take time to return to the hotel for lunch, we sit down in a Turkish restaurant. Here all the carving is done with one's hands, and everyone belches to his heart's content. Dining room and kitchen are all one, and behind you at the great fireplace little pots bubble and steam under the eye of the chef in his white turban and rolled-up sleeves. I am careful to write down the names of all the dishes and their ingredients. Also, I have made a list of all the perfumes made in Cairo–it may be very useful to me somewhere. We have hired two dragomans. In the evening an Arab storyteller comes and reads us stories, and there is an effendi whom we pay to make translations for us.

. . . .

A few days ago I spent a fine afternoon. Max stayed at home to do I forget what, and I took Hasan (the second dragoman we have temporarily hired) and paid a visit to the bishop of the Copts for the sake of a conversation with him. I entered a square courtyard surrounded by columns, with a little garden in the middle–that is, a few big trees and a bed of dark greenery, around which ran a trellised wooden divan. My dragoman, with his capacious trousers and wide-sleeved jacket, walked ahead; I behind. On one of the corners of the divan was sitting a scowling old personage with a long white beard, wearing an ample pelisse; books in a baroque kind of handwriting were strewn all about him. At a certain distance were standing three black-robed theologians, younger and also with long beards. The dragoman said: "This is a French gentleman *(cawadja fransaoui)* who is traveling all over the world in search of knowledge, and who has come to you to speak of your religion." Such is the kind of language they go in for here. Can you imagine how I talk to them? A while ago, when I was looking at seeds in a shop, a woman to whom I had given something said: "Blessings on you, my sweet lord: God grant that you return safe and sound to your native land." There is much use of such blessings and ritual formulas. When Max asked a groom if he wasn't tired, the answer was: "It's enough for me to see the pleasure in your eyes."

Caricature of Du Camp, circa 1866. In a letter sent to his mother from Cairo, Flaubert wrote that the Arabs had given him a nickname meaning "the Father of the Moustache" and Du Camp a name that meant "the man who is excessively thin" (watercolor by Eugène Giraud; cliché Bibliothèque nationale de France, Paris).

But to return to the bishop. He received me with many courtesies. Coffee was brought, and I soon began to ask questions concerning the Trinity, the Virgin, the Gospels, the Eucharist–all my old erudition of *Saint Antoine* came back in a flood. It was superb, the sky blue above us, the trees, the books spread out, the old fellow ruminating in his beard before answering me, myself sitting cross-legged beside him, gesticulating with my pencil and taking notes, while Hasan stood motionless, translating aloud, and the three other theologians, sitting on stools, nodded their heads and interjected an occasional few words. I enjoyed it deeply. That was indeed the old Orient, land of religions and flowing robes. When the bishop gave out, one of the theologians replaced him; and when I finally saw that they were all somewhat flushed, I left. I am going back, for there is much to learn in that place. The Coptic religion is the most ancient of existing Christian sects, and little or nothing is known about it in Europe (so far as I know). I'm going to talk with the Armenians, too, and the Greeks, and the Sunnites, and especially with Moslem scholars.

We're still waiting for the return of the caravan from Mecca. It is too good an event to miss, and we shall not leave for Upper Egypt until the pilgrims have arrived. There are some bizarre things to see, we have been told: priests' horses walking over prostrate bodies of the faithful, all kinds of dervishes, singers, etc.

. . . .

Max's days are entirely absorbed and consumed by photography. He is doing well, but grows desperate whenever he spoils a picture or finds that a plate has been badly washed. Really, if he doesn't take things easier he'll crack up. But he has been getting some superb results, and in consequence his spirits have been better the last few days. The day before yesterday a kicking mule almost smashed the entire equipment.

. . . .

When I think of my future (that happens rarely, for I generally think of nothing at all despite the elevated thoughts one should have in the presence of ruins!), when I ask myself: "What shall I do when I return? What path shall I follow?" and the like, I am full of doubts and indecisions. At every stage in my life I have put off facing my situation in just this same way; and I shall die at eighty before having formed any opinion concerning myself or, perhaps, without writing anything that would have shown me what I could do. Is *Saint Antoine* good or bad? That is what I often ask myself, for example: who was mistaken–I or the others? However, I worry very little about any of this. I live like a plant, suffusing myself with sun and light, with colors and fresh air. I keep eating, so to speak; afterwards the digesting will have to be done, then the shitting; and the shit had better be good! That's the important thing.

. . . You ask me whether the Orient is up to what I imagined. Yes, it is; and more than that, it extends far beyond the narrow idea I had of it. I have found, clearly delineated, everything that was hazy in my mind. Facts have taken the place of suppositions–with such perfection that it is often as though I were suddenly coming upon old forgotten dreams.

–*The Letters of Gustave Flaubert, 1830–1857,* pp. 107–109

* * *

During his sojourn in the Middle East, Flaubert filled his notebooks with observations and impressions that show the sort of details that struck him, in particular the landscapes, the sunsets, and the customs of the people he encountered. These notes were of use to Flaubert ten years later when he wrote Salammbô.

In this excerpt, written about a ten-day period in May 1850, Flaubert describes a camel journey with Du Camp and Joseph Brichetti, their dragoman, through the desert. He had imagined this experience as a twenty-one-year-old in his short romantic novel Novembre.

From Kena to Koseir and the Red Sea

Saturday, 18 May. We rise at dawn; drawn up on the beach are four slave-traders' boats. The slaves come ashore and walk in groups of fifteen to twenty, each led by two men. When I am on my camel, Hadji-Ismael runs up to give me a handshake. The man on the ground raising his arm to shake the hand of a man mounted on his camel, or to give him something, is one of the most beautiful gestures of the Orient; especially at the moment of departure there is something solemn and sad about it. The inhabitants of Kena are not yet up; the almehs, decked with golden piastres, are sweeping their doorways with palm branches and smoking their morning chibouk. The sun is dim, veiled by the *khamsin.* On the left, the cliff-like Arabian hills; ahead, the grayish desert; on the right, green plains. We follow the desert's edge, gradually leave the cultivated plain behind: it drops away to the right, and we plunge into the desert. After four hours we arrive at a small grove of *gassis* in which stands a long, one-storey building with an arcaded gallery; it is a *khan,* Bir 'Ambar. There we eat lunch, sitting on mats . . . , and take our siesta.

Reach Bir 'Ambar 9:30; leave 11:30.

Facing the arcade of the *khan* [caravansary], two long stone troughs where the camels are watered. Arabs in the shade, eating, praying, sleeping; the animals, like the humans, are under the trees, grouped haphazardly: the authentic "Travelers' Rest."

The terrain is rolling and stony, the trail arid, we are in full desert, our camel-drivers sing, and their song ends with a half-whistling, half-guttural modulation meant to excite the dromedaries. Visible on the sand are several tracks that wind parallel: these are caravan trails–each track was made by a camel. Sometimes there are fifteen to twenty such tracks; the wider the trail, the more numerous they are. Here and there, about every two or three leagues (but irregularly spaced), large plaques of yellow sand that look as if they were varnished with *terre-de-Sienne*–colored laqueur; these are the places where the camels stop to piss. It is hot; on the right a *khamsin* dust-cloud is moving our way from the direction of the Nile (of which all that we can faintly see now is a few of the palms that line the bank). The dust-cloud grows and comes straight at us–it is like an immense vertical cloud that before enveloping us is already high above us for some time, while its base, to the right, is still distant. It is red-

The Temple of Abu Simbel, visited by the travelers in March 1850. Although Flaubert noted the effects of the sun's reflections on the half-buried statues, he admitted to be "profoundly bored by Egyptian temples" (photograph by Du Camp; courtesy of the New York Public Library).

dish brown and pale red; now we are in the midst of it. A caravan passes us coming the other way; the men, swathed in *kufiyehs* [headcloths] (the women are thickly veiled) lean forward on the necks of their dromedaries; they pass very close to us, no one speaks; it is like a meeting of ghosts amid clouds. I feel something like terror and furious admiration creep along my spine; I laugh nervously; I must have been very pale, and my enjoyment of the moment was intense. As the caravan passed, it seemed to me that the camels were not touching the ground, that they were breasting ahead with a ship-like movement, that inside the dust-cloud they were raised high above the ground, as though they were wading belly-deep in clouds.

From time to time we meet other caravans. One first sees them as a long horizontal line on the horizon, barely distinguishable from the horizon itself; then that dark line rises above the other, and on it one begins to make out small dots; the small dots themselves rise up–they are the heads of camels walking abreast, swaying regularly along the entire line. Seen foreshortened, they look like the heads of ostriches.

The hot wind comes from the south; the sun looks like a tarnished silver plate; a second dust-spout comes on us. This one advances like the smoke from a conflagration, suet-colored, with jet-black tones at the base: it comes . . . and comes . . . and the curtain is on us, bulging out in volutes below, with deep black fringes. We are enveloped by it: the force of the wind is such that we have to clutch our saddles to stay on. When the worst of the storm has passed, there comes a hail of small pebbles carried by the wind: the camels turn their tails to it, stop, and lie down. We resume our way.

Towards 7:30 in the evening the dromedaries abruptly change their course and head south. A few moments later we spy in the darkness a few low-lying hovels with dromedaries sleeping around them; it is the village of Lakeita. There is a well here, good for camels. Ten or so shapeless huts built of piled-up dry stones and straw mats, inhabited by ʻAbabdehs. A few goats are hunting for a bit of grass between the stones, pigeons are pecking at the remains of the camels' straw, vultures strut around the huts. No one will sell us milk. A negress's teat–it hangs down well below her umbilicus, and so flat that it is scarcely the thickness of the two layers of skin; were she to go on all fours, it would certainly trail on the ground.

We sleep on our blankets on the ground. At three I awake; we leave at five, going on foot for the first hour.

In the middle of the day we stop for four hours at Gamseh Shems, in a small cave formed by a fallen rock; I lie down there on my back. When I raise my hand (stretching as I wake) the heat of the wind on it is like the breath of an oven; we have to wrap our handkerchiefs around the pommels of our saddles. Toward four o'clock, on the right, in the black rock, hieroglyphs overlaid with Greek inscriptions: sacrifice to Ammon the Begetter and to Horus. The space between the hills gradually narrows; we are walking in a wide corridor. In the evening, beautiful moon: the shadows of our camels' collars sway on the sand. At half-past nine we pass close to a large structure within a square walled enclosure; it is the well of Bir Hammamat, dug by the English. We push ahead and spend the night half an hour further on, after a march of eleven hours.

Monday, 20 [May]. Set out at half-past four. Mountain defile, up and down. In the middle of the trail, at a place where the mountains draw apart, a dead *gassis* stripped of its bark; a few other, small ones, in bloom, further on. One of our two camel-drivers takes an empty waterskin and runs on ahead of us; a good hour later we find him at Bir es-Sidd (Well of the Lock, Closed Well). This is an excavation in the earth, three feet in diameter, reached by sliding under a rock. There is little water, and what there is is very earthy; it is at an extremely narrow stretch of the trail as you come from Kena after it, the trail climbs. Down by the well, ten paces before it, we find an old Turk, calmly sitting there on a rug with his servants and his wives. Beside the well, a camel lying on its side and uttering its death-rattle; it broke its back falling into the well, its owner pulled it out, and it has remained there, dying, for three months. When its owner passes he feeds it, and Arabs give it water to drink; the great number of *hadjis* [pilgrims] passing by explains why it hasn't been devoured by wild beasts.

While we were there, a caravan arrives from the opposite direction: the gorge is very narrow; congestion of camels and people; everyone has to dismount and lead his camel by the halter. We go on foot for a time because of the difficulty of the trail: it is strewn with the carcasses of camels; they have their skins, but are completely gutted. This is the work of rats: the hide, dried and stretched by the sun, is intact, but has been gnawed from within until it is no thicker than an onion-skin; it covers the skeleton, which is itself scarred with scratches made by the rodents' teeth. Innumerable rat-holes in the desert.

The trail broadens again, we pass close beside a demolished *khan,* Okkel Zarga (Purple Khan). Not a sound, devouring heat, one's hands tingle as in the hot-room of a bath . . . At quarter to twelve we take shelter beneath a large pink granite rock, where a flock of desert partridges were enjoying the cool; this place is called Aby Ziram (Father of the Jars). We gobble a watermelon that Joseph bought this morning at Bir es-Sidd; we have to abandon our chickens–gone bad. The day before, at the same time, we had to throw away our leg of lamb; scarcely had it fallen to the ground when a vulture fell on it and began to devour it. All day we keep seeing large numbers of partridges.

In the evening, Joseph's camel bolts. I see it pass by on my left. Joseph terrified and shouting; his white jacket disappears into the night. We make haste to follow after him, more especially as our camels show signs of imitating his. It comes back to us at a walk. We pass ropes through the nostrils of our dromedaries, who are trembling and in a rage: we prudently stop, and spend the night in a very beautiful open spot–a kind of small plain opening out to our left in the hills of Daoui (Clear or Open Place).

Tuesday, 21 [May]. Set out at 4 a.m., descending steadily. Many more caravans; the hills are now white, with long dark streaks. At eight we reach Bir el-Beida (White Well, because of the nearby mountains), or Bir el-Inglis (Well of the English, who dug it). 'Ababdehs are encamped around the well. Hovels of straw mats and earth. This is an open place, a plain in the midst of mountains. A young man, naked except for cotton drawers, his skin gray with dirt or dust, takes my camel (gesture of his raised arm as he leaps up!) to give it a drink; he draws water into a skin at the end of a rope and pulls it up, full, or almost full, and pissing from all its holes. The well is enclosed within a curb of dry stones, wide at the base and slanting: he braces his foot against it as he draws. The camels drink slowly and in huge amounts: it is three days since they drank last. We are thirsty too, and the water is execrable. The 'Ababdehs refuse to sell us milk, their only food.

The trail bends to the left; we descend. The chalky mountains surrounding this plain recall the Mokattam. The sky is full of clouds, the air humid, one feels the sea, our clothes are moist. I long to be there; it is always the same whenever I am nearing a goal: I have patience in all things–as far as the antechamber. A few drops of rain. An hour after leaving the well we come to a place full of reeds and high grass; dromedaries and donkeys are in the midst of it, eating and enjoying themselves. Water flows at the roots of the

Philae Island in the Nile, where Flaubert and Du Camp stayed three days in April 1850 (photograph by Du Camp; courtesy of the Bibliothèque de la Société de Géographie, Paris)

grass in numerous small streams, which deposit considerable quantities of salt on the ground; this is Wadi Ambagi (Place Where There is Water). The hills subside, we turn to the right. A flat face of reddish rock, to the left, at the entrance to the broader valley which leads, first over stones, then over sand, to Koseir. In my impatience I go on foot, running over the gravel and climbing hillocks, hoping to see the sea a minute sooner. How often in the past I have eaten my heart out with impatience, as pointlessly as now! Finally I see the dark line of the Red Sea against the gray horizon. The Red Sea!

I remount my camel, and we proceed over the sand to Koseir. It is as though wind had blown the sea-sand back into this broad valley: it is like the abandoned bed of a gulf. From a distance we see the forward masts of ships . . . Birds of prey are flying about and perched on low sand-dunes. Sea and ships to the right; Koseir ahead, with its white houses. To the right, before turning, a few palms enclosed within white walls: a garden! What a blessing for the eyes!

We cross the town: our drivers take the halters and lead us; Arabs draw back on each side of the street to let us pass. We put up in the house of Père Elias, brother of Issa, of Kena. He is a Christian from Bethlehem, an old man with a white beard, open and cordial expression, the French agent in this town. On his doorstep we find M. Barthélemy, . . . attaché in the consulate at Jidda; he is untidily dressed and wears a straw hat covered with a white cotton cloth. We are installed in a small square pavilion, one window on the sea, another on the street, a third on Père Elias's courtyard, full of sacks of grain. The sea, seen from my window, is more green than blue. The Arab boats, with their outsize sterns, their frail bows and their high prow. Arrival of M. Métayssier, French consul at Jidda–his head sunk between his shoulders and giving off a musky smell, which makes me suppose that he wears a drain in his neck: garrulous, insipid, deadly, knows everything and everybody–has given advice to Casimir-Périer, to Thiers, to Louis-Philippe. Poor man! My journey wasn't yet over when I heard of the end of his: he died at Jidda after being there three months!

We make a tour of the town; it is quite clean–no longer like Egypt. Various races of negroes–some of the men look like women, especially one whom I saw on the wooden jetty . . . he had the breasts, thighs and buttocks of a woman, and his skull narrowed so sharply above the temples that it was almost pyramidal. There are, I think, even more varieties in the negro race than in the white. Compare the negro of the Senaar (Indian type, Caucasian, European, pure black) with the negro of Central Africa; the head of the negro from Guinea is a head of Jupiter beside it.

These people, naked and carrying a bowl (a hollowed-out calabash) as their only possession, come from heaven knows where; there are some who have been on the march for several years. Dr Rüppel saw some in the Kordofan who had been traveling for seven years; MM. Barthélemy and Métayssier, coming from Kena to Koseir, found one half dead from thirst on the way: he had been traveling in the desert for a year. Some come with their wives, who give birth en route. Tartars from Bukhara, in fur caps, ask us for alms; they have the faces of frightful scoundrels, especially one with two missing front teeth and a smile. We see them again later in the shade of a boat, sewing their rags. The pilgrims persecute you with their begging and crowd like famished vultures around watermelon rinds, which are devoured here down to the green. Certain negroes excessively tall and no less extraordinarily thin; they seem to be nothing but bones, and extremely weak: still one more kind of negro. The pearl-fishers' *pirogues,* which are dug-out tree-trunks; oars that are mere poles with a circular board nailed on the end. We walk along the shore, past the boats drawn up on the beach; some are made of a kind of Indian wood, yellow, very hard; all are held together with iron nails. Pitilessness of M. le Consul, who insists on prolonging the walk 'just for half an hour'; I am harassed by him and by fatigue. Of all wild beasts, one of the most dangerous is the man who likes to 'take a walk.'

Copious dinner, execrable water–and I had looked forward to slaking my thirst at Koseir! Everything is permeated by this ghastly odor of soap and rotten eggs, even the latrines, which smell of Koseir water and nothing else! Even adding a little *raki* doesn't help. M. Elias's son does not dine with us: he is a young man of about twenty, with a timid, pious look, pointed nose and pinched mouth. We are served by a young eunuch of about eighteen, Saïd, in a striped colored jacket: bare-headed, wavy hair, a small dagger stuck in his shawl-belt, bare arms, thick silver ring on one finger, pointed red shoes. His soft voice when he held out the coffee tray with his right hand, put his left hand on his hip, and said '*Tafaddal*' ['*S'il vous plaît*']. He has as fellow-servant a long imbecile named Abdallah, dressed in rags, whose intelligence isn't even up to snuffing the candles. How well I slept that night, on Père Elias's divan! What a delicious thing to rest one's body!

Wednesday, 22 [May]. Stroll in the town. The cafés are big *khans,* or rather *okkels;* they are empty during the day, then they gleam with the lighted *sheeshehs* of the pilgrims to Mecca. We visit the boat the pilgrims are to take . . . These Red Sea boats are terrifying: they reek of the plague; to step on board is frightening; thank God I don't have to sail in one. For latrines, there is a kind of wooden balcony, or armchair, fastened outside the gunwale: if the sea were a bit rough one would inevitably be washed away. The divan and cabin are in the poop–they have no flooring and are filled with freight. Men playing cards with little leather disks printed in color–there were suns, swords, etc. In the evening, at sunset, we swim. What a swim! How deliciously I lolled in the water!

Thursday. 23 [May]. We set out very early on donkeys to see Old Koseir, of which absolutely nothing remains. We are accompanied by M. Barthélemy, by Elias's son, who wears an ample brown robe that flaps in the wind and who rides his dromedary expertly, and by M. Métayssier's janissary, Reschid. He is a Kurd, was taken prisoner in the Hejaz and made to work water-wheels for seven years. His only ambition is to see Paris and enlist in the African service. He is madly in love with a woman he is taking with him to Jidda; he had already sent her away once for misconduct, but when he passed through Kena, where she was a prostitute, he took her back. He carries an arsenal on him and is pleased to take charge of our two rifles . . . M. Métayssier's second janissary, Omar Agas, tall, thin-faced, more intelligent than the other, blue robe. At Old Koseir the sea takes on fabulous colors, with no transition between them–from dark brown to limpid azure. The Red Sea looks more like the ocean than like the Mediterranean. So many shells! Maxime, who is suffering from indigestion, falls asleep on the sand. M. Barthélemy and young Elias look for shells. Smell of the sea. Large birds fly past, wings outspread. Sun, sun, and blue sea; in the sand, large pieces of mother-of-pearl.

At 4 o'clock we say goodbye to Père Elias: it was one of the moments of my life when I felt the saddest: my heart was heavy. Père Elias felt it himself: tears were in his eyes, and he kissed me.

Slept at El-Beida. I am the only one who eats–Max has his indigestion and Joseph is feverish. Violent gale all night.

Friday, 24 May. The water from Koseir, gone from bad to worse in the skins, becomes undrinkable: we

Omar's Mosque in Jerusalem, photographed by Du Camp in August 1850. Flaubert wrote to Bouilhet that he was quite surprised and impressed to see the Holy City, but that on the whole he found it dirty and sad (cliché Bibliothèque nationale de France, Paris).

The ruins of Baalbek photographed by Du Camp in September 1850. Flaubert wrote to his mother that he was in love with the columns of the temple (cliché Bibliothèque nationale de France, Paris).

have to make do with watermelons. We meet pilgrims from Alexandria going to Koseir, all by dromedary; the women are shouting, arguing, gesticulating. At 10 o'clock we stop in full sun in a wide plain, El-Mour; we tie our blankets to a *gassis* as best we can and try to sleep under them. In the evening, at a quarter to eight, we stop and sleep at El-Markar (The Cave).

Saturday, 25 [May]. At Bir es-Sidd. The poor camel is dead and partly eaten: vultures keep a greedy watch. I dip my face in a wooden bowl and swallow great gulps of the well-water–earthy, but far preferable to what we have in our waterbags. At half-past ten we sleep on the steps of the big well of Bir el-Hammamat. At eight we stop and pass the night at Kasr el-Banat (Castle of the Maidens), despite the remarks of our drivers, who tell us it is a place haunted by the devil and dangerous to stop at. During the night a jackal makes off with part of our stores that we had left out to cool.

Sunday, 26 [May]. Set out at quarter to four in the morning. Lunch at Lakeita–we eat watermelon. The old woman who sneaks in and gathers up the rinds. We go on without siesta.

At four in the afternoon we reach Bir 'Ambar. Joseph has been delirious for the last three hours. We lie down under some *gassis,* in the shade, and drink our fill–drink till we are drunk. Horses, donkeys, camels and chickens make so much noise that our night is disturbed.

Monday, 27 [May]. At a quarter to four in the morning, we set out for Kena. After two hours we begin to meet large numbers of people and sight the square pigeon-cotes of Kena. At eight we reach the *cange,* where we are given a warm welcome. Hadji Ismael is the first to greet me, as he was the last to say goodbye.

From Kena to Koseir, 45½ hours' walking time; return, 41¼ .

Go into Kena. I am exhausted. Bath. An *almeh* (Mère Maurice)–dark eyes, much lengthened by antimony; her face held up by velvet chinstraps; sunken mouth, jutting chin, smelling of butter, blue robe. She lives at the end of the street, in the last house. I see Hosna et-Taouilah again, who tells me in sign language that I have beautiful eyes and especially beautiful eyebrows. Like all *ces dames* in Egypt, she dislikes my moustache.

–*Flaubert in Egypt: A Sensibility on Tour,* pp. 180–192

The Long Journey Home

On 25 June 1850 they returned to Cairo, from which they departed on 5 July, heading to Beirut. In August, they visited Jerusalem; in September they were in Damascus and Baalbek, and then came back to Beirut. They left to go to Rhodes on 1 October, visited Constantinople in November, and reached Greece on 19 December. In February 1851 they traveled to Brindisi and then Naples. When they reached Rome, Du Camp returned directly to Paris whereas Madame Flaubert came to accompany her son until the end of the trip (together they visited Florence and Venice).

The Years of *Madame Bovary:* 1851–1857

Writing *Madame Bovary*

Shortly after Flaubert's return from his long trip abroad, he and Louise Colet met in a hotel in Rouen on 26 June 1851 and resumed the relationship they had broken off in 1848. Flaubert's letters to Colet provide the best testimony of his progress on Madame Bovary, *which he began in September, for he discusses not only his fears and pains but also his art and his literary goals. The correspondence reveals an increasing irritation developing between the lovers, especially by the end of 1853; they continued to write while seldom seeing one another until April 1854. The final, bitter breakup occurred in 1855; they never met again.*

These excerpts are from a letter Flaubert wrote on a Friday night from Croisset.

Flaubert to Louise Colet, 16 January 1852

There are in me, literarily speaking, two distinct persons: one who is infatuated with bombast, lyricism, eagle flights, sonorities of phrase and lofty ideas; and another who digs and burrows into the truth as deeply as he can, who likes to treat a humble fact as respectfully as a big one, who would like to make you feel almost *physically* the things he reproduces. The former likes to laugh, and enjoys the animal side of man.

. . . .

[In *Saint Antoine,*] having taken a subject which left me completely free as to lyricism, emotions, excesses of all kinds, I felt in my element, and had only to let myself go. Never will I rediscover such recklessness of style as I indulged in during those eighteen long months. How passionately I carved the beads of my necklace! I forgot only one thing–the string . . .

A view of Flaubert's home at Croisset, as drawn by his niece Caroline Commanville (Collections de la Bibliothèque municipale de Rouen. Cliché Thierry Ascencio-Parvy)

What seems beautiful to me, what I should like to write, is a book about nothing, a book dependent on nothing external, which would be held together by the internal strength of its style, just as the earth, suspended in the void, depends on nothing external for its support; a book which would have almost no subject, or at least in which the subject would be almost invisible, if such a thing is possible. The finest works are those that contain the least matter; the closer expression comes to thought, the closer language comes to coinciding and merging with it, the finer the result. I believe the future of Art lies in this direction. I see it, as it has developed from its beginnings, growing progressively more ethereal, from Egyptian pylons to Gothic lancets, from the 20,000-line Hindu poems to the effusions of Byron.

Form, in becoming more skillful, becomes attenuated; it leaves behind all liturgy, rule, measure; the epic is discarded in favor of the novel, verse in favor of prose; there is no longer any orthodoxy, and form is as free as the will of its creator. This progressive shedding of the burden of tradition can be observed everywhere: governments have gone through similar evolution, from oriental despotisms to the socialisms of the future.

It is for this reason that there are no noble subjects or ignoble subjects; from the standpoint of pure Art one might almost establish the axiom that there is no such thing as subject–style in itself being an absolute manner of seeing things.

I should need an entire book to develop what I want to say. I'll write about all that in my old age, when I'll have nothing better to scribble. Meanwhile, I'm working hard on my novel. Will the great days of *Saint Antoine* return? May the result be different, Lord God! I go slowly: in four days I have done five pages, but so far I find it good fun. It brings me some peace of mind. The weather is ghastly, the river like an ocean; not a cat passes under my windows. I keep a big fire going . . .

–*The Letters of Gustave Flaubert, 1830–1857,* edited by Francis Steegmuller (Cambridge, Mass.: Harvard University Press, 1980), p. 154

* * *

These excerpts are from a letter written in Croisset on a Saturday night.

Flaubert to Colet, 24 April 1852

If I haven't written sooner in reply to your sad, discouraged letter, it's because I have been in a great fit of work. The day before yesterday I went to bed at five in the morning and yesterday at three. Since last Monday I have put everything else aside, and have done nothing all week but sweat over my *Bovary,* disgruntled at making such slow progress. I have now reached my ball, which I will begin Monday. I hope that may go better. Since you last saw me I have written 25 pages in all (25 pages in six weeks). They were rough going. Tomorrow I shall read them to Bouilhet. I have gone over them so much myself, copied them, changed them, shuffled them, that for the time being I see them very confusedly. But I think they will stand up. You speak of your discouragements: if you could see mine! Sometimes I don't understand why my arms don't drop from my body with fatigue, why my brain doesn't melt away. I am leading an austere life, stripped of all external pleasure, and am sustained only by a kind of permanent frenzy, which sometimes makes me weep tears of impotence but never abates. I love my work with a love that is frantic and perverted, as an ascetic loves the hair shirt that scratches his belly.

Sometimes, when I am empty, when words don't come, when I find I haven't written a single sentence after scribbling whole pages, I collapse on my couch and lie there dazed, bogged in a swamp of despair, hating myself and blaming myself for this demented pride that makes me pant after a chimera. A quarter of an hour later, everything has changed; my heart is pounding with joy. Last Wednesday I had to get up and fetch my handkerchief; tears were streaming down my face. I had been moved by my own writing: the emotion I had conceived, the phrase that rendered it, and the satisfaction of having found the phrase–all were causing me the most exquisite pleasure. At least I think that all those elements were present in this emotion, which after all was predominantly a matter of nerves. There exist even higher emotions of this same kind: those which are devoid of the sensory element. These are superior, in moral beauty, to virtue–so independent are they of any personal factor, of any human implication. Occasionally (at great moments of illumination) I have had glimpses, in the glow of an enthusiasm that made me thrill from head to foot, of such a state of mind, superior to life itself, a state in which fame counts for nothing and even happiness is superfluous. If everything around us, instead of permanently conspiring to drown us in a slough of mud, contributed rather to keep our spirits healthy, who can tell whether we might not be able to do for aesthetics what stoicism did for morals? Greek art was not an art; it was the very constitution of an entire people, of an entire race, of the country itself. In Greece the profile of the mountains was different from elsewhere, and they were made of marble, for sculptors, etc.

The time for beauty is over. Mankind may return to it, but it has no use for it at present. The more Art develops, the more scientific it will be, just as science will become artistic. Separated in their early stages, the two will become one again when both reach their culmination. It is beyond the power of human thought today to foresee in what a dazzling intellectual light the works of the future will flower. Meanwhile we are in a shadowy corridor, groping in the dark. We are without a lever; the ground is slipping under our feet; we all lack a basis–literati and scribblers that we are. What's the good of it all? Is our chatter the answer to any need? Between the crowd and ourselves, no bond exists. Alas for the crowd; alas for us, especially. But since there is a reason for everything, and since the fancy of one individual seems to me just as valid as the appetite of a million men, and can occupy an equal place in the world, we must (regardless of material things and of mankind, which disavows us) live for our

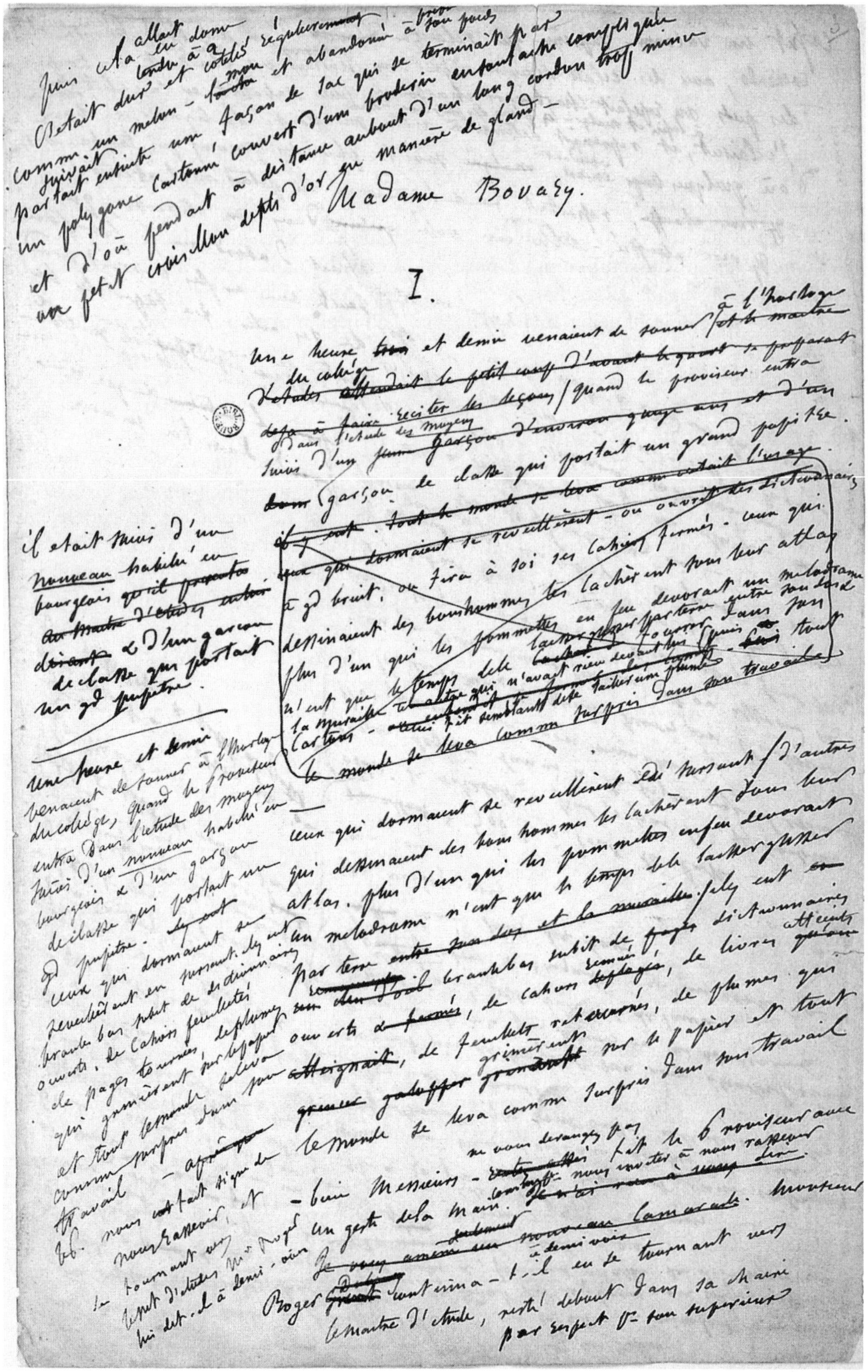
Madame Bovary

I.

One of the multiple drafts of the first page of Madame Bovary *(Collections de la Bibliothèque municipale de Rouen. Cliché Thierry Ascencio-Parvy)*

vocation, climb up our ivory tower, and there, like a bayadere with her perfumes, dwell alone with our dreams. At times I have feelings of great despair and emptiness–doubts that taunt me in the midst of my simplest satisfactions. And yet I would not exchange all this for anything, because my conscience tells me that I am fulfilling my duty, obeying a decree of fate–that I am doing what is Good, that I am in the Right.

. . . .

. . . I envision a style: a style that would be beautiful, that someone will invent some day, ten years or ten centuries from now, one that would be rhythmic as verse, precise as the language of the sciences, undulant, deep-voiced as a cello, tipped with flame: a style that would pierce your idea like a dagger, and on which your thought would sail easily ahead over a smooth surface, like a skiff before a good tail wind. Prose was born yesterday: you have to keep that in mind. Verse is the form par excellence of ancient literatures. All possible prosodic variations have been discovered; but that is far from being the case with prose.
–*The Letters of Gustave Flaubert, 1830–1857,* pp. 158–159

* * *

These excerpts are from a letter written in Croisset on a Saturday night at 1 A.M.

Flaubert to Colet, 25 June 1853

Only now have I finished my first section of Part Two,[1] the very section I had planned to have ready before our last meeting in Mantes. You see how slow I have been. I'll spend a few more days reading it over and recopying it, and a week from tomorrow will spill it all out to the Hon. Bouilhet. If it passes the test, that will be one great worry the less–and a good thing, too, believe me, for the substructure was very flimsy. Apart from that, I think the book will have a big defect, namely faulty proportions in regard to length. I already have two hundred sixty pages which are merely preliminary to the action, containing more or less disguised descriptions of character, . . . of landscapes, of places. My conclusion, which will be my little lady's death, her burial and her husband's subsequent grief, will be at least sixty pages. That leaves, for the body of the action itself, one hundred twenty to one hundred sixty pages at the most. Isn't that a great flaw? What reassures me (though only moderately) is that the book is a biography rather than a story with a complicated plot. The drama plays only a small part in it, and if this dramatic element is skillfully blended with the rest, so that a uniform, overall tonality is achieved, then perhaps the lack of harmonious development of the various phases will pass unnoticed. Besides, I think that this is rather characteristic of life itself. The sexual act may last only a minute, though it has been anticipated for months! Our passions are like volcanoes: they are always rumbling, but eruption is only intermittent.

Unfortunately the French spirit is mad for entertainment. It demands so much that is showy. It takes so little pleasure in what for me is the essence of poetry, namely exposition, whether our treatment of it is descriptive or moral, whether we stress picturesque aspects or psychological analysis . . . I would like to produce books which would entail only the writing of sentences (if I may put it that way), just as in order to live it is enough to breathe. What I dislike are the tricks inherent in the making of an outline, the arranging of effects, all the underlying calculations–which are, however, Art, for they and they alone account for the stylistic effect.

. . . .

If the book I am writing with such difficulty turns out well, I'll have established, by the very fact of having written it, these two truths, which for me are axiomatic, namely: (1) that poetry is purely subjective, that in literature there are no such things as beautiful subjects, and that therefore Yvetot is the equal of Constantinople; and (2) that consequently one can write about any one thing equally well as about any other. The artist must raise everything to a higher level: he is like a pump; he has inside him a great pipe that reaches down into the entrails of things, the deepest layers. He sucks up what was lying there below, dim and unnoticed, and brings it out in great jets to the sunlight.
–*The Letters of Gustave Flaubert, 1830–1857,* pp. 188–189

---

1. *Madame Bovary,* Part II. Chapters 1–7. From the Bovarys' arrival in Yonville to the first appearance of Rodolphe.

* * *

This excerpt is from a letter written in Croisset on a Tuesday at midnight.

Flaubert to Colet, 25 October 1853

You are lucky, you poets: you have an outlet in your verse. When something troubles you, you spit out a sonnet, and that relieves you. But we poor devils, writers of prose, who are forbidden (myself in particular) any expression of personal feelings–think of all the

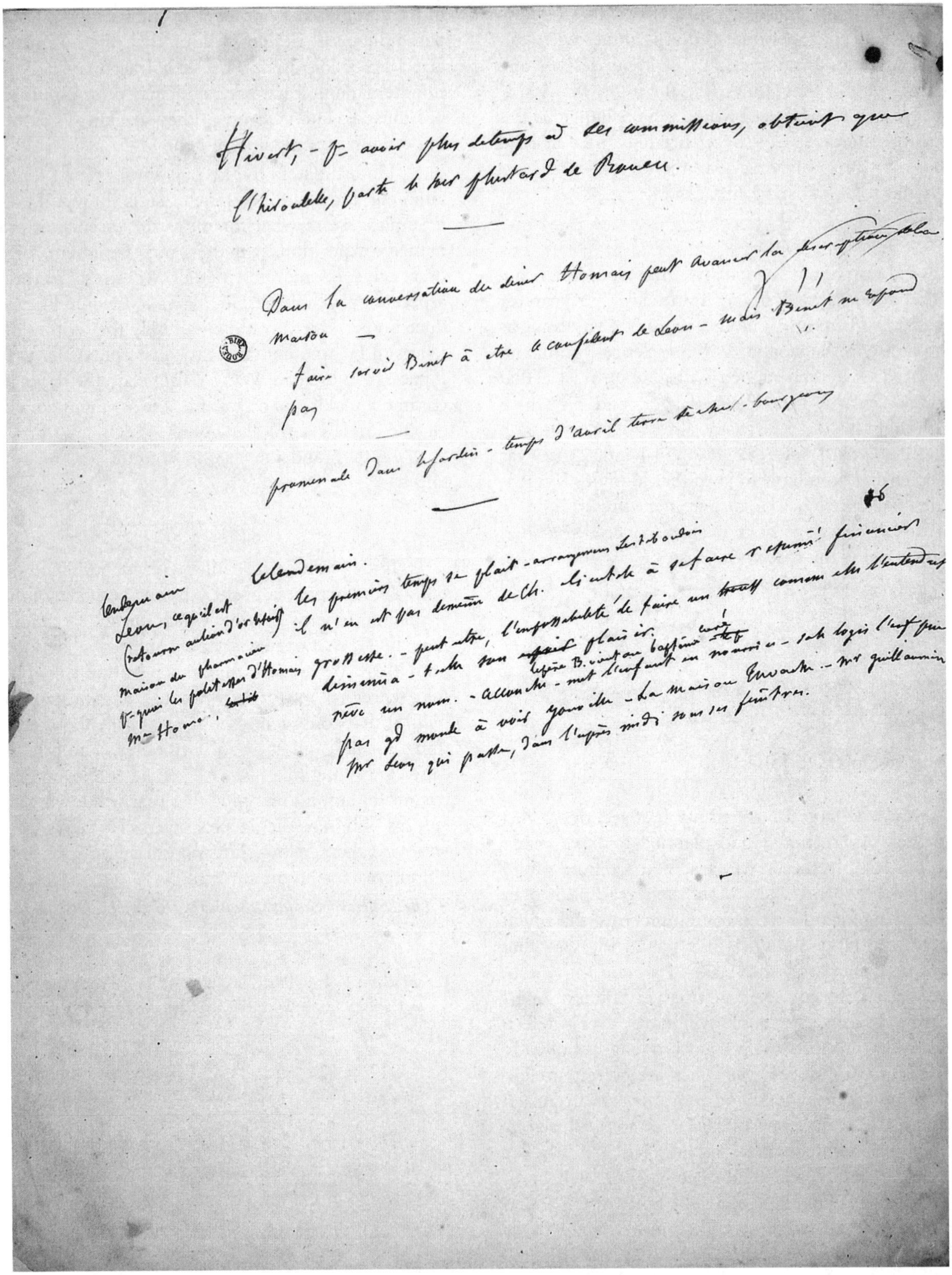

Notes for the beginning of part 2, chapter 1 of Madame Bovary *(Collections de la Bibliothèque municipale de Rouen. Cliché Thierry Ascencio-Parvy)*

bitterness that remains in our souls, all the moral mucus we gag on!

There is something faulty in my character and in my vocation. I was born a lyricist and I write no poetry. I want to shower good on those I love, and I make them weep. Look at Bouilhet: there's a man for you! Such a complete nature! If I were capable of being jealous of anyone, it would be of him. With the stultifying life he has had and the misfortunes that have befallen him, I would certainly be an imbecile by now, or deported, or hanged by my own hand. The buffetings he has suffered have only improved him. That is what happens to forests of tall trees: they keep growing ever higher in the wind, and they force their roots through silex and granite; whereas espaliers, with all their fertilizer and their straw matting, die against the wall that supports them, in full sun. Be fond of him–that is all I can say to you about him–and never doubt him for an instant.

Do you know what I talked about with my mother all last evening? About you. I told her many things she didn't know, or which she had at most half guessed. She appreciates you, and I am sure that this winter she will be glad to see you. So that question is settled.

Bovary is marching ahead again. Bouilhet was pleased on Sunday. But he was in such high spirits, and so preoccupied with Eros (not that I was the object of his passion), that perhaps he judged too favorably. I am waiting for his second reading, to be sure I am on the right track. I can't be far off it, however. This agricultural show will take me another full six weeks (a good month after my return from Paris). But the difficulties that remain are mostly in the execution. Then I will have to go over the whole thing, as the style is a little choppy. Some passages will have to be rewritten, others eliminated. So it will have taken me from July to the end of November to write *one scene!* If at least I enjoyed doing it! But I will never like this book, no matter how successfully I may bring it off. Now that I have a clear view of it as a whole, it disgusts me. But at least it will have been good training. I'll have learned how to do dialogue and portraits. I will write other books! The pleasure of criticism surely has a charm of its own, and if a fault you find in your work leads you to conceive a greater beauty, isn't this conception alone a delight in itself, almost a promise?

Adieu, à bientôt. Mille baisers. [Goodbye, see you soon. A thousand kisses.]

–*The Letters of Gustave Flaubert, 1830–1857,* p. 200

* * *

This excerpt is from a letter written in Croisset on a Friday night at 2 A.M.

Flaubert to Colet, 23 December 1853

I must love you to write you tonight, for I am *exhausted.* My skull feels encased in an iron helmet. Since two o'clock yesterday afternoon (except for about twenty-five minutes for dinner), I have been writing *Bovary.* I am in full fornication, in the very midst of it: my lovers are sweating and gasping. This has been one of the rare days of my life passed completely in illusion, from beginning to end. At six o'clock tonight, as I was writing the word "hysterics," I was so swept away, was bellowing so loudly[1] and feeling so deeply what my little Bovary was going through, that I was afraid of having hysterics myself. I got up from my table and opened the window to calm myself. My head was spinning. Now I have great pains in my knees, in my back, and in my head. I feel like a man who has been fucking too much (forgive the expression)–a kind of rapturous lassitude. And since I am in the midst of love it is only proper that I should not fall asleep before sending you a caress, a kiss, and whatever thoughts are left in me.

Will what I have written be good? I have no idea–I am hurrying a little, to be able to show Bouilhet a complete section when he comes. What is certain is that my book has been going at a lively rate for the past week. May it continue so, for I am weary of my usual snail's pace. But I fear the awakening, the disillusion that may come when the pages are copied. No matter: for better or worse, it is a delicious thing to write, to be no longer yourself but to move in an entire universe of your own creating. Today, for instance, as man and woman, both lover and mistress, I rode in a forest on an autumn afternoon under the yellow leaves, and I was also the horses, the leaves, the wind, the words my people uttered, even the red sun that made them almost close their love-drowned eyes.[2]

Is this pride or piety? Is it a foolish overflow of exaggerated self-satisfaction, or is it really a vague and noble religious instinct? But when I brood over these marvelous pleasures I have enjoyed, I would be tempted to offer God a prayer of thanks if I knew he could hear me. Praised may he be for not creating me a cotton merchant, a vaudevillian, a wit, etc.! Let us sing to Apollo as in ancient days, and breathe deeply of the fresh cold air of Parnassus; let us strum our guitars and clash our cymbals, and whirl like dervishes in the eternal hubbub of Forms and Ideas.

–*The Letters of Gustave Flaubert, 1830–1857,* p. 203

---

1. Flaubert often shouted aloud *(gueulait)* the sentences he was writing. He called his study his *gueuloir.*
2. *Madame Bovary,* Part II, Chapter 9.

* * *

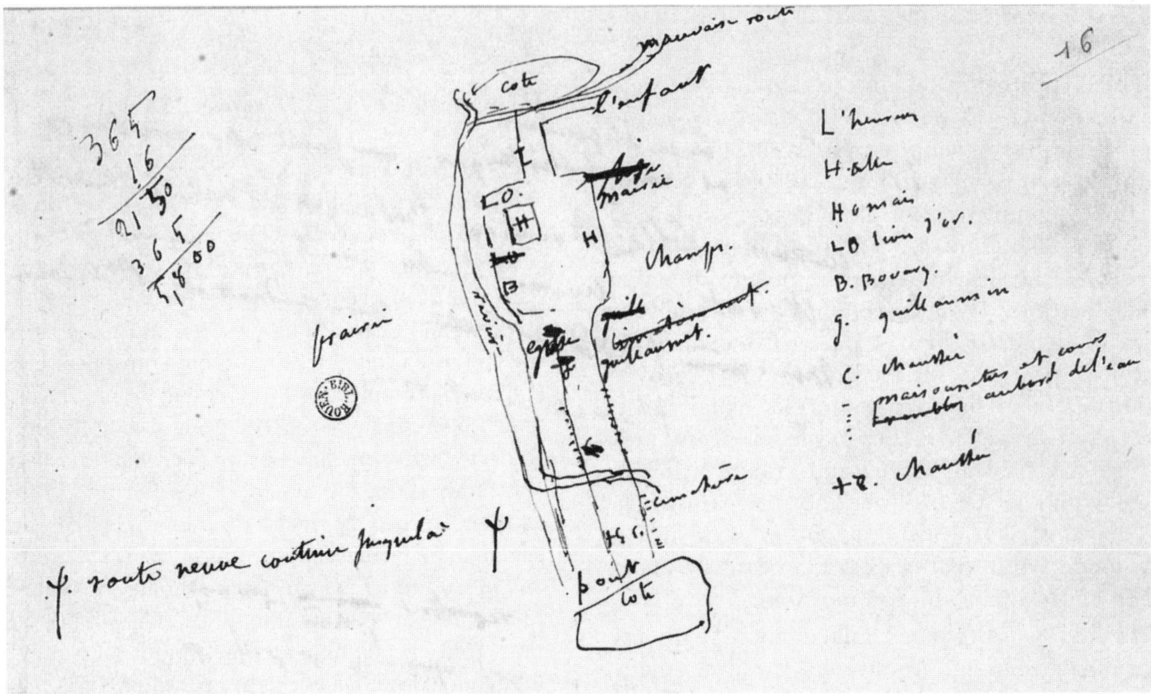

Flaubert invented Yonville-l'Abbaye, a country town to which the Bovary couple moves at the beginning of the second part of Madame Bovary *(map drawn by Flaubert; Collections de la Bibliothèque municipale de Rouen. Cliché Thierry Ascencio-Parvy).*

This excerpt is from a letter written in Croisset on a Friday night at 1 A.M.

Flaubert to Colet, 13 January 1854

In your note that came this morning, you ask me to reply to your letter of last Friday. I have just reread it; it is here, lying open on my table. What kind of answer can I give you? You must know me as well as I know myself, and you keep bringing up things we've discussed a hundred times without getting anywhere. You even reproach me for the affectionate expressions–you call them "bizarre"–that I use in my letters to you (though it seems to me I do not overindulge in sentimentalities). I will be even more sparing of them in the future, since they "make you gag." Let us go back, start over again. I will be categorical, explicit:

1. About my mother. Yes: your guess is correct. It is because I am persuaded that if she were to see you she would behave coldly toward you, less than politely, as you put it, that I prefer you not to see one another. Besides, I dislike this confusion, this bringing together of two very dissimilar kinds of affection. (You can picture what kind of woman my mother is, in this respect, when I tell you that she will never visit her elder son without invitation.) Besides: what would be her pretext for calling on you? When I told you she would visit you, I had at last overcome a tremendous obstacle, after several days of parleying, because I wanted to please you. You took no account of that, and rushed most inopportunely to reopen an irritating subject, one extremely antipathetic to me, on which I had expended great effort. I would have gone on, but you told me not to. Too bad. Now once again I beg you: leave this alone. When the time is ripe and an occasion presents itself, I will know what to do. Your persistence in this matter strikes me as very odd. Your continually asking to meet my mother, wanting me to bring her to your house, wanting her to see you, seems to me just as peculiar as though she, on her side, were to want me not to see you, not to have anything to do with you, because, because, etc. And I assure you that if she were to open her mouth concerning such matters she would soon shut it again.

Next question: financial. I am not "sulking" about this at all. I am not playing a game. I never hide my money (when I have some). There are few people as meagerly off as I who have such an air of wealth about them. (I do give the impression of being rich: that is quite true.) This is unfortunate, as it can cause me to be taken for a miser. You seem to consider me niggardly because I don't offer assistance when I am not asked. But when did I ever refuse? (No one knows the trouble I have sometimes gone to to oblige a friend.) You say I never feel a spontaneous urge to be generous? I say that is not true, that I am quite capable of such impulses. But this is no doubt a strange delusion. Didn't Du Camp, too, once tell me: "Your purse strings are stiff from disuse?"

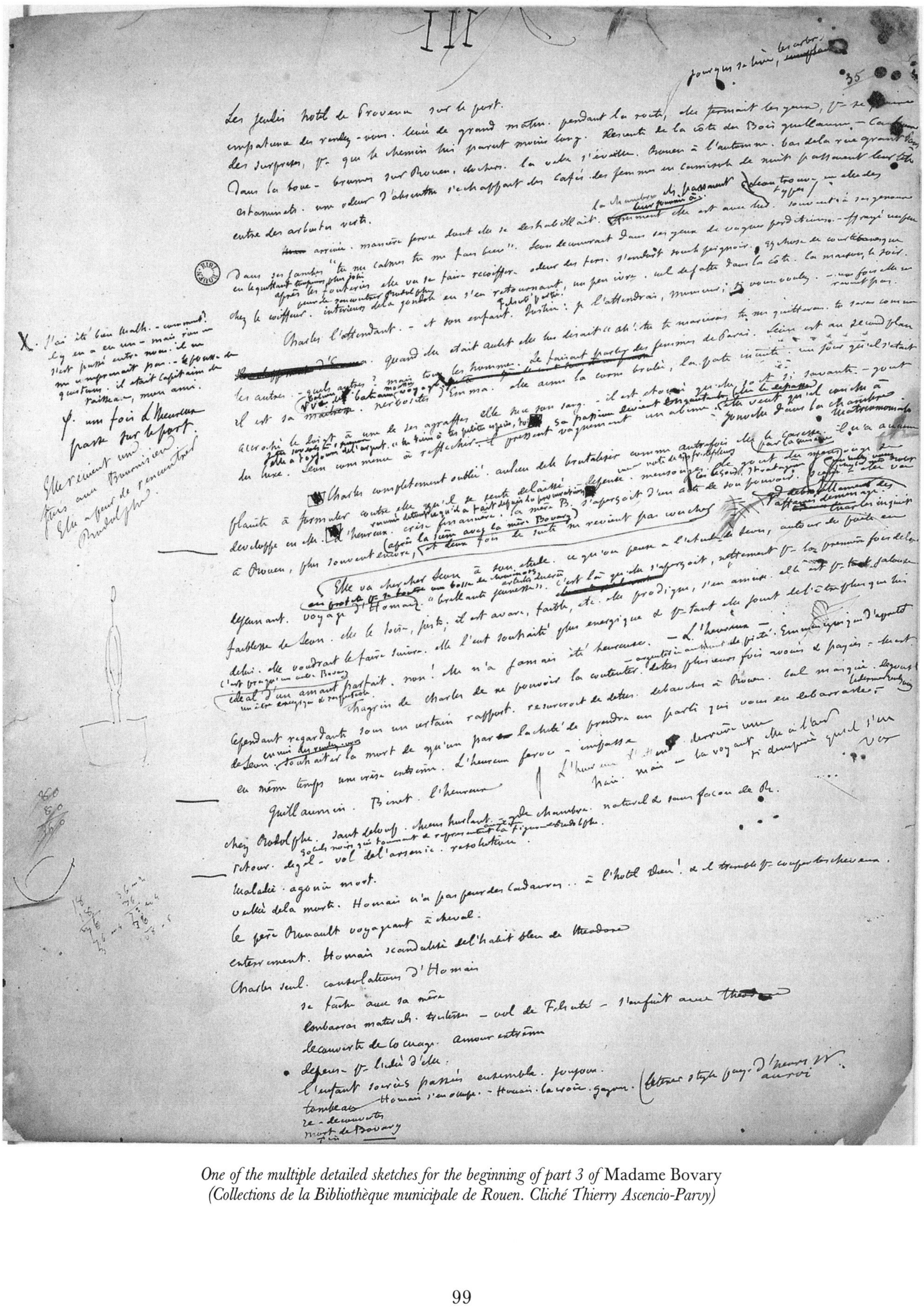

One of the multiple detailed sketches for the beginning of part 3 of Madame Bovary
(Collections de la Bibliothèque municipale de Rouen. Cliché Thierry Ascencio-Parvy)

To sum up: I told you that I will *always* oblige you, and yet I keep saying I haven't a sou. That seems suspect to you, but I deny none of it, and I repeat it again. Let me explain. It is quite true that I haven't a farthing. (At the moment, 20 francs must carry me through till February.) Don't you think I would buy 100 copies of Leconte's book, etc. if I could? But one must first pay one's debts. Of the 2000 francs I have coming to me this year,[1] I already owe almost 1200. On top of that there are my trips to Paris. Next year, in order to live in Paris I shall have to dig deep into my capital. *That is unavoidable.* I have decided on a certain sum for living expenses in the city. Once that is used up, I'll have to resume my present existence, unless I earn something–a supposition I find absurd.

But, but!–pay close attention to this *but:* if you needed it, I would find money for you anyway, even if I had to pawn the family silver. Do you understand me now?

As for finishing *Bovary,* I have already set myself so many dates, and been mistaken so often, that I refuse not only to speak of it, but to think of it. I no longer have any idea, and can only trust in God. It will be finished in its own good time, even if I die of vexation and impatience–which might very well happen were it not for the fury that sustains me. Meanwhile I will come to see you every two months, as I promised.

Now, poor dear Louise, do you want me to tell you what I really think, or rather what you really feel? I think that your love is wavering. Your dissatisfactions, the sufferings I inflict on you, can have only that cause; for as I am now, so I have always been. But now you see me more clearly, and your judgment is a reasonable one, perhaps. I don't know. However, when you love a person *completely* you love him just as he is, with his faults and his monstrousnesses; you adore even his scabs, and the hump on his back; you love to inhale the breath that poisons you. The same is true of the spiritual aspect. Now, I am "warped, squalid, selfish," etc. You know, you'll end up by making me insufferably proud, always finding fault with me as you do. I think there cannot be a mortal on this earth less commended than I; but I will not change. I will not reform. I have already erased, corrected, blotted out or suppressed so many things in myself that I am weary of it. Everything has its end, and I think I'm now a big enough boy to consider my education complete. Now I have other things to think about. I was born with all the vices. I have radically suppressed some, and kept the rest on a starvation diet. God alone knows the martyrdoms I have undergone in this psychological training-school; but now I give up. That path leads to the grave, and I want to live through three or four more books; so behold me crystallized, immobile. You say I am made of granite. I admit it. But if my

The Boulevard du Temple in Paris during the 1850s. As he was reaching the end of Madame Bovary, *Flaubert rented an apartment at 42, Boulevard du Temple, where he started to spend winter months; he kept this apartment from 1855 until 1869 (cliché Bibliothèque nationale de France, Paris).*

heart is inflexible, it is at least firm, and never gives way. Desertions and injustices do not change what is engraved on it. Everything that is there remains; and the thought of you, whatever you or I may do, will not be effaced.

Adieu–a long kiss on your beloved forehead.

–*The Letters of Gustave Flaubert, 1830–1857,* pp. 208–209

---

1. Flaubert's personal income came from property left him by his father; he had no expenses while living at home. In her letter of "last Friday," Louise had characterized her many complaints as "further proof of [my] love." Flaubert had lent her 800 francs, which she had so far been unable to repay.

The End of the Affair

Colet recounted her relationship with Flaubert in two autobiographical novels, Une Histoire de soldat *(*The Story of a Soldier*, 1856) and* Lui *(1859; translated as* Lui. A View of Him*, 1986). In* Lui*, she takes her revenge on Flaubert through her portrayal of Léonce, a remote lover and egoistic writer, locked up in his countryside and art. These excerpts present a lonely and neglected Marquise Stéphanie de Rostand, Léonce's mistress, as she begins to turn away from him in favor of a relationship with the old poet Albert de Linceul–an affair based on Colet's liaison with the poet Alfred de Musset.*

A View of Flaubert

By now I had an income of only two thousand francs. After the fortune I was used to, it was almost destitution, but I possessed two opulent splendors which towered over all the vulgar, petty constraints–radiating upon them like a sun beaming upon the moors. I had a magnificent child, a seven-year-old son who spread laughter and life around me, and I had a deep love in my heart, blind as hope and strong as faith. I expected everything from this love, and I believed in it the way the faithful believe in God! You can imagine how much energy I drew from it to live in what the world called poverty and how much indifference I felt for anything not bearing on that happiness or on my maternal joy. However, the man I loved was a kind of myth for my friends. He was seen at my place only at rare intervals. He lived at some distance in the country, working on a great book like a fanatic in a cult of art, he said. I was the confidante of this unknown genius. I received his letters every day, and every two months when a part of his task was completed, I became once more his fond reward, his shimmering sensuality, the passing frenzy of his heart, which, strange to say, opened and closed to these powerful sensations at will.

I had been overwhelmed by so much disillusionment during the dreary years of my marriage. I had lived until thirty in such gloomy isolation that in the beginning this love affair consumed me entirely and seemed to me the feast of life I had so vainly longed for.

I was coming out of the night. This flame stunned and blinded me. It had first shone on me like a forbidden happiness when I was still bound. When I was free, I rushed headlong towards it as if to the hearth of all warmth and light. Narrating this story compels me to touch that image, in ashes now, and give it substance. I shall do so discreetly because if it is sinister to call forth the dead from the tomb, it is even more so to call forth the dead from the living.

I found in that love an atmosphere of ethereal exaltation which made me savor only the joys which flowed from it. Receiving his letters every day when I awoke, writing to him every evening, spinning in the vortex of his ideas, whirling them around me, plunging into them until I was dizzy, such was my life.

He seemed so indifferent, both for others and for himself, to anything that wasn't the abstraction of art and beauty, that, given the distance we lived from each other, he acquired a special grandeur and prestige. How would someone like him, who esteemed only the ideas of things, have noticed my straitened circumstances?

–Louise Colet, *Lui. A View of Him,* translated by Marilyn Gaddis Rose (Athens & London: University of Georgia Press, 1986), pp. 14–15

* * *

Flaubert on *Lui*

When Colet's novel was published in 1859, Flaubert wrote to Amélie Bosquet, a novelist from Rouen:

My liaison with Mme Colet left me with no lasting 'wound,' in the usual emotional and deep sense of the word. What remains is rather the memory (and, even now, the sensation) of prolonged irritation. Her book has been the crowning touch. Add to it the comments, questions, jokes, and allusions I have been subjected to since the publication of said work. When I saw that you, too, were joining in the game I lost my patience a little, I admit, because in public I keep my dignity.

–*The Letters of Gustave Flaubert, 1857–1880* (1982), pp. 17–18

Although Colet and Flaubert did not meet again after their final breakup, it is said that she saw him one day in 1863 at the Collège de France and told her daughter Henriette: "My God! How ugly he is! Look how ugly he is!"

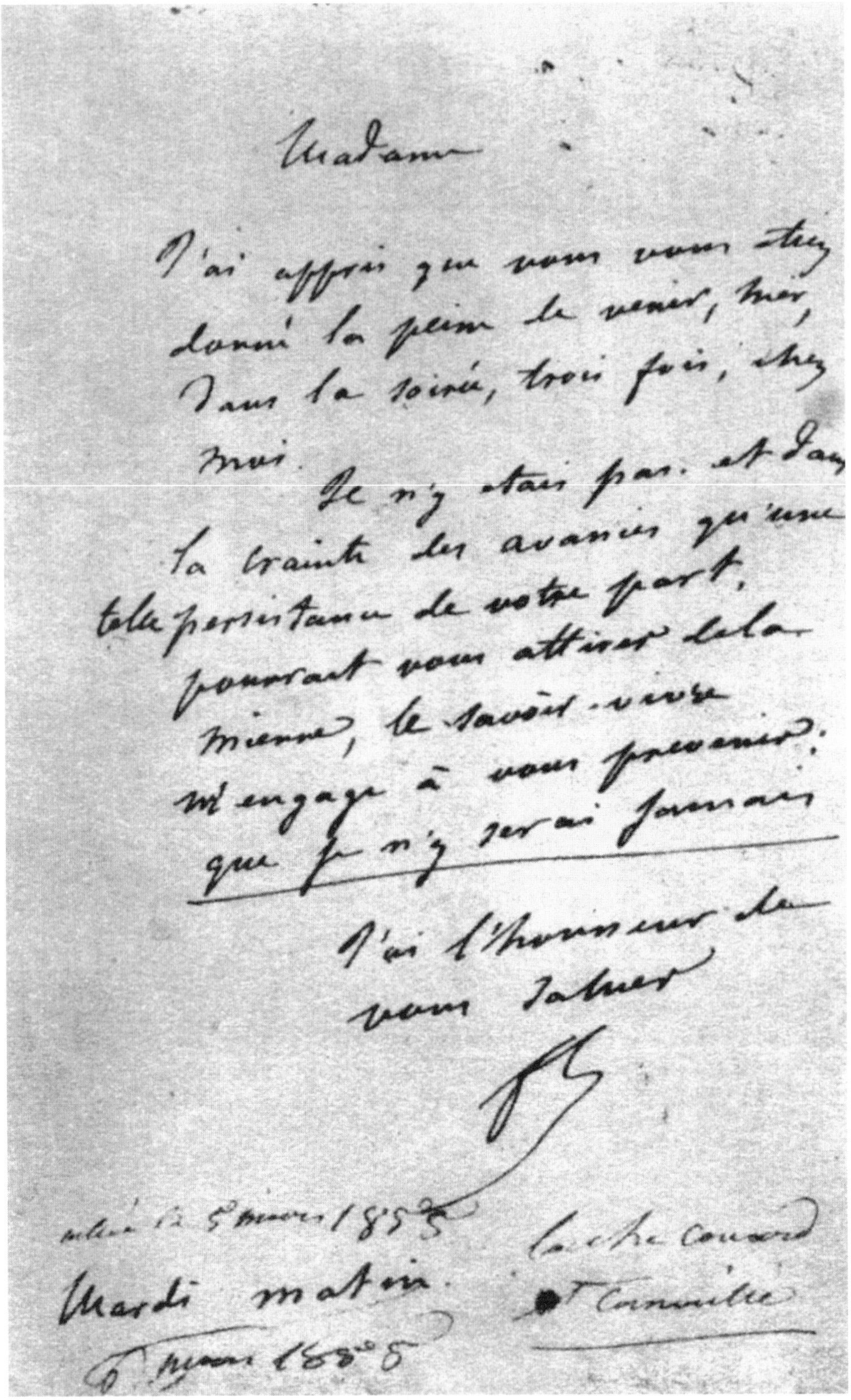

Madame

J'ai appris que vous vous êtes donné la peine de venir, hier, dans la soirée, trois fois, chez moi.

Je n'y étais pas. Et dans la crainte des avanies qu'une telle persistance de votre part pourrait vous attirer de la mienne, le savoir-vivre m'engage à vous prévenir: que je n'y serai jamais

J'ai l'honneur de vous saluer

G F

reçu le 5 mars 1855

Mardi matin.

6 mars 1855

lâche couard et canaille

Last letter from Flaubert to Colet, dated 6 March 1855: "Madame: I was told that you took the trouble to come here to see me three times last evening. I was not in. And, fearing lest persistence expose you to humiliation, I am bound by the rules of politeness to warn you that I shall never be in. *Yours, G.F." At the bottom right of the page, Colet wrote: "coward, poltroon* and scum*"* (The Letters of Gustave Flaubert, 1830–1857; *courtesy of the Musée Calvet, Avignon).*

Chapter IX

I had met Albert de Lincel at the end of winter. Spring had come quickly with fine days at first, as so often happens in Paris.

A woman is especially susceptible to this rapid transition from one season to the next. To go from the icy chills of winter to a warm temperature, to feel in yourself the sap of the trees and plants budding and blooming when you are near the man you love, you yourself blossom in intoxication and pride. But in solitude, this overabundance of being is transformed into suffering and torture. What can you do with a heart that is full to bursting? What is the purpose served by the sudden flushes coloring your cheeks? The sharper flames darting from your eyes? What is the good of feeling stronger and looking better if there is no beloved to enjoy your beauty and energy?

Léonce had promised to visit in the spring, but now he wrote me that finishing the first part of the great book he was working on would chain him to his lonely desk for another month. I should feel sorry for him, he said, since a powerful abstraction was like religion, like martyrdom, and he owed himself to it entirely. After the harsh labor was completed, just like the devout believer who has paradise for his reward, he would savor all the more intensely the immense joy of love.

These letters caused me pain and irritation. Such quietude, real or feigned, seemed cruel to me. Sometimes I even saw in it the negation of love. But then my despair would be so great that in order to keep on believing I would cling to his words, tender, occasionally passionate, which concealed from me the cold, unshakable priority of that heart of steel. He would reply to my cries of pain with cries of passion. He was suffering more than I, he claimed, but suffering was grandeur in itself. He delighted in comparing himself to the Desert Fathers, consumed with desire but immolating their heart and flesh for the jealous god of Thabor. For him Art was the jealous god which can be possessed and assimilated only when you dedicate yourself entirely to him in solitude.

I was broken by his obstinacy, and sometimes I simply gave up trying to express my anguish, but then my letters emitted such dejection that he would become alarmed. Then he would advise me to seek distractions, to see my friends more often, to work at attracting Albert who should be cured at any price.

How often I used to cry reading these stoical letters! How often when midnight struck and I could hear around me only my son breathing in his sleep and the treetops rustling in the winds of the night, I would stand in front of my mirror, letting down my hair before tying it up to sleep. Then how often I would be seized by an overwhelming desire to see him! I wanted to go to him, surprise him in his nocturnal labor, throw my arms around him, and say to him between sobs, "Let's not be separated again. Old age will come quickly. Death will follow. Why spend in tears of anticipation these brief, happy days, so soon passed, when body and soul celebrate their prime? Oh, if you don't spend your youth when you're in love, you're like the miser who dies of hunger next to his treasure or like the invalid who knows the secrets that can save him but prefers to die."

While the man to whom I had given my life left me prey to all the anxieties of love, Albert, who found in my company a tranquilizing distraction, gradually fell into the habit of coming to see me every day. Sometimes his visits calmed me down. Sometimes they made me nervous. My heart was obsessed by its secret torment.

Well, what did a man I couldn't love matter to me? I wasn't waiting for him. I wanted youth, handsomeness, strength. I wanted the man whom banal passions had not damaged, whose lofty severity held me in his sway. Albert, love's sickly, frail, broken and withered remains, interested me like a brother and touched me like a child. But as for being the complement of my own being, my master, he was not, not then, and probably never would have been. In our basic natures we shared too many sensitive fibers, too much parity of ideas and imagination. Like and like make brethren, but the tormented union of lovers requires opposites.

I am going to risk a complete confession. Sometimes in the despair Léonce reduced me to, I almost wished that Albert would inspire a more romantic attraction, that my heart would beat faster hearing him come in, that I would feel near him a turmoil that could lead to infidelity. He always succeeded in distracting me with his wit, but he never alleviated my distress. Sometimes I was brusque and unreasonable with him, and since he was determined to be with me, he redoubled his kind and imaginative efforts to entertain me for a few hours.

My son had become very fond of him. Whenever Albert came in, he would throw his arms around him. Sometimes he would say to me, "Mommy, you're treating him very badly. He's so pale and looks so sick you just have to love him. I like him much better myself than that tall dark-haired man who comes here every two months and doesn't even look at me."

– *Lui. A View of Him,* pp. 84–86

* * *

Alfred de Musset (1810–1857) as a young man. Musset, Victor Hugo, Alphonse-Marie-Louis de Prat de Lamartine, and Alfred de Vigny are considered the four great poets of the Romantic Movement in France. Musset was a dissipated forty-two when he met Colet (Henry Dwight Sedgwick, Alfred de Musset *[Indianapolis: Bobbs-Merrill, 1931]).*

Chapter XXI

I couldn't get to sleep until daybreak, and at the hour my son usually got up, I was awakened from this brief, troubled sleep by Marguerite coming into my room. I shook off my malaise and began at once to write to Léonce. I didn't want to wait until evening to tell him the story Albert had confided in me. I was under the sway of blind love. That is why during the great poet's own lifetime I entrusted his painful and secret confessions to another heart. But that other heart no longer contains anything but dead ashes, colder than the dust in coffins. So I won't call on that heart to confirm the truth of my testimony. For all those who have lived by both heart and mind, its truth throbs sufficiently both in the overall outline and in the details I've just related.

If this narrative were a fiction meant for a book, perhaps the rules of what we call art would require ending it here. But in my opinion, real concern outweighs imaginary concern, and the unforeseeable attraction of a real action outweighs the contrived effect of a clever composition. Then, too, nothing which bears on a truly great person is trivial. Nothing is irrelevant if it was part of a life that was dear to us. So I will tell you Albert's last emotions, mixed in, as they are, with events of my own life.

I had written to Léonce without either restraint or uneasiness because secure as he was of having all my love, what I told him about Albert's enthusiastic feelings for me could indeed somewhat upset him, but never frighten or hurt him.

I waited calmly for his reply, while I was overwrought and hence preoccupied with what I could say to Albert. How could he be brought down from his keyed-up state of the night before by the pointblank confession of my love for Léonce? This love affair, which he refused to believe, how could I insist on its reality and make that cruel conviction penetrate his wounded and loving heart? To reject him as a lover was to lose him as a friend, to forgo forever our heartfelt camaraderie, our fellowship of kindred minds which meant so much to me. I was well aware that he wouldn't want my friendship. From the moment love strikes, all other feelings disappear, consumed, so to speak. It's the spark that sets the flame ablaze. And still I felt hesitating would show bad faith on my part. To say nothing was to deceive both Albert and Léonce, for leaving one of them room for hope meant removing the other's sense of security.

I was in the grips of this nagging dilemma when the doorbell rang. It had to be Albert. I thought I was going to faint, but I felt immediately relieved to see his servant instead. He came to tell me that his master was indisposed and wouldn't be able to come to see me either during the day or in the evening.

"Is he seriously ill," I asked, "since he didn't write? If this is the case, I'll go to see him."

His servant dissuaded me, informing me that during such nervous attacks which his master suffered once or twice a month, he insisted on keeping completely to himself. "He keeps completely still and doesn't talk," he added, "taking what he calls his 'bath of silence and repose,' and in twenty-four hours he's over it."

"Tell him anyway that if he wants to see me, I'll run over," I repeated as the man went off.

As soon as I was alone I realized that my message, when quoted, would make Albert think I loved him.

I spent the rest of the day inexpressibly agitated. I didn't know what course to take or what form to give my confession. If I wrote Albert about my passion for Léonce, it would be like sending him a cold-blooded dismissal. For the written word always has something fixed and unpardonable about it, while what comes from the voice, no matter how grievous the meaning, responds to the feelings of the listener. So I finally decided to wait until Albert visited and let the moment be my guide.

The next morning, I heard from Léonce.

There had never been a novel, he said, which interested him so much as the story of Antonia and Albert's romance. That man had put into his passion the grandeur, intensity, and duration which made it truly beautiful. But it was doubtful that after so many painful incidents and so many repeated and deleterious attempts at consolation in debauchery, Albert could still love as he once had. This second love he was offering me would be only a pale and grimacing simulacrum of the first. I deserved something better than the vestiges of a damaged heart and dormant genius. Albert was famous and he himself was unknown, but he, at least, was giving me his entire soul where no image obscured my own. I would always be the only woman, the inspiration of his solitude, the beloved bond of his youth, the gentle light hovering over his decline, like Mohammed's first wife. She was the prophet's destined mate, loved to very last days, old and whitehaired, preferred to the fresh young brides who never had his heart.

He was too proud, he continued, to add anything more, but he waited for the decision of my love with an impatience which was disturbing his work and solitude. In closing, he begged me to continue unreservedly to give him reports on Albert. Albert was, he said, a living case study of unparalleled interest, and in satisfying his curiosity, I would give him genuine proof of my love!

I crumpled that letter convulsively. Nowhere did I find a cry from the heart. Oh, my God, I thought, what held him back? Why didn't he show spontaneous feeling? How could he leave me alone when my soul was in such a state of distress? The last sentence affected me like a scalpel which would have cut into living flesh. He wanted to know everything about Albert, whose noble genius had become an object of analysis for his cold, reclusive intellect. Well, no! I thought, I would not continue with the dissection of that great wounded heart. That would be like treason. I would stop. On the first day I ought to have refused to expose Albert's drama. And yet could I have done anything else? To conceal part of my life from Léonce was to love him only halfway and consequently not to love him, because according to the profound injunction of the *Imitation,* "Let my love know no bounds." He whose love has limits, doesn't love at all.[1]

But did he have an unlimited love for me? Alas, I didn't see any sign of it in that letter. But other letters were more tender. They had made my heart expand and filled it with contentment. It wasn't a dream. I really was loved. I was convinced in his arms and reassured in his letters. Suddenly I was seized by a violent desire to reread them. I pulled out several at random

George Sand in 1838. Musset met and fell in love with Sand, six years his senior, in 1833 and wrote of their tempestuous affair in Confession d'un enfant du siècle *(1836; translated as* The Confession of a Child of the Century, *1892). In* Lui. A View of Him *Colet refers to a fictional parallel of this memoir when she has Léonce praise "the story of Antonia and Albert's romance" (detail of painting by Auguste Charpentier; courtesy of the Musée Carnavalet, Paris).*

from the strongbox I kept them in, and as their calm, measured tenderness took hold of me, I felt my serenity return. He loves me! I repeated with sweet tears, and in that confidence I found the strength to tell Albert everything. I was ready to confess my love the way the first Christians confessed their faith.

At that moment I heard Albert's voice. Marguerite had met him on the staircase and was going to let him in my study. My first impulse was to hide Léonce's letters. But that was followed at once by another idea, and I left the letters scattered over my worktable.

Albert came in. He was a little wan, but his very studied manner of dress gave him an appearance of health.

"So, you wanted to come see me," he said with a kiss. "Sending that kind thought cured me, and I have come to see you and thank you. But, my dear, are you ill yourself?" he added, studying me carefully. "You're as white and cold as a marble bust. And you have tears in your eyes. Why are you crying? I want to know."

"You shall," I exclaimed, "you shall know everything. Albert, listen to me without getting angry and don't take away your friendship. Several times already I've wanted to tell you, and you haven't wanted to hear me out. Albert, I can't love you as a lover, because I love someone else, someone who loves me, and from whom nothing could separate me!"

He staggered and became so ghastly pale that I was afraid of the injury I might have done.

"Oh," he murmured slowly, "You're worth no more than *she* was. You, too; I give you love, and you make me suffer."

"Is it my fault," I asked, pressing his hands in mine, "if before meeting you I had given away my heart? Are you going to resent me for telling the truth the way you resented Antonia for telling lies? Was I supposed to deceive you? . . ."

"Yes, rather than snatch away that dream that was going to let me live again. So good-bye forever. I don't want to know anything more."

"You are harsh," I told him. "And you ill repay my loyalty. Was I supposed to treat you like a child who can't bear to have anyone step in between his desires and their impossibility? Oh, my dearest Albert, if the confidence of a strong, sincere mind frightens you, why were you surprised when Antonia lied to you? She must have realized in the depths of her genius that men will always deny us women freedom in love and dignity in frankness."

"Oh, be quiet!" he shouted, losing his composure. "I really don't care what you say. I prefer to look at you so pale and dejected. Your looks at least lead me to believe that you suffer from the pain you're inflicting."

"Oh yes," I agreed, kissing him as I would have kissed my son, "I suffer to see you unhappy. I would so much rather change it into happiness."

"You have the persuasiveness of kindness," he replied. "And you make me see that I wasn't rational. It is true. I can't keep you from loving someone else, but what I could have done, what I certainly would have done when I was younger and better looking is take his place. Let's see. This isn't possible. This lover is not a husband. He is not even an assiduous lover, since he lets you languish like this."

His voice had suddenly taken on considerable detachment. He seemed to be smiling with lust.

"How about it, my dear? Shall we try a bit of love-making? Afterwards, you may prefer me to this terrible absentee."

"No!" I cried, hurt but fortified by his change in tone. "He alone attracts me. He alone is my type."

"Ah, well, I understand," he said, looking at himself in the mirror. "I have the same effect on you that Antonia had on me at our last meeting. But if that's the way it is, why don't you avoid me? Why, on the contrary, do you keep after me? And why do you weep over me?"

"Because in your genius there is something eternally young and handsome, which, distinct from romantic love, exerts a powerful seduction, an ideal attraction. I would not want to betray him, but I would not want to lose you; you are my beloved poet. You hold my trembling soul in your hands. Don't you realize that?"

"You're a kind creature," he said. "I'll try to forget my egoistic desire, and hear you out. Come now, tell me whom you love. Does he at least deserve his good fortune?"

"What I would say wouldn't let you know him very well," I answered. "I have all the bias and blindness of love. But read these letters. Be for me the judicious heart receiving the confidence of a friend."

He took himself in hand and picked up a letter at random, motivated somewhat, I suspect, by curiosity.

It was painful watching him read. My head bent towards him, I tried to figure out the impressions he was getting from his eyes, his lips, alternately smiling or pursed, the fleeting wrinkles on his forehead. He read twenty or so of them without a pause, without a word. But I saw on his face, like in a mirror, all the reactions in his soul. I saw from one moment to the next his impatience with familiarity that was too coarse; his genius' contempt of those tedious disquisitions on art and fame tactlessly mixed in with expressions of love; his mocking pity of Léonce's monstrous personality which increased continually in his isolation the way pyramids in the desert keep growing beneath the layers of sterile sand covering and compressing them. Sometimes I saw bitterness and scorn, betrayed by a cutting ironic glance that seemed to whiplash certain racial vices which Léonce's letters exposed. He had read everything, and not once did I detect a sign of involuntary sympathy for the truth of that love which had taken over my life.

"Well?" I ventured, undone by his silence, questioning him since I could see he wasn't going to speak.

"Stéphanie, my dear," he replied, studying me sadly, "you are loved by that man's brain, but not by his heart."

"Don't speak badly of him," I cried. "You would be suspect."

"Don't go suspecting me of being jealous of that Léonce," he retorted, raising his head proudly. "No, I am reassured, because I'm worth more than he is, worth more by the sincerity of my emotions. In my old, damaged heart there is more warmth and enthusiasm than in that cold, inert thirty-year-old heart. I am reassured, I repeat, and I am no longer jealous because I am certain that one day you will love me and no longer love him. There are too many differences between you. Even while your feelings try to blend, too much shocks and grates. Sooner or later you will become enemies. And then, dead or alive, you will love me. If dead, it will be a happiness to make me quiver in my casket, feeling you are all mine!"

"Albert," I implored, "you have a place in my heart, but show some mercy. Don't kill the poor love affair which has kept me alive for ten years. For ten years others besides yourself have hurled themselves against its strength and have drawn back at its steadfastness. It's an inaccessible rock where no one may tread. You can torment me with your doubts and afflict me with your predictions, but I feel within the will to love forever and the certainty of being loved. The love which you don't find in these letters, for me quivers and burns on every line. You have the diffident eye of defiance, and defiance makes you an atheist. I am confident. I believe, and I sense the hidden god!"

While I was speaking, I had seized the open letters in my hands and held them out like witnesses.

"If I explicated them in front of you," Albert continued, "you would say I am cruel. The hour hasn't struck for you to hear the truth."

"I fear nothing," I replied, "for nothing can undermine my love."

"All right, then, you will hear me out. The fight is on between that man and me, and I will not show bad sportsmanship, fighting with the arms he has furnished. He is not only odious to me because I love you but because I sense in him also the antagonist of my spirit and all my instincts. Look at this one," he said, picking up a letter and glancing through it. "Here the young man positively on fire with love regales you with a four-page apologia on solitude. You are his life, he says, and he willingly lives apart from you in order to bury himself in frenetic labor. He suppresses his heart's affections in hope of being inspired. It's absolutely as if we suppressed a lamp's oil in hopes of making it burn brighter. Think back over the lives of all our great men. They tamed their genius by loving! What do these petty Origens of art for art's sake want?[2] Do they imagine that self-mutilation will help them procreate?

"Here I find," he continued, taking up another letter, "that he presumes to surpass us all in the correctness of style. Naive arrogance! As if writing was a matter of symmetry, marquetery, and floor polish. If the idea does not make the word throb, what importance will it have anyway? If perfect pleats of material shudder on a mannequin, will I be moved?" And Albert broke into the sneering laugh that the fresh young girl slings at contrived beauty of a painted coquette.

He went on. "This man has been working for four years on a long novel which he tells you about, day in, day out. Each day he adds a painfully worked out page, and there where inspired writers experience the energizing of spiritual exhilaration, he confesses that he experiences only the agonies of the craft. He's the pedagogue who at the hour of creation feels as torpid as a bump on a log, while any schoolboy can fantasize like Cherubim.[3] I know another pedant of the same species as your Léonce, who cloistered himself for two years to imitate one of my poems, the liveliest in manner and the least didactic. In our times we have slow, sure, mathematical procedures for these imitations of Romantic literature, just as there used to be for counterfeit Classical literature. For example, Campistron aped Racine.[4] A sculptor in my set who has turned out more fine phrases than fine statues, has called my patient imitator a pawn in the Romantic chess game.[5] You may be sure that the book your lover has been gestating for forty-eight months will be a flagrant, heavy-handed compilation of Balzac!"

"Does one bestow genius upon oneself?" I cried. "Not everyone can have a creative spirit. Wishing won't make it so. But it's an effort of the intelligence having its own grandeur to pursue beauty without respite and approach it. You cannot deny that despite his lack of genius he possesses this powerful will to beauty. It's not his fault, if it's not greater."

"Well, who would dream of humiliating him," replied Albert, "if he didn't display his monstrous arrogance himself? In the letters you had me read, he's always hovering overhead like a condor, who with all his weight, imagines he's superior to an eagle! How loftily he passes judgment on all contemporary writers. He is kind enough to make an exception for Chateaubriand, Hugo, and myself, which makes little difference to me, my dear Marquise. But what disdain he heaps on great writers whom he will never equal. Sainte-Rive, for example, what a tone he takes to despise Sainte-Rive's marvelous psychological novel on love, one of the most impressive books of our times–without understanding it, of course.[6] None of this will probably hinder this presumptuous upstart, if he ever publishes his book, from going to beg Sainte-Rive for a few laudatory comments."

And Albert crumpled the letter where Léonce made fun of this famous critic.

"But none of this implicates his heart and has little to do with my love," I kept protesting.

"Are you claiming that you can cut a person in two?" Albert jeered. "No indeed, nature is more logical than your love. Everything in an organism is either a coordinate or a complement. Your Léonce's heart is the manifest and palpable corollary of his brain. His heart is an indefinably dilated organ, but it is insensitive. It's an empty gibbosity where everything goes in and nothing comes out, like Harlequin's humpback," he added, laughing harder.

–Louise Colet, *Lui. A View of Him,* 253–263

---

1. *Imitatio Christi* was written between 1390 and 1440 and is ascribed to Thomas à Kempis (1380–1471). It is alleged to be the most influential book in Christendom, aside from the Bible.
2. It is hard to find Albert's comparison especially apt. He is extremely unlikely to have read this early Egyptian defender of Christianity against paganism. Perhaps Albert considers the devotees of art for art's sake belaboring the obvious also. If Albert were aware of the unverifiable account of Origen's self-castration, he would see an analogy with Léonce, presumably immolating himself by seclusion.
3. Cherubim is a page in Beaumarchais' *Le Mariage de Figaro.*
4. Jean Galbert de Campistron (1656–1723) was a derivative dramatist.
5. Albert may be referring to Antonie Auguste Préault (1809–79) who was called Aristophanes by his friends.
6. This novel is Sainte-Beuve's *Volupté* (1834).

* * *

In one of the articles Colet wrote for the journal Le Siècle *during her trip to Egypt in 1869–assembled under the title* Les Pays lumineux *(Luminous Countries) and published posthumously in 1879–she described a curious nightmare she experienced on the boat at Giza before her cruise up the Nile.*

Haunted by Flaubert

For many hours . . . I was prey to a strange and indefinable hallucination. The defunct image of a being whom I had loved in my blind youth, buried in my heart for over twenty years, was suddenly resurrected in dominating and brutal form. His giant's body bent toward me as if to seize me; and his specter spoke to me, with a quiet voice as icy as the air that comes from a tomb closed centuries ago:

"Take care! You don't have the strength anymore to suffer through the tribulations which I once imposed on you. You might well lose your body this time, in the same manner in which you injured yourself trying to soften my heart, that tough metal compressed in the double carapace of science and debauch."

My voice, stifled by suffering, answered him with indifference:

"What do you want of me? What do I care about the nature of your heart? You have no more power over me. Your phantom is vanished in the void of time." . . .

The larval spirit weighed upon my burning chest, heavy and opaque as some brutish animal. The round porthole, through which two large stars shone, seemed to be his haggard-eyed face, at times blazing, at times dimmed in a penumbra. I closed my eyes. . . .

As I ceased to see him, I still felt his crude, obtrusive presence. Weren't those his hands, trying to strangle my wheezing throat? Wasn't that his mouth, biting at my languishing body?

Over my head, I heard a continuous noise similar to those of footsteps on a wooden floor. The biting was succeeded by a raw, intolerable itching, as if I were clawing at my body with my own hands; I shouted out in pain more than in fear, for I do not believe in ghosts; sitting up, I lit a candle I had by my bedside. . . .

Why the reappearance of that forgotten being? . . . Ah! It's quite simple. . . . Yesterday I realized that the motives inciting me to take this excursion to Upper Egypt had to do with my desire to encounter perhaps in the form of a living mummy–one of those seductive almehs who so revolted and upset me in [Flaubert's] accounts of his Egyptian Journey. The nightmare of this night may have arisen from that prospect. . . .

It was twenty years ago . . . that this man shattered and sullied with his uncouth hands the dazzling pedestal which I built to him in a temple which he ignored. . . . He chased himself out of the sacred precinct by sullying it with fleshly debauch and, worse, with a corrupt soul and ignoble vanity. . . .

You who have retained, over the years, all your youthfulness and vigor of spirit, how could you fear the apparition of this specter? Is it the memory of him which batters you and gives you this spectral air? No! It's the enormous sadness of having your most sacred beliefs lost, destroyed, profaned by him. . . . Victim, you have been heaped with outrage, executioner, he has been glorified, but the hour of reckoning is sure to come, he will not escape punishment . . .

Remember that great Arab proverb: If a man has secretly killed, the grass of the fields will tell you so. . . .

A tear is sometimes a more powerful weapon than a knife! Reveal your emotions, and you will be the victor! Woman is forever the sacrificial lamb at the mercy of love. But the lamb so bestially stabbed in secret can heal its wounds, it revives and becomes a young lion, it can attack the unpunished murderer and become the instrument of eternal justice.

–Francine du Plessix Gray, *Rage and Fire: A Life of Louise Colet* (New York: Simon & Schuster, 1994), pp. 349–351

On Colet's Death

After Colet's death on 8 March 1876, Flaubert wrote to their common friend, Edma Roger des Genettes:

You understood very well all my feelings on the death of my poor Muse. . . . This revival of her memory made me review the course of my life. But your friend has become more stoical during the past year. I have trampled on so many things, in order to stay alive! In short, after an afternoon given over to days gone by I *willed* myself to think of them no longer, and went back to work. One more thing concluded!

The family, which is Catholic, took her to Verneuil in order to avoid civil burial, and there was no scandal. The newspapers made little mention of any of it. Do you remember the little apartment in the rue de Sèvres, and all the rest? Ah! God have mercy on us!

–*The Letters of Gustave Flaubert, 1857–1880,* p. 235

Maxime Du Camp in 1853. As co-director of Revue de Paris *he arranged for the publication of* Madame Bovary *in the periodical for 2,000 francs. Although this was regarded as a fair price at the time, it amounted to about what an unskilled laborer could expect to earn in three years (courtesy of the Bibliothèque de l'Institut de France, Paris).*

The Trial of *Madame Bovary*

The manuscript of Madame Bovary *indicates the dates of the writing: September 1851–April 1856. After receiving 2,000 francs for its publication in the* Revue de Paris, *Flaubert returned to work on his unpublished work "La Tentation de saint Antoine," revising the first version he had completed in 1849. Excerpts from this work were published by Théophile Gautier in four issues of* L'Artiste *between December 1856 and February 1957. Indeed, the prosecutor in the trial of* Madame Bovary *quoted a few lines from one of these excerpts to emphasize the "vividness" of Flaubert's descriptive style.*

The directors of the Revue de Paris *had asked Flaubert to make cuts to his text, which he reluctantly did, and the first installment of* Madame Bovary *was published on 1 October 1856. When some readers complained about the work, the government asked the Department of Justice to sue the* Revue de Paris, *calling the novel an "outrage to public morals and religion." Responding to government threats, the editors of the* Revue *made new cuts on their own to the novel, an action that angered Flaubert. In December he signed a contract with Michel Lévy to publish the novel as a book. He earned 800 francs.*

Despite the self-imposed censorship of the Revue de Paris, *the government proceeded with its charges on 29 January 1857 against Flaubert as well as Léon Laurent-Pichat, the owner of the review, and Auguste-Alexis Pillet, the printer. These excerpts from the trial of* Madame Bovary *provide a fascinating insight into imperial mores and attitudes about censorship in mid-century France. In his speech for the prosecution, Imperial Attorney Ernest Pinard argues that Flaubert offended public morals with "lascivious pictures" and by mixing the profane with the sacred. He was ably opposed by Antoine-Marie-Jules Sénard, who formerly had been a lawyer in Rouen and a friend of Flaubert's father. The verdict was read on 7 February: all defendants were acquitted.*

Pinard for the Prosecution

Gentlemen, the first part of my task is fulfilled: I have told the story; now I am going to quote, and after the quotations will come the accusations on two counts–offense against public morals, offense against religious morals. The offense against public morals is in the lascivious pictures that I will place before your eyes; the offense against religious morals is in the mingling of voluptuous images with sacred things. I come now to the quotations. I shall be brief, for you will read the novel in its entirety. I will restrict myself to put before you four scenes, or rather four pictures. The first will portray her love for and her downfall with Rodolphe, the second a religious bout between the two adulteries, the third the affair with Léon, and the fourth the death of Madame Bovary.

Before uncovering for you these canvases, allow me to inquire about Monsieur Flaubert's tone and color, his brushwork, for after all, if his novel is a painting it will be necessary for us to know to what school he belongs, what colors he employs, and what manner of a portrait he has painted of his heroine.

The author's general color, permit me to say to you, is a lascivious color, before, during, and after these transgressions. Madame Bovary is a child, she is ten or twelve years old, she is at the Ursuline convent. At this age where the girl is still unformed, where the woman cannot feel the first excitements that disclose a new world, she confesses her sins:

> When she went to confession, she would invent trivial sins in order to prolong her stay there, on her knees in the shadow, hands clasped, her face at the grill as the priest whispered above her. The references to fiancé, husband, heavenly lover, and eternal marriage that recur in sermons awakened unexpected joys within her.

Is it natural for a little girl to invent trivial sins when one knows that for a child it is the smallest things that are the most difficult to tell? To show her at such an age inventing trivial sins in the shadows while the priest whispers, bringing to her mind the similes of fiancé, of husband, of heavenly lover, and of eternal marriage, which she feels like a thrill of pleasure–is this not to evoke what I have called a lascivious painting?

Now, do you want to see Madame Bovary in her simplest actions, in her natural state, without a lover, without a fault? I pass over the mention of "the next day" and over this bride "whose self-control gave no opportunity for conjecture," which is already a more than equivocal turn of phrase; but would you like to know what was the husband's state?

This bridegroom of the next day, "who could have been taken for the virgin of the night before," and this bride, "whose self-control gave no opportunity for conjecture." This husband who gets up and departs, "his heart filled with the joys of the previous night, his spirit calm, flesh content," and who goes away "pondering his happiness like those who after dinner still savor the taste of the truffles they are digesting."

I must insist, gentlemen, on showing up the hallmark of Monsieur Flaubert's literary brushstrokes. At times there are strokes that mean a great deal, and these strokes cost him nothing.

And then at the château de la Vaubyessard, do you know what draws the eye of this young woman, what strikes her most? It is always the same thing; it is the Duke de Laverdière, who was said to have "been Marie-Antoinette's lover between Messieurs de Coigny and de Lauzun" and at whom "Emma could not keep herself from staring, as on someone extraordinary and august. He had lived at Court and slept in the bed of queens!"

That is only a historical parenthesis, one might say? An unfortunate and useless parenthesis! History may be able to authorize suspicions, but it has no right to elevate them to certainties. History has spoken of the queen's necklace in any number of novels, history has spoken of a thousand things, but these are only suspicions, and, I repeat, I do not know that history has authorized anyone to transform these suspicions into certainties. And when Marie-Antoinette has died with the dignity of a sovereign and the calm of a Christian, the blood that has been shed ought to erase all faults, and even more so, suspicions. God knows, Monsieur Flaubert did need a striking image to depict his heroine, and he has chosen that particular one to express both Madame Bovary's depraved instincts and her ambition!

Madame Bovary is supposed to waltz very well, and here she is waltzing:

> They began slowly, then moved more rapidly. Everything was turning around them, the lights, furniture, paneling, and the floor, like a disk on a pivot. Passing near the doors, the hem of Emma's dress flared out against her partner's trousers; their legs intertwined; he looked down at her, she raised her eyes to him; a numbness overcame her, she stopped. They started again and the viscount, with a more rapid movement, swept her away, disappeared with her to the end of the gallery, where, out of breath, she almost fell and for one moment leaned her head on his chest. And then, still turning, but more gently now, he led her back to her place; she leaned back against the wall and put her hand before her eyes.

I know very well that people do waltz a little in this way, but that does not make it any the more moral.

Take Madame Bovary in her most simple actions. It is always the same kind of brushwork, the same on every page. Even Justin, the servant of the druggist next door, is suddenly awestruck when he is received in the privacy of this woman's dressing room. He is haunted by his voluptuous admiration even in the kitchen:

> His elbow on the long board on which she [Félicité, Madame Bovary's maid] was ironing, he would look avidly at all the female garments strewn around him: dimity petticoats, fichus, muslin collars, and pantaloons with drawstrings, voluminous around the hips and tapering near the bottom.
>
> "What's this for?" the boy would ask, stroking a crinoline or fingering some hooks.
>
> "Haven't you ever seen anything?" Félicité replied with a laugh. . . .

The husband also wonders, in the presence of this sweet-smelling woman, if the scent comes from her skin or from her petticoat:

> . . . every night he would come home to a glowing fire, the table set, the furniture arranged comfortably, and a charming woman, neatly dressed, smelling so fresh you wondered where the fragrance came from and whether it wasn't her skin lending the scent to her petticoat.

Enough quoting of details! Now you know how Madame Bovary appears in repose, when she is tantalizing no one, when she is not sinning, when she is still completely innocent, when on her return from an appointment she is not yet beside a husband whom she detests; now you understand the general color of the painting, the general appearance of Madame Bovary. The author has taken the greatest pains, has employed all the marvels of his style to paint this woman. Has he tried to show her from the point of view of intelligence? Never. Of feeling? That neither. Of mind? No. Of physical beauty? Not even that. Oh! I know very well that there is a most brilliant portrait of Madame Bovary after the adultery; but the picture is primarily lascivious, the poses are voluptuous, the beauty of Madame Bovary is the beauty of enticement.

I now come to the four principal passages; I shall quote only four; I intend to limit my field. I have said that the first concerns the love affair with Rodolphe, the second the religious conversion, the third the affair with Léon, and the fourth her death.

Let us look at the first. Madame Bovary is near to her downfall, ready to succumb: "The domestic monotony" pushed her to luxurious fancies, "the conjugal embraces evoked adulterous desires. . . . She cursed herself for not having loved him [Léon]. She thirsted for his lips."

What had first captivated Rodolphe and put the thought into his head? The billowing of Madame Bovary's dress and its clinging to her bodice as she moved! Rodolphe has brought his servant to Bovary to have him bled. The servant faints, Madame Bovary is holding the basin:

> Madame Bovary picked the basin up to put it under the table. As she bent down, her dress (a yellow summer frock with four flounces, long-waisted and wide-skirted) billowed around her over the floor. She was slightly unsteady on her legs as she stooped and stretched her arms, and the folds of the fabric collapsed in a few places in response to her gestures.

Here also are Rodolphe's thoughts:

Ernest Pinard, the Imperial Attorney at the obscenity trial of Madame Bovary. *In 1879 Flaubert was amused to learn that Pinard, who professed so much virtue and religion during the trial, was actually an author of pornographic poetry (lithograph by Sirouy from a photograph by Adam-Salomon; cliché Bibliothèque nationale de France, Paris).*

> He pictured Emma in the room, first dressed as he had seen her and then nude.

This is the first day that they speak together:

> They were looking at one another. A supreme desire was causing their dry lips to quiver. Gently, without effort, their fingers intertwined.

Those are the preliminaries to her downfall. Now we must read the downfall itself:

> When the outfit was ready, Charles wrote to Monsieur Boulanger that his wife awaited his convenience and that they were counting on his kindness.
>
> At noon the next day Rodolphe arrived at Charles's door with two riding horses. One had pink pompons on its ears and a buckskin sidesaddle.
>
> Rodolphe was wearing high soft-leather boots. He told himself that she had probably never seen their like. Emma was indeed charmed by his appearance when he

IMAGES OF EMMA

Sculptor and painter Albert Fourié (1854–1896) produced dozens of illustrations for scenes in Madame Bovary *that have been used in various editions of the novel published after Flaubert's death.*

Scene from part 1, chapter 7 (illustration by Albert Fourié; Madame Bovary. Mœurs de province, *3 volumes [Paris: Librarie Illustrée, 1900])*

Emma and Rodolphe, from part 2, chapter 9 (illustration by Albert Fourié; Madame Bovary. Mœurs de province, *3 volumes [Paris: Librarie Illustrée, 1900])*

Emma in the Hôtel de Bourgogne, from part 3, chapter 6 (illustration by Albert Fourié; Madame Bovary. Mœurs de province, *3 volumes [Paris: Librarie Illustrée, 1900])*

FLAUBERT ON ILLUSTRATIONS

During his life Flaubert did not allow any of his books to be illustrated. The issue was not raised when Madame Bovary *was first published but became a significant point of disagreement in regard to the publication of his second novel,* Salammbô *(1862), because publisher Michel Lévy believed that illustrations were appropriate for its exotic portrayal of ancient Carthage. For Flaubert, it was a question of aesthetic principle, as he explained in a 12 June 1862 letter to Ernest Duplan, who acted as his intermediary with Lévy:*

Never, as long as I'm alive, will I accept to have a novel of mine illustrated, because: the most beautiful literary description is destroyed by the worst drawing. Once a type is fixed with a pencil, it loses its general quality, its accordance with one thousand known objects that make the reader say: "I saw that" or "that must be."

When Flaubert, a few months before his death, allowed the publication of his play Le Château des cœurs *(translated as* The Castle of Hearts*) in the 24 January 1880 issue of* La Vie Moderne–*an illustrated literary journal directed by Émile Bergerat–he thought the illustrations were ridiculous and ruined his text.*

Léon Laurent-Pichat, owner and co-director with Du Camp of the Revue de Paris. *The prosecutor characterized Laurent-Pichat and his printer as "secondary defendants" in the case against Flaubert (cliché Bibliothèque nationale de France, Paris).*

appeared on the landing in his long velvet coat and his white tricot riding breeches. . . .

Emma's horse broke into a gallop as soon as it felt soft ground. Rodolphe kept alongside.

And there they are in the forest:

He led her farther along, around a small pond where the green duckweed covered the water. . . .

"I shouldn't, I shouldn't," she said. "I'm mad to listen to you."

"Why? Emma–Emma–"

"Oh, Rodolphe!" the young woman said slowly, leaning on his shoulder.

The cloth of her habit clung to the velvet of his coat. She threw back her head, her white throat swelled in a sigh, and without resisting, tears streaming, with a long shudder and her face hidden, she gave herself to him.

When she got up again, when, after having shaken off the languors of love, she returned home, to this home where she would find a husband who adored her, after her first transgression, after this first adultery, after this first fall, is it remorse, the sense of remorse that she feels in the face of this betrayed husband who adores her? No! With head held high, she returns home, glorifying adultery:

. . . when she saw her reflection in the mirror, she was astounded at her appearance. Her eyes had never been so large, so black, nor of such a depth. She was transfigured by some subtle change permeating her entire being.

She kept telling herself, "I have a lover! A lover!" relishing the thought like that of some unexpected second puberty. So she was finally going to possess those joys of love, that fever of happiness, of which she had so long despaired. She was entering into something marvelous where all would be passion, ecstasy, delirium. . .

Thus, from this first transgression, from this first fall, she makes a glory of adultery, she sings a hymn to adultery, to its poetry, its pleasures. There, gentlemen, is what I find much more dangerous, much more immoral than the downfall itself!

Gentlemen, all else pales beside this glorification of adultery, even the nighttime trysts several days later:

Rodolphe would announce his presence by throwing a handful of gravel against the shutters. She would jump up. Sometimes she had to wait because Charles had a habit of sitting by the fireside and chattering interminably.

She would rage with impatience. If looks could have done it, she would have pushed him out the window. Finally she would begin undressing, then pick up a book and start quietly reading with obvious pleasure. Charles, already in bed, would call to her.

"Emma, come to bed, it's late," he would say.

"I'm coming," she would answer.

But as the candles were too bright for his eyes, he would turn toward the wall and fall asleep. Then, holding her breath, she would sneak out of the room, a smile on her face and her heart pounding, half undressed.

Rodolphe had a voluminous cloak that he would wrap around her. He would wind his arms around her waist and lead her silently to the back of the garden.

They would stay in the arbor on the same bench of rotting wood where in the old days Léon had looked at her so lovingly in the summer nights. She rarely thought of him now.

The stars shone through the leafless jasmine branches. They could hear the river flowing behind them and an occasional crackling of dry reeds on the bank. Great masses of shadow loomed up against the obscurity, and sometimes, rising as if with a shudder, they would advance like huge black waves ready to engulf them. The cold of the night made them hold each other even more tightly; the sighs emerging from their lips seemed louder; their eyes, which they could discern only with difficulty, seemed even larger; and in the midst of the silence, their whispered words fell crystal clear on their souls and echoed and reechoed with continuing vibrations.

Gentlemen, do you know anywhere of a more expressive language? Have you ever seen a more lascivious painting? Listen further:

> Never had Madame Bovary been so beautiful as now. She had that indefinable beauty that comes from joy, enthusiasm, and success, a beauty that is but the blending of temperament with circumstances. Her desires, her regrets, her experience of sensual pleasure, and the continually youthful illusions had nurtured her gradually, as fertilizer, rain, wind, and sunshine nurture a flower, and she finally blossomed forth in all the fullness of her being. Her eyelids seemed purposely shaped for her long amorous gazes, in which the pupils disappeared, while her heavy breathing caused her delicately chiseled nostrils to flare and raised the fleshy corners of her upper lip (which was lightly shaded by a slight black down). One would have said that some artist skilled in depravity had arranged the coil of hair on the nape of her neck. It was wound carelessly, in a heavy mass, and loosened every day by the chance meetings with her lover. The inflections of her voice became more languid, and also her body. A certain penetrating subtlety detached itself even from the folds of her dress and the instep of her foot. As he had during the first days of their marriage, Charles now found her delicious and completely irresistible.

Until now this woman's beauty had consisted in her grace, in her appearance, in her clothes; at last she has been shown to you unveiled, and you can say if adultery has not made her more beautiful:

> "Take me away," she sobbed. "Take me away. Please!"
>
> She kissed him passionately, as if to draw the unexpected consent from his mouth.

There you have a portrait, gentlemen, as Monsieur Flaubert knows how to paint them. How this woman's eyes dilate! What an enchantment has been shed over her since her fall! Has her beauty ever been so dazzling as on the day after her downfall, as on the days which followed her sin? What the author is showing you is the poetry of adultery, and once more I ask you if these lascivious pages are not profoundly immoral!

I come now to the second passage. The second passage is about a religious change. Madame Bovary has been very ill, at death's door. She comes back to life, her convalescence is marked by a transitory religious period:

> Abbé Bournisien came to see her at that hour. He would ask about her health, bring her the news, and try to nudge her toward religion with some unctuous gossip that was not without charm. The very sight of his cassock comforted her.

At last she is going to take Communion. I do not very much like to find sacred matters treated in a novel, but if they are mentioned, they must at the very least not have been travestied by the language. Is there anything, in this adulterous woman who goes to Communion, of the faith of the repentant Magdalen? No, no, it is still the passionate woman looking for illusions, and who looks for them in the most sacred, the most august things.

> One day, at the height of her illness, she believed herself dying and asked for Communion; and as the preparations for the sacrament went on in her room, as they arranged the dresser with its clutter of medicine bottles into an altar and Félicité scattered dahlia petals over the floor, Emma sensed something powerful passing over her, freeing her from all her pains, from all perception and feeling. Her body, freed of its burden, no longer thought; another life was beginning; it seemed to her that her being, ascending toward God, was going to be destroyed in that love like a burning incense that is dissolved in smoke.

In what language does one pray to God with the words addressed to a lover in the effusions of adultery? We shall doubtless be told of local color, we shall hear the excuse that a romantic, fanciful woman does not, even in matters religious, do things like the rest of the world. There is no local color that excuses this mixture! Voluptuous one day, devout the next, no woman, even in other countries, even under the sky of Spain or of Italy, murmurs to God the adulterous endearments she gave to her lover: You will appraise this language, gentlemen, and you will not excuse these words of adultery introduced, as it were, into the sanctuary of the Divinity! That was the second passage; I come now to the third, which is about the continuation of adultery.

After the religious period, Madame Bovary is again ready to fall. She goes to the theater in Rouen. *Lucia di Lammermoor* was playing. Emma thought back on her past:

> Ah! If, in the freshness of her beauty, before the defilements of marriage and the disillusionments of adultery–[there are those who would have said "the disillusionments of marriage and the defilements of adultery"]–before the defilements of marriage and the disillusionments of adultery, she had been able to offer her life to some generous, solid heart. Then virtue, tenderness, sensual delights, and duty would have mingled. Never would she have fallen from such high happiness.

When she saw the actor Lagardy on the stage, "she wanted to run into his arms, to take refuge in his strength as in the incarnation of love itself, and to say to him, to cry out: 'Take me away, take me with you, let us go! I am yours, yours; all my passion and all my dreams are yours!'"

Léon was behind her:

> He stood behind her, leaning his shoulder against the wall of the box, and she quivered occasionally at the warm breath from his nostrils blowing into her hair.

A moment ago you were told of the defilements of marriage; now again adultery is going to be shown to you in all of its poetry, its ineffable charm. I have said that the author might at least have modified the expressions and said "the disillusionments of marriage and the defilements of adultery." Very often, when one is married, instead of the cloudless happiness one had expected, one encounters sacrifice and bitterness. The word "disillusionment" may therefore be justified; the word "defilement" cannot be.

Léon and Emma made a rendezvous at the cathedral. They conversed there, where people do not converse. They went out:

> A street urchin was playing on the pavement. "Get me a cab!" The child flew off like a shot . . .
>
> "Ah! Leon, really–I don't know–if I ought–" she simpered. Then, with a more serious expression: "It's very improper, you know."
>
> "How so?" answered the clerk. "It's done in Paris!" And that statement convinced her. It was an irresistible argument.

We know now, gentlemen, that her downfall did not take place in the cab. Because of scruples that do him honor, the editor of the *Revue* suppressed the passage about her downfall in the cab. But if the *Revue de Paris* draws the blinds of the cab, it allows us to enter the room where their trysts take place.

Emma wants to leave, for she had promised that she would return the same evening. "Besides, Charles was expecting her; and she already felt in her heart that

The cathedral of Rouen, 1842. In the book version of the novel, Emma commits adultery in the cab with her second lover, Léon, after being given a tour of the cathedral by an enthusiastic Swiss guide (drawing by Chapuy; cliché Bibliothèque nationale de France, Paris).

cowardly submissiveness that is, for many women, both the punishment and the atonement of their adultery."

> Léon would keep walking along the sidewalk. She would follow him to his hotel. He would go up, open the door, and go in; and then, what a passionate embrace!
>
> After the kisses came an outpouring of words. They told each other all the woes of the past week, their misgivings, their anxieties about letters; but now all that was forgotten and they looked at each other laughing with sensual delight and uttering terms of endearment.
>
> The bed was a large mahogany one shaped like a boat. The red silk curtains that hung from the ceiling were bunched very low near the bell-shaped headboard–and nothing in the world was as beautiful as her dark hair and white skin standing out against the deep red when she covered her face with her two hands in a gesture of modesty and revealed her nude arms.
>
> The warm room with its noise-muffling rug, its gay ornaments, and soft light, seemed exactly right for the intimacies of passion.

Emma and Léon in the cathedral in Rouen (illustration by Albert Fourié; Madame Bovary, *2 volumes [Philadelphia: Printed for subscribers only by George Garie & Sons, 1897])*

You see what takes place in that room. It is another passage of great importance–as a lascivious painting!

> How they loved that dear room filled with gaiety, despite its slightly faded splendor. They always found the furniture as they had left it, and sometimes even found hairpins beneath the base of the clock that she had forgotten the previous Thursday. They would sit and eat by the fire on a small table inlaid with rosewood. Emma would carve the food and put the pieces into his plate, chattering all the while, and she would laugh loudly and dissolutely when the champagne froth spilled over the fragile glass onto the rings on her fingers. They were so completely lost in each other that they actually believed they were living in their own house and would remain there until death like a couple eternally young. They said *our room, our rug, our armchairs,* she even said *our slippers.* They were a gift from Léon, in response to a whim of hers–pink satin slippers trimmed with swansdown. Her leg dangled in midair when she sat on his lap, since she was too short for it to reach the floor; and the charming backless little slipper was held on solely by the toes of her bare foot.
>
> For the first time in his life he was tasting the inexpressible subtlety of feminine grace. He had never before encountered this refinement of speech, this quiet elegance of dress, these poses of a soothed dove. He admired the raptures of her spirit and the laces of her petticoat. Moreover, wasn't she "a woman of the world"–and a married woman? In other words, a real mistress.

There, gentleman, was a description that will leave no doubt, I hope, as to the justification of our criminal charge? Here is another, or rather, here is the continuation of the same scene:

> She offered tender words and kisses that drove him mad. Where, where had she learned this corruption, so deep and yet so disguised that it appeared almost disembodied?

Oh! I can understand the disgust her husband inspired in her when he would embrace her on her return; I can understand perfectly that when meetings of this kind had taken place, she felt a horror at night at having "to sleep next to him."

This is not all; there is a last picture that I cannot omit; she had finally become wearied by passion:

> She kept promising herself a profound joy for their next meeting; then she would admit to herself that she

> had felt nothing extraordinary. This disappointment soon gave way to a renewed hope, and Emma would return to him more impassioned and avid. She would undress savagely, tearing at the thin lacing of her corset, which fell down around her hips like a gliding snake. She would tiptoe on her bare feet to see once more if the door were locked, then she would drop all her clothes in one movement–and pale, without speaking, solemn, she would fall against his chest with one long shudder.

Here I point out two things, gentlemen: a painting which is admirable with respect to talent, but a painting which is abominable from the point of view of morality. Yes, Monsieur Flaubert knows how to beautify his paintings with all the resources of art, but without the circumspection of art. With him there is no reticence, no veil; he shows nature in all of its nudity, in all of its coarseness!

Here is another passage:

> They knew each other too well to feel those mutual revelations of possession that multiply its joys a hundredfold. She was as sated with him as he was tired of her. Emma was finding in adultery all the banalities of marriage.

Banalities of marriage, poetry of adultery! Sometimes it is the defilement of marriage, sometimes it is banalities, but always it is the poetry of adultery. You see, gentlemen, the situations Monsieur Flaubert likes to portray, and unhappily he portrays them all too well.

I have related three scenes: the scene with Rodolphe, and there you have seen her downfall in the forest, the glorification of adultery, and this woman whose beauty becomes all the greater because of its poetry. I have spoken of the religious period, and there you have seen prayer borrow its language from adultery. I have spoken of the second affair, I have unrolled the scenes which took place with Léon. I have shown you the scene in the cab–which was suppressed–but I have shown you the picture of their room and of the bed. Now that we believe that our case is established, let us come to the final scene, to the scene of torment.

Many cuts have been made here, apparently by the *Revue de Paris*. Here are the terms in which Monsieur Flaubert protests against this: "For motives that I have not been able to determine, the *Revue de Paris* has felt obliged to make a deletion in the issue of December first. Their scruples having been renewed at the time of the present issue, they have thought fit to remove several further passages. In consequence, I disclaim responsibility for the lines that follow; the reader is begged therefore to regard them only as fragments and not as a whole."

And so let us pass over these fragments and come to the death scene. She poisons herself. She poisons herself, and why? "It's really quite simple to die," she thought. "I'll fall asleep and it will all be over." Then, without a regret, without a confession, without a tear of repentance for her present suicide and for her past adulteries, she is to receive the Last Sacrament. Why the Sacrament, when, in her thoughts just before, she is going into nothingness? Why, when there is not a tear, not a sigh of repentant Magdalen for her sin of disbelief, for her suicide, for her adulteries?

After this scene comes that of the Last Sacrament. These are holy and sacred words to us. It is with these words that we have closed the eyes of our forbears, of our fathers or our near ones, and it is with these same

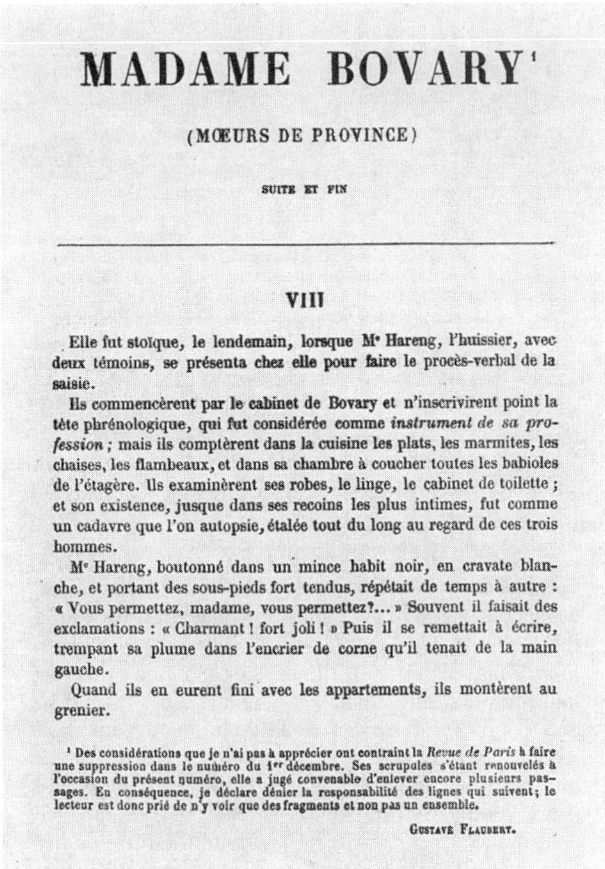

MADAME BOVARY[1]

(MŒURS DE PROVINCE)

SUITE ET FIN

VIII

Elle fut stoïque, le lendemain, lorsque Mᵉ Hareng, l'huissier, avec deux témoins, se présenta chez elle pour faire le procès-verbal de la saisie.

Ils commencèrent par le cabinet de Bovary et n'inscrivirent point la tête phrénologique, qui fut considérée comme *instrument de sa profession* ; mais ils comptèrent dans la cuisine les plats, les marmites, les chaises, les flambeaux, et dans sa chambre à coucher toutes les babioles de l'étagère. Ils examinèrent ses robes, le linge, le cabinet de toilette ; et son existence, jusque dans ses recoins les plus intimes, fut comme un cadavre que l'on autopsie, étalée tout du long au regard de ces trois hommes.

Mᵉ Hareng, boutonné dans un mince habit noir, en cravate blanche, et portant des sous-pieds fort tendus, répétait de temps à autre : « Vous permettez, madame, vous permettez?... » Souvent il faisait des exclamations : « Charmant ! fort joli ! » Puis il se remettait à écrire, trempant sa plume dans l'encrier de corne qu'il tenait de la main gauche.

Quand ils en eurent fini avec les appartements, ils montèrent au grenier.

[1] Des considérations que je n'ai pas à apprécier ont contraint la *Revue de Paris* à faire une suppression dans le numéro du 1ᵉʳ décembre. Ses scrupules s'étant renouvelés à l'occasion du présent numéro, elle a jugé convenable d'enlever encore plusieurs passages. En conséquence, je déclare dénier la responsabilité des lignes qui suivent; le lecteur est donc prié de n'y voir que des fragments et non pas un ensemble.

GUSTAVE FLAUBERT.

Page from the last installment of Flaubert's novel, in the 15 December 1856 issue of the Revue de Paris. *Flaubert insisted on the insertion of the note at the bottom of the page: "Considerations which it is not in my province to judge compelled the* Revue de Paris *to omit a passage from the issue of December 1; its scruples having been again aroused on the occasion of the present issue, it has thought proper to omit several more. Consequently, I hereby decline responsibility for the lines which follow. The reader is asked to consider them as a series of fragments, not as a whole" (*The Letters of Gustave Flaubert, 1830–1857; *cliché Bibliothèque nationale de France, Paris).*

words that our children one day will close our own eyes. If one wants to reproduce them, it must be done exactly; at the very least they must not be accompanied by sensual images from the past.

You know it, the priest makes the holy unction on the forehead, the ears, the mouth, the feet, while pronouncing the liturgy: *Quidquid per pedes, per aures, per pectus,* etc., always followed by the words *misericordia.* . . . Sin on the one hand, mercy on the other. These holy and sacred words must be reproduced exactly; if they are not reproduced exactly, at least do not introduce anything sensual.

> She turned her head slowly and seemed suffused with joy at the sudden sight of the purple stole–probably rediscovering in this instant of extraordinary peace the lost ecstasy of her first flights of mysticism and beginning to have visions of eternal bliss.
>
> The priest stood up to take hold of the crucifix. She stretched out her neck like one who is thirsty, and pressing her lips to the body of the Man-God, she placed on it, with all her fading strength, the most passionate kiss of love she had ever given. Then he recited the *Misereatur* and the *Indulgentiam,* dipped his right thumb into the oil, and began the unctions; first on the eyes, which had been so covetous of earthly splendors; then on the nostrils, avid for warm breezes and scents of love; then on the mouth, which had opened to emit lies, had groaned with pride, and had cried out in lust; then over the hands, which had reveled in sensual contacts; and finally on the soles of the feet, which had once moved so rapidly when she was hurrying to quench her desires and which now would walk no longer.

Now come the prayers for the dying, which the priest recites very low, and where at each verse the words "Christian soul, depart for a higher region" appear. They are murmured at the moment when the dying man's last breath escapes his lips. The priest recites them, etc.

> As the death rattle grew louder, the priest hurried his prayers. They mingled with Bovary's muffled sobs, and at times everything seemed to merge with the monotonous murmur of the Latin syllables that sounded like the tolling of a bell.

The author has thought fit to alternate these words, to make them into a sort of reply. He allows the intervention of a blind man on the sidewalk below, chanting a song whose profane words are a sort of response to the prayers for the dying.

> Suddenly there was a clatter of heavy clogs on the sidewalk and the tapping of a stick. Then a voice arose, singing raucously:
>
> Often the warmth of a lovely day
> Makes a girl dream of love. . . .
> There was a strong breeze that day
> And her short petticoat flew away!

It is at this moment that Madame Bovary dies.

Thus you have the picture: on the one hand the priest who recites the prayer for the dying, on the other the organ grinder who draws from the dying woman "a horrible, frenzied, despairing laugh–imagining that she could see the hideous face of the beggar standing out against the eternal darkness like a nightmare. . . . A convulsion pulled her back down on the mattress. They all drew near the bed. She was no more."

And then afterward, when the body is cold, the thing that must be respected above all is the corpse that the soul has quitted. When the husband is there, on his knees, mourning his wife, when he has drawn the winding sheet over her, anyone else would have stopped short. And this is the moment when Monsieur Flaubert gives the final brushstroke:

> The sheet sagged between her breasts and her knees and then rose again over her toes.

That was the death scene. I have shortened and arranged it, as it were. It is for you to decide and to determine if this is a mingling of the sacred and the profane, or if it would not be something worse, a mingling of the sacred and the sensual.

I have told you the story of the novel, then I made my charges against it, and if I may say so, the style Monsieur Flaubert cultivates, and which he achieves without the circumspection but with all the resources of art, is the descriptive style: it is the realistic school of painting. And you see to what lengths he goes. Recently I happened to see an issue of *L'Artiste;* there is no question here of accusing *L'Artiste,* but only of learning Monsieur Flaubert's style, and I ask your permission to read you some lines that have no connection with the present trial, but that show to what extent Monsieur Flaubert excels in painting. He likes to paint temptations, above all those temptations to which Madame Bovary succumbed. Indeed I find a model of this style in the following few lines on the temptation of Saint Anthony, signed "Gustave Flaubert," in *L'Artiste* for the month of January. God knows it is a subject on which one can say many things, but I do not think that it would be possible to give more vividness to the image, more brilliance to the apollonian portrait of Saint Anthony: "Is this wisdom? Is this glory? Would you rest your eyes on dewy jasmine? Would you feel your body plunge into the sweet flesh of ecstatic women as if into a wave?"

It is indeed the same color, the same power of brushwork, the same vividness of expression!

I must now sum up. I have analyzed the book, I have told the story without omitting a page, then I made my charge, which was the second part of my task. I have specified a few portraits, I have shown Madame Bovary in repose, in relation to her husband, in relation to those whom she should not have tempted, and I have dwelt upon the lascivious colors of her portrait! Then I analyzed several important scenes: the downfall with Rodolphe, the religious period, the affair with Léon, and the death scene, and in all of them I found offenses against public morality and against religion.

I require only two scenes; for the offense against morality, will you not see it in the downfall with Rodolphe? Will you not see it in this glorification of adultery? Will you not see it, above all, in what takes place with Léon? And then, for the offense against religious morality, I find that in the passage about her confession (p. 56), in the religious period (p. 207), and finally in the last death scene.

Gentlemen, you have three defendants before you: Monsieur Flaubert, the author of the book; Monsieur Pichat, who accepted it; and Monsieur Pillet, who printed it. In such matters there is no offense without publicity, and all who have collaborated in the publicity should be equally penalized. But we hasten to add that the owner of the *Revue* and the printer are only secondary defendants. The principal person accused is the author, Monsieur Flaubert; Monsieur Flaubert, who, when informed by the editors, protested against the deletions made in his book. After him, in second place, comes Monsieur Laurent Pichat, whom you will call to account, not for the deletions he did make, but for those that he should have made; and finally, in third place comes the printer, who is the advance guard against scandal. In all other respects, Monsieur Pillet is a reputable man and I have nothing whatever against him. In regard to him we ask only one thing, that you enforce the law. Printers must read; when they have not read a book or had it read, they print at their own risk and peril. Printers are not machines; they are licensed, they take oath, they are in a special situation, they are responsible. Again I repeat, if you permit me the expression, that they are like an advance guard; if they allow the offense to pass, it is as if they allowed the enemy to pass. Mitigate the penalty as much as you wish with regard to Pillet; be just as indulgent with regard to the director of the *Revue;* but for Flaubert, the principal culprit, for him you must reserve all your severity!

I have performed my task; we must now expect or anticipate objections. As a general objection, the defense will say to us, "But, after all, is the novel not fundamentally moral, since the adulterous woman is punished?"

To this objection there are two replies: assuming a moral work, hypothetically speaking, a moral ending could not pardon the lascivious details that could be found in it. And therefore I say the book fundamentally is not moral.

I say, gentlemen, that lascivious details cannot be screened by a moral ending, otherwise one could recount all the orgies imaginable, one could describe all the depravities of a harlot, so long as she were made to die on a pallet in the poorhouse. It would be permissible to study and to show all of her lascivious attitudes! It would be running counter to all the rules of common sense. It would be to place poison within the reach of all, and the remedy within the reach of a very few, if there is a remedy. Who is it who reads Monsieur Flaubert's novels? Are they the men engaged in social or political economy? No! The light pages of *Madame Bovary* fall into hands that are even lighter, into the hands of young girls, sometimes of married women. Well then! When the imagination will have been seduced, when this seduction will have reached into the heart, when the heart will have spoken to the senses, do you think that a very dispassionate argument will be very effective against this seduction of the senses and the feelings? And besides, man must not presume too much on his strength and on his virtue; man gets his instincts from below and his thoughts from on high, and with all of us virtue is only the result of an effort that is very often painful. Lascivious paintings generally have more influence than dispassionate arguments. That is my reply to this theory; it is my first reply, but I have a second one.

I maintain that the story of Madame Bovary, considered from a philosophical viewpoint, is not at all moral. Doubtless Madame Bovary dies poisoned, and it is true that she has suffered much; but she dies at an hour of her choosing, and she dies not because she is an adulteress, but because she has wished to die; she dies in all of the glamour of her youth and beauty; she dies after having had lovers, leaving a husband who loves her, who adores her, who will find Rodolphe's portrait, who will find his letters and Léon's, who will read the letters of a wife who was twice an adulteress, and who after that will love her even more after she is dead. Who is there in the book who can condemn this woman? No one. That is the inference. There is not one character in the book who might condemn her. If you find in it one good character, if you find in it one single principle by virtue of which the adulteress is stigmatized, I am wrong. Consequently, if in all the book there is not an idea, not a line by virtue of which the

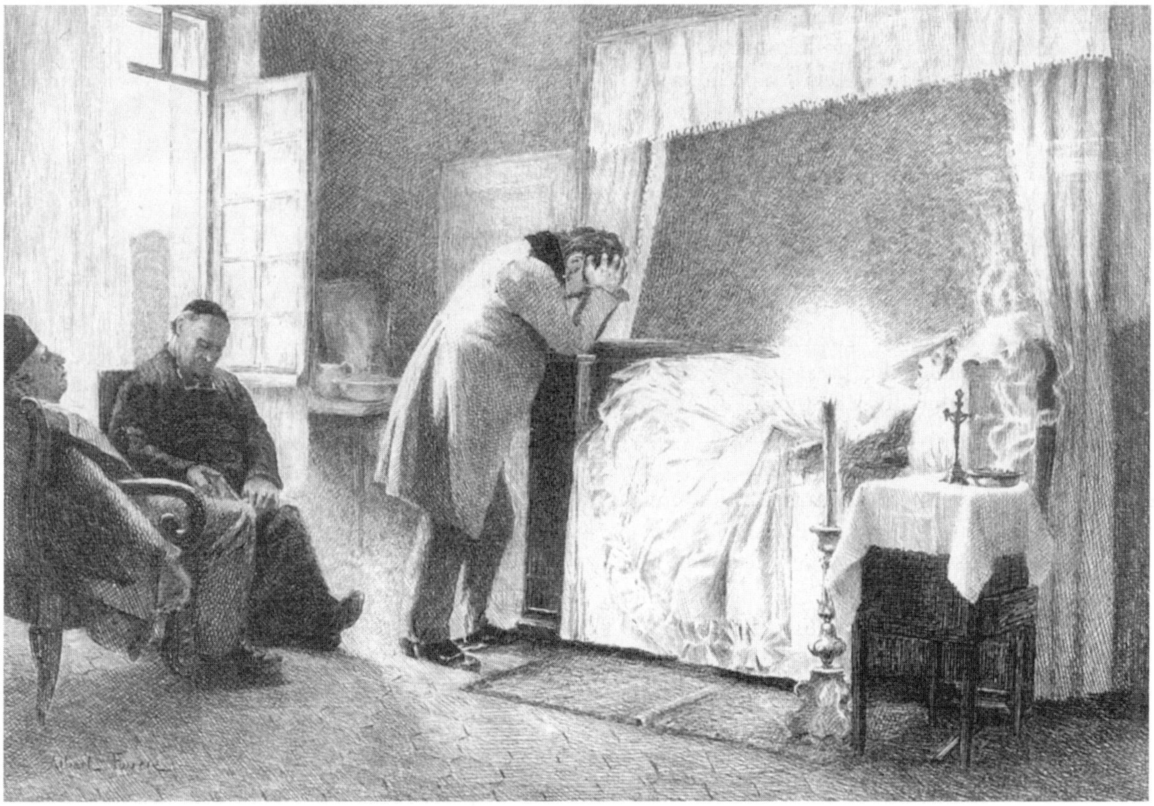

Emma's death (illustration by Albert Fourié; Madame Bovary, *2 volumes [Philadelphia: Printed for subscribers only by George Garie & Sons, 1897])*

adulteress is shamed, then it is I who am right: the book is immoral!

Might the book be condemned in the name of conjugal honor? But conjugal honor is represented by a compliant husband who, after his wife's death, on meeting Rodolphe, searches the lover's face for the features of the wife he loves (p. 321). I ask you this, can you stigmatize this woman in the name of conjugal honor when there is not a single word in the book in which the husband does not bow before the adulteress?

Would it be in the name of public opinion? But public opinion is personified by a grotesque being, by the druggist Homais, who is surrounded by ludicrous characters ruled by this woman.

Will you condemn it in the name of religious feeling? But you have this feeling personified in the Abbé Bournisien, a priest almost as grotesque as the druggist, who believes only in physical suffering, never in moral suffering, who is almost a materialist.

Will you condemn it in the name of the author's conscience? I do not know the opinion of the author's conscience, but in his Chapter IX, which is the only philosophical chapter in the book, I find the following sentence: "There is always a kind of numbness after a person's death, so difficult is it to understand this new state of nonexistence and to accept the fact that it has occurred. . . ."

This is not a cry of disbelief, but it is at least a cry of skepticism. Doubtless it is difficult to understand and to believe it, but when all is said and done, why is there this stupefaction in the face of death? Because its coming is something that is a mystery, because it is difficult to understand and to judge it, yet one must submit to it. As for myself, I say that if death is the coming of nonexistence, if the compliant husband feels his love increase on learning of his wife's adulteries, if opinion is represented by grotesque beings, if religious feeling is represented by a ludicrous priest, then one single person is in the right, prevails, rules: she is Emma Bovary. Messalina prevails against Juvenal.

That is the philosophical inference of the book, drawn not by its author, but by a man who pondered and thoroughly studied these things, by a man who searched for a character in the book who might have ruled this woman. There was none. The only character who rules is Madame Bovary. Hence one must search elsewhere than in the book, one must search in that Christian morality that is the foundation of modern civilization. In the light of this morality, everything becomes explained and clarified.

In its name, adultery is stigmatized and condemned, not because it is an imprudence that exposes one to disillusionments and to regret, but because it is a crime against the family. You stigmatize and you condemn suicide, not because it is a madness, for the madman is not responsible; not because it is a cowardly act, for it sometimes demands a certain physical courage; you condemn it because it is the contempt for one's duty in the life that is ending and the cry of disbelief in the life which is beginning.

This Christian morality stigmatizes realistic literature, not because it paints the passions: hatred, vengeance, love (the world only lives by these, and art must paint them)–but because it paints them without restraint, without bounds. Art without rules is no longer art; it is like a woman who throws off all garments. To impose upon art the single rule of public decency is not to enslave but to honor it. One grows only by a rule. Gentlemen, there you have the principles we profess; there you have the doctrine we conscientiously uphold.

–"Speech for the Prosecution," in "The Trial of *Madame Bovary,*" translated by Evelyn Gendel, *Madame Bovary* (New York: Signet, 1964), pp. 329–347

* * *

Antoine-Marie-Jules Sénard, who had been president of the Assemblée nationale as well as a minister, was at the time of the publication of Madame Bovary *a famous lawyer in Paris. It is certainly thanks to his clever speech for the defense that Flaubert and his co-defendants were acquitted. Part of Sénard's strategy was to prove with quotations that* Madame Bovary *was no more "lascivious" or "anti-religious" than works previously published by classic writers such as Samuel Richardson, Jacques-Bénigne Bossuet, and Charles de Secondat, Baron de Montesquieu as well as by important contemporary writers, such as Charles-Augustin Sainte-Beuve, Honoré de Balzac, and Prosper Mérimée. The poet Alphonse-Marie-Louis de Prat de Lamartine, who came to see Flaubert and congratulated him about his novel, promised to give him a supportive letter that could be used during the trial, which he never did; however, Sénard quotes some of Lamartine's private remarks to Flaubert. When the novel was published as a book in April 1857, Flaubert included a double dedication: the second page to Louis Bouilhet and the first to Sénard: "it is thanks to you, especially, that the novel could be published."*

Sénard for the Defense

. . . The public ministry attacks the book; I must take up the book itself in order to defend it; I must complete the quotations he has made, and for each accused passage I must show the nullity of the accusation. This will be my whole defense.

Antoine-Marie-Jules Sénard (lithograph by Fuhr for Le Panthéon des illustrations françaises au dix-neuvième siècle; *cliché Bibliothèque nationale de France, Paris)*

I shall certainly not attempt to outdo the public ministry by expressing more of the lofty, spirited, and touching opinions that surrounded all he said; the defense would not have the right to use such embellishments; it will content itself with showing the texts just as they are.

And at the outset I assert that nothing is more false than what has just been said about the lascivious tone. Lascivious tone! Just where have you found that? Has my client depicted that sort of woman in *Madame Bovary?* Eh! God knows it is sad but true, she is a young girl born decent as almost all of them are; but most of them, at least, are pretty frail when education, instead of strengthening, has weakened them or thrown them into an evil path. He has taken a young girl; has she a depraved nature? No, it is an impressionable nature, susceptible to highly charged emotions.

. . . .

Ah! You have accused us of mingling sensualism with the religious element in this picture of modern society! Rather accuse the society in which we live; do not accuse the man who, like Bossuet, cries out: "Awake and beware the danger!" Go rather and tell the fathers of families: "Take care, these are not good habits to give to your daughters; in all these mixtures of mysticism there is something that sensualizes religion." That would be to tell them the truth. It is on that account that you accuse Flaubert; it is on that account that I extol his conduct. Yes, he has done well to warn families in this way of the dangers of emotionalism to young girls attracted by petty practices instead of becoming attached to a strong and severe religion that would support them in their day of weakness. And now, you are going to see the purpose behind the trivial sins "as the priest whispers above."

> She had read *Paul and Virginia* and dreamed about the bamboo cottage, the Negro Domingo, and the dog Fidèle, but most of all about the sweet friendship of some dear little brother who gathers ripe fruit for you in huge trees taller than steeples or who runs barefoot over the sand, bringing you a bird's nest.

Is this lascivious, gentlemen?

THE IMPERIAL ATTORNEY: I have not said that this passage was lascivious.

MONSIEUR SÉNARD: I beg your pardon. It is precisely from this passage that you have plucked a lascivious phrase, and you have been able to find it lascivious only by isolating it from what precedes and follows it.

> Instead of following the Mass, she looked at the pious vignettes edged in azure in her book, and she loved the sick lamb, the Sacred Heart pierced with sharp arrows, and poor Jesus stumbling as He walked under His cross. She tried to fast one entire day to mortify her soul. She attempted to think of some vow to fulfill.

Do not forget that; if she invents trivial sins to confess and attempts to think of some vow to fulfill, as we now find in the preceding line, evidently she has had her ideas slightly warped somewhere. And I ask you now if I need to dispute your passages! But I continue:

> In the evening, before prayers, some religious selection would be read at study. During the week it was a summary of Abbé Frayssinous's religious-history lectures and on Sunday, for relaxation, passages from *Le Génie du Christianisme*. How she listened, those first times, to the sonorous lamentation of romantic melancholy being echoed throughout the world and unto eternity! Had her childhood been spent in an apartment behind a store in some business district, she might have been receptive to nature's lyric effusions that ordinarily reach us only via the interpretations of writers. But she knew the countryside too well; she knew the lowing of the flocks, the milking, and the plowing. Accustomed to the calm life, she turned away from it toward excitement. She loved the sea only for its storms, and trees only when they were scattered among ruins. She needed to derive immediate gratification from things and rejected as useless everything that did supply this satisfaction. Her temperament was more sentimental than artistic. She sought emotions and not landscapes.

Now you will see with what delicacy the author introduces that good old maid and how he teaches religion by slipping a new element into the convent–the novels that are introduced by this person from outside. Never forget that when it comes to judging the religious morality.

> There was an old maid who came to the convent for one week every month to work in the laundry. Protected by the archbishop because she belonged to an old aristocratic family ruined during the Revolution, she ate in the refectory at the good sisters' table and would chat with them for a while after dinner before returning to her work. The girls would often steal out of class to visit her. She knew the romantic songs of the past century by heart and would sing them softly as she plied her needle. She told stories, brought in news of the outside world, ran errands in the city, and would secretly lend the older girls some novel that she always kept in the pocket of her apron, of which the good creature herself devoured long chapters between tasks.

This is not only marvelous from a literary point of view: acquittal cannot be denied the man who writes such admirable passages pointing out to everyone the perils of this kind of education and showing a young woman the dangers of the life in which she is about to embark. Let us continue:

> It was always love, lovers, mistresses, persecuted women fainting in solitary little houses, postilions expiring at every relay, horses killed on every page, gloomy forests, romantic woes, oaths, sobs, tears and kisses, small boats in the moonlight, nightingales in the groves, gentlemen brave as lions, gentle as lambs, impossibly virtuous, always well dressed, who wept copiously. For six months, at the age of fifteen, Emma soiled her hands with these dusty remains of old reading rooms. Later, with Walter Scott, she grew enamored of historic events, dreamed of traveling chests, guardrooms, and minstrels. She wished that she had lived in some old manor, like those long-waisted ladies of the manor who spent their days under the trefoil of pointed arches, elbows on the rampart and chin in band, watching a cavalier with a white feather emerge from the horizon on a galloping black charger. During that period she had a passion for Mary Stuart and adored unfortunate or celebrated women. Joan of Arc, Héloise, Agnès Sorel, La Belle Ferronnière, and Clémence Isaure blazed for her like comets over the murky immensity of history, on which, still standing out in relief, but more lost in the shadow and with no relationship to each other, were Saint Louis with his

oak, the dying Bayard, a few vicious crimes of Louis XI, a bit of the Saint Bartholomew Massacre, Henri IV's plume, and the continuing memory of the painted plates praising Louis XIV.

In the ballads she sang in music class there were only tiny angels with golden wings, madonnas, lagoons, gondoliers–gentle compositions that enabled her to perceive, through the foolishness of the style and the weaknesses of the music, the attractive fantasy of sentimental realities.

What, you did not remember that? When, after returning to the farm and marrying a village doctor, this poor country girl is invited to a ball at the château–you did not remember that when you tried to draw the court's attention to the ball scene to show something lascivious in the waltz she was dancing! You did not remember her education when this invitation transported her from her husband's humble home to the château and the poor woman was dazzled by the sight of these handsome men and beautiful ladies and this old duke, who was said to have enjoyed good fortune at court . . . ! The imperial attorney indulged in a fine outburst on the subject of Queen Marie-Antoinette! Assuredly there is not one of us who does not share your

Marie-Antoinette on the way to the guillotine. Sénard rejected the prosecutor's assertion that Flaubert needlessly insulted the former queen (sketch by Jacques-Louis David; British Museum).

thought. Like you, we trembled to hear the name of this victim of the Revolution, but the subject here is not Marie-Antoinette; it is the château de la Vaubyessard.

There was an old duke there who was the object of all eyes and who–so people said–had had relations with the queen. And when this young woman was thus transported into this world and saw the realization of all the fantastic dreams of her youth, you are astonished at the intoxication she felt; you accuse her of having been lascivious! But rather accuse the waltz itself that people dance at our large modern balls, and in which, as an author has described it, "the woman leans on the shoulder of her partner, whose leg clings to hers." You find Madame Bovary lascivious as Flaubert describes her. But there is not a man, and I do not except yourselves, who, having attended a ball and seen this sort of waltz, has not wished that his wife or his daughter would forego this pleasure that contains something so wild. If one counts on a young girl's purity to protect her and sometimes allows her to give herself to this pleasure that has been sanctioned by fashion, one must count very heavily on that protection; and however heavily one counts on it, she will very possibly show the same effects Monsieur Flaubert has shown in the name of morality and purity.

There she is at the château de la Vaubyessard; there she is gazing at this old duke, observing the scene with rapture, and you cry out: "What details!" Just what can that mean? Details? Details are everywhere when one quotes only a single passage.

Madame Bovary noticed that several of the women had not put their gloves in their wineglasses.

At the upper end of the table, alone among all the women, there was one old man eating, bending over the well-filled platter with his napkin knotted in back like a child, drops of sauce dribbling from his mouth. His eyes were bloodshot and he wore a small pigtail tied with a black ribbon. It was the marquis' father-in-law, the old Duke of Laverdière, once favorite of the Count d'Artois in the days of the Marquis de Conflans's hunting parties in Vaudreuil; it was said he had been Marie-Antoinette's lover between Messieurs de Coigny and de Lauzun.

Defend the queen, defend her above all before the scaffold; say that her title deserves respect, but spare your accusations when all that has been said is that according to gossip, the duke had once been the queen's lover. Can you be serious in accusing us of having insulted the memory of this unfortunate woman?

He had led a thoroughly debauched life, filled with duels, wagers, and abductions, had run through his fortune and been the terror of his entire family. A servant behind his chair was shouting into his ear the names of dishes that the old man would point to with his finger,

> mumbling. Emma could not keep herself from staring at the slack-mouthed old man as on someone extraordinary and august. He had lived at Court and slept in the bed of queens!

Although these descriptions are undeniably charming, you see that it is not possible to pick out a line here and there from which to create a kind of lascivious tone, against which one's conscience would protest. It is not a lascivious tone; it is the tone of the book that is at the same time its literary principle and its moral principle.

There she is, this young girl who has received this education, there she is become a woman. The imperial attorney has said: "Did she even try to love her husband?" But he has not read the book; if he had read it, he would not have raised this objection.

There she is, gentlemen, this poor woman; at the outset she will indulge in daydreams. On page 60 you will see her daydreams. And there is more, there is something of which the imperial attorney has not spoken and which I must point out to you: these are her impressions on her mother's death–and you will see if that too is lascivious! Now if you will be good enough to turn to page 58 and to follow me:

> She cried a great deal the first days after her mother's death. She had a memorial picture made with the dead woman's hair, and in a letter that she sent to Les Bertaux, all filled with sad reflections about life, she asked to be buried in the same tomb when she died. Her father thought she must be ill and came to see her. Emma was inwardly pleased to feel that she had achieved at her first attempt this rare ideal of pallid existence that mediocre hearts never achieve. She let herself glide in to Lamartinian meanderings, listened to all the harps on the lake, to the songs of dying swans, to all the falling leaves, the pure virgins rising to heaven, and the voice of the Eternal reverberating in the valleys. She tired of this, didn't want to admit it, continued first out of habit, then out of vanity, and was finally surprised to find herself soothed and with as little sadness in her heart as wrinkles on her forehead.

Now I wish to reply to the imperial attorney's objection that she made no effort to love her husband.

THE IMPERIAL ATTORNEY: I have not objected to that; I said that she had not succeeded.

MONSIEUR SÉNARD: If I have misunderstood you, if you have not made this objection, that is the best reply that we could have. I thought I heard you make it; let us agree that I was mistaken. Moreover, here is what I find at the bottom of page 62:

> And yet, in line with the theories she admired, she wanted to give herself up to love. In the moonlight of the garden she would recite all the passionate poetry she knew by heart and would sing melancholy adagios to him with sighs, but she found herself as calm afterward as before and Charles didn't appear more amorous or moved because of it.
>
> After she had several times struck the flint on her heart without eliciting a single spark, incapable as she was of understanding that which she did not feel or of believing things that didn't manifest themselves in conventional forms, she convinced herself without difficulty that Charles's passion no longer offered anything extravagant. His effusions had become routine; he embraced her at certain hours. It was one habit among others, like the established custom of eating dessert after the monotony of dinner.

On page 63 we will find a mass of similar things. Now we see the danger about to begin. You know how she had been brought up; this is what I beg you not to forget for an instant.

After reading these last six pages, there is no man who would not say, the book in his hand, that Monsieur Flaubert is not only a great artist but also a man of feeling, for he has diverted all of the horror and contempt toward the wife and all of the sympathy toward the husband. He is an even greater artist because he has not transformed the husband, because he has left him to the end just as he was: a good man, common and mediocre, performing his professional duties, faithfully loving his wife, but lacking in refinement, lacking in any aspiration of mind. He is the same at his wife's deathbed. And yet there is no other character one remembers with more sympathy. Why? Because he has kept his simplicity and his goodness of heart up to the end; because up to the end he performed his duty, from which his wife had strayed. His death is as beautiful and as moving as his wife's death is hideous. The author has shown the stains left on the wife's corpse by the vomitings of poison; they have soiled the white sheet in which she will be shrouded; he wanted to make it an object of disgust. But there is a man who is sublime; he is the husband beside that grave. He is a man who is great and sublime, whose death is admirable; it is this husband, all of whose remaining illusions were successively destroyed with his wife's death, who embraces his wife with his dying thoughts. Remember this, I beg you; as Lamartine told him, the author has gone beyond what is permissable in rendering this woman's death hideous and her expiation most terrible. The author has known how to concentrate all sympathy on the man who had not swerved from the line of duty, who had kept his mediocre character, which doubtless the author could not have changed, but who also kept all his generosity of heart. And the author has heaped all horrors upon the death of the wife who deceived and ruined him, who gave herself to the moneylenders, who forged his name to promissory notes, and who finally arrived at suicide. We will see if this was the natural death for a woman who, had she not found the poison with which to end it, would have been crushed all the same under the weight of misfortune. That is what the author has done. His book would not be read if he had done otherwise, if he had not been lavish with the charming images and powerful pictures to which the prosecution objects, but which were needed to show where such a dangerous education as Madame Bovary's may lead.

Monsieur Flaubert constantly emphasizes the superiority of the husband over the wife, and what sort of superiority is this? It is that of duty fulfilled, while Emma strays from it! And then, placed as she is on the downward path of that unsuitable education, there she is after the ball scene, starting off with a young boy, Léon, as inexperienced as herself. She will flirt with him but will not dare go further; nothing will happen. Then comes Rodolphe, and he will take this woman. After having seen her for an instant, he says to himself; "She is all right, this woman!" And she will succumb to him because she is weak and inexperienced. As for her downfall, you will reread pages 159–162. I have only a word to say to you about this scene, there are no details, no description, not one image that paints the agitation of the senses; one single word indicates the fall: "She gave herself to him." Again I will beg you to be good enough to reread the details of the fall of Clarissa Harlowe, which I do not believe to have been described in a bad book. Monsieur Flaubert has substituted Rodolphe for Lovelace, and Emma for Clarissa. You will compare the two authors and the two works, and you will judge.

Samuel Richardson, the author of Clarissa *(1747–1748), a novel Sénard likens to* Madame Bovary *(portrait by Joseph Highmore; Thomas Eaves,* Samuel Richardson *[Oxford: Clarendon Press, 1971])*

But here I meet with the imperial attorney's indignation. He is shocked that remorse does not follow immediately upon the downfall and that instead of expressing bitterness she tells herself with satisfaction: "I have a lover." But the author would not be right if, while the cup was still at her lips, he made her taste all the bitterness of the enchanted potion. A man who would write as the imperial attorney expects might be moral, but he would be saying something that is not in human nature. No, it is not at the moment of the first transgression that the feeling of wrongdoing awakens; if that were so, it would not be committed. No, it is not at the moment when she is still under the intoxicating illusion that the intoxication itself may warn her of the immense wrong she has committed. She recalls only the rapture; she returns home happy and glowing, she sings in her heart: "At last I have a lover." But does this last for long? You have read pages 163 and 164. Two pages later, if you please, on page 165, the feeling of distaste for the lover has not yet appeared, but already she feels a sense of fear and anxiety. She observes, she considers, she wants never to leave Rodolphe:

> Something stronger than herself was pushing her toward him, so that one day, seeing her appear unexpectedly, he frowned as if he were annoyed.
>
> "What's the matter?" she asked. "Are you ill? Tell me!"
>
> He declared, very gravely, that her visits were becoming imprudent and that she was compromising herself.
>
> Gradually Rodolphe's fears began to affect her. At first she had been so drunk with love that she thought of nothing beyond it. But now that it was so indispensable to her life, she was terrified that it might be disturbed or even destroyed. She would look around anxiously when returning from his house, stare at every shadow on the horizon and each attic window in the village from which she might be seen. She strained her ears for the sound of footsteps, shouts, the noise of plows; and she would stop short, more pale and quivering than the poplar leaves swaying above her.

You see clearly that she is not mistaken; she feels strongly that there is something that is not what she had dreamed of. Let us take pages 169 and 170, and you will be even more convinced:

> When it rained, they took shelter in the consulting room, between the shed and the stable. She would light one of the kitchen candles, which she had hidden behind the books. Rodolphe would make himself as comfortable as if he were at home. The sight of the bookcase and the desk, of the entire room, intensified his gaiety; he could not refrain from making various jokes at Charles's expense, which Emma found embarrassing. She wanted him to be more serious and even more dramatic on occasion. Once, for example, she thought she heard approaching footsteps in the lane.
>
> "Someone's coming!" she said.
>
> He blew out the light.
>
> "Do you have your pistols?"
>
> "What for?"
>
> "To–to defend yourself," Emma said.
>
> "Against your husband? That poor fellow!" And Rodolphe finished his sentence with a gesture signifying: "I could crush him with a flick of the finger."
>
> She was amazed at his courage, although she sensed in it an indelicacy and blatant vulgarity that she thought shocking.
>
> Rodolphe thought a long while about this talk of pistols. If she had meant it seriously, it would be the height of idiocy, even odious, for he personally had no reason to hate good old Charles. Rodolphe was not a man "devoured with jealousy." Besides, in this connection Emma had made a solemn promise to him that, moreover, he did not find in the best of taste.
>
> She was also becoming quite sentimental. They had had to exchange miniatures and locks of hair and now she wanted a ring, an actual marriage band as a sign of eternal union. She would often speak to him of the bells of evening or of the "voices of nature." She would talk to him about her mother and his.

In short, she bored him.

Then on page 170:

> He [Rodolphe] no longer used words so sweet that they made her cry, as he had in the old days; nor were his caresses so ardent that they drove her mad. So the great love affair in which she had plunged seemed to diminish under her like the water of a river being absorbed into its own bed, and she began to see slime at the bottom. She didn't want to believe it and redoubled her tenderness. Rodolphe hid his indifference less and less.
>
> She did not know if she regretted having given in to him or if she wished, on the contrary, to love him even more. The humiliation of feeling how weak she was where he was concerned turned into a resentment tempered only by sensual pleasure. It was not an attachment, but a permanent seduction. He was subjugating her. She was almost afraid of him.

Emma and Rodolphe (illustration by Albert Fourié; Madame Bovary *[Paris, London & New York: Société des Beaux-Arts, 1915])*

And the imperial attorney fears that young women may read that! I am less frightened and less timid than you. For my part, I perfectly understand the father of a family who says to his daughter: "Young woman, if your heart, your conscience, your religious feeling, and the voice of duty do not suffice to show you the right path–look, my child, and see what anxiety, sorrow, pain, and grief await the woman who attempts to find happiness elsewhere than in her own home!" These words would not offend you coming from a father–very well then! Monsieur Flaubert has said nothing else; it is the truest, the most striking picture of what a woman immediately finds when she had dreamed of happiness outside her own home.

But let us go on; we are coming to all the disillusioning adventures. You object to Léon's caresses on page 250. Alas! Soon she will pay the price of adultery, and you will find it a terrible price, just a few pages after the passages you accuse. She has sought happiness in adultery, unhappy woman! But there, besides the disgust and weariness that the monotony of marriage may give the woman who does not walk in the path of duty, there she has found only disillusionment and the contempt of the man to whom she had given herself. Does anything mitigate his contempt? Oh no! Rodolphe, who has shown himself so base, gives her a final proof of egotism and cowardice. She says to him: "Take me away! Take me away! I am stifling, I can no longer breathe in my husband's house, which I have shamed and dishonored." He hesitates; she insists; finally he promises, and the next day she receives from him a crushing letter, under which she falls overwhelmed, annihilated. She falls ill, she is dying. The following installment shows her in all the convulsions of a struggling soul that may perhaps be drawn back to duty through the very intensity of its suffering. But unfortunately she soon encounters the youth with whom she had toyed when she had been still inexperienced. That is the progression of the novel, and then comes the expiation.

But the imperial attorney stops me and says: "Assuming that the work's intention is good from start to finish, would you be able to permit yourself such obscene details as those you have permitted?"

Most certainly I could not permit myself such details, but have I permitted them? Where are they? I come now to the most offending passages. I am no longer speaking of the adventure in the cab; the court has had satisfaction on that count. I come to the passages that you have pointed out as contrary to public morality and that constitute a certain number of pages in the issue of December first. And there is only one thing I need to do to demolish the entire support for your charge: I need only restore what precedes and what follows your quotations–in a word, to substitute the complete text for your fragments.

On page 265, Léon, after having been in touch with Homais the pharmacist, goes to the Hotel de Bourgogne, and then the pharmacist comes to see him.

> She had just left in exasperation. Now she detested him. His failure to keep his promise about their rendezvous seemed an outrage to her. She kept looking for other reasons to break with him: he was incapable of heroism; weak, commonplace . . .
>
> Then, calming down, she finally realized that she had probably unjustly condemned him. But the disparagement of those we love always erodes a bit of the affection. One must not touch idols; the gilt rubs off on one's hands.
>
> From now on, matters apart from their love entered into their correspondence. . . .

My God! It is because of the lines I am about to read that we are being prosecuted before you. Listen now:

> From now on, matters apart from their love entered into their correspondence. Emma's letters to him talked of flowers, poetry, the moon and the stars, naïve expedients of a weakening passion trying to revive itself by external devices. She kept promising herself a profound joy for their next meeting; then she would admit to herself that she felt nothing extraordinary. This disappointment soon gave way to a renewed hope, and Emma would return to him more impassioned and avid. She would undress savagely, tearing at the thin lacing of her corset, which fell down around her hips like a gliding snake. She would tiptoe on her bare feet to see once more if the door were locked, then she would drop all her clothes in one movement–and pale, without speaking, solemn, she would fall against his chest with one long shudder.

The imperial attorney has stopped there; permit me to continue:

Emma undressing for Léon (illustration by Albert Fourié; Madame Bovary *[Paris, London & New York: Société des Beaux-Arts, 1915])*

Yet there was something wild, something strange and tragic in this forehead covered with cold sweat, in those stammering lips and wildly staring eyes, in the embrace of those arms–something that seemed to Léon to be coming between them subtly as if to tear them apart.

You call that a lascivious tone; you say that it will give a taste for adultery; you say that those are pages that can inflame, arouse the senses–lascivious pages! But death is in these pages. You do not think of that, Mr. Imperial Attorney; you are shocked to find there the words "corset" and "she would drop all her clothes," and you cling to these three or four words of corset and dropping clothes! Would you like me to show how a corset may appear in a classic, a most classic book? This is what I shall give myself the pleasure of doing in a moment.

"She would undress–" Ah! Mr. Imperial Attorney, how you have misunderstood this passage! "She would undress savagely"–unfortunate woman–"tearing at the thin lacing of her corset, which fell down around her hips like a gliding snake . . . and pale, without speaking, solemn, she would fall against his chest with one long shudder. Yet there was something . . . strange and tragic in this forehead covered with cold sweat . . . in the embrace of those arms. . . ."

It is here that one must ask oneself where is the lascivious tone? And where is the stern tone? And if the young girl into whose hands this book may fall might find the senses aroused, inflamed–as in the reading of a classic of classics, a book that I shall quote to you shortly, that has been reprinted a thousand times, and that no attorney, imperial or royal, has ever dreamed of prosecuting. Is there anything analogous in what I am about to read to you? Or, on the contrary, does not this "something tragic that seems to come between them as if to tear them apart" arouse a horror of vice? Let us continue, if you will:

He did not dare question her; but seeing how experienced she was, he told himself that she must have known all the extremes of suffering and pleasure. What had once charmed him now frightened him a little. He was also rebelling against the increasing encroachment upon his personality. He resented Emma for this permanent victory over him, even tried not to want her; and then at the sound of her footsteps he felt himself grow weak like an alcoholic at the sight of strong liquor.

And that–is that lascivious?

And then take the last paragraph:

One day when they had parted early, she was walking alone along the boulevard. She noticed the walls of her convent and sat down on a bench in the shade of the elm trees. How calm those days had been! How wistful she was about the indescribable ideas of love she had tried to imagine for herself from books.

The first months of her marriage, her horseback rides in the forest, the viscount waltzing, and Lagardy singing–all of this passed before her eyes.

Do not forget that either, Mr. Imperial Attorney, when you would judge the author's intention, when you would absolutely insist on finding a lascivious tone where I can find only an excellent book.

And Léon suddenly appeared to be as far from her as the others. "But I love him!" she told herself. Nevertheless she was not happy, had never been happy. Why then was life so inadequate? Why did she feel this instantaneous decay of the things she relied on?

And is that lascivious?

If there existed somewhere a strong and handsome being, a valiant nature, imbued with both exaltation and refinement, the heart of a poet in the shape of an angel, a lyre with strings of bronze, sounding elegiac nuptial songs toward the heavens–why, why could she not find him? How impossible it seemed! And anyway, nothing was worth looking for; everything was a lie. Each smile hid a yawn of boredom, each joy a curse, each pleasure its aftermath of disgust, and the best of kisses left on your lips only the unattainable desire for a higher delight.

A metallic clang rang through the air and there were four strokes from the convent clock. Four o'clock! And it seemed to her that she had been there on that bench for eternity.

One must not search through one book for something to explain what is at the heart of another. I have read you the accused passage without adding a word to defend a work that is its own best defense. Let us continue our reading of this passage that has been accused of immorality.

Emma would stay in her room. No one went up. She would remain there all day long, in a torpor, only half dressed, burning incense that she had bought in Rouen in an Algerian shop. She managed by enough fussing to relegate Charles to the second floor so that she wouldn't have to sleep next to him. All night long she would read sensational books in which there were orgies and gory situations.

This makes one envy the adulteress, does it not?

Often she would be terrified by a sudden thought and scream. Charles would come running.

"Oh, go away," she would say.

> At other times, burning violently from her adulterous passion, panting and shaking, throbbing with desire, she would open her window, breathe in the cold air, let down her heavy mass of hair, and stare at the stars, yearning for the love of a prince. She would think of *him,* of Léon. At that moment she would have given anything for just one of those meetings that sated her desires.
>
> Those were her festive days–when they met. She wanted them to be splendid, and when he alone could not pay for them, she freely paid the difference. This happened nearly every time. He tried to make her understand that they would be just as comfortable elsewhere, in a more modest hotel, but she always objected.

You see how simple all of this is when one reads the whole, whereas with the imperial attorney's fragments the smallest word becomes a mountain.

THE IMPERIAL ATTORNEY: I have not quoted any one of those phrases, and even if you wish to quote what I have never accused, still you must not simply pass over page 270.

MONSIEUR SÉNARD: I am passing over nothing, I am stressing the phrases accused in the summons. We are indicted for page 271.

THE IMPERIAL ATTORNEY: I am speaking of the quotations made before the court, and I think that you are accusing me of having quoted the lines that you have just read.

MONSIEUR SÉNARD: Mr. Imperial Attorney, I have quoted all of the passages with whose aid you hoped to establish an offense that is now shattered. You developed your case before the court as you saw fit, and to you it was fair game. Happily, we have had the book; the defense knows the book–if we had not known it, allow me to say that our position would have been very strange. I was charged with defending such and such passages, and then in court other passages were substituted. Had I not the thorough knowledge of the book that I have, the defense would have been difficult. Now, I am showing you by careful analysis that far from having to be presented as lascivious, the book should, on the contrary, be considered as an eminently moral work. After having done this, I am taking the passages that inspired the criminal indictment, and after having reunited your fragments with what precedes and follows them, the minute that I read them to you the evidence becomes so weak that it shocks you yourself! Nevertheless I still have a good right to quote the same passages you pointed out as offensive an instant ago in order to make you see the nullity of your charge.

I now resume my quotation where I left it, on page 272:

> Now he [Léon] was bored when Emma would suddenly sob on his chest; and his heart, like people who can stand only a certain amount of music, languished with indifference amid the stridency of a love whose subtleties left him cold.
>
> They knew each other too well to feel those mutual revelations of possession that multiply its joys a hundredfold. She was as sated with him as he was tired of her. Emma was finding in adultery all the banalities of marriage.

The banalities of marriage. The man who plucked out this phrase has said: "What, here we have a man who says that in marriage there are only banalities! It is an attack against marriage, it is an outrage against morality!" You must agree, Mr. Imperial Attorney, that with artfully chosen fragments one can go far in pressing charges. Just what is it that the author has called the banalities of marriage? That monotony that Emma had dreaded and had wished to flee and that she had unfailingly rediscovered in adultery, and which was precisely disillusionment. And so you see very clearly that if one reads what precedes and follows instead of cutting out parts of phrases and single words, then nothing whatever remains of the accusation. And you will understand perfectly that my client, who knows his own intention, must be somewhat indignant to hear it misrepresented in this way. Let us continue:

> She was as sated with him as he was tired of her. Emma was finding in adultery all the banalities of marriage.
>
> But how could she break free? Though she felt humiliated by the base quality of such happiness, she clung to it out of habit or depravity. Each day she clung more desperately to it, thus destroying all happiness by demanding too much of it. She blamed Léon for her disappointed hopes as if he had betrayed her, and she even wished for some catastrophe that would cause their separation since she lacked the courage to bring it about herself.
>
> Nevertheless, this did not stop her from continuing to write him loving letters, in line with the idea that a woman should always be writing to her lover.
>
> But even as she wrote she perceived another man, a phantom fabricated from her most ardent memories . . .

What follows is no longer under indictment:

> . . . Then she fell back to earth, broken, for her surges of imaginary love tired her more than wild debauches.
>
> She was now living in a state of chronic and complete wretchedness. She would often receive summonses, official documents she barely glanced at. She wished she were dead, or continually asleep.

I call that an incitement to virtue by horror of vice, as the author himself declares, and which the most casual reader cannot but see unless he is unwilling.

And now something more to make you perceive the kind of man you have to judge. In order to show you, not the sort of justification I might make, but if Monsieur Flaubert had any lascivious tone at all, and where he takes his inspiration, let me give you this book he has used that inspired him to paint the wantonness, the seductions of this woman who seeks happiness in illicit pleasures and who cannot find it there, who seeks again, who seeks on and on, and who never finds it. And where has Flaubert taken his inspiration, gentlemen? From the book you see here; listen:

The Delusion of the Senses

> Whoever therefore becomes attached to the emotions must necessarily wander from object to object and become deceived, so to speak, in shifting position; thus concupiscence, which is love of pleasures, is always changing because all its fervor languishes and dies with continuity and it is only change that revives it. And so what else is the life of the senses but the alternate movement from desire to aversion, and from aversion to desire, while the soul hovers always uncertain between the abating and the rekindling passion. *Inconstantia, concupiscentia.* Inconstancy, thy name is concupiscence. There you have the life of the senses. Meanwhile, in this perpetual movement, one never ceases to be diverted by the sense of a ranging freedom.

There you have the life of the senses. And who was it who said that? Who wrote the words you have just heard on its excitements and unceasing fervors? What book is it whose pages Monsieur Flaubert constantly turns and that was his inspiration for the passages that the imperial attorney now accuses? It is Bossuet! What I have just read is a fragment of a discourse by Bossuet on *Illicit Pleasures.* I will make you see that all of these accused passages are, not plagiarized–a man who adapts an idea is not a plagiarist–but modeled on Bossuet. Would you like another example? Here it is:

On Sin

> And do not ask me, Christians, how this great alteration of our pleasures into torments takes place; the thing is proven by the Scriptures. It is the true God who tells it; it is the All Powerful who does it. And yet, if you consider the nature of the passions to which you surrender your heart, you will easily understand how they may become an intolerable torment. In themselves they all contain cruel punishments, loathings, and bitterness. They all contain a boundlessness that rages at being unable to find appeasement; a rage that sweeps them away, that degenerates into a kind of frenzy as painful as it is unreasoning. Love, if I may so name it from this pulpit, has its incertitudes, its violent agitations and irresolvable problems, and the hell of its jealousies.

Jacques-Bénigne Bossuet (1627–1704), an eminent theologian whom Sénard cited extensively as a sanction for Flaubert's handling of moral themes (cliché Musées Nationaux, Versailles)

And further on:

> Eh! What can be easier therefore than to turn our passions into the insupportable pain of our sins by removing from them, as is most just, that portion of sweetness by which they seduce us, thus leaving them only the cruel anxieties and the bitterness with which they abound? Our sins against us, our sins upon us, our sins surrounding us; an arrow piercing our breast, an insupportable weight upon our head, a poison devouring our entrails.

Is all of this not meant to show the bitterness of passion? I shall leave you this book, which is all annotated and worn by this studious man who took his ideas from it. And he who drew his inspiration from such a source, who has described adultery in the terms you have just heard–this man is prosecuted for outrage against public and religious morality!

I shall read a few more lines from Bossuet on *The Sinning Woman,* and you will see how Monsieur Flaubert, when he had to paint these passions, took inspiration from his model:

> But as we are punished for our wrongdoing without becoming disenchanted, we seek a new remedy for our mistake in change; we wander from object to object, and if we are finally held by someone, it is not that we are content with our choice, but that we are sated with our inconstancy . . .
>
> Everything in these creatures appeared to him to be empty, false, disgusting; his heart, far from rediscovering the first attractions against which it had been so difficult to defend itself, now saw in them only frivolity, danger, and vanity . . .
>
> I do not speak of an engagement of passion; what terrors are unleashed by secrecy! What precautions to be taken for the sake of the proprieties and for glory! How many eyes to avoid! How many observers to deceive! What qualms of fear as to the fidelity of the chosen servants and confidants of one's passion! What rebuffs to endure from the man for whom, perhaps, one has sacrificed happiness and freedom, and of which one would not dare complain! To all of that, add those cruel moments when slackening passion leaves us the leisure to reproach ourselves and to feel all the humiliation of our position; those moments when the heart, born for more substantial pleasures, wearies of its own idols and finds its torment in its aversion and in its inconstancy. Ungodly world! If that is your vaunted bliss, grant it to your worshipers, and in giving such happiness, punish them for the faith they have so carelessly placed in your promises!

Let me tell you this: when in the silence of the night a man has meditated upon the causes of corruption in women, when he has found them in education, and when, to express them and mistrusting his own observations, he has gone to the sources I have just mentioned; when he has taken up his pen only after having been inspired by the thoughts of Bossuet and of Massillon, may I ask if there is a word to express my surprise and distress on seeing this man summoned to police court for some passages in his book that express precisely the most noble ideas and sentiments he could have assembled! I beg you not to forget this when you think of the charge of outrage against religious morality. And then if I may, I will place before you in comparison what I myself would call an attack upon morality: the satisfaction of passions without bitterness, without those *drops of cold sweat* that fall from the brows of those who have succumbed to it. I will not quote from one of those licentious books whose authors have tried to inflame the senses; I will quote from a book that is given as a prize in our schools; I will only ask your permission not to reveal the author until after I have

*Jean-Baptiste Massillon (1663–1742), a renowned preacher Sénard named as one of Flaubert's inspirations (*Œuvres de Massillon, *volume 1 [Paris: Renovard, 1810]; courtesy of Thomas Cooper Library, University of South Carolina)*

read you a passage. I will now read the passage; then I will have the book passed to you. And I would rather see this book committed to justice than Monsieur Flaubert's.

> The next day I was led again to her apartment. There I perceived all that could enhance sensual pleasure. The most agreeable perfumes had been diffused in the room. She lay on a bed that was covered only by garlands of flowers. She appeared there in languid repose. She gave me her hand and made me sit beside her. Everything, including the veil that covered her face, had charm. I saw the lines of her beautiful body. A simple cloth stirred with her movements, by turns allowing me to lose and discover ravishing beauties.

A simple cloth, when it was drawn over a corpse, seemed to you to be a lascivious image; here it is drawn over a living woman.

> She noticed that my eyes were occupied, and as she saw them glow, the cloth seemed to fall open of itself; I saw all of the treasures of a divine beauty. In that moment she grasped my hand; my eyes roamed everywhere. I cried out: "Only my beloved Ardasire is so beautiful; but I call the gods to witness my fidelity . . ." She threw her arms around me and pressed me to her. All at once the room darkened, her veil opened; she

Charles de Secondat, Baron de Montesquieu (1689–1755), a president of the Academy of France, whose writing Sénard cited as a precedent for Flaubert's "lascivious" imagery (cliché Bibliothèque nationale de France, Paris)

> kissed me. I was utterly beside myself; a sudden flame throbbed through my veins and set all my senses afire. The thought of Ardasire receded. A trace of memory . . . but it seemed only a dream . . . I was going . . . going to herself rather than to the dream. Already my hands were on her breast; they roamed swiftly everywhere; love shows itself only by its passion; it rushed headlong to its victory; a moment more, and Ardasire could no longer defend herself.

Who has written that? It is not even the author of *La Nouvelle Héloise*–it is the president of the Academy of France: Monsieur de Montesquieu! Here there is no bitterness or disgust, all is sacrificed to literary beauty–and they give that as a prize to students of the classics, doubtless to serve as model for the exercises or the descriptions they are given to do. In *Les Lettres Persanes,* Montesquieu has described a scene that could not even be read aloud. It concerns a woman whom this author places between two men who contend for her. This woman placed thus between two men has dreams–which appear to her very agreeable.

Have we not succeeded, Mr. Imperial Attorney! Must we still quote Jean Jacques Rousseau in *Les Confessions* and elsewhere? No, I will only say to the court that if Monsieur Mérimée were prosecuted for his scene in the carriage in *La Double Méprise,* he would be acquitted at once. One would see his book only as a work of art, of great literary beauty. One would no more condemn him than one condemns paintings or sculptures that express not only the beauties of the human body but all its ardors and passions as well. I am not finished: I want your acknowledgment that Monsieur Flaubert has not exaggerated his images and that he has done only one thing–to draw the scene of degradation with a most masterly hand. He emphasized disillusionment in every line of his book, and instead of ending with something charming, he shows us this woman, after her contempt, neglect, and ruin of her house, arriving at the most appalling death. In a word, I can only repeat what I said in opening my defense, that Monsieur Flaubert is the author of a good book–a book that is an incitement to virtue through the horror of vice.

I must now examine the charge of outrage against religion. Outrage against religion committed by Monsieur Flaubert! And in what does the charge consist, if you please? The imperial attorney has thought to see in him a skeptic. I can reply to the imperial attorney that he is mistaken. I am not here to make a profession of faith; I have only the book to defend, and so I am able to confine myself to this single work. But as for the book, I defy the imperial attorney to find anything whatever that resembles an outrage against religion. You have seen how religion was introduced into Emma's education and how this religion, warped in a thousand ways, could not hold her from the downward path to which she was lured. Do you wish to know how Monsieur Flaubert speaks of religion? Listen to several lines I take from the first installment, pages 119 and 120:

> One evening as she was sitting at the open window and watching Lestiboudois, the sexton, trim the boxwood hedge, she suddenly heard the Angelus ringing.
>
> It was the beginning of April, when the primroses are in bloom; a warm wind blows over the flower beds, and the gardens, like women, seem to be dressing for the summer holidays. Through the arbor lattice and all around beyond it, the river could be seen making its meandering way through the grassy meadow. The evening mist was passing through the leafless poplars, blurring their outlines with a violet haze, paler and more transparent than a fine gauze hung on their branches. Cattle were moving about in the distance; neither their steps nor their lowing was audible; and the bell, still ringing, continued its peaceful lamentation in the air.
>
> At this repeated chiming, the young woman's thoughts strayed to her old memories of youth and school days. She remembered the candelabras, taller than the altar, the vases filled with flowers, and the tabernacle with its little columns. She wished she were still moving in that long line of white veils marked with

black by the stiff coifs of the nuns kneeling on their *prie-Dieux.*

These are the terms in which religious sentiment is expressed. And yet, to hear the imperial attorney, it is skepticism that reigns from one end to the other of Monsieur Flaubert's book. And now I ask you: where can you find skepticism there?

THE IMPERIAL ATTORNEY: I have not said that it was in that passage.

MONSIEUR SÉNARD: If it is not in that passage, then where is it? In your fragments, evidently. But here is the work in its entirety; let the court judge that and it will see that religious feeling is so strongly stamped there that the accusation of skepticism is a real calumny. And now, will the imperial attorney permit me to tell him that it was not worth the trouble to accuse the author of skepticism with such a fuss? Let us continue:

> When she lifted her head during Mass on Sunday, she would see the sweet face of the Virgin in the bluish clouds of incense that were rising. Then a tender emotion would suffuse her; she felt completely limp and abandoned like the down of a bird swirling in the tempest. Without being aware of what she was doing at that moment, she headed toward the church, prepared for any act of devotion as long as she could give her soul up there and make her entire existence disappear.

This, gentlemen, was the first appeal to religion to hold Emma from the downward path of the passions. She fell, poor woman, then was thrust down by the foot of the man to whom she had surrendered herself. She almost dies, she recovers, she revives; and now you will see what appears on page 207:

> One day, at the height of her illness, she believed herself dying and asked for Communion; and as the preparations for the sacrament went on in her room, as they arranged the dresser with its clutter of medicine bottles into an altar and Félicité scattered dahlia petals over the floor, Emma sensed something powerful passing over her, freeing her from all her pains, from all perception and feeling. Her body, freed of its burden, no longer thought; another life was beginning; it seemed to her that her being, ascending toward God . . .

You see in what terms Monsieur Flaubert speaks of religious things.

> . . . it seemed to her that her being, ascending toward God, was going to be destroyed in that love like a burning incense that is dissolved in smoke. They sprinkled holy water over the sheets; the priest took the white wafer from the holy pyx; and she nearly fainted with a celestial joy as she offered her lips to receive the body of the Saviour.

I beg pardon of the imperial attorney and of the court for interrupting this passage, but I want to say that it is the author who is speaking and to point out the terms in which he expresses himself on the mystery of the Communion; before I resume reading, I want the court to have discerned the literary value derived from this picture; and I want to emphasize these expressions that belong to the author himself:

> . . . and she nearly fainted with a celestial joy as she offered her lips to receive the body of the Saviour. The curtains of her alcove swelled out gently, like clouds, and the rays of the two candles burning on the chest of drawers seemed to her to be two dazzling haloes. Then she dropped her head, thinking she could hear the far-off song of heavenly harps and see God the Father on a golden throne in an azure sky, in the midst of saints bearing green palms, a God radiant with majesty, signaling to angels with flaming wings to descend to earth and take her off in their arms.

He continues:

> This splendid vision remained in her memory as the most beautiful dream imaginable, so much so that she kept trying to recapture the sensation, which continued with the same sweetness, albeit less intensely. Her soul, aching with pride, was at last reposing in Christian humility; she relished the pleasure of having succumbed and studied the destruction of her will within herself, which was to allow free entry of heavenly grace. And so there existed greater joys than mere happiness, another love above all other loves, with neither interruption nor end, which would grow eternally! In her illusions born of hope she envisaged a state of purity floating above the earth, blending with the heavens, into which she longed to be absorbed. She wanted to become a saint. She bought rosaries and wore amulets; she wanted an emerald-studded reliquary at her bedside so that she could kiss it every night.

There you have religious sentiments! And if you would like to reflect for an instant upon the author's principal idea, I would ask you to read these lines:

> She grew annoyed at the rules of ritual; the arrogance of the written polemics displeased her by their pitiless attacks on people she didn't know; and the secular tales, with their religious touches, seemed to have been written out of such ignorance of the world that imperceptibly they drove her away from the truths she was seeking.

There you have Monsieur Flaubert's manner of speaking. Now, if you please, let us come to another scene, the scene of the extreme unction. Oh! Mr. Imperial Attorney, how mistaken you were, when stopping short at the first words, you accused my client of mingling the sacred and the profane, when he has been content only to reproduce the beautiful phrases of the extreme unction at the moment when the priest touches the organs of our senses, at the moment in which he says, according to ritual: *Per istam unctionem, et suam puissimam misericordiam, indulgeat tibi Dominus quidquid deliquisti.*

You have said: "One must not touch upon holy things. By what right do you travesty these holy words: 'May God, in his holy mercy, pardon you for all the faults you have committed through the sight, through the taste, through the hearing, etc.'?"

Wait, I am going to read the passage to you, and that will be my entire vengeance. I dare to call it my vengeance, because the author must be avenged. Yes, Monsieur Flaubert must leave here, not only acquitted, but avenged! You will see by what readings he has been nurtured. The passage is on page 301:

> Pale as a statue, his eyes red as coals, Charles, no longer crying, stood at the foot of the bed looking at her, while the priest, on one knee, was murmuring in a low voice.

This whole picture is magnificent, and it is irresistible in the reading; but set your minds at ease, I shall not prolong it beyond measure. Here now is the passage:

> She turned her head slowly and seemed suffused with joy at the sudden sight of the purple stole–probably rediscovering in this instant of extraordinary peace the lost ecstasy of her first flights of mysticism and beginning to have visions of eternal bliss.
>
> The priest stood up to take hold of the crucifix. She stretched out her neck like one who is thirsty, and pressing her lips to the body of the Man-God, she placed on it, with all her fading strength, the most passionate kiss of love she had ever given.

The extreme unction has not yet begun, but already they reproach us with this kiss. I will not search as far as Saint Theresa, whom you perhaps know but whose figure is too distant; I will not even search in Fenelon for the mysticism of Madame Guyon, nor the more modern mysticisms in which I find many more examples. I will not ask the explanation for this kiss from these that you term schools of sensual Christianity; it is Bossuet, Bossuet himself, whom I will ask:

Honoré de Balzac and Victor Hugo, two giants of French literature whose works Sénard cited as precedents for Flaubert's less-than-respectful treatment of clergy (left, photograph by Félix Nadar; Frederick Lawson, Balzac *[London: Richards, 1910]; right, photograph by Pierre Pettit; Daniele Gasiglia,* Victor Hugo *[Paris: Birr, 1984])*

> Obey and strive moreover to enter into Jesus' feelings while taking Communion; these are the feelings of union, of possession, and of love: the whole gospel proclaims it. Jesus desires one to be with him; he desires to possess, he desires one to possess him. His holy flesh is the medium of this union and of this chaste possession: he gives himself.

I now resume my reading of the accused passage:

> . . . Then he recited the *Misereatur* and the *Indulgentiam,* dipped his right thumb into the oil, and began the unctions; first on the eyes, which had been so covetous of earthly splendors; then on the nostrils, avid for warm breezes and scents of love; then on the mouth, which had opened to emit lies, had groaned with pride, and had cried out in lust; then over the hands, which had reveled in sensual contacts; and finally on the soles of the feet, which had once moved so rapidly when she was hurrying to quench her desires and which now would walk no longer.
>
> The priest wiped his fingers, threw the oil-soaked bits of cotton into the fire, and came back to sit near the dying woman, to tell her that now she must unite her sufferings to those of Jesus Christ and give herself up to Divine mercy.
>
> As he ended his exhortations, he tried to place a consecrated candle in her hands, symbol of the celestial glories with which she would shortly be surrounded. Emma was too weak to close her fingers, and had it not been for Monsieur Bournisien, the candle would have fallen to the floor.
>
> But she was no longer so pale, and her face wore an expression of serenity, as though the sacrament had cured her.
>
> The priest did not fail to point this out. He even explained to Bovary that the Lord sometimes prolonged people's lives when He thought it necessary for their salvation; and Charles remembered the day when, as now, she was about to die and had received Holy Communion.
>
> "Maybe we shouldn't give up hope," he thought.

Now, when a woman is dying and when the priest is giving her extreme unction, when one makes a mystic scene of this, and when we reproduce the sacramental words with scrupulous fidelity–now they say that we are touching upon holy things. We have put a reckless hand upon holy things, because to the *deliquisti per oculos, per os, per aurem, per manus, et per pedes* we have added the sin that each of these organs had committed. We are not the first to have done the same. Monsieur Sainte-Beuve also places a scene of extreme unction in a book you know well, and here is how he expressed himself:

> Oh! Yea then, first to the eyes, as the most noble and the most keen of our senses; to the eyes for what they have seen, for what they have looked upon in other eyes that was too tender, perfidious, and mortal; for what they have read and reread that were too interesting and too cherished; for the futile tears they have shed for worldly possessions and for unfaithful creatures; for the sleep they have so often forgotten at night while dreaming of them!
>
> To the hearing also for what it has heard and has allowed itself to say that was too sweet, too flattering and intoxicating; for the sound the ear slowly draws from deceiving words and for the secret honey they have drunk from them!
>
> Then for the sense of smell for the too subtle and voluptuous perfumes of spring evenings deep in the forest, for the flowers received in the morning and every day that were breathed in with such satisfaction!
>
> To the lips for what they have pronounced that was too ambiguous or too open, for what they have not replied in certain moments or what they have not revealed to certain persons, for what they have sung in solitude that was too melodious and too full of tears, for their inarticulate murmuring, for their silence!
>
> To the throat in place of the breast for the heat of desire according to the holy phrase *(propter ardorem libidinis);* yea, for the pain of affection, rivalries, and the many pangs of anguish in human love; for the tears that choke a speechless throat; for all that makes a heart beat and that torments it!
>
> To the hands also for having clasped a hand with whom it had no holy tie; for having felt tears that were too burning; for having perhaps begun to write, without finishing, some illicit reply!
>
> To the feet for not having fled, for having been capable of long solitary walks, for not having wearied soon enough in the midst of conversations that ceaselessly started afresh.

You have not prosecuted that. There you have two men, each in his own sphere, who have taken the same thing and who have added to each one of the senses the sin or the offense it had committed. Would you have forbidden them to reproduce the ritual form *Quidquid deliquisti per oculos, per aurem,* etc?

Monsieur Flaubert has done what Monsieur Sainte-Beuve has done, without becoming a plagiarist on that account. He has exercised the right, which belongs to all writers, to add to what another author has said, to complete a subject.

The last scene in the novel of *Madame Bovary* has been based, like any study of this type, on religious documents. Monsieur Flaubert has based the extreme unction scene on a book lent to him by a friend who is a venerable priest–a priest who later read this scene, who was touched to tears by it, and who has not conceived that the majesty of religion could have been injured by it. This book is entitled *Historical, Dogmatic, Moral, Liturgic, and Canonic Explanation of the Catechism, With the Answer to Objections Raised Against Religion by the Sciences,* by Abbé Ambroise Guillois, priest of Notre-Dame-du-Pré at Mans, sixth edition, etc., a work approved by His Eminence Cardinal Gousset and by Their Reverences the Bishops and Archbishops of Mans, Tours, Boulogne, Cologne, etc.; volume 3, printed at Mans by Charles Monnoyer, 1851. Now you will see in this book, as you have just seen in Bossuet, the principle and, as it were, the text of the passages the imperial attorney has accused. Now it is no longer Monsieur Sainte-Beuve, an artist and a literary fantasist, whom I quote; listen now to the Church itself:

> Extreme unction can restore health to the body if this is useful to the glory of God . . .

And the priest says that this often happens. Now here is the extreme unction:

> The priest addresses a short exhortation to the invalid if he is in condition to hear it to dispose him to receive in a worthy manner the sacrament he is about to administer to him.
>
> The priest then anoints the invalid with the stylus or with the tip of the right thumb, which he dips each time into the holy oil. These unctions must be made above all to the five parts of the body that nature has given man as the organs of sensation and knowledge: to the eyes, to the ears, to the nostrils, to the mouth, and to the hands.
>
> As the priest makes these unctions–

We have followed the ritual step by step.

> –he pronounces the corresponding words *[To the eyes, on the closed eyelid]:* "With this holy unction and by His benign mercy, may God forgive you all of the sins that you have committed with the sight." At this moment the invalid must detest anew all of the sins that he has committed with the sight: so many indiscreet glances, so much guilty curiosity, so much reading that aroused a host of thoughts contrary to religion and to morals.

What has Monsieur Flaubert done? By uniting these two parts, he has placed in the priest's mouth the words that should be in his mind and at the same time in the mind of the invalid. He has copied purely and simply.

> *[To the ears]:* "With this holy unction and by His benign mercy, may God forgive you all the sins that you have committed with the sense of hearing." At this moment the invalid must detest anew all the offenses of which he has been guilty in listening with pleasure to slander, to calumny, to unseemly talk, to obscene songs.
>
> *[To the nostrils]:* "With this holy unction and by His benign mercy, may the Lord forgive you all the sins that you have committed by the sense of smell." In this moment the invalid must detest anew all the sins that he has committed by the sense of smell, all of the searching for subtle and voluptuous perfumes, all the sensualities, all that he has breathed of the odors of iniquity . . .
>
> *[To the mouth, on the lips]:* "With this holy unction and by His benign mercy, may the Lord forgive you all the sins that you have committed with the sense of taste and by the spoken word." The invalid must, at this moment, detest anew all the sins that he has committed in uttering curses and blasphemies . . . in eating and drinking to excess . . .
>
> *[On the hands]:* "With this holy unction and by His benign mercy, may the Lord forgive you all the sins that you have committed by the sense of touch." The invalid must at this moment detest anew all of the thefts, all of the wrongs of which he may have been guilty, all of the more or less guilty liberties that he has allowed himself . . . Priests receive the unction on the outside of the hands because they have already received it on the palms at the moment of their ordination, and other invalids receive it on the palms.
>
> *[On the feet]:* "With this holy unction and by His benign mercy, may God forgive you all the sins that you have committed by your steps." The invalid must at this moment detest anew all the steps that he has taken in the paths of iniquity, so many shameful walks, so many guilty meetings . . . The feet are anointed on the upper part or on the sole, according to the comfort of the invalid, and also according to the usage of the diocese. The most common practice seems to be to do it on the soles of the feet.

And finally, to the breast. Monsieur Sainte-Beuve has followed this; we have not done so because here it concerned the breast of a woman. *Propter ardorem libidinis,* etc.

> *[To the breast]:* "With this holy unction and by His benign mercy, may the Lord forgive you all the sins that you have committed by the ardor of the passions." The invalid must at this moment detest anew all the evil thoughts, all the evil desires in which he had indulged, all the feelings of hatred and vengeance that he had harbored in his heart.

And following the ritual, we might have spoken of something worse than the breast, but God knows what a holy wrath we would have aroused in the public ministry had we spoken of the loins:

> *[To the loins (ad lumbos)]:* "With this holy unction and by His benign mercy, may the Lord forgive you all the sins that you have committed through the dissolute pleasures of the flesh."

Had we said that, with what eloquence would you not have tried to crush us, Mr. Imperial Prosecutor! And nevertheless, the ritual adds:

> The invalid must at this moment detest anew so many shameful pleasures, so many carnal delights . . .

There is the ritual, and you have seen the accused work; there is no mockery in it, everything in it is genuine and moving. And I repeat, the man who gave this book to my client and who saw the use he had made of it–that man clasped his hand and was moved to tears. You see therefore, Mr. Imperial Attorney, the rashness–not to use a more precise word that would be more severe–of your charge that we had meddled with holy things. You see now that we did not mingle the profane with the sacred in adding to each of the senses the sin committed by it, since that is the language of the Church itself.

Need I now dwell upon the other details of the charge of outrage against religion? Here is what the public ministry says to me: "It is no longer religion, it is the morality of all the ages that you have outraged; you have insulted death itself!" How have I insulted death? Because at the moment when this woman dies there passes by in the street a beggar she had met more than once demanding alms beside her carriage as she returned from her adulterous assignations–the blind man she had been accustomed to see, the blind man who sang his song as the carriage slowly mounted the hill, to whom she threw a coin and whose aspect made her shudder. This man passes in the street; and at the moment when Divine mercy forgives, or promises forgiveness, to the wretched woman who is paying for the transgressions of her life by this frightful death, human mockery appears to her in the form of a song that passes beneath her window. My God! You find outrage in that; but Monsieur Flaubert has done only what Shakespeare and Goethe have done, both of whom did not fail to let us hear some song of sadness or mockery at the hour of death to remind the dying of some pleasure he will no longer enjoy or of some transgression to expiate.

Let us read:

> Indeed, she was looking all around her, slowly, like someone waking from a dream. Then, in a clear voice she asked for her mirror, and she leaned over it awhile, big tears trickling from her eyes. Then she threw her head back with a sigh and fell back on the pillow.

I cannot read it–I am like Lamartine: "For me the expiation goes beyond truth. . . ." Nevertheless, Mr. Imperial Attorney, I would not think I would be doing wrong in reading these pages to those of my daughters who are married, virtuous girls who have been given good examples, good lessons, and whom one has never, never by any indiscretion placed outside the straight and narrow path, outside of the things that can and must be understood. I find it too painful to continue this reading; I will confine myself strictly to the passages under indictment!

> He had taken her hands and was holding them tightly–

This is Charles, on her other side; Charles whom we hardly see and who is so admirable.

> –shuddering at each beat of her heart, as at the reverberation of a falling ruin. As the death rattle grew louder, the priest hurried his prayers. They mingled with Bovary's muffled sobs, and at times everything seemed to merge with the monotonous murmur of the Latin syllables that sounded like the tolling of a bell.
>
> Suddenly there was a clatter of heavy clogs on the sidewalk and the tapping of a stick. Then a voice arose, singing raucously:
>
> Often the warmth of a lovely day
> Makes a girl dream of love.
>
> Emma lifted herself up like a galvanized corpse, her hair undone, her eyes fixed and staring.
>
> To gather up the corn
> That the scythe has reaped,
> My Nanette bends to the furrow
> In which it was born.
>
> "The blind man!" she cried. And she began to laugh–a horrible, frenzied, despairing laugh–imagining that she could see the hideous face of the beggar standing out against the eternal darkness like a nightmare.
>
> There was a strong breeze that day
> And her short petticoat flew away!
>
> A convulsion pulled her back down on the mattress. They all drew near the bed. She was no more.

See, gentlemen, at the moment of death the reminder of her transgressions and remorse made in the most poignant and frightful way. This is not the fancy of an artist wishing only to show contrast without useful purpose, without a moral; this is the blind man she hears in the street singing the frightful song he used to sing as she returned all sweating and hideous from her adulterous assignations; it is the blind man she saw at each one of these assignations; it is the blind man who pursued her with his song, with his importuning; it is he who comes at the moment when Divine mercy is present to personify the human passion that pursues her at the supreme instant of death! And they call that an outrage against public morality! But I can say, on the contrary, that there you have a tribute to public morality; nothing could be more moral than that. I can say that in this book the defects in education are brought to life as they really are in the living flesh of our society and that with every line the author is putting to us this question: "Have you done all you should in the education of your daughters? Is the religion you have given them capable of sustaining them in the storms of life, or is it only a mass of sensual superstitions that will leave them unprotected when the tempest roars? Have you taught them that life is not the realization of chimerical dreams, but that it is something prosaic with which one must compromise? Have you taught them that? Have you done what you should for their happiness? Have you said to them: 'Poor children, outside the road I show you, in the pleasure that you pursue, only disgust awaits you, only neglect of your home, only agitation, disorder, squandering, upheavals, seizure.'" And you can see if anything is missing from the picture: the bailiff is there, so also is the moneylender who sold everything to satisfy the whims of this woman; the furniture is seized, the public sale is about to take place, and the husband is still unaware of it all. Nothing remains for the wretched woman but to die!

But, says the public ministry, her death is voluntary, this woman chooses her own hour.

But could she have been able to live? Was she not condemned? Had she not already drained the last dregs of shame and degradation?

Yes, in our theaters they show fallen women who are graceful, smiling, and fortunate, and I will not say what they have done. *Questum corpore fecerant.* I will merely say this. When we are shown them happy, charming, wrapped in silk, offering a gracious hand to counts, marquesses, and dukes, these women who themselves often answer to the title of marchioness or duchess–that is what you call respect for public morality. And the man who shows you the adulterous woman dying in shame–this man commits an outrage against public morality!

In effect, I will not say that you have expressed an idea that is not your own, since you have expressed it; but you have yielded to a great pressure. No, I cannot believe it; it is not possible that you–the husband and father of a family, the man I see before me–would have come here without the pressure of the indictment and of a preconceived idea to say that Monsieur Flaubert is the author of an evil book! Indeed, left to your own inspiration, your opinion would be the same as mine; I am not speaking from a literary point of view–you and I could not differ in that respect–but from the point of view of morality and religious feeling as you and I both understand it.

They also told us that we had presented a materialistic priest. But we have taken the priest as we have taken the husband. This is not an eminent clergyman; this is a simple clergyman, a country parish priest. And just as we have insulted no one, just as we have expressed no feeling or idea that might be injurious to the husband, still less have we insulted the clergyman in this book. I have only a word to say about this.

Would you like to hear of books in which clergymen play a deplorable role? Take Balzac's *Gil Blas* and *La Chanoine;* take Victor Hugo's *Notre-Dame de Paris.* If you want priests who are the shame of the clergy, you must look elsewhere–you could not find them in *Madame Bovary.* And what is it that I have shown? A country priest who in his duties as a country priest is just what Monsieur Bovary is–a simple man. Have I portrayed him as libertine, glutton, or drunkard? I have not said one word of that kind. I have portrayed him fulfilling his ministry, not with a lofty understanding, but as his nature called him to fulfill it. Next to him, and in a state of almost perpetual argument, I have placed a personality who will live–as the creation of Monsieur Prudhomme has lived–as other creations will live, for they are so well studied and true to life that there is no possibility of our forgetting them. This personality is the country pharmacist, the voltairian, the skeptic, the unbeliever, the man who is perpetually in dispute with the priest. But in these disputes with the priest, who is the one who is continually beaten, derided, and ridiculed? It is Homais who has been given the role that is the more comic because it is the more true to life, a role that best portrays our skeptical age–what we call a rabid priest-hater. Again allow me to read pages 91–92: The innkeeper's wife is offering a glass of wine to her priest:

Joseph Prudhomme, the famous caricature drawn by Henry Monnier to satirize the prosperous bourgeois class under the July monarchy. Sénard, as well as Charles-Augustin Sainte-Beuve in his review of Madame Bovary, *compared the druggist Homais to this emblem of French society (cliché Bibliothèque nationale de France, Paris).*

"May I help you, Monsieur le curé?" the landlady asked, reaching for one of the brass candlesticks lined up along the mantelpiece. "Would you like something? A drop of cassis, a glass of wine?"

The priest refused quite politely. He had come for his umbrella: he had forgotten it the other day at the Ernemont convent. After asking Madame Lefrançois to send it to him at the parish house in the evening, he headed back to the church, where the Angelus was ringing.

When the pharmacist could no longer hear the sound of his shoes in the square, he began criticizing the curé's recent conduct. The refusal of a drink seemed to him the most detestable hypocrisy. All priests tippled in secret and were trying to bring back the days of the tithe.

The landlady came to the curé's defense.

"And anyway, he could bend four of you over his knee. Last year he helped our people bring in the hay. He carried six bales at a time; that's how strong he is!"

"Bravo!" said the pharmacist. "So send your daughters to confess to such healthy brutes. Now, if I were the government, I would want the priests bled once a month. Yes, Madame Lefrançois, an extensive bloodletting every month for the sake of law and order."

"Oh, stop talking, Monsieur Homais. You're blaspheming. You have no religion."

The pharmacist answered, "I do have a religion; and it's even deeper than all of theirs with their mummery and their tricks! On the contrary, I worship God, I believe in a Supreme Being, in a Creator whoever He is, it doesn't matter, who placed us here below to fulfill our duties to family and state, but I don't need to go into a church to kiss silver plates and fatten up a bunch of fakers who eat better than we do! You can worship Him just as well in the woods or in a field or even by studying the heavens, like the ancients. God, for me, is the God of Socrates, Franklin, Voltaire, and Béranger! I am for the *Savoyard Vicar's Profession of Faith* and for the immortal principles of eighty-nine! So I cannot accept a doddering deity who parades around in his garden with a cane in his hand, sends his friend up a whale's belly, dies with a shriek, and is resurrected three days later. These things are obviously absurd, and besides, they're completely opposed to the laws of physics; which incidentally shows us that the priests have always wallowed in a shameful ignorance in which they try to engulf their entire flock!"

He stopped talking and looked around for an audience. In his fervor the pharmacist had believed himself for a moment in a Town Council plenary session. But the mistress of the inn had stopped listening to him.

What have we there? A conversation, a commotion, just as there was every time Homais had occasion to speak of priests.

Now we come to something better in the last passage, page 300:

Public attention was distracted by the appearance of Monsieur Bournisien walking through the marketplace with the holy oils.

Homais, out of obligation to his principles, compared priests to crows attracted by the smell of death. The sight of a priest was personally distasteful to him: the cassock reminded him of a shroud and he cursed the one partly out of fear of the other.

Monsieur Flaubert's old friend, the man who lent him the catechism, was very happy with this passage; he told us: "That is strikingly true. This is truly the portrait of a priest-hater, whom the cassock reminded of a shroud and he cursed the one partly out of fear of the other." Homais was impious and he detested the cloth, a little because of impiety perhaps, but more because it reminded him of the shroud.

Permit me now to summarize my argument:

I am defending a man who, had he encountered some literary criticism on the form of his book, on some phrases, on the excess of details, or on some point or other, would have accepted this literary criticism with all his heart. But to see himself accused of outrage against morality and religion! Monsieur Flaubert cannot believe it; and here before you he protests such an accusation with all the astonishment and all the force at his command.

You are not the kind of men who condemn books on a few lines; you are the kind who judge the intention and the execution above all, and you will ask yourselves the question with which I opened my defense and with which I now close: Does the reading of such a book give a love of vice or does it inspire a horror of vice? Is not so terrible an expiation an inducement and an incitement to virtue? The reading of this book cannot produce in you any impression other than the one it has produced in us, namely: that the book is excellent as a whole, and irreproachable in its parts. All of classical literature holds our precedent for paintings and scenes which go far beyond what we have permitted ourselves. In that regard we could have taken it for our model, but we have not done so; we have imposed upon ourselves a moderation which you will take into account. If, in a word here or there, Monsieur Flaubert may possibly have overstepped the bounds he imposed upon himself, I would not only remind you that this is his first work, but I would have to add that then, even had he miscalculated, his error would be without damage to public morality. And in calling him before the Criminal Court–this man whom you now know a little through his book, whom you already like a little, I am certain, and whom you would like even more if you knew him more–he is already punished enough, he is already too cruelly punished. Now it is up to you to pronounce judgment. You have judged the book as a whole and in its parts: it is not possible that you will hesitate!

–"Speech for the Defense," in "The Trial of *Madame Bovary,*" translated by Evelyn Gendel, *Madame Bovary* (New York: Signet, 1964), pp. 363–400

Flaubert on the Trial

Flaubert praised his lawyer in a 30 January 1857 letter to his brother, Achille.

Maître Sénard's speech was splendid. He crushed the attorney from the Ministry of Justice, who writhed in his seat and made no rebuttal. We flattened him with quotations from Bossuet and Massillon, smutty passages from Montesquieu, etc. The courtroom was packed. It was marvelous, and I was in fine form. At one point I allowed myself personally to contradict the attorney, who was immediately shown to be acting in bad faith, and retracted. In any case, you will see the rest of the proceedings word for word: I had a stenographer (at 60 francs an hour) taking it all down. Sénard spoke for four hours without interruption. It was a triumph for him and for me.

–*The Letters of Gustave Flaubert, 1830–1857,* p. 226

Reception of *Madame Bovary*

Madame Bovary *was an immediate and great success upon its publication. Sainte-Beuve, at that time the most respected literary critic in France, who regularly published reviews in important journals such as* La Revue des Deux Mondes, Le Constitutionnel, *and* Le Moniteur Universel, *recognized the originality of Flaubert's book in a review he first published on 4 May 1857 in* Le Moniteur Universel.

Sainte-Beuve on Flaubert's "New Literary Manner"

I have not forgotten that this work has recently been the object of a nowise literary debate; what stands out foremost in my memory, however, are the conclusions and the wisdom of the judges. Henceforth, this work belongs to the realm of art and of art alone; it is accountable to literary critics only and critics can deal with it in full independence.

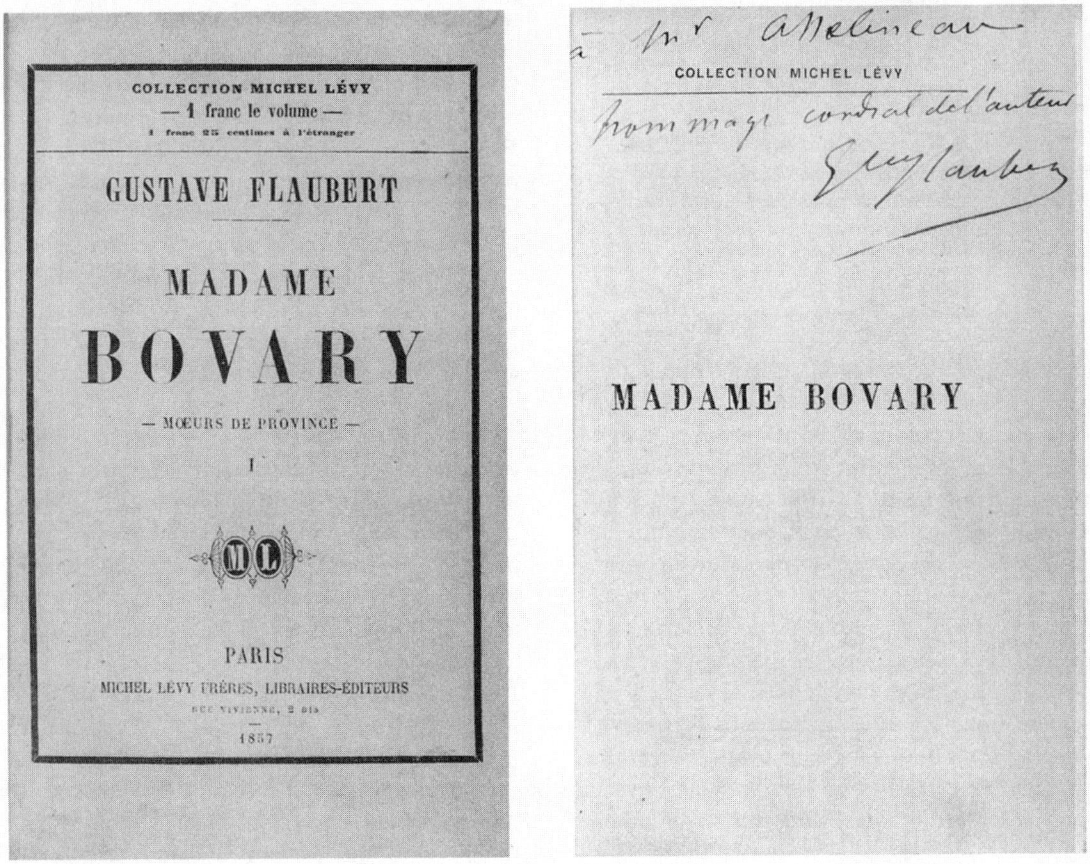

Cover and half-title inscription to Charles Asselineau, an historian of literature and friend of the author. This copy sold for $32,600 (Sotheby's, The Maurice F. Neville Collection of Modern Literature, *13 April 2004).*

Louis Bouilhet, caricature by Étienne Carjat published in Diogène, *5 April 1857. Flaubert and Bouilhet aided each other in their literary endeavors. Bouilhet's successful play* Madame de Montarcy, *like* Madame Bovary, *was published in spring 1857 by Michel Lévy (cliché Bibliothèque nationale de France, Paris).*

They can and they should. Often enough, we labor hard at resuscitating things of the past, older writers, works no longer read to which we restore a flash of interest, a semblance of life; but when genuine and live works pass within our grasp, with full canvas flying and banners floating in the breeze as if taunting with the question: *What do you think of us?*–a true critic, in whose veins flows a drop of the blood of Pope, Boileau, Johnson, Jeffrey, Hazlitt or simple M. de la Harpe, will burn with impatience, frustrated at having to remain silent, eager to speak up, to herald and salute the work as it passes by. Long ago, Pindar said about poetry: I hail old wine and youthful songs!–youthful songs: this means last night's new play, the novel of the day, all what is being discussed by the young the very moment it appears.

I had not read the first version of *Madame Bovary* when it appeared in serial form in a periodical. Striking as some parts may have been, the general idea and structure must have suffered from this mode of publication. Startled by some daring episode, the reader must have wondered if worse was still to come: he might well have assumed that the work was heading for perilous regions and that the author intended something which, in fact, he did not intend at all. Reading the book as one continuous unit, one finds each scene falling back into place. *Madame Bovary* is first and foremost a book, a carefully composed book, amply premeditated and totally coherent, in which nothing is left to chance and in which the author or, better, the painter does exactly what he intends to do from beginning to end.

The writer has obviously lived a great deal in the country, in the region of Normandy which he describes so truthfully. Generally, those who stay in the country and respond to nature with enough sensitivity to describe it well, tend to love it or, at least, to stress its beauty, especially after they have moved away; they are tempted to make it into an idyllic setting, an idealized world of nostalgically remembered happiness and well-being. As long as he lived there, Bernardin de Saint-Pierre was bored to tears by the Isle de France but, once he had left the region he fondly remembered the beauty of the landscapes, the peaceful serenity of the valleys; he made it the dwelling place of his chosen creatures and wrote *Paul and Virginia.* Without going as far as Bernardin de Sainte-Pierre, Georges Sand probably thought her Berry was pretty dull; later, however, she chose to show only the attractive aspects of the place and certainly did not try to disenchant her readers with the Creuse Valley. Even when she peopled it with passion-driven and theorizing characters, she preserved a rural, pastoral element, poetic in the Hellenic sense of the term. But here, in the case of the author of *Madame Bovary,* we come upon an altogether different manner, another kind of inspiration and, in truth, upon a different generation. The ideal is gone, the lyrical has died out; it can no longer hold us. Stern and implacable truth has entered art as the last word of experience. The author of *Madame Bovary* stayed in the provinces and in the country, in villages and small towns; he did not merely cross the region on a spring day, like the traveler mentioned by la Bruyère who, standing on a hill, composes his dream as a painter would, along the slope of the hillside–he actually lived there. And what did he see? Pettiness, poverty, conceit, stupidity, routine, monotony and boredom–and so he tells us. Those genuine and faithfully rendered landscapes inhabited by the rural spirit of the region become the setting for boorish lovers, for vulgar, prosaic, foolishly pretentious, totally ignorant or half-educated beings. One single creature capable of the nobility of dreams and aspiring to a better world is thrown into this milieu; she feels alien and oppressed; she suffers so much in solitude

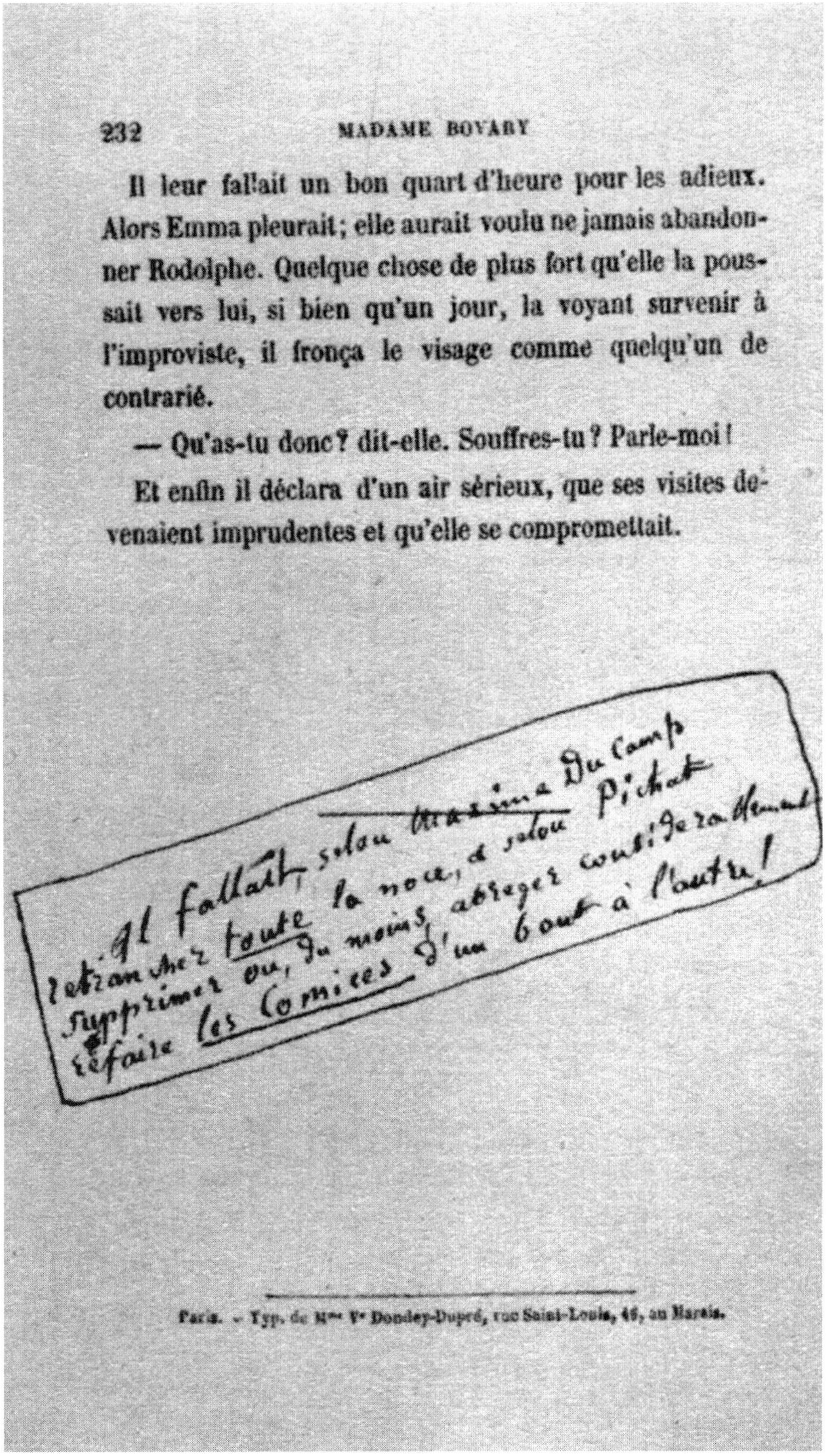
232 MADAME BOVARY

Il leur fallait un bon quart d'heure pour les adieux. Alors Emma pleurait; elle aurait voulu ne jamais abandonner Rodolphe. Quelque chose de plus fort qu'elle la poussait vers lui, si bien qu'un jour, la voyant survenir à l'improviste, il fronça le visage comme quelqu'un de contrarié.

— Qu'as-tu donc? dit-elle. Souffres-tu? Parle-moi!

Et enfin il déclara d'un air sérieux, que ses visites devenaient imprudentes et qu'elle se compromettait.

Il fallait, selon ~~Maxime~~ Du Camp retrancher toute la noce, et selon Pichat supprimer ou, du moins, abréger considérablement refaire les Comices d'un bout à l'autre!

Paris. – Typ. de Mme Ve Dondey-Dupré, rue Saint-Louis, 46, au Marais.

Page in the first edition of Madame Bovary *in which Flaubert identified passages that the editors of the* Revue de Paris *wanted to cut: "According to Maxime Du Camp, the* entire *passage recounting the wedding should have been cut, and according to Pichat, the* Agricultural fair *should have either been suppressed or, at least, entirely rewritten and abridged!" (courtesy of the Bibliothèque historique de la Ville de Paris).*

Charles-Augustin Sainte-Beuve (engraving by Bornemann from a photograph by Pierson; cliché Bibliothèque nationale de France, Paris)

that she is altered and degraded. In pursuing her false dream and absent beauty she gradually reaches ruin and depravation. Is this moral? Is it consoling? The question does not seem to have occurred to the writer; his only concern was: is this true? I presume that he himself witnessed something similar, or that, at any rate, he chose to condense on a tightly composed canvas the outcome of various observations, against a background of bitterness and irony.

Another equally surprising anomaly: among all those very real and alive characters, not a single one seems to be the kind of person the author himself would have wanted to be; the care he lavishes on them is only aimed at relentless precision; none are treated with the consideration one would show towards a friend. The novelist entirely refrains from taking sides; he is present only in order to watch, to reveal and to say everything, but not even his profile appears in a single corner of the novel. The work is entirely impersonal. This, in itself, demonstrates remarkable strength.

Next to Madame Bovary, the most important character is Monsieur Bovary. We meet the young Charles Bovary (for his father, too, is very accurately portrayed) from his very first days in school: he is a docile and well-behaved but awkward boy, a hopelessly mediocre nonentity, rather stupid, thoroughly undistinguished, tame, passive, submissively destined to follow step by step a previously mapped out path or to walk in the footsteps of his guides. Son of a somewhat rakish army surgeon, he shows none of his father's dash or vices. His mother's savings enable him to undertake rather pale studies in Rouen, leading to a painfully earned medical degree. Having to decide in which town to set up practice, he selects Tostes, a smallish place not far from Dieppe. He is married off to a much older widow rumored to have a small yearly income. He allows himself to be pushed into such arrangements without even seeming to realize how remote he remains from happiness.

One night, he finds himself summoned to les Bertaux, a farm located at a good six miles' distance from his home. He is to set the broken leg of a wealthy farmer, widowed father of a single daughter. This sequence of episodes, the trip through the night on horseback, the arrival at the large farm, his first encounter with the young girl who has nothing of the farmer's daughter, having instead been raised as a well-bred young lady in a convent, the attitude of the rich man–all this is admirably rendered in minute detail, as if we were present at the scene: it is like a Dutch or Flemish painting of Normandy. Bovary gets into the habit of returning to the Bertaux farm, more often than his attendance upon his patient requires, and he keeps going there even after Rouault is cured. Unnoticed even to himself, his frequent visits to the farm gradually grow into a habit, a delightful distraction from his painful routine.

> On these days he rose early, set off at a gallop, urging on his horse, then got down to wipe his boots in the grass and put on black gloves before entering. He liked the courtyard, seeing himself enter and noticing the gate turn against his shoulder, the cock crow on the wall, the farmboys run to meet him. He liked the granary and the stables; he liked old Roualt, who pressed his hand and called him his savior; he liked the small wooden shoes of Mademoiselle Emma on the scoured flags of the kitchen–her high heels made her a little taller; and when she walked in front of him, the wooden soles springing up quickly struck with a sharp sound against the leather of her boots.
>
> She always reconducted him to the first step of the porch. When his horse had not yet been brought round she stayed there. They had said "Good-bye"; there was no more talking. The open air wrapped her round, playing with the soft down on the back of her neck, or blew to and fro on her hips her apron-strings, that fluttered like streamers. Once, during a thaw, the bark of the trees in the yard was oozing, the snow melted on the roofs of the buildings; she stood on the threshold, went to fetch her sunshade and opened it. The parasol, made of an iridescent silk that let the sunlight sift through, colored the white skin of her face with shifting reflections. Beneath it, she smiled at the gentle warmth; drops of water fell one by one on the taut silk.

It would be hard to imagine a picture of greater freshness and precision, so well composed and delicately lighted, in which the memory of the classical is so well disguised to appear modern. The noise of the melt-

The wedding of Emma and Charles Bovary, from part 1, chapter 4 (illustration by Albert Fourié; Madame Bovary. Mœurs de province, *3 volumes [Paris: Librarie Illustrée, 1900])*

ing snow dripping down on the umbrella reminds me of a similar noise: the tinkle of ice drops as they fall from the branches on the dry leaves of the path in William Cowper's "Winter walk at noon." One invaluable quality distinguishes M. Flaubert from many other more or less talented observers who nowadays lay claim, at times legitimately, to the faithful portrayal of mere reality: he possesses style. At times, he even has too much style, and his pen may then indulge in oddities and minutiae of continued description that sometimes interfere with the general effect. His objects and his faces, even those that seem best suited to catch our eye, are somewhat flattened and overshadowed by the excessive relief of surrounding accessories. Madame Bovary herself, the Mademoiselle Emma who seemed so charming on our first encounter with her, is so often described in minute detail that I fail to visualize her physical appearance clearly in its totality, or in a distinct and decisive manner.

The first Madame Bovary soon dies and Emma becomes the second and only Madame Bovary. The chapter of the wedding at Bertaux is pictorially perfect, particularly rich in truthful details, combining spontaneity with stiff formality, at times ugly and awkward, but ribald and graceful as well, ranging from delicacy to sheer gluttony. The scene is balanced by the dance at the La Vaubyessard castle and, with the later chapter on the Agricultural Fair, the three episodes are like so many pictures which, if they had been painted on canvas, would belong in a gallery with the best works of this kind.

Emma becomes Madame Bovary, settles in the little home in Tostes, with its crammed rooms, a small garden longer than it is wide looking out over the fields. She immediately creates order, cleanliness, and an atmosphere of elegance around her. Her husband, eager to please her, buys her a secondhand carriage that will allow her to travel on the neighboring roads whenever she wishes. For the first time in his life, Charles Bovary is happy and he knows it; after looking after his patients all day, he finds joy and contentment on his return home. He is in love with his wife and only wishes this bourgeois and tranquil happiness to last forever. She, however, has known headier dreams. As a young girl, she has often wondered how to achieve happiness, and she soon realizes, even during her honeymoon, that this is not the way.

Here begins a profound, sensitive, and tightly knit analysis, a cruel dissection that will only end with the book. We enter into the heart of Madame Bovary. How to describe it?–she is woman; at first she is merely romantically inclined, by no means corrupt. Her portrayer, M. Flaubert, does not spare her. He denounces without pity the overrefined tastes of her childhood, the coquettish little girl, the dreamy schoolgirl overindulging her fancies. Shall I confess it? one often feels more tolerant towards her than the author himself. Thrust in a situation to which she ought to adjust, she always has a quality too much and a virtue too little: all her errors and her undoing stem from there. The quality she has in excess consists not only in being a romantic nature, but of having needs of heart and mind as well as ambition, aspirations towards a higher, more refined and more ornate existence than what befell her. The virtue she lacks stems from her failure to learn that the necessary condition to make life possible is the ability to tolerate *ennui,* the shapeless frustration resulting from the absence of a pleasant life better suited to our own tastes. She cannot silently and discreetly resign herself to the impossibility of finding a purpose, a meaningful course of action, in being useful to others or in the love for her child. She does not relent easily, she struggles to remain in the path of virtue; it will take her years of unsuccessful attempts before she gives in to evil. She comes closer

Emma at the Vaubyessard castle ball, from part 1, chapter 8 (illustration by Albert Fourié; Madame Bovary. Mœurs de province, *3 volumes [Paris: Librarie Illustrée, 1900])*

every day, and at last she is uncontrollably lost. But I am rationalizing, whereas the author of *Madame Bovary* merely wants to show us, day by day, minute by minute, the thoughts and actions of this heroine.

The long and melancholy days spent in loneliness as Emma is left by herself during the first months of her married life, her walks to the beechgroves of Banneville in the company of her faithful little greyhound Djali, the endless questioning of her own destiny as she asks herself *what might have been*–all this is unravelled and argued with the same delicacy and analytical subtlety we meet with in the most intimate and dream-inducing of the older novels. As in the days of René or Oberman, nature mingles at times its unpredictable and irregular movements with the longings and vague desires of the soul:

> Occasionally there came gusts of wind, breezes from the sea rolling in one sweep over the whole plateau of the Caux country, which brought to these fields a salt freshness. The rushes, close to the ground, whistled; the branches of the birch trees trembled in a swift rustling, while their crowns, ceaselessly swaying, kept up a deep murmur. Emma drew her shawl round her shoulders and rose.
>
> In the avenue a green light dimmed by the leaves lit up the short moss that crackled softly beneath her feet. The sun was setting; the sky showed red between the branches, and the trunks of the trees, uniform, and planted in a straight line, seemed a brown colonnade standing out against a background of gold. A fear took hold of her; she called Djali, and hurriedly returned to Tostes by the highroad, threw herself into an armchair, and for the rest of the evening did not speak.

It is around this time that the marquis of Andervilliers, a neighbor aspiring to political office, invites all people of note or influence in the region to a dance at the castle. He met the doctor by chance when, for lack of another surgeon, Bovary cured him of a mouth infection; on one of his visits to Tostes, he caught a glimpse of Madame Bovary and judged her sufficiently acceptable to be invited. Hence the visit of M. and Madame Bovary to the Vaubyessard castle, one of the crucial scenes of the book, and masterfully handled.

Emma is received with the politeness that a young and attractive woman is bound to encounter. On entering, she breathes the perfume of elegance and aristocracy, the chimera for which she has always been longing and which she considers her proper destiny. She waltzes without ever having been taught, guesses all there is to guess and succeeds beyond expectations in making an impression. All this will contribute to her downfall. She is poisoned by the air she has breathed there: the poison will act slowly but it has penetrated into her blood and will never leave her. All the details, even the most trivial, of this memorable evening are locked forever in her heart and will start their relentless action. "Her journey to Vaubyessard had made a gap in her life, like the huge crevasses that a thunderstorm will sometimes carve in the mountains, in the course of a single night." The morning after the dance, having left Vaubyessard in the early hours of the day, M. and Madame Bovary find themselves seated again in their small home, before their humble dinner table, with the smell of onion soup and veal stew rising from the plates; when Charles, happily rubbing his hands, exclaims, "How glad I am to be back home!" she stares at him with utter contempt. Her mind has come a long way since last night, and it has travelled in the opposite direction. When they left together, driving their carriage to the party, they were at most two very different human beings, but now, after their return, a boundless gap keeps them apart.

I summarize briefly what takes many pages and will stretch over years. It must be said in Emma's favor that her downfall is by no means speedy. She casts around for help in her effort at constraint: she looks for it in herself and in others. In herself:–she has a serious shortcoming: she lacks all capacity for sympathy as if, at an early date, the imagination has consumed all other faculties and sentiments. In others:–another misfortune! the hapless Charles, who loves her and whom she, at moments, tries to love, entirely fails to understand her. If, at least, he were an ambitious man, concerned with earning a reputation in his profession, forcing himself through study or hard work, to make his name an honored one–but he is nothing of the sort: he has neither drive, nor curiosity, none of the inner powers that propel a man beyond the circle of his daily existence, help him to move ahead and make his wife proud to hear his name. "He is not a man," she exclaims in anger. "What a sorry creature he is!" She will never forgive him for having humiliated her.

At last, she is seized by a kind of disease; they call it a nervous condition, but it is like a nostalgia, a homesickness for an *unknown country*. Always as blind as he is eager to help, Charles tries everything to cure her and can think of nothing better than a change of residence; as a result, he abandons the practice he was acquiring at Tostes for another far corner of Normandy, the town of Yonville-l'Abbaye in the county of Neufchâtel. Until now the entire novel has been a prelude; the real action only begins with the move to Yonville, and except for the continued careful analysis, it now proceeds at a somewhat faster pace.

At the moment of the move, Madame Bovary is pregnant with her first and only child, a girl. The child will bring a slight counterweight into her life; sudden and capricious outbursts of tenderness slow down the progress of evil. However, Emma's motherly feelings have been poorly prepared: her heart is already too deeply ravaged by barren passions and sterile ambitions to allow happy, natural, and self-sacrificing instincts to develop fully.

The new region where the Bovarys are settling down, bordering on the Picardie, "a mongrel area where the language is devoid of intonation, as the landscape is devoid of character," is described with pitiless truthfulness; the town and its main inhabitants, the priest, the innkeeper, the sacristan, the lawyer, etc. are taken from reality and haunt one's memory. Among those who will henceforth occupy the front of the stage and remain there till the end, filling it with their busy emptiness, we must single out M. Homais, a creation which M. Flaubert raises to the level of a type. We have all known and met M. Homais, though perhaps never in such a towering and triumphant incarnation: he is the weighty, self-important man-about-town, with a ready phrase for every situation, boastful of his own enlightenment, insistently commonplace, but devious and tricky, managing to enlist stupidity itself in the service of his interests. M. Homais is the M. Prudhomme of pseudo-science.

M. and Madame Bovary meet some of the main villagers upon their arrival at the Lion d'Or inn. One of the regular customers, M. Léon Dupuis, a lawyer's clerk, engages Madame Bovary in conversation. In a tightly handled, very natural sounding but deeply ironic dialogue, the author shows them outdoing each other in false sentiments, their taste for vague poetry and fake romanticism covering up for their real designs; it is only a beginning, but a damaging passage for those who believe in a poetry of the heart and have tried their hand at sentimental elegies: their devices are revealed, imitated and parodied, leaving one disgusted with love conversations that take themselves seriously.

Things do not quite work out as one would expect after this first encounter: the insignificant M. Léon will make headway in Madame Bovary's heart, but not so soon or so far, and not yet. For a while, Madame Bovary remains in fact an honest woman, although her secret name, as one would read it imprinted in her inner self, would already spell "betrayal" and "adultery." M. Léon, in fact, is a very small personage, but he is young, amiable, and he thinks that he is in love. At times, she thinks that she, too, loves him. All this is stimulated as well as hampered by their closely watched existences, by the difficulty of seeing each other, by their respective shyness. She wages inner battles, with no one present to appreciate the honor of her victories: "What exasperated her more than anything was that her husband seemed totally oblivious of her torture." One day, she tries to confide in the well-meaning priest, M. Bournisien, a vulgar and crude man who has no inkling of the moral distress that confronts him. Fortunately, M. Léon leaves town to pursue his studies in Paris. The embarrassed farewells, the stifled regrets, later magnified for her by memory and inflamed by the workings of her imagination, the uneven shades of feeling which they assume to be despair, all lend themselves to perfectly consistent and clearly constructed analysis. The underlying foundation is always one of irony.

The great day at Yonville-l'Abbaye comes with the agricultural fair of the Seine-Inférieure. The description of this momentous event constitutes the third large group scene in the book, and it is richly successful in its genre. Madame Bovary fulfills her destiny on this occasion. A reputedly handsome gentleman of the vicinity, the pseudo-aristocratic M. Rodolphe Boulanger de la Huchette, had noticed her at home a few days earlier, while bringing over one of his farmers to see the doctor. He is thirty-four years old, crude but with a veneer of elegance, a great chaser of women preoccupied by little else in life; her handsome eyes make him wish to add her to the list of his conquests. Although he is one of the judges, he sacrifices his official position to her company and never leaves her side on the day of the fair. This leads to a well-constructed and piquant scene: while the presiding official is delivering the inaugural address, solemnly propounding the political, economic and moral platitudes which the occasion calls for, Rodolphe, looking in from a window in the town hall, whispers in Emma's ears the eternal phrases that have so often led to the downfall of daughters of Eve. The pompous official speech, properly filled with pathos, counterpointed in a minor key by the equally banal and shopworn sentimentality of Rodolphe's cooings, make for a particularly effective and ironic scene. Convincingly enough, Madame Bovary, who withstood Léon but whose heart is shaken by the secret regret that she perhaps withstood him too well, now gives in from the very first day to this stranger–while Rodolphe is enough of a lout to think of himself as her sole conqueror. Such quirks and inconsistencies of Emma's feminine nature are excellently observed.

Once the decisive step had been taken, Madame Bovary will make up for lost time. She is hopelessly in love with Rodolphe, she pursues him and does not hesitate to compromise her reputation for his sake. From now on, we will no longer follow her so closely. The episode of the clubfoot, an inept operation undertaken and bungled by her husband, destroys once and forever whatever love or esteem she might have preserved towards him. Completely possessed by her passion, she reaches the point where she cannot stand to be away for a day from Rodolphe; she demands an elopement, begs for a cabin hidden in the woods or by the seashore. We come upon a touching and poignant scene: the unsuspecting Bovary, returning late at night from calling on his patients, dreams before the cradle of his daughter of all the happiness he foresees in her future, while next to him his wife, pretending to be asleep, dreams only of fanciful elopement in horse-drawn carriages, of romantic bliss, imaginary voyages, the Orient, Granada, Alhambra, etc. This double dream, treated as an extended juxtaposition, the abused father whose only thought is of sweet and joyful domesticity, side by side with the beautiful and determinedly destructive adulteress, is the work of an artist who, when he gets hold of a theme, extracts from it the maximum effect.

Many particularly true-to-nature phrases and expressions deserve to be singled out. One night, Rodolphe has come to visit Madame Bovary and is sitting in the empty consulting room; when a noise is heard, Emma asks him: "Have you got your gun?" The question makes him laugh. Against whom would he have to use his weapon if not against Bovary–and this is certainly the least of his intentions. All the same, the word has been

Caricature by A. Lemot of Flaubert dissecting Emma Bovary, which may have been inspired by Sainte-Beuve's remark that "Flaubert handles the pen like others the scalpel." It was published in the 5–12 September 1869 issue of La Parodie *(cliché Bibliothèque nationale de France, Paris).*

said. Madame Bovary said it without thinking, but it reveals her to be the kind of woman who, in the grip of passion, would stop at nothing. She shows it again later, after Rodolphe, who was willing enough to make love to a pretty neighbor but never even considered eloping, has abandoned her. During a trip to Rouen she meets Léon again; his former shyness has now completely disappeared and his corruption hastens Emma's. She ruins her household and goes into debt without her husband's knowledge; one day, pursued by her creditors, she urges Léon to find her 3000 francs at once: "If I were in your place, I'd know where to find them.–Where?–At your office." Madame Bovary is ready to demand murder and theft, the ultimate degradation, from her lovers, if they were willing to heed her. But Flaubert is right in merely suggesting such possibilities by means of violent utterances of this kind.

The last half of the work is not less carefully or less precisely expressed than the first, yet I must mention an all too apparent weakness: although it was certainly not the author's deliberate intention, his very method, describing everything and leaving nothing out, leads him to include many too vividly suggestive details, which come close to appealing to the reader's erotic sensuality. He should definitely not have gone so far. After all, a book is not and could never be reality itself. At certain points, description can overreach the aim, not of the moralist, but of the discriminating artist. I know that even at the most daring moments, M. Flaubert's feeling remains thoroughly critical and ironic; his tone is never seductive or tender; nothing, in fact, could be less tempting than his descriptions of sin. But he is dealing with a French reader all too eager to look for licentiousness and likely to discover it at the slightest provocation.

Madame Bovary's terrifying death, which could well be called her punishment, is presented in relentless detail. The author here dares to sound dark chords that verge on dissonance. M. Bovary's death, which follows immediately, is a touching episode and revives our sympathy for this good and unhappy man. I have mentioned earlier the presence of strikingly apt and natural phrases: in his grief at the death of his wife, Bovary, who has done the utmost not to learn of her guilt, continues to refer all events back to her person; on receiving the announcement of Léon's wedding, he exclaims, "How happy this would have made my poor wife!" Later, he finds both Léon's and Rodolphe's letters but forgives everything and never ceases to love the deceitful creature he has lost; he finally dies brokenhearted.

Frequently, in the course of the narrative, the author has the opportunity to make a character fulfill and, so to speak, redeem himself and thus to add the ideal to the real. It would have taken very little. Charles Bovary near the end, for instance: with one slight pressure of the hand, leaving a mark in the clay he was moulding into shape, the artist could have made this vulgar face into a noble and touching figure. The reader would have consented; he almost demands it. But the writer never relents; he has chosen not to.

When the old Rouault comes to the burial of his daughter, in the midst of his desperate grief, he is given a line both grotesque and sublime in its veracity: every year, he used to send Charles Bovary a turkey in memory of his cured leg; upon leaving him, with tears in his eyes, his last heartfelt words are: "Don't worry, I will keep sending you your turkey!"

Although I am fully aware of the particular bias which constitutes the method and *ars poetica* of the author, I have one reproach to make: virtue is too absent from this book; no one represents it. The little Justin, who loves Emma in silence, is the only devoted, disinterested character, but he goes by almost unnoticed. Why did Flaubert not include a single character who, by the spectacle of his virtue, would have offered some comfort, some repose to the reader and become a friendly presence? He deserves to be told: "Moralist, you know everything but you are cruel." The book is certainly not without a moral; the author has not spelled out the lesson, but the reader can reach his own frightening conclusions. Yet, is it the true function of art to refuse all consolation, to reject all clemency and gentleness for the sake of total truth? Moreover, even if truth were the only aim, can it be said that truth resides entirely with evil, with human stupidity and perverseness? Even in the provinces, full as life is of wranglings, persecutions, petty frustrations and meddling hostility, there also remain good and beautiful souls who have preserved their innocence, perhaps better and more deeply than elsewhere; instances of modesty, resignation, helpfulness extending over many years–we all know some of them. Even in your so-truthful characters, you cannot deny that you artfully collect and assemble ridiculous and evil traits; why not gather with equal art traits of virtue on at least one head, one charming or beloved brow? Hidden in the provinces, in the center of France, I have known a young woman of superior intelligence and feeling: married but childless, with no one to love or to care for, she could easily have succumbed to boredom. Instead, she adopted other children, and became the benefactor of the neighborhood, a civilizing influence in the somewhat backward region where destiny had led her. She taught the village children to read and initiated them to the principles of morality. She would walk for miles on foot accompanied by one of her pupils, and would teach him under a tree, on a footpath, in the heath. Such souls exist in the provinces and in the country: why should they not also be shown? Their presence elevates and consoles while broadening our view of humanity.

On the whole, this book bears the imprint of the times. I am told that it was begun several years ago, but it appears at the right moment. It is the right kind of book to read after hearing the precise and caustic dialogue of an Alexandre Dumas comedy, after applauding *The Fake Gentlemen,* or between two articles by Taine. In many places and under many different forms, I detect symptoms of a new literary manner: scientific, experimental, adult, powerful, a little harsh. Such are the outstanding characteristics of the leaders of the new generation. Son and brother of distinguished surgeons, M. Flaubert handles the pen like others the scalpel. Anatomists and physiologists, I meet you at every turn!

–Charles-Augustin Sainte-Beuve, "*Madame Bovary,* by Gustave Flaubert," translated by Paul de Man, in *Gustave Flaubert: Madame Bovary* (New York & London: Norton, 1965), pp. 325–336

* * *

Charles Baudelaire, circa 1860 (photograph by Étienne Carjat; courtesy of the BBC Hulton Picture Library)

Flaubert had met the poet Charles Baudelaire through their common friend, Théophile Gautier, and had congratulated him warmly in July 1857 for his collection of poems Les Fleurs du mal. *Baudelaire's important review of* Madame Bovary *was first published in the 18 October 1857 issue of* L'Artiste. *Flaubert thanked him in a letter dated 21 October 1857: "Your article gave me the greatest possible pleasure. You entered into the arcana of the book as though my brain were yours. It is understood and felt to its very depths" (*The Letters of Gustave Flaubert, 1830–1857, *p. 234).*

Baudelaire on the Greatness of *Madame Bovary*

I

In the field of criticism, the writer who comes after everybody else is not without possessing certain advantages over the prophetic reviewer who predicts, ordains and, one might say, creates success with the authority born from his courage and his loyalty.

M. Gustave Flaubert is no longer in need of loyalty, if ever he was. Some of the subtlest and most authoritative critics have added luster and distinction to his excellent book. All that remains to be done is perhaps to point out some aspects that have remained unnoticed and to emphasize certain traits and insights which, in my opinion, have not been sufficiently praised and commented upon. Moreover, as I was suggesting, the situation of the latecomer who follows in the wake of established opinion, possesses a paradoxical charm. Being alone and in no hurry, he enjoys more freedom than his predecessors; he seems to be summarizing an earlier debate; consequently, he must avoid the excesses of the prosecution as well as of the defense and seek for a new approach, with no other incitement than his love for Beauty and for Justice.

II

I have just pronounced the splendid and frightening word: Justice; may I be allowed–as it is my pleasure–to thank the magistrates of France for the splendid example of fairness and good taste which they have displayed in this circumstance. On the one hand, they confronted a blind and violent moral zeal, misguidedly acting on the wrong terrain; on the other, a novel by an as yet unknown writer–and what a novel!–the most loyal, the most objective of novels, comparable in its banality to a field in the country, soaked and lashed like nature itself by endless storms and winds. Between the two, the judges chose to be as loyal and unpartial as the book that had been offered them as a scapegoat. Better still, if we may be allowed to conjecture on the basis of the written opinions that accompanied the judgment, it now seems that even if they had discovered something truly objectionable in the book they would nevertheless have absolved it in recognition of the *Beauty* that clothes it. This striking concern for Beauty, coming from men whose faculties are primarily called upon to serve the Rightful and True, is a very moving symptom, especially if one compares it with the burning appetites of a society that has entirely forsworn all spiritual love and, forgetting its ancient entrails, now only cares for its visceral organs. It can be said, because of its highly poetic tendency, that this decision is a definitive one; the Muse has won her case in court and all writers worthy of that name have been exonerated once and forever in the person of M. Gustave Flaubert.

I do not agree with those who claim, perhaps with a slight and unconscious envy, that the book owes its popular success to the trial and subsequent acquittal. Left unmolested, it would have created the same turmoil, awakened the same curiosity and amazement. Enlightened readers had long since given it their praise. Even when an earlier version appeared in the *Revue de Paris,* marred by harmful excisions that destroyed the inner balance, it had created quite a stir. Gustave Flaubert grew famous overnight and found himself in a situation both favorable and harmful; his exceptional and genuine talent was able to overcome this equivocal predicament, caused by circumstances which I will try to analyze as well as I can.

III

Flaubert's situation can be called favorable because, ever since the death of Balzac–this prodigious meteor whose passage covered our country with a cloud of glory, like a bizarre and unusual sunlight, a polar dawn throwing its magic light over a frozen desert–all curiosity about the novel had been appeased and dormant. Some amazing experiments, it must be admitted, had been tried.

. . . .

I would be the last to reproach these writers, some of them inspired by Dickens, others molded after Byron or Bulwer, because their pride or an excess of talent prevented them from equaling even a Paul de Kock in stepping upon the unsteady threshold of popular success–this indecent slut asking only to be violated. Nor will I praise them for their failure, as little as I praise M. Gustave Flaubert for succeeding at once where others have tried for a lifetime. I see there, at most, an additional proof of strength and I will try to determine the reasons which lead the author in that particular direction rather than another.

But I also stated that the situation of the newcomer-novelist is a dangerous one due, alas, to a dismally simple reason. For many years, the interest which the public is willing to devote to matters of the spirit has considerably diminished and the allotment of its available enthusiasm has steadily decreased. The last years of Louis-Philippe's reign saw the final outbursts of a spirit still willing to be stimulated by the display of imaginative powers; the new novelist, however, is confronted with a completely worn-out public or, worse even, a stupefied and greedy audience, whose only hatred is for fiction, and only love for material possession.

In these circumstances, the reaction of a cultured mind, devoted to beauty but trained to fight in its defense, must have been to evaluate the good as well as the bad of the situation and to reason as follows:

"How can I most effectively stir up all these decrepit souls? They do not know what they would like; they only know that they positively hate greatness and consider the naïveté, the ardor of passion and the spontaneity of poetry embarrassing and insulting. Therefore, since the nineteenth century reader considers the choice of great subject-matter to be in poor taste, let us resolve to be vulgar. Let us beware above all of giving away our real feelings and of speaking in our own name. In narrating passions and adventures which would tend to kindle sympathetic fires in the ordinary reader, we will remain icily detached. We will remain objective and impersonal as the realists tell us.

"Moreover, since of late our ears have been assaulted by infantile chatter of a group of theory-makers and since we have heard of a certain literary device called *realism*–a degrading insult flung in the face of all analytical writers, a vague and overflexible term applied by indiscriminate minds to the minute description of detail rather than to a new method of literary creation–we shall take advantage of the general ignorance and confusion. We shall apply a nervous, picturesque, subtle and precise style to a banal canvas. We shall make the most trivial of plots express the most ebullient and ardent feelings. Solemn and definitive words will he uttered by the silliest of voices.

"And where we can find the breeding-ground of stupidity, the setting that produces inane absurdities and is inhabited by the most intolerant imbeciles?

"In the provinces.

"What characters, in the provinces, are particularly insufferable?

"Petty people in petty positions, with minds distorted by their actions.

"What is the tritest theme of all, worn out by repetition, by being played over and over again like a tired barrel-organ?

"Adultery.

"Neither do I have to make my 'heroine' heroic. Provided she be sufficiently handsome, daring, ambitious, irresistibly drawn to a higher world, she cannot fail to awaken interest. This will make the *tour de force* even nobler and give our sinful heroine the–comparatively speaking–rare distinction of differing entirely from the self-complacent gossips to which previous writers had accustomed us.

"I do not have to concern myself any longer with the style, the picturesque backgrounds, the description of the setting; I can do all this with almost excessive skill. I will proceed instead by fine logic and analysis, and thus demonstrate that all subjects are equally good or bad depending on how they are treated, and that the most vulgar ones can become the best of all."

Madame Bovary was born from these resolutions as the impossible task, the true *gageure,* the wager which all works of art must be.

In order to complete his exploit to the full, it remained for the author to relinquish, so to speak, his actual sex and make himself into a woman. The result is miraculous, for in spite of his zeal at wearing masks he could not help but infuse some male blood into the veins of his creation; the most energetic and ambitious, but also the most imaginative part of Madame Bovary's personality have definitely remained masculine in kind. Like weapon-bearing Pallas issuing forth from the forehead of Zeus, this bizarre and androgynous creature houses the seductiveness of a virile soul within the body of a beautiful woman.

IV

Several critics who called the book beautiful because of the precision and liveliness of its descriptions, have claimed that it lacks the central character who acts as a moral judge and expresses the author's conscience. Where can we find the proverbial and legendary figure whose task it is to explain the fable and to guide the reader's judgment? In other words, where is the lesson, the cause?

What an absurdity! The eternal and incorrigible confusion of genres and of purposes is not yet overcome! A true work of art does not need to make moral pleas. The inner logic of the work suffices for all moral implications and it is the reader's task to draw the right conclusions from its outcome.

As for the intimate, deeper center of the book, there is no doubt that it resides in the adulterous woman; she alone possesses all the attributes of a worthy hero, albeit in the guise of a disgraced victim. I have just stated that she is almost masculine and that, perhaps unconsciously, the author had bestowed upon her all the qualities of manliness.

Let the reader carefully consider the following characteristics:

1. The imagination, the highest and most tyrannical of faculties, takes the place of the heart or what is called the heart: that from which reason is generally excluded; most of the time, women, like animals, are dominated by the heart.

2. Sudden forcefulness and quickness of decision, a mystical fusion of reason and passion typical of men created for action.

3. An unlimited urge to seduce and to dominate, including a willingness to stoop to the lowest means of seduction, such as the vulgar appeal of dress, perfume and make-up–all summarized in two words: dandyism, exclusive love of domination.

And yet, Madame Bovary gives in to her lovers; carried away by the sophistry of her imagination, she gives herself with magnificent generosity, in an entirely masculine manner, to fools who don't begin to measure up to her, exactly as poets will put themselves at the mercy of foolish women.

As another proof of the masculine qualities which she carries in her arteries, one should notice that she is much less incensed by the obvious physical shortcomings of her husband or by his glaring provincialism, than by this total absence of genius, his intellectual ineptness forcefully brought home by the stupid operation of the clubfoot.

One should reread the pages that deal with this episode; some are shortsighted enough to consider it superfluous but it serves precisely to bring the cen-

Emma with Father Bournisien, from part 2, chapter 6 (illustration by Albert Fourié; Madame Bovary. Mœurs de province, *3 volumes [Paris: Librarie Illustrée, 1900])*

tral character fully into light. Her fierce anger, pent up for years, suddenly bursts into the open; doors slam; the awed husband, who was never able to give his romantically inclined wife the slightest spiritual satisfaction, is relegated to his room; he is locked up in punishment for his guilty ignorance while Madame Bovary, in despair, cries out like a smaller Lady Macbeth mismated with an inadequate captain: "Ah! if *only* I were the wife of one of those balding and stooping scholars whose eyes, sheltered by dark glasses, are forever fixed on the archives of science! I would be proud to be seen at his arm; I would be the companion of a prince of the spirit–but to be chained forever, like a convict, to a fool who is not even capable of mending a crippled foot, bah!" Caught in her petty surroundings, stifled by a narrow horizon, this woman is a truly sublime example of her kind.

I find proof of Madame Bovary's ambiguous temperament even in her convent education.

The nuns have observed that the young girl is endowed with an amazing power to enjoy life, to anticipate all the pleasures she will be able to extract from it. This characterizes the man of action.

Meanwhile, she becomes intoxicated with the color of the stained-glass windows, with the Oriental shades that the ornate windows cast on her schoolgirl prayer book; she gorges herself on the solemn music of Vespers and obeying the impulse of her nerves rather than of her mind, she substitutes in her soul for the real God a God of pure fantasy, a God of the future and of chance, a picture-God wearing spurs and mustaches. This is characteristic of the hysterical poet.

The Academy of Medicine has not as yet been able to explain the mysterious condition of hysteria. In women, it acts like a stifling ball rising in the body (I mention only the main symptom), while in nervous men it can be the cause of many forms of impotence as well as of a limitless ability at excess. Why could this physiological mystery not serve as the central subject, the true core, of a literary work?

V

When all is said, this woman has real greatness, and she provokes our pity. In spite of the author's systematic tough-mindedness, in spite of his efforts to retreat entirely from the stage and manipulate his characters rather like a puppeteer handles his puppets, all *intellectual* women owe him a debt of gratitude. By endowing them with a talent for dreaming as well as for calculating–a combination that constitutes the perfect human being–he has elevated the female species to new heights, far above the realm of the purely animal and close to the ideal realm of men.

Madame Bovary has been called ridiculous by some. Indeed, we meet her at times mistaking some species of gentleman–could he even be called a country squire?–dressed in hunting vests and contrasting dress for a hero out of Walter Scott! At another moment, she is enamored of an insignificant little clerk who is not even capable of performing a dangerous action for his mistress. Trapped finally within the narrow confines of a village, this bizarre Pasiphae, now a poor exhausted creature, still pursues the ideal in the county bars and taverns. But does it matter? Even then, we must admit, she is, like Caesar at Carpentras, in pursuit of the ideal!

I will not echo the Lycanthrope, remembered for a subversiveness which no longer prevails, when he said: "Confronted with all that is vulgar and inept in the present time, can we not take refuge in cigarettes and adultery?" But I assert that our world, even when it is weighed on precision scales, turns out to be exceedingly harsh considering it was engendered by Christ; it could hardly be entitled to throw the first stone at adultery. A few cuckolds more or less are not likely to increase the rotating speed of the spheres and to hasten by a second the final destruction of the universe. The time has come to put a stop to an increasingly contagious hypocrisy; we should expose the ridicule of men and women, themselves perverted to a point of utter triviality, who dare to attack a defenseless writer after he has deigned, with the chastity of an ancient teacher of rhetoric, to cast a mantle of glory over a bedroom-farce subject that would be repulsive and grotesque if it had not been touched by the opalescent light of poetry.

If I allowed myself to pursue this analytical bent any further, I would never finish; the book is so suggestive that one could fill a volume with one's observations. For the moment, I merely wish to indicate that the critics have overlooked or even attacked several of the most important passages in the novel. This is the case, for instance, of the section dealing with the bungled clubfoot operation. And nothing could be more authentically *modern* than the desolate and remarkable scene in which the future adulteress–for the poor woman, at that point, is still in the earliest stages of her downfall–calls on the Church for assistance. We expect the Church to be like the divine Mother, ready at all times to extend a helping hand, like a pharmacist who always has to be available. Yet Emma finds the attention of Father Bournisien, the parish priest, primarily taken up by the gymnastics of catechism pupils scattered among the stalls and chairs of the church; his candid reply to Emma is, "If you are unwell, madame, and since M. Bovary is a doctor, why don't you speak to your husband?"

Thus absolved by the ineptness of the priest, what woman would not wish to immerse herself in the swirling waters of adultery–and which one of us, in a more naïve age and in troubled circumstances, did not find himself confronted with similarly incompetent priests?

VI

Since I happen to have at hand two books by this same author (*Madame Bovary* and the as yet still uncollected fragments of the *Temptation of Saint Anthony*), my original intent had been to establish a kind of parallel between both. I meant to point out identities and correspondences. It would have been easy enough to uncover beneath the tight texture of *Madame Bovary,* the elements of high lyricism and irony that abound in the *Temptation of Saint Anthony*. Here the author appears without disguise; his Saint Anthony is Madame Bovary tempted by all the demons of illusion and heresy, by all the obscenities of matter that encompass her; harassed by all the aberrations that lead to our downfall, Saint Anthony thus becomes a stronger apologist than his smaller and fictional bourgeois equivalent. This work, which unfortunately exists only in fragments, contains dazzling passages. I am not only referring to the prodigious feast given by Nebuchadnezzar, the marvelous apparition of a frivolous Queen of Sheba dancing in miniature shape on the retina of an ascete, or the conspicuously overdone setting in which Apollonius of Tyana appears, escorted by his keeper, the idiotic millionaire whom he is dragging after him around the world. I mostly want to direct the reader's mind toward the *subcurrent* that runs through the entire book, the subterranean, rebellious painful level, the darker strain that serves as a guide in traversing this pandemonic capharnaüm of solitude.

As I said before, I could easily have shown that in *Madame Bovary* M. Flaubert deliberately muted the high ironic and lyrical faculties which he gave full rein in the *Temptation;* the latter work, truly the secret chamber of his mind, evidently remains the most interesting of the two for poets and philosophers.

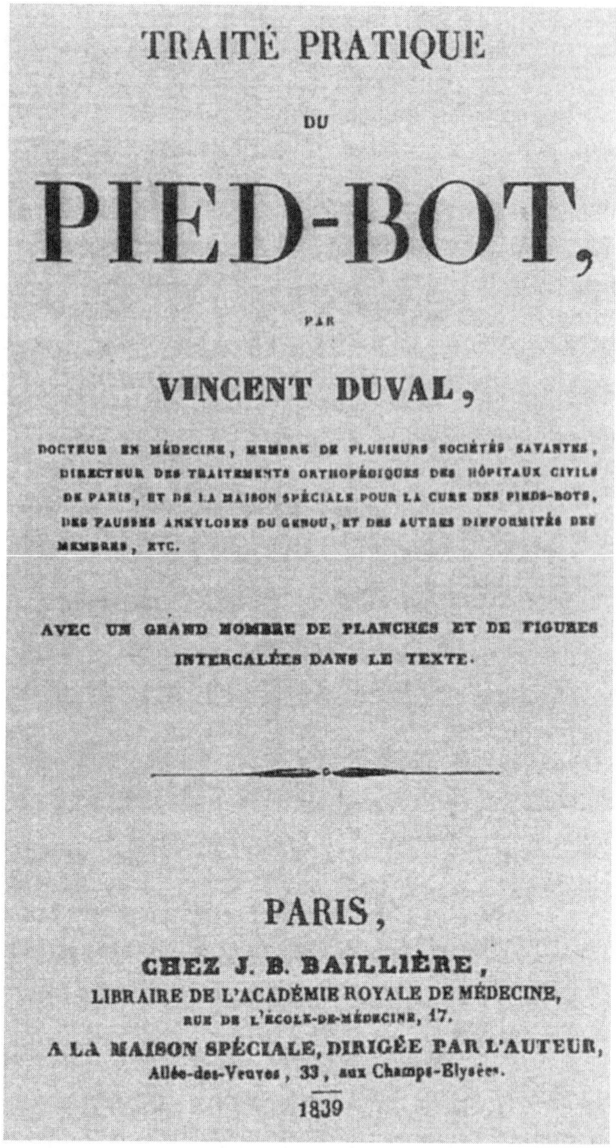
TRAITÉ PRATIQUE

DU

PIED-BOT,

PAR

VINCENT DUVAL,

DOCTEUR EN MÉDECINE, MEMBRE DE PLUSIEURS SOCIÉTÉS SAVANTES, DIRECTEUR DES TRAITEMENTS ORTHOPÉDIQUES DES HÔPITAUX CIVILS DE PARIS, ET DE LA MAISON SPÉCIALE POUR LA CURE DES PIEDS-BOTS, DES FAUSSES ANKYLOSES DU GENOU, ET DES AUTRES DIFFORMITÉS DES MEMBRES, ETC.

AVEC UN GRAND NOMBRE DE PLANCHES ET DE FIGURES INTERCALÉES DANS LE TEXTE.

PARIS,

CHEZ J. B. BAILLIÈRE,

LIBRAIRE DE L'ACADÉMIE ROYALE DE MÉDECINE,

RUE DE L'ÉCOLE-DE-MÉDECINE, 17.

A LA MAISON SPÉCIALE, DIRIGÉE PAR L'AUTEUR,

Allée-des-Veuves, 33, aux Champs-Elysées.

1839

Cover from Dr. Vincent Duval's "Practical Treatise on Club-Foot," one of the books that Flaubert used to write the clubfoot-surgery episode in part 2, chapter 11 of Madame Bovary. *Although Charles Bovary reads Dr. Duval's instructions carefully, the operation on Hippolyte's foot results in the amputation of his leg (cliché Bibliothèque nationale de France, Paris).*

Maybe I will some day have the pleasure of performing this task.

–Charles Baudelaire, "*Madame Bovary,* by Gustave Flaubert," translated by Paul de Man, in *Gustave Flaubert: Madame Bovary* (New York & London: Norton, 1965), pp. 336–343

Critical Views of *Madame Bovary*

In this excerpt, taken from an essay on Charles de Bernard and Flaubert that was first published in February 1876 by the journal Galaxy, *Henry James discusses Flaubert as a realist who approaches the world from the "outside."*

Flaubert's Disagreeable Masterpiece

. . . Practically M. Flaubert is a potent moralist; whether, when he wrote his book, he was so theoretically is a matter best known to himself. Every out-and-out realist who provokes serious meditation may claim that he is a moralist; for that, after all, is the most that the moralists can do for us. They sow the seeds of virtue; they can hardly pretend to raise the crop. Excellence in this matter consists in the tale and the moral hanging well together, and this they are certainly more likely to do when there has been a definite intention–that intention of which artists who cultivate "art for art" are usually so extremely mistrustful; exhibiting thereby, surely, a most injurious disbelief in the illimitable alchemy of art. We may say on the whole, doubtless, that the highly didactic character of "Madame Bovary" is an accident, inasmuch as the works that have followed it, both from its author's and from other hands, have been things to read much less for meditation's than for sensation's sake. M. Flaubert's theory as a novelist, briefly expressed, is to begin on the outside. Human life, we may imagine his saying, is before all things a spectacle, an occupation and entertainment for the eyes. What our eyes show us is all that we are sure of; so with this we will at any rate begin. As this is infinitely curious and entertaining, if we know how to look at it, and as such looking consumes a great deal of time and space, it is very possible that with this also we may end. We admit nevertheless that there is something else, beneath and behind, that belongs to the realm of vagueness and uncertainty, and into this we must occasionally dip. It crops up sometimes irrepressibly, and of course we do not positively count it out. On the whole we will leave it to take care of itself and let it come off as it may. If we propose to represent the pictorial side of life, of course we must do it thoroughly well–we must be complete. There must be no botching, no bungling, no scamping; it must be a very serious matter. We will "render" things–anything, everything, from a chimney-pot to the shoulders of a duchess–as painters render them. We believe there is a certain particular phrase, better than any other, for everything in the world, and the thoroughly accomplished writer ends by finding it. We care only for what *is*–we know nothing about what ought to be. Human life is interesting, because we are in it and of it; all kinds of curious things are taking place in it (we do not analyse the curious–for artists it is an ultimate fact); we select as many of them as possible. Some of the most curious are the most disagreeable, but the chance for "rendering" in the disagreeable is as great as anywhere else (some people think even greater), and moreover the disagreeable is extremely characteristic. The real is the most satisfactory thing in the world, and if we once fairly advance in this direction nothing shall frighten us back.

Some such words as those may stand as a rough sketch of the sort of intellectual conviction under which "Madame Bovary" was written. The theory in this case at least was applied with brilliant success; it produced a masterpiece. Realism seems to us with "Madame Bovary" to have said its last word. We doubt whether the same process will ever produce anything better. In M. Flaubert's own hands it has distinctly failed to do so. "L'Education Sentimentale" is in comparison mechanical and inanimate. The great good fortune of "Madame Bovary" is that here the theory seems to have been invented after the fact. The author began to describe because he had laid up a great fund of disinterested observations; he had been looking at things for years, for his own edification, in that particular way. The imitative talents in the same line, those whose highest ambition is to "do" their Balzac or their Flaubert, give us the sense of looking at the world only with the most mercenary motives–of going about to stare at things only for the sake of their forthcoming novel. M. Flaubert knew what he was describing–knew it extraordinarily well. One can hardly congratulate him on his knowledge; anything drearier, more sordid, more vulgar and desolate than the greater part of the subject-matter of this romance it would be impossible to conceive. "Mœurs de Province," the sub-title runs, and the work is the most striking possible example of the singular passion, so common among Frenchmen of talent, for disparaging their provincial life. Emma Bovary is the daughter of a small farmer, who has been able to send her to boarding-school, and to give her something of an "elegant" education. She is pretty and graceful, and she marries a small country doctor–the kindest, simplest, stupidest of husbands. He takes her to live in a squalid little country town, called Yonville-l'Abbaye, near Rouen; she is luxurious and sentimental; she wastes away with ennui, loneliness, and hatred of her narrow lot and absent opportunities, and on the very first chance she takes a lover. With him she is happy for a few months, and then he deserts her, brutally and cynically. She falls violently ill and comes near dying; then she gets well and takes another lover, of a different kind. All the world–the very little world of Yonville-l'Abbaye–sees and knows and gossips; her husband alone neither sees nor suspects. Meanwhile she has been spending money remorselessly and insanely; she has made promissory notes and she is smothered in debt. She has undermined the ground beneath her husband's feet; her second lover leaves her; she is ruined, dishonoured, utterly at bay. She goes back as a beggar to her first lover, and he refuses to give her a sou. She tries to sell herself and fails; then, in impotence and desperation, she collapses. She takes poison and dies horribly, and the bailiffs come down on her husband, who is still heroically ignorant. At last he learns the truth, and it is too much for him; he loses all courage, and dies one day on his garden-bench, leaving twelve francs fifty centimes to his little girl, who is sent to get her living in a cotton-mill. The tale is a tragedy, unillumined and unredeemed, and it might seem, on this rapid and imperfect showing, to be rather a vulgar tragedy. Women who get into trouble with the extreme facility of Emma Bovary, and by the same method, are unfortunately not rare, and the better opinion seems to be that they deserve but a limited degree of sympathy. The history of M. Flaubert's heroine is nevertheless full of substance and meaning. In spite of the elaborate system of portraiture to which she is subjected, in spite of being minutely described, in all her attitudes and all her moods, from the hem of her garment to the texture of her finger-nails, she remains a living creature, and as a living creature she interests us. The only thing that poor Charles Bovary, after her death, can find to say to her lovers is, "It's the fault of fatality." And in fact, as we enter into the situation, it is. M. Flaubert gives his readers the impression of having known few kinds of women, but he has evidently known intimately this particular kind. We see the process of her history; we see how it marches from step to step to its horrible termination, and we see that it could not have been otherwise. It is a case of the passion for luxury, for elegance, for the world's most agreeable and comfortable things, of an intense and complex imagination, corrupt almost in the germ, and finding corruption, and feeding on it, in the most unlikely and unfavouring places–it is a case of all this being pressed back upon itself with a force which makes an explosion inevitable. Madame Bovary has an insatiable hunger for pleasure, and she lives in the midst of dreariness; she is ignorant, vain, naturally depraved; of the things she dreams about not an intimation ever reaches her; so she makes her *trouée,* as the French say, bores her opening, scrapes and scratches her way out into the light, where she can. The reader may protest against a heroine who is "naturally depraved." You are welcome, he may say, to make of a heroine what you please, to carry her where you please; but in mercy do not set us down to a young lady of whom, on the first page, there is nothing better to be said than that. But all this is a question of degree. Madame Bovary is typical, like all powerfully-conceived figures in fiction. There are a great many potential Madame Bovarys, a great many young women, vain, ignorant, leading ugly, vulgar, intolerable lives, and possessed of irritable nerves and of a high natural appreciation of luxury, of admiration, of agreeable sensations, of what they consider the natural rights of pretty women; who are more or less launched upon the rapid slope which she descended to the bottom.

Henry James in the early 1880s (Houghton Library, Harvard University)

. . . .

. . . M. Flaubert keeps well out of the province of remedies; he simply relates his facts, in all their elaborate horror. The accumulation of detail is so immense, the vividness of portraiture of people, of places, of times and hours, is so poignant and convincing, that one is dragged into the very current and tissue of the story; the reader himself seems to have lived in it all, more than in any novel we can recall. At the end the intensity of illusion becomes horrible; overwhelmed with disgust and pity he closes the book.

Besides being the history of the most miserable of women, "Madame Bovary" is also an elaborate picture of small bourgeois rural life. Anything in this direction more remorseless and complete it would be hard to conceive. Into all that makes life ignoble and vulgar and sterile M. Flaubert has entered with an extraordinary penetration. The dullness and flatness of it all suffocate us; the pettiness and ugliness sicken us. Every one in the book is either stupid or mean, but against the shabby-coloured background two figures stand out in salient relief. One is Charles Bovary, the husband of the heroine; the other is M. Homais, the village apothecary. Bovary is introduced to us in his childhood, at school, and we see him afterwards at college and during his first marriage–a union with a widow of meagre charms, twenty years older than himself. He is the only good person of the book, but he is stupidly, helplessly good. At school "he had for correspondent a wholesale hardware-merchant of the Rue Ganterie, who used to fetch him away once a month, on a Sunday, send him to walk in the harbour and look at the boats, and then bring him back to college, by seven o'clock, before supper. Every Thursday evening he wrote a long letter to his mother, with red ink and three wafers; then he went over his copy books, or else read an old volume of 'Anacharsis' which was knocking about the class-room. In our walks he used to talk with the servant, who was from the country like himself." In Homais, the apothecary, M. Flaubert has really added to our knowledge of human nature–at least as human nature is modified by French social conditions. To American readers, fortunately, this figure represents nothing familiar; we do not as yet possess any such mellow perfection of charlatanism. The apothecary is that unwholesome compound, a Philistine radical–a *père de famille,* a free-thinker, a rapacious shopkeeper, a stern moralist, an ardent democrat and an abject snob. He is a complete creation; he is taken, as the French say, *sur le vif* [from life], and his talk, his accent, his pompous vocabulary, his attitudes, his vanities, his windy vacuity, are superbly rendered. Except her two lovers, M. Homais is Madame Bovary's sole male acquaintance, and her only social relaxation is to spend the evening with his wife and her own husband in his back shop. Her life has known, in the way of recreation, but two other events. Once she has been at a ball at the house of a neighbouring nobleman, for whom her husband had lanced an abscess in the cheek, and who sends the invitation as part payment–a fatal ball, which has opened her eyes to her own deprivations and intolerably quickened her desires; and once she has been to the theatre at Rouen. Both of these episodes are admirably put before us, and they play a substantial part in the tale. The book is full of expressive episodes; the most successful, in its hideous relief and reality, is the long account of the operation performed by Charles Bovary upon the club-foot of the ostler at the inn–an operation superfluous, ridiculous, abjectly unskilful and clumsy, and which results in the amputation of the poor fellow's whole leg after he

Charles, Emma, and Léon at the theater in Rouen, from part 2, chapter 15 (illustration by Albert Fourié; Madame Bovary. Mœurs de province, *3 volumes [Paris: Librarie Illustrée, 1900])*

has lain groaning under the reader's eyes and nose for a dozen pages, amid the flies and dirt, the brooms and pails, the comings and goings of his squalid corner of the tavern. The reader asks himself the meaning of this elaborate presentation of the most repulsive of incidents, and feels inclined at first to charge it to a sort of artistic bravado on the author's part–a desire to complete his theory of realism by applying his resources to that which is simply disgusting. But he presently sees that the whole episode has a kind of metaphysical value. It completes the general picture; it characterizes the daily life of a community in which such incidents assume the importance of leading events, and it gives the final touch to our sense of poor Charles Bovary's bungling mediocrity. Everything in the book is ugly; turning over its pages, our eyes fall upon only this one little passage in which an agreeable "effect" is ren-

Madame Bovary and the Battle for Zamboanga

Publisher Patrick O'Connor recalls reading Flaubert's novel during World War II.

The battle for Zamboanga, (where the monkeys have no tails) Philippine Island was far from the bloodiest battle the Forty-first Infantry Division fought but it was exciting enough for me. There were the usual five days on the open water on an L.C.I. (Landing Craft Infantry). You've seen one of them in the movies, it's the one John Wayne gets off with his bayonet fixed to the end of his rifle. You do not get off charging but you do hold your piece (Army talk for rifle) up in the air so it doesn't get wet. Before that zero minus two or three hours, the Air Force has bombed the beach to smithereens, exciting and not unlike Macy's fireworks. It's the only time the Infantry likes the Air Force, otherwise we tell stories about their dumping mail in the Pacific so they will have room to bring booze from Australia. So at Zamboanga the Air Force pulverized the beach and we casually walked off the L.C.I.'s and confusion reigned.

Meanwhile it was impossible to dig a foxhole in the coral, though several frightened rookies tried. No matter how scared you are coral doesn't give even with a pickax: I had found that out earlier.

I had found myself a little indentation in the ground and that's where my friend Sgt. Kerr found me. He was not my sergeant but my friend the sergeant who read Yeats and Pound. He reported finding me lounging on a GI blanket looking as much like Madame Récamier as a dirty infantryman could eating C-ration chocolates, and reading.

Sgt. Kerr was an aristocrat who never ever swore but he said: "Private O'Connor what the fuck are you doing?"

"I'm weeping for Emma," I said.

"The fucking world has gone crazy and this fuck is reading fucking French novels."

–Patrick O'Connor, *Don't Look Back: A Memoir* (Wakefield, R.I. & London: Moyer Bell, 1993), pp. 119–120

dered. It treats of Bovary's visits to Emma, at her father's farm, before their marriage, and it is a happy instance of the way in which this author's style arrests itself at every step in a picture. "Once, when it was thawing, the bark of the trees was reeking in the yard, the snow was melting on the roofs of the outbuildings. She was upon the threshold; she went in and fetched her umbrella and opened it. The umbrella, of iridescent silk, with the sun coming through it, lighted up her white complexion with changing reflections. Beneath it she smiled in the soft warmth, and he heard the waterdrops fall one by one upon the tense silk." To many people "Madame Bovary" will always be a hard book to read and an impossible one to enjoy. They will complain of the abuse of description, of the want of spontaneity, of the hideousness of the subject, of the dryness and coldness and cynicism of the tone. Others will continue to think it a great performance. They will admit that it is not a sentimental novel, but they will claim that it may be regarded as a philosophical one; they will insist that the descriptions are extraordinary, and that beneath them there is always an idea that holds them up and carries them along. . . .

–Henry James, "Charles de Bernard and Gustave Flaubert," in *French Poets and Novelists* (New York & London: Macmillan, 1893), pp. 201–209

* * *

For Vladimir Nabokov, Madame Bovary *was such an important novel that he included it several times in the courses he taught on literature at Cornell University. As the classes were designed for English speakers, he used Eleanor Marx Aveling's translation, though he greatly revised it. These are excerpts from lectures he gave during the late 1940s and early 1950s.*

Art Remains: Nabokov's Notes on *Madame Bovary*

We shall discuss *Madame Bovary* as Flaubert intended it to be discussed: in terms of structures (*mouvements* as he termed them), thematic lines, style, poetry, and characters. The novel consists of thirty-five chapters, each about ten pages long, and is divided into three parts set respectively in Rouen and Tostes, in Yonville, and in Yonville, Rouen, and Yonville, all of these places invented except Rouen, a cathedral city in northern France.

The main action is supposed to take place in the 1830s and 1840s, under King Louis Philippe (1830–1848). Chapter 1 begins in the winter of 1827, and in a kind of afterword the lives of some of the characters are followed up till 1856 into the reign of Napoleon III and indeed up to the date of Flaubert's completing the book. *Madame Bovary* was begun at Croisset, near Rouen, on the nineteenth of September 1851, finished in April 1856, sent out in June, and published serially at the end of the same year in the *Revue de Paris.* A hundred miles to the north of Rouen, Charles Dickens in Boulogne was finishing *Bleak House* in the summer of 1853 when Flaubert had reached part two of his novel; one year before that, in Russia, Gogol had died and Tolstoy had published his first important work, *Childhood.*

Three forces make and mold a human being: heredity, environment, and the unknown agent X. Of these the second, environment, is by far the least important, while the last, agent X, is by far the most influential. In the case of characters living in books, it is of course the author who controls, directs, and applies the three forces. The society around Madame Bovary has been manufactured by Flaubert as deliberately as Madame Bovary herself has been made by him, and to say that this Flaubertian society acted upon that Flaubertian character is to talk in circles. Everything that happens in the book happens exclusively in Flaubert's mind, no matter what the initial trivial impulse may have been, and no matter what conditions in the France of his time existed or seemed to him to exist. This is why I am opposed to those who insist upon the influence of objective social conditions upon the heroine Emma Bovary. Flaubert's novel deals with the delicate calculus of human fate, not with the arithmetic of social conditioning.

We are told that most of the characters in *Madame Bovary* are bourgeois. But one thing that we should clear up once and for all is the meaning that Flaubert gives to the term *bourgeois.* Unless it simply means *townsman,* as it often does in French, the term *bourgeois* as used by Flaubert means "philistine," people preoccupied with the material side of life and believing only in conventional values. He never uses the word *bourgeois* with any politico-economic Marxist connotation. Flaubert's bourgeois is a state of mind, not a state of pocket. In a famous scene of our book when a hardworking old woman, getting a medal for having slaved for her farmer-boss, is confronted with a committee of relaxed bourgeois beaming at her–mind you, in that scene both parties are philistines, the beaming politicians and the superstitious old peasant woman–both sides are bourgeois in Flaubert's sense. I shall clear up the term completely if I say that, for instance, today in communist Russia, Soviet literature, Soviet art, Soviet music, Soviet aspirations are fundamentally and smugly bourgeois. It is the lace curtain behind the iron one. A Soviet official, small or big, is the perfect type of bourgeois mind, of a philistine. The key to Flaubert's term is the philistinism of his Monsieur Homais. Let me add

Vladimir Nabokov (photograph by Robert L. Wegryn; Gavriel Shapiro, Nabokov at Cornell *[Ithaca, N.Y.: Cornell University Press, 2003])*

for double clarity that Marx would have called Flaubert a bourgeois in the politico-economic sense and Flaubert would have called Marx a bourgeois in the spiritual sense; and both would have been right, since Flaubert was a well-to-do gentleman in physical life and Marx was a philistine in his attitude towards the arts.

. . . .

The term *romantic* has several meanings. When discussing *Madame Bovary*–the book and the lady herself–I shall use *romantic* in the following sense: "characterized by a dreamy, imaginative habit of mind tending to dwell on picturesque possibilities derived mainly from literature." (*Romanesque* rather than romanticist.) A romantic person, mentally and emo-

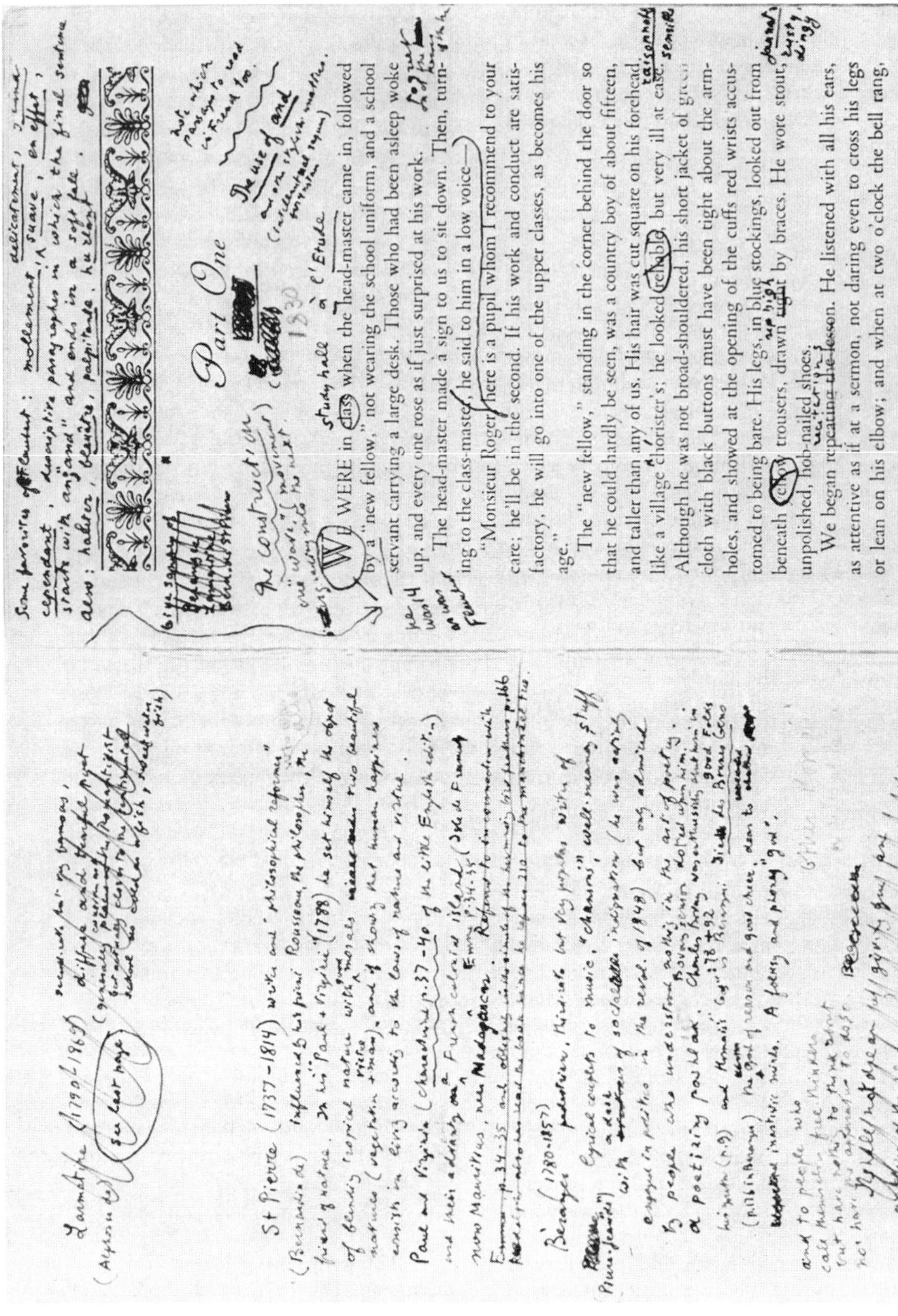

Part One

WE WERE in class when the head-master came in, followed by a "new fellow," not wearing the school uniform, and a school servant carrying a large desk. Those who had been asleep woke up, and every one rose as if just surprised at his work.

The head-master made a sign to us to sit down. Then, turning to the class-master, he said to him in a low voice—

"Monsieur Roger, here is a pupil whom I recommend to your care; he'll be in the second. If his work and conduct are satisfactory, he will go into one of the upper classes, as becomes his age."

The "new fellow," standing in the corner behind the door so that he could hardly be seen, was a country boy of about fifteen, and taller than any of us. His hair was cut square on his forehead like a village chorister's; he looked reliable, but very ill at ease. Although he was not broad-shouldered, his short jacket of green cloth with black buttons must have been tight about the armholes, and showed at the opening of the cuffs red wrists accustomed to being bare. His legs, in blue stockings, looked out from beneath yellow trousers, drawn tight by braces. He wore stout, unpolished, hob-nailed shoes.

We began repeating the lesson. He listened with all his ears, as attentive as if at a sermon, not daring even to cross his legs or lean on his elbow; and when at two o'clock the bell rang,

The opening pages of Nabokov's copy of Madame Bovary. *On the left page, Nabokov wrote notes on Alphonse-Marie-Louis de Prat de Lamartine, Bernardin de Saint-Pierre, and Pierre-Jean Béranger; on the right page, he corrected the translation and commented on Flaubert's style, such as noting recurring words and his careful use of the conjunction "et" (courtesy of the New York Public Library).*

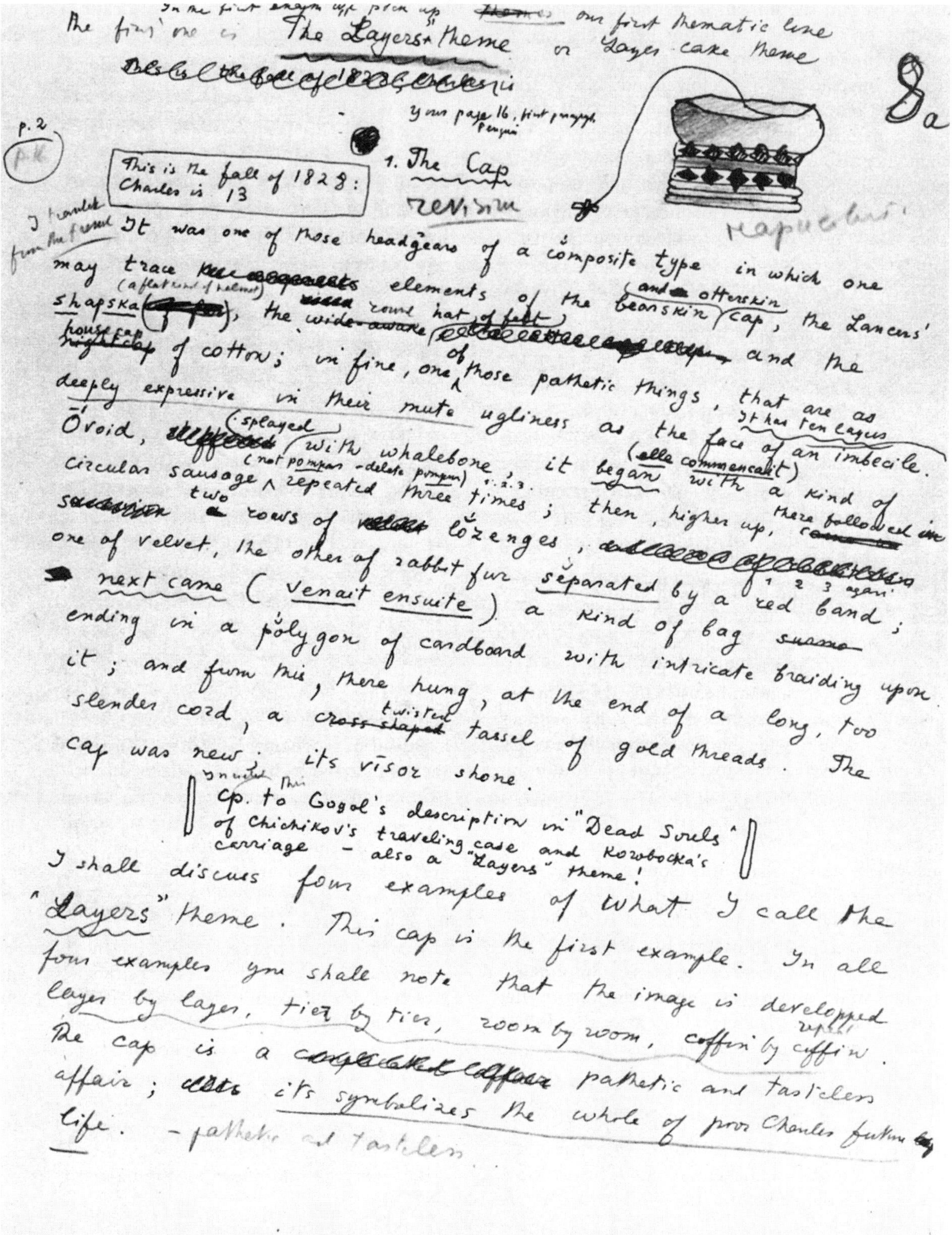

In the first chapter we pick up our first thematic line
The first one is The Layers theme or Layer cake theme

8a

p. 2

Your page 16, first paragraph Penguin

This is the fall of 1828: Charles is 13

1. The Cap

I translate from the French: It was one of those headgears of a composite type in which one may trace elements of the bearskin and otterskin cap, the Lancers' shapska (a flat kind of helmet), the round hat of felt, the house cap of cotton; in fine, one of those pathetic things, that are as deeply expressive in their mute ugliness as the face of an imbecile. Ovoid, (splayed) with whalebone, it began (elle commençait) with a kind of circular sausage repeated three times; then, higher up, there followed two rows of lozenges, one of velvet, the other of rabbit fur separated by a red band; next came (venait ensuite) a kind of bag ending in a polygon of cardboard with intricate braiding upon it; and from this, there hung, at the end of a long, too slender cord, a twisted tassel of gold threads. The cap was new; its visor shone.

It has ten layers

(not pompons - delete pompon) 1. 2. 3.

1 2 3 again

Compare this to Gogol's description in "Dead Souls" of Chichikov's traveling case and Korobochka's carriage – also a "Layers" theme!

I shall discuss four examples of what I call the "Layers" theme. This cap is the first example. In all four examples you shall note that the image is developped layer by layer, tier by tier, room by room, coffin by coffin. The cap is a pathetic and tasteless affair; its symbolizes the whole of poor Charles future life. – pathetic and tasteless

Nabokov's notes on and drawing of Charles Bovary's cap, which is described in the first chapter of the novel (courtesy of the New York Public Library)

tionally living in the unreal, is profound or shallow depending on the quality of his or her mind. Emma Bovary is intelligent, sensitive, comparatively well educated, but she has a shallow mind: her charm, beauty, and refinement do not preclude a fatal streak of philistinism in her. Her exotic daydreams do not prevent her from being small-town bourgeois at heart, clinging to conventional ideas or committing this or that conventional violation of the conventional, adultery being a most conventional way to rise above the conventional; and her passion for luxury does not prevent her from revealing once or twice what Flaubert terms a peasant hardness, a strain of rustic practicality. However, her extraordinary physical charm, her unusual grace, her birdlike, hummingbirdlike vivacity–all this is irresistibly attractive and enchanting to three men in the book, her husband and her two successive lovers, both of them heels: Rodolphe, who finds in her a dreamy childish tenderness in welcome contrast to the harlots he has been consorting with; and Léon, an ambitious mediocrity, who is flattered by having a real lady for his mistress.

Now what about the husband, Charles Bovary? He is a dull, heavy, plodding fellow, with no charm, no brains, no culture, and with a complete set of conventional notions and habits. He is a philistine, but he also is a pathetic human being. The two following points are of the utmost importance. What seduces him in Emma and what he finds in her is exactly what Emma herself is looking for and not finding in her romantic daydreams. Charles dimly, but deeply, perceives in her personality an iridescent loveliness, luxury, a dreamy remoteness, poetry, romance. This is one point, and I shall offer some samples in a moment. The second point is that the love Charles almost unwittingly develops for Emma is a real feeling, deep and true, in absolute contrast to the brutal or frivolous emotions experienced by Rodolphe and Léon, her smug and vulgar lovers. So here is the pleasing paradox of Flaubert's fairy tale: the dullest and most inept person in the book is the only one who is redeemed by a divine something in the all-powerful, forgiving, and unswerving love that he bears Emma, alive or dead. There is yet a fourth character in the book who is in love with Emma but that fourth is merely a Dickensian child, Justin. Nevertheless, I recommend him for sympathetic attention.

. . . .

The ups and downs of Emma's emotions–the longings, the passion, the frustration, the loves, the disappointments–a chequered sequence, end in a violent self-inflicted and very messy death. Yet before we part with Emma, we shall mark the essential hardness of her nature, somehow symbolized by a slight physical flaw, by the hard dry angularities of her hands; her hands were fondly groomed, delicate and white, pretty, perhaps, but not beautiful.

She is false, she is deceitful by nature: she deceives Charles from the very start before actually committing adultery. She lives among philistines, and she is a philistine herself. Her mental vulgarity is not so obvious as that of Homais. It might be too hard on her to say that the trite, ready-made pseudoprogressive aspects of Homais's nature are duplicated in a feminine pseudoromantic way in Emma; but one cannot help feeling that Homais and Emma not only phonetically echo each other but do have something in common–and that something is the vulgar cruelty of their natures. In Emma the vulgarity, the philistinism, is veiled by her grace, her cunning, her beauty, her meandering intelligence, her power of idealization, her moments of tenderness and understanding, and by the fact that her brief bird life ends in human tragedy.

Not so Homais. He is the successful philistine. And to the last, as she lies dead, poor Emma is attended by him, the busybody Homais, and the prosaic priest Bournisien. There is a delightful scene when these two–the believer in drugs and the believer in God–go to sleep in two armchairs near her dead body, facing each other, snoring in front of each other with bulging bellies and fallen jaws, twinned in sleep, united at last in the same human weakness of sleep. And what an insult to poor Emma's destiny–the epitaph Homais finds for her grave! His mind is crammed with trite Latin tags but at first he is stumped by not being able to find anything better than *sta viator;* pause, traveler (or stay, passenger). Pause where? The end of this Latin tag is *heroam calcas*–you tread on a hero's dust. But finally Homais with his usual temerity substituted for hero's dust, your beloved wife's dust. Stay, passenger, you tread upon your beloved wife–the last thing that could be said about poor Charles who, despite all his stupidity, loved Emma with a deep, pathetic adoration, a fact that she *did* realize for one brief moment before she died. And where does he die? In the very arbor where Rodolphe and Emma used to make love.

(Incidentally, in that last page of his life, not bumblebees are visiting the lilacs in that garden but bright green beetles. Oh those ignoble, treacherous, and philistine translators! One would think that Monsieur Homais, who knew a little English, was Flaubert's English translator.)

Homais has various chinks in his armor:

1. His science comes from pamphlets, his general culture from newspapers; his taste in literature is appalling, especially in the combination of authors he cites. In his ignorance, he remarks at one point "'That is the question,' as I lately read in a newspaper," not knowing that he is quoting Shakespeare and not a Rouen journalist–nor perhaps had the author of the political article in that newspaper known it either.

2. He still feels now and then that dreadful fright he got when he was almost jailed for practicing medicine.

3. He is a traitor, a cad, a toad, and does not mind sacrificing his dignity to the more serious interests of his business or to obtain a decoration.

4. He is a coward, and notwithstanding his brave words he is afraid of blood, death, dead bodies.

5. He is without mercy and poisonously vindictive.

6. He is a pompous ass, a smug humbug, a gorgeous philistine, a pillar of society as are so many philistines.

7. He does get his decoration at the end of the novel in 1856. Flaubert considered that his age was the age of philistinism, which he called *muflisme.* However, this kind of thing is not peculiar to any special government or regime; if anything, philistinism is more in evidence during revolutions and in police states than under more traditional regimes. The philistine in violent action is always more dangerous than the philistine who quietly sits before his television set.

Let us recapitulate for a moment Emma's loves, platonic and otherwise:

1. As a schoolgirl she may have had a crush on her music teacher, who passes with his encased violin in one of the retrospective paragraphs of the book.

2. As a young woman married to Charles (with whom at the beginning she is not in love), she first has an amorous friendship, a perfectly platonic one technically, with Léon Dupuis, a notary clerk.

3. Her first "affair" is with Rodolphe Boulanger, the local squire.

4. In the middle of this affair, since Rodolphe turns out to be more brutal than the romantic ideal she longed for, Emma attempts to discover an ideal in her husband; she tries seeing him as a great physician and begins a brief phase of tenderness and tentative pride.

5. After poor Charles has completely botched the operation on the poor stableboy's clubfoot–one of the greatest episodes in the book–she goes back to Rodolphe with more passion than before.

6. When Rodolphe abolishes her last romantic dream of elopement and a dream life in Italy, after a serious illness she finds a subject of romantic adoration in God.

7. She has a few minutes of daydreaming about the opera singer Lagardy.

8. Her affair with vapid, cowardly Léon after she meets him again is a grotesque and pathetic materialization of all her romantic dreams.

9. In Charles, just before she dies, she discovers his human and divine side, his perfect love for her–all that she had missed.

10. The ivory body of Jesus Christ on the cross that she kisses a few minutes before her death, this love can be said to end in something like her previous tragic disappointment since all the misery of her life takes over again when she hears the awful song of the hideous vagabond as she dies.

Who are the "good" people of the book? Obviously, the villain is Lheureux, but who, besides poor Charles, are the good characters? Somewhat obviously, Emma's father, old Rouault; somewhat unconvincingly, the boy Justin, whom we glimpse crying on Emma's grave, a bleak note; and speaking of Dickensian notes let us not forget two other unfortunate children, Emma's little daughter, and of course that other little Dickensian girl, that girl of thirteen, hunchbacked, a little bleak housemaid, a dingy nymphet, who serves Lheureux as clerk, a glimpse to ponder. Who else in the book do we have as good people? The best person is the third doctor, the great Larivière, although I have always hated the transparent tear he sheds over the dying Emma. Some might even say: Flaubert's father had been a doctor, and so this is Flaubert senior shedding a tear over the misfortunes of the character that his son has created.

––

A question: can we call *Madame Bovary realistic* or *naturalistic?* I wonder.

A novel in which a young and healthy husband night after night never wakes to find the better half of his bed empty; never hears the sand and pebbles thrown at the shutters by a lover; never receives an anonymous letter from some local busybody;

A novel in which the biggest busybody of them all, Homais–Monsieur Homais, whom we might have expected to have kept a statistical eye upon all the cuckolds of his beloved Yonville, actually never notices, never learns anything about Emma's affairs;

A novel in which little Justin–a nervous young boy of fourteen who faints at the sight of blood and smashes crockery out of sheer nervousness–should go to weep in the dead of night (where?) in a cemetery on the grave of a woman whose ghost might come to

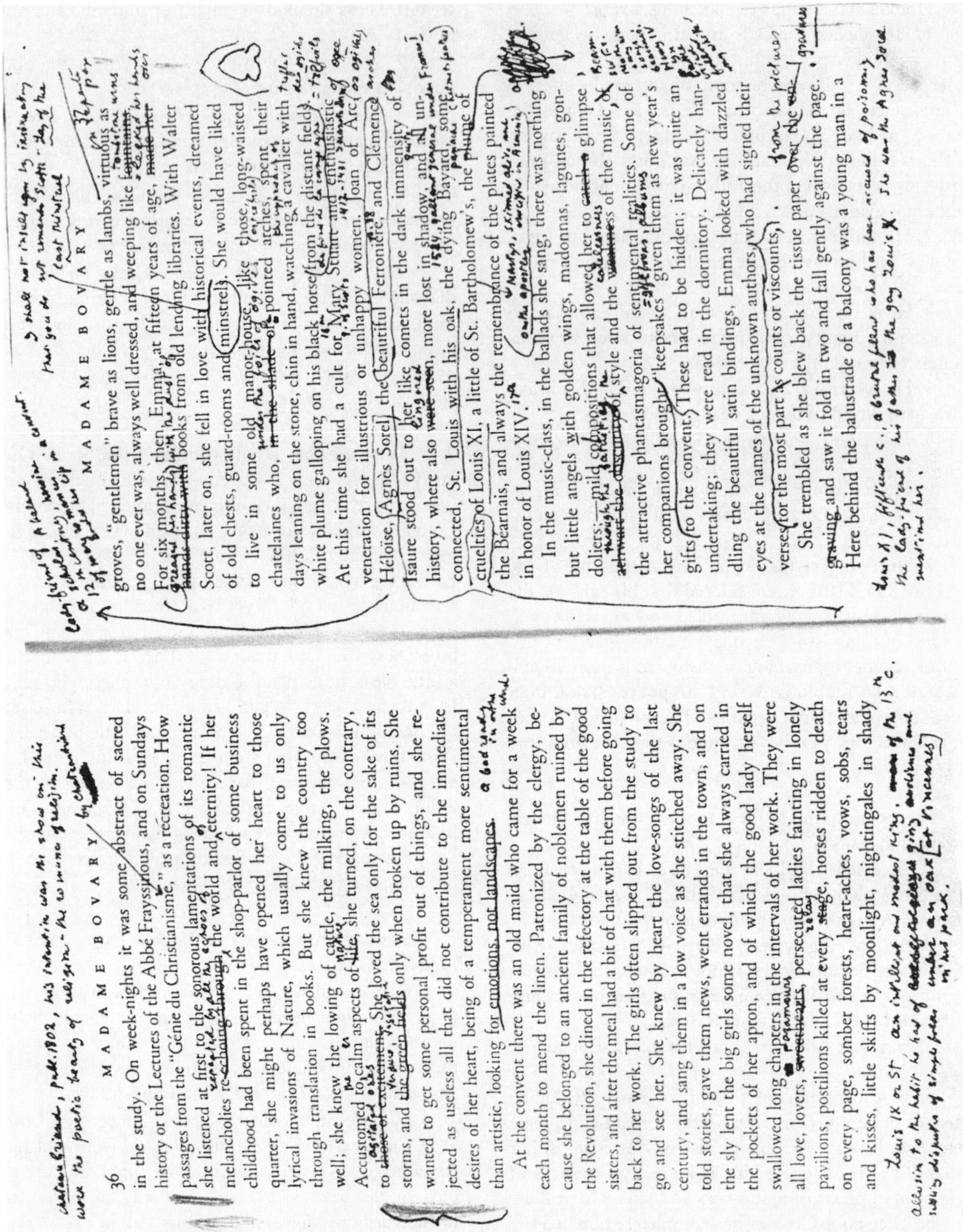

36 MADAME BOVARY

in the study. On week-nights it was some abstract of sacred history or the Lectures of the Abbé Frayssinous, and on Sundays passages from the "Génie du Christianisme," as a recreation. How she listened at first to the sonorous lamentations of its romantic melancholies re-echoing through the world and eternity! If her childhood had been spent in the shop-parlor of some business quarter, she might perhaps have opened her heart to those lyrical invasions of Nature, which usually come to us only through translation in books. But she knew the country too well; she knew the lowing of cattle, the milking, the plows. Accustomed to calm aspects of life, she turned, on the contrary, to those of excitement. She loved the sea only for the sake of its storms, and the green fields only when broken up by ruins. She wanted to get some personal profit out of things, and she rejected as useless all that did not contribute to the immediate desires of her heart, being of a temperament more sentimental than artistic, looking for emotions, not landscapes.

At the convent there was an old maid who came for a week each month to mend the linen. Patronized by the clergy, because she belonged to an ancient family of noblemen ruined by the Revolution, she dined in the refectory at the table of the good sisters, and after the meal had a bit of chat with them before going back to her work. The girls often slipped out from the study to go and see her. She knew by heart the love-songs of the last century, and sang them in a low voice as she stitched away. She told stories, gave them news, went errands in the town, and on the sly lent the big girls some novel, that she always carried in the pockets of her apron, and of which the good lady herself swallowed long chapters in the intervals of her work. They were all love, lovers, sweethearts, persecuted ladies fainting in lonely pavilions, postilions killed at every stage, horses ridden to death on every page, somber forests, heart-aches, vows, sobs, tears and kisses, little skiffs by moonlight, nightingales in shady

MADAME BOVARY

groves, "gentlemen" brave as lions, gentle as lambs, virtuous as no one ever was, always well dressed, and weeping like fountains. For six months, then, Emma, at fifteen years of age, made her hands dirty with books from old lending libraries. With Walter Scott, later on, she fell in love with historical events, dreamed of old chests, guard-rooms and minstrels. She would have liked to live in some old manor-house, like those long-waisted chatelaines who, in the shade of pointed arches, spent their days leaning on the stone, chin in hand, watching a cavalier with white plume galloping on his black horse from the distant fields. At this time she had a cult for Mary Stuart and enthusiastic veneration for illustrious or unhappy women. Joan of Arc, Héloïse, Agnès Sorel, the beautiful Ferronière, and Clémence Isaure stood out to her like comets in the dark immensity of history, where also were seen, more lost in shadow, and all unconnected, St. Louis with his oak, the dying Bayard, some cruelties of Louis XI, a little of St. Bartholomew's, the plume of the Béarnais, and always the remembrance of the plates painted in honor of Louis XIV.

In the music-class, in the ballads she sang, there was nothing but little angels with golden wings, madonnas, lagunes, gondoliers;—mild compositions that allowed her to catch a glimpse athwart the obscurity of style and the weakness of the music of the attractive phantasmagoria of sentimental realities. Some of her companions brought "keepsakes" given them as new year's gifts to the convent. These had to be hidden; it was quite an undertaking; they were read in the dormitory. Delicately handling the beautiful satin bindings, Emma looked with dazzled eyes at the names of the unknown authors, who had signed their verses for the most part as counts or viscounts.

She trembled as she blew back the tissue paper over the engraving and saw it fold in two and fall gently against the page. Here behind the balustrade of a balcony was a young man in a

Nabokov's annotations in his copy of Madame Bovary *and corrections of the translation (courtesy of the New York Public Library)*

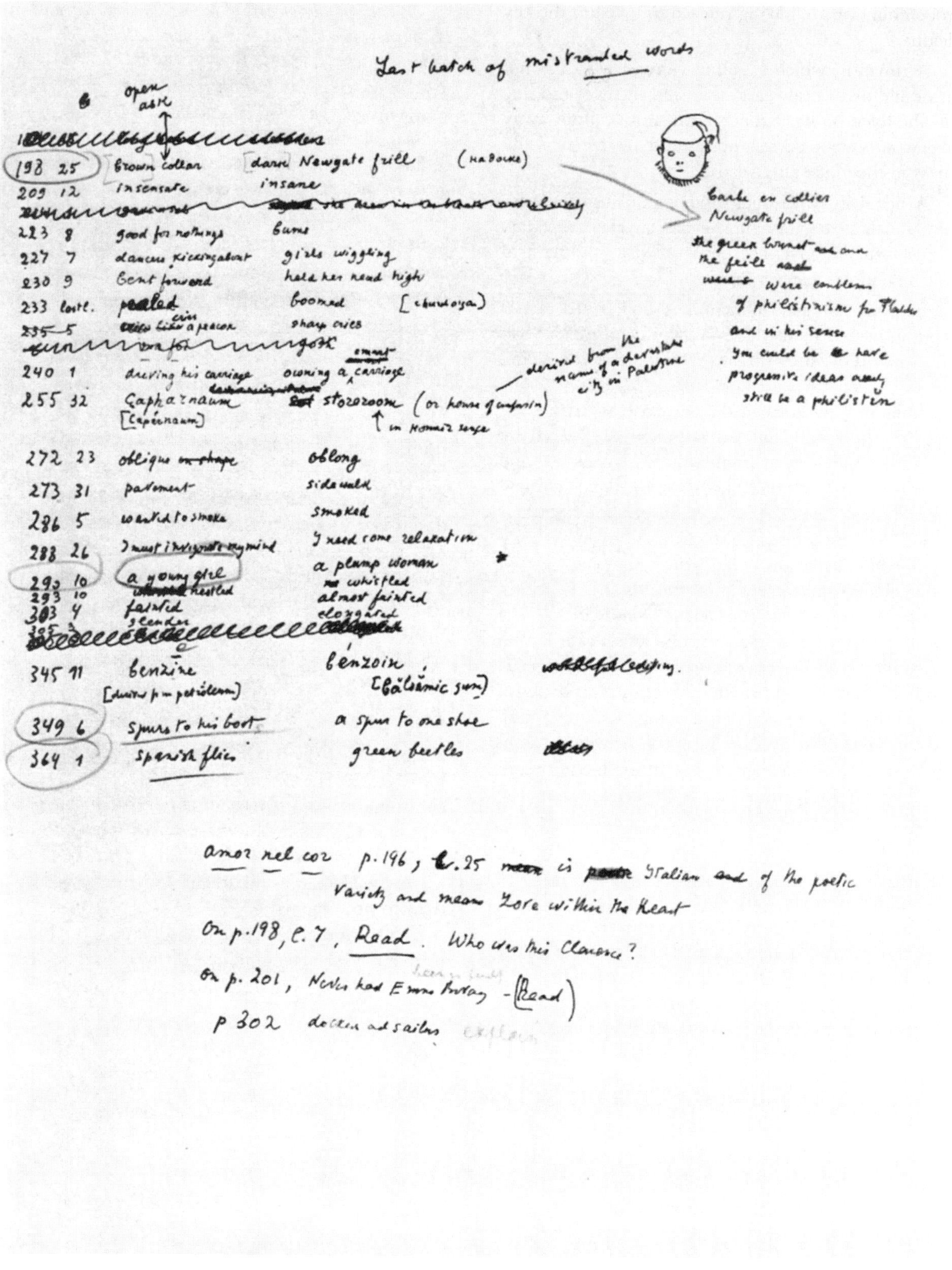

Last batch of mistranslated words

open
ask

198 25 brown collar [dark Newgate frill (набоки)
209 12 insensate insane
223 8 good for nothings bums
227 7 dancers kicking about girls wiggling
230 9 bent forward held her head high
233 last. pealed boomed [chardoyan]
235 5 cries like a peacock sharp cries
240 1 driving his carriage owning a smart carriage
255 32 Capharnaum storeroom (or house of confusion)
[Capernaum] ↑ in Homais sense
derived from the name of a dere... city in Palestine
272 23 oblique oblong
273 31 pavement sidewalk
286 5 wanted to smoke smoked
288 26 I must invigorate my mind I need some relaxation
290 10 a young girl a plump woman *
293 10 nestled whistled
303 4 fainted almost fainted
305 3 slender elongated
345 11 benzine benzoin
[derived from petroleum] [balsamic gum]
349 6 spurs to his boot a spur to one shoe
364 1 Spanish flies green beetles

barbe en collier
Newgate frill
the green bonnet and the frill were emblems of philistinism for Flaubert
and in his sense you could be have progressive ideas and still be a philistin

amor nel cor p. 196, l. 25 is Italian and of the poetic variety and mean Love within the Heart
On p. 198, l. 7, Read. Who was this Clarence?
On p. 201, Never had Emma Bovary – (Read)
p 302 doctors and sailors

reproach him for not having refused to give her the key to death;

A novel in which a young woman who has not been riding for several years–if indeed she ever did ride when she lived on her father's farm–now gallops away to the woods with perfect poise, and never feels any stiffness in the joints afterwards;

A novel in which many other implausible details abound–such as the very implausible naiveté of a certain cabdriver–such a novel has been called a landmark of so-called realism, whatever that is.

In point of fact, all fiction is fiction. All art is deception. Flaubert's world, as all worlds of major writers, is a world of fancy with its own logic, its own conventions, its own coincidences. The curious impossibilities I have listed do not clash with the pattern of the book–and indeed are only discovered by dull college professors or bright students. And you will bear in mind that all the fairy tales we have lovingly examined after *Mansfield Park* are loosely fitted by their authors into certain historical frames. All reality is comparative reality since any given reality, the window you see, the smells you perceive, the sounds you hear, are not only dependent on a crude give-and-take of the senses but also depend upon various levels of information. Flaubert may have seemed realistic or naturalistic a hundred years ago to readers brought up on the writings of those sentimental ladies and gentlemen that Emma admired. But realism, naturalism, are only comparative notions. What a given generation feels as naturalism in a writer seems to an older generation to be exaggeration of drab detail, and to a younger generation not enough drab detail. The *isms* go; the *ist* dies; art remains.

Ponder most carefully the following fact: a master of Flaubert's artistic power manages to transform what he has conceived as a sordid world inhabited by frauds and philistines and mediocrities and brutes and wayward ladies into one of the most perfect pieces of poetical fiction known, and this he achieves by bringing all the parts into harmony, by the inner force of style, by all such devices of form as the counterpoint of transition from one theme to another, of foreshadowing and echoes. Without Flaubert there would have been no Marcel Proust in France, no James Joyce in Ireland. Chekhov in Russia would not have been quite Chekhov. So much for Flaubert's literary influence.

–Vladimir Nabokov, "Gustave Flaubert: *Madame Bovary,*" *Lectures on Literature,* edited by Fredson Bowers (New York & London: Harcourt Brace Jovanovich/Bruccoli Clark, 1980), pp. 126–127, 132–133, 142–147

* * *

The appropriateness of calling Flaubert a realist–a label he always rejected–has raised many debates. In an article addressing why Madame Bovary *is still "alive" a century after it appeared, Benjamin F. Bart returns to the issue. He used his essay, originally published in* The French Review *in 1958, to conclude* Madame Bovary and the Critics: A Collection of Essays, *which he edited in 1966. All the bracketed volume and page indications in the essay refer to Flaubert's* Correspondance *as published in the Conard edition of his complete works in 1954.*

Madame Bovary after a Century

Flaubert's masterpiece is alive a century after its publication because it is the successful embodiment of a new esthetic. This esthetic has long proved confusing and still today needs redefinition. Critics who have studied it have tended to call it realism and have tried to see Flaubert as some sort of amalgam, compound, or mixture of romanticism and this new element, but this traditional approach has very serious defects. In the first place, Flaubert always rejected the claim that he was a realist; he had no use for the school [VII, 359 and 377]. In the second place, it seems very difficult to define "realism" satisfactorily in connection with Flaubert: either one makes it impossible to include those of his works which are like *Salammbô* within the definition, or one has a series of statements which are not meaningful when applied to realists other than Flaubert, for instance to William Dean Howells, who would never have written books akin to *Salammbô.* Under the circumstances, it would be wise to try for a new understanding of Flaubert's esthetic based on what he had to say about it himself while writing *Madame Bovary* and leaving aside the word "realism," which does no more than confuse the issue.

Certain of Flaubert's observations to Baudelaire form a ready starting point. He wrote to the poet: "You have found a way to rejuvenate romanticism," and "You have found a way to be a classicist while still remaining the transcendent romantic we admire" [IV, 205 and 408]. It is significant that, while Flaubert does speak of romanticism, he makes no mention at all of realism and instead names classicism as the other pole in this esthetic. And his phrasing makes it clear that he, too, believed in rejuvenating romanticism by a return to the long classical tradition. This is, in fact, his new esthetic.

To understand Flaubert's statement, one must determine what he meant by romanticism and above all by classicism: both are slippery terms. To Flaubert romanticism (at least in this context) was emotionalism unbridled by Art. A classical approach, on the other hand, was precisely that discipline which limits emotion and thereby makes Art possible, for Art has among its characteristics chasteness, precision, and ultimately serenity [II, 398, 451; III, 264, 340; IV, 164]. Flaubert would say that the writer with unbridled emotions is romantic and wrong. He prefers the author who first dominates these emotions and only then seeks the proper form to express them. Such a man is classical and right. "You must write with your head. If your heart warms it, all the better, but don't say so" [III, 50; see also IV, 5]. In point of fact, he felt that Art, to be Art at all, had to separate itself from this emotionalism. To rejuvenate romanticism, then, was in part to stop mistaking the feeling for the poem. It was, for instance, to abjure the errors of a Musset, whom Flaubert condemned for his failure to separate poetry from the sensations. It is the function of Art to complete these (and not, incidentally, to reproduce them, as the realists thought) [II, 446–47 and 460].

This classical aspect of Flaubert's esthetic has been underrated. It is what leads to mastering what he called the transcendent romanticism of Baudelaire, so as to transmute it into Art. Flaubert always felt that Beauty was calm; it was itself serene and it evoked serenity. Baudelaire's sonnet, *La Beauté,* aroused his intense admiration. Here Beauty states in part:

Je trône dans l'azur comme un sphinx incompris;
J'unis un cœur de neige à la blancheur des cygnes,
Je hais le mouvement qui déplace les lignes,
Et jamais je ne pleure et jamais je ne ris.

[I reign in the sky like a mysterious sphinx;
I join a heart of snow to the whiteness of swans,
I hate movement which upsets the lines,
And I never weep nor laugh.]

The highest goal of Art, Flaubert once asserted, was to set one to dreaming; the best works are serene of aspect and incomprehensible; and, he added, "something strangely gentle and sweet hovers over it all," "it is calm! so calm!" [III, 322, 323; see also III, 340].

Flaubert's classicism is calm, it is true, but it is not the pale ink of French nineteenth-century neo-classicism, nor is it the French seventeenth century, except incidentally. Flaubert liked La Fontaine, Boileau, Molière; but "the gentle Racine" only bemused him [II, 120, 297, 426; III, 138]. When he uses words like "classic," he really means Greece and Rome and the long tradition that fully derives from them: a true progeny, going always beyond the parents. Taking his cue from the ancient literatures–and from the romantic concept of the grotesque–Flaubert sought an all-inclusive literature. Thus he objected that Leconte de Lisle, for all his "classicism," was not a true "classicist" and therefore not a good artist, since the Parnassian poet was rejecting the modern world. Flaubert held that the ideal world of the artist, ancient or modern, is fertile only if the artist includes everything in it. Art is a work of love, not of exclusion [IV, 15; see also III, 215, 281]. Hence, to the classical tradition, Flaubert insisted on adding a modern feeling. The artist must not return to antiquity; he must rather take its procedures. One should be as artistic as the Greeks, but in other ways, because the scope of humanity had broadened since Homer's day and "the belly of Sancho Panza strains the girdle of Venus" [III, 137, 157, 281].

Various aspects of this doctrine have formed the commonplaces of critical observations on Flaubert: they all take their place within this rejuvenation of romantic emotionalism attained by controlling it so as to transmute it into a serene classical vision which would be Art. His effort to achieve comprehensiveness and universality led to a primary emphasis on impersonality and impartiality; the serenity necessitated impassivity. The absolute awareness that Beauty was the only goal of the artist led to the unremitting search for perfect form, the striving for the artistically right word, the agonies of the struggle over style. All are parts in a total process, which has meaning only when all of the parts are understood together, for the whole is an entity itself, and not just the sum of its parts.

Flaubert did not think of himself as an innovator or a revolutionary; rather he considered that he was a traditionalist. He is indeed one of the masters who moved the great line of western literature a step forward by a real return to the problem of Form. He was a classicist in the sense that he was in the Tradition, and he knew it. He was deeply irritated by those who set up little schools of the Beautiful–romantic, realistic, or classical for that matter: there was for him only one Beautiful, with varying aspects [III, 336].

Classicism was an integral part of his life and of his book *Madame Bovary*. He wanted the novel to have "a haughty, classical air" [III, 180]. Yet his was essentially a doctrine of innutrition. Born a romantic and never losing his passionate responses, he longed also to nurture himself, as Ronsard had, on the classics and to take to himself what excellences they had. One must be, he wrote, more classical than the classicists and infuriate the romantics by surpassing their intentions. He was sure it could be done, that one could be, like Baudelaire, a classicist while remaining a transcendent romantic [III, 249].

What then becomes of the familiar image of Flaubert, *chef d'école* of the French realists? It is true that he frequently asserted the absolute need for the artist to see things as they are, to penetrate into an object before writing of it. He did say, "When you can see your model clearly, you always write well . . ." [III, 269; see also III, 138]. He also wrote, "I will have produced written reality, which is rare" [III, 268]. But this does not mean that Flaubert is, after all, a realist: it is more complicated than that.

To call Flaubert a realist (as opposed to noting realistic elements in his work) is to confuse the issue seriously. It was not, he felt, a good method to look at something and then go write about it; its essence had to be digested first. He was aware that people thought him "fascinated with reality"; in fact, he hated it, he said [III, 263 and IV, 134]. This misinterpretation of his works bothered him throughout his lifetime and still troubles the critic today. Twenty-five years after writing the *Bovary,* Flaubert was still struggling to make himself understood, insisting that though he had always been incredibly scrupulous about reading all relevant documents and books, amassing all possible information and travelling wherever necessary, still he regarded all of this as secondary and inferior. So-called material reality should, he stated, never be more than a pattern used to mount higher [VIII, 374]. "Written reality," his phrase of a moment ago, is not the same thing as "reality." Art completes reality; it does not reproduce it. And this doctrine is not and cannot be called realism.

Flaubert is not a realist, nor is he a romantic; nor, for that matter, is he a naturalist or a symbolist. He sought rather to include all of these partial views of life and of Art in a larger synthesis, the Beautiful. He was preoccupied with the basic problem of the great writers of all ages, life itself: what meaning it has, what its parts really are, and (lastly) how they may be portrayed so as to display life's meaning.

Flaubert's efforts to learn what life was made up of in Normandy have been studied many times and need no lengthy rehearsal here. This is where he made his first impact. This is his documentation and the fabulous sheaves of notes. More important this is his scientism, and the prescient observation that Art would become scientific and science artistic in the future, a comment which the Freudian novel and the attitudes of an Einstein have borne out. Art was to gain in this process: gain in accuracy and truth by laying aside personal susceptibilities and affections, gain in precision by adopting a rigorous method [II, 395–96; IV, 164].

The ways Flaubert adopted to portray what he saw are perhaps his most enduring contribution. This aspect–the style–was to him the great and overriding problem of the book. He felt sure enough of his basic plan (upon which everything depended, as he well knew) so that style instead, even though a secondary issue, was the main difficulty [II, 316, 362; III, 21, 140, 248, etc.]. Truly great geniuses, he sadly confessed, often wrote badly and could readily afford it; the lesser people, like himself, were of worth only if the style were perfect. Hence he sought "style, form, indefinable Beauty, *resulting from the concept itself* and which is the splendor of the True, as Plato used to say" [IV, 165]. The *concept* of *Madame Bovary* was, unfortunately, wholly alien to Flaubert, which made the book very hard for him to write and something of a *tour de force.* He achieved it only by constantly reminding himself that there was a style for every subject and that he must find this style [II, 346, 432; III, 3, 156, 201]. This was a further aspect of Baudelaire's work which delighted him: "The originality of the style derives directly from the concept. The sentence is filled to the brim with the idea; it is almost overflowing" [IV, 205].

Problems of form–or rather, brilliant resolutions of them–have become dominant as one surveys the influence of the novel. Taking his place beside Stendhal, the earlier master of irony, there now stands Flaubert, too, evolving new dimensions and forms for the ironic view of life. Anticipating Proustian sensitivities, Flaubert, too, knew much of the passage of time and the fleeting memory: to display this required bold new forms. And towering above other mid-century French advocates of pessimism, Flaubert showed how one might work up into a novel a philosophy of despair. The use of symbols, the handling of dialogue, simile, and metaphor, problems of tempo, the place of ethics, these and innumerable other formal questions he met and resolved. But, as most of these are familiar, it is perhaps well to move beyond them, leaving to another time and place the investigation of their import after a century. In sum, style was Flaubert's chief concern; he saw clarity of concept as the true source of good form, and he rejuvenated romanticism by returning behind its looseness to the great tradition of western literature.

The question of Flaubert's view of life, the meaning he attached to it and, hence, to his book, remains to be examined. Flaubert himself directs attention to it when he says, "Everything depends on the concept" [II, 339]. What was it that he had to say? What meanings did he discover and then display with such excellence? If a work is to reach the summits and take its place on the shelf, the very small shelf, of truly world literature, its form and its content, the what as well as the how, must both be superlative and must both fuse wholly into a totality which will speak cogently to later ages. *Madame Bovary* is good enough so that one may, without absurdity, ask whether it belongs on this select shelf.

Each reader must answer for himself, and my purpose must be quite as much to provide a framework for the answers of others as it is to give my own reply. Flaubert's book had a point, and he knew it: "this novel has a perfectly clear meaning. . . ." He went on, however, to say that it was a matter of perfect indifference to him and that style alone mattered [IV, 136]. But can it properly be a matter of indifference to the rest of us, his readers, who are not writers and for whom style is therefore less important? For my own part, I must answer "No," and must further urge that Flaubert himself in his better moments knew his assertion was an exaggeration.

If, then, we ask what the message of the book is, I think we must answer that it is one of distilled hatred and disgust, for romanticism, for the bourgeois, for provincial life, for orthodox religion: for nearly everything portrayed. Some parts of the book, some paragraphs or even short episodes show Flaubert as serene as he felt the masters had been, reaching beyond the exasperation and disillusionment which are the price of wisdom, to that calm which he knew was necessary to Art. It is these moments which produced the great pages, the scene by moonlight as Emma and Rodolphe plan their trip, the Catherine Leroux episode, Doctor Larivière's visit, the death of Charles, and a host of others.

Monsieur Homais lecturing Justin, from part 3, chapter 2 (illustration by Albert Fourié; Madame Bovary. Mœurs de province, *3 volumes [Paris: Librarie Illustrée, 1900])*

Flaubert can, upon occasion, rise to the real heights of the great western tradition. Few books can ever do so, and it is great praise to say that some pages of his book do. But its essential message and its normal level are perhaps less than that: they certainly are for me, and it may be that in the pages which remain, I can suggest why.

It is Flaubert's reiterated contention in his letters that life is hateful, farcical, grotesque; that it consists of ignominy and stupidity. It is so hideous that the only way to stand it is to avoid it and to look upon the human race as "a vast assembly of monsters and rascals." He enjoys seeing humanity and all it respects "crushed, humiliated, dishonored, spat upon" [II, 321, 325, 472; III, 63, 420; IV, 33, 182]. Like Baudelaire, Flaubert sees the evil in life; but unlike the poet, he does not see anything else. His is a limited view.

This is the burden of *Madame Bovary* as well. Flaubert felt that there was no escape for Emma and his effort was to prove this "irony of fate" by closing off, one after another, every means of salvation. "Fate" is the key word of Flaubert's own philosophy, and it is used recurrently through the book at critical moments, finally and most cogently by Charles in his conversation with Rodolphe after Emma's death: "Fate is to blame." Emma is necessarily destroyed, and the world is necessarily given over to the Homais and the Lheureux of our society. Their success is even less palatable than her failure.

Any reasonable or sensitive man will reject life if this is its true and ultimate import. Flaubert asked repeatedly what meaning could possibly be attributed to this grotesque and horrible spectacle either of tears, unhappiness, and misery, or else of stupidity, infamy, cowardice, and dishonor. For his fellow man, he could feel at most a serene hatred or what he termed "so inactive a pity that it amounts to the same thing." No wonder, then, that he had to conclude that life was tolerable only providing one refused to live it: "through all the *hideousness* of existence, we must always contemplate the great blue vault of poetry. . . ." By living in Art, he once said, it seemed to him, in his conscience, that he was accomplishing his duty, that he was obeying a higher fate, that he was doing the Good, that he was in the Right [II, 396; III, 107, 108–109, 144, 251, 350].

We cannot all be artists, so what Flaubert knew of how to give dignity and meaning to life was of no value to his fellow man and he never proffered these views on Art in works he published himself. I am aware that life may be viewed as having no more significance than Flaubert attaches to it; I am aware of the pervasiveness nowadays of the doctrine of irony, which Flaubert upheld truculently. But I do believe that, upon examination, the really great books of the western tradition counsel the understanding of life and urge terms in which it may be accepted. They go beyond the bitter taste of irony to some form of love. The *Iliad* shows sure knowledge of how vicious man may be to man, but before it closes it shows the mastery of the vice it portrays, and it ends in serenity and acceptance. And this pattern, it seems to me, has been followed by all the later books which I should wish to place on my own private shelf of truly world literature. But if I would place *Madame Bovary* on the shelf below, now a century later, it would still be done affectionately and with deep respect for the man who could write in one of his letters that he would probably never be able to succeed in his attempt to write the style he imagined, that it was perhaps absurd or at best merely a worthy attempt and highly original; but that in any case, he would have passed his life in a way that was noble, and often delicious [III, 142–43].

–Benjamin F. Bart, "*Madame Bovary* after a Century," in *Madame Bovary and the Critics: A Collection of Essays,* edited by Bart (New York: New York University Press, 1966), pp. 189–197

* * *

During the 1960s Flaubert's art began to be considered from new points of view, with critics focusing mainly on Flaubert's style and techniques. In his essay "Madame Bovary *or the Book about Nothing" Jean Rousset discusses the structure of the novel and Flaubert's technique of modulation, in which the point of view subtly shifts from one character to another. In this excerpt from the essay, Rousset stresses one of the most important of Flaubert's techniques in his use of the point of view: the motif of windows, which permits an association of the character with the surrounding external background.*

Windows and the Plunging View

The Marie of *Novembre* already spent her days before her window, a spot for waiting, a vigil over the void from which a customer or an event might arise. The window is a privileged post for those Flaubertian characters who are both immobile and adrift, stuck in their inertia and given over to the vagabondage of their thoughts. In that closed place where the soul is moldering, here then is a rent through which one can be diffused in space without having to leave one's point of fixation. The window combines closing and opening, barrier and flight, confinement in the room and expansion outside, the unlimited in the circumscribed. Absent where he is, present where he is not, oscillating between contraction and dilation, as Georges Poulet has so clearly shown, the Flaubertian character was predisposed to fix his existence on this boundary point where one can both flee and stay, on this window which seems the ideal site of his reverie.

We read already in *Par les champs et par les grèves:* "Ah, air! Air! More space! Since *our constricted souls stifle and die on the window sill,* since our captive spirits, like the bear in his pit, always turn upon themselves and bump against their walls, at least grant my nostrils the perfume of all the winds of the earth, *let my eyes set off toward all the horizons.*"[1]

Emma Bovary, herself a captive between the walls of her pit, finds before her window flight "toward every horizon": "she often placed herself there" ([Dumesnil edition, Paris: Les Belles Lettres, 1945] I, 145); at Tostes it is from her window that she watches the rain fall and the monotonously repeated days of village life; from her window at Yonville she watches the notary's clerk go by, sees Rodolphe for the first time; it is from the window overlooking the garden that she hears the ringing of the angelus that stirs up mystical notions in her, and there too her eyes wander amid the clouds or across the meanders of the stream. It is at the attic window that she has her first suicidal dizziness; and after her grave illness, when she resumes contact with life, "they would push her in her chair to the window, the one that overlooked the square" (II, 54). Windows of boredom and reverie.

There are also closed windows and drawn curtains, reserved for the rare moments when Emma, in harmony with herself and the place of her existence, no longer needs to be diffused in the limitlessness of reverie, but is contained within herself in the initial and happy phase of her passions: at Rouen with Léon in the "carriage with drawn curtains . . . more tightly shut than the grave," then in the hotel room where they live shut up all day long "with shutters and doors closed"; "a hothouse atmosphere," says one of the preliminary sketches. It was the same with Rodolphe when Emma, at the beginning of their affair, went to surprise him at La Huchette in the penumbra that "the yellow curtains, hanging down the full length of the windows" cast in his room. But that first passion is habitually an open-air passion, for the forest or garden; here there are no windows at all. In this way Flaubert contrasts the characters of his two lovers while conforming to the significance of the windows in his novel.

Together with its significance for the Flaubertian character, the window offers the technician in novelistic setting and scenario structure interesting resources in perspectives, which Flaubert does not fail to utilize to vary the perspectives of narration and to obtain curious "optical effects." One thinks immediately of the brilliant "symphonic" bit of the *Comices,* presented in the visual and auditory perspective of the future lovers installed at the window of the town hall on the second storey. The downward view has a double advantage: it serves first to reinforce the ironic distance from which the author treats the agricultural gathering and, in counterpoint, the idyll that is superimposed on it and blends with it; it also expresses the movement of elevation that characterizes Emma's entrance into the life of passion; we find that movement in the following phase of the affair. In fact, the same aerial optic is used shortly afterwards, at the time of the horseback ride during which the relationship that began at the *Comices* is consummated. We arrive at the summit of a slope; Flaubert arranges there a panoramic view of the landscape, an image of the vision that Emma simultaneously has of her existence: "There was mist over the countryside. Vapors stretched out at the horizon between the outlines of the hills; and others, moving apart, rose and were dissipated. At times, *in a separation* of the clouds beneath a ray of sunlight, *one could see far off* the roofs at Yonville, with the gardens at the water's edge, the courtyards, the walls and the church steeple. Emma half closed her eyelids to recognize her house, *and that poor village where she lived had never seemed so small to her*" (I, 181). The entrance into passion is marked by an ascension above the habitual level of existence, the site of which is swallowed up and annulled beneath Emma's eyes. Yonville must diminish at a distance that the aerial perspective makes infinite, so that there can be substituted for it the imaginary space of love, depicted here as evaporating water: "From the heights where they were, the whole valley seemed an immense, pale lake, evaporating in the air." That is what becomes of the village and its houses at the moment when the author directs his exalted heroine's gaze to overlook the world beneath her: a mirage without contours or support.

When, a few pages later, Emma dreams that same evening of the new life which has just opened for her, it is still in terms in which height and the unlimited are associated in opposition to "ordinary existence," cast "beneath her," as if that afternoon's downward gaze had entered intact in the inner landscape of her mind: "She was moving into something marvelous, where all would be passion, ecstasy, delirium; a bluish vastness was all about her, the summits of sentiment sparkled beneath her thought, and ordinary existence appeared only as something far off, far beneath her, in the shadow between those heights" (I, 185).

Emma after beginning her affair with Rodolphe, from part 2, chapter 10 (illustration by Albert Fourié; Madame Bovary. Mœurs de province, *3 volumes [Paris: Librarie Illustrée, 1900])*

For this summit point above the village Flaubert reserved another use toward the end of the novel, at a moment that is not less decisive but has an opposite meaning. Madame Bovary has seen Rodolphe for the last time, she is returning to Yonville, distracted, to put an end to her life; it is no longer the climb toward passionate ecstasy, but descent toward suicide; in the course of that hallucinatory walk at nightfall, she finds herself at the summit of a slope, perhaps the same one as before, above the village; she emerges abruptly from her dizzying ecstasy: "Everything disappeared. She recognized the lights of the houses, which shone from far away in the fog.

"And now her situation, like *an abyss,* became clear to her. . . . *She ran down* the hill" (II, 168). The return from the imaginary to the real means falling toward the village, which this time emerges from the fog instead of being reabsorbed into it; it is a descent into the abyss.

Thus, at the beginning and end of this amorous odyssey, on two pages far apart but symmetrically opposed, Flaubert places his heroine in the same dominant place where he reserves for her the same plunging perspective. It is up to the attentive reader to establish the connection and to perceive the wealth with which a book so ably composed is laden. He will compare this diptych with another in which the novelist combines use of the window and the vehicle (which will play so important a role in the *Éducation*): the double view of Rouen at the arrival and departure of the diligence at the time of the Thursday rendezvous with Léon. Once more a plunging view: "Thus seen from above, all the countryside seemed motionless like a painting." And this time too, in the distorting lens of an imagination agitated by passion, the countryside, motionless at first, stirs, palpitates, dilates.

But there is an important difference: Emma's look no longer moved downward toward Yonville and her "ordinary life" but, on the contrary, toward the place where she will live her passion; also, far from appearing to her at a distance that veils it and shrinks it to the point of annulment, the site of her desire, by an inverted mirage, emerges from the mist and is magnified into a "vast capital," measured only by the wide open space before her: "Before that space her love grew greater and was filled with confusion at the vague murmuring sounds which arose. She poured it out, on the squares, on the avenues, on the streets, and the old Norman city *stretched out before her eyes like an immense capital, like a Babylon that she was entering*" (II, 112).

Windows and plunging perspectives, openings into the distance and reveries in space, all are neuralgic points in the narration, knots at which the narrative stops; they correspond to very unusual angles of vision, when the novelist relinquishes his traditional divine rights, when the subjective vision begins to dominate and the author identifies himself most with his heroine, stands behind her, and sees things through her. Their distribution in the novel is significant. They are unequally distributed. Absent from the active phases, where passion is consummated, they multiply in periods of stagnation and waiting: at Tostes after the invitation to the chateau, when one first sees Emma, the ball over, open the window and lean out;[2] it is a time of reverie that is beginning and that never ends, at Tostes as well as at Yonville, until the moment when she begins to live her great passion, returns to her husband, leaves him again after the episode of the clubfoot, prepares her flight, goes in for purchases and debts. After these chapters of action and accelerated movement the separation from Rodolphe introduces a new adagio, a new time of inertia and stagnation, announced again by a window opening before the heroine, but in a more tragic spirit, with vertigo and loss of consciousness anticipating the dénouement: the attic window where she reads the letter terminating their affair: "Opposite, over the roofs, the open countryside stretched out as far as the eye could see." She is about to go back to desiring and regretting, expanding beyond her limits, "floating" in an aerial environment which is that of her reverie and her plunging perspectives: "She stood at the very edge, almost suspended, surrounded by open space. The blue of the sky seemed to close in on her."[3]

But a relapse always follows those periodic flights constituted by the reveries before the window: "'My wife! My wife!' Charles cried out. . . . And yet he [*sic,* for 'she'] had to go down! Dinner was waiting!" (II, 46–47). Flight and fall make the rhythmical movement of the work as well as the psychological life of the heroine. Thus, at the beginning of the sixth chapter of the second part, the open window and the tinkling of the angelus stimulate Emma to rove among her memories and to feel that weightless suspension that is expressed by images of flight and of a whirling feather: "She felt weak and totally abandoned, like a bird's downy feather whirled about in the storm." Then back from church, "she *dropped* into an armchair," caught up again in the heavy, closed world of the bedroom, in the monotonous fixedness of time and motionless objects, in the opaque presence of beings that "are there" like furniture. "The furniture in its place seemed to have become more immobile. . . . The clock was still ticking. . . . Between the window and the worktable little Berthe was there. . . . Charles appeared. It was dinner time." To rejoin existence after hours of flight toward the outer world of windows is always a matter of falling, falling back into reclusion.

This double movement dominates other essential pages, like the central phase of the *Comices* where Emma, disturbed by the smell of pomade and the "far-off" view of the diligence, confuses in a sort of ecstasy lovers and times, before turning down again toward the crowd in the square and the official orator's phrases. Or like that other ecstasy, of the same amorous nature, that opens her affair with Léon in the same way that the preceding one started her passion for Rodolphe: the performance of the opera in Rouen. The box from which Emma sees the house and then the stage "from above" is an avatar of the window, a new combination of the enclosure and the opening out on an expanse where an imaginary destiny is profiled. Here it is not she who is acting it out; it is being acted for her on the stage; but she loses no time in recognizing herself and in identifying herself with the young stage heroine, sharing her desire "*to fly* into an embrace" and seeing another Rodolphe in the singer: "A madness took possession of her; he was looking at her, she was sure of it! She wanted to throw herself into his arms . . . to cry out: 'Carry me away!' The curtain *fell* . . . and she fell back into her seat" (II, 69). After the flight the brutal breaking of the dream and the aerial perspective is accompanied by inevitable descent into confinement; on this occasion Flaubert insists on the heaviness of the air and the occlusion of space: "The smell of gas was mixed with people's breath; the waving of fans made the atmosphere more stifling. Emma suddenly wanted to leave; the crowd blocked the corridors, and she fell back into her seat with suffocating palpitations."

How can we fail to foresee in this scene the death agony of the young woman, panting and choking, asking for the last time: "Open the window. . . . I am stifling" (II, 170)? In this life, each ecstasy is followed by a little death; the ultimate death is harmoniously consonant with those that have preceded and prefigured it.

All these reveries of Emma, these descents into her intimate soul, which are the moments at which Flaubert most tightly mingles his point of view with his heroine's angle of vision, abound very logically in the phases of inertia and boredom which are also the novel's adagios, where time is emptied, repeats itself, and seems to become immobile. These are the most beautiful and most novel movements of the work, and they are at the same time the most Flaubertian; they are those where Flaubert to a large extent abandons the objective vision of the universal witness.

On the other hand, when the action must proceed and there is new action to deal with, the author resumes his sovereign rights and panoramic point of view, once more moves away from his heroine, can again present an exterior view of her. This is notably the case, as we have seen, at the beginning and end of the novel or in the first chapters of a new part. Each fresh beginning requires the presence of the stage manager who erects the setting while introducing the actors. Such is the great scene at the inn in Yonville at the beginning of the second part or, for opening the third part, Emma's and Léon's conversation in the hotel room in Rouen, the meeting at the cathedral, the long ride in the cab. Here Flaubert profits from the momentary remoteness of the heroine to increase the distance still more and obtain a surprising effect of perspective. The new lovers are in the cab with its drawn curtains, but the reader is not admitted into it with them. If the preceding pages denied him entrance into the protagonist's soul, he at least could see gestures and attitudes and hear words; here even that is refused him; he no longer sees anything at all and can only follow from a distance the carriage that rolls along ahead of him. During that decisive episode he is reduced to the most indifferent point of view, that of the townspeople for whom this woman is only a stranger, and it is in that light, to which he is all the more unaccustomed because he has been and will be admitted to the very depth of her soul, that he finally sees her leave the cab: "And *a woman* got out, walking with her veil lowered and without turning her head" (II, 91). An all the more striking effect because, with our prolonged intimacy, we are able to guess everything that is hidden behind that lowered veil.

The same sort of effect of distance is created a bit later by the point of view the author has us adopt to witness Emma's desperate visit to Binet from way up in an attic where two curious neighbors have climbed. We see from a distance, are barely able to hear, and are reduced to guessing and interpreting gestures and attitudes; it is a scene from the silent screen. We can suppose that Flaubert, who has had us accompany his character very closely in the preceding hours and live her drama with her, though we are outside, is so sure of our participation that he has allowed himself this brusque disconnection to tear us out of our complicity and for an instant to present us with the heroine as she appears to the foreign gaze of an outside witness and judge. Immediately afterward we even lose sight of her, just like the gossips who see her disappear at the far end of the street, going toward the cemetery, and who are lost in speculation. After that, with a new harsh stroke, the novelist brings us brutally back to Emma arriving at the nurse's and, so to speak, drops us back into her consciousness. These violent manipulations of the reader, in keeping with the pathetic quality of that phase of the narration, surprise him all the more because they are not Flaubert's habitual manner of proceeding most often throughout the novel by gradual changes and barely perceptible modulation.

The importance assumed in Flaubert's novel by the character's point of view and her subjective vision at the expense of action observed from outside her has the consequence of increasing considerably the proportion of slow movements while reducing the importance of the objective author, who gives up a varying proportion of his rights as an impartial observer.

Probably slowness and the character's perspective are what is newest and profoundly original in Flaubert, novelist of interior vision and immobility. It is precisely these admirable virtues, so characteristic of him, that Flaubert discovers only by groping in a way that is more instinctive than voluntary, and not without some anxiety. No "action," no "movement," he states in his letters;

Emma reading Rodolphe's letter that ends their affair, from part 2, chapter 13 (illustration by Albert Fourié; Madame Bovary. Mœurs de province, *3 volumes [Paris: Librarie Illustrée, 1900])*

"fifty uninterrupted pages in which there is not a single event." If he is troubled at first to see the shape his book is taking in spite of himself, it is because he is thinking of what the novel was before him, of Balzac especially, in whom everything was movement, action, and drama.

. . . .

. . . It is part of the Flaubertian genius to prefer an event's reflection in consciousness to the event itself, to prefer the dream of passion to real passion, and to substitute for action the absence of action and for every presence a void. And that is where the art of Flaubert triumphs; what is most beautiful in his novel is what is not like usual fictional literature; it is these great empty spaces. It is not the event, which contracts under Flaubert's hands, but what is between the events, those stagnant expanses where all movement is immobilized. The miracle is that he succeeded in giving so much existence and density to those empty spaces, creating fullness out of hollowness. But this reversal implies another subversion: one that in the objective, third-person narration permits expansion of the share given to the character's perspective and to the optic of his "thought," where the heart of the matter is.

Flaubert is the great novelist of inaction, of boredom and immobility. But he did not know it or did not yet know it clearly before writing *Madame Bovary;* he discovers it as he composes his novel, and not without some anguish. He thereby reveals to us or confirms what is perhaps a law of creation: we invent only in insecurity; the new is disquieting, and the first gesture of the discoverer is a gesture of rejection. But in this groping and disturbed quest he finds what is really his own. In the act of composing he recognizes himself. And this verifies another law of creation: even in as voluntaristic an artist as Flaubert, one as convinced as he is that everything is in the conception and the plan, invention is inseparable from execution; the conception of the work is completed in the operations that bring it into being.

–Jean Rousset, "*Madame Bovary* or the Book about Nothing," translated by Raymond Giraud, in *Flaubert. A Collection of Critical Essays,* edited by Giraud (Englewood Cliffs, N.J.: Prentice-Hall, 1964), pp. 123–131

---

1. *Par les champs et par les grèves,* ed. Conard, pp. 125–126.
2. We know that Flaubert made some considerable cuts at this point: the young woman's stroll at dawn in the park and her long contemplation of the countryside through a window with colored panes (ed. Pommier-Leleu, pp. 216–217). This is a great shame. Flaubert still attached importance to these pages, and this we can understand. It is a perfect illustration of subjective vision; seen through panes of different colors, the same landscape does not change only in color, but also in form, dimensions, relationships between objects at different distances, and, finally, emotional tonality. In this way Emma will see the world through her own passion, through the diverse colors that it will assume.
3. In the rough draft: "She was on the point of floating in emptiness to escape existence," ed. Pommier-Leleu, p. 444.

* * *

In the first volume of Le Miroir qui revient *(1984; translated as* Ghosts in the Mirror, *1988), Alain Robbe-Grillet, the founder and leader of the French New Novel, discusses Flaubert and particularly* Madame Bovary, *arguing that the novelty Flaubert's style brought to literature invented the "new novel" for his own time.*

Robbe-Grillet on Flaubert

Anglo-Saxon essayists trace the birth of the novel genre back to the beginning of the eighteenth century, not before, when Defoe, then Richardson and Fielding decide that reality exists in the here and now, not elsewhere in some 'better' timeless other world characterised by its coherence. Henceforth the real world is no longer ascribed to the abstract (perfect) idea of things, of which every day life was until then at best merely a pale reflection, but it's to be found in things themselves, here on earth as each person sees them, hears them, touches them, feels them according to his lived experience.

Consequently, reality which lay exclusively in the general and the universal (the famous scholastic 'universals') is suddenly revealed to be so particular that it becomes impossible to slot it into categories of meaning–save at the cost of serious reductive distortions. What will from then on be called *novel,* to emphasise the novelty of the genre, will then stick exclusively to concrete (which doesn't mean objective) details, fragments related with meticulous simplicity even if this is to undermine (and certainly it soon does) the possibility of constructing an image of unity or any totality whatsoever.

Thus the coherence of the world begins to collapse. And yet the narrator's authority still seems at first to be unassailable; You could almost say that he has more authority since there's no longer any other world to describe but the very one he knows. We've come down to earth, but it's more than even a kind of man-god who's speaking. Now he is simply sticking close to small immediate things rather than lofty mediatised concepts.

Alain Robbe-Grillet, who was elected a member of the Academy of France in 2004 (photograph by Royal S. Brown; Anthony Fragola, The Erotic Dream Machine *[Carbondale: Southern Illinois University Press, 1992])*

It took Lawrence Sterne and Diderot for the narrative voice to claim both its total creative freedom and bold lack of authority, affirming at each twist and turn of the text with a smile of complicity: no one knows what all this means, I no more than you, and anyway what does it matter, since in any case I can invent anything? We recall the startling opening to *Jacques le fataliste* and are reminded of *L'innommable* written by Samuel Beckett nearly two centuries later.

But after that exhilarating pre-revolutionary period when the notion of truth (divine as well as human) is blithely called into question, after the chaos of bloody revolutions, regicide and so-called wars of liberation we have the inevitable back-lash: it's the bourgeoisie–monarchist and Catholic–which when all's said and done takes power in France. And the new values that they venerate demand, on the contrary, absolutely fixed meanings, the plenitude of reality, chronological and causal security, non-contradiction with no possible deviation. This is a far cry from Jacques' wanderings with their unexpected spatial dislocations, their paradoxical episodic adventures and disjointed time scheme–the clock had nonchalantly been turned back–his wanderings are certainly much farther away than they are from us now. With Balzac the coherence of the world and the narrator's authority are both pushed to the limit that had never been reached.

The 'realist' ideology is born in which the world, closed and completed in a definitive, weighty, unequivocal rigidity is entirely meaningful, where the fictional elements are classified and put into a hierarchy, where the linear plot unfolds according to the reassuring laws of reason, where the characters become types: the miserly-old-man, the young-man-of-ambition, the devoted-mother, etc. The universal comes rushing back.

And even when Balzac denounces the fragmentation of man's work and the resulting fragmentation of the whole of society and of individual consciousness (which is why the Marxist Lukàcs considers him a revolutionary writer struggling against capitalist industrialisation and subsequent alienation) he does this from the heart of a text in which, on the contrary, everything reassures the triumphant bourgeoisie: the innocent, serene continuity of the narration dispells any fear on the part of the reader of a serious (structural) flaw in the system. The undisturbed exercise of power and the annexation of the world by one class is just, necessary, since the great novelist exercises this power too, under cover of the same ideals. And, of course, the avowed subjectivity of the encyclopedist Diderot is followed by objectivity, or more accurately its mask.

Immediately, however, Flaubert appears. The first great proletarian revolt in 1848 marked the turn of the century. A clear conscience and fixed values have already to a large extent begun to break down. The 'we' that opens *Madame Bovary* as it closes it (for the last sentences of the book in the present indicative similarly clarify the position of the writer as very much inside the world he's describing and no longer in some empyrean of absolute knowledge)–the improbable meaningless objects such as Charles's monstrous cap (oh my lovely bowler hat!) the strange holes in the narrative which we'll come back to–all this shows that the novel is once more being called into question. And this time things will move fast.

And yet it's impossible to regard Balzac as a brief intermediary. He remains a supreme, conclusive example (hence the historical importance that must be accorded to this monumental work, even when it's so heavy it slips out of our hands); he has become a symbol of perfect ease at the centre of his meretricious system, 'realism'; yet it also has to be said that from that time this system has, despite everything, persisted to the present day; and it really is this literary trend that is still greeted with approval by the general public and by traditional criticism.

In fact from the middle of the nineteenth century two families of novelists will develop along parallel lines. There are those on the one hand who will persist–since bourgeois values always exist whether in Rome or Moscow, even if no one believes in them any more–in constructing narratives codified once and for all according to a sub-Balzacian realist ideology, with no contradictions or gaps in the meaningful plot. And on the other hand, those who will wish to explore, going further each decade, insoluble tensions, divisions, narrative aporia, fractures, voids, etc.–for they know that reality begins at the precise moment when meaning becomes uncertain.

And so, moved by the comforting familiarity of the world, I may very well act as if everything bore the face of Man and Reason (with capital letters). And in that case I'd write like the Sagans of this world, make film like the Truffauts. Why not? Or else, quite the reverse, shocked by the startling strangeness of the world, however anguished, I shall experiment with the absence from the depths of which I myself am speaking and soon I shall recognise that the only details making up the reality of the world in which I'm living are nothing but the gaps in the continuity of those ready-made meanings, all other details being by definition ideological. Now at last I am able to shift uneasily between the two poles.

Someone (I forget who) has said that *Madame Bovary,* in a complete break with the preceding half century where everything rests on plenitude and solidity, is the precursor of the '*nouveau roman*': 'a cross roads of gaps and misunderstandings'. And Flaubert himself writes of Emma after the famous ball which should have satisfied her fully: 'Her visit to Vaubyessard had made a gap in her life, like those great chasms that a storm sometimes hollows out of the mountains in a single night'. This theme of the void, the fault, is all the more remarkable since it will immediately reappear twice more on the very next page.

Emma is day-dreaming in front of the Vicomte's cigar case which they found on their way home. She imagines the breath of the needlewomen passing through the gaps in the stitching of the canvas stretched on its frame and the threads of coloured silk going from hole to hole, interweaving their constantly interrupted paths to form the pattern. Isn't this an accurate metaphor for the work of the modern novelist (I am Flaubert!)–on the broken thread of reality, the writing as the reading afterwards, moving from gap to gap to construct the narrative?

I'm all the more convinced of this as, twenty lines further on, Emma has just bought a street map of Paris so she can walk round the capital without leaving her room in the provinces; she traces on the paper with her fingertip multiple complex walks, stopping at the intersecting lines of streets 'in front of the blank squares indicating houses.' The author's insistent repetition of the image of an imaginary journey between 'blanks,' gaps, helps us to see to what extent the identification he claimed with his heroine is in fact something quite different from a vague, insignificant whim.

It is thanks to the holes shifting about in the texture of his novel that the text lives, like a territory in a game of 'Go' which only stays alive if you are careful to leave at least one empty space, a vacant square, what the experts call an open eye, or a freedom. If, on the contrary, all the places marked out by the intersecting lines have pieces on them, the territory is dead, the enemy could seize it simply by encircling it.

Here we find one of Einstein's fundamental ideas, popularised a few years ago by Karl Popper: the scientific criterion for testing a theory, in whatever field, is not that it can be verified as correct at each new experiment but quite the opposite, that in one case at least it can be proved wrong. Thus Marxist Leninism and orthodox psychoanalysis, Popper states, are wrongly considered by their advocates to be sciences, since these disciplines are *always* right. Closed systems, they leave no space, no area of uncertainty, no doubt as to meaning, no question without an answer. Whereas science is incompatible with such a totalitarian frame of mind: it can only be living and so there must be gaps. The same thing goes for the literature that interests me.

–Alain Robbe-Grillet, *Ghosts in the Mirror,* translated by Jo Levy (London: Calder, 1988), pp. 146–151

* * *

Dust jacket for the first English edition of Julian Barnes's second novel (Collection of Richard Layman)

Julian Barnes is a British fiction writer and critic, who has written extensively and authoritatively about the author of Madame Bovary. *In* Something to Declare *(2002), half of which is devoted to his essays about Flaubert, Barnes writes in his preface:*

> Central to me in the development of the modern sensibility is the figure of Gustave Flaubert. "I wish he'd shut up about Flaubert," Kingsley Amis, with pop-eyed truculence once complained to a friend of mine. Fat chance. Flaubert: the writer's writer par excellence, the saint and martyr of literature, the perfector of realism, the creator of the modern novel with *Madame Bovary,* and then, a quarter of a century later, the assistant creator of the modernist novel with *Bouvard et Pécuchet.*

Flaubert's Parrot *(1984) is narrated by a physician who is drawn to* Madame Bovary *in his attempts to understand the suicide of his unfaithful wife. He becomes obsessed with Flaubert's life and with the creative process that led to his greatest novel.* Flaubert's Parrot *is, finally, a study of the ways that literature has personal meaning to readers. In this passage, chapter 6 of the 15-chapter novel, Barnes provides an indictment of literary criticism demonstrating how it frequently misses the point of literature.*

Emma Bovary's Eyes

Let me tell you why I hate critics. Not for the normal reasons: that they're failed creators (they usually aren't; they may be failed critics, but that's another matter); or that they're by nature carping, jealous and vain (they usually aren't; if anything, they might better be accused of over-generosity, of upgrading the second-rate so that their own fine discriminations thereby appear the rarer). No, the reason I hate critics–well, some of the time–is that they write sentences like this:

> Flaubert does not build up his characters, as did Balzac, by objective, external description; in fact, so careless is he of their outward appearance that on one occasion he gives Emma brown eyes (14); on another deep black eyes (15); and on another blue eyes (16).

This precise and disheartening indictment was drawn up by the late Dr Enid Starkie, Reader Emeritus in French Literature at the University of Oxford, and Flaubert's most exhaustive British biographer. The numbers in her text refer to footnotes in which she spears the novelist with chapter and verse.

I once heard Dr Starkie lecture, and I'm glad to report that she had an atrocious French accent; one of those deliveries full of dame-school confidence and absolutely no ear, swerving between workaday correctness and farcical error, often within the same word. Naturally, this didn't affect her competence to teach at the University of Oxford, because until quite recently the place preferred to treat modern languages as if they were dead: this made them more respectable, more like the distant perfections of Latin and Greek. Even so, it did strike me as peculiar that someone who lived by French literature should be so calamitously inadequate at making the basic words of the language sound as they did when her subjects, her heroes (her paymasters, too, you could say) first pronounced them.

You might think this a cheap revenge on a dead lady critic simply for pointing out that Flaubert didn't have a very reliable notion of Emma Bovary's eyes. But then I don't hold with the precept *de mortuis nil nisi bonum* (I speak as a doctor, after all); and it's hard to underestimate the irritation when a critic points out something like that to you. The irritation isn't with Dr Starkie, not at first–she was only, as they say, doing her job–but with Flaubert. So that painstaking genius couldn't even keep the eyes of his most famous character a consistent colour? *Ha.* And then, unable to be cross with him for long, you shift your feelings over to the critic.

I must confess that in all the times I read *Madame Bovary,* I never noticed the heroine's rainbow eyes. Should I have? Would you? Was I perhaps too busy noticing things that Dr Starkie was missing (though what they might have been I can't for the moment think)? Put it another way: is there a perfect reader somewhere, a total reader? Does Dr Starkie's reading of *Madame Bovary* contain all the responses which I have when I read the book, and then add a whole lot more, so that my reading is in a way pointless? Well, I hope not. My reading might be pointless in terms of the history of literary criticism; but it's not pointless in terms of pleasure. I can't prove that lay readers enjoy books more than professional critics; but I can tell you one advantage we have over them. We can forget. Dr Starkie and her kind are cursed with memory: the books they teach and write about can never fade from their brains. They become family. Perhaps this is why some critics develop a faintly patronising tone towards their subjects. They act as if Flaubert, or Milton, or Wordsworth were some tedious old aunt in a rocking chair, who smelt of stale powder, was only interested in the past, and hadn't said anything new for years. Of course, it's her house, and everybody's living in it rent free; but even so, surely it is, well, you know . . . *time?*

Whereas the common but passionate reader is allowed to forget; he can go away, be unfaithful with other writers, come back and be entranced again. Domesticity need never intrude on the relationship; it may be sporadic, but when there it is always intense. There's none of the daily rancour which develops when people live bovinely together. I never find myself, fatigue in the voice, reminding Flaubert to hang up the bathmat or use the lavatory brush. Which is what Dr Starkie can't help herself doing. Look, writers aren't *perfect,* I want to cry; any more than husbands and wives are perfect. The only unfailing rule is, if they seem so, they can't be. I never thought my wife was perfect. I loved her, but I never deceived myself. I remember . . . But I'll keep that for another time.

I'll remember instead another lecture I once attended, some years ago at the Cheltenham Literary Festival. It was given by a professor from Cambridge, Christopher Ricks, and it was a very shiny performance. His bald head was shiny; his black shoes were shiny; and his lecture was very shiny indeed. Its theme was Mistakes in Literature and Whether They Matter. Yevtushenko, for example, apparently made a howler in one of his poems about the American nightingale. Pushkin was quite wrong about the sort of military dress worn at balls. John Wain was wrong about the Hiroshima pilot. Nabokov was wrong–rather surprising, this–about the phonetics of the name Lolita. There were other examples: Coleridge, Yeats and Browning were some of those caught out not knowing a hawk from a handsaw, or not even knowing what a handsaw was in the first place.

Two examples particularly struck me. The first was a remarkable discovery about *Lord of the Flies.* In the famous scene where Piggy's spectacles are used for the rediscovery of fire, William Golding got his optics wrong. Completely back to front, in fact. Piggy is shortsighted; and the spectacles he would have been prescribed for this condition could not possibly have been used as burning glasses. Which every way you held them, they would have been quite unable to make the rays of the sun coverage.

The second example concerned 'The Charge of the Light Brigade'. 'Into the valley of Death/Rode the six hundred.' Tennyson wrote the poem very quickly, after reading a report in *The Times* which included the phrase 'someone had blundered'. He also relied on an earlier account which had mentioned '607 sabres'. Subsequently, however, the number of those who took part in what Camille Rousset called *ce terrible et sanglant steeplechase* was officially corrected to 673. 'Into the valley of Death/Rode the six hundred and seventy-three'? Not quite enough swing to it, somehow. Perhaps it could have been rounded up to seven hundred–still not quite accurate, but at least more accurate? Tennyson considered the matter and decided to leave the poem as he had written it: 'Six is much better than seven hundred (as I think) metrically so keep it.'

Not putting '673' or '700' or '*c.*700' instead of '600' hardly seems to qualify as a Mistake to me. The shakiness of Golding's optics, on the other hand, must definitely be classed as an error. The next question is, Does it matter? As far as I can remember Professor Ricks's lecture, his argument was that if the factual side of literature becomes unreliable, then ploys such as irony and fantasy become much harder to use. If you don't know what's true, or what's meant to be true, then the value of what isn't true, or isn't meant to be true, becomes diminished. This seems to me a very sound argument; though I do wonder to how many cases of literary mistake it actually applies. With Piggy's glasses, I should think that a) very few people apart from oculists, opticians and bespectacled professors of English would notice; and b) when they do notice, they merely detonate the error–like blowing up a small bomb with a controlled explosion. What's more, this detonation (which takes place on a remote beach, with only a dog as witness) doesn't set fire to other parts of the novel.

Mistakes like Golding's are 'external mistakes'–disparities between what the book claims to be the case, and what we know the reality to be; often they merely indicate a lack of specific technical knowledge on the writer's part. The sin is pardonable. What, though, about 'internal mistakes', when the writer claims two incompatible things within his own creation? Emma's eyes are brown, Emma's eyes are blue. Alas, this can be put down only to incompetence, to sloppy literary habits. I read the other day a well-praised first novel in which the narrator–who is both sexually inexperienced and an amateur of French literature–comically rehearses to himself the best way to kiss a girl without being rebuffed: 'With a slow, sensual, irresistible strength, draw her gradually towards you while gazing into her eyes as if you had just been given a copy of the first, suppressed edition of *Madame Bovary*.'

I thought this was quite neatly put, indeed rather amusing. The only trouble is, there's no such thing as a 'first, suppressed edition of *Madame Bovary*'. The novel, as I should have thought was tolerably well known, first appeared serially in the *Revue de Paris;* then came the prosecution for obscenity; and only after the acquittal was the work published in book form. I expect the young novelist (it seems unfair to give his name) was thinking of the 'first, suppressed edition' of *Les Fleurs du mal.* No doubt he'll get it right in time for his second edition; if there is one.

Eyes of brown, eyes of blue. Does it matter? Not, does it matter if the writer contradicts himself; but, does it matter what colour they are anyway? I feel sorry for novelists when they have to mention women's eyes: there's so little choice, and whatever colouring is decided upon inevitably carries banal implications. Her eyes are blue: innocence and honesty. Her eyes are black: passion and depth. Her eyes are green: wildness and jealousy. Her eyes are brown: reliability and common sense. Her eyes are violet; the novel is by Raymond Chandler. How can you escape all this without some haversack of a parenthesis about the lady's character? Her eyes are mud-coloured; her eyes changed hue according to the contact lenses she wore; he never looked her in the eye. Well, take your pick. My wife's eyes were greeny-blue, which makes her story a long one. And so I suspect that in the writer's moments of private candour, he probably admits the pointlessness of describing eyes. He slowly imagines the character, moulds her into shape, and then–probably the last thing of all–pops a pair of glass eyes into those empty sockets. Eyes? Oh yes, she'd better have eyes, he reflects, with a weary courtesy.

Bouvard and Pécuchet, during their investigations into literature, find that they lose respect for an author when he strays into error. I am more surprised by how few mistakes writers make. So the Bishop of Liège dies fifteen years before he should: does this invalidate *Quentin Durward?* It's a trivial offence, something tossed to the reviewers. I see the novelist at the stern rail of a cross-Channel ferry, throwing bits of gristle from his sandwich to the hovering gulls.

I was too far away to observe what colour Enid Starkie's eyes were; all I remember of her is that she dressed like a matelot, walked like a scrum-half, and had an atrocious French accent. But I'll tell you another thing. The Reader Emeritus in French Literature at the University of Oxford and Honorary Fellow of Somerville College, who was 'well known for her studies of the lives and works of writers such as Baudelaire, Rimbaud, Gautier, Eliot and Gide' (I quote her dust-wrapper; first edition, of course), who devoted two large books and many years of her life to the author of *Madame Bovary,* chose as frontispiece to her first volume a portrait of 'Gustave Flaubert by an unknown painter'. It's the first thing we see; it is, if you like, the moment at which Dr Starkie introduces us to Flaubert. The only trouble is, it isn't him. It's a portrait of Louis Bouilhet, as everyone from the *gardienne* of Croisset onwards and upwards will tell you. So what do we make of that once we've stopped chuckling?

Perhaps you still think I'm merely being vengeful towards a dead scholar who can't answer for herself. Well, maybe I am. But then, *quis custodiet ipsos custodes?* And I'll tell you something else. I've just reread *Madame Bovary.*

> On one occasion he gives Emma brown eyes (14); on another deep black eyes (15); and on another blue eyes (16).

And the moral of it all, I suppose, is: Never take fright at a footnote. Here are the six references Flaubert makes to Emma Bovary's eyes in the course of the book. It is clearly a subject of some importance to the novelist:

1 (Emma's first appearance) 'In so far as she was beautiful, this beauty lay in her eyes: although they were brown, they would appear black because of her lashes . . .'

2 (Described by her adoring husband early in their marriage) 'Her eyes seemed bigger to him, especially when she was just waking up and fluttered her lids several times in succession; they were black when she was in shadow and dark blue in full daylight; and they seemed to contain layer upon layer of colours, which were thicker in hue deep down, and became lighter towards the enamel-like surface.'

3 (At a candlelit ball) 'Her black eyes appeared even blacker.'

4 (On first meeting Leon) 'Fixing him with her large, wide-open black eyes'.

5 (Indoors, as she appears to Rodolphe when he first examines her) 'Her black eyes'.

6 (Emma looking in a mirror, indoors, in the evening; she has just been seduced by Rodolphe) 'Her eyes had never been so large, so black, nor contained such depth.'

How did the critic put it? 'Flaubert does not build up characters, as did Balzac, by objective, external description; in fact, so careless is he of their outward appearance that . . .' It would be interesting to compare the time spent by Flaubert making sure that his heroine had the rare and difficult eyes of a tragic adulteress with the time spent by Dr Starkie in carelessly selling him short.

And one final thing, just to make absolutely sure. Our earliest substantial source of knowledge about Flaubert is Maxime du Camp's *Souvenirs littéraires* (Hachette, Paris, 1882–3, 2 vols): gossipy, vain, self-justifying and unreliable, yet historically essential. On page 306 of the first volume (Remington & Co., London, 1893, no translator credited) Du Camp describes in great detail the woman on whom Emma Bovary was based. She was, he tells us, the second wife of a medical officer from Bon-Lecours, near Rouen:

> This second wife was not beautiful; she was small, had dull yellow hair, and a face covered with freckles. She was full of pretension, and despised her husband, whom she considered a fool. Round and fair in person, her small bones were well-covered, and in her carriage and her general bearing there were flexible, undulating movements, like those of an eel. Her voice, vulgarised by its Lower Normandy accent, was full of caressing tones, and her eyes, of uncertain colour, green, grey, or blue, according to the light, had a pleading expression, which never left them.

Dr Starkie appears to have been serenely unaware of this enlightening passage. All in all, it seems a magisterial negligence towards a writer who must, one way and another, have paid a lot of her gas bills. Quite simply, it makes me furious. Now do you understand why I hate critics? I could try and describe to you the expression in my eyes at this moment; but they are far too discoloured with rage.

–Julian Barnes, "Emma Bovary's Eyes," in *Flaubert's Parrot* (London: Cape, 1984), pp. 74–81

Salammbô and Antiquity: 1857–1863

Research for a Novel of the Ancient World

With the success of Madame Bovary, *Flaubert began to spend several months a year in Paris. Back in Normandy in May 1857, he started serious research for what would become his next novel,* Salammbô. *The background of the new work was the revolt and subsequent annihilation of the unpaid mercenary army of Carthage, following that city's defeat by Rome in 241* B.C. *The title character—whose name Flaubert invented—was the daughter of the Carthaginian general Hamilcar. Flaubert read ceaselessly about antiquity, for he wanted to create a credible world, wholly in accord with what was known of ancient Carthage. Although he forced himself to write a first chapter, he had frequent misgivings about his project. On 23 January 1858 he wrote to Mlle Marie-Sophie Leroyer de Chantepie of his plan to visit the site of ancient Carthage:*

> I absolutely must make a trip to Africa; so, toward the end of March I'll return to the land of dates. I'm thrilled at the prospect. Once again I'll live on horseback and sleep under a tent. What deep breaths of air I'll treat myself to when I board my ship at Marseilles! But this trip will be a short one. I need to go only to E-Kef (thirty leagues from Tunis) and explore the environs of Carthage within a radius of twenty leagues, in order to acquaint myself thoroughly with the landscapes I'll be describing. My outline is done, and I'm a third of the way through the second chapter. The book will have fifteen.

—*The Letters of Gustave Flaubert, 1857–1880,* edited by Francis Steegmuller (Cambridge, Mass.: Harvard University Press, 1982), pp. 6–7

He left on 12 April 1858 for a trip that lasted nearly two months, visiting Philippeville, Constantine, Tunis, and Le Kef. As he had done when he traveled with Maxime Du Camp in the Middle East, Flaubert recorded his observations in travel notebooks.

Marie-Sophie Leroyer de Chantepie (1800–1888), a minor local writer who lived in Angers and corresponded with Flaubert. She first wrote to the author to praise the greatness of Madame Bovary *and the character of Emma. Although they never met, they remained faithful correspondents throughout Flaubert's life (Collections de la Bibliothèque municipale de Rouen. Cliché Thierry Ascencio-Parvy).*

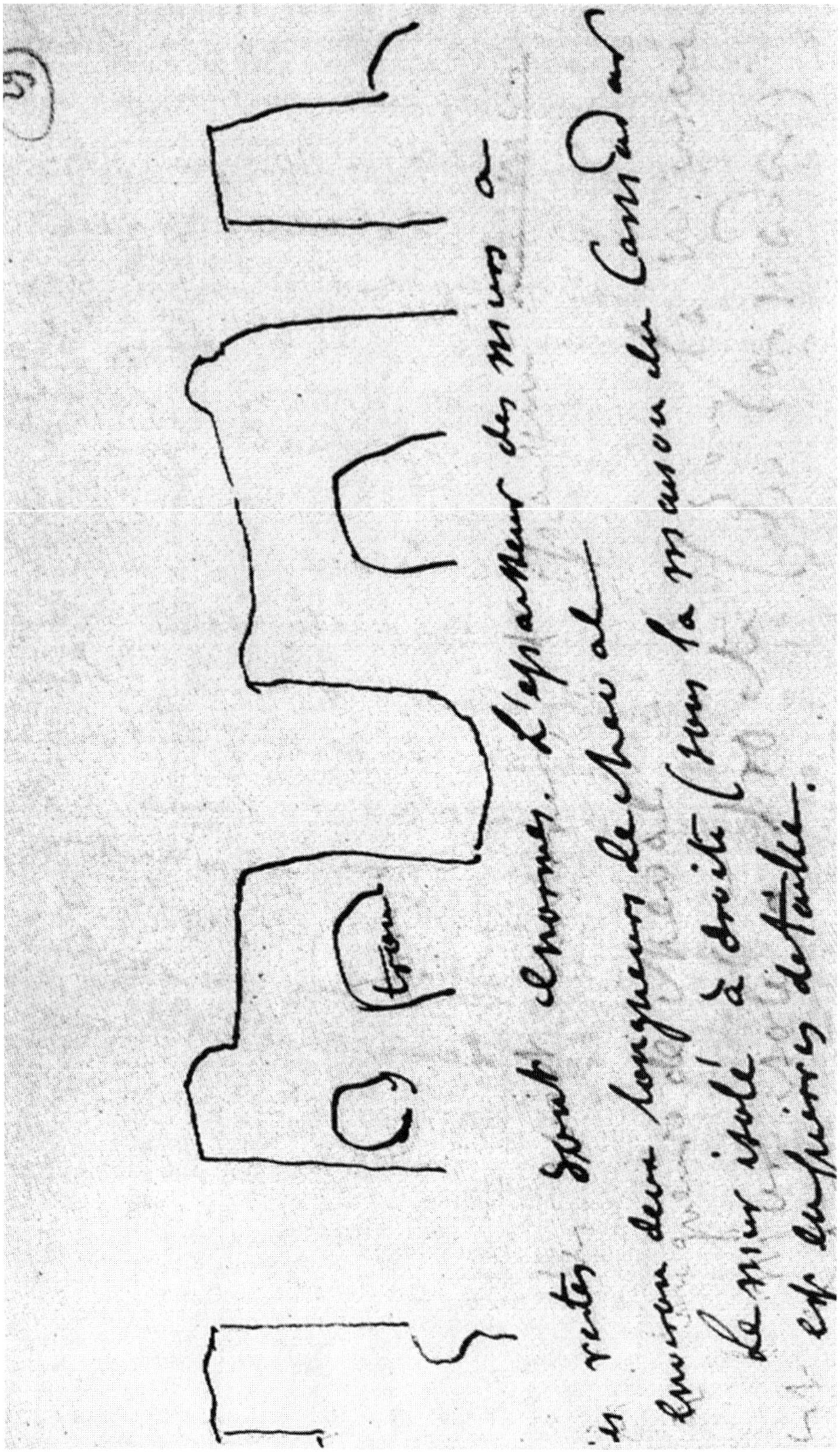

Page from Flaubert's travel book number 10, which he kept during his journey to Tunisia in spring 1858 (courtesy of the Bibliothèque historique de la Ville de Paris)

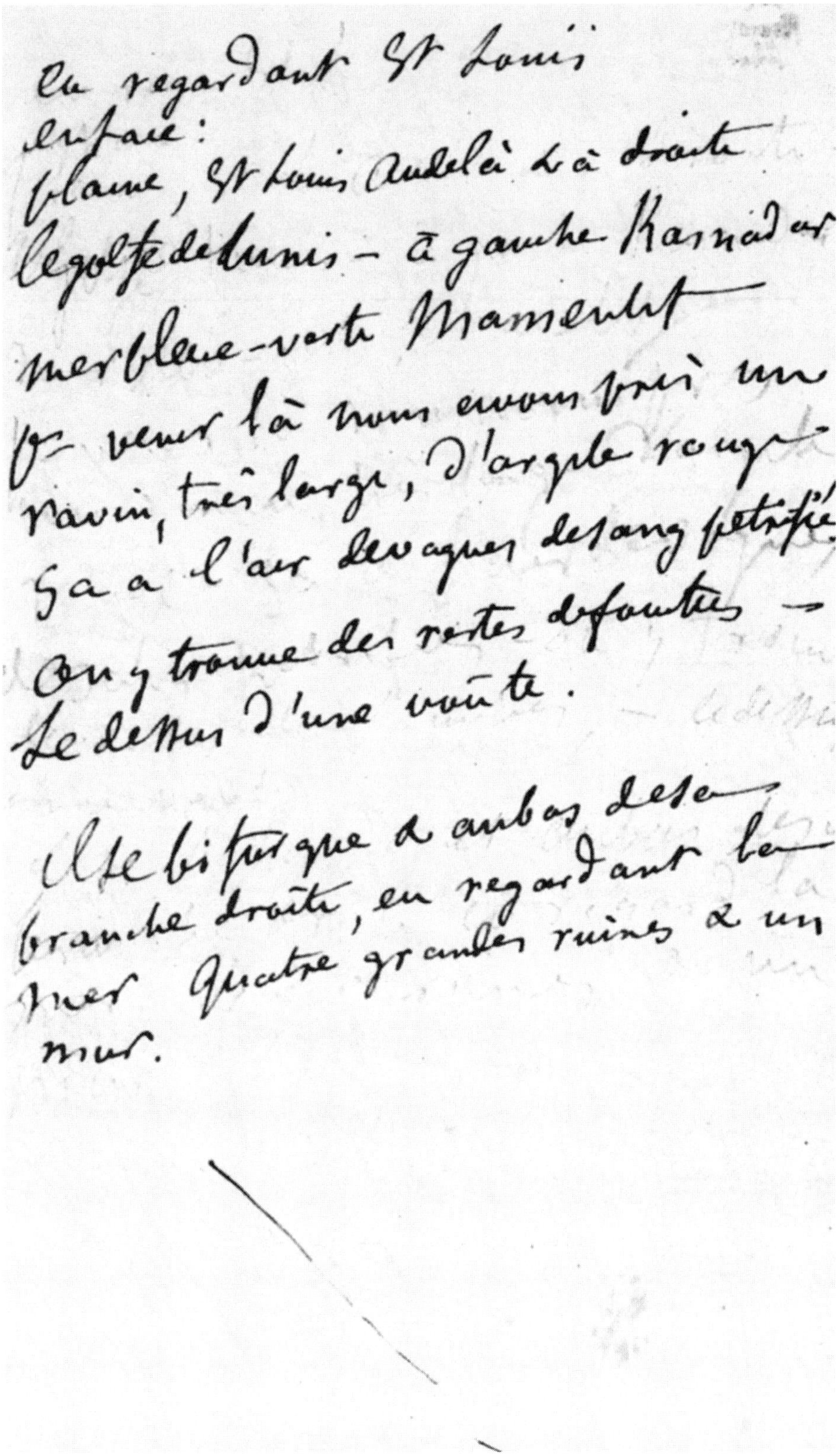
en regardant St Louis
en face:
plaine, St Louis au delà & à droite
le golfe de Tunis – à gauche Karnadar
mer bleue-verte Mamenlif
pour venir là nous avons pris un
ravin, très large, d'argile rouge
ça a l'air de vagues de sang pétrifié.
On y trouve des restes de fontes –
le dessus d'une voûte.

Il se bifurque à au bas de sa
branche droite, en regardant la
mer Quatre grandes ruines & un
mur.

Page from travel book number 10 in which Flaubert describes the landscape around the Gulf of Tunis (courtesy of the Bibliothèque historique de la Ville de Paris)

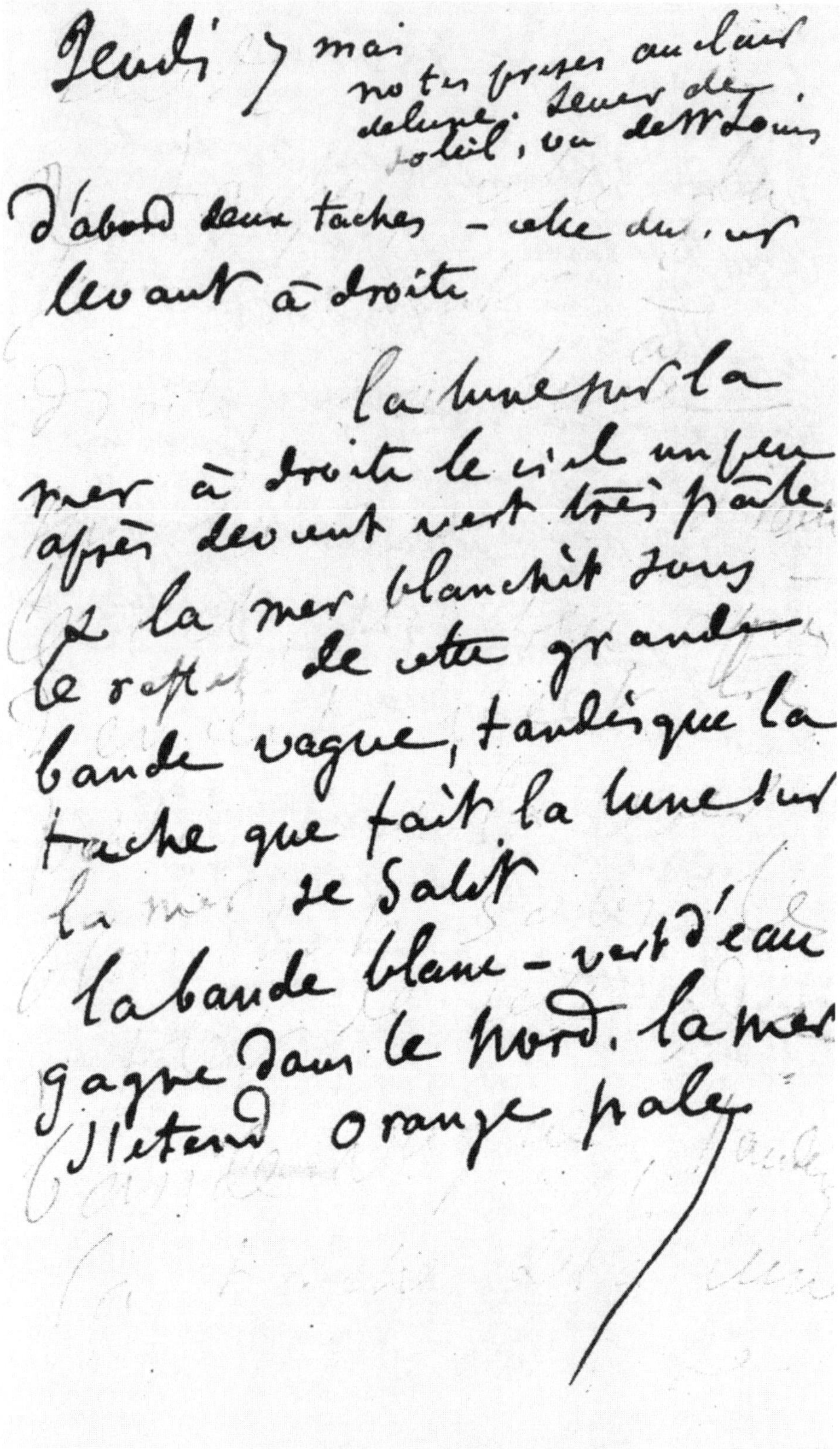
Jeudi 7 mai
notes prises au clair
de lune; lever du
soleil, vu de St Louis

d'abord deux taches – celle du [illegible]
levant à droite

la lune sur la
mer à droite le ciel un peu
après devient vert très pâle
& la mer blanchit sous
le reflet de cette grande
bande vague, tandis que la
tache que fait la lune sur
la mer se salit
la bande blanc – vert d'eau
gagne dans le Nord. la mer
s'étend orange pâle

Page from travel book number 10, written by moonlight on Thursday, 7 May 1858. Flaubert was waiting to describe the progressive color variations of the sunrise on the sea–effects that he later evoked in Salammbô *(courtesy of the Bibliothèque historique de la Ville de Paris).*

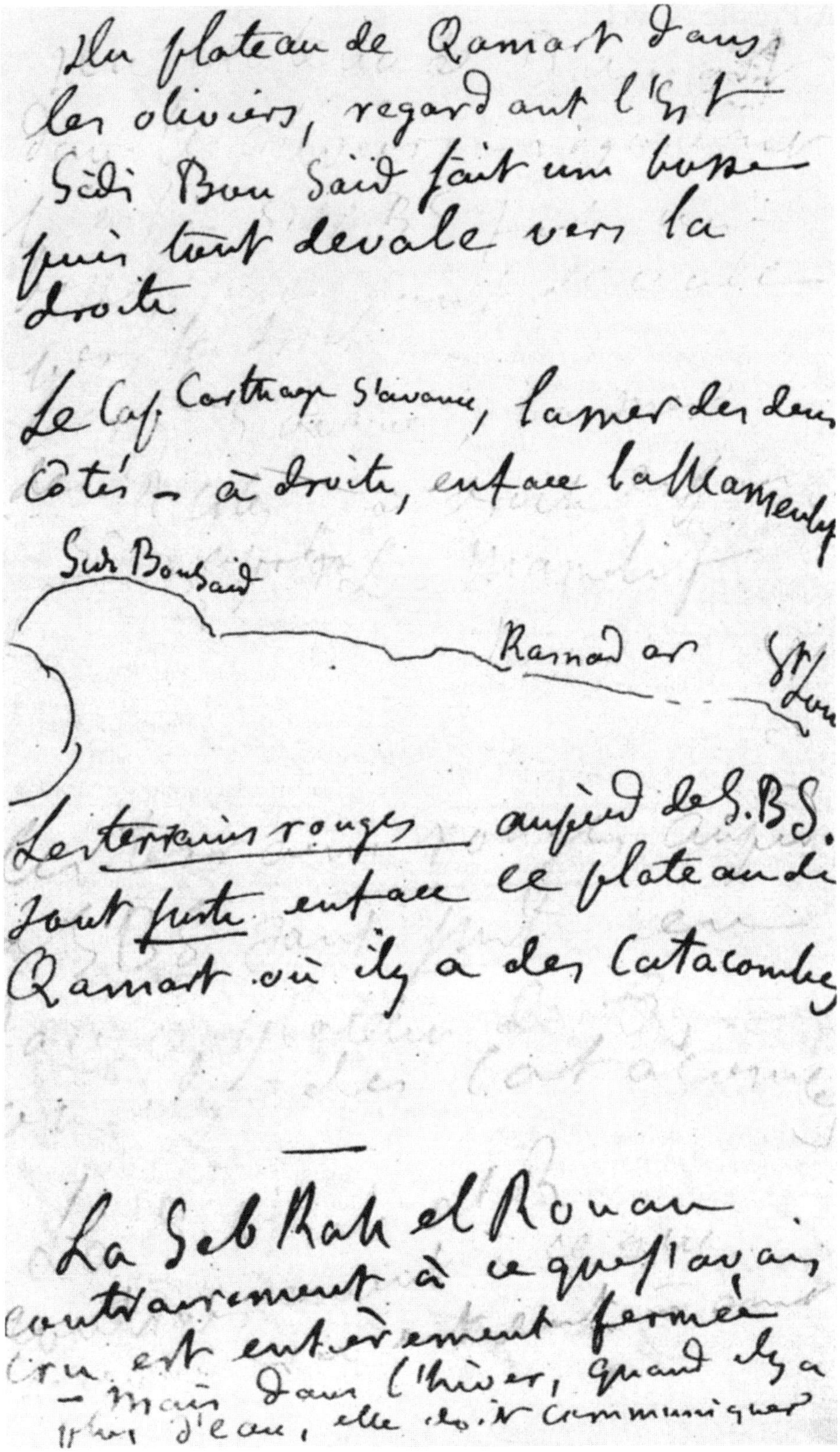

Du plateau de Qamart dans les oliviers, regardant l'Est Sidi Bou Said fait une bosse puis tout devale vers la droite

Le Cap Carthage s'avance, la mer des deux côtés – à droite, en face la Hammamelif

Sidi Bou Said

Les terrains rouges au pied de S.B.S. Tout juste en face ce plateau de Qamart où il y a des Catacombes

—

La Sebkah el Rouan contrairement à ce que j'avais cru, est entièrement fermée – mais dans l'hiver, quand il y a plus d'eau, elle doit communiquer

Page from travel book number 10 in which Flaubert describes and draws a map of the cape of ancient Carthage. He writes, "Sebkah el Rouan, contrary to what I had thought, is entirely enclosed–but in winter, when there is more water, it must communicate" (courtesy of the Bibliothèque historique de la Ville de Paris).

A Purple Novel

When he returned to Croisset on 9 June 1858, Flaubert began working intensely on the novel–staying up until four in the morning every night. In March 1861 in Paris he met his friends Edmond and Jules de Goncourt, who recorded in their journal Flaubert's remark on his work: "The story, the plot of a novel does not matter to me. When I write a novel I try to render a color, a tone. For example, in my Carthage novel, I want to do something purple." The tone of Madame Bovary, *Flaubert said, was "gray."*

In early May, Flaubert invited the Goncourts to an extended reading of his work in progress. In this excerpt from the Goncourts' Journals, *dated 6 May 1861, the brothers compare Flaubert's work to François-René Chateaubriand's Romantic prose epic,* Les Martyrs, ou le Triomphe de la religion chrétienne *(1809). The Goncourts' writing about Flaubert often shows envy and, at times, jealousy.*

A Reading of *Salammbô*

At four o'clock we arrive chez Flaubert, who has invited us to a grand reading of *Salammbô,* along with a painter whom we find there, Gleyre . . .

From four to six, Flaubert reads in that resounding, bellowing voice of his, which has the lulling effect of a purr, but a *bronze* purr. At seven we dine . . . Then, after dinner and a pipe, the reading is resumed. Certain portions he doesn't read completely, but summarizes, and we go all the way through to the last completed chapter, Salammbô's fornication with Mâtho. By this time it is two in the morning.

I am going to set down here what I sincerely think of this book by a man whom I love–there are few of whom I can say that–a man whose first book I admired.

Salammbô does not come up to what I expected of Flaubert. His personality, so very carefully concealed in *Madame Bovary* as to be in fact absent from that very impersonal book, is here revealed–inflated, melodramatic, declamatory, luxuriating in overaccentuation and in crude, almost garish, colors. Flaubert sees the Orient, and the antique Orient, in the guise of present-day Algerian decor. Some of the effects are childish, others ridiculous. His struggle with Chateaubriand is the great defect, and deprives the book of originality: the reader is constantly put in mind of *Les Martyrs.*

Immensely fatiguing are the eternal descriptions, the minute, button-by-button itemizations of every character and every costume, which destroy any possibility of grand group effects. All the effects are minuscular, concentrated on a single point; faces are obscured by trappings, feelings are lost in landscapes.

Jules and Edmond de Goncourt, who collaborated on novels and Le Journal des Goncourt, *which they began keeping in 1851 (drawing by Paul Gavarni; cliché Bibliothèque nationale de France, Paris)*

Unquestionably, immense effort, infinite patience, and rare talent have gone into this attempt to reconstruct a vanished civilization in all its detail. But this project–in my opinion doomed from the start–Flaubert has not been able to *illuminate:* there are none of those revelations by analogy which enable one to discover something of the soul of a nation no longer in existence.

. . . The feelings of his characters . . . are the banal feelings of mankind in general, not of Carthaginian mankind; and his Mâtho is basically nothing but an operatic tenor in a barbaric poem.

–The Letters of Gustave Flaubert, 1857–1880, p. 27

* * *

Flaubert finally completed the manuscript in February 1862. During the summer he worked with Louis Bouilhet on refining his novel. After complex negotiations with publisher Michel Lévy, Flaubert signed a contract for 10,000 francs, and Salammbô *was published on 24 November 1862. Flaubert sent Laure de Maupassant, the sister of his long-dead friend Alfred Le Poittevin, a copy of his book as a gift. Separated from her husband and living in the seaside town of Étretat with her two sons, she responded enthusiastically to the novel.*

Laure de Maupassant to Flaubert, 6 December 1862

I am very grateful to you, my dear Gustave, for sending me *Salammbô,* and my pleasure in first opening the book was a double one. It was proof that I was remembered by an old friend whose affection and regard I hold ever dear; and then the book, just out, was already famous, and I knew I would spend charming hours in the ancient Carthage you have so painstakingly resurrected. My first thought should have been to thank you, but I was drawn at once to your pages, and felt a compulsion to read and reread them before taking up my pen.

Here in the depths of my hermitage I lead a very active life: my sons' education, for which at the moment I am solely responsible, takes up much of my time; there are long walks, necessary to their health; and in addition, my mother is here just now. All this keeps me excessively busy, and my free moments become fewer and fewer. Still, I have pared away a bit here and there, and can now say that I know this novel, so much and so loudly spoken of in Paris that our Etretat cliffs ring with the echo. Before expressing the humble opinion of this provincial lady, before burning my bit of incense, let me say that your successes of today, as well as those of yesterday, invariably carry me back into the past, to memories of our poor Alfred, whom you too have never forgotten. Do you not feel, as I do, that he has had his part in all this, that some of it goes back to him, and to his praise–the first you had–of your early efforts? I can say things like this to you, and I am sure you agree with me that there are fond memories which occupy an increasingly greater place in our lives, instead of disappearing with time. My mother and I enjoy reliving all the past these long autumn evenings, and our hours together pass a bit sadly, but not without a certain charm. For the last few days, however, *Salammbô* has left us no time to chat: as soon as dinner is over, we sit around the fire, I take up the book, and begin to read aloud. My son Guy is by no means the least attentive member of the group: his eyes flash at your descriptions, some of them so charming and others so terrible, and I swear he hears the din of your battles and the trumpeting of your elephants. It goes without saying that my first reading was complete and for myself alone; now I am rereading it for the others as well as for myself, and very probably I shall go through it several times more. Your heroine is in my opinion a strikingly original creation: I think you fashioned her out of moonbeams. Around this woman–almost a goddess, and suffused with a mysterious perfume–the action develops, powerful, grandiose, terrible. We are present at the scenes you describe, we touch them with our fingers; and when at the end we see Mâtho fall, and see his living heart offered to the sun, we close our eyes against the unspeakable horror. It is Ribera, I think, who lent you his brush, and you will do well to keep it, for no one will be able to use it as you do. The few summer people still here are besieging me with requests to lend them *Salammbô;* everyone wants to read it; so far, I have given it to no one–to avoid stirring up jealousy.

Laure de Maupassant, circa 1860. The sister of Flaubert's best friend Alfred Le Poittevin, she was the mother of writer Guy de Maupassant (cliché Bibliothèque nationale de France, Paris).

Your dear mother has already learned from mine of some of the troubles I have had; but to all you dear friends of other days I want to say a little more. I have suffered greatly–I know you understand that: but I am one of those who can make, and keep, a resolution, and I hope you know and esteem me sufficiently to make it unnecessary for me to say that this resolution is absolutely irrevocable, and that I shall know how to preserve the dignity of my life. I am quite well situated

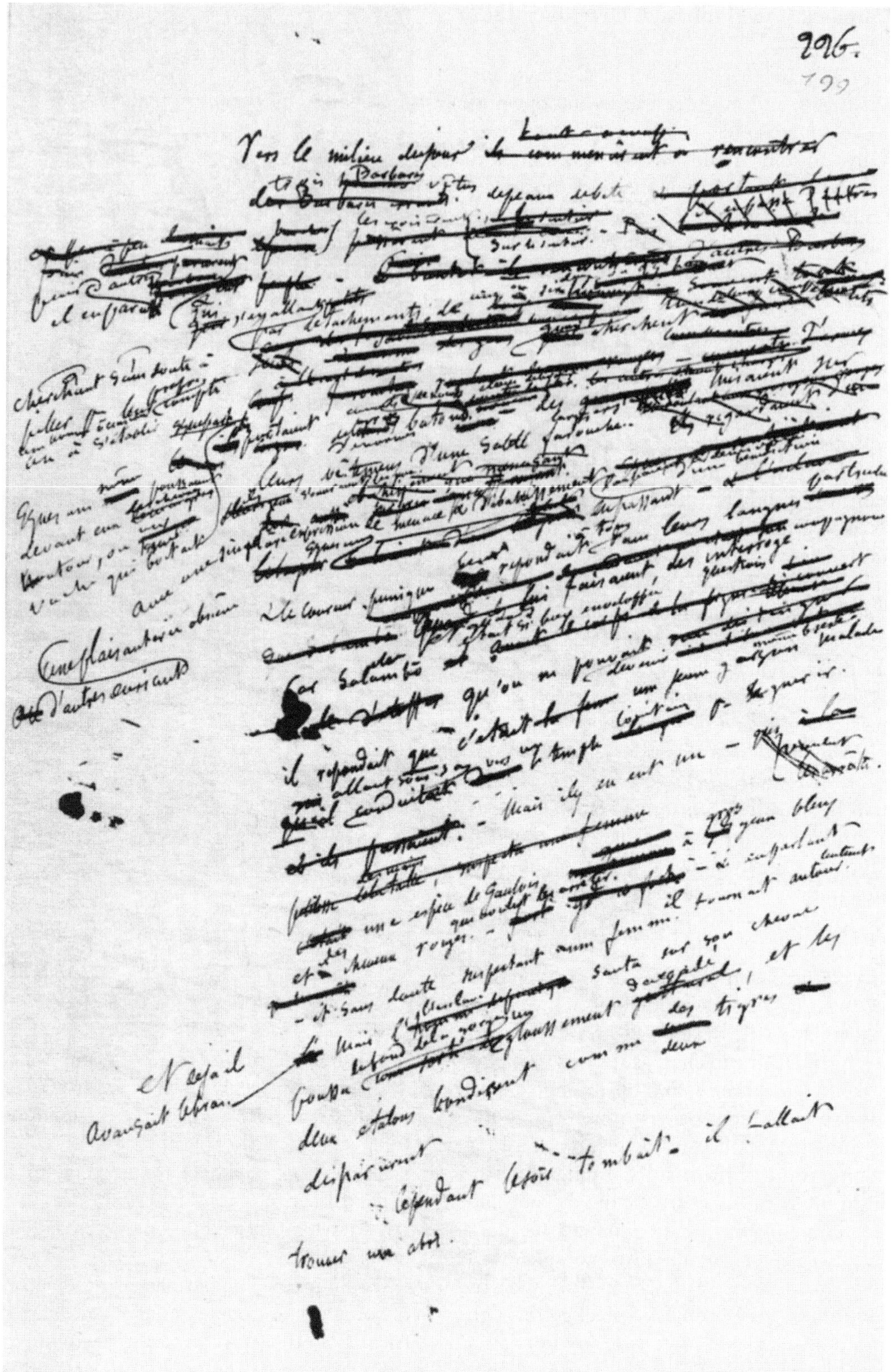

Pages from Flaubert's drafts of Mâtho's encounter with Salammbô in chapter 11, "Under the Tent" (clichés Bibliothèque nationale de France, Paris)

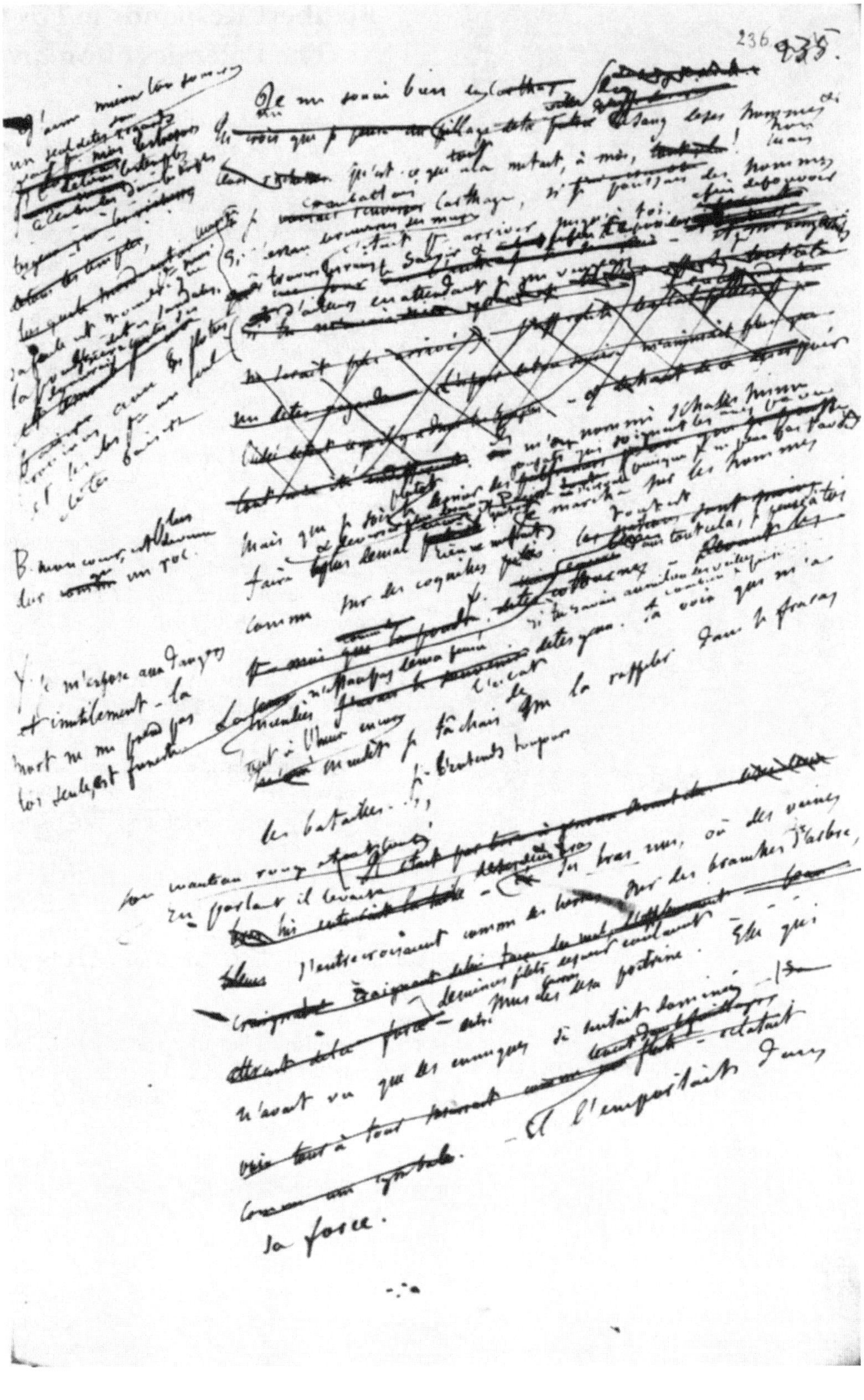

Guy de Maupassant at 10, two years before the publication of Salammbô. *When he later decided to be a writer, he became Flaubert's disciple (cliché Bibliothèque nationale de France).*

here in my pretty village, in my modest house, and in this new-found tranquillity there is a kind of happiness. My sons are growing up and developing; the elder is almost a man in his intelligence, and I have to work hard to keep up with him–I who have grown so ignorant. I have plunged into being a student again: I enjoy it, and it does me good. I have greatly improved the appearance of my house this year–painted it white, and made a garden that goes down to the Fécamp road. I greatly hope that Madame Flaubert won't fail to pay us a visit next summer; my mother is counting on all of you, and you must not deprive us of the joy your presence here would bring us.

–*The Letters of Gustave Flaubert, 1857–1880,* pp. 32–33

Flaubert Responds to His Critics: The Polemics of *Salammbô*

Although Salammbô *was a popular success, it received a mixed reaction from critics. Charles-Augustin Sainte-Beuve wrote several articles against the novel in* Le Constitutionnel, *and the archaeologist Guillaume Froehner harshly criticized Flaubert in* La Revue Contemporaine *on the grounds of his lack of knowledge on his subject. Flaubert published in newspapers replies to both of these critics–an exchange known as "the polemics of* Salammbô.*" The charges of the critics are clearly indicated in Flaubert's thorough defense of his work, which reveal his sources, his method, and the serious effort he made in doing research for his novel.*

Sainte-Beuve was impressed by Flaubert's "apologia," which was published in the fourth volume of his Nouveaux lundis *(New Mondays, 1872). He wrote Flaubert on Christmas Day, "I no longer regret having written those articles, since by doing so I induced you to bring out all your reasons. The African sun has had the singular effect of causing the humors of all of us, even our secret humors, to erupt" (*The Letters of Gustave Flaubert, 1857–1880, *p. 50).*

Flaubert to Charles-Augustin Sainte-Beuve, 23–24 December 1862

Your third article on *Salammbô* has mollified me (I was never very outraged). My friends were a bit annoyed by the two others; but remembering how frankly you told me what you thought of my big tome, I am grateful to you for the leniency of your criticism. Therefore, once again, and very sincerely, I thank you for the marks of affection you show me; and now, bypassing the usual compliments, I begin my "Apologia."

Are you quite sure, first of all, that your general judgment isn't a little overinfluenced by your emotional reaction? The world I depict in my book–barbarian, Oriental, Molochian–is displeasing to you *in itself.* You begin by doubting the verisimilitude of my reproduction of it, and then you say: "After all, it *may* be true"; and, in conclusion, "So much the worse if it *is* true!" You keep being surprised, and hold it against me that you should be. But that I cannot help! Should I have embellished the picture, sweetened, distorted, frenchified it? But you yourself reproach me for having written a poem, for being classical in the unfavorable sense of that word, and you use *Les Martyrs*[1] as a stick to beat me with.

Now, Chateaubriand's system seems to me diametrically opposed to mine. He started from a completely ideal viewpoint: he was thinking of the martyr as a certain type. Whereas I, by applying to antiquity the technique of the modern novel, wanted to capture a mirage, and I tried to be simple. Laugh as much as you like! Yes, I say *simple,* and not sober. Nothing is more complicated than a Barbarian.

But now for the points you make. I defend myself: I fight you inch by inch.

From the outset, I clash with you head-on about Hanno's *Periplus,*[2] which Montesquieu admired and I do not. Who can be persuaded to believe today that it is an "original" document? It is obviously translated, shortened, pruned, and arranged by a Greek. Never did an Oriental, whoever he might be, write in that style. Witness the inscription of Eshmunazar,[3] so bombastic and redundant. People who have themselves called "son of God," "eye of God" (see Hamaker's inscriptions)[4] are not simple in the way you mean. And then you will grant me that the Greeks understood nothing about the barbarian world. If they had understood something about it, they would not have been Greeks. The Orient was repugnant to the Hellenic spirit. What travesties they made of everything that came to them from abroad! The same is true of Polybius. He is for me an incontestable authority as to facts; but for anything he has not seen (or which he omits intentionally, for he too had a preconceived framework and belonged to a "school") I am perfectly entitled to look elsewhere. Hanno's *Periplus* is thus not a "Carthaginian monument," let alone the "only one," as you say it is. One true Carthaginian monument is the inscription at Marseilles,[5] written in real Punic. That one is "simple," I admit, because it is a list of charges; and even so, it is less "simple" than the famous *Periplus,* in which a touch of the marvelous comes through the Greek–to mention only those gorilla-skins, mistaken for human skins, that hung in the temple of Moloch (i.e. Saturn), and whose description I spared you. (You can thank me for that.) So: one point settled. I will even tell you, entre nous, that Hanno's *Periplus* is completely odious to me, the result of my having read and reread it together with Bougainville's four dissertations (in the *Mémoires* of the Academy of Inscriptions), not to mention many a doctoral thesis, the *Periplus* being a thesis subject.[6]

As for my heroine, I do not defend her. According to you, she resembles a "sentimental Elvire," Velléda, Mme Bovary.[7] No: Velléda is active, intelligent, European; Mme Bovary is the prey of many passions; Salammbô, on the contrary, remains adamantine, immobilized by her obsession. She is a maniac, a kind of Saint Teresa. No matter! I am not sure how real she is; for neither I, nor you, nor anyone, whether ancient or modern, can understand the Oriental woman, for the reason that association with her is impossible.

You accuse me of lacking logic, and you ask: "Why did the Carthaginians massacre the Balearics?" The reason is very simple: they hate all the Mercenaries; they happen to have that one group of them, the Balearics, in their power; they are stronger, and they kill them. But, you say: "The news could reach the camp from one moment to the next." How? Who would have brought it? The Carthaginians? What would have been their purpose? Or some of the Barbarians? But there were none left in the city. Foreigners? Persons unconcerned? But I was careful to show that there was no communication between Carthage and the army.

As for Hanno[8] . . . (The "bitches' milk," let me say in passing, is not a "joke." It was, and *still is,* a remedy against leprosy. See the *Dictionnaire des sciences médicales,* article "Leprosy"–a poor article, by the way: I corrected parts of it from my own observations in Damascus and Nubia.) Hanno escapes because the Mercenaries deliberately let him escape. They are not yet "unleashed" against him. They become indignant later, when they reconsider the matter: they are slow to grasp all the perfidy of which the Elders are capable. (See the beginning of my Chapter IV.) Mâtho "prowls like a madman" around Carthage. "Madman" is the right word. As conceived by the ancients, wasn't love a madness, a curse, a sickness sent by the gods? Polybius would be "astonished," you say, to see his Mâtho so depicted. I do not think so, nor would M. de Voltaire have shared this astonishment. Remember what he has the old woman in *Candide* say about the violence of passions in Africa: "Like fire, vitriol, etc."

Concerning the aqueduct: "Here the reader is up to his neck in improbability." Yes, cher maître, you are right, and even more so than you think; but not in the way you think. I will tell you further along what I think about this episode, introduced not to describe the aqueduct itself (which gave me a lot of trouble), but to enable my two heroes to enter Carthage. Actually, it is taken from an anecdote recounted by Polyaenus[9] (*Strategica*)–the story of Theodorus, the friend of Cleon, at the capture of Sestos by the people of Abydos.

"One needs a dictionary." This is a reproach that I consider supremely unfair. I could have bored the reader to death with technical terms. Far from doing so, I was careful to translate everything into French. I used not a single special term without immediately furnishing an explanation. I except the names of coins, measurements, and the months, which are indicated by the context. But surely, when you encounter on a page such words as "kreutzer," "yard," "piastre," or "penny," they are not beyond your understanding? What would you have said had I called Moloch "Melek," Hannibal "Han-Baal,"

Carthage "Karthadhadtha," and if instead of saying that the slaves in the mill wore muzzles, I had written "pausicapes"?! As for the names of perfumes and precious stones, it is true that I had to take names that are in Theophrastus, Pliny, and Athenaeus. For plants, I used Latin names–commonly accepted names–instead of Arab or Phoenician. Thus I said "Lausonia" instead of "Henneb," and I was even considerate enough to write "Lausonia" with a "u," which is wrong, and not to add "inermis," which would have been more precise. The same for "Rokh'eul," which I call "antimony," sparing you "sulphide," oh ungrateful one! But out of respect for the French reader I cannot write "Hannibal" and "Hamilcar" without the "H" (since there is a "rough breathing" on the *alpha*), and remain faithful to Rollin.[10] Be a bit gentle with me, please!

As for the temple of Tanit, I am confident that I reconstruct it correctly, on the basis of the treatise on the Syrian Goddess,[11] the duc de Luynes' medals, our knowledge of the temple at Jerusalem, a passage from St. Jerome quoted by Selden[12] (*de Diis Syriis*), the plan of the temple at Gozo[13] (which is certainly Carthaginian), and the ruins of the temple of Thugga,[14] which I have seen with my own eyes and which, so far as I know, is mentioned by no traveler or antiquarian. "No matter," you will say, "it is a strange-sounding place." Granted. The description itself, from the literary point of view, I find perfectly comprehensible. And it does not impede the action: Spendius and Mâtho remain in the foreground; the reader never loses sight of them. The descriptions in my book are never isolated or gratuitous: they all serve some purpose relating to my characters, and sooner or later they are seen to play a role in the plot.

Nor do I accept the word "chinoiserie" as applied to Salammbô's bedroom, despite the "exquisite" you add to take the curse off it (like "devouring" applied to "dogs" in the famous Dream),[15] because I have not included a single detail that is not in the Bible or not still to be seen in the Orient. You tell me more than once that the Bible is not a guide to Carthage (a debatable point); but surely the Hebrews were closer to the Carthaginians than were the Chinese! Besides, there are climatic considerations, which are eternal. For furniture and costumes, I refer you to the texts included in the twenty-first dissertation by the Abbé Mignot (*Mémoires* of the Academy of Inscriptions, Volume LX or XLI, I forget which).

As for everything in the book having a flavor of "opera, pomp, and bombast," why should you think that things were not like that then, considering that that is how they are now? Ceremonies, state visits, obeisances, panegyrics, and all the rest were not invented by Mohammed, I suppose.

The same applies to Hannibal. Why do you maintain that I have made his childhood "fabulous"? Because he kills an eagle? A miracle indeed, in a land where eagles abound! If the scene had been Gaul, I would have made it an owl, a wolf, or a fox. Being French, you are accustomed, automatically, to think of the eagle as a noble bird, more symbol than living thing. However, eagles do exist.

You ask me where I derived "such an idea of the Council of Carthage." But in all situations of the kind, in periods of revolution, from our own Convention to the American Parliament,[16] where until quite recently there were duels with canes and pistols, said canes and pistols (like my daggers) were brought in hidden in coatsleeves. And even my Carthaginians were more seemly than the Americans, since the public was not admitted to the Council. Against me you quote a weighty authority: Aristotle. But Aristotle lived more than eighty years before my period, and carries no weight here. Besides, the Stagirite is grossly mistaken when he states that "in Carthage there was never an uprising or a tyrant." Would you like a few dates? Carthalo's conspiracy in 530 B.C.; the usurpation of the two Magos, 460; Hanno's conspiracy, 337; Bomilcar's conspiracy, 307. But here I go beyond Aristotle's time. On to something else.

You scold me about the "carbuncles formed by lynxes' urine." That is from Theophrastus, *On Stones*. So: poor Theophrastus![17]

I was forgetting Spendius. No, cher maître, his stratagem is neither "bizarre" nor "strange." It is almost a stereotype. I took it from Aelianus (*History of Animals*) and Polyaenus (*Strategica*). In fact, it was so well known following the siege of Megara by Antipater (or Antigonus) that pigs were deliberately fed alongside elephants in order that the larger animals not be frightened by the smaller. In short, it was a common device, probably often used in Spendius's day. I didn't have to go back as far as Samson, because I avoided, as much as possible, details belonging to legendary periods.

Now I come to Hamilcar's treasure. This description, whatever you say, is not in the foreground: Hamilcar himself is the dominant figure, and I think the description is well warranted. The magistrate's anger gradually increases as he sees the depredations made in his house. Far from being "continuously beside himself," he doesn't explode until the end, when he is insulted personally. That he "does not gain in stature from this visit" is quite all right with me, since I am not writing his panegyric; but I do not think that in this scene I "caricature him, to the detriment of the rest of his characterization." The man who later kills the Mercenaries in the way I have shown (his son Hannibal went in for the same charming behavior, in Italy), is

The Popularity of *Salammbô*

Such was the popular success of the novel that Paris became obsessed with it and with the character of Salammbô. Caricatures of characters and depictions of scenes from the novel were published in newspapers. The novel affected the world of fashion as even Empress Eugénie expressed interest in Salammbô's clothing. Flaubert, who would not allow illustrations in his books, offered advice to the women's magazine L'Illustrateur des dames, *which published drawings of the four Salammbô costumes described in the narrative. The journal inserted a note explaining that, despite the fact that everyone in Paris had been talking for weeks about the costumes described by Flaubert, no newspaper had given any illustration of them. So* L'Illustrateur des dames *published them for the first time in the hope that they would be useful for costume balls. Although the empress apparently decided not to wear a Salammbô costume, Madame Barbe Rimsky-Korsakoff, a young Russian lady, made a splash in an outfit created by the fashion designer Worth at a ball given by Count Walewski, minister of state.*

Drawings of Salammbô's costumes that were published in the 22 February 1863 issue of L'Illustrateur des dames *(engravings by Henri Valentin; clichés Bibliothèque nationale de France, Paris)*

very much the same man who orders his merchandise to be adulterated and his slaves to be whipped unsparingly.

You quibble about the "eleven thousand three hundred ninety-six men" who form his army, asking me "How do you know this number? Who told you?" But you have just seen that for yourself, since I mentioned the number of men in the different corps of the Punic army. It is simply the sum total: not a figure recklessly invented to create an effect of precision.

There is nothing "sly" or "depraved" in the scene of the serpent, no "bagatelle."[18] This chapter is a kind of rhetorical precaution, to attenuate the effect of the chapter about the tent. The latter has not shocked readers; but it would have, had it not been preceded by the snake. I preferred a salacious scene with a snake (if there is salaciousness here) to one with a man. Before leaving her house, Salammbô embraces the genius of her family, the very religion of her country and its most ancient symbol. That is all. Quite possibly it would be "unseemly in an Iliad or a Pharsalia"; but I make no claim to be writing the Iliad or the Pharsalia.

Nor is it my fault if there are frequent storms in Tunis at the end of the summer. Chateaubriand no more invented storms than he did sunsets; and both, it seems to me, are everyone's property. Besides, please note that the heart of this story is Moloch–Fire, Thunder. Here the god himself acts, in one of his forms: he subdues Salammbô. Thus the thunder is appropriate: it is the voice of Moloch, speaking from without. Furthermore, you must admit that I spared you the "classic description of a storm." Besides, my poor storm occupies only *three lines*–separated, at that. The fire that follows was inspired by an episode in the story of Massinissa,[19] by another in the story of Agathocles,[20] and by a passage in Hirtius[21] – all three in analogous circumstances. As you see, I don't stray from the milieu, from the very country in which my action takes place.

About Salammbô's perfumes: you credit me with more imagination than I possess. Just take a whiff of Judith and Esther in the Bible. They literally soaked themselves, poisoned themselves, with perfumes. Which is what I was careful to say at the beginning, as soon as there was a question of Salammbô's sickness.

Why do you object to "the disappearance of the zaïmpf being a factor" in the loss of the battle, since the army of Mercenaries included men who believed in the zaïmph? I indicate the principal reasons (three military movements) for this defeat; then I add the other, as a secondary, final reason.

To say that I "invented tortures" at the funeral of the Barbarians is not true. Hendrich (*Carthago, seu Carth. respublica,* 1664) assembled texts to prove that it was a custom of the Carthaginians to mutilate the corpses of their enemies. And you are surprised that the Barbarians, defeated, desperate, enraged, should retaliate in kind, doing so on this one occasion only? Must I remind you of Mme de Lamballe, of the Garde Mobile in '48, and what is taking place this very moment in the United States?[22] In fact I have been moderate and very considerate.

And since you and I are exchanging truths, I confess to you frankly, cher maître, that your "element of sadistic imagination" wounded me a little. Every word you write is serious. Such words from you, when they are printed, become almost a stigma. Are you forgetting that I once sat on a bench in Criminal Court, accused of offences against public decency, and that fools and knaves use any weapons that come to hand? So do not be surprised if one of these days you read in the *Figaro*[23] some such words as these: "M. G. Flaubert is a disciple of Sade. His friend, his sponsor, a master critic, has said so himself, quite clearly, although with that finesse and laughing good humor which, etc." What would I reply–or do?

I bow before the following. You are right, cher maître: I did add finishing touches; I did do violence to history; as you so well say, I had "made up my mind to depict a siege." But with a military subject, what is wrong with that? And then I did not completely invent this siege. I merely laid it on a bit thick. That is my only sin.

But concerning the "passage in Montesquieu" about immolating children, I rebel. This horror does not "raise a doubt" in my mind. (Remember that human sacrifices were not completely abolished in Greece at the time of the battle of Leuctra, 370 B.C.) Despite the condition imposed by Gelon (480), in the war against Agathocles (392) two hundred children were burned, according to Diodorus; and as for later periods, I refer you to Silius Italicus, to Eusebius, and especially to St. Augustine, who states that such things sometimes took place in his day.

You regret that among the Greeks I have not included a philosopher, a dialectician who would be portrayed as giving a course in morals, or as performing good actions–a gentleman, in short, who "feels as we do." Come, now! Would that have been possible? Aratus,[24] whom you mention, was in fact the very person I thought of when imagining Spendius. He was a man of ruses and sudden assaults, capable of killing sentinels at night, and a man who had attacks of vertigo in broad daylight. True, I sidestepped a contrast, but such a contrast would have been a facile one, forced and false.

So much for your "analysis." Now as to your "judgment."

You are perhaps right in your reflections concerning the historical novel as applied to antiquity, and quite possibly I have failed.[25] However, judging from my own impressions, it seems to me quite probable that the picture I have painted does resemble Carthage. But that is not the question. I care nothing for archaeology. If the color is not unified, if details jar, if the ways of life I depict are not what can be derived from what we know of the religion, or the action from what we know of human passions, if the delineations of character are not consistent, if the costumes are inappropriate to the life of the people and the architecture to the climate–if, in a word, harmony is lacking–then my book is wrong. If not, not: it is all of a piece.

But you find the milieu itself detestable. I know you do, or rather I sense that you do. Instead of continuing to regard it from your viewpoint, your viewpoint as a man of letters, as a modern, a Parisian, why not come and look at it from mine? The human soul is not the same everywhere, whatever M. Levallois[26] may say. The briefest glance at the world provides sufficient proof of the opposite. Actually, I think I have been less hard on humanity in *Salammbô* than in *Madame Bovary.* The curiosity and love that impelled me to deal with religions and people that are no more has something moral and sympathetic about it, I think.

As to style, I sacrificed less in this book than in the other to rounding out my phrases and my periods. Metaphors are few, and epithets are factual. If I put "blue" beside "stones," it is because "blue" is the right word, believe me; and you may be equally sure that it is indeed possible to distinguish the color of stones by starlight. Ask any traveler in the Orient, or go and see for yourself.

And since you reproach me for certain words–"*énorme,*" for example, which I will not defend (even though excessive silence does give the effect of clamor)–let me in turn object to some of your expressions. I did not understand the quotation from Désaugiers,[27] or why you included it. Your "Carthaginian knickknacks" made me frown, as did your calling the zaïmph "a kind of crazy cloak," your speaking of Salammbô's "romping with the snake" as being a kind of "spicy come-on," your calling my Libyan a "handsome rogue" when he is neither handsome nor a rogue, and your reference to Schahabarim's "libertine" imagination.

One last question, oh maître–an unseemly question. Why do you find Schahabarim [the high priest] almost comic, and yet take your friends at Port-Royal[28] so seriously? For me, your M. Singlin is deadly, compared with my elephants. I regard the tattooed Barbarians as less inhuman, less "special," less ludicrous, less exceptional, than men living a communal life who address each other as "Monsieur" to the end of their days. And it is precisely because they are remote from me that I admire your talent for making me understand them. For I *believe* your picture of Port-Royal, and I would enjoy living there even less than in Carthage. Port-Royal, too, was an exclusive group, unnatural, forced, all of a piece–and yet true. Why will you not allow two truths to exist, two diametrically opposed examples of excess, two different monstrosities?

I am almost done. Be patient a bit longer! Are you curious to know the *enormous* defect ("*énorme*" is used properly here) that I find in my book? It is this:

1. The pedestal is too big for the statue. Or rather, since "too little," rather than "too much," is the great sin, there should have been a hundred pages more, devoted to Salammbô alone.

2. A few transitions are lacking. I had them, but removed them or overpruned them, for fear of being boring.

3. In Chapter VI, everything relating to Gisco is of the same tonality as the second part of Chapter II (Hanno). The situation is the same, and the effect is not enhanced.

4. Everything from the battle of the Macar to the serpent, and all of Chapter XIII, up to the enumeration of the Barbarians, sink out of sight, vanish from the reader's memory. These are areas of middle ground, dull and of ephemeral effect. Unfortunately I could not avoid them, and they give a heaviness to the book despite my best efforts at briskness. Those are the parts that gave me the most trouble; I like them the least, and yet they are the ones I am proudest of.

5. The aqueduct. A confession! My *secret* opinion is that there was no aqueduct at Carthage at that period, despite the ruined aqueduct we see today. Therefore I was careful to anticipate possible objections with a hypocritical sentence intended for archaeologists–a clumsy reminder that aqueducts were a Roman invention, new at the time, and that the aqueduct one sees now was a new construction, on the foundations of an older one. I was obsessed by the memory of Belisarius cutting the Roman aqueduct at Carthage;[29] and besides, it made such a splendid entrance for Spendius and Mâtho! But no question, my aqueduct *is* an evasion. *Confiteor!*

6. One more, final, fraud: Hanno. For the sake of keeping the picture clear, I falsified the story of his death. He was indeed crucified by the Mercenaries, but in Sardinia. The general crucified at Tunis, opposite Spendius, was named Hannibal. Think of the confusion that would have caused the reader![30]

Such, cher maître, are what I consider the worst features of my book. I will not tell you what I think the good ones. But you may be sure that my Carthage is no

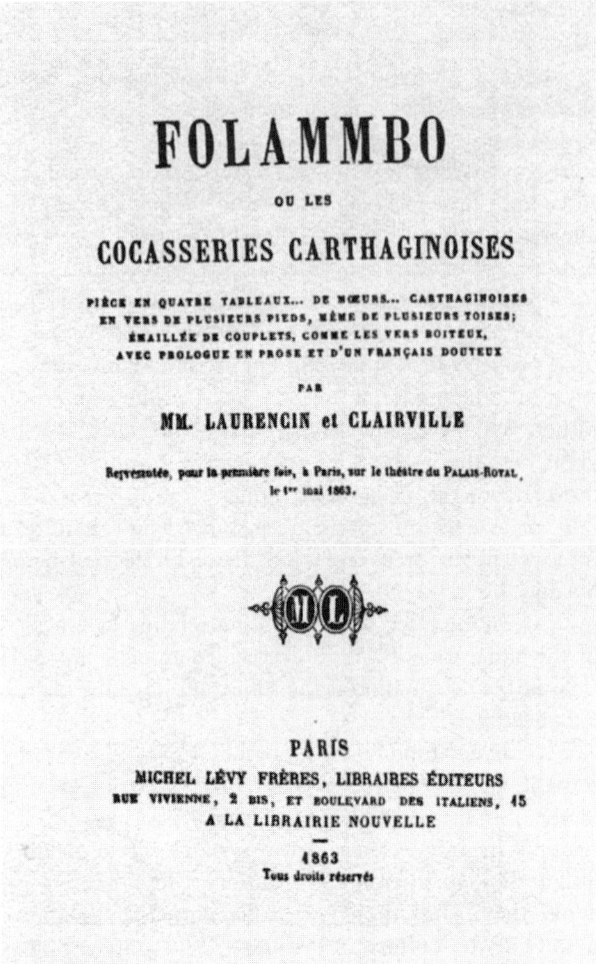

FOLAMMBO

OU LES

COCASSERIES CARTHAGINOISES

PIÈCE EN QUATRE TABLEAUX... DE MŒURS... CARTHAGINOISES
EN VERS DE PLUSIEURS PIEDS, MÊME DE PLUSIEURS TOISES;
ÉMAILLÉE DE COUPLETS, COMME LES VERS BOITEUX,
AVEC PROLOGUE EN PROSE ET D'UN FRANÇAIS DOUTEUX

PAR

MM. LAURENCIN et CLAIRVILLE

Représentée, pour la première fois, à Paris, sur le théâtre du PALAIS-ROYAL,
le 1er mai 1863.

PARIS
MICHEL LÉVY FRÈRES, LIBRAIRES ÉDITEURS
RUE VIVIENNE, 2 BIS, ET BOULEVARD DES ITALIENS, 15
A LA LIBRAIRIE NOUVELLE

1863
Tous droits réservés

Title page for the four-act parody that was staged for the first time in May 1863 at the theater of the Palais-Royal in Paris (cliché Bibliothèque nationale de France, Paris)

mere fantasy. Documents on Carthage exist, and not all of them are in Movers.[31] They must be sought for a bit further. For example, Ammianus Marcellinus[32] provided me with the exact form of a gate; a poem by Corippus[33] (the *Johannis*) with many details about African tribes, etc.

And besides: few will be following my example. So where is the danger? The Leconte de Lisles and the Baudelaires are less to be feared than the Nadauds and the Clairvilles[34] in this dear land of France, where superficiality is a *quality* and where the banal, the facile, and the foolish are invariably applauded, adopted, and adored. One does not risk corrupting anyone when one aspires to greatness. Am I forgiven?

I end by thanking you once again, mon cher maître. You have clawed me, but you have also given me the handshake of affection; and though you have mocked me a little, you have nevertheless given me three great salutes–three long articles, very detailed, very distinguished, which must have been more painful for you than they are for me. It is for that, especially, that I am grateful. Your closing advice[35] will not be forgotten, and you will see that you have not been dealing with a fool or an ingrate.

–*The Letters of Gustave Flaubert, 1857–1880,* pp. 39–50

---

1. Chateaubriand's Romantic prose epic, *Les Martyrs, ou le Triomphe de la religion chrétienne* (1809).
2. The *Periplus* is an account of a voyage around Africa, written in the Punic language by a Carthaginian (Hanno was a common Carthaginian name) and later translated into Greek.
3. Eshmunazar (the name means "the god Eshmun has helped") was a king of Sidon, about the early fifth century B.C. The inscription is on his sarcophagus, discovered in 1855.
4. Hendrik Arent Hamaker, a Dutch orientalist (1789–1835), published works on Phoenician and Punic inscriptions.
5. The so-called Marseilles Tariff, a third- or second-century B.C. stone inscription in Punic listing sacrifices and dues, found at Marseilles in 1845 and thought to have come from Carthage.
6. That is, permitted as a subject for theses in French universities.
7. Elvire is Lamartine's idealized heroine in his Romantic *Méditations poétiques* (1820). Velléda is a druidess in *Les Martyrs.*
8. This Hanno is a Carthaginian general and magistrate, a character in the novel.
9. Greek author of a book on military stratagems.
10. Charles Rollin (1661–1741), historian, Rector of the University of Paris, where he reintroduced the study of Greek. "Rough breathing" and "smooth breathing" are terms referring to the pronunciation of ancient Greek.
11. Lucian: *De dea syria.*
12. John Selden (1584–1654), English jurist and oriental scholar. The book consulted by Flaubert was his *De dis syris syntagmata II* (London, 1617). Flaubert would later be scolded for his misspelling of the title (see letter to Froehner, January 21, 1863, note 14).
13. The second-largest island in the Maltese group.
14. In Tunisia. Sometimes written Dougga. When Sainte-Beuve published Flaubert's letter, with permission, as a note to his review as reprinted in a volume of *Nouveaux Lundis,* he appended the following footnote: "M. Flaubert, whom I asked to reread this passage of his letter, has agreed that he was neither the first nor the only writer, as he had previously thought, to speak of the temple of Thugga."
15. The dream in Racine's *Athalie,* II, 5.
16. One supposes Flaubert means the Congress. The reference might be to the beating of Charles Sumner in the Senate in 1856.
17. Sainte-Beuve had jeered at Flaubert's description of Hamilcar's collection of gems: "Here we have to do with

an auctioneer, amusing himself in this underground treasure house by reeling off for us a list of all the mineralogical marvels imaginable, even including 'carbuncles formed by lynxes' urine.' This is too much, and shows up the author as a dilettante who is making sport of us."

André Gide wrote more understandingly of this aspect of *Salammbô* in his *Journal* (April 9, 1908): "It seems to me that in the texts he used as sources, Flaubert was seeking less for documentation than for authorization. In his horror of daily reality, he was enchanted by everything in these texts that differed from it. Did he really believe that carbuncles were 'formed by lynxes' urine'? Certainly not! But he was delighted that a passage in Theophrastus authorized him to pretend to believe so; and so on throughout the book."

This inner, or secret, way of the artist, Flaubert would not, or perhaps could not, explain to someone who, like Sainte-Beuve, did not sense it.

18. "Bagatelle" in the eighteenth-century sense: the act of coition.
19. King of Numidia (c. 238–149 B.C.), vassal and ally of Carthage, who was married to Sophinisba, daughter of the Carthaginian Hasdrubal, transferred his allegiance to Rome.
20. Sicilian tyrant (d. 289 B.C.).
21. Roman historian (d. 43 B.C.).
22. The Princesse de Lamballe, friend of Queen Marie-Antoinette, met an atrocious end at the hands of a mob during the September massacres of 1792. The Garde Mobile (a portion of the National Guard) mowed down demonstrating workmen during the "June Days" of 1848; Flaubert refers to the National Guard again in his letter of September 29, 1868, to George Sand, and it plays a large role in *L'Éducation sentimentale*. Bulletins concerning the events of the American Civil War were appearing in the newspapers Flaubert read.
23. "in the *Figaro*." Responding to Flaubert's request that in his letter as printed the name of the newspaper be omitted, Sainte-Beuve substituted "in some little scandal sheet."
24. Achaean general, ally and then enemy of Philip of Macedon.
25. In his review, Sainte-Beuve had written: "On this subject chosen by M. Flaubert, little information is provided either by monuments or by books. What he tried to accomplish was thus a complete tour de force, and it is little wonder that, in my opinion, he has failed."
26. Jules Levallois (1829–1903), Sainte-Beuve's former secretary, had written unfavorably about *Salammbô* in the *Opinion Nationale*.
27. Antoine Désaugiers (1772–1827), composer of light songs. Sainte-Beuve, whose taste in humor was not always the most appropriate, had quoted, quite ineptly, some jolly lines from Désaugiers "as a relief from the solemnity and monotony" of *Salammbô*.
28. The reference is to Sainte-Beuve's *Port-Royal,* his study of the community of seventeenth-century Jansenists.
29. In A.D. 534–approximately eight hundred years after the events recounted in *Salammbô*.
30. That is, they would probably have thought that Flaubert was speaking of the younger, greater, Hannibal.
31. Franz Karl Movers (1806–1856), German orientalist. His *Die Phönizier,* one of Flaubert's sources for Carthaginian names and other particulars, was published in two separate parts: Bonn, 1841, and Berlin, 1856.
32. Roman historian in the age of Julian.
33. Flavius Cresconius Corippus, Roman epic poet of the sixth century A.D.
34. Gustave Nadaud (1829–1893), composer of light songs; and Louis-François Nicolaie, called Clairville (1811–1879), composer and *vaudevilliste*. Flaubert was probably unaware, when writing his "Apologia," that a few months later a vaudeville by Clairville and a collaborator, entitled *Folammbô, ou les Cocasseries carthaginoises,* would open at the Théâtre du Palais-Royal, then as now the home of the farce.
35. Sainte-Beuve's "closing advice" to the author of *Salammbô* had been: "A new book by him is due us, and let us hope that this time we shall not have to wait so long. To men–even to the most genuine talents–few years of fertility are granted: one must know how to make use of them, in order to establish oneself before it is too late–anchor oneself in the hearts and memory of one's contemporaries. Besides, that is the surest route to posterity. So let him give us, without too much delay, and without excessive concern for that style of which he is such a master that he can afford to relax a little, a strong, powerful, well-observed, vital work. Certainly it must have some of the bitter, refined qualities of his first novel; it must be earmarked with his originality and his inimitable nature (no one wishes him to abdicate!); but one hopes it will contain at least one vein that will please all of us, if only as a measure of consolation."

Perhaps Flaubert was referring to that "closing advice" when he wrote to his niece, on Sainte-Beuve's death seven years later: "I wrote *L'Éducation sentimentale* in part for Sainte-Beuve."

* * *

Froehner was an assistant curator in the Department of Antiquities at the Louvre museum. Flaubert's letter in response to his criticisms was first published in the 24 January 1863 issue of L'Opinion Nationale.

Flaubert to Guillaume Froehner, 21 January 1863

Monsieur,

I have just read your article on *Salammbô*[1] in the *Revue Contemporaine* of December 31, 1862. Despite my practice of never replying to reviews, I find yours unacceptable. It is very courteous, and contains many things extremely flattering to me; but since it casts doubt on the sincerity of my studies, you will kindly allow me to use this space to challenge a number of your assertions.

Let me first ask you, Monsieur, why you so obstinately link me with the Campana collection,[2] claiming that it was my source, my continual inspiration. The fact is that I completed *Salammbô* last March, six weeks before the opening of that museum. Already an error, you see: we shall be finding others, more serious.

I have, Monsieur, no pretensions to archaeology. My book is presented as a novel, without preface and without notes, and I marvel that a man of your eminence should waste his time and effort on such light literature! However, I know enough to risk saying that you err completely, from the beginning of your article to the end, on every one of your eighteen pages, in every paragraph, and in almost every line.

You reprimand me for not having consulted either Falbe or Dureau de la Malle,[3] from whom I "might have profited." A thousand pardons! I have read them–more often than you, perhaps, and amid the ruins of Carthage itself. It is indeed quite possible that you "know of no satisfactory work dealing with the configuration of the city or with its principal districts"; others, however, better informed, do not at all share your skepticism. We may lack information as to the whereabouts of the suburb Aclas, or the place called Fuscianus, or concerning the exact sites of the principal gates whose names we have, etc.; but we do know, and quite well, the position of the city, the architectonic construction of the walls, the Taenia, the Mole, and the Cothon.[4] We know that the houses were faced with tar and the streets paved with blocks; we have an idea of the Ancô,[5] described in my Chapter XV; we have heard about Malqua, about Byrsa, about Megara, about the Mappalia and the Catacombs, and about the temple of Eshmun, situated on the Acropolis, and that of Tanit, a little to the right as one stood with one's back to the sea. All that is to be found (not to mention Appian, Pliny, and Procopius) in that same Dureau de la Malle whom you accuse me of not knowing. So it is really regrettable, Monsieur, that you did not, as you put it, "go into tedious detail" to prove that I had no idea of the situation and

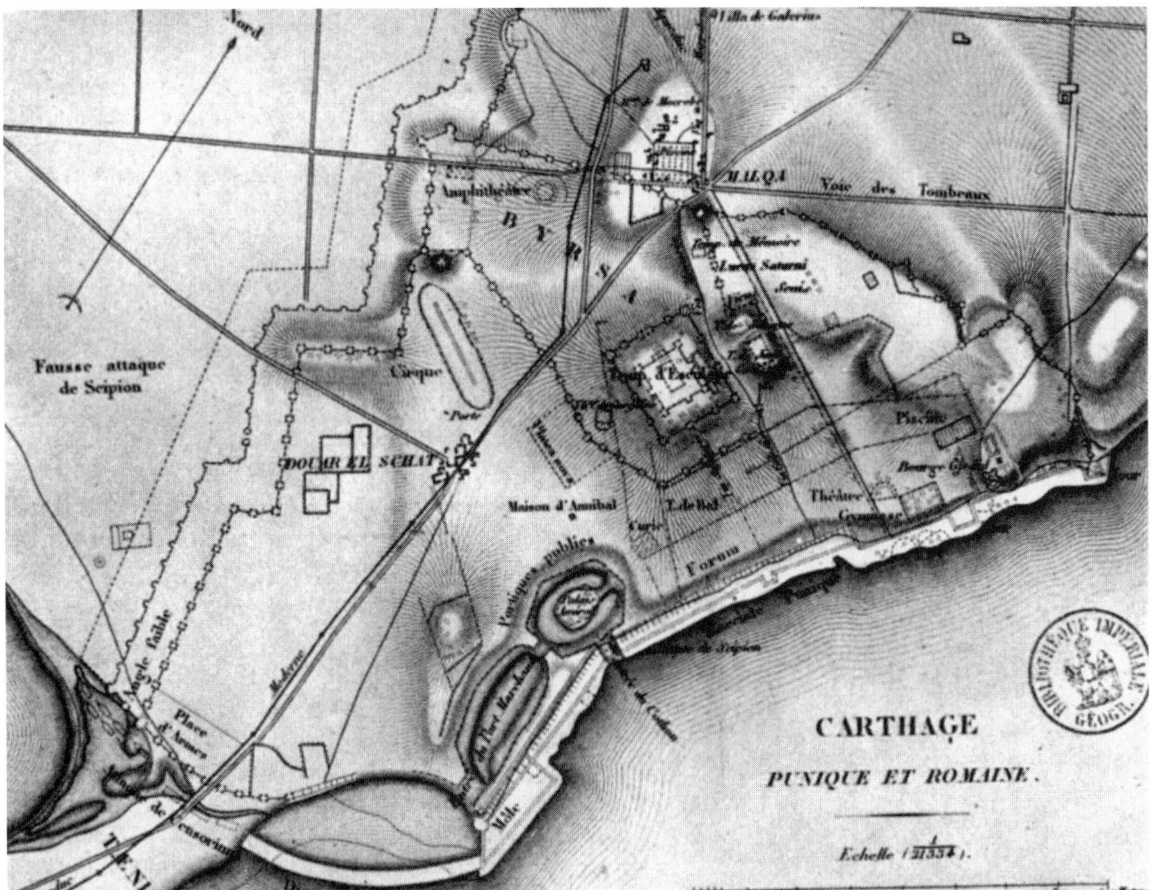

A map of ancient Carthage drawn by Dureau de la Malle, whose book Recherches sur la topographie de Carthage *(1833) was useful to Flaubert. In his reply to Froehner, he wrote that he read it "amid the ruins of Carthage itself" (cliché Bibliothèque nationale de France, Paris).*

plan of ancient Carthage "even less than Dureau de la Malle," you add. What is one to believe? On whom is one to rely?–since you have so far not had the kindness to reveal your own system with respect to Carthaginian topography.

It is true that I can quote no text to prove that there existed a street of the Tanners, or of the Perfumers, or of the Dyers. Still, you must agree that it is a likely hypothesis. But I most certainly did not invent Kinisdo and Cynasyn–"names," you say, "whose structure is foreign to the spirit of the Semitic languages." Not so foreign as all that, however, since they are in Gesenius.[6] Almost all my Punic names ("disfigured," according to you) were taken from Gesenius (*Scripturae lingaeque phoeniciae* [*monumenta quotquot supersunt*]) [1837], or from Falbe, whom I assure you I did consult.

An orientalist of your erudition, Monsieur, should have been a bit more indulgent concerning the Numidian name Naravasse, which I write Narr'Havas, from Nar-el-haouah, *feu du souffle.*[7] You could have guessed that the two *m*'s in Salammbô were put there on purpose, so that the name would be pronounced Sala*m* and not as in Salan;[8] and you might have had the charity to suppose that Égates, instead of Ægates, was a typographical error–corrected, incidentally, in the second edition of my book, which appeared a fortnight before the article in which you offer me advice. The same goes for Scissites, instead of Syssites, and for the word Kabires, which has always been printed without an *h* (horrors!) even in the most serious works, such as Maury's *Les Religions de la Grèce antique.* As for Schalischim, if I did not write (as I should have) Rosh-eisch-Schalischim, it was to shorten a name that I found too forbidding–it not having occurred to me that I would be quizzed by philologists. But since you choose to descend to these chicaneries about words, I will take you up on two (among others) of your own: (1) *Compendieusement,* which you employ in the opposite sense from its meaning, making it signify "abundantly," "prolixly"; and (2) *carthachinoiserie,*[9] an excellent jest, but not your own: you took it from the little newspaper in which it appeared early last month. As you see, Monsieur, if you are sometimes unacquainted with my authors, I know yours. But it might have been better had you passed over "those minutiae," as you so properly call them, "which do not survive critical examination."

One more such, however. Why did you underline the *and* in this sentence (a little shortened) from my page 156: "Buy me some Cappadocians *and* some Asiatics"? Was it because you wanted to impress a few ignoramuses, to make them think that I don't distinguish Cappadocia from Asia Minor? But I know the country, Monsieur: I have seen it, I have ridden through it![10]

You have read me with so little care that almost always you *quote me incorrectly.* Nowhere did I say that the priests formed a particular caste, nor, on page 109, that the Libyan soldiers "were possessed by the desire to drink iron," but that the Barbarians threatened to make the Carthaginians "drink iron";[11] nor, on page 108, that the guards of the Legion "wore, in the middle of the forehead, a silver horn to make them look like rhinoceroses," but that *their great horses* were so adorned; nor, on page 29, that the peasants amused themselves one day by crucifying two hundred lions. The same goes for those unfortunate Syssites,[12] which, according to you, I spoke of "doubtless not knowing that the term signified special guilds." Your "doubtless" is charming. But doubtless I did know what those guilds were, and the etymology of the word, since I translate it into French the first time it appears in my book, on page 7: "Syssites, companies (of merchants) who ate together." Furthermore, you have falsified a passage from Plautus: his *Poenulus* does not at all prove that "the Carthaginians knew all languages" (which would be a curious privilege for an entire nation); the prologue reads simply (line 112): "*Is omnes linguas scit,*" which must be translated as "*This man* knows all languages"–the Carthaginian in question, not all Carthaginians.

It is not true to say that "Hanno was not crucified in the war of the Mercenaries, since he was still commanding armies long afterward": for you will find in Polybius, Monsieur, Book I, Chapter XVII, that he was indeed captured by the rebels and crucified (in Sardinia, it is true, but at this same time). Thus it is not a question of "that gentleman" having "grounds for complaint against M. Flaubert," but rather of Polybius having grounds for complaint against M. Froehner.

As for the sacrificing of children, it is very far from "impossible" that they were being burned alive at the time of Hamilcar, since they were still being so sacrificed at the time of Julius Caesar and Tiberius, if one is to trust Cicero (*Pro Balbo*) and Strabo (Book III). "The statue of Moloch," you say, "does not resemble the hellish device described in *Salammbô.* This figure, composed of seven compartments, one above the other, for the confinement of victims, belongs to the Gallic religion. M. Flaubert has no pretext for making the analogy: his audacious transposition is unjustified." No! I have no *pre*text: quite true. But I have a *text,* namely *the* text, the actual description by Diodorus,[13] which you may recall, and which is the source of mine–as you may verify should you care to reread, or read, Book XX in Diodorus, Chapter IV, to which please add the Chaldean paraphrase by Paul Fage,[14] which you do not mention, and which is quoted by Selden, *De diis syriis,* pp. 164–170, along with Eusebius, *Preparatio evangelica,* Book I.

How can it be that "history makes no mention of the miraculous mantle,"[15] since you yourself state that "it was exhibited in the temple of Venus, but much later, and only at the time of the Roman emperors"? Now I find in Athenaeus, XII, 58, a very minute description of this mantle of which "history makes no mention." It was bought from Dionysius the Elder for 120 talents, brought to Rome by Scipio Aemilianus, returned to Carthage by Caius Gracchus, brought again to Rome under Heliogabalus, and then again returned to Carthage. All of which is found also in Dureau de la Malle, from whom I most decidedly did "profit."

Three lines further down, you affirm, with the same–candor, that "most of the other gods invoked in *Salammbô* are completely invented," and you add: "Who has ever heard of an Aptouknos?" Who? D'Avezac[16] (in his *Cyrénaique*), in connection with a temple near Cyrene.–"Of a Schaoûl?" But that is a name I give to a slave (see my page 91).–"Or of a Matisman?" He is mentioned as a god by Corippus.[17] (See his *Johannis* and *Mémoires de l'Académie des Inscriptions,* Vol. XII, p. 181). "Who doesn't know that Micipsa was not a divinity, but a man?" But that is what I say, Monsieur, and very clearly, on that same page 91, when Salammbô calls her slaves: "Help! Help! . . . Kroûm, Ewa, Micipsa, Schaoûl!"

You accuse me of taking Astareth and Astarté to be two distinct divinities. But early in the book, page 48, when Salammbô invokes Tanit, she invokes her by all her names at once: "Anaïtis! Astarté! Derceto! Astareth! Tiratha!" And I was even careful to say, a little further on, page 52, that she repeated "all these names, which had no distinct meaning for her." Are you perhaps like Salammbô in this? I am tempted to think so, since you make Tanit the goddess of war rather than of love, of the female, humid, fecund element: you do so despite Tertullian, and despite the very name Tiratha, of which you will find the scarcely decent, but very explicit, explanation in Movers,[18] *Phenic.*, Book I, page 574.

Next, you are astonished by my apes consecrated to the moon and horses consecrated to the sun. "These details"–you are sure "are found in no ancient author nor in any authentic monument." But let me remind you, Monsieur, that baboons were consecrated to the moon in Egypt, as one still sees on the walls of the temples, and that Egyptian cults had penetrated into Libya and the oases. As for the horses, I do not say that they were consecrated to Aesculapius, but to Eshmun–who was assimilated to Aesculapius, Iolas, Apollo, the Sun. Horses consecrated to the sun are mentioned in Pausanius (Book I, Chapter I), and in the Bible (II Kings 23:11). But perhaps you will deny that the Egyptian temples are authentic monuments, and that the Bible and Pausanias are ancient authorities?

Apropos of the Bible, I will take another vast liberty, Monsieur, and draw your attention to Volume II of Cahen's translation,[19] page 186, where you will read this: "Around their necks they wore, suspended from a gold chain, a small figure made of precious stones, which they called The Truth. Debates opened when the president set before himself the image of The Truth." That is a text from Diodorus. Here is another, from Aelian:[20] "The eldest among them was their chief, and the judge of all; around his neck he wore an image carved in sapphire. This image was called The Truth." So be it, then, that [as you say], "this 'Truth' is a very pretty invention by M. Flaubert."

But everything surprises you: malobathrum, which is quite properly written (if you have no objection) either "malobathrum" or "malabathrum"–the gold powder that is still gathered today, as in the past, on Carthaginian beaches; the elephants' ears painted blue; the men who daub themselves with vermilion (cinnabar) and eat vermin and apes; the Lydian men in women's dress, the carbuncles formed by lynxes' urine;[21] the mandragoras (which are in Hippocrates); the ankle-chainlet[22] (which is in the *Song of Songs*–Cahen, Volume XVI, 37); the sprinkling of pomegranate trees with silphium; bound beards; crucified lions, etc.–everything!

Well, no, Monsieur, I did *not* "borrow all those details from the negroes of Senegambia." I refer you, concerning the elephants, to the work by Armandi,[23] page 256, and to the authorities he indicates, such as Florus, Diodorus, Ammianus Marcellinus, and other such Senegambian Negroes.

As for the nomads who eat apes, munch lice, and daub themselves with vermilion: since you might be "asked from what source the author has drawn these precious bits of information," and would be, as you confess, "very embarrassed as to know what to say," let me humbly give you a few hints that may help you in your research.

"The Maxyans . . . paint their bodies with vermilion." "The Gyzantians all paint themselves with vermilion, and eat apes." "Their women [the women of the Adyrmachidae] . . . if they are bitten by a louse, take it up, bite it, etc." You will find all this in the Fourth Book of Herodotus, Chapters CXCI, CXCIV, and CLXVIII.[24] (I feel no "embarrassment" in telling you this.)

It was Herodotus from whom I learned (in his description of Xerxes' army) that the Lydians wore women's dress. Athenaeus, also, in his chapter on the

Etruscans and their resemblance to the Lydians, says that they wore women's dress. Finally, the Lydian Bacchus is always portrayed in feminine costume. Is that enough about the Lydians and their garb?

Beards bound up as a sign of mourning are mentioned in Cahen (Ezekiel 24:17),[25] and are found on Egyptian colossi, such as those at Abu Simbel; carbuncles formed by lynxes' urine, in Theophrastus's treatise *On Stones* and in Pliny, Book VIII, Chapter LVII. And as regards the crucified lions (you increase their number to two hundred, no doubt to impute to me an absurdity not my own), do me the favor of consulting Pliny yet again–same book, Chapter XVIII–where you will learn that Scipio Aemilianus and Polybius, riding together in the countryside near Carthage, saw several strung up in that position. "*Quia ceteri metu poenae similis absterrerentur eadem noxa.*"[26] Are those, Monsieur, some of the passages taken indiscriminately (as you suggest) from the *Univers pittoresque,* and "which the higher criticism has tellingly used against M. Flaubert"? What is the "higher criticism" you speak of? Your own?

You make very merry about the pomegranate trees sprinkled with silphium. But this detail is not my invention, Monsieur. It is in Pliny, Book XVII, Chapter XLVII. And I am very sorry to have to spoil your joke about the hellebore that "should be grown at Charenton";[27] but as you yourself say, "the most penetrating mind cannot make up for the lack of acquired knowledge." Of which, by the way, you display a complete lack in affirming that "among the precious stones in Hamilcar's treasury more than one properly belongs to Christian legend and superstition." No, Monsieur: they are *all* in Pliny and Theophrastus.

The emerald steles at the temple entrance, which make you laugh (you have a delightful sense of humor), are mentioned by Philostratus (*Life of Apollonius*) and by Theophrastus (treatise *On Stones*), whom Heeren[28] (Volume II) quotes as follows: "The largest Bactrian emerald is at Tyre, in the temple of Hercules. It is a column of considerable size." Another passage from Theophrastus (Hill's translation): "In their temple of Jupiter there was an obelisk composed of four emeralds."

Despite your "acquired knowledge," you confuse jade, which is a greenish-brown nephrite and comes from China, with jasper, a variety of quartz found in Europe *and* in Sicily. Had you chanced to open the *Dictionnaire de l'Académie française* at the word *jaspe*, you would have discovered without looking further that there is black, red, and white jasper. You would then perhaps have moderated your marvelous mirth and not heaped hilarious reproaches on my master and friend Théophile Gautier for giving a woman (in his *Roman de la Momie*) "green feet"–when the feet he gives her are white. Thus it is not he, but you, who have made "a ridiculous error." If you were a bit less disdainful of travel,[29] you could have seen in the Turin museum the very arm of this mummy, brought from Egypt by M. Passalacqua, and in the gesture described by Th. Gautier–"a gesture" which, according to you, "is certainly not Egyptian."[30]

Théophile Gautier, circa 1856, one of Flaubert's closest literary friends. He also wrote a novel inspired by Egyptian antiquity, Le Roman de la momie *(photograph by Félix Nadar; cliché Bibliothèque nationale de France, Paris).*

Even without being an engineer you would have learned the functioning of the sakiehs which carry water into the houses, and would have been convinced that I was not mistaken in speaking of black clothing: it is generally worn in those countries, where women of the upper classes never go out except swathed in black. But since you prefer written testimony, let one recommend, in the matter of women's clothing, Isaiah 3:18–24; the Mishna ("de Sabbatho"); Samuel 13:18; St. Clement of Alexandria, *Paedagogus*, II, 13; and Abbé Mignot's dissertations in the *Mémoires de l'Académie des Inscriptions*, Vol. XLII. And as for that abundance of ornamentation which so astonishes you, I am certainly correct in attributing it to a people who encrusted the floors of their apartments with precious stones. (See Cahen, Ezekiel 28:14). But you are unlucky, as regards precious stones.[31]

In closing, let me thank you, Monsieur, for your charming manners–a rare thing nowadays. I have called attention to only the grossest of your inaccuracies, those relating to specific points. As to your vague criticisms, your personal allusions, and your consideration of my book from a literary point of view, I have left them unmentioned. I have kept strictly to your own territory–erudition; and I repeat once more that there I am but middling strong. I know neither Hebrew, nor Arabic, nor German, nor Greek, nor Latin, and I make no boast of knowing French. I have often used translations; on occasion, the originals. In my uncertainties I have consulted the men who in France are considered the most competent, and if I have not been "better guided" it is because I have not had the honor, the advantage, of knowing you: forgive me! Had I taken advice from you, would I "have been more successful"? I doubt it. In any case, I would have been deprived of those proofs of benevolence which you display throughout your article, and I would have spared you the kind of remorse which you express at the close. But let me reassure you, Monsieur: though you seem to be terrified of your own strength, and though you seriously think that you have "torn my book to shreds," have no "fear": set your mind at rest! For you have not been "cruel": you have merely been–trivial.[32]

–*The Letters of Gustave Flaubert, 1857–1880,* pp. 52–62

---

1. More accurately, the article, entitled "Le Roman archéologique en France," was "on" three publications: principally *Salammbô,* but also Théophile Gautier's *Le Roman de la momie,* and Ernest Desjardins' *Promenade dans les galeries du Musée Napoléon III.*
2. Le Musée Campana, also called Le Musée Napoléon III, was an assemblage of antiquities bought by the French state from an Italian collector, the Marchese Campana, and opened to the public in Paris in April 1862. For complex legal reasons it was forced to close, amid some scandal, after only a few months. It was dispersed, and some of its contents are now in the Louvre.

   Froehner had strangely called *Salammbô* "the natural daughter of *Les Misérables* . . . and of the Campana collection." Flaubert's riposte has been questioned because of what he wrote to Mlle Leroyer de Chantepie on April 24: "Last Sunday . . . I finally finished my novel *Salammbô.*" But a novel is apt to be "finished" several times. Flaubert possibly meant something like: "Six weeks before the Musée Campana opened, everything that would appear in *Salammbô* was down on paper." Indeed in that same letter of April 24 he mentions that the Musée Campana has opened.
3. Christian Tuxen Falbe, *Recherches sur l'Emplacement de Carthage, avec le plan topographique du Terrain et des Ruines de la Ville* (Paris, 1833); Adolphe-Jules-César-Auguste Dureau de la Malle, *Recherches sur la topographie de Carthage* (Paris, 1835).
4. These and the following are identifiable sections or landmarks of Punic Carthage. The Taenia ("ribbon") was the strip of land, south of the city, dividing the present Lake of Tunis from the sea; the Cothon was the military harbor, and so on.
5. The Ancô, which is not mentioned by name in Chapter XV or elsewhere in the novel, is identified by Flaubert in one of his working notes as the dungeon, hollowed in the rock of the Acropolis, where Mâtho is held in solitary confinement and from which he emerges, on the day of his execution, "bowed almost double, with the bewildered air of wild beasts when they are suddenly released from captivity."
6. Heinrich Friedrich Wilhelm Gesenius (1786–1842), German orientalist and biblical scholar.
7. On introducing Narr'Havas, the Numidian prince, in the early pages of *Salammbô,* Flaubert emphasizes his "blazing, staring eyes." *Feu du souffle* can be translated "fire of the breath," or perhaps "fiery current." One wonders whether Faubert was aware that *haouah* is also a form of a word meaning "passion." It seems likely that had he known this he would have profited from the word's double intensity.
8. Meaning that the *m* should be pronounced hard, rather than merely giving the syllable a nasal sound, as when *m* or *n,* preceded by a vowel, is written singly.
9. A humorous word coined from the French *chinoiserie,* literally "Chinese knickknacks," but in common use as "foolish intricacies," "stuff and nonsense." This was one of many journalistic lampoonings of *Salammbô.*
10. The point here seems to be a distinction between Cappadocia, the name of the Roman province north of Cilicia, and the narrow antique application of the name "Asia" to the country around Ephesus. Flaubert had ridden through both regions with Maxime DuCamp in 1850.
11. Probably a metaphor: "to cut their throats." But the more literal "to make them drink [molten] iron" would not be out of place in the *Salammbô* torture repertoire.
12. The Syssites were doubly unfortunate in the printed French spellings of their name. There was the misprint in the first edition, already alluded to; and furthermore, as Froehner had properly shown (a point ignored by Flaubert), the correct French spelling would be "Syssities" (from the Greek *Syssitia*). In English it is usually written "Syssitia." Flaubert's definition of the term is correct. (D.M.)
13. Diodorus Siculus, Greek historian of the first century B.C.
14. Froehner, in his riposte, makes fun of Flaubert's gallicization of the name of the seventeenth-century German scholar "Paulus Fagius"–which was, he says, in itself a latinization of the original "Paul Bucheim." Froehner also corrects Flaubert's "De diis syriis" to "De dis syriis." Selden's title page says "De dis syris."
15. The "zaïmph," the sacred veil, or mantle, of the goddess Tanit, stolen, in the novel, from her temple by the giant Mâtho and retrieved by *Salammbô* in Mâtho's tent at the price (ecstatically paid) of her virginity.

16. Marie-Armand-Pascal d'Avezac-Macaya (1799–1875), French geographer.
17. See letter to Sainte-Beuve, note 33.
18. For Movers see letter to Sainte-Beuve, note 31. The "explanation," as given in Movers' original German text (p. 583), is left in Latin: *pudendum muliebre.*
19. The hebraicist Samuel Cahen (1796–1862) published his French translation of the Old Testament in eighteen volumes (1831–1851). They include the Hebrew text and ample notes by Cahen. The passages from Diodorus and Aelian quoted by Flaubert are in Cahen's "supplementary notes" to Exodus 28:30. ("I have just read Cahen's book from one end to the other," Flaubert had written Ernest Feydeau in August 1857. "I know perfectly well that it's very faithful, very good, very scholarly: no matter! I prefer the old Vulgate, because of the Latin! How it rumbles, beside this poor little puny consumptive French! I'll even show you two or three mistranslations, or embellishments, in the Vulgate, which are much finer than the true meaning.")
20. The anecdotal *Various History* of Claudius Aelianus (Aelian), Roman rhetorician of the age of Hadrian.
21. See letter to Sainte-Beuve, note 17.
22. This is the gold chainlet joining Salammbô's ankles, first described by Flaubert as worn "pour régler sa marche," and which later snaps when she is in Mâtho's arms. Cahen, in his note to a variant of the Song of Songs 2:7, refers to "the chainlets attached to both legs, to prevent accidents that might befall girls taking overlong strides. This kind of fetter served as a sign of virginity–a sign whose absence could give rise to great scandal at the time of marriage."
23. Pierre-Damien Armandi, *Histoire militaire des éléphants* (Paris, 1843); L. Florus (other names and exact identity uncertain), Latin historian of the age of Hadrian and Trajan: *Epitome de T. Livio Bellorum omnium annorum DCC Libri duo;* for Marcellinus, see letter to Sainte-Beuve, note 31.
24. George Rawlinson's translation of Herodotus, IV, 168 reads: "Their women . . . when they catch any vermin on their persons, bite it and throw it away."
25. Cahen's translation, ". . . ne fais pas de deuil; . . . ne te voile pas le menton" is closer to Flaubert's "beards" than is the King James: "cover not thy lips."
26. Flaubert's slightly faulty Latin has been corrected here. The meaning is: "because the others might be deterred from the same mischief by fear of the same penalty." The "Univers pittoresque" (begun in 1844) was a popular series of seventy illustrated volumes describing the countries of the world.
27. Charenton is a famous mental hospital of seventeenth-century origin in a suburb of Paris, popularly thus called by the name of its location; now officially named L'Hôpital Esquirol. The expression "bon pour Charenton" ("fit for the loony bin") is still current. Froehner's jeer at the "pomegranate trees sprinkled with silphium" reads: "I know that an infusion of this plant was a well known herbal drink . . . What would we say of a gardener who sprinkled his orange trees with linden tea? We would probably send him to grow hellebore at Charenton." (In ancient times hellebore was thought to cure madness.)
28. Arnold Hermann Ludwig Heeren (1760–1842), German author of numerous works on ancient history. It is not certain to which of them Flaubert refers. As to the huge "emeralds," both Theophrastus himself and John Hill, in his notes to his translation (London, 1746), say that they are the stuff of legend and cannot possibly be true emeralds. Flaubert had apparently read Hill carelessly. Froehner, in his riposte, continued to jeer at Flaubert's "emeralds."
29. Froehner had written of some of Flaubert's details that "they smack of the modern traveler, who is perhaps an excellent recounter of traditions picked up along the way, but whose testimony has not the slightest value when it comes to reconstituting the society of ancient Carthage." Flaubert, of course, was "the modern traveler." For example, in connection with Flaubert's mention (a few lines further on) of sakiehs, which he had seen in Egypt, Froehner had expressed doubt that they could raise water to the upper floors of Carthaginian houses, some of which were six stories high.
30. Gautier himself says, in the novel, that the gesture of his beautiful Tahoser, "celle de la Vénus de Milo," is "peu fréquent chez les momies."
31. Flaubert himself seems "unlucky" in this reference. Ezekiel 28:14 does not speak of the floors of apartments. The King James reads: ". . . thou hast walked up and down in the midst of the stones of fire." Cahen's French translation is almost identical.
32. Flaubert's word is *léger.*

Critical Views of *Salammbô*

In a critique written in 1901, Arthur Symons "sets Salammbô *above all other historical novels," praising Flaubert's ability to match his style with his historical subject.*

The Harmony of *Salammbô*

Salammbô is an attempt, as Flaubert, himself his best critic, has told us, to 'perpetuate a mirage by applying to antiquity the methods of the modern novel.' By the modern novel he means the novel as he had reconstructed it; he means *Madame Bovary.* That perfect book is perfect because Flaubert had, for once, found exactly the subject suited to his method, had made his method and his subject one. On his scientific side Flaubert is a realist, but there is another, perhaps a more intimately personal side, on which he is lyrical, lyrical in a large, sweeping way. The lyric poet in him made *La Tentation de Saint-Antoine,* the analyst made *L'Education sentimentale;* but in *Madame Bovary* we find the analyst and the lyric poet in equilibrium. It is the history of a woman, as

Arthur Symons, a biographer and critic regarded as an important interpreter of fin de siècle literature (photograph by Elliott & Fry)

carefully observed as any story that has ever been written, and observed in surroundings of the most ordinary kind. But Flaubert finds the romantic material which he loved, the materials of beauty, in precisely that temperament which he studies so patiently and so cruelly. Madame Bovary is a little woman, half vulgar and half hysterical, incapable of a fine passion; but her trivial desires, her futile aspirations after second-rate pleasures and second-hand ideals, give to Flaubert all that he wants: the opportunity to create beauty out of reality. What is common in the imagination of Madame Bovary becomes exquisite in Flaubert's rendering of it, and by that counterpoise of a commonness in the subject he is saved from any vague ascents of rhetoric in his rendering of it.

In writing *Salammbô* Flaubert set himself to renew the historical novel, as he had renewed the novel of manners. He would have admitted, doubtless, that perfect success in the historical novel is impossible, by the nature of the case. We are at best only half conscious of the reality of the things about us, only able to translate them approximately into any form of art. How much is left over, in the closest transcription of a mere line of houses in a street, of a passing steamer, of one's next-door neighbour, of the point of view of a foreigner looking along Piccadilly, of one's own state of mind, moment by moment, as one walks from Oxford Circus to the Marble Arch? Think, then, of the attempt to reconstruct no matter what period of the past, to distinguish the difference in the aspect of a world perhaps bossed with castles and ridged with ramparts, to two individualities encased within chain-armour! Flaubert chose his antiquity wisely: a period of which we know too little to confuse us, a city of which no stone is left on another, the minds of Barbarians who have left us no psychological documents. "Be sure I have made no fantastic Carthage," he says proudly, pointing to his documents: Ammianus Marcellinus, who has furnished him with 'the *exact* form of a door'; the Bible and Theophrastus, from which he obtains his perfumes and his precious stones; Gesenius, from whom he gets his Punic names; the *Mémoires de l'Académie des Inscriptions.* 'As for the temple of Tanit, I am sure of having reconstructed it as it was, with the treatise of the Syrian Goddess, with the medals of the Duc de Luynes, with what is known of the temple at Jerusalem, with a passage of St. Jerome, quoted by Seldon (*De Diis Syriis*), with the plan of the temple of Gozzo, which is quite Carthaginian, and best of all, with the ruins of the temple of Thugga, which I have seen myself, with my own eyes, and of which no traveller or antiquarian, so far as I know, has ever spoken.' But that, after all, as he admits (when, that is, he has proved point by point his minute accuracy to all that is known of ancient Carthage, his faithfulness to every indication which can serve for his guidance, his patience in grouping rather than his daring in the invention of action and details), that is not the question. "I care little enough for archæology! If the colour is not uniform, if the details are out of keeping, if the manners do not spring from the religion and the actions from the passions, if the characters are not consistent, if the costumes are not appropriate to the habits and the architecture to the climate, if, in a word, there is not harmony, I am in error. If not, no."

And there, precisely, is the definition of the one merit which can give a historical novel the right to exist, and at the same time a definition of the merit which sets *Salammbô* above all other historical novels. Everything in the book is strange, some of it might easily be bewildering, some revolting; but all is in harmony. The harmony is like that of Eastern music, not immediately conveying its charm, or even the secret of its measure, to Western ears; but a monotony coiling perpetually upon itself, after a severe law of its own. Or rather, it is like a fresco, painted gravely in hard, definite colours, firmly detached from a background of burning sky; a procession of Barbarians, each in the costume of his country, passes across the wall; there are battles, in which elephants fight with men; an army besieges a great city, or rots to death in a defile between mountains; the ground is paved with dead men; crosses, each bearing its living burden, stand against the sky; a few figures of men and women appear again and again, expressing by their gestures the soul of the story.

Flaubert himself has pointed, with his unerring self-criticism, to the main defect of his book: 'The pedestal is too large for the statue.' There should have been, as he says, a hundred pages more about Salammbô. He declares: 'There is not in my book an isolated or gratuitous description; all are useful to my characters, and have an influence, near or remote, on the action.' This is true, and yet, all the same, the pedestal is too large for the statue. Salammbô, 'always surrounded with grave and exquisite things,' has something of the somnambulism which enters into the heroism of Judith; she has a hieratic beauty, and a consciousness as pale and vague as the moon whom she worships. She passes before us, 'her body saturated with perfumes,' encrusted with jewels like an idol, her head turreted with violet hair, the gold chain tinkling between her ankles; and is hardly more than an attitude, a fixed gesture, like the Eastern women whom one sees passing, with oblique eyes and mouths painted into smiles, their faces curiously traced into a work of art, in the languid movements of a pantomimic dance. The soul behind those eyes? the temperament under that at times almost terrifying mask? Salammbô is as inarticulate for us as the serpent, to whose drowsy beauty, capable of such sudden awakenings, hers seems half akin; they move before us in a kind of hieratic pantomime, a coloured, expressive thing, signifying nothing. Mâtho, maddened with love, 'in an invincible stupor, like those who have drunk some draught of which they are to die,' has the same somnambulistic life; the prey of Venus, he has an almost literal insanity, which, as Flaubert reminds us, is true to the ancient view of that passion. He is the only quite vivid person in the book, and he lives with the intensity of a wild beast, a life 'blinded alike' from every inner and outer interruption to one or two fixed ideas. The others have their places in the picture, fall into their attitudes naturally, remain so many coloured outlines for us. The illusion is perfect; these people may not be the real people of history, but at least they have no self-consciousness, no Christian tinge in their minds.

'The metaphors are few, the epithets definite,' Flaubert tells us, of his style in this book, where, as he

Poster for the 1892 production of Salammbô *in Paris. With the continuing popularity of his novel, Flaubert was soon asked for his consent to its adaptation as an opera. Giuseppe Verdi was chosen to be the composer; however, this project was abandoned. In 1876 Flaubert agreed to an adaptation by Ernest Reyer. The opera, which was not completed until after Flaubert's death, was staged for the first time in 1890 in Brussels, where it was hugely successful (cliché Bibliothèque nationale de France, Paris).*

says, he has sacrificed less 'to the amplitude of the phrase and to the period,' than in *Madame Bovary*. The movement here is in briefer steps, with a more earnest gravity, without any of the engaging weakness of adjectives. The style is never archaic, it is absolutely simple, the precise word being put always for the precise thing; but it obtains a dignity, a historical remoteness, by the large seriousness of its manner, the absence of modern ways of thought, which, in *Madame Bovary,* bring with them an instinctively modern cadence.

Salammbô is written with the severity of history, but Flaubert notes every detail visually, as a painter notes the details of natural things. A slave is being flogged under a tree: Flaubert notes the movement of the thong as it flies, and tells us: 'The thongs, as they

Rose Caron as Salammbô and Albert Saleza as Mâtho in the final act of the 1892 Paris production of Salammbô *(cliché Bibliothèque nationale de France, Paris)*

whistled through the air, sent the bark of the plane trees flying.' Before the battle of the Macar, the Barbarians are awaiting the approach of the Carthaginian army. First 'the Barbarians were surprised to see the ground undulate in the distance.' Clouds of dust rise and whirl over the desert, through which are seen glimpses of horns, and, as it seems, wings. Are they bulls or birds, or a mirage of the desert? The Barbarians watch intently. 'At last they made out several transverse bars, bristling with uniform points. The bars became denser, larger; dark mounds swayed from side to side; suddenly square bushes came into view; they were elephants and lances. A single shout, "The Carthaginians!" arose.' Observe how all that is seen, as if the eyes, unaided by the intelligence, had found out everything for themselves, taking in one indication after another, instinctively. Flaubert puts himself in the place of his characters, not so much to think for them as to see for them.

Compare the style of Flaubert in each of his books, and you will find that each book has its own rhythm, perfectly appropriate to its subject-matter. That style, which has almost every merit and hardly a fault, becomes what it is by a process very different from that of most writers careful of form. Read Chateaubriand, Gautier, even Baudelaire, and you will find that the aim of these writers has been to construct a style which shall be adaptable to every occasion, but without structural change; the cadence is always the same. The most exquisite word-painting of Gautier can be translated rhythm for rhythm into English, without difficulty; once you have mastered the tune, you have merely to go on; every verse will be the same. But Flaubert is so difficult to translate because he has no fixed rhythm; his prose keeps step with no regular march-music. He invents the rhythm of every sentence, he changes his cadence with every mood or for the convenience of every fact. He has no theory of beauty in form apart from what it expresses. For him form is a living thing, the physical body of thought, which it clothes and interprets. 'If I call stones blue, it is because blue is the precise word, believe me,' he replies to Sainte-Beuve's criticism. Beauty comes into his words from the precision with which they express definite things, definite ideas, definite sensations. And in his book, where the material is so hard, apparently so unmalleable, it is a beauty of sheer exactitude which fills it from end to end, a beauty of measure and order, seen equally in the departure of the doves of Carthage, at the time of their flight into Sicily, and in the lions feasting on the corpses of the Barbarians, in the defile between the mountains.

–Arthur Symons, "Gustave Flaubert," in *Figures of Several Centuries* (New York: E. P. Dutton, 1916), pp. 130–140

* * *

Georg Lukács examines the Flaubert/Sainte-Beuve polemic and argues that Salammbô *marks a significant development of the historical novel. This essay was originally published in Lukács's* The Historical Novel *(1962).*

Salammbô as a Modern Historical Novel

Flaubert's *Salammbô* is the great representative work of [a] phase of development in the historical novel. It combines all the high artistic qualities of Flaubert's style. Stylistically, it is the paradigm of Flaubert's artistic aims; which is why it shows so much more clearly than the writings of the mediocre and untalented writers of this period the unresolved contradictions, the irremovable inner "problematic" of the new historical novel.

Flaubert formulated his aims programmatically. He says that he wished to apply the procedure and

Georg Lukács, an influential Marxist critic, in the late 1960s

method of the modern novel to antiquity. And this programme was fully acknowledged by the important representatives of the new trend of naturalism. Zola's criticism of *Salammbô* is essentially a realization of this statement by Flaubert. Zola admittedly finds fault with a number of details, but accepts that Flaubert has applied the methods of the new realism correctly to historical material.

Outwardly *Salammbô* has not had the outstanding success of *Madame Bovary*. Nevertheless its echo has been quite strong. The leading French critic of the period, Sainte-Beuve, devoted a whole series of articles to it. Flaubert himself considered this critique so important that in a letter to Sainte-Beuve, published later, he took up all his critic's points in detail. This controversy illuminates so sharply the new problems which had arisen in this new phase of the historical novel that we must deal at length with the main arguments of the polemic.

Sainte-Beuve's basic critical position is deprecatory, despite his respect for Flaubert's literary personality. What makes this deprecation so interesting for us is that the critic himself takes up a philosophical and literary position similar in many respects to the Flaubert he criticizes. The difference is that the older Sainte-Beuve is still somewhat bound to the traditions of the earlier period; he is more flexible and willing to compromise than Flaubert, particularly in artistic questions. Flaubert pursued his path to its logical conclusion with the radical disregard of a deeply convinced and important writer. Sainte-Beuve's criticism, therefore, of Flaubert's creative method is certainly not that of the Scott-Balzac period, as we shall see. Indeed in this period Sainte-Beuve proposed and even realized artistic views which in many respects approached those of Flaubert and sharply contrasted with those of Balzac.

Flaubert keenly felt this affinity between his own basic position and that of his critic. Thus, in his letter to Sainte-Beuve, the author of *Port Royal,* he presents his critic with the following *argumentum ad hominem:* "One last question, master, an improper question: why do you find Schahabarim almost comic and your good fellows of Port Royal so serious? For me M. Singlin is funereal beside my elephants. . . . And it is precisely because they [the characters of Port Royal] are very distant from me that I admire your talent in trying to make them intelligible to me. For I believe and wish to live in Port Royal even less than I do in Carthage. Port Royal, too, was exclusive, unnatural, forced, all of a piece and yet true. Why do you not want two truths to exist, two contrary excesses, two different monstrosities?"

It is interesting to compare Flaubert's praise for Sainte-Beuve here with Balzac's entirely negative judgment on *Port Royal.* Balzac and Flaubert are fairly close to one another in their judgment of the world which Sainte-Beuve, as an historian with artistic pretentions, presents. Both see the fragmented, eccentric, bagatelle nature of Sainte-Beuve's picture of history. But while Balzac passionately rejects such a conception of history, Flaubert regards it with an interested and sceptical curiosity. And there is no question here of simple politeness on the part of Flaubert towards the famous critic. His discussion in his correspondence of the Goncourts' historical pictures of the eighteenth century, for example, clearly proves the sincerity of these remarks, for there these Sainte-Beuve tendencies are pushed to the extreme. What comes out in all these cases is the new feeling of the leading ideologists towards history.

Of course, Flaubert's position in this process is not an average one. His literary greatness is expressed in the fact that the general tendency of the time appears in his work with an honest, passionate consistency. While in most other writers of the time, a negative attitude towards the contemporary prose of bourgeois life was simply a matter of aesthetic amusement or, frequently, of reactionary feeling, in Flaubert it is an intense disgust, a vehement hatred.

This disgust and hatred are behind Flaubert's interest in history: "I am weary of ugly things and sordid surroundings. Bovary has disgusted me with bourgeois morals for some time to come. I am going to live, for several years perhaps, inside a subject of splendour, far from the modern world of which I am heartily sick." And in another letter, also written while he was at work on *Salammbô:* "When one reads *Salammbô,* one will not, I hope, think of the Author. Few will guess how sad one had to be in order to resuscitate Carthage! There's a Thebaid to which disgust with modern life has driven me."

Thus Flaubert set himself a consistent programme: to reawaken a vanished world of no concern to us. It was precisely because of his deep hatred for modern society that he sought, passionately and paradoxically, a world which would in no way resemble it, which would have no connection with it, direct or indirect. Of course, this lack of connection–or rather the illusion of such–is at the same time the subjective factor which connects Flaubert's exotic historical subject matter with the everyday life of the present. For one must not forget that he tried to plan and execute his social novels, too, as a bystander, a non-participant. The letters he wrote while working on them testify to this again and again. And similarly one has to see that in both cases the programmatic non-partisanship, the famous "impassibilité" turns out to be an illusion: Flaubert reveals his attitude to both Emma Bovary and Salammbô through the atmosphere he creates. The only difference one can really discover in the treatment of the two themes is that the author is not in fact very emotionally involved with the masses of protectors and enemies of Carthage, while the everyday world of the contemporary novels kindles unceasing hatred and love in him. (It would be too superficial altogether to overlook this factor; it is enough to think of Dussardier in *L'Éducation Sentimentale.*) This all explains why Flaubert could think it possible to use the same artistic means for both *Salammbô* and *Madame Bovary.* At the same time, however, it also explains the completely different artistic results: the artistic fruitfulness of genuine hatred and love, however hidden and suppressed in the one case, the transformation of disinterestedness into sterile exoticism in the other.

In the attempt to solve this task artistically, the contradictions in Flaubert's position come out very plainly. Flaubert wishes to portray this world realistically, using the artistic means which he himself had discovered a few years earlier for *Madame Bovary* and there brought to perfection. But now it is not the grey everyday reality of French provincial life to which this realism of minutely observed and exactly described detail is to be applied; instead it is the alien and distant, incomprehensible but picturesque, decorative, grandiose, gorgeous, cruel and exotic world of Carthage which is to arise before us. This explains Flaubert's desperate struggle to evoke a graphic picture of old Carthage by means of exact study and exact production of archaeological detail.

Sainte-Beuve has a strong sense of the artistic discrepancy which results from this aim. He is always pointing out how the description of objects in Flaubert, the dead environment of men, overwhelms the portrayal of the men themselves: he criticizes the fact that, though all these details are correctly and brilliantly described in Flaubert, they do not add up to a whole, not even in relation to the dead objects. Flaubert describes doors, locks etc., all the components of a house, but the architect who builds the whole is nowhere to be seen. Sainte-Beuve sums up this criticism as follows: "the political side, the character of the persons, the genius of the people, the aspects whereby the particular history of this seafaring and, in its own way, civilizing people is of concern to history in general and of interest to the great current of civilization, are sacrificed here or subordinated to the exorbitant, descriptive side, to a dilettantism which, unable to apply itself to anything but rare ruins, is compelled to exaggerate them."

That these remarks hit a central defect in *Salammbô* is shown by Flaubert's despairing letters written while at work on the book. Thus he writes to a friend: "I am now full of doubts about the whole, about the general plan; I think there are too many soldiers. That is History, I know quite well. But if a novel is as tedious as a scientific potboiler, then Good Night, there's an end to Art. . . . I am beginning the siege of Carthage now. I am lost among the machines of war, the balista and the scorpions, and I understand nothing of it, neither I nor anyone else."

But what can a world thus re-awakened mean to us? Granted that Flaubert successfully solved all the problems which he raised artistically–has a world so represented any real living significance for us? Flaubert's paradoxes with regard to subjects which do not concern us, and which are artistic because they do not concern us, are very characteristic of the author's moods, but they also have their objective aesthetic consequences which are already known to us. Sainte-Beuve denies that the world of *Salammbô* has this significance for us. He uses an interesting argument, which shows that something of the old tradition of the historical novel is still alive in him. He doubts whether one can treat antiquity artistically, whether it can be made the theme of a really living historical novel. "One can reconstruct antiquity, but one cannot bring it back to life." And he refers specifically to the living, continuous relation between Scott's themes and the present, to the many living links which make it possible for us to experience even the distant Middle Ages.

But his chief objection to the theme of *Salammbô* is not confined to this general doubt. Flaubert's subject, he says, occupies a special, remote, unrelated position even among the themes of antiquity. "What do I care about the duel between Tunis and Carthage? Speak to me of the duel between Carthage and Rome, that's a different matter! There I am attentive, there I am involved. In the bitter struggle between Rome and Carthage the whole of future civilization is at stake; our own depends on it. . . ."

To this decisive objection Flaubert has no concrete answer. "Perhaps you are right in your considerations of the historical novel as applied to antiquity, and it is very possible that I have failed."

But he has nothing more concrete to say about this question and, while rejecting the artistic significance of archaeological authenticity, simply speaks of the immanent connections within the historical world he has so selected and portrayed. And he maintains that he is right or wrong according to whether he has been successful or not with regard to this immanent harmony.

Apart from which he defends his subject-matter and portrayal in a more lyrical and biographical vein. "I believe even," he says, "that I have been less hard on humanity in *Salammbô* than in *Madame Bovary*. The curiosity, the love which made me seek out vanished religions and peoples has something moral and sympathetic about it, so it seems to me."

The comparison between *Salammbô* and *Madame Bovary* does not derive from Flaubert himself; it occurs already in Sainte-Beuve's critique. Sainte-Beuve analyses the figure of *Salammbô:* "She talks to her nurse, confides to her her vague anxieties, her stifled sense of unease, her listlessness. . . . She looks for, dreams of, calls to something unknown. It is the situation of more than one daughter of Eve, Carthaginian or otherwise; to some extent it is that of *Madame Bovary* at the beginning, when life has become too tedious for her and she goes off on her own to the beech-grove of Banneville. . . . Well, poor Salammbô experiences in her own way the same feeling of vague yearning and oppressive desire. The author has only transposed, with great art, and *mythologised* this muffled lament of the heart and the senses." In another connection he compares Flaubert's general attitude to his historical characters with Chateaubriand's manner of portrayal. He says that Flaubert's Salammbô is less a sister of Hannibal than of Chateaubriand's Gallic maiden, Velléda.

The reproach of *modernization* is clearly contained in these comparisons, although Sainte-Beuve does not make an issue out of this question and often shows a great deal of tolerance toward modernization. Nor has Flaubert's protest anything to do with the general methodological problem of modernization. This he takes to be self-evident. His disagreement is only with the concrete comparisons which Sainte-Beuve makes. "As for my heroine, I do not defend her. According to you she resembles . . . Velléda, Mme Bovary. Not at all! Velléda is active, intelligent, European, Mme Bovary is stirred by multiple passions; Salammbô, on the contrary, is rooted in a fixed idea. She is a maniac, a kind of Saint Theresa. What does it matter? I am not sure of her reality, for neither I, you, nor anyone, neither ancient nor modern can know the oriental woman, because it is impossible to associate with her."

"Salammbô," a watercolor by Georges Rochegrosse (1859–1938). An artist who illustrated the work of many French writers, including Anatole France and José-Maria de Hérédia, Rochegrosse became famous in particular for his oriental art. Salammbô was a natural subject (cliché Bibliothèque nationale de France, Paris).

Thus Flaubert is protesting only against the concrete form of modernization which Sainte-Beuve has attributed to the figure of Salammbô. The modernization itself he grants as self-evident; for it is really quite immaterial whether one attributes to Hannibal's sister the psychology of a French *petite bourgeoise* of the nineteenth century or of a Spanish nun of the seventeenth.

To which must be added that Flaubert is, of course, also modernizing the psychology of Saint Theresa.

This is not a minor aspect of the work and influence of Flaubert. He chooses an historical subject whose inner social-historical nature is of no concern to him and to which he can only lend the appearance of reality in an external, decorative, picturesque manner by means of the conscientious application of archaeology. But at some point he is forced to establish a contact with both himself and the reader, and this he does by modernizing the psychology of his characters. The proud and bitter paradox which contends that the novel has nothing at all to do with the present, is simply a defensive paradox contending against the trivialities of his age. We see from Flaubert's explanations which we have already quoted that *Salammbô* was more than just an artistic experiment. It is for this reason that the modernization of the characters acquires central importance; it is the only source of movement and life in this frozen, lunar landscape of archaeological precision.

Naturally it is a ghostly illusion of life. And an illusion which dissolves the hyper-objective reality of the objects. In describing the individual objects of an historical *milieu* Flaubert is much more exact and plastic than any other writer before him. But these objects have nothing to do with the inner life of the characters. When Scott describes a medieval town or the habitat of a Scottish clan, these material things are part and parcel of the lives and fortunes of people whose whole psychology belongs to the same level of historical development and is a product of the same social-historical ensemble as these material things. This is how the older epic writers produced their "totality of objects." In Flaubert there is no such connection between the outside world and the psychology of the principal characters. And the effect of this lack of connection is to degrade the archaeological exactness of the outer world: it becomes a world of historically exact *costumes and decorations,* no more than a pictorial frame within which a purely modern story is unfolded.

The actual influence of Salammbô is in fact also connected with this modernization. Artists have admired the accomplishment of Flaubert's descriptions. But the effect of Salammbô herself was to provide a heightened image, a decorative symbol, of the hysterical longings and torments of middle-class girls in large cities. History simply provided a decorative, monumental setting for this hysteria, which in the present spends itself in petty and ugly scenes, and which thus acquired a tragic aura quite out of keeping with its real character. The effect is powerful but it shows that Flaubert, because of his embitterment with the shallow prose of his time, had become objectively untruthful and distorted the real proportions of life. The artistic superiority of his bourgeois novels lies precisely in the fact that in them the proportions between emotion and event, between desire and its translation into deeds, correspond to the real, social-historical character of emotion and desire. In *Salammbô* the emotions, in themselves quite unmonumental, are falsely and distortedly monumentalized and hence inwardly unequal to such artistic heightening. The way in which the figure of Salammbô was regarded as a symbol during the obvious decline of Royalism and the psychological reaction which set in against Zola's naturalism, is best shown by the analysis which Paul Bourget gives of her: "It is a constant law in his [Flaubert's] eyes that human effort must end abortively, first of all because external circumstances run counter to one's dreams, secondly because even favourable circumstances cannot prevent the soul from devouring itself in the gratification of its chimera. Our desire floats before us like the veil of Tanit, the embroidered *Zaïmph,* before Salammbô. While she cannot seize it, the girl languishes in despair. As soon as she touches it, she must die."

This modernizing determines the structure of the plot. Its basis is formed by two motifs which are only very externally connected: a "crown and state" conflict between Carthage and the rebellious mercenaries, and the love episode of Salammbô herself. Their involvement with one another is quite external and inevitably remains so. Salammbô is as much a stranger to the interests of her homeland, to the life-and-death struggle of her native city, as Madame Bovary is to the medical practice of her husband. But while in the bourgeois novel this indifference can be made the vehicle of a plot with Emma Bovary at the centre precisely because she is a stranger to provincial daily life, here instead we have a "crown and state" story, outwardly grandiose and requiring therefore extensive preparation, with which Salammbô's destiny has no organic connection. The links are all either pure accidents or external pretexts. But in the presentation of the story the external pretext must inevitably suppress and stifle the main theme. External occasions take up the major part of the novel; the main theme is reduced to a small episode.

This lack of relation between the human tragedy, which is what kindles the reader's interest, and the political action clearly shows the change already undergone by historical feeling in this age. The political plot is not only lifeless because it is cluttered up with descriptions of inessential objects, but because it has no discernible connection with any concrete form of popular life that we may experience. The mercenaries in this novel are the same kind of wild, irrational, chaotic mass as the inhabitants of Carthage. True, we are told in exhaustive detail how the quarrel arises, namely the fact that the mercenaries have not been paid, and by

Detail of a Punic stela engraved with the emblem of Tanit, the goddess whose sacred veil, or Zaïmph, Salammbô recovers from Mâtho. Found in the ruins of Carthage in Tunisia, this stela was given to the Musée Flaubert at Croisset in 1920 by Dr. Carton, who was at the time the mayor of Carthage (Collections de la Bibliothèque municipale de Rouen. Cliché Thierry Ascencio-Parvy).

what circumstances this quarrel grows into a war; yet we have not the least idea of the real social-historical and human driving force which causes these clashes to take place in the way they do. These remain an irrational, historical fact despite Flaubert's detailed portrayal. And since the human motives do not spring organically out of a concrete social-historical basis, but are given to isolated figures in a modernized form, they only confuse the total picture still further, reduce still further the social reality of the entire story.

This comes out at its crudest in the love episode of Mâtho. Sainte-Beuve, in his analysis of this love-maddened mercenary, rightly recalls the so-called historical novels of the seventeenth century, in which Alexander the Great, Cyrus or Genserich appeared as love-stricken heroes. "But Mâtho in love, this African Goliath, who behaves so wildly and childishly in sight of Salammbô, seems just as false to me; he is as outside nature as he is outside history."

And Sainte-Beuve rightly remarks on the feature peculiar to Flaubert here, what is new in this distortion of history as compared with the seventeenth century: whereas the lovers of the old novels had been sweet and sentimental, Mâtho has a bestially savage character. In short, those brutal and animal features are emphasized and placed at the centre, which occur later in Zola as characteristics of the life of modern workers and peasants. Thus Flaubert's portrayal is "prophetic." Not, however, in the sense in which Balzac's works were prophetic, anticipating the actual, future development of social types, but merely in a literary-historical sense, anticipating the later distortion of modern life in the works of the Naturalists.

Flaubert's defence against this criticism of Sainte-Beuve is extremely interesting, illuminating yet another aspect of his method of approach to history. This is how he defends himself against the charge of modernization in the figure of Mâtho: "Mâtho *prowls like a madman* round Carthage. Madness is the right word. Wasn't love, as conceived by the ancients, a madness, a curse, an illness sent by the gods?"

This defence bases itself apparently on historical evidence. But only apparently; for Flaubert never examines the real nature of love within the social life of antiquity, the connection of its different psychological forms with other forms of ancient life. His starting point is an analysis of the isolated *idea* of love, as we find it in certain ancient tragedies. Flaubert is right when he says for instance that the love of Phaedra in Euripides' *Hippolytus* is presented as a sudden passion, innocently visited upon her by the Gods. But it is an entirely unhistorical modernization of ancient life to take merely the subjective side of such tragic conflicts and then to blow this up into a "psychological peculiarity" of the whole of antiquity. Obviously, in certain cases individual love and passion did irrupt "suddenly" into people's lives and cause great tragic collisions. It is also true that these collisions were far more unusual in ancient life than in the period of development from the Middle Ages until modern times, when similar problems occurred, though in a different form in keeping with the changed social circumstances. The special manifestation of passion in the portrayals of the ancients is connected in the closest possible way with the special forms of the break-up of gentile society in antiquity. But this is the final ideological result of a particular development. If this result is then torn out of its social-historical context, if its subjective-psychological side is isolated from the causes which produce it, if therefore the artist's point of departure is not existence but an isolated idea, then whatever one's apparent historical evidence one's only approach to this idea is via modernization. Only in Flaubert's imagination does Mâtho embody ancient love. In reality, he is a prophetic model of the decadent drunkards and madmen of Zola.

This connection between approaching history from the standpoint of an idea and portraying it as a compound of outward exoticism and inner modernity is so important for the whole artistic development of the second half of the nineteenth century that we may be allowed to illustrate it by a further example. Richard Wagner, whose points of similarity with Flaubert Nietzsche disclosed with spiteful shrewdness, discovers the brother-and-sister love of Siegmund and Sieglinde in the Edda. This is an unusually interesting, exotic phenomenon, and is made "intelligible" by a lavish display of decorative pomp and modern psychology. Marx in few words revealed Wagner's falsification of the social-historical connections. Engels, in his *Origin of the Family,* quotes this letter of Marx: "Was it ever possible that brother embraced sister as a bride?" To these "lewd gods" of Wagner who, quite in the modern manner, spice their love intrigues with a little incest, Marx replied: "In primitive times the sister *was* the wife, and that was moral." Wagner's example shows even more clearly than Flaubert's how, by starting from an isolated idea rather than from actual existence, one inevitably ends up by misrepresenting and distorting history. What remains are the outward, soulless facts of history (here love between brother and sister) which are injected with an entirely modern sensibility, and the old story, the old occurrence serves only to give picturesqueness to this modern sensibility, to add to it a decorative grandeur which, as we have seen, it does not deserve.

This question has, however, still another side which is of exceptional importance for modern developments. As we have seen, the inner emptiness of social-historical events, left by the rift between the outward happenings and the modernized psychology of the characters, give rise to the exotic historical *milieu.* The historical event, emptied in this subjectivist manner of its inner greatness has to acquire a pseudo-monumentality by other means. For it is precisely the longing to escape from the triviality of modern bourgeois life which produces these historical themes.

One of the most important means of producing this pseudo-monumentality is the emphasis on brutality. We have already seen how the most significant and influential critics of the period, Taine and Brandes, lament the absence of such brutality in Scott. Sainte-Beuve, belonging to an older generation, notes its presence and predominance in *Salammbô* with great unease: "he cultivates atrocity. The man is good, excellent, the book is cruel. He believes that it is a proof of strength to appear inhuman in his books."

For anyone who knows *Salammbô* it is hardly necessary to quote examples. I shall simply mention the great contrast during the siege of Carthage: while Carthage's supply of water is cut off and the whole city is dying of thirst, the most terrible hunger rages in the camp of the mercenaries. Flaubert takes delight in giving detailed and cruel pictures of the sufferings of the masses in and around Carthage. There is never any humanity in this suffering; it is simply horrible, senseless torment. No single member of the masses is individually characterized, the suffering yields no single conflict or action which might humanly interest or grip us.

Here we may see the sharp opposition between the old and the new representation of history. The writers of the classical period of the historical novel were only interested in the cruel and terrible happenings of previous history insofar as they were necessary expressions of definite forms of class struggle (e.g. the cruelty of the Chouans in Balzac) and also because they gave birth of a similar necessity to great human passions and conflicts, etc. (the heroism of the Republican officers during the Chouans' massacre of them in the same novel). The placing of the cruel processes of social development in a necessary and intelligible connection and the relationship between these and the human greatness of the combatants take from the events their cruelty and brutality. Which does not mean that the cruelty and brutality are in any way ironed out or mitigated–the reproach which Taine and Brandes levelled at Scott; they are simply given their rightful place inside the total context.

Flaubert begins a development where the inhumanity of subject-matter and presentation, where atrocity and brutality become ends in themselves. These features acquire their central position owing to the weak presentation of what is the chief issue–the social development of man; indeed for the same reason they assume even more importance than even this position warrants. Since real greatness is everywhere replaced by extensiveness–the decorative splendour of the contrasts replaces the social-human connections–inhumanity, cruelty, atrocity and brutality become substitutes for the lost greatness of real history. At the same time they spring from the morbid longing of modern man to escape from the suffocating narrowness of everyday life, a longing which he projects into this pseudo-monumentality. Disgust with small and petty office intrigues produces the ideal image of the mass poisoner, Cesare Borgia.

Flaubert felt deeply hurt by Sainte-Beuve's accusation. But his objections to the critic do not exceed a feeling of injury. And this is not accidental. For the extraordinarily sensitive and highly moral Flaubert has against his will become the initiator of the inhuman in modern literature. The development of capitalism not only levels and trivializes, it also brutalizes.

This brutalization of feeling manifests itself in literature to an ever increasing extent, most clearly of all in the description and portrayal of love, where the physical-sexual side gains growing ascendancy over the passion itself. Think how the greatest portrayers of love–Shakespeare, Goethe and Balzac–confined themselves to the merest intimations in their description of the physical act itself. The interest shown by modern literature in this aspect of love on the one hand derives from the increasing brutalization of the real emotions of love, which occurs in life itself, and on the other has the consequence that writers are forced to search for more and more exquisite, abnormal, perverse, etc. themes in order to escape monotony.

Flaubert himself, in this respect, stands at the beginning of this development. And it is very characteristic both for him as well as for the entire development of the historical novel during the crisis of decline of bourgeois realism that these tendencies are much more pronounced in his historical novels than in his pictures of modern society. In both, hatred and disgust for the pettiness, triviality and meanness of modern bourgeois life are expressed with equal force, yet very differently in keeping with the difference of subject-matter. In his contemporary novels Flaubert concentrates his ironic attack on the portrayal of everyday bourgeois life and average bourgeois man. As an outstanding realist artist he thus achieves an infinitely nuanced picture of that dismal greyness which is a real aspect of this everyday life. Precisely his naturalist tendencies restrain Flaubert from any eccentricity in his treatment of the inhuman forms of capitalist life. But his historical novel, as we have seen, he considered a liberation from the fetters of this monotonous flatness. All that his naturalist conscience had forced him to renounce in his picture of contemporary reality found a place here. In terms of form–the colourfulness, the decorative monumentality of an exotic *milieu;* in terms of content–eccentric passions in their fullest extent and uniqueness. And it is here that we clearly see the social, moral and ideological limitations of this great and sincere artist: while he sincerely hates the capitalist present, his hatred has no roots in the great popular and democratic traditions either of the past or present and therefore has no future perspective. His hatred does not historically transcend its object. Thus if, in the historical novels the suppressed passions break open their fetters, it is the eccentric-individualist side of capitalist man which comes to the fore, that inhumanity which everyday life hypocritically seeks to conceal and subdue. The later decadents already portray this side of capitalist inhumanity with boastful cynicism. In Flaubert it appears in the Bengal illumination of a romantic-historical monumentality. Thus the sides which Flaubert here reveals of the new manner of portraying life do not become widespread until later and he himself was not yet aware of them as such general tendencies.

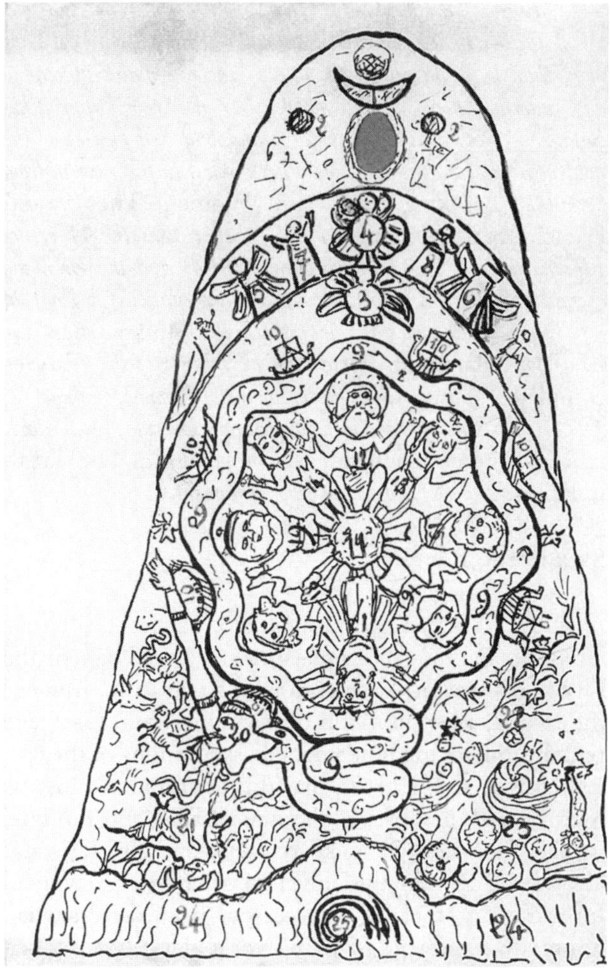

Detail of the veil made by Madame Rochegrosse from the diverse descriptions of the Zaïmph in Salammbô; *her husband, Georges Rochegrosse, gave it in October 1924 to the Musée Flaubert in Croisset (Collections de la Bibliothèque municipale de Rouen. Cliché Thierry Ascencio-Parvy).*

But the contradiction between Flaubert's ascetic disgust with modern life and these inhuman excesses of a riotous and demented imagination does not alter the fact that he appears here as one of the most important precursors of dehumanization in modern literature. This inhumanity is not, of course, in every instance a simple and straightforward capitulation to the dehumanizing tendencies of capitalism, which is the simple and most general case, in literature as in life. The important personalities of this crisis of decline, Flaubert, Baudelaire, Zola and even Nietzsche, suffer from this development and savagely oppose it; yet the manner of their opposition leads to an intensification in literature of capitalist dehumanization in life.

–Georg Lukács, "*Salammbô,*" in his *The Historical Novel,* translated by Hannah and Stanley Mitchell (London: Merlin, 1962), pp. 184–195

* * *

Even if Flaubert believed that "the pedestal is too small for the statue"–that the character Salammbô required more development than he could allow–the title character remains pivotal to any interpretation of the novel. Naomi Schor approaches Salammbô from a psychoanalytical standpoint and focuses on the golden chainlet she wears between her ankles. In this excerpt from her study Breaking the Chain: Women, Theory and French Realist Fiction *(1985), Schor uses the Garnier-Flammarion edition of* Salammbô *(1964) and the Brentano edition (1919) of Flaubert's novel for her citations in English, referring several times to the preface that Maurice Bardèche wrote for* Salammbô, *included in his edition of the* Œuvres complètes *(Paris: Club de L'Honnête Homme, volume 2, 1971). She draws on the ideas of Jacques Derrida, particularly in* La Vérité en peinture *(1978; translated as* The Truth in Painting, *1987), in making her argument.*

Salammbô Bound

. . . Whether one proposes to bracket the character of Salammbô, or emphasizes the homology of the love and war stories, or even goes so far as to privilege the sexual, the opposition of Salammbô and Carthage remains one of the fundamental assumptions of the critics. Now it seems to me that this assumption must be interrogated, because, as the manuscripts and the final version of *Salammbô* make readily apparent, it is not always so easy in this novel to separate the woman from the city, that is, the accessory from the essential, to borrow Flaubert's revealing vocabulary as it is taken up and elaborated upon by Bardèche. Indeed, basing himself on one of Flaubert's notations in an early draft–"The historical events are nothing but an *accessory* of the novel" (CHH [Club de l'Honnête Homme edition], p. 36; emphasis added)–the author of the preface notes that in the course of the successive revisions of the scenarios, the relationship between the accessory and the essential is reversed: "In the final scenario it is definitely the Mercenaries who triumph. The subject is their dramatic rebellion against Carthage, it is no longer the love of Mâtho for Salammbô. That which was initially the accessory to the novel has become the entire novel" (CHH, p. 37).

Having observed that the elaboration of the final scenario goes hand in hand with the generalization of the accessory, how can one not end up questioning the opposition of the accessory and the essential, indeed the very category of the accessory? It will perhaps be obvious to certain readers that I am here following the line of inquiry opened up by Derrida, particularly in *La Vérité en peinture,* where, in the course of a discussion of the *parergon,* that is, the ornament in Kant's aesthetic, Derrida insists on the extreme difficulty of tracing a clear boundary between the clothes and the statue, the clothes that cover a statue serving as the privileged example of the *parergon:*

> This demarcation of the center and of the integrity of the representation, of its inside and its outside, may already appear strange. One wonders besides where should the clothes be made to begin. Where does a *parergon* begin, where does it end. Are all clothes *parerga?*[1]

This is precisely the question raised by the descriptions of Salammbô, for finally Salammbô is a clothed statue and it becomes literally impossible to say where the female body ends and the clothing begins, it is as though her finery were stuck to her skin:

> Mâtho did not hear; he was staring at her, and her garments, that were for him blended with her body: the sheen of the fabrics was like the splendour of her skin, something special, peculiar to her alone: her eyes and diamonds sparkled; the polish of her finger-nails were a continuation of the lustre of jewels that bedecked her fingers. (p. 231)

> Mâtho n'entendait pas; il la contemplait, et les vêtements, pour lui, se confondaient avec le corps. La moire des étoffes était, comme la splendeur de sa peau, quelque chose de spécial et n'appartenait qu'à elle. Ses yeux, ses diamants étincelaient; le poli de ses ongles continuait la finesse des pierres qui chargeaient ses doigts.[2]

If, as I believe, in *Salammbô* synecdoche takes precedence over metonymy, entailing the invasion of the body of the novel by details that evoke the leprosy that slowly eats away at the Suffet Hanno's skin, it follows that the question of the relationship of woman and city is to be posed in terms other than those of mutual exclusion. What is more: if, as I have just shown, it is vain to attempt to separate the ornament from the ornamented, it is because what we have here is what I would call an *ornamental text.* What does this signify? I am, of course, hardly the first critic to draw attention to what Victor Brombert calls the "Parnassian aesthetic"[3] which presides over the writing of *Salammbô.* If I have proposed another expression to account for the ornate quality of the novel, it is precisely to draw attention away from *Salammbô*'s place in literary history and to attempt to think through what is covered over by the gangue of historical labels. And what is true of literary history is also true of the study of genres: to say that *Salammbô* is an ornamental text is not tantamount to proposing a generic reclassification of this reputedly unclassifiable work. Thus Bardèche speaks of the ornamental quality of *Salammbô* only to bring this limit-text under the sway of the epic. That would be fine with me were it not for the fact that, as the following quotation makes clear, this taxonomic rectification leaves intact the accessory/essential opposition under interrogation:

> The ornaments are also those of the epic. The "beauties" of *Salammbô* are battles, moonlit cemeteries, passes, orgies, extraordinary or horrifying actions . . . One feels very strongly that for him these are "major productions," whose proportions and savage grandeur are meant to ensure his book the deathless dignity of the masterpiece, and which do in fact do so. These huge mosaics are purely ornamental. *Salammbô* is like a palace one visits to contemplate them. (CHH, p. 22)

To say that a text is ornamental necessarily implies a revalorization of the ornamental, an unthinkable operation as long as a modernist aesthetic totally dedicated to a bleached writing hostile to all decorative elements held sway. *Salammbô,* a "purple" text according to Flaubert's celebrated word,[4] might well be the precursor text of postmodernism and as such requires the elaboration of a hermeneutic specially adapted to its texture. For, as E. H. Gombrich points out in his great book on decorative art, the ornamental calls into play an entirely different mode of perception or reception than either painting or speech: "Painting, like speaking, implicitly demands attention whether or not it receives it. Decoration cannot make this demand. It normally depends for its effect on the fluctuating attention we can spare while we scan our surroundings."[5] And he goes on to say: "Those critics who feel overwhelmed by the assault on their senses made by the profusion of ornament and have therefore condemned it as tasteless and barbaric may have misunderstood what was expected of them" (p. 116). Indeed, according to Gombrich, the spectator, who like the visitor to the Alhambra is confronted with a bewildering profusion of ornaments, is not expected to look at everything, to pay equal attention to all the details. On the contrary, he is free to choose his sightline, to let his gaze wander, to scan the whole until a detail catches his passing glance. And, just as the analyst's "evenly poised attention" fastens onto certain details of the analysand's discourse–details which insist or stand out–the fluctuating attention of the spectator of decorative art is attracted–and we can recognize here the Gestaltist assumptions that link Gombrich's work to that of the theoreticians of *Rezeptionsaesthetik*[6]–by any gap, any break in the decorative order: "The disturbance of regularity such as a flaw in a smooth fabric can act like a magnet to the eye" (p. 110). And Gombrich goes on to give an example of just such an eye-catching irregularity, a necklace with a missing bead: "In the case of the necklace it is the missing bead, the gap between the equal units, which obtrudes on our attention" (p. 111). Now there is in *Salammbô* just such a gap, not a broken necklace, but a broken chain, and it is on this detail that my evenly poised attention, my wandering viewpoint came to settle. This detail is, to borrow Barthes' term, the *punctum* of the novel, that which in the text "pricks me," but also, Barthes adds in a meaningful parenthesis, "bruises me, is poignant to me."[7] I am referring to the gold chainlet which Salammbô wears between her ankles "to regulate her steps" ("pour régler sa marche" [p. 14/36]). We shall learn subsequently (in the chapter entitled "In the Tent," about which more later), that this chainlet, which hobbles Salammbô's walk, serves as an index both of her rank and her virginity:

> Finally he slept; then, disengaging herself from his arms, she placed one foot on the ground, and she saw that her chainlet was broken.
>
> In great families the virgins were accustomed to respect these little shackles with almost the same reverence as if they were religious symbols. Salammbô,

Engraving of the feast of the mercenaries, from chapter 1 of Salammbô *(by Georges Rochegrosse; cliché Bibliothèque nationale de France, Paris)*

blushing, rolled around her ankles the two ends of her dishonoured gold chainlet.

Il s'endormit. Alors, en se dégageant de son bras, elle posa un pied par terre, et elle s'aperçut que sa chaînette était brisée.

On accoutumait les vierges dans les grandes familles à respecter ces entraves comme une chose presque religieuse, et Salammbô, en rougissant, roula autour de ses jambes les deux tronçons de la chaîne d'or. (p. 238/212)

It is then a *Kosmos* (order, ornament), that is, an ornament which is very precisely not *purely* ornamental. Indeed, as the Hindu art historian Ananda Coomaraswamy reminds us, the very notion of the "purely ornamental" is but a modern degradation of the original function of ornament which is always and everywhere of a magical and metaphysical order. Thus in his article on ornament he proposes to demonstrate that "most of these words which imply for us the notion of something adventitious and luxurious, added to utilities but not essential to their efficacy, originally implied a completion or fulfillment of the artifact or other object in question; [that] to 'decorate' an object or person originally meant to endow the object or person with its or his 'necessary accidents,' with a view to 'proper' operation."[8]

It is no accident if in his reading of the novel Sainte-Beuve speaks of this chainlet with supreme contempt; thus, à propos of Salammbô's first appearance in the midst of the mercenaries' feast, he writes: "She thus descends amongst the Barbarians, walking in measured steps and even a little impeded by *heaven knows what gold chainlet* she drags about between her feet" (CHH, p. 417; emphasis added). This contempt is no surprise coming from a critic who . . . flaunts his lack of interest in the character of Salammbô. The case of the author of the preface we have cited so often is more complex: while admitting his lack of interest in Salammbô, he demonstrates his interest in the chainlet. Alluding to the scene where Hamilcar, seeing his daughter return with the Zaïmph, observes that the chainlet is broken, Bardèche writes: "there remains only for us to consider with some degree of perplexity, like Hamilcar, the broken chainlet between Salammbô's ankles, to which we are free to attribute whatever meaning we please" (CHH, p. 25). The gap in the chainlet opens up the text to the plural of interpretations; it is the breach through which the interpreter enters the text, as though breaking and entering. What a shame then that the very same critic who was the first to intuit the significance of the broken chainlet should feel obliged some pages later to fill the gap and bring to a halt the free play of interpretation: "The broken chainlet attached to Salammbô's ankles is, of course, as clear a symbol for Flaubert as the pieces of paper which are thrown from the lowered windows of the fiacre in *Madame Bovary*. These 'signs' were well understood by the reading public . . . They seem a bit pale and singularly timid to today's readers [lecteurs]" (CHH, p. 37). On the contrary it seems to me–but it is true that I am a female reader and a goldsmith's daughter to boot!–that this chainlet throws into sharp relief the central enigma of this narrative aptly described as "enigmatic" by Jean Rousset, namely: what happened under the tent?[9] What matters, of course, is not to discover what *really* happened under the tent, but rather to give full play to the uncertainty that marks the central event of the story. What needs to be emphasized is that the novel is organized–and this from the earliest drafts on–around a scene of interrupted defloration, a *hymen,* in the double sense that Derrida gives to this word:

The hymen, the consummation of differends, the continuity and confusion of the coitus, merges with what it seems to be derived from: the hymen as protective screen, the jewel box of virginity, the vaginal partition, the fine, invisible veil which, in front of the hystera, stands *between* the inside and the outside of a woman, and consequently between desire and fulfillment. It is neither desire nor pleasure but between the two.[10]

What does this mean? What would a text subject to the "law" or the "logic" of the hymen be like? It would be–I am quoting Derrida–a *perverse* text: "Nothing is more vicious than this suspense, this distance played at; nothing is more perverse than this rending penetration that leaves a virgin womb intact."[11] In the end this perversion comes to mime, when it is not become one with the perversion par excellence which is fetishism, both for Freud and Lacan. Indeed, if one reads Freud's essay on "Fetishism" in the light of what Derrida has to say about it either in "The Double Session" or *Glas,* one begins to understand that the celebrated split of the fetishist, he who says of castration in the words of Octave Mannoni, "I know, but all the same" ("Je sais bien, mais quand même"), is something like the paradigm of undecidability. For the fetishist, let us recall, woman is castrated and not castrated at the same time, a situation Freud describes as follows: "It is not true that, after the child has made his observation of the woman, he has preserved unaltered his belief that women have a phallus. He has retained that belief but has also given it up."[12]

The scene under the tent is to be read as a sort of primal scene of fetishism, for it shows the original and intimate relationship that links the fetish and the shiny, the undecidable and the ornamental. Let us recall that in Freud's essay, he speaks of a young man, "who had exalted a certain 'shine on the nose' into a fetishistic precondition: the surprising explanation of this was that the patient had been brought up in an English nursery but had later come to Germany, where he forgot his mother tongue, almost completely. The fetish, which originated from his earliest childhood, had to be understood in English, not German. The 'shine on the nose' [in German '*Glanz auf der Nase*']–was in reality a '*glance* at the nose.'"[13] However seductive, Freud's explanation presents the disadvantage, as Guy Rosolato has shown, of causing the German to disappear in favor of the English, thereby obscuring the link between that which is fetishized and that which shines, a link which, again according to Rosolato, is grounded in the *Glanz* whose signifier insists in the young man's lexicon:

> We must therefore take up again the indication given earlier, along with the hidden word, to find in the *glans* itself, in the organ, the initial tegumentary brilliance, but precisely attained at the summit of erection, outside of any envelope, appearing. Let us stop at this point to emphasize how essential it is for the fetishist to find this glistening, witness to his desire.[14]

In the scene under the tent, when Mâtho contemplates Salammbô, he is fascinated–and let us note in passing that in Latin *fascinum* means male organ–by a certain gleam: "She wore for ear-rings two tiny balances of sapphires, supporting a hollow pearl filled with liquid perfume, which percolated through minute perforations, moistening her bare shoulders. Mâtho watched it slowly trickle down" ("Elle avait pour pendants d'oreilles deux petites balances de saphir supportant une perle creuse, pleine d'un parfum liquide. Par les trous de la perle, de moment en moment, une gouttelette qui tombait mouillait son épaule nue. Mâtho la regardait tomber [pp. 231–232/207]).[15]

Flaubert's fetishism is hardly news. What remains to be studied are its manifestations in their specificity, for it is in the nature of the fetish to be, like the purloined letter, both perfectly visible and totally ignored: "The meaning of the fetish is not known to other people, so the fetish is not withheld from him: it is easily accessible" (p. 154). If, then, we interrogate the specificity of the chainlet, it appears that its brilliance tends to mask its function, which is to bind Salammbô's ankles. Upon closer inspection it appears that the chainlet belongs to a very particular form of fetish mentioned by Freud at the end of his essay: the bound feet of Chinese women. "Another variant, which is also a parallel to fetishism in social psychology, might be seen in the Chinese custom of mutilating the female foot and then revering it like a fetish" (p. 157). This is perhaps the place to note that when Flaubert compares Salammbô to a statue mounted on a pedestal he should be taken quite literally. From the bound ankles of Salammbô to the bound feet of Chinese women, there is not far to go, and that would account at least in part for the veneration she elicits. When Froehner described *Salammbô* as a "*carthachinoiserie*" he was closer to the mark than he could know!

It is then surely not by chance that of all the details in *Salammbô,* it is the detail of the chainlet which caught and held my attention: what is at stake here is the fate of the female protagonist under fetishism, a regime which bears certain resemblances to the feudal regime described by Julia Kristeva in *Des Chinoises*:

> Freud saw in the custom of foot-binding the symbol of the castration of woman which Chinese civilization was unique in admitting. If by "castration" we understand the necessity for something to be excluded so that the socio-symbolic order may be built–the cutting off of one part of the whole as such may be constituted as an alliance of homogeneous parts–it is interesting to note that for Chinese feudal civilization this "superfluous" quality was found in women. Is it simply a matter of knowing that woman does not have a penis? But then the insistence of underlining what's "missing" in woman by additional symbols (crippling the foot) would tend to prove that they're not all that certain; that some doubt still persists.[16]

Kristeva's text is doubly valuable to us because it stresses both the political stakes of castration and the doubt betrayed by the supplement of the fetish. Indeed, Salammbô's destiny bears eloquent witness to the threat the doubt embodied by the daughter constitutes for the socio-symbolic order incarnated by the father. For Hamilcar–as for the critic–doubt is properly speaking unbearable. Upon returning to Carthage, Hamilcar learns of the rumors regarding Mâtho's night visit to Salammbô. As a result, the reunion of father and daughter takes place under the sign of doubt, doubt that Hamilcar is not about to resolve, since he has sworn before the Council of the Hundred that he will not speak of the incident to Salammbô: "Hamilcar struggled against his inclination to break his oath. However, he kept it from pride, or *through dread of putting an end to his uncertainty,* and scanned her full in the face, trying with all his might to discover what she hid at the bottom of her heart" ("Hamilcar combattait l'envie de rompre son serment. Il le tenait par orgueil, ou *par crainte d'en finir avec son incertitude:* et il la regardait en face, de toutes ses forces, pour saisir ce qu'elle cachait au fond de son cœur" [p. 184/142, emphasis added]). Further along in the novel, just like the critic who hastens to bring the enigmatic sign back to the fold of interpretation, Hamilcar rushes to bring his errant daughter back under his sway; in the blink of an eye he will go from the recognition that the chainlet is broken to the engagement of his daughter with Narr'Havas: "His eyes alternately scanned her and the Zaïmph; and he noticed that her chainlet was broken. Then he quivered, seized by a *terrible suspicion.* But quickly resuming his impassibility, he looked at Narr'Havas askance without turning his face" ("Ses yeux se portaient alternativement sur le zaïmph et sur elle, et il remarqua que sa chaînette était rompue. Alors il frissonna, saisi par un *soupçon terrible.* Mais reprenant vite son impassibilité, il considéra Narr'Havas obliquement, sans tourner la figure" [p. 246/217, emphasis added]).

By going to Mâtho, by submitting to his caresses, by allowing the chainlet to be broken, Salammbô breaks the social contract which subordinates her to the law of the father for, as Tony Tanner has convincingly argued in *Adultery and the Novel,* for women and especially for daughters, the relationship to the city in the sense of the *polis* is entirely mediated by the father (or paternal surrogates, such as the priest Schahabarim). To speak of woman and the city, of woman in the ancient city, is always in one way or another to speak of the father-daughter relationship. This would explain the highly significant language of the first person Salammbô meets after leaving Mâtho, old Giscon:

"The Gardens" of Hamilcar, from Salammbô *(engraving by Georges Rochegrosse; cliché Bibliothèque nationale de France, Paris)*

> –"Ah! I was there!" cried he. "I heard you panting with lust like a prostitute, and when he told you of his passion, you permitted him to kiss your hands! But if the madness of your unchastity impelled you, at least you should have done as the wild beasts, which hide themselves to couple, and not thus have displayed your shame almost before the very eyes of your father!"

> –"Ah! j'étais là!" s'écria-t-il. "Je t'ai entendue râler d'amour comme une prostituée; puis il te racontait son désir, et tu te laissais baiser les mains! Mais, si la fureur de ton impudicité te poussait, tu devais faire au moins comme les bêtes fauves qui se cachent dans leurs accouplements, et ne pas étaler ta honte jusque sous les yeux de ton père!" (p. 241/214)

Nonetheless, during the brief interval that separates the scenes under Mâtho's and Hamilcar's tents, Salammbô enjoys a rare freedom, a freedom which takes the form of a mobility in sharp contrast with her customary hieratic attitude:

> She *threw* the Zaïmph around her waist, gathered up her veils, mantle, and scarf–"*I go there*" she ejaculated, and disappeared.

> Elle *jeta* le zaïmph autour de sa taille, ramassa *vivement* ses voiles, son manteau, son écharpe. –"*J'y cours*" s'écria-t-elle; et, s'échappant, Salammbô disparut. (p. 242/214)

> . . . taking the hem of her robe between her teeth, in three *bounds* she attained the platform.

> Elle prit avec ses dents le bas de sa robe qui la gênait, et, en trois *bonds,* elle se trouva sur la plateforme. (p. 242/215)

> She *quickly* dismounted.

> Elle *sauta* vite à bas de son cheval. (p. 245/217)

Considering the unbinding of energy produced by the rupture of the chainlet and the social contract it figures–because originally the decorative and decorum are inseparable–it is hardly surprising to note that Salammbô's reinscription in the circuit of symbolic exchange goes hand in hand with the putting back into place of her yoke, results finally in her rebinding: "their thumbs were tied together with a thong of leather" ("On attacha leurs pouces l'un contre l'autre avec une lanière de bœuf" [p. 246/218]).

As Hamilcar discovers, however, it is not so easy to check the doubt and disorder spread by his daughter. Even after the engagement, Hamilcar keeps questioning Salammbô about what really happened under the tent, but he keeps coming up against her enigmatic silence:

> But the Suffet always reverted to Mâtho, under the pretext of acquiring military information. He could not understand how she had employed the hours passed in his tent. Salammbô did not mention Gisco . . . She said that the *Schalischim* appeared furious, that he had shouted a great deal, and afterwards went to sleep. Salammbô told nothing more, perhaps from shame, or possibly from an excess of innocence, which caused her to attach no importance to the kisses of the soldier.

> . . . le Suffète revenait toujours à Mâtho, sous prétexte de renseignements militaires. Il ne comprenait rien à l'emploi des heures qu'elle avait passées dans la tente. En effet, Salammbô ne parlait pas de Giscon . . . Elle disait que le schalischim paraissait furieux, qu'il avait crié beaucoup, puis qu'il s'était endormi. Salammbô n'en racontait pas davantage, par honte peut-être, ou bien par un excès de candeur faisant qu'elle n'attachait guère d'importance aux baisers du soldat. (pp. 282–283/247)

It is only in the final chapter that the work of rebinding is completed and doubt held in check, if not conjured. It is as though the chainlet had multiplied, ensheathing Salammbô's entire body; the female protagonist has become ornamental from head to toe, "*a perfect phallus for perverse desire,*" to quote Jean Baudrillard:[17]

> From her ankles to her hips she was enveloped in a network of tiny links, in imitation of the scales of a fish, and lustrous as polished mother-of-pearl . . . Her headdress was made of peacocks' plumage, starred with jewels; a wide, ample mantle, white as snow, fell behind her–her elbows were close against her body; her knees pressed together; circlets of diamonds were clasped on her arms; she sat perfectly upright in a hieratic attitude.

> Des chevilles aux hanches, elle était prise dans un réseau de mailles étroites imitant les écailles d'un poisson et qui luisaient comme de la nacre . . . Elle avait une coiffe faite avec des plumes de paon étoilées de pierreries; un large manteau, blanc comme de la neige, retombait derrière elle,–et les coudes au corps, les genoux serrés, avec des cercles de diamants au haut des bras, elle restait toute droite, dans une attitude hiératique. (pp. 362–363/306)

But this is not Salammbô's final incarnation. Shortly after this apotheosis of woman as statue, of bound woman, Salammbô crumbles as though struck by lightning. This unriveting takes place immediately after the mutilation of Mâtho's corpse by the priest Schahabarim:

> Salammbô arose, like her consort, grasping a cup in her hand, to drink also. She fell, with her head lying over the back of the throne, pallid, stiff, her lips parted–and her loosened hair hung to the ground.

> Salammbô se leva comme son époux, avec une coupe à la main, afin de boire aussi. Elle retomba, la tête en arrière, par-dessus le dossier du trône,–blême, raidie, les lèvres ouvertes,–et ses cheveux dénoués pendaient jusqu'à terre. (p. 369/311)

Of all the deaths in Flaubert's fiction, Salammbô's is by far the most spectacular, the most theatrical, and the one which has received the least attention from the critics. Yet the sentence that marks the closure of *Salammbô*–"Thus died Hamilcar's daughter, for having

"The Temple of Moloch" (engraving by Georges Rochegrosse; cliché Bibliothèque nationale de France, Paris)

touched the Veil of Tanit" ("Ainsi mourut la fille d'Hamilcar pour avoir touché au manteau de Tanit" [ibid.])–clearly indicates the significance Flaubert attributes to the *manner* in which Salammbô dies. In their haste to discover what lies hidden *behind* Tanit's cloak, the critics have not given full play to the word "thus" (ainsi"). In the light of the preceding analysis, it seems to me that the privileged detail in the description of this unnatural, or better yet, unnaturalized death, is the undoing of the hair. We know that the hair is a corporeal attribute highly prized by the fetishist. In addition, Coomaraswamy notes: "the putting of one's hair in order is primarily a matter of decorum."[18]

If, as I believe, we must attribute the same symbolic or rather semiotic value to the undoing of the hair as to the breaking of the chainlet, what then does the dénouement–in its double meaning of closure and unknotting–of *Salammbô* mean? In order to answer this question, we must return to the final sentence and more particularly to the syntagm which follows "thus died" ("ainsi mourut"), that is the periphrasis, "Hamilcar's daughter" ("la fille d'Hamilcar"). For if we fold the last sentence over the first–"It was in Hamilcar's gardens, at Megara, on the outskirts of Carthage" ("C'était à Mégara, faubourg de Carthage, dans les jardins d'Hamilcar" [p. 28/1])–we discover that in both cases, whether it be a question of the gardens or the daughter of Hamilcar, it is a question of the father as proprietor. We are under the sway of the father–at least of the paternal function–and just as Emma is first and foremost Charles' wife, Salammbô is above all Hamilcar's daughter. Her death only confirms the hegemony of the father's law: because if Salammbô dies "for having touched the Veil of Tanit"–I say "if" because no narrative voice assumes this explanation–that is tantamount to saying that she dies for having violated a taboo, and taboo, Freud repeatedly asserts, comes under the jurisdiction of the father's will. But–and it is here that the detail of the undone hair comes into play–by her extravagant death, Salammbô also subverts the patriarchal order: not only does she die making a mockery of the proprieties, she also refuses to play the role of object of value and exchange assigned by her father and the phallo-theocracy he represents.

Viewed either as a sacrifice which restores order to the city or as a deus ex machina which links the daughter of Hamilcar to the daughter of Agamemnon–Iphigenia may well be the paradigmatic daughter in Western literature–Salammbô's death interests us above all because its implausibility exposes the workings of the ornamental, that is the fetishistic text. No nineteenth-century French novelist has gone further than Flaubert in laying bare the function of the female protagonist: since Salammbô did not exist, she had to be invented, for the ornamental text is the product of the close play of binding and unbinding female energy. Salammbô's famous immobility is but a surface effect which covers over a movement which is of the order of female desire; the binding of Salammbô is the price paid for the work's polished surface and that binding is not stable. Once the novel has been written, the source of the energy tapped by the ornamental text can be sacrificed.

Let us return then in closing to our starting point: the question of perspective. It might seem that by privileging the detail of the chainlet we have done little more than follow the perceptual path traced by Flaubert in his *Correspondance* when he writes: "The detail grabs you and lays hold of you and the more it engages you the less you grasp the whole; then, gradually, things harmonize and place themselves according to all the requirements of perspective."[19] Nothing could be fur-

"The Tent," from chapter 11 of Salammbô *(engraving by Georges Rochegrosse; cliché Bibliothèque nationale de France, Paris)*

ther from the truth: in what precedes, it is not a question of bringing *Salammbô* back under the regime of perspective which has ordered observation since the Renaissance. On the contrary, it is a question of valorizing positively that which Sainte-Beuve, Froehner, and even Flaubert considered the principal flaw of the novel: the lack of a privileged vantage point. To the multiplication of perspectives *in Salammbô*–well studied by Rousset–corresponds heretofore the multiplication of perspectives *on Salammbô,* that is Carthage. For in modern philosophical discourse, "perspectivism" is linked to the city, as this quotation from Nietzsche shows: "it is another town that corresponds to each point of view, and each point of view is another town."[20] Today it is no longer a question of destroying but rather of deconstructing Carthage, which may be the only way to save it.

–Naomi Schor, "Salammbô Bound," in her *Breaking the Chain. Women, Theory, and French Realist Fiction* (New York: Columbia University Press, 1985), pp. 113–126

---

1. Jacques Derrida, *La vérité en peinture,* p. 66.
2. Gustave Flaubert, *Salammbô* (Garnier-Flammarion), p. 207. All references to the French text of the novel are drawn from this edition.
3. Victor Brombert, *Flaubert par lui-même,* p. 82.
4. "I want to make something *purple*" ("je veux faire quelque chose de *pourpre*")–remark attributed to Flaubert by Jules and Edmond de Goncourt in the March 17 entry of their *Journal,* 4:167. Cf. Roland Barthes, *The Pleasure of the Text,* p. 31 for the negative connotations of the color purple under modernism.
5. E. H. Gombrich, *The Sense of Order: A Study in the Psychology of Decorative Art,* p. 116. . . .
6. The evenly poised attention of the spectator of the decorative arts is comparable in particular to the "wandering viewpoint" of the reader in Wolfgang Iser's poetics of reading; see *The Act of Reading: A Theory of Aesthetic Response.*
7. Roland Barthes, *Camera Lucida: Reflections on Photography,* p. 27. . . .
8. Ananda K. Coomaraswamy, *Figures of Speech or Figures of Thought: Collected Essays on the Traditional or 'Normal' Views of Art,* p. 86.
9. Jean Rousset, "Positions, distances, perspectives dans 'Salammbô,' *Poétique* (1971), 6:154. . . .
10. Jacques Derrida, *Dissemination,* pp. 212–213.
11. *Ibid.,* p. 216.
12. Sigmund Freud, "Fetishism," *The Standard Edition of the Complete Psychological Works,* 21:154.
13. *Ibid.,* p. 152.
14. Guy Rosolato, "Le Fétichisme dont se 'dérobe' l'objet," p. 36. . . .
15. Cf. Flaubert, *Madame Bovary,* p. 38. If we superimpose this passage from *Salammbô* on the famous description of Charles' cap, the fetishistic network linking the glans/gland/gold, and the brilliant stands out very clearly.
16. Julia Kristeva, *About Chinese Women,* p. 83.
17. Jean Baudrillard, *Poor une critique de l'économie politique du signe,* p. 104.
18. Coomaraswamy, *Figures of Speech,* p. 64. . . .
19. Flaubert, *Correspondance,* 2:148.
20. As quoted by Vincent Descombes in *Modern French Philosophy,* p. 189.

L'Éducation sentimentale: 1863–1869

After finishing Salammbô, *Flaubert wrote* Le Château des cœurs *(The Castle of Hearts) with the collaboration of Louis Bouilhet and Charles d'Osmoy; however, the* féerie *(fairy play) was not accepted for onstage production. He then started sketching scenarios for two novels,* L'Éducation sentimentale *and* Bouvard et Pécuchet, *and after months of hesitation eventually chose the first subject, for which he elaborated the plan with the help of Bouilhet. The writing of* L'Éducation sentimentale *began on 1 September 1864 and was not completed until 16 May 1869. As usual, Flaubert did considerable research and gathered much information from friends, such as Jules Duplan, Ernest Feydeau, and Maxime Du Camp.*

The years of L'Éducation sentimentale *correspond also to a period of fame in Flaubert's life; he regularly went to the salon of Princess Mathilde, was invited to balls given by the emperor, and even received the* Légion d'honneur *on 15 August 1866. At the Magny dinners in Paris (organized by Charles-Augustin Sainte-Beuve) he met writers such as Ivan Turgenev, Hippolyte Taine, and Ernest Renan; he also met George Sand, who became one of his most faithful correspondents.*

The completion of L'Éducation sentimentale *marked the beginning of a difficult period for Flaubert: Bouilhet died on 18 July 1869, before he could read the final version of the novel; then Sainte-Beuve died on 13 October. Moreover, after it was published on 17 November 1869,* L'Éducation sentimentale *was violently criticized by the press.*

Gustave Flaubert, circa 1866 (watercolor by Eugène Giraud; cliché Bibliothèque nationale de France, Paris)

A New Novel with an Old Title

A complex novel—part bildungsroman, part historical or social novel, part love story, and in large part satire— L'Éducation sentimentale *is the story of the life and times of Frédéric Moreau, which was inspired in many respects by Flaubert's own experiences. Although Flaubert explored some of the material he had already written in the novel from his youth bearing the same title (*L'Éducation sentimentale, *1845), this work was an entirely new creation. Besides the depiction of an entire generation and Frédéric's platonic love for Madame Arnoux and love affairs with the* lorette *(half prostitute, half kept woman) Rosanette Bron, the banker's wife Madame Dambreuse, and the provincial young bourgeois Louise Roque,* L'Éducation sentimentale *presents such a negative depiction of the period—in particular the Revolution of 1848 and its consequences leading to the coup d'état and to the Second Empire—that Flaubert may well have anticipated the public's first misunderstanding and discomfort with the novel.*

Flaubert wrote this letter to Sand from Croisset as he was still wrestling with his novel. He was to be confirmed in his assessment of contemporary criticism when L'Éducation sentimentale *was published.*

Charles d'Osmoy, who with Louis Bouilhet wrote the verse passages of Le Château des cœurs *while Flaubert wrote the prose dialogue (Collections de la Bibliothèque municipale de Rouen. Cliché Thierry Ascencio-Parvy)*

Flaubert to George Sand, 2 February 1869

Ma chère maître,

Your old troubadour is the very picture of exhaustion. I spent a week in Paris verifying boring details (7 to 9 hours of cabs a day, a fine way to get rich with Literature! Ah well . . .) I have just read over my outline. The amount I still have to write overwhelms me, or rather it makes me almost vomit from discouragement. It's always like this when I get back to work. It's then that I'm bored, bored, bored. But this time it's worse than ever. That's why I so dread any interruption of the grind. I had no choice, however. I had myself carted to undertakers' establishments, to Père-Lachaise, to the valley of Montmorency, past shops selling religious paraphernalia, etc.[1]

In short, I still have four or five months' work ahead of me. What a sigh of relief I'll send up when it's done! And what a long while it will be before I tackle the bourgeois again! It's time I enjoyed myself!

I have seen both Sainte-Beuve and the Princess. And I know everything about their quarrel: it seems to me irreparable. Sainte-Beuve was angry with Dalloz,[2] and went over to *Le Temps*. The Princess begged him not to. He wouldn't listen. That's the whole story. My opinion, if you care to have it, is this: the first fault was committed by the Princess, who was intemperate: but the second and more serious offender is Sainte-Beuve, who acted ungallantly. When you have so accommodating a friend, and when this friend has provided you with an income of 30,000 livres a year, you owe her some consideration. It seems to me that in Sainte-Beuve's place I'd have said: "If you disapprove, let's say no more about it." He was bad-mannered and lacking in magnanimity. What disgusted me a little, just between ourselves, was the way he sang the praises of the Emperor. Yes: to me! Praise of Badinguet! And we were alone, too.

The Princess took things too seriously from the start. I wrote to her, siding with Sainte-Beuve, whereas he, I'm sure, found me unresponsive. That was why, to justify himself in my eyes, he protested his love for Isidore, which I found rather humiliating. For it amounted to taking me for an utter imbecile.

I think he's preparing himself for a funeral like Béranger's, and that he's jealous of old Hugo's ability to speak the language of the people. Why write for newspapers when you can write books and aren't starving to death?

He's far from being a sage; he's not like you! Your Strength charms and amazes me. I mean the Strength of your entire person, not only your brain.

You spoke of criticism in your last letter, saying it will soon disappear. I think, on the contrary, that it's only just beginning. The trend is the opposite of what it used to be, that's all. (In the days of La Harpe, critics were grammarians; in the days of Sainte-Beuve and Taine they're historians.) When will they be *artists,* only artists, but *real* artists? Where have you ever seen a piece of criticism that is concerned, intensely concerned, with the work in itself? The setting in which it was produced and the circumstances that occasioned it are very closely analyzed. But the *inner* poetics that brought it into being? Its composition? Its style? The author's point of view? *Never.*

Such criticism as that would require great imagination and great goodwill. I mean an ever-ready faculty of enthusiasm. And then taste–a quality rare even among the best, so very rare that it is no longer even mentioned.

What infuriates me daily is to see a masterpiece and a disgrace put on the same level. They put down the mighty, and exalt those of low degree.[3] Nothing could be more stupid or immoral.

Speaking of stupidity, "I permitted myself to be told" (as le sieur de Brantôme puts it) that Plessy is becoming boring and unsociable. Her friends avoid her.

In Père-Lachaise I was overcome by a deep and painful disgust for mankind. You cannot imagine the fetishism of the tombs. Your true Parisian is more idolatrous than a black. I felt like dropping down into one of the graves.

And people with "advanced ideas" can find nothing better to do than rehabilitate Robespierre! Look at Hamel's book! If there were to be another Republic they'd start blessing Liberty Trees again as a powerful contribution to politics.[4]

Give your two granddaughters my love. Je vous baise sur les deux joues, tendrement.

Your old
Gve Flaubert

When are we going to meet? I expect to be in Paris from Easter to the end of May. This summer I'll come and see you at Nohant. I promise myself.

–*Flaubert~Sand: The Correspondence,* translated and edited by Francis Steegmuller and Barbara Bray (New York: Knopf, 1993), pp. 133–135

---

1. Continuing to document himself for *L'Éducation sentimentale.*
2. Sainte-Beuve had broken with the semi-official *Moniteur universel* and its editor Paul Dalloz over the insistence that he delete an unfavourable reference to Mgr Le Courtier, bishop of Montpellier, from one of his weekly articles. He had gone over to *Le Temps,* the mouthpiece of the liberal opposition, despite Princesse Mathilde's request that he not do so. In her displeasure the princess revealed the spirit of her benefactions to Sainte-Beuve in saying that his acceptance of a senatorship (for which she had recommended him) had made him "a vassal of the Empire". (André Billy, *Sainte-Beuve, Sa vie et son temps,* Paris, 1952.)
3. A reference to *Luke,* i, 52.
4. Since the recent restoration of permission to hold public meetings, there had been a number in which orators invoked the spirit of 1789, exalting Robespierre, etc. . . .

* * *

Sand, who was working on a new novel, Pierre qui roule *(Rolling Stone, 1870), replied from her house in Nohant, located in the Indre valley.*

Sand to Flaubert, 11 February 1869

While you've been trotting about for your novel I've been doing my best not to get on with mine. I let myself indulge in *indefensible* fantasies. I get caught up in a book I read, which sets me off scribbling something that will merely lie on my desk, bringing in absolutely nothing.[1] It amused, or rather compelled, me–for it's no good my struggling against such whims. They just irrupt and take me over . . . I'm not as strong as you think, you see.

As for our friend [Sainte-Beuve], he's ungrateful, whereas our other friend [Princesse Mathilde] is too exacting. As you say, they're both in the wrong; and neither is at fault. It's the social mechanism that's to blame. The kind of gratitude, or rather obedience, that she insists on belongs to a tradition which the present age still exploits (and there's the rub) but no longer accepts as a duty. The attitudes of a person who receives a favour have changed; those of a person who bestows a favour

Princess Mathilde Bonaparte, a cousin of Napoleon III and a patron of the arts. Flaubert began visiting her home on the Rue de Courcelles in Paris in the early 1860s (photograph by A. Braun, circa 1860; Bibliothèque nationale de France, Paris).

Charles-Augustin Sainte-Beuve, who wrote prominent reviews of Flaubert's previous works, died in 1869 before the publication of L'Éducation sentimentale *(caricature by Eugène Giraud; cliché Bibliothèque nationale de France, Paris).*

ought, correspondingly, to change. A benefactress should remember that she can't buy another's moral liberty–and as for *him,* he should have realized he'd seem to be under an obligation. The simplest solution would have been not to want an income of 30,000 livres. It's so easy to do without it! We must just let them get on with it. They won't catch us at that game–we've got more sense.

You say some very good things about criticism. But it would take artists to practice it as you prescribe, and artists are too busy with their own work to delve into that of others.

Heavens, what lovely weather! I hope you at least enjoy it through your window? I wager the tulip tree is in bud. Here the peach and apricot trees are flowering. Everyone says they'll get spoiled. That doesn't stop them from being pretty and unconcerned.

We've had our family carnival. Niece, great-nephews and so on. We all wore fancy dress. No difficulty about that here–you've only got to go up to the wardrobe room and come down again as Cassandra or Scapin, Mezzetino, Figaro or Basilio. All the costumes are accurate and very handsome. The best of the lot was Lolo as young Louis XIII in crimson and white satin trimmed with silver braid. I spent three days making that extremely stylish costume, and it looked so pretty and droll on a little girl of three that we were all quite taken aback. Then we played charades, had supper, and larked about till dawn. We still have plenty of energy, you see, even if we are stuck in the back of beyond. So I put off business and going to Paris as long as I can. If you were there I wouldn't be so reluctant. But you're only going to town at the end of March and I can't hang back as long as that. Still, you do promise to come here this summer, and we're absolutely counting on it, even if I have to come and drag you by the hair. Much love in return for that welcome hope.

G. Sand

–*Flaubert~Sand: The Correspondence,* pp. 135–136

---

1. Sand had been reading a French translation of *El Condenado por Desconfidado,* by Tirso de Molina, which preached the Catholic dogma of Grace. It inspired her to write a short novel, *Lupo Liverani,* published in *La Revue des Deux Mondes* beginning 1 December 1869.

Sand as Defender

Sand and Flaubert exchanged several letters about her own positive response to the novel and the negative reaction of most reviewers. The conservative press was particularly harsh on Flaubert and, among other critiques, violently condemned the episode in part 3, chapter 1, where the character of Père Roque calmly shoots down a republican prisoner, kept in the cellar of the Tuileries, who asks for bread. However, although the political climate was not a quiet one because of the success of some republican opposition to the Second Empire (forty republicans had been elected in May 1869, all opposed to Napoleon III), Flaubert was happy to report that the sales for L'Éducation sentimentale *were quite good. He was correcting* Le Château des cœurs *once again, in the hope that the* féerie *would be accepted for production on stage, and had approached Raphaël Félix, director of the theater of the Porte-Saint-Martin.*

Sand to Flaubert, 30 November 1869

Cher ami de mon cœur,

I made a point of re-reading your book, and my daughter-in-law has read it too, as have some of my young men, all sincere and sensitive readers and not at all stupid. And we all agree it's a fine book, as forceful as the best of Balzac's novels and more real–that's to say, more faithful to the truth throughout. It takes great art, exquisite form, and rigour such as yours to be able to dispense with the ornaments of fancy. And yet, to the picture you

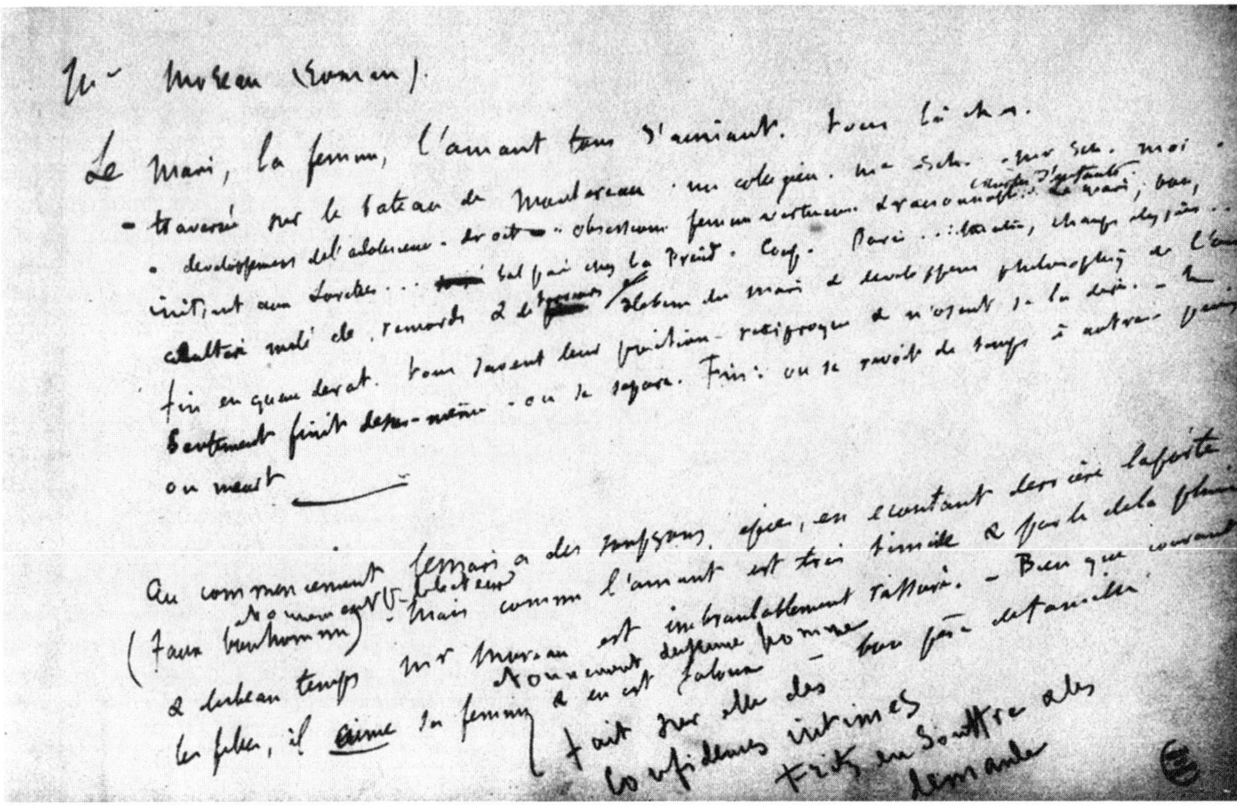

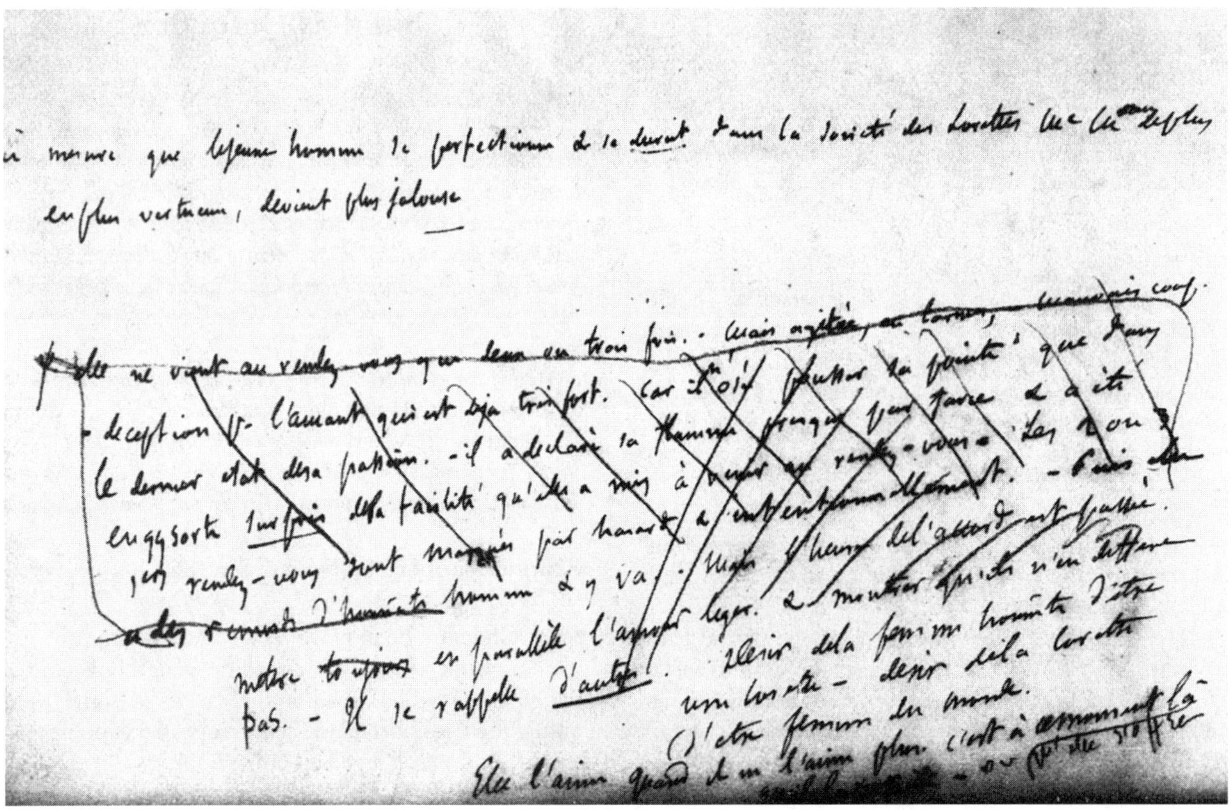

Preliminary notes that Flaubert made in 1862 when he began planning L'Éducation sentimentale
(courtesy of the Bibliothèque historique de la Ville de Paris)

depict, you add poetry with a lavish hand, whether your characters understand it or not. Rosanette doesn't know what kind of grass she's walking on at Fontainebleau, yet she's poetic all the same. All that is masterly, and your place is assured for ever. So take things as easy as possible, so that you may live long and produce much.

I've seen a couple of short articles that didn't seem too hostile to your success, but I don't really know what goes on–politics seems to be swallowing up everything else. Let me know what happens. If anyone should fail to do you justice I'd lose my temper and say what I think.

I don't know exactly when, but some time in the coming month I'll probably come and see you–and pick you up if I can tear you away from Paris. My children are still counting on it, and we all send you our praise and our love.

À toi, ton vieux troubadour

G. Sand

–*Flaubert~Sand: The Correspondence,* p. 167

* * *

Flaubert wrote from Paris.

Flaubert to Sand, 3 December 1869

Chère bon maître,

Your old troubadour is being greatly berated in the press. Look at last Monday's *Constitutionnel* and this morning's *Gaulois*–they don't mince their words. They call me a cretin and a scoundrel. Barbey d'Aurevilly's piece in the *Constitutionnel* is typical, and the one by our friend Sarcey, though less violent, is no more complimentary than the rest.[1] These gentlemen protest in the name of morality and the ideal! I have also been flayed in the *Figaro* and in *Paris,* by Cesena and Duranty.

I don't care in the least, but it does surprise me that there should be so much hatred and dishonesty.

The *Tribune,* the *Pays* and the *Opinion nationale,* on the other hand, praise me to the skies.[2]

As for my friends–people who received copies adorned with my signature–they are afraid of compromising themselves, and speak to me about everything except the book. Instances of courage are rare. Nevertheless, the book is selling very well despite the political situation, and Lévy seems satisfied.

I know that the Rouen bourgeois are furious with me because of old Roque and the cellar of the Tuileries. Their opinion is that "the publication of such books should be forbidden" (I quote verbatim), that I favour the Reds, that I am guilty of fanning revolutionary passions, etc. etc!

In short, I have gathered very few laurels so far, and have been wounded by no rose petals.[3]

I told you, didn't I, that I'm re-working the *féerie?* I am now writing a horse-racing scene,[4] and have removed everything I considered conventional. Raphaël Félix doesn't seem in any hurry to read it. *Problème!*

In a fortnight I'll be finished, and ready to set off in your direction.

Comme j'ai envie de vous embrasser!
Mille tendresses de votre vieux
Gve Flaubert

All the papers adduce as proof of my iniquity the episode of la Turque[5]–which they garble, of course; and Sarcey compares me to the marquis de Sade, whom he admits he hasn't read!

None of this destroys my composure. But I keep asking myself: what's the point of publishing?

–*Flaubert~Sand: The Correspondence,* pp. 167–168

---

1. Barbey d'Aurevilly reproached Flaubert especially for his "lack of originality" and for his "endless descriptions." Sarcey concluded his indictment by exclaiming, "What a wretched abuse of talent!"
2. Articles by Emile Zola, Paul de Léoni and Jules Levallois.
3. An allusion to one of the Roman "histories" of Claudius Aelianus (d. A.D. 140), in which the Sybarite Smindyrides complains of spending a sleepless night because one of the rose petals strewn on his bed was folded in two.
4. The final, published text of *Le Château des cœurs* contains no such episode.
5. The much discussed last scene in the book, when Moreau and Deslauriers recall the fiasco of their adolescent approach to a brothel as having been "the best moment of their lives."

* * *

As the critics continued to publish negative comments on his novel, Flaubert felt compelled to ask Sand to write a defense of L'Éducation sentimentale, *which she immediately did. After some hesitation, she sent the review to Émile de Girardin, director of* La Presse, *where the article was published on 22 December 1869. Sand praised the structure of the novel and Flaubert's mastery of detail, calling him "a great poet and an excellent writer."*

Flaubert to Sand, 7 December 1869

Chère maître,

The way they're all jumping on your old troubadour is incredible. People to whom I've sent a copy of my novel are afraid to talk to me about it,[1] either for fear of compromising themselves or out of pity for me. The most indulgent are of the opinion that what I've written is merely a series of scenes, and that composition and pattern are completely lacking. Saint-Victor, who extols the books of Arsène Houssaye, won't write about mine, finding it too bad. *Voilà.* Théo is away,[2] and no one (absolutely no one) is coming to my defence.

Therefore (you can guess what's coming), if you would care to take on that role you'd oblige me. If it embarrasses you, do nothing. No mere indulgence between us.

Another thing: yesterday Raphaël and Michel Lévy heard me read the *féerie.* Applause, enthusiasm. I felt that they were about to give me a contract on the spot. Raphaël understood the play so well that he made two or three excellent suggestions. I found him a charming fellow, by the way. He asked me to give him until Saturday for a definite answer.

But just now, a letter (very polite) from said Raphaël, in which he tells me that the *féerie* would involve him in expenses he cannot afford. Another blow! We must look elsewhere.

Nothing new at the Odéon.

Sarcey has published a second article against me. Barbey d'Aurevilly claims that I pollute a stream by washing myself in it[3] (Sic). All this upsets me not the slightest. But God! How stupid people are!

When are you coming to Paris?

Je vous embrasse.

Gve Flaubert

–*Flaubert~Sand: The Correspondence,* pp. 168–169

---

1. Of the hundred and fifty or so people to whom he had sent copies of *L'Éducation sentimentale,* Flaubert wrote to Jules Duplan on December 9, thirty at most had replied.
2. Théophile Gautier was in Egypt, sent by the *Journal officiel* to cover the festivities celebrating the opening of the Suez Canal.
3. In his second article (*Le Gaulois,* 4 December) Sarcey reproached Flaubert especially for his impassivity and superabundance of descriptions, and he ended: "*Oh, quel ennui! quel ennui!*" Barbey d'Aurevilly had written in his article in the *Constitutionnel:* "Flaubert has neither grace nor melancholy: his robustness is like that of Courbet's painting 'Women Bathing'–women washing themselves in a brook, polluting it."

* * *

Sand to Flaubert, 9–10 December 1869

Mon camarade, the thing is done. The article will go off tomorrow. I'm sending it to . . . whom? The answer, please, by telegram. I feel like sending it to Girardin, but perhaps you've a better idea–I'm not very well up in the importance and prestige of the various papers. Send me a wire with a name and the address (I've got Girardin's).

I'm not altogether pleased with what I've written. I've had a kind of sprain and a temperature the last couple of days. But I don't want to lose any time.

Je t'embrasse.

G. Sand

–*Flaubert~Sand: The Correspondence,* p. 169

* * *

Flaubert to Sand, 10 December 1869

Chère maître, bon comme du bon pain,

I have just sent you a telegram saying "To Girardin." *La Liberté* will print your article immediately.

What do you say about my friend Saint-Victor, who refused to write one, because he found the book "bad." You don't have so squeamish a conscience!

I continue to be dragged through the mud. *La Gironde* calls me Prud'homme. That's something new.

How can I thank you? I long to say all kinds of affectionate things. I have so many in my heart that none comes to my fingertips. What a kind woman you are, and what a *brave homme!* Not to mention the rest.

Je vous embrasse.

Your old troubadour,

Gve Flaubert

Take care of the sprain, and the temperature, and give me news of both.

–*Flaubert~Sand: The Correspondence,* p. 170

* * *

Sand to Flaubert, 10–11 December 1869

I've spent today and this evening rewriting my article. I'm feeling better, and it's a bit clearer. I'll expect to have your telegram tomorrow. If you don't veto it I'll send the article to Ulbach–his paper starts up on the 15th of this month[1] and I had a letter from him this morning begging me for some sort of contribution. I imagine a lot of people will read this first number, so it should be good publicity. Lévy ought to be more knowledgeable than we are about what's best to do: consult him.

You sound surprised by all the ill-will. You're being too naive. You don't realize how original your book is, and how many people it's bound to offend because of the force of the writing. And there are you fondly imagining you're producing things that will pass unnoticed!

I've laid stress on the book's construction. That's what people understand the least, yet it's the novel's strongest point. I've tried to show the unsophisticated reader how to read it: that's the kind of reader who makes a book a success. The clever ones can't bear anyone else to *have* a success. I haven't bothered with the people who are actuated by malice: it would be doing them too much honour.

[unsigned]

–*Flaubert~Sand: The Correspondence,* p. 170

---

1. *La Cloche.* The first number appeared on 19 December.

Critical Views of *L'Éducation sentimentale*

Beyond contemporary journalism and reviews, critiques of L'Éducation sentimentale *were generally negative until well into the twentieth century. Today, however, many critics consider* L'Éducation sentimentale *to be the best of Flaubert's novels. The following section provides a sampling of views.*

When Henry James in 1902 wrote a foreword to a new translation of Madame Bovary, *he still was not able to understand Flaubert's art in* L'Éducation sentimentale. *In this excerpt he cites the insights of the French critic Émile Faguet, who had written a monograph on Flaubert in 1899.*

An Epic without Air: James on *L'Éducation sentimentale*

We meet Frédéric first, we remain with him long, as a *moyen,* a provincial bourgeois of the mid-century, educated and not without fortune, thereby with freedom, in whom the life of his day reflects itself. Yet the life of his day, on Flaubert's showing, hangs together with the poverty of Frédéric's own inward or for that matter outward life; so that, the whole thing being, for scale, intention and extension, a sort of epic of the usual (with the Revolution of 1848 introduced indeed as an episode,) it affects us as an epic without air, without wings to lift it; reminds us in fact more than anything else of a huge balloon, all of silk pieces strongly sewn together and patiently blown up, but that absolutely refuses to leave the ground. The discrimination I here make as against our author is, however, the only one inevitable in a series of remarks so brief. What it really represents–and nothing could be more curious–is that Frédéric enjoys his position not only without the aid of a single "sympathetic" character of consequence, but even without the aid of one with whom we can directly communicate. Can we communicate with the central personage? or would we really if we could? A hundred times no, and if he himself can communicate with the people shown us as surrounding him this only proves him of their kind. Flaubert on his "real" side was in truth an ironic painter, and ironic to a tune that makes his final accepted state, his present literary dignity and "classic" peace, superficially anomalous. There is an explanation to which I shall immediately come; but I find myself feeling for a moment longer in presence of "L'Éducation" how much more interesting a writer may be on occasion by the given failure than by the given success. Successes pure and simple disconnect and dismiss him; failures–though I admit they must be a bit qualified–keep him in touch and in relation. Thus it is that as the work of a "grand écrivain" "L'Éducation," large, laboured, immensely "written," with beautiful passages and a general emptiness, with a kind of leak in its stored sadness, moreover, by which its moral dignity escapes–thus it is that Flaubert's ill-starred novel is a curiosity for a literary museum. Thus it is also that it suggests a hundred reflections, and suggests perhaps most of them directly to the intending labourer in the same field. If in short, as I have said, Flaubert is the novelist's novelist, this performance does more than any other toward making him so.

I have to add in the same connection that I had not lost sight of Madame Arnoux, the main ornament of "L'Éducation," in pronouncing just above on its deficiency in the sympathetic. Madame Arnoux is exactly the author's one marked attempt, here or elsewhere, to represent beauty otherwise than for the senses, beauty of character and life; and what becomes of the attempt is a matter highly significant. M. Faguet praises with justice his conception of the figure and of the relation, the relation that never bears fruit, that keeps Frédéric adoring her, through hindrance and change, from the beginning of life to the end; that keeps her, by the same constraint, forever immaculately "good," from youth to age, though deeply moved and cruelly tempted and sorely tried. Her contacts with her adorer are not even frequent, in proportion to the field of time; her conditions of fortune, of association and occupation are almost sordid, and we see them with the march of the drama, such as it is, become more and more so; besides which–I again remember that M. Faguet excellently notes it–nothing in the nature of "parts" is attributed to her; not only is she not presented as clever, she is scarce invested with a character at all. Almost nothing that she says is repeated, almost nothing that she does is shown. She is an image none the less beautiful and vague, an image of passion cherished and abjured, renouncing all sustenance and yet persisting in life. Only she has for real distinction the extreme drawback that she is offered us quite preponderantly through Frédéric's vision of her, that we see her practically in no other light. Now Flaubert unfortunately has not been able not so to discredit Frédéric's vision in general, his vision of everyone and everything, and in particular of his own life, that it makes a medium good enough to convey adequately a noble impression. Madame Arnoux is of course ever so much the best thing in his life–which is saying little; but his life is made up of such queer material that we find ourselves displeased at her being "in" it on whatever terms; all the more that she seems scarcely to affect, improve or determine it. Her creator in short never had a more awkward idea than this attempt to give us the benefit of such a conception in such a way; and even though I have still something else to say about that I may as well speak of it at once as a mistake that gravely counts against him. It is but one of three, no doubt, in all his work; but I shall not, I trust, pass for extravagant if I call it the most indicative. What makes it so is its being the least superficial; the two others are, so to speak, intellectual, while this is somehow moral. It was a mistake, as I have already hinted, to propose to register in so mean a consciousness as that of such a hero so large and so mixed a quantity of life as "L'Éducation" clearly intends; and it was a mistake of the tragic sort that is a theme mainly for silence to have embarked on "Bouvard et Pécuchet" at all, not to have given it up sooner than be given up by it. But these were at the worst not wholly compromising blunders. What *was* compromising–and the great point is that it remained so, that nothing has an equal weight against it–is the unconsciousness of error in respect to the opportunity that would have counted as his finest. We feel not so much that Flaubert misses it, for that we could bear; but that he doesn't *know* he misses it is what stamps the blunder. We do not pretend to say how he might have shown us Madame Arnoux better–that was his own affair. What is ours is that he really thought he was showing her as well as he could, or as she might be shown; at which we veil our face. For once that he had a conception quite apart, apart I mean from the array of his other conceptions and more delicate than any, he "went," as we say, and spoiled it. Let me add in all tenderness, and to make up for possibly too much insistence, that it is the only stain on his shield; let me even confess that I should not wonder if, when all is said, it is a blemish no one has ever noticed.

–Henry James, "Gustave Flaubert," in his *Notes on Novelists* (New York: Scribners, 1914), pp. 84–88

* * *

In these excerpts from a 1922 essay, John Middleton Murry misquotes the text of Flaubert's novel several times.

Stylistic Faults in *L'Éducation sentimentale*

There are two Flauberts. One was born on the 12th of December, 1821, in the surgeon's house at Rouen hospital; the other in enthusiastic minds in the last quarter of the nineteenth century. One was a broad, big-boned, lovable, rather simple-minded man, with the look and the laugh of a farmer, who spent his life in agonies over the intensive culture of half a dozen curiously assorted volumes; the other was an incorporeal giant, a symbol, a war-cry, a banner under which a youthful army marched and marches still to the rout of the bourgeois and the revolution of literature.

To distinguish these beings from each other is not so difficult as to understand how they came to be so completely interfused that the separation of the legend and the reality may appear an act of wanton iconoclasm. So much has been derived from the legendary Flaubert, so many advancing waves have borne his name on the crest of their attack, that he has acquired the dignity of an institution. We have a critic of the stature of Remy de Gourmont declaring that Flaubert is the very archetype of the creative writer, for two reasons; because he devoted his life and his personality to his work, suffering nothing to be wasted in the exigencies and delights of mere living, and because he was pre-eminently gifted with visual imagination.

It is not easy to see why the value of a writer's work should depend upon the completeness of his incineration on the altar of Art. A good writer has to make sacrifices, of course, but he need not (indeed, he had better not) burn himself to ashes. Greater writers than Flaubert have not felt the necessity. To one who is not a born Flaubertian the astonishing tortures he inflicted upon himself would naturally suggest, not that his genius was pre-eminent, but that his creative impulse was not of the strongest. While the truth about his visual imagination is that it was not of the finest quality. Flaubert adored images; he believed, truly enough, that the highest poetic faculty is mastery of metaphor; he fancied that when he was wholly free to write what pleased him–though when was he not?–he would triumphantly indulge his passion. Yet, in fact, Flaubert's use of imagery is almost invariably strained or commonplace, and often both. Take the similes with which *L'Éducation Sentimentale* begins and ends: neither is successful. Here is the first:

> "Enfin le navire partit; et les deux berges, peuplées de magasins, de chantiers et d'usines, filèrent comme deux larges rubans qu'on [*sic,* for 'que l'on'] déroule."

Élisa Schlésinger, the model for Marie Arnoux, the woman Frédéric Moreau idealizes in L'Éducation sentimentale. *Some sources say that the photograph was taken in 1864, the year Flaubert began writing his novel, while others put the year as 1872, the year Madame Schlésinger may have made her last visit to Flaubert's home in Croisset (Collections de la Bibliothèque municipale de Rouen. Cliché Thierry Ascencio-Parvy).*

[Finally the boat left; and the two banks, filled with stores, yards and factories, flew past like two wide ribbons that one unwinds.]

The image is forced, and it gives the wrong tempo to the opening movement. A torpedo-boat destroyer could not steam fast enough to justify it wholly, and this was a river-steamer on the Seine. The second simile is used by Madame Arnoux when she revisits Frédéric Moreau:

> Elle s'étonnait de sa mémoire. Cependant, elle lui dit:
>
> –Quelquefois, vos paroles me reviennent comme un écho lointain, comme le son d'un cloche apporté par le vent: et il me semble que vous êtes là, quand je lis les [*sic,* for 'des'] passages d'amour dans les livres.

> [She marveled at his memory. However, she told him:
>
> –Sometimes, your words come back to me like a remote echo, like the sound of a bell carried by the wind; and it seems to me that you are here, when I read in books passages about love.]

This is, indeed, not a visual image; but its discrepancy is not less remarkable for that. Had the words been given to the second-rate romanticism of Emma Bovary they might have been in place. But Madame Arnoux was designed to be Emma's opposite. For the sake of a worn-out poetical metaphor, Flaubert was willing to make his heroine speak out of character. It would be hard to find an absolutely convincing metaphor in the whole of his work. Some of them are really comic, as this of Rosanette. "Toutes ces images qu'elle se créait lui faisait [*sic,* for 'faisaient'] comme autant de fils qu'elle aurait perdus, *l'excès de la douleur multipliant sa maternité. . . .*" ['All these images she created were like so many sons she never had, *the excess of pain multiplying her maternity . . .* '].

The fact is that Flaubert did not possess the finest kind of literary discrimination. He had an unusual visual faculty which he turned to good account, but the use he made of it was primitive. Most of his descriptions are visual pageantry, sometimes impressive, sometimes beautiful, sometimes as tedious as the tail-end of a Lord Mayor's show when we are waiting to cross the road. Of the faculty which employs visual imagery to differentiate the subtler emotions of the soul, Flaubert had little or nothing at all. The true faculty of metaphor was denied him.

. . . .

. . . Having chosen the ivory tower, he had to justify its existence. Hating life, he had to be convinced that literature was also indifferent to it. Accordingly he tried to persuade himself that the subject-matter of a work of literature was of no account. A structure of beauty could be raised upon no matter what foundation, and beauty was absolute and incommensurable.

Two things are remarkable about this aesthetic theory of Flaubert's; the theory itself, and his manner of holding it. Though it seemed to resemble the doctrine held by other French romantics of his generation, it was profoundly different. Baudelaire, for instance, who claimed for the poet the right to deal with subjects generally held to be immoral, made this claim on behalf of what he considered to be the higher morality of art. He believed that the importance of a subject was independent of the moral estimation in which it was held, but he insisted that the subject should be important. Flaubert, on the other hand, tried to believe that the significance of a subject was an unessential quality. The writer actually endowed it with importance by the beauty of the language in which he treated it. Pressed to its logical conclusion, the theory is almost meaningless, for the writer must choose a subject and must have motives for his choice. So that it is not surprising that Flaubert never wholly satisfied himself. He wavered. At one moment he asserted that 'tout découle de la conception' ['everything stems from conception'], at another that style was 'the soul beneath the words,' at yet another that everything in literature depended on character. These beliefs do not necessarily conflict with one another, but not one of them can really be reconciled with the notion that the subject-matter is indifferent. For some reason Flaubert was incapable of thinking the question out to a conclusion. His formulated theory of writing went no farther than the injunction–valuable enough–to think clearly, express precisely, and read aloud to test the rhythm.

. . . .

A style of which the greatest writers have no need, to the want of which they owe their greatness, is a dubious light to follow. It was less dangerous for Flaubert, who saw his own limitations clearly, than for those who have blindly followed him. But probably Flaubert also paid a price for his obsession; probably it distracted his attention from the content of his work and induced him to spend energies that might have gone to the expansion of his sensibility upon the painful polishing of a hollow surface; the substance which could have made it solid his starved sensibility could not provide. One dare not dogmatise. Who knows for certain that a writer by taking thought can add a cubit

Flaubert's niece Caroline, who married Ernest Commanville, a wood merchant from Dieppe, on 6 April 1864. Flaubert encouraged the marriage because Commanville was considered a successful businessman (Collections de la Bibliothèque municipale de Rouen. Clichés Thierry Ascencio-Parvy).

to the stature of his soul? Possibly Flaubert, being the man he was, made a right choice; possibly he persevered where he could make some progress and abandoned the road along which advance was barred. But the probability and the evidence point the other way. The book whose style he laboured least–a Flaubertian minimum is not as other men's–is the one by which he is chiefly remembered. The youthful *Madame Bovary* has a validity which he was to achieve only once again, in *Un Cœur Simple. Madame Bovary* alone answers to his own definition of a great work of literature; it gathers scattered personalities into a type and brings new personalities to the consciousness of the human race. Emma Bovary and Monsieur Homais are figures of this kind; they are (except perhaps Félicie [*sic,* for 'Félicité']) the only ones in Flaubert's work.

Flaubert began his career with what is, take it all in all, a masterpiece; he was to write no other. *L'Education Sentimentale* is not one. It may be life, but it is not living; it is a work of history rather than literature. Flaubert had no certain hold of his characters, and his handling of his theme at the crucial moment falls to the level of melodrama. The most famous passage in the book is the death of Dussardier:–

> Mais, sur les marches de Tortoni, un homme–Dussardier–remarquable de loin à sa haute taille, restait sans plus bouger qu'une cariatide.
>
> Un des agents qui marchait en tête, le tricorne sur les yeux, le menaça de son épée.
>
> L'autre alors, s'avançant d'un pas, se mit à crier,–
>
> –"Vive la République!"
>
> Il tomba sur le dos, les bras en croix.
>
> Un hurlement d'horreur s'éleva de la foule. L'agent fit un cercle autour de lui avec son regard; et Frédéric, béant, reconnut Sénécal.
>
> Il voyagea.
>
> Il connut la melancolie des paquebots, les froids réveils sous la tente, l'étourdissement des paysages et des ruines, l'amertume des sympathies interrompues.
>
> Il revint.
>
> [But, on the steps of Tortoni's, a man–Dussardier–remarkable from afar because of his size, stayed as motionless as a caryatid.
>
> One of the agents who was walking in front, his three-cornered hat down over his eyes, threatened him with his sword.
>
> So the other, taking one step forward, began to shout:
>
> –"Long live the Republic!"
>
> He fell on his back, his arms spread out.
>
> A cry of horror rose from the crowd. The agent looked around him; and Frédéric, open-mouthed, recognized Sénécal.
>
> He traveled.
>
> He came to know the melancholy of steamships, the cold awakenings under the tent, the exhilaration of landscapes and ruins, the bitterness of interrupted friendships.
>
> He came back.]

'Et Frédéric, béant, reconnut Sénécal' ['And Frédéric, open-mouthed, recognized Sénécal'], has been for years the object of an esoteric admiration as a masterpiece of style. In a different book it might, indeed, have been overwhelming; in the gray monotone of *L'Education Sentimentale* it is a splash of discordant red. The dramatic artifice tears through the even texture of the narrative: it belongs to another world of seeing and feeling, and the measure of its discordance is our astonishment at Sénécal's surprising change. If a respectable solicitor were to slip behind a screen and reappear in a cardboard nose and a pair of huge moustaches, it could not be more disturbing than this *coup de théâtre* in the most laboriously realistic story ever written.

Only if style could be separated from content, the surface from the perceptions which make it solid, could Flaubert's style be praised without reserve. The distinction, as he knew, cannot be made. And Flaubert's style is sometimes perfect, sometimes bad, more often indifferent than either.

–John Middleton Murry, "Gustave Flaubert, 1821–1880," in his *Countries of the Mind: Essays in Criticism* (London: W. Collins, 1922), pp. 203–205, 207–209, 213–216

* * *

In this excerpt from his essay on the political background of Flaubert's novels, American critic Edmund Wilson praises the acuteness of the author's understanding of his society. The essay was included in Wilson's collection The Triple Thinkers *(1938), the title of which he borrowed from a remark Flaubert made in a letter to Colet, "What is an artist but a triple thinker?"*

Flaubert's Politics

. . . It is in "L'Education Sentimentale" that Flaubert's account of society comes closest to socialist theory. Indeed, his presentation here of the Revolution of 1848 parallels in so striking a manner Marx's analysis of the same events in "The Eighteenth Brumaire of Louis Napoleon" that it is worth while to bring together into the same focus the diverse figures of Flaubert and Marx in order to see how two great minds of the last century, pursuing courses so apparently divergent, arrived at identical interpretations of the happenings of their own time.

When we do this, we become aware that Marx and Flaubert started from very similar assumptions and that they were actuated by moral aims almost equally uncompromising. Both implacably hated the bourgeois, and both were resolved at any cost of worldly success to keep outside the bourgeois system. And Marx, like Flaubert, shared to some degree the romantic bias in favor of the past. Karl Marx can, of course, hardly be said to have had a very high opinion of any period of human history; but in comparison with the capitalist nineteenth century, he betrayed a certain tenderness for Greece and Rome and the Middle Ages. He pointed out that the slavery of the ancient world had at least purchased the "full development" of the masters and that a certain Antipater of Thessalonica had joyfully acclaimed the invention of the water wheel for grinding corn because it would set free the female slaves who had formerly had to do this work, whereas the bourgeois economists had seen in machinery only a means for making the workers work faster and longer in order "to transform a few vulgar and half-educated upstarts into 'eminent cotton spinners,' 'extensive sausage makers' and 'influential blacking dealers.'" And he had also a soft spot for the feudal system before the nobility had revolted against the Crown and while the rights of all classes, high and low, were still guaranteed by the king. Furthermore, the feudal lords, he insisted, had spent their money lavishly when they had it, whereas it was of the essence of capitalism that the capitalist saved his money and invested it, only to save and reinvest the profits.

Karl Marx's comment on his time was the Communist Manifesto. What is the burden of the great social novel of Flaubert? Frédéric Moreau, the hero of "L'Education Sentimentale," is a sensitive and intelligent young man with an income; but he has no stability of purpose and is capable of no emotional integrity. He becomes so aimlessly, so will-lessly, involved in love affairs with different types of women that he is unable to make anything real out of any of them: they trip each other up until in the end he is left with nothing. He is most in love from the very beginning with the virtuous wife of a sort of glorified drummer, who is engaged in more or less shady business enterprises; but, what with his timidity and her virtue, he never gets anywhere with her–and even though she loves him in return–and leaves her in the hands of the drummer. Flaubert makes it plain to us, however, that Frédéric and the vulgar husband at bottom represent the same thing: Frédéric is only the more refined as well as the more incompetent side of the middle-class mediocrity of which the promoter is the more flashy and active.

Novelist Amandine-Aurore-Lucile Dupin, who used the nom de plume George Sand (photograph by Félix Nadar, circa 1865; cliché Bibliothèque nationale de France, Paris)

And so in the case of the other characters, the representatives of journalism, art and drama and of the various political factions of the time, and the remnants of the old nobility, Frédéric finds the same shoddiness and lack of principle which are gradually revealed in himself–the same qualities which render so odious to him the banker, M. Dambreuse, the type of the rich and powerful class. M. Dambreuse is always ready to trim his sails to any political party, monarchist or republican, which seems to have a chance of success. "Most of the men who were there," Flaubert writes of the guests at M. Dambreuse's house, "had served at least four governments; and they would have sold France or the human race in order to guarantee their fortune, to spare themselves a difficulty or anxiety, or even from simple baseness, instinctive adoration of force." "*Je me moque des affaires!*" ["*I don't care about business!*"] cries Frédéric when the guests at M. Dambreuse's are complaining that criticism of the government hurts business; but he always comes back to hoping to profit by M. Dambreuse's investments and position.

The only really sympathetic characters in "L'Education Sentimentale" are, again, the representatives of the people. Rosanette, Frédéric's mistress, is the daughter of poor workers in the silk mills, who sold her at fifteen to an old bourgeois. Her liaison with Frédéric is a symbol of the disastrously unenduring union between the proletariat and the bourgeoisie, of which Marx, in "The Eighteenth Brumaire," had written. After the suppression of the workers' insurrection during the June days of '48, Rosanette gives birth to a weakly child, which dies while Frédéric is already arranging a love affair with the dull wife of the banker. Frédéric believes that Mme. Dambreuse will be able to advance his interests. And bourgeois socialism gets a very Marxist treatment–save in one respect, which we shall note in a moment–in the character of Sénécal, who is eternally making himself unpleasant about communism and the welfare of the masses, for which he is ready to fight to the last barricade. When Sénécal, however, gets a job as foreman in a pottery factory, he turns out to be an inexorable little tyrant; and when it begins to appear, after the putting down of the June riots, that the reaction is sure to triumph, he begins to decide, like our fascists today, that the strong centralization of the government is already itself a kind of communism and that authority is in itself a great thing.

On the other hand, there is the clerk Dussardier, a strapping and stupid fellow and one of the few honest characters in the book. When we first see him, he has just knocked down a policeman in a political brawl on the street. Later, when the National Guard, of which Dussardier is a member, turns against the proletariat in the interests of law and order, Dussardier fells one of the insurgents from the top of a barricade and gets at the same time a bullet in the leg, thereby becoming a great hero of the bourgeois. But Dussardier himself is unhappy. The boy he had knocked down had wrapped the tricolor around him and shouted to the National Guard: "Are you going to fire on your brothers?" Dussardier isn't at all sure that he oughtn't to have been on the other side. His last appearance is at the climax of the story, constitutes, indeed, the climax: he turns up in a proletarian street riot, which the cavalry and police are putting down. Dussardier refuses to move on, crying "*Vive la République!*"; and Frédéric comes along just in time to see one of the policemen kill him. Then he recognizes the policeman: it is the socialist, Sénécal.

"L'Education Sentimentale," unpopular when it first appeared, is likely, if we read it in our youth, to prove baffling and even repellent. It sounds as if it were going to be a love story, but the love affairs turn out so consistently to be either unfulfilled or lukewarm that we find ourselves irritated or depressed. Is it a satire? It is too real for a satire. Yet it does not seem to have the kind of vitality which we are accustomed to look for in a novel.

Yet, although we may rebel, as we first read it, against "L'Education sentimentale," we find afterwards that it has stuck in our crop. If it is true, as Bernard Shaw has said, that "Das Kapital" makes us see the nineteenth century "as if it were a cloud passing down the wind, changing its shape and fading as it goes," so that we are never afterward able to forget that "capitalism, with its wage slavery, is only a passing phase of social development, following primitive communism, chattel slavery and feudal serfdom into the past"–so Flaubert's novel plants deep in our mind an idea which we never quite get rid of–the suspicion that our middle-class society of business men, bankers and manufacturers, and people who live on or deal in investments, so far from being redeemed by its culture, has ended by cheapening and invalidating culture: politics, science and art–and not only these but the ordinary human relations: love, friendship and loyalty to cause–till the whole civilization has seemed to dwindle.

But fully to appreciate the book, one must have had time to see something of life and to have acquired a certain interest in social as distinct from personal

George Sand's First Magny Dinner

During his stays in Paris, Flaubert often had dinner at the Magny restaurant, which provided an informal setting for writers to meet. The following excerpt is a translation of Sand's 12 February 1866 diary description of her first dinner at the Magny.

Dinner chez Magny with my petits camarades. They couldn't have given me a warmer welcome. They were very brilliant, except for the great scholar Berthelot. Gautier constantly dazzling and paradoxical. Saint-Victor charming and distinguished. Flaubert, impassioned and more sympathetic to me than the others. Why? I'm still not sure. The Goncourts, too self-assured, especially the younger, who is very witty but too contentious with his elders. The best talker, and no less witty than the rest, is 'l'oncle Beuve,' as they call him. Everyone pays ten francs, the dinner is mediocre. There's a lot of smoking and loud talk, and you leave when you like. I was forgetting Louis Bouilhet, who looks like Flaubert and was modest.

–*Flaubert~Sand: The Correspondence,* p. 9

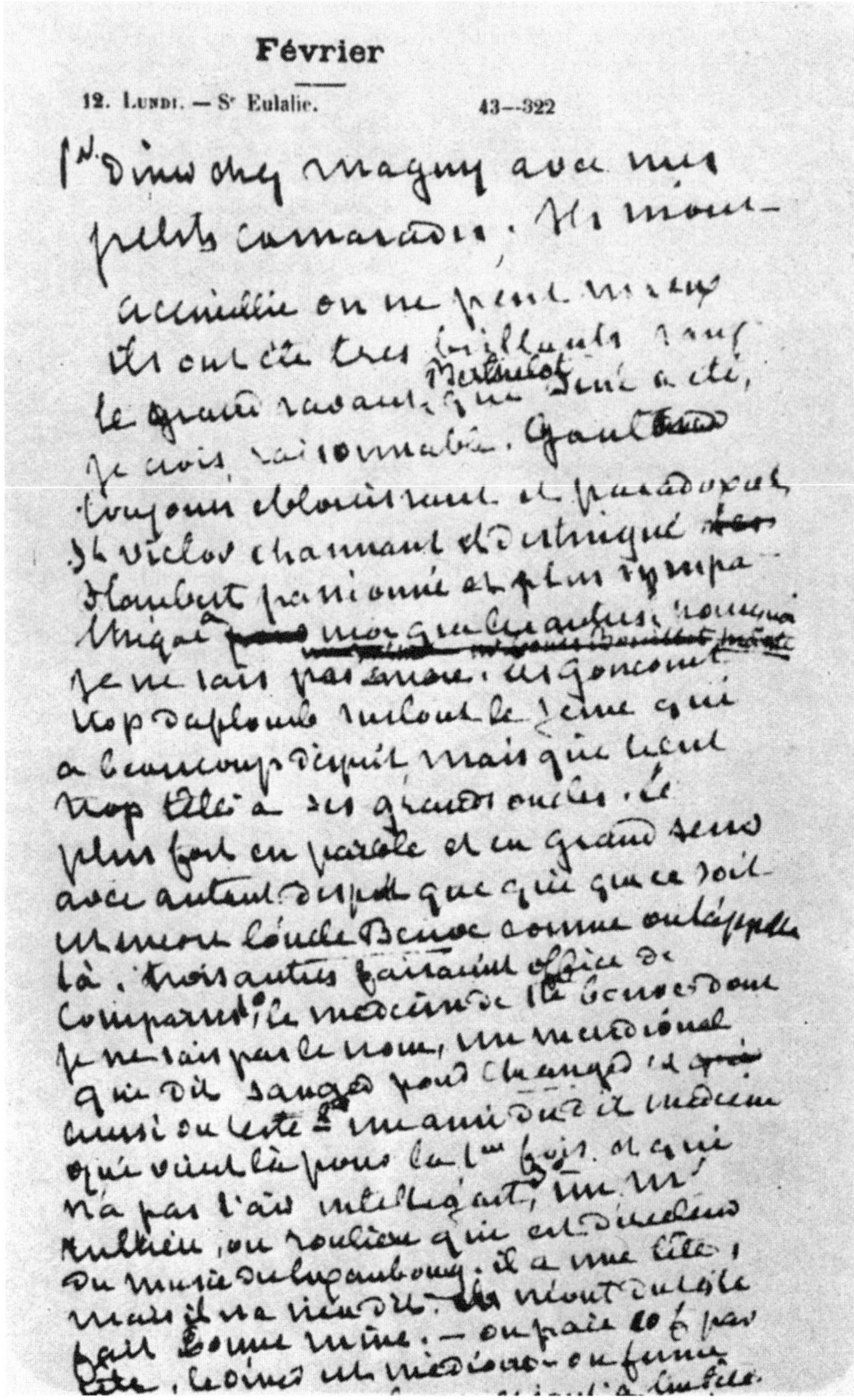

Février

12. Lundi. — Sᵗ Eulalie. 43—322

1er dîner chez Magny avec mes
petits camarades. Ils m'ont
accueillie on ne peut mieux
Ils ont été très brillants sauf
le grand savant Berthelot qui a été,
je crois, raisonnable. Gautier
toujours éblouissant et paradoxal,
St Victor charmant et distingué
Flaubert passionné est plus sympa-
thique à moi que les autres. Pourquoi
je ne sais pas encore. Les Goncourt
trop d'aplomb surtout le jeune qui
a beaucoup d'esprit, mais qui tient
trop tête à ses grands oncles. Le
plus fort en parole et en grand sens
avec autant d'esprit que qui que ce soit
Sainte-Beuve comme on l'appelle
là.

Page from George Sand's diaries dated 12 February 1866, in which she reports her impressions after the first Magny dinner she attended (cliché Bibliothèque nationale de France, Paris)

questions. Then, if we read it again, we are amazed to find that the tone no longer seems really satiric and that we are listening to a sort of muted symphony of which the timbres had been inaudible before. There are no hero, no villain, to arouse us, no clowns to amuse us, no scenes to wring our hearts. Yet the effect is deeply moving. It is the tragedy of nobody in particular, but of the poor human race itself reduced to such ineptitude, such cowardice, such commonness, such weak irresolution–arriving, with so many fine notions in its head, so many noble words on its lips, at a failure which is all the more miserable because those who have failed are hardly conscious of having done so.

Going back to "L'Education Sentimentale," we come to understand Mr. F. M. Ford's statement that you must read it fourteen times. Though it is less attractive on the surface than "Madame Bovary" and perhaps others of Flaubert's books, it is certainly the one which he put the most into. And once we have got the clue to all the immense and complex drama which unrolls itself behind the detachment and the monotony of the tone, we find it as absorbing and satisfying as a great play or a great piece of music.

The one conspicuous respect in which Flaubert's criticism of the events of 1848 *diverges* from that of Marx has been thrown into special relief by the recent events of our own time. For Marx, the evolution of the socialist into a policeman would have been due to the bourgeois in Sénécal; for Flaubert, it is a natural development of socialism. Flaubert distrusted, as I have mentioned in quoting from his letters, the authoritarian aims of the socialists. For him, Sénécal, given his bourgeois hypocrisy, was still carrying out a socialist principle–or rather, his behavior as a policeman and his yearnings toward socialist control were both derived from his impulse toward tyranny.

Today we must recognize that Flaubert had observed something of which Marx was not aware. We have had the opportunity to see how even a socialism which has come to power as the result of a proletarian revolution has bred a political police of almost unprecedented ruthlessness and all-pervasiveness–how the socialism of Marx himself, with its emphasis on dictatorship rather than on democratic processes, has contributed to produce this disaster. Here Flaubert, who believed that the artist should aim to be without social convictions, has been able to judge the tendencies of political doctrines as the greatest of doctrinaires could not; and here the role of Flaubert is justified.

–Edmund Wilson, "Flaubert's Politics," in *The Triple Thinkers: Ten Essays on Literature* (New York: Harcourt, Brace, 1938), pp. 108–115

* * *

In the following excerpt from his 1965 study of Flaubert's novels, Victor Brombert discusses the final and initial scenes of L'Éducation sentimentale *to show the sophisticated structure of the narrative.*

L'Éducation sentimentale:
Profanation and the Permanence of Dreams

The Bordello: In the End Is the Beginning

Ten years after the publication of *L'Éducation sentimentale,* Flaubert was still pained by the critics' hostile reaction. To his friend Turgenev, he wrote in 1879: "Without being a monster of pride, I consider that this book has been unfairly judged, especially the end. On this score I feel bitter toward the public."[1] Few endings of novels have indeed baffled, even outraged more readers. The hero's flat assertion that an adolescent excursion to a brothel has been the most precious experience of a lifetime confirmed suspicions that Flaubert was an incurable cynic. It was bad enough that the "hero," Frédéric Moreau, after a life distinguished by failure, returns to the somnolence of a provincial existence, a death-in-life which corresponds to a total abdication and to a permanent vocation for nothing. But did the author have to bring Frédéric and Deslauriers together in this scene, pointing up the weakness and bad faith inherent in their reconciliation? Did he have to indulge in an inventory of decay? And does the exalted expedition to the provincial bawdyhouse not cheapen whatever might have been salvaged (the very memory of Mme Arnoux!) by stressing venal love and by linking almost perversely the prurient excitement of early adolescence with the impotence of precocious senility? Yet Flaubert felt surer of the validity of this scene than of almost any other scene in the novel. Endings were for him a matter of utmost concern even when, as in *Madame Bovary* or *L'Éducation sentimentale,* they may at first appear like an unfunctional appendix. But the anticlimactic last three chapters in *Madame Bovary* are far from gratuitous. In *L'Éducation sentimentale,* the ending is even more intimately bound up with the very structure and meaning of the book. Paradoxically, it almost engenders the very beginning. It is an epilogue, no doubt: but this epilogue echoes and parallels one of the earliest passages in the book. I refer to the second chapter, which is partly a flashback to Frédéric's and Deslauriers' childhood, and partly an early conversation between the two friends as they look forward to the future, but already have a past to talk about. Thus the book can be said to begin and to close with a conversation between Frédéric and Deslauriers in which projects or reminiscences take priority over action. The immediate effect of this extension in time (the prologue

Drawings of George Sand by Thomas Couture (left; cliché Bibliothèque nationale de France, Paris) and Charles Marchal (cliché Bablin, courtesy of the Bibliothèque de l'Institut de France, Paris). Sand gave both portraits to Flaubert, who thanked her in a letter dated 29 September 1866: "Of the two portraits, I prefer the drawing by Couture. Marchal saw only the 'good woman' in you; but for me, old Romantic that I am, the other is the 'portrait of the author' who so often set me dreaming in my youth" (Flaubert~Sand. The Correspondence, *p. 25).*

carries us back to 1833, the epilogue forward to the winter of 1868) is a feeling of temporal circularity and erosion. All the dreams have come to nought. And already during the first conversation, the light the two friends can see shining from the small window of the *maison basse,* the house of ill repute, seems like a shimmering symbol of unattainable desire. "I am of the race of the disinherited," says Frédéric, convinced before the event that no worthwhile woman will ever love him. In the meantime, they do not have enough money to respond to the blinking light. But they do remember a common adventure of some years back, the same adventure that, twenty-seven years later, they will tell each other, agreeing that it had been the best moment of their lives. "C'est là ce que nous avons eu de meilleur" ["That is the best we ever had"].

If, however, we look at this last scene more closely, we must notice that the bordello motif is not exploited for its sheer anecdotal value, nor even primarily to allow for the devastating final comment. The episode, as remembered by the two friends–though it occurred some time before the events of the novel itself–does in fact sum up, in miniature fashion, a whole pattern of events and meanings. What happened is banal enough: on a late Sunday afternoon, the two boys plucked some flowers, gathered them into bouquets and proceeded furtively to the house of "La Turque."

> Frédéric presented his bouquet, like a boyfriend to his fiancée. But the heat of the day, the fear of the unknown, a kind of remorse, and even the excitement of seeing at a glance so many women at his disposal, affected him so much that he grew very pale and could neither move nor speak. They all laughed, amused at his embarrassment. Thinking that he was being made fun of, he ran away; and since he had the money, Deslauriers was forced to follow him. (III.7)

Several aspects of this passage deserve analysis. To begin with, the author provides here a subtly nuanced sketch of Frédéric's character. The naïve gesture of appearing with flowers at a brothel points up a latent and ineffectual idealism. The comparison with the boyfriend and his fiancée is touching enough, but suggests a tendency to see reality through a deforming imagination. The heat which paralyzes him reminds us of many other states of dreamy indolence in Frédéric's life. The vague sense of guilt, which, one must assume, is here related to a mother-image, is elsewhere associated with the pure and "maternal" image of Marie Arnoux. The multiplicity of women making the choice impossible corresponds not only to the constant and inconclusive wavering, within the novel, from one woman to another, but to Frédéric's basic inability to focus on anything and impose a single direction on his life. The immobility, the speechlessness and the ultimate flight underline a chronic timidity, the fear of judgment and humiliation. Thus he also tears up his first letter to Mme Arnoux: ". . . he did nothing, attempted nothing–paralyzed by the fear of failure" (I.3). And the flight itself corresponds, of course, to a flight from the realities of the capital and a return to the sheltered life of the province.

But there is more to this passage. The naïve arrival in the whorehouse, the flustered departure, the very *fiasco* of the expedition symbolize the poetic illusion that clings tenaciously to unfulfilled love. It symbolizes the orgyless orgy, the love-dream remaining pure because it was unrealized. After all, Frédéric leaves "La Turque" chaste! The debauches have been of the imagination: mere velleities. So that the final comment ("C'est là ce que nous avons eu de meilleur"), far from being exclusively a cynical remark, or a symptom of arrested development, must also be interpreted as a lasting nostalgia for innocence.[2] This preference for the past conceals another form of idealism. Memory illumines. And although both friends seem to have lost everything, this final dialogue between the man who sought Love and the man who sought Power reveals that it is the search for Love (no matter how clumsy and frustrating) which retrospectively bestows the only meaning. The episode thus combines, in the most ambiguous manner, touching illusion and adult disillusionment, flights of fancy and retreat into the self, attraction to the multiform manifestations of life and paralysis caused by the very proliferation of forms and possibilities, eternally youthful memories and the pathos of aging. In other words, it is a retrospective prolepsis of the very essence of the novel. Even the relationship of Frédéric and his friend is prefigured in the terse remark that since the one had the money, the other was obliged to follow him!

The bordello motif, or in a more general sense the image of the Prostitute and the theme of Prostitution, is at the core of *L'Éducation sentimentale*. Frédéric's erotic sensibility and erotic dreams as a boy crystallize around visions of satin-covered boudoirs where he and his friend will experience "fulgurant orgies with illustrious courtesans" (I.2). Such exotic passions are inevitably linked to dreams of success. He and Deslauriers spend so many hours constructing and peopling their harems that they are as exhausted as though they had indulged in real debauches. Later, when Frédéric actually penetrates into the world of Parisian women, he is almost overcome by the luxurious *odor di femmina*. There is, to be sure, a certain literary tradition behind this particular mystique of the senses. Romanticism had cast the eternal hetaera, whether simple *fille de joie* or high-class courtesan, in the role of initiator into the deep mysteries of life. Even social, artistic and political success–in nineteenth-century literature–is often related to one form or another of prostitution. Such literary expressions no doubt correspond to certain social and psychological patterns: the bourgeois adolescent looked at the prostitute with mixed feelings of admiration, contempt, desire to redeem and even a yearning for profanation. There is for instance a curious letter from Alfred Le Poittevin to Flaubert which tells of the young man's desire to desecrate in the company of a whore places where he has been "young and credulous."[3] As for Flaubert himself, it is clear that he is haunted by the image of the prostitute, whom he associates, in an almost Baudelairean manner, with equally complex monastic and ascetic urges.

In the novel, the bordello motif and the theme of prostitution assume in part a satiric function. The world of the *lorettes* into which Frédéric is ironically introduced by Mme Arnoux's husband, appears to him at first in the guise of a masked ball, where the most tempting display of flesh, costumes and poses inevitably brings to mind the variegated offerings of an elegant house of prostitution providing "specialties" for every whim. Frédéric is so dazzled that, during the first moments, he can distinguish only silk, velvet and naked shoulders. Then, gradually, he takes stock of the contents of this Parisian seraglio: the languorous Polish beauty, the placid and falsely modest Swiss siren, the provocative Fishwife, the Primitive with peacock feathers, the avid Bacchante, the carnival Workwoman–all the "refinements of modern love" dance before him, and the beads of perspiration on their foreheads further suggest a hothouse atmosphere (II.1). This scene, ending in a collective hangover the following morning, recalls the famous Taillefer orgy in Balzac's *La Peau de chagrin:* the same display of available carnality, the same specter of disease and death, the same garish coupling of the lascivious and the macabre. Only Flaubert is not concerned with sheer pyrotechnics. He is not out to rival Petronius' description of decadence in the *Satyricon*. His aim is neither sensational nor allegorical. He works and weaves his images patiently and deliberately into the general pattern of the novel. But there are some immediate effects, and the most noteworthy is a vertiginous proliferation of forms and gestures which ultimately transforms human beings into mechanized objects. In her drunken stupor, one of the women imitates "the oscillation of a launch."

The easy-virtued world of Rosanette is not the only one to be described in terms of lupanar images. Frédéric's suggestive vision imposes these very same images onto the assembly of elegant feminine guests in the salon of Mme Dambreuse (II.2). The upper-class ladies all sit in a row, "offering" their bosoms to the eye; the rustling of their gowns suggests that dresses are about to slip down. The lack of expression on their faces is in perverse contrast to their "provocative garments." The animal-like placidity of these ladies in décolleté evokes the "interior of a harem." Flaubert's intention becomes quite explicit, for he adds: "A more vulgar comparison came to the young man's mind." Here too, the salon provides a sampling of physical and regional types to satisfy every possible taste: English beauties with keepsake profiles, Italians with ardent eyes, three Norman sisters "fresh as apple trees in April"–an alluring and appetizing display of sophisticated impudicity. The total effect is once again dehumanization: the crescendo of feminine chatter sounds like the cackle of birds.

Even public locales (cafés, restaurants, *bals publics*) are seen as places of prostitution, for instance the Alhambra, where, according to Deslauriers, one can easily get to know "women." The exotic name corresponds to fake exotic architecture, or rather to jarring elements of architecture: Moorish galleries, the restaurant side in the form of a Gothic cloister, Venetian lanterns, a Chinese roofing over the orchestra, neoclassical painted cupids (I.5). This shocking combination is not merely a sign of vulgarity. It represents the particular attempt at facile poetry, or rather at facile estrangement, which is the special function of all purveyors of bought pleasures. In this light, the bordello becomes the convenient metaphor for any catering to the thirst for illusion. The Alhambra provides sensual pleasures for the public. The reader witnesses a collective debauchery: the last firecracker of the evening provokes an orgastic sigh. But in reality, nothing really happens. The policemen who wake up Frédéric on the boulevard bench where he has fallen asleep, and who are convinced that he has "fait la noce" ["had fun"], are as wrong as his own mother concerning his visit to "La Turque." For Frédéric, it has been an innocent orgy, combining in characteristic fashion exposure to depravity with an exacerbated yearning for ideal love. Frédéric's only activity right after the Alhambra is to stare at Mme Arnoux's window.

Ernest Feydeau, as caricatured after the production of his play Un Coup de bourse *(The Stock Market Game). Well known for stock-market trading, Feydeau answered questions about investments when Flaubert was describing Frédéric's financial troubles in* L'Éducation sentimentale *(cliché Bibliothèque nationale de France, Paris).*

This aspect of the metaphorical unity of *L'Éducation sentimentale* is further strengthened by the presence of key characters who, in one form or another, are for sale. The most important of these is Rosanette Bron, "La Maréchale." That Rosanette is a kept woman, and most often kept by several men at the same time, is of course no secret. Her true calling is perhaps never more graphically suggested than by her portrait, commissioned by M. Arnoux, eventually purchased by Frédéric, but which in the meantime stands exposed in the window of a gallery with the following words written in black letters underneath: "Mme Rose-Annette Bron, appartenant à M. Frédéric Moreau, de Nogent" (II.4). True to her vocation, she specializes, one might say, in sexual provocation. Innumerable passages in the novel stress this talent. Her laughter has a whiplike effect on Frédéric's nerves. At times, she assumes the poses of a "provocative slave." Most often, her sex appeal is less indolent: her way of pulling up her stockings, her movements, her very chignon are "like a challenge" (II.2). When she eats, and the redness of the fruit mixes with the purple of her lips, the insolence of

L'Abeille, *a steamer in the 1840s, such as the one on which Frédéric meets Madame Arnoux for the first time while returning to Nogent at the beginning of* L'Éducation sentimentale *(courtesy of the Musée Carnavalet, Paris)*

her look fills Frédéric with mad desires. As for her innumerable caprices, her disconnected cravings, they correspond to the usual versatility associated with the prostitution metaphor; only here the multiplicity of forms and possibilities is internalized. The capricious, unpredictable nature of Rosanette also corresponds to her treachery–and in a broader sense, to the theme of treason so important in this novel. Hers is partially an irresponsible type of cruelty best exemplified by her coldly abandoning Frédéric at the Café Anglais after accepting from de Cisy a bracelet with three opals.

A far more cold-blooded selfishness is the main feature of the "grande dame," the regal prostitute Mme Dambreuse. Frédéric finds that she has something "languorous" and "dry" (II.4). Her sterile cupidity appears in full light when, after the death of her husband, and in the presence of her lover, she stares, disconsolate, into the empty strong box! As for the perfidious Vatnaz, the eternal procuress, she provokes only disgust. The mere touch of her "thin, soft hand" sends shivers down Frédéric's spine. The world of Paris thus insistently proposes to Frédéric images of prostitution: *lorettes* at the hippodrome; streetwalkers under the gaslight; scenes of slave markets with lewd sultans and cheap puns in boulevard plays. At the horse races, he glimpses an obscenely made-up queen of the burlesque theater known as the "Louis XI of prostitution." Everywhere he turns, it would seem that, as in Baudelaire's *Tableaux parisiens,* "La Prostitution s'allume dans les rues" ["Prostitution lights up in the streets"].

But actual prostitution is of course not the only form of prostitution. There are less literal manifestations, all pointing to some manner of depravity. For the bordello motif is closely bound up with Frédéric's apprenticeship of life. His "education" in Paris–the subject as well as the title of the novel place it squarely in the tradition of the *Bildungsroman*–is to begin with the discovery of one type or another of pandering, cheapening or desecration. One could almost take one by one every character and every activity. The very name of Arnoux's hybrid establishment, *L'Art industriel* [Industrial Art], is like a profanation of art. And his career sadly illustrates this profanation: an amateur painter, he is in turn director of an art magazine, an art dealer, the owner of a pottery factory manufacturing "artistic" soup plates and mythological decorations for bathrooms. With every chapter he takes a step down. After designing letters for signboards and wine labels, and going bankrupt through shady deals, he has the idea of a *café chantant* [*singing café*] and of a military hat-making business, and he finally winds up dealing in beads and cheap "religious art." The very word "décadence" (III.4) aptly sums up his career. There is the same brutal deflation in the life of Pellerin, the painter who wanted to rival Veronese, then places his art in the service of politics, and ends up being a professional photographer. The actor Delmar, a coarse histrion, similarly illustrates the prostitution of art: he sells out his vulgar talent to political parties, and gives public recitals of humanitarian poetry on . . . prostitution (III.3). This propensity for selling out is most strikingly symbolized by the epitaph-like résumé of the life of the financier Dambreuse, who "had acclaimed Napoleon, the Cossacks, Louis XVIII, 1830, the working-man, every régime, adoring Power with such intensity that he would have paid in order to have the opportunity of selling himself" (III.4).

As for Frédéric himself, much could be said. In a letter to Amélie Bosquet, written some ten years before the publication of *L'Éducation sentimentale,* Flaubert makes this revealing confession: "One has spoken endlessly about the prostitution of women, but not a word has been said about that of men. I have known the tortures of prostitutes, and any man who has loved for a long time and who desired no longer to love has experienced them."[4] Unquestionably Frédéric's ambiguous situation vis-à-vis the Arnoux household, combining the duplicity of an adulterer, the frustrations of an unsuccessful suitor and the embarrassment of being Arnoux's rival not only with his wife, but with his mistress, exposes him to complex compromises and turpitudes. His dilettantish vacillations and reliance on others are almost those of a "kept" person. Frédéric is not only weak (Flaubert often depicts strong women and weak, virginal men), but passive and "feminine." He holds, for his friend Deslauriers, "un charme presque féminin" ["an almost feminine charm"] (II.5). The projected marriage to Mme Dambreuse, for money and social prestige, shows us Frédéric morally at his most depraved.

Finally, the prostitution motif provides a link between individual and collective attitudes. Society itself, as represented by various groups, corporations or institutions, is the great whore who always embraces the winner. Like Rosanette, who after despising the revolutionaries now declares herself in favor of the Republic, so do all the representative authorities–"as his lordship the Archbishop had already done, and as the magistracy, the Conseil d'État, the Institut, the marshals of France, Changarnier, M. de Falloux, all the Bonapartists, all the Legitimists, and a considerable number of Orleanists were about to do with a swiftness displaying marvelous zeal" (III.I). Politics in particular, which held a somewhat perverse fascination for the apolitical Flaubert, is viewed as a slattern. During the obscenely violent and profanatory sack of the Tuileries palace, a slut is seen, on a heap of garments, assuming the motionless, allegorical pose of the Statue of Liberty.

The bitterness of an image such as this stresses the coarseness and the fickleness of political allegiances. But it is part of a more general theme of betrayed ideals. *L'Éducation sentimentale* is a novel of bankruptcy and of pathological erosion. Certain chapters accumulate one form of betrayal on top of another, until the feeling is that of an immense desertion. Friendship, ambition, politics, love–nothing seems immune from this chronic deterioration and devaluation.[5] The most brutal manifestation of this aspect of the novel is the double betrayal of the political turncoat Sénécal, the former Socialist now turned police agent, who during the coup d'état of 1851 coldbloodedly kills the sentimental revolutionary Dussardier. This stunning act, which leaves Frédéric agape, is like an allegory of treason destroying idealism.

And it is no gratuitous coincidence that makes Frédéric the witness to this despicable deed. The images of prostitution and degradation exist primarily in relation to Frédéric's personal vision, to his longings, his sadness, his disappointments and his defeats. The bordello motif may permeate the novel as a whole and may have a universal significance within its context. It represents ersatz on all levels, transmuting almost every gesture into parody: the duel with de Cisy is no real duel; the props Pellerin uses for his "Venetian" portrait are fake props; all creative efforts are derivative. But it is in relation to Frédéric's "sentimental education" that all this counterfeit acquires dramatic meaning. No matter how obviously depraved the objective world may be, it is his sentimental life which, subjectively, is most affected by the principle of degrading vicariousness. Thus Frédéric bounces from one woman to another, permanently oscillating between contradictory desires and contradictory experiences, always driven to seek a poor substitute for the *authentic* experience he dreams of, and which, in the process, he steadily defiles. One desire awakens a contradictory desire, suggesting a repetitive discontinuity. "The frequentation of the two women provided, as it were, two strains of music in his life, the one playful, passionate, amusing; and the other almost religious . . ." (II.2). And there are not two women in his life, but four–if one includes the young girl, Louise Roque. This oscillation at times obliges Flaubert to resort to devices which appear extraneous: chance encounters, unexpected letters, coincidences which further underline the passivity of the hero and his easy surrender to the easiest path. Almost symbolically, at one point, the "strumpet" Rosanette (Flaubert actually uses the word "catin") interrupts a love scene in progress, thus making the ideal "irrevocably impossible" (III.3).

What is worse, Frédéric *uses* the image of one woman in his relationship with another. It is bad

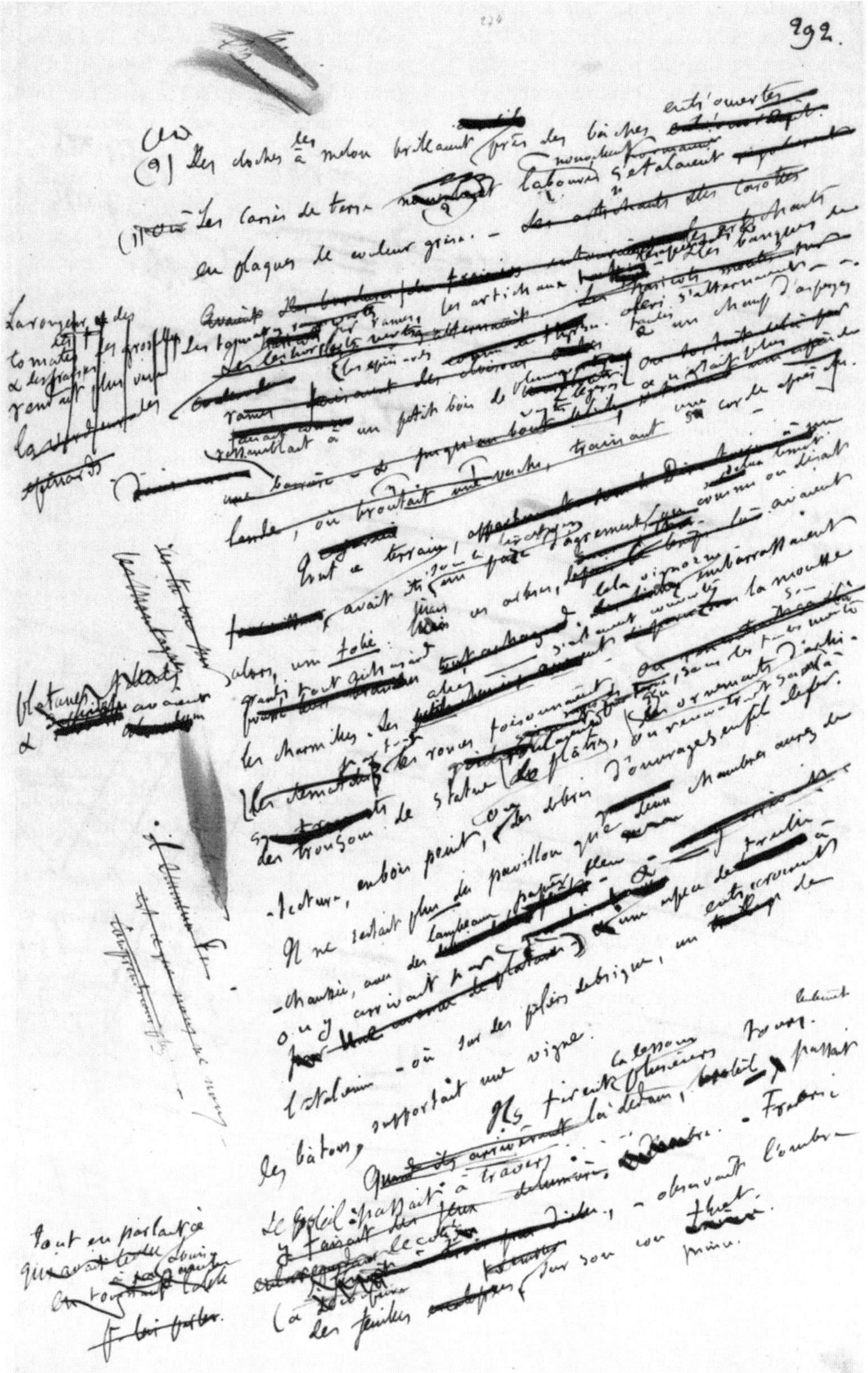

Page from a draft of the description of the town Nogent-sur-Seine, an important setting in L'Éducation sentimentale *(cliché Bibliothèque nationale de France, Paris)*

enough that he has learned to make one sentiment serve multiple purposes: in his courtship of Mme Dambreuse, he "makes use of his old passion" for Mme Arnoux (III.3); he repeats to Mme Dambreuse the very oath he just uttered to Rosanette, sends them both identical bouquets and writes them love letters simultaneously (III.4). Even more sadly, he has to rely on substitute images to stimulate himself sexually. "He found it necessary to evoke the image of Rosanette or of Mme Arnoux." (Thus Flaubert himself once told the Goncourts that "all the women he ever possessed were no more than the mattress for another woman he dreamed of.")[6] In the novel, this sexual substitution takes place quite literally when Frédéric, desperate because Mme Arnoux failed to show up at their rendezvous, makes love to Rosanette on the very bed he had so devoutly prepared for Mme Arnoux.

Such a pattern of substitution and profanation–underlined by the permanent prostitution motif–leads to contradictory results. On the one hand, we witness a strange paralysis, reminiscent of the scene in the brothel when Frédéric could not make his "choice." Life is a planned orgy which never quite amounts to one. As boys, Frédéric and Deslauriers had such extravagant dreams that they were "sad as after a great debauch" (I.2). Frédéric feels destined to accept defeat before even attempting a victory. He has a keen sense of loss before even having possessed. His imagination builds and furnishes Moorish palaces (always the exotic yearning!); he sees himself lounging on cashmere divans listening to the murmur of fountains–and these sensuous dreams become so precise "that they saddened him as though he had lost them" (I.5). Make-belief and mental aphrodisiacs turn out to be manifestations of impotence.

The other result appears as a complete contrast to this atony: a vertiginous proliferation. But this proliferation, much like the dizzying display of women at "La Turque," only leads to another form of futility. Innumerable examples in *L'Éducation sentimentale* illustrate this coupling of diversity with sterility: the different esthetic "theories," the contradictory literary projects, the cacophony of political ideas, the jarring clash of opinions and inept clichés. Polymorphism, in the Flaubertian context, is nearly always a sure sign of an almost hypnotic attraction to nothingness, a suicidal yearning for annihilation. "Exhausted, filled with contradictory desires, no longer even conscious of what he wanted, he felt an extraordinary sadness, the desire to die" (II.4).

It is significant that this allurement to nothingness, so explicitly stated, should be experienced by Frédéric while in the company of a high-class prostitute. For somehow, in Flaubert's own imagination, prostitution and an almost ascetic staring into the emptiness of existence are closely related. To Louise Colet he writes that the sight of streetwalkers and of monks "tickles" his soul in its deepest recesses, that prostitution evokes simultaneously "lewdness, bitterness, the nothingness of human relations. . . ."[7] The theme of sterility and even abortion in *L'Éducation sentimentale* is illumined by a comment such as this. Flaubert's admiration for the marquis de Sade, which he shares with Baudelaire, makes him suspect Nature and explains in part why he views the Prostitute both as an antiphysis and the very incarnation of sterility. With bitter irony, Flaubert describes the "maison de santé et d'accouchement" ["nursing and maternity home"] where Rosanette gives birth to a sickly offspring in terms that are most equivocal: the chambermaid looks like a "soubrette," the director of the establishment is called "Madame," the establishment itself (with its closed shutters and continuous sounds of piano playing) is called a "maison discrète" [discrete house] (III.4)–leaving little doubt as to the analogy the author had in mind. Originally, Flaubert had even planned to have the "Madame" explain to Frédéric how to dispose of the newborn baby! And when the sickly child soon after dies, Rosanette's grief coincides with the grief of Mme Dambreuse as she realizes that her husband has left all his wealth to someone else. "A mother grieving beside an empty cradle was not more pitiful than Mme Dambreuse at the sight of the open strong-boxes" (III.4). The theme of sterility could not possibly be pushed much further.

Profanation, betrayal, sterility . . . and yet. And yet the reader is never permitted to forget the ideally pure figure of Mme Arnoux. Frédéric may use other women, and forget himself with them; they are nothing but substitutes for an ideal. One might even say, paradoxically, that profanation is here in the service of purity. Ever since *Mémoires d'un fou,* written at the age of seventeen, Flaubert was haunted by the contrasts between idealized woman *(le ciel)* and cheap love *(la boue)*. The narrator of *Mémoires d'un fou,* still writing under the recent impact of his meeting with Mme Schlésinger, the model for Mme Arnoux, feels guilt and shame because he has lost his virginity with a promiscuous creature, "as though my love for Maria were a religion that I had profaned" (16). In *Novembre,* written at the age of twenty, he attempted to synthesize in one figure the dual visage of woman. *L'Éducation sentimentale* again insists on a polarity. It is clear that the very concept of immaculate beauty required, in Flaubert's imagination, the drama of inaccessibility, as well as the antithesis of corruption.[8]

This persistent idealism, strengthened by profanation as though made holier by it, is implicit in the bor-

Student demonstration at the Pont de la Concorde on 22 February 1848 (engraving by Dujardin; courtesy of the Musée Carnavalet, Paris)

The people assaulting the Hôtel de Ville (Paris's city hall) on 24 February 1848 (lithograph by Becquet Frères; courtesy of the Musée Carnavalet, Paris)

Scenes of Revolution

The revolution that took place in February 1848 plays an essential role in part 3, chapter 1, of L'Éducation sentimentale, *as the betrayal of the second republic parallels the betrayal of love, as Frédéric deceives the four female characters who love him.*

The burning of Louis-Philippe's throne, Place de la Bastille on 24 February 1848 (courtesy of the Musée Carnavalet, Paris)

The people in the throne room of the Tuileries palace on 24 February 1848 (lithograph by V. Adam and J. Arnout; cliché Bibliothèque nationale de France, Paris)

dello exploit, the subject of the last scene of the book. Just as the narrator of *Mémoires d'un fou* was haunted by the loss of virginity, so here Frédéric is filled with nostalgia for a lost innocence. For the memory is altogether a chaste one, and even on the level of sheer venery, the incident is marked by a sort of poetry of unrealized love. The memory, however, coming as it does at the end of the book (and especially after the ultimate, deeply moving encounter with Mme Arnoux), acquires an additional aura. And it is significant that Frédéric says not a word of this unforgettable last meeting to Deslauriers. For this is a private realm, a regal chamber open to no one. All throughout the novel it is Mme Arnoux's image that shines forth from behind the Parisian fog, keeping alive an "invincible hope." The very name Marie (the same name as in *Mémoires d'un fou* and in *Novembre*) suggests purity. And in the service of this "image," despite all his weaknesses and abdications, Frédéric acquires nobility. For the sake of this "image," he has in the long run given up everything.

In fact, Marie Arnoux is more than an image, she is a *vision.* But this carries us from the last scene back to the very first scene of the novel.

The River and the Boat: In the Beginning Is the End

On September 15, 1840, Frédéric–a young man about to begin the study of law–is traveling on a riverboat. *L'Éducation sentimentale* begins among the whirlwinds of smoke, on a vessel which is about to steam away. The destination is Nogent, where Frédéric is to remain with his mother until the fall term begins.

Flaubert was evidently in no way compelled to begin his novel with a river journey. Yet the earliest, very sketchy outline of the novel–not even twenty lines in length–already envisions this as a key scene: "traversée sur le bateau de Montereau. un collégien."[9] ["cruise on the boat to Montereau. A college boy."] The special care with which the scene was eventually written is revealed by the number of drafts–at least seven, it would seem. But such statistics are hardly needed to communicate the importance and suggestive power of these opening pages. Not only does the river journey establish the geographic poles of the novel (the capital and the provincial home), but it provides an ideal setting for the fleeting encounter with Mme Arnoux. Flaubert knew only too well the hopeless dreams that can crystallize around a figure met under ephemeral circumstances: his first meeting with Elisa Schlésinger took place on the beach in Trouville. The boat provided an even more dramatic setting.[10]

The symbolic potential of the scene is more significant still. For this is not an exotic sea voyage, with the excitement of hoped-for discoveries and possible adventures. Although there is the hustle and bustle of a real departure, nothing could be more prosaic, more commonplace, than the itinerary of the *Ville de Montereau* and the bourgeois vulgarity of its human cargo. It is a departure which fails to bring about an authentic voyage. So too, the movement of the boat is only another form of immobility. A passenger is not an active agent. But here the passivity is double: the boat itself merely follows the inevitable course of the river. Submissiveness to an ineluctable flow, the monotony of the landscape as it slowly glides by, the ability to see its details and yet the inability to hold on to impressions as they merge and fade away–these characteristics of the river navigation are exploited here as an almost prophetic symbol of Destiny and Time, and anticipate the drifting, languid and perpetually dreamy quality of Frédéric's life.[11]

For passiveness and the propensity to dream are closely bound up. The vibrations of the ship are conducive to drowsy well-being. The two banks "unroll" like "two large ribbons": the image almost suggests a film in slow motion. And there is a curious harmony between the outer landscape, slowly gliding by, and the inner landscape with its permanent mutations. To these evanescent forms the mind of Frédéric easily surrenders. Motion, real or imagined, will in fact always be for him an invitation to dream, a liberation from reality. Gaston Bachelard's observations about the excitement of railway travel could easily apply to Frédéric's experience on the boat: "The trip unfolds a film of dream houses . . . with the salutary prohibition of ever *verifying.*"[12] As the ship passes by a hill, a vineyard, a windmill–Frédéric's imagination sketches out entire novels of his many unlived lives. His mind is filled with *projects.* And this tendency, which the distance between the boat and the land brings out literally and symbolically, will remain a constant trait of his character. Frédéric "dreams his life" (as opposed to Emma Bovary, who dreams about life), explains Albert Thibaudet.[13] But at the origin of this trancelike state there is the habit of projecting himself into time and space: "he saw Mme Arnoux, ruined, crying, selling all her furniture" (II.2); he "glimpsed, as though in a flash, an immense fortune . . ." (II.2); "Already he saw himself in a waistcoat with lapels and a tricolored sash" (III.I). Often the very "projection" is closely bound up with an image of motion or travel (thus dreams engender dreams): "They would travel, they would go to Italy, to the East!" "He saw her standing on a little hill, gazing at a landscape" (II.6); "He saw himself with Her at night in a post-chaise; then on a river's bank on a summer evening" (III.I). The result is an almost self-hypnotizing, almost hallucinated state. The word "hallucination" actually occurs on several occasions. ("His daydream became so intense that he

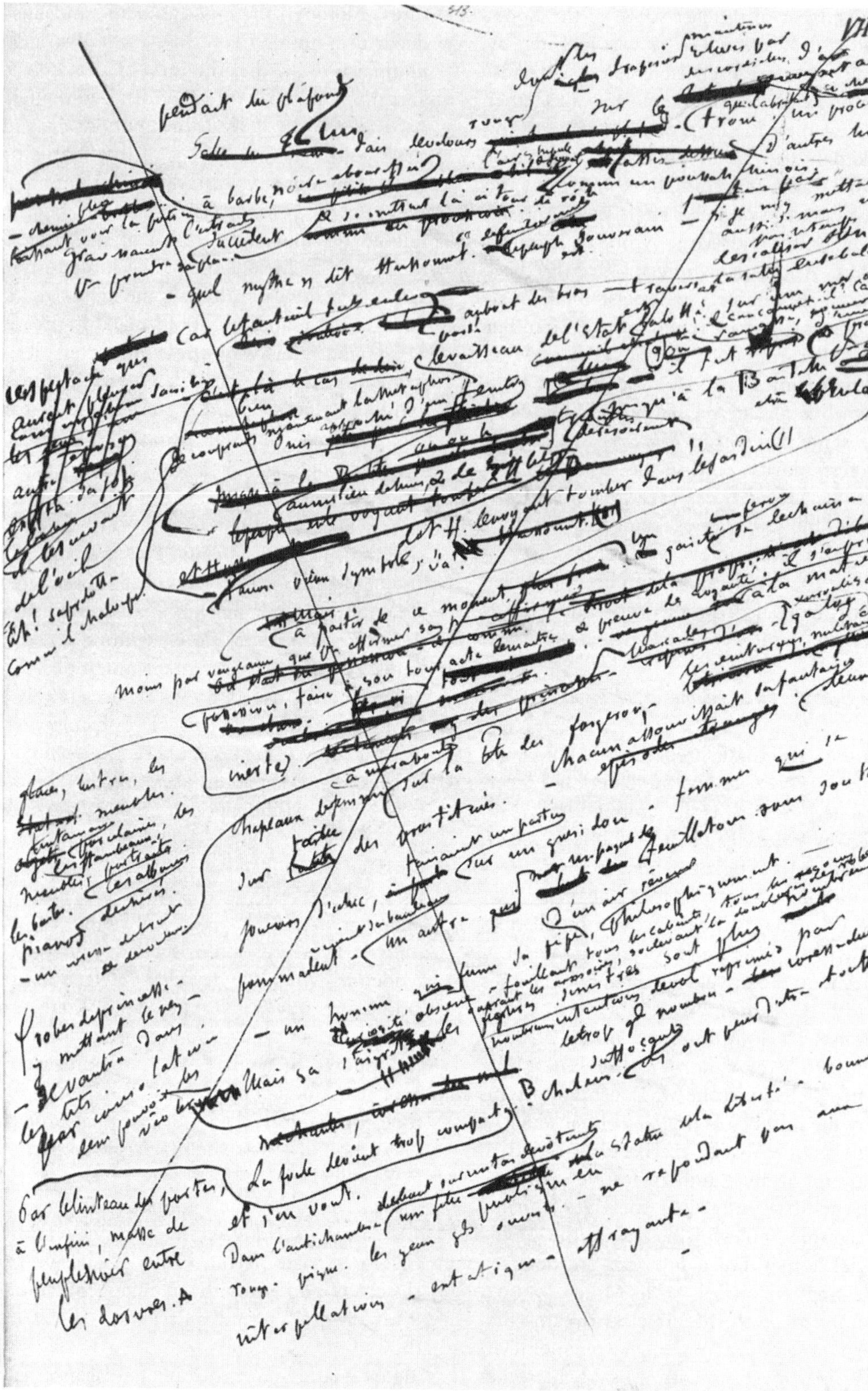

Page from a draft in which Flaubert describes the people invading the Tuileries palace during the 1848 Revolution for part 3, chapter 1, of L'Éducation sentimentale *(cliché Bibliothèque nationale de France, Paris)*

had a kind of hallucination.")[14] The riverboat, in the first scene of the book, provides an initial setting in which the capacity to dream is closely linked with the attraction to the impossible: movement and distance are inseparable.

But there is also irony in the fact that dreams take shape in the midst of the floating mediocrity of public transportation. The passengers are not exactly models of refinement. Except for a few "bourgeois" in first class, they are representative of humanity at its shabbiest. Flaubert goes to great length in describing a repulsive assembly: sordid clothes, worn-out hats, dirty shirts, torn ties. People eat and sleep pell-mell. The deck is soiled with nutshells, cigar butts and garbage. A sordid "reality" thus seems to engender the very dream-world. But does the presence of this "reality" not also soil the dream? Or does it heighten its beauty?

The fact is that Flaubert very deliberately placed this scene of grotesque filth and crudeness immediately before the dazzling first encounter with Mme Arnoux. "Ce fut comme une apparition." ["It was like a vision."] The word *apparition* must be taken here in its strongest sense: the earthly manifestation of an unworldly being. Mme Arnoux is like a vision–a vision made concrete, and yet so splendent that it immediately obliterates all that which surrounds it. She sits alone, or so it seems, for Frédéric suffers from a momentary blindness ("éblouissement") caused by too great a splendor. Everything in this passage suggests the vision of an angelic creature. The rays which emanate from her eyes, the spiritualized oval contours of the face, the features that stand out against a blue sky which here is like a background in a Fra Angelico painting, the "splendeur" of her brown skin, her delicate, almost immaterial hands through which light flows–all this, as seen through Frédéric's eyes, and Flaubert's art, transmutes a woman into an apparition, and makes of her, in the midst of a nineteenth-century scene of everyday life, a sister to Beatrice.

> e par che sia una cosa venuta
> da cielo in terra a miracol mostrare.
>
> [It is as if she had come down
> From heaven to earth to show a miracle.]

Frédéric might have recited to himself these lines from Dante's *Vita Nuova.* He, too, feels a "deeper yearning," a curiosity that knows no limits. The mystical overtones of these pages are further stressed by Frédéric's giving "alms" to the harpist, a gesture which vaguely corresponds, in his own mind, to an idea of blessing and to an almost religious impulse.

These images of spirituality are of the utmost thematic importance. One of the earliest sketches indeed sums up this initial meeting with the single word: *éblouissement* (dazzlement).[15] Throughout the novel, Mme Arnoux repeatedly "appears" as a vision (". . . Madame Arnoux parut" I.4). Her role as Madonna is brought out by a number of scenes in which she is shown together with her children in the "tranquil majesty" of a maternal pose.[16] Her hands seem forever ready to spread alms and wipe away tears. Frédéric frequently sits and merely "contemplates" her (I.5). Most often, however, her figure is associated with a particular quality of light. "Madame Arnoux was sitting on a big rock with this incandescent light at her back"–the image here is one of a halo. Her glances penetrate his soul "like those great rays of sunlight which descend to the bottom of the water" (I.5). When Frédéric meets her in the street, "the sunlight surrounded her" and her entire person seems invested with an "extraordinary splendor": an "infinite suavity" emanates from her eyes (II.6). At times Frédéric uses nothing but the capitalized personal pronoun *Elle* when he thinks of her. Her entire person is not only extraordinarily radiant (light pours from her as from a glory), but even the tiniest part of her body is infinitely precious. "Each of her fingers was for him more than a thing, almost a person."[17] In short, Frédéric places her "outside the human condition" (II.3). She fills him alternately with religious awe and with an "undefinable beatitude" (II.6). Nothing better illustrates Flaubert's skill at objectively presenting a subjectivity–and of simultaneously stressing the drama of this subjectivity–than the manner in which he idealizes Mme Arnoux through the eyes of Frédéric. One wonders how Henry James could have reproached Flaubert for what is precisely one of the main achievements of this novel: the fact that Mme Arnoux is offered us preponderantly through Frédéric's vision. Henry James obviously missed the point.[18] What matters is not whether Frédéric is a worthy medium through which to view so noble a soul, nor even whether the lady really is so sublime a creature (a futile question!)–but the tragic urge to create such a figure, to believe in her, and to cling stubbornly to the beauty of a vision engendered, as it were, by the very banality of existence.

The thematic importance of the first scene is further brought out by the fact that the image of Mme Arnoux is very frequently associated with the idea of travel. In part this corresponds to a characteristic Flaubertian yearning for the exotic. Thus already in the first scene, on the boat, exotic elements are introduced and amplified by the hero's imagination. He attributes Mme Arnoux's complexion to an Andalusian origin; when he sees her Negro servant, he imagines that she has

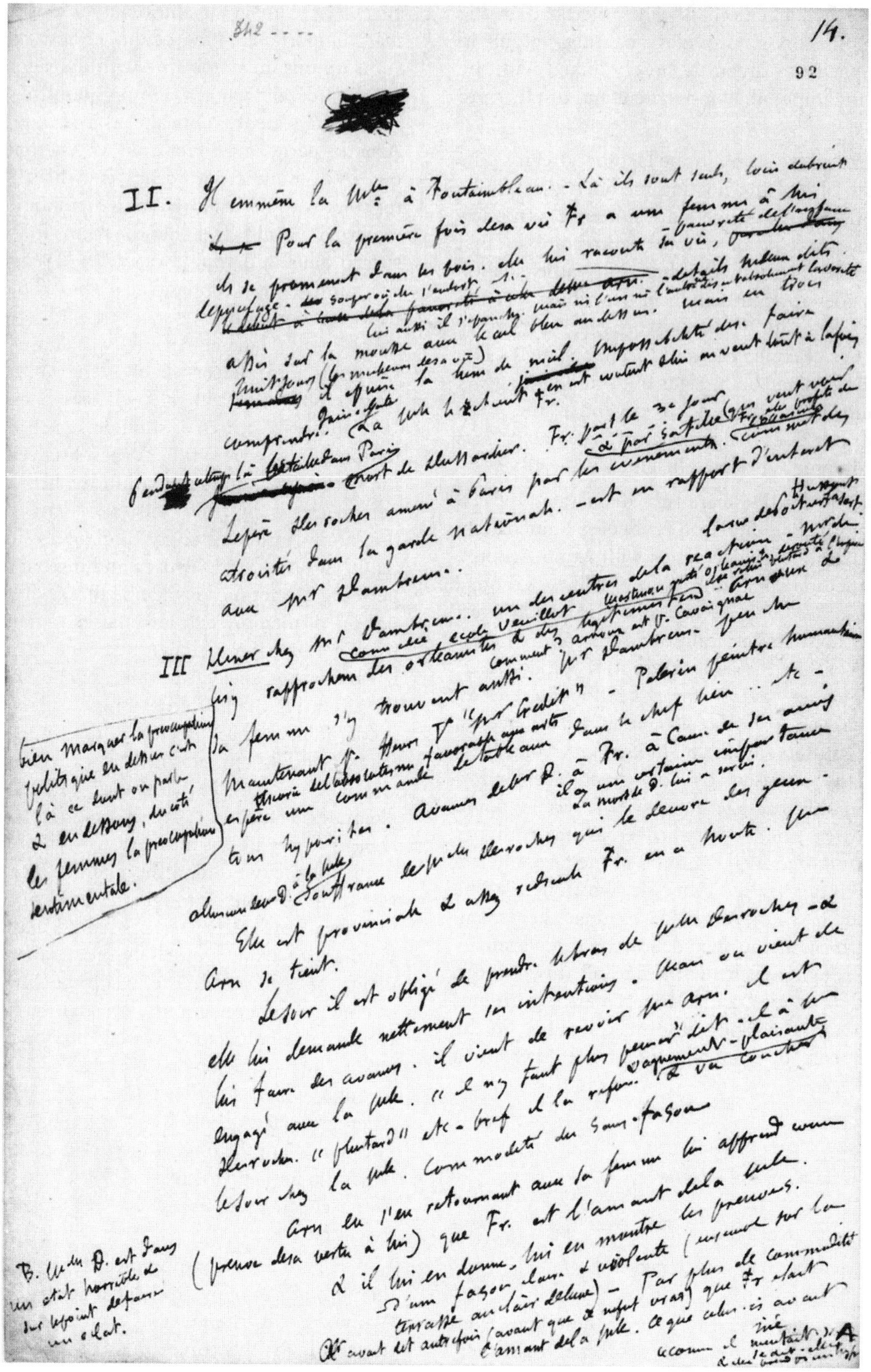

Page from a sketch for L'Éducation sentimentale, *including the episode in part 3, chapter 1, in which Frédéric and Rosanette go to Fontainebleau during June 1848, and the scene in chapter 2 of the dinner at Dambreuse's (cliché Bibliothèque nationale de France, Paris)*

brought her from the West Indies, and that she herself is a Creole. The harpist on the boat plays an "Oriental ballad" all about daggers, flowers and stars. And later in the novel when Frédéric dreams of Mme Arnoux, he sees himself traveling with her to distant lands, on dromedaries, elephants or elegant yachts. Such images are to some extent ironic, but not altogether. They also represent a genuine lyricism.[19] For Frédéric, just as for Flaubert, the ideas of love and passion are commonly associated with ideas of motion and travel to distant lands. Frédéric frequently fancies himself *in movement* with "Her." (It is in a carriage that he almost dares touch her hand!) But movement can also mean separation; travel can mean remoteness, estrangement, inaccessibility. It can mean that the loved one is elsewhere. Thus, already on the boat, Frédéric's destination and Mme Arnoux's destination are not the same: he will get off in Nogent, while she will proceed with her husband to Montereau, and from there to Switzerland. When his mother later talks to him, his mind tries to follow the image of Mme Arnoux: he pictures her sitting in a diligence, wrapped up in her shawl, her head leaning against the cloth of the coupé. There is a similar image of departure and separation almost at the end of the book: he conjures up a vision of her, sitting in a railway carriage or on the deck of a steamship "like the first time he met her" (III.5). The very reference to the first scene of the novel testifies to the permanence of the dual themes of encounter and separation. The very symbol of an exalted meeting thus tragically turns out to be a symbol of an irretrievable loss.

The travel motif is thus broadly speaking charged with a sense of poetic bitterness. Frédéric perpetually dreams of "distant countries and long voyages"–yet the only long voyage takes place during the hiatus which precedes the epilogue. He travels to forget, and appropriately the trip itself is barely mentioned: it is forgotten, swallowed by Time and meaninglessness. It is a void, a vacancy–almost an initiation to death.[20] As for his other trips, they are all derisory. His second arrival in Paris, at the beginning of Part II, is by coach. The trip begins in exhilaration, but as the heavy carriage, slowed down by rain, moves through the outskirts of the capital, the prevailing mood becomes one of ugliness and sterility, as Frédéric glimpses empty lots, branchless trees, chemical works, puddles of dirty water, sordid courtyards littered with refuse, midwives' signboards. Similar effects of disenchantment are achieved through other scenes of locomotion. The excursion to Creil to see Mme Arnoux in her husband's factory ends in discomfiture. The hedonistic journey to Fontainebleau with Rosanette (the lovers are constantly on the move) is made trivial by Rosanette's inept comments during the visit to the château. The impetuous

Time in *L'Éducation sentimentale*

Flaubert's treatment of time in L'Éducation sentimentale *is one of the marks of its modernity. In the following excerpt from his* The Theory of the Novel *(1971), György Lukács focuses on time as the carrier of epic poetry in a novel, the experience of which, he believes, is the "basis" of* L'Éducation sentimentale. *He identifies Flaubert's book as one of the major novels of "disillusionment."*

. . . Of all great works of this type, *L'Éducation sentimentale* appears to be the least composed; no attempt is made here to counteract the disintegration of outside reality into heterogeneous, brittle and fragmentary parts by some process of unification or to replace absent connections or valencies of meaning by lyrical mood-imagery: the separate fragments of reality lie before us in all their hardness, brokenness and isolation. The central figure is not made significant by means of limiting the number of characters, by the rigorous convergence of the composition upon the centre, or by any emphasis upon the central character's outstanding personality: the hero's inner life is as fragmentary as the outside world, his interiority possesses no lyrical power of scorn or pathos that might set it against the pettiness of reality. Yet this novel, of all novels of the nineteenth century, is one of the most typical of the problematic of the novel form; in the unmitigated desolation of its matter it is the only novel that attains true epic objectivity and, through it, the positiveness and affirmative energy of an accomplished form.

This victory is rendered possible by time. The unrestricted, uninterrupted flow of time is the unifying principle of the homogeneity that rubs the sharp edges off each heterogeneous fragment and establishes a relationship–albeit an irrational and inexpressible one–between them. Time brings order into the chaos of men's lives and gives it the semblance of a spontaneously flowering, organic entity; characters having no apparent meaning appear, establish relations with one another, break them off, disappear again without any meaning having been revealed. But the characters are not simply dropped into that meaningless becoming and dissolving which preceded man and will outlast him. Beyond events, beyond psychology, time gives them the essential quality of their existence: however accidental the appearance of a character may be in pragmatic and psychological terms, it emerges from an existent, experienced continuity, and the atmosphere of thus being borne upon the unique and unrepeatable stream of life cancels out the accidental nature of their experiences and the isolated nature of the events recounted.

–György Lukács, *The Theory of the Novel* (Cambridge, Mass.: MIT Press, 1971), pp. 122–129

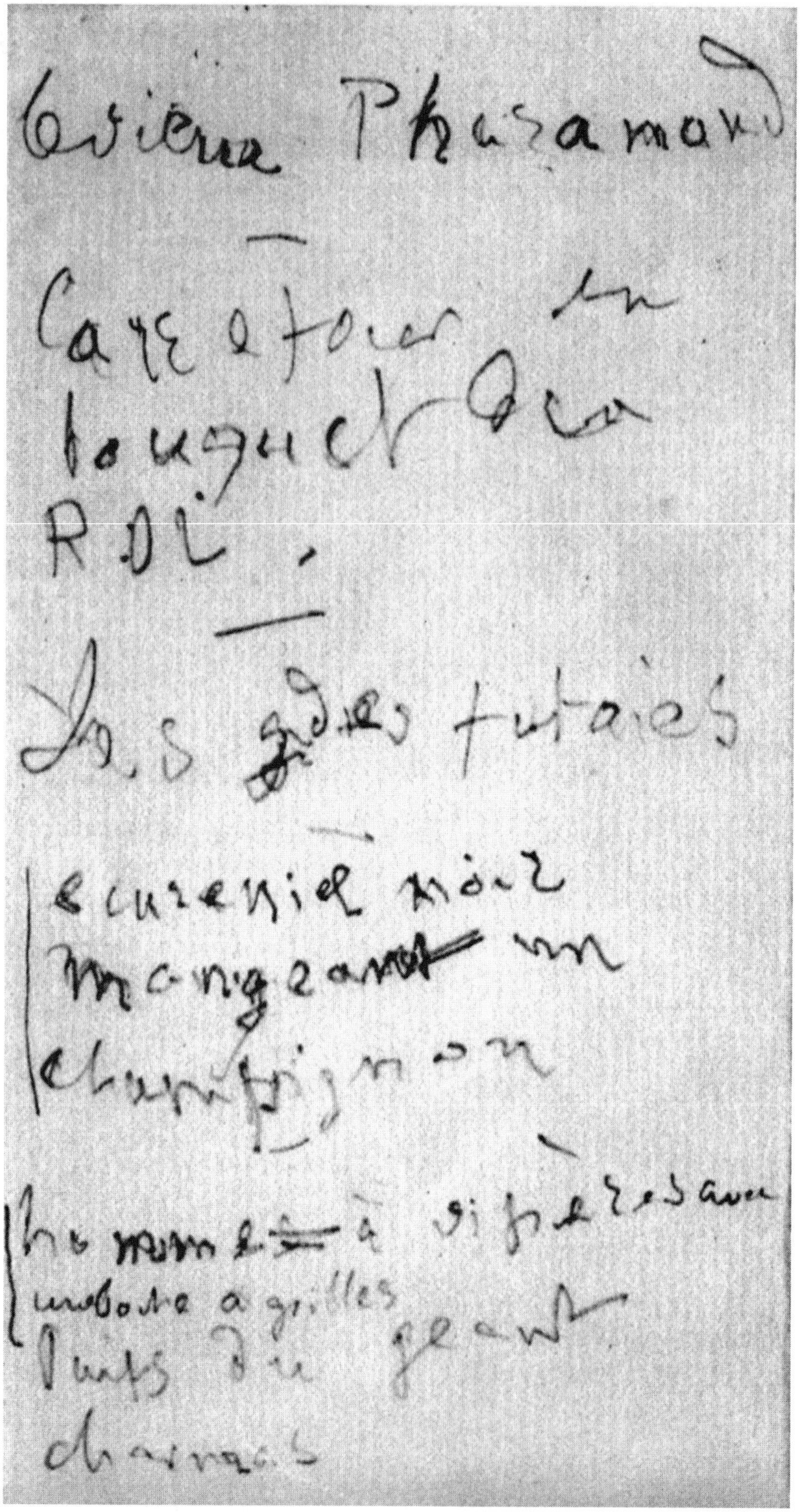

Pages from Flaubert's notebook in which he recorded observations of the Fontainebleau forest for part 3, chapter 1, of L'Éducation sentimentale. *During summer 1868 Flaubert went three times to Fontainebleau and saw the forest several times, taking notes while riding in a coach (courtesy of the Bibliothèque historique de la Ville de Paris).*

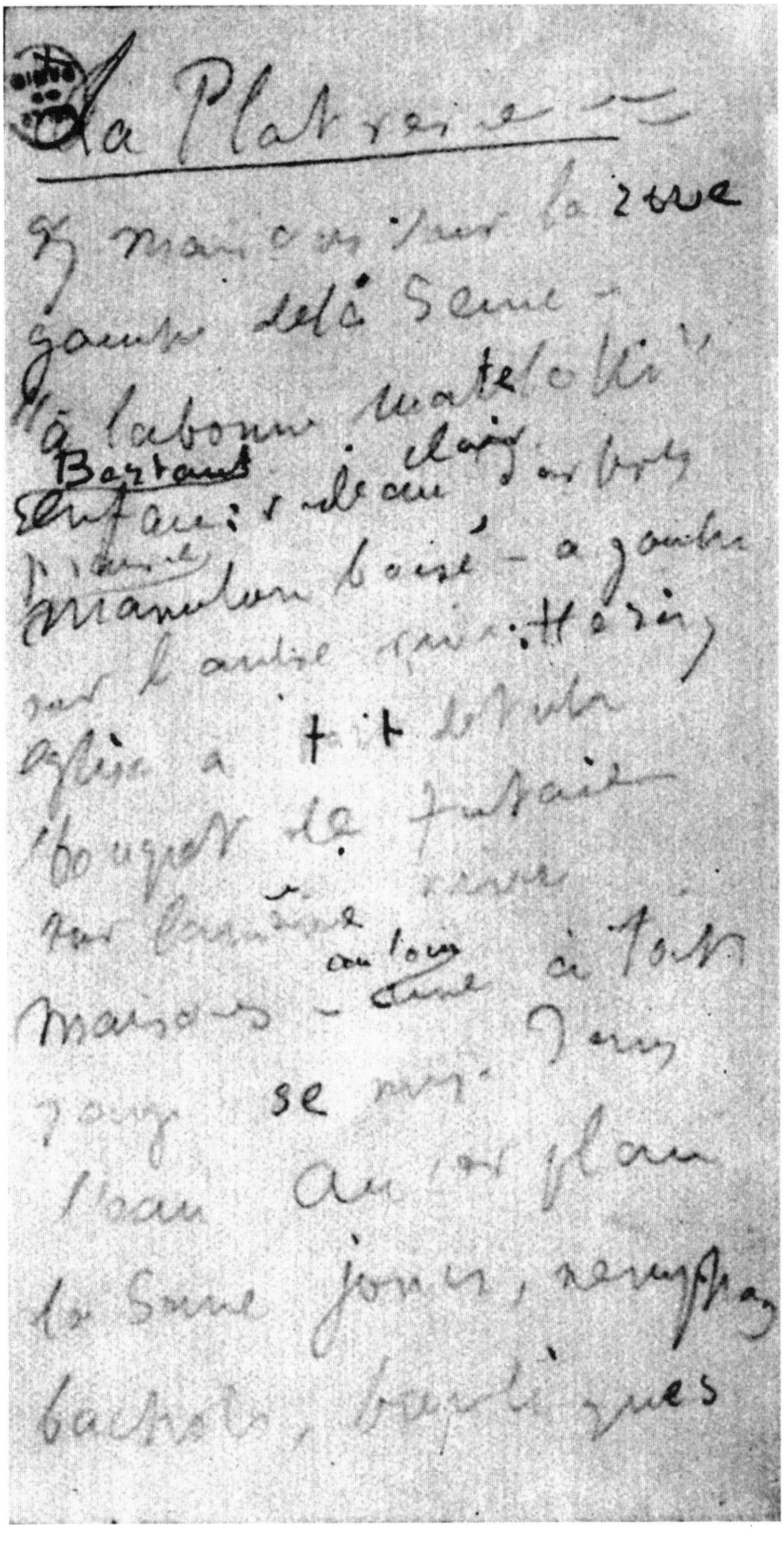

trip to Nogent after the double rupture with Rosanette and Mme Dambreuse only leads to another "defeat": Frédéric arrives just in time to witness the marriage of Louise Roque to Deslauriers. And even in town, vehicles and motion most often communicate a feeling of interrupted flow, for instance during the traffic jam after the races. The entire book seems to be conceived under the ambiguous sign of continual motion and stasis, which correspond to Frédéric's contradictory need to escape outside his solipsistic self and yet to seek refuge, to *dissolve* within it.

Images of dissolution, of liquefaction, are indeed extremely important in the metaphorical texture of the novel. *L'Éducation sentimentale* begins with a scene of travel, but it is travel by water. The Seine is where the destinies of Mme Arnoux and Frédéric meet, and it is also where, in the very first pages, they prophetically separate. The Seine is part of the Parisian landscape–and it occupied an even greater portion of the landscape Flaubert himself had constantly before his eyes from his room in Croisset. But although Flaubert was far from insensitive to its beauty, it is, in *L'Éducation sentimentale,* a river of sadness and of cruel indifference. Frédéric, in his despondent moments, watches the river flow between the somber quays blackened by the seams of the sewers. (How different from the graceful, carefree Seine of Hugo, the melodramatic Seine of Balzac, the picturesque Seine of Zola!) Flaubert's Seine has no definite color (it is "jaunâtre"–vaguely yellow). It is a river associated with loss and tragic unconcern. An old man cries; his son was probably killed during the uprising: "The Seine flowed calmly" (III.I). Tears and dirty water–they are part of the same scenery.

Albert Thibaudet has admirably shown the omnipresence of the river image in Flaubert's description of Parisian traffic and in the "liquid continuity" of the imperfect tense.[21] In fact, at one point the Champs-Élysées are quite explicitly likened to a river. But the Parisian crowds also–whether peaceful strollers on the boulevard or riotous mobs–are compared to liquid masses in motion. What Frédéric surveys near the Madeleine is an "immense flot ondulant" ["an immense undulating flow"] (I.5). The revolutionary mobs, later in the novel, are seen as "flots vertigineux" ["breathtaking flows"] (III.I): images which appropriately suggest ineluctable forces, as well as an energy that eventually flows away or evaporates.

For images of liquid in *L'Éducation sentimentale* are intimately related to images of vapor. At the beginning of the novel, a wandering haze covers the surface of the water. As the novel progresses, the poetic mist (still associated with hope in the scene where Deslauriers and Frédéric contemplate the delicate haziness in the direction of the river) becomes a tenacious fog. The characteristic weather in Flaubert's Paris is a steady drizzle and a depressing fog. At times rain becomes torrential: streets are transformed into waterways. But most often an almost anesthetizing fog seems to settle. Frédéric feels himself surrounded by "damp air" (I.4); a "humid gloom" (I.3) descends into the depths of his heart. But it is also a strangely luminous fog: from behind it shines the invisible, but effulgent figure of Mme Arnoux. This opaque luminosity is one of Flaubert's most notable achievements in *L'Éducation sentimentale.* It makes of him not only one of the outstanding poets of Paris, together with Hugo and Baudelaire, but also a brother to the Impressionist painters.[22]

This vaporous liquefaction admirably conveys states of passiveness and expectancy, and a strange mixture of stubborn hope and inherent defeatism. Thus while waiting interminably in a café, Frédéric (though not in the least bit thirsty) absorbs one "liquid" after another: a glass of rum, then a glass of kirsch, followed by a glass of curaçao, then various hot and cold grogs (II.I). Variety once more betrays futility. Drinking becomes almost literally a manner of "killing time." And repeatedly liquids and liquefaction evoke the erosive quality of Time, as well as a sense of dissolution and loss. Sitting near the river with Louise Roque, Frédéric plays with sand, letting it slip through his fingers, while close by the sound of a cascade and the bubbling whirlpools can be heard (II.5). The sand, trickling through fingers as though liquefied, no doubt signifies Time slipping away. And this dissolving quality of Time, so central to the meaning of *L'Éducation sentimentale,* is almost redundantly imparted by means of "liquid" associations. Thus while the rain pours outside, Frédéric, sitting in the café and still waiting, looks at the clock in such a manner that, if objects could be worn out by looking at them, "Frédéric would have dissolved the clock" (II.I). The same image of dissolution recurs as Frédéric waits for Mme Arnoux, who does not show up at their rendezvous: "He felt himself dissolve from utter dejection." Even the political disintegration of Louis-Philippe's regime is expressed in terms of a liquefaction (which is of course also a liquidation): "the Monarchy was melting away in rapid dissolution" (III.I).

L'Éducation sentimentale, viewed in this light, appears as a novel of steady flow and indefinite expectation. No final catastrophe ever interrupts the fluidity of existence. Tragedy here stems not from the brutal interruption of life, but from its hopeless and self-destructive continuity. The gradual bankruptcy of an entire generation is experienced, often circuitously, through the consciousness of an individual who himself is the victim of slow disintegration. The auction sale of Mme Arnoux's private belongings, toward the end of the novel, admirably symbolizes this impression of a whole life being liquidated. As Frédéric witnesses the profanation of her most intimate objects–her hats, her shoes, her lingerie–he experiences a sense of "dissolution," a mournful torpor akin to spiritual death (III.5). This feeling of slow disintegration, this wearing down by life itself, is perhaps one of the reasons why young readers are so often impatient with this book. But the theme of progressive deterioration is only one of the strands in *L'Éducation sentimentale.* The poetic power of the novel is largely to be attributed to its inner contradictions reflected in the enigmatic double ending of the epilogue, which juxtaposes a scene of transcending love and one which almost smugly surveys a life of defeats. And there is a double irony here. For just as the dreams associated with lovely images of travel and water are doomed to a fiasco, so the apparently cynical memories of the brothel in the final scene mask a never defeated and never satisfied craving for innocence and beauty.

–Victor Brombert, "*L'Éducation sentimentale:* Profanation and the Permanence of Dreams," in his *The Novels of Flaubert. A Study of Themes and Techniques* (Princeton: Princeton University Press, 1966), pp. 125–150

---

1. Flaubert, *Lettres inédites à Tourgueneff* [Monaco: Éditions du Rocher, 1946], p. 206.
2. A nostalgia for innocence which, as Harry Levin suggests, goes hand in hand with the need to be "sheltered from the contingencies of adult existence" (*The Gates of Horn* [New York: Oxford University Press, 1963], p. 229).
3. Le Poittevin, *Une Promenade de Bélial et œuvres inédites* [Paris: Les Presses Françaises, 1924], pp. 194–195.
4. Flaubert, *Correspondence* [9 volumes; Paris: Conard, 1926–1933], IV, 352.
5. For instance, in chapter 2, Part II, Rosanette betrays both Arnoux and Frédéric, Arnoux betrays his wife, and Frédéric betrays the confidence of Arnoux.
6. Goncourt, *Journal* [22 volumes; Monaco: Éditions de l'Imprimerie Nationale de Monaco, 1956–1958], VI, 172.
7. Flaubert, *Corresp.,* III, 216.
8. From the notebooks published by Marie-Jeanne Durry [*Flaubert et ses projets inédits.* Paris: Nizet, 1950], it is obvious that these two elements are associated in the earliest stages of the novel's genesis. . . .
9. Durry, *Flaubert et ses projets inédits,* p. 137.
10. Elsewhere in the novel Flaubert himself associates travel, especially ship travel, with the "amertume des sympathies interrompues" ["bitterness of interrupted friendships"] (III.6).
11. Albert Thibaudet, who rightly insists on the water imagery of this beginning, speaks of the "images flottantes de la vie qui se décompose" ["floating images of decaying life"] (*Gustave Flaubert* [Paris: Gallimard, 1935], p. 143).
12. Bachelard, *La Poétique de l'espace* [Paris: PUF, 1957], p. 69.
13. Thibaudet, *Gustave Flaubert,* p. 145.
14. D. L. Demorest, with the support of striking quotations, has shown that the tendency to exaltation at times leads to states akin to "somnambulism" (*L'Expression figurée et symbolique dans l'œuvre de Gustave Flaubert* [Paris: Les Presses Modernes, 1931], pp. 531–532). Flaubert himself seems to associate such states with movement. See the comparison, in *L'Éducation sentimentale* (II.I): "He felt somewhat stunned, like a man who gets off a ship." . . .
15. Durry, *Flaubert et ses projets inédits,* p. 163.
16. One of Flaubert's most striking early impressions of Elisa Schlésinger was the sight of her nursing her baby.
17. II.6. Is it not likely that this remark concerning Madame Arnoux's fingers corresponds to the curious notation in Flaubert's notebooks which baffled Marie-Jeanne Durry: "toutes les dents sont des personnes" (*Flaubert et ses projets inédits,* pp. 192-193)?
18. James, *Notes on Novelists* [New York: Scribner, 1914], p. 86. . . .
19. On the non-ironic qualities of exoticism in *L'Éducation sentimentale,* see Raymond Giraud's *The Unheroic Hero* [New Brunswick, N.J.: Rutgers University Press], pp. 159–160.
20. It is significant that Marcel Proust should have prized above all in *L'Éducation sentimentale* this "blank" which communicates by means of a stupendous "change of gears," the poetical qualities in the rhythmical fluctuations of time (*Chroniques* [Paris: Éditions de la Nouvelle Revue Française], p. 205).
21. Thibaudet, *Gustave Flaubert,* p. 144.
22. Harry Levin, in a perceptive discussion of this city-poetry, links Flaubert's art with that of Monet, Degas, Renoir and Pissaro (*The Gates of Horn,* pp. 230–231).

* * *

In this excerpt from his 1981 rhetorical study of French prose styles, John Porter Houston analyzes Flaubert's use of punctuation and tenses, where rhythmic effects abound, as well as subtle imitative sounds. Houston's approach, as well as other stylistic and genetic studies, suggest the degree of close study that is necessary to give a real account of Flaubert's art.

The Rhetoric of *L'Éducation sentimentale*

Of course, certain basic principles do not change in Flaubert's books after *Madame Bovary.* He remained sensitive to the clatter of *qui* and *que* [*which* and *that*] choosing often to substitute present participles for relative clauses in a way unknown in the previous two centuries of French prose; *le soleil se couchant* [the setting sun] and analogous expressions sometimes seem like merely idiosyncratic variations and sometimes have a hard-to-define grammatical beauty. The period frequently contains no hypotactic elements, the avoidance of explanations in representational narrative technique diminishing the need for subordinate clauses. Sometimes there are new prepositional substitutes for

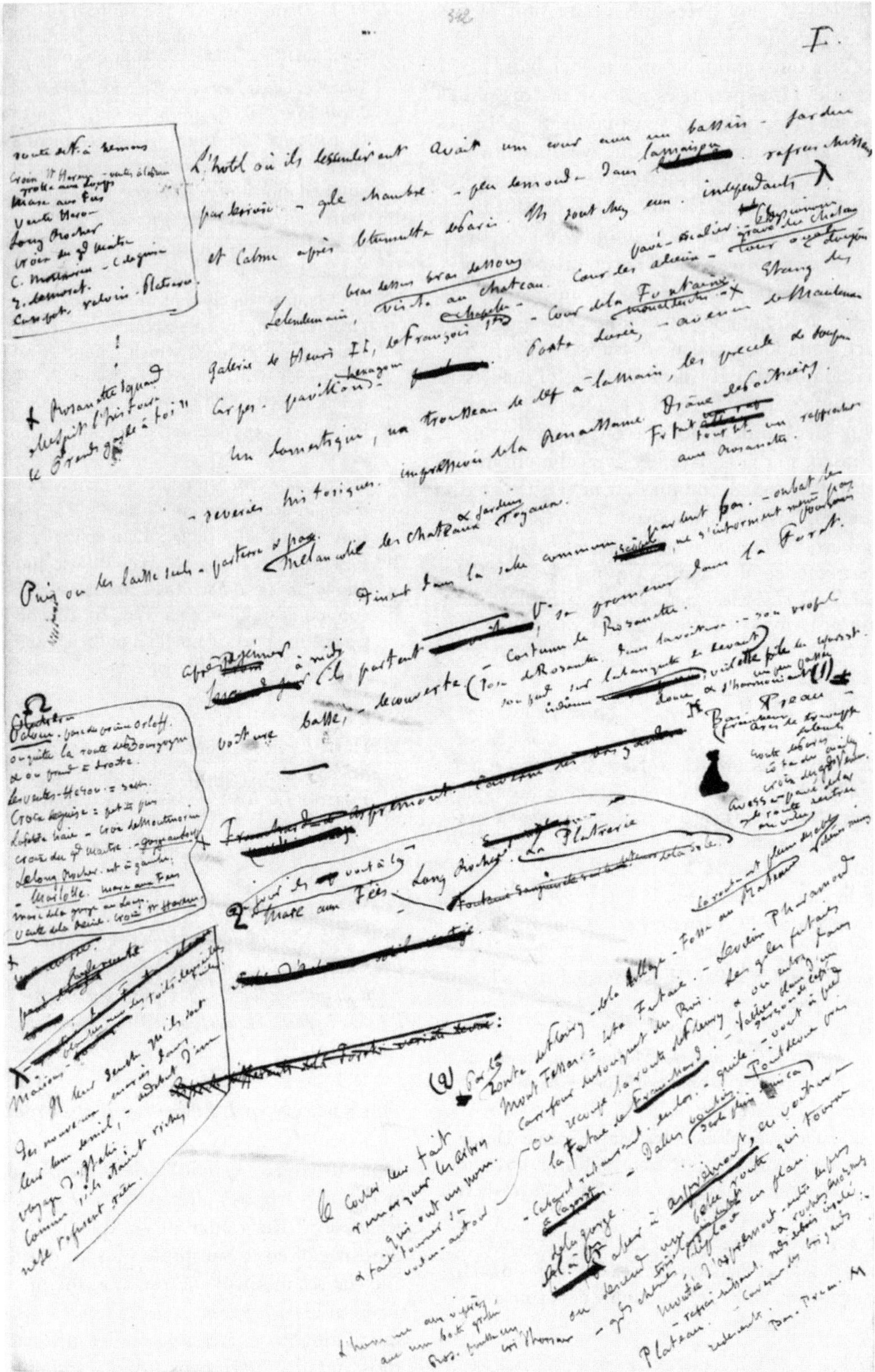

Page from a sketch of the Fontainebleau episode, in which Flaubert describes the castle and the forest in part 3, chapter 1, of L'Éducation sentimentale. *The additions in the margin are from his notebook (cliché Bibliothèque nationale de France, Paris).*

Page from a draft of the last encounter between Frédéric and Madame Arnoux at the end of L'Éducation sentimentale, *part 3, chapter 6 (cliché Bibliothèque nationale de France, Paris)*

clauses, as in "Mais les hommes de Caussidière, avec leur sabre et leur écharpe, l'effrayaient un peu."[1] ["But the men of Caussidière, with their swords and sashes, scared him a little."] In general, however, Flaubert does not lean to an excessively nominal syntax in which finite verbs are avoided. Despite seemingly anticipatory expressions in *Bovary* like *Il y eut une agitation sur l'estrade [There was a movement on the dais]* or *les lendemains de mariage ont de plus suaves paresses [Days following marriages have smoother laziness],* the verbal noun and the plural of nouns not normally taking a plural do not increase in Flaubert's later work, as they increased in French prose generally after 1860. Flaubert, like Hugo, was an early user of such constructions, but their occurrence is quite exceptional. Only once in a while, as in a phrase like *le reflet des ors décorant la nervure des pendititfs* [*the reflection of the gold paint decorating the rib of the pendentives*] (*Education sentimentale,* III, 4), does the combination of the odd plural with the peculiar participle and the rare substantives suggest the eccentric art-prose of the later nineteenth century.

In general there is less minute segmentation of the sentence in *L'Éducation sentimentale* than before, and adverbial expressions are placed less often directly after the subject. Metaphors and similes become uncommon, and there is a certain increase in phrase length. These features cohere in a new continuity of style, which, like that of *Bovary,* takes precedence over all technical questions of point of view in fiction and even, interestingly, of representational narrative method itself.

The larger number of characters, the important ideological subject matter forming a counterbalance to Frédéric's sentimental education, make the gradual revelation of character we see in *Madame Bovary* impracticable in the later novel. Psychological commentary is frequent and found from the beginning; we know that Frédéric is enthusiastic and melancholy. Since his background and verbal culture are superior to Emma's, there is little need of the tentative, exploratory method used in the earlier novel. Nor are Frédéric's fits of boredom and despondency at such a vague, generalized level of consciousness as Emma's; it is usually quite clear what, in the realm of possibility, might relieve them. Finally, the irony is of a different, less mordant kind than that of *Madame Bovary:* whereas there is an extreme discrepancy between Emma's social condition and her dreams, Frédéric is a privileged person whose aspirations are by no means out of keeping with his station in life. Even his exotic daydreams, for example, are not impossibilities: in later life he travels, like Flaubert, to what appears to be Italy, Greece, and the Near East. Irony in *L'Éducation sentimentale* comes from the ambiguous relative value of Frédéric's experiences and, in the case of his friends, from the contrast between ideology and human nature.

If representational narrative is not consistently the means of rendering Frédéric's consciousness, another kind of representation assumes enormous importance in *L'Éducation sentimentale:* the conveying of movement through rhythmic means. While it has been claimed that there are imitative effects of sound in *Madame Bovary,* these are far more elusive than the rendering of a ship's movement, carriages stopping and starting, a crowd's various actions, fencing motions, a train arriving at a station, and so forth. The first page of *L'Éducation sentimentale* contains an especially brilliant example of imitative sound: "Des gens arrivaient hors d'haleine; des barriques, des câbles, des corbeilles de linge gênaient la circulation; les matelots ne répondaient à personne; on se heurtait; les colis montaient entre les deux tambours, et le tapage s'absorbait dans le bruissement de la vapeur, qui, s'échappant par des plaques de tôle, enveloppait tout d'une nuée blanchâtre, tandis que la cloche, en avant, tintait sans discontinuer." ["Some people were arriving, out of breath; barrels, cables, laundry baskets were in everyone's way; sailors ignored all questions; one bumped into one another; packages were raised between the two paddle-wheels, and the uproar merged with the hissing of the steam, which, escaping through iron plates, wrapped everything in a whitish cloud, while the bell, in the front, continuously tolled."] Flaubert makes careful distinctions between the cumulative period, in which sentences are separated by semicolons, and disjunct actions marked by periods. Here we are building up to the ship's departure. The short phrases through *les colis [packages]* . . . render breathlessness, the chaos on the deck, and bluntly bumping into someone. With the *et* comes the hiss and release of steam: a long clause of fifteen syllables is followed by two medium length ones *(s'échappant . . .; enveloppait . . .)* [(escaping . . .; wrapped . . .)] for additional whistles of steam. The bell sound is contained in the nasal vowels and nasal consonants of *tinter* and *discontinuer* [*chime* and *continuously*].

Flaubert's entertainment is not over yet, however. First a one-sentence paragraph depicts, with a long phrase after shorter ones, the ship's gliding out into and up the river: "Enfin le navire partit; et les deux berges, peuplées de magasins, de chantiers et d'usines, filèrent comme deux larges rubans que l'on déroule." ["Finally the boat left; and the two banks, filled with stores, yards and factories, flew past like two wide ribbons that one unwinds."]

Next some quiet comes in short phrases followed by a long phrase depicting smoke: "Le tumulte s'apaisait; tous avaient pris leur place; quelques-uns, debout, se chauffaient autour de la machine, et la cheminée crachait avec un râle lent et rhythmique son panache de fumée noire; des gouttelettes de rosée coulaient sur les cuivres; le pont tremblait sous une petite vibration intérieure, et les deux roues, tournant rapidement, battaient l'eau." ["The uproar was calming down; they had all taken their places; some of them, standing, were warming themselves around the engine, and the funnel spat, with a slow and regular groan, its plume of black smoke; droplets of dew ran down the brass; the deck shook from a small internal vibration, and the two paddle-wheels, turning rapidly, beat the water."] The splash of water is conveyed by the concluding short phrases.

We must elaborate briefly on the principles of Flaubert's phrasing. While relativity is important in one's perception of phrase lengths, and sense and tone certainly contribute to one's impression, I would say that here short and long phrases lie on either side of a mean of ten syllables. With the long ones we have a further distinction to make. When intonational phrases break without a pause, Flaubert uses no punctuation; this is, of course, true most of all with the break between a substantial noun subject and its verb, where the shift of phrasing (marked often by a comma in the seventeenth century) entails no pause. In general, in *L'Éducation sentimentale* the really long sequences of words without commas consist of phrases continuous in time, much like the phrases meeting at the unpunctuated cesura of many classically constructed alexandrines. I shall refer, however, for convenience, to anything enclosed in punctuation marks as one phrase. For Flaubert the comma, and even more so the semicolon, is not a casual, conventional unemphatic sign but an important articulation of rhythm and sense. When we encounter a commaless clause like *et la cheminée crachait avec un râle lent et rhythmique son panache de fumée noire [and the funnel spat, with a slow and regular groan, its plume of black smoke],* its three sections, which depict the long plume of smoke, must be connected.

The relation of syntax and rhythm is nicely illustrated by the paragraph immediately following the above one: "La rivière était bordée par des grèves de sables. On rencontrait des trains de bois qui se mettaient à onduler sous le remous des vagues, ou bien, dans un bateau sans voiles, un homme assis pêchait; puis les brumes errantes se fondirent, le soleil parut, la colline qui suivait à droite le cours de la Seine peu à peu s'abaissa, et il en surgit une autre, plus proche, sur la rive opposée." ["The river was bordered by banks of sand. One came across wood rafts which began to rock in the swirl of the waves, or, in a boat with no sails, a man sitting fishing; then the wandering mists melted away, the sun came out, the hill which followed the course of the Seine on the right grew lower little by little, and another one came up, closer, on the opposite bank."] The first unemphatic sentences with imperfect tenses conclude with short equal phrases, in an alexandrine cadence. But a great sense of movement follows; in phrases of widely varying lengths, *passé simple [past historic]* verbs are grouped in close pairs. The phrasing, in conjunction with the verbs, is designed to suggest first speed *(fondirent, parut)* [(melted away, came out)], then a suspenseful tension broken by the shifting of hills from one bank to another; quiet returns at the end. Although the boat perhaps moves no faster, the changing banks give the sense of heightened motion. The stylistic method is one of contrasting phrase lengths sharpened by punctual tenses.

Elsewhere tense and phrase length are used for similar effect: "Un coupé bleu, attelé d'un cheval noir, stationnait devant le perron. La portière s'ouvrit, une dame y monta et la voiture, avec un bruit sourd, se mit à rouler sur le sable." ["A blue brougham, with a black harnessed horse, was standing beside the steps. The door opened, a lady climbed in and the coach, with a muffled noise, began to move on the sand."] The carriage stops at the concierge's loge and Frédéric looks inside it: "Les vêtements de la dame l'emplissaient; il s'échappait de cette petite boîte capitonnée un parfum d'iris et comme une vague senteur d'élégances féminines. Le cocher lâcha les rênes, le cheval frôla la borne brusquement, et tout disparut." ["The lady's clothes filled it; from this little padded box escaped a perfume of iris and like a vague scent of feminine elegance. The coachman loosened the reins, the horse suddenly skimmed past the corner-stone, and everything disappeared."] As Frédéric inhales the scent of Mme Dambreuse's boudoir-vehicle, the phrase lengthens, only to end with her departure in short phrases and *passé simple* verbs. In two substantial passages in *L'Éducation sentimentale,* Flaubert describes, with rhythmic devices, carriages filling the Champs-Élysées, coming to a halt in the jam, and starting to move once more (I, 3, and II, 4).

The indications furnished by punctuation can be significant, as in this series of mostly short phrases (the populace has entered the Tuileries Palace in the 1848 revolution): "On n'entendait plus que les piétinements de tous les souliers, avec le clapotement des voix. La foule inoffensive se contentait de regarder. Mais, de temps à autre, un coude trop à l'étroit enfonçait une vitre; ou bien un vase, une statuette déroulait d'une console, par terre. Les boiseries pressées craquaient. Tous les visages étaient rouges; la sueur en coulait à larges gouttes; Hussonnet fit cette remarque: 'Les héros ne sentent pas bon!'" ["One could hear nothing but the stamping of all shoes, with the lapping of voices. The crowd, inoffensive, was content to stare. But, from time to time, an elbow, cramped for room, smashed a window; or else a vase, a statuette rolled off a console down to the floor. The wainscoting, pressured, creaked. All the faces were red; the sweat was dripping in large drops; Hussonnet made this remark: 'Heroes don't smell nice!'"] The full stops are disjunctions, holes in the fabric of events. With the words *tous les visages [all the faces],* a focus suddenly occurs, a rudimentary period forms. The use of punctua-

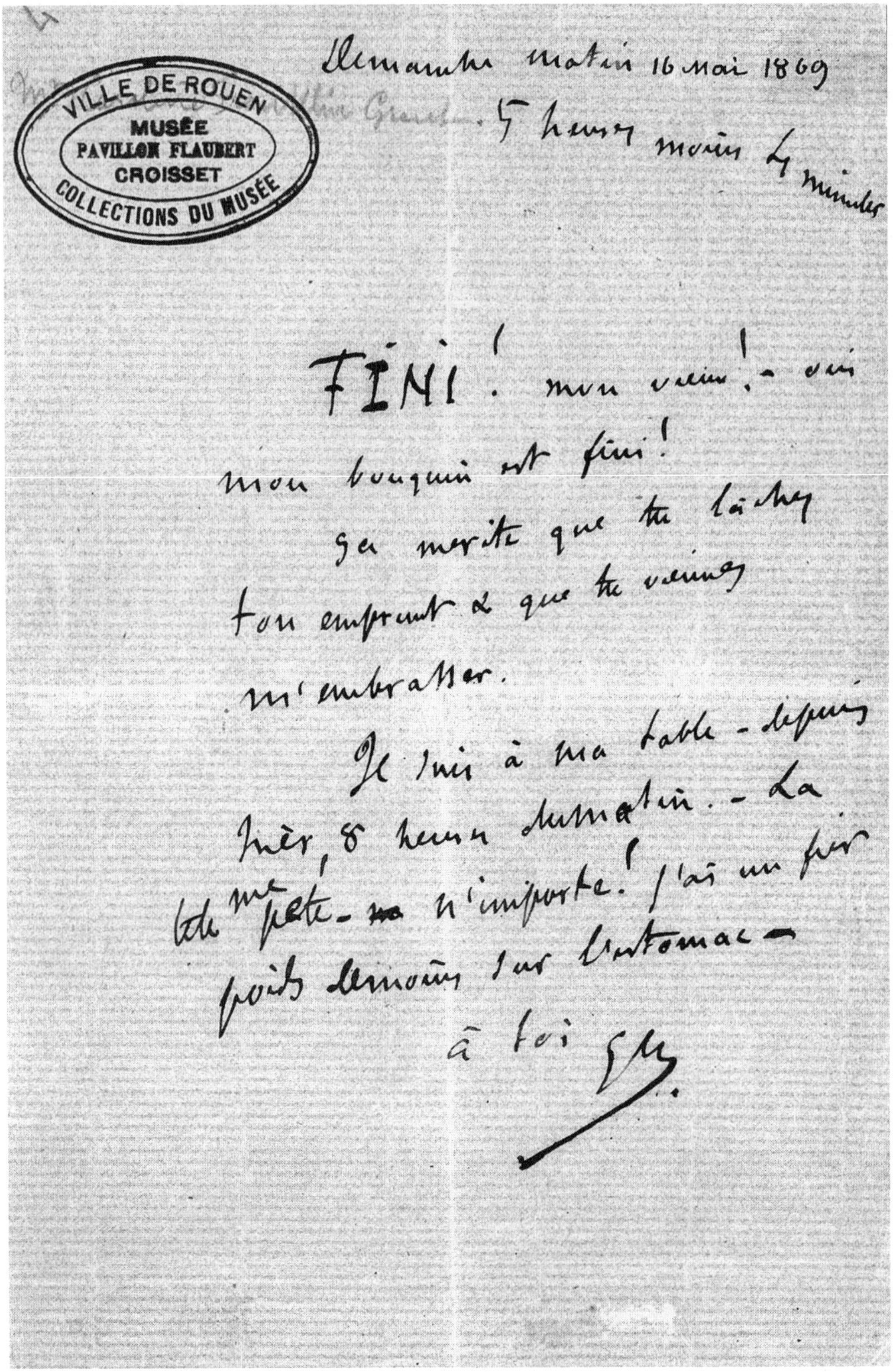

Dimanche matin 16 Mai 1869
5 heures moins 4 minutes

FINI! mon vieux! – oui
mon bouquin est fini!
Ça mérite que tu lâches
ton emprunt & que tu viennes
m'embrasser.
Je suis à ma table – depuis
hier, 8 heures du matin. – La
tête me pète – n'importe! j'ai un fier
poids de moins sur l'estomac –
à toi Gve.

The letter Flaubert sent to his friend Jules Duplan when he reached the end of L'Éducation sentimentale *on "Sunday morning, 16 May 1869, four minutes to five": "Fini! mon vieux! Yes, my book is finished! This calls for your stopping work and coming to embrace me. I've been at my desk since 8 o'clock yesterday morning. My head is bursting. No matter–there's a tremendous weight off my stomach! A toi"* (The Letters of Gustave Flaubert, 1857–1880, *p. 129; Collections de la Bibliothèque municipale de Rouen. Cliché Thierry Ascencio-Parvy)*

Jules Duplan, who helped Flaubert many times with his research and became one of his closest friends. He died in March 1870 (cliché Bibliothèque nationale de France, Paris).

tion is of especial interest in all the passages depicting crowds in the opening months of the Second Republic.

As much ingenuity as Flaubert uses in mimicking action in sentence rhythms, this aspect of his style is less remarkable than the imitation of psychological states or events in *L'Éducation sentimentale*. There is, of course, no necessary simple correspondence preestablished between states of mind and prose rhythm; the art lies, once a context is established, in manipulating long, medium, and short phrases so that they seem, momentarily at least, to have a necessary correlation. We do not have difficulty in seeing languor depicted in the following sentences: "Il y avait dans le ciel de petits nuages blancs arrêtés, et l'ennui, vaguement répandu, semblait alanguir la marche du bateau et rendre l'aspect des voyageurs plus insignifiant encore" ["There were some little motionless clouds in the sky, and boredom, vaguely spread out, seemed to slow down the movement of the boat and rendered the passengers even more insignificant"] and "Ainsi les jours s'écoulaient, dans la répétition des mêmes ennuis et des habitudes contractées." ["So days flew by, with the repetition of the same boredom and habits"]. On the other hand, the long phrase suggests in this case that Frédéric is impressed by the importance of Arnoux's review, *L'Art Industriel:* "Frédéric avait vu ce titre-là, plusieurs fois, à l'étalage du libraire de son pays natal, sur d'immenses prospectus, où le nom de Jacques Arnoux se développait magistralement." ["Frédéric had seen that title, several times, in the window of his local bookshop, on huge handbills, where the name of Jacques Arnoux was written in a grand manner"] Long adverbs, disdained as awkward and heavy by writers before Flaubert, play an important role in the prose of *L'Éducation sentimentale.* Sometimes the adverb is like a decisive clause in itself: "Il avait ordre de ramener Frédéric, définitivement." ["He had orders to bring Frédéric back, definitely."]

More interesting though than isolated sentences are places where Flaubert chooses different rhythmic means to convey similar effects. In I, 2, in successive paragraphs, Flaubert wants to express the after-effects of excitement: ". . . ils travailleraient ensemble, ne se quitteraient pas; et, comme délassement à leurs travaux, ils auraient des amours de princesses dans des boudoirs de satin, ou de fulgurantes orgies avec des courtisanes illustres. Des doutes succédaient à leurs emportements d'espoir. Après des crises de gaieté verbeuse, ils tombaient dans des silences profonds." [" . . . they would work together, would not leave each other; and, as a relaxation from their labors, they would have love affairs with princesses in satin boudoirs, or dazzling orgies with illustrious courtesans. Doubts followed their transports of hope. After fits of wordy gaiety, they relapsed into profound silences."] After the ample *ils auraient . . . illustres [they would have . . . illustrious],* the shorter clauses render doubts, the weariness that overcomes Frédéric and Deslauriers after imaginary debauches. The mechanism is clear: a short phrase after a long one means failing power. But in the next paragraph we find a description of the boys returning to the *collège* after lying in the fields dreaming of their future life: ". . . les rues désertes sonnaient sous leurs pas; la grille s'ouvrait, on remontait l'escalier; et ils étaient tristes comme après de grandes débauches." [" . . . the empty streets echoed their footsteps; the gate opened, one climbed the stairs; and they were sad, as after great debauchery."] Here a long phrase clearly indicates the worn-out, supine body and imagination. As it works out, long phrases have contradictory associations. On the positive side they are a full release of energy after constraint, confidence, a desired result, and grandeur; the negative connotations, on the other hand, include a drop of intensity, melancholy, resignation, and lack of vitality. Short phrases are also paradoxical in effect, and for both long and short phrases there exists a possible dimension of ironic meaning.

Frédéric's life as a student in Paris is at first far from agreeable, thanks to its contrast with his cozy, comfortable, adequately staffed home in Nogent: "Mille choses nouvelles ajoutaient à sa tristesse. Il lui fallait compter son linge et subir le concierge, rustre à tournure d'infirmier, qui venait le matin retaper son lit, en sentant l'alcool et en grommelant. Son appartement, orné d'une pendule d'albâtre, lui déplaisait. Les cloisons étaient minces; il entendait les étudiants faire du punch, rire, chanter." ["One thousand new things added to his sadness. He had take care of his laundry and deal with the concierge, a boorish fellow looking like a male nurse, who came every morning to make his bed, smelling of alcohol and grumbling. His apartment, adorned with an alabaster lamp, was unpleasant to him. The partitions were thin; he heard the students making punch, laughing, singing."] Only the first phrase of the second sentence is of real length; the subdued movement of parataxis and general brevity represents Frédéric's disgruntlement. When he goes to look up Martinon, an acquaintance from school, he finds him placidly installed, with mistress, in a *pension bourgeoise* and not very comprehending: "Comme les ennuis de Frédéric n'avaient point de cause raisonnable et qu'il ne pouvait arguer d'aucun malheur, Martinon ne comprit rien à ses lamentations sur l'existence. Lui, il allait tous les matins à l'Ecole, se promenait ensuite dans le Luxembourg, prenait le soir sa demi-tasse au café, et, avec quinze cents francs par an et l'amour de cette ouvrière, il se trouvait parfaitement heureux." ["Since Frédéric's boredom had no rational cause and since he could not himself claim any misfortune, Martinon understood nothing in his lamentations about life. He, for his part, went to the School every morning, then took a walk in the Luxembourg, in the evening had half a cup at a café, and, with fifteen hundred francs a year and the love of this working-class woman, he found himself perfectly happy."] Here, a few lines from the preceding paragraph, the expansive voice of reason, with its language of cause and effect, explains away Frédéric's moodiness; two long phrases setting forth the premises of any sound conclusion *(Comme les ennuis . . .; avec quinze cents francs . . .) [(Since Frédéric's boredom . . .; with fifteen hundred francs . . .)]* are followed by relatively shorter phrases, which here seem decisive and logical in virtue of their comparative brevity. The last one, above all, is almost aphoristic in its confident demonstration of how happiness is possible. "'Quel bonheur!' exclama intérieurement Frédéric." ["'What happiness!' exclaimed Frédéric inwardly."]

Short phrases nicely render awkwardness and irritation when Frédéric calls on Arnoux in the absence of the latter's wife and while a woman is concealed somewhere in the apartment: "Ils ne trouvèrent, ensuite, absolument rien à se dire. Arnoux, qui s'était fait une cigarette, tournait autour de la table, en soufflant. . . . Un morceau de journal, roulé en boule, traînait par terre, dans l'antichambre; Arnoux le prit; et, se haussant sur la pointe des pieds, il l'enfonça dans la sonnette, pour continuer, dit-il, sa sieste interrompue. Puis, en lui donnant une poignée de main: 'Avertissez le concierge, s'il vous plaît, que je n'y suis pas!'" ["They found, then, absolutely nothing to talk about. Arnoux, who had rolled himself a cigarette, was walking around the table, puffing away. . . . A piece of newspaper, rolled into a ball, was lying on the floor, in the antechamber; Arnoux picked it up; and, standing on his tiptoes, pushed it into the bell to continue, he said, his interrupted nap. Then, shaking his hand: 'Tell the concierge, please, that I'm not here!'"] In one memorable passage in short phrases Frédéric meets soldiers as he enters Paris during the June, 1848, insurrection: "Quatre barricades formaient, au bout des quatre voies, d'énormes talus de pavés; des torches çà et là grésillaient; malgré la poussière qui s'élevait, il distingua des fantassins de la ligne et des gardes nationaux, tous le visage noir, débraillés, hagards. Ils venaient de prendre la place, avaient fusillé plusieurs hommes; leur colère durait encore." ["Four barricades formed, at the end of the four streets, enormous ramparts of cobble-stones; here and there torches sputtered; in spite of the dust floating around, he could distinguish infantrymen and National Guards, all with black faces, sloppy, haggard. They had just taken the place, had shot down several men; their anger was unabated."] In this depiction of physical threat, asyndeton combines strikingly with short phrases to produce a tense, terse effect.

Long phrases and short can make interesting combinations when their value shifts. Here is Frédéric poverty stricken, resigned to living in Nogent and working as a law clerk: "Ces lamentations se répétèrent vingt fois par jour, durant trois mois; et, en même temps, les délicatesses du foyer le corrompaient; il jouissait d'avoir un lit plus mou, des serviettes sans déchirures; si bien que, lassé, énervé, vaincu enfin par la terrible force de la douceur, Frédéric se laissa conduire chez maître Prouharam." ["These laments were repeated twenty times a day, during three months; and, at the same time, the comfort of the home corrupted him; he enjoyed having a softer bed, towels which were not torn; so that, exhausted, worn out, finally defeated by the terrible force of gentleness, he let himself be taken to Maître Prouharam."] The long concluding phrases express Frédéric's surrender of his dreams of living in Paris, but in the next paragraph the long phrase depicts the exaggerated expectations of his fellow *nogentais:* "Il n'y montra ni science ni aptitude. On l'avait considéré jusqu'alors comme un jeune homme

The grave of Louis Bouilhet at the Cimetière monumental in Rouen, square M, second row. He died of a kidney ailment at forty-seven. Flaubert, who described Bouilhet as "my counselor, my guide, my companion of thirty seven years," was later buried in the same area (photograph by Éric Le Calvez).

de grands moyens qui devait être la gloire du département. Ce fut une déception publique." ["There he showed neither knowledge nor skill. One had considered him, until now, as a young man of great ability who was supposed to be the distinction of the department. It was a public deception."] Here the final short phrase has no energy, but merely a dropping effect–an example of the influence of meaning on the value of rhythm.

For short phrases conveying determination, there is Frédéric's frame of mind before his duel with Cisy: "Il fut pris d'un paroxysme de bravoure, d'une soif carnassière. Un bataillon ne l'eût pas fait reculer. Cette fièvre calmée, il se sentit, avec joie, inébranlable." ["He was seized with a rush of bravery, a bloodthirsty craving. A battalion would not have made him step back. This fever calmed down; he felt, with joy, unshakable."] Whereas Frédéric is depicted in *style coupé [broken style],* in Cisy's juxtaposed lament the phrases are not so much long as connected syntactically, as his mind races on in fear and anguish: "Il souhaita que Frédéric, pendant la nuit, mourût d'une attaque d'apoplexie, ou qu'une émeute survenant, il y eût le lendemain assez de barricades pour fermer tous les abords du bois de Boulogne, ou qu'un événement empêchât un des témoins de s'y rendre; car le duel faute de témoins manquerait." ["He wished that Frédéric, during the night, would die of a stroke, or that an insurrection would break out, so that the following day there would be enough barricades to block all approaches to the Bois de Boulogne, or that some event would prevent one of the seconds from showing up, for without seconds the duel could not take place."] This device of shifting styles with a change of paragraph to produce some ironic effect is highly characteristic of Flaubert's method, which relies a good deal on suggestion by context and contrast.

We have been observing a kind of local rhythmic effect, but there is a larger, more general aspect of prose rhythm in *L'Education sentimentale.* We are aware, right from the first line, of a very special voice speaking, well before Frédéric's consciousness is focused upon; the opening sentence is cast in the grand Chateaubrianesque mold with four delaying, shorter phrases followed by a longer final one divided symmetrically: "Le 15 septembre 1840, vers six heures du matin, la *Ville-de-Montereau,* près de partir, fumait à gros tourbillons devant le quai Saint-Bernard." ["On the 15th of September 1840, around six o'clock in the morning, the *Ville-de-Monteau,* ready to leave, sent off whirls of smoke along the Quai Saint-Bernard."] We perceive a disparity between the magnificence of the rhythm–usually saved in Chateaubriand for special, poetic moments–and the commonplaceness of the subject matter. We hear the same voice in many descriptions in the novel, such as this one of Frédéric's table, when he is about to receive his friends after his inheritance: "Un domestique en longues guêtres ouvrit la porte, et l'on aperçut la salle à manger avec sa haute plinthe en chêne relevée d'or et ses deux dressoirs chargés de vaisselle. Les bouteilles chauffaient sur le poêle; les lames des couteaux neufs miroitaient près des huîtres; il y avait dans le ton laiteux des verres-mousseline comme une douceur engageante, et la table disparaissait sous du gibier, des fruits, des choses extraordinaires." ["A servant in long leggings opened the door, and one could take a glimpse at the dining-room with its lofty dado of oak adorned with gold and its two cupboards loaded with dishes. The bottles were warming on the stove; the blades of the new knives were glittering close to the oysters; there was, in the milky tint of the muslin glass, almost an inviting softness, and the table disappeared under game, fruit, extraordinary things."] In the description of Frédéric's table, one is struck by the heterogeneity of the exact remark on the high molding in oak and gold and the more general terms that follow, until the last words, *choses extraordinaires [extraordinary things],* could hardly be less descriptive in a concrete sense. There is an interesting question here of the esthetic of the description in *L'Education sentimentale.* Besides the rather iconographic image of Madame Arnoux, some beautiful depictions of weather with great insistence on effects of light, and the pictures of the Seine, Flaubert tends in *L'Education sentimentale* to describe unevenly, a few striking details mingling with the most approximate terms. The office of *L'Art Industriel,* the Dambreuses' reception rooms, and Rosanette's apartment are all presented in this way. In general, sensory notations count less than rhythmic effects, and we observe that the memorable image in the *chute de phrase [end of the sentence],* so characteristic of *Madame Bovary,* is absent from the later novel. There are reasons for this: Frédéric is sensitive to visual details, having a certain esthetic culture, but he is not quite an artist in his perceptions; things play an enormous role in the novel, not so much as beautiful objects in themselves, but as reminders that bourgeois society is founded on the notion of property and that one's identity is one's things; and, finally, the controlling, authorial voice in *L'Education sentimentale* conveys its meaning often through a disparity between vocabulary and rhythm.

The imagery of the ugly is quite striking, especially in the descriptions of the passengers on the boat and the outskirts of Paris as Frédéric returns to the city by stagecoach, at the beginning of Part II. The solemn grandeur of the latter is memorable: "Puis, la double ligne de maisons ne discontinua plus; et, sur la nudité de leurs façades, se détachait, de loin en loin, un gigantesque cigare de fer-blanc, pour indiquer un débit de tabac. . . . Des affiches couvraient l'angle des murs, et, aux trois quarts déchirées tremblaient au vent comme des guenilles. Des ouvriers en blouse passaient, et des haquets de brasseurs, des fourgons de blanchisseuses, des carrioles de bouchers; une pluie fine tombait, il faisait froid, le ciel était pâle, mais deux yeux qui valaient pour lui le soleil resplendissaient derrière la brume." ["Then the double line of houses became continuous; and, on the bare façades stood out, here and there, a huge tin cigar indicating a tobacconist's shop . . . Posters covered the corners of the walls, and, three-quarters torn off, fluttered in the wind like rags. Workmen in smocks were passing by, and brewers' drays, laundry carriages; a fine rain was falling, it was cold, the sky was pale, but two eyes which for him were worth the sun were shining behind the mist."] Elaborate devices are present: the balancing phrase *un gigantesque . . . tabac [a huge . . . tobacconist's shop],* the inversion of subject and verb, and the hinge expression ; *plus et plus [more and more];* three short noun phrases *(des haquets . . .)* [*(drays . . .)*] elegantly precede three short clauses (*une pluie fine . . .*) [*(a fine rain . . .)*], and the final clause stretches out in a magnificent conclusion. Flaubert is specifically trying to render the contrast between concrete reality and Frédéric's inner excitement; but, more generally, he is conveying the contrast that results from a great sensibility, represented by the rhythmic aspect of the prose, acting on the inferior material which is life. Over and over again in the novel we find this effect, which is established right in the opening pages, of the grand spreading out or dying away rhythms depicting undistinguished sights and events. "La misère des propos se trouvait comme renforcée par le luxe des choses ambiantes" ["The pettiness of the talks was reinforced by the luxury of the surrounding things"]; the remark, made of one of Mme Dambreuse's receptions, has a certain general validity for the subject matter and rhythms of the novel.

While rhythmic luxury is often used ironically in the depiction of the second-rate, as in the many portraits in the novel, it also at times paints the truly beautiful or stately; but here we encounter Flaubert's important stylistic decision not to allow too brilliant a sensory vocabulary to distract from the controlling rhythms of the book or to form purple patches contrasting with their context. The presentation of the chateau and forest at Fontainebleau is an excellent example. The look of the rooms in the chateau is cursorily described rather than evoked in detail, Flaubert tending to summarize and comment: "Les résidences royales ont en elles une mélancolie particulière, qui tient sans doute à leurs dimensions trop considérables pour le petit nombre de leurs hôtes, au silence qu'on est surpris d'y trouver après tant de fanfares, à leur luxe immobile prouvant par sa vieillesse la fugacité des dynasties, l'éternelle misère de tout; et cette exhalaison des siècles, engourdissante et funèbre comme un parfum de momie, se fait sentir même aux têtes naïves." ["Royal residences have in themselves a particular melancholy, stemming probably from their dimensions which are disproportionate for the small number of guests, from the silence one finds with surprise after so many fanfares, from their motionless luxury, proving by its old age the transience of dynasties, the eternal misery of everything; and this exhalation from centuries, as overpowering and funereal as the scent of a mummy, affects even naïve minds."] Both parts of the period conclude with relatively short clauses, and the second sentence as a whole is less long than the first. Diminishing, dying away rhythmic effects become almost regular and continue on into the description of the forest. The description, while it first may seem somewhat lengthy and unrelieved, shows Flaubert working to produce his most subtle effects. Long ago, Thibaudet pointed out that in the description of the trees the various elements in the sentence, both pictorial and grammatical, shift places from clause to clause:[2] "La diversité des arbres faisait un spectacle changeant. Les hêtres, à l'écorce blanche et lisse, entremêlaient leurs couronnes; des frênes courbaient mollement leurs glauques ramures; dans les cépées de charmes, des houx pareils à du bronze se hérissaient; puis venait une file de minces bouleaux, inclinés dans des attitudes élégiaques; et les pins, symétriques comme des tuyaux d'orgue, en se balançant continuellement, semblaient chanter." ["The diversity of the trees made a changing spectacle. The beeches, with their white and smooth bark, mingled their crowns; ashes softly curved their blue-green boughs; in the hornbeam coppices holly-bushes looking like bronze bristled; then came a line of thin birches, bent in elegiac attitudes; and the pines, as symmetrical as organ-pipes, while continuously swaying, seemed to sing."] As we continue to read the paragraph, a new facet of the passage emerges. Whereas dying rhythms are half again as frequent as lengthening ones in the description of the forest, here we encounter mostly the latter.

> Il y avait des chênes rugueux, énormes, qui se convulsaient, s'étiraient du sol, s'étreignaient les uns les autres, et, fermes sur leurs troncs, pareils à des torses, se lançaient avec leurs bras nus des appels de désespoir, des menaces furibondes, comme un groupe de Titans immobilisés dans leur colère. Quelque chose de plus lourd, une langueur fiévreuse planait au-dessus des mares, découpant la nappe de leurs eaux entre des buissons d'épines; les lichens de leurs berges, où les loups viennent boire, sont couleur de soufre, brûlés comme par le pas des sorcières, et le coassement in-interrompu des grenouilles répond au cri des corneilles qui tournoient.

> [There were huge, rough oaks which rose out of the ground with convulsions, embraced one another, and, solid on their trunks similar to torsos, threw out with their bare arms desperate appeals, enraged threats, like a group of Titans struck motionless in their anger. Something heavier, a feverish atmosphere hung over the ponds, indenting the still surface of their waters between thorn-bushes; the moss on their banks, where wolves come to drink, are sulphur-colored, as if it had been burnt by the footsteps of witches, and the uninterrupted croaking of the frogs echoes the cry of the crows which wheel around.]

In the whole of the paragraph, which I have not quoted, seven periods as against three are of the augmenting sort: Flaubert is making this section of the forest description stand out as the high point before resuming the former, diminishing rhythmic structure.

Émile Zola, who wrote one of the rare enthusiastic articles on L'Éducation sentimentale *(photograph by Nadar; cliché Bibliothèque nationale de France, Paris)*

The most famous passage of *L'Education sentimentale* makes use of the broadest contrast between the short clause and the long. It begins with a pronoun reference back to the preceding chapter, a device Proust pointed out as an extraordinary example of stylistic continuity between units and which links many paragraphs in the novel.[3]

> Il voyagea.
>
> Il connut la mélancolie des paquebots, les froids réveils sous la tente, l'étourdissement des paysages et des ruines, l'amertume des sympathies interrompues.
>
> Il revint.
>
> Il fréquenta le monde, et il eut d'autres amours encore. Mais le souvenir continuel du premier les lui rendait insipides; et puis la véhémence du désir, la fleur même de la sensation était perdue. Ses ambitions d'esprit avaient également diminué. Des années passèrent; et il supportait le désœuvrement de son intelligence et l'inertie de son cœur.

George Sand's house at Nohant, which Flaubert visited several times during the 1870s. In December 1869, disgusted by the negative reviews of L'Éducation sentimentale, *Flaubert left Paris to spend Christmas vacation with Sand in Nohant (photograph by Éric Le Calvez).*

[He traveled.

He came to know the melancholy of steamships, the cold awakenings under the tent, the exhilaration of landscapes and ruins, the bitterness of interrupted friendships.

He came back.

He went into society, and had yet other loves. But the continuous memory of the first made them insipid; and besides, the violence of desire, the very flower of feeling was lost. His spiritual ambitions had equally diminished. Years went by; and he endured the idleness of his mind and the inertia of his heart.]

It is characteristic of Flaubert to have avoided anything too simply or too obviously Flaubertian in this passage; there are no ternary groups for example: the second sentence has four complements, and binary periods occur later. In the sentence beginning *Il connut,* the complements are not only four in number, they are partly isocolonic, so that neither spreading nor diminishing effects occur; it is too soon for Flaubert to use a conclusive cadence, this paragraph being left open as the fourth one is closed. Typically the prepositional phrases modifying *mélancolie, réveils, étourdissement,* and *sympathies* [*melancholy, awakenings, exhilaration,* and *friendships*] are varied in form. Heterocolon takes over with the paragraph beginning *Il fréquenta,* and increases till the last sentence. Verb position varies, but the most interesting device is the placing of the complex *rendait insipides [made them insipid]* and the forms *était perdue, diminué,* and *passèrent* in the *chute de phrase* [*was lost, diminished,* and *went by* in the *end of the sentence*], which, containing the verb, produces a more striking effect of dying away than anything we have considered up to now. Likewise the languorous, spreading clause of the end of the fourth paragraph is extreme in its effect, being all of twenty-three syllables long, as opposed to the immediately preceding six.

Proust called Flaubert's style a *trottoir roulant [rolling sidewalk],* alluding to a means of conveyance invented for the visitors to one of the Paris Expositions Universelles. In a sense, the slow but steady-seeming pace at which events occur as Frédéric and his friends drift down the river of life justifies the comparison, but actually, as we have seen, the sentences seem to reflect another water movement, ebb and flow. Rhythmic oscillation between long and short, within or between sentences and paragraphs, is much more its motion, and, in fact, this is the real movement of Frédéric's life: he oscillates between love of Mme Arnoux and pique or indifference. Connected, but somewhat independent, is the alternation between psychic energy and languor, and, of course, there are lesser oscillations involving Deslauriers, Rosanette, and the Dambreuses. All of his shifts of direction are presented as virtually involuntary, like the many coincidences of which the plot is made. Frédéric can scarcely have a broad enough point of view to encompass the whole picture, and thus we have the authorial presence in specific passages of commentary and everywhere in the controlling rhythms. Even in the free indirect discourse, there is a tendency to modulate into something more eloquent than what could have been actually said, as we saw in the passage dealing with Martinon's reactions to Frédéric's self-pity. Free indirect discourse moves between the extremes of the character's words and the author's, and frequently Flaubert inclines toward the latter.

Many other passages in *L'Education sentimentale* have remarkable features, such as the portrait of Sénécal all in bipartite constructions to render his heavy, rigid, emphatic mind, or that of Rosanette principally in verbs to render her flighty temperament; but we have seen sufficiently the range of Flaubert's style to draw one important conclusion: Flaubert worked out a whole rhetoric for the novel–not just a stylistic manner suitable to one or two subjects, but an elaborate mimesis of action. The extent of Flaubert's influence, deep and pervasive, shows the broad usefulness of his devices, the completeness of his ensemble of techniques. These include the possibility of a high style, the first real one after Chateaubriand, and in this respect also, Flaubert's work stands out from that of other romantics. In *Bovary,* to be sure, we are still close to the grotesque and ironic principles first set forth by Hugo; Emma's death scene with the depiction of extreme unction, drawing on allusions to the appropriate prayers and constituting the grandest passage in the novel, concludes with the appearance of the leprous beggar, in an effect that probably seemed to Flaubert quite Shakespearean but which appears to us more in the romantic macabre vein. The heightened passages in *L'Education sentimentale,* however, such as that beginning *Il voyagea,* are strictly dependent for their effect on reference to the whole of the novel; there are no anthology pieces.

–John Porter Houston, "Flaubert," in *The Traditions of French Prose Style: A Rhetorical Study* (Baton Rouge & London: Louisiana State University Press, 1981), pp. 217–230

---

1. See Marcel Cressot, *La Phrase et le Vocabulaire de J.-K. Huysmans* (Paris: Droz, 1938), 58–59. One alternative form of the sentence could be *Mais le sabre et l'écharpe que portaient les hommes de Caussidière l'effrayaient un peu.*
2. See Albert Thibaudet, *Gustave Flaubert* (Paris: Gallimard, 1935), 234–236.
3. Marcel Proust, "A propos du style de Flaubert," in *Contre Sainte-Beuve précédé de Pastiches et Mélanges et suivi d'Essais et Articles,* Bibliothèque de la Pléiade (Paris: Gallimard, 1971), 588.

La Tentation de saint Antoine, a Lifetime's Work: 1870–1874

As soon as L'Éducation sentimentale *was completed, Flaubert returned to* La Tentation de saint Antoine, *which he rewrote while continuing his research into the life of the saint and his era. When the Franco-Prussian War broke out and the Prussians invaded Normandy in December 1870, Flaubert and his mother were forced to leave Croisset to go to Rouen, and he wrote his niece Caroline how humiliated he felt. In 1872 Flaubert's mother, who had become more and more neurasthenic since the war, died on 6 April. Although Flaubert was devastated, he managed to finish* La Tentation *at the end of June, but he decided to postpone its publication and began planning* Bouvard et Pécuchet. *In April 1873 he went to see George Sand in Nohant, and they were joined by Ivan Turgenev. Later that year he wrote* Le Candidat, *a play that he completed on 22 November.* Le Candidat, *which premiered on 11 March 1874, and* La Tentation de saint Antoine *were published at the end of the month. For Flaubert, the appearance of his new works became a double failure: he withdrew the play from the stage after the fourth show, and the press violently criticized* La Tentation de saint Antoine.

Gustave Flaubert, circa 1870 (photograph by Félix Nadar; cliché Bibliothèque nationale de France, Paris)

The Legacy of Louis Bouilhet

From 1871 to 1873, while he was continuing with his own projects, Flaubert was also busy with the works of his deceased friend Louis Bouilhet: he intervened to have the verse drama Mademoiselle Aïssé *produced at the Odéon, where it failed in January 1872, and in 1873 he finished* Le Sexe faible, *which Bouilhet had left incomplete.*

He also wrote a preface to Bouilhet's Dernières chansons *(Last Songs), which was published by Lévy in 1872. In this excerpt from what is the only piece of literary criticism ever officially published by Flaubert, he explains Bouilhet's artistic goals—that is, his own.*

Preface to the *Last Songs* of Louis Bouilhet

Who has the right to classify the talents of his contemporaries, and, thinking himself superior to all, say: "This one comes first, that one second, and this other third"? Fame's sudden changes are numerous. There are irretrievable failures; some long, obscure periods, and some triumphant reappearances. Was not Ronsard forgotten before Sainte-Beuve? In days gone by, Saint-Amant was considered inferior as a poet to Jacques Delille. *Don Quixote, Gil Blas, Manon Lescaut, La Cousine Bette* and other masterpieces, have never had the success of *Uncle Tom.* In my youth, I heard comparisons made between Casimir Delavigne and Victor Hugo, and it seems that "our great national poet" was declining. Let us

Louis Bouilhet, circa 1860 (cliché Bibliothèque nationale de France, Paris)

then be careful, or posterity will misjudge us–perhaps laugh at our bitterness–still more, perhaps, at our adulations; for the fame of an author does not spring from public approbation, but from the verdict of a few intellects, who, in the course of time, impose it upon the public.

Some will say that I have given my friend too high a place; but they know not, no more do I, what place he will retain. Because his first book is written in stanzas of six lines each, with triple rhymes, like *Naouma,* and begins like this: "Of all the men that ever walked through Rome, in Grecian buskins and linen toga, from Suburra to the Capitoline hill, the handsomest was Paulus," somewhat similar to this: "Of all the libertines in Paris, the first, oldest and most prolific in vice, where debauchery is so easily found, the lewdest of all was Jacques Rolla," without more ado, and ignoring the dissimilarity of execution, poetry, and nature, it was declared that the author of *Melœnis* imitated Alfred de Musset! He was condemned on the spot; a farce–it is so easy to label a thing so as to be able to put it aside.

I do not wish to be unfair: but where has Musset, in any part of his works, harmonized description, dialogue, and intrigue in more than two thousand consecutive rhymes, with such results of composition, such choice of language, in short, where is there a work of such magnitude? What wonderful ability was needed to reproduce Roman society, without affectation, yet keeping within the narrow confines of a dramatic fable!

If you look for the primitive idea, the general element in Louis Bouilhet's poems, you will find a kind of naturalism that reminds you of the Renaissance. His hatred of commonplace saved him from platitudes; his inclination towards the heroic was tempered by his wit–he was very witty. This part of his talent was almost unknown; he kept it somewhat in the shadow, thinking it of no consequence; but now nothing hinders me from acknowledging that he excelled in epigrams, sonnets, rondeaux and other jests, written for distraction or pastime, and also through sheer good-nature. I discovered some official speeches for functionaries, New-Year verses for a little girl, some stanzas for a barber, for the christening of a bell, for the visit of a king. He dedicated to one of our friends, wounded in 1848, an ode on the patron of *The Taking of Namur,* where emphasis reached the pinnacle of dullness. To another who killed a viper with his whip he sent a piece entitled: *The struggle of a monster and a genius,* which contained enough imperfect metaphors and ridiculous periphrasis to serve as a model or as a scarecrow. But his best was a masterpiece, in Béranger's style, entitled *The Nightcap!* His intimate friends will always remember it. It praised glory, the ladies, and philosophy so highly,–it was enough to make all the members of the Caveau burst with the desire of emulating him.

He had the gift of being entertaining–a rare thing for a poet. Compare his Chinese with his Roman plays, *Neera* with *Lied Norman, Pastel* with *Clair de Lune, Chronique de Printemps* with *Sombre Eglogue, Le Navire* with *Une Soirée,* and you will see how productive and ingenious he was.

He has dramatised all human passions; he has written about the mummies, the triumphs of the unknown, the sadness of the stones, has unearthed worlds, described barbaric peoples and biblical scenes, and written lullabies. The scope of his imagination is sufficiently proven in *Les Fossiles,* which Theophile Gautier called "the most difficult subject ever attempted by any poet!" I may add that it is the only scientific poem in all French literature that is really poetical. The stanzas at the end, on the future man, show how well he understood the most transcendent utopias. Among religious works, his *Colombe* will perhaps live as the declaration of faith of the nineteenth century. His individuality manifests itself plainly in *Dernière Nuit, A Une Femme, Quand vous m'avez quitté, Boudeuse,* etc., where he is by turns dismal and ironical; whereas in *La fleur rouge* it bursts out in a singularly sharp and almost savage manner.

He does not look for effect; follows no school but his own individual style, which is versatile, fluent, violent, full of imagination and always musical. He possesses all the secrets of poetry; that is the reason that his works abound with good lines, good all the way through, as in *Le Lutrin* and *Les Châtiments.* Take, for instance: "Is long like a crocodile, with bird-like extremities." "A big, brown bear, wearing a golden helmet." "He was a muleteer from Capua." "The sky was as blue as a calm sea." "The thousand things one sees when mingling with a crowd."

And this one of the Virgin Mary: "Forever pale from carrying her God."

In one sense of the word, he is classical. His *l'Oncle Million* is written in the most excellent French. "A poem! Make rhymes! It is insanity! I have seen saner men put into a padded cell! Zounds! Who speaks in rhymes? What a farce! Am I imaginative? Do I make verses? Do you know, my boy, what I have had to endure to give you the extreme pleasure of watching, lyre in hand, which way the winds blow? Wisely considered, these frivolities are well enough at odd moments. I myself knew a clerk that wrote verses."

Then further: "I say Léon is not even a poet! He a poet, come! You are joking. Why, I saw him when he was no higher than that! What has he out of the ordinary? He is a rattle-brained, stupid fool, and I warrant you he will be a business man, or I will know the reason why!"

This style goes straight to the point. The meaning comes out so clearly that the words are forgotten; that is, while clinging to it, they do not impede or alter its purport.

But you will say these accomplishments are of no use for the stage; that he was not a successful playwright. The sixty-eight performances of *Montarcy,* ninety of *Hélène*

Monument located on the left corner of the entrance to the Bibliothèque municipale de Rouen, of which Bouilhet had become a librarian in May 1867. Soon after Bouilhet's death, a committee (chaired by Flaubert) was formed in July 1869 to organize the erection of a monument in honor of the poet's work. Despite Flaubert's best efforts, the city council rejected the proposal of the committee in December 1871. Flaubert wrote a long and outraged letter to the "Conseil Municipal de Rouen," which was published in Le Temps *on 26 January 1872. This monument to Bouilhet was inaugurated in August 1882, more than two years after Flaubert's death (photograph by Éric Le Calvez).*

Peyron, and five hundred of *La Conjuration d'Ambroise,* prove the contrary. One must really know what is suitable for the stage, and, above all things, acknowledge that the dominant question is spontaneous and lucrative success. The most experienced are at sea, not being able to follow the vagaries of public taste. In olden times, one went to the theatre to hear beautiful thoughts put into beautiful language. In 1830, furious and roaring passion was the rage; later, such rapidity of action, that the heroes had not time to speak; then, thesis; after that, witty sallies; and now the reproduction of stupid vulgarism appears to monopolize the public favour.

Bouilhet cared nothing for thesis; he hated insipid phrases, and considered what is called "realism" a monstrosity. Stunning effects not being acquired by mild colouring, he preferred bold descriptions, violent situations–that is what made his poems really tragic. His plots weakened sometimes towards the middle, but, for a play in verse, were it more concise, it would crowd out all poetry. *La Conjuration d'Ambroise* and *Mademoiselle Aïssé* show some progress in this respect; but I am not blind; I censure his Louis XIV in *Madame de Montarcy* as too unreal; in *l'Oncle Million* the feigned illness of the notary; in *Hélène Peyron* the too prolix scene in the fourth act, and in *Dolorès* the lack of harmony between vagueness and precision. In short, his personages are too poetical. He knew how to bring out sensational effects, however. For instance, the reappearance of Marcelline at Dubret's, the entrance of Dom Pedro in the third act of *Dolorès,* the Countess of Brissot in the dungeon, the commander in the last act of *Aïssé,* and the ghostly reappearance of Cassius before the Empress Faustine. This book was unjustly criticised; nor was the atticism understood in *l'Oncle Million,* it being perhaps the best written of all his plays, as *Faustine* is the most labouriously contrived. They are all very pathetic at the end, filled with exquisite things and real passion. How well suited to the voice his poems are! How virile his words, which make one shiver! Their impulsion resembles the flap of a great bird's wings!

The heroic style of his dramas secured them an enthusiastic reception; but his triumphs did not turn his head, as he knew that the best part of a work is not always understood, and he might owe his success to the weaker. If he had written the same plays in prose, perhaps his dramatic talent would have been extolled; but, unfortunately, he used a medium that is generally disliked. "No comedy in verse!" was the first cry, and later, "No verses on the stage!" Why not confess that we desire none at all?

He never wrote prose; rhymes were his natural dialect. He thought in rhymes, and he loved them so that he read all sorts with equal attention. When we love a thing we love every part of it. Play-goers love the green-room; gourmands love to smell cooking; mothers love to bathe their children. Disillusion is a sign of weakness. Beware of the fastidious, for they are usually powerless!

Art, he thought, was a serious thing, its aim being to create a vague exaltation; that alone being its morality. From a memorandum I take the following notes:

> "In poetry, one need not consider whether the morals are good, but whether they adapt themselves to the person described; thus will it describe with equal indifference good and bad actions, without suggesting the latter as an example."–PIERRE CORNEILLE.

> "Art, in its creations, must strive to please only those who have the right to judge it; otherwise it will follow the wrong path."–GOETHE.

> "All the intellectual beauties and details of a tale (if it is well written) are so many useful facts, and are perhaps more precious to the public mind than the main points that make up the subject."–BUFFON.

Therefore art, being its own motive, must not be considered an expedient. No matter how much genius we might use in the development of a story used as an example, another might prove the contrary. A climax is not a conclusion. We must not infer generalities from one particular case; those who think themselves progressive in doing so are working against modern science, which demands that we gather all the facts before proclaiming a law.

Bouilhet did not like that moralising art which teaches and corrects; he liked still less the frivolous art, which strives to divert the mind or stir the feelings; he did not follow democratic art, being convinced that, to be accessible to all, it must descend to the lowest level; as, at this civilised period, when we try to be artless we become silly. As to official art, he refused all its advantages, not wishing to defend causes that are so short-lived.

He avoided paradoxes, oddities, and all deviations; he followed a straight road; that is, the generous feelings, the immutable side of the human soul. As "thoughts are the foundation of language," he tried to think well so as to write well. Although he wrote emotional dramas, he never said: "If Margot wept, the melodrama is good," as he did not believe in replacing emotion by trickery. He hated the new maxim that says, "One must write as one speaks." It is true, the old way of wasting time in making researches, the trouble taken when bringing out a book, would seem ridiculous nowadays; we are above all those things, we overflow with fluency and genius!

Not that he lacked genius, however; he often made corrections while a rehearsal was in progress.

Inspiration, he held, cannot be made, but must come naturally. He followed Buffon's advice, expressing each thought by an image, and made his conceptions as vivid as possible; but the *bourgeois* declared that "atmosphere" was too material a thing to express sentiment; and fearing their sound French judgment might be disturbed and carried beyond its limits, they exclaimed "too much metaphor"!– as if they had any to spare!

Few authors take such pains in choosing their words, in phrasing. He did not give the title of author to those who possess only certain elements of style. Many of the most praised would have been unable to combine analysis, description, and dialogue!

He loved rhythm, in verse as well as in prose. He considered that language without rhythm was tedious, and unfit to stand the test of being read aloud. He was very liberal; Shakespeare and Boileau were equally admired by him; he read Rabelais continually, loved Corneille and La Fontaine, and, although very romantic, he praised Voltaire. In Greek literature, he preferred first of all the Odyssey, then Aristophanes; in Latin, Tacitus and Juvenal. He had also studied Apuleius a great deal.

He despised public speeches, whether addressed to God or to the people; the bigot's style, as that of the labourer; all things that reek of the sewer or of cheap perfume. Many things were unknown to him; such as the fanaticism of the seventeenth century, the infatuation for Calvin, the continuous lamentations on the decline of the arts. He cared little for M. de Maistre, nor did Prudhon [*sic*] dazzle him. In his estimation, sober minds were nothing else than inferior minds; he hated affected good taste, thinking it more execrable than bad; and all discussions on the arts, the gossip of the critics. He would rather have died than write a preface. The following page, taken from a notebook and entitled *Notes et Projets,* will give a better idea: "This century is essentially pedagogic. There is no scribbler, no book, be they never so paltry, that does not press itself upon the public; as to form, it is outlawed. If you happen to write well, you are accused of lacking ideas. Heavens! One must be stupid indeed to want for ideas at the price they bring! By simply using these three words future, progress, society, no matter who you are, you are a poet. How easy to encourage the fools and console the envious! Mediocre, profitable poetry, school-room literature, aesthetic prattle, economical refuse, scrofulous products of an exhausted nation, oh! how I detest you all from the bottom of my heart! You are not gangrene, you are putrescence!"

The day after his death Théophile Gautier wrote: "He carried with pride the old tattered banner, which had seen so many battles; we can make a shroud of it, the valiant followers of Hernani are no more." How true! He devoted his entire life to ideals, loving literature for itself; as the last fanatic loves a religion nearly or quite extinct.

"Second-rate genius," you will say; but fourth-rate ones are not so plentiful now! We are getting wide of the mark. We are so engrossed in stupidity and vulgarism that we shun delicacy and loftiness of mind; we think it a bore to show respect to great men. Perhaps we shall lose, with literary tradition, that ethereal element which represented life as more sublime than it really is; but if we wish our works to live after us, we must not sneer at fame. By cultivating the mind we acquire some wit. Witnessing beautiful actions makes us more noble.

If there should be somewhere two young men who spend their Sundays reading poetry together, telling each other what they have written and what they would like to write, and, while indifferent to all else, conceal this passion from all eyes–if so, my advice to them is this:

Go side by side, through the woods, reciting poetry; mingle your souls with the sap of the trees and the eternity of God's creations; abandon yourselves to reverie and the torpors of sublimity! Give up your youth to the Muse; it will replace all other loves. When you have experienced the world's miseries; when everything, including your own existence, seems to point towards one purpose; when you are ready for any sacrifice, any test,–then, publish your works. After that, no matter what happens, you will look on the wretchedness of your rivals without indignation, and on their success without envy. As the less favoured will be consoled by the other's success, the one with a stouter heart will encourage the weaker one; each will contribute his particular gift; this mutual help will avert pride and delay declination.

When one of you dies–as we must all die–let the other treasure his memory; let him use it as a bulwark against weakness, or, better, as a private altar where he can open his heart and pour out his grief. Many times, in the stillness of night, will he look vainly for his friend's shadow, ready to question him: "Am I doing right? What must I do? Answer me!"–and if this memory be a constant reminder of his sorrow, it will at least be a companion in his solitude.

–Gustave Flaubert, "Preface to the *Last Songs* of Louis Bouilhet," in *The Complete Works of Gustave Flaubert,* volume 10 (New York & London: Walter Dunne, 1904), pp. 12–22

The mortuary mask of Madame Flaubert, cast by Félix Bonet in April 1872 (Collections de la Bibliothèque municipale de Rouen. Cliché Thierry Ascencio-Parvy)

Flaubert's mother in old age (Collections de la Bibliothèque municipale de Rouen. Cliché Thierry Ascencio-Parvy)

The grave of Madame Flaubert at the Cimetière monumental in Rouen (photograph by Éric Le Calvez)

The Failure of *Le Candidat*

Flaubert wrote to Sand from Paris the day after Le Candidat *premiered at the Vaudeville theater. The action takes place in a small provincial town, where everyone tells Monsieur Rousselin (the main character) that he should be a candidate to become a deputy. He thinks and even dreams about it until he tries, by every means, to obtain votes, going to the point of sacrificing his own daughter, Louise, to his political ambitions. This political satire, characterized by the writer Auguste Villiers de l'Isle-Adam as a "photograph of stupidity" (in a review published in* Revue du Monde Nouveau, *1 February 1874), was condemned by all political parties, which Sand explained by saying the play was "too true" for the public of the time. Referring to himself as "Cruchard" (a nickname he gave to himself–which he also used to sign some letters when he was in a negative state of mind–derived from a pun on the word* cruche, *which means* pitcher *but also* dumb *or* idiot*), Flaubert mentions the theater director Léon Carvaille, known as Carvalho.*

Flaubert to Sand, 12 March 1874

Chère maître,

If ever there was a Flop! People wanting to flatter me insist that the play will catch on with the general public, but I don't believe it for a second.

I know the defects of my play better than anyone. If Carvalho hadn't driven me crazy for a month making one foolish "correction" after another (all of which I rejected), I'd have done some retouching, or rather made some changes myself that might have altered the final result. But, as it was, I grew so disgusted with the whole business that I wouldn't have changed a line for a million francs. In a word, I'm sunk.

Besides, it has to be said that the audience was detestable, all fops and stockbrokers who had no understanding of what words *mean.* Anything poetic they took as a joke. A poet says: "I'm a man of the 1830s, you know. I learned to read from *Hernani* and would have liked to be Lara."[1] That brought a roar of ironic laughter. And more of the same.

And then the public was misled by the title. They were expecting another *Rabagas.* The Conservatives were annoyed because I didn't attack the Republicans, and the Communards would have liked me to throw a few insults at the Legitimists.

My actors played superbly, Saint-Germain among the rest. Delannoy, who carries the entire play, is much distressed, and I don't know how to console him.

As for Cruchard, he is calm, very calm! He dined very well before the performance, and after it supped even better. Menu: two dozen Ostend oysters, a bottle of iced champagne, three slices of roatsbeaf [sic], truffle salad, coffee, liqueur.

Cruchard is sustained by his Religion and his Stomach.

I confess I'd have liked to make some money. But since my fiasco has nothing to do with art or feeling, I really don't give a damn. I tell myself, "At last it's over," and feel much relieved.

The worst of all was the scandal about tickets. Note that I was given 12 seats in the stalls and one box (the *Figaro* had 18 stalls and 3 boxes). I never even *saw* the chef de claque.[2] It's almost as though the management of the Vaudeville set things up for a failure. Their dream came true.

I didn't have a quarter of the seats I'd have liked to dispose of. And I bought a number–for people who then proceeded to knife me during the intervals. The "bravos" of a few faithful supporters were quickly drowned in a sea of "Shhhs." At the mention of my name after the final curtain there was some applause (for the man, not the play), together with two rounds of boos from the top gallery. And that's the truth.

This morning's newspapers–the minor press–are polite. I can't ask more of them than that.

Adieu, chère bon maitre. Don't feel sorry for me. Because I don't feel pitiable. I've been having a frightful grippe, like your little girls. But I'm better.

Et je vous embrasse trétous.[3]

Votre vieux

Gve Flaubert

My man said something nice as he handed me your letter this morning. Recognizing your handwriting, he sighed, and said: "Ah, the best one wasn't there last night."

My sentiments precisely.

–*Flaubert~Sand. The Correspondence,* translated by Francis Steegmuller and Barbara Bray, edited by Steegmuller (New York: Knopf, 1993), pp. 335–337

---

1. The unworldly Flaubert is surprised that a boulevard (corresponding to "West End" or "Broadway") theatre audience should laugh at references to Romantic poetry in the midst of a satirical comedy. (*Hernani,* drama in verse by Victor Hugo, 1830; *Lara, a Tale,* poem by Byron, 1814.)
2. The *claque* was a set of applauders hired by the theatre. The author of the play was expected to reward them via their leader.
3. *trétous:* a Flaubertian verbal invention, combining *très* ("very") and *tous* ("all of you").

* * *

Two views of the Vaudeville theater in Paris, where Le Candidat *was produced. Flaubert withdrew it after the fourth night (drawings by Bertrand; clichés Bibliothèque nationale de France, Paris).*

Sand wrote from Nohant.

Sand to Flaubert, 14 March 1874

I've had the same experience a couple of dozen times myself, and the worst is the disgust you speak of. One never sees or hears one's own play; it's become unrecognizable, and one's ceased to have any feelings about it. Hence the philosophy with which writers who happen to be artists accept the verdict, whatever it may be.

I'd already heard something about the opening. The audience wasn't well-disposed. The subject was too near the bone. People don't like seeing themselves as they are. There's no room in the theatre now for anything but either idealism or smut. There's an audience only for the two extremes. Any study of morals upsets those whose ways are immoral, and, as these may well be the only ways left, people dismiss as boring what they in fact find uncomfortable. Anyhow, you're not taking it to heart, and that's the right attitude to adopt until you can get your own back.

I don't know anything about the play except that it was a work of enormous talent (as Saint-Germain wrote to me recently, though he did say he didn't expect it would be to the taste of present-day audiences). Do send it to me when it's published, and then I'll tell you whether it's Cruchard or the public who got it wrong. See how the next two performances go. See if the reactions of different sections of the public say anything useful.

As for the habit of doling out tickets to everyone except the author, that's how it's always been for me too. We're too easy-going. And as for friends stabbing one in the back, it happens to everybody.

Je t'embrasse et je t'aime. Get your revenge soon; I have no worries about the future.

Love from all of us. Tell your man he's right and that he's a good fellow. The little ones are better. I'm working.

[unsigned]

–*Flaubert~Sand. The Correspondence,* p. 337

* * *

Flaubert to Sand, 15 March 1874

Since there would have had to be a fight, and since Cruchard detests the idea of a struggle, I have withdrawn my play, even though there was 5 thousand francs' worth of advance sales. Too bad, but I won't have my actors hissed and booed. The second night, when I saw Delannoy coming off the stage with tears in his eyes, I felt like a criminal and decided that was enough. (I'm touched by the distress of three people–Delannoy, Turgenev, and my manservant.) So it's over. I'm having the play printed; you'll receive it by the end of the week.

I'm being flayed by all parties–the *Figaro* and the *Rappel.*[1] It's unanimous. People for whom I bought tickets or did other favours are calling me a cretin–for example Monselet, who *asked* his paper to let him write an article against me.[2] All of which leaves me untouched. Never have I been less upset. I'm astonished by my own stoicism (or pride). And when I seek the reason for this I wonder whether you, chère maître, aren't partly responsible.

I remember the first night of *Villemer,* which was a triumph, and the first night of *Les Don Juan du Village,* which was a defeat. You don't know how much I admired you on those two occasions. The nobility of your character (a thing rarer even than genius) was truly edifying! And I said a prayer: "O, that I might be like her under such circumstances!" Who knows? Was I perhaps sustained by your example? Forgive the comparison.

Well, I don't give a damn, and that's the truth.

But I do confess I regret the several thousand francs I might have earned. My little money-box is empty. I had wanted to buy some new furniture for Croisset. Nothing doing!

My dress rehearsal was deadly. The entire Parisian press! They took everything as a joke. In your copy I'll underline the passages they pounced on.[3]

Yesterday and the day before, those passages no longer bothered anybody. Anyway, too late now. Perhaps Cruchard's pride carried him away.

And they wrote articles about my house, my slippers, and my dog.[4] They described my apartment, where they saw "pictures and bronzes on the walls". In fact there is nothing at all on my walls. I know that one critic was indignant with me for not paying him a call: this morning an intermediary came to tell me that, and asked, "What answer shall I give him?"–"*Merde.*"–"But Dumas and Sardou and even Victor Hugo aren't like you."–"Oh, I'm quite aware of that."–"Well, then, don't be surprised if . . ." Etc.

Adieu, chère bon maître. Amitiés aux vôtres, baisers aux chères petites et à vous toutes mes tendresses.

Gve Flaubert

–*Flaubert~Sand. The Correspondence,* pp. 337–339

---

1. A. Vitu, in the *Figaro* for 14 March, reproached Flaubert particularly for having included no sympathetic characters in his play–a criticism recurrently levelled against certain works by Flaubert. The review in *Le Rappel* of the same day spoke of the "*ennui glacial*" caused by the play's "puerility, naiveté, and total lack of interest".
2. Charles Monselet, dramatic critic on *L'Evénement,* wrote that "Six lines of *Madame Bovary*, chosen at random, are worth more than all of *Le Candidat.*" He spoke warmly of Flaubert's human and literary qualities.

3. However, the *Figaro,* in its report of the dress rehearsal, had predicted a great success.
4. One of the reporters wrote of "the hermitage at Croisset", where Flaubert worked "shut away for weeks on end, writing at night, and sleeping on a rug during the day, with his great dog Salambô [sic], for company".

* * *

Flaubert sent Sand copies of Le Candidat, *published on 28 March, and* La Tentation de saint Antoine, *published on 31 March. In her response Sand refers to Flaubert's ongoing research for* Bouvard et Pécuchet, *the deux bonshommes (two fellows).*

Sand to Flaubert, 3 April 1874

We've read *Le Candidat* and we're going to re-read *Antoine.* I have no difficulty about the latter: it's a masterpiece. I'm not so happy with *Le Candidat.* It's not something that can be seen by "you", the spectator, watching events unfold and trying to take an interest in them. The subject itself is off-putting; too real for the stage, and treated too realistically. From the point of view of the theatre a real rose tree is ineffective–you need a *painted* rose tree. And there's no advantage in having one painted by a master, either. What's needed is just a rough likeness, a kind of cheat. And this applies to the play. It isn't amusing to read. On the contrary, it's depressing. It's so true to life it doesn't make one laugh, and since one can't take an interest in any of the characters one isn't interested in the action. That's not to say you can't or shouldn't write for the theatre. On the contrary, I believe you will, and do it very well. But writing to be acted is difficult, much more difficult, a hundred times more difficult than writing to be *read.* Unless one is Molière and has a well-defined society to depict, eighteen out of every twenty attempts are bound to fail. But that doesn't matter. As you've seen for yourself, one is philosophical, one soon gets used to this hand-to-hand battle, and just carries on until one hits the enemy, the public, the blockheads. If it was easy, if we were sure to succeed every time, there'd be no merit in engaging in this diabolical struggle of one against all.

You see, mon chéri–I say what I think. So you can be sure of my sincerity when I back you up unreservedly. I haven't read what the newspapers say about you. I care as little for what they think about you as for what they think about me. Individual judgments are neither here nor there. Theatre makes its impact collectively, and I've tried to read your play as a member of the public *as a whole.* Even if you'd had a success, I'd have been pleased with the success, but not with the play. Certainly, from the point of view of the writing, it shows talent: it couldn't do otherwise. But it's a case of good construction being used to build a house on an unsuitable piece of land. The architect has picked the wrong site. The subject lends itself to caricature, as in *M. Prud'homme,* or to tragedy, as in *Richard d'Arlington.*[1] But you treat it *exactly,* which means that the art of the theatre disappears: for exactness belongs to photography. Very few people can produce a perfectly accurate photograph; but even then it isn't art. And you are an artist par excellence! Have another go and do better! as the peasants say.

I'm writing a play at the moment[2] and I think it's very good. But as soon as it's exposed to the scrutiny of rehearsal I'll find it quite dreadful. And in reality it's just as likely to be excellent as worthless. One never knows oneself what one's doing and what one's worth, and one's best friends don't know either. They can be enchanted by a play of ours when they read it, and disenchanted when they see it on the stage. That doesn't mean they've betrayed us. They've merely been affected differently. They want to applaud, but their hands fall back in their laps. The electricity has gone. The author was mistaken, and so were they. But what does it matter? When the author's an artist, and an artist like you, he wants to try again, the wiser for the experience. I'd rather see you trying again straight away than buried in your *deux bonshommes.* I fear, from what you've told me about the subject, that it may be another case of something too true, too well observed and too accurately rendered. You have the talents for that; but you have other, greatly superior capacities as well–intuition, largeness of vision and genuine power. I notice that in the past you've employed sometimes the one set of talents and sometimes the other, amazing everyone with the extraordinary contrast. Why not combine the realistic and the poetic, the true and the fictional? Isn't the most comprehensive art an amalgam of both? You have two publics–one for *Madame Bovary* and another for *Salammbô.* Put them together in one auditorium and force them to get on with one another.

Bonsoir mon troubadour, je t'aime et je t'embrasse, nous t'embrassons tous.

G. Sand

–*Flaubert~Sand. The Correspondence,* pp. 339–341

---

1. *Richard d'Arlington,* drama in 3 acts, in prose, by the elder Dumas in collaboration with J.-F. Beudin and P.-P. Goubaux, had opened at the Théâtre de la Porte-Saint-Martin on 10 December 1831.
2. Sand read her play *Salcède* to the management of the Odéon the following 31 May. It was accepted, but "with alterations to be made by the author". It was never produced.

* * *

Flaubert to Sand, 8 April 1874

Chère maître,

Thank you for your long letter about *Le Candidat.* Now let me add a few critical remarks of my own.

1 The curtain should have come down after the electoral meeting, and the second half of the 3rd act should have constituted the opening of the 4th.

2 Omit the anonymous letter–it's superfluous, since Arabella tells Rousselin that his wife has a lover.

3 Reverse the order of the scenes in the 4th act: that is, begin with the announcement of Mme R[ousselin]'s rendezvous with Julien, and make Rousselin a bit more jealous. He would like to catch his wife committing adultery, but is too busy with the elections.

The exploiters aren't sufficiently developed. There should have been 10 instead of 3! Then he sacrifices his daughter. That's the end of everything. And just as he becomes aware of his own rottenness, he's elected. His dream comes true. But it brings him no happiness.

That way there would have been dramatic development, and a moral.

Whatever you may say, I think the *subject* a good one.

But I bungled it. Not one of the critics pointed out how. But I know. And that consoles me.

What do you say to La Rounat's begging me, in his article, "in the name of our old friendship", not to have the play published, because he finds it so "stupid and badly written"? And he goes on to draw a parallel between me and Gondinet.[1]

One of the most comic aspects of our time is the arcana of the theatre. Anyone would think that the art of the stage was a realm inaccessible to mere human intelligence, a secret known only to those who write like cab-drivers. The element of "instant success" takes precedence over all else. It's a veritable school for demoralization! If my play had been given proper support by the management, it could have made money like any other. But would it have been any better? You know I wasn't given *a single ticket,* I never even saw the chef de claque, and I was booed by one of the managers of the theatre.

Your friend Saint-Germain so disparaged me before, during, and after my 4 performances that I didn't send him the printed text. He found that shocking. I wonder why he should have, since he thought the audience was right to go for me about lines I consider excellent. Charpentier came close to showing him the door, so violent were his diatribes against yours truly. Please believe me–I don't give a damn about all this. But one mustn't be a simpleton: one must know whom one is dealing with.

Since we're having a gossip, let me tell you that the clerk at our friend Lévy's is assuring customers that "Mme Sand thinks *La Tentation de Saint Antoine* detestable." But there are some customers who won't have that, and contradict him–Turgenev, for example: in fact it was to Turgenev that the clerk made his remark.

La Tentation seems to be doing well anyway. The first printing of 2 thousand copies is sold out. Tomorrow the second will be in the shops. I've been torn to pieces in the minor newspapers, and praised to the skies by two or three people. Nothing of consequence has appeared as yet, and I suspect nothing may ever appear. Renan no longer writes in the *Débats,* he tells me, and Taine is busy with his new house at Annecy.

I've been denounced by Villemessant and Buloz,[2] both of whom can be counted on to do everything possible to make things disagreeable for me. Villemessant blames me for "not getting myself killed by the Prussians"! It's all enough to make you vomit.

And you want me to overlook human Stupidity! And to forego the pleasure of portraying it! But the Comic is Virtue's sole consolation. And besides, there's a lofty way of taking it. That's what I'm going to try to do in my *Deux bonshommes.* Have no fear that this book will be too realistic! On the contrary: I'm afraid it may seem impossible, so excessively will it be concerned with ideas. This little task that I'll be beginning in six weeks will take me four or five years: it will have *that* virtue, at least!

Adieu, chère bon maître. Amitiés aux vôtres, et à vous toutes les tendresses de

Cruchard

–*Flaubert~Sand. The Correspondence,* pp. 341–343

---

1. Edmond Gondinet's *Le Chef de division,* a satirical comedy about bureaucracy, had opened a few months before.
2. The reason for Buloz' hostility–if it really existed–is not known. Villemessant, editor of *Le Figaro,* appears to have been hostile to Flaubert because of the latter's republican sympathies.

* * *

Sand to Flaubert, 10 April 1874

Anyone who says I don't think *Saint Antoine* is a fine and excellent work is lying, as I need hardly say. And I don't know how I'm supposed to have confided in Lévy's clerk, whom I've never even met! I do remember telling Lévy himself last summer[1] that I found the book superb and of the highest distinction.

I'd have written you an article if I hadn't refused to do one for Meurice in the last few days on V. H[ugo]'s *Quatrevingt-Treize.* I told him I was ill. The fact is, I don't know how to write articles, and I've done so many for Hugo already I've exhausted the subject. I wonder why he's never written one for me: I'm no more a journalist than he is, and I could do with his support more than he with mine.

Anyway, articles serve no more purpose nowadays than having friends in the theatre. As I said, it's a battle of all against one, and the secret, if there is one, is how to produce an electric current. The subject is therefore very important in the theatre. With a novel you have time to draw the reader to you. A completely different matter! I don't agree that there's nothing mysterious about the theatre. In one way it's *very* mysterious: you can't judge your effects in advance, and even the cleverest playwrights are wrong more often than not. You say yourself that you made mistakes. I'm working on a play now, and it's impossible for me to tell if I'm going the right way about it. And when *shall* I know? The day after the first performance, if I have it put on, which isn't certain. The only thing that's amusing is work that hasn't yet been read to anyone. All the rest is a chore and part of the "job". Horrible!

Just laugh at all the gossip. The most blameworthy people are those who relay it. I find it very strange that they say all those things against you to your friends. No one ever says anything to me; they know I wouldn't stand for it.

Be brave and glad because *Saint Antoine* is doing and selling well. What does it matter if they slate you in some paper or other? Once upon a time it did matter. But not now. The public is no longer what it was, and journalism hasn't the slightest influence on literature any more. Everyone is a critic and forms his own opinion. No one ever writes me any articles for my novels. I don't even notice.

Je t'embrasse et nous t'aimons.
Ton vieux
troubadour

–*Flaubert~Sand. The Correspondence,* p. 343

---

1. Michel Lévy had been a guest at Nohant from 9 to 12 July 1873.

Critical Views of *La Tentation de saint Antoine*

Part novel, part drama, and wholly original, Flaubert's La Tentation de saint Antoine, *a seven-part work consisting primarily of descriptions of Antoine's religious visions or hallucinations and the saint's interaction with them, was published in Paris on 31 March 1874 to a mixed reception.*

Although Henry James called Flaubert "the novelist of novelists," he did not understand La Tentation de saint Antoine, *as he had not understood* L'Éducation sentimentale. *In a review that was published in the 4 June 1874 issue of the American journal* The Nation, *James acknowledges Flaubert's descriptive strength but finds the work a "really painful failure."*

Flaubert's *Temptation of Saint Anthony*

Saint Anthony, as most readers know, was an Egyptian monk who, toward the end of the third century, hid himself in the desert to pray, and was visited by a series of hallucinations painfully irrelevant to this occupation. His visions and his stout resistance to them have long been famous–so famous that here is M. Gustave Flaubert, fifteen hundred years afterwards, publishing a large octavo about them, and undertaking to describe them in every particular. This volume, we confess, has been a surprise to us. Announced for publication three or four years ago, it seemed likely to be a novel of that realistic type which the author had already vigorously cultivated, with Saint Anthony and his temptation standing simply as a symbol of the argument. We opened it with the belief that we were to find, not a ragged old cenobite struggling to preserve his virtue amid Egyptian sands, but a portrait of one of the author's own contemporaries and fellow-citizens engaged in this enterprise in the heart of the French capital. M. Flaubert's strong side has not been hitherto the portrayal of resistance to temptation, and we were much in doubt as to whether the dénouement of the novel was to correspond to that of the legend; but it was very certain that, whatever the upshot, the temptation itself would be elaborately represented. So, in fact, it has been; but it is that of the dim-featured founder of monasticism, and not of a gentleman beset by our modern importunities. The work has the form of a long monologue by the distracted saint, interrupted by voluminous pictorial representations of his visions and by his imagined colloquies with the creatures who people them. We may frankly say that it strikes us as a ponderous failure; but it is an interesting failure as well, and it suggests a number of profitable reflections.

In so far as these concern M. Gustave Flaubert himself, they are decidedly melancholy. Many American readers probably have followed his career, and will readily recall it as an extraordinary example of a writer outliving his genius. There have been poets and novelists in abundance who are people of a single work, who have had their one hour of inspiration, and gracefully accept the certainty that it would never strike again. There are other careers in which a great success has been followed by a period of inoffensive mediocrity, and, if not confirmed, at least not flagrantly discredited. But we imagine there are few writers who have been at such extraordinary pains as M. Flaubert to undermine an apparently substantial triumph. Some fifteen years ago he published 'Madame Bovary,' a novel which, if it cannot be said

The Temptation of Saint Anthony: *top, the painting attributed to Peter Brueghel the Younger (Flaubert,* The Temptation of Saint Anthony *[London: Secker & Warburg, 1980]); bottom, an etching made by Jacques Callot in 1635. Flaubert was so impressed by Brueghel's painting, which he saw in Genoa, that, after his return to Normandy in August 1846, he bought a copy of Callot's etching (cliché Bibliothèque nationale de France, Paris).*

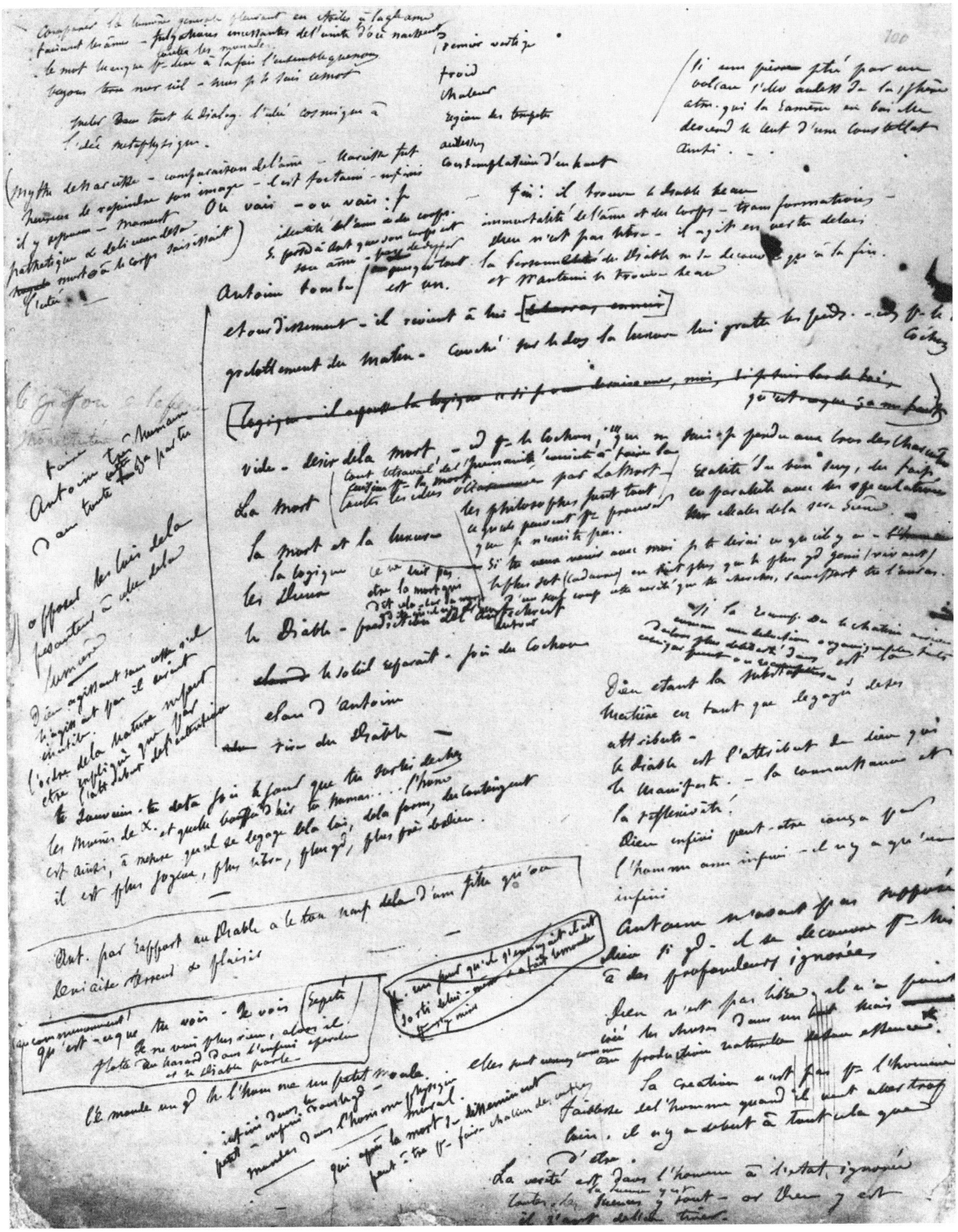

Page from Flaubert's notes for La Tentation de saint Antoine *(cliché Bibliothèque nationale de France, Paris)*

exactly to have taken its place in the "standard literature" of his country, must yet have fixed itself in the memory of most readers as a revelation of what the imagination may accomplish under a powerful impulse to mirror the unmitigated realities of life. 'Madame Bovary,' we confess, has always seemed to us a great work, and capable really of being applied to educational purposes. It is an elaborate picture of vice, but it represents it as so indefeasibly commingled with misery that in a really enlightened system of education it would form exactly the volume to put into the hands of young persons in whom vicious tendencies had been distinctly perceived, and who were wavering as to which way they should let the balance fall.

The facts in 'Madame Bovary' were elaborate marvels of description, but they were also, by good luck, extremely interesting in themselves, whereas the facts in 'Salammbô,' in 'L'Éducation sentimentale,' and in the performance before us, appeal so very meagrely to our sympathy that they completely fail in their appeal to our credulity. And yet we would not for the world have had M. Flaubert's novels unwritten. Lying there before us so unmistakably still-born, they are a capital refutation of the very dogma in defence of which they appeared. The fatal charmlessness of each and all of them is an eloquent plea for the ideal. M. Flaubert's peculiar talent is the description–minute, incisive, exhaustive–of material objects, and it must be admitted that he has carried it very far. He succeeds wonderfully well in making an image, in finding and combining just the words in which the *look* of his object resides. The scenery and properties in his dramas are made for the occasion; they have not served in other pieces. "The sky [in St. Anthony's landscape] is red, the earth completely black; under the gusts of wind the sand-drifts rise up like shrouds and then fall down. In a gap, suddenly, pass a flight of birds in a triangular battalion, like a piece of metal, trembling only on the edges." This is a specimen, taken at random, of the author's constant appeal to observation; he would claim, doubtless, for his works that they are an unbroken tissue of observations, that this is their chief merit, and that nothing is further from his pretension than to conclude to philosophize or to moralize. He proceeds upon the assumption that these innumerable marvels of observation will hold together without the underlying moral unity of what is called a "purpose," and that the reader will proceed eagerly from point to point, stopping just sufficiently short of complete hallucination to remember the author's cleverness.

The reader has, at least, in *La Tentation de Saint Antoine,* the satisfaction of expecting a subject combining with a good deal of chance for color a high moral interest. M. Flaubert describes, from beginning to end, the whole series of the poor hermit's visions; the undertaking implies no small imaginative energy. In one sense, it has been bravely carried out; it swarms with ingenious, audacious, and erudite detail, and leaves nothing to be desired in the way of completeness. There is generally supposed to be a certain vagueness about visions; they are things of ambiguous shapes and misty edges. But vagueness of portrayal has never been our author's failing, and St. Anthony's hallucinations under his hands become a gallery of photographs, executed with the aid of the latest improvements in the art. He is visited successively by all the religions, idolatries, superstitions, rites and ceremonies, priests and potentates, of the early world–by Nebuchadnezzar and the Queen of Sheba, the Emperor Constantine and the Pope Calixtus, the swarm of the early Christian fanatics, martyrs, and philosophers–Origen, Tertullian, Arius, Hermogenes, Ebionites and Encratites, Theodotians and Marcosians, by Helen of Troy and Appollonius of Rhodes, by the Buddha in person, by the Devil in person, by Ormuzd and Ahriman, by Diana of the Ephesians, by Cybele, Atys, Isis, by the whole company of the gods of Greece and by Venus in particular, by certain unnamable Latin deities, whom M. Flaubert not only names but dramatizes, by the figures of Luxury and Death, by the Sphinx and the Chimæra, by the Pigmies and the Cynocephali, by the "Sadhuzag" and the unicorn, by all the beasts of the sea, and finally by Jesus Christ. We are not precisely given to understand how much time is supposed to roll over the head of the distracted anchorite while these heterogeneous images are passing before him, but, in spite of the fact that he generally swoons away in the *entr-acte,* as it were, we receive an impression that he is getting a good deal at one sitting, and that the toughest part of his famous struggle came off on a single night. To the reader who is denied the occasional refreshment of a swoon, we recommend taking up the book at considerable intervals. Some of the figures in our list are minutely described, others are briefly sketched, but all have something to say. We fancy that both as a piece of description and a piece of dramatization M. Flaubert is especially satisfied with his Queen of Sheba:

> "Her dress, in golden brocade, divided regularly by furbelows of pearls, of jet, and of sapphire, compresses her waist into a narrow bodice, ornamented with applied pieces in color representing the twelve signs of

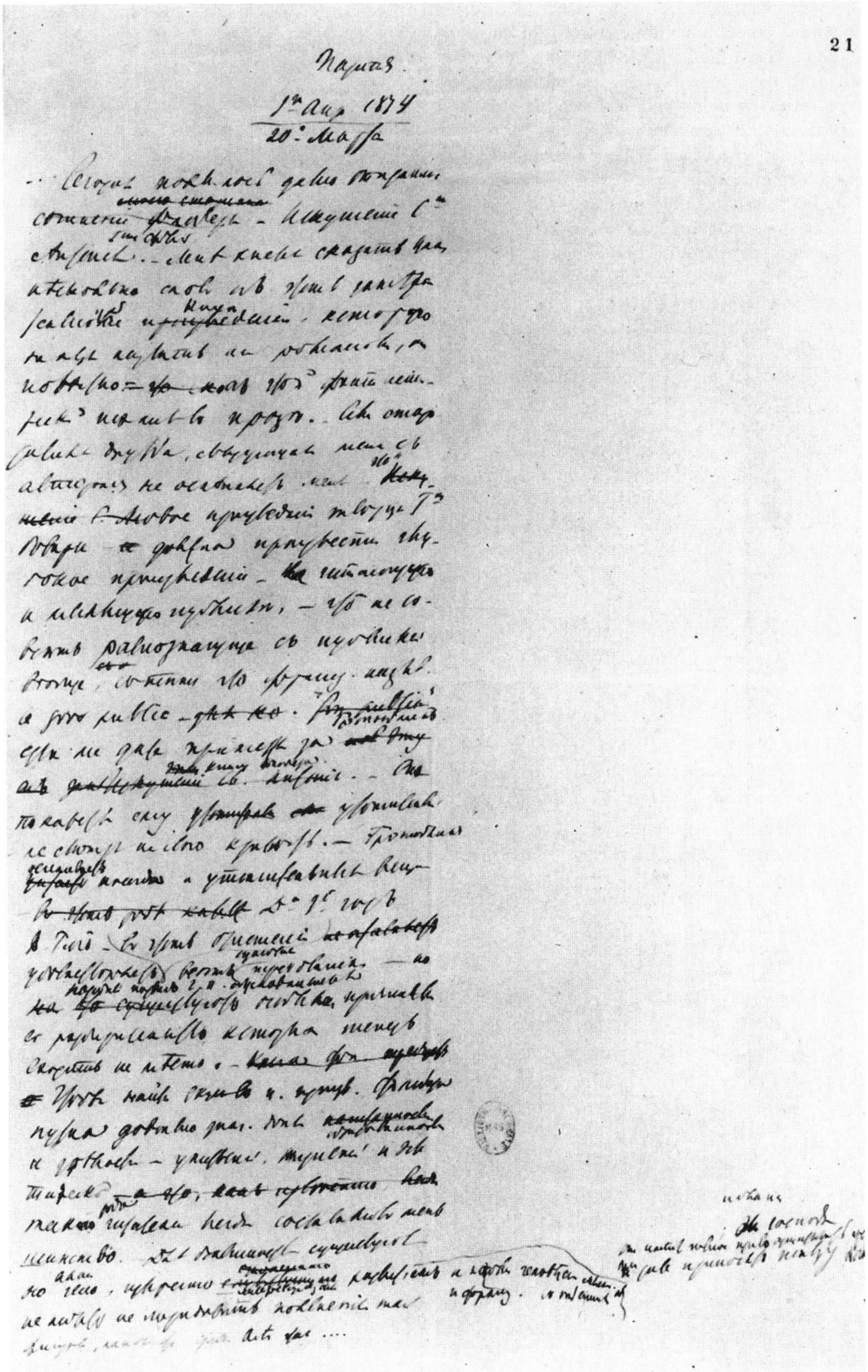
21

Париж.

1е Апр. 1874
20 Марта

Page from the manuscript for Ivan Turgenev's article in Russian on La Tentation de saint Antoine, *a review he began on 1 April 1874 but never finished. Turgenev found the work "remarkable" and impossible to classify, calling it "a fantastic prose poem" that requires from its readers "a certain level of instruction, maturity of mind, and taste" (cliché Bibliothèque de France, Paris).*

the zodiac. She wears high skates, of which one is black and spangled with silver stars, with the crescent of the moon, while the other is white, and covered with little drops in gold, with the sun in the middle. Her wide sleeves, covered with emeralds and with feathers of birds, expose the nakedness of her little round arm, ornamented at the wrist by a bracelet of ebony; and her hands, laden with rings, terminate in nails so pointed that the ends of her fingers look almost like needles. A flat gold chain, passing under her chin, ascends beside her cheeks, rolls in a spiral around her hair, which is powdered with blue powder, then, falling, grazes her shoulder and comes and fastens itself on her bosom in a scorpion in diamonds which thrusts out its tongue between her breasts. Two great blood pearls drag down her ears. The edges of her eyelids are painted black. She has on her left cheek-bone a natural brown mole, and she breathes, opening her mouth, as if her bodice hurt her. She shakes as she walks, a green parasol surrounded with gilt bells, and twelve little woolly-headed negroes carry the long train of her dress, held at the end by a monkey, who occasionally lifts it up. She says: *'Ah, bel ermite! bel ermite! mon cœur défaille!'*"

This is certainly a "realistic" Queen of Sheba, and Nebuchadnezzar is almost equally so. Going on from figure to figure and scene to scene in this bewildering panorama, we ask ourselves exactly what it is that M. Flaubert has proposed to accomplish. Not a prose-poem from the saint's own moral point of view, with his spiritual sufferings and vagaries for its episode, and his ultimate expulsion of all profane emotions for its dénouement; for St. Anthony throughout remains the dimmest of shadows, and his commentary upon his hallucination is meagre and desultory. Not, on the other hand, a properly historical presentment of the various types he evokes, for fancy is called in at every turn to supplement the scanty testimony of history. What is M. Flaubert's historic evidence for the mole on the Queen of Sheba's cheek and the blue powder in her hair? He has simply wished to be tremendously pictorial, and the opportunity for spiritual analysis has been the last thing in his thoughts. It is matter of regret that a writer with the pluck and energy to grapple with so pregnant a theme should have been so indifferent to its most characteristic side. It is probable that, after M. Flaubert's big volume, we shall not have, in literature, for a long time, any more 'Temptations of Saint Anthony'; and yet there is obviously a virtue in the subject which has by no means been exhausted. Tremendously pictorial M. Flaubert has certainly succeeded in being, and we stand amazed at his indefatigable ingenuity. He has accumulated a mass of curious learning; he has interfused it with a mass of still more curious conjecture; and he has resolved the whole into a series of pictures which, considering the want of models and precedents, may be said to be very handsomely executed. But what, the reader wonders, has been his inspiration, his motive, his *souffle,* as the French say? Of any abundant degree of imagination we perceive little in the work. Here and there we find a touch of something like poetry, as in the scene of the Christian martyrs huddled in one of the vaults of the circus, and watching through the bars of the opposite vault the lions and tigers to whom they are about to be introduced. Here and there is a happy dramatic turn in the talk of the hermit's visionary interlocutor or a vague approach to a "situation" in the attitude of the saint. But for the most part M. Flaubert's picturesque is a strangely artificial and cold-blooded picturesque–abounding in the grotesque and the repulsive, the abnormal and the barely conceivable, but seeming to have attained to it all by infinite labor, ingenuity, and research–never by one of the fine intuitions of a joyous and generous invention. It is all hard, inanimate, superficial, and inexpressibly disagreeable. When the author has a really beautiful point to treat–as the assembly of the Greek deities fading and paling away in the light of Christianity–he becomes singularly commonplace and ineffective.

His book being, with its great effort and its strangely absent charm, the really painful failure it seems to us, it would not have been worth while to call attention to it if it were not that it pointed to more things than the author's own deficiencies. It seems to us to throw a tolerably vivid light on the present condition of the French literary intellect. M. Flaubert and his contemporaries have pushed so far the education of the senses and the cultivation of the grotesque in literature and the arts that it has left them morally stranded and helpless. In the perception of the materially curious, in fantastic refinement of taste and marked ingenuity of expression, they seem to us now to have reached the limits of the possible. Behind M. Flaubert stands a whole society of æsthetic *raffinés,* demanding stronger and stronger spices in its intellectual diet. But we doubt whether he or any of his companions can permanently satisfy their public, for the simple reason that the human mind, even in indifferent health, does after all need to be *nourished,* and thrives but scantily on a regimen of pigments and sauces. It needs sooner or later–to prolong our metaphor–to detect a body-flavor, and we shall be very much surprised if it ever detects one in 'La Tentation de Saint Antoine.'

–Henry James, "Flaubert's *Temptation of St. Anthony,*" *The Nation* (4 June 1874)

* * *

In this excerpt from his discussion of Flaubert in Creative Spirits of the Nineteenth Century *(1923), Danish literary historian Georg Brandes praises the boldness and originality of* La Tentation de saint Antoine *while acknowledging its serious flaws. In "the last vision of St. Antonius" the critic hears Flaubert's "stifled wail over the imperfection of his entire life-work, and this master-work of his life in especial."*

The Last Confession of Flaubert

VI

The year 1874 finally brought the work which Flaubert himself considered his *chef d'œuvre,*–a work on which he had labored for twenty years, and which furnished the sharpest definition in his mind,–a most startling work. When it was first rumored that a French novelist had written "The Temptation of St. Antonius," at least nine-tenths of the public entertained not the slightest doubt that the title was to be accepted facetiously or symbolically. Who could surmise that the work was a thoroughly serious history of the temptation of the ancient Egyptian hermit!

No novelist, indeed no poet of any kind, had ever attempted anything similar. It is true, Goethe had written "Die classische Walpurgisnacht" (The Classic Walpurgis Night); Byron in the second act of "Cain" had furnished a model for certain portions; Turgenief, in "Visions," had treated in a masterly way, a remotely related subject within a very small framework. A drama in seven parts, however, consisting of one long drawn out monologue, or, more accurately speaking, a detailed presentation of what had passed during a night of terror, through the brain of one single mortal who had become a prey to hallucinations; such a work had never before been written. And yet this work, failure though it is in some respects, displayed a quiet grandeur, in its melancholy monotony, and an absolutely modern stamp, attained by but few poetic works of French literature.

St. Antonius stands on the threshold of his hut on a mountain in Egypt. A tall cross is planted in the earth; an old twisted palm-tree bends over the edge of the precipice; the Nile forms a lake at the foot of the mountain. The sun is setting. The hermit, exhausted from a day passed in fasting, labor, and self-torture, feels his spiritual strength give way, as darkness falls upon the earth. A dreary yearning for the external world fills his heart. Now sensual, now proud, now idyllic and laughing memories allure and torment him.

First of all Antonius yearns for his childhood, for Ammonaria, a young maiden whom he once loved; he thinks of his charming pupil, Hilarion, who has forsaken him; he curses his solitary life. The migratory birds that pass over his head awaken within him the desire to fly onward as they do. He deplores his lot; he begins to lament and groan with anguish. Why had not he become a peaceful monk in a cell? Why had not he chosen the calm and useful life of a priest? He wishes that he were a grammarian or a philosopher, a toll-keeper on a bridge, a rich married merchant, or a brave, jovial soldier; his physical strength would then have had employment. He is overcome with despair at his position, bursts into tears, and seeks consolation and edification in the Holy Scriptures. Opening at the Acts of the Apostles, he reads the passage where Peter is permitted to eat all animals, clean or unclean, while he, Antonius, is tormenting himself with strict fasting. Turning to the Old Testament at the same time, he reads how the right is given to the Jews to kill all their enemies, to slaughter them by the wholesale, while he is commanded to forgive his enemies; he reads of Nebuchadnezzar, and envies him his festivals; of Ezekias, and shudders with desire when he thinks of all his precious perfumes and golden treasures; of the beautiful Queen of Sheba, and asks himself how she could possibly hope to lead the wise Solomon into temptation; and it seems to him that the shadows which the two arms of the cross cast on the earth, approach each other like two horns. He calls upon God, and the two shadows assume their old places once more. Vainly does he seek to humiliate himself; he thinks with pride of his long martyrdom; his heart swells when he recalls the honor that has been shown him from every quarter, for even the emperor has written to him three times; and then he sees that his water-jug is empty and his bread consumed. Hunger and thirst gnaw at his vitals.

He remembers the envy and the hatred which the Church Fathers showed toward him at the Council of Nice, and his soul cries for revenge. He dreams of the aristocratic women who formerly visited him so often in his wilderness, in order to confess to him and entreat him to permit them to remain with him, the saint. He is absorbed in these dreams so long that they become realities to him. He sees the fine ladies from the city approach, borne in their sedan chairs; he extinguishes his torch in hopes of dispelling the apparitions, and now for the first time clearly beholds the visions in the dark canopy of the night sky, like scarlet images on a ground of ebony, whirling past him in bewildering haste.

Voices which resound from the obscurity proffer him beautiful women, heaps of gold, and scenes of splendor. This is the beginning of the temptation, the thirst of animal instincts. Then he dreams that he is the confidant of the emperor, the prime minister, with

Two watercolors of Croisset by Georges Rochegrosse, one of Flaubert's study and the other of the Seine viewed from the pavilion, located at the entrance to the Flauberts' property. They were painted in October 1874, when Rochegrosse accompanied his father-in-law, the poet Théodore de Banville, who was Flaubert's friend, on a brief visit to Croisset (Collections de la Bibliothèque municipale de Rouen. Cliché Thierry Ascencio-Parvy).

the reins of power in his hands. The emperor crowns him with his diadem. He avenges himself cruelly on his enemies among the Church Fathers, wades in their blood, and suddenly finds himself in the midst of one of Nebuchadnezzar's festivals, in a glittering palace, where the viands and drinks form mountains and streams. Anointed, and decorated with precious stones, the emperor sits upon his throne, while Antonius from afar reads upon his brow his haughty, ambitious thoughts. He penetrates him so thoroughly, that suddenly he himself becomes Nebuchadnezzar, and amidst all his revelling feels the need of becoming an animal. Flinging himself down, he creeps on the ground, bellowing like a steer, and then he scratches his hand on a stone and awakens. He lashes himself so long in punishment for this vision, that the pain becomes a rapturous delight, and suddenly the Queen of Sheba appears before him. Her hair is powdered blue; she is all radiant with gold and diamonds, and she offers herself to him with wanton coquetry. She is all women in one, and he knows that if he were to touch her shoulder with one finger a stream of liquid fire would shoot through his veins. There she stands, all fragrant with the perfume of the Orient. Her words ring upon his ear like singularly captivating music, and, seized with burning desire, he stretches forth his arms toward her. Then he controls himself and orders her from his presence. She and her whole train vanish. And now the devil assumes the form of his pupil, Hilarion, who comes to shake his faith.

The little, withered Hilarion, to his alarm, calls his attention to the fact that in fancy he has been mastered by the enjoyments which in real life he has renounced, assuring him that God is no Moloch, who forbids the enjoyment of life, and that the endeavor to understand God is worth more than all the self-torture in the world. He first points out to Antonius the contradictions between the Old and the New Testament, then the various contradictions of the New. And Hilarion grows. Then there arise in the brain of Antonius recollections of all the heresies of which he has heard and read in Alexandria and elsewhere, and has victoriously overcome: the hundreds upon hundreds of heresies of the early Christian sects; views, of which one is more monstrous than the other, are howled in his ears by the heretics themselves. They clamor about him like so many hyenas. Each one belches out its madness upon him. Hysterical women and the sweethearts of the martyrs cast themselves wailing upon the ashes of the dead. Antonius sees heretics who emasculate themselves, heretics who burn themselves. Apollonius of Tyre reveals himself to him as a miracle-worker in no respect inferior to Christ. And Hilarion continues to grow. Following in the train of the heretics come the gods of the different religions in a monstrous procession, from the most abhorrent and grotesque stone idols and wooden fetiches of ancient times, to the blood-thirsty gods of Eastern lands, and the gods of beauty of Greece. They all move swiftly past, and uttering a loud wail of lamentation, disappear with a wild leap in the great vacuum. He sees gods that fall into a swoon, others that are whirled away, others that are crushed, torn to pieces, and precipitated into a black hole; gods that are drowned or dissolved into air, and gods that are guilty of self-destruction. Among them looms up Buddha, who in everything that he narrates concerning himself bears the most startling resemblance to the Saviour. Finally Crepitus, that Roman god of digestion, and Jehovah, the Lord of Hosts, make the leap down into the abyss.

A terrible silence, a deep night ensues.

"They are all gone," says Antonius.

"I still remain," replies a voice.

And Hilarion stands before him, by far larger than before, transfigured, beautiful as an archangel, radiant as the sun, and so tall that Antonius is compelled to throw back his head in order to see him.

"Who are you?"

Hilarion replies: "My kingdom is as large as the world, and my desire knows no bounds. I am always marching forward, freeing minds and weighing worlds, without fear, without pity, without love, and without God. They call me Science."

Antonius recoils in horror. "You are, rather, the devil!"

"Do you wish to see him?" A horse's hoof shows itself, the devil takes the saint on his horns and bears him through space, through the heavens of modern science, wherein the planets are as abundant as grains of dust. And the firmament expands with the thoughts of Antonius. "Higher, higher!" he exclaims. Infinity reveals itself to his gaze. Timidly he inquires of the devil for God. The devil answers him with new queries, new doubts. "What you call form is perhaps but a delusion of your senses," he says; "what you call substance is only a conceit of your mind. Who knows if the world is not an eternal stream of facts and occurrences, the semblance the only truth, the illusion the only reality!"

"Adore me!" suddenly exclaims the devil, "and curse the mockery you have called God!" He vanishes, and Antonius awakens, lying on his back on the brink of his rock.

But his teeth are chattering, he is ill; he has no longer either bread or water in his hut, and his hallucinations begin anew. He loses himself in the swarm

"The Devil carrying him [Saint Anthony] into the midst of the stars," a scene from part 6 of La Tentation de saint Antoine *(wood engraving by Ilse Bischoff; frontispiece,* The Temptation of Saint Antony *[New York: Ives Washburn, 1930], Thomas Cooper Library, University of South Carolina)*

of fabulous animals that throng about him, the fantastic monsters of the earth. He finds himself on a strand amid the inhabitants and plants of the sea and land, and he can no longer distinguish plants and animals. The twining plants wind and curve like serpents; he confuses the vegetable and mineral world with that of mortals. The gourds look like human breasts; the Babylonian tree Dedaim, bears human heads as its fruit; pebbles seem like skulls; diamonds glitter like eyes. He experiences the pantheistic yearning to blend with universal nature, and this is his last wail:–

"I have a desire to fly, to swim, to bark, to roar, to howl. Would that I had wings, a horny plate, a shell, a beak! Would that I could coil my body like a serpent, divide myself, be in everything, be wafted around like a perfume, unfold myself like a plant, sound like a tune, shine like a light, conceal myself in all forms and penetrate every atom!"

The night is at an end. It was only a new incubus. The sun rises, and in its disk the face of Christ beams upon him. Then follows the last discreet irony of the author. Antonius makes the sign of the cross, and begins anew the prayer that was interrupted by these visions.

In this work of fiction we have Flaubert complete, with his sluggish blood, his gloomy imagination, his intrusive erudition, and his need of bringing to a level old and new illusions, ancient and modern faiths. The almost savage vehemence of his temperament reveals itself when he thrusts the god Crepitus before the God Jehovah. That he chose the legend of St. Antonius as a medium through which to free his mind, and utter some bitter truths to mankind, was because he was brought into contact by this material with antiquity and the Orient which he loved. Through it he could use the large cities and landscapes of Egypt as a background on which to lavish brilliant colors and gigantic forms. And with this theme he no longer painted the helplessness and stupidity of a society, but of a world. He depicted, quite impersonally, humanity as having waded up to its ankles until that hour of its existence, in mire and in blood, and pointed to science–which is as much shunned and dreaded as the devil–as the sole salvation.

The idea was as grand as it was new. The execution by no means attained the level of the plan. The book was crushed by the material used in its preparation. It is not a poetic work; it is partly a theogony, partly a piece of church history, and it is moulded in the form of a psychology of frenzy. There is in it an enumeration of details that is as wearisome as the ascent of an almost perpendicular mountain wall. Certain parts in it, indeed, are only thoroughly intelligible to savants, and seem almost unreadable to the general public. The great author had gradually passed into abstract erudition and abstract style. "It was a sorrowful sight," Émile Zola has pertinently remarked, "to see this powerful talent become petrified like the forms of antique mythology. Very slowly, from the feet to the girdle, from the girdle to the head, Flaubert became a marble statue."

VII

I have delayed speaking of the last vision of St. Antonius because it seems to me the most remarkable of all, and was undoubtedly the poet's own vision. After all the gods have vanished, and the journey through the heavens has come to an end, Antonius beholds, upon the opposite shore of the Nile, the

Sphinx, lying on its belly, with outstretched claws. But springing, flying, howling, snorting fire through its nostrils, and beating its wings and its dragon's tail, Chimera is circling about the Sphinx. What is the Sphinx? What else than the gloomy riddle that is chained to earth, the eternal question,–brooding science! What is the Chimera? What else than the winged imagination, which speeds through space, and touches the stars with the tips of its wings.

The Sphinx (the word is of the masculine gender in French) says: "Stand still, Chimera! Do not run so fast, do not fly so high, do not howl so loud. Cease snorting thy flames into my face; thou canst not possibly melt my granite."

The Chimera replies, "I never stand still. Thou canst never grasp me, thou dread Sphinx."

The Chimera gallops through the corridor of the labyrinth, flies across the sea, and holds fast with its teeth to the sailing clouds.

The Sphinx lies motionless, tracing the alphabet in the sand with its claws, musing and calculating; and while the sea ebbs and flows, the grain waves to and fro, caravans pass by, and cities fall to decay, it keeps its firm gaze bent fixedly on the horizon.

Finally it exclaims, "O phantasy! lift me up on thy pinions, out of my deadly ennui!"

And Chimera replies, "Thou unknown one! I am enamored with thine eyes; like an inflamed hyena I circle about thee. Oh, embrace me! Fructify me!"

The Sphinx rises up; but Chimera flees in terror of being crushed beneath the stony weight. "Impossible!" says the Sphinx, and sinks into the deep sand.

I see in this scene the last confession of Flaubert, his stifled wail over the imperfection of his entire life-work, and this master-work of his life in especial. The Sphinx and the Chimera, science and poetry, desire each other in him, seek each other again and again, circle about each other with passionate yearning and ardor; but the true impregnation of poetry through science he did not accomplish.

Not that his principle was unsound or incorrect. On the contrary, the future of poetry is embodied in it; this I most truly believe, for in it was its past. The greatest poets, an Æschylus, a Dante, a Shakespeare, a Goethe, possessed all the essential knowledge of their day, and deposited it in their poetry. True, erudition and scientific culture, in and for themselves, have no poetic value. They can never in the world take the place of poetic sentiment and artistic creative power. When the poetic endowment, however, exists, the gaze is sharpened by an acquaintance with the laws of nature and the human soul and expanded by the study of history. In our day, when modern science is reconstructed in every direction, however, it is undoubtedly far more difficult than ever to span the materials of science without being overwhelmed, and Flaubert did not possess that native harmony of spirit which renders difficult things easy, and reconciles the profound antitheses of the world of ideas.

"La Tentation de St. Antoine" was disposed of in Paris with a merry boulevard jest. Few people, indeed, had the patience to enter thoroughly into the volume, and the public at large was soon ready with its judgment: the book was mortally tedious. How could the author expect that such a work would entertain the Parisians? Now "Madame Bovary" was quite another thing. Why did not Flaubert repeat himself (as all poor writers do)? Why did not he write ten new "Madame Bovarys"?

–Georg Brandes, "Gustave Flaubert," in his *Creative Spirits of the Nineteenth Century,* translated by Rasmus B. Anderson (New York: Crowell, 1923), pp. 257–265

* * *

In this excerpt from his preface to "Tales from Flaubert" (1928), George Saintsbury argues that through his revision of the "raw" earlier versions of La Tentation de saint Antoine *Flaubert was able to create its "definitive" form in 1874, which Saintsbury believes is "by far Flaubert's greatest work."*

Improving *La Tentation de saint Antoine*

When, some dozen years ago, Flaubert's representatives at last made up their minds to publish the mass of his early (and by himself suppressed, or rather never uttered) novice-work, there were those who thought they did well to be angry: and perhaps they were not wrong. It is always rather doubtful business to publish what an author has not published: but in Flaubert's case there seemed to be worse than doubt. It was perfectly well known, from his own confessions as well as from the testimony of those who knew him, that though he was not, in the German phrase, one "who could never be ready", he was probably *the* one of all men of letters who took most trouble in getting himself ready, and was most ruthless in sacrificing what he thought was *not* ready. The extraordinarily silly as well as vulgar taunt of Edmond de Goncourt that Flaubert just got the best epithets *de tout le monde* [of everyone], while he, Edmond, and his brother, Jules, only used such as were their own private invention, is in reality an almost grovelling admission of his greatness. Any clever fool can, as Miss Edgeworth's little boy, not at all foolishly, says, "call his hat Cadwallader", but it takes more or less of a genius to select the best epithet *de tout le monde* for a particular hat in a particular context.

From more than one side the objections were justified. By far the greater part of the *Œuvres Premières* had no value except for a curiosity which, in the better class of readers, probably felt a little ashamed of itself. Not that there was anything discreditable in the work: it was simply an obvious failure. Much of it had the extravagant diablerie, horror, griminess, etc., which was the wrong hall-mark, as we may call it, of the earlier Romanticism of the lower class, like Janin's *Âne Mort* and Borel's *Champavert,* with which Flaubert's own stuff was nearly contemporary. Almost all of it, to a reader who was not a child or a fool, was quite evidently that half-done work which proverbially ought not to be shown or told to children and fools themselves, and from which even those who are not children or fools can derive only a sort of pseudo-scientific, not an honestly aesthetic, pleasure. One does indeed see, from the first version of the *Éducation Sentimentale,* how he could improve things; and can at least guess how much he *would* have improved *Bouvard et Pécuchet:* but this was hardly *tanti* [a lot].

The comparison, however, of the earlier (1849–56) versions of the *Tentation de Saint Antoine* with its final form in 1874 is an altogether different matter: and though probably only a few readers would care to have the complete texts side by side, as they ought to be for full critical appreciation of the facts, it may be worth while, before taking account of the "definitive" form *as* definitive, to consider "the excellent differences"–a Shakespearean phrase which applies here itself excellently. It must be remembered that in this case there was actual or partial publication and republication; that instead of rejection there was simply amelioration. Of course, there have been the usual eccentrics–perhaps occasionally sincere but much more often not–who have pretended to prefer the first form. If you only take the good old *Respice finem* [look at the end] for guide, that matter ought to be easily settled. All ending–all real ending–should be quiet, by whatever disquiet it is preceded. This is managed consummately in the latest form: it is not so in the first. I hardly know anything of the kind finer than the conclusion as we now have it. Sunrise and silent prayer, the terrors of the night having vanished, and the face of Christ dominating all. To use a homely parallel, the ingredients of the early version are not thoroughly mixed and, though not uncooked, not thoroughly cooked: there is still a sort of rawness about them.

It was, of course, necessary to read the two versions together carefully while preparing this Preface to the later one, and to give full weight to what M. Louis Bertrand's editorial care did for the earlier some twenty years ago, before Flaubert's still earlier attempts were released or dug up, whichever phrase may be preferred. His chief argument–true in its facts, though questionable in its effect–is that this earlier one, some fragments of which had always been known as having appeared in the *Artiste* under Gautier's editorship, had more pure Early Romanticism in it than the later. It certainly has, and in fact was certain to have. But it has also much more of the faults of 1830, as it was also certain to have: and it has a good deal of one of the worst of those faults–the attempt to reach the great Romantic vague by a sort of higgledy-piggledy disorder. It seems, from a most interesting pair of quotations from Flaubert's manuscripts, one original, the other copied from his friend George Sand's *Mlle la Quintinie,* that he had (at least at first) intended to depict a general tone *d'abrutissement* [dumbness], *d'idiotisme, et de fatigue* in the Saint, on which George Sand comments and which she explains George-Sandically. Now something of this undoubtedly suits the situation of Anthony, being confronted with all these mysteries and terrors in the first place with the Devil among and behind them; and with

Depiction of the image of Christ that appears to Saint Anthony at the end of La Tentation de saint Antoine *(lithograph by Odilon Redon; photograph © SPADEM, Paris; from* La Tentation de saint Antoine, *edited by Édouard Maynial [Paris: Éditions Garnier Frères, 1954], Thomas Cooper Library, University of South Carolina)*

"the awful rose of Dawn" and God Himself in it, behind and over all. But in the earlier version this situation and this attitude have not got "disembroiled" enough. The incidents and the personification are in the hands of the group of Seven Deadly Sins, *plus* Logic, and in some way stage-managed by the Devil; the Saint is in a state of undignified fussiness too often; his pig, though a relief, seems generally superfluous, and at least once makes a plusquam-piggish and merely nasty speech; while the episode of Apollonius and Damis, which even in the final form one may think a little overdone, seems more disproportionate and out of place than ever.

Above all, there is no Hilarion.

Now it is no extravagance to say that it is worth while to read this first version if for nothing else than because you cannot perceive the full importance of this character unless you know that he is a *new* character, and can appreciate not merely what he *is* but what he *does.* It is, of course, possible that Flaubert might have found some other ways of getting rid of the defects of 1849–56: but he could hardly have found a better. The part supplies a sort of concatenation or mortar to the other parts. Anthony's supposed familiarity with the person (a former disciple of his) steadies the Saint, and gives, if a dangerous, a useful mouthpiece for the treacherous and ungodly suggestions which come much better from the other than from those chattering Deadlies and that most illogical Logic. As a scholar and a divine he serves as a special excuse for all the Heresiarchs and their crews who in the earlier version turn up rather too promiscuously. But more of him presently.

On the other hand, the abolition of "Science" who appears in the earlier version as a separate *persona,* is, though a less constant gain, a considerable one. She is quite out of place in such a scene, such a company, and such a time: nor is she, as perhaps by some *tour de force* she might have been, adjusted to all three. All through, moreover, there are touches of what I believe it is fashionable now to call architectonic–which certainly had not been achieved in '49, but which were delightfully visible in '74. I have always thought the *Tentation* by far Flaubert's greatest work: but I certainly should not have thought so if it had been only represented by the earlier version. Indeed the *Artiste* fragments–that about Nebuchadnezzar and others–would, if they had stood by themselves, have given a false impression. They might have made one think the rest of the *Tentation* better than it was, but then they could hardly have suggested that the author would make that rest so triumphantly good as it actually is.

Of course, the use of such a word as "triumphantly" will shock or disgust or amuse people who agree with M. Faguet as to Gautier's *La Morte Amoureuse* being a *diablerie puérile,* with our Modernists as to the supernatural element in Religion being merely "magic", and so on; but of them and with them we do not reason. It is permissible, as a certain ancient saying has it, for Dorians to speak Doric: and Literature, which is a somewhat supernatural thing itself, has proved long ago in a decidedly triumphant fashion that it is permissible for it to speak of the supernatural. But it must, by the same general tenor of law, speak of the supernatural, as of everything else, in a literary manner–that manner involving the observance of certain principles and methods, some at least of which have been discovered and set forth by persons from Aristotle of Stagira down to men of the present day: but many of which are not quite formulable, and are rather to be recognised by and in their results than indicated *a priori.*

Besides the great improvement of the introduction of Hilarion, the later version enjoys a much larger imparting of the elaborate stage-direction.

I have not the least idea whether Mr. Hardy derived from Flaubert any suggestion of the magnificent things of this kind in *The Dynasts:* but I know no third example of anything like such success in the use of a device which might be simply a bore; which might also be made a mere substitute for something else; but which can be and is here made to support and, as it were, present that "something else" with fullest dramatic effect. I can conceive objection being taken to the length of the Saint's preliminary discourse: but it seems to me essentially right. He has got to survey his life: and the reader or spectator (for there are not many actual dramas which present what is presented by them so forcibly as this) has to have it surveyed for him in order that the cause of the *Tentation*–that mixture of tedium of life and regret for it which gives the Devil standpoint and grip-hold–may arise. It arises: the passages chosen as *Sortes Biblicae* [the words of the Bible] being cunningly adjusted to fit the danger.

In the earlier version the temptations had been immediate and direct: they are here less so, and are preceded by a sort of dream which shows him that the life, as to the actual course of which he had been half grumbling, half regretting, might have been one of splendour in Church and State. He has seen a vision of Nebuchadnezzar in pomp, but he wakes and, as a form of penitence, flogs himself. This ambiguous process results in the first personal temptation–no less than the appearance of the Queen of Sheba. The sign of the cross saves him, but only just: and Balkis departs with a mixture of sigh and sneer. But she leaves–Hilarion.

The way in which the Tempter (for such the old disciple really is) insinuates himself after a slightly uncanny overture which sustains the uncanniness of the whole atmosphere, is admirable. He is familiar with the Saint's ways; they have talked of all these things before; he can edge in doubts, *aporias,*[1] simple questions, quite naturally. And so the ghostly congregation and procession of the Heresiarchs comes on the stage quite appropriately, though the figures vary from personages who hardly deserve to be called Christians at all, like Manes and the wilder Gnostics, to "Fathers" by something more than courtesy, but obviously questionable on points, like Tertullian and Origen. Gymnosophists, Simon Magus and his "Ennoia"[2] (pretended successor of Helen), follow and are followed by Apollonius of Tyana and his faithful Damis. I have, I think, said before that Apollonius does not so much appeal to me: but only the cross itself, embraced, and not merely signed for, saves Anthony; and his reflections after the Tyanian disappears are rather doubtful. He admits indeed that the splendours of Nebuchadnezzar had not dazzled him, nor the charms of Balkis allured him so much. He begins to speculate on various forms and notions of Divinity: and this lets Hilarion in again.

The reader will hardly want much guide or comment along the way in which he, who is now almost declaredly Hilarion-Satanas, avails himself of this dangerous mood of displaying *all* religions, from the clumsiest idols to Buddha (the fiend occasionally making Mephistophelian suggestions of Christian parallels), through Oannes, Belus, Ormuzd, the Ephesian Diana, Cybele, Isis, and so to Olympus itself–for a moment in all its glory, attracting Anthony's admiration. But Hilarion makes the mistake of too open propaganda: and the Saint with a sort of wrench, though sighing at each clause, pronounces the Lord's Prayer. Whereat the cross throws its shadow on the sky and there follows a *Götterdämmerung* which I have always liked to compare with Heine's (not the poem under that title, but the one specially called *Die Götter Griechenlands*) in the *Buch der Lieder.* Minor Divinities follow and even the special deity of the Jews as the "Lord of Hosts" is made to pass, in order probably to give an entrance to the Devil himself *as* the Devil, but in his archangelic form. He carries the Saint through space, shows him its vastness, and only at last, when all other hope of safety seems gone, makes the demand for Adoration of himself, and denial or blasphemy of God. But Anthony does not comply; and, apparently abandoned in the Void, wakes to find himself in front of his own cave–alive but exhausted, and by no means even yet in a hallowed state of mind. I suppose that it is at this point that a certain kind of criticism finds most fault with the *Tentation* as we have it. The refusal of Adoration should have settled the matter and given a satisfactory "curtain". As a matter of fact it does not do so: there are two scenes to come before the great if almost eventless close which has been spoken of above. The first, which one might think something of a repetition, is a last and concentrated effort on the part of the two temptresses, Suicide and Voluptuousness, to get Anthony, one or the other, for their prey. It is very powerfully done and can be pleaded for. He has seen all worlds, all faiths, all philosophies. They are all vanity. Why not finish with it all? or, if not, be content with that sensual pleasure which, whatever may be said against it, and whatever payment for itself it may exact, is at any rate *something?*

But he succumbs to neither; and they finally wrestle with and defeat each other, leaving him rather proud than anything else. (In the earlier version Pride appears constantly throughout as the chief tempter.) They are succeeded by another quaint duel of the Sphinx and a Chimera (negation and delusion) half fighting, half making love: while these in turn give place to phantasmagoria of less important and famous monsters, from pygmies and Cynocephali through Basilisks and Griffins to the Catoblepas and the Martichoras (I always liked the spelling Ma*n*tichor*a* better), who figure in the furthest Fauna of Fancy. These appearances of animals change to birds, fishes, even vegetables, if not bacilli, and Anthony seems to recover animation at the presence (if with a sort of pan-theistical suggestion) of life, even in a bewildering multitude of infinitesimal forms, descending to the lowest. Then and not till then comes the end, glanced at before: the Saint returning, with the light and under the face of Christ, to the quiet prayer to which at first and throughout he has been unable to resign himself. In comparison with this, the end of the earlier version, where the Devil, though acknowledging himself beaten for the time, departs with jeers and threats to return, seems distinctly inferior: and that not merely on the strength of preference for a "happy ending". There are some interesting fragments of the first draft: or rather there are some passages which M. Bertrand thought best not to incorporate in but add to the presentation of that draft or series of drafts which he gave. And some people may regret the expulsion of the pig, specially when he wakes and feels the sun and says, "What a jolly sun! I was in such a funk to-night." But the thing could never have been brought off as a mystery-farce: and it *has* been at last brought off as a mystery-romance.

–George Saintsbury, "Tales from Flaubert," in his *Prefaces and Essays,* edited by Oliver Elton (London: Macmillan, 1933), pp. 416–426

---

1. We want an English word for this. "Difficulty" is thus meant but is not quite good enough. "Poser" is near but undignified.
2. Thought personified–very much personified.

* * *

As has been the case with other works by Flaubert, La Tentation de saint Antoine *has been rediscovered by twentieth-century critics who are less interested in judging the work than in Flaubert's groundbreaking approach and techniques. In this excerpt from his essay originally published as "Un 'Fantastique' de bibliothèque" (translated as "Fantasia of the Library," 1977) in the March 1967 issue of Cahiers Renand-Barrault philosopher Michel Foucault writes of the bookishness of* La Tentation de saint Antoine *and examines its intricate organization.*

A Monument to Erudition

II

We readily understand *The Temptation* as setting out the formal progression of unconfined reveries. It would be to literature what Bosch, Breughel [*sic*], or the Goya of the *Capricios* were at one time to painting. The first readers (or audience) were bored by the monotonous progression of grotesques: Maxime Du Camp remarked: "We listened to the words of the Sphinx, the chimera, the Queen of Sheba, of Simon the Magician. . . . A bewildered, somewhat simpleminded, and, I would even say, foolish Saint Anthony sees, parading before him, different forms of temptation."[1] His friends were enraptured by the "richness of his vision" (François Coppée), "by its forest of shadows and light" (Victor Hugo), and by its "hallucinatory mechanism" (Hippolyte Taine). But stranger still, Flaubert himself invoked madness, phantasms; he felt he was shaping the fallen trees of a dream: "I spend my afternoons with the shutters closed, the curtains drawn, and without a shirt, dressed as a carpenter. I bawl out! I sweat! It's superb! There are moments when this is decidedly more than delirium." As the book nears completion: "I plunged furiously into *Saint Anthony* and began to enjoy the most terrifying exaltation. I have never been more excited."

In time, we have learned as readers that *The Temptation* is not the product of dreams and rapture, but a monument to meticulous erudition.[2] To construct the scene of the heresiarchs, Flaubert drew extensively from Tillemont's *Mémoires Ecclésiastiques,* Matter's four-volume *Histoire du gnosticisme,* the *Histoire de Manichée* by Beausobre, Reuss's *Théologie chrétienne,* and also from Saint Augustine and, of course, from Migne's *Patralogie* (Athanasius, Jerome, and Epiphanus). The gods that populate the text were found in Burnouf, Anquetil-Duperron, in the works of Herbelot and Hottinger, in the volumes of the *Univers Pittoresque,* in the work of the Englishman, Layard, and, particularly, in Creutzer's translation, the *Religions de l'Antiquité.* For information on monsters, he read Xivrey's *Traditions tératologiques,* the *Physiologus* re-edited by Cahier and Martin, Boaïstrau's *Histoires prodigieuses,* and the Duret text devoted to plants and their "admirable history." Spinoza inspired his metaphysical meditation on extended substance.[3] Yet, this list is far from exhaustive. Certain evocations in the text seem totally dominated by the machinery of dreams: for example, the magisterial Diana of Ephesus, with lions at her shoulders and with fruits, flowers, and stars interlaced on her bosom, with a cluster of breasts, and griffins and bulls springing from the sheath which tightly encircles her waist. Nevertheless, this "fantasy" is an exact reproduction of plate 88 in Creutzer's last volume: if we observe the details of the print, we can appreciate Flaubert's diligence. Cybele and Atys (with his languid pose, his elbow against a tree, his flute, and his costume cut into diamond shapes) are both found in plate 58 of the same work; similarly, the portrait of Ormuz is in Layard and the medals of Oraios, Sabaoth, Adonaius, and Knouphus are easily located in Matter. It is indeed surprising that such erudite precision strikes us as a phantasmagoria. More exactly, we are astounded that Flaubert experienced the scholar's patience, the very patience necessary to knowledge, as the liveliness of a frenzied imagination.

Possibly, Flaubert was responding to an experience of the fantastic which was singularly modern and relatively unknown before his time, to the discovery of a new imaginative space in the nineteenth century. This domain of phantasms is no longer the night, the sleep of reason, or the uncertain void that stands before desire, but, on the contrary, wakefulness, untiring attention, zealous erudition, and constant vigilance. Henceforth, the visionary experience arises from the black and white surface of printed signs, from the closed and dusty volume that opens with a flight of forgotten words; fantasies are carefully deployed in the hushed library, with its columns of books, with its titles aligned on shelves to form a tight enclosure, but within confines that also liberate impossible worlds. The imaginary now resides between the book and the lamp. The fantastic is no longer a property of the heart, nor is it found among the incongruities of nature; it evolves from the accuracy of knowledge, and its treasures lie dormant in documents. Dreams are no longer summoned with closed eyes, but in reading; and a true image is now a product of learning: it derives from words spoken in the past, exact recensions, the amassing of minute facts, monuments reduced to infinitesimal fragments, and the reproductions of reproductions. In the modern experience, these elements contain the power of the impossible. Only the assiduous clamor created by repetition can transmit to us what only happened once. The imaginary is not formed in opposition to reality as its denial or compensation; it grows among signs, from book to book, in the interstice of repetitions and commentaries;

The god Vichnou, plate IX, fig. 47, from Creuzer's Les Religions de l'antiquité, *translated in four volumes from 1829 to 1851. Flaubert relied on Creuzer's work in his research for* La Tentation de saint Antoine *(cliché Bibliothèque nationale de France, Paris).*

it is born and takes shape in the interval between books. It is a phenomenon of the library.

Both Michelet (in the *Sorcière*) and Edgar Quinet (in *Ahasvérus*) had explored these forms of erudite dreams, but *The Temptation* is not a scholarly project which evolved into an artistically coherent whole. As a work, its form relies on its location within the domain of knowledge: it exists by virtue of its essential relationship to books. This explains why it may represent more than a mere episode in the history of Western imagination; it opens a literary space wholly dependent on the network formed by the books of the past: as such, it serves to circulate the fiction of books. Yet, we should not confuse it with apparently similar works, with *Don Quixote* or the works of Sade, because the link between the former and the tales of knight-errantry or between the *Nouvelle Justine* and the virtuous novels of the eighteenth century is maintained through irony; and, more importantly, they remain books regardless of their intention. *The Temptation,* however, is linked in a completely serious manner to the vast world of print and develops within the recognizable institution of writing. It may appear as merely another new book to be shelved alongside all the others, but it serves, in actuality, to extend the space that existing books can occupy. It recovers other books; it hides and displays them and, in a single movement, it causes them to glitter and disappear. It is not simply the book that Flaubert dreamed of writing for so long; it dreams other books, all other books that dream and that men dream of writing–books that are taken up, fragmented, displaced, combined, lost, set at an unapproachable distance by dreams, but also brought closer to the imaginary and sparkling realization of desires. In writing *The Temptation,* Flaubert produced the first literary work whose exclusive domain is that of books: following Flaubert, Mallarmé is able to write *Le Livre* and modern literature is activated–Joyce, Roussel, Kafka, Pound, Borges. The library is on fire.

Déjeuner sur l'Herbe and *Olympia* were perhaps the first "museum" paintings, the first paintings in European art that were less a response to the achievement of Giorgione, Raphael, and Velasquez than an acknowledgement (supported by this singular and obvious connection, using this legible reference to cloak its operation) of the new and substantial relationship of painting to itself, as a manifestation of the existence of museums and the particular reality and interdependence that paintings acquire in museums. In the same period, *The Temptation* was the first literary work to comprehend the greenish institutions where books are accumulated and where the slow and incontrovertible vegetation of learning quietly proliferates. Flaubert is to the library what Manet is to the museum. They both produced works in a self-conscious relationship to earlier paintings or texts–or rather to the aspect in painting or writing that remains indefinitely open. They erect their art within the archive.[4] They were not meant to foster the lamentations–the lost youth, the absence of vigor, and the decline of inventiveness–through which we reproach our Alexandrian age, but to unearth an essential aspect of our culture: every painting now belongs within the squared and massive surface of painting and all literary works are confined to the indefinite murmur of writing. Flaubert and Manet are responsible for the existence of books and paintings within works of art.

III

The presence of the book in *The Temptation,* its manifestation and concealment, is indicated in a strange way: it immediately contradicts itself as a book. From the start, it challenges the priority of its printed signs and takes the form of a theatrical presentation: the transcription of a text that is not meant to be read, but recited and staged. At one time, Flaubert had wanted to transform *The Temptation* into a kind of epic drama, a *Faust* capable of swallowing the entire world of religion and gods. He soon gave up this idea but retained within the text the indications marking a possible performance: division into dialogues and scenes, descriptions of the place of action, the scenic elements, and their modifications, blocking directions for the "actors" on stage–all given according to a traditional typographical arrangement (smaller type and wider margins for stage directions, a character's name in large letters above the speeches, etc.). In a significant redoubling, the first indicated setting–the site of all future modifications–has the form of a natural theater: the hermit's retreat has been placed "at the top of a mountain, on a platform rounded in the form of a half-moon and enclosed by large boulders." The text describes a stage which, itself, represents a "platform" shaped by natural forces and upon which new scenes will in turn impose their sets. But these indications do not suggest a future performance (they are largely incompatible with an actual presentation); they simply designate the specific mode of existence of the text. Print can only be an unobtrusive aid to the visible; an insidious spectator takes the reader's place and the act of reading is dissolved in the triumph of another form of sight. The book disappears in the theatricality it creates.

But it will immediately reappear within a scenic space. No sooner have the first signs of temptation emerged from the gathering shadows, no sooner have the disquieting faces appeared in the night, than Saint Anthony lights a torch to protect himself and opens a "large book." This posture is consistent with the iconographic tradition: in the painting of Breughel [*sic*] the Younger, the painting that so impressed Flaubert when he visited the Balbi collection in Genoa and that he felt had incited him to write *The Temptation,* the hermit, in the lower right-hand corner of the canvas, is kneeling before an immense volume, his head slightly bowed, and his eyes intent on the written lines. Surrounding him on all sides are naked women with open arms, lean Gluttony stretching her giraffe's neck, barrel-like men creating an uproar, and nameless beasts devouring each other; at his back is a procession of the grotesques that populate the earth–bishops, kings, and tyrants. But this assembly is lost on the saint, absorbed in his reading. He sees nothing of this great uproar, unless perhaps through the corner of his eye, unless he seeks to protect himself by invoking the enigmatic powers of a magician's book. It may be, on the contrary, that the mumbling recitation of written signs has summoned these poor shapeless figures that no language has ever named, that no book can contain, but that anonymously invade the weighty pages of the volume. It may be, as well, that these creatures of unnatural issue escaped from the book, from the gaps between the open pages or the blank spaces between the letters. More fertile than the sleep of reason, the book perhaps engenders an infinite brood of monsters. Far from being a protection, it has liberated an obscure swarm of creatures and created a suspicious shadow through the mingling of images and knowledge. In any case, setting aside this discussion of the open folio in Breughel's [*sic*] painting, Flaubert's Saint Anthony seizes his book to ward off the evil that begins to obsess him and reads at random five passages from Scriptures. But, by a trick of the text, there immediately arises in the evening air the odors of gluttony, the scent of blood and anger, and the incense of pride, aromas worth more than their weight in gold, and the sinful perfumes of Oriental queens. The book–but not any book–is the site of temptation. Where the first passage read by the hermit is taken from the "Acts of the Apostles," the last four, significantly, come from the Old Testament[5]–from God's Scripture, from the supreme book.

The two earlier versions of *The Temptation* excluded the reading of sacred texts. Attacked by the canonical figures of evil, the hermit immediately seeks refuge in his chapel; goaded by Satan, the Seven Deadly Sins are set against the Virtues and, led by Pride, they make repeated assaults upon the protected enclosure. This imagery of the portal and the staging of a mystery are absent from the published text. In the final version, evil is not given as the property of characters, but incorporated in words. A book intended to lead to the gates of salvation also opens the gates of Hell. The full range of fantastic apparitions that eventually unfold before the hermit–orgiastic palaces, drunken emperors, unfettered heretics, misshapen forms of the gods in agony, abnormalities of nature–arise from the opening of a book, as they issued from the libraries that Flaubert consulted. It is appropriate, in this context, that Flaubert dropped from the definitive text the symmetrical and opposing figures of logic and the swine, the original leaders of the pageant, and replaced them with Hilarion, the learned disciple who was initiated into the reading of sacred texts by Saint Anthony.

The presence of the book in *The Temptation,* initially in a theatrical spectacle and then more prominently as the source of a pageant, which, in turn, obscures its presence, gives rise to an extremely complicated space. We are apparently presented with a frieze of colorful characters set against cardboard scenery; on the edge of the stage, in a corner, sits the hooded figure of the motionless saint. The scene is reminiscent of a puppet theater. As a child, Flaubert saw *The Mystery of Saint Anthony* performed numerous times by Père Legrain in his puppet theater; he later brought Georges [*sic,* for George] Sand to a performance. The first two versions of *The Temptation* retained elements from this source (most obviously, the pig, but also the personification of sin, the assault on the chapel, and the image of the virgin). In the definitive text, only the linear succession of the visions remains to suggest an effect of "marionettes": sins, temptations, divinities, and monsters are paraded before the laconic hermit–each emerging, in turn, from the hellish confines of the box where they were kept. But this is only a surface effect constructed upon a staging in depth (it is the flat surface that is deceptive in this context).

As support for these successive visions, to set them up in their illusory reality, Flaubert arranged a limited number of stages, which extends, in a perpendicular direction, the pure and straightforward reading of the printed phrases. The first intersection is the reader (1)–the actual reader of the text–and the book lies before him (1*a*); from the first lines (*it is in the Thebaid . . . the hermit's cabin appears in the background*) the text invites the reader to become a spectator (2) of a stage whose scenery is carefully described (2*a*); at center stage, the spectator sees the hermit (3) seated with his legs crossed: he will shortly rise and turn to his book (3*a*) from which disturbing visions will gradually escape–banquets, palaces, a voluptuous queen, and finally Hilarion, the insidious discipline [*sic*] (4). Hilarion leads the saint into a space filled with visions (4*a*); this opens a world of heresies and gods, and a world where improbable creatures proliferate (5). Moreover, the heretics are also capable of speech and recount their shameless rites; the gods recall their past glories and the cults that were devoted to them; and the monsters proclaim their proper bestiality. Derived from the power of their words or from their mere presence, a new dimension is realized, a vision that lies within that produced by the satanic disciple (5*a*), a vision that contains the abject cult of the Ophites, the miracles of Apollonius, the temptations of Buddha, and the ancient and blissful reign of Isis (6). Beginning as actual readers, we successively encounter five distinct levels, five different orders of language (indicated by *a*): that of the book, a theater, a sacred text, visions, and visions that evolve into further visions. There are also five series of characters, of figures, of landscapes, and of forms: the invisible spectator, Saint Anthony in his retreat, Hilarion, the heretics, the gods and the monsters, and finally, the shadows propagated by their speeches or through their memories.

This organization, which develops through successive enclosures, is modified by two others. (In actuality, it finds its confirmation and completion in two others.) The first is that of a retrospective encasement. Where the figures on the sixth level (visions of visions) should be the palest and least accessible to direct perception, they appear forcefully on the scene, as dense, colorful, and insistent as the figures that precede them or as Saint Anthony himself. It is as if the clouded memories and secret desires, which produced these visions from the first, have the power of acting without mediation in the scenic space, upon the landscape where the hermit pursues his imaginary dialogue with his disciple, or upon the stage that the fictitious spectator is meant to behold during the acting out of this semi-mystery. Thus, the fictions of the last level fold back upon themselves, envelop the figures from which they arose, quickly surpass the disciple and the anchorite, and finish by inscribing themselves within the supposed materiality of the theater. Through this retrospective envelopment, the most ephemeral fictions are presented in the most direct language, through the stage directions, indicated by the author, whose task is an external definition of the characters.

This arrangement allows the reader (1) to see Saint Anthony (3) over the shoulder of the implied spectator (2) who is an accomplice to the dramatic presentation: the effect is to identify the reader with the spectator. Consequently, the spectator sees Anthony on the stage, but he also sees over his shoulder the apparitions presented to the hermit, apparitions that are as substantial as the saint: Alexandria, Constantinople, the Queen of Sheba, Hilarion. The spectator's glance dissolves into the hallucinated gaze of the hermit. Anthony then leans over Hilarion's shoulder, and sees with his eyes the figures evoked by the evil disciple; and Hilarion, through the arguments of the heretics, perceives the face of the gods and the snarling monsters, contemplates the images that haunt them. Developed from one figure to another, a wreath is constructed which links the characters in a series of knots independent of their proper intermediaries, so that their identities are gradually merged and their different perceptions blended into a single dazzling sight.

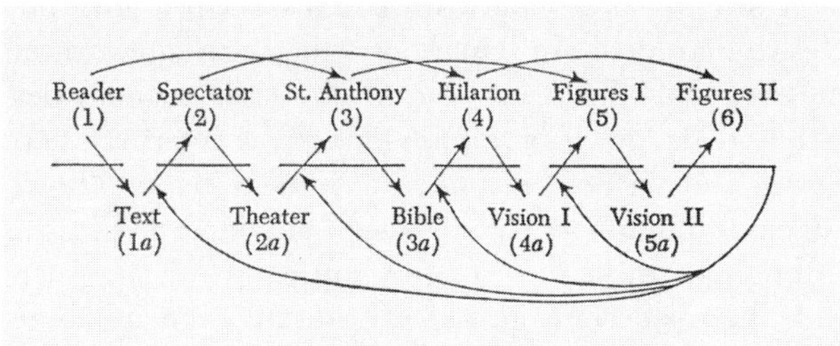

An immense distance lies between the reader and the ultimate visions that entrance the imaginary figures: orders of language placed according to degrees of subordination, relay-characters gazing over each other's shoulders and withdrawing to the depths of this "text-representation," and a population abounding in illusions. But two movements counter this distance: the first, affecting the different orders of language, renders the invisible elements visible through a direct style, and the second, which concerns the figures, gradually adopts the vision and the light fixed upon the characters and brings forward the most distant images until they emerge from the sides of the scene. It is this double movement that makes a vision actually tempting: the most indirect and encased elements of the vision are given with a brilliance compatible with the foreground; and the visionary, attracted by the sights placed before him, rushes into this simultaneously empty and overpopulated space, identifies himself with this figure of shadow and light, and begins to see, in turn, with unearthly eyes. The profundity of these boxed apparitions and the linear and naive succession of figures are not in any way contradictory. Rather, they form the perpendicular intersections that constitute the paradoxical shape and the singular domain of *The Temptation.* The frieze of marionnettes and the stark, colored surface of these figures who jostle one another in the shadows offstage are not the effects of childhood memories or the residue of vivid impressions: they are the composite result of a vision that develops on successive and gradually more distant levels and a temptation that attracts the visionary to the place he has seen and that suddenly envelops him in his own visions.

IV

The Temptation is like a discourse whose function is to maintain not a single and exclusive meaning (by excising all the others), but the simultaneous existence of multiple meanings. The visible sequence of scenes is extremely simple: first, the memories of the aging monk, the hallucinations and sins summarized by the figure of an ancient queen who arrives from the Orient (Chapters I and II); then, the disciple who initiates the rapid multiplication of heresies through his debate on Scripture (III and IV); followed by the emergence of the gods who successively appear on the stage (V); with the depopulation of the earth, Anthony is free to return to it guided by his disciple who has become both Satan and Knowledge, free to gauge its expanse and to observe the tangled and infinite growth of monsters (VI, VII). This visible sequence is supported by a number of underlying series.

1. Temptation is conceived in the hermit's heart; it hesitantly evokes his companions during his retreat and the passing caravans; from this, it extends into vaster regions: overpopulated Alexandria, the Christian Orient torn by theological conflicts, all those Mediterranean civilizations ruled by gods who emerged from Asia, and, finally, the limitless expanses of the universe–the distant stars at night, the imperceptible cell from which life awakens. But this ultimate scintillation only serves to return the hermit to the material principle of his first desires. Having reached the limits of the world, the grand and tempting itinerary returns to its point of departure. In the first two versions of the text, the Devil explained to Anthony "that sins were in his heart and sorrows in his mind." These explanations are now inessential: pushed to the limits of the universe, the arching waves of the temptation return to those things that are nearest. In the minute organism where the primordial desires of life are awakened, Anthony recaptures his ancient heart, his badly controlled appetites, but no longer experiences their charged fantasies. Before his eyes, there lies the material truth. Under this red light, the larva of desire is gently formed. The center of temptation has not shifted: or rather, it has been displaced very slightly from the top to the bottom–passing from the heart to the sinews, from a dream to the cell, from a bright image to matter. Those things that haunted the imagination of the hermit from inside can now become the object of enraptured contemplation; and where he had pushed them aside in fear, they now attract and invite him to a dormant identification: "to descend to the very depths of matter, to become matter."[6] It is only in appearance that the temptation wrenches the hermit from his solitude and populates his field of vision with men, gods, and monsters, for, along its curved expanse, it gives rise to a number of distinct movements: a progressive expansion to the confines of

the universe; a loop bringing desire back to its truth; a shift that causes a violent phantasm to subside in the soft repose of matter; a passage from the inside to the outside–from heartfelt nostalgia to the vivid spectacle of life; the transformation of fear into the desire for identification.

2. Sitting on the doorstep of his cabin, the hermit is obsessed by the memories of an old man: formerly, isolation was less painful, work less tedious, and the river not as distant as now. He had enjoyed his youth–the young girls who congregated at the fountain–and also his retreat, and the opportunity for companionship, particularly with his favorite disciple. His memories flood back upon him in this slight wavering of the present at the hour of dusk. It is a total inversion of time: first, the images of twilight in the city humming with activity before dark–the port, shouting in the streets, the tambourines in the taverns; followed by Alexandria in the period of the massacres, Constantinople during the Council; this suddenly gives way to the heretics whose affronts originated with the founding of Christianity; behind them are the gods who once had a following of faithful and whose temples range from India to the Mediterranean; and finally, the appearance of figures as old as time itself–the distant stars, brute matter, lust and death, the recumbent Sphinx, chimeras, all those things that, in a single movement, create life and its illusions. Further, beyond this primordial cell from which life evolved, Anthony desires an impossible return to the passive state prior to life: the whole of his existence is consequently laid to rest where it recovers its innocence and awakens once again to the sounds of animals, the bubbling fountain, and the glittering stars. The highest temptation is the longing to be another, to be all others; it is to renew identifications and to achieve the principle of time in a return that completes the circle. The vision of Engadine approaches.[7]

An ambiguous figure–simultaneously a form of duration and eternity, acting as conclusion and a fresh start–introduces each stage of this return through time. The heresies are introduced by Hilarion–as small as a child and withered like an old man, as young as awakening knowledge and as old as well-pondered learning. Apollonius introduces the gods: he is familiar with their unending metamorphoses, their creation and death, but he is also able to regain instantly "the Eternal, the Absolute, and Being."[8] Lust and Death lead the dance of life because they undoubtedly control the end and new beginnings, the disintegration of forms and the origin of all things. The larva-skeleton, the eternal Thaumaturge, and the old child each function within the book as "alternators" of duration; through the time of history, myth, and the entire universe, they guarantee the hermit's recapture of the cellular principle of life. The night of *The Temptation* can greet the unchanged novelty of a new day, because the earth has turned back upon its axis.

3. The resurgence of time also produces a prophetic vision of the future. Within his recollections, Anthony encountered the ancient imagination of the Orient: deep within this memory, which no longer belongs to him, he saw a form arising that represented the temptation of the wisest of the kings of Israel–the Queen of Sheba. Standing behind her, he recognized in the shape of an ambiguous dwarf, her servant and his own disciple, a disciple who is indissociably linked to Desire and Wisdom. Hilarion is the incarnation of all the dreams of the Orient, but he possesses as well a perfect knowledge of Scriptures and their interpretation. Greed and science are united in him–covetous knowledge and damnable facts. This gnome increases in size throughout the course of the liturgy; by the last episode, he has become gigantic, "beautiful as an archangel and luminous as the sun." His kingdom now includes the universe as he becomes the Devil in the lightning flash of truth. Serving as an embryonic stage in the development of Western thought, he first introduces theology and its infinite disputes; then, he revives ancient civilizations and their gods whose rule was so quickly reduced to ashes; he inaugurates a rational understanding of the world; he demonstrates the movement of the stars and reveals the secret powers of life. All of European culture is deployed in this Egyptian night where the spector, the ancient history, of the Orient still haunts the imagination: the theology of the Middle Ages, the erudition of the Renaissance, and the scientific bent of the modern period. *The Temptation* acts as a nocturnal sun whose trajectory is from east to west, from desire to knowledge, from imagination to truth, from the oldest longings to the findings of modern science. The appearance of Egypt converted to Christianity (and with it Alexandria) and the appearance of Anthony represent the zero point between Asia and Europe; both seem to arise from a fold in time, at the point where Antiquity, at the summit of its achievement, begins to vacillate and collapses, releasing its hidden and forgotten monsters; they also plant the seed of the modern world with its promise of endless knowledge. We have arrived at the hollow of history.

The "temptation" of Saint Anthony is the double fascination exercised upon Christianity by the sumptuous spectacle of its past and the limitless acquisitions of its future. The definitive text excludes Abraham's God, the Virgin, and the virtues (who appear in the first two versions), but not to save them from profanation; they were incorporated in figures that represent them–in Buddha, the tempted god, in Apollonius the thau-

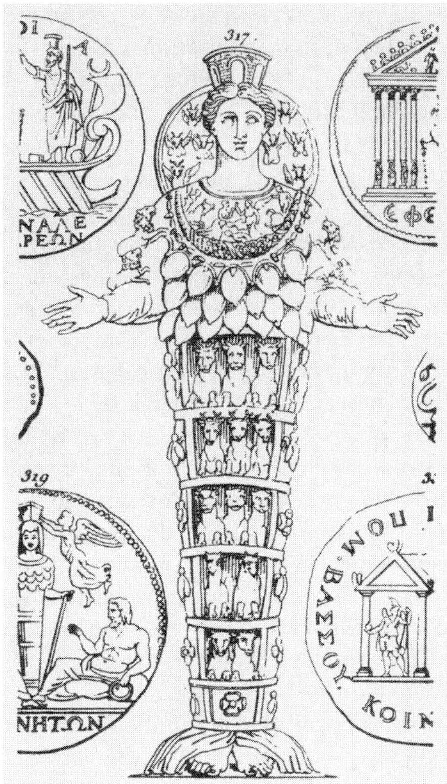

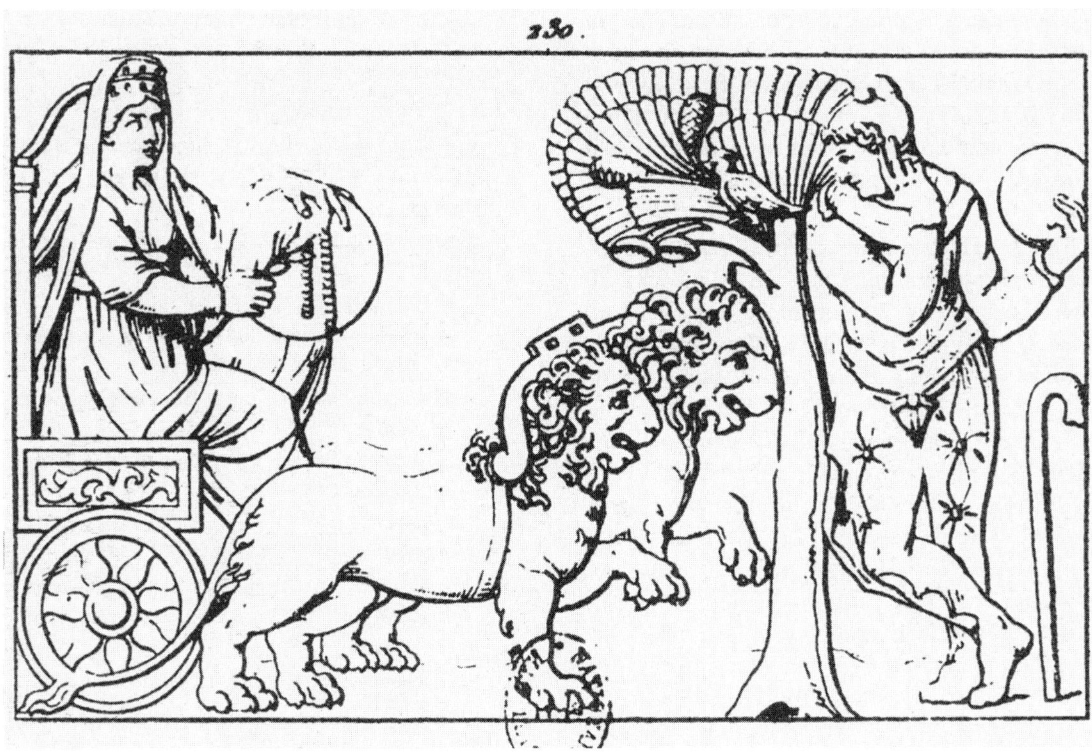

Diana of Ephesus, plate LXXXVIII, fig. 317, and Cybele and Atys, plate LVIII, fig. 230, from Creuzer's Les Religions de l'antiquité*–illustrations that Michel Foucault says Flaubert precisely describes in* La Tentation de saint Antoine *(clichés Bibliothèque nationale de France, Paris)*

maturge who resembles Christ, and in Isis the mother of sorrows. *The Temptation* does not mask reality in its glittering images, but reveals the image of an image in the realm of truth. Even in its state of primitive purity, Christianity was formed by the dying reflections of an older world, formed by the feeble light it projected upon the still grey shadows of a nascent world.

4. The two earlier versions of *The Temptation* began with the battle of the Seven Deadly Sins against the three theological virtues (Faith, Hope, and Charity), but this traditional imagery of the mysteries disappears in the published text. The sins appear only in the form of illusions and the virtues are given a secret existence as the organizing principles of the sequences. The endless revival of heresies places Faith at the mercy of overpowering error; the agony of the gods, which makes them disappear as glimmers of imagination, transforms Hope into a futile quest; and nature in repose or with its savage forces unleashed reduces Charity to a mockery. The three supreme virtues have been vanquished; and turning away from Heaven, the saint "lies flat on his stomach, and leaning upon his elbows, he watches breathlessly. Withered ferns begin to flower anew."[9] At the sight of this small palpitating cell, Charity is transformed into dazzling curiosity ("O joy! O bliss! I have seen the birth of life; I have seen motion begin."),[10] Hope is transformed into an uncontrollable desire to dissolve into the violence of the world ("I long to fly, to swim, to bark, to shout, to howl."),[11] and Faith becomes an identification with brute nature, the soft and somber stupidity of things ("I wish to huddle upon these forms, to penetrate each atom, to descend to the depths of matter–to become pure matter.").[12]

This book, which initially appears as a progression of slightly incoherent fantasies, can claim originality only with respect to its meticulous organization. What appears as fantasy is no more than the simple transcription of documents, the reproductions of drawings or texts, but their sequence conforms to an extremely complex composition. By assigning a specific location to each documentary element, it is also made to function within several simultaneous series. The linear and visible sequence of sins, heresies, divinities, and monsters is merely the superficial crest of an elaborate vertical structure. This succession of figures, crowded like puppets dancing the farandole, also functions as: a trinity of canonical virtues; the geodesic line of a culture born in the dreams of the Orient and completed in the knowledge of the West; the return of History to the origin of time and the beginning of things; a pulsating space that expands to the outer limits of the universe and suddenly recedes to return to the simplest element of life. Each element and each character has its place not only in the visible procession, but in the organization of Christian allegories, the development of culture and knowledge, the reverse chronology of the world, and the spatial configurations of the universe.

In addition, *The Temptation* develops the encapsulated visions in depth as they recede, through a series of stages, to the distance; it constitutes a volume behind the thread of its speeches and under its line of successions. Each element (setting, character, speech, alteration of scenery) is effectively placed at a definite point in the linear sequence, but each element also has its vertical system of correspondences and is situated at a specific depth in the fiction. This explains why *The Temptation* can be the book of books: it unites in a single "volume" a series of linguistic elements that derive from existing books and that are, by virtue of their specific documentary character, the repetition of things said in the past. The library is opened, catalogued, sectioned, repeated, and rearranged in a new space; and this "volume" into which Flaubert has forced it is both the thickness of a book that develops according to the necessarily linear thread of its text and a procession of marionnettes that, in deploying its boxed visions, also opens a domain in depth.

–Michel Foucault, *Language, Counter-Memory, Practice: Selected Essays and Interviews,* edited by Donald F. Bouchard, translated by Donald F. Bouchard and Sherry Simon (Ithaca, N.Y.: Cornell University Press, 1977), pp. 88–105

---

1. *Souvenirs littéraires* (Paris, 1882); Du Camp, who was among the first to listen to Flaubert's recitation, discouraged his efforts.
2. As a result of the remarkable studies by Jean Seznec–FOUCAULT.
3. Jacques Suffel, in a Preface to *The Temptation* (Paris: Garnier-Flammarion, 1967), p. 19, discusses Flaubert's preoccupation with *The Ethics.*
4. See Foucault's discussion of the "archive" in *The Archaeology of Knowledge,* pp. 126–31.
5. Acts of the Apostles 10:11; Daniel 2:46; 2 Kings 20:13; 1 Kings 10:1 – FOUCAULT.
6. *The Temptation of Saint Anthony,* trans. Lafcadio Hearn (New York: Grosset & Dunlap, [No date]), p. 164.
7. Engadine is an Alpine valley in Switzerland where Nietzsche spent his summers between 1879 and 1888.
8. *The Temptation,* p. 97.
9. *The Temptation,* p. 163.
10. Ibid.
11. Ibid.
12. Ibid., p. 164.

* * *

In this excerpt from chapter 4 of The Literary Dream in French Romanticism: A Psychoanalytic Interpretation *(1979), Laurence M. Porter examines the psychologically astute changes Flaubert made as he revised and rewrote* La Tentation de saint Antoine.

Projection as Ego Defense: Flaubert's *Tentation de saint Antoine*

. . . By presenting Anthony's memories of his past as sources of his visions, Flaubert gradually moved from a conventionally medieval Christian, comic-epic episode in the unending struggle between good and evil to an inner, psychological depiction of the saint. Near the beginning of the second of three parts in the 1856 version, Anthony recalls his parents' house and his old mother weeping at his departure. And in 1856 Flaubert added a passage (later suppressed) which demonstrates his lucid understanding of the psychic mechanism of projection, the generative principle of the hallucinations which make up the *Tentation.* Anthony exclaims: "It seems to me that outside objects are penetrating my person, or rather that my thoughts are escaping from it like lightning bolts from a cloud, and assuming corporeal form of themselves, there . . . in front of me! Perhaps that's how God conceived the Creation?"[1] But it was Taine's queries concerning the nature of the artistic imagination which incited Flaubert, in 1866, explicitly to link hallucinations with memory: he says his own epileptic visions occurred "suddenly, like lightning, an invasion or rather an instantaneous bursting in *of memory,* for the true hallucination is nothing other than that–for me, at least. It's a sickness of the memory, an unloosing of its hidden contents. You feel images escaping from you like jets of blood."[2]

Critic, historian, and philosopher Hippolyte Taine, who attended Flaubert's Sunday afternoon meetings in Paris and exchanged several letters with him regarding hallucinations and the artistic imagination (cliché Bibliothèque nationale de France, Paris)

So as he began composing the final version of the *Tentation* late in July 1869, Flaubert was able to hope to find a logical connection between the saint's various hallucinations, without sacrificing the dramatic interest of his story.[3] He described Anthony's past experiences in much greater detail than in the 1856 version. He expanded the cursory mentions of Anthony's mother and of his childhood playmate Ammonaria into detailed scenes, into the quasi-explicit indications of the sources of his fantasias of lust and death in Part VII. Three letters received from Constantine, and Anthony's humiliation in theological debate at the Nicean Council, motivate his fantasies of power and revenge in Part II. The Bible reading introduced in 1856, now shifted to the beginning of the work, provides a "day residue" (an experience remembered from the previous waking period, and incorporated into a dream) to explain the origin of Anthony's visions of Nebuchadnezzar and the Queen of Sheba. His longing for his favorite disciple, Hilarion, prepares the reader for the events of Part III. His memories of heretics preaching in Alexandria anticipates the dream of the assembly of heretics in Part IV. His memories of wall paintings at the temple of Heliopolis, and of the ranks of idols carried by the barbarians who were making a treaty with the emperor, at the beginning of Part V, announce the procession of the gods which follows. In Part VI, the Devil's supreme attempt to destroy Anthony's belief in a personal god employs, as the saint later realizes, the arguments of the pre-Socratic philosophers concerning the infinite, the Creation, and the impossibility of attaining certitude.[4] The monstrous mural paintings he had seen at Belus, and a mosaic at Carthage, announce the visions of the Sphinx and Chimera and monsters in Part VII. In sum, the 1874 version provides a source in Anthony's lived experience for almost every major vision.[5] Once the coherence of the work had been assured in this fashion, Flaubert could reintroduce the powerful episodes which he had considered omitting or truncating in 1869 because they seemed to overshadow the depiction of the personality of the saint: Simon, Apollonius, the pagan gods, the monsters.

Physiological stimuli on the other hand, remain a constant, albeit minor, source of visions throughout the three versions. Anthony's hunger and thirst stimulate dreams of gluttony, and the final assault of La Luxure is caused by what Flaubert identified, in a note from 1849, as "la bandaison matinale" [morning hard-on].[6] He later added the moonlit Nile as the catalyst for the vision of the Ophites' serpent, and the fire which singed the saint's beard as the stimulus for his dream of the Gymnosophist's funeral pyre (pp. 106, 120). For all his belief in the Devil, Saint Anthony acknowledges at least once, in the 1874 version, that the temptations he endures derive from his own body: "Pourquoi ces choses? Elles viennent des soulèvements de la chair" ("Why these things? They come from restless stirrings of the flesh" [pp. 38–39]). But as Flaubert progressively eliminated from the work the personified, exaggerated, schematized versions of Anthony's baser instincts, strengths, and weaknesses–the pig, the virtues, the sins, the Devil–and attenuated the comical physical descriptions of these entities and the quarrels among them (see pp. 212–22, 318ff., and 357–58 in the 1849 version), he multiplied indications that preconscious memories were the sources of Anthony's visions. These changes allowed him to decrease the number of other sorts of suggestions that Anthony's was a mental drama. So the proportion of his metaphors which explicitly evoke the saint's inner world diminishes from 57 percent in 1849 to 46 percent in 1856 and 24 percent in 1874. Those which survive are the less striking.[7] In compensation, from one draft to the next Flaubert made Anthony's subjective world more predominant by carefully eliminating many expressions which overtly shifted the focus of the visions and thus betrayed the structuring hand of the author. The margins of the final 1874 version bear the reminders "too many 'then's,' and the *suddenly*"; "too many *suddenly*'s, 'but's,' 'then's'"; "watch out for *little* and *suddenly*."[8] Moreover, after 1849 he prepared the reader much more carefully for Anthony's visions. The 1849 version introduces hallucinatory voices on page two; the pig talks on page four. The considerably shorter 1856 version describes wind noises which become voices only on page twenty-three (page nine of the 1874 manuscript), and the first apparitions appear only on page forty-three.

All three versions, however, employ the *mise en abyme* construction to imply the coexistence of conscious and unconscious mental levels, and the invasion of the former by the latter. The physical setting of the hermit's hut (Level I) contains elements–Bible, river, birds and animals, bread and water, torch, pebble, knife–which lead to memories and visions of Anthony's past, of biblical characters, of Satan, temptations, and heretics (Level II). Some of these beings describe their own visions (Level III), which include pagan gods who themselves speak (Level IV). At this same level, Satan attempts to supplant them and the Christian God as the ultimate reality, but he dissolves into the twofold phantom of Lust and Death, a phantom which is itself an illusion. At last (Level V) Saint Anthony makes contact with the primordial reality of life, embodied in monsters who themselves address him.[9] Fascinated and mentally engulfed, as it were, by their seething, pulsating mass, like Jonah by his whale, Anthony undergoes a sort of Night Sea Journey which, at daybreak, restores him to the vision of Christ or the integrated personality. The spatial and temporal confines of Anthony's visions, which have steadily expanded during his arrogant attempt to apprehend the transcendent through reason, suddenly retract to the minute scale of the biological cell, the ultimate secret (p. 275). Contemplating the cell finally opens before Anthony's gaze a heaven no longer void, but charged with meaning.

Those historical inaccuracies which Flaubert allowed to stand in 1874 enrich the psychological implications of the *Tentation.* That this Anthony can read, although the real saint could not, creates a secondary source of fantasies through Constantine's letters and the biblical passages. The exaggeration of repellent behavior in the depictions of the heretics expresses Anthony's resistance to heretical thoughts within himself. His location on a cliff above the Nile, though not historically correct, dramatizes the alluring terror of self-destruction. The poignant scene of family rupture at Anthony's departure–the weeping mother, reproachful sister, and desperate playmate (whom some sentimental critics inaccurately identify as Anthony's fiancée)–emphasizes the drama of self-definition and the quest for independence in Flaubert's version of the saint's life. In reality, Anthony's parents died before he left his native village, and he continued to live there for some years after their death. When his parents died, he arranged for his sister to be lodged in a religious establishment, and he had no known romantic attachment, nor any surrogate father to lead him away.[10]

Increasingly from one version to the next the Devil functions as a Jungian "Shadow," as the repressed "unworthy" part of Anthony's personality embodying all his repressed doubts and resistance to the will of God. Anthony's need to dissociate himself from his own impulses calls the Devil into being.[11] Once one recognizes the Devil as part of Saint Anthony, and the series of temptations as an inner debate, one can dismiss such literal-minded complaints as those of Paul Valéry, Jonathan Culler, and Michel Butor. Valéry complained that Anthony as a character is weak and uninteresting, overwhelmed by a mass of historical detail: "he scarcely exists. His reactions are disconcertingly weak. . . . He is tediously passive. . . . His responses are defeats. . . . It's as if Flaubert had been intoxicated by secondary issues at the expense of the main subject"; he missed his chance to be profound by studying the psychology of temptation.[12] Butor concurs, adding that nothing in particular happens to Anthony; his situation does not change; the next night the same temptations will no doubt return. Flaubert, claims Butor, arranged the incidents like a parade, aiming for a contrast and variety which would have the maximum effect upon the reader rather than upon the saint. He makes the Seven Deadly Sins return repeatedly in approximately the same order, creating a "spiral" structure.

On the contrary, however, Anthony's paralysis throughout most of the *Tentation* results from and expresses his inner conflicts. The Devil embodies his *libidio sciendi* and rebellious mental surge toward self-sufficiency which clashes with his desire to submit to God. In the guise of Hilarion, the Devil grows in stature and impressiveness throughout the work. The setting of the visions, too, expands steadily from the local to the cosmic, from the historic to the mythic, from the personal to the universal, reflecting the hubristic efforts of the human intellect to subject externality to a system of thought. Having renounced active involvement with the world, the saint unconsciously craves a compensatory mastery of the world of ideas. When he achieves self-understanding, which includes the recognition of his mental limitations, the temptation ends (in its 1874 version) with the successful integration of the two sides of his personality. Having served his function of crystallizing Anthony's self-dissatisfaction, issuing an imperative call to self-examination, and being the catalyst for a constructive personality change, the Devil becomes expendable and disappears, like those devils who appear to Goethe's Faust and Dostoevsky's Ivan.

The earlier version of the *Tentation* had three parts: first the apparition of the personified sins and the heresiarchs; then Anthony's resulting fantasies of power, lust, and self-abasement; and finally the direct confrontation with Satan. The 1874 version has seven parts to suggest the Seven Deadly Sins. In Part I there are internal assaults on Anthony's virtue, arising from tendencies in his own personality. Voluntarily removed from society in the desert, then visually isolated from his surroundings by descending night, he weakens in his religious resolve. He regrets the lost possibilities for involvement with others in the past; nostalgic memories of companionship overwhelm him. Then he begins to hear hallucinatory voices. In Part II external assaults on Anthony's virtue begin. Temptations suggesting the Seven Deadly Sins assail him (they are defensively dissociated from himself through the psychic mechanism of projection). Sloth prepares the way for the others. Hallucinatory visions begin. In Part III internal assaults on Christian doctrine begin. The saint's own weakness in the face of temptation makes him doubt the faith he holds. Disguised as Anthony's favorite disciple, Hilarion, the Devil comes forward to ask insidious questions about the foundations of the saint's belief. Part IV depicts external assaults upon Christian doctrine. Projected outward, Anthony's doubts assume the form of heretics preaching their doctrines. Distressingly similar

"The old palm-tree becomes the torso of a woman leaning over the abyss," from part I, "A Holy Saint" (wood engraving by Ilse Bischoff; from The Temptation of Saint Antony *[New York: Ives Washburn, 1930], Thomas Cooper Library, University of South Carolina)*

to Christians, they too have their martyrs and their scripture. Therefore Saint Anthony's ego ideal is threatened in Part V. His attempts to personify the guiding forces of the universe (in the form of the Holy Trinity) are mocked and parodied by a grotesque procession of barbaric gods. In Part VI Satan completes Anthony's alienation from the supernatural by taking him on a voyage through outer space to show that the transcendent has no personality: it cannot be apprehended by the human intellect. Thus, in Part VII, Anthony must confront the human condition without God–no grace, no afterlife–as represented by the twin phantoms of Lust and Death. But he succeeds in recognizing them as illusions concealing the continuity of all life. He renounces pride, associates himself with this continuity, and finally achieves psychic wholeness through a vision of Christ's face in the rising sun.

Flaubert's initial description suggests a polarity between Anthony's ascetic ambition and his weakness. The saint's cabin of mud and reeds–the baseness and frailty of the human condition–is located at the summit of a cliff–a precarious attempt at spiritual elevation. The empty desert below the cliff and the prominent book on a lectern within the cabin suggest that this will be an intellectual drama divorced from a social context. The river running through the desert below hints at mental depths from which unexpected thoughts may emerge; the absence of a door on the cabin implies that Anthony will have no way to shut these thoughts out. The opposition of spiritual aspiration and human frailty recurs in the third paragraph, which describes a tall cross planted in the ground–the idealized self-image–and a twisted old tree leaning over the abyss.[13]

Characteristically for romantic literature, sunset in the opening scene creates a change in lighting which corresponds to a transition from rational waking thought to an *état second* of involuntary impressions. But mentions and metaphors of dryness show that Anthony has lost contact with his unconscious–his tenderness and need for companionship. In his first speech he says that upon arising he used to pray; then he descended to bring back water from the river; then he prayed again: "Les deux bras étendus je sentais comme une fontaine de miséricorde qui s'épanchait du haut du ciel dans mon cœur. Elle est tarie, maintenant" ("Praying with my arms outstretched, I felt a fountain of mercy, as it were, flowing down to my heart from the heights of heaven. Now that fountain has run dry" [p. 3]). At the beginning of Part II we learn that Anthony's water jug is empty and his water pitcher broken (p. 24). In short, the saint is undergoing the final crisis of human development: the struggle to achieve a sense of integrity rather than self-contempt. In old age, looking back over his entire life, he must convince himself that all his sacrifice has been worthwhile; that, despite his isolation, he exists in meaningful solidarity with other men, including those of other times and places; that his own life, a limited cycle which gives way to future generations, still contributes something irreplaceable to them.[14] The text states each alternative. Formerly, says Anthony, "mes moindres actions me semblaient alors des devoirs qui n'avaient rien de pénible" ("my least actions seemed to me at that time like duties which were not the least bit arduous" [p. 3]). But at the depths of his crisis, when Death says "Tu dois être fatigué par la monotonie des mêmes actions, la durée des jours, la laideur du monde, la bêtise du soleil!" ("You must be tired of the monotony of the same actions, the length of the days, the ugliness of the world, the stupidity of the sun!"), he answers "Oh! oui, tout ce qu'il éclaire me déplaît!" ("Oh! yes, everything it shines on displeases me!" [p. 252]). Chronic displeasure with the world masks disgust with oneself.

Adrift in the present, the saint seeks an identity in the past. He recalls the first, decisive suppression of the instinctual in his life: his departure from home and the three women–mother, sister and Ammonaria–who loved him. The well beside which he met Ammonaria each evening, and her tears, associate her with the symbolic motif of water as emotional fulfillment. Because Anthony repressed all feelings about women after he left home, his feelings for the three he remembers from childhood will assume an enormous importance in his psychic life.[15] His next association, between Ammonaria and a memory of a voluptuous naked woman being flogged (pp. 6, 40) reveals his unconscious connection between asceticism and repressed sexuality. Hilarion later draws an explicit parallel:

> Hypocrite qui s'enfonce dans la solitude pour se livrer mieux au débordement de ses convoitises! Tu te prives de viandes, de vin, d'étuves, d'esclaves et d'honneurs; mais comme tu laisses ton imagination t'offrir des banquets, des parfums, des femmes nues et des foules applaudissantes! Ta chasteté n'est qu'une corruption plus subtile, et ce mépris du monde l'impuissance de ta haine contre lui! [P. 59]

> [Hypocrite, you bury yourself in solitude the better to yield to your superabundant lusts! You deny yourself meat, wine, bathhouses, slaves, and honors; but how complaisantly you allow your imagination to offer you banquets, perfume, naked women, and applauding crowds! Your chastity is merely a more subtle form of corruption, and your contempt for the world, the powerlessness of your hatred for it.]

In response, the saint breaks into sobs.

Saint Anthony feels intensely lonely. The escapism at first embodied in his reminiscences becomes more explicit when he longs to join the passing birds or to sail on the boats he used to watch. As his desire for companionship grows, his fantasies become increasingly secular. At first he wishes that he had joined the monastic community at Nitria; then he thinks of being a priest among lay persons; finally he dreams of wordly occupations. After imagining a merchant kissing his wife, his desire for physical affection becomes so strong that he wishes to caress one of the jackals in a passing troop. In this first phase of temptation, Anthony acknowledges his own weakness as the source of his unworthy thoughts (p. 10) and reads the Bible in an attempt to redirect them. But his repressed impulses of gluttony, anger, pride, and avarice return through the very instrument of their repression: the passages Anthony notices seem to justify these impulses. So a new food of fantasies wells up. They culminate in a series of lustful memories of the wealthy female penitents who used to visit him.

In the second phase of his temptation, Saint Anthony unwittingly exteriorizes his thoughts and dissociates himself from responsibility for them. This makes them less controllable. He imagines that the sound of the wind is harness bells tinkling in a procession which is bringing a female penitent to him. Momentarily ashamed when he calls out and then realizes the procession was imaginary, he quickly loses self-awareness again: the wind noise becomes hallucinatory voices cajoling him. Sharply defined visual hallucinations follow, bright and isolated against the night sky, very like the epileptic visions which Flaubert himself experienced and described. Anthony collapses into helpless passivity.

He enters a third phase of temptation as the second section of Flaubert's dream narrative begins. With the appearance of the Devil as "a vast shadow, more insubstantial than a natural shadow" while Anthony's eyes remain closed, Flaubert signals a modulation in the saint's perceptions from the natural-external to the supernatural-internal. No longer do the visions have an ostensible cause in the real world, yet their origin has now been personified as Satan, an external figure with whose activities the saint can deny any voluntary connection. At the same time, by dreaming that he is an Egyptian hermit–as he is in fact–he attempts to deny his real situation.

Incited by desire and consummated by repression, the resultant doubling of the self progressively becomes more marked. First the saint hallucinates rich food: his desires direct part of himself toward an external object. As soon as he manages to reject this temptation, a cornucopia of coins and jewels replaces it. More an intellectual than a sensualist, the saint becomes intoxicated with this false wealth. But when he throws himself upon it, it vanishes. This time he does not have the excuse of physical need, and the second stage of succumbing to temptation, the delectation of the mind, has given way to the third, the consent of the will.

As Saint Anthony realizes what he has done, his self-contempt becomes unendurable. He must project it outward, in the term of hostility against others more wealthy and comfortable than he: "On n'est pas plus imbécile et plus infâme. Je voudrais me battre, ou plutôt m'arracher de mon corps! Il y a trop longtemps que je me contiens! J'ai besoin de me venger, de frapper, de tuer! c'est comme si j'avais dans l'âme un troupeau de bêtes féroces" ("You can't be more stupid and vile. I'd like to strike myself, or better yet, tear myself out of my body! I've been holding myself in too long. I need to avenge myself, to lash out, to kill! It's as if I had a pack of wild beasts in my soul" [p. 29]). He seizes his knife to lash out at an imagined crowd, but collapses, "cataleptic" (p. 29), and the same movement through greed to vengeful repression recurs in another form. Anthony dreams that he is enjoying the rich novelty and diversity of city life in Alexandria. Then an invading army of desert monks destroys the city and massacres the inhabitants. He himself becomes one of the monks, meets all his enemies, and slaughters them. Trembling with pleasure, he wades in blood. He inhales its vapors and delights in feeling the bloody folds of his tunic clinging to his legs. His longing for civilized luxuries and his violent repression of this longing are successively enacted.

But repression creates frustration. This feeling is relieved by fantasies of power which transform the saint into the chief confidant of the emperor Constantine, while his rivals are humiliated. He then becomes the heathen king Nebuchadnezzar, planning to rebuild the Tower of Babel and dethrone God. Waking abruptly, the saint realizes he has sinned in thought. He flagellates himself, but the return of the repressed transforms the pain into voluptuous delight. First he imagines himself being beaten next to the naked woman he had remembered earlier; then the apparition of the amorous Queen of Sheba transposes the chain of visions from history to legend. She is simultaneously an archetypal *anima*-figure who can take the form of all women (p. 51) and the first incarnation of the Devil which is directly visible to Anthony. When the Shadow has been repressed, Shadow and *anima* combine in the unconscious. Their union may be expressed as a rape, as a kidnapping, as a marriage of the heroine by the villain (as in *Aurélia* and generally in melodrama), or, as it is here, by presenting woman in the guise of a demonic temptress.[16] The saint makes the sign of the cross and drives her away.

A dwarfish *puer senex* from the queen's train remains behind. The dwarf symbolizes the emerging contents of the unconscious. As child, he embodies the potential future self, here implying the hope for personal immortality through one's influence on others. His aged, wretched appearance threatens this hope. As Part III begins, he identities himself as Anthony's former disciple Hilarion. This episode was added in the 1874 version, absorbing conversations with La Logique and La Science. It provides an effective transition between the erotic temptation of Part II and the heretical temptations of Part IV: it suggests that Anthony's potentialities for loving women and raising children were sublimated as affection for his disciples. In his first reminiscences he says Hilarion was like a son to him (p. 7). That Hilarion has emerged from the saint's preconscious through psychic projection is underlined by Flaubert, who has Hilarion say: "Apprends même que je ne t'ai jamais quitté. Mais tu passes de longues périodes sans m'apercevoir" ("Know, indeed, that I have never left you. But you spend long periods without noticing me" [p. 55]).

The disciple embodies an apparently harmless and even admirable form of Saint Anthony's pride in his intellect and desire to influence others by providing a model of religious devotion and an understanding of Christian doctrine for his pupils. But insofar as he wishes his disciples' loyalty and admiration to remain attached to him personally, he risks becoming infatuated with his own singularity at the expense of his service to God. Ahistorically, Flaubert makes pride in intellect and an excessive intellectual curiosity be Anthony's weakest point. When Hilarion tries to stimulate Anthony's vanity by denigrating his prominent disciple and biographer Athanasius, the saint vigorously rejects all the slanders. But Hilarion then calls Athanasius so limited intellectually that he admits he can understand nothing concerning the nature of the Word. In response, Anthony smiles, pleased at his own superiority, and agrees that Athanasius' mind is not very profound (p. 58).

So Hilarion encourages a debauchery of the mind. With specious humility, he points to internal contradictions in Christian dogma and revelation. Anthony admits that he has long been struggling against the doubts Hilarion has raised. They return so persistently, he says, that at times he fears he is damned. Hilarion promises that once Anthony employs his reason rather than trusting in revealed religion, the face of the unknown shall be revealed. He claims that mortification of the flesh in an attempt to obtain God's mercy is inferior, as a spiritual discipline, to efforts to understand the nature of God; that the religious person's only merit is his thirst for truth; and that outside the purview of

"The Devil resting against the roof of the cell and carrying under his wings the Seven Deadly Sins," from part II, "The Temptation of Love and Power" (wood engraving by Ilse Bischoff; from The Temptation of Saint Antony *[New York: Ives Washburn, 1930], Thomas Cooper Library, University of South Carolina)*

dogma, there are no restrictions on intellectual speculation. Anthony responds eagerly that he senses his thought straining to burst free of the prison of the body. He thinks it may succeed. The saint does not yet realize the dangers of the Gnostic temptation of knowledge: reason may lead him into the sin of demanding that the transcendent God reveal himself and justify his ways to man, under penalty of ceasing to exist. This danger will emerge slowly.

Throughout Part IV, a parade of representatives of the heresies of the early Christian period addresses the saint. Hilarion uses them to attack tradition as a basis for belief. The heretics embody Saint Anthony's doubts: Flaubert locates this scene inside a building (an immense basilica), which suggests that the entire spectacle is happening inside the saint's head. He evokes all the major Gnostic heresies one by one, while disclosing their devastating influence on faith and morals.[17]

The general movement of the beginning of the fourth section reproduces that of the second one: repression; yielding to the flesh; a disgusted reaction of redoubled restraint; self-contempt destructively projected upon the outside world. But the visions are transposed from an individual and predominantly physical plane to a collective, intellectual one. The Manichean heretics' denial of the flesh (pp. 71–74) is justified by a series of spokesmen for other heresies who condemn the physical order as the creation of the Devil or of a deranged god (pp. 76–77). This same conviction leads still other heretics to debauchery until Tertullian appears. He harshly insists on subduing both body and mind: "Priez, jeûnez, pleurez, mortifiez-vous! Pas de philosophie! pas de livres! après Jésus, la science est inutile!" ("Pray, fast, weep, mortify yourselves! No philosophy! no books! after Jesus, knowledge is useless!" [p. 84]).[18] The vision culminates in the Circoncellions' frenzy of universal destruction. The heretics join in a howling chorus. Challenged by Anthony, they produce their apocryphal, uncanonical gospels to refute the claim that they possess no revelation.

The heretics surround Anthony and close in as if demanding that he acknowledge them as a repressed side of himself. Then the swelling coils of the serpent whom the Ophites believe is Christ fill the room where Anthony finds himself, and start drawing tightly around him. Rather than recognize this Shadow, he faints and drifts into a defensive counter-vision of Christian self-sacrifice in which he is among Christian martyrs at the Roman coliseum. The weeping, imprisoned martyrs suggest Anthony's condition of self-imposed sequestration in the ascetic life, in contrast to the joyous, active crowds outside the arena. The encircling animal menace has been transformed from the serpent into pacing, expectant beasts of prey. At first Anthony, transported with love, is eager to face them and die for the Lord. But his resolve weakens until he feels he would prefer any other death (pp. 108–11). The lion, which in conventional iconography can represent either Satan or Christ, stands for the morally ambiguous, indeterminate nature of one's own unrecognized unconscious.

This motif of the protagonist surrounded by animals, which may be either benevolent or hostile, recurs throughout Flaubert's career.[19] The heretics crowding around Anthony in Part IV, and the monsters in Part VII, constitute similar invitations to self-knowledge. At times the *anima*-figure is added at the center. For instance, in an 1845 dream Flaubert and his mother are taking a walk when monkeys suddenly surround them. After Flaubert, repelled by the creatures, has shot and wounded one of them, his mother reproachfully identifies them as his brothers. A similar image recurred in the *Tentation* from draft to draft, and was removed only at the last moment (NAF, 23667, fol. 73, which would have appeared on p. 143, line 12): Apollonius says that at the world's end he found monkeys gorged with milk (perfectly fulfilled in union with the feminine principle), with the Indian Venus dancing quite naked amidst them. The protagonist must realize that the *anima*'s bond with the animalistic Shadow expresses his own desire for her: then his unconscious may be integrated with ego consciousness.

"The Christians stagger and their brethren push them forward," from part IV, "The Fiery Trial" (wood engraving by Ilse Bischoff; from The Temptation of Saint Antony *[New York: Ives Washburn, 1930], Thomas Cooper Library, University of South Carolina)*

The following scene, added only in April 1871, shows a visit of surviving relatives to the martyrs' graves, which degenerates into a sexual orgy. Fantasies of martyrdom by animals followed by an orgy symbolize a defective relationship between ego consciousness and the Shadow (perceived as a dangerous beast intent on devouring one), superseded by self-knowledge and the union of "male" and "female" principles of the psyche. But on the conscious level, the event signifies that exemplary self-sacrifice does not ensure that one's followers will be worthy and persevere in the faith. This is precisely what Anthony, who has withdrawn from society in order to regenerate it, has been worried about. He attempts to escape his dilemma, in fantasy, by imagining the self-sufficient gymnosophist, whose voluntary self-immolation does not depend on the behavior of followers to preserve its full meaning (pp. 117–19).

Yet Anthony has become calmer and more enlightened through this encounter with his unconscious. Rather than rejecting the heretics with horror as he did at first, he now recognizes the quest for God as a unity underlying all their extravagances (p. 121). The temptation of doubt gives way to that of pride. Apparitions of the supreme heretics Simon the Magician (rival to Saint Peter) and Apollonius of Tyana (rival to Christ) embody his ambition to become a miracle worker and to possess ultimate truth. Apollonius boasts of knowing all gods, all rites, all prayers and prophecies (p. 154). This claim provokes Anthony's curiosity concerning the pagan gods, leading to the parade of these in Part V (p. 161). And until the 1869 version (which preserves a trace of it on fol. 28), Flaubert gave Anthony a prideful reaction as he watched Apollonius depart which clearly anticipated the flight through space in Part VI: "Une ambition tumultueuse m'enlève à des hauteurs qui m'épouvantent, le sol fuit comme une onde, ma tête éclate" ("A tumultuous ambition raises me to fearsome heights; the ground is rushing away like a wave; my head is bursting").[20]

By moving the procession of the gods from the end of the *Tentation* to the middle in 1874, Flaubert freed Anthony's personal drama from its subordination to the sweep of religious history. The saint comes to represent human religious experience in general, not just one phase of it. He reflects the interest of Flaubert and his contemporaries, particularly since Chateaubriand and Constant, in the relativity of religious beliefs and their underlying resemblances. Non-Christian religions are seen not as impostures, but as the provisional forms of an eternal ideal. Such was the opinion of Parnassian poetry; of Renan (a major influence on the *Tentation*); of the opening pages of Quinet's *Génie des religions* (1841); of Jacobi's *Dictionnaire mythologique* (translated in 1846); and of the major source for Flaubert's Part V, Creuzer's *Les Religions de l'antiquité considérées principalement dans leurs formes symboliques et mythologiques* (translated in 1825 to 1851). Flaubert's *Tentation* reflects the ever-increasing influence in his day

"Anthony remains motionless between the pair, contemplating them," from part VII, "The Chimera and the Sphinx" (wood engraving by Ilse Bischoff; from The Temptation of Saint Antony *[New York: Ives Washburn, 1930], Thomas Cooper Library, University of South Carolina)*

of the discipline of comparative religion: in 1849, the saint's only reaction to the dying gods is to say, "so mine will pass also"; in 1856 he makes comparisons among them; and in 1874 Hilarion offers a virtual course in comparative mythology.[21]

. . . .

Critics who interpret the ending of the 1874 version as a defeat for Anthony forget that Flaubert's manuscript notes show he always intended to have the saint win, exhausting by his resistance all the Devil's stratagems.[22] Flaubert knew that the historical Anthony, as Harry Levin points out, "emerged from his trials in the desert to strengthen the faithful and confound the heretics of Alexandria. In the monastery he had organized, among those who were attracted to the stringencies of his rule, he died a serene and natural death at the age of a hundred and five."[23] In the final draft, Flaubert removed the adversative "mais" which set the apparition of Christ's face against the apparition of the monsters. He also removed the phrase "la tentation est finie" which suggested that the saint's final effusion was part of the temptation. And by shifting the appearance of Christ, "the classical symbol for the unity and divinity of the self,"[24] from the procession of the dying gods to the end, where He replaced the three Theological Virtues, Flaubert made the *Tentation* more clearly a drama of personality.

For Christ to appear in the sun, of course, meant no apotheosis to Flaubert. Other gods had appeared there too, only to fade. In the 1849 *Tentation,* Uranus complained: "Saturn has mutilated me, and God's face no longer appears in the disk of the sun."[25] And until the last draft, the 1874 *Tentation* suggested a physiological explanation for such visions, in Tertullian's description of the soul: "It has a human face, and is transparent like those aerial disks which sometimes float between your eyelids and the sun."[26] What really matters is not what one sees, but how. So long as Anthony insists on trying to impose his own intellectual structures on the universe, he generates the Devil, vainglorious self-sufficiency writ large. Once Anthony renounces his secret desire for rational explanations, the entire universe becomes for him a mediator through which God is mystically knowable. He then shares Flaubert's own experience: "Are we not composed of the emanations of the Universe? . . . And if atoms are infinite in number and pass into Forms like an eternal river flowing between its banks, then what holds back thoughts or connects them? Sometimes, by dint of contemplating a pebble, an animal, a picture, I have felt myself enter into it. Communication between people is no more intense than that."[27]

–Laurence M. Porter, "Projection as Ego Defense: Flaubert's *Tentation de saint Antoine,*" in his *The Literary Dream in French Romanticism: A Psychoanalytic Interpretation* (Detroit: Wayne State University Press, 1979), pp. 49–67

---

1. Flaubert, *Œuvres complètes* (Paris: Louis Conard, 1910–54), vol. 17, p. 589. This volume contains the 1849 and 1856 versions of the *Tentation* as appendices to the 1874 text.
2. *Œuvres* [ed. Maurice Nadaud, 18 vols., Lausanne, Editions Rencontre], vol. 12, p. 159.
3. Letter to George Sand, *ibid.,* vol. 12, p. 405.
4. Flaubert, *La Tentation de saint Antoine,* ed. Édouard Maynial (Paris: Garnier, 1968), p. 245. In this chapter, page numbers in parentheses refer to this edition [English translations by L. M. Porter–ed.].
5. Two famous recent critics have created a distorted image of an excessively bookish Flaubert and saint. Michel Foucault exaggerates grossly by saying that all the saint's fantasies derive from the biblical passages he read, and that in the 1874 version evil has assumed an exclusively verbal form; see his "Un 'Fantastique' de bibliothèque" [*Cahiers Renaud-Barrault,* 59 (March 1967)], p. 15. Michel Butor quite misleadingly claims that there is no "day residue" specifically related to the temptations which assail Anthony; see "La Spirale des sept péchés," *Critique,* 26 (May 1970): 393.
6. NAF, 23671, fol. 107.
7. See Don-L. Demorest, *L'Expression figurée et symbolique dans l'œuvre de Gustave Flaubert* (Geneva: Slatkine Reprints, 1967), pp. 323–24.
8. NAF, 23667, fols. 19, 44, 59.
9. Foucault discusses the nesting layers of the *Tentation* lucidly on pp. 16–26 of his article cited . . . above, although he exaggerates their complexity.
10. For an excellent evaluation of the historical accuracy of Flaubert's *Tentation,* see the *Œuvres complètes,* vol. 17, pp. 655–65. Accounts of the saint's life are found in the *Catholic Encyclopedia* and in Hastings' *Encyclopaedia of Religion and Ethics.* The primary source is the saint's life by his disciple Athanasius.
11. See Jung, *PT* [*Psychological Types of the Psychology of Individuation,* London: Kegan Paul, 1946], p. 441, and *Aion* [*Researches in the Phenomenology of the Self, Collected Works,* 2d ed. Princeton: Princeton University Press, 1968, vol. 9, part 2], p. 42; Freud, "Negation," *SE* [*The Standard Edition of the Complete Psychological Works of Sigmund Freud,* ed. Lytton Strachey, 24 vols. London: Hogarth, 1953–74], vol. 19, pp. 235, 239. "The devil is certainly nothing else than the personification of the repressed unconscious instinctual life," Freud claimed in "Character and Anal Eroticism," *SE,* vol. 9, p. 174, repeated in "Dreams in Folklore," *SE,* vol. 12, p. 188.
12. Paul Valéry, "La Tentation de (saint) Flaubert," *Variété V* (Paris: Gallimard, 1944), pp. 204–5. See also Jonathan Culler, *Flaubert: The Uses of Uncertainty* (Ithaca, N.Y.: Cornell University Press, 1974), p. 181, who claims "The Saint has no psychology," and his pp. 136–37.
13. "Psychic growth . . . is in dreams frequently symbolized by the tree, whose slow, powerful, involuntary growth fulfills a definite pattern" (Jung, *MAHS* [*Man and His Symbols,* Garden City, N.Y.: Doubleday, 1964], p. 161).
14. Erick H. Erickson, *Identity and the Life Cycle* [New York: International Universities Press, 1959], pp. 99–100.
15. The 1856 version associated sexual feelings more directly with memories of the mother. Immediately after Anthony hallucinated her, he imagined the encounter of a shepherd and a whore with veiled face (the faceless woman is a common disguise for the mother in incestuously tinged fantasies). Then he had a vision of a group of frolicking, naked nymphs. Their multiplicity means that Anthony is defending himself against his sexual feelings by making their object diffuse. Finally he saw the Queen of Sheba. She is safely remote from Anthony's life because she is a

legend from the past, yet her royal status suggests a maternal figure as viewed by the child.

16. There is an excellent treatment of this episode by André Chastel in his "L'Épisode de la Reine de Saba dans la *Tentation de saint Antoine* de Flaubert," *Romanic Review* 40 (December 1949): 261–67.
17. Jean Seznec, *Nouvelles études sur "La Tentation de saint Antoine"* (London: Warburg Institute, 1949), pp. 19–21, comments illuminatingly on this scene.
18. See Jung, *PT,* pp. 18–33, 70–75, for an overview of the Gnostic heresies which dominated the Alexandrian period; for a discussion of Tertullian and Origen; for speculations concerning how the Gnosis (like alchemy after it) anticipated depth psychology; and for comment on how Anthony's battles against demons, as reported by Athanasius, constituted an attempted repression of the personal unconscious.
19. For a definitive discussion see Benjamin F. Bart, "Psyche into Myth" [*Kentucky Romance Quarterly,* 20 (1973)], pp. 317–42; and his *Flaubert* [Syracuse, N.Y.: Syracuse University Press, 1967], pp. 670–75.
20. NAF, 23665, fol. 71A. In the psychosexual sphere, Anthony's recurrent visions of prostitutes like the Ennoia who accompanies Simon, and the latent homosexuality manifest in his effusions concerning Damis and Apollonius (Anthony says Apollonius charmed him more profoundly than the Queen of Sheba, and was worth all Hell put together as a temptation), derive from the fixation of libido on the mother, and its consequent diversion from ordinary heterosexual outlets. See Reik, *Flaubert* [*Flaubert und seine "Versuchung des heiligen Antonius": Ein Beitrag zur Künstlerpsychologie,* Minden: J. C. C. Bruns, 1912], pp. 182–83.
21. See Jean Seznec, *Les Sources de l'épisode des dieux dans "La Tentation de saint Antoine"* (Paris: Vrin, 1940), pp. 10–31.
22. NAF, 23669, fol. 290/432; NAF, 23671, fol. 107.
23. Levin, "Flaubert" [*Kenyon Review,* 10 (1948)], p. 43.
24. Jung, "Individual Dream Symbolism in Relation to Alchemy: A Study of the Unconscious Processes at Work in Dreams," in his *Psychology and Alchemy, CW2,* vol. 12, pp. 83–84. The early Christians sometimes identified the rising sun with Christ. . . .
25. NAF, 23664, fol. 461.
26. NAF, 23667, fol. 46.
27. Letter to Louise Colet, May 27, 1853; *O,* vol. 6, p. 146. For a collection of similar statements with a lucid commentary, see Alison Fairlie, "Flaubert et la conscience du réel," *Essays in French Literature* 4 (1967): 1–12, esp. pp. 2–3.

Final Years: 1874–1880

After he finished La Tentation de saint Antoine, *Flaubert began planning* Bouvard et Pécuchet, *the "encyclopedic novel" that had long been in his mind. As early as a 4 September 1850 letter to Bouilhet, Flaubert had mentioned his idea for* Le Dictionnaire des idées reçues—*which later became part of his plan for the second volume of the novel.*

Over many years, with the help of friends, in particular Jules Duplan, Flaubert compiled lists of words with their definitions for an alphabetized "dictionary." This project was driven by Flaubert's obsession with bêtise *(stupidity) and language, as many of the entries are based on fixed linguistic forms and provide false definitions that are commonly accepted as true (received ideas). In the entry on "champignons" (mushrooms), for example, the reader is advised to "ne manger que ceux qui viennent du marché" ("eat only those that come from the market"). Flaubert intended to place the dictionary in the second volume of* Bouvard et Pécuchet; *it is not known whether the two copy clerks—the Bouvard and Pécuchet of the title—were to compile it themselves or to have found it as it is. In his research for* Bouvard et Pécuchet, *Flaubert read voluminously, often in fields, such as chemisty, in which he had little expertise. In 1880 he reported to his longtime correspondent Edma Roger des Genettes that he had read and annotated more than 1,500 books in order to imagine the story of the two clerks' long journey into human knowledge and* bêtise *(stupidity).*

The last years of Flaubert's life were difficult ones. Overwhelmed by the scope of his novel as well as saddened by the deaths of friends and dispirited by physical and financial woes, Flaubert for a time abandoned Bouvard et Pécuchet *and believed he was finished as a writer. And yet he courageously continued to work, publishing the stories of* Trois Contes *in 1877 before returning to the novel that he left unfinished at his death.*

Gustave Flaubert, drawing by Ed. Liphart printed in an article published after Flaubert's death in the 15 May 1880 issue of La Vie moderne *(Collections de la Bibliothèque municipale de Rouen. Cliché Thierry Ascencio-Parvy)*

Beginning *Bouvard et Pécuchet*

Flaubert discussed his misgivings as well as his hopes for his novel with his friend, the Russian novelist Ivan Turgenev, in this letter he wrote from Dieppe.

Flaubert to Turgenev, 25 July 1874

My good old Turgenev,

I shall be back at Croisset on Friday (the day after tomorrow) and on Saturday 1 August I at last start *Bouvard and Pécuchet!* I have taken a vow! There's no going back! But how scared I am! I'm on tenterhooks! I feel as if I were setting off on a very long journey into unknown territory, and that I shan't come back.

In spite of the immense respect I have for your critical judgement (for in you the critic is on the same level as the Creator, which is saying a lot) I don't share your opinion as to how the subject should be dealt with. If it's done briefly, with a concise, light touch, it will be a more or less witty fantasy, but will lack impact and verisimilitude, whereas if it's detailed and developed, it will look as though I believe in my story, and it can become a serious and even a frightening thing. The great danger is monotony and boredom. That's what I'm afraid of, however . . . but then, I can always

Ivan Turgenev, one of Flaubert's most important literary correspondents in the last years of his life (drawing by E. Hedouin; cliché Bibliothèque nationale de France, Paris)

tighten it up or abridge it later. Moreover, it's impossible for me to produce anything short. I can't express an idea without going the whole way.

Something else. Do you remember a play by me and Bouilhet: *The Weaker Sex?* Well, after being accepted by the Vaudeville and reworked by me, the Vaudeville changed its mind, then Perrin turned it down on the grounds of indecency, Duquesnel said it would have to be "completely rewritten," the Cluny Theatre finds it excellent and the manager of these inferior boards counts on making a lot of money with it. Admire the contradictions in all these judgements! What do you say to all these fools, these highly experienced cretins? And how to draw any practical conclusion from their opinions! And to think that Mme Sand believes these men and listens to their views! In any case, the play will go on after Zola's,[1] probably in November. So I shall be in rehearsal towards the middle of October. That'll make me lose two months and perhaps bring me more insults. But I don't care in the least. The shortest sentence of *B. and P.* worries me more than the whole of *The Weaker Sex* put together.

Your last letter seems tinged with melancholy? If I let myself go, I could reply in similar vein. Because I also feel terribly fed up with everything, and mainly with myself. At times I think I'm going mad, that I have no ideas left, and that my skull is like an empty beer jug. My stay (or rather my crass idleness) at the Rigi has stupefied me. One should never rest, for from the moment one stops doing things, one thinks about oneself and becomes ill, or one thinks one's ill, which is the same thing.

And you, my poor old fellow? How is the gout? Since Karlsbad did you a lot of good last year why shouldn't it be the same this year?

If you come back towards the beginning of September, it's possible I might see you in Paris, as I shall be there for two or three days then. Otherwise I'm counting on you this autumn at Croisset. My book will be started and we'll be able to talk about it until we've exhausted every possibility.

Politics are becoming incomprehensibly stupid. I don't believe that the Assembly will be dissolved. On the subject of politics I saw a curious thing in Geneva: old Gaillard's beer shop, he who was a bootmaker and former general of the Commune. I'll describe it to you. *It's another world,* the world dreamed of by democracy, and which I shall never see, thank God. What will dominate for the next two to three centuries is enough to make a man of taste vomit. It's time we went.

Adieu, my good dear old fellow. Send me your news and come back cured.

I embrace you vigorously.

Your

G. Flaubert

–*Flaubert & Turgenev. The Complete Correspondence,* translated and edited by Barbara Beaumont (New York & London: Norton, 1985), pp. 90–92

---

1. *Les Héritiers Rabourdin.*

* * *

This letter was written from Croisset.

Flaubert to Turgenev, 22 September 1874

Do send me your news, my dear old fellow. It's a month now since I heard anything from you, and I am afraid you may be too ill to write. As for me, for several days I've had violent dysentery which I've managed to cure with bismuth and laudanum.

I feel more confident about *Bouvard and Pécuchet* now. It's going better. I think I'm getting it about right. I shall soon have finished the first chapter.

The rehearsals for *The Weaker Sex* will doubtless begin in a month's time. So I'll come to Paris about then for the whole winter; but between now and then I should like to have finished the introduction to my two old fellows.

As you are a reader of Buloz's rag, did you savour *The Story of a Diamond* by P. de Musset?[1] What a work! I defy you to write one like that.

I recommend you to go into the lobby of Nadar the photographer's (*near Old England*). There you will see a lifesize photograph of Alexandre Dumas, and alongside it a terra-cotta bust of the same Dumas. He's supposed to be bringing out prefaces to *Manon Lescaut* and *Paul et Virginie!* And to think he has no idea how ridiculous he is!

Have you heard from Mme Sand? She doesn't write to me any more.

I embrace you.

Your old
G. Flaubert

–*Flaubert & Turgenev. The Complete Correspondence,* p. 92

---

1. This story appeared in the *Revue des Deux Mondes,* vol. 5 (1874).

The Commanville Collapse

In 1875 Flaubert was working on the difficult third chapter of Bouvard et Pécuchet *on sciences, when suddenly disaster struck: the husband of his niece Caroline, Ernest Commanville, came close to bankruptcy. In order to save his niece, Flaubert sold the farm in Deauville, which he had inherited from his mother, and almost brought himself to financial ruin. The situation remained precarious, and he feared they would have to sell Croisset, the home that had afforded him the peace of mind he required to write. In order to save money, he left his apartment in Paris on rue Murillo to share Caroline's at 240, rue du Faubourg Saint-Honoré. Flaubert had a nervous breakdown and health problems; for a time he was incapable of any work and abandoned the painful writing of* Bouvard et Pécuchet.

George Sand wrote from her estate in Nohant.

Sand to Flaubert, 15 August 1875

Mon pauvre cher vieux,

I heard only today, in a letter from our dear lazy Turgenev, of your niece's misfortune. Is it really irreparable? Her husband is young and intelligent–can't he start again, or get some employment that will mend matters? They haven't any children, and they're both young and healthy, so they don't need a fortune to live. Turgenev says your own resources are damaged by the débâcle. If it's only a question of damage, it's a serious setback, but you'll bear it philosophically. You have no vices or ambitions to cater for, and I'm sure you can adjust your life to your means. The worst trial will be the suffering of the young woman who is like a daughter to you, but you will give her courage and consolation. Now is the time to rise above your own troubles in order to lessen other people's. I'm sure that even as I write you have already calmed her mind and touched her heart. And perhaps the disaster isn't as great as it seemed to begin with. Things may lighten a little, and a new way of dealing with them emerge. That's how it usually works out, and people's worth is reflected in their energy and their hopes, always an indication of strength and intelligence. Many a man has overcome adversity by his own efforts. Be sure that better days will come, and keep telling them so, for it's true. You mustn't let your own moral and physical health be harmed by this reversal. Think about curing the people you love and forget yourself. *We'll* be thinking of you instead, and suffering for you. I am truly distressed that in the midst of your spleen you should have yet another cause for sadness.

So come, cher excellent vieux, brighten up, write us a good successful novel, and think of those who love you and whose hearts bleed when you are depressed. Love them, love us, and your energy and verve will come back to you.

Nous t'embrassons tous bien tendrement. Don't write if you don't feel like it, just send a word saying I'm better and I love you all.

G. Sand

–*Flaubert~Sand. The Correspondence,* translated by Francis Steegmuller and Barbara Bray, edited by Steegmuller (New York: Knopf, 1993), pp. 369–370

* * *

Flaubert wrote from Croisset.

Flaubert to Sand, 18 August 1875

Chère bon maître,

I haven't written to you because my news was too sad. Throughout the past year I continually sensed the approach of some great misfortune. My spleen had no other cause. Now it has come to pass. My poor niece is completely ruined, and I three quarters so. At the very best we shall have barely enough to live on, and poorly at that.

Ever since I was young I have sacrificed everything to my peace of mind. Now that's gone forever. You know that I'm not a *poseur.* Well, I long to die as soon as possible, because I am *finished,* emptied out, and older than if I were a hundred. To carry on I would have to be fired by an idea, by a subject for a book. But I no longer have *Faith.* And work of any kind has become impossible for me.

So, not only am I worried about my material future: my literary future seems to me blasted.

The logical thing would be to seek employment immediately, to find some lucrative occupation. But what could I do? Remember: I'm 54 years old, and at that age one doesn't change one's habits; one doesn't start a new life!

I've braced myself against misfortune. I've tried to be stoical. Every day I make an immense effort to work. Impossible! Impossible. My poor brain is pulverized.

Since I need to get away (it's now four months that I've been agonizing here with my poor niece), it's possible that in a fortnight's time I'll go to Concarneau, where I'll stay as long as possible. I'll be with Georges Pouchet,[1] who is continuing Coste's experiments with fish-breeding there. Perhaps the sea air will do me good and I'll come back stronger.

I fear I may have to leave Croisset. That would be the coup de grâce.

Embrassez pour moi les chères petites, et à vous toutes mes tendresses. Votre troubadour bien embêté

Gve Flaubert

–*Flaubert~Sand. The Correspondence,* p. 370

---

1. Georges Pouchet, director of the Laboratory of Marine Biology at Concarneau, a branch of the Museum of Natural History in Paris. . . .

Flaubert's depression intensified, and in September 1875 he left Croisset to join Georges Pouchet, a naturalist friend of his, to visit Concarneau in Brittany. Little by little he managed to calm down and started to work on a short story he had first considered writing in the 1850s, "La Légende de saint Julien l'Hospitalier." He continued work on the story when he was back in Paris in November and finished the tale in early 1876. Flaubert then began "Un cœur simple," another story he had sketched in the 1850s, recounting the simple life of Félicité, an old servant in Normandy.

Flaubert wrote this letter from Concarneau.

Flaubert to Sand, 3 October 1875

Chère maître,

I still hesitate to write to you these days, because I'm afraid of wearying you with my laments–a man shedding tears about his money doesn't merit much attention. But what can I tell you? I'm neither a Stoic nor a Christian. And I feel utterly prostrated. I'll never recover from this blow. Adversity is good for nothing, however much hypocrites may assert its virtue.

My nephew has devoured half my small capital. To prevent his going bankrupt I have compromised all the

Drawing of the "Julian window" in the cathedral of Rouen by Espérance Langlois. It was published in a book written by her father, Eustache-Hyacinthe Langlois: Essai historique et descriptif sur la peinture sur verre ancienne et moderne *(Historic and Descriptive Essay on Old and Modern Painting on Glass, 1832). Flaubert owned a copy of the work, which was one of the sources that inspired him to write "La Légende de saint Julien l'Hospitalier." Langlois was a friend of the Flaubert family and had drawn Flaubert as a child of nine (cliché Bibliothèque nationale de France, Paris).*

rest. And now I don't know how I am to live. Nothing more can be asked of me.

To put on a good front, after all that, and console myself with words like "devotion," "duty," "sacrifice"– No! No! I have been accustomed to great independence of mind, to being completely unconcerned with the material side of existence. At my age one can't start a new life. One can't change one's habits. My heart is broken and my imagination destroyed. That's how things stand with me.

I'm seeking a subject for a novel, and not finding one to my taste. Because I've abandoned my two *bonshommes.* Shall I ever take them up again? I doubt it. I've grown very timid, very lazy, a sterile coward, a brute beast. Nevertheless, to keep myself occupied I'm going to try to "put into writing" the legend of St Julian the Hospitaller. It will be very short–perhaps thirty pages.

I go to bed at 10, get up at 9, stuff myself with lobster, and walk along the shore, mulling over my memories and my griefs, deploring my wasted life–and the next day it all begins again. I watch my companion, G. Pouchet, as he dissects molluscs and explains things in which I attempt to interest myself. I eat at the table d'hôte and hear the local bourgeois talk about hunting and sardines. Every day these gentlemen spend six hours in the café. I envy them, because they seem happy. I read *Le Siècle* and *Le Temps* regularly! Great stuff! But none of this does me good.

I've read somewhere that one of your plays is to be revived at the Français.[1] Is it true? In that case will you be coming to Paris this winter? When would it be? I shan't be there before mid-November. I have no reason to be there: quite the contrary. I dread next winter, which will be no fun for my niece and me. Perhaps she will have to sell Croisset? And I may have to look for a "job"–yes, a job, in order to live. We must await the result of the liquidation. But here I go, talking about accursed *business.* Forgive my bad manners. And continue to love

votre vieux troubadour
bien démoli

Gve Flaubert

Embrassez bien fort pour moi les chères petites. Ah! If I had one of my own to hug! Maurice has the

Detail from the "Julian window" in the cathedral of Rouen. The window is difficult to see well as it is located high in the cathedral and usually receives poor light (photograph by Éric Le Calvez).

right idea! He arranged his life well. Why didn't I do the same?

–*Flaubert~Sand. The Correspondence,* pp. 373–374

---

1. *Le Marquis de Villemer,* at the Comédie-Française, with a cast to include Mme Arnould-Plessy and Sarah Bernhardt.

* * *

Sand to Flaubert, 8 October 1875

There now! Your health's improving in spite of you, if you're sleeping so long at night. The sea air forces you to live, and you've made progress–you've abandoned a subject that wouldn't have been a success. Write something more down to earth that suits everybody.

Tell me what would be for sale at Croisset if it had to be sold. Is it just a house and garden, or is there a farm and land? If it wasn't beyond my means I'd buy it and you could live there for the rest of your life. I haven't any cash, but I could try to transfer some capital. Please give me a serious answer. If I can do it, it shall be done.

This green stuffed parrot may have been the one that Flaubert borrowed from the museum of natural history in Rouen in order to "fill his soul with the parrot" when he was writing "Un cœur simple" (cliché Bruno Maurey, courtesy of the Musée Flaubert et d'Histoire de la Médecine).

I've been ill all summer–that's to say, I've been constantly unwell, but I've worked all the harder to distract myself.[1] Yes, they are going to revive *Villemer* and *Victorine* at the Théâtre-Français. But there are no definite details yet, and I don't know at what point in the autumn or winter I shall have to be in Paris.[2] When I do come I shall find you in good form and hopeful, shan't I? I believe that if out of kindness and devotion you've made a great sacrifice for your niece, who is to all intents and purposes your daughter, you will and so I think you'll be able to put all that behind you and start life again like a young man. One isn't old unless one wants to be old. Stay by the sea as long as you can. The main thing is to furbish up the physical mechanism.

It's as hot here as in high summer. I hope you'll go on having sunshine where you are. Learn about life from the molluscs! They're cleverer creatures than they're given credit for, and I personally would love to go on an excursion with Georges Pouchet! Natural history is an inexhaustible source of pleasant occupation even for those who seek only amusement, and if you got interested it would be the saving of you. But you'll save yourself anyway: you're a person of consequence, and couldn't go to pieces like some ruined grocer.

Nous t'embrassons tous du meilleur de nos cœurs.

G. Sand

–*Flaubert~Sand. The Correspondence,* pp. 374–375

---

1. George Sand's right arm still gave her trouble, and intestinal disorders often kept her from eating. But she continued to work steadily: new tales, additions to her *Contes d'une grand'mère,* were appearing in *Le Temps* and in *La Revue des Deux Mondes;* she corrected proofs for the publication, in book form, of *Flamarande* and *Les Deux Frères.* She was now writing *La Tour de Percemont,* which *La Revue des Deux Mondes* started to publish 1 December 1875.
2. *Le Mariage de Victorine,* a comedy in three acts, first performed in 1851, was revived at the Théâtre-Français on 7 March 1876, and *Le Marquis de Villemer* on 4 June 1877.

* * *

Flaubert wrote from Concarneau.

Flaubert to Sand, 11 October 1875

Ah, chère maître! What a great heart you have! Your letter moved me to tears. You are adorable, simply adorable. How can I thank you? What I long to do is give you a great hug.

Well, this is how things stand. My nephew has devoured half my fortune, and with the remainder I indemnified one of his creditors who wanted to put him into receivership. Once the liquidation is completed, I hope to recover approximately the amount I have risked. From now until then, we can keep going.

Croisset belongs to my niece. We have definitely decided not to sell it except in the last extremity. It is worth a hundred thousand francs (the equivalent of an annual yield of five thousand), but it brings in no income, as the upkeep is expensive. Anything that might come in from the stables, gardens, etc. is counterbalanced by the gardener's wages and the maintenance of the buildings.

My niece was married under the *régime dotal*,[1] and therefore she cannot sell a piece of land unless she immediately re-invests the proceeds in real estate or securities. So, as things stand, she cannot give Croisset to me. To help her husband, she has pledged her entire income–the only resource she had.

As you see, the situation is complicated. To live, I need 6 or 7 thousand francs a year (at least) *and* Croisset.

I may perhaps recoup the six or seven thousand francs at the end of the winter.[2] As for Croisset, we'll decide about it later. That is the present state of affairs. It will be a great grief to me if I have to leave this old house, so full of tender memories. For all your goodwill, I fear there is nothing you can do. Since there is no urgency at the moment, I prefer not to think about it. Like a coward, I dismiss, or rather would like to dismiss, from my mind all thoughts of the future and of "business". Am I fed up with it! And have been for five months–good God!

I continue to work a little, and take walks. But now it's growing cold and rainy. Even so, I shan't return to Paris before the 8th or 10th of November.

You approve of my abandoning my bitch of a novel. It was too much for me, I realize. And that discovery is another blow. Despite all my efforts to harden myself against fate, I feel very feeble.

Merci encore une fois, chère bon maître, je vous aime bien, vous le savez.

Votre vieux

Cruchard

more than ever a stupid old wreck

–*Flaubert~Sand. The Correspondence*, pp. 375–376

---

1. A legal financial clause limiting her use of her dowry.
2. As usual, Flaubert is vague when writing about finances. He probably means that he may recover some income-producing capital if the liquidation of Commanville's assets, the sawmill and the adjoining land, brings in sufficient funds.

Sand's Death and *Trois Contes*

Flaubert wrote "Un cœur simple" partly to please Sand; however, she died on 7 June 1876, before she was able to read the not-yet-completed story. Flaubert went to Nohant for the last time to attend her funeral and then returned to his work on his tales.

Turgenev wrote from the Spasskoye Mtsensk Province of Oryol in central Russia.

Turgenev to Flaubert, 18 June 1876

My dear friend,

Since this morning, I have been at my Patmos–and it has the effect of a wet blanket. (Have you noticed that it's generally at such times that one writes to one's best friends?) The temperature is 32 degrees Réaumur in the shade–and added to that–thanks to a frost of minus 9 degrees below zero on 21 May–all the greenery in the garden is streaked with little dead leaves that make me think vaguely of the corpses of small children–and my old lime trees give only a thin and sparse shade that is pitiful to see. Add to that the fact that my brother who was supposed to be waiting for me here to arrange some money matters that are very important to me, left for Carlsbad five days ago, that I think I'm going to have an attack of gout (which happened to me at the same time and in the same place two years ago); that I have almost certain proof that my bailiff is robbing me–and that I shan't be able to get rid of him–you see the situation! The death of Mme Sand has also distressed me greatly, very greatly. I know that you went to Nohant for the funeral, and I wanted to send a telegramme of condolence in the name of the Russian reading public, but a sort of ridiculous modesty held me back, through fear of the *Figaro* and of the publicity–stupid things, all in all! The Russian readership is amongst those on which Mme Sand has had the greatest influence–and it needed to be said, by God–and I didn't have the right–after all. But there you are!!

Poor dear Mme Sand! She loved us both–you especially–that was only natural. What a heart of gold she had! Such an absence of all low, petty or false sentiments–what a good fellow she was and what a fine woman! And now all of that is there, in the horrible relentless hole in the ground, silent, stupid–and it doesn't even know what it is it's devouring!

Come–there's nothing to be done about it and let us try to keep our chins above water.

I'm writing to you at Croisset–I assume you are there–have you got back down to work? If I do noth-

George Sand's grave in the cemetery of Nohant. Flaubert was greatly moved by the funeral, which he told Turgenev "was like a chapter from one of her books" (photograph by Éric Le Calvez).

ing here–that must mean it's all up with me. There is a silence here, which you can't possibly imagine; not a single neighbour in a radius of twenty kilometers–everything languishes, is motionless! The house is wretched–but not too hot–and the furniture is good. A writing desk–fine–and an armchair with a double rush seat! And for example, there is a dangerous sofa, as soon as one is on it, one falls asleep. I shall try to avoid it. I shall start by finishing St Julian.

Before me in a corner of the room there is an old Byzantine icon, all blackened, in a silver frame, nothing but a huge stiff and gloomy face–it troubles me rather–but I can't have it taken down, my manservant would take me for a pagan, and here that's no joking matter.

Send me a couple of lines more cheerful than these.

I embrace you and am your old friend

Iv. Turgenev

–*Flaubert & Turgenev. The Complete Correspondence,* pp. 101–102

* * *

Flaubert wrote from Croisset.

Flaubert to Turgenev, 25 June 1876

How I seized upon your letter yesterday, my dear old man, as soon as I recognised your handwriting! For I was starting to miss you badly! So having embraced, let us talk.

I am distressed to hear that you have money problems and fears for your health. Let us hope that you are wrong and that the gout will leave you alone.

The death of poor old mother Sand caused me infinite pain. I blubbered shamelessly at her funeral, and that twice over: the first time on kissing her granddaughter Aurore (whose eyes were so much like hers that day, that it seemed almost like a reincarnation) and the second as her coffin passed in front of me. There was some scandal of course! So as not to offend "public opinion," its eternal, execrable voice, they carried her off to the church. I must tell you all the details of this contemptible action. My heart was heavy and I could positively have murdered M. Adrien Marx.[1] The very sight of him took away all my appetite for dinner that evening at Châteauroux. Oh what a tyrant the *Figaro* is! What a public pestilence. I suffocate with rage whenever I think about those fools.

My companions on the journey, Renan and the Prince Napoleon,[2] were charming, the former perfect in his tact and respect, and he saw through it all from the beginning better than either of us.

You are right to regret the loss of our friend, for she loved you dearly and never spoke of you without calling you "good Turgenev". But why pity her? She lacked nothing and will remain a great figure.

The good country people wept a great deal round her grave. We were up to our ankles in mud in that little country cemetery. A gentle rain was falling. Her funeral was like a chapter from one of her books.

Forty-eight hours later, I was back at my Croisset, where *I am amazingly glad to be*. I enjoy the greenness, the trees and the silence in quite a new way. I have taken up cold-water treatment (ferocious hydrotherapy) again and I'm working like a madman.

My *Story of a Simple Soul* will doubtless be finished towards the end of August. After that I shall embark on *Hérodias!* But how difficult it is! By God it's difficult! The further I get, the more aware of it I become. It seems to me that French prose can achieve a *beauty* that we can't even imagine. Don't you find that our friends don't care over much for Beauty? And yet it is the most important thing in the world!

And what about you? Are you working? Is *St Julian* coming on? What I'm going to say is silly, but I

Frieze on the western portal of the cathedral of Rouen. Flaubert was inspired by its depiction of Salome's dance leading to the decapitation of Saint John the Baptist, which he narrates in the third section of "Hérodias" (photograph by Éric Le Calvez).

really *want to see* it printed in Russian! Besides the fact that a translation by you "tickles the proud weakness of my heart", the only resemblance between Agamemnon and me.

When you left Paris, you hadn't read Renan's new book.[3] It seems charming to me. "Charming" is the right word. Do you share my opinion? However, I have no idea what has been happening in the world for the last two weeks, not once having read a single newspaper. Fromentin sent me his book on "old masters".[4] As I know very little about Dutch painting, it doesn't have the same interest for me as it will for you. It's clever, but too long, too long! The said Fromentin seems to me to be greatly influenced by Taine. Ah! I was forgetting! The poet Mallarmé[5] (the author of *The Faun*) made me a present of a book he is editing: *Vathek,* an oriental story, written in French by an Englishman at the end of the last century. It's curious.

I drift off into dreams (and desires) when I think that this sheet of paper will go to you in your house that I shall never know! And I'm cross that I don't have a more precise idea of your surroundings.

If you're hot where you are, we are not exactly suffering from cold here either. I spend the whole day behind closed shutters, in exclusive solitude. At mealtimes, I have for distraction the sight of my faithful Émile and my greyhound.

My niece, to whom I shall convey your greetings, is going off at the end of the month to Eaux-Bonnes with her husband, and I shan't leave here until the end of September, when I go to Daudet's first night. But by then you will have been back at Les Frênes for some time.

You'll be pleased to learn that my nephew's affairs seem to have taken a turn for the better. At least there is some blue sky on the horizon.

Yes my dear old fellow, let us try, in spite of everything, to keep our [heads] above water. Look after yourself, work well and come back soon.

I embrace you tenderly and vigorously.

Your

G. Flaubert

–*Flaubert & Turgenev. The Complete Correspondence,* pp. 102–104

---

1. A journalist covering G. Sand's funeral for *Le Figaro.*
2. Nephew of Napoleon Bonaparte and brother of the Princess Mathilde.
3. *Dialogues et fragments philosophiques.*
4. E. Fromentin, *Les Maîtres d'autrefois* (1876).
5. Stéphane Mallarmé (1842-98), symbolist poet, had published his famous *Après-midi d'un faune* the previous year.

* * *

After finishing "Un cœur simple" in August, Flaubert spent a couple of weeks at Princess Mathilde's in September. He then began his usual research for his third tale, "Hérodias"–the story of John the Baptist under the reign of Herod Antipus–which he wrote with great difficulties from November 1876 to February 1877. The three tales were first printed separately in journals and on 24 April 1877, Charpentier published them in a single volume, Trois contes. *It did not sell very well at first but obtained critical success. Critics praised Flaubert's original style or, rather, the three different styles and tones he had invented in order to match these three different stories and periods.*

This letter was written in Paris.

Turgenev to Flaubert, 19 December 1876

My dear old man,

I've just got back from making a very virtuous family visit which took three days–and which was pretty boring. So here I am now answering your letter. Let's sort out the question of the three stories first.

St Julian is translated, and with the publisher–and will be paid for at my usual rate–i.e. you'll get 300 rubles (the ruble varies between 2 francs 85 centimes and 3 francs 30 centimes) per printer's sheet (16 pages). But there's the snag. I had to make a formal promise to my publisher and to the reading public (in a note that I was foolish enough to allow to be published) to let *nothing appear* under my name before my great devil of a novel. I have finished this novel, and I've sent it to St Petersburg, and it's being printed at this moment; only my publisher, who is as cunning as a snake, instead of printing it as a whole (which he promised categorically) is cutting it in half–so that it will come out in the two editions of 1–13 January and 1–13 February–and he has so succeeded in twisting me round his little finger (you know what a *soggy* pear I am) that I have agreed to this mutilation, which puts poor *Julian* off until 1–13 March. The two other stories would then have to be published in the 1–13 April edition; in any case, the *Simple Soul shouldn't appear on its own.* That would not be impossible according to what you say in your letter. I have given *A Simple Soul* to a Russian lady of letters who handles the language very well (she is here in Paris)–and if she does a creditable job, I could entrust Hérodiade [*sic*] to her as well. Naturally I shall check the translation most carefully–I'll copy it out if necessary, for my name must be on it! Otherwise people will say: if he translated the first story, why didn't he translate the others? Are they less good then? We wouldn't get a good price that way. But–another hitch! I'm leaving for Petersburg (keep this to yourself) on *15 February* for a month. It's probable that you won't have finished by then, or if you have, I could only take the original, without having time to have a translation made; well, in that case, I'd have to find someone in Petersburg–which is not impossible. *Final Result*: try to finish Hérodiade in the first few days of February. And then we'll see!

. . . .

And now I embrace you.

Your

I.T.

–*Flaubert & Turgenev. The Complete Correspondence,* pp. 115–117

* * *

Flaubert wrote from Croisset.

Flaubert to Turgenev, 24 December 1876

Ouf! I have just completed a session of *ten hours at a stretch* hammering away at my work. So, for a breath of air, I shall be going shortly to midnight mass with the nuns at the Convent of Saint Barbara. See my good fellow! Can one be more romantic than that?

But this present communication (commercial style) is only to thank you in respect of the translations. Really, if I could get this volume out in the spring, after having published it as a serial (i) in Russia and (ii) in the Parisian journals, it would be a great help.

If you're only leaving at the end of February, everything will be ready, or very nearly so. In any case, there would still be time if it were 13 May (!), since I have the right, don't I, to publish elsewhere, and as I see fit, immediately afterwards. But if it's after that, it would mean waiting until winter.

What with such *phrenetic* work[1] (all the more as I haven't changed my ways) you can imagine that I shan't be in Paris before the end of January, or even the first few days of the following month.

. . . .

Thereupon I embrace you and wish you a Happy New Year.

All the best.

Your old

G. Flaubert

–*Flaubert & Turgenev. The Complete Correspondence,* p. 117

---

1. Flaubert's neologism.

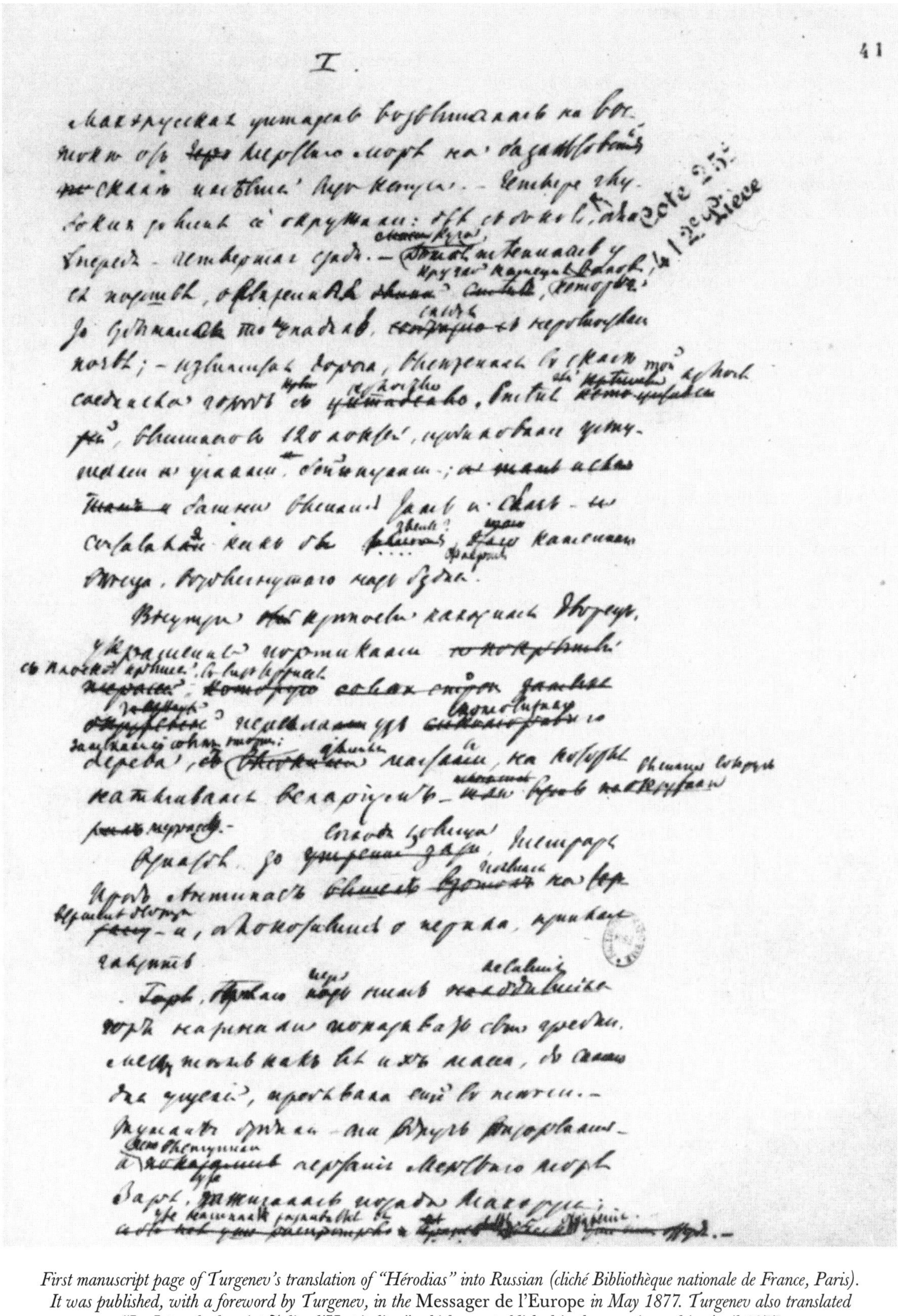

First manuscript page of Turgenev's translation of "Hérodias" into Russian (cliché Bibliothèque nationale de France, Paris). It was published, with a foreword by Turgenev, in the Messager de l'Europe *in May 1877. Turgenev also translated "La Légende de saint Julien l'Hospitalier," which was published in the same journal in April 1877.*

Last Years

Flaubert's financial state and health were still precarious, but he managed to return to Bouvard et Pécuchet *in July 1877, which meant for him new readings, new doubts, and pain. His friends tried, with no success, to intervene and find a sincere for him at the Mazarine Library in Paris.*

This letter was written in Croisset.

Flaubert to Turgenev, 19 July 1877

It was very kind of you to write to me as soon as you got back, my good dear old fellow; but now I would like a few more details as to your large and exquisite person. And first of all, how is the foot? Has the swelling gone down? Is the attack over at last?

Did you get done in Russia what you wanted to do? Are you happy with the arrangements concerning your fortune? And holy literature, what's she up to in all this?

I await to see the famous *dressing-gown* before weeping with gratitude. But even now I thank you effusively: nothing could give me more pleasure, and *I'm dying* to try it on.

My medicine is finished (I'm talking about *B. and P.*). For the moment I'm working on the geology and archaeology (of Falaise and district). When this is finished, I shall make quite a long trip into Lower Normandy, then I shall come back here, to write the ending of this terrible Chapter II, which will have just about finished me off. And when it's finished (towards the New Year?) I shall be about a quarter of the way! One has to be mad to embark on such a work! Moreover this one may well be idiotic? In any case, it will be out of the ordinary.

What's more, I'm reading nothing outside of my immediate studies–what about you?

I should like to be at the elections to see the faces of the Macmahonites. Moral Order in the provinces goes so far as to ban charity meetings that aren't of a clerical nature. Oh Human Stupidity!

Farewell, my good dear old chap.

I embrace you.

Your
G. Flaubert

–*Flaubert & Turgenev. The Complete Correspondence,* pp. 125–126

* * *

Turgenev wrote from Paris.

Turgenev to Flaubert, 24 July 1877

My dear old fellow,

I didn't answer you straightaway as I was vaguely hoping to go to Croisset to bring you your dressing-gown myself; but this hope has faded away–for the moment–so I am writing to you and sending the dressing-gown by the railway. My foot is better–but it would still be impossible for me to walk much–I think I shall end up trying the new remedy that is much vaunted in the newspapers–its name begins with *sal* and ends in *ate*.[1] This blackguard gout is becoming semi-chronic and semi-accute in me, which is annoying. It's a pity B. and P. have *finished* their medical studies. I would have consulted them.

In Russia I got done a quarter of what I wanted to do–which is something. Naturally I didn't do the essential: I didn't see my brother. That's only normal.

I wish this war[2] would end, so that the exchange rate against the ruble would go back up. The present situation is completely paralysing my finances.

You are working–that's good; and your business affairs–the matter–you remember–that seemed so promising–how is it going?

My literature is for the moment in the depths of the deepest abyss.

I read Zola's little short story in *L'Écho universel*.[3] The beginning especially is remarkable. My greetings to all.

I embrace you.

I.T.

P.S. Let me know when you get the dressing-gown.

–*Flaubert & Turgenev. The Complete Correspondence,* p. 126

---

1. Salicylate is a basic component of aspirin.
2. The Russo-Turkish War.
3. Émile Zola's *Une Histoire d'amour* appeared in *L'Écho Universel* on 27 April 1877.

* * *

Flaubert to Turgenev, 27 July 1877

Splendid!

I'm overwhelmed by it. Thank you, my good dear old fellow. That really is a present! I would have

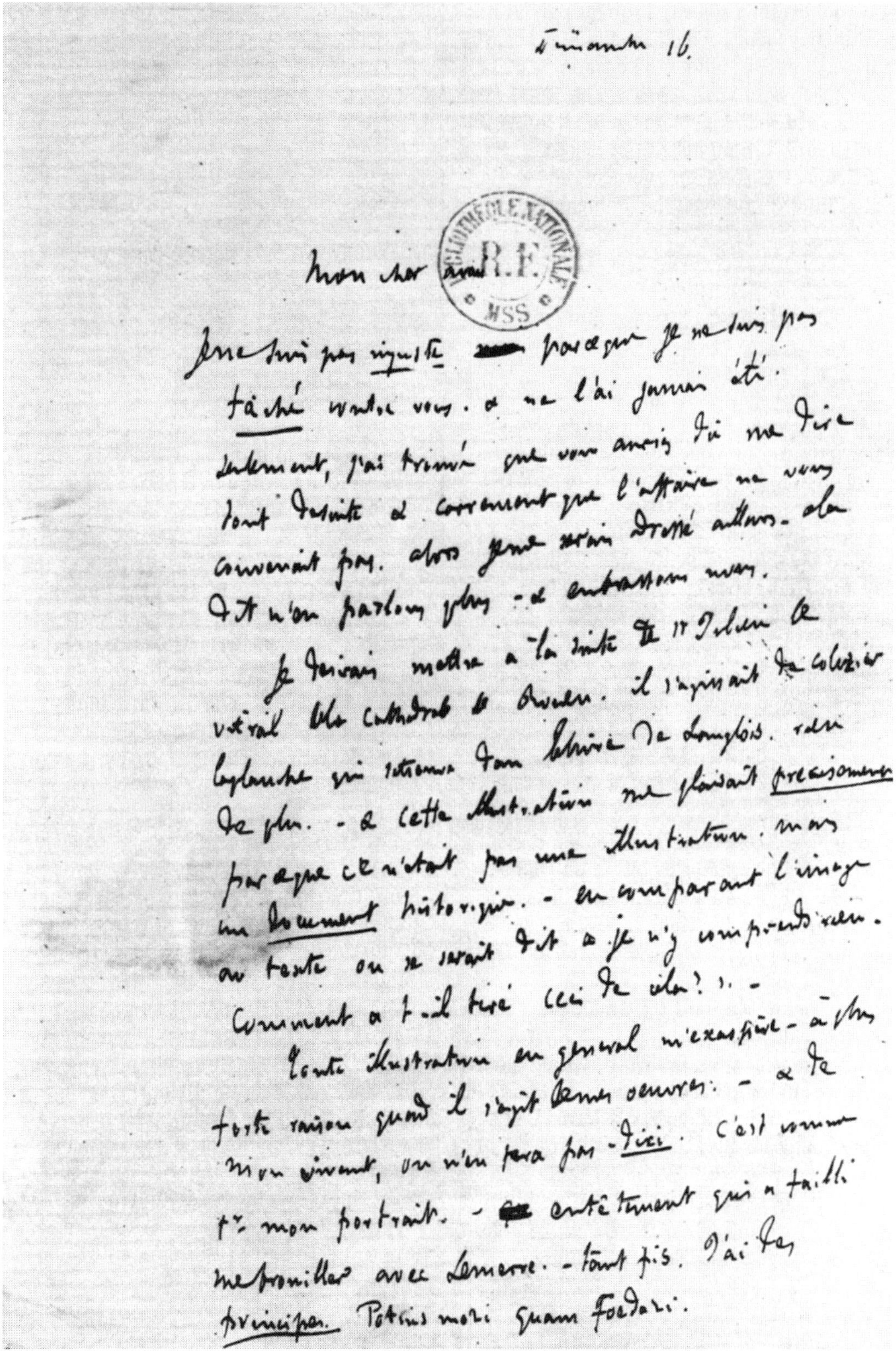

Dimanche 16.

Mon cher ami

Je ne suis pas injuste parce que je ne suis pas fâché contre vous. & ne l'ai jamais été. Seulement, j'ai trouvé que vous auriez dû me dire tout de suite & carrément que l'affaire ne vous convenait pas. alors je me serais adressé ailleurs. Et n'en parlons plus – & embrassons nous.

Je désirais mettre à la suite de St Julien le vitrail de la cathédrale de Rouen. il s'agissait de colorier la planche qui se trouve dans l'ouvrage de Langlois. rien de plus. – & cette illustration me plaisait précisément parce que ce n'était pas une illustration, mais un document historique. – en comparant l'image au texte on se serait dit & je n'y comprends rien. Comment a-t-il tiré ceci de cela? – –

Toute illustration en général m'exaspère – à plus forte raison quand il s'agit de mes œuvres: – & de mon vivant, on n'en fera pas – Dixi. C'est comme pour mon portrait. – cet entêtement qui a failli me brouiller avec Lemerre. – Tant pis. J'ai des principes. Potius mori quam foedari.

The 16 February 1879 letter from Flaubert to his publisher Georges Charpentier regarding the possible publication of a luxury edition of "La Légende de saint Julien l'Hospitalier," which never appeared. Flaubert said that he wanted to place a reproduction of the Julian window at the end of the tale: "I liked this illustration precisely because it was not an illustration, but a historical document. When comparing the image with the text, the reader would have thought: 'I don't understand anything. How did he get this from that?'" (cliché Bibliothèque nationale de France, Paris).

answered you sooner if the railway brought parcels as far as here. But they don't, which means a delay of twenty-four if not thirty-six hours. (The station-master only wrote to me last night.)

This royal garment plunges me into dreams of absolutism and luxury. I should like to be naked underneath and harbour Circassian women inside it. Although the weather is stormy at the moment and I'm too hot, I'm wearing the said covering, and am thinking of how useful it will be to me this winter. Frankly you couldn't have given me a finer present.

I'm working on *B. and P.*'s geology; and on Monday I start writing again. When I've finished that chapter I shall give a great sigh of relief!

It's possible that I shall come and see you at Bougival towards the end of August. I'm not inviting you to Croisset at the moment, as your room is going to be taken by a friend of Caroline's. She'll stay for two weeks.

In September I shall make the archaeological and geological excursions in Lower Normandy, still all for my two fools. I'm afraid of being one myself. What a book! What an abyss (a wasps' nest or a latrine) I have stuffed myself into! There's no going back now.

But this autumn, the devil take it, you must come here and *stay!* An apparition of twenty-four or thirty-six hours is a cruel thing that upsets me in advance.

As for business affairs, they are dragging. The worst is over however. But the last 200 thousand francs are hard to find.

I'm reading *The Nabob* in *Le Temps*.[1] What do you think of it? I find the style rather slovenly, a bit childish.

The war in the East which doesn't concern me in the least annoys me. I wish the children of the Prophet a hearty thrashing, and let it be quick, so that we can have peace.

Were you, like me, outraged by Mme Gras?[2] She is the greatest criminal I know of.

No news from our friends, except for young Guy. He wrote to me recently. . . . That's all very well but. . . . We are no longer at that stage, my good fellow!

Friendly greetings to all; and for you, a thousand tendernesses from your old

G. Flaubert

P.S. Indeed I succumb under the weight of your magnificence. I'm going to take the dressing-gown off. What is its local name and its homeland? Bokhara isn't it?

–*Flaubert & Turgenev. The Complete Correspondence,* pp. 127–128

---

1. Daudet's *Le Nabob* was serialized in *Le Temps* between 12 July and 21 October 1877.

2. Mme Gras, a widow who blinded her young lover with sulphuric acid in order to obtain administration of his considerable fortune. The case came up for trial in July 1877.

* * *

Henry James met Flaubert in 1876 when he was living in Paris. He was introduced to him by Turgenev and came to like the man more than the artist. In this excerpt from a 1902 essay, James wrote about his memories of the Sunday meetings in Flaubert's apartment.

Sundays with Flaubert

His complications were of the spirit, of the literary vision, and though he was thoroughly profane he was yet essentially anchoretic. I perhaps miss a point, however, in not finally subjoining that he was liberally accessible to his friends during the months he regularly spent in Paris. Sensitive, passionate, perverse, not less than *immediately* sociable–for if he detested his collective contemporaries this dropped, thanks to his humanising shyness, before the individual encounter–he was in particular and superexcellently not *banal,* and he attached men perhaps more than women, inspiring a marked, a by no means colourless shade of respect; a respect not founded, as the air of it is apt to be, on the vague presumption, but addressed almost in especial to his disparities and oddities and thereby, no doubt, none too different from affection. His friends at all events were a rich and eager *cénacle,* among whom he was on occasion, by his picturesque personality, a natural and overtopping centre; partly perhaps because he was so much and so familiarly at home. He wore, up to any hour of the afternoon, that long, colloquial dressing-gown, with trousers to match, which one has always associated with literature in France–the uniform really of freedom of talk. Freedom of talk abounded by his winter fire, for the *cénacle* was made up almost wholly of the more finely distinguished among his contemporaries; of philosophers, men of letters and men of affairs belonging to his own generation and the next. He had at the time I have in mind a small perch, far aloft, at the distant, the then almost suburban, end of the Faubourg Saint-Honoré, where on Sunday afternoons, at the very top of an endless flight of stairs, were to be encountered in a cloud of conversation and smoke most of the novelists of the general Balzac tradition. Others of a different birth and complexion were markedly not of the number, were not even conceivable as present; none of those, unless I misremember, whose fictions were at that time "serialised" in the Revue des Deux Mondes. In spite of Renan and Taine and two or three more, the contributor to the Revue would indeed at no time have found in the circle in question his foot on his native heath. One could recall if one would two or three vivid allusions to him, not of the most quotable, on the lips of the most famous of "naturalists"–allusions to him as represented for instance by M. Victor Cherbuliez and M. Octave Feuillet. The author of these pages recalls a concise qualification of this last of his fellows on the lips of Émile Zola, which that absorbed auditor had too directly, too rashly asked for; but which is alas not reproducible here. There was little else but the talk, which had extreme intensity and variety; almost nothing, as I remember, but a painted and gilded idol, of considerable size, a relic and a memento, on the chimney-piece. Flaubert was huge and diffident, but florid too and resonant, and my main remembrance is of a conception of courtesy in him, an accessibility to the human relation, that only wanted to be sure of the way taken or to take. The uncertainties of the French for the determination of intercourse have often struck me as quite matching the sharpness of their certainties, as we for the most part feel these latter, which sometimes in fact throw the indeterminate into almost touching relief. I have thought of them at such times as the people in the world one may have to go more of the way to meet than to meet any other, and this, as it were, through their being seated and embedded, provided for at home, in a manner that is all their own and that has bred them to the positive preacceptance of interest on their behalf. We at least of the Anglo-American race, more abroad in the world, perching everywhere, so far as grounds of intercourse are concerned, more vaguely and superficially, as well as less intelligently, are the more ready by that fact with inexpensive accommodations, rather conscious that these themselves forbear from the claim to fascinate, and advancing with the good nature that is the mantle of our obtuseness to any point whatever where entertainment may be offered us. My recollection is at any rate simplified by the fact of the presence almost always, in the little high room of the Faubourg's end, of other persons and other voices. Flaubert's own voice is clearest to me from the uneffaced sense of a winter week-day afternoon when I found him by exception alone and when something led to his reading me aloud, in support of some judgment he had thrown off, a poem of Théophile Gautier's. He cited it as an example of verse intensely and distinctively French, and French in its melancholy, which neither Goethe nor Heine nor Leopardi, neither Pushkin nor Tennyson nor, as he said, Byron, could at all have matched in *kind.* He converted me at the moment to this perception, alike by the sense of the thing and by his large utterance of it; after which it is dreadful to have to confess not only that the poem was then new to me, but that, hunt as I will in every volume of its author, I am never able to recover it. This is perhaps after all happy, causing Flaubert's own full tone, which was the note of the occasion, to linger the more unquenched. But for the rhyme in fact I could have believed him to be spouting to me something strange and sonorous of his own. The thing really rare would have been to hear him do that–hear him *gueuler,* as he liked to call it. Verse, I felt, we had always with us, and almost any idiot of goodwill could give it a value. The value of so many a passage of "Salammbô" and of "L'Éducation" was on the other hand exactly such as gained when he allowed himself, as had by the legend ever been frequent *dans l'intimité,* to "bellow" it to its fullest effect. . . .

–Henry James, "Gustave Flaubert," in his *Notes on Novelists* (New York: Scribners, 1914), pp. 70–74

* * *

In 1879, Jules Ferry, the minister of education and fine arts, granted Flaubert a pension of 3,000 francs a year for his literary work. While continuing his work on Bouvard et Pécuchet, *Flaubert corrected the text of* L'Éducation sentimentale, *which was reprinted by Charpentier in November 1879.*

Flaubert to Turgenev, 9 August 1879

Ah, at last! I have news of you, my dear good old fellow! So you are very fed up–but I prefer the *lavatorial* state of your soul to the gouty state of your body.

Perhaps your moral sufferings come from your Doctoral mortarboard? Or from the fact that you haven't had the opportunity to break your word to me? I'm still awaiting an explanation for your last piece of treachery, for you were supposed to dine at my place one Saturday in the month of June. Since then, no sign of the fellow!

As for me, *B. and P.* are wearing me out. I have only four pages to go to finish the Philosophy chapter. After which I shall start the penultimate chapter. These last two will take me up to March or April. Then there'll be the second volume! In short I shall still be at it in a year's time. One needs to be a master of asceticism to inflict such labours on oneself! On certain days it seems to me that all the blood is drained from my limbs and that my death is imminent. Then I bounce back, and things are all right *all the same*. There you are.

You will be pleased to learn that there is a little blue sky on the financial horizon of my life. Commanville has managed to set up a sawmill again. He is launched anew. Provided he doesn't sink again! But I don't think so: the business seems to me a good one.

My niece isn't very well. She is anaemic and subject to almost constant migraines.

No news from our friends.

If you are in Paris towards the middle of September, I hope to see you there when I'm at Saint-Gratien at the princess's.

You don't seem very busy. *So,* there's nothing to stop you writing me a long letter. Do it, it would be a charitable act.

Friendly greetings and my respects to all at your place. I embrace you tenderly.

Your old
G. Flaubert

–*Flaubert & Turgenev. The Complete Correspondence,* p. 165

* * *

The rhythm of Flaubert's readings and writing did not slow down from the moment he returned to Bouvard et Pécuchet *to the beginning of 1880. In January 1880 Flaubert started writing the tenth chapter of the novel, which was intended*

Deuxième Année. N° 4. Samedi 24 Janvier 1880.

LA VIE MODERNE

ART SOMMAIRE LITTERATURE

LE THÉATRE DE LA « VIE MODERNE »

LE CHATEAU DES CŒURS, GRANDE FÉERIE INÉDITE

PAR GUSTAVE FLAUBERT, LOUIS BOUILHET ET CHARLES D'OSMOY

Rideau par H. SCOTT.

First page from the initial 1880 installment of Le Château des cœurs *in* La Vie Moderne. *Although Flaubert collaborated on the play in 1863, it was never accepted for production on stage (illustration by H. Scott; cliché Bibliothèque nationale de France, Paris).*

to be the last of the first volume. His letters show, however, that he was still overwhelmed by the enormous task on which he had begun working eight years earlier.

Flaubert to Turgenev, 7 April 1880

My good dear old fellow,

I rejoice in the thought that I shall see you again in about a month. All the worries you had have disappeared, thank God! And soon we shall be able to talk about them at length.

Were your ears burning on Easter Sunday? Here we drank a toast to Turgenev and regretted his absence. Those who clinked their champagne glasses to your health were: (i) your humble servant, then Zola, Charpentier, A. Daudet, Goncourt, Fortin my doctor and "that little rascal Maupassant" as Lagier says. On the subject of Maupassant, he's not in such a bad way as I feared; he has nothing organically wrong, but this young man has chronic gout, is ultra-rheumatic and is a complete nervous wreck. After dining here these gentlemen spent the night and left the following day after lunch. I had a job to stop myself reading something from *B. and P.* to them.

When Pradier was working at the Invalides in 1848, he used to say "The Emperor's tomb will become my own",[1] so weary was he with the task. And I can say it's time my book were finished, otherwise I shall be. Frankly it's driving me mad, and I'm exhausted by it. It's becoming a chore! And I've still got three months to go without counting the second volume which will take me six! All in all I'm afraid that the result won't have been worth the effort that has gone into it, and I feel so worn out that the ending could well be insipid and a flop. Moreover, I no longer understand any of it, and my limbs feel as if they've taken a thrashing, I have stomach cramps and I barely sleep these days. But that's enough moaning!

This is how I plan my existence: I hope to be in Paris towards 10 May and to stay there until the end of June, to spend two months at Croisset making Extracts for my second volume, then to return to Paris in September and to stay for a long time.

. . . .

La Vie Moderne continues to disgrace me with the illustrations for *Le Château des Coeurs*. My poor fairy play has had no luck. But then why did I listen to the advice of Other People? Why did I give in!

I read none of the books that are sent to me, consequently I can give you no literary news.

Dr. Charles-André Fortin, Flaubert's friend and physician (Collections de la Bibliothèque municipale de Rouen. Cliché Thierry Ascencio-Parvy)

I am now principally indignant against Botanists.[2] It is impossible to get them to understand a question that seems as clear as anything to me! You'll see for yourself, and you will be amazed at how small the faculty of judgement is in these brains.

Try to find a few minutes to write to me. That would be kind. Don't delay your return to us.

I embrace you with open arms, my dear old fellow.

Your
G. Flaubert

–*Flaubert & Turgenev. The Complete Correspondence,* pp. 176–177

---

1. The sculptor Pradier who worked on the tomb of Napoleon Bonaparte.
2. Flaubert needed some botanical details for *Bouvard and Pécuchet.* A professor at the Jardin des Plantes in Paris had confirmed Flaubert's own *intuitive* notion over the view of Baudry, a local Rouen naturalist.

The Last Saint Polycarp Dinner

Flaubert wrote to his niece Caroline on 28 April 1880 about the St. Polycarp dinner. Very early on in his life, Flaubert liked to compare himself to Saint Polycarp (a bishop of Smyrne, who became a martyr in 167 A.D.); in a letter dated 21 August 1853, Flaubert wrote to his mistress Louise Colet: "Where can I go and live! Saint Polycarp used to say, escaping the place where he stayed: 'In what century, my God, was I born!' I am becoming like Saint Polycarp." There were two Saint Polycarp dinners in Rouen, organized by Flaubert's friends Charles Lapierre and his wife: the first one in April 1879 and the second in April 1880.

The St. Polycarp celebration left me speechless! . . . As presents, I was given a pair of silk socks, a foulard, three bouquets, a wreath, a portrait (Spanish) of St. Polycarp, a tooth (relic of the saint); and a box of flowers is on its way from Nice! An orchestra had been hired, but failed to put in an appearance. Letters from Raoul Duval and his two daughters. A poem by Mme Brainne's son. All the letters (including Mme Régnier's) were adorned with the likeness of my patron saint. I was forgetting a menu composed of dishes all named for my books. . . .

–*The Letters of Gustave Flaubert, 1857–1880* (Cambridge, Mass.: Harvard University Press, 1982), p. 274

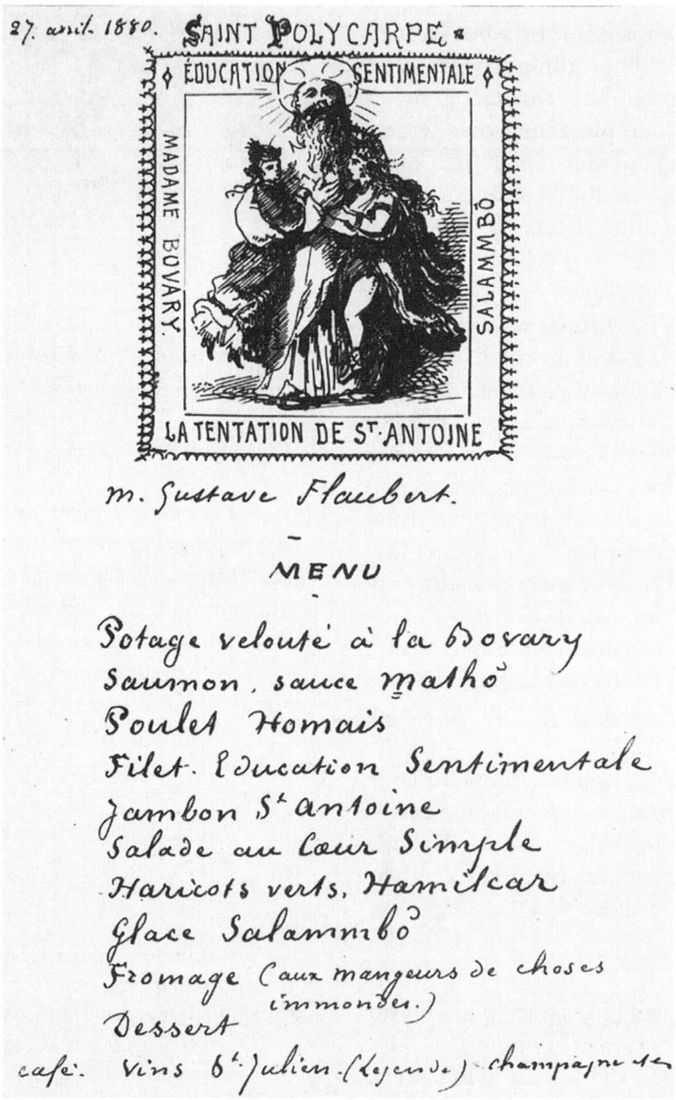

The menu for the last "Saint Polycarp" celebration, which took place on 27 April 1880 (Collections de la Bibliothèque municipale de Rouen. Cliché Thierry Ascencio-Parvy)

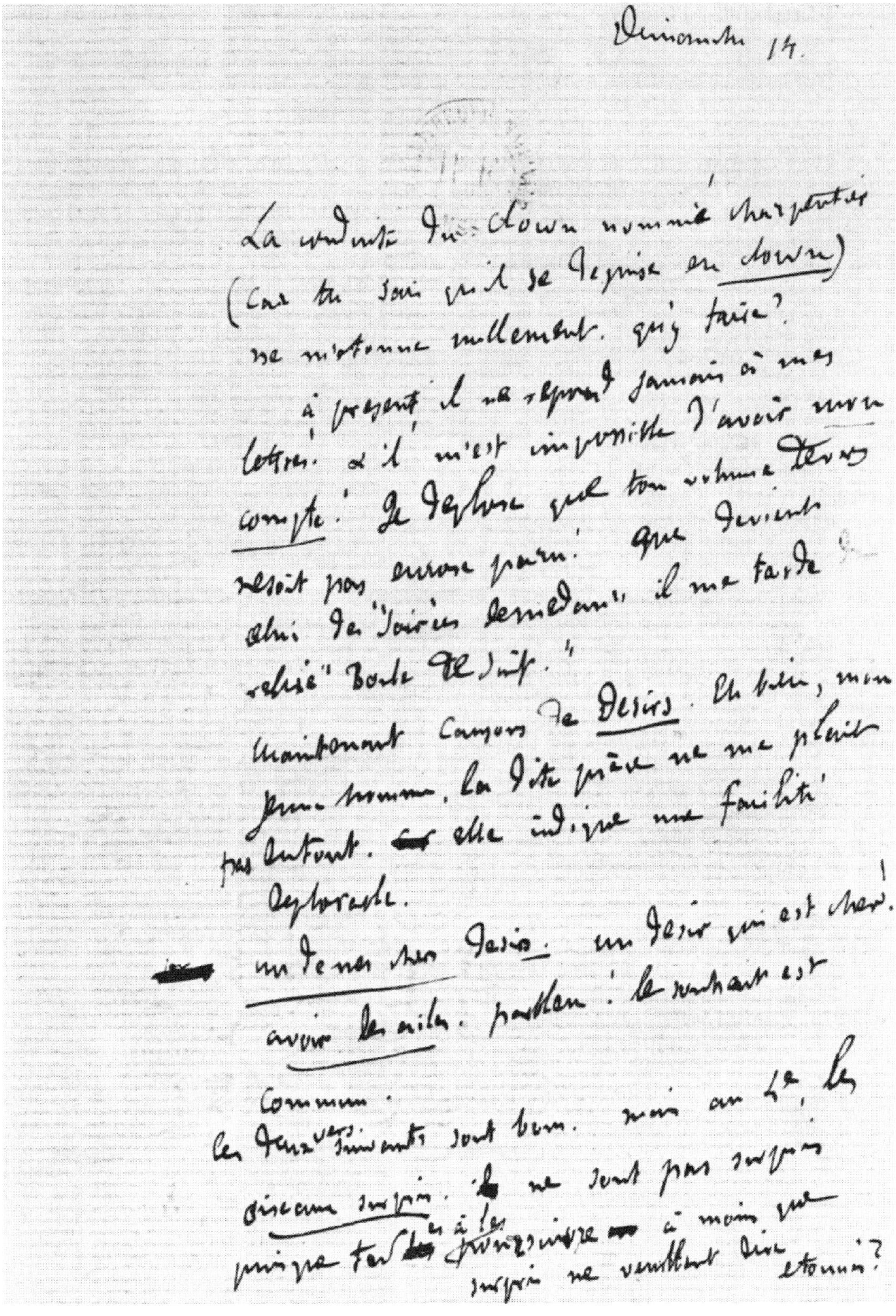

Dimanche 14.

La conduite du clown nommé Charpentier (car ce soir qu'il se déguise en clown) ne m'étonne nullement. qu'y faire? à présent il ne répond jamais à mes lettres. et il m'est impossible d'avoir mon compte! Je déplore que ton volume [illegible] n'est pas encore paru! que devient celui des "Soirées de Médan" il me tarde relire "Boule de suif."

Maintenant causons de Désirs. Eh bien, mon jeune homme, la dite pièce ne me plaît pas du tout. car elle indique une facilité déplorable!

un de nos chers désirs. un désir qui est cher! avoir les ailes. pardon! le souhait est commun.

les deux vers suivants sont bons. mais au 4e, les oiseaux surpris. ils ne sont pas surpris puisque tout à les surprise [illegible] à moins que surpris ne veuillent dire étonnés?

One of Flaubert's last letters, in which he asks Guy de Maupassant when Les Soirées de Médan *(Evenings at Médan) will be published, for he cannot wait to read "Boule de suif." Then, he criticizes a poem by Maupassant, "Désirs" (cliché Bibliothèque nationale de France, Paris).*

Flaubert's Death

Flaubert never saw Turgenev again: while he was planning his visit to Paris in May he suddenly died from apoplexy on 8 May 1880, leaving the tenth chapter of his novel unfinished. In a letter to Turgenev, Guy de Maupassant, whose short story "Boule de suif" Flaubert had praised as a masterpiece, recounts the circumstances of the writer's final moments.

Guy de Maupassant to Turgenev, 25 May 1880

Dear Master and Friend,

I am still prostrated by this calamity, and his dear face follows me everywhere. His voice haunts me, phrases keep coming back, the disappearance of his affection seems to have emptied the world around me.

At three-thirty in the afternoon on Saturday, May eighth, I received a telegram from Mme Commanville: "Flaubert apoplexy. No hope. Leaving at six." I joined the Commanvilles at six o'clock at the station; but stopping at my apartment on the way I found two other telegrams from Rouen announcing his death. We made the horrible journey in the dark, sunk in black and cruel grief. At Croisset we found him on his bed, looking almost unchanged, except that his neck was dark and swollen from the apoplexy. We learned details. He had been very well during the preceding days, happy to be nearing the end of his novel; and he was to leave for Paris on Sunday the ninth. He looked forward to enjoying himself–having, he said, "hidden a nest-egg in a pot." It wasn't a very large nest-egg, and he had earned it by his writing. He had eaten a very good dinner on Friday, spent the evening reciting Corneille with his doctor and neighbor, M. Fortin; had slept until eight the next morning, taken a long bath, made his toilet, and read his mail. Then, feeling a little unwell, he called his maid; she was slow in coming, and he called to her out the window to fetch M. Fortin–but he, it turned out, had just left for Rouen by boat. When the maid arrived she found him standing, quite dizzy but not at all alarmed. He said, "I think I'm going to have a kind of fainting fit; it's lucky it should happen today; it would have been a great nuisance tomorrow, in the train." He opened a bottle of eau de Cologne and rubbed some on his forehead, and let himself down quietly onto a large divan, murmuring, "Rouen–we're not far from Rouen–Hellot–I know the Hellots–" And then he fell back, his hands clenched, his face darkened and swollen with blood, stricken by the death he had not for a second suspected.

His last words, which the newspapers interpreted as a reference to Victor Hugo, who lives in the Avenue d'Eylau, seem to me unquestionably to have meant: "Go to Rouen, we're not far from Rouen, and bring Dr. Hellot. I know the Hellots."

I spent three days beside him. With Georges Pouchet and M. Fortin I wrapped him in his shroud. And on Tuesday morning we took him to the cemetery, from which one has a perfect view of Croisset, with the great curve of the river and the house he so loved.

The days when we consider ourselves happy don't atone for days like those.

At the cemetery were many friends from Paris, especially his younger friends, *all* the young people he knew, and even some whom nobody knew; but not Victor Hugo, nor Renan, nor Taine, nor Maxime DuCamp, nor Frédéric Baudry, nor Dumas, nor Augier, nor Vacquerie, etc.

That's all, my dear master and friend. But I shall have many more things to tell you. We shall attend to the novel when the heirs have settled their affairs. You'll be needed for everything.

I wrote the very day of the calamity to Mme Viardot, asking her to tell you, because I didn't know your address in Russia. I preferred you should learn this sad news from friends rather than from a newspaper.

I shake your hands sadly, mon cher maître, and hope to see you soon.

Your entirely devoted
Guy de Maupassant

–*The Letters of Gustave Flaubert, 1857–1880,* edited by Francis Steegmuller (Cambridge, Mass.: Harvard University Press, 1982), pp. 275–277

Guy de Maupassant, Flaubert's "disciple" (Collections de la Bibliothèque municipale de Rouen. Cliché Thierry Ascencio-Parvy)

The graves of the Flaubert family, with a close-up view of the author's tombstone at the Cimetière monument in Rouen, square M, second row (photographs by Éric Le Calvez)

View of the city of Rouen and the spire of its cathedral from the Cimetière monumental near Flaubert's grave (photograph by Éric Le Calvez)

Critical Views of *Trois Contes* and *Bouvard et Pécuchet*

Trois Contes *is acknowledged as one of Flaubert's masterpieces. This essay by Raymonde Debray Genette was written in French and translated for inclusion in* Flaubert and Postmodernism *(1984).*

Profane, Sacred: Disorder of Utterance in *Trois Contes*

Critics have never tired of demonstrating the fact that Flaubert, whether seen as a writer or a storyteller, is always at odds with language. *Trois Contes* constitutes a perfect example of this, as it is a condensation of many forms of this confrontation. But in comparing the short stories to Flaubert's other fictional pieces, we find that the religious reflection running through *Trois Contes* calls into question the relationship between language and the sacred more specifically than it does in the other works. It should be noted in this regard that the status of utterance differs from one story to the next in *Trois Contes,* although the narrative and discursive modes are often identical. It is the frequency and the context in which it is used that change its functional value. Though all three of the *Contes* are written with the same kind of technical virtuosity, their aesthetic and philosophic yield differs for this reason. Utterance in *Trois contes,* from its most infrequent to its most omnipresent manifestation, is always characterized by a specific kind of disorder, which in turn is either the product or the cause of a more general disintegration of the relationship of the individual to the world.[1] For lack of space here, however, one panel will be missing from my analysis: the primary diverting of sexuality toward religion, or rather the sacred, will not be spoken of in this paper. Many thematic and psychoanalytic critics have already dealt with this aspect of the problem. As I am more concerned with forms of narrative discourse, I have chosen to sketch out the lines of confrontation between sacred utterance and its profane counterpart.

In referring to utterance in the narrative, I am thinking not only of speech in its literary sense, as in the monologue, the dialogue, or the quotation (in general, quoted discourse); but I am also thinking of all narrated forms of elocution, be they physical or mental, the responsibility for which is adopted to a greater or lesser extent by the narration. These range from, on the one hand, the naming of an act, which implies that one speaks or speaks to oneself, to, on the other hand, indirect discourse, free indirect discourse, and italicized discourse. I will be following Dorrit Cohn's categories of interiority in this discussion (psycho-narration, quoted monologue, narrated monologue), applying them to narratives which propose a global representation of life.[2] In particular, the psycho-narration is an accounting of utterance in the form of narrative event. As is also the case with silence, utterance–at times hidden, but more frequently mentioned in Flaubert as figure of its own absence or failure–is one of the primary event-centered forms of narrative. From a methodological standpoint, it is not feasible to limit oneself to a linguistically based analysis of all of these forms, unless it be to point out, as Ann Banfield has done, the irreducible nature of literary discourse.[3] On the other hand, what is being studied here will not be revealed by pure thematic analysis that bypasses formal literary aspects either. Narratively speaking, that which is divine and prophetic manifests itself in specific aspects of the language, like direct discourse, figurative expression, or the proleptic mode. Consequently, the theoretical path I have chosen may seem narrow and paved with thin narrative detail. In the end, however, the narrative speaks for itself: nourished with language, it produces among other things a fiction that can be called utterance.

This discussion will be organized in accordance with the order in which the stories were written, for one may well conceive of the group in terms of the repetition and contrast that result from the compositional genesis of the work, with *Hérodias* constituting the most difficult of the three. I will, therefore, return to an interpretation respectful of the order of publication. Consequently, we shall begin with *Saint Julian,* or *sacrificial utterance*. It would seem here that human utterance is sacrificed in favor of a sacrificial Voice. By *Voice* [*voix*], we mean the utterance of sacred origin (the Voice of God, of Jesus, of the Holy Spirit, or of the prophets and diviners), while by *parole* we are referring to the *utterance* which is human in origin. From a linguistic point of view, this distinction would appear to be without basis. Whereas pragmatically, Voice pertains to the performative domain, utterance is affiliated with the constative–though reversals in these functions are of course possible. From a narrative standpoint, however, this distinction corresponds to several clear-cut narrative techniques that appear in *Saint Julian.*

Saint Julian is the least prolix of the three stories, but this is due to the fact that it belongs to the strict, even restrictive generic category of the legend. Insomuch as the legend is or pretends to be an oral phenomenon, it does not contain many utterances that are attributable to its characters. Instead, the narrator-speaker tends to control the enunciation as much as possible. Interventions are rapid though incisive because they occur in the first person singular or plural and are addressed to an overall community of listener-narratees. "Our father Adam," "Our Saviour Jesus Christ," and the celebrated ending "And this is the story of Saint Julian Hospitator, more or less as it is depicted in a stained-glass window in a church in my part of the world"[4] all function this way. Another, even more devious way that the narrator has of depriving the hero of access to utterance is through the process of exaggeration. Carried away by a kind of ardent enthusiasm that recalls that of Don Quixote, the narrator insists upon the truth of his own words: "it was he, and no other, who slew the viper of Milan and the Dragon of Oberbirbach!" (p. 70). The entire first section of chapter 2 ("He enlisted in a troup of soldiers of fortune which were passing by" [p. 69]) is in fact a marvelous pastiche of the chivalric novel. This doubling of the narrator has the effect of further obscuring the enunciation and causes a kind of fading of the fundamental line of the legend to take place.

What then is left for the characters? In general, we find an efficacious utterance geared toward action rather than representation. There are nineteen instances of direct discourse in this story, though most of these are attributable to beings with supernatural qualities. The hermit, the bohemian, and the deer form a prophetic trilogy: you shall be a saint, you shall be an emperor, you shall be a parricide. And along with them stands the leper, the relentless beggar, before he is transformed into Christ. The main characters, on the other hand, intervene very rarely: Julian's wife speaks three times briefly, and Julian himself only five times–four of which are actually inner thoughts. I will not elaborate on these instances in detail, but I will make a few general statements about them. Two comments are in order: all literary sources of Saint Julian–be they Latin or Romantic–contain a great deal of direct discourse.[5] In Flaubert's version, however, this form of narration is not only reduced; it is also frequently invented. This does not mean that utterance is unimportant, but rather that its role is extremely well defined and limited. As for the Voice, its role is quite obviously to announce various stages of the legend and their contradictory outcomes as well. Curiously, in the 1856 draft of Flaubert's text, Julian's own utterance incorporates the Voice as well: "Mother, I have been told that I

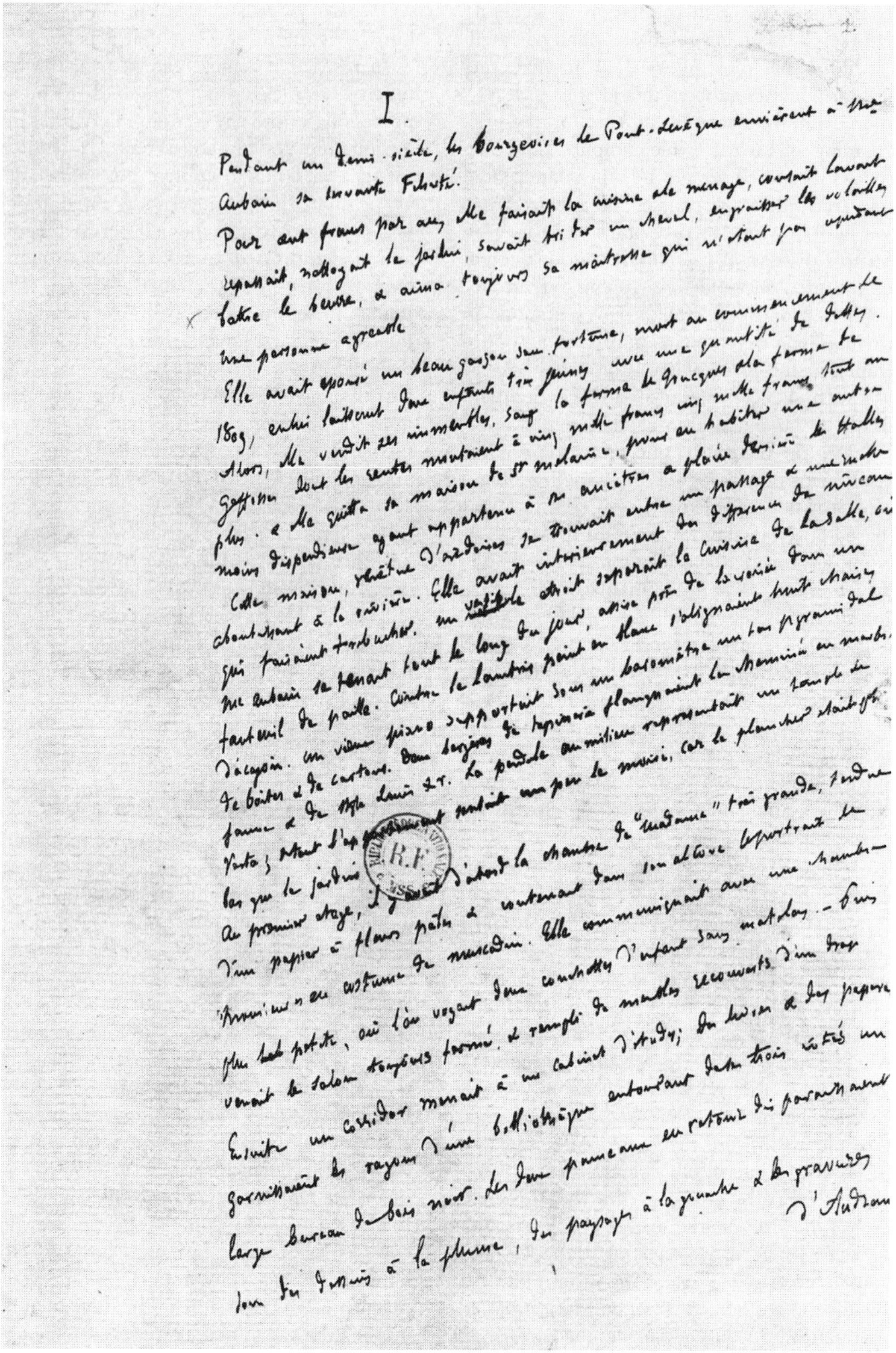

First page of the final manuscript for "Un cœur simple" (cliché Bibliothèque nationale de France, Paris)

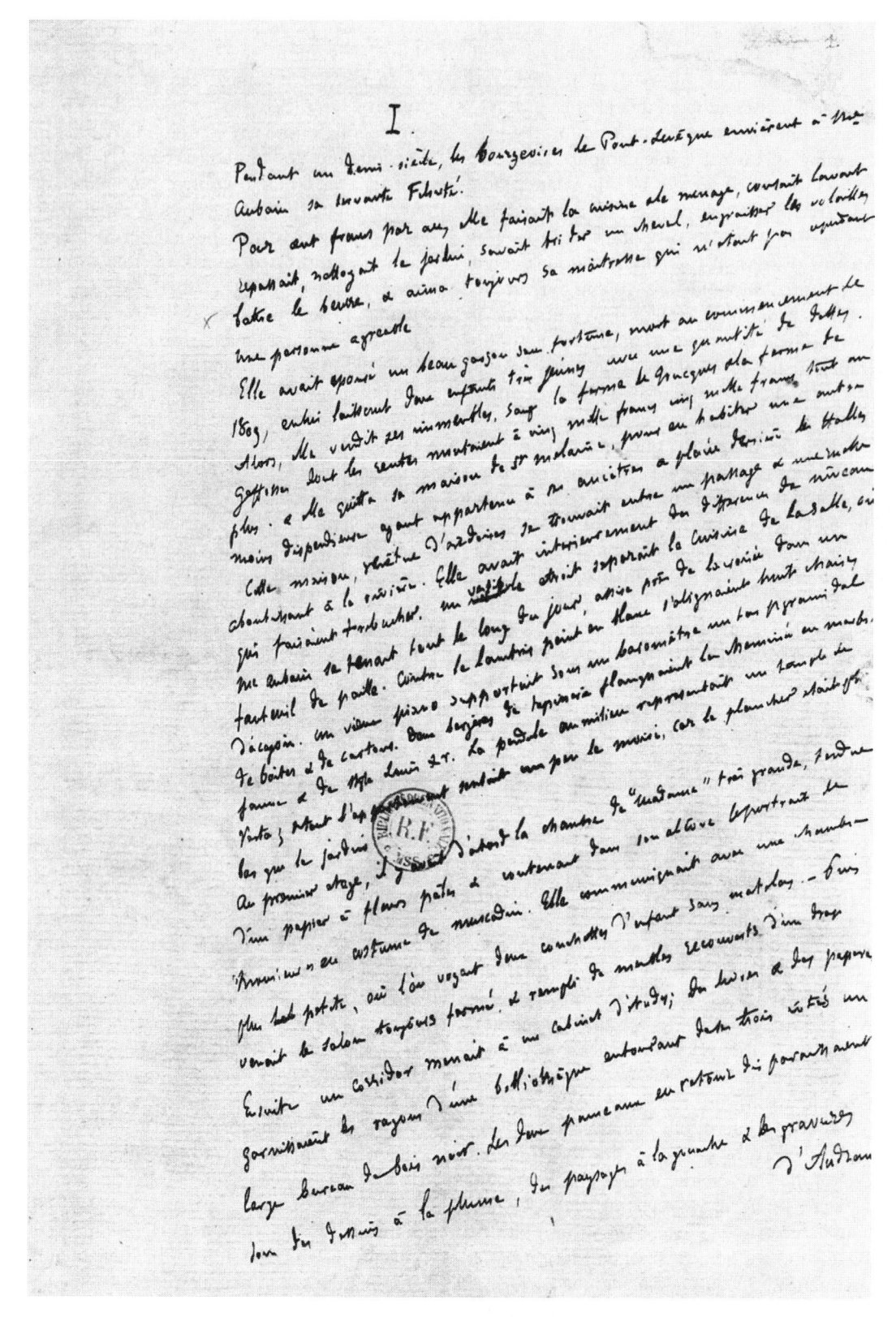

would kill you." The final text isolates the Voice and attributes a more subtle role to utterance.

It is worth mentioning that each of the three stories, even in their earliest forms, grows out of a central event that is verbal, without the occurrence of which nothing would come to pass. We have already seen this in *Saint Julian.* In the earliest version of *Un Cœur simple,* entitled *Perroquet,* possibly also dating from 1856, the structure of the story is based on a fully deployed dialogue between Félicité and the priest which serves as a starting point for the confusion between the sacred and the profane ("It seemed to me that the small chains of the censers made the sound of his chain–is this a sin, my father?–no, my child"). In *Hérodias* it is the myth, or *mythos,* that we will be examining. In each case, narrative developments should be read as corollaries growing out of the key utterances in question. The outward expansion is literal in the case of *Saint Julian:* what was predicted comes to pass. In *Un Cœur simple,* it was metonymic at first, metaphoric afterwards: the confusion is carried through to its final metaphoric resolution. The expansion in *Hérodias* verges on the allegoric, though this tendency is never fully actualized: instead, realization of the figurative utterance transforms it into a consumable myth.

It is the narration, of course, that dominates in the overall design of *Saint Julian,* and, to a lesser extent, description rather than dialogue. What Flaubert refers to as "analysis" does not occur until the third chapter, after the murder has already been accomplished. At this point, all communication, human and animal, is blocked. The forms most frequently used to translate interior life are, first, verbs expressing opinions or sentiments, and second, indirect constructions. Flaubert's celebrated free indirect discourse ("indirect libre"– I′ as it shall be referred to here) is in fact relatively infrequent. It is set off grammatically and appears most predominantly in chapter 2 in the discreet debate between the influence of Julian's wife and the renewed attractions of the hunt. Here it constitutes a résumé of the conversations, reflections, and orders that Julian gives before becoming a mendicant. One example among others seems to me to illustrate the role of utterance particularly well by means of a triple opposition. Julian "told [his wife] of his dreadful fear" (p. 73). This résumé of utterances is apotropaic. Even more perverse is the response of his wife, which appears in a sequence of I′: "She fought against it [this thought] reasoning very soundly: his father and mother were probably dead, but if he were ever to see them again, what chance or purpose could possibly lead him to commit such a horrible crime? His fear was completely groundless, and he ought to take up hunting again" (p. 73). The use of I′ partially shifts responsibility from the wife to the transcribing narrator. Direct discourse would on the other hand shift the burden of guilt in her direction. It is not surprising then that the only case in which Julian addresses himself directly to his wife permits him to succumb to the temptation of the hunt: "I am obeying your orders," he said; "I shall be back at sunrise" (p. 73). The subtlety of the three-part usage of the various modes of representation of utterance is visible here: they avoid the expression of the murderous desire, exonerating Julian, and all the same trap him by the very fact of this circumlocution.

Among the many deceptive forms of utterance, one might well expect to encounter the irresponsible italics, a discursive form which does not carry the mark of its source. There is, however, not a single instance of this in *Saint Julian.* Perhaps, this is because there is no real social discourse at work here–there is only that discourse which the narrator needs to affirm the existence of a communal spirit among the readers. The narrator speaks of the "Good Lord," of "charming paintings," and of Julian as a child "who looked like an Infant Jesus" (p. 60). Such mental quotations are not set off by quotation marks; they represent a fictional and heroic vox populi. On the other hand, we will see further on how important citations set off by quotation marks are in *Un Cœur simple.* Julian, for his part, is actually alone and settling a personal score. Granted, he is born within a social context. His father, for example, speaks of or has read or recited the exploits of former warriors and the adventures of pilgrims to him. Julian listens to them. Even as a young child, he already knows by heart "all there was to be known about the chase" (p. 62).

As for Julian's mother, she speaks a different, more secret language that is at the same time more lyrical than the father's: there are prayers, and the crowing of the cocks, the voices of the angels, and the singing of the church bells become audible. The mother teaches Julian to sing. But the silence, which is even stronger than these sounds, takes over the protagonist very early in his life–and it is a guilty silence: "About the murder of the little mouse, he said nothing to anyone" (p. 61). The silence comes along with the padded, dampening effect of the château belonging to Julian's wife; it is also the result of that wife's choosing not to speak. She does not reveal the reasons for Julian's departure to his parents.

Everything changes, however, when the murder occurs. Julian howls while committing the act, and it is with a voice wholly different from his normal voice, according to the text, that he takes leave of his wife and the world. The latter takes fitting revenge on Julian by preventing him from confessing his deed. It will be recalled how, as a beggar, Julian tries to deliver himself by utterance, to tell his story: people listen to him in

A map in Auguste Parent's Machaerous *(1868), one of many sources that Flaubert consulted in writing "Hérodias" (cliché Bibliothèque nationale de France, Paris)*

horror and drive him away with shouts and threats. He silences himself in turn, but wishes at least to listen: "The triviality of their conversation froze his heart" (p. 81). Even worse than this is the fact that while Julian agrees to accept absolute solitude, he is unable to attain total silence for himself. Evil noises resound in him: death-rattles, the dripping of his blood, sobs come forth. At last, all that is heard in the final moments of this dispossession is the Voice which cries out in the tempest, which moans and supplicates in the hovel, and reaches its goal without drawing a response. This is a tyrannical voice, and Julian carries out its instructions quite literally and automatically without grasping its significance. In the end, he becomes absorbed by the Voice, though he no longer has recourse to the utterance he has misused. The fact that ultimately Julian is carried off to heaven is a sublimation of his loss of power over utterance and over its receptacle. As much as the ending tries to appear optimistic, this new version of the Oedipus story tells us above all the lethal power of utterance, be it silent or pronounced.

Contrary to what one might expect, there is no real sacrifice of utterance by the charitable Félicité. All of those who have written about her have noted it: Félicité has little gift in this area, or at least few such gifts are allowed here, and those that are seem poor in quality. Yet she does express herself more than is usually indicated, and hardly can be said to have recourse alone to the kind of psittacism (whose inverse is violence) which has already been so excellently commented upon by others that I would hardly want to begin to parrot it here.[6] I would, however, like to elaborate. First, Félicité speaks far more than one realizes: sixteen direct responses, though only from one to twelve words in length, are to be found here. This means that Félicité speaks as much by herself as all the other characters of *Saint Julian* put together. Her interventions range from the modest "Ah" expressed in the company of Théodore to the tender "Is he all right?" (p. 55) directed toward Loulou by Félicité *in articulo mortis,* and includes the accusatory challenge: "It doesn't matter a bit, not to them it doesn't!" (p. 28). This particular remark concerns the death of Victor, but it could as well refer to the entire life of Félicité, as it has been lived up to this point. Félicité's mistress speaks almost as much.

These utterances, in addition to those of the minor characters and the parrot's four interventions, total thirty-six instances of direct discourse (if my calculations are correct). Thus there is a lifelike presence here testifying to the existence of the linguistic universe. But a majority of the conversations are truncated, generally being absorbed by descriptive passages that follow or precede them. For example, the narrator describes at length Félicité's sister and her two children, one of whom is a young cabin boy. Yet the next paragraph reads: "Madame Aubain sent her off after a quarter of an hour" (p. 28). This is representative of the status of social discourse in general in this story: we are given only a small hint of reality. Also, in marked contrast to what we shall see in *Hérodias,* direct discourse contributes little information–with the exception of the announcement of the nephew's death, where a kind of reticence predominates: "'They have some bad news for you . . . your nephew . . .' He was dead. Nothing more was said" (p. 36). What are such passages expressive of? Are they indicative of a stylistic trait or a personality at least? It would seem not, for there appears to be nothing individual or revealing about them–we find just one popular expression ("Poor little lad!" [p. 36]) and orders having come in particular from others, spread here and there like cartoon captions. The actual substance of the story is not vehicled by these instances of utterance, but rather by other narrative techniques.

Nonetheless, brief occurrences of direct quotation, interspersed in the narrative proper, do prolong the dialogue with the world, do maintain the effect of direct discourse, at least until the death of the parrot. This type of rapid intervention allows some of Félicité's idiolect to appear: "To use her own words, she was 'eaten up inside'" (p. 32), and in another example, "To 'occupy her mind,' she asked if her nephew Victor might come and see her" (p. 32). This emphasizes Félicité's naïveté: "Was it possible, she wondered, 'in case of need' to come back by land?" (p. 36) (note the insertion of direct discourse in the sequence of I'). Finally, this technique allows Félicité to adopt the role of respectful servant: "'Madame's bedroom'" (p. 18), "a portrait of 'Monsieur'" (p. 18), "the style of the house" (p. 21), "in remembrance of 'her' [Virginie]" (p. 40). The more typical Flaubertian cliché of politeness, such as we find spoken by Mère Liébard, can be left aside, as well as the unctuous euphemisms of the nun and the gossip about Bourais. It would seem that Flaubert focuses more on the speech act itself than on the cliché. This undoubtedly explains why there is only one italicized expression repeated: "*those* Rochefeuille girls" (p. 44). Thus one is dealing here less with social discourse per se than with the bits of speech which refer to the presence of characters, of Félicité especially, in fragmentary fashion.

Even the I' type of discourse underlines this citational forcefulness. It occurs more frequently than is usually recognized, though it is scattered and often very brief. Also, at least five such instances, and not the least important of them at that, render the thoughts of Félicité herself. Note that I do not intend to reinstitute the more than fifty years of grammatical, stylistic, and now even psychoanalytic debate concerning the basis and effects of free indirect discourse.[7] As the use of this style is purely literary, we should be attentive here above all to the question of its effects. Paradoxically, when utilized to reveal in part Félicité's thoughts, the I′ is indicative of an attempt to establish an autonomy of the utterance that direct discourse either cannot or does not want to accomplish. Will Félicité manage to elucidate her way of thinking? That part of the story where she receives instruction in the catechism and reflects upon it is of primary importance in this respect. Beginning with a singulative narrative ("The priest began with a brief outline of sacred history"), the narration then shifts to the discourse of Félicité herself, making use of the all-important verb to gain access to an interiority, without actually entering on this inward path: "Félicité saw in imagination" (p. 29). The I′ form of discourse in the following sentence allows Félicité to interpret the life of Jesus as emanating from the life of the fields.

At this point in the text, there are three voices intertwined; Félicité's voice of course is one: "Why had they crucified Him, when He loved children, fed the multitudes, healed the blind?" (p. 29). There is also the voice of the narrator, which carries out the substitutions of the profane for the sacred. Finally, there is the voice of the Gospels, whose traces we find here and there, seeming so natural in the mouth of Félicité: "Seeds," "harvest," "pressing of the grapes," "lambs," "doves" (pp. 29–30). These words seem to fall upon her ear and sanctify her heart as if the Host were being offered to her. They constitute such an intimate part of Félicité that her reflections about the Holy Ghost are expressed through a present-tense monologue. Except for the fact that there is no direct manifestation of the first person, the technique here resembles that of the most modern of novels: "She wondered whether that was its light she had seen flitting about the edge of the marshes at night, whether that was its breath she had felt driving the clouds across the sky, whether that was its voice she had heard in the sweet music of the bells" (p. 30). Here Félicité speaks, or rather speaks to herself of abundance. Naturally, she is no more capable of aiming for the purity and property of her discourse than are any other Flaubertian characters. *Breaths, clouds, bells* are all words coming from Romantic discourse and grafted onto peasant superstitions. In this respect, Félicité resembles Emma Bovary. Thus we find a qualitative rather than a quantitative insufficiency in her: a lack of expressivity, along with fragmented quotations, and a diverting of her discourse in its sincerest, most intimate forms.

Félicité's salvation in the end will come from her being deaf, which in turn is the outgrowth of Loulou's pranks. Sheltered from the words of the world ("Every living thing moved about in a ghostly silence" [p. 46]), Félicité first takes great joy in listening to the parrot. Critics have already explored not only the type of words, but also the sounds this voice reproduces. The next step comes when–"They held conversations with each other" (p. 47)–Félicité begins to discover a language of her own: "words which were just as disconnected, but which came from the heart" (ibid). Though deaf, Félicité does not always remain silent, as the first chapter would have us believe. Admittedly, during her mourning work for the dead Loulou, Félicité sanctifies the bird, and an iconic form of identification is established. But the most telling passage, written in I′, is doubly related to language: "God the Father could not have chosen a dove as a means of expressing Himself, since doves cannot talk, but rather one of Loulou's ancestors" (p. 50). If "it is language which makes Félicité vulnerable," as Shoshana Felman has so convincingly demonstrated,[8] if it is by means of language that she is exploited, it should nonetheless be recognized that once this point has been reached, Félicité–in the midst of her tears and mourning–has only simple words to speak. Yet it is because of this very simplicity that these words are sublime. Being sick, she suffers "like Madame," she forgives Fabu, she devotes all that she thinks and says to Loulou. As for the parrot, having lost or rather returned the borrowed gift of language, he is transformed from mere voice to the voiceless Verb. The parrot's silence consequently offers Félicité access to a Holy Ghost that is "intelligible," incarnate. Yet he is also seen to be stuffed, a deteriorated and thoroughly destroyed form. Félicité dies adoring an image of the Word [*Verbe*], a sheaf of utterance; but in the end, what we hear is the gentle sound of her heart–the most profound thing she has to say.

Thus Félicité's liberation from utterance comes about through a progressive muting of the Word. In *Hérodias,* much to the contrary, it is a noisy combat between utterance and the Word, between utterances and the Voice, that takes place. Narratively speaking, this story is based on the expansive development and necessary realization of what Flaubert called "myth," this as early on as the scenarios. The myth in this case, it should be said, is a figurative phrase that makes reference to a sacred event: "In order for him to grow, I must be diminished." In the Book of John (3:30), this expression is pronounced by John the Baptist as he tries to explain the humility of his role to his disciples. Flaubert's Iaokanaan repeats the formula in the darkness of his prison. He does not seem to be the originator of these words and needs to justify them to himself. Nonetheless, he experiences them as a parable. In contrast to this, when the same words are spoken by Mannaëi, they remain enigmatic and empty for him, as they do for Antipas. Also, the use of such words is in marked contrast to those at work within the prophetic system in *Saint Julian.* Iaokanann is not alone in his preoccupation with this utterance, for he serves as vehicle for an Other. An intervention from outside is needed in order for the utterance to be filled. Thus the prophet is neither author nor master of his fate. It is most likely for this reason that he is represented only by a voice–a voice that is skillfully modulated. First, it is a voice in the silence. Then, in chapter 2, it is a "diabolical machine," a thundering that transmits the prophecies of doom "like mighty blows," one after the other. And at another moment, it is instead an enchanted voice bringing the news of future happiness. In the third act, contrary to all indications in the first scenarios, Iaokanaan no longer has the right to participate. Not only does this character constitute a voice because of his physical power but also because of the fact that he is incapable of speaking in his own name.

The narrative here, all of which is rendered in direct discourse (for were Iaokanaan to speak in I′, the entire face of the heavens would be transformed), is a tissue of biblical quotations, generally taken from the Books of the Prophets and chosen for their violence and vivid character. The intertextuality is very powerful here and so well executed that the reader retains only the excess, as if it were a caricature of the Old Testament. The prophet too is reduced to a voice, for he soliloquizes; no one responds; he resembles the coryphacus more closely than he does a character. "The voice grew louder and stronger, rolling and roaring like thunder, and as the mountains sent it back, it broke over Machaerus in repeated echoes" (p. 109). There is a bit of Loulou in Iaokanaan. The Syrian interpreter, a kind of parrot in his own right, even indicates this: "The Tetrarch and Herodias were forced to endure them twice over" (p. 108). Thus Iaokanaan constitutes the Voice of God before the incarnation of the Word becomes known.

Interposed between this voice and Antipas, we find Phanuel–a mediator of sorts. Phanuel is a mediator first of all in that he attempts to reconcile the interests of the prisoner with those of Antipas. He plays a mediatory role even more so because he is situated at a midway point–not between the sacred and the profane–but between the pagan sacred and the Christian sacred, which he communicates without understanding even though his ideas and actions seem to grow out of it. He is thus an oracle of sorts. We do not know what it is that inspires him when he says at the end of chapter 1: "If you ill-treat him, you will be punished," or "He will go among the Arabs, the Gauls, the Scythians. His work must extend to the ends of the earth!" (p. 98). He is always very near the other truth; he burns; he is only mistaken as to the person. At the same time, he has difficulty in delivering his own astronomical-astrological message, which is put off from the end of chapter 1 to the end of chapter 2. And for the one and only time in *Trois Contes,* the oracular utterance is rendered in I′: "From all this he augured the death of an important man that very night in Machaerous" (p. 111). The I′ type of discourse implies interiority: Phanuel no longer constitutes a single voice, but rather a character which is the human, more engaging double for the intractable Iaokanaan. As the indefinite article ("a man") indicates, he is not sheltered from doubts by his purity. Of course, Antipas will try to take advantage of his hesitation, thinking it possible to change destiny. Having failed to understand the prophecy, he turns to the oracle. Phanuel, on the other hand, will be the only one, along with his two disciples, to be enlightened by the end of the story. For there is one utterance never to be spoken in the course of the tale, which is nonetheless ever present: "At the very moment that the sun rose, two men who had been sent out by Iokanaan sometime before returned with the long-awaited reply. They confided it to Phanuel, who received it with transports of delight" (p. 124). The response that Matthew gave (11:4-6) appears nowhere directly: "John is Elijah and Jesus the Messiah." The story retains this last bit of mystery. Caught midway between the human and the divine interpretations, it finds its ultimate resolution in myth. Although it goes beyond the purely historic, it is never transformed into the allegoric mode. The messages of the Voices, among others, are not directly figured.

Antipas, receiving these words directly or indirectly, is traversed by them, but understands neither their sense nor their character. He cuts short their impact. For example, all that he retains of them is a threat of death. The rest remains a fog of sorts, which seems to dissipate like Arab tents at sunrise. In one sense we might say that the semiotics of a character such as Antipas are the opposite of the semiotics of Félicité. Whereas Félicité understood what were merely spoken or written signs to be icons, Antipas takes all that is meant as symbol to be sign and utterance. At other moments, however, superstition reverses his interpretive system and refers back to Félicité's. No sooner has the name Iaokanaan been pronounced than he falls backward "as if he had been struck full in the chest" (p. 116). He obstructs the free circulation of these symbolic messages as much as possible. As for the crowd, although it repeats them, it has an equally distorted grasp of the meaning of these messages. To name Elie is to unleash all kinds of visions in the crowd. This complex of semiotic confusion is paralleled by linguistic confusion.

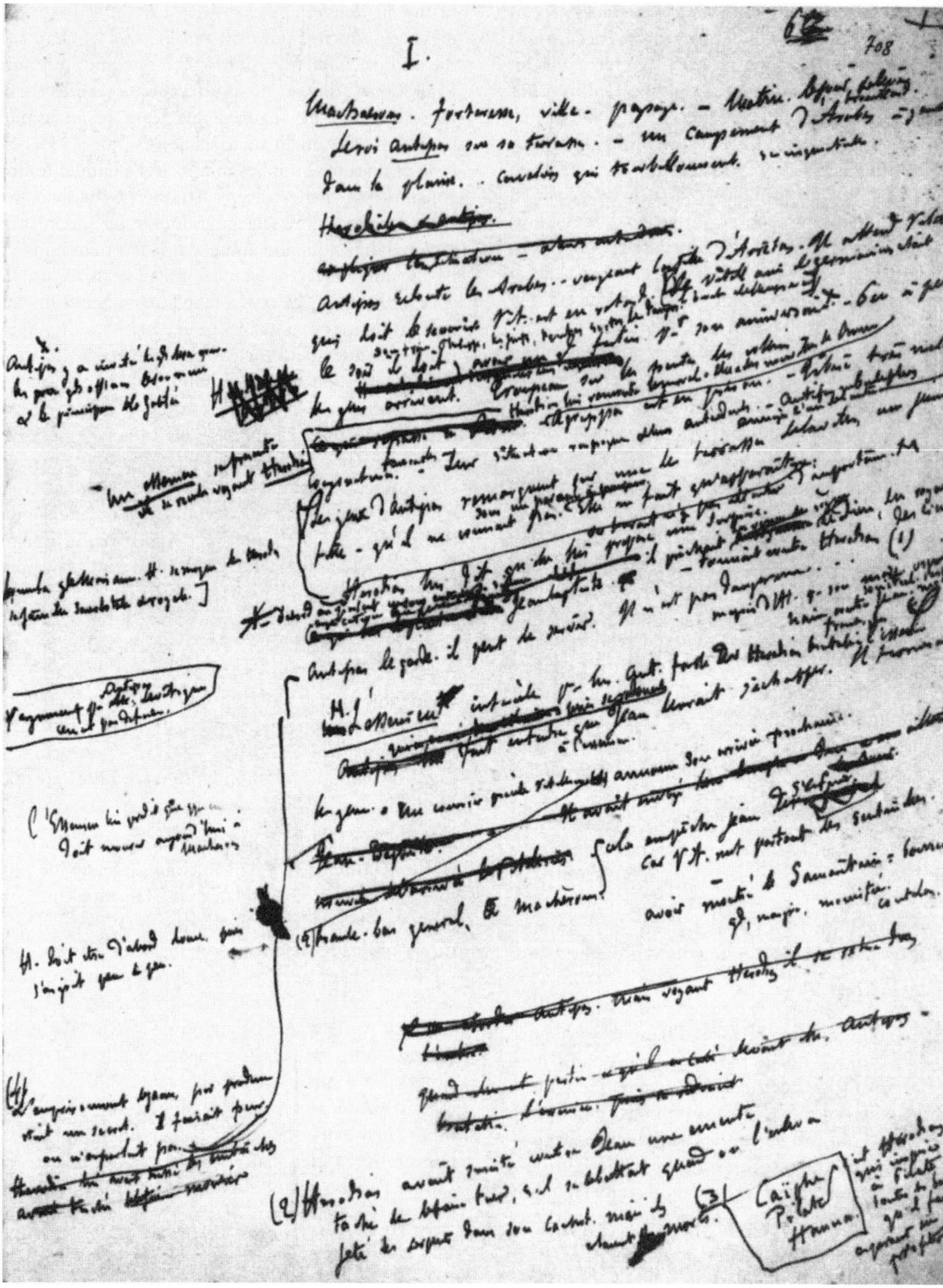

Two of the sketches Flaubert wrote during his preparation for "Hérodias" (clichés Bibliothèque nationale de France, Paris)

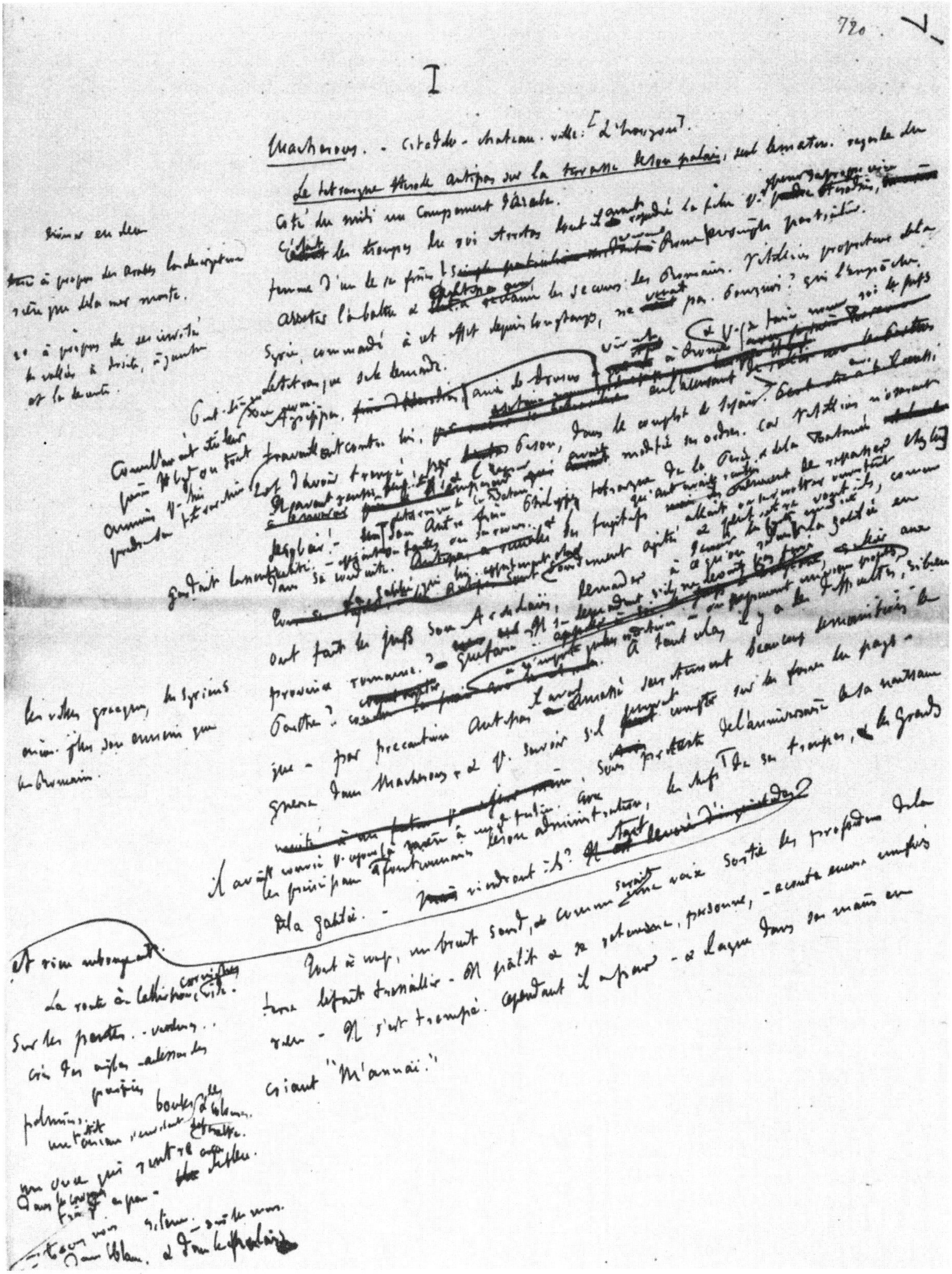

Flaubert presents all this in a kind of theater of words (*théâtre de paroles*). He is once again tempted to create a dramatic form of discourse, just as Mallarmé with his "Hérodiade." Far removed from the realist dramatic form, this work looks toward symbolic theater as its model; and contrary to what we might expect, the historicity of this writing does not inhibit its theatricality in the least. The need to amplify the use of direct response, already indicated in the preliminary drafts, and the existence of a widely spaced mise-en-scène, made up of paragraphs that have been broken apart into fragmented incidents, are characteristic of this story. The traditional style of ancient history provides much liberty of discourse. I am referring here to the Latins, to Tacitus and Suetonius primarily, but also to Livy, whose style is recalled most of all by the I' type of discourse, and this at times to the point of pastiche. The marriage of the two models–the historic and the dramatic–is in fact what gives the story its greatest originality.[9]

Flaubert has constructed a modern drama upon the foundation of ancient phrasing, a drama where utterance is protean. The following is one of many examples of this. Hérodias greets Vitellius, and she speaks to him of her brother Agrippa, who has just been imprisoned in Rome: "She added: 'It is because he wanted Caïus to be Emperor!' While living on their charity, Agrippa had been trying to obtain the title of king, which they coveted just as much as he did. But in future they would have no cause for fear! 'The dungeons of Tiberius are hard to open,' said Herodias, 'and life inside them is sometimes far from safe!'" (p. 93). In this passage, we move successively from a verb of speech to a segment of truncated direct discourse, then to the narrator's explanation of the state of affairs, next to a second instance of direct discourse (with neither dashes nor quotation marks, but only an exclamation mark), and finally to a genuine direct reply. All of this appears in the absence of any manifestation of the first person, which accounts for the exemplary character of utterance. It is because of this kind of well-controlled variation from one form of discourse to the next that history seems to reinstate discourse and vice-versa. But all of the techniques of reinstatement originate in the writing process itself and are designed to cloud the sources of enunciation. The movements of the crowds, for example, provoke uproars, vociferations, and sometimes even laughter that would seem unattributable: "Murmurs of disapproval interrupted him [Jacob]. It was generally believed that Elias had only disappeared" (p. 116). I will not take up a discussion of the banquet here that Victor Brombert has already so astutely analyzed elsewhere.[10] It is useful to retain, however, the idea that one cannot attribute a clear-cut position to Flaubert in this matter. Although there is sufficient distance at work in the text for us to experience utterance as a kind of cacophony, there is at the same time enough presence for that utterance to function in a wholly efficacious way. There is a fundamental sense of frustration that remains with the reader as well as the characters. No one is responsible, though each word stands as a fragment of the drama as a whole. Except for the descriptions, which are of prime importance, all else–the summary and analysis–disappears, merges into the fabric of the generalized discourse, of this verbal anomaly.

There is indeed a current passing from the sacred utterance (myth, Voice, or oracle) to the human, disordered utterance, but through a catastrophically faulty circuit. The manner in which human utterance comes into contact with the sacred texts and *verba* provokes all kinds of sacrileges, the most extreme of which is the murder of Iokanaan. What we find here is a struggle between two distinct powers: utterance always reveals a bit too much, the Word apparently not quite enough. Hérodias thinks it possible to benefit from this conflict–first by creating a zone of reticence and secrecy around Salomé and then by allowing her a seemingly inoffensive power of speech. Salomé forgets, rediscovers, and lisps. Nonetheless, thanks to her delicate speech, she charms words out of Antipas, draws the Voice out of the prophet. In this way, she permits the realization of the myth to come about, which in turn allows the Word to rediscover a means of expression–an expression whose murderous power we have already seen in the case of Julian, whose pathetic nature was evident in the story of Félicité. From this point on, the Christian myth takes on the role which Lévi-Strauss has spoken of: "to legitimate a social order and a world view by means of an original vision of things, to explain what things are on the basis of what they were, to find a justification for their present state in their past and conceive of the future as a function of the present and the past."[11]

This hardly means that Flaubert adheres to the contents of this myth, but that he draws attention to its use, and, in a pessimistic vein, to the necessity of its effects as well. This at least is as one particular reading of *Trois Contes*–one that respects the order in which the stories were published–would have it. Man is constantly delegating his power of speech, his very being, to one form of divinity or another, and this in an ever more degraded way. All that he worships diminishes him, with the exception perhaps of art, which as Flaubert would say, attempts to counter this loss with the power of man's own utterance.

–Raymonde Debray-Genette, "Profane, Sacred: Disorder of Utterance in *Trois Contes*," translated by Susan Huston, in *Flaubert and Postmodernism*, edited by Naomi Schor and Henry F. Majewski (Lincoln & London: University of Nebraska Press, 1984), pp. 13–29

---

1. Throughout the text *parole* will be translated as "utterance." "Utterance" would seem to be a more accurate translation of *parole* than either "speech" or "word," since it is used here to convey nonvocal or nonvoiced as well as voiced types of communication.–TRANS.
2. Dorrit Cohn, *Transparent Minds* (Princeton, N.J.: Princeton University Press, 1978).
3. Ann Banfield "Le style narratif et la grammaire du discours direct et indirect," *Change* 16–17 (September 1973): 188–226; and "Où l'épistémologie, le style et la grammaire rencontrent l'histoire littéraire: Le développement de la parole et de la pensée représentées," *Langue française* 44 (December 1979): 9–26.
4. Gustave Flaubert, *Three Tales,* trans. Robert Baldick (Harmondsworth: Penguin Books, 1975), p. 87. All page references cited in the text are to this edition. Texts quoted other than those of Flaubert are translated by the translator.–EDS.
5. See Benjamin F. Bart and Robert F. Cook, *The Legendary Sources of Flaubert's Saint Julian,* (Toronto: University of Toronto Press, 1977).
6. Marc Bertrand, "Parole et silence dans les *Trois Contes* de Flaubert," *Stanford French Review* 1 (1977): 191–203.
7. Claude Perruchot, "Le Style indirect libre et la question du sujet dans *Madame Bovary,*" in *La Production du sens chez Flaubert,* ed. Claudine Gothot-Mersch (Paris: Union Générale d'Éditions, 1975); and D. G. Laporte, "Le lieu commun," *Ornicar,* nos. 20–21 (1980), pp. 281–306.
8. Shoshana Felman, *La Folie et la chose littéraire* (Paris: Seuil, 1978), pp. 159–169.
9. See Michael Issacharoff, "Hérodias et la symbolique combinatoire des *Trois Contes,*" and "Trois Contes et le problème de la non-linéarité," in *L'Espace et la nouvelle* (Paris: Corti, 1976), pp. 21–59.
10. Victor Brombert, *The Novels of Flaubert* (Princeton, N.J.: Princeton University Press, 1966).
11. Claude Lévi-Strauss, *Le Nouvel Observateur,* no. 818 (15 July 1980).

* * *

Flaubert considered Bouvard et Pécuchet *his "testament." The unfinished version was first printed in* La Nouvelle revue *from 15 December 1880 to 1 March 1881. In March, it was published as a volume by Lemerre. Readers of the time found it strange and did not understand the work. Barbey d'Aurevilly, Flaubert's old enemy, even wrote that it was "unreadable and unbearable," but Flaubert's friends, including Sabatier, Maupassant, and Céard, tried to defend the novel and wrote positive articles.*

Beyond the conjectures on what the second volume should have been from the huge amount of notes and the thousands of pages Flaubert left after his death, twentieth-century scholars have approached the novel from a variety of standpoints. In this excerpt from his essay collected in Flaubert and Postmodernism, *Charles Bernheimer analyzes the "fetishism" of the characters in their quest for knowledge.*

Fetishism and Allegory in *Bouvard et Pécuchet*

. . . The clerks' successive fetishes are the codes of signification proposed by the society and by the library. Not surprisingly, one of the first of these to operate in the text is the code defining the signs of sexual difference. The encounter of Bouvard and Pécuchet is explicitly placed in the great Romantic tradition of the *coup de foudre*[1] [*love at first sight*]. Angular Pécuchet, still virgin at forty-seven, afraid of draughts and spices, deferential toward religion, prudish, plays the female role, while rotund Bouvard, bon vivant, liberal, pipe-smoking, ribald, atheistic, has the male lead. Sexual identities thus appear more metaphorical than physical, more a product of society's conventional attitudes than of anatomical destiny. The very conventionality of these attitudes, however, undercuts the distinctions they maintain. The mutual attraction of Bouvard and Pécuchet is not based on the one's appreciating the strong femininity or masculinity of the other. Rather, it is based on their sharing the same artificial set of clichéd opinions and received ideas, within which are included certain views about male-female difference. Thus even though Pécuchet is a shy virgin and Bouvard a lusty widower, they agree that women are "frivolous, bad-tempered, and stubborn" and go on to make the well-balanced observation that "despite that [women] were often better than men; at other times they were worse" and to conclude that "in short, it was better to live without them" (p. 53). So the reader's response to Pécuchet's sensibility as feminine enters into a network of commonplace definitions of women that makes any conclusion about the nature of sexual difference seem as arbitrary as the clerks' decision to do without the so-called opposite sex.

In a probing article, Claudine Gothot-Mersch studies the various scenarios for the novel in order to determine whether Flaubert conceived of his characters consistently in terms of a romantic couple.[2] She finds many notations that point in this direction, such as: "The lovers look at each other," or "They cherish each other. The marriage is made." But other textual indications suggest that Flaubert did not bother to maintain the coherence of those clichéd codes that he provisionally used to construct character. Gothot-Mersch observes that Bouvard is more sentimental than Pécuchet (in regard to Gorju and the children) and that he cries more easily (at the time of the fire, in front of the broken chest, confronted with the decaying carcass). Moreover, in one of the scenarios for the penultimate chapter, Flaubert wrote: "Pécuchet took responsibility for Victor. Bouvard, gentler, more feminine, for Victorine." Indeed, there is a certain *flottement du sens* [*wavering of meaning*] perceptible in these contradictory suggestions as to sex roles, but the meaning of that *flottement* is clear: it points precisely to the arbitrariness of all received ideas about gender. (Are women really more sentimental than men? Do they cry more easily?)

However, the plot itself suggests that there may be pragmatic wisdom in the clerks' apparently groundless decision to avoid women. The presence of actual women entails disease (Pécuchet's fate with Mélie) or financial loss (Bouvard's experience with Madame Bordin) and confirms the clerks in their initial resolve ("No more women, okay? Let's live without them!" [p. 272]). It would appear that the clerks can maintain a certain fluid indeterminacy of gender identity only by retreating from the physical realities of sexual difference. With Pécuchet as symbolic woman, love can flourish, for sexual difference is not a bodily fact, but the arbitrary product of a shared social code.

Subsequently, the clerks replace the code of clichés that initially served to cement their friendship (and which included the mainspring of the plot: "What a good time we could have in the country!" [p. 52]) with a succession of books. Each of these books contains a specialized vocabulary, a hermeneutic code, that they adopt and cathect with erotic energy. The function they expect the book to perform is fetishistic in that its role is to signify and systematize difference precisely by denying the *reality* of difference. The book should, in other words, perform analogously to the code that allowed their romance to flourish at the outset.

Ideally, the clerks want all signification to be translatable into substitute signs within a hermeneutic totality. Thus they are never more happy than on the few occasions when they manage to become both subjects and objects of the code they currently favor. For instance, Pécuchet, during pauses in his gardening, studies his manual while imitating the pose of the gardener pictured on its frontispiece. "This resemblance," we are told, "even flattered him very much. It raised the author in his esteem" (p. 47). Having adopted the technical vocabulary of gardening ("They talked incessantly about sap and cambium, paling, fracture, thinning of buds" [p. 96]), carefully numbered each of his saplings to coincide with his list of their names, and dressed himself in the characteristic costume of the profession, Pécuchet regards himself as fully integrated into the code of signs elaborated in his technical manual. He even seems to consider himself the original model of what he is in fact imitating, as if his sense of origin were a function of his being able to read himself as a sign belonging to a systematic code.

That the translation of a problematic physical reality into purely linguistic formulations has something to do with fetishism is suggested by the case Freud cites in the second paragraph of his essay on fetishism. In this curious case, the phrase from the patient's mother tongue, English, *a glance at the nose,* had been transformed in German into a *Glanz auf den Nase,* that is, "a shine on the nose," and this special brilliance had been exalted into a fetishistic condition. As Guy Rosolato has pointed out, the word that is omitted from Freud's account of this extraordinary case, although it cannot help be heard in the interplay of *glance* and *Glanz,* is the Latin word for penis, *glans.*[3] Rosolato observes that the occulted Latin word acts in Freud's text as a kind of universal signifier, untranslatable itself while it supports and gives meaning to the process of translation between the English and German homophones. Thus the text's *exemplary* denial of the Latin word *glans,* of the word that explicitly evokes the fantasy of the mother's penis, is the equivalent of the fetishist's denial of the difference between the sexes. The absence of *glans,* where the real meaning lies, promotes the movement of translation between languages, while it retains the hidden fantasy of the ultimate inclusion of all semantic differences in one universal language.

Now it is precisely this fantasy that seems to me to determine the structure of Bouvard and Pécuchet's existence. They are constantly attempting to find the rule that will enable them to translate specialized languages either into material reality or into other specialized languages. Were the clerks psychologically plausible characters, one might argue that their fetishistic devotion to books prevents their relationship from becoming overtly homosexual. But the whole psychological framework of analysis collapses as soon as we realize that the clerks' model for continuity and sameness exists much less in the order of biological life than it does in that of bibliography. The fetishist's fantasy of a universal sexual organ is displaced in the clerks' case by a fantasy of a universal library. Whereas the explicitly erotic fetish refers metonymically to sexual uniformity, the book as fetish refers metonymically to what Baudrillard calls "the systematicity of signs."[4] The erotic fantasy that sustains the clerks' enterprises is the conception of a fully interpreted and intelligible world that would dissolve all difference between nature and culture by assimilating both into a uniform code of signification. Such a fantasy resembles Borges's Library of Babel, which "includes all verbal structures, all variations permitted by the twenty-five orthographical symbols, but not a

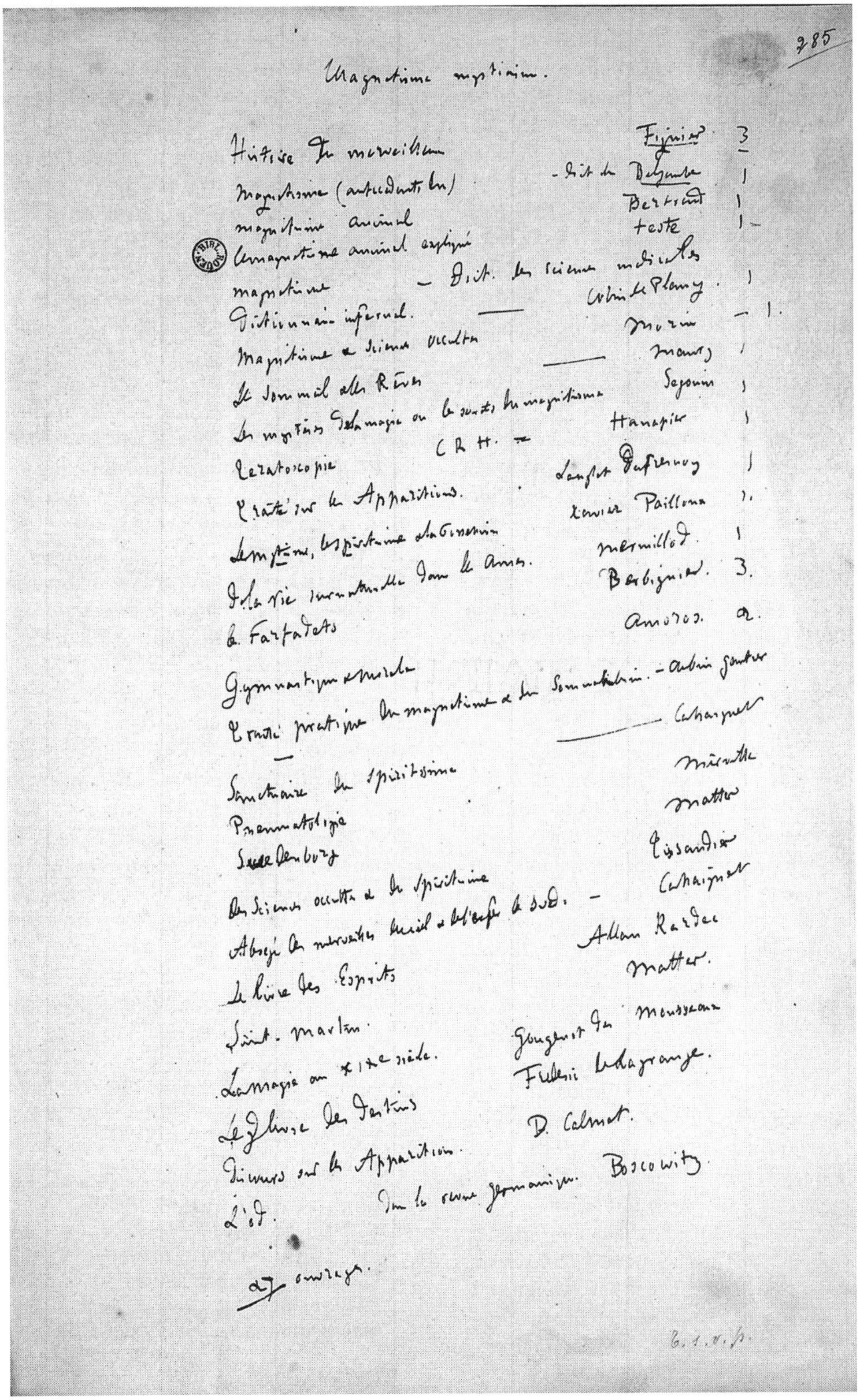

Flaubert made lists of the volumes he read to prepare Bouvard et Pécuchet. *Here he noted the books he needed and annotated for the writing of the passage on "magnetism" and "mysticism" in chapter 8; at the bottom of the page Flaubert wrote: "27 books" (Collections de la Bibliothèque municipale de Rouen. Cliché Thierry Ascencio-Parvy).*

single example of absolute nonsense."[5] The universal library is like the mother's *glans*. It allows for the meaningful determination of differences only by abstracting the signifier from the signified. As maintained in the face of experience, the fantasy of the mother's penis signifies castration, but the signifier, the fetish itself, restores the threatened sense of continuity by a kind of reflexive mirroring, the *glance* reflected back by the shiny *Glanz*.

It is this kind of reflexiveness, or translatability, that the clerks expect each of their bookish codes to be able to produce, as if by contagious magic. Indeed, the ideological fetishism of the signifier is the late capitalistic version of the primitive belief in the magic of names and the omnipotence of thoughts. As Freud points out, the survival of such beliefs in modern man is symptomatic of obsessional neurosis.[6] The obsessive separates himself defensively from the world by retreating into systems and categories whereby a threatening reality is represented and ordered. That this reality is defined most specifically as the difference between the sexes is made clear from Freud's case histories of both the Rat-man and the Wolf-man. The compulsive defends against the fearful implications of sexual difference by considering difference the product of an intellectual act, by making it a purely structural function.

No object of interpretation has significance for the clerks unless it refers as a part to the maternal totality of meaning, unless it serves to bridge the gaps of temporal experience and reconstitute the illusion of sameness and continuity. But the clerks' fetishes repeatedly fail to perform their desired homogenizing function. Even the phallus as universal symbol proves inadequate to the task (remember the moment when "for Bouvard and Pécuchet everything became a phallus" [p. 180]). Unlike Frédéric and Madame Arnoux, they find no code to signify the union of "flesh and spirit." Nature's manner of transforming itself in time remains totally alien to the linguistic code of changes invented to translate natural phenomena into cultural signification. The clerks' study of geology, for instance, convinces them that "everything decays, crumbles, changes form. Creation is put together in a fluctuating and transient manner" (p. 159). Later in the novel when they take on speculative disciplines such as aesthetics, philosophy, and religion, these purely cultural creations seem just as resistant to translation into a single differential code as had the uncertain fluctuations of nature. Thus, having studied the major philosophers, Bouvard concludes: "The proofs of God's existence given by Descartes, Kant, and Leibniz are not the same and mutually cancel each other out" (pp. 308–9).

Instead of achieving translation, integration, and ultimate sameness, the clerks' activities result in the revelation of unbridgeable difference and the proliferation of ruins. Their discovery of semantic arbitrariness, irreducible heterogeneity, and temporal flux in every field of knowledge they explore signals the collapse of the fetishistic mechanism that determines their existence. Yet the clerks do not respond to this collapse with the castration anxiety the psychoanalytic model for their conduct would lead one to expect. They are occasionally discouraged by their failures, but most often they move on without regret to the next supposedly authoritative code. This apparent advance is not progressive, however. The clerks make no instructive connections between their various failures. Each remains isolated, and their very lives seem to reflect this fragmented and discontinuous structure. It is as if their subjectivities were recreated with each new code they fetishize and existed only as long as the unifying function of that code remained in force. They have no psychological history, no past lives that permeate the present. Admittedly, we are given the barest outlines of Bouvard's and Pécuchet's biographies, but these supposedly lived pasts play no significant role in the present of the narrative and could just as well be the reductive digests of two books they have read. Thus for the reader their existence as coherent psychological subjects is as problematic as is the coherence of any one of the hermeneutic codes they adopt. Their fetishism seems to have an almost entirely structural function in the text, as the vehicle of the desire for structure.

The results of the clerks' obsession with structure are nowhere more brilliantly displayed than in their ornamental garden. This is how the garden appears to the clerks' astonished guests when, after dinner, the curtains are drawn apart:

> In the twilight it was something quite frightening. The rock, like a mountain, occupied the lawn, the tomb formed a cube in the middle of the spinach, the Venetian bridge a circumflex accent over the kidney beans–and the cabin beyond made a large black smudge, for they had burned its roof to make it more poetic. The yews, trimmed into the shapes of stags or armchairs, stretched one after the other as far as the blasted tree, which extended diagonally from the arbor to the bower, where love apples hung like stalactites. A sunflower here and there displayed its yellow disc. The Chinese pagoda, painted red, looked like a lighthouse on the mound. The peacocks' beaks, caught by the sun, sent sparks of light back and forth, and behind the fence, cleared of its boards, the completely flat countryside closed the horizon. [Pp. 106–7]

This surreal landscape collects in one space objects belonging to at least two disparate conceptions of what constitutes a garden. On the one hand are some familiar components of a vegetable garden: spinach, kidney beans, love apples (tomatoes), to which one could perhaps link the sunflower. On the other hand are the widely divergent elements belonging to the clerks' fetishizing interpretation of the symbolic code for ornamental gardens found in Pierre Boitard's book *L'Architecte des jardins* (1852). These are the rock, tomb, Venetian bridge, burnt cabin, blasted tree, and Chinese pagoda. The first series of elements has a coherence we recognize from our experience of vegetable gardens; the second series is an entirely incoherent mixture born of the clerks' response to the arbitrary symbolic equivalences invented by Boitard.

The juxtaposition of these two systems, the one homogeneous, the other heterogeneous, gives rise to a third system of images, which are the metaphoric transformations of elements from the first two: mountain, cube, circumflex accent, large black smudge, stalactites, disc, lighthouse. These metaphors apparently reflect the impressions of the clerks' guests who are viewing the garden for the first time. The paragraph is introduced by the sentence "The curtains parted and the garden appeared" (p. 106) and followed by a single-sentence paragraph, "The astonishment of their guests filled Bouvard and Pécuchet with true delight" (p. 107). However, we may well wonder how any of the guests could have known that the turned-up tin hat on red stilts was meant to be a pagoda, that what was described earlier as "a quadrilateral of black plaster, six feet high, resembling a dog kennel" (p. 101) was indeed a tomb, that the bridge was Venetian, or that the black smudge had once been a cabin. Observing this, one might conclude that the metaphors belong to the narrator, who is putting himself momentarily in the place of the clerks' guests and condensing their collective response to the scene into his own terms. Yet his terms are intended to explain the guests' astonishment, so the origin of the series of metaphors vacillates and ultimately remains undecidable.

The metaphoric images themselves, however, have just as much presence in the paragraph as do the images of perceptible objects. They do not serve to unify the scene in relation to a perceiving subject, but appear as separate entities in a kind of unstable collage. In fact, by the end of the passage the reader's confident assumption that perception determines reality has effectively been destroyed. Does anyone actually *see* a Chinese pagoda or the beaks of peacocks? The various elements come to seem equally derealized in a landscape that juxtaposes some of the components of a traditional still life to the geometric forms of abstract art (cube, circumflex accent, black splotch, yellow disc). Finally, all of the nouns in the paragraph, be they "spinach" (actual garden vegetable) "stags" (shape given to yew trees), "stalactites" (appearance of love apples, already a figurative description for tomatoes), or "lighthouse" (metaphor for the "Chinese pagoda," itself an obscure symbolic construction), are absorbed into the sparkling play of reflections between the peacocks' beaks (cones made of an unspecified substance) and ultimately flattened out on the plane of the horizon.

If the clerks initially experience a kind of erotic *jouissance* at the response of their guests to their fantastic exhibit, it is because they imagine that the guests have been able to read the garden's meaning and that they are all united in a shared enjoyment of the victory of ideology over nature. Moments later, however, they find that the code has not been understood after all: "The tomb was not understood, nor the burned cabin, nor the ruined wall" (p. 107). And the guests even permit themselves various critical remarks, based on their own ideological viewpoints, about what they find lacking or excessive. But whereas the clerks fail to absorb difference into universal signification, another kind of absorption takes place through the agency of Flaubert's style. Indeed, the process of equalization and leveling that occurs in the description of the garden perfectly fulfills Roman Jakobson's description of the poetic function: the metaphoric principle of equivalence has been projected onto the metonymic axis of succession.[7] The clerks are agents of metaphoric structurality: their desire is to translate the world into representational codes bound within a hermeneutic totality. Their defeat comes as this ideal is projected onto the metonymic axis of temporal succession, or, in Jakobson's phrase, as "similarity is superinduced upon contiguity."[8]

The effect of such projection, as Joel Fineman has brilliantly argued, is essentially allegorical.[9] The allegorical quest, in Fineman's view, is motivated formally by the desire to recuperate the fracture in some original hermeneutic totality caused by the inevitable metonymic component of any metaphoric structure. Flaubert makes this quest seem particularly futile in that the clerks' fetishism suggests the purely phantasmatic nature of the very notion of totality. Metonymy for them is a figure for bonding structure to a lost origin, the perfect systematicity of all signs; it is not a figure for temporal succession, but one for regressive nostalgia. Opposed to this desire is the conception of metonymy embodied in Flaubert's style. His writing conveys temporality as the repetitive accumulation in space of isolated fragments and disjunctive pieces, the creation, one could say, of ever more gaps. "Allegories," says Walter Benjamin in a memorable formulation, "are, in the realm of thoughts, what ruins are in the realm of things."[10]

Spread out on the metonymic axis, signs in *Bouvard et Pécuchet* seem to become part of a *danse macabre* celebrating their emancipation from the maternal con-

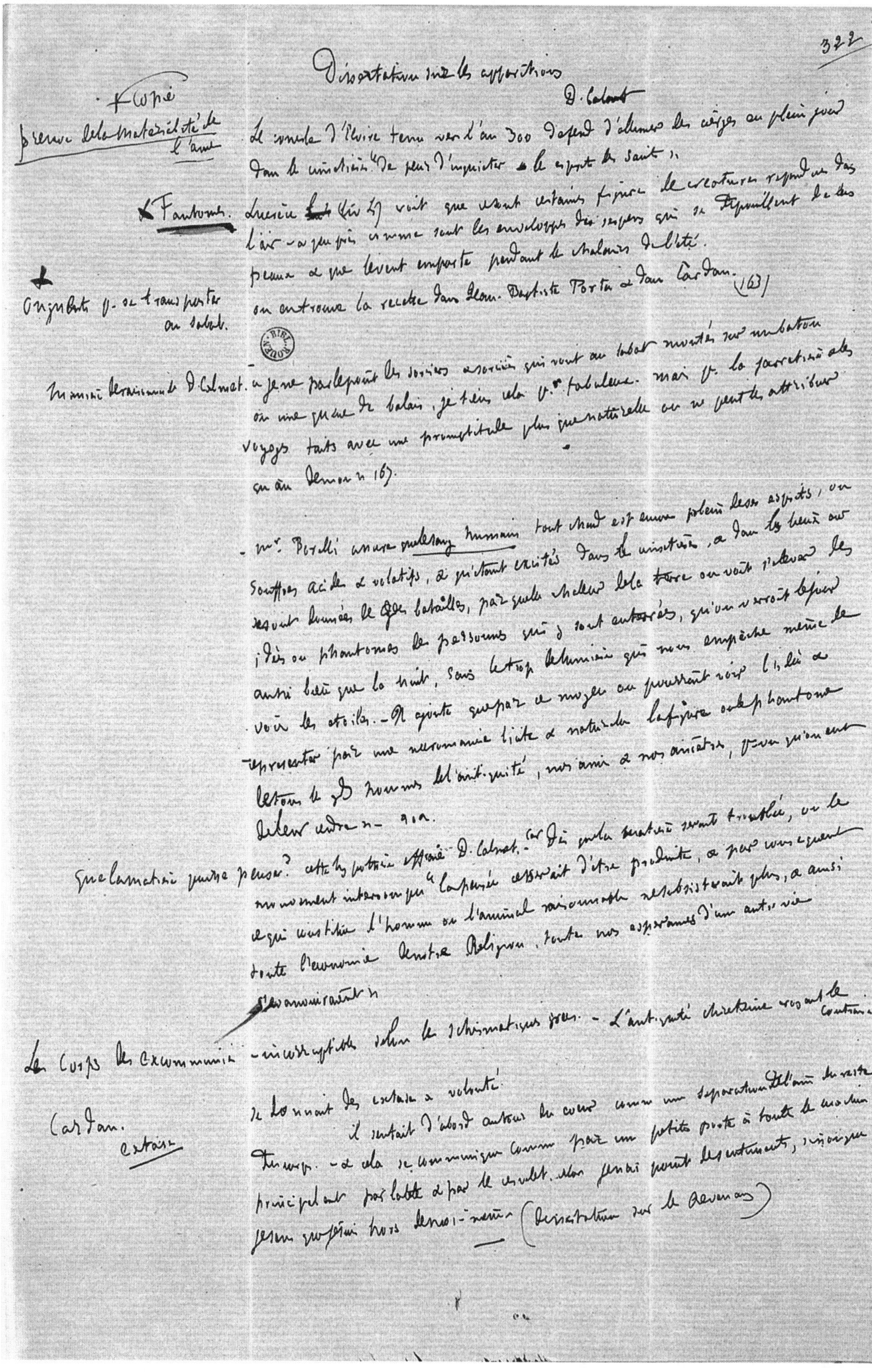

322

Dissertation sur les apparitions

D. Calmet

Preuve de la matérialité de l'âme

A page of Flaubert's notes on Dom Calmet's book about ghosts and spirits, Dissertation sur les apparitions, *which Flaubert read before writing the episode in which Bouvard and Pécuchet want to experiment with magic in chapter 8 of the novel (Collections de la Bibliothèque municipale de Rouen. Cliché Thierry Ascencio-Parvy)*

text of the library, or any other unifying context, and their subjection to materiality and death. Indeed, this movement of deconstruction and designification may be understood quite precisely in psychoanalytic terms as a function of the death instinct, whose aim, Freud declared, "is to undo connections and so to destroy things."[11] The death instinct works to diminish tensions to a zero point, to a point where all significant differences are reduced to their common denominator in inorganic matter.[12]

Flaubert's technique of flattening out onto a single plane discrete images isolated from their normal context is a manifestation of this mode of reduction, one that is typical of allegorical practice. Angus Fletcher remarks: "An allegorical world gives us objects all lined up, as it were, on the frontal plane of a mosaic, each with its 'true,' unchanging size and shape. . . . Allegory has an idealizing consistency of thematic content because, in spite of the visual absurdity of much allegorical imagery, the relations between ideas are under strong logical control."[13] Flaubert's logical control could not be stronger. But the ideal his logic is serving, the truth of the images he presents in the discontinuous, surrealistic surface of his text, does not fill the gaps between unrelated images with redeeming meaning. Rather, it insists on those gaps as being themselves the revelation of the final truth. It is one of the most radical aspects of Walter Benjamin's theory of allegory that he considers this insistence, whereby "allegory goes away empty handed,"[14] as determining what is most specific to the allegorical universe.

The clerks' obsession with structure, and with its loss, gives them the unnatural Faustian energy, the antisocial tendencies, and the quasi-scientific curiosity about the order of things that Fletcher associates with the allegorical hero. Their lives, however, are subject to the destructuring violence that flattens them out as effectively as the elements of their garden are equalized in the reflections of the peacocks' beaks. These reflections thus perform a function directly opposed to those functions I discussed earlier between *Glanz* and *glance*. The fetish, I noted, permits the decoding of the significant difference between homophones and the meaningful translation between languages. In contrast, Flaubert's style foregrounds words in their essential untranslatability as things. In allegory, comments Benjamin, "word, syllable, and sound are emancipated from any context of traditional meaning and are flaunted as objects."[15] This objectification makes translation impossible, while it creates a pervasive sense of substitutability, any word seeming to be of equal value to the next, as if their relation to reality were as arbitrary as the assignation of proper names. That arbitrariness defines the radical difference that, in allegory, separates a creation at once "fluctuating and transient" from its signification, indeed even from its proper nomination.

The possibility of such nominal dissociation is suggested in the opening scene of the novel when each clerk reads the other's name in the hat he has just removed and placed by his side on the bench. The proper referent for the name is indicated by the metonymic proximity of hat and person and on the basis of the social convention through which you signify ownership by inscribing your name. But there is, of course, no necessary link between the names and the individuals who have just removed (their?) hats. Either man might have borrowed his headpiece, perhaps from a friend who had been given the hat by someone else, who in turn might conceivably have written his father-in-law's name in it as a mnemonic device. In any case, by the end of the novel the clerks have repeatedly experienced the arbitrariness of names–their failure to demonstrate possession or signify origin. At that point they decide to treat any name, be it found in a hat, museum, or library, as mere language subject to copy.

According to Flaubert's plan for the conclusion to the second volume, their last act would have been to reproduce the rough draft of a letter, found by chance amidst masses of discarded writing, in which the clerks themselves are designated as "inoffensive imbeciles" (p. 443). The clerks ask themselves what to do with it and decide: "No reflections! Let's copy it! The page must fill up, 'the monument' must be completed–equality of everything, of the good and the bad, the beautiful and the ugly, the insignificant and the characteristic. Only phenomena are true" (p. 443). From fetishists of the signifier, the clerks have become memorialists of the signifier's demise. First among the differences that are canceled out through the activity of transcription is the code that established their own sexual difference. In one of the scenarios, Flaubert noted at the end of the novel: "In the joy of copying and the community of passion they become the same man and . . . resemble each other physically."[16] This collapse of physical difference reflects the collapse of nominal specificity that makes the clerks' names appear in the *copie* as just two syllabic combinations (with the same etymological meaning: *bos* = *pecus* [ox-herd]) among countless others–Taranis, Pacchioni, Borelli, Clodowig, Fécamp, Cambrian, Gabrielle de Vergy, Agamemnon, Mont Faunes, Foureau, Béchet, Buffon, Becquerel, Bouvard, Marescot, Marmontel, Marianne–so many names out of a mad hatter's hat, signifying nothing.

Or perhaps they do signify something, in the manner in which a relic signifies the death of a whole being and by its presence, albeit as a fragment, even a repulsive one, assures against the reality of our own death. Indeed, the relic plays the same role in relation to the death instinct that the fetish does in relation to Eros. What is denied by the fetish is the reality of castration; what is denied by the relic is the reality of the putrefying corpse.[17] Yet the relic also participates in the uncanny power of death's otherness, just as the fetish gains its efficacy from that female otherness that it serves at once to forget and to re-member. Thus the clerks' monument is not only a pyramid in which the epistemological claims of the library are laid to rest. The monument is actually made up of rests, fragments that have survived the destructive process, whose survival suggests the possibility of mastering death. This is why "'the monument' must be completed." It may be an ironic monument (hence the quotation marks between which Flaubert places the word) in that it is composed of bits and pieces of the dead. But as monument it has a chance to hold firm and erect through time. Its creation, like that of the fetish, is a symptom of obsessional neurosis. The monument brings structure back into the chaos of fragments. (We need only think of the clerks'–and Flaubert's–numerous *classements*). In terms of this return of structure, the *copie* represents that moment of *Umschwung,* of turnabout, that Benjamin describes when allegory "denies the void in which it is represented [and] faithlessly leaps forward to the idea of resurrection."[18] Flaubert's leap is much less extravagant: he imagines that a monument to death can survive the death it memorializes.

–Charles Bernheimer, "Fetishism and Allegory in Bouvard et Pécuchet," in *Flaubert and Postmodernism,* edited by Naomi Schor and Henry F. Majewski (Lincoln & London: University of Nebraska Press, 1984), pp. 163–176

---

1. Flaubert, *Bouvard et Pécuchet,* ed. Claudine Gothot-Mersch (Paris: Gallimard, 1979), p. 59. Subsequent references in my text are to this edition, the most accurate currently available. The text of the Seuil L'Intégrale edition is not reliable.
2. Claudine Gothot-Mersch, "*Bouvard et Pécuchet:* Sur la genèse des personnages," in *Flaubert à l'œuvre* (Paris: Flammarion, 1980).
3. Guy Rosolato, "Le Fétichisme dont se dérobe l'objet," *Nouvelle Revue de psychanalyse,* no. 2 (Fall 1970), pp. 31–39.
4. Baudrillard, "Fétichisme et idéologie" [*Nouvelle Revue de psychanalyse,* no. 2 (Fall 1970)], p. 217.
5. Jorge Luis Borges, *Labyrinths: Selected Stories and Other Writings,* ed. Donald A. Yates and James E. Irby (New York: New Directions, 1964), p. 57.
6. See Sigmund Freud, *Totem and Taboo,* trans. James Strachey (New York: Norton, 1950), pp. 86–90.
7. See Roman Jakobson, "Linguistics and Poetics," in *The Structuralists from Marx to Lévi-Strauss,* ed. Richard and Fernande De George (New York: Anchor Books, 1972), p. 95.
8. Ibid., p. 111.
9. Joel Fineman, "The Structure of Allegorical Desire," in *Allegory and Representation: Selected Papers From the English Institute, 1979–80,* ed. Stephen Greenblatt (Baltimore, Md.: Johns Hopkins University Press, 1981), pp. 26–60.
10. Walter Benjamin, *The Origin of German Tragic Drama,* trans. John Osborne (London: New Left Books, 1977), p. 178.
11. Sigmund Freud, *An Outline of Psychoanalysis,* trans. James Strachey (New York: Norton, 1949), p. 5.
12. Eugenio Donato has suggested that Flaubert conceived of the force that defeats the clerks' desire on a model analogous to the second law of thermodynamics. This law states that energy goes from a differentiated to an undifferentiated state. Time is understood as moving toward an abolition of differences through a slow but inexorable process of corruption and decay. Such a conception bears an evident similarity to the Freudian death instinct, which works to reduce tensions and return the differentiated organism to an inanimate state. See Eugenio Donato, "The Museum's Furnace: Notes toward a Contextual Reading of *Bouvard and Pécuchet,*" in *Textual Strategies: Perspectives in Post-Structuralist Criticism,* ed. Josué Harari (Ithaca, N.Y.: Cornell University Press, 1979), pp. 213–38.
13. Angus Fletcher, *Allegory: The Theory of a Symbolic Mode* (Ithaca, N.Y.: Cornell University Press, 1964), pp. 104–5.
14. Benjamin, *The Origin of German Tragic Drama,* p. 233. . . .
15. Benjamin, *The Origin of German Tragic Drama,* p. 207.
16. Quoted by Gothot-Mersch, *"Bouvard et Pécuchet,"* p. 151.
17. Pierre Fédida makes this point in his article "La Relique et le travail du deuil," *Nouvelle Revue de psychanalyse,* no. 2 (Fall 1970): "The relic, which in itself is a ridiculous and repulsive remnant, puts the corpse and its putrefaction outside the sphere of representation" (p. 252).
18. Benjamin, *The Origin of German Tragic Drama,* p. 233.

* * *

Flaubert always said that he hated the artificiality of "dialogues" in narratives, and the issue of speech and discourse has been addressed many times in Flaubertian criticism. In this article, Stirling Haig examines Flaubert's technique of free indirect discourse in Bouvard et Pécuchet, *which has changed radically since* Madame Bovary.

Bouvard et Pécuchet and the End of Dialogue

The difference between *L'Éducation sentimentale* and *Bouvard et Pécuchet* would seem to mark the boundary between a nineteenth-century confidence in fiction's signifying power, however ironically articulated, and an unmitigated rejection of the novel as a valid mimetic form. Indeed, *Bouvard et Pécuchet* appears to constitute an attack on all culture, and a recognition that the novel has reached an esthetic deadend. And, as if to repel once and for all the label

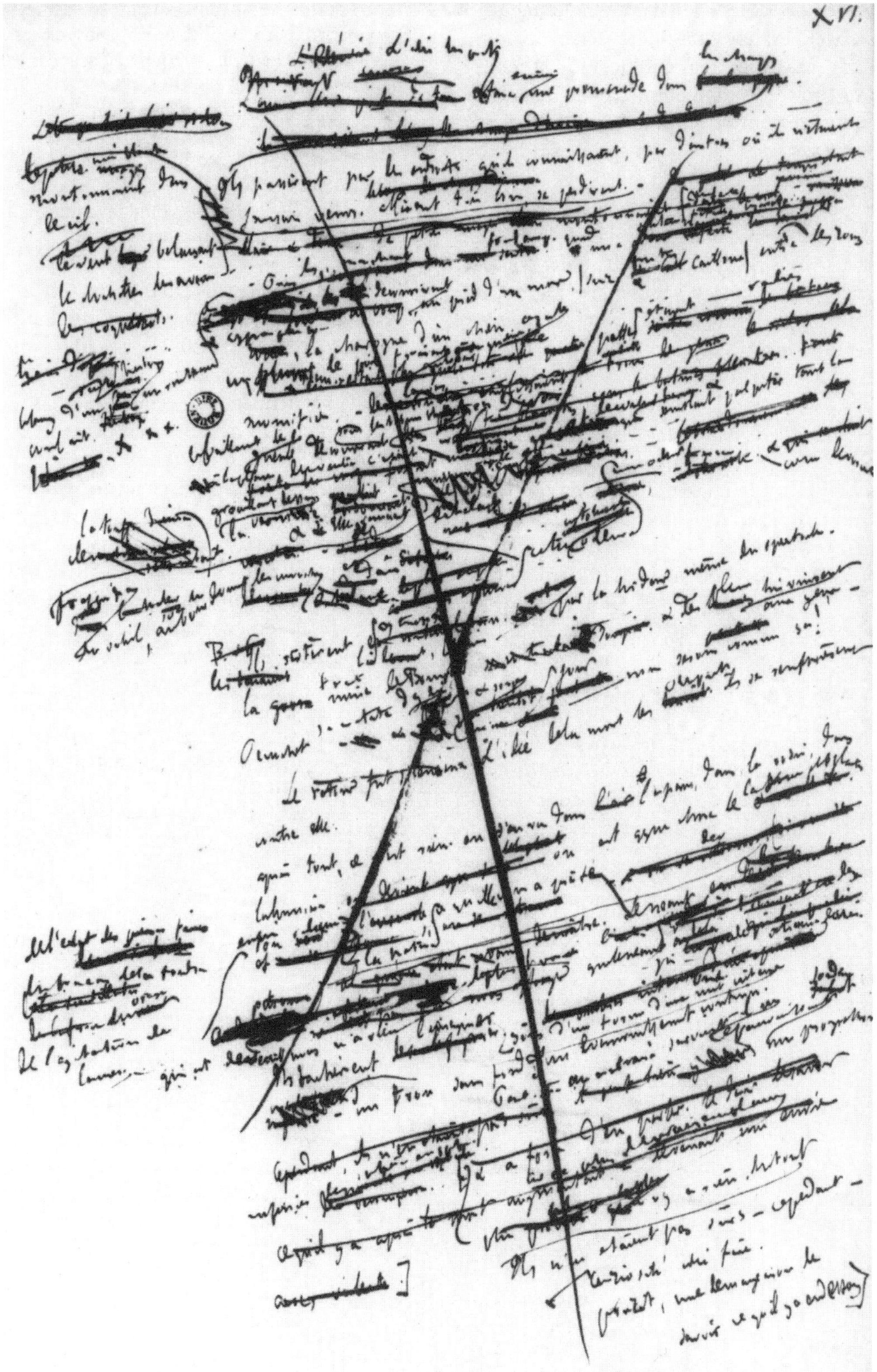

Page from a draft for the scene in which Bouvard and Pécuchet find the carcass of a dog at the end of chapter 8. Flaubert's handwriting, always difficult to decipher, was particulary bad in his late work on Bouvard et Pécuchet, *written when he was depressed and exhausted (Collections de la Bibliothèque municipale de Rouen).*

of *réaliste* that he so loathed, Flaubert would seem to have written a deliberately non-referential work, one whose reading retraces its own composition, thereby referring readers to the 1,500 volumes that the author claimed to have devoured during his preparatory work. "The very writing of the book can be said to be its subject," states Victor Brombert.[1]

Yet the novelty of *Bouvard et Pécuchet* is not so great that it has not been constantly related, by virtue of its encyclopedism, to *La Tentation de Saint Antoine,* the work that Flaubert himself obsessively "retraced" three times during his lifetime. *Bouvard et Pécuchet* would be the modern counterpart of the Saint's story, and "aura les prétentions d'être comique" ["will have the pretension to be comic"] (1 July 1872).[2]

The ties with *L'Éducation sentimentale* are nearly as strong, though. After finishing *Salammbô,* Flaubert had pondered his next undertaking, hesitating between *L'Éducation* and "Les Deux Cloportes" ["The Two Woodlice"] (an early title of *Bouvard et Pécuchet;* and he once wrote that in *Madame Bovary* he had tried to give the impression of a woodlouse's existence). Both books share strong historical and intellectual underpinning in the 1848 Revolution, as Claudine Gothot-Mersch has noted in her excellent edition of the work.[3] There is the same satire of Utopian socialist writings and reactionary ravings, pastiches of political speechifying (accompanied as always with mentions of dung heaps), a futile attempt at suicide, a clumsy visit to a bordello ending in flight (Pécuchet ran away in order to preserve himself for the wife "he would later have"), and most of all, the same recommencement: the end of each book returns to its beginning, completing the circularity that constitutes the grand figuration or trajectory of all Flaubert's major works.

Once more, two fast friends self-consciously embark upon an education of sorts, leading to repeated cycles of opposition between literature and life, love and power, knowledge and action, and yielding in the end only the failure–or perhaps consolation–of reinscription.[4] The two "cretins," copy-clerks at the outset of their intellectual adventure, return to copying in Flaubert's plans for the unfinished last chapter. They have a double desk made for them, purchase copybooks, sand sprinklers, erasers, and then–"Ils s'y mettent" ["They begin"]. Theirs truly are unnourishing occupations that validate another of Flaubert's early titles for the book, one that it shares with *L'Éducation,* "Les Fruits secs" ["Dry Fruits"].[5]

Bouvard et Pécuchet begins conventionally enough, with the chance yet fateful meeting of the two clerks and a conversation launched by the discovery of a text, something written in their hats: their names.

> –Tiens, dit-il, nous avons eu la même idée, celle d'inscrire notre nom dans nos couvre-chefs.
> –Mon Dieu, oui, on pourrait prendre le mien à mon bureau!
> –C'est comme moi, je suis employé.
>
> [–So, he said, we had the same idea, that is, write our names in our hats.
> –My God, yes, one could take mine at my office.
> –It's like me, I'm a clerk.]

At this stage of their story, the two friends are interchangeable, with the exception that Bouvard is tall and Pécuchet short. But they could easily be a pair of pathetic Beckettian clowns, Mutt 'n' Jeff, or an Ionesco couple, so identical and redundant that they must wear huge name cards around their necks. It is impossible, in the excerpt just quoted, to say with certainty who speaks first. Both are forty-seven years old, both copyists! Such discoveries unite them in a sympathy that is inexplicable; *it is:* "Ce qu'on appelle le coup de foudre est vrai pour toutes les passions" ["What is called love at first sight is true for all passions"] (II, 204). Their characters interpenetrate, as they express mutual disgust for their hopeless situation:

> Pécuchet contracta la brusquerie de Bouvard, Bouvard prit quelque chose de la morosité de Pécuchet.
> –J'ai envie de me faire saltimbanque sur les places publiques! disait l'un.
> –Autant être chiffonnier! s'écriait l'autre.
> Quelle situation abominable! Et nul moyen d'en sortir! Pas même d'espérance! (II, 205)
>
> [Pécuchet contracted the abruptness of Bouvard, Bouvard took something from Pécuchet's gloominess.
> –I want to become an acrobat on public squares! one said.
> –You might as well be a rag collector! exclaimed the other.
> What an abominable situation! And no way to get out of it! Not even hope!]

This lament illustrates the interchangeable nature of the voices. The text, in order to underscore this, does not trouble to particularize the *inquit* phrases, which remain completely unspecified: "disait l'un, s'écriait l'autre" ["one said, exclaimed the other"] FID [Free Indirect Discourse] (here voiceless) obviously plumps for the effect of a comic duet, and indeed choral responses are one of the most striking features of dialogue in *Bouvard et Pécuchet.* When the clerks do find a way out, thanks to Bouvard's inheritance, they dream of leaving Paris for the freedom of the countryside: "–Nous ferons tout ce qui nous plaira! nous laisserons pousser notre barbe!" ["–We will do anything that will please us! We will let our beards grow out!"] they exclaim in unison, in a satirical assumption of petty bourgeois liberty. Throughout the book, though their perspectives may differ, they are united through an ineradicable compulsion to seek knowledge, and their voices will yield, as we shall see, to the discourse of science and "wisdom."

In this respect, the handling of FID in *Bouvard et Pécuchet* is instructive. Its status is totally different from that in *Madame Bovary,* where it was an instrument of retrieval and redemption, rescuing Emma's inner discourse from platitudinous gushings or regurgitations of passages lifted from Romantic novels. Emma, when she speaks, does indeed sound like a book, but . . . the narrator intervened to point out the tragic inadequation of speech to feeling. Through FID, he sought to lyricize the cliché and Emma's tenacious belief, which reinvigorated her moribund Romantic idols. It was an intensely subjective phenomenon. In *Bouvard et Pécuchet,* however, FID plays so restricted a role that it virtually disappears before a larger, enigmatic type of pseudo-authoritative discourse. Bouvard and Pécuchet's inner existence, unlike Emma's, is so shallow that there are few depths to tap, and FID here is generally restricted to a synoptical function, as a means of rapid summarizing. It has become a purely grammatical phenomenon that is close to indirect discourse. Thus Bouvard and Pécuchet, in the midst of their study of organic chemistry, discover that humans and minerals contain the same elements:

> Quelle merveille que de retrouver chez les êtres vivants les mêmes substances qui composent les minéraux! (II, 219)

> [What a marvel to find among living beings the same substances which make up minerals!]

Few basic distinctions separate this choral FID from numerous other choral responses cast in direct speech. From *Madame Bovary* through *L'Éducation sentimentale* to *Bouvard et Pécuchet,* the history of FID is its progressive effacement, its reduction from a device of great psychological import to an indistinctive stylistic flourish, from chord to grace note.[6] The consequence of this subsidence of the phenomenon of the dual voice is no less than the decline, almost the death, of the narrator, for the two idiots–and the texts they study–survive as the only sources of sign production. The vestigial uses of FID are often mere "interferences." Thus when Pécuchet finds it impossible to purchase horse manure for the compost heap he dreams of, he sets out on the road in search of it:

This little pavilion, turned into the Musée Flaubert at the beginning of the twentieth century, is all that remains from Flaubert's residence in Croisset. Flaubert's niece Caroline sold the property in May 1881, one year after her uncle's death. The main house was completely destroyed and replaced by a building that successively served as a distillery, a chemical factory, and finally a paper manufacturer (photograph by Éric Le Calvez).

> Enfin, après beaucoup de recherches, malgré les instances de Bouvard et abjurant toute pudeur, il prit le parti «d'aller lui-même au crottin!» (II, 209)

> Finally, after much research, in spite of any advice of Bouvard and giving up all decency, he took upon himself to «go himself for horse manure!»

The curious transformation of **moi-même* [*myself*] into *lui-même* [*himself*] within the quoted speech marked by *guillemets* [*quotation marks*] can only be attributed to a latent reflexive shift of pronouns from first to third person that operates within FID formation. Thus the *guillemets* [*quotation marks*] are either a "mistake," or more likely, Flaubert wished to foreground *crottin,* the word for horse droppings. Italics might have been expected to point to this vulgarity in earlier works, but italics, except for titles and Latin phrases, have also disappeared from *Bouvard et Pécuchet,* where the grand and the grotesque flow into one another. Discourse here is experienced chiefly as *alterity*–it has become something else, and dialogue has actually evanesced, been absorbed into an alien text. Let us consider the following:

> Les jachères, selon Bouvard, étaient un préjugé gothique. Cependant Leclerc note les cas où elles sont presque indispensables. Gasparin cite un Lyonnais qui, pendant un demi-siècle, a cultivé des céréales sur le même champ: cela renverse la théorie des assolements. Tull exalte les labours au préjudice des engrais; et voilà le major Beetson qui supprime les engrais avec les labours! (II, 211)

> [Fallows, according to Bouvard, were a gothic prejudice. However, Leclerc notes cases where they are almost indispensable. Gasparin cites a man from Lyon who, for half a century, cultivated grain in the same field: that overturns the theory of rotations. Tull exalts plowings in the detriment of fertilizers; and here Major Beetson suppresses fertilizers with plowings!]

In an irritated reaction to such passages as this in Chapter 2 of *Bouvard et Pécuchet,* Margaret Tillett complains that "Flaubert's researches into farming and gardening have been exactly the same as those he suggests to his heroes."[7] Precisely! The passage is an excellent example of what we might call Flaubert's "citational style," his structural nesting of text within text, a form of *emboîtement* [*fitting together*] that is peculiar to this strange novel. Here the primary, or citing text, is constituted itself by a host of intertextual latencies that emerge in the form of quoted summaries. The protagonists' voices (by now we can see that their choral responses amount to a new sort of "dual" voice) are *overspoken* by mutually contradictory experts: Leclerc, Gasparin, Tull, Major Beetson. We have something like a voiced text, but we do not have the possibility of knowing for certain the source of that voice. The "cependant" ["however"] and the exclamation point at the end would seem to mark a certain affectivity or subjectivity emanating from the character. But other information could just as easily be construed as having been provided by the narrator, or merely as one-line summaries of the books themselves.

Now summaries are a disturbing feature of *Bouvard et Pécuchet,* and they are crucial to critical debates over what the novel's definitive form might have been. We have an accurate idea of Chapters 9 and 10 from Flaubert's plans. But there was also to have been a second volume to *Bouvard et Pécuchet,* a volume consisting "presque entièrement en citations" ["almost entirely in citations"] (25 January 1880). Flaubert also spoke to various people about this second volume: Edmond de Goncourt, Maupassant, Henry Céard. Based on what they recollected, and what Flaubert himself wrote, the second volume would have been a transcription of notes taken on the autodidacts' readings mentioned in volume one. These quotations would have brought out the contradictions and *bêtise* [*stupidity*] of these works. We certainly have a taste of what this might have yielded in the contradictory passage on fertilizing and ploughing cited above, and in the texts bearing the collective title of *Sottisier.* An often quoted example from this compendium of foolish sayings, stylistic infelicities, and factual errors, is this excerpt from Eugène Scribe's reception speech to the Académie Française (Flaubert's comment is given in italics):

> La comédie de Molière nous instruit-elle des grands événements du siècle de Louis XIV? Nous dit-elle un mot des erreurs, des faiblesses ou des fautes du grand roi? Nous parle-t-elle de la Révocation de l'Édit de Nantes? (*Molière mort en 1673. Révocation de l'Édit de Nantes en 1685.*)

> [Do Molière's comedies teach us important events from the century of Louis XIV? Do they say a word on the errors, the weakness or the mistakes of the grand king? Do they speak to us of the Revocation of the Edict of Nantes? (*Molière dead in 1673. Revocation of the Edict of Nantes in 1685*).]

Several passages touch upon language: "Il est une langue européenne qui a beaucoup d'analogie avec la langue écrite des Chinois, c'est la langue anglaise" ["There is a European language which has many analogies with the written Chinese language, it is the English language"] (Buchez); "Les langues des sauvages ne peuvent être que des débris de langues antiques, ruinées, s'il est permis de s'exprimer ainsi, et dégradées comme les hommes qui les parlent" ["Languages of the savages can only be the debris of old languages, ruined, if it is permitted to thus express oneself, and degraded like the men who speak them"] (De Maistre); "Van Helmont croyait la langue hébraïque, la langue naturelle de l'homme" ["Van Helmont believed that the Hebrew language was the natural language of mankind"] (Gérando); "Les pharmaciens américains fournissent des spécifiques pour faire parler hébreu, grec et latin" ["American druggists provide medications to make you speak Hebrew, Greek and Latin"] (Rogers).

Claudine Gothot-Mersch finds it hard to believe in the very concept of a second volume that would have been nearly three hundred pages of unrelieved quotations.[8] She notes that Flaubert's scenarios demonstrate an increasing concern for maintaining a narrative, a "story" component in the second volume. He would have told what had happened in the village since Bouvard and Pécuchet began their copying (Chapter 11) and invented this "conclusion" in Chapter 12:

> Un jour, ils trouvent (dans les vieux papiers de la manufacture) le brouillon d'une lettre de Vaucorbeil à M. le Préfet.
>
> Le Préfet lui avait demandé si Bouvard et Pécuchet n'étaient pas des fous dangereux. La lettre du docteur est un rapport confidentiel expliquant que ce sont deux imbéciles inoffensifs. En résumant toutes leurs actions et pensées, elle doit pour le lecteur, être la critique du roman.
>
> –«Qu'allons-nous en faire?»–Pas de réflexion! Copions! Il faut que la page s'emplisse, que le «monument» se complète.–égalité de tout, du bien et du mal, du Beau et du laid, de l'insignifiant et du caractéristique. Il n'y a de vrai que les phénomènes.–
>
> Finir sur la vue des deux bonshommes penchés sur leur pupitre, et copiant.[9]
>
> [One day, they find (among old papers from the manufactory) the draft of a letter from Vaucorbeil to M. le Préfet.
>
> M. le Préfet had asked him if Bouvard et Pécuchet were not dangerous madmen. The doctor's letter is a confidential report explaining that they are two inoffensive imbeciles. Summarizing all their actions and thoughts, it should be, for the reader, the critique of the novel.
>
> –«What are we going to do with it?»–No comment! Let's copy! The page needs to be filled out, the «monument» must complete itself.–equality of everything, good and evil, Beauty and ugly, insignificant and characteristic. There is nothing true but phenomena.
>
> Finish with a view of the two men bent over their desk, and copying.]

According to D. L. Demorest, however, Chapters 11 and 12 would have been the *introduction* to the second volume, the bulk of the novel to be formed by Bouvard and Pécuchet's copy.[10] Alberto Cento's refutation of Demorest does not advance the reader of *Bouvard et Pécuchet* very much.[11] In the absence of conclusive proof as to Flaubert's intentions, the present-day reader, used to reading inside a single cover the novel plus some annexes (usually the *Dictionnaire des idées reçues,* sometimes the *Dictionnaire* and *Catalogue des idées chic* and/or the *Sottisier*) is safe to surmise that with this he has a roughly accurate idea of what the definitive volume might have been like.

The disturbing factor of *Bouvard et Pécuchet* is the absence of a clearly demarcated, *locatable* narrative instance. As mentioned above, the summaries of the characters' readings are often impossible to ascribe to a single source–character, treatise, narrator. The encyclopedic bits, the discourse of "knowledge," are left suspended in a kind of narrative no man's land. Roland Barthes wrote of the *logosphere:*

> Tout ce que nous lisons et entendons nous recouvre comme une nappe, nous entoure et nous enveloppe comme un milieu: c'est la logosphère. Cette logosphère nous est donnée par notre époque, notre classe, notre métier: c'est une "donnée" de notre sujet.[12]
>
> [Everything we read and hear covers us like a sheet, surrounds us and envelopes us like a milieu: this is the logosphere. This logosphere is given to us by our era, our class, our work: it is a «given» belonging to us.

The logosphere of *Bouvard et Pécuchet* is perturbed by a discourse that *disoriginates* itself. Utterances become freefloating, and there results a strange sort of enunciative "jamming" that lends itself to disorienting effects *resembling* parody or ironic pastiche. In a brilliant study of this phenomenon, Jean-Pierre Moussaron has discussed the various ways in which (pseudo-)scientific discourse, of undecidable origin, produces the *simulation* of an imitation, of a "mimésis sans fond" ["endless mimesis"].[13] By upsetting the foundations of classical mimesis, in which copy and model, imitator and imitated are clearly situated with respect to one another, this language displaces the very concept of origin and truth:

> À l'écart de toute présence de la parole du manuel attestée comme telle, ces occurences proposent de pseudo-références à des modèles, fragments possibles de manuels, qui n'existent dans le texte que par l'effet de leur feinte copie, fausse citation. En ce jeu d'écriture, «les instances du modèle et de la copie ne sont pas abolies,» mais déportées l'une avec l'autre dans un espace neutre (ni de l'une, ni de l'autre) de langage, ou s'échangent et se perdent les attributs de propriété entre l'original, plausible, et le facsimilé, apparent. De sorte que de telles scènes de mots ne donnent à lire que l'infinie *capacité du discours d'imiter du discours,* jusque dans la simulation de l'imitation même. (p. 103)
>
> [Beyond any presence of the speech of the manual attested as such, these occurrences offer pseudo-references to models, possible fragments of manuals, which only exist in the text by the effect of their feigned copies, false citations. In this writing game, «occurrences of the model and the copy are not abolished,» but displaced one with the other to a neutral space (neither from one nor the other) of language, or exchange and lose their attributes between the plausible original and the apparent facsimile. So that such scenes only give to read the infinite *capacity of speech to imitate,* up until the simulation of imitation itself.]

This then is the novel of (re)circulation, of a stirring *up* whose consequence is to prevent meaning from settling *down,* and signs from stabilizing. Examples of disoriginating discourse abound in *Bouvard et Pécuchet.*

The monument by Chapu in honor of Flaubert was dedicated in Rouen on 23 November 1890, in the gardens of the Musée des Beaux-arts. It has lately been transferred to the Musée Flaubert et d'Histoire de la Médecine at the Hôtel-Dieu (51, rue Lecat), in the garden where medicinal plants are still grown (courtesy of the Musée Flaubert et d'Histoire de la Médecine).

Thus one typical passage reports on Swedenborg's stellar peregrinations:

> Swedenborg y [in the "espaces lumineux"] a fait de grands voyages. Car, en moins d'un an, il a exploré Vénus, Mars, Saturne et vingt-trois fois Jupiter. De plus, il a vu à Londres Jésus-Christ, il a vu Saint-Paul, il a vu saint Jean, il a vu Moïse, et, en 1736, il a même vu le jugement dernier.
>
> Aussi nous donne-t-il des descriptions du ciel.
>
> On y trouve des fleurs, des palais, des marchés et des églises absolument comme chez nous. (II, 267)
>
> [Swedenborg made there [in the 'luminous space'] great journeys. Indeed, in less than a year, he explored, Venus, Mars, Saturn and twenty-three times Jupiter. Moreover, he saw Jesus Christ in London, he saw Saint Paul, he saw Saint John, he saw Moses, and in 1736, he even saw the last judgment.
>
> So he gives us descriptions of heaven.
>
> One finds there flowers, palaces, markets and churches absolutely like here on earth.]

Summary, transcription, parody? Text, voice, narration? The hand is the hand of Flaubert, but the voice is the echo of the voice of Voltaire. In the absence of textual indicators of the relationship between model and copy, we are baffled in our attempt to seize the locus of enunciative authority. There is perhaps a trace of irony in the insistent repetition of "il a vu" ["he saw"] that would point to disparity between signifier and signified, but the flatness of the tone here can be counted as belonging equally to "sincere" affirmation or tongue-in-cheek irony. Our context is missing.[14]

Passages inserted in the present tense are problematic as well, for the resulting absence of temporal perspective postpones any sense of progress. Once again, the quest for the origin of the following utterances, their truth status, yields simply confusion and contradiction:

> Thierry démontre, à propos des Barbares, combien il est sot de rechercher si tel prince fut bon ou fut mauvais. Pourquoi ne pas suivre cette méthode dans l'examen des époques plus récentes? Mais l'histoire doit venger la morale; on est reconnaissant à Tacite d'avoir déchiré Tibère. Après tout, que la reine ait eu des amants; que Dumouriez, dès Valmy, se proposât de trahir; en prairial, que ce soit la Montagne ou la Gironde qui ait commencé, et en Thermidor les Jacobins ou la Plaine, qu'importe au développement de la Révolution, dont les origines sont profondes et les résultats incalculables? (II, 239)
>
> [Thierry demonstrates, with regard to the Barbarians, how much it is foolish to research if such a prince was good or bad. Why not follow this method in examining more recent times? But history must take revenge of the moral: one is grateful to Tacite to have torn up Tibère. After all, that the queen had lovers; that Dumouriez, since Valmy, proposed to betray; in Prairial whether it be the Montagne party or the Gironde party that started, and in Thermidor the Jacobins or the Plaine party, what importance to the development of the Revolution, whose origins are deep and the results incalculable?]

The first sentence in this excerpt deriving from Bouvard and Pécuchet's study of history might pass as summary, narration, or direct speech without quotation marks. That the second sentence is close to the reported words of one of the characters seems nearly certain—a certainty aided by the infinitive phrasing, but left in doubt by the absence of quotation indicators (dashes or *guillemets*). Claudine Gothot-Mersch has coined the term *style direct libre* to designate this peculiar formation. She further cites this instance from *Bouvard et Pécuchet:*

> un jour Bouvard jeta son havresac par terre, en déclarant qu'il n'irait pas plus loin.
>
> La géologie est trop défectueuse! A peine connaissons-nous quelques endroits de l'Europe. Quant au reste, avec le fond des océans, on l'ignorera toujours.
>
> Enfin Pécuchet ayant prononcé le mot de règne minéral:
>
> –«Je n'y crois pas, au règne minéral! . . .» (II, 231)
>
> [one day Bouvard threw his bag on the ground, declaring that he would not go any further.
>
> Geology is too defective! We hardly know a few places in Europe. As for the rest, with the depth of the oceans, one will always ignore it.
>
> Finally Pécuchet having pronounced the words mineral kingdom:
>
> –«I don't believe in mineral kingdom! . . . »]

The second paragraph, she notes, is not set off by *guillemets,* and is not a reply spoken by a character; nor is the narrator speaking. The text indicates rather that there has been a long speech by Pécuchet ("Enfin Pécuchet ayant prononcé le mot de règne minéral . . ."), or perhaps a long dialogue which this passage in the present tense *takes the place of* ("tient lieu"); it sums up that dialogue, and represents it without reproducing it. This is the *style direct libre.*[15]

While the dissolution, or absorption of dialogue into the perplexing citational style is the most intriguing technical feature of *Bouvard et Pécuchet,* much dialogue is nevertheless *reproduced* (in the sense intended by Gothot-Mersch) in the familiar forms of the earlier novels. If dialogue was earlier given as cliché (Emma and Homais), now it is subject to a variation of the repetitive pattern. Repetition in Flaubert certainly reaches its apex here, as we know from the projected outcome of the double copying desk. *Copying* and *doubling* become codes that command a significant number of speech acts in *Bouvard et Pécuchet.* Thus the humorous inanity of a repetition forms the basis for one of the pair's first tours of their farm. Under the branches of the arbor, Bouvard discovers a plaster statue. With two fingers, a lady holds her skirt aside, her knees bent, her head tilted on her shoulder as though afraid of being surprised. Bouvard exclaims, wittily:

> –Ah! pardon! ne vous gênez pas!
>
> Et cette plaisanterie les amusa tellement que, vingt fois par jour, pendant plus de trois semaines, ils la répétèrent. (II, 208)
>
> [–Oh pardon! Well don't mind us!
>
> And this joke amused them so much that, twenty times a day, for more than three weeks, they repeated it.]

In such scenes, language is content with reproducing *itself,* discovering its status as the signifier of a signifier.

The echo phenomenon is literally displayed shortly after this incident in another scene of linguistic repression. The companions decide to fix up their garden, and having duly consulted *L'Architecte des jardins* (The Garden Architect), they opt for the "Terrible" genre: overhanging rocks and shattered trees are among its chief features. Their task ended, Bouvard stands on the steps of the house to survey their handiwork, and calls out:

> –Ici! on voit mieux!
> –Voit mieux, fut répété dans l'air.
> –Pécuchet répondit:
> –J'y vais!
> –Y vais!
> –Tiens, un écho!
> –Écho! (II, 215)
>
> [–Here! One can see better!
> –See better, was repeated in the air.
> –Pécuchet replied:
> –I'm going!
> –Going!
> –Hey, an echo!
> –Echo!]

This constitutes a double *mise en abyme* –the phenomenon of textual self-mirroring–to the extent that each of these interchangeable friends finds his *co-respondent* both in his own voice (the echo) and in that of his comrade.[16]

The chapter on literature is another example of textual doubling. In assessing Balzac, Pécuchet complains of his encyclopedic embrace, his inflation of the insignificant:

> Pourquoi gonfler ce qui est plat, et décrire tant de sottises! Il a fait un roman sur la chimie, un autre sur la Banque, un autre sur les machines à imprimer . . . Nous en aurions sur tous les métiers et sur toutes les provinces, puis sur toutes les villes et les étages de chaque maison et chaque individu, ce qui ne sera plus de la littérature, mais de la statistique ou de l'ethnographie. (II, 244)
>
> [Why swell what is flat, and describe so many idiocies! He wrote a novel on chemistry, another on the Bank, another on printing machines . . . We would have novels on every trade and on every province, then on every town and the floors of every house and each individual, which will no longer be literature, but statistics or ethnography.]

Thus Bouvard and Pecuchet will ultimately abandon literature as well. But the mention of Balzac's novel on chemistry reminds us that it was the friends' own study of chemistry (as the result of an exploded still) that was the first subject matter in the long series (medicine, natural sciences, history) that led them to literature. Their search for first principles is a never-ending one, parallel to the infinite regress of signifiers. In fine, their abhorrence of *bêtise* ("Alors une faculté pitoyable se développa dans leur esprit, celle de voir la bêtise et de ne plus la tolérer" ["So a pitiful power developed in their spirit, that to see stupidity and to no longer tolerate it"] [II, 275]) is matched by their disgust for the priest's clichés.

> Il croyait aux sortilèges, faisait des plaisanteries sur les idoles, affirmait que tous les idiomes sont dérivés de l'hébreu [cf. the Gérando quotation in the *Sottisier*]; sa rhétorique manquait d'imprévu . . . (II, 286)

> [He believed in spells, made jokes of the idols, affirmed that all idioms are derived from Hebrew [cf. the Gérando quotation in the *Sottisier*]; his rhetoric lacked the unforeseen.]

Lionel Trilling asserted that *Bouvard et Pécuchet* was less to be compared "with any other literary work than with the stand of Roland at Roncesvalles."[17] But if Flaubert's task was indeed to divert or stem a cultural "flood of swinishness," he learned that he was faced with an epistemological rearguard action as well. The only stopping of cliché lay, paradoxically, in the amassing of it, in participation in the storehousing of words, in *copying*. Speech is drawn into the same phenomenon, as we have seen. Direct speech–"natural" speech–is upended and dissolved into a citational mix where all opposition between the written and the spoken becomes irrelevant. The discursive has become discourse. Thus *Bouvard et Pécuchet* is the first truly "writerly" text: it not only resists all reader effort to recuperate meaning, it foregrounds that resistance and makes of it its very subject. Escape lies in the representation of the very process of cliché-making, *clichage*. In this way, wrote Barthes (in a passage so often quoted that Anne Herschberg-Pierrot wonders if it has not become a cliché itself), "*on ne sait jamais s'il* [Flaubert] *est responsable de ce qu'il écrit* (s'il y a un sujet *derrière* son langage); car l'être de l'écriture (le sens du travail qui la constitue) est d'empêcher de jamais répondre à cette question: *Qui parle?* " ["*one never knows if he* [Flaubert] *is responsible for what he writes (if there is a subject behind his language);* since the matter of writing (the meaning of the work which constitutes it) is to prevent from ever answering this question: *Who is talking?*"][18] And finally, *Bouvard et Pécuchet* is Flaubert's solution to the problem he himself posed in a letter to George Sand: "Quelle forme faut-il prendre pour exprimer parfois son opinion sur les choses de ce monde, sans risquer de passer, plus tard, pour un imbécile?" ["What form does one have to take to sometimes express one's opinion on things in this world without risking, later, to be taken for an imbecile?"] (18–19 December 1867).

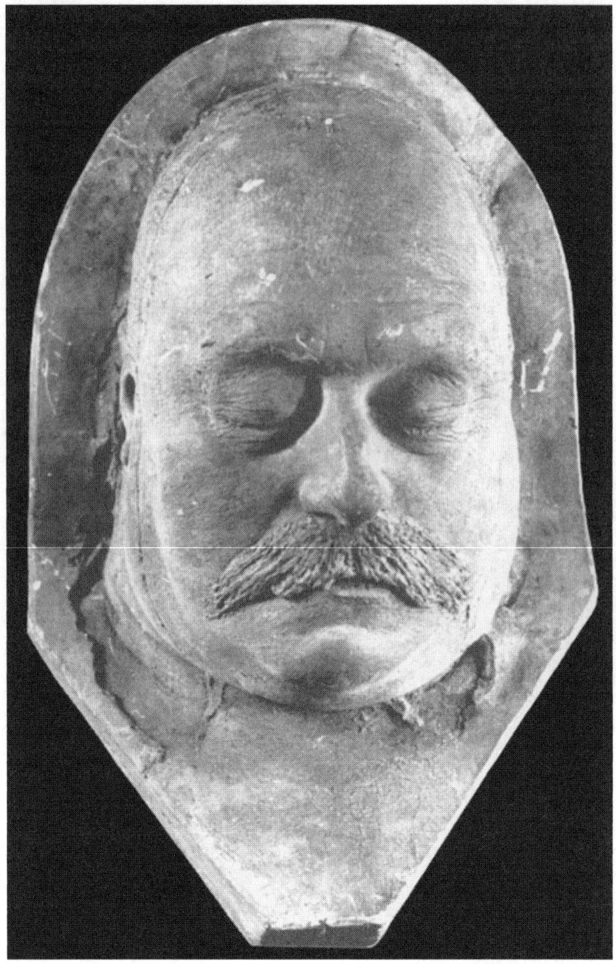

Flaubert's mortuary mask, cast from a mold taken the morning he died. It was made by Félix Bonet, a sculptor from Rouen who had cast the mortuary mask of Flaubert's mother in 1872 (courtesy of the Musée Carnavalet, Paris).

–Stirling Haig, "*Bouvard et Pécuchet* and the End of Dialogue," in *Flaubert and the Gift of Speech. Dialogue and Discourse in Four Modern Novels* (Cambridge: Cambridge University Press, 1986), pp. 160–169

---

1. *The Novels of Flaubert*, p. 259.
2. Flaubert had praised Homer and Rabelais for being "des encyclopédies de leur époque" ["encyclopedias from their time"] (7 April 1854).
3. *Bouvard et Pécuchet, avec un choix des scénarios, du Sottisier, L'Album de la Marquise* et *Le Dictionnaire des idées reçues* (Paris: Gallimard, 1979).

4. Thus Harry Levin called *Bouvard et Pécuchet* a "Bildungsroman in reverse" (*The Gates of Horn,* p. 298).
5. This image of failure is made explicit in Chapter 6: "Fruit sec des concours, il regrettait Paris, et c'était la conscience de sa vie manquée qui lui donnait un air morose" ["Dry fruit of competitions, he regretted Paris, and it was the consciousness of his missed life that gave him a morose appearance"] (II, 251).
6. It still retains its dissimulative function; that is, it indicates hesitation, roundabout approaches, and feelings the characters are loath to express directly.
7. Margaret Tillett, *On Reading Flaubert* (London: Oxford University Press, 1961), p. 111.
8. Claudine Gothot-Mersch, Introduction to her edition of *Bouvard et Pécuchet* (Paris: Gallimard, 1979); the same arguments are presented with even more clarity in her article, "Le Roman interminable: un aspect de la structure de *Bouvard et Pécuchet,*" in *Nouvelles Recherches sur "Bouvard et Pécuchet" de Flaubert* (Paris: Société d'Édition d'Enseignement Supérieur, 1981), esp. pp. 20–1.
9. *Bouvard et Pécuchet,* ed. Claudine Gothot-Mersch, p. 443.
10. D. L. Demorest, *À travers les plans, manuscrits et dossiers de "Bouvard et Pécuchet"* (Paris: Les Presses Modernes, 1931).
11. Alberto Cento, *Commentaire de "Bouvard et Pécuchet"* (Naples: Liguori, 1973).
12. Roland Barthes, "Brecht et le discours," in *L'Autre Scène,* no. 8–9 (Paris: L'Arche, 1975), p. 6.
13. Jean-Pierre Moussaron, "Une étrange greffe," in *Flaubert et le comble de l'art* (Paris: Société d'Édition d'Enseignement Supérieur, 1981), pp. 89–109.
14. Alberto Cento had noted that Flaubert's use of "document" in *L'Éducation sentimentale* as incontrovertible, damning evidence, was an indication of his contempt for the *bêtise* of the modern world (*Il Realismo documentario nell' "Éducation sentimentale"*), p. 68.
15. Claudine Gothot-Mersch, "De *Madame Bovary* à *Bouvard et Pécuchet.* La parole des personnages dans les romans de Flaubert," *Revue d'Histoire Littéraire de la France,* 81 (juillet–octobre, 1981), 559. See also her "Sur le narrateur chez Flaubert," *Nineteenth-Century French Studies,* 12, 3 (Spring 1984), 349.
16. An example of visual echoing can be observed in the description of Pécuchet reading his gardener's manual "avec sa bêche auprès de lui, dans la pose du jardinier qui décorait le frontispice du livre" ["with his spade close to him, in the pose of the gardener who was decorating the frontispiece of the book"] (II, 214).
17. Lionel Trilling, Introduction, *Bouvard and Pécuchet* (Norfolk, Conn.: New Directions, 1954), p. vi.
18. Roland Barthes, *S/Z* (Paris: Seuil, 1970), p. 146; Anne Herschberg-Pierrot, "Problématiques du cliché–sur Flaubert," *Poétique,* 11 (septembre 1980), 334–45.

Checklist of Further Readings

Bart, Benjamin F. *Flaubert.* Syracuse, N.Y.: Syracuse University Press, 1967.

Bart. "Flaubert's Concept of the Novel," *PMLA,* 80 (1965): 84–89.

Bart. "Is Maxime Du Camp a Reliable Witness?" *Modern Language Review,* 48 (1953): 17–25.

Bart, ed. *Madame Bovary and the Critics: a Collection of Essays.* New York: New York University Press, 1966.

Barthes, Roland. "The reality effect," in *French Literary Theory Today: A Reader,* edited by Tzveten Todorov. Cambridge: Cambridge University Press / Paris: Éditions de la Maison des Sciences de l'Homme, 1982, pp. 11–17.

Bem, Jeanne. *Désir et savoir dans l'œuvre de Flaubert. Étude de* La Tentation de saint Antoine. Neuchâtel: La Baconnière, 1979.

Bersani, Leo. "Flaubert and the Threats of Imagination," in *Balzac to Beckett: Center and Circumference in French Fiction.* New York: Oxford University Press, 1970, pp. 140–191.

Bersani. "Flaubert's Encyclopedism," *Novel,* 21 (1988): 140–146.

Bourdieu, Pierre. *The Rules of Art: Genesis and Structure of the Literary Field,* translated by Susan Emanuel. Stanford, Cal.: Stanford University Press, 1996.

Brandes, Georg. "Gustave Flaubert," in *Creative Spirits of the Nineteenth Century,* translated by Rasmus B. Anderson. New York: Crowell, 1923, pp. 223–266.

Brombert, Victor. *The Novels of Flaubert: A Study of Themes and Techniques.* Princeton: Princeton University Press, 1966.

Bruneau, Jean. *Les Débuts littéraires de Gustave Flaubert, 1831–1845.* Paris: Armand Colin, 1962.

Chambers, Ross. *Story and Situation: Narrative Seduction and the Power of Fiction.* Minneapolis: University of Minnesota Press, 1984.

Cortland, Peter. *A Reader's Guide to Flaubert: An Analysis of the Texts and Discussions of Current Criticism.* New York: Helios Books, 1968.

Culler, Jonathan. *Flaubert: The Uses of Uncertainty,* revised edition. Ithaca, N.Y.: Cornell University Press, 1985.

De Biasi, Pierre-Marc. *La Génétique des textes.* Paris: Nathan, 2000.

De Biasi, ed. *Carnets de Travail.* Paris: Balland, 1988.

Debray-Genette, Raymonde. *Métamorphoses du récit. Autour de Flaubert.* Paris: Seuil, Poétique, 1988.

Felman, Shoshana. *Writing and Madness.* Ithaca, N.Y.: Cornell University Press, 1985.

Foucault, Michel. "Fantasia of the Library" in *Language, Counter-Memory, Practice: Selected Essays and Interviews,* translated by Donald Bouchard. Ithaca, N.Y.: Cornell University Press, 1977, pp. 87–109.

Gans, Eric. *The Discovery of Illusion: Flaubert's Early's Works, 1835–37.* Berkeley: University of California Press, 1971.

Gaultier, Jules de. *Bovarysm,* translated by Gerald M. Spring. New York: Philosophical Library, 1970.

Ginsburg, Michal Peled. *Flaubert Writing: A Study in Narrative Strategies.* Stanford, Cal.: Stanford University Press, 1986.

Giraud, Raymond, ed. *Flaubert: A Collection of Critical Essays.* Englewood Cliffs, N.J.: Prentice-Hall, 1964.

Gothot-Mersch, Claudine. *La Genèse de* Madame Bovary. Paris: Corti, 1966.

Gray, Francine du Plessix. *Rage and Fire: A Life of Louise Colet.* New York: Simon & Schuster, 1994.

Haig, Stirling. *Flaubert and the Gift of Speech: Dialogue and Discourse in Four Modern Novels.* Cambridge: Cambridge University Press, 1986.

Houston, John Porter. *The Traditions of French Prose Style: A Rhetorical Study.* Baton Rouge: Louisiana State University Press, 1981.

Jackson, Ernest. *The Critical Reception of Gustave Flaubert in the United States, 1860–1960.* The Hague: Mouton, 1966.

James, Henry. "Charles de Bernard and Gustave Flaubert," in *French Poets and Novelists.* New York: Grosset & Dunlap, 1964, pp. 186–210.

James. "Flaubert's *Temptation of St. Anthony,*" in *Literary Reviews and Essays,* edited by Albert Mordell. New York: Twayne, 1957, pp. 145–150.

James. "Gustave Flaubert," in *Notes on Novelists.* New York: Biblio and Tannen Booksellers and Publishers, 1942, pp. 65–108.

LaCapra, Dominique. *Madame Bovary on Trial.* Ithaca, N.Y.: Cornell University Press, 1982.

Le Calvez, Éric. *Flaubert topographe:* L'Éducation sentimentale. *Essai de poétique génétique.* Amsterdam & Atlanta: Rodopi, Faux Titre, 1997.

Le Calvez. *La Production du descriptif. Exogenèse et endogenèse de* L'Éducation sentimentale. Amsterdam & New York: Rodopi, Faux Titre, 2002.

Leclerc, Yvan. *La Spirale et le monument. Essai sur* Bouvard et Pécuchet *de Flaubert.* Paris: CDU-Sédès, 1988.

Levin, Harry. *The Gates of Horn: A Study of Five French Realists.* New York: Oxford University Press, 1963.

Lottman, Herbert. *Gustave Flaubert.* Boston, Toronto & London: Little, Brown, 1989.

Lukacs, Georg. *The Historical Novel,* translated by Hannah Mitchell and Stanley Mitchell. London: Merlin Press, 1962; Boston: Beacon, 1963.

Maurois, André. "Gustave Flaubert. *Madame Bovary,*" in *The Art of Writing,* translated by Gerard Hopkins. New York: Dutton, 1960, pp. 116–135.

Murry, J. Middleton. "Flaubert" (1921) in *Countries of the Mind: Essays in Literary Criticism,* second edition. London: Oxford University Press, 1931, pp. 158–173.

Nabokov, Vladimir. "Gustave Flaubert: *Madame Bovary*," in *Lectures on Literature,* edited by Fredson Bowers. New York: Harcourt Brace Jovanovitch/Bruccoli Clark, 1980, pp. 125–177.

Porter, Laurence M. "Projection as Ego Defense: Flaubert's *Tentation de saint Antoine*," in *The Literary Dream in French Romanticism: A Psychoanalytic Interpretation.* Detroit: Wayne State University Press, 1979, pp. 47–67.

Porter, ed. *Critical Essays on Gustave Flaubert.* Boston: G. K. Hall, 1986, pp. 150–164.

Porter, ed. *A Gustave Flaubert Encyclopedia.* Westport, Conn.: Greenwood Press, 2001.

Poulet, Georges. "Flaubert," in *Studies in Human Time.* Baltimore: Johns Hopkins University Press, 1956, pp. 248–261.

Ramazani, Vaheed. *The Free Indirect Mode: Flaubert and the Poetics of Irony.* Charlottesville: University Press of Virginia, 1988.

Richard, Jean-Pierre. *Littérature et sensation.* Paris: Seuil, Points Essais, 1954.

Saintsbury, George. "Tales from Flaubert," in *Prefaces and Essays.* Freeport, N.Y.: Books for Libraries Press, Essay Index Reprint Series, 1969, pp. 416–431.

Sarraute, Nathalie. "Flaubert," *Partisan Review,* 33 (Spring 1966): 193–208.

Sartre, Jean-Paul. *The Family Idiot,* 5 volumes, translated by Carol Cosman. Chicago: University of Chicago Press, 1981–1993.

Schor, Naomi. "Salammbô Bound," in *Breaking the Chain: Women, Theory, and French Realist Fiction.* New York: Columbia University Press, 1985, pp. 111–126.

Schor and Majewski, Henry F., eds. *Flaubert and Postmodernism.* Lincoln: University of Nebraska Press, 1984.

Spencer, Philip Herbert. *Flaubert, A Biography.* London: Faber & Faber, 1952.

Starkie, Enid. *Flaubert. The Making of the Master.* New York: Atheneum, 1967.

Starkie. *Flaubert, The Master.* New York: Atheneum, 1971.

Symons, Arthur. *Figures of Several Centuries.* London: Constable, 1916.

Ullmann, Stephen. "Reported Speech and Internal Monologue in Flaubert," in *Style in the French Novel.* New York: Barnes, 1964, pp. 94–120.

Manuscripts:

Bibliothèque nationale de France, Paris; Bibliothèque historique de la Ville de Paris; Bibliothèque municipale de Rouen.

Cumulative Index

Dictionary of Literary Biography, Volumes 1-301
Dictionary of Literary Biography Yearbook, 1980-2002
Dictionary of Literary Biography Documentary Series, Volumes 1-19
Concise Dictionary of American Literary Biography, Volumes 1-7
Concise Dictionary of British Literary Biography, Volumes 1-8
Concise Dictionary of World Literary Biography, Volumes 1-4

Cumulative Index

DLB before number: *Dictionary of Literary Biography,* Volumes 1-301
Y before number: *Dictionary of Literary Biography Yearbook,* 1980-2002
DS before number: *Dictionary of Literary Biography Documentary Series,* Volumes 1-19
CDALB before number: *Concise Dictionary of American Literary Biography,* Volumes 1-7
CDBLB before number: *Concise Dictionary of British Literary Biography,* Volumes 1-8
CDWLB before number: *Concise Dictionary of World Literary Biography,* Volumes 1-4

A

Aakjær, Jeppe 1866-1930 . . . . DLB-214
Aarestrup, Emil 1800-1856 . . . . DLB-300
Abbey, Edward 1927-1989 . . . . DLB-256, 275
Abbey, Edwin Austin 1852-1911 . . . . DLB-188
Abbey, Maj. J. R. 1894-1969 . . . . DLB-201
Abbey Press DLB-49
The Abbey Theatre and Irish Drama, 1900-1945 . . . . DLB-10
Abbot, Willis J. 1863-1934 . . . . DLB-29
Abbott, Edwin A. 1838-1926 . . . . DLB-178
Abbott, Jacob 1803-1879 . . . . DLB-1, 42, 243
Abbott, Lee K. 1947- DLB-130
Abbott, Lyman 1835-1922 . . . . DLB-79
Abbott, Robert S. 1868-1940 . . . . DLB-29, 91
Abe Kōbō 1924-1993 . . . . DLB-182
Abelaira, Augusto 1926- DLB-287
Abelard, Peter circa 1079-1142? DLB-115, 208
Abelard-Schuman DLB-46
Abell, Arunah S. 1806-1888 . . . . DLB-43
Abell, Kjeld 1901-1961 . . . . DLB-214
Abercrombie, Lascelles 1881-1938 . . . . DLB-19
  The Friends of the Dymock Poets Y-00
Aberdeen University Press Limited DLB-106
Abish, Walter 1931- DLB-130, 227
Ablesimov, Aleksandr Onisimovich 1742-1783 . . . . DLB-150
Abraham à Sancta Clara 1644-1709 . . . . . . DLB-168
Abrahams, Peter 1919- DLB-117, 225; CDWLB-3
Abrams, M. H. 1912- DLB-67
Abramson, Jesse 1904-1979 . . . . DLB-241
Abrogans circa 790-800 . . . . DLB-148
Abschatz, Hans Aßmann von 1646-1699 . . . . DLB-168
Abse, Dannie 1923- DLB-27, 245
Abutsu-ni 1221-1283 . . . . DLB-203
Academy Chicago Publishers DLB-46
Accius circa 170 B.C.-circa 80 B.C. DLB-211
Accrocca, Elio Filippo 1923-1996 . . . . DLB-128
Ace Books DLB-46
Achebe, Chinua 1930- DLB-117; CDWLB-3
Achtenberg, Herbert 1938- DLB-124
Ackerman, Diane 1948- DLB-120
Ackroyd, Peter 1949- DLB-155, 231
Acorn, Milton 1923-1986 . . . . DLB-53
Acosta, Oscar Zeta 1935?-1974? DLB-82
Acosta Torres, José 1925- DLB-209
Actors Theatre of Louisville DLB-7
Adair, Gilbert 1944- DLB-194
Adair, James 1709?-1783? DLB-30
Aðalsteinn Kristmundsson (see Steinn Steinarr)
Adam, Graeme Mercer 1839-1912 . . . . DLB-99
Adam, Robert Borthwick, II 1863-1940 . . . . DLB-187
Adame, Leonard 1947- DLB-82
Adameşteanu, Gabriel 1942- DLB-232
Adamic, Louis 1898-1951 . . . . DLB-9
Adams, Abigail 1744-1818 . . . . DLB-183, 200
Adams, Alice 1926-1999 . . . . DLB-234; Y-86
Adams, Bertha Leith (Mrs. Leith Adams, Mrs. R. S. de Courcy Laffan) 1837?-1912 . . . . DLB-240
Adams, Brooks 1848-1927 . . . . DLB-47
Adams, Charles Francis, Jr. 1835-1915 . . . . DLB-47
Adams, Douglas 1952-2001 . . . . DLB-261; Y-83
Adams, Franklin P. 1881-1960 . . . . DLB-29
Adams, Hannah 1755-1832 . . . . DLB-200
Adams, Henry 1838-1918 . . . . DLB-12, 47, 189
Adams, Herbert Baxter 1850-1901 . . . . DLB-47
Adams, James Truslow 1878-1949 . . . . DLB-17; DS-17
Adams, John 1735-1826 . . . . DLB-31, 183
Adams, John Quincy 1767-1848 . . . . DLB-37
Adams, Léonie 1899-1988 . . . . DLB-48
Adams, Levi 1802-1832 . . . . DLB-99
Adams, Richard 1920- DLB-261
Adams, Samuel 1722-1803 . . . . DLB-31, 43
Adams, Sarah Fuller Flower 1805-1848 . . . . DLB-199
Adams, Thomas 1582/1583-1652 . . . . DLB-151
Adams, William Taylor 1822-1897 . . . . DLB-42
J. S. and C. Adams [publishing house] DLB-49
Adamson, Harold 1906-1980 . . . . DLB-265
Adamson, Sir John 1867-1950 . . . . DLB-98
Adamson, Robert 1943- DLB-289
Adcock, Arthur St. John 1864-1930 . . . . . . DLB-135
Adcock, Betty 1938- DLB-105
  "Certain Gifts" DLB-105
  Tribute to James Dickey Y-97
Adcock, Fleur 1934- DLB-40
Addison, Joseph 1672-1719 . . . . DLB-101; CDBLB-2
Ade, George 1866-1944 . . . . DLB-11, 25
Adeler, Max (see Clark, Charles Heber)
Adlard, Mark 1932- DLB-261
Adler, Richard 1921- DLB-265
Adonias Filho 1915-1990 . . . . DLB-145
Adorno, Theodor W. 1903-1969 . . . . DLB-242
Adoum, Jorge Enrique 1926- DLB-283
Advance Publishing Company DLB-49
Ady, Endre 1877-1919 . . . . . . DLB-215; CDWLB-4
AE 1867-1935 . . . . DLB-19; CDBLB-5
Ælfric circa 955-circa 1010 . . . . DLB-146
Aeschines circa 390 B.C.-circa 320 B.C. DLB-176
Aeschylus 525-524 B.C.-456-455 B.C. DLB-176; CDWLB-1
Aesthetic Papers DLB-1
Aesthetics
  Eighteenth-Century Aesthetic Theories DLB-31
  African Literature
    Letter from Khartoum Y-90
African American
  Afro-American Literary Critics: An Introduction DLB-33
  The Black Aesthetic: Background DS-8
  The Black Arts Movement, by Larry Neal DLB-38
  Black Theaters and Theater Organizations in America, 1961-1982: A Research List DLB-38
  Black Theatre: A Forum [excerpts] DLB-38
  Callaloo [journal] Y-87
  Community and Commentators: Black Theatre and Its Critics DLB-38

The Emergence of Black Women Writers DS-8
The Hatch-Billops Collection DLB-76
A Look at the Contemporary Black Theatre Movement DLB-38
The Moorland-Spingarn Research Center DLB-76
"The Negro as a Writer," by G. M. McClellan DLB-50
"Negro Poets and Their Poetry," by Wallace Thurman DLB-50
Olaudah Equiano and Unfinished Journeys: The Slave-Narrative Tradition and Twentieth-Century Continuities, by Paul Edwards and Pauline T. Wangman DLB-117
PHYLON (Fourth Quarter, 1950), The Negro in Literature: The Current Scene DLB-76
The Schomburg Center for Research in Black Culture DLB-76
Three Documents [poets], by John Edward Bruce DLB-50
After Dinner Opera Company Y-92
Agassiz, Elizabeth Cary 1822-1907 . . . . . . DLB-189
Agassiz, Louis 1807-1873 . . . . DLB-1, 235
Agee, James 1909-1955 . . . . DLB-2, 26, 152; CDALB-1
The Agee Legacy: A Conference at the University of Tennessee at Knoxville Y-89
Aguilera Malta, Demetrio 1909-1981 . . . . DLB-145
Agustini, Delmira 1886-1914 . . . . DLB-290
Ahlin, Lars 1915-1997 . . . . DLB-257
Ai 1947- DLB-120
Aichinger, Ilse 1921- DLB-85, 299
Aickman, Robert 1914-1981 . . . . DLB-261
Aidoo, Ama Ata 1942- DLB-117; CDWLB-3
Aiken, Conrad 1889-1973 . . . . DLB-9, 45, 102; CDALB-5
Aiken, Joan 1924- DLB-161
Aikin, Lucy 1781-1864 . . . . DLB-144, 163
Ainsworth, William Harrison 1805-1882 . . . . DLB-21
Aistis, Jonas 1904-1973 . . . . . DLB-220; CDWLB-4
Aitken, George A. 1860-1917 . . . . DLB-149
Robert Aitken [publishing house] DLB-49
Akenside, Mark 1721-1770 . . . . DLB-109
Akhamatova, Anna Andreevna 1889-1966 . . . . DLB-295
Akins, Zoë 1886-1958 . . . . DLB-26
Aksakov, Ivan Sergeevich 1823-1826 . . . . . DLB-277
Aksakov, Sergei Timofeevich 1791-1859 . . . . DLB-198
Akunin, Boris (Grigorii Shalvovich Chkhartishvili) 1956- DLB-285
Akutagawa Ryūnsuke 1892-1927 . . . . DLB-180
Alabaster, William 1568-1640 . . . . DLB-132
Alain de Lille circa 1116-1202/1203 . . . . . DLB-208
Alain-Fournier 1886-1914 . . . . DLB-65
Alanus de Insulis (see Alain de Lille)
Alarcón, Francisco X. 1954- DLB-122
Alarcón, Justo S. 1930- DLB-209
Alba, Nanina 1915-1968 . . . . DLB-41
Albee, Edward 1928- . . . DLB-7, 266; CDALB-1
Albert, Octavia 1853-ca. 1889 . . . . DLB-221
Albert the Great circa 1200-1280 . . . . DLB-115
Alberti, Rafael 1902-1999 . . . . DLB-108
Albertinus, Aegidius circa 1560-1620 . . . . DLB-164
Alcaeus born circa 620 B.C. DLB-176
Alcoforado, Mariana, the Portuguese Nun 1640-1723 . . . . DLB-287
Alcott, Amos Bronson 1799-1888 . . . . DLB-1, 223; DS-5
Alcott, Louisa May 1832-1888 . . . DLB-1, 42, 79, 223, 239; DS-14; CDALB-3
Alcott, William Andrus 1798-1859 . . . . DLB-1, 243
Alcuin circa 732-804 . . . . DLB-148
Alden, Henry Mills 1836-1919 . . . . DLB-79
Alden, Isabella 1841-1930 . . . . DLB-42
John B. Alden [publishing house] DLB-49
Alden, Beardsley, and Company DLB-49
Aldington, Richard 1892-1962 . . . . DLB-20, 36, 100, 149
Aldis, Dorothy 1896-1966 . . . . DLB-22
Aldis, H. G. 1863-1919 . . . . DLB-184
Aldiss, Brian W. 1925- DLB-14, 261, 271
Aldrich, Thomas Bailey 1836-1907 . . . . DLB-42, 71, 74, 79
Alegría, Ciro 1909-1967 . . . . DLB-113
Alegría, Claribel 1924- DLB-145, 283
Aleixandre, Vicente 1898-1984 . . . . DLB-108
Aleksandravičius, Jonas (see Aistis, Jonas)
Aleksandrov, Aleksandr Andreevich (see Durova, Nadezhda Andreevna)
Alekseeva, Marina Anatol'evna (see Marinina, Aleksandra)
Aleramo, Sibilla (Rena Pierangeli Faccio) 1876-1960 . . . . DLB-114, 264
Aleshkovsky, Petr Markovich 1957- . . . DLB-285
Alexander, Cecil Frances 1818-1895 . . . . . DLB-199
Alexander, Charles 1868-1923 . . . . DLB-91
Charles Wesley Alexander [publishing house] DLB-49
Alexander, James 1691-1756 . . . . DLB-24
Alexander, Lloyd 1924- DLB-52
Alexander, Sir William, Earl of Stirling 1577?-1640 . . . . DLB-121
Alexie, Sherman 1966- DLB-175, 206, 278
Alexis, Willibald 1798-1871 . . . . DLB-133
Alfred, King 849-899 . . . . DLB-146
Alger, Horatio, Jr. 1832-1899 . . . . DLB-42
Algonquin Books of Chapel Hill DLB-46
Algren, Nelson 1909-1981 . . . . . . DLB-9; Y-81, 82; CDALB-1
Nelson Algren: An International Symposium Y-00
Aljamiado Literature DLB-286
Allan, Andrew 1907-1974 . . . . DLB-88
Allan, Ted 1916-1995 . . . . DLB-68
Allbeury, Ted 1917- DLB-87
Alldritt, Keith 1935- DLB-14
Allen, Dick 1939- DLB-282
Allen, Ethan 1738-1789 . . . . DLB-31
Allen, Frederick Lewis 1890-1954 . . . . DLB-137
Allen, Gay Wilson 1903-1995 . . . . . DLB-103; Y-95
Allen, George 1808-1876 . . . . DLB-59
Allen, Grant 1848-1899 . . . . DLB-70, 92, 178
Allen, Henry W. 1912-1991 . . . . Y-85
Allen, Hervey 1889-1949 . . . . DLB-9, 45
Allen, James 1739-1808 . . . . DLB-31
Allen, James Lane 1849-1925 . . . . DLB-71
Allen, Jay Presson 1922- DLB-26
John Allen and Company DLB-49
Allen, Paula Gunn 1939- DLB-175
Allen, Samuel W. 1917- DLB-41
Allen, Woody 1935- DLB-44
George Allen [publishing house] DLB-106
George Allen and Unwin Limited DLB-112
Allende, Isabel 1942- DLB-145; CDWLB-3
Alline, Henry 1748-1784 . . . . DLB-99
Allingham, Margery 1904-1966 . . . . DLB-77
The Margery Allingham Society Y-98
Allingham, William 1824-1889 . . . . DLB-35
W. L. Allison [publishing house] DLB-49
The *Alliterative Morte Arthure and the Stanzaic Morte Arthur* circa 1350-1400 . . . . DLB-146
Allott, Kenneth 1912-1973 . . . . DLB-20
Allston, Washington 1779-1843 . . . . . . DLB-1, 235
John Almon [publishing house] DLB-154
Alonzo, Dámaso 1898-1990 . . . . DLB-108
Alsop, George 1636-post 1673 . . . . DLB-24
Alsop, Richard 1761-1815 . . . . DLB-37
Henry Altemus and Company DLB-49
Altenberg, Peter 1885-1919 . . . . DLB-81
Althusser, Louis 1918-1990 . . . . DLB-242
Altolaguirre, Manuel 1905-1959 . . . . DLB-108
Aluko, T. M. 1918- DLB-117
Alurista 1947- DLB-82
Alvarez, A. 1929- DLB-14, 40
Alvarez, Julia 1950- DLB-282
Alvaro, Corrado 1895-1956 . . . . DLB-264
Alver, Betti 1906-1989 . . . . . DLB-220; CDWLB-4
Amadi, Elechi 1934- DLB-117
Amado, Jorge 1912-2001 . . . . DLB-113
Ambler, Eric 1909-1998 . . . . DLB-77
The Library of America DLB-46
The Library of America: An Assessment After Two Decades Y-02
America: or, A Poem on the Settlement of the British Colonies, by Timothy Dwight DLB-37
American Bible Society Department of Library, Archives, and Institutional Research Y-97

American Conservatory
Theatre DLB-7

American Culture
American Proletarian Culture:
The Twenties and Thirties. DS-11

Studies in American Jewish Literature. Y-02

The American Library in Paris Y-93

American Literature
The Literary Scene and Situation and . . .
(Who Besides Oprah) Really Runs
American Literature? Y-99

Who Owns American Literature, by
Henry Taylor Y-94

Who Runs American Literature? Y-94

American News Company. DLB-49

A Century of Poetry, a Lifetime of Collecting:
J. M. Edelstein's Collection of Twentieth-
Century American Poetry. Y-02

The American Poets' Corner: The First
Three Years (1983-1986). Y-86

American Publishing Company. DLB-49

American Spectator
[Editorial] Rationale From the Initial
Issue of the American Spectator
(November 1932). DLB-137

American Stationers' Company. DLB-49

The American Studies Association
of Norway. Y-00

American Sunday-School Union DLB-49

American Temperance Union. DLB-49

American Tract Society DLB-49

The American Trust for the British Library . . Y-96

American Writers Congress
The American Writers Congress
(9-12 October 1981) Y-81

The American Writers Congress: A Report
on Continuing Business Y-81

Ames, Fisher 1758-1808. . . . . .DLB-37

Ames, Mary Clemmer 1831-1884 . . . . .DLB-23

Ames, William 1576-1633 . . . . .DLB-281

Amiel, Henri-Frédéric 1821-1881. . . . . . . .DLB-217

Amini, Johari M. 1935- DLB-41

Amis, Kingsley 1922-1995
. . . . . . DLB-15, 27, 100, 139, Y-96; CDBLB-7

Amis, Martin 1949- DLB-14, 194

Ammianus Marcellinus
circa A.D. 330-A.D. 395 . . . . .DLB-211

Ammons, A. R. 1926-2001 . . . . .DLB-5, 165

Amory, Thomas 1691?-1788 . . . . .DLB-39

Anania, Michael 1939- DLB-193

Anaya, Rudolfo A. 1937- DLB-82, 206, 278

Ancrene Riwle circa 1200-1225. . . . . .DLB-146

Andersch, Alfred 1914-1980 . . . . .DLB-69

Andersen, Benny 1929- DLB-214

Andersen, Hans Christian 1805-1875 . . . .DLB-300

Anderson, Alexander 1775-1870. . . . . .DLB-188

Anderson, David 1929- DLB-241

Anderson, Frederick Irving 1877-1947 . . . .DLB-202

Anderson, Margaret 1886-1973 . . . . .DLB-4, 91

Anderson, Maxwell 1888-1959 . . . . DLB-7, 228

Anderson, Patrick 1915-1979. . . . . .DLB-68

Anderson, Paul Y. 1893-1938 . . . . .DLB-29

Anderson, Poul 1926-2001 . . . . .DLB-8

Tribute to Isaac Asimov Y-92

Anderson, Robert 1750-1830. . . . . .DLB-142

Anderson, Robert 1917- DLB-7

Anderson, Sherwood
1876-1941 . . . . .DLB-4, 9, 86; DS-1; CDALB-4

Andreae, Johann Valentin 1586-1654 . . . .DLB-164

Andreas Capellanus
flourished circa 1185. . . . . .DLB-208

Andreas-Salomé, Lou 1861-1937 . . . . .DLB-66

Andreev, Leonid Nikolaevich
1871-1919 . . . . .DLB-295

Andres, Stefan 1906-1970 . . . . .DLB-69

Andresen, Sophia de Mello Breyner
1919- DLB-287

Andreu, Blanca 1959- DLB-134

Andrewes, Lancelot 1555-1626 . . . . . DLB-151, 172

Andrews, Charles M. 1863-1943. . . . . DLB-17

Andrews, Miles Peter ?-1814 . . . . .DLB-89

Andrews, Stephen Pearl 1812-1886 . . . . . .DLB-250

Andrian, Leopold von 1875-1951 . . . . .DLB-81

Andrić, Ivo 1892-1975 . . . . . . DLB-147; CDWLB-4

Andrieux, Louis (see Aragon, Louis)

Andrus, Silas, and Son. DLB-49

Andrzejewski, Jerzy 1909-1983 . . . . .DLB-215

Angell, James Burrill 1829-1916 . . . . .DLB-64

Angell, Roger 1920- DLB-171, 185

Angelou, Maya 1928- DLB-38; CDALB-7

Tribute to Julian Mayfield. Y-84

Anger, Jane flourished 1589. . . . . .DLB-136

Angers, Félicité (see Conan, Laure)

The Anglo-Saxon Chronicle
circa 890-1154 . . . . .DLB-146

Angus and Robertson (UK) Limited DLB-112

Anhalt, Edward 1914-2000 . . . . .DLB-26

Anissimov, Myriam 1943- DLB-299

Anker, Nini Roll 1873-1942. . . . . .DLB-297

Annenkov, Pavel Vasil'evich
1813?-1887 . . . . .DLB-277

Annensky, Innokentii Fedorovich
1855-1909 . . . . .DLB-295

Henry F. Anners [publishing house] DLB-49

Annolied between 1077 and 1081. . . . . .DLB-148

Anscombe, G. E. M. 1919-2001. . . . . .DLB-262

Anselm of Canterbury 1033-1109 . . . . . . .DLB-115

Anstey, F. 1856-1934. . . . . DLB-141, 178

Anthologizing New Formalism DLB-282

Anthony, Michael 1932- DLB-125

Anthony, Piers 1934- DLB-8

Anthony, Susanna 1726-1791. . . . . .DLB-200

Antin, David 1932- DLB-169

Antin, Mary 1881-1949 . . . . DLB-221; Y-84

Anton Ulrich, Duke of Brunswick-Lüneburg
1633-1714 . . . . .DLB-168

Antschel, Paul (see Celan, Paul)

Antunes, António Lobo 1942- DLB-287

Anyidoho, Kofi 1947- DLB-157

Anzaldúa, Gloria 1942- DLB-122

Anzengruber, Ludwig 1839-1889 . . . . . . .DLB-129

Apess, William 1798-1839 . . . . DLB-175, 243

Apodaca, Rudy S. 1939- DLB-82

Apollinaire, Guillaume 1880-1918. . . . . . .DLB-258

Apollonius Rhodius third century B.C. . . . DLB-176

Apple, Max 1941- DLB-130

Appelfeld, Aharon 1932- DLB-299

D. Appleton and Company DLB-49

Appleton-Century-Crofts. DLB-46

Applewhite, James 1935- DLB-105

Tribute to James Dickey Y-97

Apple-wood Books. DLB-46

April, Jean-Pierre 1948- DLB-251

Apukhtin, Aleksei Nikolaevich
1840-1893 . . . . DLB-277

Apuleius circa A.D. 125-post A.D. 164
. . . . DLB-211; CDWLB-1

Aquin, Hubert 1929-1977 . . . . .DLB-53

Aquinas, Thomas 1224/1225-1274 . . . . . . DLB-115

Aragon, Louis 1897-1982. . . . . DLB-72, 258

Aragon, Vernacular Translations in the
Crowns of Castile and 1352-1515. . . . DLB-286

Aralica, Ivan 1930- DLB-181

Aratus of Soli
circa 315 B.C.-circa 239 B.C. DLB-176

Arbasino, Alberto 1930- DLB-196

Arbor House Publishing Company DLB-46

Arbuthnot, John 1667-1735 . . . . DLB-101

Arcadia House. DLB-46

Arce, Julio G. (see Ulica, Jorge)

Archer, William 1856-1924 . . . . .DLB-10

Archilochhus
mid seventh century B.C.E. DLB-176

The Archpoet circa 1130?-?. DLB-148

Archpriest Avvakum (Petrovich)
1620?-1682 . . . . DLB-150

Arden, John 1930- DLB-13, 245

Arden of Faversham. DLB-62

Ardis Publishers. Y-89

Ardizzone, Edward 1900-1979. . . . . DLB-160

Arellano, Juan Estevan 1947- DLB-122

The Arena Publishing Company. DLB-49

Arena Stage DLB-7

Arenas, Reinaldo 1943-1990 . . . . DLB-145

Arendt, Hannah 1906-1975 . . . . .DLB-242

Arensberg, Ann 1937- Y-82

Arghezi, Tudor 1880-1967. . . DLB-220; CDWLB-4

Arguedas, José María 1911-1969 . . . . DLB-113

Argueta, Manlio 1936- DLB-145

Arias, Ron 1941- .DLB-82

Arishima Takeo 1878-1923 . . . . DLB-180

Aristophanes circa 446 B.C.-circa 386 B.C.
. . . . DLB-176; CDWLB-1

Aristotle 384 B.C.-322 B.C. DLB-176; CDWLB-1
Ariyoshi Sawako 1931-1984 .... DLB-182
Arland, Marcel 1899-1986 .... DLB-72
Arlen, Michael 1895-1956 .... DLB-36, 77, 162
Armah, Ayi Kwei 1939- DLB-117; CDWLB-3
Armantrout, Rae 1947- DLB-193
Der arme Hartmann ?-after 1150 .... DLB-148
Armed Services Editions DLB-46
Armitage, G. E. (Robert Edric) 1956- DLB-267
Armstrong, Martin Donisthorpe 1882-1974 .... DLB-197
Armstrong, Richard 1903- DLB-160
Armstrong, Terence Ian Fytton (see Gawsworth, John)
Arnauld, Antoine 1612-1694 .... DLB-268
Arndt, Ernst Moritz 1769-1860 .... DLB-90
Arnim, Achim von 1781-1831 .... DLB-90
Arnim, Bettina von 1785-1859 .... DLB-90
Arnim, Elizabeth von (Countess Mary Annette Beauchamp Russell) 1866-1941 .... DLB-197
Arno Press DLB-46
Arnold, Edwin 1832-1904 .... DLB-35
Arnold, Edwin L. 1857-1935 .... DLB-178
Arnold, Matthew 1822-1888 .... DLB-32, 57; CDBLB-4
Preface to *Poems* (1853) DLB-32
Arnold, Thomas 1795-1842 .... DLB-55
Edward Arnold [publishing house] DLB-112
Arnott, Peter 1962- DLB-233
Arnow, Harriette Simpson 1908-1986 .... DLB-6
Arp, Bill (see Smith, Charles Henry)
Arpino, Giovanni 1927-1987 .... DLB-177
Arrebo, Anders 1587-1637 .... DLB-300
Arreola, Juan José 1918-2001 .... DLB-113
Arrian circa 89-circa 155 .... DLB-176
J. W. Arrowsmith [publishing house] DLB-106
Art
John Dos Passos: Artist Y-99
The First Post-Impressionist Exhibition DS-5
The Omega Workshops DS-10
The Second Post-Impressionist Exhibition DS-5
Artaud, Antonin 1896-1948 .... DLB-258
Artel, Jorge 1909-1994 .... DLB-283
Arthur, Timothy Shay 1809-1885 .... DLB-3, 42, 79, 250; DS-13
Artmann, H. C. 1921-2000 .... DLB-85
Artsybashev, Mikhail Petrovich 1878-1927 .... DLB-295
Arvin, Newton 1900-1963 .... DLB-103
Asch, Nathan 1902-1964 .... DLB-4, 28
Nathan Asch Remembers Ford Madox Ford, Sam Roth, and Hart Crane Y-02
Ascham, Roger 1515/1516-1568 .... DLB-236
Aseev, Nikolai Nikolaevich 1889-1963 .... DLB-295
Ash, John 1948- DLB-40
Ashbery, John 1927- DLB-5, 165; Y-81
Ashbridge, Elizabeth 1713-1755 .... DLB-200
Ashburnham, Bertram Lord 1797-1878 .... DLB-184
Ashendene Press DLB-112
Asher, Sandy 1942- Y-83
Ashton, Winifred (see Dane, Clemence)
Asimov, Isaac 1920-1992 .... DLB-8; Y-92
Tribute to John Ciardi Y-86
Askew, Anne circa 1521-1546 .... DLB-136
Aspazija 1865-1943 .... DLB-220; CDWLB-4
Asselin, Olivar 1874-1937 .... DLB-92
The Association of American Publishers Y-99
The Association for Documentary Editing Y-00
The Association for the Study of Literature and Environment (ASLE) Y-99
Astell, Mary 1666-1731 .... DLB-252
Astley, Thea 1925- DLB-289
Astley, William (see Warung, Price)
Asturias, Miguel Ángel 1899-1974 .... DLB-113, 290; CDWLB-3
Atava, S. (see Terpigorev, Sergei Nikolaevich)
Atheneum Publishers DLB-46
Atherton, Gertrude 1857-1948 .... DLB-9, 78, 186
Athlone Press DLB-112
Atkins, Josiah circa 1755-1781 .... DLB-31
Atkins, Russell 1926- DLB-41
Atkinson, Kate 1951- DLB-267
Atkinson, Louisa 1834-1872 .... DLB-230
The Atlantic Monthly Press DLB-46
Attaway, William 1911-1986 .... DLB-76
Atwood, Margaret 1939- DLB-53, 251
Aubert, Alvin 1930- DLB-41
Aubert de Gaspé, Phillipe-Ignace-François 1814-1841 .... DLB-99
Aubert de Gaspé, Phillipe-Joseph 1786-1871 .... DLB-99
Aubin, Napoléon 1812-1890 .... DLB-99
Aubin, Penelope 1685-circa 1731 .... DLB-39
Preface to *The Life of Charlotta du Pont* (1723) DLB-39
Aubrey-Fletcher, Henry Lancelot (see Wade, Henry)
Auchincloss, Louis 1917- DLB-2, 244; Y-80
Auden, W. H. 1907-1973 .... DLB-10, 20; CDBLB-6
Audio Art in America: A Personal Memoir Y-85
Audubon, John James 1785-1851 .... DLB-248
Audubon, John Woodhouse 1812-1862 .... DLB-183
Auerbach, Berthold 1812-1882 .... DLB-133
Auernheimer, Raoul 1876-1948 .... DLB-81
Augier, Emile 1820-1889 .... DLB-192
Augustine 354-430 .... DLB-115
Aulnoy, Marie-Catherine Le Jumel de Barneville, comtesse d' 1650/1651-1705 .... DLB-268
Aulus Gellius circa A.D. 125-circa A.D. 180? DLB-211
Austen, Jane 1775-1817 .... DLB-116; CDBLB-3
Auster, Paul 1947- DLB-227
Austin, Alfred 1835-1913 .... DLB-35
Austin, J. L. 1911-1960 .... DLB-262
Austin, Jane Goodwin 1831-1894 .... DLB-202
Austin, John 1790-1859 .... DLB-262
Austin, Mary Hunter 1868-1934 .... DLB-9, 78, 206, 221, 275
Austin, William 1778-1841 .... DLB-74
Australie (Emily Manning) 1845-1890 .... DLB-230
Authors and Newspapers Association DLB-46
Authors' Publishing Company DLB-49
Avallone, Michael 1924-1999 .... Y-99
Tribute to John D. MacDonald Y-86
Tribute to Kenneth Millar Y-83
Tribute to Raymond Chandler Y-88
Avalon Books DLB-46
Avancini, Nicolaus 1611-1686 .... DLB-164
Avendaño, Fausto 1941- DLB-82
Averroës 1126-1198 .... DLB-115
Avery, Gillian 1926- DLB-161
Avicenna 980-1037 .... DLB-115
Ávila Jiménez, Antonio 1898-1965 .... DLB-283
Avison, Margaret 1918-1987 .... DLB-53
Avon Books DLB-46
Avyžius, Jonas 1922-1999 .... DLB-220
Awdry, Wilbert Vere 1911-1997 .... DLB-160
Awoonor, Kofi 1935- DLB-117
Ayckbourn, Alan 1939- DLB-13, 245
Ayer, A. J. 1910-1989 .... DLB-262
Aymé, Marcel 1902-1967 .... DLB-72
Aytoun, Sir Robert 1570-1638 .... DLB-121
Aytoun, William Edmondstoune 1813-1865 .... DLB-32, 159

B

B.V. (see Thomson, James)
Babbitt, Irving 1865-1933 .... DLB-63
Babbitt, Natalie 1932- DLB-52
John Babcock [publishing house] DLB-49
Babel, Isaak Emmanuilovich 1894-1940 .... DLB-272
Babits, Mihály 1883-1941 .... DLB-215; CDWLB-4
Babrius circa 150-200 .... DLB-176
Babson, Marian 1929- DLB-276
Baca, Jimmy Santiago 1952- DLB-122
Bacchelli, Riccardo 1891-1985 .... DLB-264
Bache, Benjamin Franklin 1769-1798 .... DLB-43
Bachelard, Gaston 1884-1962 .... DLB-296
Bacheller, Irving 1859-1950 .... DLB-202
Bachmann, Ingeborg 1926-1973 .... DLB-85
Bačinskaitė-Bučienė, Salomėja (see Nėris, Salomėja)
Bacon, Delia 1811-1859 .... DLB-1, 243

Bacon, Francis
1561-1626 . . . . .DLB-151, 236, 252; CDBLB-1
Bacon, Sir Nicholas circa 1510-1579 . . . . .DLB-132
Bacon, Roger circa 1214/1220-1292 . . . . .DLB-115
Bacon, Thomas circa 1700-1768. . . . . .DLB-31
Bacovia, George
1881-1957 . . . . .DLB-220; CDWLB-4
Richard G. Badger and Company DLB-49
Bagaduce Music Lending Library Y-00
Bage, Robert 1728-1801. . . . . .DLB-39
Bagehot, Walter 1826-1877 . . . . .DLB-55
Baggesen, Jens 1764-1826. . . . . .DLB-300
Bagley, Desmond 1923-1983 . . . . .DLB-87
Bagley, Sarah G. 1806-1848?. DLB-239
Bagnold, Enid 1889-1981. . . DLB-13, 160, 191, 245
Bagryana, Elisaveta
1893-1991 . . . . .DLB-147; CDWLB-4
Bahr, Hermann 1863-1934 . . . . .DLB-81, 118
Bailey, Abigail Abbot 1746-1815 . . . . .DLB-200
Bailey, Alfred Goldsworthy 1905- DLB-68
Bailey, H. C. 1878-1961. . . . . .DLB-77
Bailey, Jacob 1731-1808. . . . . .DLB-99
Bailey, Paul 1937- DLB-14, 271
Bailey, Philip James 1816-1902 . . . . .DLB-32
Francis Bailey [publishing house]. DLB-49
Baillargeon, Pierre 1916-1967 . . . . .DLB-88
Baillie, Hugh 1890-1966 . . . . .DLB-29
Baillie, Joanna 1762-1851. . . . . .DLB-93
Bailyn, Bernard 1922- DLB-17
Bain, Alexander
English Composition and Rhetoric (1866)
[excerpt] DLB-57
Bainbridge, Beryl 1933- DLB-14, 231
Baird, Irene 1901-1981 . . . . .DLB-68
Baker, Augustine 1575-1641 . . . . .DLB-151
Baker, Carlos 1909-1987 . . . . .DLB-103
Baker, David 1954- DLB-120
Baker, George Pierce 1866-1935 . . . . .DLB-266
Baker, Herschel C. 1914-1990. . . . . .DLB-111
Baker, Houston A., Jr. 1943- DLB-67
Baker, Howard
Tribute to Caroline Gordon Y-81
Tribute to Katherine Anne Porter. Y-80
Baker, Nicholson 1957- DLB-227; Y-00
Review of Nicholson Baker's *Double Fold: Libraries and the Assault on Paper* Y-00
Baker, Samuel White 1821-1893 . . . . .DLB-166
Baker, Thomas 1656-1740. . . . . .DLB-213
Walter H. Baker Company
("Baker's Plays") DLB-49
The Baker and Taylor Company DLB-49
Bakhtin, Mikhail Mikhailovich
1895-1975 . . . . .DLB-242
Bakunin, Mikhail Aleksandrovich
1814-1876 . . . . .DLB-277
Balaban, John 1943- DLB-120
Bald, Wambly 1902- DLB-4
Balde, Jacob 1604-1668 . . . . .DLB-164
Balderston, John 1889-1954. . . . . .DLB-26
Baldwin, James 1924-1987
. . . . . .DLB-2, 7, 33, 249, 278; Y-87; CDALB-1
Baldwin, Joseph Glover
1815-1864 . . . . .DLB-3, 11, 248
Baldwin, Louisa (Mrs. Alfred Baldwin)
1845-1925 . . . . .DLB-240
Baldwin, William circa 1515-1563. . . . . . .DLB-132
Richard and Anne Baldwin
[publishing house] DLB-170
Bale, John 1495-1563. . . . . .DLB-132
Balestrini, Nanni 1935- DLB-128, 196
Balfour, Sir Andrew 1630-1694 . . . . .DLB-213
Balfour, Arthur James 1848-1930 . . . . . . .DLB-190
Balfour, Sir James 1600-1657 . . . . .DLB-213
Ballantine Books DLB-46
Ballantyne, R. M. 1825-1894. . . . . .DLB-163
Ballard, J. G. 1930- DLB-14, 207, 261
Ballard, Martha Moore 1735-1812. . . . . . .DLB-200
Ballerini, Luigi 1940- DLB-128
Ballou, Maturin Murray (Lieutenant Murray)
1820-1895 . . . . .DLB-79, 189
Robert O. Ballou [publishing house] DLB-46
Bal'mont, Konstantin Dmitrievich
1867-1942. . . . . .DLB-295
Balzac, Guez de 1597?-1654. . . . . .DLB-268
Balzac, Honoré de 1799-1855 . . . . .DLB-119
Bambara, Toni Cade
1939-1995 . . . . .DLB-38, 218; CDALB-7
Bamford, Samuel 1788-1872. . . . . .DLB-190
A. L. Bancroft and Company DLB-49
Bancroft, George 1800-1891 . . . DLB-1, 30, 59, 243
Bancroft, Hubert Howe 1832-1918 . . . DLB-47, 140
Bandelier, Adolph F. 1840-1914. . . . . .DLB-186
Bang, Herman 1857-1912. . . . . .DLB-300
Bangs, John Kendrick 1862-1922. . . . . . DLB-11, 79
Banim, John 1798-1842 . . . . DLB-116, 158, 159
Banim, Michael 1796-1874. . . . . .DLB-158, 159
Banks, Iain (M.) 1954- DLB-194, 261
Banks, John circa 1653-1706 . . . . .DLB-80
Banks, Russell 1940- DLB-130, 278
Bannerman, Helen 1862-1946. . . . . .DLB-141
Bantam Books DLB-46
Banti, Anna 1895-1985 . . . . DLB-177
Banville, John 1945- DLB-14, 271
Banville, Théodore de 1823-1891 . . . . DLB-217
Baraka, Amiri
1934- DLB-5, 7, 16, 38; DS-8; CDALB-1
Barańczak, Stanisław 1946- DLB-232
Baratynsky, Evgenii Abramovich
1800-1844 . . . . .DLB-205
Barba-Jacob, Porfirio 1883-1942 . . . . .DLB-283
Barbauld, Anna Laetitia
1743-1825 . . . . DLB-107, 109, 142, 158
Barbeau, Marius 1883-1969. . . . . .DLB-92
Barber, John Warner 1798-1885 . . . . .DLB-30
Bàrberi Squarotti, Giorgio 1929- DLB-128
Barbey d'Aurevilly, Jules-Amédée
1808-1889 . . . . .DLB-119
Barbier, Auguste 1805-1882 . . . . .DLB-217
Barbilian, Dan (see Barbu, Ion)
Barbour, John circa 1316-1395 . . . . .DLB-146
Barbour, Ralph Henry 1870-1944 . . . . .DLB-22
Barbu, Ion 1895-1961 . . . . . . DLB-220; CDWLB-4
Barbusse, Henri 1873-1935 . . . . .DLB-65
Barclay, Alexander circa 1475-1552. . . . . .DLB-132
E. E. Barclay and Company DLB-49
C. W. Bardeen [publishing house]. DLB-49
Barham, Richard Harris 1788-1845. . . . . .DLB-159
Barich, Bill 1943- DLB-185
Baring, Maurice 1874-1945 . . . . .DLB-34
Baring-Gould, Sabine 1834-1924. . . . DLB-156, 190
Barker, A. L. 1918- DLB-14, 139
Barker, Clive 1952- DLB-261
Barker, Dudley (see Black, Lionel)
Barker, George 1913-1991. . . . . .DLB-20
Barker, Harley Granville 1877-1946 . . . . . . DLB-10
Barker, Howard 1946- DLB-13, 233
Barker, James Nelson 1784-1858 . . . . DLB-37
Barker, Jane 1652-1727 . . . . .DLB-39, 131
Barker, Lady Mary Anne 1831-1911. . . . .DLB-166
Barker, Pat 1943- DLB-271
Barker, William circa 1520-after 1576 . . . .DLB-132
Arthur Barker Limited. DLB-112
Barkov, Ivan Semenovich 1732-1768 . . . . .DLB-150
Barks, Coleman 1937- DLB-5
Barlach, Ernst 1870-1938. . . . . .DLB-56, 118
Barlow, Joel 1754-1812 . . . . .DLB-37
The Prospect of Peace (1778) DLB-37
Barnard, John 1681-1770 . . . . .DLB-24
Barnard, Marjorie (M. Barnard Eldershaw)
1897-1987 . . . . .DLB-260
Barnard, Robert 1936- DLB-276
Barne, Kitty (Mary Catherine Barne)
1883-1957 . . . . .DLB-160
Barnes, Barnabe 1571-1609 . . . . .DLB-132
Barnes, Djuna 1892-1982 . . . . DLB-4, 9, 45; DS-15
Barnes, Jim 1933- DLB-175
Barnes, Julian 1946- DLB-194; Y-93
Notes for a Checklist of Publications Y-01
Barnes, Margaret Ayer 1886-1967 . . . . .DLB-9
Barnes, Peter 1931- DLB-13, 233
Barnes, William 1801-1886 . . . . .DLB-32
A. S. Barnes and Company DLB-49
Barnes and Noble Books DLB-46
Barnet, Miguel 1940- DLB-145
Barney, Natalie 1876-1972 . . . . .DLB-4; DS-15
Barnfield, Richard 1574-1627. . . . . DLB-172
Richard W. Baron [publishing house] DLB-46
Barr, Amelia Edith Huddleston
1831-1919 . . . . .DLB-202, 221

Barr, Robert 1850-1912 . . . . DLB-70, 92
Barral, Carlos 1928-1989 . . . . DLB-134
Barrax, Gerald William 1933- DLB-41, 120
Barrès, Maurice 1862-1923. . . . . DLB-123
Barreno, Maria Isabel (see The Three Marias: A Landmark Case in Portuguese Literary History)
Barrett, Eaton Stannard 1786-1820. . . . . . DLB-116
Barrie, J. M. 1860-1937. . . . . . DLB-10, 141, 156; CDBLB-5
Barrie and Jenkins. DLB-112
Barrio, Raymond 1921- DLB-82
Barrios, Gregg 1945- DLB-122
Barry, Philip 1896-1949 . . . . .DLB-7, 228
Barry, Robertine (see Françoise)
Barry, Sebastian 1955- DLB-245
Barse and Hopkins DLB-46
Barstow, Stan 1928- DLB-14, 139, 207
Tribute to John Braine. Y-86
Barth, John 1930- DLB-2, 227
Barthelme, Donald 1931-1989 . . . . .DLB-2, 234; Y-80, 89
Barthelme, Frederick 1943- DLB-244; Y-85
Barthes, Roland 1915-1980. . . . . DLB-296
Bartholomew, Frank 1898-1985 . . . . DLB-127
Bartlett, John 1820-1905. . . . . DLB-1, 235
Bartol, Cyrus Augustus 1813-1900. . . . DLB-1, 235
Barton, Bernard 1784-1849. . . . . DLB-96
Barton, John ca. 1610-1675. . . . . DLB-236
Barton, Thomas Pennant 1803-1869 . . . . DLB-140
Bartram, John 1699-1777 . . . . DLB-31
Bartram, William 1739-1823. . . . . DLB-37
Barykova, Anna Pavlovna 1839-1893 . . . .DLB-277
Basic Books. DLB-46
Basille, Theodore (see Becon, Thomas)
Bass, Rick 1958- DLB-212, 275
Bass, T. J. 1932- Y-81
Bassani, Giorgio 1916-2000 . . . . DLB-128, 177, 299
Basse, William circa 1583-1653 . . . . DLB-121
Bassett, John Spencer 1867-1928. . . . . DLB-17
Bassler, Thomas Joseph (see Bass, T. J.)
Bate, Walter Jackson 1918-1999. . . . . .DLB-67, 103
Bateman, Stephen circa 1510-1584 . . . . . . DLB-136
Christopher Bateman [publishing house] DLB-170
Bates, H. E. 1905-1974 . . . . DLB-162, 191
Bates, Katharine Lee 1859-1929 . . . . DLB-71
Batiushkov, Konstantin Nikolaevich 1787-1855 . . . . DLB-205
B. T. Batsford [publishing house] DLB-106
Battiscombe, Georgina 1905- DLB-155
The Battle of Maldon circa 1000. . . . . DLB-146
Baudelaire, Charles 1821-1867 . . . . DLB-217
Baudrillard, Jean 1929- DLB-296
Bauer, Bruno 1809-1882. . . . . DLB-133
Bauer, Wolfgang 1941- DLB-124
Baum, L. Frank 1856-1919. . . . . DLB-22
Baum, Vicki 1888-1960 . . . . DLB-85
Baumbach, Jonathan 1933- Y-80
Bausch, Richard 1945- DLB-130
Tribute to James Dickey Y-97
Tribute to Peter Taylor Y-94
Bausch, Robert 1945- DLB-218
Bawden, Nina 1925- DLB-14, 161, 207
Bax, Clifford 1886-1962 . . . . .DLB-10, 100
Baxter, Charles 1947- DLB-130
Bayer, Eleanor (see Perry, Eleanor)
Bayer, Konrad 1932-1964 . . . . DLB-85
Bayle, Pierre 1647-1706. . . . . DLB-268
Bayley, Barrington J. 1937- DLB-261
Baynes, Pauline 1922- DLB-160
Baynton, Barbara 1857-1929. . . . . DLB-230
Bazin, Hervé (Jean Pierre Marie Hervé-Bazin) 1911-1996 . . . . DLB-83
The BBC Four Samuel Johnson Prize for Non-fiction Y-02
Beach, Sylvia 1887-1962. . . . . DLB-4; DS-15
Beacon Press. DLB-49
Beadle and Adams DLB-49
Beagle, Peter S. 1939- Y-80
Beal, M. F. 1937- Y-81
Beale, Howard K. 1899-1959 . . . . DLB-17
Beard, Charles A. 1874-1948 . . . . DLB-17
Beat Generation (Beats)
As I See It, by Carolyn Cassady DLB-16
A Beat Chronology: The First Twenty-five Years, 1944-1969. . . . . DLB-16
The Commercialization of the Image of Revolt, by Kenneth Rexroth . . . DLB-16
Four Essays on the Beat Generation . . DLB-16
in New York City DLB-237
in the West. DLB-237
Outlaw Days DLB-16
Periodicals of DLB-16
Beattie, Ann 1947- DLB-218, 278; Y-82
Beattie, James 1735-1803 . . . . DLB-109
Beatty, Chester 1875-1968 . . . . DLB-201
Beauchemin, Nérée 1850-1931 . . . . DLB-92
Beauchemin, Yves 1941- DLB-60
Beaugrand, Honoré 1848-1906 . . . . DLB-99
Beaulieu, Victor-Lévy 1945- DLB-53
Beaumont, Francis circa 1584-1616 and Fletcher, John 1579-1625. . . . . DLB-58; CDBLB-1
Beaumont, Sir John 1583?-1627 . . . . DLB-121
Beaumont, Joseph 1616-1699 . . . . DLB-126
Beauvoir, Simone de 1908-1986. . . . .DLB-72; Y-86
Personal Tribute to Simone de Beauvoir . . . Y-86
Beaver, Bruce 1928- DLB-289
Becher, Ulrich 1910-1990. . . . . DLB-69
Becker, Carl 1873-1945 . . . . DLB-17
Becker, Jurek 1937-1997 . . . . DLB-75, 299
Becker, Jurgen 1932- DLB-75
Beckett, Samuel 1906-1989 . . . . DLB-13, 15, 233; Y-90; CDBLB-7
Beckford, William 1760-1844. . . . . . . DLB-39, 213
Beckham, Barry 1944- DLB-33
Bećković, Matija 1939- DLB-181
Becon, Thomas circa 1512-1567. . . . . DLB-136
Becque, Henry 1837-1899. . . . . DLB-192
Beddoes, Thomas 1760-1808 . . . . DLB-158
Beddoes, Thomas Lovell 1803-1849 . . . . . DLB-96
Bede circa 673-735 . . . . DLB-146
Bedford-Jones, H. 1887-1949 . . . . DLB-251
Bedregal, Yolanda 1913-1999. . . . . DLB-283
Beebe, William 1877-1962 . . . . .DLB-275
Beecher, Catharine Esther 1800-1878. DLB-1, 243
Beecher, Henry Ward 1813-1887. . . . . DLB-3, 43, 250
Beer, George L. 1872-1920. . . . . DLB-47
Beer, Johann 1655-1700 . . . . DLB-168
Beer, Patricia 1919-1999. . . . . DLB-40
Beerbohm, Max 1872-1956 . . . . .DLB-34, 100
Beer-Hofmann, Richard 1866-1945 . . . . . . DLB-81
Beers, Henry A. 1847-1926. . . . . DLB-71
S. O. Beeton [publishing house] DLB-106
Begley, Louis 1933- DLB-299
Bégon, Elisabeth 1696-1755 . . . . DLB-99
Behan, Brendan 1923-1964 . . . . DLB-13, 233; CDBLB-7
Behn, Aphra 1640?-1689 . . . . DLB-39, 80, 131
Behn, Harry 1898-1973 . . . . DLB-61
Behrman, S. N. 1893-1973 . . . . .DLB-7, 44
Beklemishev, Iurii Solomonvich (see Krymov, Iurii Solomonovich)
Belaney, Archibald Stansfeld (see Grey Owl)
Belasco, David 1853-1931 . . . . DLB-7
Clarke Belford and Company DLB-49
Belgian Luxembourg American Studies Association. Y-01
Belinsky, Vissarion Grigor'evich 1811-1848 . . . . DLB-198
Belitt, Ben 1911- DLB-5
Belknap, Jeremy 1744-1798. . . . . .DLB-30, 37
Bell, Adrian 1901-1980. . . . . DLB-191
Bell, Clive 1881-1964 . . . . .DS-10
Bell, Daniel 1919- DLB-246
Bell, Gertrude Margaret Lowthian 1868-1926 . . . . .DLB-174
Bell, James Madison 1826-1902 . . . . DLB-50
Bell, Madison Smartt 1957- DLB-218, 278
Tribute to Andrew Nelson Lytle Y-95
Tribute to Peter Taylor Y-94
Bell, Marvin 1937- DLB-5
Bell, Millicent 1919- DLB-111
Bell, Quentin 1910-1996. . . . . DLB-155
Bell, Vanessa 1879-1961 . . . . .DS-10
George Bell and Sons DLB-106

Robert Bell [publishing house] DLB-49
Bellamy, Edward 1850-1898 . . . . DLB-12
Bellamy, Joseph 1719-1790 . . . . DLB-31
John Bellamy [publishing house] DLB-170
La Belle Assemblée 1806-1837 . . . . DLB-110
Bellezza, Dario 1944-1996 . . . . DLB-128
Belli, Carlos Germán 1927- DLB-290
Belli, Gioconda 1948- DLB-290
Belloc, Hilaire 1870-1953 . . . . DLB-19, 100, 141, 174
Belloc, Madame (see Parkes, Bessie Rayner)
Bellonci, Maria 1902-1986 . . . . DLB-196
Bellow, Saul 1915- DLB-2, 28, 299; Y-82; DS-3; CDALB-1
Tribute to Isaac Bashevis Singer Y-91
Belmont Productions DLB-46
Bels, Alberts 1938- DLB-232
Belševica, Vizma 1931- DLB-232; CDWLB-4
Bely, Andrei 1880-1934 . . . . DLB-295
Bemelmans, Ludwig 1898-1962 . . . . DLB-22
Bemis, Samuel Flagg 1891-1973 . . . . DLB-17
William Bemrose [publishing house] DLB-106
Ben no Naishi 1228?-1271? DLB-203
Benchley, Robert 1889-1945 . . . . DLB-11
Bencúr, Matej (see Kukučin, Martin)
Benedetti, Mario 1920- DLB-113
Benedict, Pinckney 1964- DLB-244
Benedict, Ruth 1887-1948 . . . . DLB-246
Benedictus, David 1938- DLB-14
Benedikt Gröndal 1826-1907 . . . . DLB-293
Benedikt, Michael 1935- DLB-5
Benediktov, Vladimir Grigor'evich 1807-1873 . . . . DLB-205
Benét, Stephen Vincent 1898-1943 . . . . DLB-4, 48, 102, 249
Stephen Vincent Benét Centenary Y-97
Benét, William Rose 1886-1950 . . . . DLB-45
Benford, Gregory 1941- Y-82
Benítez, Sandra 1941- DLB-292
Benjamin, Park 1809-1864 . . . . . DLB-3, 59, 73, 250
Benjamin, Peter (see Cunningham, Peter)
Benjamin, S. G. W. 1837-1914 . . . . DLB-189
Benjamin, Walter 1892-1940 . . . . DLB-242
Benlowes, Edward 1602-1676 . . . . DLB-126
Benn, Gottfried 1886-1956 . . . . DLB-56
Benn Brothers Limited DLB-106
Bennett, Arnold 1867-1931 . . . . DLB-10, 34, 98, 135; CDBLB-5
The Arnold Bennett Society Y-98
Bennett, Charles 1899-1995 . . . . DLB-44
Bennett, Emerson 1822-1905 . . . . DLB-202
Bennett, Gwendolyn 1902-1981 . . . . DLB-51
Bennett, Hal 1930- DLB-33
Bennett, James Gordon 1795-1872 . . . . DLB-43
Bennett, James Gordon, Jr. 1841-1918 . . . . . DLB-23
Bennett, John 1865-1956 . . . . DLB-42
Bennett, Louise 1919- DLB-117; CDWLB-3
Benni, Stefano 1947- DLB-196
Benoit, Jacques 1941- DLB-60
Benson, A. C. 1862-1925 . . . . DLB-98
Benson, E. F. 1867-1940 . . . . DLB-135, 153
The E. F. Benson Society Y-98
The Tilling Society Y-98
Benson, Jackson J. 1930- DLB-111
Benson, Robert Hugh 1871-1914 . . . . DLB-153
Benson, Stella 1892-1933 . . . . DLB-36, 162
Bent, James Theodore 1852-1897 . . . . DLB-174
Bent, Mabel Virginia Anna ?-? DLB-174
Bentham, Jeremy 1748-1832 . . . DLB-107, 158, 252
Bentley, E. C. 1875-1956 . . . . DLB-70
Bentley, Phyllis 1894-1977 . . . . DLB-191
Bentley, Richard 1662-1742 . . . . DLB-252
Richard Bentley [publishing house] DLB-106
Benton, Robert 1932- and Newman, David 1937- DLB-44
Benziger Brothers DLB-49
Beowulf circa 900-1000 or 790-825 .DLB-146; CDBLB-1
Berent, Wacław 1873-1940 . . . . DLB-215
Beresford, Anne 1929- DLB-40
Beresford, John Davys 1873-1947 . . . . DLB-162, 178, 197
"Experiment in the Novel" (1929) [excerpt] DLB-36
Beresford-Howe, Constance 1922- DLB-88
R. G. Berford Company DLB-49
Berg, Elizabeth 1948- DLB-292
Berg, Stephen 1934- DLB-5
Bergengruen, Werner 1892-1964 . . . . DLB-56
Berger, John 1926- DLB-14, 207
Berger, Meyer 1898-1959 . . . . DLB-29
Berger, Thomas 1924- DLB-2; Y-80
A Statement by Thomas Berger Y-80
Bergman, Hjalmar 1883-1931 . . . . DLB-259
Bergman, Ingmar 1918- DLB-257
Berkeley, Anthony 1893-1971 . . . . DLB-77
Berkeley, George 1685-1753 . . . . DLB-31, 101, 252
The Berkley Publishing Corporation DLB-46
Berlin, Irving 1888-1989 . . . . DLB-265
Berlin, Lucia 1936- DLB-130
Berman, Marshall 1940- DLB-246
Bernal, Vicente J. 1888-1915 . . . . DLB-82
Bernanos, Georges 1888-1948 . . . . DLB-72
Bernard, Catherine 1663?-1712 . . . . DLB-268
Bernard, Harry 1898-1979 . . . . DLB-92
Bernard, John 1756-1828 . . . . DLB-37
Bernard of Chartres circa 1060-1124? DLB-115
Bernard of Clairvaux 1090-1153 . . . . DLB-208
Bernard, Richard 1568-1641/1642 . . . . DLB-281
Bernard Silvestris flourished circa 1130-1160 . . . . DLB-208
Bernari, Carlo 1909-1992 . . . . DLB-177
Bernhard, Thomas 1931-1989 . . . . DLB-85, 124; CDWLB-2
Berniéres, Louis de 1954- DLB-271
Bernstein, Charles 1950- DLB-169
Berriault, Gina 1926-1999 . . . . DLB-130
Berrigan, Daniel 1921- DLB-5
Berrigan, Ted 1934-1983 . . . . DLB-5, 169
Berry, Wendell 1934- DLB-5, 6, 234, 275
Berryman, John 1914-1972 . . . .DLB-48; CDALB-1
Bersianik, Louky 1930- DLB-60
Thomas Berthelet [publishing house] DLB-170
Berto, Giuseppe 1914-1978 . . . . DLB-177
Bertocci, Peter Anthony 1910-1989 . . . . . . DLB-279
Bertolucci, Attilio 1911-2000 . . . . DLB-128
Berton, Pierre 1920- DLB-68
Bertrand, Louis "Aloysius" 1807-1841 . . . . DLB-217
Besant, Sir Walter 1836-1901 . . . . . . DLB-135, 190
Bessa-Luís, Agustina 1922- DLB-287
Bessette, Gerard 1920- DLB-53
Bessie, Alvah 1904-1985 . . . . DLB-26
Bester, Alfred 1913-1987 . . . . DLB-8
Besterman, Theodore 1904-1976 . . . . DLB-201
Beston, Henry (Henry Beston Sheahan) 1888-1968 . . . . DLB-275
Best-Seller Lists
An Assessment Y-84
What's Really Wrong With Bestseller Lists Y-84
Bestuzhev, Aleksandr Aleksandrovich (Marlinsky) 1797-1837 . . . . DLB-198
Bestuzhev, Nikolai Aleksandrovich 1791-1855 . . . . DLB-198
Betham-Edwards, Matilda Barbara (see Edwards, Matilda Barbara Betham-)
Betjeman, John 1906-1984 . . . . .DLB-20; Y-84; CDBLB-7
Betocchi, Carlo 1899-1986 . . . . DLB-128
Bettarini, Mariella 1942- DLB-128
Betts, Doris 1932- DLB-218; Y-82
Beveridge, Albert J. 1862-1927 . . . . DLB-17
Beverley, Robert circa 1673-1722 . . . . . . DLB-24, 30
Bevilacqua, Alberto 1934- DLB-196
Bevington, Louisa Sarah 1845-1895 . . . . . DLB-199
Beyle, Marie-Henri (see Stendhal)
Białoszewski, Miron 1922-1983 . . . . DLB-232
Bianco, Margery Williams 1881-1944 . . . . DLB-160
Bibaud, Adèle 1854-1941 . . . . DLB-92
Bibaud, Michel 1782-1857 . . . . DLB-99
Bibliography
Bibliographical and Textual Scholarship Since World War II Y-89
Center for Bibliographical Studies and Research at the University of California, Riverside Y-91
The Great Bibliographers Series Y-93
Primary Bibliography: A Retrospective . . Y-95
Bichsel, Peter 1935- DLB-75
Bickerstaff, Isaac John 1733-circa 1808 . . . . DLB-89

Drexel Biddle [publishing house] DLB-49
Bidermann, Jacob 1577 or 1578-1639 . . . . DLB-164
Bidwell, Walter Hilliard 1798-1881 . . . . . . DLB-79
Biehl, Charlotta Dorothea 1731-1788 . . . . DLB-300
Bienek, Horst 1930-1990 . . . . DLB-75
Bierbaum, Otto Julius 1865-1910 . . . . DLB-66
Bierce, Ambrose 1842-1914? DLB-11, 12, 23, 71, 74, 186; CDALB-3
Bigelow, William F. 1879-1966 . . . . DLB-91
Biggle, Lloyd, Jr. 1923- DLB-8
Bigiaretti, Libero 1905-1993 . . . . .DLB-177
Bigland, Eileen 1898-1970. . . . . DLB-195
Biglow, Hosea (see Lowell, James Russell)
Bigongiari, Piero 1914-1997 . . . . DLB-128
Bilenchi, Romano 1909-1989 . . . . DLB-264
Billinger, Richard 1890-1965 . . . . DLB-124
Billings, Hammatt 1818-1874 . . . . DLB-188
Billings, John Shaw 1898-1975 . . . . DLB-137
Billings, Josh (see Shaw, Henry Wheeler)
Binding, Rudolf G. 1867-1938 . . . . DLB-66
Bingay, Malcolm 1884-1953. . . . . DLB-241
Bingham, Caleb 1757-1817 . . . . DLB-42
Bingham, George Barry 1906-1988 . . . . . DLB-127
Bingham, Sallie 1937- DLB-234
William Bingley [publishing house] DLB-154
Binyon, Laurence 1869-1943 . . . . DLB-19
Biographia Brittanica DLB-142
Biography
Biographical Documents Y-84, 85
A Celebration of Literary Biography Y-98
Conference on Modern Biography Y-85
The Cult of Biography Excerpts from the Second Folio Debate: "Biographies are generally a disease of English Literature" Y-86
New Approaches to Biography: Challenges from Critical Theory, USC Conference on Literary Studies, 1990 . . . . Y-90
"The New Biography," by Virginia Woolf, *New York Herald Tribune,* 30 October 1927 . . . . DLB-149
"The Practice of Biography," in *The English Sense of Humour and Other Essays,* by Harold Nicolson DLB-149
"Principles of Biography," in *Elizabethan and Other Essays,* by Sidney Lee . . DLB-149
Remarks at the Opening of "The Biographical Part of Literature" Exhibition, by William R. Cagle. Y-98
Survey of Literary Biographies Y-00
A Transit of Poets and Others: American Biography in 1982. . . . . Y-82
The Year in Literary Biography Y-83–01
Biography, The Practice of:
An Interview with B. L. Reid. Y-83
An Interview with David Herbert Donald . . Y-87
An Interview with Humphrey Carpenter . . . Y-84
An Interview with Joan Mellen Y-94
An Interview with John Caldwell Guilds Y-92
An Interview with William Manchester. . . Y-85
John Bioren [publishing house]. DLB-49
Bioy Casares, Adolfo 1914-1999 . . . . DLB-113
Bird, Isabella Lucy 1831-1904 . . . . DLB-166
Bird, Robert Montgomery 1806-1854 . . . DLB-202
Bird, William 1888-1963 . . . . DLB-4; DS-15
The Cost of the *Cantos:* William Bird to Ezra Pound Y-01
Birken, Sigmund von 1626-1681 . . . . DLB-164
Birney, Earle 1904-1995. . . . . DLB-88
Birrell, Augustine 1850-1933 . . . . DLB-98
Bisher, Furman 1918- DLB-171
Bishop, Elizabeth 1911-1979. . . . . DLB-5, 169; CDALB-6
The Elizabeth Bishop Society. Y-01
Bishop, John Peale 1892-1944 . . . . . . DLB-4, 9, 45
Bismarck, Otto von 1815-1898. . . . . DLB-129
Bisset, Robert 1759-1805 . . . . DLB-142
Bissett, Bill 1939- DLB-53
Bitzius, Albert (see Gotthelf, Jeremias)
Bjørnboe, Jens 1920-1976 . . . . DLB-297
Bjørnvig, Thorkild 1918- DLB-214
Black, David (D. M.) 1941- DLB-40
Black, Gavin (Oswald Morris Wynd) 1913-1998 . . . . .DLB-276
Black, Lionel (Dudley Barker) 1910-1980 . . . . .DLB-276
Black, Winifred 1863-1936. . . . . DLB-25
Walter J. Black [publishing house] DLB-46
Blackamore, Arthur 1679-? DLB-24, 39
Blackburn, Alexander L. 1929- Y-85
Blackburn, John 1923-1993 . . . . DLB-261
Blackburn, Paul 1926-1971. . . . . .DLB-16; Y-81
Blackburn, Thomas 1916-1977. . . . . DLB-27
Blacker, Terence 1948- DLB-271
Blackmore, R. D. 1825-1900 . . . . DLB-18
Blackmore, Sir Richard 1654-1729 . . . . . . DLB-131
Blackmur, R. P. 1904-1965. . . . . DLB-63
Basil Blackwell, Publisher. DLB-106
Blackwood, Algernon Henry 1869-1951 . . . . .DLB-153, 156, 178
Blackwood, Caroline 1931-1996. . . . . .DLB-14, 207
William Blackwood and Sons, Ltd. DLB-154
Blackwood's Edinburgh Magazine 1817-1980. . . . . DLB-110
Blades, William 1824-1890. . . . . DLB-184
Blaga, Lucian 1895-1961 . . . . DLB-220
Blagden, Isabella 1817?-1873 . . . . DLB-199
Blair, Eric Arthur (see Orwell, George)
Blair, Francis Preston 1791-1876. . . . . DLB-43
Blair, Hugh
Lectures on Rhetoric and Belles Lettres (1783), [excerpts] DLB-31
Blair, James circa 1655-1743 . . . . DLB-24
Blair, John Durburrow 1759-1823 . . . . DLB-37
Blais, Marie-Claire 1939- DLB-53
Blaise, Clark 1940- DLB-53
Blake, George 1893-1961 . . . . DLB-191
Blake, Lillie Devereux 1833-1913. . . . DLB-202, 221
Blake, Nicholas (C. Day Lewis) 1904-1972. . . . . DLB-77
Blake, William 1757-1827 . . . . . . DLB-93, 154, 163; CDBLB-3
The Blakiston Company DLB-49
Blanchard, Stephen 1950- DLB-267
Blanchot, Maurice 1907-2003 . . . . DLB-72, 296
Blanckenburg, Christian Friedrich von 1744-1796 . . . . DLB-94
Blandiana, Ana 1942- DLB-232; CDWLB-4
Blanshard, Brand 1892-1987 . . . . .DLB-279
Blaser, Robin 1925- DLB-165
Blaumanis, Rudolfs 1863-1908. . . . . DLB-220
Bleasdale, Alan 1946- DLB-245
Bledsoe, Albert Taylor 1809-1877. . . . . .DLB-3, 79, 248
Bleecker, Ann Eliza 1752-1783 . . . . DLB-200
Blelock and Company DLB-49
Blennerhassett, Margaret Agnew 1773-1842. . . . . DLB-99
Geoffrey Bles [publishing house] DLB-112
Blessington, Marguerite, Countess of 1789-1849. . . . . DLB-166
Blew, Mary Clearman 1939- DLB-256
Blicher, Steen Steensen 1782-1848 . . . . . . DLB-300
The Blickling Homilies circa 971 . . . . DLB-146
Blind, Mathilde 1841-1896. . . . . DLB-199
Blish, James 1921-1975. . . . . DLB-8
E. Bliss and E. White [publishing house] DLB-49
Bliven, Bruce 1889-1977. . . . . .DLB-137
Blixen, Karen 1885-1962 . . . . DLB-214
Bloch, Ernst 1885-1977. . . . . DLB-296
Bloch, Robert 1917-1994. . . . . DLB-44
Tribute to John D. MacDonald Y-86
Block, Lawrence 1938- DLB-226
Block, Rudolph (see Lessing, Bruno)
Blok, Aleksandr Aleksandrovich 1880-1921 . . . . DLB-295
Blondal, Patricia 1926-1959 . . . . DLB-88
Bloom, Harold 1930- DLB-67
Bloomer, Amelia 1818-1894. . . . . DLB-79
Bloomfield, Robert 1766-1823 . . . . DLB-93
Bloomsbury Group. .DS-10
The *Dreadnought* Hoax DS-10
Blotner, Joseph 1923- DLB-111
Blount, Thomas 1618?-1679. . . . . DLB-236
Bloy, Léon 1846-1917. . . . . DLB-123
Blume, Judy 1938- DLB-52
Tribute to Theodor Seuss Geisel. Y-91
Blunck, Hans Friedrich 1888-1961. . . . . . . DLB-66
Blunden, Edmund 1896-1974. . . .DLB-20, 100, 155
Blundeville, Thomas 1522?-1606. . . . . . . DLB-236

Blunt, Lady Anne Isabella Noel 1837-1917 . . . DLB-174
Blunt, Wilfrid Scawen 1840-1922 . . . DLB-19, 174
Bly, Nellie (see Cochrane, Elizabeth)
Bly, Robert 1926- . . . DLB-5
Blyton, Enid 1897-1968 . . . DLB-160
Boaden, James 1762-1839 . . . DLB-89
Boas, Frederick S. 1862-1957 . . . DLB-149
The Bobbs-Merrill Company . . . DLB-46, 291
The Bobbs-Merrill Archive at the Lilly Library, Indiana University . . . Y-90
Boborykin, Petr Dmitrievich 1836-1921 . . DLB-238
Bobrov, Semen Sergeevich 1763?-1810 . . . DLB-150
Bobrowski, Johannes 1917-1965 . . . DLB-75
Bocage, Manuel Maria Barbosa du 1765-1805 . . . DLB-287
Bodenheim, Maxwell 1892-1954 . . . DLB-9, 45
Bodenstedt, Friedrich von 1819-1892 . . . DLB-129
Bodini, Vittorio 1914-1970 . . . DLB-128
Bodkin, M. McDonnell 1850-1933 . . . DLB-70
Bodley, Sir Thomas 1545-1613 . . . DLB-213
Bodley Head . . . DLB-112
Bodmer, Johann Jakob 1698-1783 . . . DLB-97
Bodmershof, Imma von 1895-1982 . . . DLB-85
Bodsworth, Fred 1918- . . . DLB-68
Böðvar Guðmundsson 1939- . . . DLB-293
Boehm, Sydney 1908- . . . DLB-44
Boer, Charles 1939- . . . DLB-5
Boethius circa 480-circa 524 . . . DLB-115
Boethius of Dacia circa 1240-? . . . DLB-115
Bogan, Louise 1897-1970 . . . DLB-45, 169
Bogarde, Dirk 1921-1999 . . . DLB-14
Bogdanov, Aleksandr Aleksandrovich 1873-1928 . . . DLB-295
Bogdanovich, Ippolit Fedorovich circa 1743-1803 . . . DLB-150
David Bogue [publishing house] . . . DLB-106
Bohjalian, Chris 1960- . . . DLB-292
Böhme, Jakob 1575-1624 . . . DLB-164
H. G. Bohn [publishing house] . . . DLB-106
Bohse, August 1661-1742 . . . DLB-168
Boie, Heinrich Christian 1744-1806 . . . DLB-94
Boileau-Despréaux, Nicolas 1636-1711 . . . DLB-268
Bok, Edward W. 1863-1930 . . . DLB-91; DS-16
Boland, Eavan 1944- . . . DLB-40
Boldrewood, Rolf (Thomas Alexander Browne) 1826?-1915 . . . DLB-230
Bolingbroke, Henry St. John, Viscount 1678-1751 . . . DLB-101
Böll, Heinrich 1917-1985 . . . DLB-69; Y-85; CDWLB-2
Bolling, Robert 1738-1775 . . . DLB-31
Bolotov, Andrei Timofeevich 1738-1833 . . . DLB-150
Bolt, Carol 1941- . . . DLB-60
Bolt, Robert 1924-1995 . . . DLB-13, 233
Bolton, Herbert E. 1870-1953 . . . DLB-17
Bonaventura . . . DLB-90
Bonaventure circa 1217-1274 . . . DLB-115
Bonaviri, Giuseppe 1924- . . . DLB-177
Bond, Edward 1934- . . . DLB-13
Bond, Michael 1926- . . . DLB-161
Albert and Charles Boni [publishing house] . . . DLB-46
Boni and Liveright . . . DLB-46
Bonnefoy, Yves 1923- . . . DLB-258
Bonner, Marita 1899-1971 . . . DLB-228
Bonner, Paul Hyde 1893-1968 . . . DS-17
Bonner, Sherwood (see McDowell, Katharine Sherwood Bonner)
Robert Bonner's Sons . . . DLB-49
Bonnin, Gertrude Simmons (see Zitkala-Ša)
Bonsanti, Alessandro 1904-1984 . . . DLB-177
Bontempelli, Massimo 1878-1960 . . . DLB-264
Bontemps, Arna 1902-1973 . . . DLB-48, 51
The Book Buyer (1867-1880, 1884-1918, 1935-1938 . . . DS-13
The Book League of America . . . DLB-46
Book Reviewing
The American Book Review: A Sketch . . . Y-92
Book Reviewing and the Literary Scene . . . Y-96, 97
Book Reviewing in America . . . Y-87–94
Book Reviewing in America and the Literary Scene . . . Y-95
Book Reviewing in Texas . . . Y-94
Book Reviews in Glossy Magazines . . . Y-95
Do They or Don't They? Writers Reading Book Reviews . . . Y-01
The Most Powerful Book Review in America [*New York Times Book Review*] . . . Y-82
Some Surprises and Universal Truths . . . Y-92
The Year in Book Reviewing and the Literary Situation . . . Y-98
Book Supply Company . . . DLB-49
The Book Trade History Group . . . Y-93
The Booker Prize . . . Y-96–98
Address by Anthony Thwaite, Chairman of the Booker Prize Judges Comments from Former Booker Prize Winners . . . Y-86
Boorde, Andrew circa 1490-1549 . . . DLB-136
Boorstin, Daniel J. 1914- . . . DLB-17
Tribute to Archibald MacLeish . . . Y-82
Tribute to Charles Scribner Jr. . . . Y-95
Booth, Franklin 1874-1948 . . . DLB-188
Booth, Mary L. 1831-1889 . . . DLB-79
Booth, Philip 1925- . . . Y-82
Booth, Wayne C. 1921- . . . DLB-67
Booth, William 1829-1912 . . . DLB-190
Bor, Josef 1906-1979 . . . DLB-299
Borchardt, Rudolf 1877-1945 . . . DLB-66
Borchert, Wolfgang 1921-1947 . . . DLB-69, 124
Bording, Anders 1619-1677 . . . DLB-300
Borel, Pétrus 1809-1859 . . . DLB-119
Borgen, Johan 1902-1979 . . . DLB-297
Borges, Jorge Luis 1899-1986 . . . DLB-113, 283; Y-86; CDWLB-3
The Poetry of Jorge Luis Borges . . . Y-86
A Personal Tribute . . . Y-86
Borgese, Giuseppe Antonio 1882-1952 . . . DLB-264
Börne, Ludwig 1786-1837 . . . DLB-90
Bornstein, Miriam 1950- . . . DLB-209
Borowski, Tadeusz 1922-1951 . . . DLB-215; CDWLB-4
Borrow, George 1803-1881 . . . DLB-21, 55, 166
Bosanquet, Bernard 1848-1923 . . . DLB-262
Bosch, Juan 1909-2001 . . . DLB-145
Bosco, Henri 1888-1976 . . . DLB-72
Bosco, Monique 1927- . . . DLB-53
Bosman, Herman Charles 1905-1951 . . . DLB-225
Bossuet, Jacques-Bénigne 1627-1704 . . . DLB-268
Bostic, Joe 1908-1988 . . . DLB-241
Boston, Lucy M. 1892-1990 . . . DLB-161
Boston Quarterly Review . . . DLB-1
Boston University
Editorial Institute at Boston University . . . Y-00
Special Collections at Boston University . . Y-99
Boswell, James 1740-1795 . . . DLB-104, 142; CDBLB-2
Boswell, Robert 1953- . . . DLB-234
Bosworth, David . . . Y-82
Excerpt from "Excerpts from a Report of the Commission," in *The Death of Descartes* . . . Y-82
Bote, Hermann circa 1460-circa 1520 . . . DLB-179
Botev, Khristo 1847-1876 . . . DLB-147
Botkin, Vasilii Petrovich 1811-1869 . . . DLB-277
Botta, Anne C. Lynch 1815-1891 . . . DLB-3, 250
Botto, Ján (see Krasko, Ivan)
Bottome, Phyllis 1882-1963 . . . DLB-197
Bottomley, Gordon 1874-1948 . . . DLB-10
Bottoms, David 1949- . . . DLB-120; Y-83
Tribute to James Dickey . . . Y-97
Bottrall, Ronald 1906- . . . DLB-20
Bouchardy, Joseph 1810-1870 . . . DLB-192
Boucher, Anthony 1911-1968 . . . DLB-8
Boucher, Jonathan 1738-1804 . . . DLB-31
Boucher de Boucherville, Georges 1814-1894 . . . DLB-99
Boudreau, Daniel (see Coste, Donat)
Bouhours, Dominique 1628-1702 . . . DLB-268
Bourassa, Napoléon 1827-1916 . . . DLB-99
Bourget, Paul 1852-1935 . . . DLB-123
Bourinot, John George 1837-1902 . . . DLB-99
Bourjaily, Vance 1922- . . . DLB-2, 143
Bourne, Edward Gaylord 1860-1908 . . . DLB-47
Bourne, Randolph 1886-1918 . . . DLB-63
Bousoño, Carlos 1923- . . . DLB-108
Bousquet, Joë 1897-1950 . . . DLB-72

Bova, Ben 1932- Y-81
Bovard, Oliver K. 1872-1945 . . . . DLB-25
Bove, Emmanuel 1898-1945. . . . . DLB-72
Bowen, Elizabeth 1899-1973. . . . . DLB-15, 162; CDBLB-7
Bowen, Francis 1811-1890 . . . . DLB-1, 59, 235
Bowen, John 1924- DLB-13
Bowen, Marjorie 1886-1952 . . . . DLB-153
Bowen-Merrill Company DLB-49
Bowering, George 1935- DLB-53
Bowers, Bathsheba 1671-1718. . . . . DLB-200
Bowers, Claude G. 1878-1958 . . . . DLB-17
Bowers, Edgar 1924-2000. . . . . DLB-5
Bowers, Fredson Thayer 1905-1991 . . . . DLB-140; Y- 91
The Editorial Style of Fredson Bowers . . . Y-91
Fredson Bowers and Studies in Bibliography . . . . Y- 91
Fredson Bowers and the Cambridge Beaumont and Fletcher . . . . Y- 91
Fredson Bowers as Critic of Renaissance Dramatic Literature. . . . . Y- 91
Fredson Bowers as Music Critic. Y-91
Fredson Bowers, Master Teacher . . . . . . Y- 91
An Interview [on Nabokov] Y-80
Working with Fredson Bowers Y-91
Bowles, Paul 1910-1999 . . . . . .DLB-5, 6, 218; Y-99
Bowles, Samuel, III 1826-1878 . . . . DLB-43
Bowles, William Lisle 1762-1850 . . . . DLB-93
Bowman, Louise Morey 1882-1944 . . . . . . DLB-68
Bowne, Borden Parker 1847-1919 . . . . . . .DLB-270
Boyd, James 1888-1944 . . . . DLB-9; DS-16
Boyd, John 1919- DLB-8
Boyd, Martin 1893-1972. . . . . DLB-260
Boyd, Thomas 1898-1935 . . . . DLB-9; DS-16
Boyd, William 1952- DLB-231
Boye, Karin 1900-1941. . . . . DLB-259
Boyesen, Hjalmar Hjorth 1848-1895 . . . . .DLB-12, 71; DS-13
Boylan, Clare 1948- DLB-267
Boyle, Kay 1902-1992 DLB-4, 9, 48, 86; DS-15; Y-93
Boyle, Roger, Earl of Orrery 1621-1679. . . DLB-80
Boyle, T. Coraghessan 1948- DLB-218, 278; Y-86
Božić, Mirko 1919- DLB-181
Brackenbury, Alison 1953- DLB-40
Brackenridge, Hugh Henry 1748-1816. DLB-11, 37
The Rising Glory of America. DLB-37
Brackett, Charles 1892-1969. . . . . DLB-26
Brackett, Leigh 1915-1978 . . . . DLB-8, 26
John Bradburn [publishing house] DLB-49
Bradbury, Malcolm 1932-2000. . . . . . DLB-14, 207
Bradbury, Ray 1920- DLB-2, 8; CDALB-6
Bradbury and Evans. DLB-106
Braddon, Mary Elizabeth 1835-1915 . . . . .DLB-18, 70, 156
Bradford, Andrew 1686-1742 . . . . DLB-43, 73
Bradford, Gamaliel 1863-1932 . . . . DLB-17
Bradford, John 1749-1830. . . . . DLB-43
Bradford, Roark 1896-1948 . . . . DLB-86
Bradford, William 1590-1657. . . . . DLB-24, 30
Bradford, William, III 1719-1791 . . . . . DLB-43, 73
Bradlaugh, Charles 1833-1891 . . . . DLB-57
Bradley, David 1950- DLB-33
Bradley, F. H. 1846-1924 . . . . DLB-262
Bradley, Katherine Harris (see Field, Michael)
Bradley, Marion Zimmer 1930-1999 . . . . . . DLB-8
Bradley, William Aspenwall 1878-1939 . . . . DLB-4
Ira Bradley and Company DLB-49
J. W. Bradley and Company DLB-49
Bradshaw, Henry 1831-1886 . . . . DLB-184
Bradstreet, Anne 1612 or 1613-1672 . . . . DLB-24; CDALB-2
Bradūnas, Kazys 1917- DLB-220
Bradwardine, Thomas circa 1295-1349 . . DLB-115
Brady, Frank 1924-1986. . . . . DLB-111
Frederic A. Brady [publishing house] DLB-49
Bragg, Melvyn 1939- DLB-14, 271
Brahe, Tycho 1546-1601 . . . . DLB-300
Charles H. Brainard [publishing house] . . . DLB-49
Braine, John 1922-1986 . DLB-15; Y-86; CDBLB-7
Braithwait, Richard 1588-1673 . . . . DLB-151
Braithwaite, William Stanley 1878-1962. DLB-50, 54
Bräker, Ulrich 1735-1798 . . . . DLB-94
Bramah, Ernest 1868-1942. . . . . DLB-70
Branagan, Thomas 1774-1843 . . . . DLB-37
Brancati, Vitaliano 1907-1954. . . . . DLB-264
Branch, William Blackwell 1927- DLB-76
Brand, Christianna 1907-1988 . . . . .DLB-276
Brand, Max (see Faust, Frederick Schiller)
Brandão, Raul 1867-1930 . . . . DLB-287
Branden Press. DLB-46
Brandes, Georg 1842-1927 . . . . DLB-300
Branner, H.C. 1903-1966. . . . . DLB-214
Brant, Sebastian 1457-1521 . . . . .DLB-179
Brassey, Lady Annie (Allnutt) 1839-1887. . . . . DLB-166
Brathwaite, Edward Kamau 1930- DLB-125; CDWLB-3
Brault, Jacques 1933- DLB-53
Braun, Matt 1932- DLB-212
Braun, Volker 1939- DLB-75, 124
Brautigan, Richard 1935-1984 . . . . .DLB-2, 5, 206; Y-80, 84
Braxton, Joanne M. 1950- DLB-41
Bray, Anne Eliza 1790-1883 . . . . DLB-116
Bray, Thomas 1656-1730 . . . . DLB-24
Brazdžionis, Bernardas 1907- DLB-220
George Braziller [publishing house] DLB-46
The Bread Loaf Writers' Conference 1983 . . . Y-84
Breasted, James Henry 1865-1935 . . . . DLB-47
Brecht, Bertolt 1898-1956 . . . . .DLB-56, 124; CDWLB-2
Bredel, Willi 1901-1964 . . . . DLB-56
Bregendahl, Marie 1867-1940. . . . . DLB-214
Breitinger, Johann Jakob 1701-1776 . . . . . . DLB-97
Brekke, Paal 1923-1993 . . . . DLB-297
Bremser, Bonnie 1939- DLB-16
Bremser, Ray 1934-1998 . . . . DLB-16
Brennan, Christopher 1870-1932 . . . . DLB-230
Brentano, Bernard von 1901-1964 . . . . DLB-56
Brentano, Clemens 1778-1842 . . . . DLB-90
Brentano, Franz 1838-1917. . . . . DLB-296
Brentano's. DLB-49
Brenton, Howard 1942- DLB-13
Breslin, Jimmy 1929-1996 . . . . DLB-185
Breton, André 1896-1966 . . . . DLB-65, 258
Breton, Nicholas circa 1555-circa 1626. . . DLB-136
The Breton Lays 1300-early fifteenth century. DLB-146
Brett, Simon 1945- DLB-276
Brewer, Luther A. 1858-1933. . . . . .DLB-187
Brewer, Warren and Putnam DLB-46
Brewster, Elizabeth 1922- DLB-60
Breytenbach, Breyten 1939- DLB-225
Bridge, Ann (Lady Mary Dolling Sanders O'Malley) 1889-1974 . . . . DLB-191
Bridge, Horatio 1806-1893. . . . . DLB-183
Bridgers, Sue Ellen 1942- DLB-52
Bridges, Robert 1844-1930 . . . . DLB-19, 98; CDBLB-5
The Bridgewater Library DLB-213
Bridie, James 1888-1951. . . . . DLB-10
Brieux, Eugene 1858-1932 . . . . DLB-192
Brigadere, Anna 1861-1933 . . . . DLB-220; CDWLB-4
Briggs, Charles Frederick 1804-1877. DLB-3, 250
Brighouse, Harold 1882-1958. . . . . DLB-10
Bright, Mary Chavelita Dunne (see Egerton, George)
Brightman, Edgar Sheffield 1884-1953. . . .DLB-270
B. J. Brimmer Company. DLB-46
Brines, Francisco 1932- DLB-134
Brink, André 1935- DLB-225
Brinley, George, Jr. 1817-1875 . . . . DLB-140
Brinnin, John Malcolm 1916-1998 . . . . DLB-48
Brisbane, Albert 1809-1890 . . . . DLB-3, 250
Brisbane, Arthur 1864-1936. . . . . DLB-25
British Academy. DLB-112
The British Critic 1793-1843 . . . . DLB-110
British Library
The American Trust for the British Library. Y-96
The British Library and the Regular Readers' Group. Y-91

Building the New British Library at St Pancras Y-94
British Literary Prizes DLB-207; Y-98
British Literature
The "Angry Young Men" DLB-15
Author-Printers, 1476-1599 . . . . DLB-167
The Comic Tradition Continued DLB-15
Documents on Sixteenth-Century Literature DLB-167, 172
Eikon Basilike 1649 . . . . DLB-151
Letter from London Y-96
A Mirror for Magistrates DLB-167
"Modern English Prose" (1876), by George Saintsbury DLB-57
Sex, Class, Politics, and Religion [in the British Novel, 1930-1959] DLB-15
Victorians on Rhetoric and Prose Style DLB-57
The Year in British Fiction Y-99–01
"You've Never Had It So Good," Gusted by "Winds of Change": British Fiction in the 1950s, 1960s, and After DLB-14
British Literature, Old and Middle English
Anglo-Norman Literature in the Development of Middle English Literature DLB-146
The *Alliterative Morte Arthure and the Stanzaic Morte Arthur* circa 1350-1400 . . . . DLB-146
Ancrene Riwle circa 1200-1225 . . . . DLB-146
The Anglo-Saxon Chronicle circa 890-1154 . . . . DLB-146
The Battle of Maldon circa 1000 . . . . DLB-146
Beowulf circa 900-1000 or 790-825 . . . . DLB-146; CDBLB-1
The Blickling Homilies circa 971 . . . . . DLB-146
The Breton Lays 1300-early fifteenth century DLB-146
The Castle of Perserverance circa 1400-1425 . . . . DLB-146
The Celtic Background to Medieval English Literature DLB-146
The Chester Plays circa 1505-1532; revisions until 1575 . . . . DLB-146
Cursor Mundi circa 1300 . . . . DLB-146
The English Language: 410 to 1500 . . . . DLB-146
The Germanic Epic and Old English Heroic Poetry: *Widsith, Waldere,* and *The Fight at Finnsburg* DLB-146
Judith circa 930 . . . . DLB-146
The Matter of England 1240-1400 . . . DLB-146
The Matter of Rome early twelfth to late fifteenth centuries DLB-146
Middle English Literature: An Introduction DLB-146
The Middle English Lyric DLB-146
Morality Plays: *Mankind* circa 1450-1500 and *Everyman* circa 1500 . . . . DLB-146
N-Town Plays circa 1468 to early sixteenth century DLB-146
Old English Literature: An Introduction DLB-146
Old English Riddles eighth to tenth centuries DLB-146
The Owl and the Nightingale circa 1189-1199 . . . . DLB-146
The Paston Letters 1422-1509 . . . . DLB-146
The Seafarer circa 970 . . . . DLB-146
The *South English Legendary* circa thirteenth to fifteenth centuries DLB-146
The British Review and London Critical Journal 1811-1825 . . . . DLB-110
Brito, Aristeo 1942- DLB-122
Brittain, Vera 1893-1970 . . . . DLB-191
Briusov, Valerii Iakovlevich 1873-1924 . . . DLB-295
Brizeux, Auguste 1803-1858 . . . . DLB-217
Broadway Publishing Company DLB-46
Broch, Hermann 1886-1951 . . . . DLB-85, 124; CDWLB-2
Brochu, André 1942- DLB-53
Brock, Edwin 1927-1997 . . . . DLB-40
Brockes, Barthold Heinrich 1680-1747 . . . DLB-168
Brod, Max 1884-1968 . . . . DLB-81
Brodber, Erna 1940- DLB-157
Brodhead, John R. 1814-1873 . . . . DLB-30
Brodkey, Harold 1930-1996 . . . . DLB-130
Brodsky, Joseph (Iosif Aleksandrovich Brodsky) 1940-1996 . . . . DLB-285; Y-87
Nobel Lecture 1987 . . . . Y-87
Brodsky, Michael 1948- DLB-244
Broeg, Bob 1918- DLB-171
Brøgger, Suzanne 1944- DLB-214
Brome, Richard circa 1590-1652 . . . . DLB-58
Brome, Vincent 1910- DLB-155
Bromfield, Louis 1896-1956 . . . . DLB-4, 9, 86
Bromige, David 1933- DLB-193
Broner, E. M. 1930- DLB-28
Tribute to Bernard Malamud Y-86
Bronk, William 1918-1999 . . . . DLB-165
Bronnen, Arnolt 1895-1959 . . . . DLB-124
Brontë, Anne 1820-1849 . . . . DLB-21, 199
Brontë, Charlotte 1816-1855 . . . . . . DLB-21, 159, 199; CDBLB-4
Brontë, Emily 1818-1848 . . . . . . DLB-21, 32, 199; CDBLB-4
The Brontë Society Y-98
Brook, Stephen 1947- DLB-204
Brook Farm 1841-1847 . . . . DLB-1; 223; DS-5
Brooke, Frances 1724-1789 . . . . DLB-39, 99
Brooke, Henry 1703?-1783 . . . . DLB-39
Brooke, L. Leslie 1862-1940 . . . . DLB-141
Brooke, Margaret, Ranee of Sarawak 1849-1936 . . . . DLB-174
Brooke, Rupert 1887-1915 . . . . DLB-19, 216; CDBLB-6
The Friends of the Dymock Poets Y-00
Brooker, Bertram 1888-1955 . . . . DLB-88
Brooke-Rose, Christine 1923- DLB-14, 231
Brookner, Anita 1928- DLB-194; Y-87
Brooks, Charles Timothy 1813-1883 . . DLB-1, 243
Brooks, Cleanth 1906-1994 . . . . DLB-63; Y-94
Tribute to Katherine Anne Porter Y-80
Tribute to Walker Percy Y-90
Brooks, Gwendolyn 1917-2000 . . . . DLB-5, 76, 165; CDALB-1
Tribute to Julian Mayfield Y-84
Brooks, Jeremy 1926- DLB-14
Brooks, Mel 1926- DLB-26
Brooks, Noah 1830-1903 . . . . DLB-42; DS-13
Brooks, Richard 1912-1992 . . . . DLB-44
Brooks, Van Wyck 1886-1963 . . . DLB-45, 63, 103
Brophy, Brigid 1929-1995 . . . . DLB-14, 70, 271
Brophy, John 1899-1965 . . . . DLB-191
Brorson, Hans Adolph 1694-1764 . . . . DLB-300
Brossard, Chandler 1922-1993 . . . . DLB-16
Brossard, Nicole 1943- DLB-53
Broster, Dorothy Kathleen 1877-1950 . . . . DLB-160
Brother Antoninus (see Everson, William)
Brotherton, Lord 1856-1930 . . . . DLB-184
Brougham, John 1810-1880 . . . . DLB-11
Brougham and Vaux, Henry Peter Brougham, Baron 1778-1868 . . . . DLB-110, 158
Broughton, James 1913-1999 . . . . DLB-5
Broughton, Rhoda 1840-1920 . . . . DLB-18
Broun, Heywood 1888-1939 . . . . DLB-29, 171
Brown, Alice 1856-1948 . . . . DLB-78
Brown, Bob 1886-1959 . . . . DLB-4, 45; DS-15
Brown, Cecil 1943- DLB-33
Brown, Charles Brockden 1771-1810 . . . . DLB-37, 59, 73; CDALB-2
Brown, Christy 1932-1981 . . . . DLB-14
Brown, Dee 1908-2002 . . . . Y-80
Brown, Frank London 1927-1962 . . . . DLB-76
Brown, Fredric 1906-1972 . . . . DLB-8
Brown, George Mackay 1921-1996 . . . . DLB-14, 27, 139, 271
Brown, Harry 1917-1986 . . . . DLB-26
Brown, Larry 1951- DLB-234, 292
Brown, Lew 1893-1958 . . . . DLB-265
Brown, Marcia 1918- DLB-61
Brown, Margaret Wise 1910-1952 . . . . DLB-22
Brown, Morna Doris (see Ferrars, Elizabeth)
Brown, Oliver Madox 1855-1874 . . . . DLB-21
Brown, Sterling 1901-1989 . . . . DLB-48, 51, 63
Brown, T. E. 1830-1897 . . . . DLB-35
Brown, Thomas Alexander (see Boldrewood, Rolf)
Brown, Warren 1894-1978 . . . . DLB-241
Brown, William Hill 1765-1793 . . . . DLB-37
Brown, William Wells 1815-1884 . . . . DLB-3, 50, 183, 248
Brown University
The Festival of Vanguard Narrative Y-93
Browne, Charles Farrar 1834-1867 . . . . DLB-11
Browne, Frances 1816-1879 . . . . DLB-199

Browne, Francis Fisher 1843-1913 . . . . DLB-79
Browne, Howard 1908-1999 . . . . DLB-226
Browne, J. Ross 1821-1875 . . . . DLB-202
Browne, Michael Dennis 1940- DLB-40
Browne, Sir Thomas 1605-1682 . . . . DLB-151
Browne, William, of Tavistock 1590-1645 . . . . DLB-121
Browne, Wynyard 1911-1964 . . . . . . DLB-13, 233
Browne and Nolan DLB-106
Brownell, W. C. 1851-1928 . . . . DLB-71
Browning, Elizabeth Barrett 1806-1861 . . . . DLB-32, 199; CDBLB-4
Browning, Robert 1812-1889 . . . . DLB-32, 163; CDBLB-4
Essay on Chatterron DLB-32
Introductory Essay: *Letters of Percy Bysshe Shelley* (1852) DLB-32
"The Novel in [Robert Browning's] 'The Ring and the Book'" (1912), by Henry James DLB-32
Brownjohn, Allan 1931- DLB-40
Tribute to John Betjeman Y-84
Brownson, Orestes Augustus 1803-1876 . . . . DLB-1, 59, 73, 243; DS-5
Bruccoli, Matthew J. 1931- DLB-103
Joseph [Heller] and George [V. Higgins] . . . Y-99
Response [to Busch on Fitzgerald] Y-96
Tribute to Albert Erskine Y-93
Tribute to Charles E. Feinberg Y-88
Working with Fredson Bowers Y-91
Bruce, Charles 1906-1971 . . . . DLB-68
Bruce, John Edward 1856-1924
Three Documents [African American poets] DLB-50
Bruce, Leo 1903-1979 . . . . DLB-77
Bruce, Mary Grant 1878-1958 . . . . DLB-230
Bruce, Philip Alexander 1856-1933 . . . . . . DLB-47
Bruce-Novoa, Juan 1944- DLB-82
Bruckman, Clyde 1894-1955 . . . . DLB-26
Bruckner, Ferdinand 1891-1958 . . . . DLB-118
Brundage, John Herbert (see Herbert, John)
Brunner, John 1934-1995 . . . . DLB-261
Tribute to Theodore Sturgeon Y-85
Brutus, Dennis 1924- DLB-117, 225; CDWLB-3
Bryan, C. D. B. 1936- DLB-185
Bryant, Arthur 1899-1985 . . . . DLB-149
Bryant, William Cullen 1794-1878 . . . . DLB-3, 43, 59, 189, 250; CDALB-2
Bryce, James 1838-1922 . . . . DLB-166, 190
Bryce Echenique, Alfredo 1939- DLB-145; CDWLB-3
Bryden, Bill 1942- DLB-233
Brydges, Sir Samuel Egerton 1762-1837 . . . . DLB-107, 142
Bryskett, Lodowick 1546?-1612 . . . . DLB-167
Buchan, John 1875-1940 . . . . DLB-34, 70, 156
Buchanan, George 1506-1582 . . . . DLB-132
Buchanan, Robert 1841-1901 . . . . DLB-18, 35
"The Fleshly School of Poetry and Other Phenomena of the Day" (1872) DLB-35
"The Fleshly School of Poetry: Mr. D. G. Rossetti" (1871), by Thomas Maitland DLB-35
Buchler, Justus 1914-1991 . . . . DLB-279
Buchman, Sidney 1902-1975 . . . . DLB-26
Buchner, Augustus 1591-1661 . . . . DLB-164
Büchner, Georg 1813-1837 . . . . DLB-133; CDWLB-2
Bucholtz, Andreas Heinrich 1607-1671 . . . . DLB-168
Buck, Pearl S. 1892-1973 . . DLB-9, 102; CDALB-7
Bucke, Charles 1781-1846 . . . . DLB-110
Bucke, Richard Maurice 1837-1902 . . . . . . DLB-99
Buckingham, Edwin 1810-1833 . . . . DLB-73
Buckingham, Joseph Tinker 1779-1861 . . . DLB-73
Buckler, Ernest 1908-1984 . . . . DLB-68
Buckley, Vincent 1925-1988 . . . . DLB-289
Buckley, William F., Jr. 1925- DLB-137; Y-80
Publisher's Statement From the Initial Issue of *National Review* (19 November 1955) DLB-137
Buckminster, Joseph Stevens 1784-1812 . . . . DLB-37
Buckner, Robert 1906- DLB-26
Budd, Thomas ?-1698 . . . . DLB-24
Budrys, A. J. 1931- DLB-8
Buechner, Frederick 1926- Y-80
Buell, John 1927- DLB-53
Bufalino, Gesualdo 1920-1996 . . . . DLB-196
Job Buffum [publishing house] DLB-49
Bugnet, Georges 1879-1981 . . . . DLB-92
Buies, Arthur 1840-1901 . . . . DLB-99
Bukiet, Melvin Jules 1953- DLB-299
Bukowski, Charles 1920-1994 . . . DLB-5, 130, 169
Bulatović, Miodrag 1930-1991 . . . . DLB-181; CDWLB-4
Bulgakov, Mikhail Afanas'evich 1891-1940 . . . . .DLB-272
Bulgarin, Faddei Venediktovich 1789-1859 . . . . DLB-198
Bulger, Bozeman 1877-1932 . . . . .DLB-171
Bull, Olaf 1883-1933 . . . . DLB-297
Bullein, William between 1520 and 1530-1576 . . . . DLB-167
Bullins, Ed 1935- DLB-7, 38, 249
Bulwer, John 1606-1656 . . . . DLB-236
Bulwer-Lytton, Edward (also Edward Bulwer) 1803-1873 . . . . DLB-21
"On Art in Fiction "(1838) DLB-21
Bumpus, Jerry 1937- Y-81
Bunce and Brother DLB-49
Bunner, H. C. 1855-1896 . . . . .DLB-78, 79
Bunting, Basil 1900-1985 . . . . DLB-20
Buntline, Ned (Edward Zane Carroll Judson) 1821-1886 . . . . DLB-186
Bunyan, John 1628-1688 . . . . . DLB-39; CDBLB-2
The Author's Apology for His Book DLB-39
Burch, Robert 1925- DLB-52
Burciaga, José Antonio 1940- DLB-82
Burdekin, Katharine (Murray Constantine) 1896-1963 . . . . DLB-255
Bürger, Gottfried August 1747-1794 . . . . . . DLB-94
Burgess, Anthony (John Anthony Burgess Wilson) 1917-1993 . . . . . . DLB-14, 194, 261; CDBLB-8
The Anthony Burgess Archive at the Harry Ransom Humanities Research Center Y-98
Anthony Burgess's *99 Novels:* An Opinion Poll Y-84
Burgess, Gelett 1866-1951 . . . . DLB-11
Burgess, John W. 1844-1931 . . . . DLB-47
Burgess, Thornton W. 1874-1965 . . . . DLB-22
Burgess, Stringer and Company DLB-49
Burgos, Julia de 1914-1953 . . . . DLB-290
Burick, Si 1909-1986 . . . . .DLB-171
Burk, John Daly circa 1772-1808 . . . . DLB-37
Burk, Ronnie 1955- DLB-209
Burke, Edmund 1729?-1797 . . . . DLB-104, 252
Burke, James Lee 1936- DLB-226
Burke, Johnny 1908-1964 . . . . DLB-265
Burke, Kenneth 1897-1993 . . . . DLB-45, 63
Burke, Thomas 1886-1945 . . . . .DLB-197
Burley, Dan 1907-1962 . . . . DLB-241
Burley, W. J. 1914- DLB-276
Burlingame, Edward Livermore 1848-1922 . . . . DLB-79
Burman, Carina 1960- DLB-257
Burnet, Gilbert 1643-1715 . . . . DLB-101
Burnett, Frances Hodgson 1849-1924 . . . . .DLB-42, 141; DS-13, 14
Burnett, W. R. 1899-1982 . . . . DLB-9, 226
Burnett, Whit 1899-1973 . . . . .DLB-137
Burney, Fanny 1752-1840 . . . . DLB-39
Dedication, *The Wanderer* (1814) DLB-39
Preface to *Evelina* (1778) DLB-39
Burns, Alan 1929- DLB-14, 194
Burns, Joanne 1945- DLB-289
Burns, John Horne 1916-1953 . . . . Y-85
Burns, Robert 1759-1796 . . . . DLB-109; CDBLB-3
Burns and Oates DLB-106
Burnshaw, Stanley 1906- DLB-48; Y-97
James Dickey and Stanley Burnshaw Correspondence Y-02
Review of Stanley Burnshaw: The Collected Poems and Selected Prose Y-02
Tribute to Robert Penn Warren Y-89
Burr, C. Chauncey 1815?-1883 . . . . DLB-79
Burr, Esther Edwards 1732-1758 . . . . DLB-200
Burroughs, Edgar Rice 1875-1950 . . . . DLB-8
The Burroughs Bibliophiles Y-98
Burroughs, John 1837-1921 . . . . .DLB-64, 275
Burroughs, Margaret T. G. 1917- DLB-41

Burroughs, William S., Jr. 1947-1981 . . . . . DLB-16
Burroughs, William Seward 1914-1997 . . . . DLB-2, 8, 16, 152, 237; Y-81, 97
Burroway, Janet 1936- DLB-6
Burt, Maxwell Struthers 1882-1954 . . . . . DLB-86; DS-16
A. L. Burt and Company DLB-49
Burton, Hester 1913- DLB-161
Burton, Isabel Arundell 1831-1896 . . . . . DLB-166
Burton, Miles (see Rhode, John)
Burton, Richard Francis 1821-1890 . . . . . DLB-55, 166, 184
Burton, Robert 1577-1640 . . . . . DLB-151
Burton, Virginia Lee 1909-1968 . . . . . DLB-22
Burton, William Evans 1804-1860 . . . . . DLB-73
Burwell, Adam Hood 1790-1849 . . . . . DLB-99
Bury, Lady Charlotte 1775-1861 . . . . . DLB-116
Busch, Frederick 1941- DLB-6, 218
Excerpts from Frederick Busch's USC Remarks [on F. Scott Fitzgerald] Y-96
Tribute to James Laughlin Y-97
Tribute to Raymond Carver Y-88
Busch, Niven 1903-1991 . . . . . DLB-44
Bushnell, Horace 1802-1876 . . . . . DS-13
Business & Literature
The Claims of Business and Literature: An Undergraduate Essay by Maxwell Perkins Y-01
Bussières, Arthur de 1877-1913 . . . . . DLB-92
Butler, Charles circa 1560-1647 . . . . . DLB-236
Butler, Guy 1918- DLB-225
Butler, Joseph 1692-1752 . . . . . DLB-252
Butler, Josephine Elizabeth 1828-1906 . . . . . DLB-190
Butler, Juan 1942-1981 . . . . . DLB-53
Butler, Judith 1956- DLB-246
Butler, Octavia E. 1947- DLB-33
Butler, Pierce 1884-1953 . . . . . DLB-187
Butler, Robert Olen 1945- DLB-173
Butler, Samuel 1613-1680 . . . . . DLB-101, 126
Butler, Samuel 1835-1902 . . . . . DLB-18, 57, 174; CDBLB-5
Butler, William Francis 1838-1910 . . . . . DLB-166
E. H. Butler and Company DLB-49
Butor, Michel 1926- DLB-83
Nathaniel Butter [publishing house] DLB-170
Butterworth, Hezekiah 1839-1905 . . . . . DLB-42
Buttitta, Ignazio 1899-1997 . . . . . DLB-114
Butts, Mary 1890-1937 . . . . . DLB-240
Buzo, Alex 1944- DLB-289
Buzzati, Dino 1906-1972 . . . . . DLB-177
Byars, Betsy 1928- DLB-52
Byatt, A. S. 1936- DLB-14, 194
Byles, Mather 1707-1788 . . . . . DLB-24
Henry Bynneman [publishing house] DLB-170
Bynner, Witter 1881-1968 . . . . . DLB-54
Byrd, William circa 1543-1623 . . . . . DLB-172
Byrd, William, II 1674-1744 . . . . . DLB-24, 140
Byrne, John Keyes (see Leonard, Hugh)
Byron, George Gordon, Lord 1788-1824 . . . . . DLB-96, 110; CDBLB-3
The Byron Society of America Y-00
Byron, Robert 1905-1941 . . . . . DLB-195

C

Caballero Bonald, José Manuel 1926- DLB-108
Cabañero, Eladio 1930- DLB-134
Cabell, James Branch 1879-1958 . . . . . DLB-9, 78
Cabeza de Baca, Manuel 1853-1915 . . . . . DLB-122
Cabeza de Baca Gilbert, Fabiola 1898- DLB-122
Cable, George Washington 1844-1925 . . . . . DLB-12, 74; DS-13
Cable, Mildred 1878-1952 . . . . . DLB-195
Cabral, Manuel del 1907-1999 . . . . . DLB-283
Cabrera, Lydia 1900-1991 . . . . . DLB-145
Cabrera Infante, Guillermo 1929- DLB-113; CDWLB-3
Cadell [publishing house] DLB-154
Cady, Edwin H. 1917- DLB-103
Caedmon flourished 658-680 . . . . . DLB-146
Caedmon School circa 660-899 . . . . . DLB-146
Caesar, Irving 1895-1996 . . . . . DLB-265
Cafés, Brasseries, and Bistros DS-15
Cage, John 1912-1992 . . . . . DLB-193
Cahan, Abraham 1860-1951 . . . . . DLB-9, 25, 28
Cahn, Sammy 1913-1993 . . . . . DLB-265
Cain, George 1943- DLB-33
Cain, James M. 1892-1977 . . . . . DLB-226
Caird, Edward 1835-1908 . . . . . DLB-262
Caird, Mona 1854-1932 . . . . . DLB-197
Čaks, Aleksandrs 1901-1950 . . . . . DLB-220; CDWLB-4
Caldecott, Randolph 1846-1886 . . . . . DLB-163
John Calder Limited [Publishing house] DLB-112
Calderón de la Barca, Fanny 1804-1882 . . . . . DLB-183
Caldwell, Ben 1937- DLB-38
Caldwell, Erskine 1903-1987 . . . . . DLB-9, 86
H. M. Caldwell Company DLB-49
Caldwell, Taylor 1900-1985 . . . . . DS-17
Calhoun, John C. 1782-1850 . . . . . DLB-3, 248
Călinescu, George 1899-1965 . . . . . DLB-220
Calisher, Hortense 1911- DLB-2, 218
Calkins, Mary Whiton 1863-1930 . . . . . DLB-270
Callaghan, Mary Rose 1944- DLB-207
Callaghan, Morley 1903-1990 . . . . . DLB-68; DS-15
Callahan, S. Alice 1868-1894 . . . . . DLB-175, 221
Callaloo [journal] Y-87
Callimachus circa 305 B.C.-240 B.C. DLB-176
Calmer, Edgar 1907- DLB-4
Calverley, C. S. 1831-1884 . . . . . DLB-35
Calvert, George Henry 1803-1889 . . . . . DLB-1, 64, 248
Calvino, Italo 1923-1985 . . . . . DLB-196
Cambridge, Ada 1844-1926 . . . . . DLB-230
Cambridge Press DLB-49
Cambridge Songs (Carmina Cantabrigensia) circa 1050 . . . . . DLB-148
Cambridge University
Cambridge and the Apostles DS-5
Cambridge University Press DLB-170
Camden, William 1551-1623 . . . . . DLB-172
Camden House: An Interview with James Hardin Y-92
Cameron, Eleanor 1912-2000 . . . . . DLB-52
Cameron, George Frederick 1854-1885 . . . . . DLB-99
Cameron, Lucy Lyttelton 1781-1858 . . . . . DLB-163
Cameron, Peter 1959- DLB-234
Cameron, William Bleasdell 1862-1951 . . . DLB-99
Camm, John 1718-1778 . . . . . DLB-31
Camões, Luís de 1524-1580 . . . . . DLB-287
Camon, Ferdinando 1935- DLB-196
Camp, Walter 1859-1925 . . . . . DLB-241
Campana, Dino 1885-1932 . . . . . DLB-114
Campbell, Bebe Moore 1950- DLB-227
Campbell, David 1915-1979 . . . . . DLB-260
Campbell, Gabrielle Margaret Vere (see Shearing, Joseph, and Bowen, Marjorie)
Campbell, James Dykes 1838-1895 . . . . . DLB-144
Campbell, James Edwin 1867-1896 . . . . . DLB-50
Campbell, John 1653-1728 . . . . . DLB-43
Campbell, John W., Jr. 1910-1971 . . . . . DLB-8
Campbell, Ramsey 1946- DLB-261
Campbell, Roy 1901-1957 . . . . . DLB-20, 225
Campbell, Thomas 1777-1844 . . . . . DLB-93, 144
Campbell, William Edward (see March, William)
Campbell, William Wilfred 1858-1918 . . . . DLB-92
Campion, Edmund 1539-1581 . . . . . DLB-167
Campion, Thomas 1567-1620 . . . . . DLB-58, 172; CDBLB-1
Campo, Rafael 1964- DLB-282
Campton, David 1924- DLB-245
Camus, Albert 1913-1960 . . . . . DLB-72
Camus, Jean-Pierre 1584-1652 . . . . . DLB-268
The Canadian Publishers' Records Database . . Y-96
Canby, Henry Seidel 1878-1961 . . . . . DLB-91
Cancioneros DLB-286
Candelaria, Cordelia 1943- DLB-82
Candelaria, Nash 1928- DLB-82
Canetti, Elias 1905-1994 . . . . . DLB-85, 124; CDWLB-2
Canham, Erwin Dain 1904-1982 . . . . . DLB-127
Canitz, Friedrich Rudolph Ludwig von 1654-1699 . . . . . DLB-168
Cankar, Ivan 1876-1918 . . . . . DLB-147; CDWLB-4
Cannan, Gilbert 1884-1955 . . . . . DLB-10, 197
Cannan, Joanna 1896-1961 . . . . . DLB-191

Cannell, Kathleen 1891-1974 . . . . DLB-4
Cannell, Skipwith 1887-1957. . . . . DLB-45
Canning, George 1770-1827 . . . . DLB-158
Cannon, Jimmy 1910-1973 . . . . .DLB-171
Cano, Daniel 1947- DLB-209
Old Dogs / New Tricks? New Technologies, the Canon, and the Structure of the Profession Y-02
Cantú, Norma Elia 1947- DLB-209
Cantwell, Robert 1908-1978 . . . . DLB-9
Jonathan Cape and Harrison Smith [publishing house] DLB-46
Jonathan Cape Limited. DLB-112
Čapek, Karel 1890-1938 . . . . DLB-215; CDWLB-4
Capen, Joseph 1658-1725 . . . . DLB-24
Capes, Bernard 1854-1918 . . . . DLB-156
Capote, Truman 1924-1984 . . . . .DLB-2, 185, 227; Y-80, 84; CDALB-1
Capps, Benjamin 1922- DLB-256
Caproni, Giorgio 1912-1990. . . . . DLB-128
Caragiale, Mateiu Ioan 1885-1936 . . . . . . DLB-220
Cardarelli, Vincenzo 1887-1959 . . . . DLB-114
Cardenal, Ernesto 1925- DLB-290
Cárdenas, Reyes 1948- DLB-122
Cardinal, Marie 1929-2001. . . . . DLB-83
Cardoza y Aragón, Luis 1901-1992 . . . . . DLB-290
Carew, Jan 1920- DLB-157
Carew, Thomas 1594 or 1595-1640 . . . . DLB-126
Carey, Henry circa 1687-1689-1743 . . . . . . DLB-84
Carey, Mathew 1760-1839 . . . . .DLB-37, 73
M. Carey and Company DLB-49
Carey, Peter 1943- DLB-289
Carey and Hart DLB-49
Carlell, Lodowick 1602-1675 . . . . DLB-58
Carleton, William 1794-1869 . . . . DLB-159
G. W. Carleton [publishing house]. DLB-49
Carlile, Richard 1790-1843 . . . . DLB-110, 158
Carlson, Ron 1947- DLB-244
Carlyle, Jane Welsh 1801-1866 . . . . DLB-55
Carlyle, Thomas 1795-1881. . . . . DLB-55, 144; CDBLB-3
"The Hero as Man of Letters: Johnson, Rousseau, Burns" (1841) [excerpt] DLB-57
The Hero as Poet. Dante; Shakspeare (1841) DLB-32
Carman, Bliss 1861-1929 . . . . DLB-92
Carmina Burana circa 1230. . . . . DLB-138
Carnap, Rudolf 1891-1970 . . . . .DLB-270
Carnero, Guillermo 1947- DLB-108
Carossa, Hans 1878-1956 . . . . DLB-66
Carpenter, Humphrey 1946- DLB-155; Y-84, 99
Carpenter, Stephen Cullen ?-1820? DLB-73
Carpentier, Alejo 1904-1980 . . . . DLB-113; CDWLB-3
Carr, Emily (1871-1945) DLB-68
Carr, Marina 1964- DLB-245
Carr, Virginia Spencer 1929- DLB-111; Y-00
Carrera Andrade, Jorge 1903-1978. . . . . . DLB-283
Carrier, Roch 1937- DLB-53
Carrillo, Adolfo 1855-1926. . . . . DLB-122
Carroll, Gladys Hasty 1904- DLB-9
Carroll, John 1735-1815 . . . . DLB-37
Carroll, John 1809-1884. . . . . DLB-99
Carroll, Lewis 1832-1898 . . . . . .DLB-18, 163, 178; CDBLB-4
The Lewis Carroll Centenary Y-98
The Lewis Carroll Society of North America Y-00
Carroll, Paul 1927- DLB-16
Carroll, Paul Vincent 1900-1968 . . . . DLB-10
Carroll and Graf Publishers DLB-46
Carruth, Hayden 1921- DLB-5, 165
Tribute to James Dickey Y-97
Tribute to Raymond Carver Y-88
Carryl, Charles E. 1841-1920. . . . . DLB-42
Carson, Anne 1950- DLB-193
Carson, Rachel 1907-1964 . . . . .DLB-275
Carswell, Catherine 1879-1946. . . . . DLB-36
Cartagena, Alfonso de ca. 1384-1456 . . . . DLB-286
Cartagena, Teresa de 1425?-? DLB-286
Cărtărescu, Mirea 1956- DLB-232
Carter, Angela 1940-1992. . . . . . .DLB-14, 207, 261
Carter, Elizabeth 1717-1806 . . . . DLB-109
Carter, Henry (see Leslie, Frank)
Carter, Hodding, Jr. 1907-1972. . . . . DLB-127
Carter, Jared 1939- DLB-282
Carter, John 1905-1975. . . . . DLB-201
Carter, Landon 1710-1778. . . . . DLB-31
Carter, Lin 1930-1988 . . . . Y-81
Carter, Martin 1927-1997 . . . .DLB-117; CDWLB-3
Carter, Robert, and Brothers DLB-49
Carter and Hendee. DLB-49
Cartwright, Jim 1958- DLB-245
Cartwright, John 1740-1824 . . . . DLB-158
Cartwright, William circa 1611-1643 . . . . DLB-126
Caruthers, William Alexander 1802-1846 . . . . DLB-3, 248
Carver, Jonathan 1710-1780 . . . . DLB-31
Carver, Raymond 1938-1988. . . DLB-130; Y-83,88
First Strauss "Livings" Awarded to Cynthia Ozick and Raymond Carver An Interview with Raymond Carver . . . Y-83
Carvic, Heron 1917?-1980 . . . . .DLB-276
Cary, Alice 1820-1871 . . . . DLB-202
Cary, Joyce 1888-1957 . . . DLB-15, 100; CDBLB-6
Cary, Patrick 1623?-1657 . . . . DLB-131
Casal, Julián del 1863-1893 . . . . DLB-283
Case, John 1540-1600. . . . . DLB-281
Casey, Gavin 1907-1964. . . . . DLB-260
Casey, Juanita 1925- DLB-14
Casey, Michael 1947- DLB-5
Cassady, Carolyn 1923- DLB-16
"As I See It" DLB-16
Cassady, Neal 1926-1968 . . . . .DLB-16, 237
Cassell and Company. DLB-106
Cassell Publishing Company DLB-49
Cassill, R. V. 1919- DLB-6, 218; Y-02
Tribute to James Dickey Y-97
Cassity, Turner 1929- DLB-105; Y-02
Cassius Dio circa 155/164-post 229 . . . . . .DLB-176
Cassola, Carlo 1917-1987 . . . . .DLB-177
Castellano, Olivia 1944- DLB-122
Castellanos, Rosario 1925-1974. . . . . .DLB-113, 290; CDWLB-3
Castelo Branco, Camilo 1825-1890 . . . . . DLB-287
Castile, Protest Poetry in DLB-286
Castile and Aragon, Vernacular Translations in Crowns of 1352-1515 . . . . DLB-286
Castillo, Ana 1953- DLB-122, 227
Castillo, Rafael C. 1950- DLB-209
The Castle of Perserverance circa 1400-1425 . . . . DLB-146
Castlemon, Harry (see Fosdick, Charles Austin)
Čašule, Kole 1921- DLB-181
Caswall, Edward 1814-1878 . . . . DLB-32
Catacalos, Rosemary 1944- DLB-122
Cather, Willa 1873-1947 . . . . DLB-9, 54, 78, 256; DS-1; CDALB-3
The Willa Cather Pioneer Memorial and Education Foundation Y-00
Catherine II (Ekaterina Alekseevna), "The Great," Empress of Russia 1729-1796. . . . . . . DLB-150
Catherwood, Mary Hartwell 1847-1902. . . DLB-78
Catledge, Turner 1901-1983 . . . . .DLB-127
Catlin, George 1796-1872 . . . . DLB-186, 189
Cato the Elder 234 B.C.-149 B.C. DLB-211
Cattafi, Bartolo 1922-1979 . . . . DLB-128
Catton, Bruce 1899-1978 . . . . .DLB-17
Catullus circa 84 B.C.-54 B.C. DLB-211; CDWLB-1
Causley, Charles 1917- DLB-27
Caute, David 1936- DLB-14, 231
Cavendish, Duchess of Newcastle, Margaret Lucas 1623?-1673. . . . . DLB-131, 252, 281
Cawein, Madison 1865-1914 . . . . DLB-54
William Caxton [publishing house] DLB-170
The Caxton Printers, Limited DLB-46
Caylor, O. P. 1849-1897. . . . . DLB-241
Cayrol, Jean 1911- DLB-83
Cecil, Lord David 1902-1986. . . . . DLB-155
Cela, Camilo José 1916-2002 . . . . Y-89
Nobel Lecture 1989 . . . . Y-89
Celan, Paul 1920-1970 . . . . . . DLB-69; CDWLB-2
Celati, Gianni 1937- DLB-196
Celaya, Gabriel 1911-1991. . . . . DLB-108
Céline, Louis-Ferdinand 1894-1961 . . . . . . DLB-72
Celtis, Conrad 1459-1508. . . . . .DLB-179

Cendrars, Blaise 1887-1961 . . . . DLB-258
The Steinbeck Centennial Y-02
Censorship
The Island Trees Case: A Symposium on School Library Censorship Y-82
Center for Bibliographical Studies and Research at the University of California, Riverside Y-91
Center for Book Research Y-84
The Center for the Book in the Library of Congress Y-93
A New Voice: The Center for the Book's First Five Years Y-83
Centlivre, Susanna 1669?-1723 . . . . DLB-84
The Centre for Writing, Publishing and Printing History at the University of Reading Y-00
The Century Company DLB-49
A Century of Poetry, a Lifetime of Collecting: J. M. Edelstein's Collection of Twentieth-Century American Poetry Y-02
Cernuda, Luis 1902-1963 . . . . DLB-134
Cerruto, Oscar 1912-1981 . . . . DLB-283
Cervantes, Lorna Dee 1954- DLB-82
de Céspedes, Alba 1911-1997 . . . . DLB-264
Ch., T. (see Marchenko, Anastasiia Iakovlevna)
Chaadaev, Petr Iakovlevich 1794-1856 . . . . DLB-198
Chabon, Michael 1963- DLB-278
Chacel, Rosa 1898-1994 . . . . DLB-134
Chacón, Eusebio 1869-1948 . . . . DLB-82
Chacón, Felipe Maximiliano 1873-? DLB-82
Chadwick, Henry 1824-1908 . . . . DLB-241
Chadwyck-Healey's Full-Text Literary Databases: Editing Commercial Databases of Primary Literary Texts Y-95
Challans, Eileen Mary (see Renault, Mary)
Chalmers, George 1742-1825 . . . . DLB-30
Chaloner, Sir Thomas 1520-1565 . . . . DLB-167
Chamberlain, Samuel S. 1851-1916 . . . . DLB-25
Chamberland, Paul 1939- DLB-60
Chamberlin, William Henry 1897-1969 . . . . DLB-29
Chambers, Charles Haddon 1860-1921 . . . DLB-10
Chambers, María Cristina (see Mena, María Cristina)
Chambers, Robert W. 1865-1933 . . . . DLB-202
W. and R. Chambers [publishing house] DLB-106
Chamisso, Adelbert von 1781-1838 . . . . DLB-90
Champfleury 1821-1889 . . . . DLB-119
Chandler, Harry 1864-1944 . . . . DLB-29
Chandler, Norman 1899-1973 . . . . DLB-127
Chandler, Otis 1927- DLB-127
Chandler, Raymond 1888-1959 . . . . DLB-226, 253; DS-6; CDALB-5
Raymond Chandler Centenary Y-88
Channing, Edward 1856-1931 . . . . DLB-17
Channing, Edward Tyrrell 1790-1856 . . . . DLB-1, 59, 235
Channing, William Ellery 1780-1842 . . . . DLB-1, 59, 235
Channing, William Ellery, II 1817-1901 . . . . DLB-1, 223
Channing, William Henry 1810-1884 . . . . DLB-1, 59, 243
Chapelain, Jean 1595-1674 . . . . DLB-268
Chaplin, Charlie 1889-1977 . . . . DLB-44
Chapman, George 1559 or 1560-1634 . . . . DLB-62, 121
Chapman, Olive Murray 1892-1977 . . . . . DLB-195
Chapman, R. W. 1881-1960 . . . . DLB-201
Chapman, William 1850-1917 . . . . DLB-99
John Chapman [publishing house] DLB-106
Chapman and Hall [publishing house] . . . DLB-106
Chappell, Fred 1936- DLB-6, 105
"A Detail in a Poem" DLB-105
Tribute to Peter Taylor Y-94
Chappell, William 1582-1649 . . . . DLB-236
Char, René 1907-1988 . . . . DLB-258
Charbonneau, Jean 1875-1960 . . . . DLB-92
Charbonneau, Robert 1911-1967 . . . . DLB-68
Charles, Gerda 1914- DLB-14
William Charles [publishing house] DLB-49
Charles d'Orléans 1394-1465 . . . . DLB-208
Charley (see Mann, Charles)
Charskaia, Lidiia 1875-1937 . . . . DLB-295
Charteris, Leslie 1907-1993 . . . . DLB-77
Chartier, Alain circa 1385-1430 . . . . DLB-208
Charyn, Jerome 1937- Y-83
Chase, Borden 1900-1971 . . . . DLB-26
Chase, Edna Woolman 1877-1957 . . . . DLB-91
Chase, James Hadley (René Raymond) 1906-1985 . . . . DLB-276
Chase, Mary Coyle 1907-1981 . . . . DLB-228
Chase-Riboud, Barbara 1936- DLB-33
Chateaubriand, François-René de 1768-1848 . . . . DLB-119
Chatterton, Thomas 1752-1770 . . . . DLB-109
Essay on Chatterton (1842), by Robert Browning DLB-32
Chatto and Windus DLB-106
Chatwin, Bruce 1940-1989 . . . . DLB-194, 204
Chaucer, Geoffrey 1340?-1400 . . . . DLB-146; CDBLB-1
New Chaucer Society Y-00
Chaudhuri, Amit 1962- DLB-267
Chauncy, Charles 1705-1787 . . . . DLB-24
Chauveau, Pierre-Joseph-Olivier 1820-1890 . . . . DLB-99
Chávez, Denise 1948- DLB-122
Chávez, Fray Angélico 1910-1996 . . . . DLB-82
Chayefsky, Paddy 1923-1981 . . . . DLB-7, 44; Y-81
Cheesman, Evelyn 1881-1969 . . . . DLB-195
Cheever, Ezekiel 1615-1708 . . . . DLB-24
Cheever, George Barrell 1807-1890 . . . . DLB-59
Cheever, John 1912-1982 . . . . DLB-2, 102, 227; Y-80, 82; CDALB-1
Cheever, Susan 1943- Y-82
Cheke, Sir John 1514-1557 . . . . DLB-132
Chekhov, Anton Pavlovich 1860-1904 . . . DLB-277
Chelsea House DLB-46
Chênedollé, Charles de 1769-1833 . . . . . . DLB-217
Cheney, Brainard
Tribute to Caroline Gordon Y-81
Cheney, Ednah Dow 1824-1904 . . . . . . DLB-1, 223
Cheney, Harriet Vaughan 1796-1889 . . . . . DLB-99
Chénier, Marie-Joseph 1764-1811 . . . . DLB-192
Chernyshevsky, Nikolai Gavrilovich 1828-1889 . . . . DLB-238
Cherry, Kelly 1940 . . . . Y-83
Cherryh, C. J. 1942- Y-80
Chesebro', Caroline 1825-1873 . . . . DLB-202
Chesney, Sir George Tomkyns 1830-1895 . . . . DLB-190
Chesnut, Mary Boykin 1823-1886 . . . . . . DLB-239
Chesnutt, Charles Waddell 1858-1932 . . . . DLB-12, 50, 78
Chesson, Mrs. Nora (see Hopper, Nora)
Chester, Alfred 1928-1971 . . . . DLB-130
Chester, George Randolph 1869-1924 . . . . DLB-78
The Chester Plays circa 1505-1532; revisions until 1575 . . . . DLB-146
Chesterfield, Philip Dormer Stanhope, Fourth Earl of 1694-1773 . . . . DLB-104
Chesterton, G. K. 1874-1936 . . DLB-10, 19, 34, 70, 98, 149, 178; CDBLB-6
"The Ethics of Elfland" (1908) DLB-178
Chettle, Henry circa 1560-circa 1607 . . . . DLB-136
Cheuse, Alan 1940- DLB-244
Chew, Ada Nield 1870-1945 . . . . DLB-135
Cheyney, Edward P. 1861-1947 . . . . DLB-47
Chiara, Piero 1913-1986 . . . . DLB-177
Chicanos
Chicano History DLB-82
Chicano Language DLB-82
Chicano Literature: A Bibliography . . DLB-209
A Contemporary Flourescence of Chicano Literature Y-84
Literatura Chicanesca: The View From Without DLB-82
Child, Francis James 1825-1896 . . . . DLB-1, 64, 235
Child, Lydia Maria 1802-1880 . . . . DLB-1, 74, 243
Child, Philip 1898-1978 . . . . DLB-68
Childers, Erskine 1870-1922 . . . . DLB-70
Children's Literature
Afterword: Propaganda, Namby-Pamby, and Some Books of Distinction . . . DLB-52
Children's Book Awards and Prizes . . . DLB-61
Children's Book Illustration in the Twentieth Century DLB-61
Children's Illustrators, 1800-1880 . . . . DLB-163
The Harry Potter Phenomenon Y-99
Pony Stories, Omnibus Essay on DLB-160
The Reality of One Woman's Dream: The de Grummond Children's Literature Collection Y-99

School Stories, 1914-1960 . . . . DLB-160
The Year in Children's Books. Y-92–96, 98–01
The Year in Children's Literature Y-97
Childress, Alice 1916-1994 . . . . .DLB-7, 38, 249
Childress, Mark 1957- DLB-292
Childs, George W. 1829-1894 . . . . DLB-23
Chilton Book Company DLB-46
Chin, Frank 1940- DLB-206
Chinweizu 1943- DLB-157
Chitham, Edward 1932- DLB-155
Chittenden, Hiram Martin 1858-1917 . . . . DLB-47
Chivers, Thomas Holley 1809-1858. . . DLB-3, 248
Chkhartishvili, Grigorii Shalvovich (see Akunin, Boris)
Chocano, José Santos 1875-1934 . . . . DLB-290
Cholmondeley, Mary 1859-1925 . . . . DLB-197
Chomsky, Noam 1928- DLB-246
Chopin, Kate 1850-1904. . . DLB-12, 78; CDALB-3
Chopin, René 1885-1953 . . . . DLB-92
Choquette, Adrienne 1915-1973 . . . . DLB-68
Choquette, Robert 1905-1991 . . . . DLB-68
Choyce, Lesley 1951- DLB-251
Chrétien de Troyes circa 1140-circa 1190 . . . . DLB-208
Christensen, Inger 1935- DLB-214
Christensen, Lars Saabye 1953- DLB-297
The Christian Examiner DLB-1
The Christian Publishing Company. DLB-49
Christie, Agatha 1890-1976. . . . . . . .DLB-13, 77, 245; CDBLB-6
Christine de Pizan circa 1365-circa 1431 . . . . DLB-208
Christopher, John (Sam Youd) 1922- . . DLB-255
Christus und die Samariterin circa 950 . . . . . . DLB-148
Christy, Howard Chandler 1873-1952 . . . DLB-188
Chulkov, Mikhail Dmitrievich 1743?-1792 . . . . DLB-150
Church, Benjamin 1734-1778 . . . . DLB-31
Church, Francis Pharcellus 1839-1906 . . . . DLB-79
Church, Peggy Pond 1903-1986. . . . . DLB-212
Church, Richard 1893-1972 . . . . DLB-191
Church, William Conant 1836-1917 . . . . . DLB-79
Churchill, Caryl 1938- DLB-13
Churchill, Charles 1731-1764 . . . . DLB-109
Churchill, Winston 1871-1947 . . . . DLB-202
Churchill, Sir Winston 1874-1965. . . . . . . DLB-100; DS-16; CDBLB-5
Churchyard, Thomas 1520?-1604 . . . . . . DLB-132
E. Churton and Company DLB-106
Chute, Marchette 1909-1994 . . . . DLB-103
Ciardi, John 1916-1986. . . . . DLB-5; Y-86
Cibber, Colley 1671-1757 . . . . DLB-84
Cicero 106 B.C.-43 B.C. DLB-211, CDWLB-1
Cima, Annalisa 1941- DLB-128
Čingo, Živko 1935-1987. . . . . DLB-181
Cioran, E. M. 1911-1995 . . . . DLB-220
Čipkus, Alfonsas (see Nyka-Niliūnas, Alfonsas)
Cirese, Eugenio 1884-1955. . . . . DLB-114
Cīrulis, Jānis (see Bels, Alberts)
Cisneros, Antonio 1942- DLB-290
Cisneros, Sandra 1954- DLB-122, 152
City Lights Books. DLB-46
Civil War (1861–1865)
Battles and Leaders of the Civil War. . DLB-47
Official Records of the Rebellion DLB-47
Recording the Civil War DLB-47
Cixous, Hélène 1937- DLB-83, 242
Clampitt, Amy 1920-1994 . . . . DLB-105
Tribute to Alfred A. Knopf Y-84
Clancy, Tom 1947- DLB-227
Clapper, Raymond 1892-1944 . . . . DLB-29
Clare, John 1793-1864 . . . . DLB-55, 96
Clarendon, Edward Hyde, Earl of 1609-1674. . . . . DLB-101
Clark, Alfred Alexander Gordon (see Hare, Cyril)
Clark, Ann Nolan 1896- DLB-52
Clark, C. E. Frazer, Jr. 1925-2001 . .DLB-187; Y-01
C. E. Frazer Clark Jr. and Hawthorne Bibliography. DLB-269
The Publications of C. E. Frazer Clark Jr.. . . . . DLB-269
Clark, Catherine Anthony 1892-1977. . . . . DLB-68
Clark, Charles Heber 1841-1915 . . . . DLB-11
Clark, Davis Wasgatt 1812-1871 . . . . DLB-79
Clark, Douglas 1919-1993 . . . . .DLB-276
Clark, Eleanor 1913- DLB-6
Clark, J. P. 1935- DLB-117; CDWLB-3
Clark, Lewis Gaylord 1808-1873. . . . . .DLB-3, 64, 73, 250
Clark, Walter Van Tilburg 1909-1971. DLB-9, 206
Clark, William 1770-1838. . . . . DLB-183, 186
Clark, William Andrews, Jr. 1877-1934 . . . . DLB-187
C. M. Clark Publishing Company DLB-46
Clarke, Sir Arthur C. 1917- DLB-261
Tribute to Theodore Sturgeon. Y-85
Clarke, Austin 1896-1974 . . . . DLB-10, 20
Clarke, Austin C. 1934- DLB-53, 125
Clarke, Gillian 1937- DLB-40
Clarke, James Freeman 1810-1888 . . . . DLB-1, 59, 235; DS-5
Clarke, John circa 1596-1658 . . . . DLB-281
Clarke, Lindsay 1939- DLB-231
Clarke, Marcus 1846-1881 . . . . DLB-230
Clarke, Pauline 1921- DLB-161
Clarke, Rebecca Sophia 1833-1906 . . . . . . DLB-42
Clarke, Samuel 1675-1729 . . . . DLB-252
Robert Clarke and Company. DLB-49
Clarkson, Thomas 1760-1846. . . . . DLB-158
Claudel, Paul 1868-1955 . . . . DLB-192, 258
Claudius, Matthias 1740-1815 . . . . DLB-97
Clausen, Andy 1943- DLB-16
Claussen, Sophus 1865-1931 . . . . DLB-300
Clawson, John L. 1865-1933 . . . . .DLB-187
Claxton, Remsen and Haffelfinger DLB-49
Clay, Cassius Marcellus 1810-1903 . . . . . . DLB-43
Clayton, Richard (seed Haggard, William)
Cleage, Pearl 1948- DLB-228
Cleary, Beverly 1916- DLB-52
Cleary, Kate McPhelim 1863-1905. . . . . . DLB-221
Cleaver, Vera 1919-1992 and Cleaver, Bill 1920-1981 . . . . DLB-52
Cleeve, Brian 1921- DLB-276
Cleland, John 1710-1789 . . . . DLB-39
Clemens, Samuel Langhorne (Mark Twain) 1835-1910 . . . . DLB-11, 12, 23, 64, 74, 186, 189; CDALB-3
Comments From Authors and Scholars on their First Reading of *Huck Finn* Y-85
Huck at 100: How Old Is Huckleberry Finn? Y-85
Mark Twain on Perpetual Copyright Y-92
A New Edition of *Huck Finn*. Y-85
Clement, Hal 1922- DLB-8
Clemo, Jack 1916- DLB-27
Clephane, Elizabeth Cecilia 1830-1869 . . DLB-199
Cleveland, John 1613-1658 . . . . DLB-126
Cliff, Michelle 1946- DLB-157; CDWLB-3
Clifford, Lady Anne 1590-1676 . . . . DLB-151
Clifford, James L. 1901-1978 . . . . DLB-103
Clifford, Lucy 1853?-1929 . . . . .DLB-135, 141, 197
Clift, Charmian 1923-1969. . . . . DLB-260
Clifton, Lucille 1936- DLB-5, 41
Clines, Francis X. 1938- DLB-185
Clive, Caroline (V) 1801-1873 . . . . DLB-199
Edward J. Clode [publishing house] DLB-46
Clough, Arthur Hugh 1819-1861 . . . . DLB-32
Cloutier, Cécile 1930- DLB-60
Clouts, Sidney 1926-1982. . . . . DLB-225
Clutton-Brock, Arthur 1868-1924 . . . . DLB-98
Coates, Robert M. 1897-1973 . . . . .DLB-4, 9, 102; DS-15
Coatsworth, Elizabeth 1893-1986. . . . . DLB-22
Cobb, Charles E., Jr. 1943- DLB-41
Cobb, Frank I. 1869-1923 . . . . DLB-25
Cobb, Irvin S. 1876-1944 . . . . DLB-11, 25, 86
Cobbe, Frances Power 1822-1904 . . . . . . DLB-190
Cobbett, William 1763-1835. . . . . DLB-43, 107, 158
Cobbledick, Gordon 1898-1969 . . . . .DLB-171
Cochran, Thomas C. 1902- DLB-17
Cochrane, Elizabeth 1867-1922 . . . . . DLB-25, 189
Cockerell, Sir Sydney 1867-1962 . . . . DLB-201
Cockerill, John A. 1845-1896 . . . . DLB-23
Cocteau, Jean 1889-1963 . . . . DLB-65, 258
Coderre, Emile (see Jean Narrache)
Cody, Liza 1944- DLB-276

Coe, Jonathan 1961- DLB-231
Coetzee, J. M. 1940- DLB-225
Coffee, Lenore J. 1900?-1984............DLB-44
Coffin, Robert P. Tristram 1892-1955.....DLB-45
Coghill, Mrs. Harry (see Walker, Anna Louisa)
Cogswell, Fred 1917- DLB-60
Cogswell, Mason Fitch 1761-1830........DLB-37
Cohan, George M. 1878-1942..........DLB-249
Cohen, Arthur A. 1928-1986............DLB-28
Cohen, Leonard 1934- DLB-53
Cohen, Matt 1942- DLB-53
Cohen, Morris Raphael 1880-1947......DLB-270
Colbeck, Norman 1903-1987...........DLB-201
Colden, Cadwallader
1688-1776 ....DLB-24, 30, 270
Colden, Jane 1724-1766...............DLB-200
Cole, Barry 1936- DLB-14
Cole, George Watson 1850-1939........DLB-140
Colegate, Isabel 1931- DLB-14, 231
Coleman, Emily Holmes 1899-1974 ....DLB-4
Coleman, Wanda 1946- DLB-130
Coleridge, Hartley 1796-1849 ....DLB-96
Coleridge, Mary 1861-1907..........DLB-19, 98
Coleridge, Samuel Taylor
1772-1834 ....DLB-93, 107; CDBLB-3
Coleridge, Sara 1802-1852.............DLB-199
Colet, John 1467-1519 ....DLB-132
Colette 1873-1954 ....DLB-65
Colette, Sidonie Gabrielle (see Colette)
Colinas, Antonio 1946- DLB-134
Coll, Joseph Clement 1881-1921 ....DLB-188
A Century of Poetry, a Lifetime of Collecting:
J. M. Edelstein's Collection of
Twentieth-Century American Poetry Y-02
Collier, John 1901-1980............ DLB-77, 255
Collier, John Payne 1789-1883..........DLB-184
Collier, Mary 1690-1762 ....DLB-95
Collier, Robert J. 1876-1918.............DLB-91
P. F. Collier [publishing house] DLB-49
Collin and Small DLB-49
Collingwood, R. G. 1889-1943 ....DLB-262
Collingwood, W. G. 1854-1932.........DLB-149
Collins, An floruit circa 1653...........DLB-131
Collins, Anthony 1676-1729............DLB-252
Collins, Merle 1950- DLB-157
Collins, Michael 1964- DLB-267
Tribute to John D. MacDonald......... Y-86
Tribute to Kenneth Millar............. Y-83
Why I Write Mysteries: Night and Day .. Y-85
Collins, Mortimer 1827-1876 ....DLB-21, 35
Collins, Tom (see Furphy, Joseph)
Collins, Wilkie
1824-1889 ....DLB-18, 70, 159; CDBLB-4
"The Unknown Public" (1858)
[excerpt] DLB-57
The Wilkie Collins Society Y-98
Collins, William 1721-1759 ....DLB-109
Isaac Collins [publishing house]..........DLB-49
William Collins, Sons and Company DLB-154
Collis, Maurice 1889-1973.............DLB-195
Collyer, Mary 1716?-1763? DLB-39
Colman, Benjamin 1673-1747 ....DLB-24
Colman, George, the Elder 1732-1794.....DLB-89
Colman, George, the Younger
1762-1836 ....DLB-89
S. Colman [publishing house] DLB-49
Colombo, John Robert 1936- DLB-53
Colquhoun, Patrick 1745-1820 ....DLB-158
Colter, Cyrus 1910-2002 ....DLB-33
Colum, Padraic 1881-1972..............DLB-19
The Columbia History of the American Novel
A Symposium on.................... Y-92
Columella fl. first century A.D..........DLB-211
Colvin, Sir Sidney 1845-1927 ....DLB-149
Colwin, Laurie 1944-1992........ DLB-218; Y-80
Comden, Betty 1915- and
Green, Adolph 1918- DLB-44, 265
Comi, Girolamo 1890-1968............DLB-114
Comisso, Giovanni 1895-1969 ....DLB-264
Commager, Henry Steele 1902-1998......DLB-17
Commynes, Philippe de
circa 1447-1511 ....DLB-208
Compton, D. G. 1930- DLB-261
Compton-Burnett, Ivy 1884?-1969 ....DLB-36
Conan, Laure (Félicité Angers)
1845-1924.......................DLB-99
Concord, Massachusetts
Concord History and Life..........DLB-223
Concord: Literary History
of a Town..................DLB-223
The Old Manse, by Hawthorne DLB-223
The Thoreauvian Pilgrimage: The
Structure of an American Cult ...DLB-223
Conde, Carmen 1901-1996 ....DLB-108
Congreve, William
1670-1729 ....DLB-39, 84; CDBLB-2
Preface to *Incognita* (1692) DLB-39
W. B. Conkey Company...............DLB-49
Conn, Stewart 1936- DLB-233
Connell, Evan S., Jr. 1924- DLB-2; Y-81
Connelly, Marc 1890-1980 ....DLB-7; Y-80
Connolly, Cyril 1903-1974 ....DLB-98
Connolly, James B. 1868-1957...........DLB-78
Connor, Ralph (Charles William Gordon)
1860-1937 ....DLB-92
Connor, Tony 1930- DLB-40
Conquest, Robert 1917- DLB-27
Conrad, Joseph
1857-1924 ....DLB-10, 34, 98, 156; CDBLB-5
John Conrad and Company DLB-49
Conroy, Jack 1899-1990 .... Y-81
A Tribute [to Nelson Algren] Y-81
Conroy, Pat 1945- DLB-6
Considine, Bob 1906-1975.............DLB-241
Consolo, Vincenzo 1933- DLB-196
Constable, Henry 1562-1613...........DLB-136
Archibald Constable and Company DLB-154
Constable and Company Limited DLB-112
Constant, Benjamin 1767-1830..........DLB-119
Constant de Rebecque, Henri-Benjamin de
(see Constant, Benjamin)
Constantine, David 1944- DLB-40
Constantine, Murray (see Burdekin, Katharine)
Constantin-Weyer, Maurice 1881-1964....DLB-92
Contempo (magazine)
Contempo Caravan:
Kites in a Windstorm Y-85
The Continental Publishing Company DLB-49
A Conversation between William Riggan
and Janette Turner Hospital Y-02
Conversations with Editors Y-95
Conway, Anne 1631-1679 ....DLB-252
Conway, Moncure Daniel
1832-1907 ....DLB-1, 223
Cook, Ebenezer circa 1667-circa 1732 .....DLB-24
Cook, Edward Tyas 1857-1919.........DLB-149
Cook, Eliza 1818-1889................DLB-199
Cook, George Cram 1873-1924.........DLB-266
Cook, Michael 1933-1994 ....DLB-53
David C. Cook Publishing Company DLB-49
Cooke, George Willis 1848-1923 ....DLB-71
Cooke, John Esten 1830-1886 ....DLB-3, 248
Cooke, Philip Pendleton
1816-1850 ....DLB-3, 59, 248
Cooke, Rose Terry 1827-1892........DLB-12, 74
Increase Cooke and Company DLB-49
Cook-Lynn, Elizabeth 1930- DLB-175
Coolbrith, Ina 1841-1928 ....DLB-54, 186
Cooley, Peter 1940- DLB-105
"Into the Mirror" DLB-105
Coolidge, Clark 1939- DLB-193
Coolidge, Susan
(see Woolsey, Sarah Chauncy)
George Coolidge [publishing house] DLB-49
Cooper, Anna Julia 1858-1964 ....DLB-221
Cooper, Edith Emma 1862-1913........DLB-240
Cooper, Giles 1918-1966...............DLB-13
Cooper, J. California 19??- DLB-212
Cooper, James Fenimore
1789-1851 ....DLB-3, 183, 250; CDALB-2
The Bicentennial of James Fenimore Cooper:
An International Celebration Y-89
The James Fenimore Cooper Society Y-01
Cooper, Kent 1880-1965 ....DLB-29
Cooper, Susan 1935- DLB-161, 261
Cooper, Susan Fenimore 1813-1894 .....DLB-239
William Cooper [publishing house]...... DLB-170
J. Coote [publishing house] DLB-154
Coover, Robert 1932- DLB-2, 227; Y-81
Tribute to Donald Barthelme Y-89
Tribute to Theodor Seuss Geisel Y-91

Copeland and Day DLB-49
Ćopić, Branko 1915-1984 . . . . DLB-181
Copland, Robert 1470?-1548 . . . . DLB-136
Coppard, A. E. 1878-1957 . . . . DLB-162
Coppée, François 1842-1908 . . . . DLB-217
Coppel, Alfred 1921- Y-83
Tribute to Jessamyn West Y-84
Coppola, Francis Ford 1939- DLB-44
Copway, George (Kah-ge-ga-gah-bowh) 1818-1869 . . . . DLB-175, 183
Copyright
The Development of the Author's Copyright in Britain DLB-154
The Digital Millennium Copyright Act: Expanding Copyright Protection in Cyberspace and Beyond Y-98
Editorial: The Extension of Copyright . . . Y-02
Mark Twain on Perpetual Copyright Y-92
Public Domain and the Violation of Texts Y-97
The Question of American Copyright in the Nineteenth Century
Preface, by George Haven Putnam
The Evolution of Copyright, by Brander Matthews
Summary of Copyright Legislation in the United States, by R. R. Bowker
Analysis of the Provisions of the Copyright Law of 1891, by George Haven Putnam
The Contest for International Copyright, by George Haven Putnam
Cheap Books and Good Books, by Brander Matthews DLB-49
Writers and Their Copyright Holders: the WATCH Project Y-94
Corazzini, Sergio 1886-1907 . . . . DLB-114
Corbett, Richard 1582-1635 . . . . DLB-121
Corbière, Tristan 1845-1875 . . . . DLB-217
Corcoran, Barbara 1911- DLB-52
Cordelli, Franco 1943- DLB-196
Corelli, Marie 1855-1924 . . . . DLB-34, 156
Corle, Edwin 1906-1956 . . . . Y-85
Corman, Cid 1924- DLB-5, 193
Cormier, Robert 1925-2000 . . . DLB-52; CDALB-6
Tribute to Theodor Seuss Geisel Y-91
Corn, Alfred 1943- DLB-120, 282; Y-80
Corneille, Pierre 1606-1684 . . . . DLB-268
Cornford, Frances 1886-1960 . . . . DLB-240
Cornish, Sam 1935- DLB-41
Cornish, William circa 1465-circa 1524 . . . . DLB-132
Cornwall, Barry (see Procter, Bryan Waller)
Cornwallis, Sir William, the Younger circa 1579-1614 . . . . DLB-151
Cornwell, David John Moore (see le Carré, John)
Coronel Urtecho, José 1906-1994 . . . . DLB-290
Corpi, Lucha 1945- DLB-82
Corrington, John William 1932-1988 . . . . DLB-6, 244
Corriveau, Monique 1927-1976 . . . . DLB-251
Corrothers, James D. 1869-1917 . . . . DLB-50
Corso, Gregory 1930-2001 . . . . .DLB-5, 16, 237
Cortázar, Julio 1914-1984 . . . .DLB-113; CDWLB-3
Cortéz, Carlos 1923- DLB-209
Cortez, Jayne 1936- DLB-41
Corvinus, Gottlieb Siegmund 1677-1746 . . . . DLB-168
Corvo, Baron (see Rolfe, Frederick William)
Cory, Annie Sophie (see Cross, Victoria)
Cory, Desmond (Shaun Lloyd McCarthy) 1928- DLB-276
Cory, William Johnson 1823-1892 . . . . DLB-35
Coryate, Thomas 1577?-1617 . . . . . . .DLB-151, 172
Ćosić, Dobrica 1921- DLB-181; CDWLB-4
Cosin, John 1595-1672 . . . . DLB-151, 213
Cosmopolitan Book Corporation DLB-46
Costa, Maria Velho da (see The Three Marias: A Landmark Case in Portuguese Literary History)
Costain, Thomas B. 1885-1965 . . . . DLB-9
Coste, Donat (Daniel Boudreau) 1912-1957 . . . . DLB-88
Costello, Louisa Stuart 1799-1870 . . . . DLB-166
Cota-Cárdenas, Margarita 1941- DLB-122
Côté, Denis 1954- DLB-251
Cotten, Bruce 1873-1954 . . . . DLB-187
Cotter, Joseph Seamon, Jr. 1895-1919 . . . . DLB-50
Cotter, Joseph Seamon, Sr. 1861-1949 . . . . DLB-50
Joseph Cottle [publishing house] DLB-154
Cotton, Charles 1630-1687 . . . . DLB-131
Cotton, John 1584-1652 . . . . DLB-24
Cotton, Sir Robert Bruce 1571-1631 . . . . . DLB-213
Coulter, John 1888-1980 . . . . DLB-68
Cournos, John 1881-1966 . . . . DLB-54
Courteline, Georges 1858-1929 . . . . DLB-192
Cousins, Margaret 1905-1996 . . . . DLB-137
Cousins, Norman 1915-1990 . . . . DLB-137
Couvreur, Jessie (see Tasma)
Coventry, Francis 1725-1754 . . . . DLB-39
Dedication, *The History of Pompey the Little* (1751) DLB-39
Coverdale, Miles 1487 or 1488-1569 . . . . DLB-167
N. Coverly [publishing house] DLB-49
Covici-Friede DLB-46
Cowan, Peter 1914-2002 . . . . DLB-260
Coward, Noel 1899-1973 . . . . DLB-10, 245; CDBLB-6
Coward, McCann and Geoghegan DLB-46
Cowles, Gardner 1861-1946 . . . . DLB-29
Cowles, Gardner "Mike", Jr. 1903-1985 . . . . DLB-127, 137
Cowley, Abraham 1618-1667 . . . . . . DLB-131, 151
Cowley, Hannah 1743-1809 . . . . DLB-89
Cowley, Malcolm 1898-1989 . . . . . . .DLB-4, 48; DS-15; Y-81, 89
Cowper, Richard (John Middleton Murry Jr.) 1926-2002 . . . . DLB-261
Cowper, William 1731-1800 . . . . .DLB-104, 109
Cox, A. B. (see Berkeley, Anthony)
Cox, James McMahon 1903-1974 . . . . . . .DLB-127
Cox, James Middleton 1870-1957 . . . . .DLB-127
Cox, Leonard circa 1495-circa 1550 . . . . . DLB-281
Cox, Palmer 1840-1924 . . . . DLB-42
Coxe, Louis 1918-1993 . . . . DLB-5
Coxe, Tench 1755-1824 . . . . DLB-37
Cozzens, Frederick S. 1818-1869 . . . . DLB-202
Cozzens, James Gould 1903-1978 . . . . DLB-9, 294; Y-84; DS-2; CDALB-1
Cozzens's *Michael Scarlett* Y-97
Ernest Hemingway's Reaction to James Gould Cozzens Y-98
James Gould Cozzens–A View from Afar Y-97
James Gould Cozzens: How to Read Him Y-97
James Gould Cozzens Symposium and Exhibition at the University of South Carolina, Columbia Y-00
Mens Rea (or Something) Y-97
Novels for Grown-Ups Y-97
Crabbe, George 1754-1832 . . . . DLB-93
Crace, Jim 1946- DLB-231
Crackanthorpe, Hubert 1870-1896 . . . . . . DLB-135
Craddock, Charles Egbert (see Murfree, Mary N.)
Cradock, Thomas 1718-1770 . . . . DLB-31
Craig, Daniel H. 1811-1895 . . . . DLB-43
Craik, Dinah Maria 1826-1887 . . . . . . DLB-35, 163
Cramer, Richard Ben 1950- DLB-185
Cranch, Christopher Pearse 1813-1892 . . . . DLB-1, 42, 243; DS-5
Crane, Hart 1899-1932 . . . . . DLB-4, 48; CDALB-4
Nathan Asch Remembers Ford Madox Ford, Sam Roth, and Hart Crane Y-02
Crane, R. S. 1886-1967 . . . . DLB-63
Crane, Stephen 1871-1900 . . . . DLB-12, 54, 78; CDALB-3
Stephen Crane: A Revaluation, Virginia Tech Conference, 1989 . . . . Y-89
The Stephen Crane Society Y-98, 01
Crane, Walter 1845-1915 . . . . DLB-163
Cranmer, Thomas 1489-1556 . . . . . DLB-132, 213
Crapsey, Adelaide 1878-1914 . . . . DLB-54
Crashaw, Richard 1612/1613-1649 . . . . . DLB-126
Craven, Avery 1885-1980 . . . . .DLB-17
Crawford, Charles 1752-circa 1815 . . . . . . DLB-31
Crawford, F. Marion 1854-1909 . . . . DLB-71
Crawford, Isabel Valancy 1850-1887 . . . . . DLB-92
Crawley, Alan 1887-1975 . . . . DLB-68
Crayon, Geoffrey (see Irving, Washington)
Crayon, Porte (see Strother, David Hunter)
Creamer, Robert W. 1922- DLB-171
Creasey, John 1908-1973 . . . . DLB-77
Creative Age Press DLB-46
Creative Nonfiction Y-02
William Creech [publishing house] DLB-154

Thomas Creede [publishing house] DLB-170
Creel, George 1876-1953 . . . . DLB-25
Creeley, Robert 1926- DLB-5, 16, 169; DS-17
Creelman, James 1859-1915 . . . . DLB-23
Cregan, David 1931- DLB-13
Creighton, Donald 1902-1979 . . . . DLB-88
Crémazie, Octave 1827-1879 . . . . DLB-99
Crémer, Victoriano 1909?- DLB-108
Crescas, Hasdai circa 1340-1412? DLB-115
Crespo, Angel 1926-1995 . . . . DLB-134
Cresset Press DLB-112
Cresswell, Helen 1934- DLB-161
Crèvecoeur, Michel Guillaume Jean de 1735-1813 . . . . DLB-37
Crewe, Candida 1964- DLB-207
Crews, Harry 1935- DLB-6, 143, 185
Crichton, Michael (John Lange, Jeffrey Hudson, Michael Douglas) 1942- DLB-292; Y-81
Crispin, Edmund (Robert Bruce Montgomery) 1921-1978 . . . . DLB-87
Cristofer, Michael 1946- DLB-7
Criticism
Afro-American Literary Critics: An Introduction DLB-33
The Consolidation of Opinion: Critical Responses to the Modernists DLB-36
"Criticism in Relation to Novels" (1863), by G. H. Lewes DLB-21
The Limits of Pluralism DLB-67
Modern Critical Terms, Schools, and Movements DLB-67
"Panic Among the Philistines": A Postscript, An Interview with Bryan Griffin Y-81
The Recovery of Literature: Criticism in the 1990s: A Symposium Y-91
The Stealthy School of Criticism (1871), by Dante Gabriel Rossetti. DLB-35
Crnjanski, Miloš 1893-1977 . . . . DLB-147; CDWLB-4
Crocker, Hannah Mather 1752-1829. . . . . DLB-200
Crockett, David (Davy) 1786-1836 . . . . DLB-3, 11, 183, 248
Croft-Cooke, Rupert (see Bruce, Leo)
Crofts, Freeman Wills 1879-1957. . . . . DLB-77
Croker, John Wilson 1780-1857. . . . . DLB-110
Croly, George 1780-1860. . . . . DLB-159
Croly, Herbert 1869-1930 . . . . DLB-91
Croly, Jane Cunningham 1829-1901 . . . . . . DLB-23
Crompton, Richmal 1890-1969 . . . . DLB-160
Cronin, A. J. 1896-1981. . . . . DLB-191
Cros, Charles 1842-1888 . . . . DLB-217
Crosby, Caresse 1892-1970 and Crosby, Harry 1898-1929 and . . . DLB-4; DS-15
Crosby, Harry 1898-1929 . . . . DLB-48
Crosland, Camilla Toulmin (Mrs. Newton Crosland) 1812-1895. . . . . DLB-240
Cross, Gillian 1945- DLB-161
Cross, Victoria 1868-1952. . . . . DLB-135, 197
Crossley-Holland, Kevin 1941- DLB-40, 161
Crothers, Rachel 1870-1958. . . . . DLB-7, 266
Thomas Y. Crowell Company DLB-49
Crowley, John 1942- Y-82
Crowley, Mart 1935- DLB-7, 266
Crown Publishers DLB-46
Crowne, John 1641-1712 . . . . DLB-80
Crowninshield, Edward Augustus 1817-1859 . . . . DLB-140
Crowninshield, Frank 1872-1947. . . . . DLB-91
Croy, Homer 1883-1965 . . . . DLB-4
Crumley, James 1939- DLB-226; Y-84
Cruse, Mary Anne 1825?-1910 . . . . DLB-239
Cruz, Migdalia 1958- DLB-249
Cruz, Victor Hernández 1949- DLB-41
Csokor, Franz Theodor 1885-1969 . . . . DLB-81
Csoóri, Sándor 1930- DLB-232; CDWLB-4
Cuadra, Pablo Antonio 1912-2002 . . . . . . DLB-290
Cuala Press DLB-112
Cudworth, Ralph 1617-1688 . . . . DLB-252
Cugoano, Quobna Ottabah 1797-?. Y-02
Cullen, Countee 1903-1946 . . . . DLB-4, 48, 51; CDALB-4
Culler, Jonathan D. 1944- DLB-67, 246
Cullinan, Elizabeth 1933- DLB-234
Culverwel, Nathaniel 1619?-1651? DLB-252
Cumberland, Richard 1732-1811. . . . . DLB-89
Cummings, Constance Gordon 1837-1924 . . . . DLB-174
Cummings, E. E. 1894-1962 . . . . DLB-4, 48; CDALB-5
The E. E. Cummings Society Y-01
Cummings, Ray 1887-1957 . . . . DLB-8
Cummings and Hilliard. DLB-49
Cummins, Maria Susanna 1827-1866 . . . . . DLB-42
Cumpián, Carlos 1953- DLB-209
Cunard, Nancy 1896-1965 . . . . DLB-240
Joseph Cundall [publishing house]. DLB-106
Cuney, Waring 1906-1976. . . . . DLB-51
Cuney-Hare, Maude 1874-1936. . . . . DLB-52
Cunningham, Allan 1784-1842 . . . . . DLB-116, 144
Cunningham, J. V. 1911-1985 . . . . DLB-5
Cunningham, Michael 1952- DLB-292
Cunningham, Peter (Peter Lauder, Peter Benjamin) 1947- DLB-267
Peter F. Cunningham [publishing house] DLB-49
Cunquiero, Alvaro 1911-1981 . . . . DLB-134
Cuomo, George 1929- Y-80
Cupples, Upham and Company DLB-49
Cupples and Leon DLB-46
Cuppy, Will 1884-1949 . . . . DLB-11
Curiel, Barbara Brinson 1956- DLB-209
Edmund Curll [publishing house] DLB-154
Currie, James 1756-1805 . . . . DLB-142
Currie, Mary Montgomerie Lamb Singleton, Lady Currie (see Fane, Violet)
Cursor Mundi circa 1300 . . . . DLB-146
Curti, Merle E. 1897-1996 . . . . DLB-17
Curtis, Anthony 1926- DLB-155
Curtis, Cyrus H. K. 1850-1933 . . . . DLB-91
Curtis, George William 1824-1892 . . . . DLB-1, 43, 223
Curzon, Robert 1810-1873. . . . . DLB-166
Curzon, Sarah Anne 1833-1898 . . . . DLB-99
Cusack, Dymphna 1902-1981 . . . . DLB-260
Cushing, Eliza Lanesford 1794-1886 . . . . . . DLB-99
Cushing, Harvey 1869-1939 . . . . DLB-187
Custance, Olive (Lady Alfred Douglas) 1874-1944 . . . . DLB-240
Cynewulf circa 770-840 . . . . DLB-146
Cyrano de Bergerac, Savinien de 1619-1655 . . . . DLB-268
Czepko, Daniel 1605-1660. . . . . DLB-164
Czerniawski, Adam 1934- DLB-232

D

Dabit, Eugène 1898-1936 . . . . DLB-65
Daborne, Robert circa 1580-1628 . . . . DLB-58
Dąbrowska, Maria 1889-1965 . . . . DLB-215; CDWLB-4
Dacey, Philip 1939- DLB-105
"Eyes Across Centuries: Contemporary Poetry and 'That Vision Thing,'" DLB-105
Dach, Simon 1605-1659. . . . . DLB-164
Dagerman, Stig 1923-1954. . . . . DLB-259
Daggett, Rollin M. 1831-1901 . . . . DLB-79
D'Aguiar, Fred 1960- DLB-157
Dahl, Roald 1916-1990 . . . . DLB-139, 255
Tribute to Alfred A. Knopf. Y-84
Dahlberg, Edward 1900-1977 . . . . DLB-48
Dahn, Felix 1834-1912. . . . . DLB-129
Dal', Vladimir Ivanovich (Kazak Vladimir Lugansky) 1801-1872 . . . . DLB-198
Dale, Peter 1938- DLB-40
Daley, Arthur 1904-1974 . . . . DLB-171
Dall, Caroline Healey 1822-1912 . . . . . DLB-1, 235
Dallas, E. S. 1828-1879 . . . . DLB-55
The Gay Science [excerpt](1866) DLB-21
The Dallas Theater Center DLB-7
D'Alton, Louis 1900-1951 . . . . DLB-10
Dalton, Roque 1935-1975 . . . . DLB-283
Daly, Carroll John 1889-1958 . . . . DLB-226
Daly, T. A. 1871-1948 . . . . DLB-11
Damon, S. Foster 1893-1971 . . . . DLB-45
William S. Damrell [publishing house] DLB-49
Dana, Charles A. 1819-1897 . . . . . . DLB-3, 23, 250
Dana, Richard Henry, Jr. 1815-1882 . . . . DLB-1, 183, 235
Dandridge, Ray Garfield DLB-51
Dane, Clemence 1887-1965 . . . . DLB-10, 197

Danforth, John 1660-1730 . . . . DLB-24
Danforth, Samuel, I 1626-1674 . . . . DLB-24
Danforth, Samuel, II 1666-1727 . . . . DLB-24
Daniel, John M. 1825-1865 . . . . DLB-43
Daniel, Samuel 1562 or 1563-1619 . . . . DLB-62
Daniel Press DLB-106
Daniells, Roy 1902-1979 . . . . DLB-68
Daniels, Jim 1956- DLB-120
Daniels, Jonathan 1902-1981 . . . . DLB-127
Daniels, Josephus 1862-1948 . . . . DLB-29
Daniels, Sarah 1957- DLB-245
Danilevsky, Grigorii Petrovich 1829-1890 . . . . DLB-238
Dannay, Frederic 1905-1982 . . . . DLB-137
Danner, Margaret Esse 1915- DLB-41
John Danter [publishing house] DLB-170
Dantin, Louis (Eugene Seers) 1865-1945 . . . . DLB-92
Danto, Arthur C. 1924- DLB-279
Danzig, Allison 1898-1987 . . . . DLB-171
D'Arcy, Ella circa 1857-1937 . . . . DLB-135
Darío, Rubén 1867-1916 . . . . DLB-290
Dark, Eleanor 1901-1985 . . . . DLB-260
Darke, Nick 1948- DLB-233
Darley, Felix Octavious Carr 1822-1888 . . . . DLB-188
Darley, George 1795-1846 . . . . DLB-96
Darmesteter, Madame James (see Robinson, A. Mary F.)
Darwin, Charles 1809-1882 . . . . DLB-57, 166
Darwin, Erasmus 1731-1802 . . . . DLB-93
Daryush, Elizabeth 1887-1977 . . . . DLB-20
Dashkova, Ekaterina Romanovna (née Vorontsova) 1743-1810 . . . . DLB-150
Dashwood, Edmée Elizabeth Monica de la Pasture (see Delafield, E. M.)
Daudet, Alphonse 1840-1897 . . . . DLB-123
d'Aulaire, Edgar Parin 1898- and d'Aulaire, Ingri 1904- DLB-22
Davenant, Sir William 1606-1668 . . . DLB-58, 126
Davenport, Guy 1927- DLB-130
Tribute to John Gardner Y-82
Davenport, Marcia 1903-1996 . . . . DS-17
Davenport, Robert ?-? DLB-58
Daves, Delmer 1904-1977 . . . . DLB-26
Davey, Frank 1940- DLB-53
Davidson, Avram 1923-1993 . . . . DLB-8
Davidson, Donald 1893-1968 . . . . DLB-45
Davidson, Donald 1917- DLB-279
Davidson, John 1857-1909 . . . . DLB-19
Davidson, Lionel 1922- DLB-14, 276
Davidson, Robyn 1950- DLB-204
Davidson, Sara 1943- DLB-185
Davið Stefánsson frá Fagraskógi 1895-1964 . . . . DLB-293
Davie, Donald 1922- DLB-27
Davie, Elspeth 1919-1995 . . . . DLB-139
Davies, Sir John 1569-1626 . . . . DLB-172
Davies, John, of Hereford 1565?-1618 . . . DLB-121
Davies, Rhys 1901-1978 . . . . DLB-139, 191
Davies, Robertson 1913-1995 . . . . DLB-68
Davies, Samuel 1723-1761 . . . . DLB-31
Davies, Thomas 1712?-1785 . . . . DLB-142, 154
Davies, W. H. 1871-1940 . . . . DLB-19, 174
Peter Davies Limited DLB-112
Davin, Nicholas Flood 1840?-1901 . . . . DLB-99
Daviot, Gordon 1896?-1952 . . . . DLB-10 (see also Tey, Josephine)
Davis, Arthur Hoey (see Rudd, Steele)
Davis, Charles A. (Major J. Downing) 1795-1867 . . . . DLB-11
Davis, Clyde Brion 1894-1962 . . . . DLB-9
Davis, Dick 1945- DLB-40, 282
Davis, Frank Marshall 1905-1987 . . . . DLB-51
Davis, H. L. 1894-1960 . . . . DLB-9, 206
Davis, John 1774-1854 . . . . DLB-37
Davis, Lydia 1947- DLB-130
Davis, Margaret Thomson 1926- DLB-14
Davis, Ossie 1917- DLB-7, 38, 249
Davis, Owen 1874-1956 . . . . DLB-249
Davis, Paxton 1925-1994 . . . . Y-89
Davis, Rebecca Harding 1831-1910 . . . . DLB-74, 239
Davis, Richard Harding 1864-1916 . . . . DLB-12, 23, 78, 79, 189; DS-13
Davis, Samuel Cole 1764-1809 . . . . DLB-37
Davis, Samuel Post 1850-1918 . . . . DLB-202
Davison, Frank Dalby 1893-1970 . . . . DLB-260
Davison, Peter 1928- DLB-5
Davydov, Denis Vasil'evich 1784-1839 . . . . DLB-205
Davys, Mary 1674-1732 . . . . DLB-39
Preface to *The Works of Mrs. Davys* (1725) DLB-39
DAW Books DLB-46
Dawe, Bruce 1930- DLB-289
Dawson, Ernest 1882-1947 . . . . DLB-140; Y-02
Dawson, Fielding 1930- DLB-130
Dawson, Sarah Morgan 1842-1909 . . . . . DLB-239
Dawson, William 1704-1752 . . . . DLB-31
Day, Angel flourished 1583-1599 . . . . DLB-167, 236
Day, Benjamin Henry 1810-1889 . . . . DLB-43
Day, Clarence 1874-1935 . . . . DLB-11
Day, Dorothy 1897-1980 . . . . DLB-29
Day, Frank Parker 1881-1950 . . . . DLB-92
Day, John circa 1574-circa 1640 . . . . DLB-62
Day, Thomas 1748-1789 . . . . DLB-39
John Day [publishing house] DLB-170
The John Day Company DLB-46
Mahlon Day [publishing house] DLB-49
Day Lewis, C. (see Blake, Nicholas)
Dazai Osamu 1909-1948 . . . . DLB-182
Deacon, William Arthur 1890-1977 . . . . . . DLB-68
Deal, Borden 1922-1985 . . . . DLB-6
de Angeli, Marguerite 1889-1987 . . . . DLB-22
De Angelis, Milo 1951- DLB-128
Debord, Guy 1931-1994 . . . . DLB-296
De Bow, J. D. B. 1820-1867 . . . . DLB-3, 79, 248
de Bruyn, Günter 1926- DLB-75
de Camp, L. Sprague 1907-2000 . . . . DLB-8
De Carlo, Andrea 1952- DLB-196
De Casas, Celso A. 1944- DLB-209
Dechert, Robert 1895-1975 . . . . DLB-187
Dedications, Inscriptions, and Annotations Y-01–02
Dee, John 1527-1608 or 1609 . . . . . . DLB-136, 213
Deeping, George Warwick 1877-1950 . . . DLB-153
Defoe, Daniel 1660-1731 . . . . DLB-39, 95, 101; CDBLB-2
Preface to *Colonel Jack* (1722) DLB-39
Preface to *The Farther Adventures of Robinson Crusoe* (1719) DLB-39
Preface to *Moll Flanders* (1722) DLB-39
Preface to *Robinson Crusoe* (1719) DLB-39
Preface to *Roxana* (1724) DLB-39
de Fontaine, Felix Gregory 1834-1896 . . . . DLB-43
De Forest, John William 1826-1906 . . DLB-12, 189
DeFrees, Madeline 1919- DLB-105
"The Poet's Kaleidoscope: The Element of Surprise in the Making of the Poem" DLB-105
DeGolyer, Everette Lee 1886-1956 . . . . . . DLB-187
de Graff, Robert 1895-1981 . . . . Y-81
de Graft, Joe 1924-1978 . . . . DLB-117
De Heinrico circa 980? DLB-148
Deighton, Len 1929- DLB-87; CDBLB-8
DeJong, Meindert 1906-1991 . . . . DLB-52
Dekker, Thomas circa 1572-1632 . . . . . DLB-62, 172; CDBLB-1
Delacorte, George T., Jr. 1894-1991 . . . . . . DLB-91
Delafield, E. M. 1890-1943 . . . . DLB-34
Delahaye, Guy (Guillaume Lahaise) 1888-1969 . . . . DLB-92
de la Mare, Walter 1873-1956 . . . . DLB-19, 153, 162, 255; CDBLB-6
Deland, Margaret 1857-1945 . . . . DLB-78
Delaney, Shelagh 1939- DLB-13; CDBLB-8
Delano, Amasa 1763-1823 . . . . DLB-183
Delany, Martin Robinson 1812-1885 . . . . . DLB-50
Delany, Samuel R. 1942- DLB-8, 33
de la Roche, Mazo 1879-1961 . . . . DLB-68
Delavigne, Jean François Casimir 1793-1843 . . . . DLB-192
Delbanco, Nicholas 1942- DLB-6, 234
Delblanc, Sven 1931-1992 . . . . DLB-257
Del Castillo, Ramón 1949- DLB-209
Deledda, Grazia 1871-1936 . . . . DLB-264
De León, Nephtal 1945- DLB-82
Deleuze, Gilles 1925-1995 . . . . DLB-296
Delfini, Antonio 1907-1963 . . . . DLB-264

Delgado, Abelardo Barrientos 1931- DLB-82
Del Giudice, Daniele 1949- DLB-196
De Libero, Libero 1906-1981...........DLB-114
DeLillo, Don 1936- DLB-6, 173
de Lint, Charles 1951- DLB-251
de Lisser H. G. 1878-1944.............DLB-117
Dell, Floyd 1887-1969 ....DLB-9
Dell Publishing Company..............DLB-46
delle Grazie, Marie Eugene 1864-1931 ....DLB-81
Deloney, Thomas died 1600...........DLB-167
Deloria, Ella C. 1889-1971.............DLB-175
Deloria, Vine, Jr. 1933- DLB-175
del Rey, Lester 1915-1993...............DLB-8
Del Vecchio, John M. 1947- DS-9
Del'vig, Anton Antonovich 1798-1831....DLB-205
de Man, Paul 1919-1983...............DLB-67
DeMarinis, Rick 1934- DLB-218
Demby, William 1922- DLB-33
De Mille, James 1833-1880.........DLB-99, 251
de Mille, William 1878-1955...........DLB-266
Deming, Philander 1829-1915...........DLB-74
Deml, Jakub 1878-1961...............DLB-215
Demorest, William Jennings 1822-1895....DLB-79
De Morgan, William 1839-1917........DLB-153
Demosthenes 384 B.C.-322 B.C.........DLB-176
Henry Denham [publishing house]......DLB-170
Denham, Sir John 1615-1669........DLB-58, 126
Denison, Merrill 1893-1975.............DLB-92
T. S. Denison and Company...........DLB-49
Dennery, Adolphe Philippe 1811-1899 ...DLB-192
Dennie, Joseph 1768-1812 ..... DLB-37, 43, 59, 73
Dennis, C. J. 1876-1938...............DLB-260
Dennis, John 1658-1734...............DLB-101
Dennis, Nigel 1912-1989........DLB-13, 15, 233
Denslow, W. W. 1856-1915...........DLB-188
Dent, J. M., and Sons.................DLB-112
Dent, Tom 1932-1998.................DLB-38
Denton, Daniel circa 1626-1703..........DLB-24
DePaola, Tomie 1934- DLB-61
De Quille, Dan 1829-1898.............DLB-186
De Quincey, Thomas 1785-1859 ....DLB-110, 144; CDBLB-3
"Rhetoric" (1828; revised, 1859) [excerpt] DLB-57
"Style" (1840; revised, 1859) [excerpt] DLB-57
Derby, George Horatio 1823-1861.......DLB-11
J. C. Derby and Company..............DLB-49
Derby and Miller.....................DLB-49
De Ricci, Seymour 1881-1942..........DLB-201
Derleth, August 1909-1971.........DLB-9; DS-17
Derrida, Jacques 1930- DLB-242
The Derrydale Press..................DLB-46
Derzhavin, Gavriil Romanovich 1743-1816 ....DLB-150
Desai, Anita 1937- DLB-271
Desaulniers, Gonzalve 1863-1934........DLB-92
Desbordes-Valmore, Marceline 1786-1859 ....DLB-217
Descartes, René 1596-1650............DLB-268
Deschamps, Emile 1791-1871...........DLB-217
Deschamps, Eustache 1340?-1404.......DLB-208
Desbiens, Jean-Paul 1927- DLB-53
des Forêts, Louis-Rene 1918-2001........DLB-83
Desiato, Luca 1941- DLB-196
Desjardins, Marie-Catherine (see Villedieu, Madame de)
Desnica, Vladan 1905-1967............DLB-181
Desnos, Robert 1900-1945.............DLB-258
DesRochers, Alfred 1901-1978...........DLB-68
Desrosiers, Léo-Paul 1896-1967..........DLB-68
Dessaulles, Louis-Antoine 1819-1895 .....DLB-99
Dessì, Giuseppe 1909-1977............DLB-177
Destouches, Louis-Ferdinand (see Céline, Louis-Ferdinand)
DeSylva, Buddy 1895-1950............DLB-265
De Tabley, Lord 1835-1895............DLB-35
Deutsch, Babette 1895-1982............DLB-45
Deutsch, Niklaus Manuel (see Manuel, Niklaus)
André Deutsch Limited...............DLB-112
Devanny, Jean 1894-1962.............DLB-260
Deveaux, Alexis 1948- DLB-38
De Vere, Aubrey 1814-1902............DLB-35
Devereux, second Earl of Essex, Robert 1565-1601 ....DLB-136
The Devin-Adair Company............DLB-46
De Vinne, Theodore Low 1828-1914 ....DLB-187
Devlin, Anne 1951- DLB-245
DeVoto, Bernard 1897-1955.........DLB-9, 256
De Vries, Peter 1910-1993..........DLB-6; Y-82
Tribute to Albert Erskine Y-93
Dewart, Edward Hartley 1828-1903......DLB-99
Dewdney, Christopher 1951- DLB-60
Dewdney, Selwyn 1909-1979...........DLB-68
Dewey, John 1859-1952...........DLB-246, 270
Dewey, Orville 1794-1882.............DLB-243
Dewey, Thomas B. 1915-1981.........DLB-226
DeWitt, Robert M., Publisher...........DLB-49
DeWolfe, Fiske and Company DLB-49
Dexter, Colin 1930- DLB-87
de Young, M. H. 1849-1925............DLB-25
Dhlomo, H. I. E. 1903-1956 .... DLB-157, 225
Dhuoda circa 803-after 843............DLB-148
The Dial 1840-1844 ....DLB-223
The Dial Press.......................DLB-46
Diamond, I. A. L. 1920-1988...........DLB-26
Dibble, L. Grace 1902-1998............DLB-204
Dibdin, Thomas Frognall 1776-1847 ....DLB-184
Di Cicco, Pier Giorgio 1949- DLB-60
Dick, Philip K. 1928-1982...............DLB-8
Dick and Fitzgerald...................DLB-49
Dickens, Charles 1812-1870....DLB-21, 55, 70, 159, 166; DS-5; CDBLB-4
Dickey, Eric Jerome 1961- DLB-292
Dickey, James 1923-1997........... DLB-5, 193; Y-82, 93, 96, 97; DS-7, 19; CDALB-6
James Dickey and Stanley Burnshaw Correspondence................. Y-02
James Dickey at Seventy–A Tribute..... Y-93
James Dickey, American Poet.......... Y-96
The James Dickey Society............. Y-99
The Life of James Dickey: A Lecture to the Friends of the Emory Libraries, by Henry Hart.................. Y-98
Tribute to Archibald MacLeish......... Y-82
Tribute to Malcolm Cowley........... Y-89
Tribute to Truman Capote............ Y-84
Tributes [to Dickey] Y-97
Dickey, William 1928-1994..............DLB-5
Dickinson, Emily 1830-1886...........DLB-1, 243; CDALB-3
Dickinson, John 1732-1808.............DLB-31
Dickinson, Jonathan 1688-1747..........DLB-24
Dickinson, Patric 1914- DLB-27
Dickinson, Peter 1927- DLB-87, 161, 276
John Dicks [publishing house]..........DLB-106
Dickson, Gordon R. 1923-2001...........DLB-8
Dictionary of Literary Biography *Annual Awards for Dictionary of Literary Biography Editors and Contributors*................... Y-98–02
Dictionary of Literary Biography Yearbook Awards Y-92–93, 97–02
The Dictionary of National Biography........DLB-144
Didion, Joan 1934- DLB-2, 173, 185; Y-81, 86; CDALB-6
Di Donato, Pietro 1911- DLB-9
Die Fürstliche Bibliothek Corvey Y-96
Diego, Gerardo 1896-1987............DLB-134
Dietz, Howard 1896-1983.............DLB-265
Digby, Everard 1550?-1605............DLB-281
Digges, Thomas circa 1546-1595........DLB-136
The Digital Millennium Copyright Act: Expanding Copyright Protection in Cyberspace and Beyond.............. Y-98
Diktonius, Elmer 1896-1961...........DLB-259
Dillard, Annie 1945- DLB-275, 278; Y-80
Dillard, R. H. W. 1937- DLB-5, 244
Charles T. Dillingham Company DLB-49
G. W. Dillingham Company DLB-49
Edward and Charles Dilly [publishing house]................DLB-154
Dilthey, Wilhelm 1833-1911...........DLB-129
Dimitrova, Blaga 1922- ... DLB-181; CDWLB-4
Dimov, Dimitr 1909-1966.............DLB-181
Dimsdale, Thomas J. 1831?-1866.......DLB-186
Dinescu, Mircea 1950- DLB-232
Dinesen, Isak (see Blixen, Karen)

Dingelstedt, Franz von 1814-1881 . . . . . . DLB-133

Dinis, Júlio (Joaquim Guilherme Gomes Coelho) 1839-1871 . . . . DLB-287

Dintenfass, Mark 1941- Y-84

Diogenes, Jr. (see Brougham, John)

Diogenes Laertius circa 200 . . . . .DLB-176

DiPrima, Diane 1934- DLB-5, 16

Disch, Thomas M. 1940- DLB-8, 282

Diski, Jenny 1947- DLB-271

Disney, Walt 1901-1966 . . . . DLB-22

Disraeli, Benjamin 1804-1881 . . . . DLB-21, 55

D'Israeli, Isaac 1766-1848 . . . . DLB-107

DLB Award for Distinguished Literary Criticism Y-02

Ditlevsen, Tove 1917-1976 . . . . DLB-214

Ditzen, Rudolf (see Fallada, Hans)

Dix, Dorothea Lynde 1802-1887 . . . . . DLB-1, 235

Dix, Dorothy (see Gilmer, Elizabeth Meriwether)

Dix, Edwards and Company DLB-49

Dix, Gertrude circa 1874-? DLB-197

Dixie, Florence Douglas 1857-1905 . . . . . . .DLB-174

Dixon, Ella Hepworth 1855 or 1857-1932 . . . . DLB-197

Dixon, Paige (see Corcoran, Barbara)

Dixon, Richard Watson 1833-1900 . . . . . . DLB-19

Dixon, Stephen 1936- DLB-130

DLB Award for Distinguished Literary Criticism Y-02

Dmitriev, Andrei Viktorovich 1956- . . . DLB-285

Dmitriev, Ivan Ivanovich 1760-1837 . . . . . DLB-150

Dobell, Bertram 1842-1914 . . . . DLB-184

Dobell, Sydney 1824-1874 . . . . DLB-32

Dobie, J. Frank 1888-1964 . . . . DLB-212

Dobles Yzaguirre, Julieta 1943- DLB-283

Döblin, Alfred 1878-1957 . . . . DLB-66; CDWLB-2

Dobroliubov, Nikolai Aleksandrovich 1836-1861 . . . . .DLB-277

Dobson, Austin 1840-1921 . . . . DLB-35, 144

Dobson, Rosemary 1920- DLB-260

Doctorow, E. L. 1931- DLB-2, 28, 173; Y-80; CDALB-6

Dodd, Susan M. 1946- DLB-244

Dodd, William E. 1869-1940 . . . . DLB-17

Anne Dodd [publishing house] DLB-154

Dodd, Mead and Company DLB-49

Doderer, Heimito von 1896-1966 . . . . DLB-85

B. W. Dodge and Company DLB-46

Dodge, Mary Abigail 1833-1896 . . . . DLB-221

Dodge, Mary Mapes 1831?-1905 . . . . DLB-42, 79; DS-13

Dodge Publishing Company DLB-49

Dodgson, Charles Lutwidge (see Carroll, Lewis)

Dodsley, Robert 1703-1764 . . . . DLB-95

R. Dodsley [publishing house] DLB-154

Dodson, Owen 1914-1983 . . . . DLB-76

Dodwell, Christina 1951- DLB-204

Doesticks, Q. K. Philander, P. B. (see Thomson, Mortimer)

Doheny, Carrie Estelle 1875-1958 . . . . . . DLB-140

Doherty, John 1798?-1854 . . . . DLB-190

Doig, Ivan 1939- DLB-206

Doinaş, Ştefan Augustin 1922- DLB-232

Domínguez, Sylvia Maida 1935- DLB-122

Donaghy, Michael 1954- DLB-282

Patrick Donahoe [publishing house] DLB-49

Donald, David H. 1920- DLB-17; Y-87

Donaldson, Scott 1928- DLB-111

Doni, Rodolfo 1919- DLB-177

Donleavy, J. P. 1926- DLB-6, 173

Donnadieu, Marguerite (see Duras, Marguerite)

Donne, John 1572-1631 . . . . DLB-121, 151; CDBLB-1

Donnelly, Ignatius 1831-1901 . . . . DLB-12

R. R. Donnelley and Sons Company DLB-49

Donoghue, Emma 1969- DLB-267

Donohue and Henneberry DLB-49

Donoso, José 1924-1996 . . . . .DLB-113; CDWLB-3

M. Doolady [publishing house] DLB-49

Dooley, Ebon (see Ebon)

Doolittle, Hilda 1886-1961 . . . . . DLB-4, 45; DS-15

Doplicher, Fabio 1938- DLB-128

Dor, Milo 1923- DLB-85

George H. Doran Company DLB-46

Dorgelès, Roland 1886-1973 . . . . DLB-65

Dorn, Edward 1929-1999 . . . . DLB-5

Dorr, Rheta Childe 1866-1948 . . . . DLB-25

Dorris, Michael 1945-1997 . . . . .DLB-175

Dorset and Middlesex, Charles Sackville, Lord Buckhurst, Earl of 1643-1706 . . . .DLB-131

Dorsey, Candas Jane 1952- DLB-251

Dorst, Tankred 1925- DLB-75, 124

Dos Passos, John 1896-1970 . . . . DLB-4, 9; DS-1, 15; CDALB-5

John Dos Passos: A Centennial Commemoration Y-96

John Dos Passos: Artist Y-99

John Dos Passos Newsletter Y-00

U.S.A. (Documentary) DLB-274

Dostoevsky, Fyodor 1821-1881 . . . . DLB-238

Doubleday and Company DLB-49

Doubrovsky, Serge 1928- DLB-299

Dougall, Lily 1858-1923 . . . . DLB-92

Doughty, Charles M. 1843-1926 . . . . DLB-19, 57, 174

Douglas, Lady Alfred (see Custance, Olive)

Douglas, Ellen (Josephine Ayres Haxton) 1921- DLB-292

Douglas, Gavin 1476-1522 . . . . DLB-132

Douglas, Keith 1920-1944 . . . . DLB-27

Douglas, Norman 1868-1952 . . . . DLB-34, 195

Douglass, Frederick 1817-1895 . . . . DLB-1, 43, 50, 79, 243; CDALB-2

Frederick Douglass Creative Arts Center Y-01

Douglass, William circa 1691-1752 . . . . DLB-24

Dourado, Autran 1926- DLB-145

Dove, Arthur G. 1880-1946 . . . . DLB-188

Dove, Rita 1952- DLB-120; CDALB-7

Dover Publications DLB-46

Doves Press DLB-112

Dovlatov, Sergei Donatovich 1941-1990 . DLB-285

Dowden, Edward 1843-1913 . . . . DLB-35, 149

Dowell, Coleman 1925-1985 . . . . DLB-130

Dowland, John 1563-1626 . . . . .DLB-172

Downes, Gwladys 1915- DLB-88

Downing, J., Major (see Davis, Charles A.)

Downing, Major Jack (see Smith, Seba)

Dowriche, Anne before 1560-after 1613 . . . . .DLB-172

Dowson, Ernest 1867-1900 . . . . DLB-19, 135

William Doxey [publishing house] DLB-49

Doyle, Sir Arthur Conan 1859-1930 . . .DLB-18, 70, 156, 178; CDBLB-5

The Priory Scholars of New York Y-99

Doyle, Kirby 1932- DLB-16

Doyle, Roddy 1958- DLB-194

Drabble, Margaret 1939- DLB-14, 155, 231; CDBLB-8

Tribute to Graham Greene Y-91

Drach, Albert 1902-1995 . . . . DLB-85

Drachmann, Holger 1846-1908 . . . . DLB-300

Dragojević, Danijel 1934- DLB-181

Drake, Samuel Gardner 1798-1875 . . . . . . .DLB-187

Drama (*See* Theater)

The Dramatic Publishing Company DLB-49

Dramatists Play Service DLB-46

Drant, Thomas early 1540s?-1578 . . . . DLB-167

Draper, John W. 1811-1882 . . . . DLB-30

Draper, Lyman C. 1815-1891 . . . . DLB-30

Drayton, Michael 1563-1631 . . . . DLB-121

Dreiser, Theodore 1871-1945 . . . . .DLB-9, 12, 102, 137; DS-1; CDALB-3

The International Theodore Dreiser Society Y-01

Notes from the Underground of *Sister Carrie* Y-01

Dresser, Davis 1904-1977 . . . . DLB-226

Drew, Elizabeth A. "A Note on Technique" [excerpt] (1926) DLB-36

Drewitz, Ingeborg 1923-1986 . . . . DLB-75

Drieu La Rochelle, Pierre 1893-1945 . . . . . DLB-72

Drinker, Elizabeth 1735-1807 . . . . DLB-200

Drinkwater, John 1882-1937 . . . . .DLB-10, 19, 149

The Friends of the Dymock Poets Y-00

Droste-Hülshoff, Annette von 1797-1848 . . . . .DLB-133; CDWLB-2

The Drue Heinz Literature Prize Excerpt from "Excerpts from a Report of the Commission," in David Bosworth's *The Death of Descartes* An Interview with David Bosworth Y-82

Drummond, William, of Hawthornden 1585-1649 . . . . DLB-121, 213
Drummond, William Henry 1854-1907 . . . DLB-92
Druzhinin, Aleksandr Vasil'evich 1824-1864 . . . . DLB-238
Dryden, Charles 1860?-1931 . . . . DLB-171
Dryden, John 1631-1700 . . . . . . DLB-80, 101, 131; CDBLB-2
Držić, Marin circa 1508-1567 . . . . DLB-147; CDWLB-4
Duane, William 1760-1835 . . . . DLB-43
Dubé, Marcel 1930- DLB-53
Dubé, Rodolphe (see Hertel, François)
Dubie, Norman 1945- DLB-120
Dubin, Al 1891-1945 . . . . DLB-265
Dubois, Silvia 1788 or 1789?-1889 . . . . DLB-239
Du Bois, W. E. B. 1868-1963 . . . . DLB-47, 50, 91, 246; CDALB-3
Du Bois, William Pène 1916-1993 . . . . DLB-61
Dubrovina, Ekaterina Oskarovna 1846-1913 . . . . DLB-238
Dubus, Andre 1936-1999 . . . . DLB-130
Tribute to Michael M. Rea Y-97
Dubus, Andre, III 1959- DLB-292
Ducange, Victor 1783-1833 . . . . DLB-192
Du Chaillu, Paul Belloni 1831?-1903 . . . . . DLB-189
Ducharme, Réjean 1941- DLB-60
Dučić, Jovan 1871-1943 . . . . . DLB-147; CDWLB-4
Duck, Stephen 1705?-1756 . . . . DLB-95
Gerald Duckworth and Company Limited DLB-112
Duclaux, Madame Mary (see Robinson, A. Mary F.)
Dudek, Louis 1918-2001 . . . . DLB-88
Dudley-Smith, Trevor (see Hall, Adam)
Duell, Sloan and Pearce DLB-46
Duerer, Albrecht 1471-1528 . . . . DLB-179
Duff Gordon, Lucie 1821-1869 . . . . DLB-166
Dufferin, Helen Lady, Countess of Gifford 1807-1867 . . . . DLB-199
Duffield and Green DLB-46
Duffy, Maureen 1933- DLB-14
Dufief, Nicholas Gouin 1776-1834 . . . . DLB-187
Dufresne, John 1948- DLB-292
Dugan, Alan 1923- DLB-5
Dugard, William 1606-1662 . . . . DLB-170, 281
William Dugard [publishing house] DLB-170
Dugas, Marcel 1883-1947 . . . . DLB-92
William Dugdale [publishing house] DLB-106
Duhamel, Georges 1884-1966 . . . . DLB-65
Dujardin, Edouard 1861-1949 . . . . DLB-123
Dukes, Ashley 1885-1959 . . . . DLB-10
Dumas, Alexandre *fils* 1824-1895 . . . . DLB-192
Dumas, Alexandre *père* 1802-1870 . . . . . DLB-119, 192
Dumas, Henry 1934-1968 . . . . DLB-41
du Maurier, Daphne 1907-1989 . . . . DLB-191
Du Maurier, George 1834-1896 . . . . . DLB-153, 178
Dummett, Michael 1925- DLB-262
Dunbar, Paul Laurence 1872-1906 . . . . DLB-50, 54, 78; CDALB-3
Introduction to *Lyrics of Lowly Life* (1896), by William Dean Howells DLB-50
Dunbar, William circa 1460-circa 1522 . . . . DLB-132, 146
Duncan, Dave 1933- DLB-251
Duncan, David James 1952- DLB-256
Duncan, Norman 1871-1916 . . . . DLB-92
Duncan, Quince 1940- DLB-145
Duncan, Robert 1919-1988 . . . . DLB-5, 16, 193
Duncan, Ronald 1914-1982 . . . . DLB-13
Duncan, Sara Jeannette 1861-1922 . . . . DLB-92
Dunigan, Edward, and Brother DLB-49
Dunlap, John 1747-1812 . . . . DLB-43
Dunlap, William 1766-1839 . . . . DLB-30, 37, 59
Dunlop, William "Tiger" 1792-1848 . . . . . . DLB-99
Dunmore, Helen 1952- DLB-267
Dunn, Douglas 1942- DLB-40
Dunn, Harvey Thomas 1884-1952 . . . . . . DLB-188
Dunn, Stephen 1939- DLB-105
"The Good, The Not So Good" DLB-105
Dunne, Finley Peter 1867-1936 . . . . DLB-11, 23
Dunne, John Gregory 1932- Y-80
Dunne, Philip 1908-1992 . . . . DLB-26
Dunning, Ralph Cheever 1878-1930 . . . . DLB-4
Dunning, William A. 1857-1922 . . . . DLB-17
Duns Scotus, John circa 1266-1308 . . . . . . DLB-115
Dunsany, Lord (Edward John Moreton Drax Plunkett, Baron Dunsany) 1878-1957 . . . . DLB-10, 77, 153, 156, 255
Dunton, W. Herbert 1878-1936 . . . . DLB-188
John Dunton [publishing house] DLB-170
Dupin, Amantine-Aurore-Lucile (see Sand, George)
Dupuy, Eliza Ann 1814-1880 . . . . DLB-248
Durack, Mary 1913-1994 . . . . DLB-260
Durand, Lucile (see Bersianik, Louky)
Duranti, Francesca 1935- DLB-196
Duranty, Walter 1884-1957 . . . . DLB-29
Duras, Marguerite (Marguerite Donnadieu) 1914-1996 . . . . DLB-83
Durfey, Thomas 1653-1723 . . . . DLB-80
Durova, Nadezhda Andreevna (Aleksandr Andreevich Aleksandrov) 1783-1866 . . . . DLB-198
Durrell, Lawrence 1912-1990 . . . . DLB-15, 27, 204; Y-90; CDBLB-7
William Durrell [publishing house] DLB-49
Dürrenmatt, Friedrich 1921-1990 . . . . DLB-69, 124; CDWLB-2
Duston, Hannah 1657-1737 . . . . DLB-200
Dutt, Toru 1856-1877 . . . . DLB-240
E. P. Dutton and Company DLB-49
Duun, Olav 1876-1939 . . . . DLB-297
Duvoisin, Roger 1904-1980 . . . . DLB-61
Duyckinck, Evert Augustus 1816-1878 . . . . DLB-3, 64, 250
Duyckinck, George L. 1823-1863 . . . . DLB-3, 250
Duyckinck and Company DLB-49
Dwight, John Sullivan 1813-1893 . . . . . DLB-1, 235
Dwight, Timothy 1752-1817 . . . . DLB-37
America: or, A Poem on the Settlement of the British Colonies, by Timothy Dwight DLB-37
Dybek, Stuart 1942- DLB-130
Tribute to Michael M. Rea Y-97
Dyer, Charles 1928- DLB-13
Dyer, Sir Edward 1543-1607 . . . . DLB-136
Dyer, George 1755-1841 . . . . DLB-93
Dyer, John 1699-1757 . . . . DLB-95
Dyk, Viktor 1877-1931 . . . . DLB-215
Dylan, Bob 1941- DLB-16

E

Eager, Edward 1911-1964 . . . . DLB-22
Eagleton, Terry 1943- DLB-242
Eames, Wilberforce 1855-1937 . . . . DLB-140
Earle, Alice Morse 1853-1911 . . . . DLB-221
Earle, John 1600 or 1601-1665 . . . . DLB-151
James H. Earle and Company DLB-49
East Europe
Independence and Destruction, 1918-1941 . . . . DLB-220
Social Theory and Ethnography: Languageand Ethnicity in Western versus Eastern Man DLB-220
Eastlake, William 1917-1997 . . . . DLB-6, 206
Eastman, Carol ?- DLB-44
Eastman, Charles A. (Ohiyesa) 1858-1939 . . . . DLB-175
Eastman, Max 1883-1969 . . . . DLB-91
Eaton, Daniel Isaac 1753-1814 . . . . DLB-158
Eaton, Edith Maude 1865-1914 . . . . DLB-221
Eaton, Winnifred 1875-1954 . . . . DLB-221
Eberhart, Richard 1904- DLB-48; CDALB-1
Tribute to Robert Penn Warren Y-89
Ebner, Jeannie 1918- DLB-85
Ebner-Eschenbach, Marie von 1830-1916 . . . . DLB-81
Ebon 1942- DLB-41
E-Books' Second Act in Libraries Y-02
Ecbasis Captivi circa 1045 . . . . DLB-148
Ecco Press DLB-46
Eckhart, Meister circa 1260-circa 1328 . . . DLB-115
The Eclectic Review 1805-1868 . . . . DLB-110
Eco, Umberto 1932- DLB-196, 242
Eddison, E. R. 1882-1945 . . . . DLB-255
Edel, Leon 1907-1997 . . . . DLB-103
Edelfeldt, Inger 1956- DLB-257
A Century of Poetry, a Lifetime of Collecting: J. M. Edelstein's Collection of Twentieth-Century American Poetry Y-02

Edes, Benjamin 1732-1803 . . . . DLB-43
Edgar, David 1948- DLB-13, 233
Viewpoint: Politics and Performance DLB-13
Edgerton, Clyde 1944- DLB-278
Edgeworth, Maria 1768-1849. . . . . .DLB-116, 159, 163
The Edinburgh Review 1802-1929 . . . . DLB-110
Edinburgh University Press DLB-112
Editing
Conversations with Editors Y-95
Editorial Statements DLB-137
The Editorial Style of Fredson Bowers . . . Y-91
Editorial: The Extension of Copyright . . . Y-02
We See the Editor at Work Y-97
Whose *Ulysses?* The Function of Editing . . Y-97
The Editor Publishing Company DLB-49
Editorial Institute at Boston University Y-00
Edmonds, Helen Woods Ferguson (see Kavan, Anna)
Edmonds, Randolph 1900-1983 . . . . DLB-51
Edmonds, Walter D. 1903-1998. . . . . DLB-9
Edric, Robert (see Armitage, G. E.)
Edschmid, Kasimir 1890-1966 . . . . DLB-56
Edson, Margaret 1961- DLB-266
Edson, Russell 1935- DLB-244
Edwards, Amelia Anne Blandford 1831-1892 . . . . .DLB-174
Edwards, Dic 1953- DLB-245
Edwards, Edward 1812-1886 . . . . DLB-184
Edwards, Jonathan 1703-1758. . . . . . . .DLB-24, 270
Edwards, Jonathan, Jr. 1745-1801. . . . . DLB-37
Edwards, Junius 1929- DLB-33
Edwards, Matilda Barbara Betham 1836-1919. . . . . .DLB-174
Edwards, Richard 1524-1566 . . . . DLB-62
Edwards, Sarah Pierpont 1710-1758 . . . . . DLB-200
James Edwards [publishing house] DLB-154
Effinger, George Alec 1947- DLB-8
Egerton, George 1859-1945 . . . . DLB-135
Eggleston, Edward 1837-1902. . . . . DLB-12
Eggleston, Wilfred 1901-1986 . . . . DLB-92
Eglītis, Anšlavs 1906-1993 . . . . DLB-220
Eguren, José María 1874-1942 . . . . DLB-290
Ehrenreich, Barbara 1941- DLB-246
Ehrenstein, Albert 1886-1950 . . . . DLB-81
Ehrhart, W. D. 1948- DS-9
Ehrlich, Gretel 1946- DLB-212, 275
Eich, Günter 1907-1972. . . . . DLB-69, 124
Eichendorff, Joseph Freiherr von 1788-1857 . . . . DLB-90
Eifukumon'in 1271-1342. . . . . DLB-203
Eigner, Larry 1926-1996. . . . . DLB-5, 193
Eikon Basilike 1649 . . . . DLB-151
Eilhart von Oberge circa 1140-circa 1195 . . . . DLB-148
Einar Benediktsson 1864-1940 . . . . DLB-293
Einar Kárason 1955- DLB-293
Einar Már Guðmundsson 1954- DLB-293
Einhard circa 770-840. . . . . DLB-148
Eiseley, Loren 1907-1977 . . . . .DLB-275, DS-17
Eisenberg, Deborah 1945- DLB-244
Eisenreich, Herbert 1925-1986. . . . . DLB-85
Eisner, Kurt 1867-1919. . . . . DLB-66
Ekelöf, Gunnar 1907-1968 . . . . DLB-259
Eklund, Gordon 1945- Y-83
Ekman, Kerstin 1933- DLB-257
Ekwensi, Cyprian 1921- . . .DLB-117; CDWLB-3
Elaw, Zilpha circa 1790-? DLB-239
George Eld [publishing house] DLB-170
Elder, Lonne, III 1931- DLB-7, 38, 44
Paul Elder and Company. DLB-49
Eldershaw, Flora (M. Barnard Eldershaw) 1897-1956. . . . . DLB-260
Eldershaw, M. Barnard (see Barnard, Marjorie and Eldershaw, Flora)
The Electronic Text Center and the Electronic Archive of Early American Fiction at the University of Virginia Library. Y-98
Eliade, Mircea 1907-1986 . . . DLB-220; CDWLB-4
Elie, Robert 1915-1973 . . . . DLB-88
Elin Pelin 1877-1949 . . . . .DLB-147; CDWLB-4
Eliot, George 1819-1880 . . . . DLB-21, 35, 55; CDBLB-4
The George Eliot Fellowship Y-99
Eliot, John 1604-1690. . . . . DLB-24
Eliot, T. S. 1888-1965 . . . . .DLB-7, 10, 45, 63, 245; CDALB-5
T. S. Eliot Centennial: The Return of the Old Possum. Y-88
The T. S. Eliot Society: Celebration and Scholarship, 1980-1999 . . . . Y-99
Eliot's Court Press DLB-170
Elizabeth I 1533-1603. . . . . DLB-136
Elizabeth von Nassau-Saarbrücken after 1393-1456 . . . . .DLB-179
Elizondo, Salvador 1932- DLB-145
Elizondo, Sergio 1930- DLB-82
Elkin, Stanley 1930-1995 . . . . DLB-2, 28, 218, 278; Y-80
Elles, Dora Amy (see Wentworth, Patricia)
Ellet, Elizabeth F. 1818?-1877 . . . . DLB-30
Elliot, Ebenezer 1781-1849 . . . . DLB-96, 190
Elliot, Frances Minto (Dickinson) 1820-1898 . . . . DLB-166
Elliott, Charlotte 1789-1871 . . . . DLB-199
Elliott, George 1923- DLB-68
Elliott, George P. 1918-1980. . . . . DLB-244
Elliott, Janice 1931-1995. . . . . DLB-14
Elliott, Sarah Barnwell 1848-1928 . . . . . . DLB-221
Elliott, Sumner Locke 1917-1991 . . . . DLB-289
Elliott, Thomes and Talbot DLB-49
Elliott, William, III 1788-1863 . . . . DLB-3, 248
Ellis, Alice Thomas (Anna Margaret Haycraft) 1932- DLB-194
Ellis, Bret Easton 1964- DLB-292
Ellis, Edward S. 1840-1916. . . . . DLB-42
Ellis, George E. "The New Controversy Concerning Miracles. DS-5
Ellis, Havelock 1859-1939 . . . . DLB-190
Frederick Staridge Ellis [publishing house] DLB-106
The George H. Ellis Company. DLB-49
Ellison, Harlan 1934- DLB-8
Tribute to Isaac Asimov. Y-92
Ellison, Ralph 1914-1994 . . .DLB-2, 76, 227; Y-94; CDALB-1
Ellmann, Richard 1918-1987 . . . . . .DLB-103; Y-87
Ellroy, James 1948- DLB-226; Y-91
Tribute to John D. MacDonald Y-86
Tribute to Raymond Chandler Y-88
Eluard, Paul 1895-1952 . . . . DLB-258
Elyot, Thomas 1490?-1546 . . . . DLB-136
Emanuel, James Andrew 1921- DLB-41
Emecheta, Buchi 1944- DLB-117; CDWLB-3
Emerson, Ralph Waldo 1803-1882 . . . . . DLB-1, 59, 73, 183, 223, 270; DS-5; CDALB-2
Ralph Waldo Emerson in 1982 . . . . Y-82
The Ralph Waldo Emerson Society Y-99
Emerson, William 1769-1811 . . . . DLB-37
Emerson, William R. 1923-1997 . . . . Y-97
Emin, Fedor Aleksandrovich circa 1735-1770. . . . . DLB-150
Emmanuel, Pierre 1916-1984. . . . . DLB-258
Empedocles fifth century B.C. DLB-176
Empson, William 1906-1984 . . . . DLB-20
Enchi Fumiko 1905-1986 . . . . DLB-182
Ende, Michael 1929-1995. . . . . DLB-75
Endō Shūsaku 1923-1996. . . . . DLB-182
Engel, Marian 1933-1985 . . . . DLB-53
Engel'gardt, Sof'ia Vladimirovna 1828-1894 . . . . .DLB-277
Engels, Friedrich 1820-1895. . . . . DLB-129
Engle, Paul 1908- DLB-48
Tribute to Robert Penn Warren Y-89
English, Thomas Dunn 1819-1902. . . . . . DLB-202
Ennius 239 B.C.-169 B.C. DLB-211
Enquist, Per Olov 1934- DLB-257
Enright, Anne 1962- DLB-267
Enright, D. J. 1920- DLB-27
Enright, Elizabeth 1909-1968 . . . . DLB-22
Epictetus circa 55-circa 125-130 . . . . .DLB-176
Epicurus 342/341 B.C.-271/270 B.C. DLB-176
Epps, Bernard 1936- DLB-53
Epshtein, Mikhail Naumovich 1950- . . DLB-285
Epstein, Julius 1909-2000 and Epstein, Philip 1909-1952 . . . . DLB-26
Epstein, Leslie 1938- DLB-299
Editors, Conversations with. Y-95

Equiano, Olaudah
circa 1745-1797 . . . . . . DLB-37, 50; CDWLB-3
Olaudah Equiano and Unfinished Journeys: The Slave-Narrative Tradition and Twentieth-Century Continuities DLB-117
Eragny Press DLB-112
Erasmus, Desiderius 1467-1536 . . . . DLB-136
Erba, Luciano 1922- DLB-128
Erdman, Nikolai Robertovich
1900-1970 . . . . DLB-272
Erdrich, Louise
1954- DLB-152, 175, 206; CDALB-7
Erenburg, Il'ia Grigor'evich 1891-1967 . . . DLB-272
Erichsen-Brown, Gwethalyn Graham (see Graham, Gwethalyn)
Eriugena, John Scottus circa 810-877 . . . . . DLB-115
Ernst, Paul 1866-1933 . . . . DLB-66, 118
Erofeev, Venedikt Vasil'evich
1938-1990 . . . . DLB-285
Erofeev, Viktor Vladimirovich 1947- . . . DLB-285
Ershov, Petr Pavlovich 1815-1869 . . . . DLB-205
Erskine, Albert 1911-1993 . . . . Y-93
At Home with Albert Erskine Y-00
Erskine, John 1879-1951 . . . . DLB-9, 102
Erskine, Mrs. Steuart ?-1948 . . . . DLB-195
Ertel', Aleksandr Ivanovich
1855-1908 . . . . DLB-238
Ervine, St. John Greer 1883-1971 . . . . DLB-10
Eschenburg, Johann Joachim
1743-1820 . . . . DLB-97
Escoto, Julio 1944- DLB-145
Esdaile, Arundell 1880-1956 . . . . DLB-201
Esenin, Sergei Aleksandrovich
1895-1925 . . . . DLB-295
Eshleman, Clayton 1935- DLB-5
Espaillat, Rhina P. 1932- DLB-282
Espanca, Florbela 1894-1930 . . . . DLB-287
Espriu, Salvador 1913-1985 . . . . DLB-134
Ess Ess Publishing Company DLB-49
Essex House Press DLB-112
Esson, Louis 1878-1943 . . . . DLB-260
Essop, Ahmed 1931- DLB-225
Esterházy, Péter 1950- DLB-232; CDWLB-4
Estes, Eleanor 1906-1988 . . . . DLB-22
Estes and Lauriat DLB-49
Estleman, Loren D. 1952- DLB-226
Eszterhas, Joe 1944- DLB-185
Etherege, George 1636-circa 1692 . . . . DLB-80
Ethridge, Mark, Sr. 1896-1981 . . . . DLB-127
Ets, Marie Hall 1893-1984 . . . . DLB-22
Etter, David 1928- DLB-105
Ettner, Johann Christoph
1654-1724 . . . . DLB-168
Eudora Welty Remembered in
Two Exhibits Y-02
Eugene Gant's Projected Works Y-01
Eupolemius flourished circa 1095 . . . . DLB-148
Euripides circa 484 B.C.-407/406 B.C.
. . . . DLB-176; CDWLB-1
Evans, Augusta Jane 1835-1909 . . . . DLB-239
Evans, Caradoc 1878-1945 . . . . DLB-162
Evans, Charles 1850-1935 . . . . DLB-187
Evans, Donald 1884-1921 . . . . DLB-54
Evans, George Henry 1805-1856 . . . . DLB-43
Evans, Hubert 1892-1986 . . . . DLB-92
Evans, Mari 1923- DLB-41
Evans, Mary Ann (see Eliot, George)
Evans, Nathaniel 1742-1767 . . . . DLB-31
Evans, Sebastian 1830-1909 . . . . DLB-35
Evans, Ray 1915- DLB-265
M. Evans and Company DLB-46
Evaristi, Marcella 1953- DLB-233
Everett, Alexander Hill 1790-1847 . . . . DLB-59
Everett, Edward 1794-1865 . . . . DLB-1, 59, 235
Everson, R. G. 1903- DLB-88
Everson, William 1912-1994 . . . . . . DLB-5, 16, 212
Ewald, Johannes 1743-1781 . . . . DLB-300
Ewart, Gavin 1916-1995 . . . . DLB-40
Ewing, Juliana Horatia
1841-1885 . . . . DLB-21, 163
The Examiner 1808-1881 . . . . DLB-110
Exley, Frederick 1929-1992 . . . . DLB-143; Y-81
Editorial: The Extension of Copyright Y-02
von Eyb, Albrecht 1420-1475 . . . . DLB-179
Eyre and Spottiswoode DLB-106
Ezera, Regīna 1930- DLB-232
Ezzo ?-after 1065 . . . . DLB-148

F

Faber, Frederick William 1814-1863 . . . . . . DLB-32
Faber and Faber Limited DLB-112
Faccio, Rena (see Aleramo, Sibilla)
Facsimiles
The Uses of Facsimile: A Symposium. . . . Y-90
Fadeev, Aleksandr Aleksandrovich
1901-1956 . . . . DLB-272
Fagundo, Ana María 1938- DLB-134
Fainzil'berg, Il'ia Arnol'dovich (see Il'f, Il'ia and Petrov, Evgenii)
Fair, Ronald L. 1932- DLB-33
Fairfax, Beatrice (see Manning, Marie)
Fairlie, Gerard 1899-1983 . . . . DLB-77
Faldbakken, Knut 1941- DLB-297
Falkberget, Johan (Johan Petter Lillebakken)
1879-1967 . . . . DLB-297
Fallada, Hans 1893-1947 . . . . DLB-56
Fancher, Betsy 1928- Y-83
Fane, Violet 1843-1905 . . . . DLB-35
Fanfrolico Press DLB-112
Fanning, Katherine 1927- DLB-127
Fanon, Frantz 1925-1961 . . . . DLB-296
Fanshawe, Sir Richard 1608-1666 . . . . DLB-126
Fantasy Press Publishers DLB-46
Fante, John 1909-1983 . . . . DLB-130; Y-83
Al-Farabi circa 870-950 . . . . DLB-115
Farabough, Laura 1949- DLB-228
Farah, Nuruddin 1945- . . . DLB-125; CDWLB-3
Farber, Norma 1909-1984 . . . . DLB-61
Fargue, Léon-Paul 1876-1947 . . . . DLB-258
Farigoule, Louis (see Romains, Jules)
Farjeon, Eleanor 1881-1965 . . . . DLB-160
Farley, Harriet 1812-1907 . . . . DLB-239
Farley, Walter 1920-1989 . . . . DLB-22
Farmborough, Florence 1887-1978 . . . . DLB-204
Farmer, Penelope 1939- DLB-161
Farmer, Philip José 1918- DLB-8
Farnaby, Thomas 1575?-1647 . . . . DLB-236
Farningham, Marianne (see Hearn, Mary Anne)
Farquhar, George circa 1677-1707 . . . . DLB-84
Farquharson, Martha (see Finley, Martha)
Farrar, Frederic William 1831-1903 . . . . . . DLB-163
Farrar, Straus and Giroux DLB-46
Farrar and Rinehart DLB-46
Farrell, J. G. 1935-1979 . . . . DLB-14, 271
Farrell, James T. 1904-1979 . . . . DLB-4, 9, 86; DS-2
Fast, Howard 1914- DLB-9
Faulkner, William 1897-1962
. . . DLB-9, 11, 44, 102; DS-2; Y-86; CDALB-5
Faulkner and Yoknapatawpha Conference, Oxford, Mississippi Y-97
Faulkner Centennial Addresses Y-97
"Faulkner 100–Celebrating the Work," University of South Carolina, Columbia Y-97
Impressions of William Faulkner Y-97
William Faulkner and the People-to-People Program Y-86
William Faulkner Centenary Celebrations Y-97
The William Faulkner Society Y-99
George Faulkner [publishing house] DLB-154
Faulks, Sebastian 1953- DLB-207
Fauset, Jessie Redmon 1882-1961 . . . . DLB-51
Faust, Frederick Schiller (Max Brand)
1892-1944 . . . . DLB-256
Faust, Irvin
1924- DLB-2, 28, 218, 278; Y-80, 00
I Wake Up Screaming [Response to Ken Auletta] Y-97
Tribute to Bernard Malamud Y-86
Tribute to Isaac Bashevis Singer Y-91
Tribute to Meyer Levin Y-81
Fawcett, Edgar 1847-1904 . . . . DLB-202
Fawcett, Millicent Garrett 1847-1929 . . . . . DLB-190
Fawcett Books DLB-46
Fay, Theodore Sedgwick 1807-1898 . . . . . DLB-202
Fearing, Kenneth 1902-1961 . . . . DLB-9
Federal Writers' Project DLB-46
Federman, Raymond 1928- Y-80

Fedin, Konstantin Aleksandrovich 1892-1977 . . . . DLB-272
Fedorov, Innokentii Vasil'evich (see Omulevsky, Innokentii Vasil'evich)
Feiffer, Jules 1929- DLB-7, 44
Feinberg, Charles E. 1899-1988 . . . . DLB-187; Y-88
Feind, Barthold 1678-1721 . . . . DLB-168
Feinstein, Elaine 1930- DLB-14, 40
Feirstein, Frederick 1940- DLB-282
Feiss, Paul Louis 1875-1952 . . . . DLB-187
Feldman, Irving 1928- DLB-169
Felipe, Léon 1884-1968 . . . . DLB-108
Fell, Frederick, Publishers DLB-46
Fellowship of Southern Writers Y-98
Felltham, Owen 1602?-1668 . . . . DLB-126, 151
Felman, Shoshana 1942- DLB-246
Fels, Ludwig 1946- DLB-75
Felton, Cornelius Conway 1807-1862 . . . . DLB-1, 235
Mothe-Fénelon, François de Salignac de la 1651-1715 . . . . DLB-268
Fenn, Harry 1837-1911 . . . . DLB-188
Fennario, David 1947- DLB-60
Fenner, Dudley 1558?-1587? DLB-236
Fenno, Jenny 1765?-1803 . . . . DLB-200
Fenno, John 1751-1798 . . . . DLB-43
R. F. Fenno and Company DLB-49
Fenoglio, Beppe 1922-1963 . . . . DLB-177
Fenton, Geoffrey 1539?-1608 . . . . DLB-136
Fenton, James 1949- DLB-40
The Hemingway/Fenton Correspondence Y-02
Ferber, Edna 1885-1968 . . . . . . DLB-9, 28, 86, 266
Ferdinand, Vallery, III (see Salaam, Kalamu ya)
Ferguson, Sir Samuel 1810-1886 . . . . DLB-32
Ferguson, William Scott 1875-1954 . . . . . . DLB-47
Fergusson, Robert 1750-1774 . . . . DLB-109
Ferland, Albert 1872-1943 . . . . DLB-92
Ferlinghetti, Lawrence 1919- DLB-5, 16; CDALB-1
Tribute to Kenneth Rexroth Y-82
Fermor, Patrick Leigh 1915- DLB-204
Fern, Fanny (see Parton, Sara Payson Willis)
Ferrars, Elizabeth (Morna Doris Brown) 1907-1995 . . . . DLB-87
Ferré, Rosario 1942- DLB-145
Ferreira, Vergílio 1916-1996 . . . . DLB-287
E. Ferret and Company DLB-49
Ferrier, Susan 1782-1854 . . . . DLB-116
Ferril, Thomas Hornsby 1896-1988 . . . . . DLB-206
Ferrini, Vincent 1913- DLB-48
Ferron, Jacques 1921-1985 . . . . DLB-60
Ferron, Madeleine 1922- DLB-53
Ferrucci, Franco 1936- DLB-196
Fet, Afanasii Afanas'evich 1820?-1892 . . . . DLB-277
Fetridge and Company DLB-49
Feuchtersleben, Ernst Freiherr von 1806-1849 . . . . DLB-133
Feuchtwanger, Lion 1884-1958 . . . . DLB-66
Feuerbach, Ludwig 1804-1872 . . . . DLB-133
Feuillet, Octave 1821-1890 . . . . DLB-192
Feydeau, Georges 1862-1921 . . . . DLB-192
Fibiger, Mathilde 1830-1872 . . . . DLB-300
Fichte, Johann Gottlieb 1762-1814 . . . . DLB-90
Ficke, Arthur Davison 1883-1945 . . . . DLB-54
Fiction
American Fiction and the 1930s DLB-9
Fiction Best-Sellers, 1910-1945 . . . . DLB-9
Postmodern Holocaust Fiction DLB-299
The Year in Fiction Y-84, 86, 89, 94–99
The Year in Fiction: A Biased View Y-83
The Year in U.S. Fiction Y-00, 01
The Year's Work in Fiction: A Survey . . . Y-82
Fiedler, Leslie A. 1917- DLB-28, 67
Tribute to Bernard Malamud Y-86
Tribute to James Dickey Y-97
Field, Barron 1789-1846 . . . . DLB-230
Field, Edward 1924- DLB-105
Field, Eugene 1850-1895 . DLB-23, 42, 140; DS-13
Field, John 1545?-1588 . . . . DLB-167
Field, Joseph M. 1810-1856 . . . . DLB-248
Field, Marshall, III 1893-1956 . . . . DLB-127
Field, Marshall, IV 1916-1965 . . . . DLB-127
Field, Marshall, V 1941- DLB-127
Field, Michael (Katherine Harris Bradley) 1846-1914 . . . . DLB-240
"The Poetry File" DLB-105
Field, Nathan 1587-1619 or 1620 . . . . DLB-58
Field, Rachel 1894-1942 . . . . DLB-9, 22
Fielding, Helen 1958- DLB-231
Fielding, Henry 1707-1754 . . . . DLB-39, 84, 101; CDBLB-2
"Defense of *Amelia*" (1752) DLB-39
The History of the Adventures of Joseph Andrews [excerpt] (1742) DLB-39
Letter to [Samuel] Richardson on *Clarissa* (1748) DLB-39
Preface to *Joseph Andrews* (1742) DLB-39
Preface to Sarah Fielding's *Familiar Letters* (1747) [excerpt] DLB-39
Preface to Sarah Fielding's *The Adventures of David Simple* (1744) . . . DLB-39
Review of *Clarissa* (1748) DLB-39
Tom Jones (1749) [excerpt] DLB-39
Fielding, Sarah 1710-1768 . . . . DLB-39
Preface to *The Cry* (1754) DLB-39
Fields, Annie Adams 1834-1915 . . . . DLB-221
Fields, Dorothy 1905-1974 . . . . DLB-265
Fields, James T. 1817-1881 . . . . DLB-1, 235
Fields, Julia 1938- DLB-41
Fields, Osgood and Company DLB-49
Fields, W. C. 1880-1946 . . . . DLB-44
Fierstein, Harvey 1954- DLB-266
Figes, Eva 1932- DLB-14, 271
Figuera, Angela 1902-1984 . . . . DLB-108
Filmer, Sir Robert 1586-1653 . . . . DLB-151
Filson, John circa 1753-1788 . . . . DLB-37
Finch, Anne, Countess of Winchilsea 1661-1720 . . . . DLB-95
Finch, Annie 1956- DLB-282
Finch, Robert 1900- DLB-88
Findley, Timothy 1930-2002 . . . . DLB-53
Finlay, Ian Hamilton 1925- DLB-40
Finley, Martha 1828-1909 . . . . DLB-42
Finn, Elizabeth Anne (McCaul) 1825-1921 . . . . DLB-166
Finnegan, Seamus 1949- DLB-245
Finney, Jack 1911-1995 . . . . DLB-8
Finney, Walter Braden (see Finney, Jack)
Firbank, Ronald 1886-1926 . . . . DLB-36
Firmin, Giles 1615-1697 . . . . DLB-24
First Edition Library/Collectors' Reprints, Inc. Y-91
Fischart, Johann 1546 or 1547-1590 or 1591 . . . . DLB-179
Fischer, Karoline Auguste Fernandine 1764-1842 . . . . DLB-94
Fischer, Tibor 1959- DLB-231
Fish, Stanley 1938- DLB-67
Fishacre, Richard 1205-1248 . . . . DLB-115
Fisher, Clay (see Allen, Henry W.)
Fisher, Dorothy Canfield 1879-1958 . . . DLB-9, 102
Fisher, Leonard Everett 1924- DLB-61
Fisher, Roy 1930- DLB-40
Fisher, Rudolph 1897-1934 . . . . DLB-51, 102
Fisher, Steve 1913-1980 . . . . DLB-226
Fisher, Sydney George 1856-1927 . . . . DLB-47
Fisher, Vardis 1895-1968 . . . . DLB-9, 206
Fiske, John 1608-1677 . . . . DLB-24
Fiske, John 1842-1901 . . . . DLB-47, 64
Fitch, Thomas circa 1700-1774 . . . . DLB-31
Fitch, William Clyde 1865-1909 . . . . DLB-7
FitzGerald, Edward 1809-1883 . . . . DLB-32
Fitzgerald, F. Scott 1896-1940 . . . . DLB-4, 9, 86; Y-81, 92; DS-1, 15, 16; CDALB-4
F. Scott Fitzgerald: A Descriptive Bibliography, Supplement (2001) Y-01
F. Scott Fitzgerald Centenary Celebrations Y-96
F. Scott Fitzgerald Inducted into the American Poets' Corner at St. John the Divine; Ezra Pound Banned Y-99
"F. Scott Fitzgerald: St. Paul's Native Son and Distinguished American Writer": University of Minnesota Conference, 29-31 October 1982 . . . . Y-82
First International F. Scott Fitzgerald Conference Y-92
The Great Gatsby (Documentary DLB-219
Tender Is the Night (Documentary) DLB-273
Fitzgerald, Penelope 1916- DLB-14, 194

Fitzgerald, Robert 1910-1985 . . . . Y-80
FitzGerald, Robert D. 1902-1987 . . . . DLB-260
Fitzgerald, Thomas 1819-1891 . . . . DLB-23
Fitzgerald, Zelda Sayre 1900-1948 . . . . Y-84
Fitzhugh, Louise 1928-1974 . . . . DLB-52
Fitzhugh, William circa 1651-1701 . . . . DLB-24
Flagg, James Montgomery 1877-1960 . . . . . DLB-188
Flanagan, Thomas 1923-2002 . . . . Y-80
Flanner, Hildegarde 1899-1987 . . . . DLB-48
Flanner, Janet 1892-1978 . . . . DLB-4; DS-15
Flannery, Peter 1951- DLB-233
Flaubert, Gustave 1821-1880 . . . . DLB-119, 301
Flavin, Martin 1883-1967 . . . . DLB-9
Fleck, Konrad (flourished circa 1220) DLB-138
Flecker, James Elroy 1884-1915 . . . . DLB-10, 19
Fleeson, Doris 1901-1970 . . . . DLB-29
Fleißer, Marieluise 1901-1974 . . . . DLB-56, 124
Fleischer, Nat 1887-1972 . . . . DLB-241
Fleming, Abraham 1552?-1607 . . . . DLB-236
Fleming, Ian 1908-1964 . . . DLB-87, 201; CDBLB-7
Fleming, Joan 1908-1980 . . . . DLB-276
Fleming, May Agnes 1840-1880 . . . . DLB-99
Fleming, Paul 1609-1640 . . . . DLB-164
Fleming, Peter 1907-1971 . . . . DLB-195
Fletcher, Giles, the Elder 1546-1611 . . . . . DLB-136
Fletcher, Giles, the Younger
1585 or 1586-1623 . . . . DLB-121
Fletcher, J. S. 1863-1935 . . . . DLB-70
Fletcher, John 1579-1625 . . . . DLB-58
Fletcher, John Gould 1886-1950 . . . . DLB-4, 45
Fletcher, Phineas 1582-1650 . . . . DLB-121
Flieg, Helmut (see Heym, Stefan)
Flint, F. S. 1885-1960 . . . . DLB-19
Flint, Timothy 1780-1840 . . . . DLB-73, 186
Fløgstad, Kjartan 1944- DLB-297
Florensky, Pavel Aleksandrovich
1882-1937 . . . . DLB-295
Flores, Juan de fl. 1470-1500 . . . . DLB-286
Flores-Williams, Jason 1969- DLB-209
Florio, John 1553?-1625 . . . . DLB-172
Fludd, Robert 1574-1637 . . . . DLB-281
Fo, Dario 1926- Y-97
Nobel Lecture 1997: Contra Jogulatores
Obloquentes Y-97
Foden, Giles 1967- DLB-267
Fofanov, Konstantin Mikhailovich
1862-1911 . . . . DLB-277
Foix, J. V. 1893-1987 . . . . DLB-134
Foley, Martha 1897-1977 . . . . DLB-137
Folger, Henry Clay 1857-1930 . . . . DLB-140
Folio Society DLB-112
Follain, Jean 1903-1971 . . . . DLB-258
Follen, Charles 1796-1840 . . . . DLB-235
Follen, Eliza Lee (Cabot) 1787-1860 . . . . DLB-1, 235
Follett, Ken 1949- DLB-87; Y-81
Follett Publishing Company DLB-46
John West Folsom [publishing house] DLB-49
Folz, Hans
between 1435 and 1440-1513 . . . . DLB-179
Fonseca, Manuel da 1911-1993 . . . . DLB-287
Fontane, Theodor
1819-1898 . . . . DLB-129; CDWLB-2
Fontenelle, Bernard Le Bovier de
1657-1757 . . . . DLB-268
Fontes, Montserrat 1940- DLB-209
Fonvisin, Denis Ivanovich
1744 or 1745-1792 . . . . DLB-150
Foote, Horton 1916- DLB-26, 266
Foote, Mary Hallock
1847-1938 . . . . DLB-186, 188, 202, 221
Foote, Samuel 1721-1777 . . . . DLB-89
Foote, Shelby 1916- DLB-2, 17
Forbes, Calvin 1945- DLB-41
Forbes, Ester 1891-1967 . . . . DLB-22
Forbes, Rosita 1893?-1967 . . . . DLB-195
Forbes and Company DLB-49
Force, Peter 1790-1868 . . . . DLB-30
Forché, Carolyn 1950- DLB-5, 193
Ford, Charles Henri 1913-2002 . . . . DLB-4, 48
Ford, Corey 1902-1969 . . . . DLB-11
Ford, Ford Madox
1873-1939 . . . . DLB-34, 98, 162; CDBLB-6
Nathan Asch Remembers Ford Madox
Ford, Sam Roth, and Hart Crane Y-02
J. B. Ford and Company DLB-49
Ford, Jesse Hill 1928-1996 . . . . DLB-6
Ford, John 1586-? DLB-58; CDBLB-1
Ford, R. A. D. 1915- DLB-88
Ford, Richard 1944- DLB-227
Ford, Worthington C. 1858-1941 . . . . DLB-47
Fords, Howard, and Hulbert DLB-49
Foreman, Carl 1914-1984 . . . . DLB-26
Forester, C. S. 1899-1966 . . . . DLB-191
The C. S. Forester Society Y-00
Forester, Frank (see Herbert, Henry William)
Anthologizing New Formalism DLB-282
The Little Magazines of the
New Formalism DLB-282
The New Narrative Poetry DLB-282
Presses of the New Formalism and
the New Narrative DLB-282
The Prosody of the New Formalism DLB-282
Younger Women Poets of the
New Formalism DLB-282
Forman, Harry Buxton 1842-1917 . . . . DLB-184
Fornés, María Irene 1930- DLB-7
Forrest, Leon 1937-1997 . . . . DLB-33
Forsh, Ol'ga Dmitrievna 1873-1961 . . . . . . DLB-272
Forster, E. M.
1879-1970 . . . . DLB-34, 98, 162, 178, 195;
DS-10; CDBLB-6
"Fantasy," from *Aspects of the Novel*
(1927) DLB-178
Forster, Georg 1754-1794 . . . . DLB-94
Forster, John 1812-1876 . . . . DLB-144
Forster, Margaret 1938- DLB-155, 271
Forsyth, Frederick 1938- DLB-87
Forsyth, William
"Literary Style" (1857) [excerpt] DLB-57
Forten, Charlotte L. 1837-1914 . . . . . . DLB-50, 239
Pages from Her Diary DLB-50
Fortini, Franco 1917-1994 . . . . DLB-128
Fortune, Mary ca. 1833-ca. 1910 . . . . DLB-230
Fortune, T. Thomas 1856-1928 . . . . DLB-23
Fosdick, Charles Austin 1842-1915 . . . . DLB-42
Fosse, Jon 1959- DLB-297
Foster, David 1944- DLB-289
Foster, Genevieve 1893-1979 . . . . DLB-61
Foster, Hannah Webster
1758-1840 . . . . DLB-37, 200
Foster, John 1648-1681 . . . . DLB-24
Foster, Michael 1904-1956 . . . . DLB-9
Foster, Myles Birket 1825-1899 . . . . DLB-184
Foucault, Michel 1926-1984 . . . . DLB-242
Robert and Andrew Foulis
[publishing house] DLB-154
Fouqué, Caroline de la Motte 1774-1831 . . . DLB-90
Fouqué, Friedrich de la Motte
1777-1843 . . . . DLB-90
Four Seas Company DLB-46
Four Winds Press DLB-46
Fournier, Henri Alban (see Alain-Fournier)
Fowler, Christopher 1953- DLB-267
Fowler, Connie May 1958- DLB-292
Fowler and Wells Company DLB-49
Fowles, John
1926- DLB-14, 139, 207; CDBLB-8
Fox, John 1939- DLB-245
Fox, John, Jr. 1862 or 1863-1919 . . . . DLB-9; DS-13
Fox, Paula 1923- DLB-52
Fox, Richard Kyle 1846-1922 . . . . DLB-79
Fox, William Price 1926- DLB-2; Y-81
Remembering Joe Heller Y-99
Richard K. Fox [publishing house] DLB-49
Foxe, John 1517-1587 . . . . DLB-132
Fraenkel, Michael 1896-1957 . . . . DLB-4
France, Anatole 1844-1924 . . . . DLB-123
France, Richard 1938- DLB-7
Francis, Convers 1795-1863 . . . . DLB-1, 235
Francis, Dick 1920- DLB-87; CDBLB-8
Francis, Sir Frank 1901-1988 . . . . DLB-201
Francis, Jeffrey, Lord 1773-1850 . . . . DLB-107
C. S. Francis [publishing house] DLB-49
Franck, Sebastian 1499-1542 . . . . DLB-179
Francke, Kuno 1855-1930 . . . . DLB-71
Françoise (Robertine Barry) 1863-1910 . . . . DLB-92
François, Louise von 1817-1893 . . . . DLB-129
Frank, Bruno 1887-1945 . . . . DLB-118
Frank, Leonhard 1882-1961 . . . . DLB-56, 118

Frank, Melvin 1913-1988 . . . . DLB-26
Frank, Waldo 1889-1967 . . . . DLB-9, 63
Franken, Rose 1895?-1988 . . . . . .DLB-228, Y-84
Franklin, Benjamin 1706-1790 . . . . DLB-24, 43, 73, 183; CDALB-2
Franklin, James 1697-1735. . . . . DLB-43
Franklin, John 1786-1847 . . . . DLB-99
Franklin, Miles 1879-1954. . . . . DLB-230
Franklin Library DLB-46
Frantz, Ralph Jules 1902-1979. . . . . DLB-4
Franzos, Karl Emil 1848-1904 . . . . DLB-129
Fraser, Antonia 1932- DLB-276
Fraser, G. S. 1915-1980 . . . . DLB-27
Fraser, Kathleen 1935- DLB-169
Frattini, Alberto 1922- DLB-128
Frau Ava ?-1127 . . . . DLB-148
Fraunce, Abraham 1558?-1592 or 1593 . . DLB-236
Frayn, Michael 1933- DLB-13, 14, 194, 245
Frazier, Charles 1950- DLB-292
Fréchette, Louis-Honoré 1839-1908 . . . . . . DLB-99
Frederic, Harold 1856-1898 . . . DLB-12, 23; DS-13
Freed, Arthur 1894-1973. . . . . DLB-265
Freeling, Nicolas 1927- DLB-87
Tribute to Georges Simenon Y-89
Freeman, Douglas Southall 1886-1953 . . . . .DLB-17; DS-17
Freeman, Judith 1946- DLB-256
Freeman, Legh Richmond 1842-1915. . . . . DLB-23
Freeman, Mary E. Wilkins 1852-1930 . . . . .DLB-12, 78, 221
Freeman, R. Austin 1862-1943 . . . . DLB-70
Freidank circa 1170-circa 1233 . . . . DLB-138
Freiligrath, Ferdinand 1810-1876 . . . . DLB-133
Fremlin, Celia 1914- DLB-276
Frémont, Jessie Benton 1834-1902 . . . . . . DLB-183
Frémont, John Charles 1813-1890. . . . . DLB-183, 186
French, Alice 1850-1934 . . . . DLB-74; DS-13
French, David 1939- DLB-53
French, Evangeline 1869-1960 . . . . DLB-195
French, Francesca 1871-1960 . . . . DLB-195
James French [publishing house]. DLB-49
Samuel French [publishing house] DLB-49
Samuel French, Limited DLB-106
French Literature
Epic and Beast Epic DLB-208
French Arthurian Literature. DLB-208
Lyric Poetry DLB-268
Other Poets DLB-217
Poetry in Nineteenth-Century France: Cultural Background and Critical Commentary DLB-217
Roman de la Rose: Guillaume de Lorris 1200 to 1205-circa 1230, Jean de Meun 1235/1240-circa 1305 . . . . DLB-208
Saints' Lives DLB-208
Troubadours, *Trobaíritz,* and Trouvères DLB-208
French Theater
Medieval French Drama DLB-208
Parisian Theater, Fall 1984: Toward a New Baroque Y-85
Freneau, Philip 1752-1832 . . . . .DLB-37, 43
The Rising Glory of America. DLB-37
Freni, Melo 1934- DLB-128
Freshfield, Douglas W. 1845-1934 . . . . . . .DLB-174
Freud, Sigmund 1856-1939. . . . . DLB-296
Freytag, Gustav 1816-1895. . . . . DLB-129
Frída Á. Sigurðardóttir 1940- DLB-293
Fridegård, Jan 1897-1968 . . . . DLB-259
Fried, Erich 1921-1988 . . . . DLB-85
Friedan, Betty 1921- DLB-246
Friedman, Bruce Jay 1930- DLB-2, 28, 244
Friedman, Carl 1952- DLB-299
Friedman, Kinky 1944- DLB-292
Friedrich von Hausen circa 1171-1190 . . . DLB-138
Friel, Brian 1929- DLB-13
Friend, Krebs 1895?-1967?. DLB-4
Fries, Fritz Rudolf 1935- DLB-75
Frisch, Max 1911-1991 . . . . .DLB-69, 124; CDWLB-2
Frischlin, Nicodemus 1547-1590. . . . . .DLB-179
Frischmuth, Barbara 1941- DLB-85
Fritz, Jean 1915- DLB-52
Froissart, Jean circa 1337-circa 1404 . . . . . DLB-208
Fromm, Erich 1900-1980 . . . . DLB-296
Fromentin, Eugene 1820-1876 . . . . DLB-123
Frontinus circa A.D. 35-A.D. 103/104 . . . DLB-211
Frost, A. B. 1851-1928 . . . . DLB-188; DS-13
Frost, Robert 1874-1963. . . . . DLB-54; DS-7; CDALB-4
The Friends of the Dymock Poets Y-00
Frostenson, Katarina 1953- DLB-257
Frothingham, Octavius Brooks 1822-1895 . . . . DLB-1, 243
Froude, James Anthony 1818-1894 . . . . .DLB-18, 57, 144
Fruitlands 1843-1844 . . . . DLB-1, 223; DS-5
Fry, Christopher 1907- DLB-13
Tribute to John Betjeman. Y-84
Fry, Roger 1866-1934. . . . . .DS-10
Fry, Stephen 1957- DLB-207
Frye, Northrop 1912-1991 . . . . . . .DLB-67, 68, 246
Fuchs, Daniel 1909-1993 . . . . .DLB-9, 26, 28; Y-93
Tribute to Isaac Bashevis Singer Y-91
Fuentes, Carlos 1928- DLB-113; CDWLB-3
Fuertes, Gloria 1918-1998 . . . . DLB-108
Fugard, Athol 1932- DLB-225
The Fugitives and the Agrarians: The First Exhibition. Y-85
Fujiwara no Shunzei 1114-1204 . . . . DLB-203
Fujiwara no Tameaki 1230s?-1290s? DLB-203
Fujiwara no Tameie 1198-1275. . . . . DLB-203
Fujiwara no Teika 1162-1241. . . . . DLB-203
Fuks, Ladislav 1923-1994. . . . . DLB-299
Fulbecke, William 1560-1603?. DLB-172
Fuller, Charles 1939- DLB-38, 266
Fuller, Henry Blake 1857-1929 . . . . DLB-12
Fuller, John 1937- DLB-40
Fuller, Margaret (see Fuller, Sarah)
Fuller, Roy 1912-1991 . . . . DLB-15, 20
Tribute to Christopher Isherwood. Y-86
Fuller, Samuel 1912-1997 . . . . DLB-26
Fuller, Sarah 1810-1850 . . . . DLB-1, 59, 73, 183, 223, 239; DS-5; CDALB-2
Fuller, Thomas 1608-1661 . . . . DLB-151
Fullerton, Hugh 1873-1945. . . . . .DLB-171
Fullwood, William flourished 1568 . . . . . DLB-236
Fulton, Alice 1952- DLB-193
Fulton, Len 1934- Y-86
Fulton, Robin 1937- DLB-40
Furbank, P. N. 1920- DLB-155
Furetière, Antoine 1619-1688. . . . . .DLB-268
Furman, Laura 1945- Y-86
Furmanov, Dmitrii Andreevich 1891-1926 . . . . .DLB-272
Furness, Horace Howard 1833-1912 . . . . . DLB-64
Furness, William Henry 1802-1896 . . . . DLB-1, 235
Furnivall, Frederick James 1825-1910. . . . DLB-184
Furphy, Joseph (Tom Collins) 1843-1912 . . . . DLB-230
Furthman, Jules 1888-1966. . . . . DLB-26
Shakespeare and Montaigne: A Symposium by Jules Furthman Y-02
Furui Yoshikichi 1937- DLB-182
Fushimi, Emperor 1265-1317 . . . . DLB-203
Futabatei Shimei (Hasegawa Tatsunosuke) 1864-1909 . . . . DLB-180
Fyleman, Rose 1877-1957 . . . . DLB-160

G

Gaarder, Jostein 1952- DLB-297
Gadallah, Leslie 1939- DLB-251
Gadamer, Hans-Georg 1900-2002 . . . . . . DLB-296
Gadda, Carlo Emilio 1893-1973. . . . . .DLB-177
Gaddis, William 1922-1998 . . . . .DLB-2, 278
William Gaddis: A Tribute Y-99
Gág, Wanda 1893-1946 . . . . DLB-22
Gagarin, Ivan Sergeevich 1814-1882 . . . . DLB-198
Gagnon, Madeleine 1938- DLB-60
Gaiman, Neil 1960- DLB-261
Gaine, Hugh 1726-1807 . . . . DLB-43
Hugh Gaine [publishing house] DLB-49
Gaines, Ernest J. 1933- DLB-2, 33, 152; Y-80; CDALB-6
Gaiser, Gerd 1908-1976 . . . . DLB-69
Gaitskill, Mary 1954- DLB-244
Galarza, Ernesto 1905-1984 . . . . DLB-122

Galaxy Science Fiction Novels DLB-46
Galbraith, Robert (or Caubraith) circa 1483-1544 . . . . DLB-281
Gale, Zona 1874-1938 . . . . DLB-9, 228, 78
Galen of Pergamon 129-after 210 . . . . DLB-176
Gales, Winifred Marshall 1761-1839 . . . . . DLB-200
Medieval Galician-Portuguese Poetry DLB-287
Gall, Louise von 1815-1855 . . . . DLB-133
Gallagher, Tess 1943- DLB-120, 212, 244
Gallagher, Wes 1911- DLB-127
Gallagher, William Davis 1808-1894 . . . . . . DLB-73
Gallant, Mavis 1922- DLB-53
Gallegos, María Magdalena 1935- DLB-209
Gallico, Paul 1897-1976 . . . . DLB-9, 171
Gallop, Jane 1952- DLB-246
Galloway, Grace Growden 1727-1782 . . . . DLB-200
Gallup, Donald 1913-2000 . . . . DLB-187
Galsworthy, John 1867-1933 . . . . . . DLB-10, 34, 98, 162; DS-16; CDBLB-5
Galt, John 1779-1839 . . . . DLB-99, 116, 159
Galton, Sir Francis 1822-1911 . . . . DLB-166
Galvin, Brendan 1938- DLB-5
Gambit DLB-46
Gamboa, Reymundo 1948- DLB-122
Gammer Gurton's Needle DLB-62
Gan, Elena Andreevna (Zeneida R-va) 1814-1842 . . . . DLB-198
Gandlevsky, Sergei Markovich 1952- . . DLB-285
Gannett, Frank E. 1876-1957 . . . . DLB-29
Gao Xingjian 1940- Y-00
Nobel Lecture 2000: "The Case for Literature" Y-00
Gaos, Vicente 1919-1980 . . . . DLB-134
García, Andrew 1854?-1943 . . . . DLB-209
García, Cristina 1958- DLB-292
García, Lionel G. 1935- DLB-82
García, Richard 1941- DLB-209
García Márquez, Gabriel 1928- DLB-113; Y-82; CDWLB-3
The Magical World of Macondo Y-82
Nobel Lecture 1982: The Solitude of Latin America Y-82
A Tribute to Gabriel García Márquez Y-82
García Marruz, Fina 1923- DLB-283
García-Camarillo, Cecilio 1943- DLB-209
Gardam, Jane 1928- DLB-14, 161, 231
Gardell, Jonas 1963- DLB-257
Garden, Alexander circa 1685-1756 . . . . DLB-31
Gardiner, John Rolfe 1936- DLB-244
Gardiner, Margaret Power Farmer (see Blessington, Marguerite, Countess of)
Gardner, John 1933-1982 . . . . DLB-2; Y-82; CDALB-7
Garfield, Leon 1921-1996 . . . . DLB-161
Garis, Howard R. 1873-1962 . . . . DLB-22
Garland, Hamlin 1860-1940 . . DLB-12, 71, 78, 186
The Hamlin Garland Society Y-01
Garneau, François-Xavier 1809-1866 . . . . . DLB-99
Garneau, Hector de Saint-Denys 1912-1943 . . . . DLB-88
Garneau, Michel 1939- DLB-53
Garner, Alan 1934- DLB-161, 261
Garner, Hugh 1913-1979 . . . . DLB-68
Garnett, David 1892-1981 . . . . DLB-34
Garnett, Eve 1900-1991 . . . . DLB-160
Garnett, Richard 1835-1906 . . . . DLB-184
Garrard, Lewis H. 1829-1887 . . . . DLB-186
Garraty, John A. 1920- DLB-17
Garrett, Almeida (João Baptista da Silva Leitão de Almeida Garrett) 1799-1854 . . . . DLB-287
Garrett, George 1929- DLB-2, 5, 130, 152; Y-83
Literary Prizes Y-00
My Summer Reading Orgy: Reading for Fun and Games: One Reader's Report on the Summer of 2001 . . . . . Y-01
A Summing Up at Century's End Y-99
Tribute to James Dickey Y-97
Tribute to Michael M. Rea Y-97
Tribute to Paxton Davis Y-94
Tribute to Peter Taylor Y-94
Tribute to William Goyen Y-83
A Writer Talking: A Collage Y-00
Garrett, John Work 1872-1942 . . . . DLB-187
Garrick, David 1717-1779 . . . . DLB-84, 213
Garrison, William Lloyd 1805-1879 . . . . DLB-1, 43, 235; CDALB-2
Garro, Elena 1920-1998 . . . . DLB-145
Garshin, Vsevolod Mikhailovich 1855-1888 . . . . DLB-277
Garth, Samuel 1661-1719 . . . . DLB-95
Garve, Andrew 1908-2001 . . . . DLB-87
Gary, Romain 1914-1980 . . . . DLB-83, 299
Gascoigne, George 1539?-1577 . . . . DLB-136
Gascoyne, David 1916-2001 . . . . DLB-20
Gash, Jonathan (John Grant) 1933- DLB-276
Gaskell, Elizabeth Cleghorn 1810-1865 . . . . . . DLB-21, 144, 159; CDBLB-4
The Gaskell Society Y-98
Gaskell, Jane 1941- DLB-261
Gaspey, Thomas 1788-1871 . . . . DLB-116
Gass, William H. 1924- DLB-2, 227
Gates, Doris 1901-1987 . . . . DLB-22
Gates, Henry Louis, Jr. 1950- DLB-67
Gates, Lewis E. 1860-1924 . . . . DLB-71
Gatto, Alfonso 1909-1976 . . . . DLB-114
Gault, William Campbell 1910-1995 . . . . . DLB-226
Tribute to Kenneth Millar Y-83
Gaunt, Mary 1861-1942 . . . . DLB-174, 230
Gautier, Théophile 1811-1872 . . . . DLB-119
Gautreaux, Tim 1947- DLB-292
Gauvreau, Claude 1925-1971 . . . . DLB-88
The *Gawain*-Poet flourished circa 1350-1400 . . . . DLB-146
Gawsworth, John (Terence Ian Fytton Armstrong) 1912-1970 . . . . DLB-255
Gay, Ebenezer 1696-1787 . . . . DLB-24
Gay, John 1685-1732 . . . . DLB-84, 95
Gayarré, Charles E. A. 1805-1895 . . . . DLB-30
Charles Gaylord [publishing house] DLB-49
Gaylord, Edward King 1873-1974 . . . . DLB-127
Gaylord, Edward Lewis 1919- DLB-127
Gébler, Carlo 1954- DLB-271
Geda, Sigitas 1943- DLB-232
Geddes, Gary 1940- DLB-60
Geddes, Virgil 1897- DLB-4
Gedeon (Georgii Andreevich Krinovsky) circa 1730-1763 . . . . DLB-150
Gee, Maggie 1948- DLB-207
Gee, Shirley 1932- DLB-245
Geibel, Emanuel 1815-1884 . . . . DLB-129
Geiogamah, Hanay 1945- DLB-175
Geis, Bernard, Associates DLB-46
Geisel, Theodor Seuss 1904-1991 . . . DLB-61; Y-91
Gelb, Arthur 1924- DLB-103
Gelb, Barbara 1926- DLB-103
Gelber, Jack 1932- DLB-7, 228
Gélinas, Gratien 1909-1999 . . . . DLB-88
Gellert, Christian Füerchtegott 1715-1769 . . . . DLB-97
Gellhorn, Martha 1908-1998 . . . . Y-82, 98
Gems, Pam 1925- DLB-13
Genet, Jean 1910-1986 . . . . DLB-72; Y-86
Genette, Gérard 1930- DLB-242
Genevoix, Maurice 1890-1980 . . . . DLB-65
Genis, Aleksandr Aleksandrovich 1953- DLB-285
Genovese, Eugene D. 1930- DLB-17
Gent, Peter 1942- Y-82
Geoffrey of Monmouth circa 1100-1155 . . . . DLB-146
George, Henry 1839-1897 . . . . DLB-23
George, Jean Craighead 1919- DLB-52
George, W. L. 1882-1926 . . . . DLB-197
George III, King of Great Britain and Ireland 1738-1820 . . . . DLB-213
Georgslied 896? DLB-148
Gerber, Merrill Joan 1938- DLB-218
Gerhardie, William 1895-1977 . . . . DLB-36
Gerhardt, Paul 1607-1676 . . . . DLB-164
Gérin, Winifred 1901-1981 . . . . DLB-155
Gérin-Lajoie, Antoine 1824-1882 . . . . DLB-99
German Literature
A Call to Letters and an Invitation to the Electric Chair DLB-75
The Conversion of an Unpolitical Man DLB-66
The German Radio Play DLB-124
The German Transformation from the Baroque to the Enlightenment DLB-97

Germanophilism. DLB-66
A Letter from a New Germany Y-90
The Making of a People. DLB-66
The Novel of Impressionism DLB-66
Pattern and Paradigm: History as Design DLB-75
Premisses DLB-66
The 'Twenties and Berlin DLB-66
Wolfram von Eschenbach's *Parzival:* Prologue and Book 3. . . . . DLB-138
Writers and Politics: 1871-1918 . . . . . . DLB-66
German Literature, Middle Ages
Abrogans circa 790-800 . . . . DLB-148
Annolied between 1077 and 1081. . . . . DLB-148
The Arthurian Tradition and Its European Context DLB-138
Cambridge Songs (Carmina Cantabrigensia) circa 1050 . . . . DLB-148
Christus und die Samariterin circa 950 . . DLB-148
De Heinrico circa 980? DLB-148
Echasis Captivi circa 1045 . . . . DLB-148
Georgslied 896? DLB-148
German Literature and Culture from Charlemagne to the Early Courtly Period DLB-148; CDWLB-2
The Germanic Epic and Old English Heroic Poetry: *Widsith, Waldere,* and *The Fight at Finnsburg*. DLB-146
Graf Rudolf between circa 1170 and circa 1185. . . . . DLB-148
Heliand circa 850. . . . . DLB-148
Das Hildesbrandslied circa 820 . . . . DLB-148; CDWLB-2
Kaiserchronik circa 1147 . . . . DLB-148
The Legends of the Saints and a Medieval Christian Worldview DLB-148
Ludus de Antichristo circa 1160 . . . . DLB-148
Ludwigslied 881 or 882 . . . . DLB-148
Muspilli circa 790-circa 850 . . . . DLB-148
Old German Genesis and *Old German Exodus* circa 1050-circa 1130 . . . . DLB-148
Old High German Charms and Blessings DLB-148; CDWLB-2
The *Old High German Isidor* circa 790-800 . . . . DLB-148
Petruslied circa 854?. DLB-148
Physiologus circa 1070-circa 1150 . . . . . DLB-148
Ruodlieb circa 1050-1075 . . . . DLB-148
"Spielmannsepen" (circa 1152 circa 1500). DLB-148
The Strasbourg Oaths 842. . . . . DLB-148
Tatian circa 830 . . . . DLB-148
Waltharius circa 825 . . . . DLB-148
Wessobrunner Gebet circa 787-815 . . . . . DLB-148
German Theater
German Drama 800-1280 . . . . DLB-138
German Drama from Naturalism to Fascism: 1889-1933 . . . . DLB-118
Gernsback, Hugo 1884-1967 . . . . DLB-8, 137
Gerould, Katharine Fullerton 1879-1944. . . . . DLB-78
Samuel Gerrish [publishing house] DLB-49
Gerrold, David 1944- DLB-8
Gersão, Teolinda 1940- DLB-287
Gershon, Karen 1923-1993. . . . . DLB-299
Gershwin, Ira 1896-1983 . . . . DLB-265
The Ira Gershwin Centenary. Y-96
Gerson, Jean 1363-1429 . . . . DLB-208
Gersonides 1288-1344 . . . . DLB-115
Gerstäcker, Friedrich 1816-1872. . . . . DLB-129
Gertsen, Aleksandr Ivanovich (see Herzen, Alexander)
Gerstenberg, Heinrich Wilhelm von 1737-1823 . . . . DLB-97
Gervinus, Georg Gottfried 1805-1871. . . . . DLB-133
Gery, John 1953- DLB-282
Geßner, Solomon 1730-1788. . . . . DLB-97
Geston, Mark S. 1946- DLB-8
Al-Ghazali 1058-1111 . . . . DLB-115
Gibbings, Robert 1889-1958. . . . . DLB-195
Gibbon, Edward 1737-1794. . . . . DLB-104
Gibbon, John Murray 1875-1952 . . . . DLB-92
Gibbon, Lewis Grassic (see Mitchell, James Leslie)
Gibbons, Floyd 1887-1939 . . . . DLB-25
Gibbons, Kaye 1960- DLB-292
Gibbons, Reginald 1947- DLB-120
Gibbons, William ?-? DLB-73
Gibson, Charles Dana 1867-1944. . . . . DLB-188; DS-13
Gibson, Graeme 1934- DLB-53
Gibson, Margaret 1944- DLB-120
Gibson, Margaret Dunlop 1843-1920. . . . .DLB-174
Gibson, Wilfrid 1878-1962 . . . . DLB-19
The Friends of the Dymock Poets Y-00
Gibson, William 1914- DLB-7
Gibson, William 1948- DLB-251
Gide, André 1869-1951 . . . . DLB-65
Giguère, Diane 1937- DLB-53
Giguère, Roland 1929- DLB-60
Gil de Biedma, Jaime 1929-1990 . . . . DLB-108
Gil-Albert, Juan 1906-1994 . . . . DLB-134
Gilbert, Anthony 1899-1973 . . . . DLB-77
Gilbert, Elizabeth 1969- DLB-292
Gilbert, Sir Humphrey 1537-1583. . . . . . . DLB-136
Gilbert, Michael 1912- DLB-87
Gilbert, Sandra M. 1936- DLB-120, 246
Gilchrist, Alexander 1828-1861 . . . . DLB-144
Gilchrist, Ellen 1935- DLB-130
Gilder, Jeannette L. 1849-1916. . . . . DLB-79
Gilder, Richard Watson 1844-1909 . . . DLB-64, 79
Gildersleeve, Basil 1831-1924. . . . . DLB-71
Giles, Henry 1809-1882 . . . . DLB-64
Giles of Rome circa 1243-1316. . . . . DLB-115
Gilfillan, George 1813-1878 . . . . DLB-144
Gill, Eric 1882-1940 . . . . DLB-98
Gill, Sarah Prince 1728-1771. . . . . DLB-200
William F. Gill Company. DLB-49
Gillespie, A. Lincoln, Jr. 1895-1950 . . . . DLB-4
Gillespie, Haven 1883-1975 . . . . DLB-265
Gilliam, Florence ?-?. DLB-4
Gilliatt, Penelope 1932-1993. . . . . DLB-14
Gillott, Jacky 1939-1980. . . . . DLB-14
Gilman, Caroline H. 1794-1888 . . . . DLB-3, 73
Gilman, Charlotte Perkins 1860-1935 . . . DLB-221
The Charlotte Perkins Gilman Society . . . Y-99
W. and J. Gilman [publishing house] DLB-49
Gilmer, Elizabeth Meriwether 1861-1951 . . . . DLB-29
Gilmer, Francis Walker 1790-1826. . . . . . . DLB-37
Gilmore, Mary 1865-1962 . . . . DLB-260
Gilroy, Frank D. 1925- DLB-7
Gimferrer, Pere (Pedro) 1945- DLB-134
Gingrich, Arnold 1903-1976. . . . . .DLB-137
Prospectus From the Initial Issue of *Esquire* (Autumn 1933). DLB-137
"With the Editorial Ken," Prospectus From the Initial Issue of *Ken* (7 April 1938) DLB-137
Ginsberg, Allen 1926-1997 . . . .DLB-5, 16, 169, 237; CDALB-1
Ginzburg, Natalia 1916-1991 . . . . .DLB-177
Ginzkey, Franz Karl 1871-1963 . . . . DLB-81
Gioia, Dana 1950- DLB-120, 282
Giono, Jean 1895-1970 . . . . DLB-72
Giotti, Virgilio 1885-1957. . . . . DLB-114
Giovanni, Nikki 1943- . . . DLB-5, 41; CDALB-7
Gipson, Lawrence Henry 1880-1971 . . . . . .DLB-17
Girard, Rodolphe 1879-1956 . . . . DLB-92
Giraudoux, Jean 1882-1944 . . . . DLB-65
Girondo, Oliverio 1891-1967 . . . . DLB-283
Gissing, George 1857-1903 . . . . . .DLB-18, 135, 184
The Place of Realism in Fiction (1895) DLB-18
Giudici, Giovanni 1924- DLB-128
Giuliani, Alfredo 1924- DLB-128
Gjellerup, Karl 1857-1919. . . . . DLB-300
Glackens, William J. 1870-1938 . . . . DLB-188
Gladkov, Fedor Vasil'evich 1883-1958. . . .DLB-272
Gladstone, William Ewart 1809-1898 . . . . .DLB-57, 184
Glaeser, Ernst 1902-1963 . . . . DLB-69
Glancy, Diane 1941- DLB-175
Glanvill, Joseph 1636-1680. . . . . DLB-252
Glanville, Brian 1931- DLB-15, 139
Glapthorne, Henry 1610-1643? DLB-58
Glasgow, Ellen 1873-1945 . . . . DLB-9, 12
The Ellen Glasgow Society Y-01
Glasier, Katharine Bruce 1867-1950 . . . . . DLB-190
Glaspell, Susan 1876-1948 . . . . . . DLB-7, 9, 78, 228
Glass, Montague 1877-1934 . . . . DLB-11
Glassco, John 1909-1981 . . . . DLB-68

Glauser, Friedrich 1896-1938 . . . . DLB-56
F. Gleason's Publishing Hall DLB-49
Gleim, Johann Wilhelm Ludwig 1719-1803 . . . . DLB-97
Glendinning, Victoria 1937- DLB-155
Glidden, Frederick Dilley (Luke Short) 1908-1975 . . . . DLB-256
Glinka, Fedor Nikolaevich 1786-1880 . . . . DLB-205
Glover, Keith 1966- DLB-249
Glover, Richard 1712-1785 . . . . DLB-95
Glück, Louise 1943- DLB-5
Glyn, Elinor 1864-1943 . . . . DLB-153
Gnedich, Nikolai Ivanovich 1784-1833 . . . DLB-205
Gobineau, Joseph-Arthur de 1816-1882 . . . DLB-123
Godber, John 1956- DLB-233
Godbout, Jacques 1933- DLB-53
Goddard, Morrill 1865-1937 . . . . DLB-25
Goddard, William 1740-1817 . . . . DLB-43
Godden, Rumer 1907-1998 . . . . DLB-161
Godey, Louis A. 1804-1878 . . . . DLB-73
Godey and McMichael DLB-49
Godfrey, Dave 1938- DLB-60
Godfrey, Thomas 1736-1763 . . . . DLB-31
Godine, David R., Publisher DLB-46
Godkin, E. L. 1831-1902 . . . . DLB-79
Godolphin, Sidney 1610-1643 . . . . DLB-126
Godwin, Gail 1937- DLB-6, 234
M. J. Godwin and Company DLB-154
Godwin, Mary Jane Clairmont 1766-1841 . . . . DLB-163
Godwin, Parke 1816-1904 . . . . DLB-3, 64, 250
Godwin, William 1756-1836 . . . . DLB-39, 104, 142, 158, 163, 262; CDBLB-3
Preface to *St. Leon* (1799) DLB-39
Goering, Reinhard 1887-1936 . . . . DLB-118
Goes, Albrecht 1908- DLB-69
Goethe, Johann Wolfgang von 1749-1832 . . . . DLB-94; CDWLB-2
Goetz, Curt 1888-1960 . . . . DLB-124
Goffe, Thomas circa 1592-1629 . . . . DLB-58
Goffstein, M. B. 1940- DLB-61
Gogarty, Oliver St. John 1878-1957 . . . . DLB-15, 19
Gogol, Nikolai Vasil'evich 1809-1852 . . . . DLB-198
Goines, Donald 1937-1974 . . . . DLB-33
Gold, Herbert 1924- DLB-2; Y-81
Tribute to William Saroyan Y-81
Gold, Michael 1893-1967 . . . . DLB-9, 28
Goldbarth, Albert 1948- DLB-120
Goldberg, Dick 1947- DLB-7
Golden Cockerel Press DLB-112
Golding, Arthur 1536-1606 . . . . DLB-136
Golding, Louis 1895-1958 . . . . DLB-195
Golding, William 1911-1993 . . . . DLB-15, 100, 255; Y-83; CDBLB-7
Nobel Lecture 1993 . . . . Y-83
The Stature of William Golding Y-83
Goldman, Emma 1869-1940 . . . . DLB-221
Goldman, William 1931- DLB-44
Goldring, Douglas 1887-1960 . . . . DLB-197
Goldschmidt, Meir Aron 1819-1887 . . . . . DLB-300
Goldsmith, Oliver 1730?-1774 . . . . DLB-39, 89, 104, 109, 142; CDBLB-2
Goldsmith, Oliver 1794-1861 . . . . DLB-99
Goldsmith Publishing Company DLB-46
Goldstein, Richard 1944- DLB-185
Gollancz, Sir Israel 1864-1930 . . . . DLB-201
Victor Gollancz Limited DLB-112
Gomberville, Marin Le Roy, sieur de 1600?-1674 . . . . DLB-268
Gombrowicz, Witold 1904-1969 . . . . DLB-215; CDWLB-4
Gómez-Quiñones, Juan 1942- DLB-122
Laurence James Gomme [publishing house] DLB-46
Goncharov, Ivan Aleksandrovich 1812-1891 . . . . DLB-238
Goncourt, Edmond de 1822-1896 . . . . DLB-123
Goncourt, Jules de 1830-1870 . . . . DLB-123
Gonzales, Rodolfo "Corky" 1928- DLB-122
Gonzales-Berry, Erlinda 1942- DLB-209
"Chicano Language" DLB-82
González, Angel 1925- DLB-108
Gonzalez, Genaro 1949- DLB-122
González, Otto-Raúl 1921- DLB-290
Gonzalez, Ray 1952- DLB-122
González de Mireles, Jovita 1899-1983 . . . . DLB-122
González Martínez, Enrique 1871-1952 . . . DLB-290
González-T., César A. 1931- DLB-82
Goodis, David 1917-1967 . . . . DLB-226
Goodison, Lorna 1947- DLB-157
Goodman, Allegra 1967- DLB-244
Goodman, Nelson 1906-1998 . . . . DLB-279
Goodman, Paul 1911-1972 . . . . DLB-130, 246
The Goodman Theatre DLB-7
Goodrich, Frances 1891-1984 and Hackett, Albert 1900-1995 . . . . DLB-26
Goodrich, Samuel Griswold 1793-1860 . . . . DLB-1, 42, 73, 243
S. G. Goodrich [publishing house] DLB-49
C. E. Goodspeed and Company DLB-49
Goodwin, Stephen 1943- Y-82
Googe, Barnabe 1540-1594 . . . . DLB-132
Gookin, Daniel 1612-1687 . . . . DLB-24
Goran, Lester 1928- DLB-244
Gordimer, Nadine 1923- DLB-225; Y-91
Nobel Lecture 1991 . . . . Y-91
Gordon, Adam Lindsay 1833-1870 . . . . . . DLB-230
Gordon, Caroline 1895-1981 . . . . DLB-4, 9, 102; DS-17; Y-81
Gordon, Charles F. (see OyamO)
Gordon, Charles William (see Connor, Ralph)
Gordon, Giles 1940- DLB-14, 139, 207
Gordon, Helen Cameron, Lady Russell 1867-1949 . . . . DLB-195
Gordon, Lyndall 1941- DLB-155
Gordon, Mack 1904-1959 . . . . DLB-265
Gordon, Mary 1949- DLB-6; Y-81
Gordone, Charles 1925-1995 . . . . DLB-7
Gore, Catherine 1800-1861 . . . . DLB-116
Gore-Booth, Eva 1870-1926 . . . . DLB-240
Gores, Joe 1931- DLB-226; Y-02
Tribute to Kenneth Millar Y-83
Tribute to Raymond Chandler Y-88
Gorey, Edward 1925-2000 . . . . DLB-61
Gorgias of Leontini circa 485 B.C.-376 B.C. DLB-176
Gor'ky, Maksim 1868-1936 . . . . DLB-295
Gorodetsky, Sergei Mitrofanovich 1884-1967 . . . . DLB-295
Gorostiza, José 1901-1979 . . . . DLB-290
Görres, Joseph 1776-1848 . . . . DLB-90
Gosse, Edmund 1849-1928 . . . . . DLB-57, 144, 184
Gosson, Stephen 1554-1624 . . . . DLB-172
The Schoole of Abuse (1579) DLB-172
Gotanda, Philip Kan 1951- DLB-266
Gotlieb, Phyllis 1926- DLB-88, 251
Go-Toba 1180-1239 . . . . DLB-203
Gottfried von Straßburg died before 1230 . . . . DLB-138; CDWLB-2
Gotthelf, Jeremias 1797-1854 . . . . DLB-133
Gottschalk circa 804/808-869 . . . . DLB-148
Gottsched, Johann Christoph 1700-1766 . . . . DLB-97
Götz, Johann Nikolaus 1721-1781 . . . . DLB-97
Goudge, Elizabeth 1900-1984 . . . . DLB-191
Gough, John B. 1817-1886 . . . . DLB-243
Gould, Wallace 1882-1940 . . . . DLB-54
Govoni, Corrado 1884-1965 . . . . DLB-114
Govrin, Michal 1950- DLB-299
Gower, John circa 1330-1408 . . . . DLB-146
Goyen, William 1915-1983 . . . . . DLB-2, 218; Y-83
Goytisolo, José Augustín 1928- DLB-134
Gozzano, Guido 1883-1916 . . . . DLB-114
Grabbe, Christian Dietrich 1801-1836 . . . . DLB-133
Gracq, Julien (Louis Poirier) 1910- DLB-83
Grady, Henry W. 1850-1889 . . . . DLB-23
Graf, Oskar Maria 1894-1967 . . . . DLB-56
Graf Rudolf between circa 1170 and circa 1185 . . . . DLB-148
Graff, Gerald 1937- DLB-246
Richard Grafton [publishing house] DLB-170
Grafton, Sue 1940- DLB-226
Graham, Frank 1893-1965 . . . . DLB-241
Graham, George Rex 1813-1894 . . . . DLB-73
Graham, Gwethalyn (Gwethalyn Graham Erichsen-Brown) 1913-1965 . . . . DLB-88
Graham, Jorie 1951- DLB-120
Graham, Katharine 1917-2001 . . . . DLB-127

Graham, Lorenz 1902-1989 . . . . DLB-76
Graham, Philip 1915-1963 . . . . DLB-127
Graham, R. B. Cunninghame 1852-1936 . . . . .DLB-98, 135, 174
Graham, Shirley 1896-1977 . . . . DLB-76
Graham, Stephen 1884-1975. . . . . DLB-195
Graham, W. S. 1918-1986 . . . . DLB-20
William H. Graham [publishing house] . . . DLB-49
Graham, Winston 1910- DLB-77
Grahame, Kenneth 1859-1932 . . .DLB-34, 141, 178
Grainger, Martin Allerdale 1874-1941 . . . . DLB-92
Gramatky, Hardie 1907-1979 . . . . DLB-22
Gramcko, Ida 1924-1994 . . . . DLB-290
Gramsci, Antonio 1891-1937 . . . . DLB-296
Grand, Sarah 1854-1943. . . . . .DLB-135, 197
Grandbois, Alain 1900-1975 . . . . DLB-92
Grandson, Oton de circa 1345-1397. . . . . DLB-208
Grange, John circa 1556-?. DLB-136
Granger, Thomas 1578-1627 . . . . DLB-281
Granich, Irwin (see Gold, Michael)
Granovsky, Timofei Nikolaevich 1813-1855. . . . . DLB-198
Grant, Anne MacVicar 1755-1838 . . . . . . DLB-200
Grant, Duncan 1885-1978. . . . . .DS-10
Grant, George 1918-1988. . . . . DLB-88
Grant, George Monro 1835-1902. . . . . DLB-99
Grant, Harry J. 1881-1963 . . . . DLB-29
Grant, James Edward 1905-1966 . . . . DLB-26
Grant, John (see Gash, Jonathan)
War of the Words (and Pictures): The Creation of a Graphic Novel. Y-02
Grass, Günter 1927- . . .DLB-75, 124; CDWLB-2
Nobel Lecture 1999: "To Be Continued . . ." Y-99
Tribute to Helen Wolff Y-94
Grasty, Charles H. 1863-1924 . . . . DLB-25
Grau, Shirley Ann 1929- DLB-2, 218
Graves, John 1920- Y-83
Graves, Richard 1715-1804. . . . . DLB-39
Graves, Robert 1895-1985 . . . .DLB-20, 100, 191; DS-18; Y-85; CDBLB-6
The St. John's College Robert Graves Trust Y-96
Gray, Alasdair 1934- DLB-194, 261
Gray, Asa 1810-1888 . . . . DLB-1, 235
Gray, David 1838-1861 . . . . DLB-32
Gray, Simon 1936- DLB-13
Gray, Thomas 1716-1771 . . . . DLB-109; CDBLB-2
Grayson, Richard 1951- DLB-234
Grayson, William J. 1788-1863. . . . DLB-3, 64, 248
The Great Bibliographers Series. Y-93
The Great Gatsby (Documentary) DLB-219
"The Greatness of Southern Literature": League of the South Institute for the Study of Southern Culture and History Y-02
Grech, Nikolai Ivanovich 1787-1867 . . . . . DLB-198
Greeley, Horace 1811-1872 . . DLB-3, 43, 189, 250
Green, Adolph 1915-2002 . . . . DLB-44, 265
Green, Anna Katharine 1846-1935 . . . . DLB-202, 221
Green, Duff 1791-1875 . . . . DLB-43
Green, Elizabeth Shippen 1871-1954 . . . . DLB-188
Green, Gerald 1922- DLB-28
Green, Henry 1905-1973 . . . . DLB-15
Green, Jonas 1712-1767. . . . . DLB-31
Green, Joseph 1706-1780. . . . . DLB-31
Green, Julien 1900-1998. . . . . DLB-4, 72
Green, Paul 1894-1981. . . . . . . DLB-7, 9, 249; Y-81
Green, T. H. 1836-1882. . . . . DLB-190, 262
Green, Terence M. 1947- DLB-251
T. and S. Green [publishing house] DLB-49
Green Tiger Press. DLB-46
Timothy Green [publishing house]. DLB-49
Greenaway, Kate 1846-1901 . . . . DLB-141
Greenberg: Publisher DLB-46
Greene, Asa 1789-1838. . . . . DLB-11
Greene, Belle da Costa 1883-1950 . . . . . . DLB-187
Greene, Graham 1904-1991 . . . . .DLB-13, 15, 77, 100, 162, 201, 204; Y-85, 91; CDBLB-7
Tribute to Christopher Isherwood. Y-86
Greene, Robert 1558-1592 . . . . DLB-62, 167
Greene, Robert Bernard (Bob), Jr. 1947- DLB-185
Benjamin H Greene [publishing house] . . . DLB-49
Greenfield, George 1917-2000 . . . . Y-91, 00
Derek Robinson's Review of George Greenfield's *Rich Dust* Y-02
Greenhow, Robert 1800-1854 . . . . DLB-30
Greenlee, William B. 1872-1953. . . . . DLB-187
Greenough, Horatio 1805-1852 . . . . . . DLB-1, 235
Greenwell, Dora 1821-1882 . . . . DLB-35, 199
Greenwillow Books DLB-46
Greenwood, Grace (see Lippincott, Sara Jane Clarke)
Greenwood, Walter 1903-1974. . . . . . DLB-10, 191
Greer, Ben 1948- DLB-6
Greflinger, Georg 1620?-1677. . . . . DLB-164
Greg, W. R. 1809-1881 . . . . DLB-55
Greg, W. W. 1875-1959 . . . . DLB-201
Gregg, Josiah 1806-1850. . . . . DLB-183, 186
Gregg Press. DLB-46
Gregory, Horace 1898-1982. . . . . DLB-48
Gregory, Isabella Augusta Persse, Lady 1852-1932 . . . . DLB-10
Gregory of Rimini circa 1300-1358 . . . . . DLB-115
Gregynog Press DLB-112
Greiff, León de 1895-1976 . . . . DLB-283
Greiffenberg, Catharina Regina von 1633-1694 . . . . DLB-168
Greig, Noël 1944- DLB-245
Grenfell, Wilfred Thomason 1865-1940. . . . . .DLB-92
Gress, Elsa 1919-1988 . . . . DLB-214
Greve, Felix Paul (see Grove, Frederick Philip)
Greville, Fulke, First Lord Brooke 1554-1628 . . . . .DLB-62, 172
Grey, Sir George, K.C.B. 1812-1898 . . . . DLB-184
Grey, Lady Jane 1537-1554 . . . . DLB-132
Grey, Zane 1872-1939 . . . . DLB-9, 212
Zane Grey's West Society Y-00
Grey Owl (Archibald Stansfeld Belaney) 1888-1938 . . . . .DLB-92; DS-17
Grey Walls Press DLB-112
Griboedov, Aleksandr Sergeevich 1795?-1829. . . . . DLB-205
Grice, Paul 1913-1988 . . . . .DLB-279
Grier, Eldon 1917- DLB-88
Grieve, C. M. (see MacDiarmid, Hugh)
Griffin, Bartholomew flourished 1596 . . . .DLB-172
Griffin, Bryan
"Panic Among the Philistines": A Postscript, An Interview with Bryan Griffin. Y-81
Griffin, Gerald 1803-1840 . . . . DLB-159
The Griffin Poetry Prize. Y-00
Griffith, Elizabeth 1727?-1793. . . . . DLB-39, 89
Preface to *The Delicate Distress* (1769) . . DLB-39
Griffith, George 1857-1906. . . . . .DLB-178
Ralph Griffiths [publishing house] DLB-154
Griffiths, Trevor 1935- DLB-13, 245
S. C. Griggs and Company DLB-49
Griggs, Sutton Elbert 1872-1930. . . . . DLB-50
Grignon, Claude-Henri 1894-1976 . . . . DLB-68
Grigor'ev, Apollon Aleksandrovich 1822-1864 . . . . .DLB-277
Grigorovich, Dmitrii Vasil'evich 1822-1899 . . . . DLB-238
Grigson, Geoffrey 1905-1985. . . . . DLB-27
Grillparzer, Franz 1791-1872. . . . . .DLB-133; CDWLB-2
Grimald, Nicholas circa 1519-circa 1562 . . . . DLB-136
Grimké, Angelina Weld 1880-1958 . . . DLB-50, 54
Grimké, Sarah Moore 1792-1873 . . . . DLB-239
Grimm, Hans 1875-1959 . . . . DLB-66
Grimm, Jacob 1785-1863 . . . . DLB-90
Grimm, Wilhelm 1786-1859. . . . . DLB-90; CDWLB-2
Grimmelshausen, Johann Jacob Christoffel von 1621 or 1622-1676 . . . . . .DLB-168; CDWLB-2
Grimshaw, Beatrice Ethel 1871-1953 . . . . .DLB-174
Grímur Thomsen 1820-1896 . . . . DLB-293
Grin, Aleksandr Stepanovich 1880-1932 . . . . .DLB-272
Grindal, Edmund 1519 or 1520-1583 . . . DLB-132
Gripe, Maria (Kristina) 1923- DLB-257
Griswold, Rufus Wilmot 1815-1857. . . . . DLB-3, 59, 250
Grosart, Alexander Balloch 1827-1899 . . . DLB-184
Grosholz, Emily 1950- DLB-282
Gross, Milt 1895-1953 . . . . DLB-11

Grosset and Dunlap DLB-49
Grosseteste, Robert circa 1160-1253 . . . . . DLB-115
Grossman, Allen 1932- DLB-193
Grossman, David 1954- DLB-299
Grossman, Vasilii Semenovich 1905-1964 . . . . DLB-272
Grossman Publishers DLB-46
Grosvenor, Gilbert H. 1875-1966 . . . . DLB-91
Groth, Klaus 1819-1899 . . . . DLB-129
Groulx, Lionel 1878-1967 . . . . DLB-68
Grove, Frederick Philip (Felix Paul Greve) 1879-1948 . . . . DLB-92
Grove Press DLB-46
Groys, Boris Efimovich 1947- DLB-285
Grubb, Davis 1919-1980 . . . . DLB-6
Gruelle, Johnny 1880-1938 . . . . DLB-22
von Grumbach, Argula 1492-after 1563? DLB-179
Grundtvig, N. F. S. 1783-1872 . . . . DLB-300
Grymeston, Elizabeth before 1563-before 1604 . . . . DLB-136
Grynberg, Henryk 1936- DLB-299
Gryphius, Andreas 1616-1664 . . . . DLB-164; CDWLB-2
Gryphius, Christian 1649-1706 . . . . DLB-168
Guare, John 1938- DLB-7, 249
Guberman, Igor Mironovich 1936- DLB-285
Guðbergur Bergsson 1932- DLB-293
Guðmundur Bödvarsson 1904-1974 . . . . . DLB-293
Guðmundur Gíslason Hagalín 1898-1985 . . . . DLB-293
Guðmundur Magnússon (see Jón Trausti)
Guerra, Tonino 1920- DLB-128
Guest, Barbara 1920- DLB-5, 193
Guèvremont, Germaine 1893-1968 . . . . DLB-68
Guglielminetti, Amalia 1881-1941 . . . . DLB-264
Guidacci, Margherita 1921-1992 . . . . DLB-128
Guillén, Jorge 1893-1984 . . . . DLB-108
Guillén, Nicolás 1902-1989 . . . . DLB-283
Guilloux, Louis 1899-1980 . . . . DLB-72
Guilpin, Everard circa 1572-after 1608? . . . DLB-136
Guiney, Louise Imogen 1861-1920 . . . . DLB-54
Guiterman, Arthur 1871-1943 . . . . DLB-11
Gumilev, Nikolai Stepanovich 1886-1921 . . . . DLB-295
Günderrode, Caroline von 1780-1806 . . . . DLB-90
Gundulić, Ivan 1589-1638 . . . DLB-147; CDWLB-4
Gunesekera, Romesh 1954- DLB-267
Gunn, Bill 1934-1989 . . . . DLB-38
Gunn, James E. 1923- DLB-8
Gunn, Neil M. 1891-1973 . . . . DLB-15
Gunn, Thom 1929- DLB-27; CDBLB-8
Gunnar Gunnarsson 1889-1975 . . . . DLB-293
Gunnars, Kristjana 1948- DLB-60
Günther, Johann Christian 1695-1723 . . . . DLB-168
Gurik, Robert 1932- DLB-60
Gurney, A. R. 1930- DLB-266
Gurney, Ivor 1890-1937 . . . . Y-02
The Ivor Gurney Society Y-98
Guro, Elena Genrikhovna 1877-1913 . . . . . DLB-295
Gustafson, Ralph 1909-1995 . . . . DLB-88
Gustafsson, Lars 1936- DLB-257
Gütersloh, Albert Paris 1887-1973 . . . . DLB-81
Guterson, David 1956- DLB-292
Guthrie, A. B., Jr. 1901-1991 . . . . DLB-6, 212
Guthrie, Ramon 1896-1973 . . . . DLB-4
Guthrie, Thomas Anstey (see Anstey, FC)
The Guthrie Theater DLB-7
Gutiérrez Nájera, Manuel 1859-1895 . . . . . DLB-290
Guttormur J. Guttormsson 1878-1966 . . . . DLB-293
Gutzkow, Karl 1811-1878 . . . . DLB-133
Guy, Ray 1939- DLB-60
Guy, Rosa 1925- DLB-33
Guyot, Arnold 1807-1884 . . . . DS-13
Gwynn, R. S. 1948- DLB-282
Gwynne, Erskine 1898-1948 . . . . DLB-4
Gyles, John 1680-1755 . . . . DLB-99
Gyllembourg, Thomasine 1773-1856 . . . . . DLB-300
Gyllensten, Lars 1921- DLB-257
Gyrðir Elíasson 1961- DLB-293
Gysin, Brion 1916-1986 . . . . DLB-16

H

H.D. (see Doolittle, Hilda)
Habermas, Jürgen 1929- DLB-242
Habington, William 1605-1654 . . . . DLB-126
Hacker, Marilyn 1942- DLB-120, 282
Hackett, Albert 1900-1995 . . . . DLB-26
Hacks, Peter 1928- DLB-124
Hadas, Rachel 1948- DLB-120, 282
Hadden, Briton 1898-1929 . . . . DLB-91
Hagedorn, Friedrich von 1708-1754 . . . . . . DLB-168
Hagelstange, Rudolf 1912-1984 . . . . DLB-69
Hagerup, Inger 1905-1985 . . . . DLB-297
Haggard, H. Rider 1856-1925 . . . . DLB-70, 156, 174, 178
Haggard, William (Richard Clayton) 1907-1993 . . . . DLB-276; Y-93
Hagy, Alyson 1960- DLB-244
Hahn-Hahn, Ida Gräfin von 1805-1880 . . DLB-133
Haig-Brown, Roderick 1908-1976 . . . . DLB-88
Haight, Gordon S. 1901-1985 . . . . DLB-103
Hailey, Arthur 1920- DLB-88; Y-82
Haines, John 1924- DLB-5, 212
Hake, Edward flourished 1566-1604 . . . . . DLB-136
Hake, Thomas Gordon 1809-1895 . . . . DLB-32
Hakluyt, Richard 1552?-1616 . . . . DLB-136
Halas, František 1901-1949 . . . . DLB-215
Halbe, Max 1865-1944 . . . . DLB-118
Halberstam, David 1934- DLB-241
Haldane, Charlotte 1894-1969 . . . . DLB-191
Haldane, J. B. S. 1892-1964 . . . . DLB-160
Haldeman, Joe 1943- DLB-8
Haldeman-Julius Company DLB-46
Hale, E. J., and Son DLB-49
Hale, Edward Everett 1822-1909 . . . . DLB-1, 42, 74, 235
Hale, Janet Campbell 1946- DLB-175
Hale, Kathleen 1898-2000 . . . . DLB-160
Hale, Leo Thomas (see Ebon)
Hale, Lucretia Peabody 1820-1900 . . . . DLB-42
Hale, Nancy 1908-1988 . . . . DLB-86; DS-17; Y-80, 88
Hale, Sarah Josepha (Buell) 1788-1879 . . . . DLB-1, 42, 73, 243
Hale, Susan 1833-1910 . . . . DLB-221
Hales, John 1584-1656 . . . . DLB-151
Halévy, Ludovic 1834-1908 . . . . DLB-192
Haley, Alex 1921-1992 . . . . DLB-38; CDALB-7
Haliburton, Thomas Chandler 1796-1865 . . . . DLB-11, 99
Hall, Adam (Trevor Dudley-Smith) 1920-1995 . . . . DLB-276
Hall, Anna Maria 1800-1881 . . . . DLB-159
Hall, Donald 1928- DLB-5
Hall, Edward 1497-1547 . . . . DLB-132
Hall, Halsey 1898-1977 . . . . DLB-241
Hall, James 1793-1868 . . . . DLB-73, 74
Hall, Joseph 1574-1656 . . . . DLB-121, 151
Hall, Radclyffe 1880-1943 . . . . DLB-191
Hall, Rodney 1935- DLB-289
Hall, Sarah Ewing 1761-1830 . . . . DLB-200
Hall, Stuart 1932- DLB-242
Samuel Hall [publishing house] DLB-49
Hallam, Arthur Henry 1811-1833 . . . . DLB-32
On Some of the Characteristics of Modern Poetry and On the Lyrical Poems of Alfred Tennyson (1831) DLB-32
Halldór Laxness (Halldór Guðjónsson) 1902-1998 . . . . DLB-293
Halleck, Fitz-Greene 1790-1867 . . . . DLB-3, 250
Haller, Albrecht von 1708-1777 . . . . DLB-168
Halliday, Brett (see Dresser, Davis)
Halliwell-Phillipps, James Orchard 1820-1889 . . . . DLB-184
Hallmann, Johann Christian 1640-1704 or 1716? DLB-168
Hallmark Editions DLB-46
Halper, Albert 1904-1984 . . . . DLB-9
Halperin, John William 1941- DLB-111
Halstead, Murat 1829-1908 . . . . DLB-23
Hamann, Johann Georg 1730-1788 . . . . DLB-97
Hamburger, Michael 1924- DLB-27
Hamilton, Alexander 1712-1756 . . . . DLB-31
Hamilton, Alexander 1755?-1804 . . . . DLB-37
Hamilton, Cicely 1872-1952 . . . . DLB-10, 197
Hamilton, Edmond 1904-1977 . . . . DLB-8
Hamilton, Elizabeth 1758-1816 . . . . . DLB-116, 158

Hamilton, Gail (see Corcoran, Barbara)
Hamilton, Gail (see Dodge, Mary Abigail)
Hamish Hamilton Limited DLB-112
Hamilton, Hugo 1953- DLB-267
Hamilton, Ian 1938-2001 . . . . DLB-40, 155
Hamilton, Janet 1795-1873 . . . . DLB-199
Hamilton, Mary Agnes 1884-1962 . . . . . . DLB-197
Hamilton, Patrick 1904-1962 . . . . DLB-10, 191
Hamilton, Virginia 1936-2002 . . .DLB-33, 52; Y-01
Hamilton, Sir William 1788-1856 . . . . DLB-262
Hamilton-Paterson, James 1941- DLB-267
Hammerstein, Oscar, 2nd 1895-1960 . . . . DLB-265
Hammett, Dashiell 1894-1961 . . . DLB-226, 280; DS-6; CDALB-5
An Appeal in *TAC* Y-91
The Glass Key and Other Dashiell Hammett Mysteries Y-96
Knopf to Hammett: The Editoral Correspondence Y-00
Hammon, Jupiter 1711-died between 1790 and 1806 . . . . DLB-31, 50
Hammond, John ?-1663 . . . . DLB-24
Hamner, Earl 1923- DLB-6
Hampson, John 1901-1955 . . . . DLB-191
Hampton, Christopher 1946- DLB-13
Hamsun, Knut 1859-1952 . . . . DLB-297
Handel-Mazzetti, Enrica von 1871-1955 . . . DLB-81
Handke, Peter 1942- DLB-85, 124
Handlin, Oscar 1915- DLB-17
Hankin, St. John 1869-1909 . . . . DLB-10
Hanley, Clifford 1922- DLB-14
Hanley, James 1901-1985 . . . . DLB-191
Hannah, Barry 1942- DLB-6, 234
Hannay, James 1827-1873 . . . . DLB-21
Hannes Hafstein 1861-1922 . . . . DLB-293
Hano, Arnold 1922- DLB-241
Hanrahan, Barbara 1939-1991 . . . . DLB-289
Hansberry, Lorraine 1930-1965 . . . . DLB-7, 38; CDALB-1
Hansen, Martin A. 1909-1955 . . . . DLB-214
Hansen, Thorkild 1927-1989 . . . . DLB-214
Hanson, Elizabeth 1684-1737 . . . . DLB-200
Hapgood, Norman 1868-1937 . . . . DLB-91
Happel, Eberhard Werner 1647-1690 . . . . DLB-168
Harbach, Otto 1873-1963 . . . . DLB-265
The Harbinger 1845-1849 . . . . DLB-1, 223
Harburg, E. Y. "Yip" 1896-1981 . . . . DLB-265
Harcourt Brace Jovanovich DLB-46
Hardenberg, Friedrich von (see Novalis)
Harding, Walter 1917- DLB-111
Hardwick, Elizabeth 1916- DLB-6
Hardy, Alexandre 1572?-1632 . . . . DLB-268
Hardy, Frank 1917-1994 . . . . DLB-260
Hardy, Thomas 1840-1928 . . . . . . DLB-18, 19, 135; CDBLB-5
"Candour in English Fiction" (1890) . . DLB-18
Hare, Cyril 1900-1958 . . . . DLB-77
Hare, David 1947- DLB-13
Hare, R. M. 1919-2002 . . . . DLB-262
Hargrove, Marion 1919- DLB-11
Häring, Georg Wilhelm Heinrich (see Alexis, Willibald)
Harington, Donald 1935- DLB-152
Harington, Sir John 1560-1612 . . . . DLB-136
Harjo, Joy 1951- DLB-120, 175
Harkness, Margaret (John Law) 1854-1923 . . . . DLB-197
Harley, Edward, second Earl of Oxford 1689-1741 . . . . DLB-213
Harley, Robert, first Earl of Oxford 1661-1724 . . . . DLB-213
Harlow, Robert 1923- DLB-60
Harman, Thomas flourished 1566-1573 . . DLB-136
Harness, Charles L. 1915- DLB-8
Harnett, Cynthia 1893-1981 . . . . DLB-161
Harnick, Sheldon 1924- DLB-265
Tribute to Ira Gershwin Y-96
Tribute to Lorenz Hart Y-95
Harper, Edith Alice Mary (see Wickham, Anna)
Harper, Fletcher 1806-1877 . . . . DLB-79
Harper, Frances Ellen Watkins 1825-1911 . . . . DLB-50, 221
Harper, Michael S. 1938- DLB-41
Harper and Brothers DLB-49
Harpur, Charles 1813-1868 . . . . DLB-230
Harraden, Beatrice 1864-1943 . . . . DLB-153
George G. Harrap and Company Limited DLB-112
Harriot, Thomas 1560-1621 . . . . DLB-136
Harris, Alexander 1805-1874 . . . . DLB-230
Harris, Benjamin ?-circa 1720 . . . . DLB-42, 43
Harris, Christie 1907-2002 . . . . DLB-88
Harris, Errol E. 1908- DLB-279
Harris, Frank 1856-1931 . . . . .DLB-156, 197
Harris, George Washington 1814-1869 . . . . DLB-3, 11, 248
Harris, Joanne 1964- DLB-271
Harris, Joel Chandler 1848-1908 . . . . .DLB-11, 23, 42, 78, 91
The Joel Chandler Harris Association Y-99
Harris, Mark 1922- DLB-2; Y-80
Tribute to Frederick A. Pottle Y-87
Harris, William Torrey 1835-1909 . . . . . . .DLB-270
Harris, Wilson 1921- DLB-117; CDWLB-3
Harrison, Mrs. Burton (see Harrison, Constance Cary)
Harrison, Charles Yale 1898-1954 . . . . DLB-68
Harrison, Constance Cary 1843-1920 . . . DLB-221
Harrison, Frederic 1831-1923 . . . . .DLB-57, 190
"On Style in English Prose" (1898) . . . DLB-57
Harrison, Harry 1925- DLB-8
James P. Harrison Company DLB-49
Harrison, Jim 1937- Y-82
Harrison, M. John 1945- DLB-261
Harrison, Mary St. Leger Kingsley (see Malet, Lucas)
Harrison, Paul Carter 1936- DLB-38
Harrison, Susan Frances 1859-1935 . . . . . . DLB-99
Harrison, Tony 1937- DLB-40, 245
Harrison, William 1535-1593 . . . . DLB-136
Harrison, William 1933- DLB-234
Harrisse, Henry 1829-1910 . . . . DLB-47
The Harry Ransom Humanities Research Center at the University of Texas at Austin Y-00
Harryman, Carla 1952- DLB-193
Harsdörffer, Georg Philipp 1607-1658 . . . DLB-164
Harsent, David 1942- DLB-40
Hart, Albert Bushnell 1854-1943 . . . . .DLB-17
Hart, Anne 1768-1834 . . . . DLB-200
Hart, Elizabeth 1771-1833 . . . . DLB-200
Hart, Julia Catherine 1796-1867 . . . . DLB-99
Hart, Lorenz 1895-1943 . . . . DLB-265
Larry Hart: Still an Influence Y-95
Lorenz Hart: An American Lyricist Y-95
The Lorenz Hart Centenary Y-95
Hart, Moss 1904-1961 . . . . .DLB-7, 266
Hart, Oliver 1723-1795 . . . . DLB-31
Rupert Hart-Davis Limited DLB-112
Harte, Bret 1836-1902 . . . . .DLB-12, 64, 74, 79, 186; CDALB-3
Harte, Edward Holmead 1922- DLB-127
Harte, Houston Harriman 1927- DLB-127
Hartlaub, Felix 1913-1945 . . . . DLB-56
Hartlebon, Otto Erich 1864-1905 . . . . DLB-118
Hartley, David 1705-1757 . . . . DLB-252
Hartley, L. P. 1895-1972 . . . . DLB-15, 139
Hartley, Marsden 1877-1943 . . . . DLB-54
Hartling, Peter 1933- DLB-75
Hartman, Geoffrey H. 1929- DLB-67
Hartmann, Sadakichi 1867-1944 . . . . DLB-54
Hartmann von Aue circa 1160-circa 1205 . . . .DLB-138; CDWLB-2
Hartshorne, Charles 1897-2000 . . . . .DLB-270
Haruf, Kent 1943- DLB-292
Harvey, Gabriel 1550?-1631 . . . DLB-167, 213, 281
Harvey, Jack (see Rankin, Ian)
Harvey, Jean-Charles 1891-1967 . . . . DLB-88
Harvill Press Limited DLB-112
Harwood, Gwen 1920-1995 . . . . DLB-289
Harwood, Lee 1939- DLB-40
Harwood, Ronald 1934- DLB-13
Hašek, Jaroslav 1883-1923 . . .DLB-215; CDWLB-4
Haskins, Charles Homer 1870-1937 . . . . . . DLB-47
Haslam, Gerald 1937- DLB-212
Hass, Robert 1941- DLB-105, 206
Hasselstrom, Linda M. 1943- DLB-256
Hastings, Michael 1938- DLB-233
Hatar, Győző 1914- DLB-215

The Hatch-Billops Collection. DLB-76
Hathaway, William 1944- DLB-120
Hatherly, Ana 1929- DLB-287
Hauch, Carsten 1790-1872. . . . . DLB-300
Hauff, Wilhelm 1802-1827 . . . . DLB-90
Hauge, Olav H. 1908-1994 . . . . DLB-297
Haugen, Paal-Helge 1945- DLB-297
Haugwitz, August Adolph von 1647-1706. . . . . DLB-168
Hauptmann, Carl 1858-1921. . . . . DLB-66, 118
Hauptmann, Gerhart 1862-1946 . . . . DLB-66, 118; CDWLB-2
Hauser, Marianne 1910- Y-83
Havel, Václav 1936- DLB-232; CDWLB-4
Haven, Alice B. Neal 1827-1863. . . . . DLB-250
Havergal, Frances Ridley 1836-1879 . . . . . DLB-199
Hawes, Stephen 1475?-before 1529 . . . . . . DLB-132
Hawker, Robert Stephen 1803-1875 . . . . . . DLB-32
Hawkes, John 1925-1998 . . . . DLB-2, 7, 227; Y-80, Y-98
John Hawkes: A Tribute. Y-98
Tribute to Donald Barthelme Y-89
Hawkesworth, John 1720-1773. . . . . DLB-142
Hawkins, Sir Anthony Hope (see Hope, Anthony)
Hawkins, Sir John 1719-1789 . . . . DLB-104, 142
Hawkins, Walter Everette 1883-? DLB-50
Hawthorne, Nathaniel 1804-1864 . . . DLB-1, 74, 183, 223, 269; DS-5; CDALB-2
The Nathaniel Hawthorne Society Y-00
The Old Manse. DLB-223
Hawthorne, Sophia Peabody 1809-1871 . . . . DLB-183, 239
Hay, John 1835-1905. . . . . DLB-12, 47, 189
Hay, John 1915- DLB-275
Hayashi Fumiko 1903-1951. . . . . DLB-180
Haycox, Ernest 1899-1950. . . . . DLB-206
Haycraft, Anna Margaret (see Ellis, Alice Thomas)
Hayden, Robert 1913-1980 . . . . DLB-5, 76; CDALB-1
Haydon, Benjamin Robert 1786-1846. . . . DLB-110
Hayes, John Michael 1919- DLB-26
Hayley, William 1745-1820 . . . . DLB-93, 142
Haym, Rudolf 1821-1901 . . . . DLB-129
Hayman, Robert 1575-1629. . . . . DLB-99
Hayman, Ronald 1932- DLB-155
Hayne, Paul Hamilton 1830-1886 . . . . DLB-3, 64, 79, 248
Hays, Mary 1760-1843. . . . . DLB-142, 158
Hayward, John 1905-1965. . . . . DLB-201
Haywood, Eliza 1693?-1756. . . . . DLB-39
Dedication of *Lasselia* [excerpt] (1723) DLB-39
Preface to *The Disguis'd Prince* [excerpt] (1723) DLB-39
The Tea-Table [excerpt]. DLB-39
Willis P. Hazard [publishing house]. DLB-49
Hazlitt, William 1778-1830. . . . . DLB-110, 158
Hazzard, Shirley 1931- DLB-289; Y-82
Head, Bessie 1937-1986 . . . . DLB-117, 225; CDWLB-3
Headley, Joel T. 1813-1897 . . . DLB-30, 183; DS-13
Heaney, Seamus 1939-. . . DLB-40; Y-95; CDBLB-8
Nobel Lecture 1994: Crediting Poetry . . . Y-95
Heard, Nathan C. 1936- DLB-33
Hearn, Lafcadio 1850-1904 . . . . . . DLB-12, 78, 189
Hearn, Mary Anne (Marianne Farningham, Eva Hope) 1834-1909 . . . . DLB-240
Hearne, John 1926- DLB-117
Hearne, Samuel 1745-1792. . . . . DLB-99
Hearne, Thomas 1678?-1735 . . . . DLB-213
Hearst, William Randolph 1863-1951 . . . . . DLB-25
Hearst, William Randolph, Jr. 1908-1993 . . . . DLB-127
Heartman, Charles Frederick 1883-1953. . DLB-187
Heath, Catherine 1924- DLB-14
Heath, James Ewell 1792-1862. . . . . DLB-248
Heath, Roy A. K. 1926- DLB-117
Heath-Stubbs, John 1918- DLB-27
Heavysege, Charles 1816-1876 . . . . DLB-99
Hebbel, Friedrich 1813-1863 . . . . DLB-129; CDWLB-2
Hebel, Johann Peter 1760-1826 . . . . DLB-90
Heber, Richard 1774-1833 . . . . DLB-184
Hébert, Anne 1916-2000 . . . . DLB-68
Hébert, Jacques 1923- DLB-53
Hecht, Anthony 1923- DLB-5, 169
Hecht, Ben 1894-1964 . . . . DLB-7, 9, 25, 26, 28, 86
Hecker, Isaac Thomas 1819-1888 . . . . . DLB-1, 243
Hedge, Frederic Henry 1805-1890 . . . . DLB-1, 59, 243; DS-5
Hefner, Hugh M. 1926- DLB-137
Hegel, Georg Wilhelm Friedrich 1770-1831 . . . . DLB-90
Heiberg, Johan Ludvig 1791-1860 . . . . DLB-300
Heiberg, Johanne Luise 1812-1890 . . . . . . DLB-300
Heide, Robert 1939- DLB-249
Heidegger, Martin 1889-1976 . . . . DLB-296
Heidish, Marcy 1947- Y-82
Heißenbüttel, Helmut 1921-1996 . . . . DLB-75
Heike monogatari DLB-203
Hein, Christoph 1944- DLB-124; CDWLB-2
Hein, Piet 1905-1996 . . . . DLB-214
Heine, Heinrich 1797-1856. . . . DLB-90; CDWLB-2
Heinemann, Larry 1944- DS-9
William Heinemann Limited DLB-112
Heinesen, William 1900-1991 . . . . DLB-214
Heinlein, Robert A. 1907-1988. . . . . DLB-8
Heinrich, Willi 1920- DLB-75
Heinrich Julius of Brunswick 1564-1613 . . DLB-164
Heinrich von dem Türlîn flourished circa 1230. . . . . DLB-138
Heinrich von Melk flourished after 1160 . . . . DLB-148
Heinrich von Veldeke circa 1145-circa 1190. . . . . DLB-138
Heinse, Wilhelm 1746-1803. . . . . DLB-94
Heinz, W. C. 1915- DLB-171
Heiskell, John 1872-1972 . . . . DLB-127
Hejinian, Lyn 1941- DLB-165
Helder, Herberto 1930- DLB-287
Heliand circa 850 . . . . DLB-148
Heller, Joseph 1923-1999 . . . . . . DLB-2, 28, 227; Y-80, 99, 02
Excerpts from Joseph Heller's USC Address, "The Literature of Despair" Y-96
Remembering Joe Heller, by William Price Fox. Y-99
A Tribute to Joseph Heller Y-99
Heller, Michael 1937- DLB-165
Hellman, Lillian 1906-1984 . . . . . DLB-7, 228; Y-84
Hellwig, Johann 1609-1674 . . . . DLB-164
Helprin, Mark 1947- Y-85; CDALB-7
Helwig, David 1938- DLB-60
Hemans, Felicia 1793-1835. . . . . DLB-96
Hemenway, Abby Maria 1828-1890 . . . . . DLB-243
Hemingway, Ernest 1899-1961 . . . . DLB-4, 9, 102, 210; Y-81, 87, 99; DS-1, 15, 16; CDALB-4
A Centennial Celebration Y-99
Come to Papa Y-99
The Ernest Hemingway Collection at the John F. Kennedy Library Y-99
Ernest Hemingway Declines to Introduce *War and Peace* Y-01
Ernest Hemingway's Reaction to James Gould Cozzens. Y-98
Ernest Hemingway's Toronto Journalism Revisited: With Three Previously Unrecorded Stories. Y-92
Falsifying Hemingway. Y-96
Hemingway Centenary Celebration at the JFK Library Y-99
The Hemingway/Fenton Correspondence Y-02
Hemingway in the JFK Y-99
The Hemingway Letters Project Finds an Editor. Y-02
Hemingway Salesmen's Dummies Y-00
Hemingway: Twenty-Five Years Later . . . Y-85
A Literary Archaeologist Digs On: A Brief Interview with Michael Reynolds. Y-99
Not Immediately Discernible . . . but Eventually Quite Clear: The *First Light* and *Final Years* of Hemingway's Centenary Y-99
Packaging Papa: *The Garden of Eden*. Y-86
Second International Hemingway Colloquium: Cuba Y-98
Hémon, Louis 1880-1913 . . . . DLB-92
Hempel, Amy 1951- DLB-218
Hempel, Carl G. 1905-1997. . . . . DLB-279
Hemphill, Paul 1936- Y-87

Hénault, Gilles 1920-1996 . . . . DLB-88
Henchman, Daniel 1689-1761. . . . . DLB-24
Henderson, Alice Corbin 1881-1949 . . . . . DLB-54
Henderson, Archibald 1877-1963 . . . . DLB-103
Henderson, David 1942- DLB-41
Henderson, George Wylie 1904-1965 . . . . DLB-51
Henderson, Zenna 1917-1983. . . . . DLB-8
Henighan, Tom 1934- DLB-251
Henisch, Peter 1943- DLB-85
Henley, Beth 1952- Y-86
Henley, William Ernest 1849-1903 . . . . . . DLB-19
Henniker, Florence 1855-1923 . . . . DLB-135
Henning, Rachel 1826-1914 . . . . DLB-230
Henningsen, Agnes 1868-1962 . . . . DLB-214
Henry, Alexander 1739-1824 . . . . DLB-99
Henry, Buck 1930- DLB-26
Henry, Marguerite 1902-1997 . . . . DLB-22
Henry, O. (see Porter, William Sydney)
Henry, Robert Selph 1889-1970 . . . . DLB-17
Henry, Will (see Allen, Henry W.)
Henry VIII of England 1491-1547 . . . . . . DLB-132
Henry of Ghent circa 1217-1229 - 1293 . . DLB-115
Henryson, Robert
1420s or 1430s-circa 1505 . . . . DLB-146
Henschke, Alfred (see Klabund)
Hensher, Philip 1965- DLB-267
Hensley, Sophie Almon 1866-1946. . . . . . . DLB-99
Henson, Lance 1944- DLB-175
Henty, G. A. 1832-1902 . . . . DLB-18, 141
The Henty Society Y-98
Hentz, Caroline Lee 1800-1856 . . . . . . DLB-3, 248
Heraclitus
flourished circa 500 B.C. DLB-176
Herbert, Agnes circa 1880-1960 . . . . .DLB-174
Herbert, Alan Patrick 1890-1971 . . . . DLB-10, 191
Herbert, Edward, Lord, of Cherbury
1582-1648 . . . . DLB-121, 151, 252
Herbert, Frank 1920-1986 . . . . . DLB-8; CDALB-7
Herbert, George 1593-1633 . . DLB-126; CDBLB-1
Herbert, Henry William 1807-1858 . . . . DLB-3, 73
Herbert, John 1926- DLB-53
Herbert, Mary Sidney, Countess of Pembroke
(see Sidney, Mary)
Herbert, Xavier 1901-1984. . . . . DLB-260
Herbert, Zbigniew
1924-1998 . . . . DLB-232; CDWLB-4
Herbst, Josephine 1892-1969 . . . . DLB-9
Herburger, Gunter 1932- DLB-75, 124
Herculano, Alexandre 1810-1877 . . . . DLB-287
Hercules, Frank E. M. 1917-1996 . . . . DLB-33
Herder, Johann Gottfried 1744-1803 . . . . . DLB-97
B. Herder Book Company DLB-49
Heredia, José-María de 1842-1905 . . . . . . DLB-217
Herford, Charles Harold 1853-1931 . . . . DLB-149
Hergesheimer, Joseph 1880-1954 . . . . . DLB-9, 102
Heritage Press. DLB-46
Hermann the Lame 1013-1054. . . . . DLB-148
Hermes, Johann Timotheu 1738-1821 . . . . DLB-97
Hermlin, Stephan 1915-1997 . . . . DLB-69
Hernández, Alfonso C. 1938- DLB-122
Hernández, Inés 1947- DLB-122
Hernández, Miguel 1910-1942 . . . . DLB-134
Hernton, Calvin C. 1932- DLB-38
Herodotus circa 484 B.C.-circa 420 B.C.
. . . . .DLB-176; CDWLB-1
Heron, Robert 1764-1807 . . . . DLB-142
Herr, Michael 1940- DLB-185
Herrera, Darío 1870-1914. . . . . DLB-290
Herrera, Juan Felipe 1948- DLB-122
E. R. Herrick and Company DLB-49
Herrick, Robert 1591-1674 . . . . DLB-126
Herrick, Robert 1868-1938. . . . . .DLB-9, 12, 78
Herrick, William 1915- Y-83
Herrmann, John 1900-1959 . . . . DLB-4
Hersey, John
1914-1993 . . .DLB-6, 185, 278, 299; CDALB-7
Hertel, François 1905-1985. . . . . DLB-68
Hervé-Bazin, Jean Pierre Marie (see Bazin, Hervé)
Hervey, John, Lord 1696-1743 . . . . DLB-101
Herwig, Georg 1817-1875 . . . . DLB-133
Herzen, Alexander (Aleksandr Ivanovich
Gersten) 1812-1870 . . . . .DLB-277
Herzog, Emile Salomon Wilhelm
(see Maurois, André)
Hesiod eighth century B.C. DLB-176
Hesse, Hermann 1877-1962 . . DLB-66; CDWLB-2
Hessus, Eobanus 1488-1540. . . . . .DLB-179
Heureka! (see Kertész, Imre and Nobel Prize
in Literature: 2002) Y-02
Hewat, Alexander circa 1743-circa 1824. . . DLB-30
Hewett, Dorothy 1923-2002. . . . . DLB-289
Hewitt, John 1907-1987. . . . . DLB-27
Hewlett, Maurice 1861-1923 . . . . DLB-34, 156
Heyen, William 1940- DLB-5
Heyer, Georgette 1902-1974. . . . . .DLB-77, 191
Heym, Stefan 1913-2001 . . . . DLB-69
Heyse, Paul 1830-1914. . . . . DLB-129
Heytesbury, William
circa 1310-1372 or 1373 . . . . DLB-115
Heyward, Dorothy 1890-1961 . . . . .DLB-7, 249
Heyward, DuBose 1885-1940 . . .DLB-7, 9, 45, 249
Heywood, John 1497?-1580? DLB-136
Heywood, Thomas 1573 or 1574-1641. . . . DLB-62
Hiaasen, Carl 1953- DLB-292
Hibberd, Jack 1940- DLB-289
Hibbs, Ben 1901-1975. . . . . DLB-137
"The Saturday Evening Post reaffirms
a policy," Ben Hibb's Statement
in *The Saturday Evening Post*
(16 May 1942). DLB-137
Hichens, Robert S. 1864-1950 . . . . DLB-153
Hickey, Emily 1845-1924. . . . . DLB-199
Hickman, William Albert 1877-1957. . . . . . DLB-92
Hicks, Granville 1901-1982 . . . . DLB-246
Hidalgo, José Luis 1919-1947. . . . . DLB-108
Hiebert, Paul 1892-1987. . . . . DLB-68
Hieng, Andrej 1925- DLB-181
Hierro, José 1922-2002. . . . . DLB-108
Higgins, Aidan 1927- DLB-14
Higgins, Colin 1941-1988. . . . . DLB-26
Higgins, George V.
1939-1999 . . . . .DLB-2; Y-81, 98–99
Afterword [in response to Cozzen's
Mens Rea (or Something)]. Y-97
At End of Day: The Last George V.
Higgins Novel Y-99
The Books of George V. Higgins:
A Checklist of Editions
and Printings Y-00
George V. Higgins in Class Y-02
Tribute to Alfred A. Knopf Y-84
Tributes to George V. Higgins Y-99
"What You Lose on the Swings You Make
Up on the Merry-Go-Round" . . . Y-99
Higginson, Thomas Wentworth
1823-1911 . . . . DLB-1, 64, 243
Highwater, Jamake 1942?- DLB-52; Y-85
Hijuelos, Oscar 1951- DLB-145
Hildegard von Bingen 1098-1179 . . . . DLB-148
Das Hildesbrandslied
circa 820. . . . . .DLB-148; CDWLB-2
Hildesheimer, Wolfgang 1916-1991. . DLB-69, 124
Hildreth, Richard 1807-1865 . . DLB-1, 30, 59, 235
Hill, Aaron 1685-1750 . . . . DLB-84
Hill, Geoffrey 1932- DLB-40; CDBLB-8
George M. Hill Company DLB-49
Hill, "Sir" John 1714?-1775 . . . . DLB-39
Lawrence Hill and Company, Publishers . DLB-46
Hill, Leslie 1880-1960. . . . . DLB-51
Hill, Reginald 1936- DLB-276
Hill, Susan 1942- DLB-14, 139
Hill, Walter 1942- DLB-44
Hill and Wang DLB-46
Hillberry, Conrad 1928- DLB-120
Hillerman, Tony 1925- DLB-206
Hilliard, Gray and Company DLB-49
Hills, Lee 1906-2000. . . . . .DLB-127
Hillyer, Robert 1895-1961 . . . . DLB-54
Hilsenrath, Edgar 1926- DLB-299
Hilton, James 1900-1954 . . . . .DLB-34, 77
Hilton, Walter died 1396 . . . . DLB-146
Hilton and Company DLB-49
Himes, Chester 1909-1984. . . .DLB-2, 76, 143, 226
Joseph Hindmarsh [publishing house] DLB-170
Hine, Daryl 1936- DLB-60
Hingley, Ronald 1920- DLB-155
Hinojosa-Smith, Rolando 1929- DLB-82
Hinton, S. E. 1948- CDALB-7
Hippel, Theodor Gottlieb von
1741-1796 . . . . DLB-97

Hippius, Zinaida Nikolaevna 1869-1945 . . . . . . DLB-295
Hippocrates of Cos flourished circa 425 B.C. DLB-176; CDWLB-1
Hirabayashi Taiko 1905-1972 . . . . . . DLB-180
Hirsch, E. D., Jr. 1928- DLB-67
Hirsch, Edward 1950- DLB-120
"Historical Novel," The Holocaust DLB-299
Hoagland, Edward 1932- DLB-6
Hoagland, Everett H., III 1942- DLB-41
Hoban, Russell 1925- DLB-52; Y-90
Hobbes, Thomas 1588-1679 . . . DLB-151, 252, 281
Hobby, Oveta 1905-1995 . . . . . . DLB-127
Hobby, William 1878-1964 . . . . . . DLB-127
Hobsbaum, Philip 1932- DLB-40
Hobsbawn, Eric (Francis Newton) 1917- DLB-296
Hobson, Laura Z. 1900- DLB-28
Hobson, Sarah 1947- DLB-204
Hoby, Thomas 1530-1566 . . . . . . DLB-132
Hoccleve, Thomas circa 1368-circa 1437 . . . . . . DLB-146
Hochhuth, Rolf 1931- DLB-124
Hochman, Sandra 1936- DLB-5
Hocken, Thomas Morland 1836-1910 . . . . DLB-184
Hocking, William Ernest 1873-1966 . . . . . DLB-270
Hodder and Stoughton, Limited DLB-106
Hodgins, Jack 1938- DLB-60
Hodgman, Helen 1945- DLB-14
Hodgskin, Thomas 1787-1869 . . . . . . DLB-158
Hodgson, Ralph 1871-1962 . . . . . . DLB-19
Hodgson, William Hope 1877-1918 . . . . . . DLB-70, 153, 156, 178
Hoe, Robert, III 1839-1909 . . . . . . DLB-187
Hoeg, Peter 1957- DLB-214
Hoel, Sigurd 1890-1960 . . . . . . DLB-297
Hoem, Edvard 1949- DLB-297
Hoffenstein, Samuel 1890-1947 . . . . . . DLB-11
Hoffman, Alice 1952- DLB-292
Hoffman, Charles Fenno 1806-1884 . . . DLB-3, 250
Hoffman, Daniel 1923- DLB-5
Tribute to Robert Graves Y-85
Hoffmann, E. T. A. 1776-1822 . . . . . . DLB-90; CDWLB-2
Hoffman, Frank B. 1888-1958 . . . . . . DLB-188
Hoffman, William 1925- DLB-234
Tribute to Paxton Davis Y-94
Hoffmanswaldau, Christian Hoffman von 1616-1679 . . . . . . DLB-168
Hofmann, Michael 1957- DLB-40
Hofmannsthal, Hugo von 1874-1929 . . . . . . DLB-81, 118; CDWLB-2
Hofmo, Gunvor 1921-1995 . . . . . . DLB-297
Hofstadter, Richard 1916-1970 . . . . . . DLB-17, 246
Hogan, Desmond 1950- DLB-14
Hogan, Linda 1947- DLB-175
Hogan and Thompson DLB-49
Hogarth Press DLB-112; DS-10
Hogg, James 1770-1835 . . . . . . DLB-93, 116, 159
Hohberg, Wolfgang Helmhard Freiherr von 1612-1688 . . . . . . DLB-168
von Hohenheim, Philippus Aureolus Theophrastus Bombastus (see Paracelsus)
Hohl, Ludwig 1904-1980 . . . . . . DLB-56
Højholt, Per 1928- DLB-214
Holan, Vladimir 1905-1980 . . . . . . DLB-215
Holberg, Ludvig 1684-1754 . . . . . . DLB-300
Holbrook, David 1923- DLB-14, 40
Holcroft, Thomas 1745-1809 . . . . . DLB-39, 89, 158
Preface to *Alwyn* (1780) DLB-39
Holden, Jonathan 1941- DLB-105
"Contemporary Verse Story-telling" . . . DLB-105
Holden, Molly 1927-1981 . . . . . . DLB-40
Hölderlin, Friedrich 1770-1843 . . . . . . DLB-90; CDWLB-2
Holdstock, Robert 1948- DLB-261
Holiday House DLB-46
Holinshed, Raphael died 1580 . . . . . . DLB-167
Holland, J. G. 1819-1881 . . . . . . DS-13
Holland, Norman N. 1927- DLB-67
Hollander, John 1929- DLB-5
Holley, Marietta 1836-1926 . . . . . . DLB-11
Hollinghurst, Alan 1954- DLB-207
Hollingsworth, Margaret 1940- DLB-60
Hollo, Anselm 1934- DLB-40
Holloway, Emory 1885-1977 . . . . . . DLB-103
Holloway, John 1920- DLB-27
Holloway House Publishing Company DLB-46
Holme, Constance 1880-1955 . . . . . . DLB-34
Holmes, Abraham S. 1821?-1908 . . . . . . DLB-99
Holmes, John Clellon 1926-1988 . . . . . DLB-16, 237
"Four Essays on the Beat Generation" DLB-16
Holmes, Mary Jane 1825-1907 . . . . . DLB-202, 221
Holmes, Oliver Wendell 1809-1894 . . . . . . DLB-1, 189, 235; CDALB-2
Holmes, Richard 1945- DLB-155
Holmes, Thomas James 1874-1959 . . . . . . DLB-187
The Holocaust "Historical Novel" DLB-299
Holocaust Fiction, Postmodern DLB-299
Holocaust Novel, The "Second-Generation" DLB-299
Holroyd, Michael 1935- DLB-155; Y-99
Holst, Hermann E. von 1841-1904 . . . . . . DLB-47
Holt, John 1721-1784 . . . . . . DLB-43
Henry Holt and Company DLB-49, 284
Holt, Rinehart and Winston DLB-46
Holtby, Winifred 1898-1935 . . . . . . DLB-191
Holthusen, Hans Egon 1913-1997 . . . . . . DLB-69
Hölty, Ludwig Christoph Heinrich 1748-1776 . . . . . . DLB-94
Holub, Miroslav 1923-1998 . . . . . . DLB-232; CDWLB-4
Holz, Arno 1863-1929 . . . . . . DLB-118
Home, Henry, Lord Kames (see Kames, Henry Home, Lord)
Home, John 1722-1808 . . . . . . DLB-84
Home, William Douglas 1912- DLB-13
Home Publishing Company DLB-49
Homer circa eighth-seventh centuries B.C. DLB-176; CDWLB-1
Homer, Winslow 1836-1910 . . . . . . DLB-188
Homes, Geoffrey (see Mainwaring, Daniel)
Honan, Park 1928- DLB-111
Hone, William 1780-1842 . . . . . . DLB-110, 158
Hongo, Garrett Kaoru 1951- DLB-120
Honig, Edwin 1919- DLB-5
Hood, Hugh 1928-2000 . . . . . . DLB-53
Hood, Mary 1946- DLB-234
Hood, Thomas 1799-1845 . . . . . . DLB-96
Hook, Sidney 1902-1989 . . . . . . DLB-279
Hook, Theodore 1788-1841 . . . . . . DLB-116
Hooker, Jeremy 1941- DLB-40
Hooker, Richard 1554-1600 . . . . . . DLB-132
Hooker, Thomas 1586-1647 . . . . . . DLB-24
hooks, bell 1952- DLB-246
Hooper, Johnson Jones 1815-1862 . . . . . . DLB-3, 11, 248
Hope, A. D. 1907-2000 . . . . . . DLB-289
Hope, Anthony 1863-1933 . . . . . . DLB-153, 156
Hope, Christopher 1944- DLB-225
Hope, Eva (see Hearn, Mary Anne)
Hope, Laurence (Adela Florence Cory Nicolson) 1865-1904 . . . . . . DLB-240
Hopkins, Ellice 1836-1904 . . . . . . DLB-190
Hopkins, Gerard Manley 1844-1889 . . . . . . DLB-35, 57; CDBLB-5
Hopkins, John ?-1570 . . . . . . DLB-132
Hopkins, John H., and Son DLB-46
Hopkins, Lemuel 1750-1801 . . . . . . DLB-37
Hopkins, Pauline Elizabeth 1859-1930 . . . . DLB-50
Hopkins, Samuel 1721-1803 . . . . . . DLB-31
Hopkinson, Francis 1737-1791 . . . . . . DLB-31
Hopkinson, Nalo 1960- DLB-251
Hopper, Nora (Mrs. Nora Chesson) 1871-1906 . . . . . . DLB-240
Hoppin, Augustus 1828-1896 . . . . . . DLB-188
Hora, Josef 1891-1945 . . . . . . DLB-215; CDWLB-4
Horace 65 B.C.-8 B.C. DLB-211; CDWLB-1
Horgan, Paul 1903-1995 . . . . . DLB-102, 212; Y-85
Tribute to Alfred A. Knopf Y-84
Horizon Press DLB-46
Horkheimer, Max 1895-1973 . . . . . . DLB-296
Hornby, C. H. St. John 1867-1946 . . . . . . DLB-201
Hornby, Nick 1957- DLB-207
Horne, Frank 1899-1974 . . . . . . DLB-51
Horne, Richard Henry (Hengist) 1802 or 1803-1884 . . . . . . DLB-32
Horne, Thomas 1608-1654 . . . . . . DLB-281
Horney, Karen 1885-1952 . . . . . . DLB-246

Hornung, E. W. 1866-1921 . . . . DLB-70

Horovitz, Israel 1939- DLB-7

Horta, Maria Teresa (see The Three Marias: A Landmark Case in Portuguese Literary History)

Horton, George Moses 1797?-1883? DLB-50

George Moses Horton Society Y-99

Horváth, Ödön von 1901-1938 . . . . . DLB-85, 124

Horwood, Harold 1923- DLB-60

E. and E. Hosford [publishing house] DLB-49

Hoskens, Jane Fenn 1693-1770? DLB-200

Hoskyns, John circa 1566-1638 . . . . DLB-121, 281

Hosokawa Yūsai 1535-1610 . . . . DLB-203

Hospers, John 1918- DLB-279

Hostovský, Egon 1908-1973 . . . . DLB-215

Hotchkiss and Company DLB-49

Hough, Emerson 1857-1923 . . . . DLB-9, 212

Houghton, Stanley 1881-1913 . . . . DLB-10

Houghton Mifflin Company DLB-49

Hours at Home DS-13

Household, Geoffrey 1900-1988 . . . . DLB-87

Housman, A. E. 1859-1936 . . . DLB-19; CDBLB-5

Housman, Laurence 1865-1959 . . . . DLB-10

Houston, Pam 1962- DLB-244

Houwald, Ernst von 1778-1845 . . . . DLB-90

Hovey, Richard 1864-1900 . . . . DLB-54

Howard, Donald R. 1927-1987 . . . . DLB-111

Howard, Maureen 1930- Y-83

Howard, Richard 1929- DLB-5

Howard, Roy W. 1883-1964 . . . . DLB-29

Howard, Sidney 1891-1939 . . . . . . .DLB-7, 26, 249

Howard, Thomas, second Earl of Arundel 1585-1646 . . . . DLB-213

Howe, E. W. 1853-1937 . . . . DLB-12, 25

Howe, Henry 1816-1893 . . . . DLB-30

Howe, Irving 1920-1993 . . . . DLB-67

Howe, Joseph 1804-1873 . . . . DLB-99

Howe, Julia Ward 1819-1910 . . . . DLB-1, 189, 235

Howe, Percival Presland 1886-1944 . . . . . DLB-149

Howe, Susan 1937- DLB-120

Howell, Clark, Sr. 1863-1936 . . . . DLB-25

Howell, Evan P. 1839-1905 . . . . DLB-23

Howell, James 1594?-1666 . . . . DLB-151

Howell, Soskin and Company DLB-46

Howell, Warren Richardson 1912-1984 . . . . DLB-140

Howells, William Dean 1837-1920 . . . . .DLB-12, 64, 74, 79, 189; CDALB-3

Introduction to Paul Laurence Dunbar's *Lyrics of Lowly Life* (1896) DLB-50

The William Dean Howells Society Y-01

Howitt, Mary 1799-1888 . . . . DLB-110, 199

Howitt, William 1792-1879 . . . . DLB-110

Hoyem, Andrew 1935- DLB-5

Hoyers, Anna Ovena 1584-1655 . . . . DLB-164

Hoyle, Fred 1915-2001 . . . . DLB-261

Hoyos, Angela de 1940- DLB-82

Henry Hoyt [publishing house] DLB-49

Hoyt, Palmer 1897-1979 . . . . DLB-127

Hrabal, Bohumil 1914-1997 . . . . DLB-232

Hrabanus Maurus 776?-856 . . . . DLB-148

Hronský, Josef Cíger 1896-1960 . . . . DLB-215

Hrotsvit of Gandersheim circa 935-circa 1000 . . . . DLB-148

Hubbard, Elbert 1856-1915 . . . . DLB-91

Hubbard, Kin 1868-1930 . . . . DLB-11

Hubbard, William circa 1621-1704 . . . . DLB-24

Huber, Therese 1764-1829 . . . . DLB-90

Huch, Friedrich 1873-1913 . . . . DLB-66

Huch, Ricarda 1864-1947 . . . . DLB-66

Huddle, David 1942- DLB-130

Hudgins, Andrew 1951- DLB-120, 282

Hudson, Henry Norman 1814-1886 . . . . . DLB-64

Hudson, Stephen 1868?-1944 . . . . DLB-197

Hudson, W. H. 1841-1922 . . . . . .DLB-98, 153, 174

Hudson and Goodwin DLB-49

Huebsch, B. W., oral history Y-99

B. W. Huebsch [publishing house] DLB-46

Hueffer, Oliver Madox 1876-1931 . . . . . . DLB-197

Huet, Pierre Daniel Preface to *The History of Romances* (1715) DLB-39

Hugh of St. Victor circa 1096-1141 . . . . . DLB-208

Hughes, David 1930- DLB-14

Hughes, Dusty 1947- DLB-233

Hughes, Hatcher 1881-1945 . . . . DLB-249

Hughes, John 1677-1720 . . . . DLB-84

Hughes, Langston 1902-1967 . . . . DLB-4, 7, 48, 51, 86, 228; ; DS-15; CDALB-5

Hughes, Richard 1900-1976 . . . . DLB-15, 161

Hughes, Ted 1930-1998 . . . . DLB-40, 161

Hughes, Thomas 1822-1896 . . . . DLB-18, 163

Hugo, Richard 1923-1982 . . . . DLB-5, 206

Hugo, Victor 1802-1885 . . . . . . .DLB-119, 192, 217

Hugo Awards and Nebula Awards DLB-8

Huidobro, Vicente 1893-1948 . . . . DLB-283

Hull, Richard 1896-1973 . . . . DLB-77

Hulda (Unnur Benediktsdóttir Bjarklind) 1881-1946 . . . . DLB-293

Hulme, T. E. 1883-1917 . . . . DLB-19

Hulton, Anne ?-1779? DLB-200

Humboldt, Alexander von 1769-1859 . . . . DLB-90

Humboldt, Wilhelm von 1767-1835 . . . . . . DLB-90

Hume, David 1711-1776 . . . . DLB-104, 252

Hume, Fergus 1859-1932 . . . . DLB-70

Hume, Sophia 1702-1774 . . . . DLB-200

Hume-Rothery, Mary Catherine 1824-1885 . . . . DLB-240

Humishuma (see Mourning Dove)

Hummer, T. R. 1950- DLB-120

Humor

American Humor: A Historical Survey DLB-11

American Humor Studies Association Y-99

The Comic Tradition Continued [in the British Novel] DLB-15

Humorous Book Illustration DLB-11

International Society for Humor Studies . . Y-99

Newspaper Syndication of American Humor DLB-11

Selected Humorous Magazines (1820-1950) DLB-11

Bruce Humphries [publishing house] DLB-46

Humphrey, Duke of Gloucester 1391-1447 . . . . DLB-213

Humphrey, William 1924-1997 . . . . .DLB-6, 212, 234, 278

Humphreys, David 1752-1818 . . . . DLB-37

Humphreys, Emyr 1919- DLB-15

Humphreys, Josephine 1945- DLB-292

Huncke, Herbert 1915-1996 . . . . DLB-16

Huneker, James Gibbons 1857-1921 . . . . . . DLB-71

Hunold, Christian Friedrich 1681-1721 . . DLB-168

Hunt, Irene 1907- DLB-52

Hunt, Leigh 1784-1859 . . . . .DLB-96, 110, 144

Hunt, Violet 1862-1942 . . . . .DLB-162, 197

Hunt, William Gibbes 1791-1833 . . . . DLB-73

Hunter, Evan 1926- Y-82

Tribute to John D. MacDonald Y-86

Hunter, Jim 1939- DLB-14

Hunter, Kristin 1931- DLB-33

Tribute to Julian Mayfield Y-84

Hunter, Mollie 1922- DLB-161

Hunter, N. C. 1908-1971 . . . . DLB-10

Hunter-Duvar, John 1821-1899 . . . . DLB-99

Huntington, Henry E. 1850-1927 . . . . DLB-140

The Henry E. Huntington Library Y-92

Huntington, Susan Mansfield 1791-1823 . DLB-200

Hurd and Houghton DLB-49

Hurst, Fannie 1889-1968 . . . . DLB-86

Hurst and Blackett DLB-106

Hurst and Company DLB-49

Hurston, Zora Neale 1901?-1960 . . . . DLB-51, 86; CDALB-7

Husserl, Edmund 1859-1938 . . . . DLB-296

Husson, Jules-François-Félix (see Champfleury)

Huston, John 1906-1987 . . . . DLB-26

Hutcheson, Francis 1694-1746 . . . . . . DLB-31, 252

Hutchinson, Ron 1947- DLB-245

Hutchinson, R. C. 1907-1975 . . . . DLB-191

Hutchinson, Thomas 1711-1780 . . . . . . DLB-30, 31

Hutchinson and Company (Publishers) Limited DLB-112

Huth, Angela 1938- DLB-271

Hutton, Richard Holt 1826-1897 . . . . DLB-57

von Hutten, Ulrich 1488-1523 . . . . .DLB-179

Huxley, Aldous 1894-1963 ...... DLB-36, 100, 162, 195, 255; CDBLB-6
Huxley, Elspeth Josceline 1907-1997 .... DLB-77, 204
Huxley, T. H. 1825-1895 .... DLB-57
Huyghue, Douglas Smith 1816-1891 ...... DLB-99
Huysmans, Joris-Karl 1848-1907 .... DLB-123
Hwang, David Henry 1957- DLB-212, 228
Hyde, Donald 1909-1966 .... DLB-187
Hyde, Mary 1912- DLB-187
Hyman, Trina Schart 1939- DLB-61

I

Iavorsky, Stefan 1658-1722 .... DLB-150
Iazykov, Nikolai Mikhailovich 1803-1846 .... DLB-205
Ibáñez, Armando P. 1949- DLB-209
Ibáñez, Sara de 1909-1971 .... DLB-290
Ibarbourou, Juana de 1892-1979 .... DLB-290
Ibn Bajja circa 1077-1138 .... DLB-115
Ibn Gabirol, Solomon circa 1021-circa 1058 .... DLB-115
Ibuse Masuji 1898-1993 .... DLB-180
Ichijō Kanera (see Ichijō Kaneyoshi)
Ichijō Kaneyoshi (Ichijō Kanera) 1402-1481 .... DLB-203
Iffland, August Wilhelm 1759-1814 .... DLB-94
Iggulden, John 1917- DLB-289
Ignatieff, Michael 1947- DLB-267
Ignatow, David 1914-1997 .... DLB-5
Ike, Chukwuemeka 1931- DLB-157
Ikkyū Sōjun 1394-1481 .... DLB-203
Iles, Francis (see Berkeley, Anthony)
Il'f, Il'ia (Il'ia Arnol'dovich Fainzil'berg) 1897-1937 .... DLB-272
Illich, Ivan 1926-2002 .... DLB-242
Illustration
Children's Book Illustration in the Twentieth Century DLB-61
Children's Illustrators, 1800-1880 .... DLB-163
Early American Book Illustration DLB-49
The Iconography of Science-Fiction Art DLB-8
The Illustration of Early German Literary Manuscripts, circa 1150-circa 1300 .... DLB-148
Minor Illustrators, 1880-1914 .... DLB-141
Illyés, Gyula 1902-1983 ..... DLB-215; CDWLB-4
Imbs, Bravig 1904-1946 .... DLB-4; DS-15
Imbuga, Francis D. 1947- DLB-157
Immermann, Karl 1796-1840 .... DLB-133
Inchbald, Elizabeth 1753-1821 .... DLB-39, 89
Indiana University Press Y-02
Ingamells, Rex 1913-1955 .... DLB-260
Inge, William 1913-1973 ... DLB-7, 249; CDALB-1
Ingelow, Jean 1820-1897 .... DLB-35, 163
Ingemann, B. S. 1789-1862 .... DLB-300
Ingersoll, Ralph 1900-1985 .... DLB-127
The Ingersoll Prizes Y-84
Ingoldsby, Thomas (see Barham, Richard Harris)
Ingraham, Joseph Holt 1809-1860 ..... DLB-3, 248
Inman, John 1805-1850 .... DLB-73
Innerhofer, Franz 1944- DLB-85
Innes, Michael (J. I. M. Stewart) 1906-1994 .... DLB-276
Innis, Harold Adams 1894-1952 .... DLB-88
Innis, Mary Quayle 1899-1972 .... DLB-88
Inō Sōgi 1421-1502 .... DLB-203
Inoue Yasushi 1907-1991 .... DLB-182
"The Greatness of Southern Literature": League of the South Institute for the Study of Southern Culture and History Y-02
International Publishers Company DLB-46
Internet (publishing and commerce)
Author Websites Y-97
The Book Trade and the Internet Y-00
E-Books Turn the Corner Y-98
The E-Researcher: Possibilities and Pitfalls Y-00
Interviews on E-publishing Y-00
John Updike on the Internet Y-97
LitCheck Website Y-01
Virtual Books and Enemies of Books Y-00
Interviews
Adoff, Arnold Y-01
Aldridge, John W. Y-91
Anastas, Benjamin Y-98
Baker, Nicholson Y-00
Bank, Melissa Y-98
Bass, T. J. Y-80
Bernstein, Harriet Y-82
Betts, Doris Y-82
Bosworth, David Y-82
Bottoms, David Y-83
Bowers, Fredson Y-80
Burnshaw, Stanley Y-97
Carpenter, Humphrey Y-84, 99
Carr, Virginia Spencer Y-00
Carver, Raymond Y-83
Cherry, Kelly Y-83
Conroy, Jack Y-81
Coppel, Alfred Y-83
Cowley, Malcolm Y-81
Davis, Paxton Y-89
Devito, Carlo Y-94
De Vries, Peter Y-82
Dickey, James Y-82
Donald, David Herbert Y-87
Editors, Conversations with Y-95
Ellroy, James Y-91
Fancher, Betsy Y-83
Faust, Irvin Y-00
Fulton, Len Y-86
Furst, Alan Y-01
Garrett, George Y-83
Gelfman, Jane Y-93
Goldwater, Walter Y-93
Gores, Joe Y-02
Greenfield, George Y-91
Griffin, Bryan Y-81
Groom, Winston Y-01
Guilds, John Caldwell Y-92
Hamilton, Virginia Y-01
Hardin, James Y-92
Harris, Mark Y-80
Harrison, Jim Y-82
Hazzard, Shirley Y-82
Herrick, William Y-01
Higgins, George V. Y-98
Hoban, Russell Y-90
Holroyd, Michael Y-99
Horowitz, Glen Y-90
Iggulden, John Y-01
Jakes, John Y-83
Jenkinson, Edward B. Y-82
Jenks, Tom Y-86
Kaplan, Justin Y-86
King, Florence Y-85
Klopfer, Donald S. Y-97
Krug, Judith Y-82
Lamm, Donald Y-95
Laughlin, James Y-96
Lawrence, Starling Y-95
Lindsay, Jack Y-84
Mailer, Norman Y-97
Manchester, William Y-85
Max, D. T. Y-94
McCormack, Thomas Y-98
McNamara, Katherine Y-97
Mellen, Joan Y-94
Menaker, Daniel Y-97
Mooneyham, Lamarr Y-82
Murray, Les Y-01
Nosworth, David Y-82
O'Connor, Patrick Y-84, 99
Ozick, Cynthia Y-83
Penner, Jonathan Y-83
Pennington, Lee Y-82
Penzler, Otto Y-96
Plimpton, George Y-99
Potok, Chaim Y-84
Powell, Padgett Y-01
Prescott, Peter S. Y-86
Rabe, David Y-91
Rechy, John Y-82

Reid, B. L. Y-83
Reynolds, Michael Y-95, 99
Robinson, Derek Y-02
Rollyson, Carl Y-97
Rosset, Barney Y-02
Schlafly, Phyllis Y-82
Schroeder, Patricia Y-99
Schulberg, Budd Y-81, 01
Scribner, Charles, III Y-94
Sipper, Ralph Y-94
Smith, Cork Y-95
Staley, Thomas F. Y-00
Styron, William Y-80
Talese, Nan Y-94
Thornton, John Y-94
Toth, Susan Allen Y-86
Tyler, Anne Y-82
Vaughan, Samuel Y-97
Von Ogtrop, Kristin Y-92
Wallenstein, Barry Y-92
Weintraub, Stanley Y-82
Williams, J. Chamberlain Y-84
Into the Past: William Jovanovich's Reflections in Publishing Y-02
Ireland, David 1927- DLB-289
The National Library of Ireland's New James Joyce Manuscripts Y-02
Irigaray, Luce 1930- DLB-296
Irving, John 1942- DLB-6, 278; Y-82
Irving, Washington 1783-1859 . . . . DLB-3, 11, 30, 59, 73, 74, 183, 186, 250; CDALB-2
Irwin, Grace 1907- DLB-68
Irwin, Will 1873-1948 . . . . DLB-25
Isaksson, Ulla 1916-2000 . . . . DLB-257
Iser, Wolfgang 1926- DLB-242
Isherwood, Christopher 1904-1986 . . . . DLB-15, 195; Y-86
The Christopher Isherwood Archive, The Huntington Library Y-99
Ishiguro, Kazuo 1954- DLB-194
Ishikawa Jun 1899-1987 . . . . DLB-182
The Island Trees Case: A Symposium on School Library Censorship
An Interview with Judith Krug
An Interview with Phyllis Schlafly
An Interview with Edward B. Jenkinson
An Interview with Lamarr Mooneyham
An Interview with Harriet Bernstein Y-82
Islas, Arturo 1938-1991 . . . . DLB-122
Issit, Debbie 1966- DLB-233
Ivanišević, Drago 1907-1981 . . . . DLB-181
Ivanov, Viacheslav Ivanovich 1866-1949 . . . . DLB-295
Ivanov, Vsevolod Viacheslavovich 1895-1963 . . . . DLB-272
Ivaska, Astrīde 1926- DLB-232
M. J. Ivers and Company DLB-49
Iwaniuk, Wacław 1915- DLB-215
Iwano Hōmei 1873-1920 . . . . DLB-180
Iwaszkiewicz, Jarosłav 1894-1980 . . . . DLB-215
Iyayi, Festus 1947- DLB-157
Izumi Kyōka 1873-1939 . . . . DLB-180

J

Jackmon, Marvin E. (see Marvin X)
Jacks, L. P. 1860-1955 . . . . DLB-135
Jackson, Angela 1951- DLB-41
Jackson, Charles 1903-1968 . . . . DLB-234
Jackson, Helen Hunt 1830-1885 . . . . DLB-42, 47, 186, 189
Jackson, Holbrook 1874-1948 . . . . DLB-98
Jackson, Laura Riding 1901-1991 . . . . DLB-48
Jackson, Shirley 1916-1965 . . . . DLB-6, 234; CDALB-1
Jacob, Max 1876-1944 . . . . DLB-258
Jacob, Naomi 1884?-1964 . . . . DLB-191
Jacob, Piers Anthony Dillingham (see Anthony, Piers)
Jacob, Violet 1863-1946 . . . . DLB-240
Jacobi, Friedrich Heinrich 1743-1819 . . . . . DLB-94
Jacobi, Johann Georg 1740-1841 . . . . DLB-97
George W. Jacobs and Company DLB-49
Jacobs, Harriet 1813-1897 . . . . DLB-239
Jacobs, Joseph 1854-1916 . . . . DLB-141
Jacobs, W. W. 1863-1943 . . . . DLB-135
The W. W. Jacobs Appreciation Society . . Y-98
Jacobsen, J. P. 1847-1885 . . . . DLB-300
Jacobsen, Jørgen-Frantz 1900-1938 . . . . . . DLB-214
Jacobsen, Josephine 1908- DLB-244
Jacobsen, Rolf 1907-1994 . . . . DLB-297
Jacobson, Dan 1929- DLB-14, 207, 225
Jacobson, Howard 1942- DLB-207
Jacques de Vitry circa 1160/1170-1240 . . . DLB-208
Jæger, Frank 1926-1977 . . . . DLB-214
William Jaggard [publishing house] DLB-170
Jahier, Piero 1884-1966 . . . . DLB-114, 264
Jahnn, Hans Henny 1894-1959 . . . . . DLB-56, 124
Jaimes, Freyre, Ricardo 1866?-1933 . . . . . DLB-283
Jakes, John 1932- DLB-278; Y-83
Tribute to John Gardner Y-82
Tribute to John D. MacDonald Y-86
Jakobína Johnson (Jakobína Sigurbjarnardóttir) 1883-1977 . . . . DLB-293
Jakobson, Roman 1896-1982 . . . . DLB-242
James, Alice 1848-1892 . . . . DLB-221
James, C. L. R. 1901-1989 . . . . DLB-125
James, George P. R. 1801-1860 . . . . DLB-116
James, Henry 1843-1916 . . . . . . .DLB-12, 71, 74, 189; DS-13; CDALB-3
"The Future of the Novel" (1899) DLB-18
"The Novel in [Robert Browning's] 'The Ring and the Book'" (1912) DLB-32
James, John circa 1633-1729 . . . . DLB-24
James, M. R. 1862-1936 . . . . DLB-156, 201
James, Naomi 1949- DLB-204
James, P. D. (Phyllis Dorothy James White) 1920- DLB-87, 276; DS-17; CDBLB-8
Tribute to Charles Scribner Jr. Y-95
James, Thomas 1572?-1629 . . . . DLB-213
U. P. James [publishing house] DLB-49
James, Will 1892-1942 . . . . DS-16
James, William 1842-1910 . . . . DLB-270
James VI of Scotland, I of England 1566-1625 . . . . DLB-151, 172
Ane Schort Treatise Conteining Some Revlis and Cautelis to Be Obseruit and Eschewit in Scottis Poesi (1584) DLB-172
Jameson, Anna 1794-1860 . . . . DLB-99, 166
Jameson, Fredric 1934- DLB-67
Jameson, J. Franklin 1859-1937 . . . . DLB-17
Jameson, Storm 1891-1986 . . . . DLB-36
Jančar, Drago 1948- DLB-181
Janés, Clara 1940- DLB-134
Janevski, Slavko 1920- DLB-181; CDWLB-4
Janowitz, Tama 1957- DLB-292
Jansson, Tove 1914-2001 . . . . DLB-257
Janvier, Thomas 1849-1913 . . . . DLB-202
Japan
"The Development of Meiji Japan" . . DLB-180
"Encounter with the West" DLB-180
Japanese Literature
Letter from Japan Y-94, 98
Medieval Travel Diaries DLB-203
Surveys: 1987-1995 . . . . DLB-182
Jaramillo, Cleofas M. 1878-1956 . . . . DLB-122
Jaramillo Levi, Enrique 1944- DLB-290
Jarman, Mark 1952- DLB-120, 282
Jarrell, Randall 1914-1965 . . . . DLB-48, 52; CDALB-1
Jarrold and Sons DLB-106
Jarry, Alfred 1873-1907 . . . . DLB-192, 258
Jarves, James Jackson 1818-1888 . . . . DLB-189
Jasmin, Claude 1930- DLB-60
Jaunsudrabiņš, Jānis 1877-1962 . . . . DLB-220
Jay, John 1745-1829 . . . . DLB-31
Jean de Garlande (see John of Garland)
Jefferies, Richard 1848-1887 . . . . DLB-98, 141
The Richard Jefferies Society Y-98
Jeffers, Lance 1919-1985 . . . . DLB-41
Jeffers, Robinson 1887-1962 . . . . DLB-45, 212; CDALB-4
Jefferson, Thomas 1743-1826 . . . . DLB-31, 183; CDALB-2
Jégé 1866-1940 . . . . DLB-215
Jelinek, Elfriede 1946- DLB-85
Jellicoe, Ann 1927- DLB-13, 233
Jemison, Mary circa 1742-1833 . . . . DLB-239
Jenkins, Dan 1929- DLB-241
Jenkins, Elizabeth 1905- DLB-155

Jenkins, Robin 1912- DLB-14, 271
Jenkins, William Fitzgerald (see Leinster, Murray)
Herbert Jenkins Limited. DLB-112
Jennings, Elizabeth 1926- DLB-27
Jens, Walter 1923- DLB-69
Jensen, Axel 1932-2003 .... DLB-297
Jensen, Johannes V. 1873-1950 .... DLB-214
Jensen, Merrill 1905-1980 .... DLB-17
Jensen, Thit 1876-1957. .... DLB-214
Jephson, Robert 1736-1803 .... DLB-89
Jerome, Jerome K. 1859-1927 .... DLB-10, 34, 135
The Jerome K. Jerome Society Y-98
Jerome, Judson 1927-1991 .... DLB-105
"Reflections: After a Tornado" DLB-105
Jerrold, Douglas 1803-1857 .... DLB-158, 159
Jersild, Per Christian 1935- DLB-257
Jesse, F. Tennyson 1888-1958 .... DLB-77
Jewel, John 1522-1571 .... DLB-236
John P. Jewett and Company. DLB-49
Jewett, Sarah Orne 1849-1909 .... DLB-12, 74, 221
The Jewish Publication Society DLB-49
Studies in American Jewish Literature Y-02
Jewitt, John Rodgers 1783-1821. .... DLB-99
Jewsbury, Geraldine 1812-1880. .... DLB-21
Jewsbury, Maria Jane 1800-1833 .... DLB-199
Jhabvala, Ruth Prawer 1927- DLB-139, 194
Jiménez, Juan Ramón 1881-1958. .... DLB-134
Jin, Ha 1956- DLB-244, 292
Joans, Ted 1928- DLB-16, 41
Jōha 1525-1602 .... DLB-203
Jóhann Sigurjónsson 1880-1919. .... DLB-293
Jóhannes úr Kötlum 1899-1972 .... DLB-293
Johannis de Garlandia (see John of Garland)
John, Errol 1924-1988 .... DLB-233
John, Eugenie (see Marlitt, E.)
John of Dumbleton circa 1310-circa 1349. .... DLB-115
John of Garland (Jean de Garlande, Johannis de Garlandia) circa 1195-circa 1272. .... DLB-208
Johns, Captain W. E. 1893-1968 .... DLB-160
Johnson, Mrs. A. E. ca. 1858-1922 ...... DLB-221
Johnson, Amelia (see Johnson, Mrs. A. E.)
Johnson, B. S. 1933-1973 .... DLB-14, 40
Johnson, Charles 1679-1748. .... DLB-84
Johnson, Charles 1948- DLB-33, 278
Johnson, Charles S. 1893-1956 .... DLB-51, 91
Johnson, Colin (Mudrooroo) 1938- DLB-289
Johnson, Denis 1949- DLB-120
Johnson, Diane 1934- Y-80
Johnson, Dorothy M. 1905–1984 .... DLB-206
Johnson, E. Pauline (Tekahionwake) 1861-1913 .... DLB-175
Johnson, Edgar 1901-1995. .... DLB-103
Johnson, Edward 1598-1672 .... DLB-24
Johnson, Eyvind 1900-1976 .... DLB-259
Johnson, Fenton 1888-1958 .... DLB-45, 50
Johnson, Georgia Douglas 1877?-1966 .... DLB-51, 249
Johnson, Gerald W. 1890-1980 .... DLB-29
Johnson, Greg 1953- DLB-234
Johnson, Helene 1907-1995 .... DLB-51
Jacob Johnson and Company DLB-49
Johnson, James Weldon 1871-1938 .... DLB-51; CDALB-4
Johnson, John H. 1918- DLB-137
"Backstage," Statement From the Initial Issue of *Ebony* (November 1945. .... DLB-137
Johnson, Joseph [publishing house] DLB-154
Johnson, Linton Kwesi 1952- DLB-157
Johnson, Lionel 1867-1902. .... DLB-19
Johnson, Nunnally 1897-1977 .... DLB-26
Johnson, Owen 1878-1952. .... Y-87
Johnson, Pamela Hansford 1912-1981. .... DLB-15
Johnson, Pauline 1861-1913. .... DLB-92
Johnson, Ronald 1935-1998. .... DLB-169
Johnson, Samuel 1696-1772 ... DLB-24; CDBLB-2
Johnson, Samuel 1709-1784 .... DLB-39, 95, 104, 142, 213
Rambler, no. 4 (1750) [excerpt] DLB-39
The BBC Four Samuel Johnson Prize for Non-fiction. Y-02
Johnson, Samuel 1822-1882. .... DLB-1, 243
Johnson, Susanna 1730-1810 .... DLB-200
Johnson, Terry 1955- DLB-233
Johnson, Uwe 1934-1984. .... DLB-75; CDWLB-2
Benjamin Johnson [publishing house] DLB-49
Benjamin, Jacob, and Robert Johnson [publishing house] DLB-49
Johnston, Annie Fellows 1863-1931. ...... DLB-42
Johnston, Basil H. 1929- DLB-60
Johnston, David Claypole 1798?-1865. ... DLB-188
Johnston, Denis 1901-1984 .... DLB-10
Johnston, Ellen 1835-1873 .... DLB-199
Johnston, George 1912-1970 .... DLB-260
Johnston, George 1913- DLB-88
Johnston, Sir Harry 1858-1927 .... DLB-174
Johnston, Jennifer 1930- DLB-14
Johnston, Mary 1870-1936. .... DLB-9
Johnston, Richard Malcolm 1822-1898 .... DLB-74
Johnstone, Charles 1719?-1800? DLB-39
Johst, Hanns 1890-1978 .... DLB-124
Jökull Jakobsson 1933-1978 .... DLB-293
Jolas, Eugene 1894-1952 .... DLB-4, 45
Jón Stefán Sveinsson or Svensson (see Nonni)
Jón Trausti (Guðmundur Magnússon) 1873-1918 .... DLB-293
Jón úr Vör (Jón Jónsson) 1917-2000 ..... DLB-293
Jónas Hallgrímsson 1807-1845. .... DLB-293
Jones, Alice C. 1853-1933 .... DLB-92
Jones, Charles C., Jr. 1831-1893 .... DLB-30
Jones, D. G. 1929- DLB-53
Jones, David 1895-1974 .... DLB-20, 100; CDBLB-7
Jones, Diana Wynne 1934- DLB-161
Jones, Ebenezer 1820-1860 .... DLB-32
Jones, Ernest 1819-1868. .... DLB-32
Jones, Gayl 1949- DLB-33, 278
Jones, George 1800-1870 .... DLB-183
Jones, Glyn 1905-1995. .... DLB-15
Jones, Gwyn 1907- DLB-15, 139
Jones, Henry Arthur 1851-1929 .... DLB-10
Jones, Hugh circa 1692-1760 .... DLB-24
Jones, James 1921-1977 .... DLB-2, 143; DS-17
James Jones Papers in the Handy Writers' Colony Collection at the University of Illinois at Springfield Y-98
The James Jones Society Y-92
Jones, Jenkin Lloyd 1911- DLB-127
Jones, John Beauchamp 1810-1866 ...... DLB-202
Jones, Joseph, Major (see Thompson, William Tappan)
Jones, LeRoi (see Baraka, Amiri)
Jones, Lewis 1897-1939 .... DLB-15
Jones, Madison 1925- DLB-152
Jones, Marie 1951- DLB-233
Jones, Preston 1936-1979. .... DLB-7
Jones, Rodney 1950- DLB-120
Jones, Thom 1945- DLB-244
Jones, Sir William 1746-1794 .... DLB-109
Jones, William Alfred 1817-1900 .... DLB-59
Jones's Publishing House. DLB-49
Jong, Erica 1942- DLB-2, 5, 28, 152
Jonke, Gert F. 1946- DLB-85
Jonson, Ben 1572?-1637 .... DLB-62, 121; CDBLB-1
Johsson, Tor 1916-1951. .... DLB-297
Jordan, June 1936- DLB-38
Jorgensen, Johannes 1866-1956 .... DLB-300
Joseph, Jenny 1932- DLB-40
Joseph and George. Y-99
Michael Joseph Limited DLB-112
Josephson, Matthew 1899-1978 .... DLB-4
Josephus, Flavius 37-100. .... DLB-176
Josephy, Alvin M., Jr. Tribute to Alfred A. Knopf. Y-84
Josiah Allen's Wife (see Holley, Marietta)
Josipovici, Gabriel 1940- DLB-14
Josselyn, John ?-1675 .... DLB-24
Joudry, Patricia 1921-2000 .... DLB-88
Jouve, Pierre Jean 1887-1976 .... DLB-258
Jovanovich, William 1920-2001. .... Y-01
Into the Past: William Jovanovich's Reflections on Publishing Y-02
[Response to Ken Auletta]. Y-97
The Temper of the West: William Jovanovich Y-02

Tribute to Charles Scribner Jr. Y-95
Jovine, Francesco 1902-1950 . . . . DLB-264
Jovine, Giuseppe 1922- DLB-128
Joyaux, Philippe (see Sollers, Philippe)
Joyce, Adrien (see Eastman, Carol)
Joyce, James 1882-1941 . . . . DLB-10, 19, 36, 162, 247; CDBLB-6
Danis Rose and the Rendering of *Ulysses* . . Y-97
James Joyce Centenary: Dublin, 1982 . . . . Y-82
James Joyce Conference Y-85
A Joyce (Con)Text: Danis Rose and the Remaking of *Ulysses* Y-97
The National Library of Ireland's New James Joyce Manuscripts Y-02
The New *Ulysses* Y-84
Public Domain and the Violation of Texts Y-97
The Quinn Draft of James Joyce's Circe Manuscript Y-00
Stephen Joyce's Letter to the Editor of *The Irish Times* Y-97
Ulysses, Reader's Edition: First Reactions . . Y-97
We See the Editor at Work Y-97
Whose *Ulysses?* The Function of Editing . . Y-97
Jozsef, Attila 1905-1937 . . . . . DLB-215; CDWLB-4
Juarroz, Roberto 1925-1995 . . . . DLB-283
Orange Judd Publishing Company DLB-49
Judd, Sylvester 1813-1853 . . . . DLB-1, 243
Judith circa 930 . . . . DLB-146
Juel-Hansen, Erna 1845-1922 . . . . DLB-300
Julian of Norwich 1342-circa 1420 . . . . . DLB-1146
Julius Caesar 100 B.C.-44 B.C. DLB-211; CDWLB-1
June, Jennie (see Croly, Jane Cunningham)
Jung, Carl Gustav 1875-1961 . . . . DLB-296
Jung, Franz 1888-1963 . . . . DLB-118
Jünger, Ernst 1895- DLB-56; CDWLB-2
Der jüngere Titurel circa 1275 . . . . DLB-138
Jung-Stilling, Johann Heinrich 1740-1817 . . . . DLB-94
Junqueiro, Abílio Manuel Guerra 1850-1923 . . . . DLB-287
Justice, Donald 1925- Y-83
Juvenal circa A.D. 60-circa A.D. 130 . . . . DLB-211; CDWLB-1
The Juvenile Library (see M. J. Godwin and Company)

K

Kacew, Romain (see Gary, Romain)
Kafka, Franz 1883-1924 . . . . . DLB-81; CDWLB-2
Kahn, Gus 1886-1941 . . . . DLB-265
Kahn, Roger 1927- DLB-171
Kaikō Takeshi 1939-1989 . . . . DLB-182
Káinn (Kristján Níels Jónsson/Kristjan Niels Julius) 1860-1936 . . . . DLB-293
Kaiser, Georg 1878-1945 . . . . DLB-124; CDWLB-2
Kaiserchronik circa 1147 . . . . DLB-148
Kaleb, Vjekoslav 1905- DLB-181
Kalechofsky, Roberta 1931- DLB-28
Kaler, James Otis 1848-1912 . . . . DLB-12, 42
Kalmar, Bert 1884-1947 . . . . DLB-265
Kamensky, Vasilii Vasil'evich 1884-1961 . . . . DLB-295
Kames, Henry Home, Lord 1696-1782 . . . . DLB-31, 104
Kamo no Chōmei (Kamo no Nagaakira) 1153 or 1155-1216 . . . . DLB-203
Kamo no Nagaakira (see Kamo no Chōmei)
Kampmann, Christian 1939-1988 . . . . DLB-214
Kandel, Lenore 1932- DLB-16
Kanin, Garson 1912-1999 . . . . DLB-7
A Tribute (to Marc Connelly) Y-80
Kaniuk, Yoram 1930- DLB-299
Kant, Hermann 1926- DLB-75
Kant, Immanuel 1724-1804 . . . . DLB-94
Kantemir, Antiokh Dmitrievich 1708-1744 . . . . DLB-150
Kantor, MacKinlay 1904-1977 . . . . DLB-9, 102
Kanze Kōjirō Nobumitsu 1435-1516 . . . . DLB-203
Kanze Motokiyo (see Zeimi)
Kaplan, Fred 1937- DLB-111
Kaplan, Johanna 1942- DLB-28
Kaplan, Justin 1925- DLB-111; Y-86
Kaplinski, Jaan 1941- DLB-232
Kapnist, Vasilii Vasilevich 1758?-1823 . . . DLB-150
Karadžić, Vuk Stefanović 1787-1864 . . . . DLB-147; CDWLB-4
Karamzin, Nikolai Mikhailovich 1766-1826 . . . . DLB-150
Karinthy, Frigyes 1887-1938 . . . . DLB-215
Karmel, Ilona 1925-2000 . . . . DLB-299
Karsch, Anna Louisa 1722-1791 . . . . DLB-97
Kasack, Hermann 1896-1966 . . . . DLB-69
Kasai Zenzō 1887-1927 . . . . DLB-180
Kaschnitz, Marie Luise 1901-1974 . . . . DLB-69
Kassák, Lajos 1887-1967 . . . . DLB-215
Kaštelan, Jure 1919-1990 . . . . DLB-147
Kästner, Erich 1899-1974 . . . . DLB-56
Kataev, Evgenii Petrovich (see Il'f, Il'ia and Petrov, Evgenii)
Kataev, Valentin Petrovich 1897-1986 . . . . DLB-272
Katenin, Pavel Aleksandrovich 1792-1853 . . . . DLB-205
Kattan, Naim 1928- DLB-53
Katz, Steve 1935- Y-83
Ka-Tzetnik 135633 (Yehiel Dinur) 1909-2001 . . . . DLB-299
Kauffman, Janet 1945- DLB-218; Y-86
Kauffmann, Samuel 1898-1971 . . . . DLB-127
Kaufman, Bob 1925-1986 . . . . DLB-16, 41
Kaufman, George S. 1889-1961 . . . . DLB-7
Kaufmann, Walter 1921-1980 . . . . DLB-279
Kavan, Anna (Helen Woods Ferguson Edmonds) 1901-1968 . . . . DLB-255
Kavanagh, P. J. 1931- DLB-40
Kavanagh, Patrick 1904-1967 . . . . DLB-15, 20
Kaverin, Veniamin Aleksandrovich (Veniamin Aleksandrovich Zil'ber) 1902-1989 . . . . DLB-272
Kawabata Yasunari 1899-1972 . . . . DLB-180
Kay, Guy Gavriel 1954- DLB-251
Kaye-Smith, Sheila 1887-1956 . . . . DLB-36
Kazin, Alfred 1915-1998 . . . . DLB-67
Keane, John B. 1928- DLB-13
Keary, Annie 1825-1879 . . . . DLB-163
Keary, Eliza 1827-1918 . . . . DLB-240
Keating, H. R. F. 1926- DLB-87
Keatley, Charlotte 1960- DLB-245
Keats, Ezra Jack 1916-1983 . . . . DLB-61
Keats, John 1795-1821 . . . DLB-96, 110; CDBLB-3
Keble, John 1792-1866 . . . . DLB-32, 55
Keckley, Elizabeth 1818?-1907 . . . . DLB-239
Keeble, John 1944- Y-83
Keeffe, Barrie 1945- DLB-13, 245
Keeley, James 1867-1934 . . . . DLB-25
W. B. Keen, Cooke and Company DLB-49
The Mystery of Carolyn Keene Y-02
Kefala, Antigone 1935- DLB-289
Keillor, Garrison 1942- Y-87
Keith, Marian (Mary Esther MacGregor) 1874?-1961 . . . . DLB-92
Keller, Gary D. 1943- DLB-82
Keller, Gottfried 1819-1890 . . . . DLB-129; CDWLB-2
Kelley, Edith Summers 1884-1956 . . . . DLB-9
Kelley, Emma Dunham ?-? DLB-221
Kelley, William Melvin 1937- DLB-33
Kellogg, Ansel Nash 1832-1886 . . . . DLB-23
Kellogg, Steven 1941- DLB-61
Kelly, George E. 1887-1974 . . . . DLB-7, 249
Kelly, Hugh 1739-1777 . . . . DLB-89
Kelly, Piet and Company DLB-49
Kelly, Robert 1935- DLB-5, 130, 165
Kelman, James 1946- DLB-194
Kelmscott Press DLB-112
Kelton, Elmer 1926- DLB-256
Kemble, E. W. 1861-1933 . . . . DLB-188
Kemble, Fanny 1809-1893 . . . . DLB-32
Kemelman, Harry 1908-1996 . . . . DLB-28
Kempe, Margery circa 1373-1438 . . . . DLB-146
Kempner, Friederike 1836-1904 . . . . DLB-129
Kempowski, Walter 1929- DLB-75
Kenan, Randall 1963- DLB-292
Claude Kendall [publishing company] DLB-46
Kendall, Henry 1839-1882 . . . . DLB-230
Kendall, May 1861-1943 . . . . DLB-240
Kendell, George 1809-1867 . . . . DLB-43
Keneally, Thomas 1935- DLB-289, 299

Kenedy, P. J., and Sons DLB-49
Kenkō circa 1283-circa 1352 . . . . DLB-203
Kenna, Peter 1930-1987 . . . . DLB-289
Kennan, George 1845-1924 . . . . DLB-189
Kennedy, A. L. 1965- DLB-271
Kennedy, Adrienne 1931- DLB-38
Kennedy, John Pendleton 1795-1870 . . . DLB-3, 248
Kennedy, Leo 1907-2000 . . . . DLB-88
Kennedy, Margaret 1896-1967 . . . . DLB-36
Kennedy, Patrick 1801-1873 . . . . DLB-159
Kennedy, Richard S. 1920- DLB-111; Y-02
Kennedy, William 1928- DLB-143; Y-85
Kennedy, X. J. 1929- DLB-5
Tribute to John Ciardi Y-86
Kennelly, Brendan 1936- DLB-40
Kenner, Hugh 1923- DLB-67
Tribute to Cleanth Brooks Y-80
Mitchell Kennerley [publishing house] DLB-46
Kenny, Maurice 1929- DLB-175
Kent, Frank R. 1877-1958 . . . . DLB-29
Kenyon, Jane 1947-1995 . . . . DLB-120
Kenzheev, Bakhyt Shkurullaevich 1950- DLB-285
Keough, Hugh Edmund 1864-1912 . . . . . . DLB-171
Keppler and Schwartzmann DLB-49
Ker, John, third Duke of Roxburghe 1740-1804 . . . . DLB-213
Ker, N. R. 1908-1982 . . . . DLB-201
Kerlan, Irvin 1912-1963 . . . . DLB-187
Kermode, Frank 1919- DLB-242
Kern, Jerome 1885-1945 . . . . DLB-187
Kernaghan, Eileen 1939- DLB-251
Kerner, Justinus 1786-1862 . . . . DLB-90
Kerouac, Jack 1922-1969 . . . DLB-2, 16, 237; DS-3; CDALB-1
Auction of Jack Kerouac's *On the Road* Scroll Y-01
The Jack Kerouac Revival Y-95
"Re-meeting of Old Friends": The Jack Kerouac Conference Y-82
Statement of Correction to "The Jack Kerouac Revival" Y-96
Kerouac, Jan 1952-1996 . . . . DLB-16
Charles H. Kerr and Company DLB-49
Kerr, Orpheus C. (see Newell, Robert Henry)
Kersh, Gerald 1911-1968 . . . . DLB-255
Kertész, Imre DLB-299; Y-02
Kesey, Ken 1935-2001 . . . . DLB-2, 16, 206; CDALB-6
Kessel, Joseph 1898-1979 . . . . DLB-72
Kessel, Martin 1901-1990 . . . . DLB-56
Kesten, Hermann 1900-1996 . . . . DLB-56
Keun, Irmgard 1905-1982 . . . . DLB-69
Key, Ellen 1849-1926 . . . . DLB-259
Key and Biddle DLB-49
Keynes, Sir Geoffrey 1887-1982 . . . . DLB-201
Keynes, John Maynard 1883-1946 . . . . DS-10
Keyserling, Eduard von 1855-1918 . . . . DLB-66
Khan, Ismith 1925-2002 . . . . DLB-125
Kharitonov, Evgenii Vladimirovich 1941-1981 . . . . DLB-285
Kharitonov, Mark Sergeevich 1937- DLB-285
Khaytov, Nikolay 1919- DLB-181
Khemnitser, Ivan Ivanovich 1745-1784 . . . . DLB-150
Kheraskov, Mikhail Matveevich 1733-1807 . . . . DLB-150
Khlebnikov, Velimir 1885-1922 . . . . DLB-295
Khomiakov, Aleksei Stepanovich 1804-1860 . . . . DLB-205
Khristov, Boris 1945- DLB-181
Khvoshchinskaia, Nadezhda Dmitrievna 1824-1889 . . . . DLB-238
Khvostov, Dmitrii Ivanovich 1757-1835 . . . . DLB-150
Kibirov, Timur Iur'evich (Timur Iur'evich Zapoev) 1955- DLB-285
Kidd, Adam 1802?-1831 . . . . DLB-99
William Kidd [publishing house] DLB-106
Kidde, Harald 1878-1918 . . . . DLB-300
Kidder, Tracy 1945- DLB-185
Kiely, Benedict 1919- DLB-15
Kieran, John 1892-1981 . . . . DLB-171
Kierkegaard, Søren 1813-1855 . . . . DLB-300
Kies, Marietta 1853-1899 . . . . DLB-270
Kiggins and Kellogg DLB-49
Kiley, Jed 1889-1962 . . . . DLB-4
Kilgore, Bernard 1908-1967 . . . . DLB-127
Kilian, Crawford 1941- DLB-251
Killens, John Oliver 1916-1987 . . . . DLB-33
Tribute to Julian Mayfield Y-84
Killigrew, Anne 1660-1685 . . . . DLB-131
Killigrew, Thomas 1612-1683 . . . . DLB-58
Kilmer, Joyce 1886-1918 . . . . DLB-45
Kilroy, Thomas 1934- DLB-233
Kilwardby, Robert circa 1215-1279 . . . . . . DLB-115
Kilworth, Garry 1941- DLB-261
Kim, Anatolii Andreevich 1939- DLB-285
Kimball, Richard Burleigh 1816-1892 . . . . DLB-202
Kincaid, Jamaica 1949- DLB-157, 227; CDALB-7; CDWLB-3
Kinck, Hans Ernst 1865-1926 . . . . DLB-297
King, Charles 1844-1933 . . . . DLB-186
King, Clarence 1842-1901 . . . . DLB-12
King, Florence 1936- Y-85
King, Francis 1923- DLB-15, 139
King, Grace 1852-1932 . . . . DLB-12, 78
King, Harriet Hamilton 1840-1920 . . . . . . DLB-199
King, Henry 1592-1669 . . . . DLB-126
Solomon King [publishing house] DLB-49
King, Stephen 1947- DLB-143; Y-80
King, Susan Petigru 1824-1875 . . . . DLB-239
King, Thomas 1943- DLB-175
King, Woodie, Jr. 1937- DLB-38
Kinglake, Alexander William 1809-1891 . . . . DLB-55, 166
Kingo, Thomas 1634-1703 . . . . DLB-300
Kingsbury, Donald 1929- DLB-251
Kingsley, Charles 1819-1875 . . . . DLB-21, 32, 163, 178, 190
Kingsley, Henry 1830-1876 . . . . DLB-21, 230
Kingsley, Mary Henrietta 1862-1900 . . . . . DLB-174
Kingsley, Sidney 1906-1995 . . . . DLB-7
Kingsmill, Hugh 1889-1949 . . . . DLB-149
Kingsolver, Barbara 1955- DLB-206; CDALB-7
Kingston, Maxine Hong 1940- DLB-173, 212; Y-80; CDALB-7
Kingston, William Henry Giles 1814-1880 . . . . DLB-163
Kinnan, Mary Lewis 1763-1848 . . . . DLB-200
Kinnell, Galway 1927- DLB-5; Y-87
Kinsella, Thomas 1928- DLB-27
Kipling, Rudyard 1865-1936 . . . . DLB-19, 34, 141, 156; CDBLB-5
Kipphardt, Heinar 1922-1982 . . . . DLB-124
Kirby, William 1817-1906 . . . . DLB-99
Kircher, Athanasius 1602-1680 . . . . DLB-164
Kireevsky, Ivan Vasil'evich 1806-1856 . . . DLB-198
Kireevsky, Petr Vasil'evich 1808-1856 . . . DLB-205
Kirk, Hans 1898-1962 . . . . DLB-214
Kirk, John Foster 1824-1904 . . . . DLB-79
Kirkconnell, Watson 1895-1977 . . . . DLB-68
Kirkland, Caroline M. 1801-1864 . . . . DLB-3, 73, 74, 250; DS-13
Kirkland, Joseph 1830-1893 . . . . DLB-12
Francis Kirkman [publishing house] DLB-170
Kirkpatrick, Clayton 1915- DLB-127
Kirkup, James 1918- DLB-27
Kirouac, Conrad (see Marie-Victorin, Frère)
Kirsch, Sarah 1935- DLB-75
Kirst, Hans Hellmut 1914-1989 . . . . DLB-69
Kiš, Danilo 1935-1989 . . . . . . DLB-181; CDWLB-4
Kita Morio 1927- DLB-182
Kitcat, Mabel Greenhow 1859-1922 . . . . . DLB-135
Kitchin, C. H. B. 1895-1967 . . . . DLB-77
Kittredge, William 1932- DLB-212, 244
Kiukhel'beker, Vil'gel'm Karlovich 1797-1846 . . . . DLB-205
Kizer, Carolyn 1925- DLB-5, 169
Kjaerstad, Jan 1953- DLB-297
Klabund 1890-1928 . . . . DLB-66
Klaj, Johann 1616-1656 . . . . DLB-164
Klappert, Peter 1942- DLB-5
Klass, Philip (see Tenn, William)
Klein, A. M. 1909-1972 . . . . DLB-68
Kleist, Ewald von 1715-1759 . . . . DLB-97
Kleist, Heinrich von 1777-1811 . . . . DLB-90; CDWLB-2
Klíma, Ivan 1931- DLB-232; CDWLB-4

Klimentev, Andrei Platonovic (see Platonov, Andrei Platonovich)

Klinger, Friedrich Maximilian 1752-1831 . . . . DLB-94

Kliuev, Nikolai Alekseevich 1884-1937 . . DLB-295

Kliushnikov, Viktor Petrovich 1841-1892 . . . . DLB-238

Klopfer, Donald S. Impressions of William Faulkner Y-97

Oral History Interview with Donald S. Klopfer Y-97

Tribute to Alfred A. Knopf Y-84

Klopstock, Friedrich Gottlieb 1724-1803 . . . . DLB-97

Klopstock, Meta 1728-1758 . . . . DLB-97

Kluge, Alexander 1932- DLB-75

Kluge, P. F. 1942- Y-02

Knapp, Joseph Palmer 1864-1951 . . . . DLB-91

Knapp, Samuel Lorenzo 1783-1838 . . . . . . DLB-59

J. J. and P. Knapton [publishing house] . . DLB-154

Kniazhnin, Iakov Borisovich 1740-1791 . . DLB-150

Knickerbocker, Diedrich (see Irving, Washington)

Knigge, Adolph Franz Friedrich Ludwig, Freiherr von 1752-1796 . . . . DLB-94

Charles Knight and Company DLB-106

Knight, Damon 1922-2002 . . . . DLB-8

Knight, Etheridge 1931-1992 . . . . DLB-41

Knight, John S. 1894-1981 . . . . DLB-29

Knight, Sarah Kemble 1666-1727 . . . . DLB-24, 200

Knight-Bruce, G. W. H. 1852-1896 . . . . . .DLB-174

Knister, Raymond 1899-1932 . . . . DLB-68

Knoblock, Edward 1874-1945 . . . . DLB-10

Knopf, Alfred A. 1892-1984 . . . . Y-84

Knopf to Hammett: The Editoral Correspondence Y-00

Alfred A. Knopf [publishing house] DLB-46

Knorr von Rosenroth, Christian 1636-1689 . . . . DLB-168

Knowles, John 1926- DLB-6; CDALB-6

Knox, Frank 1874-1944 . . . . DLB-29

Knox, John circa 1514-1572 . . . . DLB-132

Knox, John Armoy 1850-1906 . . . . DLB-23

Knox, Lucy 1845-1884 . . . . DLB-240

Knox, Ronald Arbuthnott 1888-1957 . . . . . DLB-77

Knox, Thomas Wallace 1835-1896 . . . . . DLB-189

Knudsen, Jakob 1858-1917 . . . . DLB-300

Kobayashi Takiji 1903-1933 . . . . DLB-180

Kober, Arthur 1900-1975 . . . . DLB-11

Kobiakova, Aleksandra Petrovna 1823-1892 . . . . DLB-238

Kocbek, Edvard 1904-1981 . .DLB-147; CDWLB-4

Koch, C. J. 1932- DLB-289

Koch, Howard 1902-1995 . . . . DLB-26

Koch, Kenneth 1925-2002 . . . . DLB-5

Kōda Rohan 1867-1947 . . . . DLB-180

Koehler, Ted 1894-1973 . . . . DLB-265

Koenigsberg, Moses 1879-1945 . . . . DLB-25

Koeppen, Wolfgang 1906-1996 . . . . DLB-69

Koertge, Ronald 1940- DLB-105

Koestler, Arthur 1905-1983 . . . . . . Y-83; CDBLB-7

Kohn, John S. Van E. 1906-1976 . . . . DLB-187

Kokhanovskaia (see Sokhanskaia, Nadezhda Stepanova)

Kokoschka, Oskar 1886-1980 . . . . DLB-124

Kolb, Annette 1870-1967 . . . . DLB-66

Kolbenheyer, Erwin Guido 1878-1962 . . . . DLB-66, 124

Kolleritsch, Alfred 1931- DLB-85

Kolodny, Annette 1941- DLB-67

Kol'tsov, Aleksei Vasil'evich 1809-1842 . . DLB-205

Komarov, Matvei circa 1730-1812 . . . . . . DLB-150

Komroff, Manuel 1890-1974 . . . . DLB-4

Komunyakaa, Yusef 1947- DLB-120

Kondoleon, Harry 1955-1994 . . . . DLB-266

Koneski, Blaže 1921-1993 . . . DLB-181; CDWLB-4

Konigsburg, E. L. 1930- DLB-52

Konparu Zenchiku 1405-1468? DLB-203

Konrád, György 1933- DLB-232; CDWLB-4

Konrad von Würzburg circa 1230-1287 . . DLB-138

Konstantinov, Aleko 1863-1897 . . . . DLB-147

Konwicki, Tadeusz 1926- DLB-232

Koontz, Dean 1945- DLB-292

Kooser, Ted 1939- DLB-105

Kopit, Arthur 1937- DLB-7

Kops, Bernard 1926?- DLB-13

Kornbluth, C. M. 1923-1958 . . . . DLB-8

Körner, Theodor 1791-1813 . . . . DLB-90

Kornfeld, Paul 1889-1942 . . . . DLB-118

Korolenko, Vladimir Galaktionovich 1853-1921 . . . . DLB-277

Kosinski, Jerzy 1933-1991 . . . . . .DLB-2, 299; Y-82

Kosmač, Ciril 1910-1980 . . . . DLB-181

Kosovel, Srečko 1904-1926 . . . . DLB-147

Kostrov, Ermil Ivanovich 1755-1796 . . . . . DLB-150

Kotzebue, August von 1761-1819 . . . . DLB-94

Kotzwinkle, William 1938- DLB-173

Kovačić, Ante 1854-1889 . . . . DLB-147

Kovalevskaia, Sof'ia Vasil'evna 1850-1891 . . . . DLB-277

Kovič, Kajetan 1931- DLB-181

Kozlov, Ivan Ivanovich 1779-1840 . . . . . . DLB-205

Kracauer, Siegfried 1889-1966 . . . . DLB-296

Kraf, Elaine 1946- Y-81

Kramer, Jane 1938- DLB-185

Kramer, Larry 1935- DLB-249

Kramer, Mark 1944- DLB-185

Kranjčević, Silvije Strahimir 1865-1908 . . DLB-147

Krasko, Ivan 1876-1958 . . . . DLB-215

Krasna, Norman 1909-1984 . . . . DLB-26

Kraus, Hans Peter 1907-1988 . . . . DLB-187

Kraus, Karl 1874-1936 . . . . DLB-118

Krause, Herbert 1905-1976 . . . . DLB-256

Krauss, Ruth 1911-1993 . . . . DLB-52

Kreisel, Henry 1922-1991 . . . . DLB-88

Krestovsky V. (see Khvoshchinskaia, Nadezhda Dmitrievna)

Krestovsky, Vsevolod Vladimirovich 1839-1895 . . . . DLB-238

Kreuder, Ernst 1903-1972 . . . . DLB-69

Krėvė-Mickevičius, Vincas 1882-1954 . . . DLB-220

Kreymborg, Alfred 1883-1966 . . . . DLB-4, 54

Krieger, Murray 1923- DLB-67

Krim, Seymour 1922-1989 . . . . DLB-16

Kripke, Saul 1940- DLB-279

Kristensen, Tom 1893-1974 . . . . DLB-214

Kristeva, Julia 1941- DLB-242

Kristján Níels Jónsson/Kristjan Niels Julius (see Káinn)

Kritzer, Hyman W. 1918-2002 . . . . Y-02

Krivulin, Viktor Borisovich 1944-2001 . . DLB-285

Krleža, Miroslav 1893-1981 . . . . .DLB-147; CDWLB-4

Krock, Arthur 1886-1974 . . . . DLB-29

Kroetsch, Robert 1927- DLB-53

Kropotkin, Petr Alekseevich 1842-1921 . . .DLB-277

Kross, Jaan 1920- DLB-232

Kruchenykh, Aleksei Eliseevich 1886-1968 . . . . DLB-295

Krúdy, Gyula 1878-1933 . . . . DLB-215

Krutch, Joseph Wood 1893-1970 . . . . .DLB-63, 206, 275

Krylov, Ivan Andreevich 1769-1844 . . . . . DLB-150

Krymov, Iurii Solomonovich (Iurii Solomonovich Beklemishev) 1908-1941 . . . . .DLB-272

Kubin, Alfred 1877-1959 . . . . DLB-81

Kubrick, Stanley 1928-1999 . . . . DLB-26

Kudrun circa 1230-1240 . . . . DLB-138

Kuffstein, Hans Ludwig von 1582-1656 . . DLB-164

Kuhlmann, Quirinus 1651-1689 . . . . DLB-168

Kuhn, Thomas S. 1922-1996 . . . . .DLB-279

Kuhnau, Johann 1660-1722 . . . . DLB-168

Kukol'nik, Nestor Vasil'evich 1809-1868 . . . . DLB-205

Kukučín, Martin 1860-1928 . . . . .DLB-215; CDWLB-4

Kumin, Maxine 1925- DLB-5

Kuncewicz, Maria 1895-1989 . . . . DLB-215

Kundera, Milan 1929- DLB-232; CDWLB-4

Kunene, Mazisi 1930- DLB-117

Kunikida Doppo 1869-1908 . . . . DLB-180

Kunitz, Stanley 1905- DLB-48

Kunjufu, Johari M. (see Amini, Johari M.)

Kunnert, Gunter 1929- DLB-75

Kunze, Reiner 1933- DLB-75

Kupferberg, Tuli 1923- DLB-16

Kuprin, Aleksandr Ivanovich 1870-1938 . . . . DLB-295

Kuraev, Mikhail Nikolaevich 1939- . . . DLB-285

Kurahashi Yumiko 1935- DLB-182

Kureishi, Hanif 1954- DLB-194, 245
Kürnberger, Ferdinand 1821-1879 . . . . . . .DLB-129
Kurz, Isolde 1853-1944 . . . . .DLB-66
Kusenberg, Kurt 1904-1983. . . . . .DLB-69
Kushchevsky, Ivan Afanas'evich 1847-1876. . . . . .DLB-238
Kushner, Tony 1956- DLB-228
Kuttner, Henry 1915-1958. . . . . .DLB-8
Kuzmin, Mikhail Alekseevich 1872-1936 . . . . .DLB-295
Kuznetsov, Anatoli 1929-1979 . . . . .DLB-299
Kyd, Thomas 1558-1594. . . . . .DLB-62
Kyffin, Maurice circa 1560?-1598 . . . . . . .DLB-136
Kyger, Joanne 1934- DLB-16
Kyne, Peter B. 1880-1957 . . . . .DLB-78
Kyōgoku Tamekane 1254-1332. . . . . .DLB-203
Kyrklund, Willy 1921- DLB-257

L

L. E. L. (see Landon, Letitia Elizabeth)
Laberge, Albert 1871-1960. . . . . .DLB-68
Laberge, Marie 1950- DLB-60
Labiche, Eugène 1815-1888. . . . . .DLB-192
Labrunie, Gerard (see Nerval, Gerard de)
La Bruyère, Jean de 1645-1696. . . . . DLB-268
La Calprenède 1609?-1663 . . . . DLB-268
Lacan, Jacques 1901-1981 . . . . .DLB-296
La Capria, Raffaele 1922- DLB-196
Lacombe, Patrice (see Trullier-Lacombe, Joseph Patrice)
Lacretelle, Jacques de 1888-1985 . . . . .DLB-65
Lacy, Ed 1911-1968. . . . . .DLB-226
Lacy, Sam 1903- DLB-171
Ladd, Joseph Brown 1764-1786 . . . . .DLB-37
La Farge, Oliver 1901-1963 . . . . .DLB-9
Lafayette, Marie-Madeleine, comtesse de 1634-1693 . . . . DLB-268
Laffan, Mrs. R. S. de Courcy (see Adams, Bertha Leith)
Lafferty, R. A. 1914-2002 . . . . .DLB-8
La Flesche, Francis 1857-1932 . . . . DLB-175
La Fontaine, Jean de 1621-1695 . . . . DLB-268
Laforge, Jules 1860-1887 . . . . .DLB-217
Lagerkvist, Pär 1891-1974 . . . . .DLB-259
Lagerlöf, Selma 1858-1940 . . . . .DLB-259
Lagorio, Gina 1922- DLB-196
La Guma, Alex 1925-1985 . . . . DLB-117, 225; CDWLB-3
Lahaise, Guillaume (see Delahaye, Guy)
Lahontan, Louis-Armand de Lom d'Arce, Baron de 1666-1715?. DLB-99
Laing, Kojo 1946- DLB-157
Laird, Carobeth 1895-1983 . . . . Y-82
Laird and Lee DLB-49
Lake, Paul 1951- DLB-282
Lalić, Ivan V. 1931-1996 . . . . .DLB-181
Lalić, Mihailo 1914-1992 . . . . .DLB-181
Lalonde, Michèle 1937- DLB-60
Lamantia, Philip 1927- DLB-16
Lamartine, Alphonse de 1790-1869 . . . . .DLB-217
Lamb, Lady Caroline 1785-1828 . . . . .DLB-116
Lamb, Charles 1775-1834 . . . . . . DLB-93, 107, 163; CDBLB-3
Lamb, Mary 1764-1874 . . . . .DLB-163
Lambert, Angela 1940- DLB-271
Lambert, Betty 1933-1983 . . . . .DLB-60
Lamm, Donald
Goodbye, Gutenberg? A Lecture at the New York Public Library, 18 April 1995 . . . . Y-95
Lamming, George 1927- DLB-125; CDWLB-3
La Mothe Le Vayer, François de 1588-1672 . . . . .DLB-268
L'Amour, Louis 1908-1988 . . . . DLB-206; Y-80
Lampman, Archibald 1861-1899 . . . . DLB-92
Lamson, Wolffe and Company DLB-49
Lancer Books. DLB-46
Lanchester, John 1962- DLB-267
Lander, Peter (see Cunningham, Peter)
Landesman, Jay 1919- and Landesman, Fran 1927-. DLB-16
Landolfi, Tommaso 1908-1979 . . . . DLB-177
Landon, Letitia Elizabeth 1802-1838 . . . . . .DLB-96
Landor, Walter Savage 1775-1864. . . . DLB-93, 107
Landry, Napoléon-P. 1884-1956 . . . . DLB-92
Landvik, Lorna 1954- DLB-292
Lane, Charles 1800-1870 . . . . . . .DLB-1, 223; DS-5
Lane, F. C. 1885-1984 . . . . .DLB-241
Lane, Laurence W. 1890-1967. . . . . .DLB-91
Lane, M. Travis 1934- DLB-60
Lane, Patrick 1939- DLB-53
Lane, Pinkie Gordon 1923- DLB-41
John Lane Company DLB-49
Laney, Al 1896-1988 . . . . DLB-4, 171
Lang, Andrew 1844-1912 . . . . . .DLB-98, 141, 184
Langer, Susanne K. 1895-1985 . . . . DLB-270
Langevin, André 1927- DLB-60
Langford, David 1953- DLB-261
Langgässer, Elisabeth 1899-1950. . . . . .DLB-69
Langhorne, John 1735-1779 . . . . DLB-109
Langland, William circa 1330-circa 1400. . DLB-146
Langton, Anna 1804-1893. . . . . .DLB-99
Lanham, Edwin 1904-1979 . . . . .DLB-4
Lanier, Sidney 1842-1881 . . . . .DLB-64; DS-13
Lanyer, Aemilia 1569-1645 . . . . DLB-121
Lapointe, Gatien 1931-1983. . . . . .DLB-88
Lapointe, Paul-Marie 1929- DLB-88
Larcom, Lucy 1824-1893. . . . . .DLB-221, 243
Lardner, John 1912-1960. . . . . DLB-171
Lardner, Ring 1885-1933 . . . . . . DLB-11, 25, 86, 171; DS-16; CDALB-4
Lardner 100: Ring Lardner Centennial Symposium. Y-85
Lardner, Ring, Jr. 1915-2000. . . . . . . DLB-26, Y-00
Larkin, Philip 1922-1985 . . . . . .DLB-27; CDBLB-8
The Philip Larkin Society Y-99
La Roche, Sophie von 1730-1807. . . . . .DLB-94
La Rochefoucauld, François duc de 1613-1680 . . . . .DLB-268
La Rocque, Gilbert 1943-1984. . . . . .DLB-60
Laroque de Roquebrune, Robert (see Roquebrune, Robert de)
Larrick, Nancy 1910- DLB-61
Lars, Claudia 1899-1974 . . . . .DLB-283
Larsen, Nella 1893-1964 . . . . .DLB-51
Larsen, Thøger 1875-1928. . . . . .DLB-300
Larson, Clinton F. 1919-1994 . . . . .DLB-256
La Sale, Antoine de circa 1386-1460/1467 . . . . .DLB-208
Lasch, Christopher 1932-1994. . . . . .DLB-246
Lasker-Schüler, Else 1869-1945. . . . . . DLB-66, 124
Lasnier, Rina 1915-1997 . . . . .DLB-88
Lassalle, Ferdinand 1825-1864. . . . . .DLB-129
Late-Medieval Castilian Theater DLB-286
Latham, Robert 1912-1995 . . . . .DLB-201
Lathrop, Dorothy P. 1891-1980 . . . . .DLB-22
Lathrop, George Parsons 1851-1898. . . . . . DLB-71
Lathrop, John, Jr. 1772-1820 . . . . DLB-37
Latimer, Hugh 1492?-1555 . . . . .DLB-136
Latimore, Jewel Christine McLawler (see Amini, Johari M.)
Latin Literature, The Uniqueness of DLB-211
La Tour du Pin, Patrice de 1911-1975. . . .DLB-258
Latymer, William 1498-1583. . . . . .DLB-132
Laube, Heinrich 1806-1884. . . . . .DLB-133
Laud, William 1573-1645 . . . . .DLB-213
Laughlin, James 1914-1997 . . . . . DLB-48; Y-96, 97
A Tribute [to Henry Miller] Y-80
Tribute to Albert Erskine Y-93
Tribute to Kenneth Rexroth Y-82
Tribute to Malcolm Cowley Y-89
Laumer, Keith 1925-1993 . . . . .DLB-8
Lauremberg, Johann 1590-1658 . . . . .DLB-164
Laurence, Margaret 1926-1987 . . . . .DLB-53
Laurentius von Schnüffis 1633-1702 . . . . .DLB-168
Laurents, Arthur 1918- DLB-26
Laurie, Annie (see Black, Winifred)
Laut, Agnes Christiana 1871-1936. . . . . . . .DLB-92
Lauterbach, Ann 1942- DLB-193
Lautréamont, Isidore Lucien Ducasse, Comte de 1846-1870 . . . . DLB-217
Lavater, Johann Kaspar 1741-1801 . . . . DLB-97
Lavin, Mary 1912-1996. . . . . .DLB-15
Law, John (see Harkness, Margaret)
Lawes, Henry 1596-1662. . . . . .DLB-126

Lawler, Ray 1921- DLB-289
Lawless, Anthony (see MacDonald, Philip)
Lawless, Emily (The Hon. Emily Lawless) 1845-1913 .... DLB-240
Lawrence, D. H. 1885-1930 ..... DLB-10, 19, 36, 98, 162, 195; CDBLB-6
The D. H. Lawrence Society of North America Y-00
Lawrence, David 1888-1973 .... DLB-29
Lawrence, Jerome 1915- DLB-228
Lawrence, Seymour 1926-1994 .... Y-94
Tribute to Richard Yates Y-92
Lawrence, T. E. 1888-1935 .... DLB-195
The T. E. Lawrence Society Y-98
Lawson, George 1598-1678 .... DLB-213
Lawson, Henry 1867-1922 .... DLB-230
Lawson, John ?-1711 .... DLB-24
Lawson, John Howard 1894-1977 ...... DLB-228
Lawson, Louisa Albury 1848-1920 ...... DLB-230
Lawson, Robert 1892-1957 .... DLB-22
Lawson, Victor F. 1850-1925 .... DLB-25
Layard, Austen Henry 1817-1894 .... DLB-166
Layton, Irving 1912- DLB-88
LaZamon flourished circa 1200 .... DLB-146
Lazarević, Laza K. 1851-1890 .... DLB-147
Lazarus, George 1904-1997 .... DLB-201
Lazhechnikov, Ivan Ivanovich 1792-1869 .... DLB-198
Lea, Henry Charles 1825-1909 .... DLB-47
Lea, Sydney 1942- DLB-120, 282
Lea, Tom 1907-2001 .... DLB-6
Leacock, John 1729-1802 .... DLB-31
Leacock, Stephen 1869-1944 .... DLB-92
Lead, Jane Ward 1623-1704 .... DLB-131
Leadenhall Press DLB-106
"The Greatness of Southern Literature": League of the South Institute for the Study of Southern Culture and History Y-02
Leakey, Caroline Woolmer 1827-1881 ... DLB-230
Leapor, Mary 1722-1746 .... DLB-109
Lear, Edward 1812-1888 ...... DLB-32, 163, 166
Leary, Timothy 1920-1996 .... DLB-16
W. A. Leary and Company DLB-49
Léautaud, Paul 1872-1956 .... DLB-65
Leavis, F. R. 1895-1978 .... DLB-242
Leavitt, David 1961- DLB-130
Leavitt and Allen DLB-49
Le Blond, Mrs. Aubrey 1861-1934 .... DLB-174
le Carré, John (David John Moore Cornwell) 1931- DLB-87; CDBLB-8
Tribute to Graham Greene Y-91
Tribute to George Greenfield Y-00
Lécavelé, Roland (see Dorgeles, Roland)
Lechlitner, Ruth 1901- DLB-48
Leclerc, Félix 1914-1988 .... DLB-60
Le Clézio, J. M. G. 1940- DLB-83
Leder, Rudolf (see Hermlin, Stephan)
Lederer, Charles 1910-1976 .... DLB-26
Ledwidge, Francis 1887-1917 .... DLB-20
Lee, Dennis 1939- DLB-53
Lee, Don L. (see Madhubuti, Haki R.)
Lee, George W. 1894-1976 .... DLB-51
Lee, Harper 1926- DLB-6; CDALB-1
Lee, Harriet 1757-1851 and Lee, Sophia 1750-1824 .... DLB-39
Lee, Laurie 1914-1997 .... DLB-27
Lee, Leslie 1935- DLB-266
Lee, Li-Young 1957- DLB-165
Lee, Manfred B. 1905-1971 .... DLB-137
Lee, Nathaniel circa 1645-1692 .... DLB-80
Lee, Robert E. 1918-1994 .... DLB-228
Lee, Sir Sidney 1859-1926 .... DLB-149, 184
"Principles of Biography," in *Elizabethan and Other Essays* DLB-149
Lee, Tanith 1947- DLB-261
Lee, Vernon 1856-1935 ....DLB-57, 153, 156, 174, 178
Lee and Shepard DLB-49
Le Fanu, Joseph Sheridan 1814-1873 ....DLB-21, 70, 159, 178
Leffland, Ella 1931- Y-84
le Fort, Gertrud von 1876-1971 .... DLB-66
Le Gallienne, Richard 1866-1947 .... DLB-4
Legaré, Hugh Swinton 1797-1843 ....DLB-3, 59, 73, 248
Legaré, James Mathewes 1823-1859 ... DLB-3, 248
Léger, Antoine-J. 1880-1950 .... DLB-88
Leggett, William 1801-1839 .... DLB-250
Le Guin, Ursula K. 1929- DLB-8, 52, 256, 275; CDALB-6
Lehman, Ernest 1920- DLB-44
Lehmann, John 1907-1989 ....DLB-27, 100
John Lehmann Limited DLB-112
Lehmann, Rosamond 1901-1990 .... DLB-15
Lehmann, Wilhelm 1882-1968 .... DLB-56
Leiber, Fritz 1910-1992 .... DLB-8
Leibniz, Gottfried Wilhelm 1646-1716 ... DLB-168
Leicester University Press DLB-112
Leigh, Carolyn 1926-1983 .... DLB-265
Leigh, W. R. 1866-1955 .... DLB-188
Leinster, Murray 1896-1975 .... DLB-8
Leiser, Bill 1898-1965 .... DLB-241
Leisewitz, Johann Anton 1752-1806 ...... DLB-94
Leitch, Maurice 1933- DLB-14
Leithauser, Brad 1943- DLB-120, 282
Leland, Charles G. 1824-1903 .... DLB-11
Leland, John 1503?-1552 .... DLB-136
Lemay, Pamphile 1837-1918 .... DLB-99
Lemelin, Roger 1919-1992 .... DLB-88
Lemercier, Louis-Jean-Népomucène 1771-1840 .... DLB-192
Le Moine, James MacPherson 1825-1912 . DLB-99
Lemon, Mark 1809-1870 .... DLB-163
Le Moyne, Jean 1913-1996 .... DLB-88
Lemperly, Paul 1858-1939 ....DLB-187
L'Engle, Madeleine 1918- DLB-52
Lennart, Isobel 1915-1971 .... DLB-44
Lennox, Charlotte 1729 or 1730-1804 .... DLB-39
Lenox, James 1800-1880 .... DLB-140
Lenski, Lois 1893-1974 .... DLB-22
Lentricchia, Frank 1940- DLB-246
Lenz, Hermann 1913-1998 .... DLB-69
Lenz, J. M. R. 1751-1792 .... DLB-94
Lenz, Siegfried 1926- DLB-75
Leonard, Elmore 1925- DLB-173, 226
Leonard, Hugh 1926- DLB-13
Leonard, William Ellery 1876-1944 ...... DLB-54
Leonov, Leonid Maksimovich 1899-1994 ....DLB-272
Leonowens, Anna 1834-1914 .... DLB-99, 166
Leont'ev, Konstantin Nikolaevich 1831-1891 ....DLB-277
Leopold, Aldo 1887-1948 ....DLB-275
LePan, Douglas 1914-1998 .... DLB-88
Lepik, Kalju 1920-1999 .... DLB-232
Leprohon, Rosanna Eleanor 1829-1879 ... DLB-99
Le Queux, William 1864-1927 .... DLB-70
Lermontov, Mikhail Iur'evich 1814-1841. DLB-205
Lerner, Alan Jay 1918-1986 .... DLB-265
Lerner, Max 1902-1992 .... DLB-29
Lernet-Holenia, Alexander 1897-1976 ..... DLB-85
Le Rossignol, James 1866-1969 .... DLB-92
Lescarbot, Marc circa 1570-1642 .... DLB-99
LeSeur, William Dawson 1840-1917 ..... DLB-92
LeSieg, Theo. (see Geisel, Theodor Seuss)
Leskov, Nikolai Semenovich 1831-1895 .. DLB-238
Leslie, Doris before 1902-1982 .... DLB-191
Leslie, Eliza 1787-1858 .... DLB-202
Leslie, Frank (Henry Carter) 1821-1880 ....DLB-43, 79
Frank Leslie [publishing house] DLB-49
Leśmian, Bolesław 1878-1937 .... DLB-215
Lesperance, John 1835?-1891 .... DLB-99
Lessing, Bruno 1870-1940 .... DLB-28
Lessing, Doris 1919- DLB-15, 139; Y-85; CDBLB-8
Lessing, Gotthold Ephraim 1729-1781 ....DLB-97; CDWLB-2
The Lessing Society Y-00
Lettau, Reinhard 1929-1996 .... DLB-75
The Hemingway Letters Project Finds an Editor Y-02
Lever, Charles 1806-1872 .... DLB-21
Lever, Ralph ca. 1527-1585 .... DLB-236
Leverson, Ada 1862-1933 .... DLB-153
Levertov, Denise 1923-1997 .... DLB-5, 165; CDALB-7
Levi, Peter 1931-2000 .... DLB-40

Levi, Primo 1919-1987 . . . . DLB-177, 299
Levien, Sonya 1888-1960 . . . . DLB-44
Levin, Meyer 1905-1981 . . . . DLB-9, 28; Y-81
Levin, Phillis 1954- DLB-282
Lévinas, Emmanuel 1906-1995 . . . . DLB-296
Levine, Norman 1923- DLB-88
Levine, Philip 1928- DLB-5
Levis, Larry 1946- DLB-120
Lévi-Strauss, Claude 1908- DLB-242
Levitov, Aleksandr Ivanovich 1835?-1877 . . . . DLB-277
Levy, Amy 1861-1889 . . . . DLB-156, 240
Levy, Benn Wolfe 1900-1973 . . . . . . DLB-13; Y-81
Lewald, Fanny 1811-1889 . . . . DLB-129
Lewes, George Henry 1817-1878 . . . . . DLB-55, 144
"Criticism in Relation to Novels" (1863) DLB-21
The Principles of Success in Literature (1865) [excerpt] DLB-57
Lewis, Agnes Smith 1843-1926 . . . . DLB-174
Lewis, Alfred H. 1857-1914 . . . . DLB-25, 186
Lewis, Alun 1915-1944 . . . . DLB-20, 162
Lewis, C. Day (see Day Lewis, C.)
Lewis, C. I. 1883-1964 . . . . DLB-270
Lewis, C. S. 1898-1963 . . . . DLB-15, 100, 160, 255; CDBLB-7
The New York C. S. Lewis Society Y-99
Lewis, Charles B. 1842-1924 . . . . DLB-11
Lewis, David 1941-2001 . . . . DLB-279
Lewis, Henry Clay 1825-1850 . . . . DLB-3, 248
Lewis, Janet 1899-1999 . . . . Y-87
Tribute to Katherine Anne Porter Y-80
Lewis, Matthew Gregory 1775-1818 . . . . DLB-39, 158, 178
Lewis, Meriwether 1774-1809 . . . . . . DLB-183, 186
Lewis, Norman 1908- DLB-204
Lewis, R. W. B. 1917- DLB-111
Lewis, Richard circa 1700-1734 . . . . DLB-24
Lewis, Sinclair 1885-1951 . . . . . . DLB-9, 102; DS-1; CDALB-4
Sinclair Lewis Centennial Conference Y-85
The Sinclair Lewis Society Y-99
Lewis, Wilmarth Sheldon 1895-1979 . . . . . DLB-140
Lewis, Wyndham 1882-1957 . . . . DLB-15
Time and Western Man [excerpt] (1927) DLB-36
Lewisohn, Ludwig 1882-1955 . . . DLB-4, 9, 28, 102
Leyendecker, J. C. 1874-1951 . . . . DLB-188
Leyner, Mark 1956- DLB-292
Lezama Lima, José 1910-1976 . . . . . . DLB-113, 283
L'Heureux, John 1934- DLB-244
Libbey, Laura Jean 1862-1924 . . . . DLB-221
Libedinsky, Iurii Nikolaevich 1898-1959 . . . . DLB-272
Library History Group Y-01
E-Books' Second Act in Libraries Y-02
The Library of America DLB-46
The Library of America: An Assessment After Two Decades Y-02
Licensing Act of 1737 . . . . DLB-84
Leonard Lichfield I [publishing house] . . . DLB-170
Lichtenberg, Georg Christoph 1742-1799 . . . . DLB-94
The Liddle Collection Y-97
Lidman, Sara 1923- DLB-257
Lieb, Fred 1888-1980 . . . . DLB-171
Liebling, A. J. 1904-1963 . . . . DLB-4, 171
Lieutenant Murray (see Ballou, Maturin Murray)
Lighthall, William Douw 1857-1954 . . . . . . DLB-92
Lihn, Enrique 1929-1988 . . . . DLB-283
Lilar, Françoise (see Mallet-Joris, Françoise)
Lili'uokalani, Queen 1838-1917 . . . . DLB-221
Lillo, George 1691-1739 . . . . DLB-84
Lilly, J. K., Jr. 1893-1966 . . . . DLB-140
Lilly, Wait and Company DLB-49
Lily, William circa 1468-1522 . . . . DLB-132
Limited Editions Club DLB-46
Limón, Graciela 1938- DLB-209
Lincoln and Edmands DLB-49
Lind, Jakov 1927- DLB-299
Linda Vilhjálmsdóttir 1958- DLB-293
Lindesay, Ethel Forence (see Richardson, Henry Handel)
Lindgren, Astrid 1907-2002 . . . . DLB-257
Lindgren, Torgny 1938- DLB-257
Lindsay, Alexander William, Twenty-fifth Earl of Crawford 1812-1880 . . . . DLB-184
Lindsay, Sir David circa 1485-1555 . . . . . . DLB-132
Lindsay, David 1878-1945 . . . . DLB-255
Lindsay, Jack 1900-1990 . . . . Y-84
Lindsay, Lady (Caroline Blanche Elizabeth Fitzroy Lindsay) 1844-1912 . . . . DLB-199
Lindsay, Norman 1879-1969 . . . . DLB-260
Lindsay, Vachel 1879-1931 . . . . DLB-54; CDALB-3
Linebarger, Paul Myron Anthony (see Smith, Cordwainer)
Link, Arthur S. 1920-1998 . . . . DLB-17
Linn, Ed 1922-2000 . . . . DLB-241
Linn, John Blair 1777-1804 . . . . DLB-37
Lins, Osman 1924-1978 . . . . DLB-145
Linton, Eliza Lynn 1822-1898 . . . . DLB-18
Linton, William James 1812-1897 . . . . DLB-32
Barnaby Bernard Lintot [publishing house] DLB-170
Lion Books DLB-46
Lionni, Leo 1910-1999 . . . . DLB-61
Lippard, George 1822-1854 . . . . DLB-202
Lippincott, Sara Jane Clarke 1823-1904 . . . . DLB-43
J. B. Lippincott Company DLB-49
Lippmann, Walter 1889-1974 . . . . DLB-29
Lipton, Lawrence 1898-1975 . . . . DLB-16
Lisboa, Irene 1892-1958 . . . . DLB-287
Liscow, Christian Ludwig 1701-1760 . . . . . . DLB-97
Lish, Gordon 1934- DLB-130
Tribute to Donald Barthelme Y-89
Tribute to James Dickey Y-97
Lisle, Charles-Marie-René Leconte de 1818-1894 . . . . DLB-217
Lispector, Clarice 1925-1977 . . . . DLB-113; CDWLB-3
LitCheck Website Y-01
Literary Awards and Honors Y-81–02
Booker Prize Y-86, 96–98
The Drue Heinz Literature Prize Y-82
The Elmer Holmes Bobst Awards in Arts and Letters Y-87
The Griffin Poetry Prize Y-00
Literary Prizes [British] DLB-15, 207
National Book Critics Circle Awards Y-00–01
The National Jewish Book Awards Y-85
Nobel Prize Y-80–02
Winning an Edgar Y-98
The Literary Chronicle and Weekly Review 1819-1828 . . . . DLB-110
Literary Periodicals:
Callaloo Y-87
Expatriates in Paris DS-15
New Literary Periodicals: A Report for 1987 . . . . Y-87
A Report for 1988 . . . . Y-88
A Report for 1989 . . . . Y-89
A Report for 1990 . . . . Y-90
A Report for 1991 . . . . Y-91
A Report for 1992 . . . . Y-92
A Report for 1993 . . . . Y-93
Literary Research Archives
The Anthony Burgess Archive at the Harry Ransom Humanities Research Center Y-98
Archives of Charles Scribner's Sons DS-17
Berg Collection of English and American Literature of the New York Public Library Y-83
The Bobbs-Merrill Archive at the Lilly Library, Indiana University Y-90
Die Fürstliche Bibliothek Corvey Y-96
Guide to the Archives of Publishers, Journals, and Literary Agents in North American Libraries Y-93
The Henry E. Huntington Library Y-92
The Humanities Research Center, University of Texas Y-82
The John Carter Brown Library Y-85
Kent State Special Collections Y-86
The Lilly Library Y-84
The Modern Literary Manuscripts Collection in the Special Collections of the Washington University Libraries Y-87
A Publisher's Archives: G. P. Putnam . . . Y-92

Special Collections at Boston University Y-99
The University of Virginia Libraries Y-91
The William Charvat American Fiction Collection at the Ohio State University Libraries. Y-92
Literary Societies Y-98–02
The Margery Allingham Society Y-98
The American Studies Association of Norway Y-00
The Arnold Bennett Society. Y-98
The Association for the Study of Literature and Environment (ASLE). Y-99
Belgian Luxembourg American Studies Association Y-01
The E. F. Benson Society. Y-98
The Elizabeth Bishop Society. Y-01
The [Edgar Rice] Burroughs Bibliophiles Y-98
The Byron Society of America. Y-00
The Lewis Carroll Society of North America Y-00
The Willa Cather Pioneer Memorial and Education Foundation Y-00
New Chaucer Society. Y-00
The Wilkie Collins Society Y-98
The James Fenimore Cooper Society. Y-01
The Stephen Crane Society Y-98, 01
The E. E. Cummings Society. Y-01
The James Dickey Society Y-99
John Dos Passos Newsletter. Y-00
The Priory Scholars [Sir Arthur Conan Doyle] of New York Y-99
The International Theodore Dreiser Society Y-01
The Friends of the Dymock Poets Y-00
The George Eliot Fellowship Y-99
The T. S. Eliot Society: Celebration and Scholarship, 1980-1999 . . . . Y-99
The Ralph Waldo Emerson Society. Y-99
The William Faulkner Society Y-99
The C. S. Forester Society Y-00
The Hamlin Garland Society. Y-01
The [Elizabeth] Gaskell Society Y-98
The Charlotte Perkins Gilman Society . . . Y-99
The Ellen Glasgow Society Y-01
Zane Grey's West Society Y-00
The Ivor Gurney Society Y-98
The Joel Chandler Harris Association Y-99
The Nathaniel Hawthorne Society. Y-00
The [George Alfred] Henty Society Y-98
George Moses Horton Society Y-99
The William Dean Howells Society. Y-01
WW2 HMSO Paperbacks Society. Y-98
American Humor Studies Association Y-99
International Society for Humor Studies . . Y-99
The W. W. Jacobs Appreciation Society . . Y-98
The Richard Jefferies Society Y-98
The Jerome K. Jerome Society Y-98
The D. H. Lawrence Society of North America Y-00
The T. E. Lawrence Society Y-98
The [Gotthold] Lessing Society Y-00
The New York C. S. Lewis Society Y-99
The Sinclair Lewis Society Y-99
The Jack London Research Center Y-00
The Jack London Society. Y-99
The Cormac McCarthy Society. Y-99
The Melville Society Y-01
The Arthur Miller Society Y-01
The Milton Society of America Y-00
International Marianne Moore Society . . . Y-98
International Nabokov Society. Y-99
The Vladimir Nabokov Society. Y-01
The Flannery O'Connor Society Y-99
The Wilfred Owen Association Y-98
Penguin Collectors' Society Y-98
The [E. A.] Poe Studies Association. Y-99
The Katherine Anne Porter Society. Y-01
The Beatrix Potter Society. Y-98
The Ezra Pound Society Y-01
The Powys Society. Y-98
Proust Society of America Y-00
The Dorothy L. Sayers Society Y-98
The Bernard Shaw Society. Y-99
The Society for the Study of Southern Literature. Y-00
The Wallace Stevens Society Y-99
The Harriet Beecher Stowe Center Y-00
The R. S. Surtees Society. Y-98
The Thoreau Society Y-99
The Tilling [E. F. Benson] Society Y-98
The Trollope Societies Y-00
H. G. Wells Society Y-98
The Western Literature Association Y-99
The William Carlos Williams Society Y-99
The Henry Williamson Society Y-98
The [Nero] Wolfe Pack Y-99
The Thomas Wolfe Society. Y-99
Worldwide Wodehouse Societies Y-98
The W. B. Yeats Society of N.Y. Y-99
The Charlotte M. Yonge Fellowship Y-98
Literary Theory
The Year in Literary Theory. Y-92–Y-93
Literature at Nurse, or Circulating Morals (1885), by George Moore. DLB-18
Litt, Toby 1968- DLB-267
Littell, Eliakim 1797-1870 . . . . DLB-79
Littell, Robert S. 1831-1896 . . . . DLB-79
Little, Brown and Company. DLB-49
Little Magazines and Newspapers DS-15
Selected English-Language Little Magazines and Newspapers [France, 1920-1939]. DLB-4
The Little Magazines of the New Formalism DLB-282
The Little Review 1914-1929. . . . . DS-15
Littlewood, Joan 1914-2002 . . . . DLB-13
Lively, Penelope 1933- DLB-14, 161, 207
Liverpool University Press. DLB-112
The Lives of the Poets (1753). DLB-142
Livesay, Dorothy 1909-1996 . . . . DLB-68
Livesay, Florence Randal 1874-1953 . . . . . DLB-92
Livings, Henry 1929-1998 . . . . DLB-13
Livingston, Anne Howe 1763-1841 . . . DLB-37, 200
Livingston, Jay 1915-2001 . . . . DLB-265
Livingston, Myra Cohn 1926-1996 . . . . . . DLB-61
Livingston, William 1723-1790. . . . . DLB-31
Livingstone, David 1813-1873 . . . . DLB-166
Livingstone, Douglas 1932-1996 . . . . DLB-225
Livshits, Benedikt Konstantinovich 1886-1938 or 1939. . . . . DLB-295
Livy 59 B.C.-A.D. 17 . . . . . . .DLB-211; CDWLB-1
Liyong, Taban lo (see Taban lo Liyong)
Lizárraga, Sylvia S. 1925- DLB-82
Llewellyn, Richard 1906-1983 . . . . DLB-15
Lloréns Torres, Luis 1876-1944 . . . . DLB-290
Edward Lloyd [publishing house]. DLB-106
Lobel, Arnold 1933- DLB-61
Lochridge, Betsy Hopkins (see Fancher, Betsy)
Locke, Alain 1886-1954 . . . . DLB-51
Locke, David Ross 1833-1888 . . . . DLB-11, 23
Locke, John 1632-1704 . . . . .DLB-31, 101, 213, 252
Locke, Richard Adams 1800-1871 . . . . DLB-43
Locker-Lampson, Frederick 1821-1895 . . . . DLB-35, 184
Lockhart, John Gibson 1794-1854. . . . . DLB-110, 116 144
Lockridge, Ross, Jr. 1914-1948. . . . .DLB-143; Y-80
Locrine and Selimus DLB-62
Lodge, David 1935- DLB-14, 194
Lodge, George Cabot 1873-1909 . . . . DLB-54
Lodge, Henry Cabot 1850-1924. . . . . DLB-47
Lodge, Thomas 1558-1625. . . . . .DLB-172
Defence of Poetry (1579) [excerpt] DLB-172
Loeb, Harold 1891-1974. . . . . DLB-4; DS-15
Loeb, William 1905-1981. . . . . .DLB-127
Loesser, Frank 1910-1969. . . . . DLB-265
Lofting, Hugh 1886-1947 . . . . DLB-160
Logan, Deborah Norris 1761-1839. . . . . . DLB-200
Logan, James 1674-1751 . . . . DLB-24, 140
Logan, John 1923-1987. . . . . DLB-5
Logan, Martha Daniell 1704?-1779. . . . . . DLB-200
Logan, William 1950- DLB-120
Logau, Friedrich von 1605-1655 . . . . DLB-164
Logue, Christopher 1926- DLB-27

Lohenstein, Daniel Casper von 1635-1683 . . . . DLB-168
Lo-Johansson, Ivar 1901-1990 . . . . DLB-259
Lokert, George (or Lockhart) circa 1485-1547 . . . . DLB-281
Lomonosov, Mikhail Vasil'evich 1711-1765. . . . . DLB-150
London, Jack 1876-1916 . . . . . DLB-8, 12, 78, 212; CDALB-3
The Jack London Research Center. Y-00
The Jack London Society Y-99
The London Magazine 1820-1829 . . . . DLB-110
Long, David 1948- DLB-244
Long, H., and Brother DLB-49
Long, Haniel 1888-1956 . . . . DLB-45
Long, Ray 1878-1935. . . . . DLB-137
Longfellow, Henry Wadsworth 1807-1882 . . . . DLB-1, 59, 235; CDALB-2
Longfellow, Samuel 1819-1892 . . . . DLB-1
Longford, Elizabeth 1906-2002 . . . . DLB-155
Tribute to Alfred A. Knopf Y-84
Longinus circa first century DLB-176
Longley, Michael 1939- DLB-40
T. Longman [publishing house] DLB-154
Longmans, Green and Company DLB-49
Longmore, George 1793?-1867 . . . . DLB-99
Longstreet, Augustus Baldwin 1790-1870. . . . . DLB-3, 11, 74, 248
D. Longworth [publishing house] DLB-49
Lønn, Øystein 1936- DLB-297
Lonsdale, Frederick 1881-1954 . . . . DLB-10
Loos, Anita 1893-1981. . . . . DLB-11, 26, 228; Y-81
Lopate, Phillip 1943- Y-80
Lopes, Fernão 1380/1390?-1460?. DLB-287
Lopez, Barry 1945- DLB-256, 275
López, Diana (see Isabella, Ríos)
López, Josefina 1969- DLB-209
López de Mendoza, Íñigo (see Santillana, Marqués de)
López Velarde, Ramón 1888-1921 . . . . . . DLB-290
Loranger, Jean-Aubert 1896-1942 . . . . DLB-92
Lorca, Federico García 1898-1936 . . . . DLB-108
Lord, John Keast 1818-1872. . . . . DLB-99
Lorde, Audre 1934-1992 . . . . DLB-41
Lorimer, George Horace 1867-1937. . . . . . . DLB-91
A. K. Loring [publishing house]. DLB-49
Loring and Mussey DLB-46
Lorris, Guillaume de (see *Roman de la Rose*)
Lossing, Benson J. 1813-1891 . . . . DLB-30
Lothar, Ernst 1890-1974 . . . . DLB-81
D. Lothrop and Company. DLB-49
Lothrop, Harriet M. 1844-1924. . . . . DLB-42
Loti, Pierre 1850-1923 . . . . DLB-123
Lotichius Secundus, Petrus 1528-1560. . . . DLB-179
Lott, Emmeline ?-?. DLB-166
Louisiana State University Press Y-97
Lounsbury, Thomas R. 1838-1915 . . . . DLB-71
Louÿs, Pierre 1870-1925 . . . . DLB-123
Løveid, Cecile 1951- DLB-297
Lovejoy, Arthur O. 1873-1962. . . . . DLB-270
Lovelace, Earl 1935- DLB-125; CDWLB-3
Lovelace, Richard 1618-1657. . . . . DLB-131
John W. Lovell Company DLB-49
Lovell, Coryell and Company. DLB-49
Lover, Samuel 1797-1868. . . . . DLB-159, 190
Lovesey, Peter 1936- DLB-87
Tribute to Georges Simenon. Y-89
Lovinescu, Eugen 1881-1943 . . . . DLB-220; CDWLB-4
Lovingood, Sut (see Harris, George Washington)
Low, Samuel 1765-? DLB-37
Lowell, Amy 1874-1925. . . . . DLB-54, 140
Lowell, James Russell 1819-1891 . . . . . . DLB-1, 11, 64, 79, 189, 235; CDALB-2
Lowell, Robert 1917-1977. . . . . DLB-5, 169; CDALB-7
Lowenfels, Walter 1897-1976. . . . . DLB-4
Lowndes, Marie Belloc 1868-1947. . . . . DLB-70
Lowndes, William Thomas 1798-1843 . . . DLB-184
Humphrey Lownes [publishing house] . . . DLB-170
Lowry, Lois 1937- DLB-52
Lowry, Malcolm 1909-1957. . . .DLB-15; CDBLB-7
Lowther, Pat 1935-1975. . . . . DLB-53
Loy, Mina 1882-1966 . . . . DLB-4, 54
Loynaz, Dulce María 1902-1997 . . . . DLB-283
Lozeau, Albert 1878-1924 . . . . DLB-92
Lubbock, Percy 1879-1965. . . . . DLB-149
Lucan A.D. 39-A.D. 65 . . . . DLB-211
Lucas, E. V. 1868-1938 . . . . DLB-98, 149, 153
Fielding Lucas Jr. [publishing house] DLB-49
Luce, Clare Booth 1903-1987 . . . . DLB-228
Luce, Henry R. 1898-1967 . . . . DLB-91
John W. Luce and Company. DLB-46
Lucena, Juan de ca. 1430-1501 . . . . DLB-286
Lucian circa 120-180 . . . . DLB-176
Lucie-Smith, Edward 1933- DLB-40
Lucilius circa 180 B.C.-102/101 B.C.. . . . . DLB-211
Lucini, Gian Pietro 1867-1914 . . . . DLB-114
Lucretius circa 94 B.C.-circa 49 B.C. DLB-211; CDWLB-1
Luder, Peter circa 1415-1472 . . . . DLB-179
Ludlam, Charles 1943-1987. . . . . DLB-266
Ludlum, Robert 1927-2001 . . . . Y-82
Ludus de Antichristo circa 1160 . . . . DLB-148
Ludvigson, Susan 1942- DLB-120
Ludwig, Jack 1922- DLB-60
Ludwig, Otto 1813-1865 . . . . DLB-129
Ludwigslied 881 or 882 . . . . DLB-148
Luera, Yolanda 1953- DLB-122
Luft, Lya 1938- DLB-145
Lugansky, Kazak Vladimir (see Dal', Vladimir Ivanovich)
Lugn, Kristina 1948- DLB-257
Lugones, Leopoldo 1874-1938. . . . . DLB-283
Lukács, Georg (see Lukács, György)
Lukács, György 1885-1971 . . . . DLB-215, 242; CDWLB-4
Luke, Peter 1919- DLB-13
Lummis, Charles F. 1859-1928 . . . . DLB-186
Lundkvist, Artur 1906-1991 . . . . DLB-259
Lunts, Lev Natanovich 1901-1924 . . . . . . DLB-272
F. M. Lupton Company. DLB-49
Lupus of Ferrières circa 805-circa 862 . . . . DLB-148
Lurie, Alison 1926- DLB-2
Lussu, Emilio 1890-1975 . . . . DLB-264
Lustig, Arnošt 1926- DLB-232, 299
Luther, Martin 1483-1546 . . . DLB-179; CDWLB-2
Luzi, Mario 1914- DLB-128
L'vov, Nikolai Aleksandrovich 1751-1803. . . . . DLB-150
Lyall, Gavin 1932- DLB-87
Lydgate, John circa 1370-1450. . . . . DLB-146
Lyly, John circa 1554-1606 . . . . DLB-62, 167
Lynch, Patricia 1898-1972 . . . . DLB-160
Lynch, Richard flourished 1596-1601 . . . . DLB-172
Lynd, Robert 1879-1949 . . . . DLB-98
Lyon, Matthew 1749-1822. . . . . DLB-43
Lyotard, Jean-François 1924-1998 . . . . DLB-242
Lyricists
Additional Lyricists: 1920-1960 . . . . . DLB-265
Lysias circa 459 B.C.-circa 380 B.C. DLB-176
Lytle, Andrew 1902-1995 . . . . DLB-6; Y-95
Tribute to Caroline Gordon Y-81
Tribute to Katherine Anne Porter. Y-80
Lytton, Edward (see Bulwer-Lytton, Edward)
Lytton, Edward Robert Bulwer 1831-1891. . . . . DLB-32

M

Maass, Joachim 1901-1972. . . . . DLB-69
Mabie, Hamilton Wright 1845-1916 . . . . . . DLB-71
Mac A'Ghobhainn, Iain (see Smith, Iain Crichton)
MacArthur, Charles 1895-1956. . . . . DLB-7, 25, 44
Macaulay, Catherine 1731-1791. . . . . DLB-104
Macaulay, David 1945- DLB-61
Macaulay, Rose 1881-1958 . . . . DLB-36
Macaulay, Thomas Babington 1800-1859 . . . . .DLB-32, 55; CDBLB-4
Macaulay Company DLB-46
MacBeth, George 1932-1992 . . . . DLB-40
Macbeth, Madge 1880-1965 . . . . DLB-92
MacCaig, Norman 1910-1996 . . . . DLB-27
MacDiarmid, Hugh 1892-1978 . . . . .DLB-20; CDBLB-7
MacDonald, Cynthia 1928- DLB-105
MacDonald, George 1824-1905. . . . DLB-18, 163, 178

MacDonald, John D. 1916-1986..... DLB-8; Y-86
MacDonald, Philip 1899?-1980 .... DLB-77
Macdonald, Ross (see Millar, Kenneth)
Macdonald, Sharman 1951- DLB-245
MacDonald, Wilson 1880-1967 .... DLB-92
Macdonald and Company (Publishers) .. DLB-112
MacEwen, Gwendolyn 1941-1987 ... DLB-53, 251
Macfadden, Bernarr 1868-1955 ...... DLB-25, 91
MacGregor, John 1825-1892 .... DLB-166
MacGregor, Mary Esther (see Keith, Marian)
Macherey, Pierre 1938- DLB-296
Machado, Antonio 1875-1939.......... DLB-108
Machado, Manuel 1874-1947 .... DLB-108
Machar, Agnes Maule 1837-1927 .... DLB-92
Machaut, Guillaume de circa 1300-1377.................. DLB-208
Machen, Arthur Llewelyn Jones 1863-1947................DLB-36, 156, 178
MacIlmaine, Roland fl. 1574........... DLB-281
MacInnes, Colin 1914-1976 .... DLB-14
MacInnes, Helen 1907-1985 .... DLB-87
Mac Intyre, Tom 1931- DLB-245
Mačiulis, Jonas (see Maironis, Jonas)
Mack, Maynard 1909- DLB-111
Mackall, Leonard L. 1879-1937 .... DLB-140
MacKay, Isabel Ecclestone 1875-1928 .... DLB-92
MacKaye, Percy 1875-1956 .... DLB-54
Macken, Walter 1915-1967 .... DLB-13
Mackenzie, Alexander 1763-1820........ DLB-99
Mackenzie, Alexander Slidell 1803-1848 .... DLB-183
Mackenzie, Compton 1883-1972 .... DLB-34, 100
Mackenzie, Henry 1745-1831 .... DLB-39
The Lounger, no. 20 (1785) DLB-39
Mackenzie, Kenneth (Seaforth Mackenzie) 1913-1955...................... DLB-260
Mackenzie, William 1758-1828......... DLB-187
Mackey, Nathaniel 1947- DLB-169
Mackey, Shena 1944- DLB-231
Mackey, William Wellington 1937- DLB-38
Mackintosh, Elizabeth (see Tey, Josephine)
Mackintosh, Sir James 1765-1832 .... DLB-158
Macklin, Charles 1699-1797 .... DLB-89
Maclaren, Ian (see Watson, John)
MacLaverty, Bernard 1942- DLB-267
MacLean, Alistair 1922-1987 ....DLB-276
MacLean, Katherine Anne 1925- DLB-8
Maclean, Norman 1902-1990 .... DLB-206
MacLeish, Archibald 1892-1982 ....DLB-4, 7, 45; Y-82; DS-15; CDALB-7
MacLennan, Hugh 1907-1990 .... DLB-68
MacLeod, Alistair 1936- DLB-60
Macleod, Fiona (see Sharp, William)
Macleod, Norman 1906-1985............ DLB-4
Mac Low, Jackson 1922- DLB-193
Macmillan and Company............. DLB-106
The Macmillan Company DLB-49
Macmillan's English Men of Letters, First Series (1878-1892) DLB-144
MacNamara, Brinsley 1890-1963 .... DLB-10
MacNeice, Louis 1907-1963 .... DLB-10, 20
Macphail, Andrew 1864-1938 .... DLB-92
Macpherson, James 1736-1796 .... DLB-109
Macpherson, Jay 1931- DLB-53
Macpherson, Jeanie 1884-1946.......... DLB-44
Macrae Smith Company............... DLB-46
MacRaye, Lucy Betty (see Webling, Lucy)
John Macrone [publishing house]....... DLB-106
MacShane, Frank 1927-1999........... DLB-111
Macy-Masius DLB-46
Madden, David 1933- DLB-6
Madden, Sir Frederic 1801-1873........ DLB-184
Maddow, Ben 1909-1992 .... DLB-44
Maddux, Rachel 1912-1983 ....DLB-234; Y-93
Madgett, Naomi Long 1923- DLB-76
Madhubuti, Haki R. 1942- DLB-5, 41; DS-8
Madison, James 1751-1836............. DLB-37
Madsen, Svend Åge 1939- DLB-214
Madrigal, Alfonso Fernández de (El Tostado) ca. 1405-1455................... DLB-286
Maeterlinck, Maurice 1862-1949 .... DLB-192
Mafūz, Najīb 1911- Y-88
Nobel Lecture 1988 .... Y-88
The Little Magazines of the New Formalism DLB-282
Magee, David 1905-1977 .... DLB-187
Maginn, William 1794-1842 ....DLB-110, 159
Magoffin, Susan Shelby 1827-1855...... DLB-239
Mahan, Alfred Thayer 1840-1914 .... DLB-47
Maheux-Forcier, Louise 1929- DLB-60
Mahin, John Lee 1902-1984............ DLB-44
Mahon, Derek 1941- DLB-40
Maiakovsky, Vladimir Vladimirovich 1893-1930 .... DLB-295
Maikov, Apollon Nikolaevich 1821-1897.......................DLB-277
Maikov, Vasilii Ivanovich 1728-1778 .... DLB-150
Mailer, Norman 1923- DLB-2, 16, 28, 185, 278; Y-80, 83, 97; DS-3; CDALB-6
Tribute to Isaac Bashevis Singer Y-91
Tribute to Meyer Levin............... Y-81
Maillart, Ella 1903-1997 .... DLB-195
Maillet, Adrienne 1885-1963 .... DLB-68
Maillet, Antonine 1929- DLB-60
Maillu, David G. 1939- DLB-157
Maimonides, Moses 1138-1204 .... DLB-115
Main Selections of the Book-of-the-Month Club, 1926-1945 .... DLB-9
Mainwaring, Daniel 1902-1977.......... DLB-44
Mair, Charles 1838-1927 .... DLB-99
Mair, John circa 1467-1550............ DLB-281
Maironis, Jonas 1862-1932 .. DLB-220; CDWLB-4
Mais, Roger 1905-1955 .....DLB-125; CDWLB-3
Maitland, Sara 1950- DLB-271
Major, Andre 1942- DLB-60
Major, Charles 1856-1913 .... DLB-202
Major, Clarence 1936- DLB-33
Major, Kevin 1949- DLB-60
Major Books......................... DLB-46
Makanin, Vladimir Semenovich 1937- DLB-285
Makarenko, Anton Semenovich 1888-1939 ....DLB-272
Makemie, Francis circa 1658-1708 .... DLB-24
The Making of Americans Contract............ Y-98
Maksimović, Desanka 1898-1993 ....DLB-147; CDWLB-4
Malamud, Bernard 1914-1986 ....DLB-2, 28, 152; Y-80, 86; CDALB-1
Bernard Malamud Archive at the Harry Ransom Humanities Research Center Y-00
Mălăncioiu, Ileana 1940- DLB-232
Malaparte, Curzio (Kurt Erich Suckert) 1898-1957..... DLB-264
Malerba, Luigi 1927- DLB-196
Malet, Lucas 1852-1931 .... DLB-153
Mallarmé, Stéphane 1842-1898 ....DLB-217
Malleson, Lucy Beatrice (see Gilbert, Anthony)
Mallet-Joris, Françoise (Françoise Lilar) 1930- DLB-83
Mallock, W. H. 1849-1923...........DLB-18, 57
"Every Man His Own Poet; or, The Inspired Singer's Recipe Book" (1877) DLB-35
"Le Style c'est l'homme" (1892)...... DLB-57
Memoirs of Life and Literature (1920), [excerpt]................. DLB-57
Malone, Dumas 1892-1986 ....DLB-17
Malone, Edmond 1741-1812............ DLB-142
Malory, Sir Thomas circa 1400-1410 - 1471 ... DLB-146; CDBLB-1
Malouf, David 1934- DLB-289
Malpede, Karen 1945- DLB-249
Malraux, André 1901-1976............. DLB-72
Malthus, Thomas Robert 1766-1834...................DLB-107, 158
Maltz, Albert 1908-1985.............. DLB-102
Malzberg, Barry N. 1939- DLB-8
Mamet, David 1947- DLB-7
Mamin, Dmitrii Narkisovich 1852-1912.. DLB-238
Manaka, Matsemela 1956- DLB-157
Manchester University Press DLB-112
Mandel, Eli 1922-1992 .... DLB-53
Mandel'shtam, Osip Emil'evich 1891-1938 .... DLB-295
Mandeville, Bernard 1670-1733 .... DLB-101
Mandeville, Sir John mid fourteenth century DLB-146
Mandiargues, André Pieyre de 1909-1991 .... DLB-83

Manea, Norman 1936- DLB-232
Manfred, Frederick 1912-1994. . . . DLB-6, 212, 227
Manfredi, Gianfranco 1948- DLB-196
Mangan, Sherry 1904-1961 . . . . DLB-4
Manganelli, Giorgio 1922-1990 . . . . DLB-196
Manilius fl. first century A.D. DLB-211
Mankiewicz, Herman 1897-1953 . . . . DLB-26
Mankiewicz, Joseph L. 1909-1993 . . . . DLB-44
Mankowitz, Wolf 1924-1998 . . . . DLB-15
Manley, Delarivière 1672?-1724. . . . . . . DLB-39, 80
Preface to *The Secret History, of Queen Zarah, and the Zarazians* (1705) DLB-39
Mann, Abby 1927- DLB-44
Mann, Charles 1929-1998 . . . . Y-98
Mann, Emily 1952- DLB-266
Mann, Heinrich 1871-1950 . . . . DLB-66, 118
Mann, Horace 1796-1859. . . . . DLB-1, 235
Mann, Klaus 1906-1949. . . . . DLB-56
Mann, Mary Peabody 1806-1887 . . . . DLB-239
Mann, Thomas 1875-1955. . . . DLB-66; CDWLB-2
Mann, William D'Alton 1839-1920. . . . . . DLB-137
Mannin, Ethel 1900-1984 . . . . DLB-191, 195
Manning, Emily (see Australie)
Manning, Frederic 1882-1935 . . . . DLB-260
Manning, Laurence 1899-1972 . . . . DLB-251
Manning, Marie 1873?-1945 . . . . DLB-29
Manning and Loring DLB-49
Mannyng, Robert flourished 1303-1338 . . DLB-146
Mano, D. Keith 1942- DLB-6
Manor Books DLB-46
Manrique, Gómez 1412?-1490. . . . . DLB-286
Manrique, Jorge ca. 1440-1479. . . . . DLB-286
Mansfield, Katherine 1888-1923 . . . . DLB-162
Mantel, Hilary 1952- DLB-271
Manuel, Niklaus circa 1484-1530 . . . . DLB-179
Manzini, Gianna 1896-1974. . . . . DLB-177
Mapanje, Jack 1944- DLB-157
Maraini, Dacia 1936- DLB-196
March, William (William Edward Campbell) 1893-1954 . . . . DLB-9, 86
Marchand, Leslie A. 1900-1999. . . . . DLB-103
Marchant, Bessie 1862-1941 . . . . DLB-160
Marchant, Tony 1959- DLB-245
Marchenko, Anastasiia Iakovlevna 1830-1880 . . . . DLB-238
Marchessault, Jovette 1938- DLB-60
Marcinkevičius, Justinas 1930- DLB-232
Marcus, Frank 1928- DLB-13
Marcuse, Herbert 1898-1979 . . . . DLB-242
Marden, Orison Swett 1850-1924 . . . . DLB-137
Marechera, Dambudzo 1952-1987. . . . . . . DLB-157
Marek, Richard, Books DLB-46
Mares, E. A. 1938- DLB-122
Margulies, Donald 1954- DLB-228
Mariani, Paul 1940- DLB-111
Marie de France flourished 1160-1178. . . . DLB-208
Marie-Victorin, Frère (Conrad Kirouac) 1885-1944 . . . . DLB-92
Marin, Biagio 1891-1985 . . . . DLB-128
Marinetti, Filippo Tommaso 1876-1944 . . . . DLB-114, 264
Marinina, Aleksandra (Marina Anatol'evna Alekseeva) 1957- DLB-285
Marinković, Ranko 1913- DLB-147; CDWLB-4
Marion, Frances 1886-1973 . . . . DLB-44
Marius, Richard C. 1933-1999 . . . . Y-85
Markevich, Boleslav Mikhailovich 1822-1884 . . . . DLB-238
Markfield, Wallace 1926-2002. . . . . DLB-2, 28
Markham, Edwin 1852-1940. . . . . DLB-54, 186
Markle, Fletcher 1921-1991 . . . . DLB-68; Y-91
Marlatt, Daphne 1942- DLB-60
Marlitt, E. 1825-1887. . . . . DLB-129
Marlowe, Christopher 1564-1593 . . . . DLB-62; CDBLB-1
Marlyn, John 1912- DLB-88
Marmion, Shakerley 1603-1639. . . . . DLB-58
Der Marner before 1230-circa 1287. . . . . . DLB-138
Marnham, Patrick 1943- DLB-204
The *Marprelate Tracts* 1588-1589 . . . . DLB-132
Marquand, John P. 1893-1960. . . . . DLB-9, 102
Marques, Helena 1935- DLB-287
Marqués, René 1919-1979 . . . . DLB-113
Marquis, Don 1878-1937 . . . . DLB-11, 25
Marriott, Anne 1913-1997 . . . . DLB-68
Marryat, Frederick 1792-1848 . . . . DLB-21, 163
Marsh, Capen, Lyon and Webb DLB-49
Marsh, George Perkins 1801-1882 . . . . DLB-1, 64, 243
Marsh, James 1794-1842 . . . . DLB-1, 59
Marsh, Narcissus 1638-1713 . . . . DLB-213
Marsh, Ngaio 1899-1982 . . . . DLB-77
Marshall, Alan 1902-1984 . . . . DLB-260
Marshall, Edison 1894-1967 . . . . DLB-102
Marshall, Edward 1932- DLB-16
Marshall, Emma 1828-1899. . . . . DLB-163
Marshall, James 1942-1992 . . . . DLB-61
Marshall, Joyce 1913- DLB-88
Marshall, Paule 1929- DLB-33, 157, 227
Marshall, Tom 1938-1993. . . . . DLB-60
Marsilius of Padua circa 1275-circa 1342 . . . . DLB-115
Mars-Jones, Adam 1954- DLB-207
Marson, Una 1905-1965 . . . . DLB-157
Marston, John 1576-1634. . . . . DLB-58, 172
Marston, Philip Bourke 1850-1887 . . . . DLB-35
Martens, Kurt 1870-1945. . . . . DLB-66
Martí, José 1853-1895 . . . . DLB-290
Martial circa A.D. 40-circa A.D. 103 . . . . DLB-211; CDWLB-1
William S. Martien [publishing house]. DLB-49
Martin, Abe (see Hubbard, Kin)
Martin, Catherine ca. 1847-1937 . . . . DLB-230
Martin, Charles 1942- DLB-120, 282
Martin, Claire 1914- DLB-60
Martin, David 1915-1997. . . . . DLB-260
Martin, Jay 1935- DLB-111
Martin, Johann (see Laurentius von Schnüffis)
Martin, Thomas 1696-1771 . . . . DLB-213
Martin, Violet Florence (see Ross, Martin)
Martin du Gard, Roger 1881-1958 . . . . DLB-65
Martineau, Harriet 1802-1876 . . . . DLB-21, 55, 159, 163, 166, 190
Martínez, Demetria 1960- DLB-209
Martínez de Toledo, Alfonso 1398?-1468 . . . . DLB-286
Martínez, Eliud 1935- DLB-122
Martínez, Max 1943- DLB-82
Martínez, Rubén 1962- DLB-209
Martinson, Harry 1904-1978 . . . . DLB-259
Martinson, Moa 1890-1964 . . . . DLB-259
Martone, Michael 1955- DLB-218
Martyn, Edward 1859-1923 . . . . DLB-10
Marvell, Andrew 1621-1678 . . . . .DLB-131; CDBLB-2
Marvin X 1944- DLB-38
Marx, Karl 1818-1883 . . . . DLB-129
Marzials, Theo 1850-1920. . . . . DLB-35
Masefield, John 1878-1967 . . . DLB-10, 19, 153, 160; CDBLB-5
Masham, Damaris Cudworth, Lady 1659-1708 . . . . DLB-252
Masino, Paola 1908-1989 . . . . DLB-264
Mason, A. E. W. 1865-1948 . . . . DLB-70
Mason, Bobbie Ann 1940- DLB-173; Y-87; CDALB-7
Mason, William 1725-1797 . . . . DLB-142
Mason Brothers DLB-49
The Massachusetts Quarterly Review 1847-1850 . . . . DLB-1
Massey, Gerald 1828-1907 . . . . DLB-32
Massey, Linton R. 1900-1974 . . . . DLB-187
Massie, Allan 1938- DLB-271
Massinger, Philip 1583-1640 . . . . DLB-58
Masson, David 1822-1907 . . . . DLB-144
Masters, Edgar Lee 1868-1950 .DLB-54; CDALB-3
Masters, Hilary 1928- DLB-244
Mastronardi, Lucio 1930-1979. . . . . DLB-177
Matevski, Mateja 1929- . . . DLB-181; CDWLB-4
Mather, Cotton 1663-1728 . . . . DLB-24, 30, 140; CDALB-2
Mather, Increase 1639-1723. . . . . DLB-24
Mather, Richard 1596-1669. . . . . DLB-24
Matheson, Annie 1853-1924 . . . . DLB-240
Matheson, Richard 1926- DLB-8, 44
Matheus, John F. 1887- DLB-51
Mathews, Cornelius 1817?-1889 . . . DLB-3, 64, 250
Elkin Mathews [publishing house]. DLB-112

Mathews, John Joseph 1894-1979 . . . . .DLB-175
Mathias, Roland 1915- DLB-27
Mathis, June 1892-1927 . . . . DLB-44
Mathis, Sharon Bell 1937- DLB-33
Matković, Marijan 1915-1985. . . . . DLB-181
Matoš, Antun Gustav 1873-1914 . . . . DLB-147
Matos Paoli, Francisco 1915-2000 . . . . . . DLB-290
Matsumoto Seichō 1909-1992 . . . . DLB-182
The Matter of England 1240-1400 . . . . . . DLB-146
The Matter of Rome early twelfth to late fifteenth century. DLB-146
Matthew of Vendôme circa 1130-circa 1200 . . . . DLB-208
Matthews, Brander 1852-1929 . .DLB-71, 78; DS-13
Matthews, Jack 1925- DLB-6
Matthews, Victoria Earle 1861-1907. . . . . DLB-221
Matthews, William 1942-1997 . . . . DLB-5
Matthías Jochumsson 1835-1920 . . . . DLB-293
Matthías Johannessen 1930- DLB-293
Matthiessen, F. O. 1902-1950 . . . . DLB-63
Matthiessen, Peter 1927- DLB-6, 173, 275
Maturin, Charles Robert 1780-1824 . . . . . .DLB-178
Maugham, W. Somerset 1874-1965 . . . . . DLB-10, 36, 77, 100, 162, 195; CDBLB-6
Maupassant, Guy de 1850-1893 . . . . DLB-123
Maupin, Armistead 1944- DLB-278
Mauriac, Claude 1914-1996 . . . . DLB-83
Mauriac, François 1885-1970 . . . . DLB-65
Maurice, Frederick Denison 1805-1872 . . . DLB-55
Maurois, André 1885-1967. . . . . DLB-65
Maury, James 1718-1769. . . . . DLB-31
Mavor, Elizabeth 1927- DLB-14
Mavor, Osborne Henry (see Bridie, James)
Maxwell, Gavin 1914-1969. . . . . DLB-204
Maxwell, William 1908-2000. . . . . .DLB-218, 278; Y-80
Tribute to Nancy Hale. Y-88
H. Maxwell [publishing house]. DLB-49
John Maxwell [publishing house] DLB-106
May, Elaine 1932- DLB-44
May, Karl 1842-1912 . . . . DLB-129
May, Thomas 1595/1596-1650. . . . . DLB-58
Mayer, Bernadette 1945- DLB-165
Mayer, Mercer 1943- DLB-61
Mayer, O. B. 1818-1891 . . . . DLB-3, 248
Mayes, Herbert R. 1900-1987. . . . . DLB-137
Mayes, Wendell 1919-1992 . . . . DLB-26
Mayfield, Julian 1928-1984. . . . . DLB-33; Y-84
Mayhew, Henry 1812-1887 . . . . . DLB-18, 55, 190
Mayhew, Jonathan 1720-1766. . . . . DLB-31
Mayne, Ethel Colburn 1865-1941 . . . . . . DLB-197
Mayne, Jasper 1604-1672 . . . . DLB-126
Mayne, Seymour 1944- DLB-60
Mayor, Flora Macdonald 1872-1932 . . . . . DLB-36
Mayröcker, Friederike 1924- DLB-85
Mazrui, Ali A. 1933- DLB-125
Mažuranić, Ivan 1814-1890 . . . . DLB-147
Mazursky, Paul 1930- DLB-44
McAlmon, Robert 1896-1956. . . DLB-4, 45; DS-15
"A Night at Bricktop's" Y-01
McArthur, Peter 1866-1924 . . . . DLB-92
McAuley, James 1917-1976 . . . . DLB-260
Robert M. McBride and Company DLB-46
McCabe, Patrick 1955- DLB-194
McCaffrey, Anne 1926- DLB-8
McCann, Colum 1965- DLB-267
McCarthy, Cormac 1933- DLB-6, 143, 256
The Cormac McCarthy Society. Y-99
McCarthy, Mary 1912-1989. . . . . .DLB-2; Y-81
McCarthy, Shaun Lloyd (see Cory, Desmond)
McCay, Winsor 1871-1934. . . . . DLB-22
McClane, Albert Jules 1922-1991 . . . . .DLB-171
McClatchy, C. K. 1858-1936 . . . . DLB-25
McClellan, George Marion 1860-1934 . . . . DLB-50
"The Negro as a Writer" DLB-50
McCloskey, Robert 1914- DLB-22
McClung, Nellie Letitia 1873-1951 . . . . DLB-92
McClure, James 1939- DLB-276
McClure, Joanna 1930- DLB-16
McClure, Michael 1932- DLB-16
McClure, Phillips and Company DLB-46
McClure, S. S. 1857-1949 . . . . DLB-91
A. C. McClurg and Company DLB-49
McCluskey, John A., Jr. 1944- DLB-33
McCollum, Michael A. 1946- Y-87
McConnell, William C. 1917- DLB-88
McCord, David 1897-1997 . . . . DLB-61
McCord, Louisa S. 1810-1879 . . . . DLB-248
McCorkle, Jill 1958- DLB-234; Y-87
McCorkle, Samuel Eusebius 1746-1811 . . . DLB-37
McCormick, Anne O'Hare 1880-1954. . . . DLB-29
McCormick, Kenneth Dale 1906-1997. . . . . . . Y-97
McCormick, Robert R. 1880-1955. . . . . . . DLB-29
McCourt, Edward 1907-1972 . . . . DLB-88
McCoy, Horace 1897-1955. . . . . DLB-9
McCrae, Hugh 1876-1958 . . . . DLB-260
McCrae, John 1872-1918 . . . . DLB-92
McCullagh, Joseph B. 1842-1896 . . . . DLB-23
McCullers, Carson 1917-1967 . . . . . .DLB-2, 7, 173, 228; CDALB-1
McCulloch, Thomas 1776-1843 . . . . DLB-99
McDermott, Alice 1953- DLB-292
McDonald, Forrest 1927- DLB-17
McDonald, Walter 1934- DLB-105, DS-9
"Getting Started: Accepting the Regions You Own–or Which Own You". DLB-105
Tribute to James Dickey Y-97
McDougall, Colin 1917-1984 . . . . DLB-68
McDowell, Katharine Sherwood Bonner 1849-1883 . . . . DLB-202, 239
Obolensky McDowell [publishing house] DLB-46
McEwan, Ian 1948- DLB-14, 194
McFadden, David 1940- DLB-60
McFall, Frances Elizabeth Clarke (see Grand, Sarah)
McFarland, Ron 1942- DLB-256
McFarlane, Leslie 1902-1977 . . . . DLB-88
McFee, William 1881-1966. . . . . DLB-153
McGahern, John 1934- DLB-14, 231
McGee, Thomas D'Arcy 1825-1868 . . . . . DLB-99
McGeehan, W. O. 1879-1933. . . . . . . .DLB-25, 171
McGill, Ralph 1898-1969 . . . . DLB-29
McGinley, Phyllis 1905-1978 . . . . DLB-11, 48
McGinniss, Joe 1942- DLB-185
McGirt, James E. 1874-1930. . . . . DLB-50
McGlashan and Gill DLB-106
McGough, Roger 1937- DLB-40
McGrath, John 1935- DLB-233
McGrath, Patrick 1950- DLB-231
McGraw-Hill DLB-46
McGuane, Thomas 1939- DLB-2, 212; Y-80
Tribute to Seymour Lawrence. Y-94
McGuckian, Medbh 1950- DLB-40
McGuffey, William Holmes 1800-1873 . . . DLB-42
McGuinness, Frank 1953- DLB-245
McHenry, James 1785-1845 . . . . DLB-202
McIlvanney, William 1936- DLB-14, 207
McIlwraith, Jean Newton 1859-1938 . . . . . DLB-92
McInerney, Jay 1955- DLB-292
McIntosh, Maria Jane 1803-1878 . . . DLB-239, 248
McIntyre, James 1827-1906 . . . . DLB-99
McIntyre, O. O. 1884-1938 . . . . DLB-25
McKay, Claude 1889-1948. . . . .DLB-4, 45, 51, 117
The David McKay Company. DLB-49
McKean, William V. 1820-1903. . . . . DLB-23
McKenna, Stephen 1888-1967 . . . . .DLB-197
The McKenzie Trust Y-96
McKerrow, R. B. 1872-1940. . . . . DLB-201
McKinley, Robin 1952- DLB-52
McKnight, Reginald 1956- DLB-234
McLachlan, Alexander 1818-1896 . . . . DLB-99
McLaren, Floris Clark 1904-1978. . . . . DLB-68
McLaverty, Michael 1907- DLB-15
McLean, Duncan 1964- DLB-267
McLean, John R. 1848-1916. . . . . DLB-23
McLean, William L. 1852-1931 . . . . DLB-25
McLennan, William 1856-1904 . . . . DLB-92
McLoughlin Brothers DLB-49
McLuhan, Marshall 1911-1980 . . . . DLB-88
McMaster, John Bach 1852-1932 . . . . DLB-47
McMillan, Terri 1951- DLB-292

McMurtry, Larry 1936- DLB-2, 143, 256; Y-80, 87; CDALB-6
McNally, Terrence 1939- DLB-7, 249
McNeil, Florence 1937- DLB-60
McNeile, Herman Cyril 1888-1937 . . . . DLB-77
McNickle, D'Arcy 1904-1977. . . . . . . DLB-175, 212
McPhee, John 1931- DLB-185, 275
McPherson, James Alan 1943- DLB-38, 244
McPherson, Sandra 1943- Y-86
McTaggart, J. M. E. 1866-1925 . . . . DLB-262
McWhirter, George 1939- DLB-60
McWilliam, Candia 1955- DLB-267
McWilliams, Carey 1905-1980 . . . . DLB-137
"*The Nation's* Future," Carey McWilliams's Editorial Policy in *Nation* DLB-137
Mda, Zakes 1948- DLB-225
Mead, George Herbert 1863-1931. . . . . . . DLB-270
Mead, L. T. 1844-1914 . . . . DLB-141
Mead, Matthew 1924- DLB-40
Mead, Taylor ?- DLB-16
Meany, Tom 1903-1964 . . . . DLB-171
Mechthild von Magdeburg circa 1207-circa 1282 . . . . DLB-138
Medieval Galician-Portuguese Poetry DLB-287
Medill, Joseph 1823-1899. . . . . DLB-43
Medoff, Mark 1940- DLB-7
Meek, Alexander Beaufort 1814-1865 . . DLB-3, 248
Meeke, Mary ?-1816? DLB-116
Mei, Lev Aleksandrovich 1822-1862 . . . . . DLB-277
Meinke, Peter 1932- DLB-5
Mejia Vallejo, Manuel 1923- DLB-113
Melanchthon, Philipp 1497-1560 . . . . DLB-179
Melançon, Robert 1947- DLB-60
Mell, Max 1882-1971 . . . . DLB-81, 124
Mellow, James R. 1926-1997 . . . . DLB-111
Mel'nikov, Pavel Ivanovich 1818-1883 . . . DLB-238
Meltzer, David 1937- DLB-16
Meltzer, Milton 1915- DLB-61
Melville, Elizabeth, Lady Culross circa 1585-1640 . . . . DLB-172
Melville, Herman 1819-1891 . . . . DLB-3, 74, 250; CDALB-2
The Melville Society Y-01
Melville, James (Roy Peter Martin) 1931- DLB-276
Mena, Juan de 1411-1456 . . . . DLB-286
Mena, María Cristina 1893-1965. . . . DLB-209, 221
Menander 342-341 B.C.-circa 292-291 B.C. DLB-176; CDWLB-1
Menantes (see Hunold, Christian Friedrich)
Mencke, Johann Burckhard 1674-1732 . . . DLB-168
Mencken, H. L. 1880-1956 . . . . DLB-11, 29, 63, 137, 222; CDALB-4
"Berlin, February, 1917" Y-00
From the Initial Issue of *American Mercury* (January 1924) DLB-137
Mencken and Nietzsche: An Unpublished Excerpt from H. L. Mencken's *My Life as Author and Editor* Y-93
Mendelssohn, Moses 1729-1786. . . . . DLB-97
Mendes, Catulle 1841-1909 . . . . DLB-217
Méndez M., Miguel 1930- DLB-82
The Mercantile Library of New York Y-96
Mercer, Cecil William (see Yates, Dornford)
Mercer, David 1928-1980 . . . . DLB-13
Mercer, John 1704-1768 . . . . DLB-31
Mercer, Johnny 1909-1976. . . . . DLB-265
Meredith, George 1828-1909 . . . . DLB-18, 35, 57, 159; CDBLB-4
Meredith, Louisa Anne 1812-1895 . . DLB-166, 230
Meredith, Owen (see Lytton, Edward Robert Bulwer)
Meredith, William 1919- DLB-5
Meres, Francis *Palladis Tamia, Wits Treasurie* (1598) [excerpt] DLB-172
Merezhkovsky, Dmitrii Sergeevich 1865-1941 . . . . DLB-295
Mergerle, Johann Ulrich (see Abraham ä Sancta Clara)
Mérimée, Prosper 1803-1870 . . . . DLB-119, 192
Merivale, John Herman 1779-1844 . . . . DLB-96
Meriwether, Louise 1923- DLB-33
Merleau-Ponty, Maurice 1908-1961 . . . . . DLB-296
Merlin Press DLB-112
Merriam, Eve 1916-1992 . . . . DLB-61
The Merriam Company DLB-49
Merril, Judith 1923-1997 . . . . DLB-251
Tribute to Theodore Sturgeon Y-85
Merrill, James 1926-1995. . . . . . . DLB-5, 165; Y-85
Merrill and Baker DLB-49
The Mershon Company DLB-49
Merton, Thomas 1915-1968 . . . . DLB-48; Y-81
Merwin, W. S. 1927- DLB-5, 169
Julian Messner [publishing house] DLB-46
Mészöly, Miklós 1921- DLB-232
J. Metcalf [publishing house] DLB-49
Metcalf, John 1938- DLB-60
The Methodist Book Concern. DLB-49
Methuen and Company. DLB-112
Meun, Jean de (see *Roman de la Rose*)
Mew, Charlotte 1869-1928 . . . . DLB-19, 135
Mewshaw, Michael 1943- Y-80
Tribute to Albert Erskine Y-93
Meyer, Conrad Ferdinand 1825-1898 . . . . DLB-129
Meyer, E. Y. 1946- DLB-75
Meyer, Eugene 1875-1959 . . . . DLB-29
Meyer, Michael 1921-2000 . . . . DLB-155
Meyers, Jeffrey 1939- DLB-111
Meynell, Alice 1847-1922. . . . . DLB-19, 98
Meynell, Viola 1885-1956 . . . . DLB-153
Meyrink, Gustav 1868-1932 . . . . DLB-81
Mézières, Philipe de circa 1327-1405 . . . . . DLB-208
Michael, Ib 1945- DLB-214
Michael, Livi 1960- DLB-267
Michaëlis, Karen 1872-1950. . . . . DLB-214
Michaels, Anne 1958- DLB-299
Michaels, Leonard 1933- DLB-130
Michaux, Henri 1899-1984 . . . . DLB-258
Micheaux, Oscar 1884-1951 . . . . DLB-50
Michel of Northgate, Dan circa 1265-circa 1340. . . . . DLB-146
Micheline, Jack 1929-1998. . . . . DLB-16
Michener, James A. 1907?-1997. . . . . DLB-6
Micklejohn, George circa 1717-1818 . . . . . . DLB-31
Middle Hill Press DLB-106
Middleton, Christopher 1926- DLB-40
Middleton, Richard 1882-1911 . . . . DLB-156
Middleton, Stanley 1919- DLB-14
Middleton, Thomas 1580-1627 . . . . DLB-58
Miegel, Agnes 1879-1964. . . . . DLB-56
Mieželaitis, Eduardas 1919-1997 . . . . DLB-220
Miguéis, José Rodrigues 1901-1980. . . . . . DLB-287
Mihailović, Dragoslav 1930- DLB-181
Mihalić, Slavko 1928- DLB-181
Mikhailov, A. (see Sheller, Aleksandr Konstantinovich)
Mikhailov, Mikhail Larionovich 1829-1865 . . . . DLB-238
Mikhailovsky, Nikolai Konstantinovich 1842-1904 . . . . DLB-277
Miles, Josephine 1911-1985 . . . . DLB-48
Miles, Susan (Ursula Wyllie Roberts) 1888-1975 . . . . DLB-240
Miliković, Branko 1934-1961 . . . . DLB-181
Milius, John 1944- DLB-44
Mill, James 1773-1836 . . . . DLB-107, 158, 262
Mill, John Stuart 1806-1873 . . . . . .DLB-55, 190, 262; CDBLB-4
Thoughts on Poetry and Its Varieties (1833) DLB-32
Andrew Millar [publishing house] DLB-154
Millar, Kenneth 1915-1983 . . . . DLB-2, 226; Y-83; DS-6
Millay, Edna St. Vincent 1892-1950 . . . . .DLB-45, 249; CDALB-4
Millen, Sarah Gertrude 1888-1968 . . . . . . DLB-225
Miller, Andrew 1960- DLB-267
Miller, Arthur 1915- DLB-7, 266; CDALB-1
The Arthur Miller Society. Y-01
Miller, Caroline 1903-1992 . . . . DLB-9
Miller, Eugene Ethelbert 1950- DLB-41
Tribute to Julian Mayfield. Y-84
Miller, Heather Ross 1939- DLB-120
Miller, Henry 1891-1980 . . . . DLB-4, 9; Y-80; CDALB-5
Miller, Hugh 1802-1856 . . . . DLB-190
Miller, J. Hillis 1928- DLB-67
Miller, Jason 1939- DLB-7

Miller, Joaquin 1839-1913 . . . . DLB-186
Miller, May 1899-1995 . . . . DLB-41
Miller, Paul 1906-1991 . . . . DLB-127
Miller, Perry 1905-1963 . . . . DLB-17, 63
Miller, Sue 1943- DLB-143
Miller, Vassar 1924-1998 . . . . DLB-105
Miller, Walter M., Jr. 1923-1996 . . . . DLB-8
Miller, Webb 1892-1940 . . . . DLB-29
James Miller [publishing house] DLB-49
Millett, Kate 1934- DLB-246
Millhauser, Steven 1943- DLB-2
Millican, Arthenia J. Bates 1920- DLB-38
Milligan, Alice 1866-1953 . . . . DLB-240
Mills, Magnus 1954- DLB-267
Mills and Boon DLB-112
Milman, Henry Hart 1796-1868 . . . . DLB-96
Milne, A. A. 1882-1956 . . . . . DLB-10, 77, 100, 160
Milner, Ron 1938- DLB-38
William Milner [publishing house] DLB-106
Milnes, Richard Monckton (Lord Houghton) 1809-1885 . . . . DLB-32, 184
Milton, John 1608-1674 . . . . . DLB-131, 151, 281; CDBLB-2
The Milton Society of America Y-00
Miłosz, Czesław 1911- . . . DLB-215; CDWLB-4
Minakami Tsutomu 1919- DLB-182
Minamoto no Sanetomo 1192-1219 . . . . . DLB-203
Minco, Marga 1920- DLB-299
The Minerva Press DLB-154
Minnesang circa 1150-1280 . . . . DLB-138
The Music of *Minnesang* DLB-138
Minns, Susan 1839-1938 . . . . DLB-140
Minton, Balch and Company DLB-46
Mirbeau, Octave 1848-1917 . . . . DLB-123, 192
Mirk, John died after 1414? DLB-146
Miró, Ricardo 1883-1940 . . . . DLB-290
Miron, Gaston 1928-1996 . . . . DLB-60
A Mirror for Magistrates DLB-167
Mishima Yukio 1925-1970 . . . . DLB-182
Mistral, Gabriela 1889-1957 . . . . DLB-283
Mitchel, Jonathan 1624-1668 . . . . DLB-24
Mitchell, Adrian 1932- DLB-40
Mitchell, Donald Grant 1822-1908 . . . . DLB-1, 243; DS-13
Mitchell, Gladys 1901-1983 . . . . DLB-77
Mitchell, James Leslie 1901-1935 . . . . DLB-15
Mitchell, John (see Slater, Patrick)
Mitchell, John Ames 1845-1918 . . . . DLB-79
Mitchell, Joseph 1908-1996 . . . . DLB-185; Y-96
Mitchell, Julian 1935- DLB-14
Mitchell, Ken 1940- DLB-60
Mitchell, Langdon 1862-1935 . . . . DLB-7
Mitchell, Loften 1919- DLB-38
Mitchell, Margaret 1900-1949 . . DLB-9; CDALB-7
Mitchell, S. Weir 1829-1914 . . . . DLB-202
Mitchell, W. J. T. 1942- DLB-246
Mitchell, W. O. 1914-1998 . . . . DLB-88
Mitchison, Naomi Margaret (Haldane) 1897-1999 . . . . DLB-160, 191, 255
Mitford, Mary Russell 1787-1855 . . . .DLB-110, 116
Mitford, Nancy 1904-1973 . . . . DLB-191
Mittelholzer, Edgar 1909-1965 . . . . .DLB-117; CDWLB-3
Mitterer, Erika 1906- DLB-85
Mitterer, Felix 1948- DLB-124
Mitternacht, Johann Sebastian 1613-1679 . . . . DLB-168
Miyamoto Yuriko 1899-1951 . . . . DLB-180
Mizener, Arthur 1907-1988 . . . . DLB-103
Mo, Timothy 1950- DLB-194
Moberg, Vilhelm 1898-1973 . . . . DLB-259
Modern Age Books DLB-46
Modern Language Association of America
The Modern Language Association of America Celebrates Its Centennial . . . Y-84
The Modern Library DLB-46
Modiano, Patrick 1945- DLB-83, 299
Moffat, Yard and Company DLB-46
Moffet, Thomas 1553-1604 . . . . DLB-136
Mofolo, Thomas 1876-1948 . . . . DLB-225
Mohr, Nicholasa 1938- DLB-145
Moix, Ana María 1947- DLB-134
Molesworth, Louisa 1839-1921 . . . . DLB-135
Molière (Jean-Baptiste Poquelin) 1622-1673 . . . . DLB-268
Møller, Poul Martin 1794-1838 . . . . DLB-300
Möllhausen, Balduin 1825-1905 . . . . DLB-129
Molnár, Ferenc 1878-1952 . . DLB-215; CDWLB-4
Molnár, Miklós (see Mészöly, Miklós)
Momaday, N. Scott 1934- DLB-143, 175, 256; CDALB-7
Monkhouse, Allan 1858-1936 . . . . DLB-10
Monro, Harold 1879-1932 . . . . DLB-19
Monroe, Harriet 1860-1936 . . . . DLB-54, 91
Monsarrat, Nicholas 1910-1979 . . . . DLB-15
Montagu, Lady Mary Wortley 1689-1762 . . . . DLB-95, 101
Montague, C. E. 1867-1928 . . . . DLB-197
Montague, John 1929- DLB-40
Montale, Eugenio 1896-1981 . . . . DLB-114
Montalvo, Garci Rodríguez de ca. 1450?-before 1505 . . . . DLB-286
Montalvo, José 1946-1994 . . . . DLB-209
Monterroso, Augusto 1921-2003 . . . . DLB-145
Montesquiou, Robert de 1855-1921 . . . . . DLB-217
Montgomerie, Alexander circa 1550?-1598 . . . . DLB-167
Montgomery, James 1771-1854 . . . . . . DLB-93, 158
Montgomery, John 1919- DLB-16
Montgomery, Lucy Maud 1874-1942 . . . . DLB-92; DS-14
Montgomery, Marion 1925- DLB-6
Montgomery, Robert Bruce (see Crispin, Edmund)
Montherlant, Henry de 1896-1972 . . . . DLB-72
The Monthly Review 1749-1844 . . . . DLB-110
Montigny, Louvigny de 1876-1955 . . . . . . DLB-92
Montoya, José 1932- DLB-122
Moodie, John Wedderburn Dunbar 1797-1869 . . . . DLB-99
Moodie, Susanna 1803-1885 . . . . DLB-99
Moody, Joshua circa 1633-1697 . . . . DLB-24
Moody, William Vaughn 1869-1910 . . . .DLB-7, 54
Moorcock, Michael 1939- DLB-14, 231, 261
Moore, Alan 1953- DLB-261
Moore, Brian 1921-1999 . . . . DLB-251
Moore, Catherine L. 1911-1987 . . . . DLB-8
Moore, Clement Clarke 1779-1863 . . . . DLB-42
Moore, Dora Mavor 1888-1979 . . . . DLB-92
Moore, G. E. 1873-1958 . . . . DLB-262
Moore, George 1852-1933 . . . . DLB-10, 18, 57, 135
Literature at Nurse, or Circulating Morals (1885) DLB-18
Moore, Lorrie 1957- DLB-234
Moore, Marianne 1887-1972 . . . . DLB-45; DS-7; CDALB-5
International Marianne Moore Society . . . Y-98
Moore, Mavor 1919- DLB-88
Moore, Richard 1927- DLB-105
"The No Self, the Little Self, and the Poets" DLB-105
Moore, T. Sturge 1870-1944 . . . . DLB-19
Moore, Thomas 1779-1852 . . . . DLB-96, 144
Moore, Ward 1903-1978 . . . . DLB-8
Moore, Wilstach, Keys and Company DLB-49
Moorehead, Alan 1901-1983 . . . . DLB-204
Moorhouse, Frank 1938- DLB-289
Moorhouse, Geoffrey 1931- DLB-204
The Moorland-Spingarn Research Center DLB-76
Moorman, Mary C. 1905-1994 . . . . DLB-155
Mora, Pat 1942- DLB-209
Moraga, Cherríe 1952- DLB-82, 249
Morales, Alejandro 1944- DLB-82
Morales, Mario Roberto 1947- DLB-145
Morales, Rafael 1919- DLB-108
Morality Plays: *Mankind* circa 1450-1500 and *Everyman* circa 1500 . . . . DLB-146
Morand, Paul (1888-1976) DLB-65
Morante, Elsa 1912-1985 . . . . .DLB-177
Morata, Olympia Fulvia 1526-1555 . . . . . .DLB-179
Moravia, Alberto 1907-1990 . . . . .DLB-177
Mordaunt, Elinor 1872-1942 . . . . .DLB-174
Mordovtsev, Daniil Lukich 1830-1905 . . . DLB-238
More, Hannah 1745-1833 . . . . DLB-107, 109, 116, 158
More, Henry 1614-1687 . . . . DLB-126, 252
More, Sir Thomas 1477/1478-1535 . . . . DLB-136, 281
Morejón, Nancy 1944- DLB-283
Morency, Pierre 1942- DLB-60

Moreno, Dorinda 1939- DLB-122
Moretti, Marino 1885-1979 . . . . DLB-114, 264
Morgan, Berry 1919- DLB-6
Morgan, Charles 1894-1958 . . . . DLB-34, 100
Morgan, Edmund S. 1916- DLB-17
Morgan, Edwin 1920- DLB-27
Morgan, John Pierpont 1837-1913 . . . . DLB-140
Morgan, John Pierpont, Jr. 1867-1943 . . . . DLB-140
Morgan, Robert 1944- DLB-120, 292
Morgan, Sydney Owenson, Lady 1776?-1859. . . . . DLB-116, 158
Morgner, Irmtraud 1933-1990. . . . . DLB-75
Morhof, Daniel Georg 1639-1691 . . . . DLB-164
Mori Ōgai 1862-1922 . . . . DLB-180
Móricz, Zsigmond 1879-1942. . . . . DLB-215
Morier, James Justinian 1782 or 1783?-1849 . . . . DLB-116
Mörike, Eduard 1804-1875 . . . . DLB-133
Morin, Paul 1889-1963 . . . . DLB-92
Morison, Richard 1514?-1556 . . . . DLB-136
Morison, Samuel Eliot 1887-1976. . . . . DLB-17
Morison, Stanley 1889-1967 . . . . DLB-201
Moritz, Karl Philipp 1756-1793 . . . . DLB-94
Moriz von Craûn circa 1220-1230. . . . . DLB-138
Morley, Christopher 1890-1957. . . . . DLB-9
Morley, John 1838-1923 . . . . DLB-57, 144, 190
Moro, César 1903-1956. . . . . DLB-290
Morris, George Pope 1802-1864 . . . . DLB-73
Morris, James Humphrey (see Morris, Jan)
Morris, Jan 1926- DLB-204
Morris, Lewis 1833-1907 . . . . DLB-35
Morris, Margaret 1737-1816. . . . . DLB-200
Morris, Mary McGarry 1943- DLB-292
Morris, Richard B. 1904-1989 . . . . DLB-17
Morris, William 1834-1896 . . . . DLB-18, 35, 57, 156, 178, 184; CDBLB-4
Morris, Willie 1934-1999. . . . . Y-80
Tribute to Irwin Shaw. Y-84
Tribute to James Dickey Y-97
Morris, Wright 1910-1998 . . . . DLB-2, 206, 218; Y-81
Morrison, Arthur 1863-1945 . . . . DLB-70, 135, 197
Morrison, Charles Clayton 1874-1966. . . . . DLB-91
Morrison, John 1904-1998. . . . . DLB-260
Morrison, Toni 1931- DLB-6, 33, 143; Y-81, 93; CDALB-6
Nobel Lecture 1993. . . . . Y-93
Morrissy, Mary 1957- DLB-267
William Morrow and Company DLB-46
Morse, James Herbert 1841-1923 . . . . DLB-71
Morse, Jedidiah 1761-1826. . . . . DLB-37
Morse, John T., Jr. 1840-1937 . . . . DLB-47
Morselli, Guido 1912-1973. . . . . DLB-177
Morte Arthure, the *Alliterative* and the *Stanzaic* circa 1350-1400 . . . . DLB-146
Mortimer, Favell Lee 1802-1878 . . . . DLB-163
Mortimer, John 1923- DLB-13, 245, 271; CDBLB-8
Morton, Carlos 1942- DLB-122
Morton, H. V. 1892-1979 . . . . DLB-195
John P. Morton and Company DLB-49
Morton, Nathaniel 1613-1685 . . . . DLB-24
Morton, Sarah Wentworth 1759-1846. . . . . DLB-37
Morton, Thomas circa 1579-circa 1647 . . . . DLB-24
Moscherosch, Johann Michael 1601-1669 . . . . DLB-164
Humphrey Moseley [publishing house] DLB-170
Möser, Justus 1720-1794 . . . . DLB-97
Mosley, Nicholas 1923- DLB-14, 207
Moss, Arthur 1889-1969 . . . . DLB-4
Moss, Howard 1922-1987 . . . . DLB-5
Moss, Thylias 1954- DLB-120
Motion, Andrew 1952- DLB-40
Motley, John Lothrop 1814-1877 . . . . DLB-1, 30, 59, 235
Motley, Willard 1909-1965 . . . . DLB-76, 143
Mott, Lucretia 1793-1880. . . . . DLB-239
Benjamin Motte Jr. [publishing house] DLB-154
Motteux, Peter Anthony 1663-1718. . . . . . . DLB-80
Mottram, R. H. 1883-1971. . . . . DLB-36
Mount, Ferdinand 1939- DLB-231
Mouré, Erin 1955- DLB-60
Mourning Dove (Humishuma) between 1882 and 1888?-1936 . . . . DLB-175, 221
Movies
Fiction into Film, 1928-1975: A List of Movies Based on the Works of Authors in British Novelists, 1930-1959. DLB-15
Movies from Books, 1920-1974. . . . . DLB-9
Mowat, Farley 1921- DLB-68
A. R. Mowbray and Company, Limited DLB-106
Mowrer, Edgar Ansel 1892-1977 . . . . DLB-29
Mowrer, Paul Scott 1887-1971 . . . . DLB-29
Edward Moxon [publishing house] DLB-106
Joseph Moxon [publishing house] DLB-170
Moyes, Patricia 1923-2000. . . . . DLB-276
Mphahlele, Es'kia (Ezekiel) 1919- DLB-125, 225; CDWLB-3
Mrożek, Sławomir 1930- . . . DLB-232; CDWLB-4
Mtshali, Oswald Mbuyiseni 1940- DLB-125, 225
Mucedorus DLB-62
Mudford, William 1782-1848 . . . . DLB-159
Mudrooroo (see Johnson, Colin)
Mueller, Lisel 1924- DLB-105
Muhajir, El (see Marvin X)
Muhajir, Nazzam Al Fitnah (see Marvin X)
Mühlbach, Luise 1814-1873. . . . . DLB-133
Muir, Edwin 1887-1959 . . . . DLB-20, 100, 191
Muir, Helen 1937- DLB-14
Muir, John 1838-1914 . . . . DLB-186, 275
Muir, Percy 1894-1979 . . . . DLB-201
Mujū Ichien 1226-1312 . . . . DLB-203
Mukherjee, Bharati 1940- DLB-60, 218
Mulcaster, Richard 1531 or 1532-1611 . . . DLB-167
Muldoon, Paul 1951- DLB-40
Mulisch, Harry 1927- DLB-299
Müller, Friedrich (see Müller, Maler)
Müller, Heiner 1929-1995 . . . . DLB-124
Müller, Maler 1749-1825 . . . . DLB-94
Muller, Marcia 1944- DLB-226
Müller, Wilhelm 1794-1827 . . . . DLB-90
Mumford, Lewis 1895-1990 . . . . DLB-63
Munby, A. N. L. 1913-1974. . . . . DLB-201
Munby, Arthur Joseph 1828-1910. . . . . DLB-35
Munday, Anthony 1560-1633 . . . . DLB-62, 172
Mundt, Clara (see Mühlbach, Luise)
Mundt, Theodore 1808-1861 . . . . DLB-133
Munford, Robert circa 1737-1783. . . . . DLB-31
Mungoshi, Charles 1947- DLB-157
Munk, Kaj 1898-1944 . . . . DLB-214
Munonye, John 1929- DLB-117
Munro, Alice 1931- DLB-53
George Munro [publishing house]. DLB-49
Munro, H. H. 1870-1916 . . . . DLB-34, 162; CDBLB-5
Munro, Neil 1864-1930 . . . . DLB-156
Norman L. Munro [publishing house]. DLB-49
Munroe, Kirk 1850-1930. . . . . DLB-42
Munroe and Francis. DLB-49
James Munroe and Company DLB-49
Joel Munsell [publishing house] DLB-49
Munsey, Frank A. 1854-1925 . . . . DLB-25, 91
Frank A. Munsey and Company. DLB-49
Murakami Haruki 1949- DLB-182
Murav'ev, Mikhail Nikitich 1757-1807. . . . DLB-150
Murdoch, Iris 1919-1999 . . . . DLB-14, 194, 233; CDBLB-8
Murdock, James
From *Sketches of Modern Philosophy*. DS-5
Murdoch, Rupert 1931- DLB-127
Murfree, Mary N. 1850-1922 . . . . DLB-12, 74
Murger, Henry 1822-1861. . . . . DLB-119
Murger, Louis-Henri (see Murger, Henry)
Murnane, Gerald 1939- DLB-289
Murner, Thomas 1475-1537 . . . . DLB-179
Muro, Amado 1915-1971. . . . . DLB-82
Murphy, Arthur 1727-1805 . . . . DLB-89, 142
Murphy, Beatrice M. 1908-1992 . . . . DLB-76
Murphy, Dervla 1931- DLB-204
Murphy, Emily 1868-1933 . . . . DLB-99
Murphy, Jack 1923-1980 . . . . DLB-241
Murphy, John H., III 1916- DLB-127
Murphy, Richard 1927-1993 . . . . DLB-40
John Murphy and Company DLB-49

Murray, Albert L. 1916- DLB-38
Murray, Gilbert 1866-1957. . . . . DLB-10
Murray, Jim 1919-1998 . . . . DLB-241
John Murray [publishing house] DLB-154
Murray, Judith Sargent 1751-1820 . . . . DLB-37, 200
Murray, Les 1938- DLB-289
Murray, Pauli 1910-1985 . . . . DLB-41
Murry, John Middleton 1889-1957. . . . . . DLB-149
"The Break-Up of the Novel" (1922) DLB-36
Murry, John Middleton, Jr. (see Cowper, Richard)
Musäus, Johann Karl August 1735-1787 . . . DLB-97
Muschg, Adolf 1934- DLB-75
Musil, Robert 1880-1942 . . . . DLB-81, 124; CDWLB-2
Muspilli circa 790-circa 850 . . . . DLB-148
Musset, Alfred de 1810-1857 . . . . . . .DLB-192, 217
Benjamin B. Mussey and Company DLB-49
Mutafchieva, Vera 1929- DLB-181
Mutis, Alvaro 1923- DLB-283
Mwangi, Meja 1948- DLB-125
Myers, Frederic W. H. 1843-1901 . . . . . . DLB-190
Myers, Gustavus 1872-1942 . . . . DLB-47
Myers, L. H. 1881-1944 . . . . DLB-15
Myers, Walter Dean 1937- DLB-33
Myerson, Julie 1960- DLB-267
Mykle, Agnar 1915-1994 . . . . DLB-297
Mykolaitis-Putinas, Vincas 1893-1967. . . . . DLB-220
Myles, Eileen 1949- DLB-193
Myrdal, Jan 1927- DLB-257
Mystery
1985: The Year of the Mystery: A Symposium Y-85
Comments from Other Writers Y-85
The Second Annual New York Festival of Mystery Y-00
Why I Read Mysteries. Y-85
Why I Write Mysteries: Night and Day, by Michael Collins Y-85

N

Na Prous Boneta circa 1296-1328. . . . . . . DLB-208
Nabl, Franz 1883-1974 . . . . DLB-81
Nabakov, Véra 1902-1991 . . . . Y-91
Nabokov, Vladimir 1899-1977 . . DLB-2, 244, 278; Y-80, 91; DS-3; CDALB-1
International Nabokov Society. Y-99
An Interview [On Nabokov], by Fredson Bowers Y-80
Nabokov Festival at Cornell. Y-83
The Vladimir Nabokov Archive in the Berg Collection of the New York Public Library: An Overview Y-91
The Vladimir Nabokov Society Y-01
Nádaši, Ladislav (see Jégé)
Naden, Constance 1858-1889. . . . . DLB-199
Nadezhdin, Nikolai Ivanovich 1804-1856 . . . . DLB-198
Nadson, Semen Iakovlevich 1862-1887 . . .DLB-277
Naevius circa 265 B.C.-201 B.C. DLB-211
Nafis and Cornish DLB-49
Nagai Kafū 1879-1959 . . . . DLB-180
Nagel, Ernest 1901-1985. . . . . .DLB-279
Nagrodskaia, Evdokiia Apollonovna 1866-1930 . . . . DLB-295
Naipaul, Shiva 1945-1985. . . . . .DLB-157; Y-85
Naipaul, V. S. 1932- DLB-125, 204, 207; Y-85, Y-01; CDBLB-8; CDWLB-3
Nobel Lecture 2001: "Two Worlds" Y-01
Nakagami Kenji 1946-1992 . . . . DLB-182
Nakano-in Masatada no Musume (see Nijō, Lady)
Nałkowska, Zofia 1884-1954 . . . . DLB-215
Namora, Fernando 1919-1989 . . . . DLB-287
Joseph Nancrede [publishing house] DLB-49
Naranjo, Carmen 1930- DLB-145
Narbikova, Valeriia Spartakovna 1958- DLB-285
Narezhny, Vasilii Trofimovich 1780-1825. . . . . DLB-198
Narrache, Jean (Emile Coderre) 1893-1970. . . . . DLB-92
Nasby, Petroleum Vesuvius (see Locke, David Ross)
Eveleigh Nash [publishing house] DLB-112
Nash, Ogden 1902-1971 . . . . DLB-11
Nashe, Thomas 1567-1601? DLB-167
Nason, Jerry 1910-1986 . . . . DLB-241
Nasr, Seyyed Hossein 1933- DLB-279
Nast, Condé 1873-1942 . . . . DLB-91
Nast, Thomas 1840-1902 . . . . DLB-188
Nastasijević, Momčilo 1894-1938 . . . . DLB-147
Nathan, George Jean 1882-1958. . . . . DLB-137
Nathan, Robert 1894-1985 . . . . DLB-9
National Book Critics Circle Awards Y-00–01
The National Jewish Book Awards. Y-85
Natsume Sōseki 1867-1916 . . . . DLB-180
Naughton, Bill 1910-1992. . . . . DLB-13
Navarro, Joe 1953- DLB-209
Naylor, Gloria 1950- DLB-173
Nazor, Vladimir 1876-1949 . . . . DLB-147
Ndebele, Njabulo 1948- DLB-157, 225
Neagoe, Peter 1881-1960 . . . . DLB-4
Neal, John 1793-1876 . . . . DLB-1, 59, 243
Neal, Joseph C. 1807-1847 . . . . DLB-11
Neal, Larry 1937-1981 . . . . DLB-38
The Neale Publishing Company DLB-49
Nebel, Frederick 1903-1967 . . . . DLB-226
Nebrija, Antonio de 1442 or 1444-1522. . DLB-286
Nedreaas, Torborg 1906-1987 . . . . DLB-297
F. Tennyson Neely [publishing house] DLB-49
Negoițescu, Ion 1921-1993 . . . . DLB-220
Negri, Ada 1870-1945 . . . . DLB-114
Neihardt, John G. 1881-1973 . . . . . DLB-9, 54, 256
Neidhart von Reuental circa 1185-circa 1240 . . . . DLB-138
Neilson, John Shaw 1872-1942 . . . . DLB-230
Nekrasov, Nikolai Alekseevich 1821-1877. . . . . .DLB-277
Neledinsky-Meletsky, Iurii Aleksandrovich 1752-1828. . . . . DLB-150
Nelligan, Emile 1879-1941 . . . . DLB-92
Nelson, Alice Moore Dunbar 1875-1935 . . DLB-50
Nelson, Antonya 1961- DLB-244
Nelson, Kent 1943- DLB-234
Nelson, Richard K. 1941- DLB-275
Nelson, Thomas, and Sons [U.K.] DLB-106
Nelson, Thomas, and Sons [U.S.]. DLB-49
Nelson, William 1908-1978 . . . . DLB-103
Nelson, William Rockhill 1841-1915 . . . . . DLB-23
Nemerov, Howard 1920-1991 . . . . .DLB-5, 6; Y-83
Németh, László 1901-1975 . . . . DLB-215
Nepos circa 100 B.C.-post 27 B.C. DLB-211
Nėris, Salomėja 1904-1945 . . DLB-220; CDWLB-4
Neruda, Pablo 1904-1973 . . . . DLB-283
Nerval, Gérard de 1808-1855. . . . . .DLB-217
Nervo, Amado 1870-1919. . . . . DLB-290
Nesbit, E. 1858-1924 . . . . .DLB-141, 153, 178
Ness, Evaline 1911-1986. . . . . DLB-61
Nestroy, Johann 1801-1862 . . . . DLB-133
Nettleship, R. L. 1846-1892 . . . . DLB-262
Neugeboren, Jay 1938- DLB-28
Neukirch, Benjamin 1655-1729 . . . . DLB-168
Neumann, Alfred 1895-1952 . . . . DLB-56
Neumann, Ferenc (see Molnár, Ferenc)
Neumark, Georg 1621-1681. . . . . DLB-164
Neumeister, Erdmann 1671-1756 . . . . DLB-168
Nevins, Allan 1890-1971. . . . . .DLB-17; DS-17
Nevinson, Henry Woodd 1856-1941. . . . DLB-135
The New American Library. DLB-46
New Directions Publishing Corporation . . DLB-46
The New Monthly Magazine 1814-1884 . . . . DLB-110
New York Times Book Review. Y-82
John Newbery [publishing house]. DLB-154
Newbolt, Henry 1862-1938 . . . . DLB-19
Newbound, Bernard Slade (see Slade, Bernard)
Newby, Eric 1919- DLB-204
Newby, P. H. 1918- DLB-15
Thomas Cautley Newby [publishing house] DLB-106
Newcomb, Charles King 1820-1894. . . DLB-1, 223
Newell, Peter 1862-1924. . . . . DLB-42
Newell, Robert Henry 1836-1901 . . . . DLB-11
Newhouse, Samuel I. 1895-1979. . . . . .DLB-127
Newman, Cecil Earl 1903-1976 . . . . .DLB-127
Newman, David 1937- DLB-44
Newman, Frances 1883-1928 . . . . Y-80
Newman, Francis William 1805-1897. . . . DLB-190
Newman, John Henry 1801-1890. . DLB-18, 32, 55

Mark Newman [publishing house] DLB-49
Newmarch, Rosa Harriet 1857-1940 . . . . . DLB-240
George Newnes Limited DLB-112
Newsome, Effie Lee 1885-1979 . . . . DLB-76
Newton, A. Edward 1864-1940 . . . . DLB-140
Newton, Sir Isaac 1642-1727 . . . . DLB-252
Nexø, Martin Andersen 1869-1954 . . . . . . DLB-214
Nezval, Vítěslav
1900-1958 . . . . DLB-215; CDWLB-4
Ngugi wa Thiong'o
1938- DLB-125; CDWLB-3
Niatum, Duane 1938- DLB-175
The *Nibelungenlied* and the *Klage*
circa 1200 . . . . DLB-138
Nichol, B. P. 1944-1988 . . . . DLB-53
Nicholas of Cusa 1401-1464 . . . . DLB-115
Nichols, Ann 1891?-1966 . . . . DLB-249
Nichols, Beverly 1898-1983 . . . . DLB-191
Nichols, Dudley 1895-1960 . . . . DLB-26
Nichols, Grace 1950- DLB-157
Nichols, John 1940- Y-82
Nichols, Mary Sargeant (Neal) Gove
1810-1884 . . . . DLB-1, 243
Nichols, Peter 1927- DLB-13, 245
Nichols, Roy F. 1896-1973 . . . . DLB-17
Nichols, Ruth 1948- DLB-60
Nicholson, Edward Williams Byron
1849-1912 . . . . DLB-184
Nicholson, Geoff 1953- DLB-271
Nicholson, Norman 1914- DLB-27
Nicholson, William 1872-1949 . . . . DLB-141
Ní Chuilleanáin, Eiléan 1942- DLB-40
Nicol, Eric 1919- DLB-68
Nicolai, Friedrich 1733-1811 . . . . DLB-97
Nicolas de Clamanges circa 1363-1437 . . . DLB-208
Nicolay, John G. 1832-1901 and
Hay, John 1838-1905 . . . . DLB-47
Nicole, Pierre 1625-1695 . . . . DLB-268
Nicolson, Adela Florence Cory (see Hope, Laurence)
Nicolson, Harold 1886-1968 . . . . DLB-100, 149
"The Practice of Biography," in
*The English Sense of Humour and
Other Essays* DLB-149
Nicolson, Nigel 1917- DLB-155
Niebuhr, Reinhold 1892-1971 . . . . . DLB-17; DS-17
Niedecker, Lorine 1903-1970 . . . . DLB-48
Nieman, Lucius W. 1857-1935 . . . . DLB-25
Nietzsche, Friedrich
1844-1900 . . . . DLB-129; CDWLB-2
Mencken and Nietzsche: An Unpublished
Excerpt from H. L. Mencken's *My Life
as Author and Editor* Y-93
Nievo, Stanislao 1928- DLB-196
Niggli, Josefina 1910-1983 . . . . Y-80
Nightingale, Florence 1820-1910 . . . . DLB-166
Nijō, Lady (Nakano-in Masatada no Musume)
1258-after 1306 . . . . DLB-203
Nijō Yoshimoto 1320-1388 . . . . DLB-203
Nikitin, Ivan Savvich 1824-1861 . . . . DLB-277
Nikitin, Nikolai Nikolaevich 1895-1963 . . DLB-272
Nikolev, Nikolai Petrovich 1758-1815 . . . . DLB-150
Niles, Hezekiah 1777-1839 . . . . DLB-43
Nims, John Frederick 1913-1999 . . . . DLB-5
Tribute to Nancy Hale Y-88
Nin, Anaïs 1903-1977 . . . . DLB-2, 4, 152
Nína Björk Árnadóttir 1941-2000 . . . . DLB-293
Niño, Raúl 1961- DLB-209
Nissenson, Hugh 1933- DLB-28
Niven, Frederick John 1878-1944 . . . . DLB-92
Niven, Larry 1938- DLB-8
Nixon, Howard M. 1909-1983 . . . . DLB-201
Nizan, Paul 1905-1940 . . . . DLB-72
Njegoš, Petar II Petrović
1813-1851 . . . . DLB-147; CDWLB-4
Nkosi, Lewis 1936- DLB-157, 225
Noah, Mordecai M. 1785-1851 . . . . DLB-250
Noailles, Anna de 1876-1933 . . . . DLB-258
Nobel Peace Prize
The Nobel Prize and Literary Politics Y-88
Elie Wiesel Y-86
Nobel Prize in Literature
Joseph Brodsky Y-87
Camilo José Cela Y-89
Dario Fo Y-97
Gabriel García Márquez Y-82
William Golding Y-83
Nadine Gordimer Y-91
Günter Grass Y-99
Seamus Heaney Y-95
Imre Kertész Y-02
Najīb Mahfūz Y-88
Toni Morrison Y-93
V. S. Naipaul Y-01
Kenzaburō Ōe Y-94
Octavio Paz Y-90
José Saramago Y-98
Jaroslav Seifert Y-84
Claude Simon Y-85
Wole Soyinka Y-86
Wisława Szymborska Y-96
Derek Walcott Y-92
Gao Xingjian Y-00
Nobre, António 1867-1900 . . . . DLB-287
Nodier, Charles 1780-1844 . . . . DLB-119
Noël, Marie (Marie Mélanie Rouget)
1883-1967 . . . . DLB-258
Noel, Roden 1834-1894 . . . . DLB-35
Nogami Yaeko 1885-1985 . . . . DLB-180
Nogo, Rajko Petrov 1945- DLB-181
Nolan, William F. 1928- DLB-8
Tribute to Raymond Chandler Y-88
Noland, C. F. M. 1810?-1858 . . . . DLB-11
Noma Hiroshi 1915-1991 . . . . DLB-182
Nonesuch Press DLB-112
Creative Nonfiction Y-02
Nonni (Jón Stefán Sveinsson or Svensson)
1857-1944 . . . . DLB-293
Noon, Jeff 1957- DLB-267
Noonan, Robert Phillipe (see Tressell, Robert)
Noonday Press DLB-46
Noone, John 1936- DLB-14
Nora, Eugenio de 1923- DLB-134
Nordan, Lewis 1939- DLB-234
Nordbrandt, Henrik 1945- DLB-214
Nordhoff, Charles 1887-1947 . . . . DLB-9
Norén, Lars 1944- DLB-257
Norfolk, Lawrence 1963- DLB-267
Norman, Charles 1904-1996 . . . . DLB-111
Norman, Marsha 1947- DLB-266; Y-84
Norris, Charles G. 1881-1945 . . . . DLB-9
Norris, Frank
1870-1902 . . . . DLB-12, 71, 186; CDALB-3
Norris, Helen 1916- DLB-292
Norris, John 1657-1712 . . . . DLB-252
Norris, Leslie 1921- DLB-27, 256
Norse, Harold 1916- DLB-16
Norte, Marisela 1955- DLB-209
North, Marianne 1830-1890 . . . . DLB-174
North Point Press DLB-46
Nortje, Arthur 1942-1970 . . . . DLB-125, 225
Norton, Alice Mary (see Norton, Andre)
Norton, Andre 1912- DLB-8, 52
Norton, Andrews 1786-1853 . . . . DLB-1, 235; DS-5
Norton, Caroline 1808-1877 . . . . DLB-21, 159, 199
Norton, Charles Eliot 1827-1908 . . . DLB-1, 64, 235
Norton, John 1606-1663 . . . . DLB-24
Norton, Mary 1903-1992 . . . . DLB-160
Norton, Thomas 1532-1584 . . . . DLB-62
W. W. Norton and Company DLB-46
Norwood, Robert 1874-1932 . . . . DLB-92
Nosaka Akiyuki 1930- DLB-182
Nossack, Hans Erich 1901-1977 . . . . DLB-69
Notker Balbulus circa 840-912 . . . . DLB-148
Notker III of Saint Gall circa 950-1022 . . . DLB-148
Notker von Zweifalten ?-1095 . . . . DLB-148
Nourse, Alan E. 1928- DLB-8
Novak, Slobodan 1924- DLB-181
Novak, Vjenceslav 1859-1905 . . . . DLB-147
Novakovich, Josip 1956- DLB-244
Novalis 1772-1801 . . . . DLB-90; CDWLB-2
Novaro, Mario 1868-1944 . . . . DLB-114
Novás Calvo, Lino 1903-1983 . . . . DLB-145
Novelists
Library Journal Statements and
Questionnaires from First Novelists Y-87
Novels
The Columbia History of the American Novel
A Symposium on Y-92
The Great Modern Library Scam Y-98

Novels for Grown-Ups Y-97
The Proletarian Novel DLB-9
Novel, The "Second-Generation" Holocaust DLB-299
The Year in the Novel Y-87–88, Y-90–93
Novels, British
"The Break-Up of the Novel" (1922), by John Middleton Murry DLB-36
The Consolidation of Opinion: Critical Responses to the Modernists DLB-36
"Criticism in Relation to Novels" (1863), by G. H. Lewes DLB-21
"Experiment in the Novel" (1929) [excerpt], by John D. Beresford . . . DLB-36
"The Future of the Novel" (1899), by Henry James DLB-18
The Gay Science (1866), by E. S. Dallas [excerpt] DLB-21
A Haughty and Proud Generation (1922), by Ford Madox Hueffer . . DLB-36
Literary Effects of World War II DLB-15
"Modern Novelists –Great and Small" (1855), by Margaret Oliphant DLB-21
The Modernists (1932), by Joseph Warren Beach DLB-36
A Note on Technique (1926), by Elizabeth A. Drew [excerpts] DLB-36
Novel-Reading: *The Works of Charles Dickens; The Works of W. Makepeace Thackeray* (1879), by Anthony Trollope DLB-21
Novels with a Purpose (1864), by Justin M'Carthy DLB-21
"On Art in Fiction" (1838), by Edward Bulwer DLB-21
The Present State of the English Novel (1892), by George Saintsbury DLB-18
Representative Men and Women: A Historical Perspective on the British Novel, 1930-1960 . . . . . DLB-15
"The Revolt" (1937), by Mary Colum [excerpts] DLB-36
"Sensation Novels" (1863), by H. L. Manse DLB-21
Sex, Class, Politics, and Religion [in the British Novel, 1930-1959] DLB-15
Time and Western Man (1927), by Wyndham Lewis [excerpts] . . . DLB-36
Noventa, Giacomo 1898-1960 . . . . DLB-114
Novikov, Nikolai Ivanovich 1744-1818 . . DLB-150
Novomeský, Laco 1904-1976 . . . . DLB-215
Nowlan, Alden 1933-1983 . . . . DLB-53
Noyes, Alfred 1880-1958 . . . . DLB-20
Noyes, Crosby S. 1825-1908 . . . . DLB-23
Noyes, Nicholas 1647-1717 . . . . DLB-24
Noyes, Theodore W. 1858-1946 . . . . DLB-29
Nozick, Robert 1938-2002 . . . . .DLB-279
N-Town Plays circa 1468 to early sixteenth century DLB-146
Nugent, Frank 1908-1965 . . . . DLB-44
Nušić, Branislav 1864-1938 . .DLB-147; CDWLB-4
David Nutt [publishing house] DLB-106
Nwapa, Flora 1931-1993 . . . DLB-125; CDWLB-3
Nye, Edgar Wilson (Bill) 1850-1896 . . . . DLB-11, 23, 186
Nye, Naomi Shihab 1952- DLB-120
Nye, Robert 1939- DLB-14, 271
Nyka-Niliūnas, Alfonsas 1919- DLB-220

O

Oakes, Urian circa 1631-1681 . . . . DLB-24
Oakes Smith, Elizabeth 1806-1893 . . . . DLB-1, 239, 243
Oakley, Violet 1874-1961 . . . . DLB-188
Oates, Joyce Carol 1938- DLB-2, 5, 130; Y-81; CDALB-6
Tribute to Michael M. Rea Y-97
Ōba Minako 1930- DLB-182
Ober, Frederick Albion 1849-1913 . . . . . . DLB-189
Ober, William 1920-1993 . . . . Y-93
Oberholtzer, Ellis Paxson 1868-1936 . . . . . DLB-47
The Obituary as Literary Form Y-02
Obradović, Dositej 1740?-1811 . . . . DLB-147
O'Brien, Charlotte Grace 1845-1909 . . . . DLB-240
O'Brien, Edna 1932- . . . DLB-14, 231; CDBLB-8
O'Brien, Fitz-James 1828-1862 . . . . DLB-74
O'Brien, Flann (see O'Nolan, Brian)
O'Brien, Kate 1897-1974 . . . . DLB-15
O'Brien, Tim 1946- DLB-152; Y-80; DS-9; CDALB-7
O'Casey, Sean 1880-1964 . . . . . DLB-10; CDBLB-6
Occom, Samson 1723-1792 . . . . .DLB-175
Occomy, Marita Bonner 1899-1971 . . . . . . DLB-51
Ochs, Adolph S. 1858-1935 . . . . DLB-25
Ochs-Oakes, George Washington 1861-1931 . . . . DLB-137
O'Connor, Flannery 1925-1964 . . . . DLB-2, 152; Y-80; DS-12; CDALB-1
The Flannery O'Connor Society Y-99
O'Connor, Frank 1903-1966 . . . . DLB-162
O'Connor, Joseph 1963- DLB-267
Octopus Publishing Group DLB-112
Oda Sakunosuke 1913-1947 . . . . DLB-182
Odell, Jonathan 1737-1818 . . . . DLB-31, 99
O'Dell, Scott 1903-1989 . . . . DLB-52
Odets, Clifford 1906-1963 . . . . .DLB-7, 26
Odhams Press Limited DLB-112
Odio, Eunice 1922-1974 . . . . DLB-283
Odoevsky, Aleksandr Ivanovich 1802-1839 . . . . DLB-205
Odoevsky, Vladimir Fedorovich 1804 or 1803-1869 . . . . DLB-198
O'Donnell, Peter 1920- DLB-87
O'Donovan, Michael (see O'Connor, Frank)
O'Dowd, Bernard 1866-1953 . . . . DLB-230
Ōe, Kenzaburō 1935- DLB-182; Y-94
Nobel Lecture 1994: Japan, the Ambiguous, and Myself Y-94
Oehlenschläger, Adam 1779-1850 . . . . DLB-300
O'Faolain, Julia 1932- DLB-14, 231
O'Faolain, Sean 1900-1991 . . . . DLB-15, 162
Off-Loop Theatres DLB-7
Offord, Carl Ruthven 1910- DLB-76
O'Flaherty, Liam 1896-1984 . . .DLB-36, 162; Y-84
Ogarev, Nikolai Platonovich 1813-1877 . . .DLB-277
J. S. Ogilvie and Company DLB-49
Ogilvy, Eliza 1822-1912 . . . . DLB-199
Ogot, Grace 1930- DLB-125
O'Grady, Desmond 1935- DLB-40
Ogunyemi, Wale 1939- DLB-157
O'Hagan, Howard 1902-1982 . . . . DLB-68
O'Hara, Frank 1926-1966 . . . . .DLB-5, 16, 193
O'Hara, John 1905-1970 . . . . DLB-9, 86; DS-2; CDALB-5
John O'Hara's Pottsville Journalism Y-88
O'Hegarty, P. S. 1879-1955 . . . . DLB-201
Ohio State University
The William Charvat American Fiction Collection at the Ohio State University Libraries Y-92
Okara, Gabriel 1921- DLB-125; CDWLB-3
O'Keeffe, John 1747-1833 . . . . DLB-89
Nicholas Okes [publishing house] DLB-170
Okigbo, Christopher 1930-1967 . . . . .DLB-125; CDWLB-3
Okot p'Bitek 1931-1982 . . . . .DLB-125; CDWLB-3
Okpewho, Isidore 1941- DLB-157
Okri, Ben 1959- DLB-157, 231
Ólafur Jóhann Sigurðsson 1918-1988 . . . . DLB-293
Old Dogs / New Tricks? New Technologies, the Canon, and the Structure of the Profession Y-02
Old Franklin Publishing House DLB-49
Old German Genesis and *Old German Exodus* circa 1050-circa 1130 . . . . DLB-148
The *Old High German Isidor* circa 790-800 . . . . DLB-148
Older, Fremont 1856-1935 . . . . DLB-25
Oldham, John 1653-1683 . . . . DLB-131
Oldman, C. B. 1894-1969 . . . . DLB-201
Olds, Sharon 1942- DLB-120
Olearius, Adam 1599-1671 . . . . DLB-164
O'Leary, Ellen 1831-1889 . . . . DLB-240
O'Leary, Juan E. 1879-1969 . . . . DLB-290
Olesha, Iurii Karlovich 1899-1960 . . . . . . .DLB-272
Oliphant, Laurence 1829?-1888 . . . . . DLB-18, 166
Oliphant, Margaret 1828-1897 . . .DLB-18, 159, 190
"Modern Novelists–Great and Small" (1855) DLB-21
Oliveira, Carlos de 1921-1981 . . . . DLB-287
Oliver, Chad 1928-1993 . . . . DLB-8
Oliver, Mary 1935- DLB-5, 193
Ollier, Claude 1922- DLB-83
Olsen, Tillie 1912/1913- DLB-28, 206; Y-80; CDALB-7
Olson, Charles 1910-1970 . . . . .DLB-5, 16, 193
Olson, Elder 1909- DLB-48, 63

Olson, Sigurd F. 1899-1982 . . . . DLB-275
The Omega Workshops DS-10
Omotoso, Kole 1943- DLB-125
Omulevsky, Innokentii Vasil'evich 1836 [or 1837]-1883 . . . . DLB-238
Ondaatje, Michael 1943- DLB-60
O'Neill, Eugene 1888-1953 . . . . .DLB-7; CDALB-5
Eugene O'Neill Memorial Theater Center DLB-7
Eugene O'Neill's Letters: A Review Y-88
Onetti, Juan Carlos 1909-1994 . . . . DLB-113; CDWLB-3
Onions, George Oliver 1872-1961 . . . . DLB-153
Onofri, Arturo 1885-1928 . . . . DLB-114
O'Nolan, Brian 1911-1966 . . . . DLB-231
Oodgeroo of the Tribe Noonuccal (Kath Walker) 1920-1993 . . . . DLB-289
Opie, Amelia 1769-1853 . . . . DLB-116, 159
Opitz, Martin 1597-1639 . . . . DLB-164
Oppen, George 1908-1984 . . . . DLB-5, 165
Oppenheim, E. Phillips 1866-1946 . . . . DLB-70
Oppenheim, James 1882-1932 . . . . DLB-28
Oppenheimer, Joel 1930-1988 . . . . DLB-5, 193
Optic, Oliver (see Adams, William Taylor)
Orczy, Emma, Baroness 1865-1947 . . . . DLB-70
Oregon Shakespeare Festival Y-00
Origo, Iris 1902-1988 . . . . DLB-155
O'Riordan, Kate 1960- DLB-267
Orlovitz, Gil 1918-1973 . . . . DLB-2, 5
Orlovsky, Peter 1933- DLB-16
Ormond, John 1923- DLB-27
Ornitz, Samuel 1890-1957 . . . . DLB-28, 44
O'Rourke, P. J. 1947- DLB-185
Orozco, Olga 1920-1999 . . . . DLB-283
Orten, Jiří 1919-1941 . . . . DLB-215
Ortese, Anna Maria 1914- DLB-177
Ortiz, Simon J. 1941- DLB-120, 175, 256
Ortnit and *Wolfdietrich* circa 1225-1250 . . . . DLB-138
Orton, Joe 1933-1967 . . . . DLB-13; CDBLB-8
Orwell, George (Eric Arthur Blair) 1903-1950 . . . DLB-15, 98, 195, 255; CDBLB-7
The Orwell Year Y-84
(Re-)Publishing Orwell Y-86
Ory, Carlos Edmundo de 1923- DLB-134
Osbey, Brenda Marie 1957- DLB-120
Osbon, B. S. 1827-1912 . . . . DLB-43
Osborn, Sarah 1714-1796 . . . . DLB-200
Osborne, John 1929-1994 . . . . DLB-13; CDBLB-7
Osgood, Frances Sargent 1811-1850 . . . . . DLB-250
Osgood, Herbert L. 1855-1918 . . . . DLB-47
James R. Osgood and Company DLB-49
Osgood, McIlvaine and Company DLB-112
O'Shaughnessy, Arthur 1844-1881 . . . . DLB-35
Patrick O'Shea [publishing house] DLB-49
Osipov, Nikolai Petrovich 1751-1799 . . . . . DLB-150
Oskison, John Milton 1879-1947 . . . . DLB-175
Osler, Sir William 1849-1919 . . . . DLB-184
Osofisan, Femi 1946- DLB-125; CDWLB-3
Ostenso, Martha 1900-1963 . . . . DLB-92
Ostrauskas, Kostas 1926- DLB-232
Ostriker, Alicia 1937- DLB-120
Ostrovsky, Aleksandr Nikolaevich 1823-1886 . . . . DLB-277
Ostrovsky, Nikolai Alekseevich 1904-1936 . . . . DLB-272
Osundare, Niyi 1947- DLB-157; CDWLB-3
Oswald, Eleazer 1755-1795 . . . . DLB-43
Oswald von Wolkenstein 1376 or 1377-1445 . . . . DLB-179
Otero, Blas de 1916-1979 . . . . DLB-134
Otero, Miguel Antonio 1859-1944 . . . . DLB-82
Otero, Nina 1881-1965 . . . . DLB-209
Otero Silva, Miguel 1908-1985 . . . . DLB-145
Otfried von Weißenburg circa 800-circa 875? DLB-148
Otis, Broaders and Company DLB-49
Otis, James (see Kaler, James Otis)
Otis, James, Jr. 1725-1783 . . . . DLB-31
Ottaway, James 1911-2000 . . . . DLB-127
Ottendorfer, Oswald 1826-1900 . . . . DLB-23
Ottieri, Ottiero 1924- DLB-177
Otto-Peters, Louise 1819-1895 . . . . DLB-129
Otway, Thomas 1652-1685 . . . . DLB-80
Ouellette, Fernand 1930- DLB-60
Ouida 1839-1908 . . . . DLB-18, 156
Outing Publishing Company DLB-46
Overbury, Sir Thomas circa 1581-1613 . . . . DLB-151
The Overlook Press DLB-46
Ovid 43 B.C.-A.D. 17 . . . . . . DLB-211; CDWLB-1
Owen, Guy 1925- DLB-5
Owen, John 1564-1622 . . . . DLB-121
John Owen [publishing house] DLB-49
Peter Owen Limited DLB-112
Owen, Robert 1771-1858 . . . . DLB-107, 158
Owen, Wilfred 1893-1918 . . . . DLB-20; DS-18; CDBLB-6
A Centenary Celebration Y-93
The Wilfred Owen Association Y-98
The Owl and the Nightingale circa 1189-1199 . . . . DLB-146
Owsley, Frank L. 1890-1956 . . . . DLB-17
Oxford, Seventeenth Earl of, Edward de Vere 1550-1604 . . . . DLB-172
OyamO (Charles F. Gordon) 1943- DLB-266
Ozerov, Vladislav Aleksandrovich 1769-1816 . . . . DLB-150
Ozick, Cynthia 1928- . . . DLB-28, 152, 299; Y-82
First Strauss "Livings" Awarded to Cynthia Ozick and Raymond Carver An Interview with Cynthia Ozick Y-83
Tribute to Michael M. Rea Y-97

P

Pace, Richard 1482?-1536 . . . . DLB-167
Pacey, Desmond 1917-1975 . . . . DLB-88
Pacheco, José Emilio 1939- DLB-290
Pack, Robert 1929- DLB-5
Padell Publishing Company DLB-46
Padgett, Ron 1942- DLB-5
Padilla, Ernesto Chávez 1944- DLB-122
L. C. Page and Company DLB-49
Page, Louise 1955- DLB-233
Page, P. K. 1916- DLB-68
Page, Thomas Nelson 1853-1922 . . . . DLB-12, 78; DS-13
Page, Walter Hines 1855-1918 . . . . DLB-71, 91
Paget, Francis Edward 1806-1882 . . . . DLB-163
Paget, Violet (see Lee, Vernon)
Pagliarani, Elio 1927- DLB-128
Pain, Barry 1864-1928 . . . . DLB-135, 197
Pain, Philip ?-circa 1666 . . . . DLB-24
Paine, Robert Treat, Jr. 1773-1811 . . . . DLB-37
Paine, Thomas 1737-1809 . . . . DLB-31, 43, 73, 158; CDALB-2
Painter, George D. 1914- DLB-155
Painter, William 1540?-1594 . . . . DLB-136
Palazzeschi, Aldo 1885-1974 . . . . DLB-114, 264
Palei, Marina Anatol'evna 1955- DLB-285
Palencia, Alfonso de 1424-1492 . . . . DLB-286
Palés Matos, Luis 1898-1959 . . . . DLB-290
Paley, Grace 1922- DLB-28, 218
Paley, William 1743-1805 . . . . DLB-252
Palfrey, John Gorham 1796-1881 . . . DLB-1, 30, 235
Palgrave, Francis Turner 1824-1897 . . . . . . DLB-35
Palmer, Joe H. 1904-1952 . . . . DLB-171
Palmer, Michael 1943- DLB-169
Palmer, Nettie 1885-1964 . . . . DLB-260
Palmer, Vance 1885-1959 . . . . DLB-260
Paltock, Robert 1697-1767 . . . . DLB-39
Paludan, Jacob 1896-1975 . . . . DLB-214
Paludin-Müller, Frederik 1809-1876 . . . . . DLB-300
Pan Books Limited DLB-112
Panaev, Ivan Ivanovich 1812-1862 . . . . . . DLB-198
Panaeva, Avdot'ia Iakovlevna 1820-1893 . . . . DLB-238
Panama, Norman 1914- and Frank, Melvin 1913-1988 . . . . DLB-26
Pancake, Breece D'J 1952-1979 . . . . DLB-130
Panduro, Leif 1923-1977 . . . . DLB-214
Panero, Leopoldo 1909-1962 . . . . DLB-108
Pangborn, Edgar 1909-1976 . . . . DLB-8
Panizzi, Sir Anthony 1797-1879 . . . . DLB-184
Panneton, Philippe (see Ringuet)
Panshin, Alexei 1940- DLB-8
Pansy (see Alden, Isabella)
Pantheon Books DLB-46

Papadat-Bengescu, Hortensia 1876-1955 . . . . DLB-220

Papantonio, Michael 1907-1976 . . . . DLB-187

Paperback Library DLB-46

Paperback Science Fiction. DLB-8

Papini, Giovanni 1881-1956. . . . . DLB-264

Paquet, Alfons 1881-1944. . . . . DLB-66

Paracelsus 1493-1541 . . . . .DLB-179

Paradis, Suzanne 1936- DLB-53

Páral, Vladimír, 1932- DLB-232

Pardoe, Julia 1804-1862 . . . . DLB-166

Paredes, Américo 1915-1999 . . . . DLB-209

Pareja Diezcanseco, Alfredo 1908-1993 . . DLB-145

Parents' Magazine Press DLB-46

Parfit, Derek 1942- DLB-262

Parise, Goffredo 1929-1986 . . . . .DLB-177

Parish, Mitchell 1900-1993. . . . . DLB-265

Parizeau, Alice 1930-1990. . . . . DLB-60

Park, Ruth 1923?- DLB-260

Parke, John 1754-1789 . . . . DLB-31

Parker, Dan 1893-1967. . . . . DLB-241

Parker, Dorothy 1893-1967 . . . . . . DLB-11, 45, 86

Parker, Gilbert 1860-1932 . . . . DLB-99

Parker, James 1714-1770 . . . . DLB-43

Parker, John [publishing house] DLB-106

Parker, Matthew 1504-1575 . . . . DLB-213

Parker, Stewart 1941-1988 . . . . DLB-245

Parker, Theodore 1810-1860 . . . DLB-1, 235; DS-5

Parker, William Riley 1906-1968. . . . . . . DLB-103

J. H. Parker [publishing house]. DLB-106

Parkes, Bessie Rayner (Madame Belloc) 1829-1925 . . . . DLB-240

Parkman, Francis 1823-1893 . . . . .DLB-1, 30, 183, 186, 235

Parks, Gordon 1912- DLB-33

Parks, Tim 1954- DLB-231

Parks, William 1698-1750. . . . . DLB-43

William Parks [publishing house]. DLB-49

Parley, Peter (see Goodrich, Samuel Griswold)

Parmenides late sixth-fifth century B.C. . . .DLB-176

Parnell, Thomas 1679-1718. . . . . DLB-95

Parnicki, Teodor 1908-1988. . . . . DLB-215

Parnok, Sofiia Iakovlevna (Parnokh) 1885-1933 . . . . DLB-295

Parr, Catherine 1513?-1548 . . . . DLB-136

Parra, Nicanor 1914- DLB-283

Parrington, Vernon L. 1871-1929. . . . . .DLB-17, 63

Parrish, Maxfield 1870-1966. . . . . DLB-188

Parronchi, Alessandro 1914- DLB-128

Parshchikov, Aleksei Maksimovich (Raiderman) 1954- DLB-285

Parton, James 1822-1891 . . . . DLB-30

Parton, Sara Payson Willis 1811-1872. . . . . DLB-43, 74, 239

S. W. Partridge and Company DLB-106

Parun, Vesna 1922- DLB-181; CDWLB-4

Pascal, Blaise 1623-1662. . . . . DLB-268

Pasinetti, Pier Maria 1913- DLB-177

Tribute to Albert Erskine. Y-93

Pasolini, Pier Paolo 1922-1975 . . . . . .DLB-128, 177

Pastan, Linda 1932- DLB-5

Paston, George (Emily Morse Symonds) 1860-1936 . . . . .DLB-149, 197

The Paston Letters 1422-1509 . . . . DLB-146

Pastorius, Francis Daniel 1651-circa 1720 . . . . DLB-24

Patchen, Kenneth 1911-1972 . . . . DLB-16, 48

Pater, Walter 1839-1894. . .DLB-57, 156; CDBLB-4

Aesthetic Poetry (1873) DLB-35

"Style" (1888) [excerpt] DLB-57

Paterson, A. B. "Banjo" 1864-1941. . . . . . DLB-230

Paterson, Katherine 1932- DLB-52

Patmore, Coventry 1823-1896 . . . . DLB-35, 98

Paton, Alan 1903-1988. . . . . DLB-225; DS-17

Paton, Joseph Noel 1821-1901 . . . . DLB-35

Paton Walsh, Jill 1937- DLB-161

Patrick, Edwin Hill ("Ted") 1901-1964 . . DLB-137

Patrick, John 1906-1995 . . . . DLB-7

Pattee, Fred Lewis 1863-1950. . . . . DLB-71

Patterson, Alicia 1906-1963 . . . . DLB-127

Patterson, Eleanor Medill 1881-1948 . . . . . DLB-29

Patterson, Eugene 1923- DLB-127

Patterson, Joseph Medill 1879-1946 . . . . . . DLB-29

Pattillo, Henry 1726-1801. . . . . DLB-37

Paul, Elliot 1891-1958 . . . . DLB-4; DS-15

Paul, Jean (see Richter, Johann Paul Friedrich)

Paul, Kegan, Trench, Trubner and Company Limited DLB-106

Peter Paul Book Company. DLB-49

Stanley Paul and Company Limited. DLB-112

Paulding, James Kirke 1778-1860. . . . . .DLB-3, 59, 74, 250

Paulin, Tom 1949- DLB-40

Pauper, Peter, Press DLB-46

Paustovsky, Konstantin Georgievich 1892-1968 . . . . .DLB-272

Pavese, Cesare 1908-1950 . . . . .DLB-128, 177

Pavić, Milorad 1929- DLB-181; CDWLB-4

Pavlov, Konstantin 1933- DLB-181

Pavlov, Nikolai Filippovich 1803-1864 . . . . DLB-198

Pavlova, Karolina Karlovna 1807-1893 . . . . DLB-205

Pavlović, Miodrag 1928- DLB-181; CDWLB-4

Paxton, John 1911-1985 . . . . DLB-44

Payn, James 1830-1898. . . . . DLB-18

Payne, John 1842-1916. . . . . DLB-35

Payne, John Howard 1791-1852. . . . . DLB-37

Payson and Clarke DLB-46

Paz, Octavio 1914-1998 . . . . . . .DLB-290; Y-90, 98

Nobel Lecture 1990 . . . . Y-90

Pazzi, Roberto 1946- DLB-196

Pea, Enrico 1881-1958 . . . . DLB-264

Peabody, Elizabeth Palmer 1804-1894 . . . . DLB-1, 223

Preface to *Record of a School: Exemplifying the General Principles of Spiritual Culture* DS-5

Elizabeth Palmer Peabody [publishing house] DLB-49

Peabody, Josephine Preston 1874-1922 . . DLB-249

Peabody, Oliver William Bourn 1799-1848. . . . . DLB-59

Peace, Roger 1899-1968. . . . . .DLB-127

Peacham, Henry 1578-1644? DLB-151

Peacham, Henry, the Elder 1547-1634. . . . . .DLB-172, 236

Peachtree Publishers, Limited. DLB-46

Peacock, Molly 1947- DLB-120

Peacock, Thomas Love 1785-1866. . . DLB-96, 116

Pead, Deuel ?-1727 . . . . DLB-24

Peake, Mervyn 1911-1968 . . . . . .DLB-15, 160, 255

Peale, Rembrandt 1778-1860 . . . . DLB-183

Pear Tree Press DLB-112

Pearce, Philippa 1920- DLB-161

H. B. Pearson [publishing house] DLB-49

Pearson, Hesketh 1887-1964. . . . . DLB-149

Peattie, Donald Culross 1898-1964 . . . . . .DLB-275

Pechersky, Andrei (see Mel'nikov, Pavel Ivanovich)

Peck, George W. 1840-1916. . . . . DLB-23, 42

H. C. Peck and Theo. Bliss [publishing house] DLB-49

Peck, Harry Thurston 1856-1914. . . . . .DLB-71, 91

Peden, William 1913-1999 . . . . DLB-234

Tribute to William Goyen Y-83

Peele, George 1556-1596 . . . . .DLB-62, 167

Pegler, Westbrook 1894-1969 . . . . .DLB-171

Péguy, Charles 1873-1914 . . . . DLB-258

Peirce, Charles Sanders 1839-1914. . . . . . .DLB-270

Pekić, Borislav 1930-1992 . . .DLB-181; CDWLB-4

Pelevin, Viktor Olegovich 1962- DLB-285

Pellegrini and Cudahy DLB-46

Pelletier, Aimé (see Vac, Bertrand)

Pelletier, Francine 1959- DLB-251

Pellicer, Carlos 1897?-1977. . . . . DLB-290

Pemberton, Sir Max 1863-1950 . . . . DLB-70

de la Peña, Terri 1947- DLB-209

Penfield, Edward 1866-1925 . . . . DLB-188

Penguin Books [U.K.]. DLB-112

Fifty Penguin Years Y-85

Penguin Collectors' Society Y-98

Penguin Books [U.S.] DLB-46

Penn, William 1644-1718 . . . . DLB-24

Penn Publishing Company. DLB-49

Penna, Sandro 1906-1977. . . . . DLB-114

Pennell, Joseph 1857-1926 . . . . DLB-188

Penner, Jonathan 1940- Y-83

Pennington, Lee 1939- Y-82

Penton, Brian 1904-1951 . . . . DLB-260

Pepper, Stephen C. 1891-1972 . . . . DLB-270
Pepys, Samuel
1633-1703 . . . . DLB-101, 213; CDBLB-2
Percy, Thomas 1729-1811 . . . . DLB-104
Percy, Walker 1916-1990 . . . . DLB-2; Y-80, 90
Tribute to Caroline Gordon Y-81
Percy, William 1575-1648 . . . . DLB-172
Perec, Georges 1936-1982 . . . . DLB-83, 299
Perelman, Bob 1947- DLB-193
Perelman, S. J. 1904-1979 . . . . DLB-11, 44
Pérez de Guzmán, Fernán
ca. 1377-ca. 1460 . . . . DLB-286
Perez, Raymundo "Tigre" 1946- DLB-122
Peri Rossi, Cristina 1941- DLB-145, 290
Perkins, Eugene 1932- DLB-41
Perkins, Maxwell
The Claims of Business and Literature:
An Undergraduate Essay Y-01
Perkins, William 1558-1602 . . . . DLB-281
Perkoff, Stuart Z. 1930-1974 . . . . DLB-16
Perley, Moses Henry 1804-1862 . . . . DLB-99
Permabooks DLB-46
Perovsky, Aleksei Alekseevich
(Antonii Pogorel'sky) 1787-1836 . . . . . DLB-198
Perrault, Charles 1628-1703 . . . . DLB-268
Perri, Henry 1561-1617 . . . . DLB-236
Perrin, Alice 1867-1934 . . . . DLB-156
Perry, Anne 1938- DLB-276
Perry, Bliss 1860-1954 . . . . DLB-71
Perry, Eleanor 1915-1981 . . . . DLB-44
Perry, Henry (see Perri, Henry)
Perry, Matthew 1794-1858 . . . . DLB-183
Perry, Sampson 1747-1823 . . . . DLB-158
Perse, Saint-John 1887-1975 . . . . DLB-258
Persius A.D. 34-A.D. 62 . . . . DLB-211
Perutz, Leo 1882-1957 . . . . DLB-81
Pesetsky, Bette 1932- DLB-130
Pessanha, Camilo 1867-1926 . . . . DLB-287
Pessoa, Fernando 1888-1935 . . . . DLB-287
Pestalozzi, Johann Heinrich 1746-1827 . . . . . DLB-94
Peter, Laurence J. 1919-1990 . . . . DLB-53
Peter of Spain circa 1205-1277 . . . . DLB-115
Peterkin, Julia 1880-1961 . . . . DLB-9
Peters, Ellis (Edith Pargeter) 1913-1995 . . . DLB-276
Peters, Lenrie 1932- DLB-117
Peters, Robert 1924- DLB-105
"Foreword to *Ludwig of Baviria*" DLB-105
Petersham, Maud 1889-1971 and
Petersham, Miska 1888-1960 . . . . DLB-22
Peterson, Charles Jacobs 1819-1887 . . . . DLB-79
Peterson, Len 1917- DLB-88
Peterson, Levi S. 1933- DLB-206
Peterson, Louis 1922-1998 . . . . DLB-76
Peterson, T. B., and Brothers DLB-49
Petitclair, Pierre 1813-1860 . . . . DLB-99
Petrescu, Camil 1894-1957 . . . . DLB-220
Petronius circa A.D. 20-A.D. 66
. . . . DLB-211; CDWLB-1
Petrov, Aleksandar 1938- DLB-181
Petrov, Evgenii (Evgenii Petrovich Kataev)
1903-1942 . . . . DLB-272
Petrov, Gavriil 1730-1801 . . . . DLB-150
Petrov, Valeri 1920- DLB-181
Petrov, Vasilii Petrovich 1736-1799 . . . . . . DLB-150
Petrović, Rastko
1898-1949 . . . . DLB-147; CDWLB-4
Petrushevskaia, Liudmila Stefanovna
1938- DLB-285
Petruslied circa 854? DLB-148
Petry, Ann 1908-1997 . . . . DLB-76
Pettie, George circa 1548-1589 . . . . DLB-136
Pétur Gunnarsson 1947- DLB-293
Peyton, K. M. 1929- DLB-161
Pfaffe Konrad flourished circa 1172 . . . . . . DLB-148
Pfaffe Lamprecht flourished circa 1150 . . . DLB-148
Pfeiffer, Emily 1827-1890 . . . . DLB-199
Pforzheimer, Carl H. 1879-1957 . . . . DLB-140
Phaedrus circa 18 B.C.-circa A.D. 50 . . . . . DLB-211
Phaer, Thomas 1510?-1560 . . . . DLB-167
Phaidon Press Limited DLB-112
Pharr, Robert Deane 1916-1992 . . . . DLB-33
Phelps, Elizabeth Stuart 1815-1852 . . . . . . DLB-202
Phelps, Elizabeth Stuart 1844-1911 . . . DLB-74, 221
Philander von der Linde
(see Mencke, Johann Burckhard)
Philby, H. St. John B. 1885-1960 . . . . DLB-195
Philip, Marlene Nourbese 1947- DLB-157
Philippe, Charles-Louis 1874-1909 . . . . DLB-65
Philips, John 1676-1708 . . . . DLB-95
Philips, Katherine 1632-1664 . . . . DLB-131
Phillipps, Sir Thomas 1792-1872 . . . . DLB-184
Phillips, Caryl 1958- DLB-157
Phillips, David Graham 1867-1911 . . . . . DLB-9, 12
Phillips, Jayne Anne 1952- DLB-292; Y-80
Tribute to Seymour Lawrence Y-94
Phillips, Robert 1938- DLB-105
"Finding, Losing, Reclaiming: A Note
on My Poems" DLB-105
Tribute to William Goyen Y-83
Phillips, Stephen 1864-1915 . . . . DLB-10
Phillips, Ulrich B. 1877-1934 . . . . DLB-17
Phillips, Wendell 1811-1884 . . . . DLB-235
Phillips, Willard 1784-1873 . . . . DLB-59
Phillips, William 1907-2002 . . . . DLB-137
Phillips, Sampson and Company DLB-49
Phillpotts, Adelaide Eden (Adelaide Ross)
1896-1993 . . . . DLB-191
Phillpotts, Eden 1862-1960 . . DLB-10, 70, 135, 153
Philo circa 20-15 B.C.-circa A.D. 50 . . . . . DLB-176
Philosophical Library DLB-46
Philosophy
Eighteenth-Century Philosophical
Background DLB-31
Philosophic Thought in Boston DLB-235
Translators of the Twelfth Century:
Literary Issues Raised and
Impact Created DLB-115
Elihu Phinney [publishing house] DLB-49
Phoenix, John (see Derby, George Horatio)
PHYLON (Fourth Quarter, 1950),
The Negro in Literature:
The Current Scene DLB-76
Physiologus circa 1070-circa 1150 . . . . DLB-148
Piccolo, Lucio 1903-1969 . . . . DLB-114
Pickard, Tom 1946- DLB-40
William Pickering [publishing house] DLB-106
Pickthall, Marjorie 1883-1922 . . . . DLB-92
Picoult, Jodi 1966- DLB-292
Pictorial Printing Company DLB-49
Piel, Gerard 1915- DLB-137
"An Announcement to Our Readers,"
Gerard Piel's Statement in *Scientific American* (April 1948) DLB-137
Pielmeier, John 1949- DLB-266
Piercy, Marge 1936- DLB-120, 227
Pierro, Albino 1916-1995 . . . . DLB-128
Pignotti, Lamberto 1926- DLB-128
Pike, Albert 1809-1891 . . . . DLB-74
Pike, Zebulon Montgomery 1779-1813 . . . DLB-183
Pillat, Ion 1891-1945 . . . . DLB-220
Pil'niak, Boris Andreevich (Boris Andreevich
Vogau) 1894-1938 . . . . DLB-272
Pilon, Jean-Guy 1930- DLB-60
Pinar, Florencia fl. ca. late
fifteenth century DLB-286
Pinckney, Eliza Lucas 1722-1793 . . . . DLB-200
Pinckney, Josephine 1895-1957 . . . . DLB-6
Pindar circa 518 B.C.-circa 438 B.C.
. . . . DLB-176; CDWLB-1
Pindar, Peter (see Wolcot, John)
Pineda, Cecile 1942- DLB-209
Pinero, Arthur Wing 1855-1934 . . . . DLB-10
Piñero, Miguel 1946-1988 . . . . DLB-266
Pinget, Robert 1919-1997 . . . . DLB-83
Pinkney, Edward Coote 1802-1828 . . . . . . DLB-248
Pinnacle Books DLB-46
Piñon, Nélida 1935- DLB-145
Pinsky, Robert 1940- Y-82
Reappointed Poet Laureate Y-98
Pinter, Harold 1930- DLB-13; CDBLB-8
Writing for the Theatre DLB-13
Pinto, Fernão Mendes 1509/1511?-1583 . . DLB-287
Piontek, Heinz 1925- DLB-75
Piozzi, Hester Lynch [Thrale]
1741-1821 . . . . DLB-104, 142
Piper, H. Beam 1904-1964 . . . . DLB-8
Piper, Watty DLB-22
Pirandello, Luigi 1867-1936 . . . . DLB-264
Pirckheimer, Caritas 1467-1532 . . . . DLB-179
Pirckheimer, Willibald 1470-1530 . . . . DLB-179

Pires, José Cardoso 1925-1998 . . . . DLB-287
Pisar, Samuel 1929- Y-83
Pisarev, Dmitrii Ivanovich 1840-1868 . . . .DLB-277
Pisemsky, Aleksei Feofilaktovich 1821-1881 . . . . DLB-238
Pitkin, Timothy 1766-1847 . . . . DLB-30
Pitter, Ruth 1897- DLB-20
Pix, Mary 1666-1709 . . . . DLB-80
Pixerécourt, René Charles Guilbert de 1773-1844 . . . . DLB-192
Pizarnik, Alejandra 1936-1972 . . . . DLB-283
Plá, Josefina 1909-1999 . . . . DLB-290
Plaatje, Sol T. 1876-1932 . . . . DLB-125, 225
Plante, David 1940- Y-83
Platen, August von 1796-1835 . . . . DLB-90
Plantinga, Alvin 1932- DLB-279
Plath, Sylvia 1932-1963 . . . . DLB-5, 6, 152; CDALB-1
Plato circa 428 B.C.-348-347 B.C. DLB-176; CDWLB-1
Plato, Ann 1824?-? DLB-239
Platon 1737-1812 . . . . DLB-150
Platonov, Andrei Platonovich (Andrei Platonovich Klimentev) 1899-1951 . . DLB-272
Platt, Charles 1945- DLB-261
Platt and Munk Company DLB-46
Plautus circa 254 B.C.-184 B.C. DLB-211; CDWLB-1
Playboy Press DLB-46
John Playford [publishing house] DLB-170
Der Pleier flourished circa 1250 . . . . DLB-138
Pleijel, Agneta 1940- DLB-257
Plenzdorf, Ulrich 1934- DLB-75
Pleshcheev, Aleksei Nikolaevich 1825?-1893 . . . . .DLB-277
Plessen, Elizabeth 1944- DLB-75
Pletnev, Petr Aleksandrovich 1792-1865 . . . . DLB-205
Pliekšāne, Elza Rozenberga (see Aspazija)
Pliekšāns, Jānis (see Rainis, Jānis)
Plievier, Theodor 1892-1955 . . . . DLB-69
Plimpton, George 1927-2003. . .DLB-185, 241; Y-99
Pliny the Elder A.D. 23/24-A.D. 79 . . . . . DLB-211
Pliny the Younger circa A.D. 61-A.D. 112 . . . . DLB-211
Plomer, William 1903-1973 . . . . DLB-20, 162, 191, 225
Plotinus 204-270 . . . . .DLB-176; CDWLB-1
Plowright, Teresa 1952- DLB-251
Plume, Thomas 1630-1704 . . . . DLB-213
Plumly, Stanley 1939- DLB-5, 193
Plumpp, Sterling D. 1940- DLB-41
Plunkett, James 1920- DLB-14
Plutarch circa 46-circa 120 . . . . . . .DLB-176; CDWLB-1
Plymell, Charles 1935- DLB-16
Pocket Books DLB-46
Poe, Edgar Allan 1809-1849 . . . . .DLB-3, 59, 73, 74, 248; CDALB-2
    The Poe Studies Association Y-99
Poe, James 1921-1980 . . . . DLB-44
The Poet Laureate of the United States Y-86
    Statements from Former Consultants in Poetry Y-86
Poetry
    Aesthetic Poetry (1873) DLB-35
    A Century of Poetry, a Lifetime of Collecting: J. M. Edelstein's Collection of Twentieth-Century American Poetry Y-02
    "Certain Gifts," by Betty Adcock. . . . DLB-105
    Contempo Caravan: Kites in a Windstorm Y-85
    "Contemporary Verse Story-telling," by Jonathan Holden DLB-105
    "A Detail in a Poem," by Fred Chappell DLB-105
    "The English Renaissance of Art" (1908), by Oscar Wilde DLB-35
    "Every Man His Own Poet; or, The Inspired Singer's Recipe Book" (1877), by H. W. Mallock DLB-35
    "Eyes Across Centuries: Contemporary Poetry and 'That Vision Thing,'" by Philip Dacey DLB-105
    A Field Guide to Recent Schools of American Poetry Y-86
    "Finding, Losing, Reclaiming: A Note on My Poems, by Robert Phillips" DLB-105
    "The Fleshly School of Poetry and Other Phenomena of the Day" (1872) . . . DLB-35
    "The Fleshly School of Poetry: Mr. D. G. Rossetti" (1871) DLB-35
    The G. Ross Roy Scottish Poetry Collection at the University of South Carolina . . Y-89
    "Getting Started: Accepting the Regions You Own–or Which Own You," by Walter McDonald DLB-105
    "The Good, The Not So Good," by Stephen Dunn DLB-105
    The Griffin Poetry Prize Y-00
    The Hero as Poet. Dante; Shakspeare (1841), by Thomas Carlyle DLB-32
    "Images and 'Images,'" by Charles Simic DLB-105
    "Into the Mirror," by Peter Cooley . . DLB-105
    "Knots into Webs: Some Autobiographical Sources," by Dabney Stuart. DLB-105
    "L'Envoi" (1882), by Oscar Wilde . . . DLB-35
    "Living in Ruin," by Gerald Stern . . . DLB-105
    Looking for the Golden Mountain: Poetry Reviewing Y-89
    Lyric Poetry (French) DLB-268
    Medieval Galician-Portuguese Poetry DLB-287
    "The No Self, the Little Self, and the Poets," by Richard Moore. DLB-105
    On Some of the Characteristics of Modern Poetry and On the Lyrical Poems of Alfred Tennyson (1831) DLB-32
    The Pitt Poetry Series: Poetry Publishing Today Y-85
    "The Poetry File," by Edward Field. DLB-105
    Poetry in Nineteenth-Century France: Cultural Background and Critical Commentary DLB-217
    The Poetry of Jorge Luis Borges Y-86
    "The Poet's Kaleidoscope: The Element of Surprise in the Making of the Poem" by Madeline DeFrees. . . . DLB-105
    The Pre-Raphaelite Controversy DLB-35
    Protest Poetry in Castile DLB-286
    "Reflections: After a Tornado," by Judson Jerome DLB-105
    Statements from Former Consultants in Poetry Y-86
    Statements on the Art of Poetry. DLB-54
    The Study of Poetry (1880), by Matthew Arnold DLB-35
    A Survey of Poetry Anthologies, 1879-1960 . . . . DLB-54
    Thoughts on Poetry and Its Varieties (1833), by John Stuart Mill DLB-32
    Under the Microscope (1872), by A. C. Swinburne DLB-35
    The Unterberg Poetry Center of the 92nd Street Y. Y-98
    Victorian Poetry: Five Critical Views DLBV-35
    Year in Poetry Y-83–92, 94–01
    Year's Work in American Poetry. Y-82
Poets
    The Lives of the Poets (1753) DLB-142
    Minor Poets of the Earlier Seventeenth Century. DLB-121
    Other British Poets Who Fell in the Great War. DLB-216
    Other Poets [French] DLB-217
    Second-Generation Minor Poets of the Seventeenth Century. DLB-126
    Third-Generation Minor Poets of the Seventeenth Century. DLB-131
Pogodin, Mikhail Petrovich 1800-1875. . . DLB-198
Pogorel'sky, Antonii (see Perovsky, Aleksei Alekseevich)
Pohl, Frederik 1919- DLB-8
    Tribute to Isaac Asimov. Y-92
    Tribute to Theodore Sturgeon. Y-85
Poirier, Louis (see Gracq, Julien)
Poláček, Karel 1892-1945. . . .DLB-215; CDWLB-4
Polanyi, Michael 1891-1976 . . . . DLB-100
Pole, Reginald 1500-1558. . . . . DLB-132
Polevoi, Nikolai Alekseevich 1796-1846. . DLB-198
Polezhaev, Aleksandr Ivanovich 1804-1838 . . . . DLB-205
Poliakoff, Stephen 1952- DLB-13
Polidori, John William 1795-1821 . . . . . . DLB-116
Polite, Carlene Hatcher 1932- DLB-33
Pollard, Alfred W. 1859-1944 . . . . DLB-201
Pollard, Edward A. 1832-1872 . . . . DLB-30

Pollard, Graham 1903-1976 . . . . DLB-201
Pollard, Percival 1869-1911 . . . . DLB-71
Pollard and Moss DLB-49
Pollock, Sharon 1936- DLB-60
Polonsky, Abraham 1910-1999 . . . . DLB-26
Polonsky, Iakov Petrovich 1819-1898 . . . . DLB-277
Polotsky, Simeon 1629-1680 . . . . DLB-150
Polybius circa 200 B.C.-118 B.C. DLB-176
Pomialovsky, Nikolai Gerasimovich 1835-1863 . . . . DLB-238
Pomilio, Mario 1921-1990 . . . . DLB-177
Ponce, Mary Helen 1938- DLB-122
Ponce-Montoya, Juanita 1949- DLB-122
Ponet, John 1516?-1556 . . . . DLB-132
Ponge, Francis 1899-1988 . . . . DLB-258; Y-02
Poniatowska, Elena 1933- DLB-113; CDWLB-3
Ponsard, François 1814-1867 . . . . DLB-192
William Ponsonby [publishing house] DLB-170
Pontiggia, Giuseppe 1934- DLB-196
Pontoppidan, Henrik 1857-1943 . . . . DLB-300
Pony Stories, Omnibus Essay on DLB-160
Poole, Ernest 1880-1950 . . . . DLB-9
Poole, Sophia 1804-1891 . . . . DLB-166
Poore, Benjamin Perley 1820-1887 . . . . DLB-23
Popa, Vasko 1922-1991 . . . . . DLB-181; CDWLB-4
Pope, Abbie Hanscom 1858-1894 . . . . DLB-140
Pope, Alexander 1688-1744 . . . . . . DLB-95, 101, 213; CDBLB-2
Popov, Aleksandr Serafimovich (see Serafimovich, Aleksandr Serafimovich)
Popov, Evgenii Anatol'evich 1946- DLB-285
Popov, Mikhail Ivanovich 1742-circa 1790 . . . . DLB-150
Popović, Aleksandar 1929-1996 . . . . DLB-181
Popper, Karl 1902-1994 . . . . DLB-262
Popular Culture Association/ American Culture Association Y-99
Popular Library DLB-46
Poquelin, Jean-Baptiste (see Molière)
Porete, Marguerite ?-1310 . . . . DLB-208
Porlock, Martin (see MacDonald, Philip)
Porpoise Press DLB-112
Porta, Antonio 1935-1989 . . . . DLB-128
Porter, Anna Maria 1780-1832 . . . . . . DLB-116, 159
Porter, Cole 1891-1964 . . . . DLB-265
Porter, David 1780-1843 . . . . DLB-183
Porter, Eleanor H. 1868-1920 . . . . DLB-9
Porter, Gene Stratton (see Stratton-Porter, Gene)
Porter, Hal 1911-1984 . . . . DLB-260
Porter, Henry ?-? DLB-62
Porter, Jane 1776-1850 . . . . DLB-116, 159
Porter, Katherine Anne 1890-1980 . . . . . . DLB-4, 9, 102; Y-80; DS-12; CDALB-7
The Katherine Anne Porter Society Y-01
Porter, Peter 1929- DLB-40, 289
Porter, William Sydney (O. Henry) 1862-1910 . . . . DLB-12, 78, 79; CDALB-3
Porter, William T. 1809-1858 . . . . . DLB-3, 43, 250
Porter and Coates DLB-49
Portillo Trambley, Estela 1927-1998 . . . . . DLB-209
Portis, Charles 1933- DLB-6
Medieval Galician-Portuguese Poetry DLB-287
Posey, Alexander 1873-1908 . . . . DLB-175
Postans, Marianne circa 1810-1865 . . . . . . DLB-166
Postgate, Raymond 1896-1971 . . . . DLB-276
Postl, Carl (see Sealsfield, Carl)
Postmodern Holocaust Fiction DLB-299
Poston, Ted 1906-1974 . . . . DLB-51
Potekhin, Aleksei Antipovich 1829-1908 . . DLB-238
Potok, Chaim 1929-2002 . . . . DLB-28, 152
A Conversation with Chaim Potok Y-84
Tribute to Bernard Malamud Y-86
Potter, Beatrix 1866-1943 . . . . DLB-141
The Beatrix Potter Society Y-98
Potter, David M. 1910-1971 . . . . DLB-17
Potter, Dennis 1935-1994 . . . . DLB-233
John E. Potter and Company DLB-49
Pottle, Frederick A. 1897-1987 . . . . . DLB-103; Y-87
Poulin, Jacques 1937- DLB-60
Pound, Ezra 1885-1972 . . . . DLB-4, 45, 63; DS-15; CDALB-4
The Cost of the *Cantos:* William Bird to Ezra Pound Y-01
The Ezra Pound Society Y-01
Poverman, C. E. 1944- DLB-234
Povich, Shirley 1905-1998 . . . . DLB-171
Powell, Anthony 1905-2000 . . . DLB-15; CDBLB-7
The Anthony Powell Society: Powell and the First Biennial Conference Y-01
Powell, Dawn 1897-1965
Dawn Powell, Where Have You Been All Our Lives? Y-97
Powell, John Wesley 1834-1902 . . . . DLB-186
Powell, Padgett 1952- DLB-234
Powers, J. F. 1917-1999 . . . . DLB-130
Powers, Jimmy 1903-1995 . . . . DLB-241
Pownall, David 1938- DLB-14
Powys, John Cowper 1872-1963 . . . . . DLB-15, 255
Powys, Llewelyn 1884-1939 . . . . DLB-98
Powys, T. F. 1875-1953 . . . . DLB-36, 162
The Powys Society Y-98
Poynter, Nelson 1903-1978 . . . . DLB-127
Prado, Pedro 1886-1952 . . . . DLB-283
Prados, Emilio 1899-1962 . . . . DLB-134
Praed, Mrs. Caroline (see Praed, Rosa)
Praed, Rosa (Mrs. Caroline Praed) 1851-1935 . . . . DLB-230
Praed, Winthrop Mackworth 1802-1839 . . . DLB-96
Praeger Publishers DLB-46
Praetorius, Johannes 1630-1680 . . . . DLB-168
Pratolini, Vasco 1913-1991 . . . . DLB-177
Pratt, E. J. 1882-1964 . . . . DLB-92
Pratt, Samuel Jackson 1749-1814 . . . . DLB-39
Preciado Martin, Patricia 1939- DLB-209
Préfontaine, Yves 1937- DLB-53
Prelutsky, Jack 1940- DLB-61
Prentice, George D. 1802-1870 . . . . DLB-43
Prentice-Hall DLB-46
Prescott, Orville 1906-1996 . . . . Y-96
Prescott, William Hickling 1796-1859 . . . . DLB-1, 30, 59, 235
Prešeren, Francè 1800-1849 . . . . DLB-147; CDWLB-4
Presses (*See also* Publishing)
Small Presses in Great Britain and Ireland, 1960-1985 . . . . DLB-40
Small Presses I: Jargon Society Y-84
Small Presses II: The Spirit That Moves Us Press Y-85
Small Presses III: Pushcart Press Y-87
Preston, Margaret Junkin 1820-1897 . . . . DLB-239, 248
Preston, May Wilson 1873-1949 . . . . DLB-188
Preston, Thomas 1537-1598 . . . . DLB-62
Prévert, Jacques 1900-1977 . . . . DLB-258
Price, Anthony 1928- DLB-276
Price, Reynolds 1933- DLB-2, 218, 278
Price, Richard 1723-1791 . . . . DLB-158
Price, Richard 1949- Y-81
Prichard, Katharine Susannah 1883-1969 . . . . DLB-260
Prideaux, John 1578-1650 . . . . DLB-236
Priest, Christopher 1943- DLB-14, 207, 261
Priestley, J. B. 1894-1984 . . . . DLB-10, 34, 77, 100, 139; Y-84; CDBLB-6
Priestley, Joseph 1733-1804 . . . . DLB-252
Prigov, Dmitrii Aleksandrovich 1940- . . DLB-285
Prime, Benjamin Young 1733-1791 . . . . DLB-31
Primrose, Diana floruit circa 1630 . . . . DLB-126
Prince, F. T. 1912- DLB-20
Prince, Nancy Gardner 1799-? DLB-239
Prince, Thomas 1687-1758 . . . . DLB-24, 140
Pringle, Thomas 1789-1834 . . . . DLB-225
Printz, Wolfgang Casper 1641-1717 . . . . . . DLB-168
Prior, Matthew 1664-1721 . . . . DLB-95
Prisco, Michele 1920- DLB-177
Prishvin, Mikhail Mikhailovich 1873-1954 . . . . DLB-272
Pritchard, William H. 1932- DLB-111
Pritchett, V. S. 1900-1997 . . . . DLB-15, 139
Probyn, May 1856 or 1857-1909 . . . . DLB-199
Procter, Adelaide Anne 1825-1864 . . . DLB-32, 199
Procter, Bryan Waller 1787-1874 . . . . . DLB-96, 144
Proctor, Robert 1868-1903 . . . . DLB-184
Prokopovich, Feofan 1681?-1736 . . . . DLB-150
Prokosch, Frederic 1906-1989 . . . . DLB-48
Pronzini, Bill 1943- DLB-226

Propertius circa 50 B.C.-post 16 B.C. DLB-211; CDWLB-1

Propper, Dan 1937- DLB-16

Prose, Francine 1947- DLB-234

Protagoras circa 490 B.C.-420 B.C. DLB-176

Protest Poetry in Castile ca. 1445-ca. 1506 .... DLB-286

Proud, Robert 1728-1813 .... DLB-30

Proust, Marcel 1871-1922 .... DLB-65

Marcel Proust at 129 and the Proust Society of America Y-00

Marcel Proust's *Remembrance of Things Past:* The Rediscovered Galley Proofs Y-00

Prutkov, Koz'ma Petrovich 1803-1863....DLB-277

Prynne, J. H. 1936- DLB-40

Przybyszewski, Stanislaw 1868-1927 ..... DLB-66

Pseudo-Dionysius the Areopagite floruit circa 500 .... DLB-115

Public Lending Right in America

PLR and the Meaning of Literary Property Y-83

Statement by Sen. Charles McC. Mathias, Jr. PLR Y-83

Statements on PLR by American Writers . Y-83

Public Lending Right in the United Kingdom

The First Year in the United Kingdom ... Y-83

Publishers [listed by individual names]

Publishers, Conversations with:

An Interview with Charles Scribner IIIY-94

An Interview with Donald Lamm Y-95

An Interview with James Laughlin Y-96

An Interview with Patrick O'Connor Y-84

Publishing

The Art and Mystery of Publishing: Interviews Y-97

Book Publishing Accounting: Some Basic Concepts Y-98

1873 Publishers' Catalogues DLB-49

The Literary Scene 2002: Publishing, Book Reviewing, and Literary Journalism .. Y-02

Main Trends in Twentieth-Century Book Clubs DLB-46

Overview of U.S. Book Publishing, 1910-1945 .... DLB-9

The Pitt Poetry Series: Poetry Publishing Today Y-85

Publishing Fiction at LSU Press Y-87

The Publishing Industry in 1998: *Sturm-und-drang.com* Y-98

The Publishing Industry in 1999 .... Y-99

Publishers and Agents: The Columbia Connection Y-87

Responses to Ken Auletta Y-97

Southern Writers Between the Wars ... DLB-9

The State of Publishing Y-97

Trends in Twentieth-Century Mass Market Publishing DLB-46

The Year in Book Publishing Y-86

Pückler-Muskau, Hermann von 1785-1871 ....DLB-133

Pufendorf, Samuel von 1632-1694 ...... DLB-168

Pugh, Edwin William 1874-1930 .... DLB-135

Pugin, A. Welby 1812-1852 .... DLB-55

Puig, Manuel 1932-1990.....DLB-113; CDWLB-3

Pulgar, Hernando del (Fernando del Pulgar) ca. 1436-ca. 1492 .... DLB-286

Pulitzer, Joseph 1847-1911 .... DLB-23

Pulitzer, Joseph, Jr. 1885-1955 .... DLB-29

Pulitzer Prizes for the Novel, 1917-1945 .... DLB-9

Pulliam, Eugene 1889-1975 .... DLB-127

Purcell, Deirdre 1945- DLB-267

Purchas, Samuel 1577?-1626 .... DLB-151

Purdy, Al 1918-2000 .... DLB-88

Purdy, James 1923- DLB-2, 218

Purdy, Ken W. 1913-1972 .... DLB-137

Pusey, Edward Bouverie 1800-1882 ...... DLB-55

Pushkin, Aleksandr Sergeevich 1799-1837 .... DLB-205

Pushkin, Vasilii L'vovich 1766-1830 .... DLB-205

Putnam, George Palmer 1814-1872 ....DLB-3, 79, 250, 254

G. P. Putnam [publishing house] DLB-254

G. P. Putnam's Sons [U.K.] DLB-106

G. P. Putnam's Sons [U.S.] DLB-49

A Publisher's Archives: G. P. Putnam Y-92

Putnam, Hilary 1926- DLB-279

Putnam, Samuel 1892-1950 .... DLB-4; DS-15

Puttenham, George 1529?-1590 .... DLB-281

Puzo, Mario 1920-1999 .... DLB-6

Pyle, Ernie 1900-1945 .... DLB-29

Pyle, Howard 1853-1911 .... DLB-42, 188; DS-13

Pyle, Robert Michael 1947- DLB-275

Pym, Barbara 1913-1980 ......DLB-14, 207; Y-87

Pynchon, Thomas 1937- DLB-2, 173

Pyramid Books DLB-46

Pyrnelle, Louise-Clarke 1850-1907 .... DLB-42

Pythagoras circa 570 B.C.-? DLB-176

Q

Quad, M. (see Lewis, Charles B.)

Quaritch, Bernard 1819-1899 .... DLB-184

Quarles, Francis 1592-1644 .... DLB-126

The Quarterly Review 1809-1967 .... DLB-110

Quasimodo, Salvatore 1901-1968 .... DLB-114

Queen, Ellery (see Dannay, Frederic, and Manfred B. Lee)

Queen, Frank 1822-1882 .... DLB-241

The Queen City Publishing House DLB-49

Queirós, Eça de 1845-1900 .... DLB-287

Queneau, Raymond 1903-1976 ..... DLB-72, 258

Quennell, Peter 1905-1993 .... DLB-155, 195

Quental, Antero de 1842-1891 .... DLB-287

Quesada, José Luis 1948- DLB-290

Quesnel, Joseph 1746-1809 .... DLB-99

Quiller-Couch, Sir Arthur Thomas 1863-1944 ....DLB-135, 153, 190

Quin, Ann 1936-1973 .... DLB-14, 231

Quinault, Philippe 1635-1688 ....DLB-268

Quincy, Samuel, of Georgia ?-? DLB-31

Quincy, Samuel, of Massachusetts 1734-1789 .... DLB-31

Quindlen, Anna 1952- DLB-292

Quine, W. V. 1908-2000 ....DLB-279

Quinn, Anthony 1915-2001 .... DLB-122

Quinn, John 1870-1924 ....DLB-187

Quiñónez, Naomi 1951- DLB-209

Quintana, Leroy V. 1944- DLB-82

Quintana, Miguel de 1671-1748

A Forerunner of Chicano Literature DLB-122

Quintilian circa A.D. 40-circa A.D. 96 .... DLB-211

Quintus Curtius Rufus fl. A.D. 35 .... DLB-211

Harlin Quist Books DLB-46

Quoirez, Françoise (see Sagan, Françoise)

R

Raabe, Wilhelm 1831-1910 .... DLB-129

Raban, Jonathan 1942- DLB-204

Rabe, David 1940- DLB-7, 228; Y-91

Raboni, Giovanni 1932- DLB-128

Rachilde 1860-1953 .... DLB-123, 192

Racin, Kočo 1908-1943 ....DLB-147

Racine, Jean 1639-1699 ....DLB-268

Rackham, Arthur 1867-1939 .... DLB-141

Raczymow, Henri 1948- DLB-299

Radauskas, Henrikas 1910-1970 .... DLB-220; CDWLB-4

Radcliffe, Ann 1764-1823 ....DLB-39, 178

Raddall, Thomas 1903-1994 .... DLB-68

Radford, Dollie 1858-1920 .... DLB-240

Radichkov, Yordan 1929- DLB-181

Radiguet, Raymond 1903-1923 .... DLB-65

Radishchev, Aleksandr Nikolaevich 1749-1802 .... DLB-150

Radnóti, Miklós 1909-1944 ....DLB-215; CDWLB-4

Radványi, Netty Reiling (see Seghers, Anna)

Rahv, Philip 1908-1973 ....DLB-137

Raich, Semen Egorovich 1792-1855 ..... DLB-205

Raičković, Stevan 1928- DLB-181

Raiderman (see Parshchikov, Aleksei Maksimovich)

Raimund, Ferdinand Jakob 1790-1836 .... DLB-90

Raine, Craig 1944- DLB-40

Raine, Kathleen 1908- DLB-20

Rainis, Jānis 1865-1929 .... DLB-220; CDWLB-4

Rainolde, Richard circa 1530-1606 .... DLB-136, 236

Rainolds, John 1549-1607 .... DLB-281

Rakić, Milan 1876-1938 .....DLB-147; CDWLB-4

Rakosi, Carl 1903- DLB-193
Ralegh, Sir Walter 1554?-1618 . . . . DLB-172; CDBLB-1
Raleigh, Walter *Style* (1897) [excerpt] DLB-57
Ralin, Radoy 1923- DLB-181
Ralph, Julian 1853-1903. . . . . DLB-23
Ramat, Silvio 1939- DLB-128
Ramée, Marie Louise de la (see Ouida)
Ramírez, Sergío 1942- DLB-145
Ramke, Bin 1947- DLB-120
Ramler, Karl Wilhelm 1725-1798. . . . . DLB-97
Ramon Ribeyro, Julio 1929-1994 . . . . DLB-145
Ramos, Manuel 1948- DLB-209
Ramos Sucre, José Antonio 1890-1930 . . . DLB-290
Ramous, Mario 1924- DLB-128
Rampersad, Arnold 1941- DLB-111
Ramsay, Allan 1684 or 1685-1758. . . . . DLB-95
Ramsay, David 1749-1815 . . . . DLB-30
Ramsay, Martha Laurens 1759-1811 . . . . . DLB-200
Ramsey, Frank P. 1903-1930. . . . . DLB-262
Ranch, Hieronimus Justesen 1539-1607 . . . . DLB-300
Ranck, Katherine Quintana 1942- DLB-122
Rand, Avery and Company. DLB-49
Rand, Ayn 1905-1982 . . . DLB-227, 279; CDALB-7
Rand McNally and Company DLB-49
Randall, David Anton 1905-1975. . . . . DLB-140
Randall, Dudley 1914- DLB-41
Randall, Henry S. 1811-1876 . . . . DLB-30
Randall, James G. 1881-1953. . . . . DLB-17
The Randall Jarrell Symposium: A Small Collection of Randall Jarrells Y-86
Excerpts From Papers Delivered at the Randall Jarrel Symposium Y-86
Randall, John Herman, Jr. 1899-1980 . . . . DLB-279
Randolph, A. Philip 1889-1979 . . . . DLB-91
Anson D. F. Randolph [publishing house] DLB-49
Randolph, Thomas 1605-1635 . . . . . . DLB-58, 126
Random House DLB-46
Rankin, Ian (Jack Harvey) 1960- DLB-267
Henry Ranlet [publishing house] DLB-49
Ransom, Harry 1908-1976. . . . . DLB-187
Ransom, John Crowe 1888-1974 . . . . DLB-45, 63; CDALB-7
Ransome, Arthur 1884-1967 . . . . DLB-160
Raphael, Frederic 1931- DLB-14
Raphaelson, Samson 1896-1983 . . . . DLB-44
Rare Book Dealers
Bertram Rota and His Bookshop Y-91
An Interview with Glenn Horowitz. Y-90
An Interview with Otto Penzler Y-96
An Interview with Ralph Sipper Y-94
New York City Bookshops in the 1930s and 1940s: The Recollections of Walter Goldwater. Y-93
Rare Books
Research in the American Antiquarian Book Trade Y-97
Two Hundred Years of Rare Books and Literary Collections at the University of South Carolina Y-00
Rashi circa 1040-1105 . . . . DLB-208
Raskin, Ellen 1928-1984 . . . . DLB-52
Rastell, John 1475?-1536 . . . . DLB-136, 170
Rattigan, Terence 1911-1977 . . . . DLB-13; CDBLB-7
Raven, Simon 1927-2001 . . . . DLB-271
Ravnkilde, Adda 1862-1883 . . . . DLB-300
Rawicz, Piotr 1919-1982 . . . . DLB-299
Rawlings, Marjorie Kinnan 1896-1953 . . . . DLB-9, 22, 102; DS-17; CDALB-7
Rawlinson, Richard 1690-1755 . . . . DLB-213
Rawlinson, Thomas 1681-1725 . . . . DLB-213
Rawls, John 1921-2002 . . . . DLB-279
Raworth, Tom 1938- DLB-40
Ray, David 1932- DLB-5
Ray, Gordon Norton 1915-1986 . . . . DLB-103, 140
Ray, Henrietta Cordelia 1849-1916. . . . . . . DLB-50
Raymond, Ernest 1888-1974 . . . . DLB-191
Raymond, Henry J. 1820-1869 . . . . DLB-43, 79
Raymond, René (see Chase, James Hadley)
Razaf, Andy 1895-1973 . . . . DLB-265
Rea, Michael 1927-1996. . . . . Y-97
Michael M. Rea and the Rea Award for the Short Story Y-97
Reach, Angus 1821-1856. . . . . DLB-70
Read, Herbert 1893-1968 . . . . DLB-20, 149
Read, Martha Meredith. DLB-200
Read, Opie 1852-1939. . . . . DLB-23
Read, Piers Paul 1941- DLB-14
Reade, Charles 1814-1884. . . . . DLB-21
Reader's Digest Condensed Books DLB-46
Readers Ulysses Symposium Y-97
Reading, Peter 1946- DLB-40
Reading Series in New York City Y-96
Reaney, James 1926- DLB-68
Rebhun, Paul 1500?-1546 . . . . DLB-179
Rèbora, Clemente 1885-1957. . . . . DLB-114
Rebreanu, Liviu 1885-1944 . . . . DLB-220
Rechy, John 1931- DLB-122, 278; Y-82
Redding, J. Saunders 1906-1988 . . . . . . DLB-63, 76
J. S. Redfield [publishing house]. DLB-49
Redgrove, Peter 1932- DLB-40
Redmon, Anne 1943- Y-86
Redmond, Eugene B. 1937- DLB-41
Redol, Alves 1911-1969. . . . . DLB-287
James Redpath [publishing house] DLB-49
Reed, Henry 1808-1854. . . . . DLB-59
Reed, Henry 1914-1986. . . . . DLB-27
Reed, Ishmael 1938- DLB-2, 5, 33, 169, 227; DS-8
Reed, Rex 1938- DLB-185
Reed, Sampson 1800-1880. . . . . DLB-1, 235
Reed, Talbot Baines 1852-1893. . . . . DLB-141
Reedy, William Marion 1862-1920 . . . . DLB-91
Reese, Lizette Woodworth 1856-1935. . . . . DLB-54
Reese, Thomas 1742-1796 . . . . DLB-37
Reeve, Clara 1729-1807 . . . . DLB-39
Preface to *The Old English Baron* (1778) DLB-39
The Progress of Romance (1785) [excerpt] DLB-39
Reeves, James 1909-1978. . . . . DLB-161
Reeves, John 1926- DLB-88
Reeves-Stevens, Garfield 1953- DLB-251
Régio, José (José Maria dos Reis Pereira) 1901-1969 . . . . DLB-287
Henry Regnery Company. DLB-46
Rehberg, Hans 1901-1963 . . . . DLB-124
Rehfisch, Hans José 1891-1960 . . . . DLB-124
Reich, Ebbe Kløvedal 1940- DLB-214
Reid, Alastair 1926- DLB-27
Reid, B. L. 1918-1990 . . . . DLB-111
Reid, Christopher 1949- DLB-40
Reid, Forrest 1875-1947 . . . . DLB-153
Reid, Helen Rogers 1882-1970 . . . . DLB-29
Reid, James ?-?. DLB-31
Reid, Mayne 1818-1883. . . . . DLB-21, 163
Reid, Thomas 1710-1796 . . . . DLB-31, 252
Reid, V. S. (Vic) 1913-1987. . . . . DLB-125
Reid, Whitelaw 1837-1912. . . . . DLB-23
Reilly and Lee Publishing Company DLB-46
Reimann, Brigitte 1933-1973 . . . . DLB-75
Reinmar der Alte circa 1165-circa 1205. . . DLB-138
Reinmar von Zweter circa 1200-circa 1250. . . . . DLB-138
Reisch, Walter 1903-1983 . . . . DLB-44
Reizei Family DLB-203
Religion
A Crisis of Culture: The Changing Role of Religion in the New Republic. DLB-37
Remarque, Erich Maria 1898-1970 . . . . DLB-56; CDWLB-2
Remington, Frederic 1861-1909 . . . . DLB-12, 186, 188
Remizov, Aleksei Mikhailovich 1877-1957. . . . . DLB-295
Renaud, Jacques 1943- DLB-60
Renault, Mary 1905-1983 . . . . Y-83
Rendell, Ruth (Barbara Vine) 1930- DLB-87, 276
Rensselaer, Maria van Cortlandt van 1645-1689 . . . . DLB-200
Repplier, Agnes 1855-1950 . . . . DLB-221
Reshetnikov, Fedor Mikhailovich 1841-1871 . . . . DLB-238
Rettenbacher, Simon 1634-1706 . . . . DLB-168
Retz, Jean-François-Paul de Gondi, cardinal de 1613-1679. . . . . DLB-268
Reuchlin, Johannes 1455-1522. . . . . DLB-179

Reuter, Christian 1665-after 1712....... DLB-168
Fleming H. Revell Company........... DLB-49
Reverdy, Pierre 1889-1960............ DLB-258
Reuter, Fritz 1810-1874............... DLB-129
Reuter, Gabriele 1859-1941............ DLB-66
Reventlow, Franziska Gräfin zu
1871-1918....................... DLB-66
Review of Reviews Office............. DLB-112
Rexroth, Kenneth 1905-1982
.......DLB-16, 48, 165, 212; Y-82; CDALB-1
The Commercialization of the Image
of Revolt.................... DLB-16
Rey, H. A. 1898-1977................. DLB-22
Reynal and Hitchcock................ DLB-46
Reynolds, G. W. M. 1814-1879......... DLB-21
Reynolds, John Hamilton 1794-1852..... DLB-96
Reynolds, Sir Joshua 1723-1792........ DLB-104
Reynolds, Mack 1917-1983.............. DLB-8
Reznikoff, Charles 1894-1976........ DLB-28, 45
Rhetoric
Continental European Rhetoricians, 1400-1600, and Their Influence in Reaissance England........ DLB-236
A Finding Guide to Key Works on Microfilm............... DLB-236
Glossary of Terms and Definitions of Rhetoic and Logic........... DLB-236
Rhett, Robert Barnwell 1800-1876....... DLB-43
Rhode, John 1884-1964............... DLB-77
Rhodes, Eugene Manlove 1869-1934.... DLB-256
Rhodes, James Ford 1848-1927.......... DLB-47
Rhodes, Richard 1937-............. DLB-185
Rhys, Jean 1890-1979
.....DLB-36, 117, 162; CDBLB-7; CDWLB-3
Ribeiro, Bernadim
fl. ca. 1475/1482-1526/1544........ DLB-287
Ricardo, David 1772-1823.........DLB-107, 158
Ricardou, Jean 1932-................ DLB-83
Rice, Anne (A. N. Roquelare, Anne Rampling)
1941-....................... DLB-292
Rice, Christopher 1978-............ DLB-292
Rice, Elmer 1892-1967............... DLB-4, 7
Rice, Grantland 1880-1954..........DLB-29, 171
Rich, Adrienne 1929-.... DLB-5, 67; CDALB-7
Richard, Mark 1955-............... DLB-234
Richard de Fournival
1201-1259 or 1260............... DLB-208
Richards, David Adams 1950-........ DLB-53
Richards, George circa 1760-1814....... DLB-37
Richards, I. A. 1893-1979.............. DLB-27
Richards, Laura E. 1850-1943.......... DLB-42
Richards, William Carey 1818-1892..... DLB-73
Grant Richards [publishing house]...... DLB-112
Richardson, Charles F. 1851-1913....... DLB-71
Richardson, Dorothy M. 1873-1957...... DLB-36
The Novels of Dorothy Richardson
(1918), by May Sinclair......... DLB-36
Richardson, Henry Handel
(Ethel Florence Lindesay Robertson)
1870-1946...................DLB-197, 230
Richardson, Jack 1935-............... DLB-7
Richardson, John 1796-1852............ DLB-99
Richardson, Samuel
1689-1761.......... DLB-39, 154; CDBLB-2
Introductory Letters from the Second Edition of *Pamela* (1741)......... DLB-39
Postscript to [the Third Edition of] *Clarissa* (1751)............. DLB-39
Preface to the First Edition of *Pamela* (1740)................. DLB-39
Preface to the Third Edition of *Clarissa* (1751) [excerpt]......... DLB-39
Preface to Volume 1 of *Clarissa* (1747)....................... DLB-39
Preface to Volume 3 of *Clarissa* (1748)....................... DLB-39
Richardson, Willis 1889-1977........... DLB-51
Riche, Barnabe 1542-1617............ DLB-136
Richepin, Jean 1849-1926............. DLB-192
Richler, Mordecai 1931-2001........... DLB-53
Richter, Conrad 1890-1968......... DLB-9, 212
Richter, Hans Werner 1908-1993....... DLB-69
Richter, Johann Paul Friedrich
1763-1825............. DLB-94; CDWLB-2
Joseph Rickerby [publishing house]..... DLB-106
Rickword, Edgell 1898-1982........... DLB-20
Riddell, Charlotte 1832-1906.......... DLB-156
Riddell, John (see Ford, Corey)
Ridge, John Rollin 1827-1867...........DLB-175
Ridge, Lola 1873-1941................ DLB-54
Ridge, William Pett 1859-1930......... DLB-135
Riding, Laura (see Jackson, Laura Riding)
Ridler, Anne 1912-................. DLB-27
Ridruego, Dionisio 1912-1975......... DLB-108
Riel, Louis 1844-1885................. DLB-99
Riemer, Johannes 1648-1714........... DLB-168
Rifbjerg, Klaus 1931-.............. DLB-214
Riffaterre, Michael 1924-............ DLB-67
A Conversation between William Riggan and Janette Turner Hospital........... Y-02
Riggs, Lynn 1899-1954................DLB-175
Riis, Jacob 1849-1914................. DLB-23
John C. Riker [publishing house]........ DLB-49
Riley, James 1777-1840............... DLB-183
Riley, John 1938-1978................. DLB-40
Rilke, Rainer Maria
1875-1926............. DLB-81; CDWLB-2
Rimanelli, Giose 1926-..............DLB-177
Rimbaud, Jean-Nicolas-Arthur
1854-1891..................... DLB-217
Rinehart and Company............... DLB-46
Ringuet 1895-1960................... DLB-68
Ringwood, Gwen Pharis 1910-1984...... DLB-88
Rinser, Luise 1911-................. DLB-69
Ríos, Alberto 1952-................ DLB-122
Ríos, Isabella 1948-................ DLB-82
Ripley, Arthur 1895-1961.............. DLB-44
Ripley, George 1802-1880.....DLB-1, 64, 73, 235
The Rising Glory of America:
Three Poems.................... DLB-37
The Rising Glory of America: Written in 1771 (1786), by Hugh Henry Brackenridge and Philip Freneau.............. DLB-37
Riskin, Robert 1897-1955.............. DLB-26
Risse, Heinz 1898-................. DLB-69
Rist, Johann 1607-1667............... DLB-164
Ristikivi, Karl 1912-1977............. DLB-220
Ritchie, Anna Mowatt 1819-1870..... DLB-3, 250
Ritchie, Anne Thackeray 1837-1919...... DLB-18
Ritchie, Thomas 1778-1854............ DLB-43
The Ritz Paris Hemingway Award.......... Y-85
Mario Varga Llosa's Acceptance Speech.. Y-85
Rivard, Adjutor 1868-1945............. DLB-92
Rive, Richard 1931-1989......... DLB-125, 225
Rivera, José 1955-................. DLB-249
Rivera, Marina 1942-.............. DLB-122
Rivera, Tomás 1935-1984............. DLB-82
Rivers, Conrad Kent 1933-1968......... DLB-41
Riverside Press...................... DLB-49
Rivington, James circa 1724-1802........ DLB-43
Charles Rivington [publishing house].... DLB-154
Rivkin, Allen 1903-1990............... DLB-26
Roa Bastos, Augusto 1917-.......... DLB-113
Robbe-Grillet, Alain 1922-........... DLB-83
Robbins, Tom 1936-.................. Y-80
Roberts, Charles G. D. 1860-1943....... DLB-92
Roberts, Dorothy 1906-1993........... DLB-88
Roberts, Elizabeth Madox
1881-1941.................DLB-9, 54, 102
Roberts, John (see Swynnerton, Thomas)
Roberts, Keith 1935-2000............. DLB-261
Roberts, Kenneth 1885-1957............ DLB-9
Roberts, Michèle 1949-............. DLB-231
Roberts, Theodore Goodridge
1877-1953....................... DLB-92
Roberts, Ursula Wyllie (see Miles, Susan)
Roberts, William 1767-1849........... DLB-142
James Roberts [publishing house]....... DLB-154
Roberts Brothers.................... DLB-49
A. M. Robertson and Company......... DLB-49
Robertson, Ethel Florence Lindesay
(see Richardson, Henry Handel)
Robertson, William 1721-1793......... DLB-104
Robin, Leo 1895-1984............... DLB-265
Robins, Elizabeth 1862-1952...........DLB-197
Robinson, A. Mary F. (Madame James Darmesteter, Madame Mary Duclaux) 1857-1944.............. DLB-240
Robinson, Casey 1903-1979............ DLB-44
Robinson, Derek...................... Y-02
Robinson, Edwin Arlington
1869-1935............. DLB-54; CDALB-3

Review by Derek Robinson of George Greenfield's *Rich Dust* Y-02
Robinson, Henry Crabb 1775-1867 . . . . . . DLB-107
Robinson, James Harvey 1863-1936 . . . . . . DLB-47
Robinson, Lennox 1886-1958 . . . . DLB-10
Robinson, Mabel Louise 1874-1962. . . . . . . DLB-22
Robinson, Marilynne 1943- DLB-206
Robinson, Mary 1758-1800 . . . . DLB-158
Robinson, Richard circa 1545-1607 . . . . . . DLB-167
Robinson, Therese 1797-1870. . . . . DLB-59, 133
Robison, Mary 1949- DLB-130
Roblès, Emmanuel 1914-1995 . . . . DLB-83
Roccatagliata Ceccardi, Ceccardo 1871-1919 . . . . DLB-114
Rocha, Adolfo Correira da (see Torga, Miguel)
Roche, Billy 1949- DLB-233
Rochester, John Wilmot, Earl of 1647-1680 . . . . DLB-131
Rochon, Esther 1948- DLB-251
Rock, Howard 1911-1976 . . . . DLB-127
Rockwell, Norman Perceval 1894-1978 . . . DLB-188
Rodgers, Carolyn M. 1945- DLB-41
Rodgers, W. R. 1909-1969 . . . . DLB-20
Rodney, Lester 1911- DLB-241
Rodríguez, Claudio 1934-1999 . . . . DLB-134
Rodríguez, Joe D. 1943- DLB-209
Rodríguez, Luis J. 1954- DLB-209
Rodriguez, Richard 1944- DLB-82, 256
Rodríguez Julia, Edgardo 1946- DLB-145
Roe, E. P. 1838-1888. . . . . DLB-202
Roethke, Theodore 1908-1963 . . . . .DLB-5, 206; CDALB-1
Rogers, Jane 1952- DLB-194
Rogers, Pattiann 1940- DLB-105
Rogers, Samuel 1763-1855. . . . . DLB-93
Rogers, Will 1879-1935 . . . . DLB-11
Rohmer, Sax 1883-1959 . . . . DLB-70
Roiphe, Anne 1935- Y-80
Rojas, Arnold R. 1896-1988 . . . . DLB-82
Rojas, Fernando de ca. 1475-1541 . . . . DLB-286
Rolfe, Frederick William 1860-1913 . . . . DLB-34, 156
Rolland, Romain 1866-1944 . . . . DLB-65
Rolle, Richard circa 1290-1300 - 1340. . . . DLB-146
Rölvaag, O. E. 1876-1931 . . . . DLB-9, 212
Romains, Jules 1885-1972 . . . . DLB-65
A. Roman and Company. DLB-49
Roman de la Rose: Guillaume de Lorris 1200/1205-circa 1230, Jean de Meun 1235-1240-circa 1305 . . . . DLB-208
Romano, Lalla 1906-2001 . . . . DLB-177
Romano, Octavio 1923- DLB-122
Rome, Harold 1908-1993 . . . . DLB-265
Romero, Leo 1950- DLB-122
Romero, Lin 1947- DLB-122
Romero, Orlando 1945- DLB-82
Rook, Clarence 1863-1915 . . . . DLB-135
Roosevelt, Theodore 1858-1919 . . . . DLB-47, 186, 275
Root, Waverley 1903-1982 . . . . DLB-4
Root, William Pitt 1941- DLB-120
Roquebrune, Robert de 1889-1978 . . . . DLB-68
Rorty, Richard 1931- DLB-246, 279
Rosa, João Guimarães 1908-1967. . . . . . . DLB-113
Rosales, Luis 1910-1992 . . . . DLB-134
Roscoe, William 1753-1831 . . . . DLB-163
Rose, Reginald 1920-2002 . . . . DLB-26
Rose, Wendy 1948- DLB-175
Rosegger, Peter 1843-1918 . . . . DLB-129
Rosei, Peter 1946- DLB-85
Rosen, Norma 1925- DLB-28
Rosenbach, A. S. W. 1876-1952. . . . . DLB-140
Rosenbaum, Ron 1946- DLB-185
Rosenbaum, Thane 1960- DLB-299
Rosenberg, Isaac 1890-1918 . . . . DLB-20, 216
Rosenfeld, Isaac 1918-1956 . . . . DLB-28
Rosenthal, Harold 1914-1999 . . . . DLB-241
Jimmy, Red, and Others: Harold Rosenthal Remembers the Stars of the Press Box Y-01
Rosenthal, M. L. 1917-1996. . . . . DLB-5
Rosenwald, Lessing J. 1891-1979. . . . . DLB-187
Ross, Alexander 1591-1654. . . . . DLB-151
Ross, Harold 1892-1951 . . . . DLB-137
Ross, Jerry 1926-1955 . . . . DLB-265
Ross, Leonard Q. (see Rosten, Leo)
Ross, Lillian 1927- DLB-185
Ross, Martin 1862-1915. . . . . DLB-135
Ross, Sinclair 1908-1996 . . . . DLB-88
Ross, W. W. E. 1894-1966 . . . . DLB-88
Rosselli, Amelia 1930-1996 . . . . DLB-128
Rossen, Robert 1908-1966. . . . . DLB-26
Rosset, Barney. Y-02
Rossetti, Christina 1830-1894 . . . DLB-35, 163, 240
Rossetti, Dante Gabriel 1828-1882 . . . . DLB-35; CDBLB-4
The Stealthy School of Criticism (1871) DLB-35
Rossner, Judith 1935- DLB-6
Rostand, Edmond 1868-1918 . . . . DLB-192
Rosten, Leo 1908-1997 . . . . DLB-11
Rostenberg, Leona 1908- DLB-140
Rostopchina, Evdokiia Petrovna 1811-1858 . . . . DLB-205
Rostovsky, Dimitrii 1651-1709 . . . . DLB-150
Rota, Bertram 1903-1966. . . . . DLB-201
Bertram Rota and His Bookshop Y-91
Roth, Gerhard 1942- DLB-85, 124
Roth, Henry 1906?-1995 . . . . DLB-28
Roth, Joseph 1894-1939. . . . . DLB-85
Roth, Philip 1933- DLB-2, 28, 173; Y-82; CDALB-6
Rothenberg, Jerome 1931- DLB-5, 193
Rothschild Family DLB-184
Rotimi, Ola 1938- DLB-125
Rotrou, Jean 1609-1650 . . . . DLB-268
Routhier, Adolphe-Basile 1839-1920 . . . . . . DLB-99
Routier, Simone 1901-1987 . . . . DLB-88
George Routledge and Sons DLB-106
Roversi, Roberto 1923-. DLB-128
Rowe, Elizabeth Singer 1674-1737 . . . . . DLB-39, 95
Rowe, Nicholas 1674-1718. . . . . DLB-84
Rowlands, Samuel circa 1570-1630 . . . . . . DLB-121
Rowlandson, Mary circa 1637-circa 1711 . . . . DLB-24, 200
Rowley, William circa 1585-1626 . . . . DLB-58
Rowling, J. K. The Harry Potter Phenomenon Y-99
Rowse, A. L. 1903-1997. . . . . DLB-155
Rowson, Susanna Haswell circa 1762-1824 . . . . DLB-37, 200
Roy, Camille 1870-1943 . . . . DLB-92
The G. Ross Roy Scottish Poetry Collection at the University of South Carolina Y-89
Roy, Gabrielle 1909-1983 . . . . DLB-68
Roy, Jules 1907-2000 . . . . DLB-83
The Royal Court Theatre and the English Stage Company. DLB-13
The Royal Court Theatre and the New Drama. DLB-10
The Royal Shakespeare Company at the Swan Y-88
Royall, Anne Newport 1769-1854 . . . . DLB-43, 248
Royce, Josiah 1855-1916 . . . . DLB-270
The Roycroft Printing Shop DLB-49
Royde-Smith, Naomi 1875-1964 . . . . DLB-191
Royster, Vermont 1914-1996 . . . . DLB-127
Richard Royston [publishing house] DLB-170
Rozanov, Vasilii Vasil'evich 1856-1919 . . . . DLB-295
Różewicz, Tadeusz 1921- DLB-232
Ruark, Gibbons 1941- DLB-120
Ruban, Vasilii Grigorevich 1742-1795 . . . . DLB-150
Rubens, Bernice 1928- DLB-14, 207
Rubina, Dina Il'inichna 1953- DLB-285
Rubinshtein, Lev Semenovich 1947- . . . DLB-285
Rudd and Carleton DLB-49
Rudd, Steele (Arthur Hoey Davis) DLB-230
Rudkin, David 1936- DLB-13
Rudnick, Paul 1957- DLB-266
Rudnicki, Adolf 1909-1990 . . . . DLB-299
Rudolf von Ems circa 1200-circa 1254 . . . DLB-138
Ruffin, Josephine St. Pierre 1842-1924 . . . . DLB-79
Ruganda, John 1941- DLB-157
Ruggles, Henry Joseph 1813-1906. . . . . DLB-64
Ruiz de Burton, María Amparo 1832-1895 . . . . DLB-209, 221
Rukeyser, Muriel 1913-1980 . . . . DLB-48
Rule, Jane 1931- DLB-60

Cumulative Index

Rulfo, Juan 1918-1986 ..... DLB-113; CDWLB-3
Rumaker, Michael 1932- DLB-16
Rumens, Carol 1944- DLB-40
Rummo, Paul-Eerik 1942- DLB-232
Runyon, Damon 1880-1946 ....DLB-11, 86, 171
Ruodlieb circa 1050-1075 .... DLB-148
Rush, Benjamin 1746-1813 .... DLB-37
Rush, Rebecca 1779-? DLB-200
Rushdie, Salman 1947- DLB-194
Rusk, Ralph L. 1888-1962 .... DLB-103
Ruskin, John 1819-1900...... DLB-55, 163, 190; CDBLB-4
Russ, Joanna 1937- DLB-8
Russell, Benjamin 1761-1845 .... DLB-43
Russell, Bertrand 1872-1970 .... DLB-100, 262
Russell, Charles Edward 1860-1941...... DLB-25
Russell, Charles M. 1864-1926......... DLB-188
Russell, Eric Frank 1905-1978 .... DLB-255
Russell, Fred 1906-2003 .... DLB-241
Russell, George William (see AE)
Russell, Countess Mary Annette Beauchamp (see Arnim, Elizabeth von)
Russell, Willy 1947- DLB-233
B. B. Russell and Company DLB-49
R. H. Russell and Son................ DLB-49
Rutebeuf flourished 1249-1277......... DLB-208
Rutherford, Mark 1831-1913 .... DLB-18
Ruxton, George Frederick 1821-1848 .... DLB-186
R-va, Zeneida (see Gan, Elena Andreevna)
Ryan, James 1952- DLB-267
Ryan, Michael 1946- Y-82
Ryan, Oscar 1904- DLB-68
Ryder, Jack 1871-1936 .... DLB-241
Ryga, George 1932-1987 .... DLB-60
Rylands, Enriqueta Augustina Tennant 1843-1908 .... DLB-184
Rylands, John 1801-1888 .... DLB-184
Ryle, Gilbert 1900-1976 .... DLB-262
Ryleev, Kondratii Fedorovich 1795-1826...................... DLB-205
Rymer, Thomas 1643?-1713........... DLB-101
Ryskind, Morrie 1895-1985 .... DLB-26
Rzhevsky, Aleksei Andreevich 1737-1804...................... DLB-150

S

The Saalfield Publishing Company DLB-46
Saba, Umberto 1883-1957 .... DLB-114
Sábato, Ernesto 1911- DLB-145; CDWLB-3
Saberhagen, Fred 1930- DLB-8
Sabin, Joseph 1821-1881.............. DLB-187
Sacer, Gottfried Wilhelm 1635-1699 .... DLB-168
Sachs, Hans 1494-1576 ......DLB-179; CDWLB-2
Sá-Carneiro, Mário de 1890-1916 ...... DLB-287
Sack, John 1930- DLB-185
Sackler, Howard 1929-1982 .... DLB-7
Sackville, Lady Margaret 1881-1963 .... DLB-240
Sackville, Thomas 1536-1608 and Norton, Thomas 1532-1584......... DLB-62
Sackville, Thomas 1536-1608.......... DLB-132
Sackville-West, Edward 1901-1965 ..... DLB-191
Sackville-West, V. 1892-1962....... DLB-34, 195
Sá de Miranda, Francisco de 1481-1588?..................... DLB-287
Sadlier, Mary Anne 1820-1903.......... DLB-99
D. and J. Sadlier and Company DLB-49
Sadoff, Ira 1945- DLB-120
Sadoveanu, Mihail 1880-1961 .... DLB-220
Sadur, Nina Nikolaevna 1950- DLB-285
Sáenz, Benjamin Alire 1954- DLB-209
Saenz, Jaime 1921-1986 .... DLB-145, 283
Saffin, John circa 1626-1710 .... DLB-24
Sagan, Françoise 1935- DLB-83
Sage, Robert 1899-1962 .... DLB-4
Sagel, Jim 1947- DLB-82
Sagendorph, Robb Hansell 1900-1970 ... DLB-137
Sahagún, Carlos 1938- DLB-108
Sahkomaapii, Piitai (see Highwater, Jamake)
Sahl, Hans 1902-1993................. DLB-69
Said, Edward W. 1935- DLB-67
Saigyō 1118-1190 .... DLB-203
Saiko, George 1892-1962 .... DLB-85
Sainte-Beuve, Charles-Augustin 1804-1869 .... DLB-217
Saint-Exupéry, Antoine de 1900-1944 .... DLB-72
St. John, J. Allen 1872-1957............ DLB-188
St John, Madeleine 1942- DLB-267
St. Johns, Adela Rogers 1894-1988....... DLB-29
St. Omer, Garth 1931- DLB-117
Saint Pierre, Michel de 1916-1987 .... DLB-83
St. Dominic's Press.................. DLB-112
The St. John's College Robert Graves Trust . . Y-96
St. Martin's Press DLB-46
St. Nicholas 1873-1881 ....DS-13
Saintsbury, George 1845-1933 ....DLB-57, 149
"Modern English Prose" (1876)...... DLB-57
The Present State of the English Novel (1892),................ DLB-18
Saiokuken Sōchō 1448-1532........... DLB-203
Saki (see Munro, H. H.)
Salaam, Kalamu ya 1947- DLB-38
Šalamun, Tomaž 1941- ... DLB-181; CDWLB-4
Salas, Floyd 1931- DLB-82
Sálaz-Marquez, Rubén 1935- DLB-122
Salemson, Harold J. 1910-1988........... DLB-4
Salesbury, William 1520?-1584? DLB-281
Salinas, Luis Omar 1937- DLB-82
Salinas, Pedro 1891-1951 .... DLB-134
Salinger, J. D. 1919- DLB-2, 102, 173; CDALB-1
Salkey, Andrew 1928- DLB-125
Sallust circa 86 B.C.-35 B.C. DLB-211; CDWLB-1
Salt, Waldo 1914-1987 .... DLB-44
Salter, James 1925- DLB-130
Salter, Mary Jo 1954- DLB-120
Saltus, Edgar 1855-1921.............. DLB-202
Saltykov, Mikhail Evgrafovich 1826-1889 .... DLB-238
Salustri, Carlo Alberto (see Trilussa)
Salverson, Laura Goodman 1890-1970.... DLB-92
Samain, Albert 1858-1900 ....DLB-217
Sampson, Richard Henry (see Hull, Richard)
Samuels, Ernest 1903-1996............ DLB-111
Sanborn, Franklin Benjamin 1831-1917..................... DLB-1, 223
Sánchez de Arévalo, Rodrigo 1404-1470....................... DLB-286
Sánchez, Luis Rafael 1936- DLB-145
Sánchez, Philomeno "Phil" 1917- DLB-122
Sánchez, Ricardo 1941-1995............ DLB-82
Sánchez, Saúl 1943- DLB-209
Sanchez, Sonia 1934- DLB-41; DS-8
Sand, George 1804-1876...........DLB-119, 192
Sandburg, Carl 1878-1967............DLB-17, 54; CDALB-3
Sandel, Cora (Sara Fabricius) 1880-1974....................... DLB-297
Sandemose, Aksel 1899-1965 .... DLB-297
Sanders, Edward 1939- DLB-16, 244
Sanderson, Robert 1587-1663.......... DLB-281
Sandoz, Mari 1896-1966............ DLB-9, 212
Sandwell, B. K. 1876-1954 .... DLB-92
Sandy, Stephen 1934- DLB-165
Sandys, George 1578-1644 .... DLB-24, 121
Sangster, Charles 1822-1893 .... DLB-99
Sanguineti, Edoardo 1930- DLB-128
Sanjōnishi Sanetaka 1455-1537......... DLB-203
San Pedro, Diego de fl. ca. 1492........ DLB-286
Sansay, Leonora ?-after 1823 .... DLB-200
Sansom, William 1912-1976........... DLB-139
Santayana, George 1863-1952 ......DLB-54, 71, 246, 270; DS-13
Santiago, Danny 1911-1988 .... DLB-122
Santillana, Marqués de (Íñigo López de Mendoza) 1398-1458 .... DLB-286
Santmyer, Helen Hooven 1895-1986 .... Y-84
Sanvitale, Francesca 1928- DLB-196
Sapidus, Joannes 1490-1561 ....DLB-179
Sapir, Edward 1884-1939.............. DLB-92
Sapper (see McNeile, Herman Cyril)
Sappho circa 620 B.C.-circa 550 B.C. DLB-176; CDWLB-1
Saramago, José 1922- DLB-287; Y-98
Nobel Lecture 1998: How Characters Became the Masters and the Author Their Apprentice................. Y-98
Sarban (John W. Wall) 1910-1989...... DLB-255

Sardou, Victorien 1831-1908 . . . . DLB-192
Sarduy, Severo 1937-1993 . . . . DLB-113
Sargent, Pamela 1948- DLB-8
Saro-Wiwa, Ken 1941- DLB-157
Saroyan, Aram
Rites of Passage [on William Saroyan] . . . Y-83
Saroyan, William
1908-1981 . . . . . DLB-7, 9, 86; Y-81; CDALB-7
Sarraute, Nathalie 1900-1999 . . . . DLB-83
Sarrazin, Albertine 1937-1967 . . . . DLB-83
Sarris, Greg 1952- DLB-175
Sarton, May 1912-1995 . . . . DLB-48; Y-81
Sartre, Jean-Paul 1905-1980 . . . . DLB-72, 296
Sassoon, Siegfried
1886-1967 . . . . DLB-20, 191; DS-18
A Centenary Essay Y-86
Tributes from Vivien F. Clarke and
Michael Thorpe Y-86
Sata Ineko 1904- DLB-180
Saturday Review Press DLB-46
Saunders, James 1925- DLB-13
Saunders, John Monk 1897-1940 . . . . DLB-26
Saunders, Margaret Marshall
1861-1947 . . . . DLB-92
Saunders and Otley DLB-106
Saussure, Ferdinand de 1857-1913 . . . . DLB-242
Savage, James 1784-1873 . . . . DLB-30
Savage, Marmion W. 1803?-1872 . . . . DLB-21
Savage, Richard 1697?-1743 . . . . DLB-95
Savard, Félix-Antoine 1896-1982 . . . . DLB-68
Savery, Henry 1791-1842 . . . . DLB-230
Saville, (Leonard) Malcolm 1901-1982 . . . DLB-160
Savinio, Alberto 1891-1952 . . . . DLB-264
Sawyer, Robert J. 1960- DLB-251
Sawyer, Ruth 1880-1970 . . . . DLB-22
Sayers, Dorothy L.
1893-1957 . . . . DLB-10, 36, 77, 100; CDBLB-6
The Dorothy L. Sayers Society Y-98
Sayle, Charles Edward 1864-1924 . . . . DLB-184
Sayles, John Thomas 1950- DLB-44
Sbarbaro, Camillo 1888-1967 . . . . DLB-114
Scalapino, Leslie 1947- DLB-193
Scannell, Vernon 1922- DLB-27
Scarry, Richard 1919-1994 . . . . DLB-61
Schack, Hans Egede 1820-1859 . . . . DLB-300
Schaefer, Jack 1907-1991 . . . . DLB-212
Schaeffer, Albrecht 1885-1950 . . . . DLB-66
Schaeffer, Susan Fromberg 1941- . . . DLB-28, 299
Schaff, Philip 1819-1893 . . . . DS-13
Schaper, Edzard 1908-1984 . . . . DLB-69
Scharf, J. Thomas 1843-1898 . . . . DLB-47
Schede, Paul Melissus 1539-1602 . . . . DLB-179
Scheffel, Joseph Viktor von 1826-1886 . . . DLB-129
Scheffler, Johann 1624-1677 . . . . DLB-164
Schelling, Friedrich Wilhelm Joseph von
1775-1854 . . . . DLB-90
Scherer, Wilhelm 1841-1886 . . . . DLB-129
Scherfig, Hans 1905-1979 . . . . DLB-214
Schickele, René 1883-1940 . . . . DLB-66
Schiff, Dorothy 1903-1989 . . . . DLB-127
Schiller, Friedrich
1759-1805 . . . . DLB-94; CDWLB-2
Schirmer, David 1623-1687 . . . . DLB-164
Schlaf, Johannes 1862-1941 . . . . DLB-118
Schlegel, August Wilhelm 1767-1845 . . . . . . DLB-94
Schlegel, Dorothea 1763-1839 . . . . DLB-90
Schlegel, Friedrich 1772-1829 . . . . DLB-90
Schleiermacher, Friedrich 1768-1834 . . . . . . DLB-90
Schlesinger, Arthur M., Jr. 1917- DLB-17
Schlumberger, Jean 1877-1968 . . . . DLB-65
Schmid, Eduard Hermann Wilhelm
(see Edschmid, Kasimir)
Schmidt, Arno 1914-1979 . . . . DLB-69
Schmidt, Johann Kaspar (see Stirner, Max)
Schmidt, Michael 1947- DLB-40
Schmidtbonn, Wilhelm August
1876-1952 . . . . DLB-118
Schmitz, Aron Hector (see Svevo, Italo)
Schmitz, James H. 1911-1981 . . . . DLB-8
Schnabel, Johann Gottfried 1692-1760 . . . . DLB-168
Schnackenberg, Gjertrud 1953- DLB-120
Schnitzler, Arthur
1862-1931 . . . . DLB-81, 118; CDWLB-2
Schnurre, Wolfdietrich 1920-1989 . . . . DLB-69
Schocken Books DLB-46
Scholartis Press DLB-112
Scholderer, Victor 1880-1971 . . . . DLB-201
The Schomburg Center for Research
in Black Culture DLB-76
Schönbeck, Virgilio (see Giotti, Virgilio)
Schönherr, Karl 1867-1943 . . . . DLB-118
Schoolcraft, Jane Johnston 1800-1841 . . . . DLB-175
School Stories, 1914-1960 . . . . DLB-160
Schopenhauer, Arthur 1788-1860 . . . . DLB-90
Schopenhauer, Johanna 1766-1838 . . . . DLB-90
Schorer, Mark 1908-1977 . . . . DLB-103
Schottelius, Justus Georg 1612-1676 . . . . . DLB-164
Schouler, James 1839-1920 . . . . DLB-47
Schoultz, Solveig von 1907-1996 . . . . DLB-259
Schrader, Paul 1946- DLB-44
Schreiner, Olive
1855-1920 . . . . DLB-18, 156, 190, 225
Schroeder, Andreas 1946- DLB-53
Schubart, Christian Friedrich Daniel
1739-1791 . . . . DLB-97
Schubert, Gotthilf Heinrich 1780-1860 . . . . DLB-90
Schücking, Levin 1814-1883 . . . . DLB-133
Schulberg, Budd 1914- DLB-6, 26, 28; Y-81
Excerpts from USC Presentation
[on F. Scott Fitzgerald] Y-96
F. J. Schulte and Company DLB-49
Schulz, Bruno 1892-1942 . . . . DLB-215; CDWLB-4
Schulze, Hans (see Praetorius, Johannes)
Schupp, Johann Balthasar 1610-1661 . . . . . DLB-164
Schurz, Carl 1829-1906 . . . . DLB-23
Schuyler, George S. 1895-1977 . . . . DLB-29, 51
Schuyler, James 1923-1991 . . . . DLB-5, 169
Schwartz, Delmore 1913-1966 . . . . DLB-28, 48
Schwartz, Jonathan 1938- Y-82
Schwartz, Lynne Sharon 1939- DLB-218
Schwarz, Sibylle 1621-1638 . . . . DLB-164
Schwarz-Bart, Andre 1928- DLB-299
Schwerner, Armand 1927-1999 . . . . DLB-165
Schwob, Marcel 1867-1905 . . . . DLB-123
Sciascia, Leonardo 1921-1989 . . . . DLB-177
Science Fiction and Fantasy
Documents in British Fantasy and
Science Fiction DLB-178
Hugo Awards and Nebula Awards DLB-8
The Iconography of Science-Fiction
Art DLB-8
The New Wave DLB-8
Paperback Science Fiction DLB-8
Science Fantasy DLB-8
Science-Fiction Fandom and
Conventions DLB-8
Science-Fiction Fanzines: The Time
Binders DLB-8
Science-Fiction Films DLB-8
Science Fiction Writers of America
and the Nebula Award DLB-8
Selected Science-Fiction Magazines and
Anthologies DLB-8
A World Chronology of Important Science
Fiction Works (1818-1979) DLB-8
The Year in Science Fiction
and Fantasy Y-00, 01
Scot, Reginald circa 1538-1599 . . . . DLB-136
Scotellaro, Rocco 1923-1953 . . . . DLB-128
Scott, Alicia Anne (Lady John Scott)
1810-1900 . . . . DLB-240
Scott, Catharine Amy Dawson
1865-1934 . . . . DLB-240
Scott, Dennis 1939-1991 . . . . DLB-125
Scott, Dixon 1881-1915 . . . . DLB-98
Scott, Duncan Campbell 1862-1947 . . . . DLB-92
Scott, Evelyn 1893-1963 . . . . DLB-9, 48
Scott, F. R. 1899-1985 . . . . DLB-88
Scott, Frederick George 1861-1944 . . . . DLB-92
Scott, Geoffrey 1884-1929 . . . . DLB-149
Scott, Harvey W. 1838-1910 . . . . DLB-23
Scott, Lady Jane (see Scott, Alicia Anne)
Scott, Paul 1920-1978 . . . . DLB-14, 207
Scott, Sarah 1723-1795 . . . . DLB-39
Scott, Tom 1918- DLB-27
Scott, Sir Walter 1771-1832
. . . . . . DLB-93, 107, 116, 144, 159; CDBLB-3
Scott, William Bell 1811-1890 . . . . DLB-32
Walter Scott Publishing Company
Limited DLB-112
William R. Scott [publishing house] DLB-46

Scott-Heron, Gil 1949- DLB-41
Scribe, Eugene 1791-1861 .... DLB-192
Scribner, Arthur Hawley 1859-1932 ..... DS-13, 16
Scribner, Charles 1854-1930 .... DS-13, 16
Scribner, Charles, Jr. 1921-1995 .... Y-95
Reminiscences DS-17
Charles Scribner's Sons DLB-49; DS-13, 16, 17
Archives of Charles Scribner's Sons DS-17
Scribner's Magazine DS-13
Scribner's Monthly DS-13
Scripps, E. W. 1854-1926 .... DLB-25
Scudder, Horace Elisha 1838-1902 .... DLB-42, 71
Scudder, Vida Dutton 1861-1954 .... DLB-71
Scudéry, Madeleine de 1607-1701 .... DLB-268
Scupham, Peter 1933- DLB-40
Seabrook, William 1886-1945 .... DLB-4
Seabury, Samuel 1729-1796 .... DLB-31
Seacole, Mary Jane Grant 1805-1881 .... DLB-166
The Seafarer circa 970 .... DLB-146
Sealsfield, Charles (Carl Postl) 1793-1864 .... DLB-133, 186
Searle, John R. 1932- DLB-279
Sears, Edward I. 1819?-1876 .... DLB-79
Sears Publishing Company DLB-46
Seaton, George 1911-1979 .... DLB-44
Seaton, William Winston 1785-1866 ..... DLB-43
Martin Secker [publishing house] DLB-112
Martin Secker, and Warburg Limited ... DLB-112
The "Second Generation" Holocaust Novel DLB-299
Sedgwick, Arthur George 1844-1915 ..... DLB-64
Sedgwick, Catharine Maria 1789-1867 .... DLB-1, 74, 183, 239, 243
Sedgwick, Ellery 1872-1960 .... DLB-91
Sedgwick, Eve Kosofsky 1950- DLB-246
Sedley, Sir Charles 1639-1701 .... DLB-131
Seeberg, Peter 1925-1999 .... DLB-214
Seeger, Alan 1888-1916 .... DLB-45
Seers, Eugene (see Dantin, Louis)
Segal, Erich 1937- Y-86
Segal, Lore 1928- DLB-299
Šegedin, Petar 1909- DLB-181
Seghers, Anna 1900-1983 .... DLB-69; CDWLB-2
Seid, Ruth (see Sinclair, Jo)
Seidel, Frederick Lewis 1936- Y-84
Seidel, Ina 1885-1974 .... DLB-56
Seifert, Jaroslav 1901-1986 .... DLB-215; Y-84; CDWLB-4
Jaroslav Seifert Through the Eyes of the English-Speaking Reader Y-84
Three Poems by Jaroslav Seifert Y-84
Seifullina, Lidiia Nikolaevna 1889-1954 .. DLB-272
Seigenthaler, John 1927- DLB-127
Seizin Press DLB-112
Séjour, Victor 1817-1874 .... DLB-50
Séjour Marcou et Ferrand, Juan Victor (see Séjour, Victor)
Sekowski, Jósef-Julian, Baron Brambeus (see Senkovsky, Osip Ivanovich)
Selby, Bettina 1934- DLB-204
Selby, Hubert, Jr. 1928- DLB-2, 227
Selden, George 1929-1989 .... DLB-52
Selden, John 1584-1654 .... DLB-213
Selenić, Slobodan 1933-1995 .... DLB-181
Self, Edwin F. 1920- DLB-137
Self, Will 1961- DLB-207
Seligman, Edwin R. A. 1861-1939 .... DLB-47
Selimović, Meša 1910-1982 .... DLB-181; CDWLB-4
Sellars, Wilfrid 1912-1989 .... DLB-279
Sellings, Arthur (Arthur Gordon Ley) 1911-1968 .... DLB-261
Selous, Frederick Courteney 1851-1917 ... DLB-174
Seltzer, Chester E. (see Muro, Amado)
Thomas Seltzer [publishing house] DLB-46
Selvon, Sam 1923-1994 .... DLB-125; CDWLB-3
Semel, Nava 1954- DLB-299
Semmes, Raphael 1809-1877 .... DLB-189
Senancour, Etienne de 1770-1846 .... DLB-119
Sena, Jorge de 1919-1978 .... DLB-287
Sendak, Maurice 1928- DLB-61
Seneca the Elder circa 54 B.C.-circa A.D. 40 .... DLB-211
Seneca the Younger circa 1 B.C.-A.D. 65 .... DLB-211; CDWLB-1
Senécal, Eva 1905- DLB-92
Sengstacke, John 1912-1997 .... DLB-127
Senior, Olive 1941- DLB-157
Senkovsky, Osip Ivanovich (Józef-Julian Sekowski, Baron Brambeus) 1800-1858 .... DLB-198
Šenoa, August 1838-1881 .... DLB-147; CDWLB-4
Sepamla, Sipho 1932- DLB-157, 225
Serafimovich, Aleksandr Serafimovich (Aleksandr Serafimovich Popov) 1863-1949 .... DLB-272
Serao, Matilde 1856-1927 .... DLB-264
Seredy, Kate 1899-1975 .... DLB-22
Sereni, Vittorio 1913-1983 .... DLB-128
William Seres [publishing house] DLB-170
Sergeev-Tsensky, Sergei Nikolaevich (Sergei Nikolaevich Sergeev) 1875-1958 ..... DLB-272
Serling, Rod 1924-1975 .... DLB-26
Sernine, Daniel 1955- DLB-251
Serote, Mongane Wally 1944- ... DLB-125, 225
Serraillier, Ian 1912-1994 .... DLB-161
Serrano, Nina 1934- DLB-122
Service, Robert 1874-1958 .... DLB-92
Sessler, Charles 1854-1935 .... DLB-187
Seth, Vikram 1952- DLB-120, 271
Seton, Elizabeth Ann 1774-1821 .... DLB-200
Seton, Ernest Thompson 1860-1942 .... DLB-92; DS-13
Seton, John circa 1509-1567 .... DLB-281
Setouchi Harumi 1922- DLB-182
Settle, Mary Lee 1918- DLB-6
Seume, Johann Gottfried 1763-1810 ...... DLB-94
Seuse, Heinrich 1295?-1366 .... DLB-179
Seuss, Dr. (see Geisel, Theodor Seuss)
Severianin, Igor' 1887-1941 .... DLB-295
Severin, Timothy 1940- DLB-204
Sévigné, Marie de Rabutin Chantal, Madame de 1626-1696 .... DLB-268
Sewall, Joseph 1688-1769 .... DLB-24
Sewall, Richard B. 1908- DLB-111
Sewall, Samuel 1652-1730 .... DLB-24
Sewell, Anna 1820-1878 .... DLB-163
Sexton, Anne 1928-1974 ... DLB-5, 169; CDALB-1
Seymour-Smith, Martin 1928-1998 ..... DLB-155
Sgorlon, Carlo 1930- DLB-196
Shaara, Michael 1929-1988 .... Y-83
Shabel'skaia, Aleksandra Stanislavovna 1845-1921 .... DLB-238
Shadwell, Thomas 1641?-1692 .... DLB-80
Shaffer, Anthony 1926- DLB-13
Shaffer, Peter 1926- DLB-13, 233; CDBLB-8
Shaftesbury, Anthony Ashley Cooper, Third Earl of 1671-1713 .... DLB-101
Shaginian, Marietta Sergeevna 1888-1982 .... DLB-272
Shairp, Mordaunt 1887-1939 .... DLB-10
Shakespeare, Nicholas 1957- DLB-231
Shakespeare, William 1564-1616 ..... DLB-62, 172, 263; CDBLB-1
The New Variorum Shakespeare Y-85
Shakespeare and Montaigne: A Symposium by Jules Furthman Y-02
$6,166,000 for a *Book!* Observations on *The Shakespeare First Folio: The History of the Book* Y-01
Taylor-Made Shakespeare? Or Is "Shall I Die?" the Long-Lost Text of Bottom's Dream? Y-85
The Shakespeare Globe Trust Y-93
Shakespeare Head Press DLB-112
Shakhova, Elisaveta Nikitichna 1822-1899 .... DLB-277
Shakhovskoi, Aleksandr Aleksandrovich 1777-1846 .... DLB-150
Shange, Ntozake 1948- DLB-38, 249
Shapcott, Thomas W. 1935- DLB-289
Shapir, Ol'ga Andreevna 1850-1916 ..... DLB-295
Shapiro, Karl 1913-2000 .... DLB-48
Sharon Publications DLB-46
Sharov, Vladimir Aleksandrovich 1952- DLB-285
Sharp, Margery 1905-1991 .... DLB-161
Sharp, William 1855-1905 .... DLB-156
Sharpe, Tom 1928- DLB-14, 231
Shaw, Albert 1857-1947 .... DLB-91
Shaw, George Bernard 1856-1950 .... DLB-10, 57, 190, CDBLB-6

The Bernard Shaw Society Y-99
"Stage Censorship: The Rejected Statement" (1911) [excerpts] DLB-10
Shaw, Henry Wheeler 1818-1885 . . . . .DLB-11
Shaw, Irwin 1913-1984 . . . . . . DLB-6, 102; Y-84; CDALB-1
Shaw, Joseph T. 1874-1952 . . . . .DLB-137
"As I Was Saying," Joseph T. Shaw's Editorial Rationale in *Black Mask* (January 1927) DLB-137
Shaw, Mary 1854-1929 . . . . .DLB-228
Shaw, Robert 1927-1978. . . . . .DLB-13, 14
Shaw, Robert B. 1947- DLB-120
Shawn, Wallace 1943- DLB-266
Shawn, William 1907-1992 . . . . .DLB-137
Frank Shay [publishing house]. DLB-46
Shchedrin, N. (see Saltykov, Mikhail Evgrafovich)
Shcherbakova, Galina Nikolaevna 1932- DLB-285
Shcherbina, Nikolai Fedorovich 1821-1869 . . . . .DLB-277
Shea, John Gilmary 1824-1892 . . . . .DLB-30
Sheaffer, Louis 1912-1993 . . . . .DLB-103
Sheahan, Henry Beston (see Beston, Henry)
Shearing, Joseph 1886-1952. . . . . .DLB-70
Shebbeare, John 1709-1788. . . . . .DLB-39
Sheckley, Robert 1928- DLB-8
Shedd, William G. T. 1820-1894. . . . . .DLB-64
Sheed, Wilfrid 1930- DLB-6
Sheed and Ward [U.S.] DLB-46
Sheed and Ward Limited [U.K.] DLB-112
Sheldon, Alice B. (see Tiptree, James, Jr.)
Sheldon, Edward 1886-1946 . . . . .DLB-7
Sheldon and Company DLB-49
Sheller, Aleksandr Konstantinovich 1838-1900 . . . . .DLB-238
Shelley, Mary Wollstonecraft 1797-1851 . . . . DLB-110, 116, 159, 178; CDBLB-3
Preface to *Frankenstein; or, The Modern Prometheus* (1818) DLB-178
Shelley, Percy Bysshe 1792-1822 . . . . . .DLB-96, 110, 158; CDBLB-3
Shelnutt, Eve 1941- DLB-130
Shenshin (see Fet, Afanasii Afanas'evich)
Shenstone, William 1714-1763 . . . . .DLB-95
Shepard, Clark and Brown DLB-49
Shepard, Ernest Howard 1879-1976. . . . . .DLB-160
Shepard, Sam 1943- DLB-7, 212
Shepard, Thomas I, 1604 or 1605-1649 . . .DLB-24
Shepard, Thomas, II, 1635-1677 . . . . .DLB-24
Shepherd, Luke flourished 1547-1554 . . . . DLB-136
Sherburne, Edward 1616-1702. . . . . .DLB-131
Sheridan, Frances 1724-1766 . . . . .DLB-39, 84
Sheridan, Richard Brinsley 1751-1816 . . . . DLB-89; CDBLB-2
Sherman, Francis 1871-1926 . . . . .DLB-92
Sherman, Martin 1938- DLB-228
Sherriff, R. C. 1896-1975 . . . . . . .DLB-10, 191, 233
Sherrod, Blackie 1919- DLB-241
Sherry, Norman 1935- DLB-155
Tribute to Graham Greene Y-91
Sherry, Richard 1506-1551 or 1555. . . . . .DLB-236
Sherwood, Mary Martha 1775-1851 . . . . .DLB-163
Sherwood, Robert E. 1896-1955 . . . DLB-7, 26, 249
Shevyrev, Stepan Petrovich 1806-1864 . . .DLB-205
Shiel, M. P. 1865-1947. . . . . .DLB-153
Shiels, George 1886-1949 . . . . .DLB-10
Shiga Naoya 1883-1971 . . . . .DLB-180
Shiina Rinzō 1911-1973 . . . . .DLB-182
Shikishi Naishinnō 1153?-1201 . . . . .DLB-203
Shillaber, Benjamin Penhallow 1814-1890 . . . . .DLB-1, 11, 235
Shimao Toshio 1917-1986 . . . . .DLB-182
Shimazaki Tōson 1872-1943 . . . . .DLB-180
Shimose, Pedro 1940- DLB-283
Shine, Ted 1931- DLB-38
Shinkei 1406-1475 . . . . .DLB-203
Ship, Reuben 1915-1975 . . . . .DLB-88
Shirer, William L. 1904-1993 . . . . .DLB-4
Shirinsky-Shikhmatov, Sergii Aleksandrovich 1783-1837 . . . . .DLB-150
Shirley, James 1596-1666. . . . . .DLB-58
Shishkov, Aleksandr Semenovich 1753-1841 . . . . .DLB-150
Shockley, Ann Allen 1927- DLB-33
Sholokhov, Mikhail Aleksandrovich 1905-1984 . . . . .DLB-272
Shōno Junzō 1921- DLB-182
Shore, Arabella 1820?-1901. . . . . .DLB-199
Shore, Louisa 1824-1895 . . . . .DLB-199
Short, Luke (see Glidden, Frederick Dilley)
Peter Short [publishing house] DLB-170
Shorter, Dora Sigerson 1866-1918. . . . . . .DLB-240
Shorthouse, Joseph Henry 1834-1903 . . . . .DLB-18
Short Stories
Michael M. Rea and the Rea Award for the Short Story Y-97
The Year in Short Stories Y-87
The Year in the Short Story Y-88, 90–93
Shōtetsu 1381-1459 . . . . .DLB-203
Showalter, Elaine 1941- DLB-67
Shreve, Anita 1946- DLB-292
Shulevitz, Uri 1935- DLB-61
Shulman, Max 1919-1988 . . . . .DLB-11
Shute, Henry A. 1856-1943 . . . . .DLB-9
Shute, Nevil (Nevil Shute Norway) 1899-1960 . . . . .DLB-255
Shuttle, Penelope 1947- DLB-14, 40
Shvarts, Evgenii L'vovich 1896-1958. . . . . DLB-272
Sibbes, Richard 1577-1635 . . . . .DLB-151
Sibiriak, D. (see Mamin, Dmitrii Narkisovich)
Siddal, Elizabeth Eleanor 1829-1862 . . . . .DLB-199
Sidgwick, Ethel 1877-1970 . . . . .DLB-197
Sidgwick, Henry 1838-1900. . . . . .DLB-262
Sidgwick and Jackson Limited DLB-112
Sidney, Margaret (see Lothrop, Harriet M.)
Sidney, Mary 1561-1621 . . . . .DLB-167
Sidney, Sir Philip 1554-1586 . .DLB-167; CDBLB-1
An Apologie for Poetrie (the Olney edition, 1595, of *Defence of Poesie*) DLB-167
Sidney's Press DLB-49
Sierra, Rubén 1946- DLB-122
Sierra Club Books .DLB-49
Siger of Brabant circa 1240-circa 1284. . . . DLB-115
Sigourney, Lydia Huntley 1791-1865 . . . . . . DLB-1, 42, 73, 183, 239, 243
Silkin, Jon 1930-1997 . . . . .DLB-27
Silko, Leslie Marmon 1948- DLB-143, 175, 256, 275
Silliman, Benjamin 1779-1864 . . . . .DLB-183
Silliman, Ron 1946- DLB-169
Silliphant, Stirling 1918-1996 . . . . .DLB-26
Sillitoe, Alan 1928- DLB-14, 139; CDBLB-8
Tribute to J. B. Priestly Y-84
Silman, Roberta 1934- DLB-28
Silone, Ignazio (Secondino Tranquilli) 1900-1978 . . . . .DLB-264
Silva, Beverly 1930- DLB-122
Silva, Clara 1905-1976. . . . . .DLB-290
Silva, José Asunció 1865-1896. . . . . .DLB-283
Silverberg, Robert 1935- DLB-8
Silverman, Kaja 1947- DLB-246
Silverman, Kenneth 1936- DLB-111
Simak, Clifford D. 1904-1988 . . . . .DLB-8
Simcoe, Elizabeth 1762-1850 . . . . .DLB-99
Simcox, Edith Jemima 1844-1901 . . . . . . .DLB-190
Simcox, George Augustus 1841-1905 . . . . .DLB-35
Sime, Jessie Georgina 1868-1958 . . . . .DLB-92
Simenon, Georges 1903-1989 . . . . . . DLB-72; Y-89
Simic, Charles 1938- DLB-105
"Images and 'Images'". DLB-105
Simionescu, Mircea Horia 1928- DLB-232
Simmel, Georg 1858-1918 . . . . .DLB-296
Simmel, Johannes Mario 1924- DLB-69
Valentine Simmes [publishing house] DLB-170
Simmons, Ernest J. 1903-1972 . . . . .DLB-103
Simmons, Herbert Alfred 1930- DLB-33
Simmons, James 1933- DLB-40
Simms, William Gilmore 1806-1870 . . . . DLB-3, 30, 59, 73, 248
Simms and M'Intyre DLB-106
Simon, Claude 1913- DLB-83; Y-85
Nobel Lecture Y-85
Simon, Neil 1927- DLB-7, 266
Simon and Schuster DLB-46
Simons, Katherine Drayton Mayrant 1890-1969 . . . . Y-83
Simović, Ljubomir 1935- DLB-181
Simpkin and Marshall [publishing house] DLB-154

Simpson, Helen 1897-1940 . . . . DLB-77
Simpson, Louis 1923- DLB-5
Simpson, N. F. 1919- DLB-13
Sims, George 1923- DLB-87; Y-99
Sims, George Robert 1847-1922 . . . DLB-35, 70, 135
Sinán, Rogelio 1902-1994 . . . . DLB-145, 290
Sinclair, Andrew 1935- DLB-14
Sinclair, Bertrand William 1881-1972 . . . . . DLB-92
Sinclair, Catherine 1800-1864 . . . . DLB-163
Sinclair, Jo 1913-1995 . . . . DLB-28
Sinclair, Lister 1921- DLB-88
Sinclair, May 1863-1946 . . . . DLB-36, 135
The Novels of Dorothy Richardson (1918) DLB-36
Sinclair, Upton 1878-1968 . . . . . DLB-9; CDALB-5
Upton Sinclair [publishing house] DLB-46
Singer, Isaac Bashevis 1904-1991 . . . . DLB-6, 28, 52, 278; Y-91; CDALB-1
Singer, Mark 1950- DLB-185
Singmaster, Elsie 1879-1958 . . . . DLB-9
Sinisgalli, Leonardo 1908-1981 . . . . DLB-114
Siodmak, Curt 1902-2000 . . . . DLB-44
Sîrbu, Ion D. 1919-1989 . . . . DLB-232
Siringo, Charles A. 1855-1928 . . . . DLB-186
Sissman, L. E. 1928-1976 . . . . DLB-5
Sisson, C. H. 1914- DLB-27
Sitwell, Edith 1887-1964 . . . . . . DLB-20; CDBLB-7
Sitwell, Osbert 1892-1969 . . . . DLB-100, 195
Skácel, Jan 1922-1989 . . . . DLB-232
Skalbe, Kārlis 1879-1945 . . . . DLB-220
Skármeta, Antonio 1940- DLB-145; CDWLB-3
Skavronsky, A. (see Danilevsky, Grigorii Petrovich)
Skeat, Walter W. 1835-1912 . . . . DLB-184
William Skeffington [publishing house] . . DLB-106
Skelton, John 1463-1529 . . . . DLB-136
Skelton, Robin 1925-1997 . . . . DLB-27, 53
Škėma, Antanas 1910-1961 . . . . DLB-220
Skinner, Constance Lindsay 1877-1939 . . . . DLB-92
Skinner, John Stuart 1788-1851 . . . . DLB-73
Skipsey, Joseph 1832-1903 . . . . DLB-35
Skou-Hansen, Tage 1925- DLB-214
Skrzynecki, Peter 1945- DLB-289
Škvorecký, Josef 1924- DLB-232; CDWLB-4
Slade, Bernard 1930- DLB-53
Slamnig, Ivan 1930- DLB-181
Slančeková, Božena (see Timrava)
Slataper, Scipio 1888-1915 . . . . DLB-264
Slater, Patrick 1880-1951 . . . . DLB-68
Slaveykov, Pencho 1866-1912 . . . . DLB-147
Slaviček, Milivoj 1929- DLB-181
Slavitt, David 1935- DLB-5, 6
Sleigh, Burrows Willcocks Arthur 1821-1869 . . . . DLB-99
Sleptsov, Vasilii Alekseevich 1836-1878 . . . DLB-277
Slesinger, Tess 1905-1945 . . . . DLB-102
Slessor, Kenneth 1901-1971 . . . . DLB-260
Slick, Sam (see Haliburton, Thomas Chandler)
Sloan, John 1871-1951 . . . . DLB-188
Sloane, William, Associates DLB-46
Slonimsky, Mikhail Leonidovich 1897-1972 . . . . DLB-272
Sluchevsky, Konstantin Konstantinovich 1837-1904 . . . . DLB-277
Small, Maynard and Company DLB-49
Smart, Christopher 1722-1771 . . . . DLB-109
Smart, David A. 1892-1957 . . . . DLB-137
Smart, Elizabeth 1913-1986 . . . . DLB-88
Smart, J. J. C. 1920- DLB-262
Smedley, Menella Bute 1820?-1877 . . . . . DLB-199
William Smellie [publishing house] DLB-154
Smiles, Samuel 1812-1904 . . . . DLB-55
Smiley, Jane 1949- DLB-227, 234
Smith, A. J. M. 1902-1980 . . . . DLB-88
Smith, Adam 1723-1790 . . . . DLB-104, 252
Smith, Adam (George Jerome Waldo Goodman) 1930- DLB-185
Smith, Alexander 1829-1867 . . . . DLB-32, 55
"On the Writing of Essays" (1862) . . . DLB-57
Smith, Amanda 1837-1915 . . . . DLB-221
Smith, Betty 1896-1972 . . . . Y-82
Smith, Carol Sturm 1938- Y-81
Smith, Charles Henry 1826-1903 . . . . DLB-11
Smith, Charlotte 1749-1806 . . . . DLB-39, 109
Smith, Chet 1899-1973 . . . . DLB-171
Smith, Cordwainer 1913-1966 . . . . DLB-8
Smith, Dave 1942- DLB-5
Tribute to James Dickey Y-97
Tribute to John Gardner Y-82
Smith, Dodie 1896- DLB-10
Smith, Doris Buchanan 1934- DLB-52
Smith, E. E. 1890-1965 . . . . DLB-8
Smith, Elihu Hubbard 1771-1798 . . . . DLB-37
Smith, Elizabeth Oakes (Prince) (see Oakes Smith, Elizabeth)
Smith, Eunice 1757-1823 . . . . DLB-200
Smith, F. Hopkinson 1838-1915 . . . . DS-13
Smith, George D. 1870-1920 . . . . DLB-140
Smith, George O. 1911-1981 . . . . DLB-8
Smith, Goldwin 1823-1910 . . . . DLB-99
Smith, H. Allen 1907-1976 . . . . DLB-11, 29
Smith, Harry B. 1860-1936 . . . . DLB-187
Smith, Hazel Brannon 1914-1994 . . . . DLB-127
Smith, Henry circa 1560-circa 1591 . . . . . DLB-136
Smith, Horatio (Horace) 1779-1849 . . . . DLB-96, 116
Smith, Iain Crichton 1928-1998 . . . . . DLB-40, 139
Smith, J. Allen 1860-1924 . . . . DLB-47
Smith, James 1775-1839 . . . . DLB-96
Smith, Jessie Willcox 1863-1935 . . . . DLB-188
Smith, John 1580-1631 . . . . DLB-24, 30
Smith, John 1618-1652 . . . . DLB-252
Smith, Josiah 1704-1781 . . . . DLB-24
Smith, Ken 1938- DLB-40
Smith, Lee 1944- DLB-143; Y-83
Smith, Logan Pearsall 1865-1946 . . . . DLB-98
Smith, Margaret Bayard 1778-1844 . . . . . DLB-248
Smith, Mark 1935- Y-82
Smith, Michael 1698-circa 1771 . . . . DLB-31
Smith, Pauline 1882-1959 . . . . DLB-225
Smith, Red 1905-1982 . . . . DLB-29, 171
Smith, Roswell 1829-1892 . . . . DLB-79
Smith, Samuel Harrison 1772-1845 . . . . . . DLB-43
Smith, Samuel Stanhope 1751-1819 . . . . . . DLB-37
Smith, Sarah (see Stretton, Hesba)
Smith, Sarah Pogson 1774-1870 . . . . DLB-200
Smith, Seba 1792-1868 . . . . DLB-1, 11, 243
Smith, Stevie 1902-1971 . . . . DLB-20
Smith, Sydney 1771-1845 . . . . DLB-107
Smith, Sydney Goodsir 1915-1975 . . . . DLB-27
Smith, Sir Thomas 1513-1577 . . . . DLB-132
Smith, Wendell 1914-1972 . . . . DLB-171
Smith, William flourished 1595-1597 . . . . DLB-136
Smith, William 1727-1803 . . . . DLB-31
A General Idea of the College of Mirania (1753) [excerpts] DLB-31
Smith, William 1728-1793 . . . . DLB-30
Smith, William Gardner 1927-1974 . . . . . . DLB-76
Smith, William Henry 1808-1872 . . . . DLB-159
Smith, William Jay 1918- DLB-5
Smith, Elder and Company DLB-154
Harrison Smith and Robert Haas [publishing house] DLB-46
J. Stilman Smith and Company DLB-49
W. B. Smith and Company DLB-49
W. H. Smith and Son DLB-106
Leonard Smithers [publishing house] DLB-112
Smollett, Tobias 1721-1771 . . . . DLB-39, 104; CDBLB-2
Dedication to *Ferdinand Count Fathom* (1753) DLB-39
Preface to *Ferdinand Count Fathom* (1753) DLB-39
Preface to *Roderick Random* (1748) DLB-39
Smythe, Francis Sydney 1900-1949 . . . . . DLB-195
Snelling, William Joseph 1804-1848 . . . . . DLB-202
Snellings, Rolland (see Touré, Askia Muhammad)
Snodgrass, W. D. 1926- DLB-5
Snorri Hjartarson 1906-1986 . . . . DLB-293
Snow, C. P. 1905-1980 . . . . DLB-15, 77; DS-17; CDBLB-7
Snyder, Gary 1930- DLB-5, 16, 165, 212, 237, 275
Sobiloff, Hy 1912-1970 . . . . DLB-48
The Society for Textual Scholarship and *TEXT* Y-87
The Society for the History of Authorship, Reading and Publishing Y-92

Söderberg, Hjalmar 1869-1941 . . . . DLB-259
Södergran, Edith 1892-1923 . . . . DLB-259
Soffici, Ardengo 1879-1964 . . . . DLB-114, 264
Sofola, 'Zulu 1938- DLB-157
Sokhanskaia, Nadezhda Stepanovna (Kokhanovskaia) 1823?-1884 . . . . DLB-277
Sokolov, Sasha (Aleksandr Vsevolodovich Sokolov) 1943- DLB-285
Solano, Solita 1888-1975 . . . . DLB-4
Soldati, Mario 1906-1999. . . . . DLB-177
Soledad (see Zamudio, Adela)
Šoljan, Antun 1932-1993 . . . . DLB-181
Sollers, Philippe (Philippe Joyaux) 1936- DLB-83
Sollogub, Vladimir Aleksandrovich 1813-1882 . . . . DLB-198
Sollors, Werner 1943- DBL-246
Solmi, Sergio 1899-1981 . . . . DLB-114
Sologub, Fedor 1863-1927 . . . . DLB-295
Solomon, Carl 1928- DLB-16
Solov'ev, Sergei Mikhailovich 1885-1942 . . . . DLB-295
Solov'ev, Vladimir Sergeevich 1853-1900 . . . . DLB-295
Solstad, Dag 1941- DLB-297
Solway, David 1941- DLB-53
Solzhenitsyn, Aleksandr I. 1918-
  Solzhenitsyn and America Y-85
Some Basic Notes on Three Modern Genres: Interview, Blurb, and Obituary Y-02
Somerville, Edith Œnone 1858-1949 . . . . . DLB-135
Somov, Orest Mikhailovich 1793-1833 . . . DLB-198
Sønderby, Knud 1909-1966 . . . . DLB-214
Song, Cathy 1955- DLB-169
Sonnevi, Göran 1939- DLB-257
Sono Ayako 1931- DLB-182
Sontag, Susan 1933- DLB-2, 67
Sophocles 497/496 B.C.-406/405 B.C. DLB-176; CDWLB-1
Šopov, Aco 1923-1982 . . . . DLB-181
Sorel, Charles ca.1600-1674 . . . . DLB-268
Sørensen, Villy 1929- DLB-214
Sorensen, Virginia 1912-1991 . . . . DLB-206
Sorge, Reinhard Johannes 1892-1916 . . . . DLB-118
Sorokin, Vladimir Georgievich 1955- DLB-285
Sorrentino, Gilbert 1929- DLB-5, 173; Y-80
Sosa, Roberto 1930- DLB-290
Sotheby, James 1682-1742 . . . . DLB-213
Sotheby, John 1740-1807 . . . . DLB-213
Sotheby, Samuel 1771-1842 . . . . DLB-213
Sotheby, Samuel Leigh 1805-1861 . . . . DLB-213
Sotheby, William 1757-1833 . . . . DLB-93, 213
Soto, Gary 1952- DLB-82
Soueif, Ahdaf 1950- DLB-267
Souster, Raymond 1921- DLB-88
The *South English Legendary* circa thirteenth-fifteenth centuries DLB-146
Southerland, Ellease 1943- DLB-33
Southern, Terry 1924-1995 . . . . DLB-2
Southern Illinois University Press Y-95
Southern Literature
  Fellowship of Southern Writers Y-98
  The Fugitives and the Agrarians: The First Exhibition Y-85
  "The Greatness of Southern Literature": League of the South Institute for the Study of Southern Culture and History Y-02
  The Society for the Study of Southern Literature Y-00
  Southern Writers Between the Wars . . . DLB-9
Southerne, Thomas 1659-1746 . . . . DLB-80
Southey, Caroline Anne Bowles 1786-1854 . . . . DLB-116
Southey, Robert 1774-1843 . . . . . DLB-93, 107, 142
Southwell, Robert 1561?-1595. . . . . DLB-167
Southworth, E. D. E. N. 1819-1899 . . . . . . DLB-239
Sowande, Bode 1948- DLB-157
Tace Sowle [publishing house] DLB-170
Soyfer, Jura 1912-1939 . . . . DLB-124
Soyinka, Wole 1934- DLB-125; Y-86, Y-87; CDWLB-3
  Nobel Lecture 1986: This Past Must Address Its Present Y-86
Spacks, Barry 1931- DLB-105
Spalding, Frances 1950- DLB-155
Spanish Travel Writers of the Late Middle Ages DLB-286
Spark, Muriel 1918- DLB-15, 139; CDBLB-7
Michael Sparke [publishing house] DLB-170
Sparks, Jared 1789-1866. . . . . DLB-1, 30, 235
Sparshott, Francis 1926- DLB-60
Späth, Gerold 1939- DLB-75
Spatola, Adriano 1941-1988. . . . . DLB-128
Spaziani, Maria Luisa 1924- DLB-128
Specimens of Foreign Standard Literature 1838-1842 . . . . DLB-1
The Spectator 1828- DLB-110
Spedding, James 1808-1881 . . . . DLB-144
Spee von Langenfeld, Friedrich 1591-1635 . . . . DLB-164
Speght, Rachel 1597-after 1630 . . . . DLB-126
Speke, John Hanning 1827-1864 . . . . DLB-166
Spellman, A. B. 1935- DLB-41
Spence, Catherine Helen 1825-1910 . . . . . DLB-230
Spence, Thomas 1750-1814 . . . . DLB-158
Spencer, Anne 1882-1975. . . . . DLB-51, 54
Spencer, Charles, third Earl of Sunderland 1674-1722 . . . . DLB-213
Spencer, Elizabeth 1921- DLB-6, 218
Spencer, George John, Second Earl Spencer 1758-1834 . . . . DLB-184
Spencer, Herbert 1820-1903 . . . . DLB-57, 262
  "The Philosophy of Style" (1852). DLB-57
Spencer, Scott 1945- Y-86
Spender, J. A. 1862-1942 . . . . DLB-98
Spender, Stephen 1909-1995 . . . DLB-20; CDBLB-7
Spener, Philipp Jakob 1635-1705 . . . . DLB-164
Spenser, Edmund circa 1552-1599 . . . . DLB-167; CDBLB-1
  Envoy from *The Shepheardes Calender* . . DLB-167
  "The Generall Argument of the Whole Booke," from *The Shepheardes Calender* DLB-167
  "A Letter of the Authors Expounding His Whole Intention in the Course of this Worke: Which for that It Giueth Great Light to the Reader, for the Better Vnderstanding Is Hereunto Annexed," from *The Faerie Queene* (1590) DLB-167
  "To His Booke," from *The Shepheardes Calender* (1579) . . . DLB-167
  "To the Most Excellent and Learned Both Orator and Poete, Mayster Gabriell Haruey, His Verie Special and Singular Good Frend E. K. Commendeth the Good Lyking of This His Labour, and the Patronage of the New Poete," from *The Shepheardes Calender* DLB-167
Sperr, Martin 1944- DLB-124
Spewack, Bella Cowen 1899-1990 . . . . DLB-266
Spewack, Samuel 1899-1971 . . . . DLB-266
Spicer, Jack 1925-1965. . . . . DLB-5, 16, 193
Spiegelman, Art 1948- DLB-299
Spielberg, Peter 1929- Y-81
Spielhagen, Friedrich 1829-1911 . . . . DLB-129
"Spielmannsepen" (circa 1152-circa 1500) . . . DLB-148
Spier, Peter 1927- DLB-61
Spillane, Mickey 1918- DLB-226
Spink, J. G. Taylor 1888-1962 . . . . DLB-241
Spinrad, Norman 1940- DLB-8
  Tribute to Isaac Asimov Y-92
Spires, Elizabeth 1952- DLB-120
Spitteler, Carl 1845-1924 . . . . DLB-129
Spivak, Lawrence E. 1900- DLB-137
Spofford, Harriet Prescott 1835-1921 . . . . DLB-74, 221
Sports
  Jimmy, Red, and Others: Harold Rosenthal Remembers the Stars of the Press Box Y-01
  The Literature of Boxing in England through Arthur Conan Doyle Y-01
  Notable Twentieth-Century Books about Sports DLB-241
Sprigge, Timothy L. S. 1932- DLB-262
Spring, Howard 1889-1965 . . . . DLB-191
Squibob (see Derby, George Horatio)
Squier, E. G. 1821-1888. . . . . DLB-189
Stableford, Brian 1948- DLB-261
Stacpoole, H. de Vere 1863-1951 . . . . DLB-153
Staël, Germaine de 1766-1817 . . . . . . DLB-119, 192
Staël-Holstein, Anne-Louise Germaine de (see Staël, Germaine de)
Staffeldt, Schack 1769-1826 . . . . DLB-300
Stafford, Jean 1915-1979 . . . . DLB-2, 173

Stafford, William 1914-1993 . . . . DLB-5, 206
Stallings, Laurence 1894-1968 . . . . .DLB-7, 44
Stallworthy, Jon 1935- DLB-40
Stampp, Kenneth M. 1912- DLB-17
Stănescu, Nichita 1933-1983 . . . . DLB-232
Stanev, Emiliyan 1907-1979 . . . . DLB-181
Stanford, Ann 1916- DLB-5
Stangerup, Henrik 1937-1998 . . . . DLB-214
Stanihurst, Richard 1547-1618 . . . . DLB-281
Stanitsky, N. (see Panaeva, Avdot'ia Iakovlevna)
Stankevich, Nikolai Vladimirovich 1813-1840 . . . . DLB-198
Stanković, Borisav ("Bora") 1876-1927 . . . . .DLB-147; CDWLB-4
Stanley, Henry M. 1841-1904 . . . . DLB-189; DS-13
Stanley, Thomas 1625-1678 . . . . DLB-131
Stannard, Martin 1947- DLB-155
William Stansby [publishing house] DLB-170
Stanton, Elizabeth Cady 1815-1902 . . . . . . DLB-79
Stanton, Frank L. 1857-1927 . . . . DLB-25
Stanton, Maura 1946- DLB-120
Stapledon, Olaf 1886-1950 . . . . DLB-15, 255
Star Spangled Banner Office DLB-49
Stark, Freya 1893-1993 . . . . DLB-195
Starkey, Thomas circa 1499-1538 . . . . . . DLB-132
Starkie, Walter 1894-1976 . . . . DLB-195
Starkweather, David 1935- DLB-7
Starrett, Vincent 1886-1974 . . . . DLB-187
Stationers' Company of London, The DLB-170
Statius circa A.D. 45-A.D. 96 . . . . DLB-211
Stead, Christina 1902-1983 . . . . DLB-260
Stead, Robert J. C. 1880-1959 . . . . DLB-92
Steadman, Mark 1930- DLB-6
Stearns, Harold E. 1891-1943 . . . . . . DLB-4; DS-15
Stebnitsky, M. (see Leskov, Nikolai Semenovich)
Stedman, Edmund Clarence 1833-1908 . . . DLB-64
Steegmuller, Francis 1906-1994 . . . . DLB-111
Steel, Flora Annie 1847-1929 . . . . DLB-153, 156
Steele, Max 1922- Y-80
Steele, Richard 1672-1729 . . . . DLB-84, 101; CDBLB-2
Steele, Timothy 1948- DLB-120
Steele, Wilbur Daniel 1886-1970 . . . . DLB-86
Wallace Markfield's "Steeplechase" Y-02
Steere, Richard circa 1643-1721 . . . . DLB-24
Stefán frá Hvítadal (Stefán Sigurðsson) 1887-1933 . . . . DLB-293
Stefán Guðmundsson (see Stephan G. Stephansson)
Stefán Hörður Grímsson 1919 or 1920-2002 . . . . DLB-293
Stefanovski, Goran 1952- DLB-181
Stegner, Wallace 1909-1993 . . . . .DLB-9, 206, 275; Y-93
Stehr, Hermann 1864-1940 . . . . DLB-66
Steig, William 1907- DLB-61
Stein, Gertrude 1874-1946 . . . . DLB-4, 54, 86, 228; DS-15; CDALB-4
Stein, Leo 1872-1947 . . . . DLB-4
Stein and Day Publishers DLB-46
Steinbeck, John 1902-1968 . . . . .DLB-7, 9, 212, 275; DS-2; CDALB-5
John Steinbeck Research Center, San Jose State University Y-85
The Steinbeck Centennial Y-02
Steinem, Gloria 1934- DLB-246
Steiner, George 1929- DLB-67, 299
Steinhoewel, Heinrich 1411/1412-1479 . . . .DLB-179
Steinn Steinarr (Aðalsteinn Kristmundsson) 1908-1958 . . . . DLB-293
Steinunn Sigurðardóttir 1950- DLB-293
Steloff, Ida Frances 1887-1989 . . . . DLB-187
Stendhal 1783-1842 . . . . DLB-119
Stephan G. Stephansson (Stefán Guðmundsson) 1853-1927 . . . . DLB-293
Stephen, Leslie 1832-1904 . . . . . . DLB-57, 144, 190
Stephen Family (Bloomsbury Group) DS-10
Stephens, A. G. 1865-1933 . . . . DLB-230
Stephens, Alexander H. 1812-1883 . . . . DLB-47
Stephens, Alice Barber 1858-1932 . . . . . . DLB-188
Stephens, Ann 1810-1886 . . . . DLB-3, 73, 250
Stephens, Charles Asbury 1844?-1931 . . . . DLB-42
Stephens, James 1882?-1950 . . . . .DLB-19, 153, 162
Stephens, John Lloyd 1805-1852 . . . DLB-183, 250
Stephens, Michael 1946- DLB-234
Stephensen, P. R. 1901-1965 . . . . DLB-260
Sterling, George 1869-1926 . . . . DLB-54
Sterling, James 1701-1763 . . . . DLB-24
Sterling, John 1806-1844 . . . . DLB-116
Stern, Gerald 1925- DLB-105
"Living in Ruin" DLB-105
Stern, Gladys B. 1890-1973 . . . . DLB-197
Stern, Madeleine B. 1912- DLB-111, 140
Stern, Richard 1928- DLB-218; Y-87
Stern, Stewart 1922- DLB-26
Sterne, Laurence 1713-1768 . . . DLB-39; CDBLB-2
Sternheim, Carl 1878-1942 . . . . DLB-56, 118
Sternhold, Thomas ?-1549 . . . . DLB-132
Steuart, David 1747-1824 . . . . DLB-213
Stevens, Henry 1819-1886 . . . . DLB-140
Stevens, Wallace 1879-1955 . . . DLB-54; CDALB-5
The Wallace Stevens Society Y-99
Stevenson, Anne 1933- DLB-40
Stevenson, D. E. 1892-1973 . . . . DLB-191
Stevenson, Lionel 1902-1973 . . . . DLB-155
Stevenson, Robert Louis 1850-1894 . . . . .DLB-18, 57, 141, 156, 174; DS-13; CDBLB-5
"On Style in Literature: Its Technical Elements" (1885) . . . DLB-57
Stewart, Donald Ogden 1894-1980 . . . . DLB-4, 11, 26; DS-15
Stewart, Douglas 1913-1985 . . . . DLB-260
Stewart, Dugald 1753-1828 . . . . DLB-31
Stewart, George, Jr. 1848-1906 . . . . DLB-99
Stewart, George R. 1895-1980 . . . . DLB-8
Stewart, Harold 1916-1995 . . . . DLB-260
Stewart, J. I. M. (see Innes, Michael)
Stewart, Maria W. 1803?-1879 . . . . DLB-239
Stewart, Randall 1896-1964 . . . . DLB-103
Stewart, Sean 1965- DLB-251
Stewart and Kidd Company DLB-46
Sthen, Hans Christensen 1544-1610 . . . . . DLB-300
Stickney, Trumbull 1874-1904 . . . . DLB-54
Stieler, Caspar 1632-1707 . . . . DLB-164
Stifter, Adalbert 1805-1868 . . . . .DLB-133; CDWLB-2
Stiles, Ezra 1727-1795 . . . . DLB-31
Still, James 1906-2001 . . . . .DLB-9; Y-01
Stirling, S. M. 1953- DLB-251
Stirner, Max 1806-1856 . . . . DLB-129
Stith, William 1707-1755 . . . . DLB-31
Stivens, Dal 1911-1997 . . . . DLB-260
Elliot Stock [publishing house] DLB-106
Stockton, Annis Boudinot 1736-1801 . . . . DLB-200
Stockton, Frank R. 1834-1902 . .DLB-42, 74; DS-13
Stockton, J. Roy 1892-1972 . . . . DLB-241
Ashbel Stoddard [publishing house] DLB-49
Stoddard, Charles Warren 1843-1909 . . . DLB-186
Stoddard, Elizabeth 1823-1902 . . . . DLB-202
Stoddard, Richard Henry 1825-1903 . . . . DLB-3, 64, 250; DS-13
Stoddard, Solomon 1643-1729 . . . . DLB-24
Stoker, Bram 1847-1912 . . . . .DLB-36, 70, 178; CDBLB-5
On Writing *Dracula,* from the Introduction to *Dracula* (1897) DLB-178
Frederick A. Stokes Company DLB-49
Stokes, Thomas L. 1898-1958 . . . . DLB-29
Stokesbury, Leon 1945- DLB-120
Stolberg, Christian Graf zu 1748-1821 . . . . DLB-94
Stolberg, Friedrich Leopold Graf zu 1750-1819 . . . . DLB-94
Stone, Lucy 1818-1893 . . . . .DLB-79, 239
Stone, Melville 1848-1929 . . . . DLB-25
Stone, Robert 1937- DLB-152
Stone, Ruth 1915- DLB-105
Stone, Samuel 1602-1663 . . . . DLB-24
Stone, William Leete 1792-1844 . . . . DLB-202
Herbert S. Stone and Company DLB-49
Stone and Kimball DLB-49
Stoppard, Tom 1937- DLB-13, 233; Y-85; CDBLB-8
Playwrights and Professors DLB-13
Storey, Anthony 1928- DLB-14
Storey, David 1933- DLB-13, 14, 207, 245
Storm, Theodor 1817-1888 . . . . .DLB-129; CDWLB-2
Storni, Alfonsina 1892-1938 . . . . DLB-283

Story, Thomas circa 1670-1742 . . . . DLB-31
Story, William Wetmore 1819-1895 . . . DLB-1, 235
Storytelling: A Contemporary Renaissance . . . Y-84
Stoughton, William 1631-1701. . . . . DLB-24
Stow, John 1525-1605 . . . . DLB-132
Stow, Randolph 1935- DLB-260
Stowe, Harriet Beecher 1811-1896. . . . . . DLB-1,12, 42, 74, 189, 239, 243; CDALB-3
The Harriet Beecher Stowe Center Y-00
Stowe, Leland 1899-1994. . . . . DLB-29
Stoyanov, Dimitr Ivanov (see Elin Pelin)
Strabo 64/63 B.C.-circa A.D. 25. . . . . DLB-176
Strachey, Lytton 1880-1932. . . . . . DLB-149; DS-10
Preface to *Eminent Victorians* DLB-149
William Strahan [publishing house] DLB-154
Strahan and Company. DLB-106
Strand, Mark 1934- DLB-5
The Strasbourg Oaths 842. . . . . DLB-148
Stratemeyer, Edward 1862-1930 . . . . DLB-42
Strati, Saverio 1924- DLB-177
Stratton and Barnard DLB-49
Stratton-Porter, Gene 1863-1924 . . . . DLB-221; DS-14
Straub, Peter 1943- Y-84
Strauß, Botho 1944- DLB-124
Strauß, David Friedrich 1808-1874 . . . . . . DLB-133
The Strawberry Hill Press DLB-154
Strawson, P. F. 1919- DLB-262
Streatfeild, Noel 1895-1986 . . . . DLB-160
Street, Cecil John Charles (see Rhode, John)
Street, G. S. 1867-1936. . . . . DLB-135
Street and Smith. DLB-49
Streeter, Edward 1891-1976. . . . . DLB-11
Streeter, Thomas Winthrop 1883-1965 . . . DLB-140
Stretton, Hesba 1832-1911. . . . . DLB-163, 190
Stribling, T. S. 1881-1965 . . . . DLB-9
Der Stricker circa 1190-circa 1250 . . . . DLB-138
Strickland, Samuel 1804-1867 . . . . DLB-99
Strindberg, August 1849-1912 . . . . DLB-259
Stringer, Arthur 1874-1950 . . . . DLB-92
Stringer and Townsend DLB-49
Strittmatter, Erwin 1912-1994 . . . . DLB-69
Strniša, Gregor 1930-1987 . . . . DLB-181
Strode, William 1630-1645 . . . . DLB-126
Strong, L. A. G. 1896-1958 . . . . DLB-191
Strother, David Hunter (Porte Crayon) 1816-1888 . . . . DLB-3, 248
Strouse, Jean 1945- DLB-111
Stuart, Dabney 1937- DLB-105
"Knots into Webs: Some Autobiographical Sources" DLB-105
Stuart, Jesse 1906-1984 . . . . . DLB-9, 48, 102; Y-84
Lyle Stuart [publishing house] DLB-46
Stuart, Ruth McEnery 1849?-1917. . . . . . . DLB-202
Stub, Ambrosius 1705-1758 . . . . DLB-300
Stubbs, Harry Clement (see Clement, Hal)
Stubenberg, Johann Wilhelm von 1619-1663 . . . . DLB-164
Stuckenberg, Viggo 1763-1905. . . . . DLB-300
Studebaker, William V. 1947- DLB-256
Studies in American Jewish Literature. Y-02
Studio. DLB-112
Stump, Al 1916-1995 . . . . DLB-241
Sturgeon, Theodore 1918-1985 . . . . DLB-8; Y-85
Sturges, Preston 1898-1959 . . . . DLB-26
Styron, William 1925- DLB-2, 143, 299; Y-80; CDALB-6
Tribute to James Dickey Y-97
Suárez, Clementina 1902-1991 . . . . DLB-290
Suárez, Mario 1925- DLB-82
Such, Peter 1939- DLB-60
Suckling, Sir John 1609-1641? DLB-58, 126
Suckow, Ruth 1892-1960. . . . . DLB-9, 102
Sudermann, Hermann 1857-1928 . . . . DLB-118
Sue, Eugène 1804-1857 . . . . DLB-119
Sue, Marie-Joseph (see Sue, Eugène)
Suetonius circa A.D. 69-post A.D. 122 . . . DLB-211
Suggs, Simon (see Hooper, Johnson Jones)
Sui Sin Far (see Eaton, Edith Maude)
Suits, Gustav 1883-1956 . . . . DLB-220; CDWLB-4
Sukenick, Ronald 1932- DLB-173; Y-81
An Author's Response Y-82
Sukhovo-Kobylin, Aleksandr Vasil'evich 1817-1903 . . . . DLB-277
Suknaski, Andrew 1942- DLB-53
Sullivan, Alan 1868-1947 . . . . DLB-92
Sullivan, C. Gardner 1886-1965 . . . . DLB-26
Sullivan, Frank 1892-1976 . . . . DLB-11
Sulte, Benjamin 1841-1923 . . . . DLB-99
Sulzberger, Arthur Hays 1891-1968 . . . . . DLB-127
Sulzberger, Arthur Ochs 1926- DLB-127
Sulzer, Johann Georg 1720-1779 . . . . DLB-97
Sumarokov, Aleksandr Petrovich 1717-1777 . . . . DLB-150
Summers, Hollis 1916- DLB-6
Sumner, Charles 1811-1874. . . . . DLB-235
Sumner, William Graham 1840-1910 . . . . DLB-270
Henry A. Sumner [publishing house] DLB-49
Sundman, Per Olof 1922-1992 . . . . DLB-257
Supervielle, Jules 1884-1960 . . . . DLB-258
Surtees, Robert Smith 1803-1864. . . . . DLB-21
The R. S. Surtees Society Y-98
Sutcliffe, Matthew 1550?-1629. . . . . DLB-281
Sutcliffe, William 1971- DLB-271
Sutherland, Efua Theodora 1924-1996 . . . . DLB-117
Sutherland, John 1919-1956. . . . . DLB-68
Sutro, Alfred 1863-1933. . . . . DLB-10
Svava Jakobsdóttir 1930- DLB-293
Svendsen, Hanne Marie 1933- DLB-214
Svevo, Italo (Ettore Schmitz) 1861-1928 . . . . DLB-264
Swados, Harvey 1920-1972 . . . . DLB-2
Swain, Charles 1801-1874 . . . . DLB-32
Swallow Press DLB-46
Swan Sonnenschein Limited DLB-106
Swanberg, W. A. 1907-1992 . . . . DLB-103
Swedish Literature
The Literature of the Modern Breakthrough DLB-259
Swenson, May 1919-1989 . . . . DLB-5
Swerling, Jo 1897- DLB-44
Swift, Graham 1949- DLB-194
Swift, Jonathan 1667-1745 . . . . DLB-39, 95, 101; CDBLB-2
Swinburne, A. C. 1837-1909 . . . . DLB-35, 57; CDBLB-4
Under the Microscope (1872) DLB-35
Swineshead, Richard floruit circa 1350 . . . DLB-115
Swinnerton, Frank 1884-1982 . . . . DLB-34
Swisshelm, Jane Grey 1815-1884. . . . . DLB-43
Swope, Herbert Bayard 1882-1958 . . . . DLB-25
Swords, James ?-1844 . . . . DLB-73
Swords, Thomas 1763-1843. . . . . DLB-73
T. and J. Swords and Company DLB-49
Swynnerton, Thomas (John Roberts) circa 1500-1554. . . . . DLB-281
Sykes, Ella C. ?-1939 . . . . DLB-174
Sylvester, Josuah 1562 or 1563-1618. . . . . DLB-121
Symonds, Emily Morse (see Paston, George)
Symonds, John Addington 1840-1893 . . . . DLB-57, 144
"Personal Style" (1890). DLB-57
Symons, A. J. A. 1900-1941. . . . . DLB-149
Symons, Arthur 1865-1945 . . . . . . DLB-19, 57, 149
Symons, Julian 1912-1994 . . . . . DLB-87, 155; Y-92
Julian Symons at Eighty Y-92
Symons, Scott 1933- DLB-53
Synge, John Millington 1871-1909 . . . . DLB-10, 19; CDBLB-5
Synge Summer School: J. M. Synge and the Irish Theater, Rathdrum, County Wiclow, Ireland. Y-93
Syrett, Netta 1865-1943 . . . . DLB-135, 197
Szabó, Lőrinc 1900-1957 . . . . DLB-215
Szabó, Magda 1917- DLB-215
Szymborska, Wisława 1923- DLB-232, Y-96; CDWLB-4
Nobel Lecture 1996: The Poet and the World Y-96

T

Taban lo Liyong 1939?- DLB-125
Tablada, José Juan 1871-1945 . . . . DLB-290
Tabori, George 1914- DLB-245
Tabucchi, Antonio 1943- DLB-196
Taché, Joseph-Charles 1820-1894 . . . . DLB-99

Tachihara Masaaki 1926-1980 . . . . DLB-182
Tacitus circa A.D. 55-circa A.D. 117 . . . . DLB-211; CDWLB-1
Tadijanović, Dragutin 1905- DLB-181
Tafdrup, Pia 1952- DLB-214
Tafolla, Carmen 1951- DLB-82
Taggard, Genevieve 1894-1948 . . . . DLB-45
Taggart, John 1942- DLB-193
Tagger, Theodor (see Bruckner, Ferdinand)
Taiheiki late fourteenth century DLB-203
Tait, J. Selwin, and Sons DLB-49
Tait's Edinburgh Magazine 1832-1861 . . . . . DLB-110
The Takarazaka Revue Company Y-91
Talander (see Bohse, August)
Talese, Gay 1932- DLB-185
    Tribute to Irwin Shaw Y-84
Talev, Dimitr 1898-1966 . . . . DLB-181
Taliaferro, H. E. 1811-1875 . . . . DLB-202
Tallent, Elizabeth 1954- DLB-130
TallMountain, Mary 1918-1994 . . . . DLB-193
Talvj 1797-1870 . . . . DLB-59, 133
Tamási, Áron 1897-1966 . . . . DLB-215
Tammsaare, A. H. 1878-1940 . . . . DLB-220; CDWLB-4
Tan, Amy 1952- DLB-173; CDALB-7
Tandori, Dezső 1938- DLB-232
Tanner, Thomas 1673/1674-1735 . . . . DLB-213
Tanizaki Jun'ichirō 1886-1965 . . . . DLB-180
Tapahonso, Luci 1953- DLB-175
The Mark Taper Forum DLB-7
Taradash, Daniel 1913- DLB-44
Tarasov-Rodionov, Aleksandr Ignat'evich 1885-1938 . . . . DLB-272
Tarbell, Ida M. 1857-1944 . . . . DLB-47
Tardivel, Jules-Paul 1851-1905 . . . . DLB-99
Targan, Barry 1932- DLB-130
    Tribute to John Gardner Y-82
Tarkington, Booth 1869-1946 . . . . DLB-9, 102
Tashlin, Frank 1913-1972 . . . . DLB-44
Tasma (Jessie Couvreur) 1848-1897 . . . . DLB-230
Tate, Allen 1899-1979 . . . . . . .DLB-4, 45, 63; DS-17
Tate, James 1943- DLB-5, 169
Tate, Nahum circa 1652-1715 . . . . DLB-80
Tatian circa 830 . . . . DLB-148
Taufer, Veno 1933- DLB-181
Tauler, Johannes circa 1300-1361 . . . . .DLB-179
Tavares, Salette 1922-1994 . . . . DLB-287
Tavčar, Ivan 1851-1923 . . . . DLB-147
Taverner, Richard ca. 1505-1575 . . . . DLB-236
Taylor, Ann 1782-1866 . . . . DLB-163
Taylor, Bayard 1825-1878 . . . . . . DLB-3, 189, 250
Taylor, Bert Leston 1866-1921 . . . . DLB-25
Taylor, Charles H. 1846-1921 . . . . DLB-25
Taylor, Edward circa 1642-1729 . . . . DLB-24
Taylor, Elizabeth 1912-1975 . . . . DLB-139
Taylor, Sir Henry 1800-1886 . . . . DLB-32
Taylor, Henry 1942- DLB-5
    Who Owns American Literature Y-94
Taylor, Jane 1783-1824 . . . . DLB-163
Taylor, Jeremy circa 1613-1667 . . . . DLB-151
Taylor, John 1577 or 1578 - 1653 . . . . DLB-121
Taylor, Mildred D. 1943- DLB-52
Taylor, Peter 1917-1994 . . . DLB-218, 278; Y-81, 94
Taylor, Susie King 1848-1912 . . . . DLB-221
Taylor, William Howland 1901-1966 . . . DLB-241
William Taylor and Company DLB-49
Teale, Edwin Way 1899-1980 . . . . .DLB-275
Teasdale, Sara 1884-1933 . . . . DLB-45
Teillier, Jorge 1935-1996 . . . . DLB-283
Telles, Lygia Fagundes 1924- DLB-113
The Temper of the West: William Jovanovich. . . . Y-02
Temple, Sir William 1555?-1627 . . . . DLB-281
Temple, Sir William 1628-1699 . . . . DLB-101
Temple, William F. 1914-1989 . . . . DLB-255
Temrizov, A. (see Marchenko, Anastasia Iakovlevna)
Tench, Watkin ca. 1758-1833 . . . . DLB-230
Tender Is the Night (Documentary) DLB-273
Tenn, William 1919- DLB-8
Tennant, Emma 1937- DLB-14
Tenney, Tabitha Gilman 1762-1837 . . . DLB-37, 200
Tennyson, Alfred 1809-1892 . . DLB-32; CDBLB-4
    On Some of the Characteristics of Modern Poetry and On the Lyrical Poems of Alfred Tennyson (1831) DLB-32
Tennyson, Frederick 1807-1898 . . . . DLB-32
Tenorio, Arthur 1924- DLB-209
Tepl, Johannes von circa 1350-1414/1415 . . . . .DLB-179
Tepliakov, Viktor Grigor'evich 1804-1842 . . . . DLB-205
Terence circa 184 B.C.-159 B.C. or after DLB-211; CDWLB-1
Terhune, Albert Payson 1872-1942 . . . . DLB-9
Terhune, Mary Virginia 1830-1922 . . . . DS-13
Terpigorev, Sergei Nikolaevich (S. Atava) 1841-1895 . . . . .DLB-277
Terry, Megan 1932- DLB-7, 249
Terson, Peter 1932- DLB-13
Tesich, Steve 1943-1996 . . . . Y-83
Tessa, Delio 1886-1939 . . . . DLB-114
Testori, Giovanni 1923-1993 . . . . . . .DLB-128, 177
Texas
    The Year in Texas Literature Y-98
Tey, Josephine 1896?-1952 . . . . DLB-77
Thacher, James 1754-1844 . . . . DLB-37
Thacher, John Boyd 1847-1909 . . . . DLB-187
Thackeray, William Makepeace 1811-1863 . . DLB-21, 55, 159, 163; CDBLB-4
Thames and Hudson Limited DLB-112
Thanet, Octave (see French, Alice)
Thaxter, Celia Laighton 1835-1894 . . . . DLB-239
Thayer, Caroline Matilda Warren 1785-1844 . . . . DLB-200
Thayer, Douglas H. 1929- DLB-256
Theater
    Black Theatre: A Forum [excerpts] . . . DLB-38
    Community and Commentators: Black Theatre and Its Critics DLB-38
    German Drama from Naturalism to Fascism: 1889-1933 . . . . DLB-118
    A Look at the Contemporary Black Theatre Movement DLB-38
    The Lord Chamberlain's Office and Stage Censorship in England DLB-10
    New Forces at Work in the American Theatre: 1915-1925 . . . . DLB-7
    Off Broadway and Off-Off Broadway . . DLB-7
    Oregon Shakespeare Festival Y-00
    Plays, Playwrights, and Playgoers DLB-84
    Playwrights on the Theater DLB-80
    Playwrights and Professors DLB-13
    Producing *Dear Bunny, Dear Volodya: The Friendship and the Feud* Y-97
    Viewpoint: Politics and Performance, by David Edgar DLB-13
    Writing for the Theatre, by Harold Pinter DLB-13
    The Year in Drama Y-82–85, 87–98
    The Year in U.S. Drama Y-00
Theater, English and Irish
    Anti-Theatrical Tracts DLB-263
    The Chester Plays circa 1505-1532; revisions until 1575 . . . . DLB-146
    Dangerous Years: London Theater, 1939-1945 . . . . DLB-10
    A Defense of Actors DLB-263
    The Development of Lighting in the Staging of Drama, 1900-1945 . . . . DLB-10
    Education DLB-263
    The End of English Stage Censorship, 1945-1968 . . . . DLB-13
    Epigrams and Satires DLB-263
    Eyewitnesses and Historians DLB-263
    Fringe and Alternative Theater in Great Britain DLB-13
    The Great War and the Theater, 1914-1918 [Great Britain] DLB-10
    Licensing Act of 1737 . . . . DLB-84
    Morality Plays: *Mankind* circa 1450-1500 and *Everyman* circa 1500 . . . . DLB-146
    The New Variorum Shakespeare Y-85
    N-Town Plays circa 1468 to early sixteenth century DLB-146
    Politics and the Theater DLB-263
    Practical Matters DLB-263
    Prologues, Epilogues, Epistles to Readers, and Excerpts from Plays DLB-263
    The Publication of English Renaissance Plays DLB-62
    Regulations for the Theater DLB-263

Sources for the Study of Tudor and Stuart Drama DLB-62
Stage Censorship: "The Rejected Statement" (1911), by Bernard Shaw [excerpts] DLB-10
Synge Summer School: J. M. Synge and the Irish Theater, Rathdrum, County Wiclow, Ireland Y-93
The Theater in Shakespeare's Time . . . DLB-62
The Theatre Guild DLB-7
The Townely Plays fifteenth and sixteenth centuries DLB-146
The Year in British Drama Y-99–01
The Year in Drama: London Y-90
The Year in London Theatre Y-92
A Yorkshire Tragedy DLB-58
Theaters
The Abbey Theatre and Irish Drama, 1900-1945 . . . . DLB-10
Actors Theatre of Louisville DLB-7
American Conservatory Theatre DLB-7
Arena Stage DLB-7
Black Theaters and Theater Organizations in America, 1961-1982: A Research List DLB-38
The Dallas Theater Center DLB-7
Eugene O'Neill Memorial Theater Center DLB-7
The Goodman Theatre DLB-7
The Guthrie Theater DLB-7
The Mark Taper Forum DLB-7
The National Theatre and the Royal Shakespeare Company: The National Companies DLB-13
Off-Loop Theatres DLB-7
The Royal Court Theatre and the English Stage Company DLB-13
The Royal Court Theatre and the New Drama DLB-10
The Takarazaka Revue Company Y-91
Thegan and the Astronomer flourished circa 850 . . . . DLB-148
Thelwall, John 1764-1834 . . . . DLB-93, 158
Theocritus circa 300 B.C.-260 B.C. DLB-176
Theodorescu, Ion N. (see Arghezi, Tudor)
Theodulf circa 760-circa 821 . . . . DLB-148
Theophrastus circa 371 B.C.-287 B.C. DLB-176
Thériault, Yves 1915-1983 . . . . DLB-88
Thério, Adrien 1925- DLB-53
Theroux, Paul 1941- DLB-2, 218; CDALB-7
Thesiger, Wilfred 1910- DLB-204
They All Came to Paris DS-15
Thibaudeau, Colleen 1925- DLB-88
Thiele, Colin 1920- DLB-289
Thielen, Benedict 1903-1965 . . . . DLB-102
Thiong'o Ngugi wa (see Ngugi wa Thiong'o)
This Quarter 1925-1927, 1929-1932 . . . . DS-15
Thoma, Ludwig 1867-1921 . . . . DLB-66
Thoma, Richard 1902- DLB-4
Thomas, Audrey 1935- DLB-60
Thomas, D. M. 1935- . . . DLB-40, 207, 299; Y-82; CDBLB-8
The Plagiarism Controversy Y-82
Thomas, Dylan 1914-1953 . . . . DLB-13, 20, 139; CDBLB-7
The Dylan Thomas Celebration Y-99
Thomas, Edward 1878-1917 . . . . DLB-19, 98, 156, 216
The Friends of the Dymock Poets Y-00
Thomas, Frederick William 1806-1866 . . . DLB-202
Thomas, Gwyn 1913-1981 . . . . DLB-15, 245
Thomas, Isaiah 1750-1831 . . . . DLB-43, 73, 187
Thomas, Johann 1624-1679 . . . . DLB-168
Thomas, John 1900-1932 . . . . DLB-4
Thomas, Joyce Carol 1938- DLB-33
Thomas, Lewis 1913-1993 . . . . DLB-275
Thomas, Lorenzo 1944- DLB-41
Thomas, R. S. 1915-2000 . . . . . DLB-27; CDBLB-8
Isaiah Thomas [publishing house] DLB-49
Thomasîn von Zerclære circa 1186-circa 1259 . . . . DLB-138
Thomason, George 1602?-1666 . . . . DLB-213
Thomasius, Christian 1655-1728 . . . . DLB-168
Thompson, Daniel Pierce 1795-1868 . . . . . DLB-202
Thompson, David 1770-1857 . . . . DLB-99
Thompson, Dorothy 1893-1961 . . . . DLB-29
Thompson, E. P. 1924-1993 . . . . DLB-242
Thompson, Flora 1876-1947 . . . . DLB-240
Thompson, Francis 1859-1907 . . . . DLB-19; CDBLB-5
Thompson, George Selden (see Selden, George)
Thompson, Henry Yates 1838-1928 . . . . . DLB-184
Thompson, Hunter S. 1939- DLB-185
Thompson, Jim 1906-1977 . . . . DLB-226
Thompson, John 1938-1976 . . . . DLB-60
Thompson, John R. 1823-1873 . . . . DLB-3, 73, 248
Thompson, Lawrance 1906-1973 . . . . DLB-103
Thompson, Maurice 1844-1901 . . . . . . DLB-71, 74
Thompson, Ruth Plumly 1891-1976 . . . . . . DLB-22
Thompson, Thomas Phillips 1843-1933 . . . DLB-99
Thompson, William 1775-1833 . . . . DLB-158
Thompson, William Tappan 1812-1882 . . . . DLB-3, 11, 248
Thomson, Cockburn "Modern Style" (1857) [excerpt] DLB-57
Thomson, Edward William 1849-1924 . . . . DLB-92
Thomson, James 1700-1748 . . . . DLB-95
Thomson, James 1834-1882 . . . . DLB-35
Thomson, Joseph 1858-1895 . . . . DLB-174
Thomson, Mortimer 1831-1875 . . . . DLB-11
Thomson, Rupert 1955- DLB-267
Thon, Melanie Rae 1957- DLB-244
Thor Vilhjálmsson 1925- DLB-293
Þórarinn Eldjárn 1949- DLB-293
Þórbergur Þórðarson 1888-1974 . . . . DLB-293
Thoreau, Henry David 1817-1862 . . . DLB-1, 183, 223, 270, 298; DS-5; CDALB-2
The Thoreau Society Y-99
The Thoreauvian Pilgrimage: The Structure of an American Cult . . . DLB-223
Thorne, William 1568?-1630 . . . . DLB-281
Thornton, John F. [Repsonse to Ken Auletta] Y-97
Thorpe, Adam 1956- DLB-231
Thorpe, Thomas Bangs 1815-1878 . . . . DLB-3, 11, 248
Thorup, Kirsten 1942- DLB-214
Thotl, Birgitte 1610-1662 . . . . DLB-300
Thrale, Hester Lynch (see Piozzi, Hester Lynch [Thrale])
The Three Marias: A Landmark Case in Portuguese Literary History (Maria Isabel Barreno, 1939- ; Maria Teresa Horta, 1937- ; Maria Velho da Costa, 1938-) DLB-287
Thubron, Colin 1939- DLB-204, 231
Thucydides circa 455 B.C.-circa 395 B.C. DLB-176
Thulstrup, Thure de 1848-1930 . . . . DLB-188
Thümmel, Moritz August von 1738-1817 . . . . DLB-97
Thurber, James 1894-1961 . . . . . DLB-4, 11, 22, 102; CDALB-5
Thurman, Wallace 1902-1934 . . . . DLB-51
"Negro Poets and Their Poetry" DLB-50
Thwaite, Anthony 1930- DLB-40
The Booker Prize, Address Y-86
Thwaites, Reuben Gold 1853-1913 . . . . DLB-47
Tibullus circa 54 B.C.-circa 19 B.C. DLB-211
Ticknor, George 1791-1871 . . . DLB-1, 59, 140, 235
Ticknor and Fields DLB-49
Ticknor and Fields (revived) DLB-46
Tieck, Ludwig 1773-1853 . . . . DLB-90; CDWLB-2
Tietjens, Eunice 1884-1944 . . . . DLB-54
Tikkanen, Märta 1935- DLB-257
Tilghman, Christopher circa 1948 . . . . DLB-244
Tilney, Edmund circa 1536-1610 . . . . DLB-136
Charles Tilt [publishing house] DLB-106
J. E. Tilton and Company DLB-49
Time-Life Books DLB-46
Times Books DLB-46
Timothy, Peter circa 1725-1782 . . . . DLB-43
Timrava 1867-1951 . . . . DLB-215
Timrod, Henry 1828-1867 . . . . DLB-3, 248
Tindal, Henrietta 1818?-1879 . . . . DLB-199
Tinker, Chauncey Brewster 1876-1963 . . . DLB-140
Tinsley Brothers DLB-106
Tiptree, James, Jr. 1915-1987 . . . . DLB-8
Tišma, Aleksandar 1924- DLB-181
Titus, Edward William 1870-1952 . . . . DLB-4; DS-15
Tiutchev, Fedor Ivanovich 1803-1873 . . . . DLB-205
Tlali, Miriam 1933- DLB-157, 225

Todd, Barbara Euphan 1890-1976 . . . . . . DLB-160
Todorov, Tzvetan 1939- DLB-242
Tofte, Robert
1561 or 1562-1619 or 1620 . . . . .DLB-172
Tóibín, Colm 1955- DLB-271
Toklas, Alice B. 1877-1967 . . . . DLB-4; DS-15
Tokuda Shūsei 1872-1943 . . . . DLB-180
Toland, John 1670-1722 . . . . DLB-252
Tolkien, J. R. R.
1892-1973. . . . . . DLB-15, 160, 255; CDBLB-6
Toller, Ernst 1893-1939 . . . . DLB-124
Tollet, Elizabeth 1694-1754 . . . . DLB-95
Tolson, Melvin B. 1898-1966. . . . . DLB-48, 76
Tolstaya, Tatyana 1951- DLB-285
Tolstoy, Aleksei Konstantinovich
1817-1875 . . . . DLB-238
Tolstoy, Aleksei Nikolaevich 1883-1945 . DLB-272
Tolstoy, Leo 1828-1910 . . . . DLB-238
Tomalin, Claire 1933- DLB-155
Tómas Guðmundsson 1901-1983 . . . . . . DLB-293
Tomasi di Lampedusa, Giuseppe
1896-1957. . . . . .DLB-177
Tomlinson, Charles 1927- DLB-40
Tomlinson, H. M. 1873-1958 . . . .DLB-36, 100, 195
Abel Tompkins [publishing house] DLB-49
Tompson, Benjamin 1642-1714 . . . . DLB-24
Tomson, Graham R.
(see Watson, Rosamund Marriott)
Ton'a 1289-1372. DLB-203
Tondelli, Pier Vittorio 1955-1991. . . . . . . DLB-196
Tonks, Rosemary 1932- DLB-14, 207
Tonna, Charlotte Elizabeth 1790-1846 . . . DLB-163
Jacob Tonson the Elder
[publishing house] DLB-170
Toole, John Kennedy 1937-1969 . . . . Y-81
Toomer, Jean
1894-1967. . . . . DLB-45, 51; CDALB-4
Topsoe, Vilhelm 1840-1881 . . . . DLB-300
Tor Books. DLB-46
Torberg, Friedrich 1908-1979. . . . . DLB-85
Torga, Miguel (Adolfo Correira da Rocha)
1907-1995 . . . . DLB-287
Torrence, Ridgely 1874-1950 . . . . DLB-54, 249
Torres-Metzger, Joseph V. 1933- DLB-122
El Tostado (see Madrigal, Alfonso Fernández de)
Toth, Susan Allen 1940- Y-86
Richard Tottell [publishing house] DLB-170
"The Printer to the Reader,"
(1557) DLB-167
Tough-Guy Literature DLB-9
Touré, Askia Muhammad 1938- DLB-41
Tourgée, Albion W. 1838-1905 . . . . DLB-79
Tournemir, Elizaveta Sailhas de (see Tur, Evgeniia)
Tourneur, Cyril circa 1580-1626 . . . . DLB-58
Tournier, Michel 1924- DLB-83
Frank Tousey [publishing house] DLB-49
Tower Publications. DLB-46
Towne, Benjamin circa 1740-1793 . . . . DLB-43
Towne, Robert 1936- DLB-44
The Townely Plays fifteenth and sixteenth
centuries. DLB-146
Townsend, Sue 1946- DLB-271
Townshend, Aurelian
by 1583-circa 1651. . . . . DLB-121
Toy, Barbara 1908-2001. . . . . DLB-204
Tozzi, Federigo 1883-1920 . . . . DLB-264
Tracy, Honor 1913-1989 . . . . DLB-15
Traherne, Thomas 1637?-1674. . . . . DLB-131
Traill, Catharine Parr 1802-1899 . . . . DLB-99
Train, Arthur 1875-1945 . . . . DLB-86; DS-16
Tranquilli, Secondino (see Silone, Ignazio)
The Transatlantic Publishing Company. . . DLB-49
The Transatlantic Review 1924-1925 . . . . .DS-15
The Transcendental Club
1836-1840 . . . . DLB-1; DLB-223
Transcendentalism DLB-1; DLB-223; DS-5
"A Response from America," by
John A. Heraud DS-5
Publications and Social Movements DLB-1
The Rise of Transcendentalism,
1815-1860 . . . . .DS-5
Transcendentalists, American DS-5
"What Is Transcendentalism? By a
Thinking Man," by James
Kinnard Jr.. . . . . .DS-5
transition 1927-1938 . . . . .DS-15
Translations (Vernacular) in the Crowns of
Castile and Aragon 1352-1515. . . . . . DLB-286
Tranströmer, Tomas 1931- DLB-257
Tranter, John 1943- DLB-289
Travel Writing
American Travel Writing, 1776-1864
(checklist). DLB-183
British Travel Writing, 1940-1997
(checklist). DLB-204
Travel Writers of the Late
Middle Ages DLB-286
(1876-1909 . . . . .DLB-174
(1837-1875 . . . . DLB-166
(1910-1939 . . . . DLB-195
Traven, B. 1882?/1890?-1969?. DLB-9, 56
Travers, Ben 1886-1980 . . . . DLB-10, 233
Travers, P. L. (Pamela Lyndon)
1899-1996 . . . . DLB-160
Trediakovsky, Vasilii Kirillovich
1703-1769 . . . . DLB-150
Treece, Henry 1911-1966. . . . . DLB-160
Treitel, Jonathan 1959- DLB-267
Trejo, Ernesto 1950-1991 . . . . DLB-122
Trelawny, Edward John
1792-1881. . . . . .DLB-110, 116, 144
Tremain, Rose 1943- DLB-14, 271
Tremblay, Michel 1942- DLB-60
Trent, William P. 1862-1939 . . . . DLB-47, 71
Trescot, William Henry 1822-1898 . . . . . . DLB-30
Tressell, Robert (Robert Phillipe Noonan)
1870-1911. . . . . .DLB-197
Trevelyan, Sir George Otto
1838-1928 . . . . DLB-144
Trevisa, John circa 1342-circa 1402 . . . . . DLB-146
Trevor, William 1928- DLB-14, 139
Trierer Floyris circa 1170-1180 . . . . DLB-138
Trillin, Calvin 1935- DLB-185
Trilling, Lionel 1905-1975 . . . . DLB-28, 63
Trilussa 1871-1950 . . . . DLB-114
Trimmer, Sarah 1741-1810. . . . . DLB-158
Triolet, Elsa 1896-1970. . . . . DLB-72
Tripp, John 1927- DLB-40
Trocchi, Alexander 1925-1984. . . . . DLB-15
Troisi, Dante 1920-1989. . . . . DLB-196
Trollope, Anthony
1815-1882 . . . . . . .DLB-21, 57, 159; CDBLB-4
Novel-Reading: *The Works of Charles Dickens; The Works of W. Makepeace Thackeray* (1879) DLB-21
The Trollope Societies Y-00
Trollope, Frances 1779-1863. . . . . DLB-21, 166
Trollope, Joanna 1943- DLB-207
Troop, Elizabeth 1931- DLB-14
Trotter, Catharine 1679-1749 . . . . DLB-84, 252
Trotti, Lamar 1898-1952 . . . . DLB-44
Trottier, Pierre 1925- DLB-60
Trotzig, Birgitta 1929- DLB-257
Troupe, Quincy Thomas, Jr. 1943- DLB-41
John F. Trow and Company DLB-49
Trowbridge, John Townsend 1827-1916 . DLB-202
Trudel, Jean-Louis 1967- DLB-251
Truillier-Lacombe, Joseph-Patrice
1807-1863. . . . . DLB-99
Trumbo, Dalton 1905-1976 . . . . DLB-26
Trumbull, Benjamin 1735-1820 . . . . DLB-30
Trumbull, John 1750-1831 . . . . DLB-31
Trumbull, John 1756-1843 . . . . DLB-183
Truth, Sojourner 1797?-1883 . . . . DLB-239
Tscherning, Andreas 1611-1659. . . . . DLB-164
Tsubouchi Shōyō 1859-1935 . . . . DLB-180
Tsvetaeva, Marina Ivanovna 1892-1941 . . DLB-295
Tuchman, Barbara W.
Tribute to Alfred A. Knopf Y-84
Tucholsky, Kurt 1890-1935 . . . . DLB-56
Tucker, Charlotte Maria
1821-1893 . . . . DLB-163, 190
Tucker, George 1775-1861 . . . . DLB-3, 30, 248
Tucker, James 1808?-1866? DLB-230
Tucker, Nathaniel Beverley
1784-1851. DLB-3, 248
Tucker, St. George 1752-1827 . . . . DLB-37
Tuckerman, Frederick Goddard
1821-1873. . . . . DLB-243
Tuckerman, Henry Theodore 1813-1871. . DLB-64
Tumas, Juozas (see Vaizgantas)
Tunis, John R. 1889-1975. . . . . .DLB-22, 171

Tunstall, Cuthbert 1474-1559 . . . . DLB-132
Tunström, Göran 1937-2000 . . . . DLB-257
Tuohy, Frank 1925- DLB-14, 139
Tupper, Martin F. 1810-1889. . . . . DLB-32
Tur, Evgeniia 1815-1892 . . . . DLB-238
Turbyfill, Mark 1896-1991 . . . . DLB-45
Turco, Lewis 1934- Y-84
Tribute to John Ciardi Y-86
Turgenev, Aleksandr Ivanovich 1784-1845 . . . . DLB-198
Turgenev, Ivan Sergeevich 1818-1883. . . . DLB-238
Turnbull, Alexander H. 1868-1918 . . . . . . DLB-184
Turnbull, Andrew 1921-1970 . . . . DLB-103
Turnbull, Gael 1928- DLB-40
Turner, Arlin 1909-1980 . . . . DLB-103
Turner, Charles (Tennyson) 1808-1879 . . . DLB-32
Turner, Ethel 1872-1958 . . . . DLB-230
Turner, Frederick 1943- DLB-40
Turner, Frederick Jackson 1861-1932 . . . . DLB-17, 186
A Conversation between William Riggan and Janette Turner Hospital Y-02
Turner, Joseph Addison 1826-1868. . . . . . . DLB-79
Turpin, Waters Edward 1910-1968. . . . . . . DLB-51
Turrini, Peter 1944- DLB-124
Tutuola, Amos 1920-1997 . . . DLB-125; CDWLB-3
Twain, Mark (see Clemens, Samuel Langhorne)
Tweedie, Ethel Brilliana circa 1860-1940. . DLB-174
A Century of Poetry, a Lifetime of Collecting: J. M. Edelstein's Collection of Twentieth-Century American Poetry YB-02
Twombly, Wells 1935-1977. . . . . DLB-241
Twysden, Sir Roger 1597-1672 . . . . DLB-213
Tyler, Anne 1941- DLB-6, 143; Y-82; CDALB-7
Tyler, Mary Palmer 1775-1866 . . . . DLB-200
Tyler, Moses Coit 1835-1900 . . . . DLB-47, 64
Tyler, Royall 1757-1826. . . . . DLB-37
Tylor, Edward Burnett 1832-1917. . . . . DLB-57
Tynan, Katharine 1861-1931. . . . . . . DLB-153, 240
Tyndale, William circa 1494-1536. . . . . . . DLB-132
Tyree, Omar 1969- DLB-292

U

Uchida, Yoshika 1921-1992. . . . . CDALB-7
Udall, Nicholas 1504-1556. . . . . DLB-62
Ugrêsić, Dubravka 1949- DLB-181
Uhland, Ludwig 1787-1862 . . . . DLB-90
Uhse, Bodo 1904-1963 . . . . DLB-69
Ujević, Augustin "Tin" 1891-1955 . . . . DLB-147
Ulenhart, Niclas flourished circa 1600. . . . DLB-164
Ulfeldt, Leonora Christina 1621-1698. . . . DLB-300
Ulibarrí, Sabine R. 1919- DLB-82
Ulica, Jorge 1870-1926. . . . . DLB-82
Ulitskaya, Liudmila Evgen'evna 1943- DLB-285
Ulivi, Ferruccio 1912- DLB-196
Ulizio, B. George 1889-1969 . . . . DLB-140
Ulrich von Liechtenstein circa 1200-circa 1275 . . . . DLB-138
Ulrich von Zatzikhoven before 1194-after 1214. . . . . DLB-138
Unaipon, David 1872-1967 . . . . DLB-230
Unamuno, Miguel de 1864-1936. . . . . DLB-108
Under, Marie 1883-1980 . . . DLB-220; CDWLB-4
Underhill, Evelyn 1875-1941 . . . . DLB-240
Undset, Sigrid 1882-1949 . . . . DLB-297
Ungaretti, Giuseppe 1888-1970 . . . . DLB-114
Unger, Friederike Helene 1741-1813 . . . . . . DLB-94
United States Book Company DLB-49
Universal Publishing and Distributing Corporation DLB-46
University of Colorado Special Collections at the University of Colorado at Boulder. Y-98
Indiana University Press Y-02
The University of Iowa Writers' Workshop Golden Jubilee. Y-86
University of Missouri Press Y-01
University of South Carolina The G. Ross Roy Scottish Poetry Collection Y-89
Two Hundred Years of Rare Books and Literary Collections at the University of South Carolina Y-00
The University of South Carolina Press Y-94
University of Virginia The Book Arts Press at the University of Virginia Y-96
The Electronic Text Center and the Electronic Archive of Early American Fiction at the University of Virginia Library Y-98
University of Virginia Libraries Y-91
University of Wales Press DLB-112
University Press of Florida Y-00
University Press of Kansas Y-98
University Press of Mississippi Y-99
Unnur Benediktsdóttir Bjarklind (see Hulda)
Uno Chiyo 1897-1996 . . . . DLB-180
Unruh, Fritz von 1885-1970. . . . . DLB-56, 118
Unsworth, Barry 1930- DLB-194
Unt, Mati 1944- DLB-232
The Unterberg Poetry Center of the 92nd Street Y Y-98
T. Fisher Unwin [publishing house] DLB-106
Upchurch, Boyd B. (see Boyd, John)
Updike, John 1932- DLB-2, 5, 143, 218, 227; Y-80, 82; DS-3; CDALB-6
John Updike on the Internet Y-97
Tribute to Alfred A. Knopf. Y-84
Tribute to John Ciardi Y-86
Upīts, Andrejs 1877-1970 . . . . DLB-220
Uppdal, Kristofer 1878-1961 . . . . DLB-297
Upton, Bertha 1849-1912 . . . . DLB-141
Upton, Charles 1948- DLB-16
Upton, Florence K. 1873-1922. . . . . DLB-141
Upward, Allen 1863-1926 . . . . DLB-36
Urban, Milo 1904-1982. . . . . DLB-215
Ureña de Henríquez, Salomé 1850-1897 . . . . DLB-283
Urfé, Honoré d' 1567-1625. . . . . DLB-268
Urista, Alberto Baltazar (see Alurista)
Urquhart, Fred 1912-1995. . . . . DLB-139
Urrea, Luis Alberto 1955- DLB-209
Urzidil, Johannes 1896-1970 . . . . DLB-85
U.S.A. (Documentary) DLB-274
Usk, Thomas died 1388 . . . . DLB-146
Uslar Pietri, Arturo 1906-2001 . . . . DLB-113
Uspensky, Gleb Ivanovich 1843-1902. . . . DLB-277
Ussher, James 1581-1656. . . . . DLB-213
Ustinov, Peter 1921- DLB-13
Uttley, Alison 1884-1976 . . . . DLB-160
Uz, Johann Peter 1720-1796. . . . . DLB-97

V

Vadianus, Joachim 1484-1551. . . . . DLB-179
Vac, Bertrand (Aimé Pelletier) 1914- DLB-88
Vācietis, Ojārs 1933-1983 . . . . DLB-232
Vaculík, Ludvík 1926- DLB-232
Vaičiulaitis, Antanas 1906-1992 . . . . DLB-220
Vaičiūnaite, Judita 1937- DLB-232
Vail, Laurence 1891-1968 . . . . DLB-4
Vail, Petr L'vovich 1949- DLB-285
Vailland, Roger 1907-1965 . . . . DLB-83
Vaižgantas 1869-1933 . . . . DLB-220
Vajda, Ernest 1887-1954 . . . . DLB-44
Valdés, Gina 1943- DLB-122
Valdez, Luis Miguel 1940- DLB-122
Valduga, Patrizia 1953-. DLB-128
Vale Press DLB-112
Valente, José Angel 1929-2000 . . . . DLB-108
Valenzuela, Luisa 1938- . . . DLB-113; CDWLB-3
Valera, Diego de 1412-1488 . . . . DLB-286
Valeri, Diego 1887-1976. . . . . DLB-128
Valerius Flaccus fl. circa A.D. 92. . . . . DLB-211
Valerius Maximus fl. circa A.D. 31 . . . . . . DLB-211
Valéry, Paul 1871-1945 . . . . DLB-258
Valesio, Paolo 1939- DLB-196
Valgardson, W. D. 1939- DLB-60
Valle, Luz 1899-1971 . . . . DLB-290
Valle, Víctor Manuel 1950- DLB-122
Valle-Inclán, Ramón del 1866-1936. . . . . . DLB-134
Vallejo, Armando 1949- DLB-122
Vallejo, César Abraham 1892-1938. . . . . . DLB-290
Vallès, Jules 1832-1885 . . . . DLB-123
Vallette, Marguerite Eymery (see Rachilde)
Valverde, José María 1926-1996 . . . . DLB-108

Van Allsburg, Chris 1949- DLB-61
Van Anda, Carr 1864-1945 . . . . DLB-25
Vanbrugh, Sir John 1664-1726 . . . . DLB-80
Vance, Jack 1916?- DLB-8
Vančura, Vladislav 1891-1942 . . . . DLB-215; CDWLB-4
van der Post, Laurens 1906-1996 . . . . DLB-204
Van Dine, S. S. (see Wright, Williard Huntington)
Van Doren, Mark 1894-1972 . . . . DLB-45
van Druten, John 1901-1957. . . . . DLB-10
Van Duyn, Mona 1921- DLB-5
Tribute to James Dickey Y-97
Van Dyke, Henry 1852-1933 . . . . . DLB-71; DS-13
Van Dyke, Henry 1928- DLB-33
Van Dyke, John C. 1856-1932 . . . . DLB-186
Vane, Sutton 1888-1963 . . . . DLB-10
Vanguard Press DLB-46
van Gulik, Robert Hans 1910-1967 . . . . DS-17
van Itallie, Jean-Claude 1936- DLB-7
Van Loan, Charles E. 1876-1919 . . . . .DLB-171
Vann, Robert L. 1879-1940 . . . . DLB-29
Van Rensselaer, Mariana Griswold 1851-1934 . . . . DLB-47
Van Rensselaer, Mrs. Schuyler (see Van Rensselaer, Mariana Griswold)
Van Vechten, Carl 1880-1964 . . . . . . DLB-4, 9, 51
van Vogt, A. E. 1912-2000 . . . . DLB-8, 251
Varela, Blanca 1926- DLB-290
Vargas Llosa, Mario 1936- DLB-145; CDWLB-3
Acceptance Speech for the Ritz Paris Hemingway Award Y-85
Varley, John 1947- Y-81
Varnhagen von Ense, Karl August 1785-1858. . . . . DLB-90
Varnhagen von Ense, Rahel 1771-1833 . . . . DLB-90
Varro 116 B.C.-27 B.C. DLB-211
Vasilenko, Svetlana Vladimirovna 1956- DLB-285
Vasiliu, George (see Bacovia, George)
Vásquez, Richard 1928- DLB-209
Vásquez Montalbán, Manuel 1939- . . . DLB-134
Vassa, Gustavus (see Equiano, Olaudah)
Vassalli, Sebastiano 1941- DLB-128, 196
Vaugelas, Claude Favre de 1585-1650. . . . DLB-268
Vaughan, Henry 1621-1695 . . . . DLB-131
Vaughan, Thomas 1621-1666 . . . . DLB-131
Vaughn, Robert 1592?-1667. . . . . DLB-213
Vaux, Thomas, Lord 1509-1556 . . . . DLB-132
Vazov, Ivan 1850-1921. . . . . .DLB-147; CDWLB-4
Véa, Alfredo, Jr. 1950- DLB-209
Veblen, Thorstein 1857-1929 . . . . DLB-246
Vedel, Anders Sørensen 1542-1616 . . . . . DLB-300
Vega, Janine Pommy 1942- DLB-16
Veiller, Anthony 1903-1965 . . . . DLB-44
Velásquez-Trevino, Gloria 1949- DLB-122
Veley, Margaret 1843-1887 . . . . DLB-199
Velleius Paterculus circa 20 B.C.-circa A.D. 30. . . . . DLB-211
Veloz Maggiolo, Marcio 1936- DLB-145
Vel'tman, Aleksandr Fomich 1800-1870. . . . . DLB-198
Venegas, Daniel ?-? DLB-82
Venevitinov, Dmitrii Vladimirovich 1805-1827. . . . . DLB-205
Verbitskaia, Anastasiia Alekseevna 1861-1928 . . . . DLB-295
Verde, Cesário 1855-1886 . . . . DLB-287
Vergil, Polydore circa 1470-1555 . . . . DLB-132
Veríssimo, Erico 1905-1975 . . . . DLB-145
Verlaine, Paul 1844-1896 . . . . DLB-217
Vernacular Translations in the Crowns of Castile and Aragon 1352-1515. . . . . . DLB-286
Verne, Jules 1828-1905. . . . . DLB-123
Verplanck, Gulian C. 1786-1870. . . . . DLB-59
Very, Jones 1813-1880 . . . . DLB-1, 243; DS-5
Vesaas, Halldis Moren 1907-1995 . . . . . . DLB-297
Vesaas, Tarjei 1897-1970 . . . . DLB-297
Vian, Boris 1920-1959 . . . . DLB-72
Viazemsky, Petr Andreevich 1792-1878. . . . . DLB-205
Vicars, Thomas 1591-1638. . . . . DLB-236
Vicente, Gil 1465-1536/1540? DLB-287
Vickers, Roy 1888?-1965 . . . . DLB-77
Vickery, Sukey 1779-1821 . . . . DLB-200
Victoria 1819-1901 . . . . DLB-55
Victoria Press DLB-106
Vidal, Gore 1925- DLB-6, 152; CDALB-7
Vidal, Mary Theresa 1815-1873. . . . . DLB-230
Vidmer, Richards 1898-1978 . . . . DLB-241
Viebig, Clara 1860-1952. . . . . DLB-66
Viereck, George Sylvester 1884-1962. . . . . DLB-54
Viereck, Peter 1916- DLB-5
Vietnam War (ended 1975) Resources for the Study of Vietnam War Literature. DLB-9
Viets, Roger 1738-1811. . . . . DLB-99
Vigil-Piñon, Evangelina 1949- DLB-122
Vigneault, Gilles 1928- DLB-60
Vigny, Alfred de 1797-1863 . . . .DLB-119, 192, 217
Vigolo, Giorgio 1894-1983 . . . . DLB-114
Vik, Bjorg 1935- DLB-297
The Viking Press DLB-46
Vilde, Eduard 1865-1933 . . . . DLB-220
Vilinskaia, Mariia Aleksandrovna (see Vovchok, Marko)
Villanueva, Alma Luz 1944- DLB-122
Villanueva, Tino 1941- DLB-82
Villard, Henry 1835-1900. . . . . DLB-23
Villard, Oswald Garrison 1872-1949 . . DLB-25, 91
Villarreal, Edit 1944- DLB-209
Villarreal, José Antonio 1924- DLB-82
Villaseñor, Victor 1940- DLB-209
Villedieu, Madame de (Marie-Catherine Desjardins) 1640?-1683 . . . . .DLB-268
Villegas de Magnón, Leonor 1876-1955. . . . . DLB-122
Villehardouin, Geoffroi de circa 1150-1215 . . . . DLB-208
Villemaire, Yolande 1949- DLB-60
Villena, Enrique de ca. 1382/84-1432. . . . DLB-286
Villena, Luis Antonio de 1951- DLB-134
Villiers, George, Second Duke of Buckingham 1628-1687 . . . . DLB-80
Villiers de l'Isle-Adam, Jean-Marie Mathias Philippe-Auguste, Comte de 1838-1889 . . . . DLB-123, 192
Villon, François 1431-circa 1463?. DLB-208
Vine Press. DLB-112
Viorst, Judith ?- DLB-52
Vipont, Elfrida (Elfrida Vipont Foulds, Charles Vipont) 1902-1992 . . . . DLB-160
Viramontes, Helena María 1954- DLB-122
Virgil 70 B.C.-19 B.C. DLB-211; CDWLB-1
Vischer, Friedrich Theodor 1807-1887. . . DLB-133
Vitier, Cintio 1921- DLB-283
Vitruvius circa 85 B.C.-circa 15 B.C. DLB-211
Vitry, Philippe de 1291-1361 . . . . DLB-208
Vittorini, Elio 1908-1966 . . . . DLB-264
Vivanco, Luis Felipe 1907-1975. . . . . DLB-108
Vivian, E. Charles (Charles Henry Cannell, Charles Henry Vivian, Jack Mann, Barry Lynd) 1882-1947 . . . . DLB-255
Viviani, Cesare 1947- DLB-128
Vivien, Renée 1877-1909 . . . . .DLB-217
Vizenor, Gerald 1934- DLB-175, 227
Vizetelly and Company DLB-106
Voaden, Herman 1903-1991 . . . . DLB-88
Voß, Johann Heinrich 1751-1826. . . . . DLB-90
Vogau, Boris Andreevich (see Pil'niak, Boris Andreevich)
Voigt, Ellen Bryant 1943- DLB-120
Vojnović, Ivo 1857-1929. . . . .DLB-147; CDWLB-4
Vold, Jan Erik 1939- DLB-297
Volkoff, Vladimir 1932- DLB-83
P. F. Volland Company DLB-46
Vollbehr, Otto H. F. 1872?-1945 or 1946 . . . . .DLB-187
Vologdin (see Zasodimsky, Pavel Vladimirovich)
Voloshin, Maksimilian Aleksandrovich 1877-1932. . . . . DLB-295
Volponi, Paolo 1924-1994 . . . . .DLB-177
Vonarburg, Élisabeth 1947- DLB-251
von der Grün, Max 1926- DLB-75
Vonnegut, Kurt 1922- DLB-2, 8, 152; Y-80; DS-3; CDALB-6
Tribute to Isaac Asimov. Y-92
Tribute to Richard Brautigan. Y-84
Voranc, Prežihov 1893-1950 . . . . .DLB-147
Voronsky, Aleksandr Konstantinovich 1884-1937 . . . . .DLB-272
Vovchok, Marko 1833-1907. . . . . DLB-238

Voynich, E. L. 1864-1960 . . . . DLB-197

Vroman, Mary Elizabeth circa 1924-1967 . . DLB-33

W

Wace, Robert ("Maistre") circa 1100-circa 1175 . . . . DLB-146

Wackenroder, Wilhelm Heinrich 1773-1798. . . . . DLB-90

Wackernagel, Wilhelm 1806-1869 . . . . . . DLB-133

Waddell, Helen 1889-1965 . . . . DLB-240

Waddington, Miriam 1917- DLB-68

Wade, Henry 1887-1969 . . . . DLB-77

Wagenknecht, Edward 1900- DLB-103

Wägner, Elin 1882-1949 . . . . DLB-259

Wagner, Heinrich Leopold 1747-1779 . . . . . DLB-94

Wagner, Henry R. 1862-1957 . . . . DLB-140

Wagner, Richard 1813-1883 . . . . DLB-129

Wagoner, David 1926- DLB-5, 256

Wah, Fred 1939- DLB-60

Waiblinger, Wilhelm 1804-1830 . . . . DLB-90

Wain, John 1925-1994. . . . . DLB-15, 27, 139, 155; CDBLB-8

Tribute to J. B. Priestly Y-84

Wainwright, Jeffrey 1944- DLB-40

Waite, Peirce and Company DLB-49

Wakeman, Stephen H. 1859-1924. . . . . . . DLB-187

Wakoski, Diane 1937- DLB-5

Walahfrid Strabo circa 808-849. . . . . DLB-148

Henry Z. Walck [publishing house]. DLB-46

Walcott, Derek 1930- DLB-117; Y-81, 92; CDWLB-3

Nobel Lecture 1992: The Antilles: Fragments of Epic Memory Y-92

Robert Waldegrave [publishing house] . . . DLB-170

Waldis, Burkhard circa 1490-1556?. DLB-178

Waldman, Anne 1945- DLB-16

Waldrop, Rosmarie 1935- DLB-169

Walker, Alice 1900-1982 . . . . DLB-201

Walker, Alice 1944- . . DLB-6, 33, 143; CDALB-6

Walker, Annie Louisa (Mrs. Harry Coghill) circa 1836-1907 . . . . DLB-240

Walker, George F. 1947- DLB-60

Walker, John Brisben 1847-1931 . . . . DLB-79

Walker, Joseph A. 1935- DLB-38

Walker, Kath (see Oodgeroo of the Tribe Noonuccal)

Walker, Margaret 1915-1998. . . . . DLB-76, 152

Walker, Obadiah 1616-1699 . . . . DLB-281

Walker, Ted 1934- DLB-40

Walker, Evans and Cogswell Company . . . DLB-49

Wall, John F. (see Sarban)

Wallace, Alfred Russel 1823-1913 . . . . DLB-190

Wallace, Dewitt 1889-1981 . . . . DLB-137

Wallace, Edgar 1875-1932 . . . . DLB-70

Wallace, Lew 1827-1905 . . . . DLB-202

Wallace, Lila Acheson 1889-1984 . . . . DLB-137

"A Word of Thanks," From the Initial Issue of *Reader's Digest* (February 1922) DLB-137

Wallace, Naomi 1960- DLB-249

Wallace Markfield's "Steeplechase". Y-02

Wallace-Crabbe, Chris 1934- DLB-289

Wallant, Edward Lewis 1926-1962 . . . . DLB-2, 28, 143, 299

Waller, Edmund 1606-1687. . . . . DLB-126

Walpole, Horace 1717-1797 . . . . . DLB-39, 104, 213

Preface to the First Edition of *The Castle of Otranto* (1764) DLB-39, 178

Preface to the Second Edition of *The Castle of Otranto* (1765) DLB-39, 178

Walpole, Hugh 1884-1941. . . . . DLB-34

Walrond, Eric 1898-1966 . . . . DLB-51

Walser, Martin 1927- DLB-75, 124

Walser, Robert 1878-1956 . . . . DLB-66

Walsh, Ernest 1895-1926. . . . . DLB-4, 45

Walsh, Robert 1784-1859 . . . . DLB-59

Walters, Henry 1848-1931 . . . . DLB-140

Waltharius circa 825 . . . . DLB-148

Walther von der Vogelweide circa 1170-circa 1230 . . . . DLB-138

Walton, Izaak 1593-1683 . . . . DLB-151, 213; CDBLB-1

Wambaugh, Joseph 1937- DLB-6; Y-83

Wand, Alfred Rudolph 1828-1891 . . . . . . DLB-188

Waniek, Marilyn Nelson 1946- DLB-120

Wanley, Humphrey 1672-1726 . . . . DLB-213

War of the Words (and Pictures): The Creation of a Graphic Novel Y-02

Warburton, William 1698-1779. . . . . DLB-104

Ward, Aileen 1919- DLB-111

Ward, Artemus (see Browne, Charles Farrar)

Ward, Arthur Henry Sarsfield (see Rohmer, Sax)

Ward, Douglas Turner 1930- DLB-7, 38

Ward, Mrs. Humphry 1851-1920 . . . . DLB-18

Ward, James 1843-1925. . . . . DLB-262

Ward, Lynd 1905-1985 . . . . DLB-22

Ward, Lock and Company DLB-106

Ward, Nathaniel circa 1578-1652 . . . . DLB-24

Ward, Theodore 1902-1983 . . . . DLB-76

Wardle, Ralph 1909-1988 . . . . DLB-103

Ware, Henry, Jr. 1794-1843. . . . . DLB-235

Ware, William 1797-1852 . . . . DLB-1, 235

Warfield, Catherine Ann 1816-1877 . . . . DLB-248

Waring, Anna Letitia 1823-1910 . . . . DLB-240

Frederick Warne and Company [U.K.] DLB-106

Frederick Warne and Company [U.S.] DLB-49

Warner, Anne 1869-1913 . . . . DLB-202

Warner, Charles Dudley 1829-1900 . . . . . . DLB-64

Warner, Marina 1946- DLB-194

Warner, Rex 1905-1986 . . . . DLB-15

Warner, Susan 1819-1885 . . . . DLB-3, 42, 239, 250

Warner, Sylvia Townsend 1893-1978 . . . . DLB-34, 139

Warner, William 1558-1609 . . . . DLB-172

Warner Books DLB-46

Warr, Bertram 1917-1943 . . . . DLB-88

Warren, John Byrne Leicester (see De Tabley, Lord)

Warren, Lella 1899-1982. . . . . Y-83

Warren, Mercy Otis 1728-1814. . . . . . DLB-31, 200

Warren, Robert Penn 1905-1989 . . . . . DLB-2, 48, 152; Y-80, 89; CDALB-6

Tribute to Katherine Anne Porter. Y-80

Warren, Samuel 1807-1877 . . . . DLB-190

Die Wartburgkrieg circa 1230-circa 1280 . . . DLB-138

Warton, Joseph 1722-1800. . . . . DLB-104, 109

Warton, Thomas 1728-1790 . . . . DLB-104, 109

Warung, Price (William Astley) 1855-1911 . . . . DLB-230

Washington, George 1732-1799. . . . . DLB-31

Washington, Ned 1901-1976. . . . . DLB-265

Wassermann, Jakob 1873-1934 . . . . DLB-66

Wasserstein, Wendy 1950- DLB-228

Wassmo, Herbjorg 1942- DLB-297

Wasson, David Atwood 1823-1887. . . . DLB-1, 223

Watanna, Onoto (see Eaton, Winnifred)

Waten, Judah 1911?-1985 . . . . DLB-289

Waterhouse, Keith 1929- DLB-13, 15

Waterman, Andrew 1940- DLB-40

Waters, Frank 1902-1995 . . . . DLB-212; Y-86

Waters, Michael 1949- DLB-120

Watkins, Tobias 1780-1855. . . . . DLB-73

Watkins, Vernon 1906-1967 . . . . DLB-20

Watmough, David 1926- DLB-53

Watson, Colin 1920-1983 . . . . DLB-276

Watson, Ian 1943- DLB-261

Watson, James Wreford (see Wreford, James)

Watson, John 1850-1907 . . . . DLB-156

Watson, Rosamund Marriott (Graham R. Tomson) 1860-1911 . . . . DLB-240

Watson, Sheila 1909-1998. . . . . DLB-60

Watson, Thomas 1545?-1592 . . . . DLB-132

Watson, Wilfred 1911- DLB-60

W. J. Watt and Company DLB-46

Watten, Barrett 1948- DLB-193

Watterson, Henry 1840-1921 . . . . DLB-25

Watts, Alan 1915-1973. . . . . DLB-16

Watts, Isaac 1674-1748. . . . . DLB-95

Franklin Watts [publishing house]. DLB-46

Waugh, Alec 1898-1981 . . . . DLB-191

Waugh, Auberon 1939-2000 . . . DLB-14, 194; Y-00

Waugh, Evelyn 1903-1966 . . . . DLB-15, 162, 195; CDBLB-6

Way and Williams. DLB-49

Wayman, Tom 1945- DLB-53

Weatherly, Tom 1942- DLB-41

Weaver, Gordon 1937- DLB-130

Weaver, Robert 1921- DLB-88

Webb, Beatrice 1858-1943. . . . . DLB-190

Webb, Francis 1925-1973 . . . . DLB-260
Webb, Frank J. ?-? DLB-50
Webb, James Watson 1802-1884 . . . . DLB-43
Webb, Mary 1881-1927 . . . . DLB-34
Webb, Phyllis 1927- DLB-53
Webb, Sidney 1859-1947 . . . . DLB-190
Webb, Walter Prescott 1888-1963 . . . . DLB-17
Webbe, William ?-1591 . . . . DLB-132
Webber, Charles Wilkins 1819-1856? . . . DLB-202
Weber, Max 1864-1920 . . . . DLB-296
Webling, Lucy (Lucy Betty MacRaye) 1877-1952 . . . . DLB-240
Webling, Peggy (Arthur Weston) 1871-1949 . . . . DLB-240
Webster, Augusta 1837-1894 . . . . DLB-35, 240
Webster, John 1579 or 1580-1634? DLB-58; CDBLB-1
The Melbourne Manuscript Y-86
Webster, Noah 1758-1843 . . . . DLB-1, 37, 42, 43, 73, 243
Webster, Paul Francis 1907-1984 . . . . DLB-265
Charles L. Webster and Company DLB-49
Weckherlin, Georg Rodolf 1584-1653 . . . DLB-164
Wedekind, Frank 1864-1918 . . . . DLB-118; CDWLB-2
Weeks, Edward Augustus, Jr. 1898-1989 . . . . DLB-137
Weeks, Stephen B. 1865-1918 . . . . DLB-187
Weems, Mason Locke 1759-1825 . . . DLB-30, 37, 42
Weerth, Georg 1822-1856 . . . . DLB-129
Weidenfeld and Nicolson DLB-112
Weidman, Jerome 1913-1998 . . . . DLB-28
Weigl, Bruce 1949- DLB-120
Weil, Jiří 1900-1959 . . . . DLB-299
Weinbaum, Stanley Grauman 1902-1935 . . DLB-8
Weiner, Andrew 1949- DLB-251
Weintraub, Stanley 1929- DLB-111; Y82
Weise, Christian 1642-1708 . . . . DLB-168
Weisenborn, Gunther 1902-1969 . . . . DLB-69, 124
Weiss, John 1818-1879 . . . . DLB-1, 243
Weiss, Paul 1901-2002 . . . . DLB-279
Weiss, Peter 1916-1982 . . . . DLB-69, 124
Weiss, Theodore 1916- DLB-5
Weiß, Ernst 1882-1940 . . . . DLB-81
Weiße, Christian Felix 1726-1804 . . . . DLB-97
Weitling, Wilhelm 1808-1871 . . . . DLB-129
Welch, James 1940- DLB-175, 256
Welch, Lew 1926-1971? DLB-16
Weldon, Fay 1931- DLB-14, 194; CDBLB-8
Wellek, René 1903-1995 . . . . DLB-63
Wells, Carolyn 1862-1942 . . . . DLB-11
Wells, Charles Jeremiah circa 1800-1879 . . . . DLB-32
Wells, Gabriel 1862-1946 . . . . DLB-140
Wells, H. G. 1866-1946 . . . . DLB-34, 70, 156, 178; CDBLB-6
H. G. Wells Society Y-98
Preface to *The Scientific Romances of H. G. Wells* (1933) DLB-178
Wells, Helena 1758?-1824 . . . . DLB-200
Wells, Rebecca 1952- DLB-292
Wells, Robert 1947- DLB-40
Wells-Barnett, Ida B. 1862-1931 . . . . . DLB-23, 221
Welsh, Irvine 1958- DLB-271
Welty, Eudora 1909-2001 . . . . . . DLB-2, 102, 143; Y-87, 01; DS-12; CDALB-1
Eudora Welty: Eye of the Storyteller Y-87
Eudora Welty Newsletter Y-99
Eudora Welty's Funeral Y-01
Eudora Welty's Ninetieth Birthday Y-99
Eudora Welty Remembered in Two Exhibits Y-02
Wendell, Barrett 1855-1921 . . . . DLB-71
Wentworth, Patricia 1878-1961 . . . . DLB-77
Wentworth, William Charles 1790-1872 . . . . DLB-230
Werder, Diederich von dem 1584-1657 . . DLB-164
Werfel, Franz 1890-1945 . . . . DLB-81, 124
Werner, Zacharias 1768-1823 . . . . DLB-94
The Werner Company DLB-49
Wersba, Barbara 1932- DLB-52
Wescott, Glenway 1901-1987 . . . . DLB-4, 9, 102; DS-15
Wesker, Arnold 1932- DLB-13; CDBLB-8
Wesley, Charles 1707-1788 . . . . DLB-95
Wesley, John 1703-1791 . . . . DLB-104
Wesley, Mary 1912-2002 . . . . DLB-231
Wesley, Richard 1945- DLB-38
Wessel, Johan Herman 1742-1785 . . . . . . DLB-300
A. Wessels and Company DLB-46
Wessobrunner Gebet circa 787-815 . . . . DLB-148
West, Anthony 1914-1988 . . . . DLB-15
Tribute to Liam O'Flaherty Y-84
West, Cheryl L. 1957- DLB-266
West, Cornel 1953- DLB-246
West, Dorothy 1907-1998 . . . . DLB-76
West, Jessamyn 1902-1984 . . . . DLB-6; Y-84
West, Mae 1892-1980 . . . . DLB-44
West, Michael Lee 1953- DLB-292
West, Michelle Sagara 1963- DLB-251
West, Morris 1916-1999 . . . . DLB-289
West, Nathanael 1903-1940 . . . . DLB-4, 9, 28; CDALB-5
West, Paul 1930- DLB-14
West, Rebecca 1892-1983 . . . . DLB-36; Y-83
West, Richard 1941- DLB-185
West and Johnson DLB-49
Westcott, Edward Noyes 1846-1898 . . . . DLB-202
The Western Literature Association Y-99
The Western Messenger 1835-1841 . . . . DLB-1; DLB-223
Western Publishing Company DLB-46
Western Writers of America Y-99
The Westminster Review 1824-1914 . . . . DLB-110
Weston, Arthur (see Webling, Peggy)
Weston, Elizabeth Jane circa 1582-1612 . . . DLB-172
Wetherald, Agnes Ethelwyn 1857-1940 . . . DLB-99
Wetherell, Elizabeth (see Warner, Susan)
Wetherell, W. D. 1948- DLB-234
Wetzel, Friedrich Gottlob 1779-1819 . . . . . DLB-90
Weyman, Stanley J. 1855-1928 . . . . DLB-141, 156
Wezel, Johann Karl 1747-1819 . . . . DLB-94
Whalen, Philip 1923-2002 . . . . DLB-16
Whalley, George 1915-1983 . . . . DLB-88
Wharton, Edith 1862-1937 . . . . DLB-4, 9, 12, 78, 189; DS-13; CDALB-3
Wharton, William 1920s?- Y-80
Whately, Mary Louisa 1824-1889 . . . . . . DLB-166
Whately, Richard 1787-1863 . . . . DLB-190
Elements of Rhetoric (1828; revised, 1846) [excerpt] DLB-57
Wheatley, Dennis 1897-1977 . . . . DLB-77, 255
Wheatley, Phillis circa 1754-1784 . . . . DLB-31, 50; CDALB-2
Wheeler, Anna Doyle 1785-1848? DLB-158
Wheeler, Charles Stearns 1816-1843 . . DLB-1, 223
Wheeler, Monroe 1900-1988 . . . . DLB-4
Wheelock, John Hall 1886-1978 . . . . DLB-45
From John Hall Wheelock's Oral Memoir Y-01
Wheelwright, J. B. 1897-1940 . . . . DLB-45
Wheelwright, John circa 1592-1679 . . . . . . DLB-24
Whetstone, George 1550-1587 . . . . DLB-136
Whetstone, Colonel Pete (see Noland, C. F. M.)
Whewell, William 1794-1866 . . . . DLB-262
Whichcote, Benjamin 1609?-1683 . . . . . . DLB-252
Whicher, Stephen E. 1915-1961 . . . . DLB-111
Whipple, Edwin Percy 1819-1886 . . . . . DLB-1, 64
Whitaker, Alexander 1585-1617 . . . . DLB-24
Whitaker, Daniel K. 1801-1881 . . . . DLB-73
Whitcher, Frances Miriam 1812-1852 . . . . DLB-11, 202
White, Andrew 1579-1656 . . . . DLB-24
White, Andrew Dickson 1832-1918 . . . . . . DLB-47
White, E. B. 1899-1985 . . . DLB-11, 22; CDALB-7
White, Edgar B. 1947- DLB-38
White, Edmund 1940- DLB-227
White, Ethel Lina 1887-1944 . . . . DLB-77
White, Hayden V. 1928- DLB-246
White, Henry Kirke 1785-1806 . . . . DLB-96
White, Horace 1834-1916 . . . . DLB-23
White, James 1928-1999 . . . . DLB-261
White, Patrick 1912-1990 . . . . DLB-260
White, Phyllis Dorothy James (see James, P. D.)
White, Richard Grant 1821-1885 . . . . DLB-64
White, T. H. 1906-1964 . . . . DLB-160, 255
White, Walter 1893-1955 . . . . DLB-51
Wilcox, James 1949- DLB-292
William White and Company DLB-49

White, William Allen 1868-1944 . . . . DLB-9, 25

White, William Anthony Parker (see Boucher, Anthony)

White, William Hale (see Rutherford, Mark)

Whitechurch, Victor L. 1868-1933 . . . . DLB-70

Whitehead, Alfred North 1861-1947 . . . . DLB-100, 262

Whitehead, James 1936- Y-81

Whitehead, William 1715-1785 . . . . . . DLB-84, 109

Whitfield, James Monroe 1822-1871 . . . . . . DLB-50

Whitfield, Raoul 1898-1945 . . . . DLB-226

Whitgift, John circa 1533-1604 . . . . DLB-132

Whiting, John 1917-1963 . . . . DLB-13

Whiting, Samuel 1597-1679 . . . . DLB-24

Whitlock, Brand 1869-1934 . . . . DLB-12

Whitman, Albery Allson 1851-1901 . . . . . . DLB-50

Whitman, Alden 1913-1990 . . . . Y-91

Whitman, Sarah Helen (Power) 1803-1878 . . . . DLB-1, 243

Whitman, Walt 1819-1892 . . . . DLB-3, 64, 224, 250; CDALB-2

Albert Whitman and Company DLB-46

Whitman Publishing Company DLB-46

Whitney, Geoffrey 1548 or 1552?-1601 . . DLB-136

Whitney, Isabella flourished 1566-1573 . . . DLB-136

Whitney, John Hay 1904-1982 . . . . DLB-127

Whittemore, Reed 1919-1995 . . . . DLB-5

Whittier, John Greenleaf 1807-1892 . . . . DLB-1, 243; CDALB-2

Whittlesey House DLB-46

Wickham, Anna (Edith Alice Mary Harper) 1884-1947 . . . . DLB-240

Wickram, Georg circa 1505-circa 1561 . . . DLB-179

Wicomb, Zoë 1948- DLB-225

Wideman, John Edgar 1941- DLB-33, 143

Widener, Harry Elkins 1885-1912 . . . . DLB-140

Wiebe, Rudy 1934- DLB-60

Wiechert, Ernst 1887-1950 . . . . DLB-56

Wied, Gustav 1858-1914 . . . . DLB-300

Wied, Martina 1882-1957 . . . . DLB-85

Wiehe, Evelyn May Clowes (see Mordaunt, Elinor)

Wieland, Christoph Martin 1733-1813 . . . . DLB-97

Wienbarg, Ludolf 1802-1872 . . . . DLB-133

Wieners, John 1934- DLB-16

Wier, Ester 1910- DLB-52

Wiesel, Elie 1928- DLB-83, 299; Y-86, 87; CDALB-7

Nobel Lecture 1986: Hope, Despair and Memory Y-86

Wiggin, Kate Douglas 1856-1923 . . . . DLB-42

Wigglesworth, Michael 1631-1705 . . . . DLB-24

Wilberforce, William 1759-1833 . . . . DLB-158

Wilbrandt, Adolf 1837-1911 . . . . DLB-129

Wilbur, Richard 1921- . . . DLB-5, 169; CDALB-7

Tribute to Robert Penn Warren Y-89

Wilcox, James 1949- DLB-292

Wild, Peter 1940- DLB-5

Wilde, Lady Jane Francesca Elgee 1821?-1896 . . . . DLB-199

Wilde, Oscar 1854-1900 . . . . . . DLB-10, 19, 34, 57, 141, 156, 190; CDBLB-5

"The Critic as Artist" (1891) DLB-57

"The Decay of Lying" (1889) DLB-18

"The English Renaissance of Art" (1908) DLB-35

"L'Envoi" (1882) DLB-35

Oscar Wilde Conference at Hofstra University Y-00

Wilde, Richard Henry 1789-1847 . . . . . . DLB-3, 59

W. A. Wilde Company DLB-49

Wilder, Billy 1906- DLB-26

Wilder, Laura Ingalls 1867-1957 . . . . . DLB-22, 256

Wilder, Thornton 1897-1975 . . . . DLB-4, 7, 9, 228; CDALB-7

Thornton Wilder Centenary at Yale Y-97

Wildgans, Anton 1881-1932 . . . . DLB-118

Wiley, Bell Irvin 1906-1980 . . . . DLB-17

John Wiley and Sons DLB-49

Wilhelm, Kate 1928- DLB-8

Wilkes, Charles 1798-1877 . . . . DLB-183

Wilkes, George 1817-1885 . . . . DLB-79

Wilkins, John 1614-1672 . . . . DLB-236

Wilkinson, Anne 1910-1961 . . . . DLB-88

Wilkinson, Eliza Yonge 1757-circa 1813 . . . . DLB-200

Wilkinson, Sylvia 1940- Y-86

Wilkinson, William Cleaver 1833-1920 . . . DLB-71

Willard, Barbara 1909-1994 . . . . DLB-161

Willard, Emma 1787-1870 . . . . DLB-239

Willard, Frances E. 1839-1898 . . . . DLB-221

Willard, Nancy 1936- DLB-5, 52

Willard, Samuel 1640-1707 . . . . DLB-24

L. Willard [publishing house] DLB-49

Willeford, Charles 1919-1988 . . . . DLB-226

William of Auvergne 1190-1249 . . . . DLB-115

William of Conches circa 1090-circa 1154 . . . . DLB-115

William of Ockham circa 1285-1347 . . . . . DLB-115

William of Sherwood 1200/1205-1266/1271 . . . . DLB-115

The William Charvat American Fiction Collection at the Ohio State University Libraries Y-92

Williams, Ben Ames 1889-1953 . . . . DLB-102

Williams, C. K. 1936- DLB-5

Williams, Chancellor 1905-1992 . . . . DLB-76

Williams, Charles 1886-1945 . . . DLB-100, 153, 255

Williams, Denis 1923-1998 . . . . DLB-117

Williams, Emlyn 1905-1987 . . . . DLB-10, 77

Williams, Garth 1912-1996 . . . . DLB-22

Williams, George Washington 1849-1891 . . . . DLB-47

Williams, Heathcote 1941- DLB-13

Williams, Helen Maria 1761-1827 . . . . DLB-158

Williams, Hugo 1942- DLB-40

Williams, Isaac 1802-1865 . . . . DLB-32

Williams, Joan 1928- DLB-6

Williams, Joe 1889-1972 . . . . DLB-241

Williams, John A. 1925- DLB-2, 33

Williams, John E. 1922-1994 . . . . DLB-6

Williams, Jonathan 1929- DLB-5

Williams, Miller 1930- DLB-105

Williams, Nigel 1948- DLB-231

Williams, Raymond 1921-1988 . . . . DLB-14, 231, 242

Williams, Roger circa 1603-1683 . . . . DLB-24

Williams, Rowland 1817-1870 . . . . DLB-184

Williams, Samm-Art 1946- DLB-38

Williams, Sherley Anne 1944-1999 . . . . DLB-41

Williams, T. Harry 1909-1979 . . . . DLB-17

Williams, Tennessee 1911-1983 . . . . . DLB-7; Y-83; DS-4; CDALB-1

Williams, Terry Tempest 1955- . . . DLB-206, 275

Williams, Ursula Moray 1911- DLB-160

Williams, Valentine 1883-1946 . . . . DLB-77

Williams, William Appleman 1921- DLB-17

Williams, William Carlos 1883-1963 . . . . . . DLB-4, 16, 54, 86; CDALB-4

The William Carlos Williams Society Y-99

Williams, Wirt 1921- DLB-6

A. Williams and Company DLB-49

Williams Brothers DLB-49

Wiliamson, David 1942- DLB-289

Williamson, Henry 1895-1977 . . . . DLB-191

The Henry Williamson Society Y-98

Williamson, Jack 1908- DLB-8

Willingham, Calder Baynard, Jr. 1922-1995 . . . . DLB-2, 44

Williram of Ebersberg circa 1020-1085 . . . DLB-148

Willis, John circa 1572-1625 . . . . DLB-281

Willis, Nathaniel Parker 1806-1867 . . . DLB-3, 59, 73, 74, 183, 250; DS-13

Willkomm, Ernst 1810-1886 . . . . DLB-133

Wills, Garry 1934- DLB-246

Tribute to Kenneth Dale McCormick Y-97

Willson, Meredith 1902-1984 . . . . DLB-265

Willumsen, Dorrit 1940- DLB-214

Wilmer, Clive 1945- DLB-40

Wilson, A. N. 1950- DLB-14, 155, 194

Wilson, Angus 1913-1991 . . . . . . DLB-15, 139, 155

Wilson, Arthur 1595-1652 . . . . DLB-58

Wilson, August 1945- DLB-228

Wilson, Augusta Jane Evans 1835-1909 . . . DLB-42

Wilson, Colin 1931- DLB-14, 194

Tribute to J. B. Priestly Y-84

Wilson, Edmund 1895-1972 . . . . DLB-63

Wilson, Ethel 1888-1980 . . . . DLB-68

Wilson, F. P. 1889-1963 . . . . DLB-201

Wilson, Harriet E. 1827/1828?-1863? DLB-50, 239, 243

Wilson, Harry Leon 1867-1939 . . . . DLB-9

Wilson, John 1588-1667 . . . . DLB-24
Wilson, John 1785-1854 . . . . DLB-110
Wilson, John Anthony Burgess (see Burgess, Anthony)
Wilson, John Dover 1881-1969 . . . . DLB-201
Wilson, Lanford 1937- DLB-7
Wilson, Margaret 1882-1973 . . . . DLB-9
Wilson, Michael 1914-1978 . . . . DLB-44
Wilson, Mona 1872-1954 . . . . DLB-149
Wilson, Robert Charles 1953- DLB-251
Wilson, Robert McLiam 1964- DLB-267
Wilson, Robley 1930- DLB-218
Wilson, Romer 1891-1930 . . . . DLB-191
Wilson, Thomas 1524-1581 . . . . DLB-132, 236
Wilson, Woodrow 1856-1924 . . . . DLB-47
Effingham Wilson [publishing house] DLB-154
Wimpfeling, Jakob 1450-1528 . . . . DLB-179
Wimsatt, William K., Jr. 1907-1975 . . . . . . DLB-63
Winchell, Walter 1897-1972 . . . . DLB-29
J. Winchester [publishing house] DLB-49
Winckelmann, Johann Joachim 1717-1768 . . . . DLB-97
Winckler, Paul 1630-1686 . . . . DLB-164
Wind, Herbert Warren 1916- DLB-171
John Windet [publishing house] DLB-170
Windham, Donald 1920- DLB-6
Wing, Donald Goddard 1904-1972 . . . . . DLB-187
Wing, John M. 1844-1917 . . . . DLB-187
Allan Wingate [publishing house] DLB-112
Winnemucca, Sarah 1844-1921 . . . . DLB-175
Winnifrith, Tom 1938- DLB-155
Winsloe, Christa 1888-1944 . . . . DLB-124
Winslow, Anna Green 1759-1780 . . . . DLB-200
Winsor, Justin 1831-1897 . . . . DLB-47
John C. Winston Company DLB-49
Winters, Yvor 1900-1968 . . . . DLB-48
Winterson, Jeanette 1959- DLB-207, 261
Winther, Christian 1796-1876 . . . . DLB-300
Winthrop, John 1588-1649 . . . . DLB-24, 30
Winthrop, John, Jr. 1606-1676 . . . . DLB-24
Winthrop, Margaret Tyndal 1591-1647 . . DLB-200
Winthrop, Theodore 1828-1861 . . . . DLB-202
Wirt, William 1772-1834 . . . . DLB-37
Wise, John 1652-1725 . . . . DLB-24
Wise, Thomas James 1859-1937 . . . . DLB-184
Wiseman, Adele 1928-1992 . . . . DLB-88
Wishart and Company DLB-112
Wisner, George 1812-1849 . . . . DLB-43
Wister, Owen 1860-1938 . . . . DLB-9, 78, 186
Wister, Sarah 1761-1804 . . . . DLB-200
Wither, George 1588-1667 . . . . DLB-121
Witherspoon, John 1723-1794 . . . . DLB-31
  The Works of the Rev. John Witherspoon (1800-1801) [excerpts] DLB-31
Withrow, William Henry 1839-1908 . . . . . DLB-99
Witkacy (see Witkiewicz, Stanisław Ignacy)
Witkiewicz, Stanisław Ignacy 1885-1939 . . . . DLB-215; CDWLB-4
Wittenwiler, Heinrich before 1387-circa 1414? DLB-179
Wittgenstein, Ludwig 1889-1951 . . . . DLB-262
Wittig, Monique 1935- DLB-83
Wodehouse, P. G. 1881-1975 . . . . DLB-34, 162; CDBLB-6
  Worldwide Wodehouse Societies Y-98
Wohmann, Gabriele 1932- DLB-75
Woiwode, Larry 1941- DLB-6
  Tribute to John Gardner Y-82
Wolcot, John 1738-1819 . . . . DLB-109
Wolcott, Roger 1679-1767 . . . . DLB-24
Wolf, Christa 1929- DLB-75; CDWLB-2
Wolf, Friedrich 1888-1953 . . . . DLB-124
Wolfe, Gene 1931- DLB-8
Wolfe, Thomas 1900-1938 . . . . . DLB-9, 102, 229; Y-85; DS-2, DS-16; CDALB-5
  "All the Faults of Youth and Inexperience": A Reader's Report on Thomas Wolfe's *O Lost* Y-01
  Emendations for *Look Homeward, Angel*. . . . Y-00
  Eugene Gant's Projected Works Y-01
  Fire at the Old Kentucky Home [Thomas Wolfe Memorial] Y-98
  Thomas Wolfe Centennial Celebration in Asheville Y-00
  The Thomas Wolfe Collection at the University of North Carolina at Chapel Hill Y-97
  The Thomas Wolfe Society Y-97, 99
Wolfe, Tom 1931- DLB-152, 185
John Wolfe [publishing house] DLB-170
Reyner (Reginald) Wolfe [publishing house] DLB-170
Wolfenstein, Martha 1869-1906 . . . . DLB-221
Wolff, David (see Maddow, Ben)
Wolff, Helen 1906-1994 . . . . Y-94
Wolff, Tobias 1945- DLB-130
  Tribute to Michael M. Rea Y-97
  Tribute to Raymond Carver Y-88
Wolfram von Eschenbach circa 1170-after 1220 . . . DLB-138; CDWLB-2
  Wolfram von Eschenbach's *Parzival:* Prologue and Book 3 . . . . DLB-138
Wolker, Jiří 1900-1924 . . . . DLB-215
Wollstonecraft, Mary 1759-1797 . . . . DLB-39, 104, 158, 252; CDBLB-3
Women
  Women's Work, Women's Sphere: Selected Comments from Women Writers DLB-200
Wondratschek, Wolf 1943- DLB-75
Wong, Elizabeth 1958- DLB-266
Wood, Anthony à 1632-1695 . . . . DLB-213
Wood, Benjamin 1820-1900 . . . . DLB-23
Wood, Charles 1932-1980 . . . . DLB-13
  The Charles Wood Affair: A Playwright Revived Y-83
Wood, Mrs. Henry 1814-1887 . . . . DLB-18
Wood, Joanna E. 1867-1927 . . . . DLB-92
Wood, Sally Sayward Barrell Keating 1759-1855 . . . . DLB-200
Wood, William ?-? DLB-24
Samuel Wood [publishing house] DLB-49
Woodberry, George Edward 1855-1930 . . . . DLB-71, 103
Woodbridge, Benjamin 1622-1684 . . . . DLB-24
Woodbridge, Frederick J. E. 1867-1940 . . . DLB-270
Woodcock, George 1912-1995 . . . . DLB-88
Woodhull, Victoria C. 1838-1927 . . . . DLB-79
Woodmason, Charles circa 1720-? DLB-31
Woodress, James Leslie, Jr. 1916- DLB-111
Woods, Margaret L. 1855-1945 . . . . DLB-240
Woodson, Carter G. 1875-1950 . . . . DLB-17
Woodward, C. Vann 1908-1999 . . . . DLB-17
Woodward, Stanley 1895-1965 . . . . DLB-171
Woodworth, Samuel 1785-1842 . . . . DLB-250
Wooler, Thomas 1785 or 1786-1853 . . . . DLB-158
Woolf, David (see Maddow, Ben)
Woolf, Douglas 1922-1992 . . . . DLB-244
Woolf, Leonard 1880-1969 . . . . . . DLB-100; DS-10
Woolf, Virginia 1882-1941 . . . . DLB-36, 100, 162; DS-10; CDBLB-6
  "The New Biography," *New York Herald Tribune,* 30 October 1927 . . . . DLB-149
Woollcott, Alexander 1887-1943 . . . . DLB-29
Woolman, John 1720-1772 . . . . DLB-31
Woolner, Thomas 1825-1892 . . . . DLB-35
Woolrich, Cornell 1903-1968 . . . . DLB-226
Woolsey, Sarah Chauncy 1835-1905 . . . . . DLB-42
Woolson, Constance Fenimore 1840-1894 . . . . DLB-12, 74, 189, 221
Worcester, Joseph Emerson 1784-1865 . . . . DLB-1, 235
Wynkyn de Worde [publishing house] . . . DLB-170
Wordsworth, Christopher 1807-1885 . . . . DLB-166
Wordsworth, Dorothy 1771-1855 . . . . DLB-107
Wordsworth, Elizabeth 1840-1932 . . . . DLB-98
Wordsworth, William 1770-1850 . . . . DLB-93, 107; CDBLB-3
Workman, Fanny Bullock 1859-1925 . . . . DLB-189
World Literatue Today: A Journal for the New Millennium Y-01
World Publishing Company DLB-46
World War I (1914-1918) DS-18
  The Great War Exhibit and Symposium at the University of South Carolina . . Y-97
  The Liddle Collection and First World War Research Y-97
  Other British Poets Who Fell in the Great War DLB-216
  The Seventy-Fifth Anniversary of the Armistice: The Wilfred Owen Centenary and the Great War Exhibit at the University of Virginia Y-93

X

Y

Z

Ø

ISBN 0-7876-6838-9